The Developing Labor Law
Second Edition

The Developing Labor Law

The Board, the Courts, and the National Labor Relations Act

Second Edition

Volume I

Editor in Chief

Charles J. Morris
Professor of Law
Southern Methodist University

Editors

Allan L. Bioff
Attorney at Law
Kansas City, Mo.

Bernard T. King
Attorney at Law
Syracuse, N.Y.

Laurence J. Cohen
Attorney at Law
Washington, D.C.

Charles A. Powell III
Attorney at Law
Birmingham, Ala.

Section of Labor and Employment Law
American Bar Association

The Bureau of National Affairs, Inc., Washington, D.C.

Copyright © 1971, 1983
American Bar Association
Chicago, Ill.

Second Printing September 1983

Library of Congress Cataloging in Publication Data

Main entry under title:
The Developing labor law.

"Section of Labor and Employment Law, American Bar
Association."
    Kept up to date by annual supplements.
    Includes index.
    1. Labor laws and legislation—United States.
I. Morris, Charles J., 1923—   II. American Bar
Association. Section of Labor and Employment Law.
KF3369.D48   1983   344.73'01   83-3689
ISBN 0-87179-360-1 (set)   347.3041
ISBN 0-87179-403-9 (vol. I)
ISBN 0-87179-404-7 (vol. II)
ISBN 0-87179-405-5 (student ed.: set)
ISBN 0-87179-406-3 (student ed.: vol. I)
ISBN 0-87179-407-1 (student ed.: vol. II)

Printed in the United States of America

31

DONALD J. CAPUANO
Washington, D.C.

JAMES K. COOK
St. Louis, Mo.

HAROLD DATZ
Washington, D.C.

JOHN J. DELANEY, JR.
Boston, Mass.

WILLIAM J. EMANUEL
Los Angeles, Cal.

THEODORE T. GREEN
Washington, D.C.

JOHN IRVING
Washington, D.C.

HARRY J. KEATON
Los Angeles, Cal.

G. ROGER KING
Columbus, Ohio

WILLIAM A. KRUPMAN
New York, N.Y.

ROBERT D. KURNICK
Washington, D.C.

ALAN S. LEVINS
San Francisco, Cal.

STUART LINNICK
Los Angeles, Cal.

SORRELL LOGOTHETIS
Dayton, Ohio

MARCUS MANOFF
Philadelphia, Pa.

ARTHUR P. MENARD
Boston, Mass.

TIMOTHY P. O'REILLY
Philadelphia, Pa.

THOMAS F. PHALEN, JR.
Cincinnati, Ohio

DAVID PREVIANT
Milwaukee, Wis.

ROBERT J. RABIN
Syracuse, N.Y.

SIDNEY REITMAN
Newark, N.J.

STEPHEN B. RUBIN
Chicago, Ill.

STANLEY SCHAIR
New York, N.Y.

HOWARD S. SIMONOFF
Haddonfield, N.J.

LEONARD SINGER
Kansas City, Mo.

EVAN J. SPELFOGEL
New York, N.Y.

ROBERT L. THOMPSON
Atlanta, Ga.

IRA H. WEINSTOCK
Harrisburg, Pa.

PETER W. ZINOBER
Tampa, Fla.

CONTRIBUTING EDITORS

L. Gray Geddie, Jr.
William P. Getty
Kenneth R. Gilberg
Dennis A. Gladwell
Michael E. Gold
Gerald A. Golden
Leon L. Gorden
Denis F. Gordon
Stuart M. Gordon
Eugene B. Grafnof
Kathlyn Graves
Richard H.
   Greenberg
Arthur A.
   Greenfield
John Gregg
Brian S. Greig
Hartin Gringer
Harold E. Grotto
Russell Moyer
   Guttshall III

William Melvin Haas
   III
Neal Haber
Donald Myers Hall
Wayne W. Hanson
Kevin H. Harren
Bernard M.
   Hartnett, Jr.
Richard D. Hayes
Timothy J. Heinsz
F. George Heinze
Louis Peyton
   Hendricks
R. Kent Henslee
Wayne Alfrea Hersh
Henry William
   Heunemann
Samuel D. Hewlett
   III
Peter R. Hicks

Donald B. Hordes
Daniel L. Hornbeck
Chester A. Hurwitz
Melvin R. Hutson

Alexander M. Irvin

James A. Jackson
Robert Glenn Jarvis
Paula L. Jewell
David Dale Johnson
John Paul Jones
Phillip R. Jones

Alvin I. Kaplan
Deborah A. H.
   Karalunas
Marc G. Kartman
Daniel M. Katz
Michael E. Kennedy
Clem J. Kennington
Steven L. Kessler
Kenneth Kilimnick
Paul J. Kingston
Robert E.
   Kinnecome
Thomas J. Kircher
Norman H.
   Kirshman
Alfred Klein
Linda S. Klibanow
Daniel M. Kolkey
Frank L. Kollman
Daniel N.
   Kosanovich
David Koskinen

Cathy Lacinak
Robert J. Landsman
David W. Larrison
Alan Liebowitz

John C. Lombard
Richard L. Lotts
W. F. Lubersky
Stephen W. Lyman
Paul V. Lyons

Joseph Mack III
James C. Mallien
Ernest R. Malone,
   Jr.
Michael Marcionese
David N. Mark
John Markle, Jr.
Barry W. Marr
Gary A. Marsack
Joseph E. Mayer
Adrianne C. Mazura
John P. McAdams
Dennis McAteer
John F. McCarthy,
   Jr.
Charles H.
   McCreary
John McIntyre
Joseph M.
   McLaughlin
Robert G. Mebus
Charles D. Miller
Louis A. Minella
Michael S. Mitchell
Ar'min J. Moeller, Jr.
E. John Morehouse
Marylou Morelock
Anne K. Morrill

John J. Naun
Louella E. Nelson
Peter D. Nussbaum

Ernest B. Orsatti
William S. Ostan

Robert E. Paul
Irving Perlman
Andrew A. Peterson
Frank Peter Pinchak
Donald C. Pogue
Brian A. Powers
Penelope A. Proctor
Warren H. Pyle

Mozart G. Ratner
Douglas E. Ray
James S. Ray
Richard M. Resnick
David J. Rice
Matthew R. Robbins
Michael A. Robbins
James B. Robinson
John W. Robinson
 IV
Orlando Rodio
Louis Rosner

Theodore Sachs
Mimi C. Satter
Paul B. Schechter
Emil Schlesinger

Mark William
 Schneider
Truman G. Serle
Mark A. Shank
Richard J. Silber
Stephen M. Silvestri
Scott D. Soldon
Michael J. Soltis
Michael D. Stein
John H. Stephens
Janet Strain
Rebecca Strandberg
William G. Strock
Cynthia L. Summers
Matthew Swaya

Steven H. Taylor
Fred T. Thompson
Robert P. Tinnin, Jr.

Mary L. Vanderpan

James M. Walters
Barry J. Waters
William Wardlaw
 Watkins

David E. Watson
Charles B. Waud
Leslie Weisbrod
Robert Donald
 Weisman
L. N. D. Wells, Jr.
Priscilla Wheeler
Dermot J. White
Norman I. White
Barry R. Whitman
George K. Whyte,
 Jr.
A. Martin Wickliff,
 Jr.
Donald F. Woodcock
Edwin V. Woodsome
John Francis Wymer
 III

Ted Martin Yeiser,
 Jr.

Richard A. Zansitis
Edgar Alan Zingman
Matthew Zubek

FOREWORD

Over a dozen years ago, while I was serving as Secretary of what was then styled the Section of Labor Relations Law, I had a ringside seat at the production of the first edition of THE DEVELOPING LABOR LAW. I remember counting myself thrice blessed. I had no role whatsoever to play in the impossible task Charlie Morris had undertaken. Yet if by some miracle he succeeded, I could join my fellow Council members in taking due credit for our sagacity in sponsoring such an ambitious and imaginative project. And as a teacher and researcher, I would have available a truly unique resource. All that was problematic. But on one point I was absolutely certain. The Section would have to look elsewhere for an editor for any succeeding edition. No man in his right mind would twice attempt to ride herd on such a formidable collection of mavericks as had been assembled from the union, management, and public segments of the labor bar to essay this monumental feat. Obviously, I failed to reckon with the almost infinite dedication, perseverance, and patience—not to mention wiliness—of Professor Morris.

The first edition, which then-Dean Michael Sovern confessed in the Foreword had left him "in awe of the accomplishment," has been with us for more than a decade. Now its successor has arrived, with some different faces among the contributors but with the same indomitable figure holding the reins. The new edition covers much the same ground as its predecessor, and is similarly organized. It is nearly twice as long, however, reflecting a considerably more refined and exhaustive analysis of the material. The superiority of the current work is epitomized by its keener, more thorough treatment of such subtle and controversial topics as mandatory subjects of bargaining and the relationship of the National Labor Relations Board to the arbitration process. Indeed, THE DEVELOPING LABOR LAW (Second Edition) can fairly be described as the most comprehensive, reliable, and objective study ever published on the National Labor Relations Act.

That last sentence is of course intended as high praise. Yet indirectly it suggests the intrinsic limitations as well as the strengths of this imposing set of books. The very objectivity of this collaborative effort, which makes it an ideal starting point for research and ensures that it will continually be cited in both management and union briefs, also means that it lacks some of the critical punch and creative thrust that characterize the best writing of the freewheeling individual scholar or advocate, including quite specifically the often-provocative Professor Morris and some of his often-provocative colleagues. Neutrality is plainly the price of a joint endeavor like this one, however, and the results are well worth the price. Few law review articles arguing an idiosyncratic thesis come close to packing as much usable information into every page as does THE DEVELOPING LABOR LAW. And no single labor specialist could hope to match the combined expertise represented in these volumes.

The mildly misleading title invites mention of another limitation (not defect) of the work. Its actual scope is better defined in its subtitle, "The Board, the Courts, and the National Labor Relations Act." That puts the emphasis on the regulation of the union-management relationship, which was the primary focus of labor law for the three decades beginning with the New Deal era. Probably the most significant development in the whole field during the past two decades has been the shift of the spotlight from more conventional labor relations, with heavy stress on voluntary collective bargaining, to what might be termed the employment relationship, with much more direct governmental regulation of employer-employee relations and to a lesser extent of union-employee relations. The contemporary retreat from voluntarism began with Landrum-Griffin, and continued with the Equal Pay Act, Title VII of the 1964 Civil Rights Act, the Occupational Safety and Health Act, and the Employee Retirement Income Security Act. The states have recently furthered the trend with an increasing number of modifications of the at-will employment doctrine. Even the renaming of our Section in 1978 as the Section of Labor and Employment Law was in keeping with this new pattern.

Quite properly, the editors of THE DEVELOPING LABOR LAW have not diluted their product by trying to encompass this vast body of fresh material, although they have superbly treated "the mutual aid and protection" coverage which the NLRA provides for nonunion as well as unionized employees. Nevertheless, at a time when union membership in the United States has dipped below 20 percent of the total labor force, and when half the standing substantive committees of our Section do not deal directly with collective bargaining, we must recognize that "labor law" today embraces far more than the application of the NLRA. If it is conceivable that there exist within the Section the counterparts of Professor Morris and his doughty band, there is work aplenty for them to do. At any rate I no longer feel my initial twinge of regret that the present publication was not put off until 1985, when it would have coincided with the fiftieth anniversary of the Wagner Act. In some respects it is just as fitting that the work should be published on the fiftieth anniversary of that important path-breaking transitional statute, the National Industrial Recovery Act.

What is the overall impression conveyed by these weighty tomes concerning the state of the NLRA as it rounds out its first half century? In 1970 Dean Sovern found much stability, and indeed some stodginess, amidst labor law's fabled volatility. But he also remarked that even such a settled doctrine as federal preemption "has a way of coming unglued." That dual theme of a relatively stable framework housing a frequently swinging pendulum is still with us. There is more consensus than ever on the right of employees to be free from all manner and kind of economic coercion or direct interference by employers and unions. At the same time our Editor in Chief must frantically juggle page proof to take account of the Labor Board's latest gyrations on the effect of an employer's misrepresentations preceding a union election. The most substantial empirical study ever carried out on a labor law problem has apparently done little to resolve disputes about the appropriate treatment of employer and union speech and conduct during representation campaigns. Participants and decision makers in the labor law community still seem to prefer in many instances to base their judgments on their hunches or their politics, rather than on an effort to dig out the hard facts. What I said years ago before this Section about the first term of the Burger Court thus remains generally true of the Board and the courts in dealing with the NLRA: "Plus ça change, plus c'est la même chose!" ("The more things change, the more they stay the same!")

I tell my students there are three reasons they should practice labor law rather than one of those dreary other specialties. It is intellectually exciting; it treats of profound social values; and it involves real (and often colorful) human beings. Anyone who peruses the present text will find ample evidence of the first factor; those who read between the lines will sense the second; and all one need do is meet a few of the editors and contributors to be convinced of the third. Finally, the active practitioner, whether specialist or generalist, could not hope for a more satisfactory guide than these volumes to the intricacies of the law governing union-management relations. Professor Morris, his associates, and the Section deserve plaudits for a signal achievement and a major contribution to the profession.

THEODORE J. ST. ANTOINE*

March 1983

---

*James E. & Sarah A. Degan Professor of Law, University of Michigan

INTRODUCTION

The Section of Labor and Employment Law of the American Bar Association is proud to introduce this Second Edition of THE DEVELOPING LABOR LAW, edited by Charles J. Morris, Professor of Law at Southern Methodist University.

For the balanced objectivity, the high standard of scholarship, and the fine expository, yet analytical, style of the book, Professor Morris must be given primary credit. The plan of organization of the book is the work of Professor Morris, the Editor in Chief. The final editing was his responsibility. The Council, the Section of Labor and Employment Law, and the American Bar Association are greatly indebted to him for the thousands of hours of work he devoted to the book.

THE DEVELOPING LABOR LAW has become a very respected work in the labor relations field. It was the first book to chronicle the development of the law under the National Labor Relations Act, and to state the present decisional law, not only with exactness but also in relation to its historical background. It has been kept current by annual supplements prepared by the Section's Committee on the Development of Law Under the National Labor Relations Act. This Second Edition will also be supplemented on an annual basis through the work of that Committee. It is hoped that this new volume will be as invaluable an aid as was its predecessor—not only to every lawyer who specializes in the labor relations field but also to the general practitioner who needs a comprehensive source of reference.

This Second Edition is the result of the intellectual and physical efforts of many members of the Section's Committee on the Development of Law Under the National Labor Relations Act. The overall coordination of this effort was carried out, under the guidance and direction of Professor Morris, by Allan L. Bioff of Kansas City, Mo., Laurence J. Cohen of Washington, D.C., Bernard T. King of Syracuse, N.Y., and Charles A. Powell

III of Birmingham, Ala. The Section is deeply grateful to each of them for their tireless efforts on this project over a three-year period.

To the Editor in Chief, the members of the Committee on the Development of Law Under the National Labor Relations Act, past and present, and all other contributors, we render our thanks for their efforts and the resulting contribution to their profession, this Section, and the American Bar Association. A thank-you is also due to Southern Methodist University for making Professor Morris and its facilities available to the Section for this project.

Finally, our personal thanks go to Howard Schulman, Fred Elarbee, Robert Connerton, and Charles Bakaly, who have served as Section Chairmen during the more difficult years of this project. Without their prior efforts, the book's completion would have been more burdensome for us.

BERNARD F. ASHE
    Chairman, Section of Labor
    and Employment Law

EUGENE L. HARTWIG
    Chairman-Elect, Section of
    Labor and Employment Law

March 1983

PREFACE TO SECOND EDITION

The general description of the scope of this treatise contained in the preface to the first edition remains valid. However, this new edition is intended to be more than an updated version of the law of the National Labor Relations Act. While the material has of course been updated, the entire text and the footnotes have also been expanded and rewritten to improve the coverage, style, and accuracy of the work. Save for minor modifications, which I shall note later, the organizational structure remains the same. Although this second edition, like the first, is designed to fill the need for a comprehensive and analytical study which both chronicles the historical development of the law and presents a practical compendium of the details of its current status, it is my personal hope that it will also serve some other useful ends.

I. CONCERNING PURPOSE

I have long held the view that American labor law is sorely in need of rationalization. Indeed, the law of the National Labor Relations Act has evolved into an unduly complex system to which efficient access is difficult to achieve. But I stubbornly refuse to believe that such complexity is inherent in the statute. The time which I invested in this project—more than four years for the first edition and almost the same amount of time for this edition—thus represents my wager that it is feasible to present this law in a manner that will advance the public interest embodied in the congressional mandates written into the amended Act.

If my colleagues and I have done our work well, this second edition might help to attain the following lofty objectives: (1) to make this law easier to understand; (2) to move toward a "restatement" of this law; (3) to assist the National Labor Relations Board in its efforts to obtain better operating efficiency and greater achievement of statutory objectives; (4) to realize, indirectly, some reduction in polarization between labor and management by helping to dispel ignorance of this law; (5) to make it easier for advocates and decision makers to base their choices on an understanding of developments that have already transpired; and (6) to stimulate the creative process of finding new or improved ways to make our industrial relations system more responsive to the public need.

Underlying all of our efforts was a conscious attempt to present a clear statement of the law—a statement which would present the law's ramifications in a simple and easily understandable manner so that the benefits and obligations of this important statute might become more accessible to the parties in the industrial relations community whom the Act was intended to serve. Anything which tends to dispel the mystery that seems to surround the organization of employee representation and the rights and duties of the parties at the workplace should be deemed in the public interest.

I am therefore optimistic that these volumes will be useful not only to labor law specialists but also to other lawyers who may only occasionally seek the hidden keys to the labor law kingdom. And many nonlawyers, the active participants in the day-to-day workings of the industrial relations system, might also profit from this presentation of the "do's" and "don'ts" and "maybe's" which accompany the descriptions of the fact situations from which the adjudicated rules of law are drawn.

As has been demonstrated in other fields of developing law, particularly in traditional common-law fields, a restatement of the law can sometimes serve to clarify basic principles and shed light on obscure areas that require further definition. Although THE DEVELOPING LABOR LAW, as even its title indicates, is not a restatement of the law, it nevertheless moves in that direction to the extent that it provides a measure of codification where none existed before. This may serve an important purpose. Over the years, the National Labor Relations Board has eschewed utilizing the formal rule-making processes authorized by Section 6 of the National Labor Relations Act and by the Administrative Procedure Act. Instead, the Board has employed an adjudicatory process as the primary—indeed almost the exclusive—means for promulgating substantive rules under the statute. Notwithstanding the obvious benefits derived from the latter approach, for example, the ability to employ trial-and-error methods and to develop doctrines in an evolutionary manner, the adjudicatory approach is not without its shortcomings. One, to which this treatise is in part directed, concerns the means whereby the interested public is advised of the basic rules governing what is permitted, what is prohibited, and what is required. The proliferation of almost half a century of case law—thousands of Board and court decisions contained in hundreds of volumes of reports—has complicated the educational process. Accordingly, there has been a perceived need for a legal compendium such as this work. As the Board continues to grind out its rules on a case-by-case basis, often continually reinventing the wheel in the doing, my colleagues and I have sought to bring some order to what might appear to be chaos to an outsider.

I would even cautiously hope that if the full potential of these volumes is realized, the NLRB and the law which it administers might function a little more efficiently. My own observation of the Board since passage of the Taft-Hartley Act has convinced me that its heavy case load and, indirectly, its time-consuming decisional methods, are closely related to two factors: In the first place, many participants—whether they be employees, managers, or union representatives—simply do not know what the law allows. If they did, there would be fewer violations. In the second place, some unfair labor practices are undoubtedly committed by violators who feel that either the law is ineffective or that the Board's remedial devices are so relatively impotent that the law may be ignored with little risk. Ready access to a fairly complete, and hopefully understandable, statement of the law's requirements and its remedies for violations might conceivably have a deterrent effect on the commission of certain unfair labor practices.

It has become routine for scholars and other observers, including myself, to bemoan the fact that excessive polarization characterizes American labor relations. Much of that polarization is surely a by-product of the uncertainty and insecurity which employers and unions feel when confronting each other. Although the roots of such feelings may be deeply embedded in our collective social and economic psyche, some of that polarity probably stems simply from a commonplace fear of the unknown. Part of the ideal behind my own interest in this treatise is a hope that these volumes will help to dispel much of the prevailing ignorance of the labor laws and thereby dispel some of the fear of the unknown. Because the industrial system in this country has the unique capacity to provide flexible and democratic procedures, American industry and American workers should be capable of finding improved ways to organize their joint efforts to maximize mutual gain. I hope these volumes will help explain the unknown to those who need to know. Knowing how the system operates is important to its effective operation.

Although this work will probably have its heaviest usage as a convenient legal manual for labor law practitioners and decision makers, it will hopefully serve yet a broader educational purpose. The discussion of historical development which accompanies virtually all of the legal doctrines in these volumes should provide the student—and all of us who work in this field are students—with an important sense of perspective. Congress chose to use sparse language to describe the rights, obligations, and prohibitions that would govern private sector labor relations under this Act. The Labor Board was thus invested with a wide discretion for interpreting the bare bones of statutory language and fleshing out the interstices in ways deemed suitable for effectuating the policies of the Act. Historical reminders can play a significant role in the formulation of policy. Revealing documentation concerning policy-oriented developments— readily available reference to what has gone before—may make it easier for advocates and decision makers to assert rational choices.

As this work goes to press, the American economy is struggling to climb up from the bottom of a recession. More than ever before there is widespread recognition of a need for rethinking and reworking various aspects of the several relationships which comprise the field of employee relations: relationships between employers and individual employees, between employers and unions, and between unions and employees. However these objectives be defined—whether in terms of greater efficiency, higher productivity, managerial and entrepreneurial flexibility, greater worker participation, or increased cooperation between labor and management—real knowledge of how the labor relations system works is critical for effective use of the system. If my colleagues and I have succeeded in our basic objective, it may become easier for both lawyers and laypersons to understand the American industrial relations system. And I would like to believe that, in turn, creative processes may thus be stimulated to help find new or improved ways to make that system more responsive to the public interest.

The foregoing disclosure of noble and salutory purposes is a statement of personal faith. I have faith that the system's singular features which are derived from and are dependent upon the National Labor Relations Act can be used more advantageously toward achieving the objectives which Congress mandated. This is the goal to which I dedicate the efforts which I have invested in these volumes.

II. CONCERNING ORGANIZATION

As I have noted, the organizational structure of this edition is basically the same as in the first edition, and the original preface generally describes that structure. One change, however, reflects the enhanced importance of the relation of arbitration to the Board's processes. *Arbitration and the Act* is now treated as a distinct subject area in Part V. Another change is found in Chapters 6 and 9, which cover subjects that were treated together in Chapter 5 in the first edition. That material has been divided into two chapters in order to separate unfair labor practice "interference" (Chapter 6) from violations of "laboratory conditions" relating to preelection conduct which does not constitute unfair labor practices (Chapter 9). Additionally, the chapter on the union duty of fair representation (Chapter 28) now precedes the chapter on union security (Chapter 29), a reversal of order from the original edition.

III. CONCERNING CONTRIBUTORS

As is readily apparent from the listing of the more than 300 attorneys who contributed directly to these volumes, this work was a team project. The magnitude of the case material and the rapidity with which the Board and the courts have produced such material have made the team approach essential. No small group, and certainly not a single author, could have assembled this mass of material with sufficient accuracy and detail. Time waits for no man, or woman, and certainly not for the Board and the courts, for the decisional law proliferates week after week without respite. These volumes could be written only because a small army of dedicated but busy labor law specialists were willing to contribute generously of their time and talent to the project. I am grateful to all of them for the excellence of their contributions and for the cooperation and patience which they demonstrated in our working together.

Credit is due not only to the contributors whose names appear in this edition, but also to those who joined me in writing the first edition. Although almost all of the current contributors are new, there were some notable personal links between the two editions which deserve special mention. Stuart Linnick, as a young lawyer, worked with me as a valued editorial assistant on the original volume. And on this edition he ably served as an assistant editor responsible for a draft chapter. A. John Harper II, who worked on the first edition as my student at Southern Methodist University School of Law, was also responsible for a fine draft chapter in this current edition, for which he served as an associate editor. Others, all of whom are named in the first edition, have also made their mark in this edition, because in writing the current version we were able to build upon the strong foundation of the original volume. I am indebted to each of them.

Many other persons were also essential to the success of this undertaking. The late A. J. Thomas, former Dean Ad Interim, and Jeswald Salacuse, the present Dean, exemplified the splendid support which SMU School of Law provided for this project. Professor Earl Borgeson, Law Librarian, was especially helpful in providing a research environment so necessary to the success of this undertaking; Fred Taylor, the School's financial officer, made financial and logistical arrangements pleasant and possible. And special thanks go to the word processor operators who so efficiently converted dirty manuscript into clean copy: Jill Dickson and Kathleen Mooney.

I cannot imagine any author or editor having better publishing support than that which was provided by the dedicated BNA editorial staff. I am especially grateful to Don Farwell and Mary Miner. And to Mildred Cary I can only say, "We could not have done it without you."

And finally, gratitude which cannot be adequately expressed in words is due to Minnette, my wife. She suffered with me and provided understanding and support during the tedious years which preceded publication. She also gave valuable assistance in proofreading manuscript, as did also two of my sons, Joe and John. I recognize with deep appreciation the support and inspiration provided by my entire family.

CHARLES J. MORRIS

February 1983

PREFACE TO FIRST EDITION

The DEVELOPING LABOR LAW is a book about the National Labor Relations Act, *i.e.*, the Wagner Act of 1935, as amended by the Taft-Hartley Act of 1947 and the Landrum-Griffin Act of 1959. It is about a statute whose contours have directly shaped labor relations for the greater part of the private sector in the United States and have indirectly influenced the newly forming patterns in labor relations for the public sector. This volume was written in an effort to fill a need for a comprehensive and analytical treatise on this important subject.

In 1966, when the American Bar Association Section of Labor Relations Law, of which Ted Smoot was then Chairman, graciously invited me to serve as general editor of the project from which this work emerged, none of us involved in the early planning could foresee the complexity of the task which we were about to undertake.

During the first year of the project it became apparent that fulfillment of our ambitious goal would require much more than writing and editing a collection of essays on various aspects of the statute; so we decided to commence an intensive study of the thousands of decisions and rules which had been unfolding since 1935 in the National Labor Relations Board and in the courts. Here was a magnificent opportunity to chronicle the legislative and common-law development of this body of jurisprudence that had become deeply woven into the institutional fabric of our society in a relatively short period of time.

The opportunity was within our reach because we could and did draw from a rich reservoir of legal talent that was uniquely available in the Labor Relations Law Section. At the final counting, a total of 72 persons have contributed to the research, writing, and editing of this volume—nine professors of labor law, 53 practicing labor lawyers, and 10 senior law students. This group of lawyers and scholars proceeded in its task of uncovering and recording the evolutionary movements in the pertinent case law and the more abrupt changes wrought by congressional action. Our intent was to produce a volume which would provide, in historical perspective, a clear view of the ever-changing landscape covered by this statute. We attempted to make visible—generally as to the entire Act and its amendments, but specifically as to each rule of law for which the statute is a primary or significant source—all important changes in the law and also the interplay between the NLRB and the courts that provided the principal medium for these changes.

The book was designed, however, to be more than a history of past events; we also intended that it would be a practical compendium of the current state of the law under and concerning the National Labor Relations Act. In this regard, we have tried to be concise and objective. If the text draws value judgments or enunciates policies, these are the judgments and policies of the Congress, the Board, and the courts. At least this has been our intention, for we have tried to present objectively whatever the law was and whatever it now is.

Of course we write on shifting sands. The title of the book is a testament to the transitory quality of the subject matter. Yet there is more stability in many labor law doctrines than some popular critics may be willing to concede, and this volume demonstrates that teaching. But as to large areas where the law is undergoing change, we are again fortunate in being able to rely on the considerable talent found in the Labor Relations Law Section of the ABA, for that Section's Committee on Development of Law under the National Labor Relations Act will key its future reports to the organization of this volume, and those reports will be published as annual supplements.

This book is organized along functional lines. It is divided into seven parts, the first being devoted to historical materials and the last to administration of the statute. The parts in between follow a rough chronology coinciding with the development of prototypical labor relations: Part II, employee rights (including treatment of organizational and preelection activity and discrimination in employment); Part III, the representation process and union recognition; Part IV, the collective bargaining process; Part V, economic activity; and Part VI, relations between the employee and the union. We trust this organizational structure will help the reader to find some order from the seeming chaos of thousands of labor law decisions and hundreds of law review articles which have been written about subjects under this Act. The reader must judge for himself the extent to which we have succeeded in achieving our objectives.

I wish to express profound indebtedness to the many persons who made this book possible—first and foremost to my academic and professional colleagues and to my students who contributed so generously of their time and talent in valuable research and writing. I also want to thank scores of other unnamed but not unappreciated lawyers and law students who assisted in myriad tasks associated with our effort to achieve accuracy in citation and reporting. I also acknowledge the generosity of Texas Instruments, Inc., in making unlimited Xerox facilities available for the project. And special thanks are due to Hibernia Turbeville, Law Librarian of Southern Methodist University, for her ready assistance in securing research materials, and to Lois Blackburn, my secretary, for typing reams of manuscript and helping in many ways. Thanks are extended also to Ogden W. Fields, Executive Secretary of the National Labor Relations Board, for providing full texts of all NLRB decisions promptly upon issuance; and to Donald F. Farwell, Howard J. Anderson, and other members of the BNA staff for their editorial assistance and infinite patience.

For my wife and children—who managed to put up with me during the four years of the project—there are no words adequate to express my appreciation for their vital contributions. I am very grateful to them.

Though this book is a cooperative venture, I alone am responsible for weaknesses in its organizational structure and any errors in reporting. Nothing herein should be deemed to represent the view or action of the American Bar Association or its Section of Labor Relations Law, unless and until adopted by the Association or Section pursuant to their bylaws.

CHARLES J. MORRIS

December 1970

SUMMARY TABLE OF CONTENTS

VOLUMES I AND II

PART I

HISTORY OF THE
NATIONAL LABOR RELATIONS ACT

PART II

PROTECTED EMPLOYEE ACTIVITY

PART III

THE REPRESENTATION PROCESS
AND UNION RECOGNITION

PART IV

THE COLLECTIVE BARGAINING PROCESS

PART V

ARBITRATION AND THE ACT

PART VII

RELATIONS BETWEEN EMPLOYEE AND UNION

Part VIII

ADMINISTRATION OF THE ACT

DETAILED TABLE OF CONTENTS

VOLUME I

PART I

HISTORY OF THE
NATIONAL LABOR RELATIONS ACT

PART II

PROTECTED EMPLOYEE ACTIVITY

PART III

THE REPRESENTATION PROCESS
AND UNION RECOGNITION

PART V

ARBITRATION AND THE ACT

HISTORY OF THE
NATIONAL LABOR RELATIONS ACT

Chapter 1

HISTORICAL BACKGROUND OF THE WAGNER ACT

By the early 1930s organized labor had been a part of the American scene for over a century.[1] In the resulting lush progression of crises and governmental countermeasures, it is fairly easy to pick out, with a comfortable perspective of five decades, three major themes:

1. The case law afforded a cumulative demonstration that the courts were not institutionally capable of formulating or implementing a workable labor policy.

2. The course of legislative and judicial action revealed increasing awareness that the role of organized labor presented a question of national proportions that no state was capable of answering definitively.

3. There was the development of two mutually incompatible national policies towards organized labor: one regarding it as creating market restraints inimical to the national economy, and the other regarding it as necessary to a regime of industrial peace based upon a balanced bargaining relationship between employers wielding the combined power of incorporated capital wealth and unions wielding the power of organized labor.

I. The Inadequacies of Judicial Regulation

The inability of the courts to provide viable solutions to the problems presented by the labor movement was twofold. First,

---

[1]The "first" American labor case, known as the Philadelphia Cordwainer's case, was decided in 1806. *See* C. Gregory, Labor and the Law 22 (2d rev. ed., 1961). For a detailed account of the trial, *see* Lieberman, Unions Before the Bar 1-15 (rev. ed., 1960).

the process of case-by-case adjudication was an inadequate instrument for the formulation of a cohesive policy or rational substantive norms of conduct. The industrial revolution, and the combinations of capital and of labor that it called to life, presented problems that called for broad legislative solutions. The courts were unable to develop any workable standards for governing concerted employee conduct; they did not even try to establish any standard to regulate the behavior of employers towards labor organizations. Second, court procedures proved too cumbersome and judicial remedies too inflexible, to effectuate whatever substantive standards the courts announced.

American courts engaged in an early flirtation with the proposition that any concerted employee action, even to raise wages, was indictable as criminal conspiracy, even though the motivating purpose and the means utilized would be legal if similar action were taken by individuals. During the first 40 years of the nineteenth century, numerous convictions were upheld ostensibly upon the conspiracy theory, although many of the decisions in fact involved violence or coercion, or contained language suggesting that the crime in question required either a motivating purpose or resort to means that would be illegal under some established category of common law.[2] Chief Justice Shaw of Massachusetts drew these threads together in his 1842 opinion in *Commonwealth* v. *Hunt*,[3] in which the conspiracy doctrine was narrowed and rationalized as requiring either an illegal purpose or resort to illegal means.

The *Hunt* decision also provided a bridge between declining use of the conspiracy doctrine, whose criminal sanctions produced overwhelmingly adverse public reaction,[4] and judicial use of civil remedies to regulate union activity. Since *Hunt*, "American legal history is a steady accumulation of instances where the line has been drawn between purposes and acts permitted, and purposes and acts forbidden."[5] But after *Hunt*, the evolution of these standards occurred primarily in the context of civil proceedings for damages or injunctions, rather than in criminal prosecutions.

---

[2]The Philadelphia Cordwainers' case, *see* F. Frankfurter & N. Greene, THE LABOR INJUNCTION 2-3 (1930).
[3]4 Met. 111 (1842).
[4]Gregory, *supra* note 1 at 27.
[5]Frankfurter & Greene, *supra* note 2 at 4-5.

Even this basic analytical division into purposes and means was not without its difficulties. In many instances, it merely provided alternative avenues for judicial condemnation of union activity. Inducing a strike against *A* to discourage *A* from doing business with *B* may have been condemned upon the theory that its secondary purpose was illegal or, quite as easily, upon the theory that the secondary boycott was an illegal means.[6] Similarly, federal courts were inclined to make the legality of an organizational strike depend upon the manner in which it was conducted, while "in Massachusetts, the rationale for decision [shifted] almost completely to an emphasis upon the issue of justifiable ends."[7]

Aside from the ambiguity inherent in the easy interchangeability of the two tests of "ends" and "means," in the administration of each test serious problems were encountered. Even when the means test was utilized to condemn such clearly reprehensible conduct as threatening physical injury to person or property, there was a tendency toward judicial subjectivity. As late as 1900, for example, the Supreme Court of Massachusetts suggested that a threat to strike was illegal because it necessarily implied accompanying violence and injury, "however mild the language or suave the manner in which the threat to strike is made."[8]

It was in judging the legality of purposes of labor activity that the gravest difficulties were encountered. Although a few courts briefly entertained contentions to the contrary,[9] the view quickly and overwhelmingly prevailed that intentional infliction of economic harm, even by means that were not illegal, was actionable unless justified by some legitimate purpose creating a defense of privilege.[10] The difficulty was that judges were unable to agree as to what purposes were sufficient to justify the infliction of harm. Some adopted the position that any economic self-

---

[6]The "objectives" test was adopted in Massachusetts under the persuasive aegis of Holmes, C. J., in Plant v. Woods, 176 Mass 492 (1900) (although Holmes himself dissented in this case); the "means" test found favor in certain federal courts, *e.g.*, Atchison, Topeka & Sante Fe Ry. Co. v. Gee, 139 F 582 (SD Iowa, 1905) (peaceful picketing compared with chaste vulgarity); Frankfurter & Greene, *supra* note 2 at 24-46.

[7]Frankfurter & Greene, *supra* note 2 at 27.

[8]Plant v. Woods, 176 Mass 492, 497 (1900).

[9]Gregory, *supra* note 1 at 76-82, in which this minority view is called the "civil rights" view.

[10]Vegelahn v. Guntner, 167 Mass 92, 105 (1896) (Holmes, J., dissenting); *see* Restatement of Torts §775 (1939).

interest was an adequate justification. Their thesis was that competition was worth more to society than it cost, or at any rate that this was a basic value judgment of the common law, the alteration of which was the proper business of legislators but not of judges.[11] Other judges undertook to assess the importance of the union's asserted interest and to weigh it against competing interests of other segments of society, and frequently found organized labor on the light side of the scales.[12]

Needless to say, the economic sophistication and bias of an individual judge were often pivotal when such balancing was undertaken. Between the pure bargaining strike by employees against their own employer, which came to be quite generally accepted,[13] and the many forms of secondary boycott, which were condemned with equal generality on a wide variety of rationales,[14] there was a diversity of judicial opinion as to the legitimacy of almost all peaceful forms of concerted employee conduct.[15] Thus, one judge might conclude that a concerted refusal to work for the purpose of expanding union membership was not justified by any legitimate purpose; another judge, attributing greater weight to the importance to the union of a strong bargaining position, might find that the same strike was for the ultimate purpose of raising wages, and therefore privileged.[16]

On the remedial side, other institutional shortcomings of judicial regulation became evident. Broad use of criminal sanctions imposed for peaceful labor activity quickly proved unacceptable to the public at large and was abandoned. Money damages, the standard remedy in actions at law, imposed an inordinately heavy sanction for peaceful conduct condemned upon such unreliable criteria as those just discussed, especially since a business enterprise's capacity for economic injury so far exceeds the usual employee's ability to pay damages.[17] Because of the uncertain legality of much proposed union action under the substan-

---

[11]Vegelahn v. Guntner, *supra* note 10 at 106 (Holmes, J., dissenting); Duplex Printing Press Co. v. Deering, 254 US 443, 488 (1921) (Brandeis, J., dissenting).
[12]Vegelahn v. Guntner, *supra* note 10; Plant v. Woods, *supra* note 8.
[13]Gregory, *supra* note 1 at 60.
[14]Frankfurter & Greene, *supra* note 2 at 43.
[15]*Id.* at 26-27.
[16]*Compare* the majority opinion by Hammond, J., in Plant v. Woods, *supra* note 6, *with* the dissent by Chief Justice Holmes in the same case, *id.* at 504.
[17]*E.g.,* in Loewe v. Lawlor, 208 US 274 (1908), plaintiffs were seeking $80,000 in damages from union members. *See* Chapter 31 *infra* at notes 338-39.

tive law, the deterrent effect of either criminal penalties or damages was too undiscriminating; in close cases, deterrence operated with equal effect whether the proposed concerted action would ultimately be determined to have been permissible or not. The only traditionally judicial remedy that transcended these limitations was the equitable remedy of injunction, and American courts turned increasingly to its use during the last two decades of the nineteenth century.[18]

The injunction was used in the labor field almost exclusively at the behest of employers to prevent injury by restraining concerted labor activity.[19] It easily lent itself to this role, since it provided prompt provisional restraint of the activity complained of, unlike criminal and common-law sanctions. But where the substantive law was uncertain, the availability of temporary injunctive relief became more important as a practical matter than the substantive law ultimately applied, since the momentum of a temporarily enjoined strike could not normally be regained even if the injunction ultimately was vacated.[20] There were other objectionable features of labor injunctions. They were frequently so vaguely worded as to be unintelligible. Contempt sanctions enabled courts to punish violations by criminal penalties without the intercession of a jury or even of a judge, other than the author of the prohibition. And all this coercive machinery could be set in motion by an ex parte application for provisional relief supported only by affidavits of interested parties.[21] The resulting "government by injunction" became a national political issue as early as 1896.[22]

By the 1930s, it had been clear for some time that the courts could not be expected to provide answers to the problems presented by the labor movement. They were not the appropriate institution to formulate a rational basis for discriminating between tolerable and intolerable concerted employee activity, with the single exception of nonpeaceful conduct. Although they had extrapolated from precedent in an attempt to regulate union activity, it would probably have been preferable had they not

---

[18]In re Debs, 158 US 564 (1895); Frankfurter & Green, *supra* note 2 at 17-18, 23.
[19]On rare occasion a union successfully obtained injunctive relief; *see* Frankfurter & Greene, *supra* note 2 at 108.
[20]*See* In re Debs, *supra* note 18; Frankfurter & Greene, *supra* note 2 at 17.
[21]A. Cox & D. Bok, LABOR LAW CASES AND MATERIALS 100-101 (6th ed., 1965); Frankfurter & Greene, *supra* note 2 at 53-60.
[22]Frankfurter & Greene, *supra* note 2 at 1.

done so, and certainly no one had ever expected them to make a similar effort in order to formulate norms for employer conduct. Thus, by the time a controversy reached the courts, industrial strife usually already had occurred, and the remedies available limited the range of judicial decision to the question whether the union activity in question should be punished or suppressed, and, if so, by what sanction.

II. THE RISE OF FEDERAL REGULATION

Federal courts played two roles in regulating labor disputes before the Wagner Act. In exercising their diversity-of-citizenship jurisdiction, they were major participants in the unsuccessful attempt to make common-law precedents answer the challenge of organized labor. In exercising federal-question jurisdiction under several federal statutes, for a time they imported much of this unfortunate common-law precedent into national policy, and they marked out—in what proved to be a tentative fashion—the permissible limits of federal governmental action to regulate labor disputes.

Under the doctrine of *Swift* v. *Tyson*,[23] federal courts deciding questions of state common law were not bound to follow decisions of state courts as precedents. Federal judges, enjoying tenure for life as a practical matter,[24] were on the whole far less sensitive to the demands of organized labor than their brothers on the state bench whose tenure frequently was less secure. Thus in many instances an employer might expect a more favorable result in federal than in state court. And employers, as plaintiffs, were able to manipulate the matter of citizenship with considerable success to enable themselves to maintain suit in federal court. Consequently there grew a large body of federal "common law" applicable to labor disputes. Further, federal equity practice, which had always been independent of state law, provided fertile soil for the development of labor injunctions.[25]

As late as 1930, it appears, a majority of the labor cases in federal courts were there because of diversity jurisdiction.[26] But

---

[23]41 US 1 (1842).
[24]U.S. CONST. art. III, § 1.
[25]Frankfurter & Greene, *supra* note 2 at 5-17.
[26]*Id.* at 210.

beginning before 1900, an increasing number of cases—many of them extremely influential—were brought into federal court by virtue of federal legislation. In 1895, in the landmark case of *In re Debs*,[27] the Supreme Court upheld the jurisdiction of a federal court to enjoin labor violence in a railroad strike, at the instance of the United States, on the basis of statutes prohibiting obstruction of the mails and regulating interstate commerce. The latter of these, the Interstate Commerce Act,[28] was used as the basis of federal intervention in a number of labor cases marked by uncertainty as to the applicability of the common-law tests of illegal means and illegal ends.[29]

This problem never had to be resolved; even before the *Debs* case, lower federal courts had commenced to use another statute as a basis for federal-question jurisdiction to intervene in labor disputes.[30] This was the Sherman Act,[31] enacted in 1890. Section 1 of the Act rendered illegal "every contract, combination in the form of trust or otherwise, or conspiracy, in restraint of trade or commerce among the several states." The Act created a cause of action for treble damages for persons injured by violations, authorized injunctions and criminal prosecution of violations, at the instance of the United States, and created federal jurisdiction over all such proceedings.

The Supreme Court avoided the question of the Sherman Act's role in labor cases in the *Debs* litigation, but ultimately faced it in a series of decisions beginning in 1908 with *Loewe* v. *Lawlor*,[32] the celebrated *Danbury Hatters'* case. A threshold question in this respect, which has been extensively and acrimoniously debated, was whether the Sherman Act was applicable to labor unions at all.[33] The Act was intended primarily "as a safeguard against the social and economic consequences of massed capital,"[34] but its substantive provisions are worded broadly enough to encompass violations by labor organizations, and a proposed amendment to exempt them specifically was advanced in the Senate but never incorporated into the statute. In any

---

[27]158 US 564 (1895).
[28]24 Stat 379 (1887), 49 USC §§ 1-22 (1964).
[29]Toledo, A.A. & N.M. Ry. Co. v. Pennsylvania Co., 54 F 730 (ND Ohio, 1893); Knudson v. Benn, 123 F 636 (D Minn, 1903).
[30]United States v. Debs, 64 F 724 (ND Ill, 1894).
[31]26 Stat 209 (1890), 15 USC §§ 1-7 (1964). *See generally* Chapter 31 *infra*.
[32]208 US 274 (1908).
[33]*See* H. Millis & E. Brown, FROM THE WAGNER ACT TO TAFT-HARTLEY 9 (1949).
[34]Frankfurter & Greene, *supra* note 2 at 8.

event, the question was resolved in favor of applicability in the *Danbury Hatters'* decision.

Without more, the Supreme Court's decision that labor organizations were not excluded from the category of potential violators of the Sherman Act meant merely that it would be possible for an employer to state a claim for treble damages against a union and its adherents "arising under" the Act and thus within the jurisdiction of federal courts, and that there similarly would be judicial cognizance of government proceedings to impose injunctive or penal sanctions. But deciding this did not decide what ingredients were essential to a violation of the statute in a labor dispute.

As muddy as the common law was in its application to labor activity, it seems clear that Congress intended the Court to turn to the common law to determine the scope of the Sherman Act's prohibitions.[35] It thus seems odd that the Court did not accept this invitation to indulge its own economic and social ideas in determining what purposes and means of concerted action should or should not render it prohibited under the Act. Several decisions and further action by Congress were required for the Court to reach something approximating this result. In its first application of the Sherman Act to organized labor in the *Danbury Hatters'* case, the Court indicated that it would be enough to establish a violation if the employees' concerted action obstructed the flow of the employer's product in interstate commerce.[36] The activity actually before the Court in the case could for the most part have been condemned on narrower grounds; in an attempt to insulate its gains from price competition by nonunion products, the union was utilizing primary and secondary consumer boycotts to organize a nonunion manufacturer. All this pressure might have been condemned under the means and objectives tests at common law; but the rule adopted by the Court was much broader.

A degree of flexibility was added to the rule in two decisions in 1921 and 1922, with the result that federal regulation of union activity under the Sherman Act conformed somewhat more closely with the results reached at common law. The first of these involved the Clayton Act,[37] which, as a result of union

---

[35]Gregory, *supra* note 1 at 205.
[36]Loewe v. Lawlor, *supra* note 32 at 292-93.
[37]38 Stat 730 (1914), 15 USC §§ 12-27 (1964). *See* notes 39 and 40 *infra* for cases.

lobbying in response to the *Danbury Hatters'* decision, contained two provisions that were widely thought to relieve the strictures that case had imposed upon union activity. These provisions, Sections 6 and 20 of the Clayton Act, are discussed subsequently.[38] It is enough here to say that they were very narrowly construed by the Supreme Court in *Duplex Printing Press Co.* v. *Deering*[39] and held to exempt only concerted activity already regarded as lawful at common law, and then only when engaged in by employees in an effort to settle a labor dispute with their own employer. With this exception, any concerted action was a violation of the Sherman Act if it produced a disruption in the flow of goods in interstate commerce. The activity involved in *Duplex* was a secondary labor boycott; again it seems that the Court might have condemned it on the narrower ground that it would have been illegal under the means or objectives tests at common law. As it was, the *Duplex* decision imported into the Sherman Act a line of distinction—between pressure upon one's employer and pressure exerted upon others—closely akin to the distinction utilized by common law to condemn secondary boycotts.

A closer conformity between the Sherman Act and the common law was achieved one year later in *United Mine Workers* v. *Coronado Coal Co.*[40] As in the two boycott cases, the union ultimately was concerned with elimination of price competition from non-union-produced commodities. The concerted action took the form of a strike accompanied by violence and property destruction, the effect of which was to halt the mining of coal, and thereby, of course, to disrupt the flow of the employer's product in interstate commerce. The Court chose to differentiate between this kind of disruption, caused by interference with manufacturing or mining the product, and the disruptions caused by boycotts which inhibited demand for the product. The former was characterized as an "indirect" obstruction to interstate commerce; the Court took the view that such an indirect restraint would violate the Sherman Act only if used to further an intention to create a market restraint or monopoly in interstate commerce.[41] This was in fact the ultimate purpose in the two boycott cases as well as in the *Coronado* case. But

---

[38]*See* Chapter 31*infra* at notes 334-418.
[39]254 US 443 (1921).
[40]259 US 344 (1922).
[41]*Id.* at 410-11.

in the latter, since the obstruction to interstate commerce was "indirect," proving the purpose became crucial. This meant that, given adequate proof of this subjective purpose, the federal courts had a means of condemning organizational strikes while leaving purely bargaining strikes uncondemned by the Sherman Act.[42]

Thus the Supreme Court ultimately conformed its applications of the Sherman Act to organized labor to a pattern not greatly different from that reached by many courts at common law. The major differences, aside from the requirement of a disruption of interstate commerce, were (1) that the Sherman Act, as amended by the Clayton Act, gave to employers the remedy of treble damages as well as the injunction and (2) that the United States was empowered to sue for injunctions and to institute criminal prosecutions for violations of the Sherman Act.

At best, all this amounted to in terms of substantive law was a step backward. Partially counterbalancing this, however, is the consideration that some degree of federal power to regulate labor disputes under the Commerce Clause was thoroughly established. Indeed, even an "indirect" obstruction caused by a cessation of mining or manufacturing had been recognized as a sufficient link to validate regulation by Congress. From this it was only a step—albeit not an easy one—to recognition of Congress' power to regulate labor policies of employers engaged in interstate commerce, as well as organized employee activities.

III. AN AFFIRMATIVE NATIONAL LABOR POLICY: THE ANCESTRY OF THE WAGNER ACT

While the federal courts were pursuing their unsuccessful quest for an answer to the challenge posed by the labor movement, the two other branches of the federal government became increasingly sensitive to the same challenge and slowly began to articulate their own policies toward organized labor. The judicial policy in essence was one of selective suppression of organized labor's activities whenever they trenched too heav-

---

[42]Coronado Coal Co. v. United Mine Workers, 268 US 295 (1925). The "fink" had been discovered. See Gregory, *supra* note 1 at 216.

ily upon the interests of any other segment of society. Commercial interests must not be injured by disruption of the interstate flow of goods; consumers and unorganized laborers must not be injured by wage standardization; employers and the public at large must not be injured by expansion of labor disputes through secondary boycotts. Save for the bargaining strike and accompanying picketing, very little indulgence was given to the claims of organized labor to an institutional role in the nation's economy.

The rival policy that was developed by the executive and legislative branches of government assigned an important function to organized labor in the operation of the national economy and sought to protect this function in two ways: by eliminating judicial interference with the operation of labor organizations and by affording some of these operations affirmative legal protection.

A. The Erdman Act

The history of this governmental second labor front begins with the 1894 Pullman strike, which gave rise to the *Debs* case.[43] The United States Strike Commission, appointed by President Cleveland to inquire into the matter, filed a report adopting ideas that are now a part of our national labor policy. The commission concluded that the judicial approach to labor organization was inappropriate in the light of "the rapid concentration of power and wealth, under stimulating legislative conditions, in persons, corporations, and monopolies."[44] It was suggested that organization of employees was beneficial to the employment relationship because it tended to reduce failures of communication and promote rational and responsible settlement of labor disputes by peaceful means. At least some of the courts were nonetheless "still poring over the law reports of antiquity in order to construe conspiracy out of labor unions."[45]

The commission's central conclusion was that employers should recognize and deal with labor organizations: If employers "take labor into consultation at proper times, much of the severity of strikes can be tempered and their number re-

---

[43]In re Debs, 158 US 564 (1895).
[44]UNITED STATES STRIKE COMMISSION, REPORT ON THE CHICAGO STRIKE OF JUNE-JULY 1894 XLVII (1894).
[45]*Id.*

duced."[46] "Yellow dog" contracts obligating employees to abstain from union membership should be made illegal. In response to the railway strike that had occasioned its inquiry, the commission recommended a permanent federal commission to investigate, conciliate, and if necessary decide railway labor disputes with judicial enforcement power. The parties to each dispute—employees through their unions if they so chose—should be entitled to representation in the hearing body. While proceedings were pending, and for six months thereafter, a moratorium should be imposed upon concerted union activity against the employer and upon employer discrimination against adherents of the union. More broadly, the presidential commission's report recommended that the states establish agencies to mediate and conciliate labor disputes and to encourage and facilitate arbitration, and that the states give labor organizations "standing before the law."[47]

This report became the basis of the Erdman Act, enacted by Congress in 1898.[48] Though limited to employees engaged in the operation of interstate trains, the Act suggested what was to become the basis for future legislation relating to organized labor. It imposed criminal penalties for the discharge or threatened discharge of employees for union membership, and, utilizing unions as representatives of employees, provided facilities for mediation and conciliation of railway labor disputes. The mediators were directed to encourage submission of unsettled disputes to arbitration.

The mediation provisions of the Erdman Act operated with moderate success until World War I, when the government took over the railroads.[49] The prohibition in Section 10 of the Act against anti-union discrimination, however, was held unconstitutional by the Supreme Court in *Adair* v. *United States*,[50] decided one week before the *Danbury Hatters'*[51] case in early 1908. The Court concluded that Section 10 of the Act deprived the railroads and their agents, as well as railroad employees, of liberty of contract without due process of law, in violation of the Fifth Amendment, and, further, that the commerce power did

---

[46]*Id.* at LIV.
[47]*Id.*
[48]30 Stat 424 (1898).
[49]Cox & Bok, *supra* note 21 at 70.
[50]208 US 161 (1908).
[51]Loewe v. Lawlor, 208 US 274 (1908).

not authorize Congress to make this regulation of contractual relations. A railroad employee's membership in a labor organization, the Court said,

> cannot have, *in itself* and in the eye of the law, any bearing upon the commerce with which the employé is connected by his labor and services. . . . One who engages in the service of an interstate carrier will, it must be assumed, faithfully perform his duty, whether he be a member or not a member of a labor organization.[52]

Thus, in *Adair* the Court disagreed with the factual conclusions reached by President Cleveland's commission, and by Congress as well, that disruptions in interstate transportation were traceable directly to the railroads' refusal to deal with labor organizations. A majority of the Justices could conceive of only one national policy toward organized labor, which they attributed to Congress a week later in the *Danbury Hatters'* case. Symptomatic relief of commercial disruptions was deemed a legitimate exercise of federal power, but Congress could not root out the cause by regulating the employment relationships out of which commercial disruptions arose. State legislation implementing the recommendations of the commission's report met a similar fate by application of the Due-Process Clause of the Fourteenth Amendment.[53]

B. The Clayton Act

Sections 6 and 20 of the Clayton Act,[54] which deal expressly with organized labor, may best be regarded historically as a response to the Supreme Court's *Adair* and *Danbury Hatters'* decisions. In those two cases, the Court had told Congress: first, that it had no power to protect interstate commerce against labor disruptions by regulating employers' hiring and firing practices to promote the growth of unions; and second, that Congress had, in the Sherman Act, adopted a contrary policy of suppressing the activities of organized labor when they interfered with the flow of goods in interstate commerce. On the first of these points, Congress recognized that the Supreme Court has the final say because of its power to determine the constitutionality of federal legislation. On the second, however,

---

[52]Adair v. United States, 208 US 161, 178 (1908).
[53]Coppage v. Kansas, 236 US 1 (1915).
[54]38 Stat 731 (1914), 15 USC §17 (1964); 38 Stat 738 (1914), 29 USC §52 (1964). For general discussion of the applicability of the antitrust laws to labor union activity, *see* Chapter 31 *infra*.

Congress recognized that it had the power to alter the policy attributed to it by the Court's interpretation of the Sherman Act in the *Danbury Hatters'* decision. This is what Congress sought to do in the labor provisions of the Clayton Act. Accepting the Court's admonition that affirmative promotion of unionism by regulation of employer conduct was beyond its constitutional power, Congress sought to advance the same policy in a negative fashion by limiting narrowly the circumstances in which the courts might intervene to assist an employer in resisting the organizational efforts of labor unions.

There appears to have been some fear after the *Danbury Hatters'* decision that the Supreme Court might resurrect ancient law under the Sherman Act to conclude that *all* organized labor activity interfering with the flow of goods in interstate commerce was in violation of the Act, since the basic principle of labor organization is combination to control the supply, and thereby the price, of labor in a given market.[55] Section 6 of the Clayton Act was designed to eliminate this possibility by providing that labor itself is not "an article of commerce" and that the antitrust laws do not prohibit the existence of labor organizations or their "lawfully carrying out" their "legitimate objectives."

The full meaning of Section 6 standing alone is quite nebulous; in order to determine what concerted employee activity is exempted from the antitrust laws, it is necessary to give some content to the phrase "lawfully carrying out . . . legitimate objectives." The operative words "lawfully" and "legitimate" suggest, of course, the two-part formulation of the common law: The concerted activity must not itself be an illegal means, and it must be justified by a legitimate purpose. But the content that the common law gave to these two tests was itself amorphous. Further light is cast upon the scope of the Section 6 exemption by Section 20.

Section 20 of the Clayton Act consists of two paragraphs. The first of these sought to eliminate the broad-scale use of labor injunctions by revitalizing the classical requirement of equity jurisdiction that there must be actual or threatened injury and no adequate remedy at law before an injunction will issue—a requirement that had fallen by the wayside with the growth of

---

[55]Gregory, *supra* note 1 at 205, 208.

labor-injunction practice prior to the turn of the century.[56] In this paragraph Congress referred to the cases it was dealing with as those "between an employer and employees, or between persons employed and persons seeking employment, involving, or growing out of, a dispute concerning terms or conditions of employment."

The second paragraph of Section 20 limits labor injunctions by a different technique. It describes several basic categories of concerted labor activity, and provides that none of these activities shall "be considered or held to be violations of any law of the United States," and that even if there is injury and no adequate remedy at law, so that an injunction might issue under the first paragraph of Section 20, "no such . . . injunction shall prohibit" any of the described activities. Needless to say, Congress did not intend to legitimate violent acts, physical injury to persons or property, threats of such conduct, or similar illegal means. The categories of activity legalized by the second paragraph of Section 20 reflect this at several points. Persuading others to strike must be "by peaceful means"; proselytizing for a union is limited to "any place where any such person or persons may lawfully be," and the persuasion must be exercised "peacefully." One may persuade others to cease to patronize "by peaceful and lawful means." Groups may "peaceably" assemble, "in a peaceful manner, and for lawful purposes." With the sole exception of the last-quoted phrase, Section 20 makes no reference to legality of purpose. To the contrary, the final category of activity legitimated by the section indicates that Congress intended to extend immunity without regard to the objective of the activity, so long as the activity did not fall within any established, non-labor-oriented category of illegality at common law: No one, singly or in concert, is to be restrained "from doing any act or thing which might lawfully be done in the absence of such [labor] dispute by any party thereto." The section thus appeared to remove all limitations upon the permissible purposes of concerted labor activity. Not even economic self-interest was required. The Act appeared to adopt a "civil rights" labor philosophy that had found only temporary acceptance in even the most liberal state courts.[57]

---

[56]*Id.* at 98-99; Frankfurter & Greene, *supra* note 2 at 23, 60, 200-201.
[57]Gregory, *supra* note 1 at 76-82.

The Clayton Act also amended the Sherman Act by authorizing private injunction suits to restrain violations.[58] It was such a suit that brought Sections 6 and 20 of the Clayton Act before the Supreme Court in *Duplex Printing Press Co.* v. *Deering.*[59] The defendants had imposed a secondary labor boycott in an effort to complete the organization of the newspaper-press manufacturing industry and thereby protect union gains already made in that industry against price competition from Duplex's non-union-made presses. The boycott successfully halted the movement of Duplex presses in interstate commerce, and so violated Section 1 of the Sherman Act as interpreted in the *Danbury Hatters'* case, unless the Clayton Act had changed the law.

The Supreme Court concluded that if the Clayton Act had changed the law, it had done so only to a very slight extent. The Court read the first paragraph of Section 20, requiring the absence of an adequate remedy at law, as an approval of existing practice rather than an attempt to resurrect a fallen barrier to the issuance of injunctions in labor cases. The only significance attributed to the paragraph was the restriction found to be imposed upon the second paragraph. The first paragraph's reference to cases "between an employer and employees" was read to mean between an employer and *his* employees. The second paragraph was read as legalizing the described categories of concerted activity only in such cases, since it afforded protection against injunctions issued subject to the requirements of the first paragraph. This restrictive reading was reinforced, the Court found, by the emphasis in the second paragraph "on the words 'lawful' and 'lawfully,' 'peaceful' and 'peacefully,' " in describing the activities to be afforded protection. The Court found in this emphasis legislative approval and adoption of the common law's unmanageable tests for the legality of concerted employee action, rather than a legislative command not to interfere with such action in the absence of violence or similar misconduct. Since secondary boycotts were illegal at common law, it reasoned the second paragraph of Section 20 did not mean to legalize them; this reinforced the Court's conclusion that Section 20

---

[58]38 Stat 737 (1915), 15 USC §26 (1964).
[59]254 US 443 (1921). *See* Chapter 31 *infra* at notes 341-42.

applied only to cases between an employer and his own employees.[60]

Two incompatible policies toward organized labor thus were fairly well crystallized by the Clayton Act and the *Duplex* decision. The polarity of these policies should not be obscured by the fact that the Supreme Court managed to read one policy into legislation designed to promulgate the other,[61] a distortion facilitated by the remarkable turgidity of Congress' language in Sections 6 and 20. It remained for Congress to design and enact legislation that would effectuate its policy of fostering collective bargaining in the face of opposition, not only from employers, but from the Supreme Court as well.

C. The Railway Labor Act

In *Adair* v. *United States*,[62] the Supreme Court had invalidated only Section 10 of the Erdman Act, and the statutory machinery for settlement of railway labor disputes remained intact. The report of President Cleveland's United States Strike Commission was joined by others in 1902 and 1915 making similar recommendations for the fostering of labor relations based upon collective bargaining between employers and labor organizations.[63] The Wilson Administration, under which Congress had enacted the Clayton Act provisions that Samuel Gompers had hopefully dubbed "labor's charter of freedom," extended more effective protection to the labor movement when, in 1917, government intervention to prevent labor disputes became necessary to maintain the production of war materials. President Wilson established the War Labor Conference Board in early 1918, and upon its recommendations established the National War Labor Board.

The fundamental policy adopted by the new Board was as follows:

> The right of workers to organize in trade unions and to bargain collectively, through chosen representatives, is recognized and

---

[60]*Id.* at 470-74.
[61]*Id.* at 484-86 (Brandeis, J., dissenting).
[62]208 US 161 (1908).
[63]ANTHRACITE COAL STRIKE COMM. REP., S. DOC. No. 6, 58th Cong. Spec. Sess., 63 (1902); UNITED STATES COMM. ON INDUSTRIAL RELATIONS REPORT, published in 1915, is carefully analyzed in Adams, AGE OF INDUSTRIAL VIOLENCE 1910-15 (1966).

affirmed. This right shall not be denied, abridged, or interfered with by the employers in any manner whatsoever.[64]

Employers who persisted, in defiance of orders of the Board, in tactics designed to discourage organization of their employees—such as discharge for union activities, espionage, and interrogation of employees—in several cases found their businesses seized and operated by the government.[65]

Although business and government repudiated the collective bargaining policy as a general proposition when the crisis of war was past, the Railway Shopmen's strike in 1922 ultimately produced, in 1926, a statute that successfully established the collective bargaining policy on the railroads: the Railway Labor Act.[66] In addition to machinery for settlement of minor disputes, i.e., employee grievances arising under collective agreements, the Act established a presidentially appointed board with authority to mediate contract-negotiation disputes, implementing a statutory duty imposed upon both sides to make "every reasonable effort to make and maintain agreements concerning rates of pay, rules, and working conditions." Should mediation fail and the parties be unwilling to submit to arbitration, the Board was to notify the President if the dispute threatened a disruption of interstate commerce sufficient to deprive any section of the country of essential transportation services. The President might then appoint an "emergency" board with power to investigate and report upon the dispute. During this process, the statute imposed a moratorium for up to 60 days upon any change in the status quo by either party to the dispute.

The provisions of the Railway Labor Act had been largely negotiated in advance by the railroads and the railroad brotherhoods.[67] The 60-day embargo had been conceded by labor in exchange for provisions protecting union organizational efforts. The Act provided that "collective action, without interference, influence or coercion exercised by either party over the self-organization or designation of representatives by the other" was

---

[64]NATIONAL WAR LABOR BOARD, PRINCIPLES AND RULES OF PROCEDURE 4 (1919); COX & BOK, *supra* note 21 at 81.

[65]Cox & Bok, *supra* note 21 at 81.

[66]44 Stat 577 (1926), 45 USC §§161-63 (1964).

[67]Cox & Bok, *supra* note 21 at 113.

to be the manner in which representatives of parties to labor disputes under the Act should be selected.

The Railway Labor Act was challenged in *Texas & New Orleans R.R. Co.* v. *Brotherhood of Railway & S.S. Clerks,*[68] which reached the Supreme Court in 1930. The railroad had sought to establish a company-dominated union and in so doing had engaged in a campaign of discharges for union activity and other forms of coercion. Since the Act did not provide any means of enforcement of the employees' right to select their representatives without "interference, influence or coercion" by the employer, the union brought suit in federal court to enjoin the employer's anti-union activities. The Supreme Court upheld the suit, and in doing so removed major obstacles to further legislative implementation of the policy fostering collective bargaining.

Specifically, the Court recognized that Congress, in exercising its power to regulate commerce,

> may facilitate the amicable settlements of disputes which threaten the service of the necessary agencies of interstate transportation. In shaping its legislation to this end, Congress was entitled to take cognizance of actual conditions and to address itself to practicable measures. The legality of collective action on the part of employees in order to safeguard their proper interests is not to be disputed. . . . Congress was not required to ignore this right of the employees but could safeguard it and seek to make their appropriate collective action an instrument of peace rather than of strife.[69]

Adair v. *United States*[70] was distinguished upon the unconvincing basis that, unlike the Erdman Act, the Railway Labor Act "does not interfere with the normal exercise of the right of the carrier to select its employees or to discharge them," but is aimed rather "at the interference with the right of employees to have representatives of their own choosing."[71] Freedom to engage in such interference was not a right protected by the Constitution.

D. The Norris-LaGuardia Act

The last piece of major labor legislation enacted before the advent of the New Deal was the Norris-LaGuardia Act.[72] The

---

[68]281 US 548 (1930).
[69]*Id.* at 570.
[70]208 US 161 (1908).
[71]Texas & N.O.R.R. Co. v. Bhd. of Ry. Clerks, *supra* note 68 at 571.
[72]47 Stat 70 (1932), 29 USC §§101-15 (1964).

Supreme Court's decisions upholding the constitutionality of the Railway Labor Act as an exercise of the national power to regulate interstate commerce had not overturned the Court's established view that this power did not extend to local businesses such as manufacturing and mining, and this limited vision of the commerce power was a major factor in the shaping of the new legislation. It sought not to regulate labor relations under the commerce power, but to further the policy of collective bargaining by preventing judicial interference with labor activities in an exercise of Congress' power, under Article I, Section 8, of the Constitution, to regulate the jurisdiction of the lower federal courts under Article III.

Two important sections of the statute—Sections 4 [73] and 7 [74]—are reminiscent of Section 20 of the Clayton Act, with these exceptions:

(1) They are phrased as denials of jurisdiction, rather than as prohibitions against the issuance of injunctions;

(2) Section 7 imposes more rigid restrictions upon the issuance of labor injunctions than the mere absence of an adequate remedy at law;

(3) There is no provision giving substantive legitimacy to the activities that are thus exempted from injunction; and

(4) Primarily by a broad definition of "labor dispute" in Section 13(c), the provisions of Sections 4 and 7 are made applicable "whether or not the disputants stand in the proximate relation of employer and employee," thus avoiding possible judicial emasculation such as that suffered by the Clayton Act provisions in the *Duplex* case.

Because the Norris-LaGuardia Act operated solely to restrict federal judicial intervention in labor disputes, it has been said that the point of the Act "is not what it does for organized labor but what it permits organized labor to do for itself without judicial interference."[75] Notwithstanding this laissez-faire approach, it would be inaccurate to attribute to Congress a

---

[73] 47 Stat 70 (1932), 29 USC §104 (1964).
[74] 47 Stat 71 (1932), 29 USC §107 (1964).
[75] Gregory, *supra* note 1 at 186. For a discussion of judicial adaptation of the Norris-LaGuardia Act to enforcement of collective bargaining agreements, *see* Chapter 19 *infra*.

neutral attitude toward labor disputes in the enactment of the statute. Through the medium of eliminating judicial interference, the statute was designed to promote employer recognition of unions and thus foster the practice of collective bargaining as an institution in the conduct of labor relations. It was primarily because of limitations upon its power to regulate employer conduct under the Commerce Clause, as then construed by the Supreme Court, that Congress limited itself to this method of effectuating its policy. Section 2 of the Act contains a statement of the national policy the Act was designed to advance:

> Whereas under prevailing economic conditions, developed with the aid of governmental authority for owners of property to organize in the corporate and other forms of ownership association, the individual unorganized worker is commonly helpless to exercise actual liberty of contract and to protect his freedom of labor, and thereby to obtain acceptable terms and conditions of employment, wherefore, though he should be free to decline to associate with his fellows, it is necessary that he have full freedom of association, self-organization, and designation of representatives of his own choosing, to negotiate the terms and conditions of his employment, and that he shall be free from the interference, restraint, or coercion of employers of labor, or their agents, in the designation of such representatives or in self-organization or in other concerted activities for the purpose of collective bargaining or other mutual aid or protection. . . .[76]

Additional provisions of the Act, in furtherance of this policy, render unenforceable in federal courts the "yellow-dog" contract, by which employees obligated themselves to refrain from union membership; limit the imposition of vicarious liability upon union officials and members for acts of other agents of the union; deny injunctive relief to any party who has not attempted to settle the dispute by negotiation or resort to available governmental machinery for mediation or voluntary arbitration; and impose procedural safeguards for litigants against whom contempt sanctions are sought.

The length to which Congress went to promote union organization in the Norris-LaGuardia Act is perhaps most vividly evident in the scope given the Act by the definitional provisions in Section 13.[77] The Act was made applicable to any case involving or growing out of a labor dispute. Such a case was defined

---

[76]47 Stat 70 (1932), 29 USC §102 (1964).
[77]47 Stat 73 (1932), 29 USC §113 (1964).

as one involving "persons who are engaged in the same industry, trade, craft, or occupation; or have direct or indirect interests therein," and labor dispute was broadly defined to include "any controversy concerning terms or conditions of employment, or concerning the association or representation of persons in negotiating, fixing, maintaining, changing, or seeking to arrange terms or conditions of employment, regardless of whether or not the disputants stand in the proximate relation of employer and employee." The "allowable area of economic conflict"[78] had been enlarged, for purposes of avoiding federal injunctive action, as much as organized labor had any reason to wish.[79]

---

[78]Frankfurter & Greene, *supra* note 2, Chap. I.

[79]Gregory, *supra* note 1 at 190. For an account of American labor history during the era preceding the New Deal, *see* I. Bernstein, THE LEAN YEARS—A HISTORY OF THE AMERICAN WORKER 1920-1933 (1960).

CHAPTER 2

THE WAGNER ACT PERIOD

I. THE POLITICAL CLIMATE

The Great Depression and the advent of the New Deal spawned a political climate that was favorable to—or at least tolerant of— the major federal legislation thought necessary at the time to promote the growth of organized labor. This growth was considered by many to be essential if employees in American industry were to acquire sufficient economic leverage to bargain effectively with management. It was hoped that the end result of these concurrent developments would be an equitable division between labor and management of the spoils of private enterprise and, coincidentally, an important impetus to the revitalization of the economy. The economic conditions prevailing during the early 1930s focused attention on the plight of the working man, and economists were quick to point out that low spending power among the employees of American business would prolong the depression. The infallibility of industry management was disproved by post-1929 events, and the political influence that management could marshal against pro-union legislation was considerably diminished by the abrupt change from a boom to a bust economy.

The Norris-LaGuardia Act[1] had given organized labor a shield against judicial interference with the tools of union self-help. But by itself the Act was in fact of little value in promoting the growth of organized labor and the development of collective bargaining in American industry. Similarly, Section 7(a) of the National Industrial Recovery Act (NIRA),[2] passed by Congress in 1933, had attempted to persuade industry to recognize employee rights to organize and to bargain collectively, but the

---

[1] 47 Stat 70 (1932), 29 USC §§101-115 (1964). *See* Chapter 1 *supra*.
[2] 48 Stat 198 (1933).

absence of any power to enforce these "rights" rendered them virtually useless in the face of management's understandable hesitancy to aid the growth of organized labor. Most employers rebuffed union efforts and refused recognition and collective bargaining; in the alternative, employers created company unions and agreed to bargain with these unions, but with no others.[3] In this way an employer was able to go through the motions of recognizing and cooperating with organized labor, but was able to avoid the danger inherent in the recognition of a union that had a mind of its own. Also, while employees had a "right" to organize into labor unions, employers had a commensurate "right" to inflict serious injury—in particular, discharge—upon any employee brash enough to exercise his organizational "right."[4]

II. THE ROLE OF SENATOR WAGNER

These, then, were the conditions prevailing in 1934, when Senator Robert Wagner introduced a far-reaching bill that he felt would give the needed federal support to employee organization and to collective bargaining.[5] In particular, Senator Wagner stressed the failure of mere persuasion under Section 7(a) of the NIRA and proposed in his bill the creation of a quasi-judicial tribunal with defined legal authority and the power to have its orders enforced by court decree. In the face of well-organized industry opposition, Wagner's bill had little chance of success; however, on June 19, 1934, Congress did enact a compromise measure, Resolution 44, authorizing the President's appointment of a board with the power to order and conduct elections and the power to investigate labor controversies "arising under" Section 7(a) of the NIRA or burdening the "free flow of interstate commerce."[6] But neither Senator Wagner nor others of the same view were placated by this compromise measure, and in 1935 Wagner introduced another bill, similar to his 1934 bill.

---

[3]A. Link & W. Catton, AMERICAN EPOCH 416 (1963).
[4]For a general discussion of the failure of §7(a) of the NIRA, see I. Bernstein, TURBULENT YEARS 172-85 (1970); J. Gross, THE MAKING OF THE NATIONAL LABOR RELATIONS BOARD: 1933-1937, at 23-39, 122-30 (1974).
[5]See H. Millis & E. Brown, FROM THE WAGNER ACT TO TAFT-HARTLEY 24 (1950).
[6]48 Stat 1183 (1934). For a more complete discussion of Resolution 44 and its place in the legislative developments of the early 1930s, see Madden, The Origin and Early History of the National Labor Relations Board, 29 GEO. WASH. L. REV. 234, 237-38 (1960).

As in 1934, Senator Wagner's bill met with vigorous opposition from industry, but in 1935 this opposition was unable to create in Congress a climate incompatible with the bill's passage. But another potential obstacle arose as the Administration refused to support the Wagner bill when it was first introduced.[7] Although President Roosevelt eventually joined the Wagner camp, he delayed until after the bill had been passed by the Senate and passage by the House was a certainty. In short, the bill's passage was largely dependent upon Senator Wagner's talent for coordinating the support of his colleagues and upon the sentiment of the times. Unlike other major New Deal legislation, the Wagner Act thus was the product of a single man's efforts; and, although the political circumstances of 1935 may have been favorable to these efforts, it required Wagner's energy and expertise as a legislative midwife to bring forth the origin of modern American labor law—the Wagner Act.[8]

III. THE NATIONAL LABOR RELATIONS ACT: THE BEGINNING OF AN ERA

From the outset, Wagner considered the National Labor Relations Act to be more than a weapon against the disruption of industry by labor-management disputes. This was, of course, an important function of the Act, but in the Senator's eyes its reach was far broader.[9] As was implicit in his recurrent statements on the Senate floor in support of the bill, he envisioned the proposed legislation as an "affirmative vehicle"[10] for economic and social progress.

---

[7]In addition to Administration neutrality, there was active opposition to the Wagner Bill among several high-ranking members of the Roosevelt Administration. *See* Keyserling, *The Wagner Act: Its Origin and Current Significance*, 29 GEO. WASH. L. REV. 199, 203-204 (1960); Gross, *supra* note 4 at 148.

[8]*See* Address by Judge J. Warren Madden, Section on Labor Relations Law of the ABA, Luncheon Meeting, Aug. 9, 1966, in 1966 SECTION OF LABOR RELATIONS LAW PROCEEDINGS, MONTREAL, CANADA 24 (1967).

[9]The broad reach desired by Senator Wagner was, in fact, embodied in the final version of his bill as enacted. Despite the language of §1, which described the purpose of the Act almost exclusively in terms of "industrial strife" and "burdening or obstructing commerce," the provisions of the Act created the substantive rights and federal machinery that Senator Wagner believed would produce economic and social progress. The actual language of §1 seems to have been designed primarily to give the Act a jurisdictional basis under the Commerce Clause and did not indicate a failure by Senator Wagner to achieve the broad reach that he sought. *See* Gross, *supra* note 4 at 144.

[10]Keyserling, *supra* note 7 at 218.

Caught in the labyrinth of modern industrialism and dwarfed by the size of corporate enterprise, [the employee] can attain freedom and dignity only by cooperation with others of his group.[11]

To accomplish this broad purpose, the Act created a right for employees to organize and, unlike the earlier provisions of the NIRA, made this right legally enforceable.[12] The Act also gave meaning to this organizational right by requiring employers to bargain collectively with employees[13] through representatives chosen by the employees.[14] The cornerstone of the Act was Section 7, which originally provided:

> Employees shall have the right to self-organization, to form, join or assist labor organizations, to bargain collectively through representatives of their own choosing, and to engage in concerted activities for the purpose of collective bargaining or other mutual aid or protection.

This troika of rights—(1) the right to organize, (2) the right to bargain collectively, and (3) the right to engage in strikes, picketing, and other concerted activities—was considered essential to establish a balance of bargaining power between employer and employee and thereby to avoid the pitfalls and inadequacies which had characterized earlier labor legislation.

To enforce the substantive rights given employees by Section 7 and the specific provisions implementing those rights—particularly the provisions of Section 8 defining employer unfair labor practices—the Wagner Act established the type of administrative agency which had become a hallmark for much of the New Deal legislation. Sections 3 through 6 created the National Labor Relations Board (NLRB) and set out the essential details of its operation. Section 9, in addition to introducing into labor relations the principle of majority rule, gave the NLRB exclusive jurisdiction over questions of representation. Section 10 accorded the Board exclusive jurisdiction over the unfair labor practices defined by Section 8 and also set forth the broad outlines for NLRB procedure,[15] including provisions for judicial review and court enforcement of Board orders.[16]

---

[11]79 CONG. REC. 7565 (1935) (remarks of Senator Wagner).
[12]See Chapter 33 infra.
[13]See Chapters 13-18 infra.
[14]See Chapters 10-12 infra.
[15]See Chapters 31 and 32 infra.
[16]See Chapters 33 and 34 infra.

A conspicuous characteristic of the Wagner Act, when set in the context of the shield given employee activities by the Norris-LaGuardia Act, was its one-sided nature. The prime function of the Act was to protect employees against employer tactics designed either to obstruct organizational efforts or to withhold the fruits of those efforts. Management was given no corresponding protection against union actions, and little attention was paid to the protection of employee interests from union abuse.[17] The main function of the Act was focused on the creation of a meaningful—i.e., enforceable—right to organize and to bargain collectively; and, in fulfilling this primary function, Senator Wagner and Congress had looked no further than the needs of the employee who was bent on organizing. But Congress' tunnel vision could not have been fairly criticized at the time, for in 1935 it was generally believed that the shortcomings of federal labor law arose primarily from the inability of employees to join together into units having sufficient economic leverage to bargain with their employers. Management could and did frustrate attempts at organization with its arsenal of self-help devices; the threat of discharge, for example, was a formidable weapon during the depression, when jobs were few and far between. And in 1935 the one-sided nature of the Wagner Act did not seem to be a conspicuous deficiency, for labor unions then were a force of less than awesome proportions.[18] Furthermore, one-sided legislation may have been deliberately chosen by Senator Wagner and Congress as the best means to ensure that organizational rights were, in fact, respected and enforced. If the Wagner Act had included express restrictions on union activities, the attainment of its principal goal—protecting organizational efforts—might have been jeopardized.

Today, when critics of the Wagner Act have before them evidence of 48 years of operation and two major enactments that have emphasized the fallibilities of the Act,[19] it may be easy to criticize Congress' action in 1935. But whatever stigma may

---

[17]The §9 provision for majority rule afforded some protection to the employee—at least in the initial stage when employees chose their bargaining representative. And a proviso in §9(a) seemed to guard against union inaction by extending to each employee the "right" to present grievances to his employer.

[18]*See* I. Bernstein, *supra* note 4 at 318-51, for a colorful description of the passage of the Act. For a discussion of union membership trends during the 1930s, *see* H. Millis & R. Montgomery, ORGANIZED LABOR 192-201 (1945).

[19]The Taft-Hartley amendments, discussed in Chapter 3 *infra*, and the Landrum-Griffin amendments, discussed in Chapter 4 *infra*.

attach retroactively, it is certain that the Act was the starting point for contemporary American labor law. Whatever the justification, the Wagner Act, as set against the Norris-LaGuardia backdrop, was the statute which was intended to give labor unions the power to become an important force in American industry.

IV. CRITICISM OF THE ACT:
ONE-SIDED LEGISLATION

Critics of the Wagner Act set to work immediately following its passage by Congress in 1935. Their first step was to urge the unconstitutionality of the Act in the hope that the judiciary would be less receptive to Senator Wagner's efforts than Congress had been. In 1935, a group of 58 prominent lawyers and public figures published the "Report on the Constitutionality of the National Labor Relations Act," which was essentially a brief *pro bono publico,* setting forth the opinion that the Wagner Act was unconstitutional. This Liberty League Brief, as it was called, marshaled forces along two fronts: the Due Process Clause and the Commerce Clause. It argued that Section 9(a) and its provision for majority rule deprived minority groups and individual employees of their right to negotiate with their employers, thereby infringing the constitutional requirement of due process. More basically, the brief claimed that Congress was without jurisdiction to impose the Wagner Act's provisions upon employers and employees; the Commerce Clause, it was urged, did not give Congress the carte blanche used to pass this legislation. The Supreme Court, apparently by coincidence, lent considerable support to the arguments offered by the brief when *United States* v. *Butler*[20] and *Carter* v. *Carter Coal Co.*[21] were handed down in 1936.

The NLRB was not oblivious to the constitutional threat posed by the Liberty League Brief and by the precedents of the Supreme Court; it was thus careful not to allow the constitutional issue to be presented to the Court in an unfavorable posture. Considerable effort was made to have insignificant cases settled or terminated before court action;[22] and the Board was successful

---

[20]297 US 1 (1936) (holding the Agriculture Adjustment Act, 1933, unconstitutional).
[21]298 US 238 (1936) (holding the Bituminous Coal Conservation Act of 1935 unconstitutional).
[22]*See* Madden, *supra* note 8; Gross, *supra* note 4 at 183-88.

in delaying adjudication of the constitutional issues until 1937, when five cases presenting these issues, in what the agency believed was a satisfactory context, were brought to the Court. On April 12, 1937, in *Jones & Laughlin Steel Corp.*,[23] the Court rejected the argument of the critics of the Wagner Act and held the Act constitutional. Concluding that the Commerce Clause issue was pivotal, the Court adopted a more liberal definition of the commerce power than it had accepted in its earlier opinions—for example, in *Carter Coal Co.* The constitutional criterion, the Court said, was not the locus of the actions and conditions which Congress sought to regulate; rather, it was whether or not those actions and conditions were the *source* of burdens and obstructions to the free flow of commerce. In the light of the Wagner Act's purpose and effect, which relied on the statutory phrase "affecting commerce," the Act clearly fell within the scope of congressional powers.

With the Court's settlement of the constitutional issue, the critics of the Act changed their tack, and concentrated upon particular revisions of the statutory scheme which they considered desirable. Although some continued to press for outright repeal of the Act, most believed that any chance for its complete demise was lost when the Supreme Court handed down its decision in *Jones & Laughlin.* Numerous bills were introduced in Congress to amend the regulatory scheme created by the Norris-LaGuardia and Wagner Acts. In 1940, and again in 1941, Representative Howard W. Smith of Virginia introduced bills to amend the Wagner Act, and in each instance the bill was passed by the House but thereafter failed to be reported out of committee in the Senate.[24]

Critics took the view that the Act was one-sided legislation, slanted heavily in favor of organized labor; therefore a number of "equalizing" amendments were needed. The primary spokesmen of the campaign to equalize the Act were the United States Chamber of Commerce and the National Association of Manufacturers (NAM). The American Federation of Labor (AFL) was also in favor of limited amendments during this period;[25] it

---

[23]NLRB v. Jones & Laughlin Steel Corp., 301 US 1 (1937). *See* further discussion of the Act's constitutionality in Chapter 30 *infra.*

[24]*See* Reilly, *The Legislative History of the Taft-Hartley Act,* 29 GEO. WASH. L. REV. 285, 287 (1960).

[25]Millis & Brown, *supra* note 5 at 284.

was disturbed over certain Board decisions which it felt showed favoritism toward the emerging Congress of Industrial Organizations (CIO) unions.[26]

The drive for amendment faltered as the nation busied itself with the problems of World War II. However, a series of work stoppages in the coal industry in 1943 focused public attention on the problem of labor relations. These stoppages were especially unpopular since unions were operating under a no-strike pledge for the duration of the war. The displeasure of Congress over the strikes was reflected in the passage, over the veto of President Roosevelt, of the Smith-Connally War Labor Disputes Act.[27]

When World War II ended, a renewed campaign to amend the Wagner Act gained momentum as a result of certain well-publicized activities of some labor unions. The wartime strikes of the United Mine Workers had aroused public feeling that unions were becoming irresponsible, and both employers and the general public were disturbed over friction and division within the labor movement. These controversies often resulted in "raiding" practices between unions competing to represent certain units, and in jurisdictional disputes which caught the employer in the middle. A union tactic which received considerable news-media coverage was mass picketing during strikes. In addition, certain types of secondary boycotts came under close scrutiny, as, for example, the practice of picketing or boycotting small retail outlets rather than directly organizing the workers.[28] Finally, there were isolated instances of glaring abuses in the conduct of the internal affairs of some unions, including the charging of exorbitant dues under closed-shop conditions and cases of racketeering. It was contended that certain unions practiced discrimination in choosing their membership and expelled members under vague and undemocratic circumstances.[29]

---

[26]*See, e.g.,* the *American Can* case, 13 NLRB 1252, 4 LRRM 392 (1939).

[27]The Smith-Connally Act gave the President authority to seize and operate struck plants, made instigating a strike subject to criminal penalties, and required 30 days' notice of any labor dispute that might interrupt production. On the thirtieth day the NLRB was required to conduct a secret strike vote. Act of June 25, 1943, ch. 144, §§1-11, 57 Stat 163, appendix, 50 USC §§1501-11 (1964). §8 of the War Labor Disputes Act, 57 Stat 167, §1508 of appendix, 50 USC, dealing with the function of the NLRB to take secret ballots of employees on the question of an interruption of war production, was abolished by 5 USC §133y-16, Reorg. Plan of 1946, No. 3, Part VII, 701 (1964).

[28]Millis & Brown, *supra* note 5 at 279.

[29]*Id.* at 280.

In 1946 both Houses passed the Case Bill, aimed at curbing abuse of union power under the existent statutory scheme; but the bill was vetoed, and the House was unable to muster the necessary two-thirds vote to override the veto.[30]

The publicizing of union misconduct, however random, coupled with the effective campaign still being waged by the Chamber of Commerce and the NAM, led to continued legislative activity. Indeed, prior to 1947 most of the major provisions of the Taft-Hartley Act had been introduced in Congress in one or more forms. Professors Millis and Brown have pointed out that 230 major bills dealing with amendment of the Wagner Act were introduced from 1936 to the passage of Taft-Hartley, excluding the Taft-Hartley proposals.[31] They divide these bills into several distinct categories reflecting the major criticisms of the Wagner Act in the 12-year period:

(1) *NLRB organization and procedures:* One of the most common complaints was that the NLRB combined the functions of investigation, prosecution, and adjudication. Other dissatisfactions with the Board stemmed from its handling of evidence, its treatment of employers' rights of speech in organizational campaigns, and its use of subpoena powers. Another complaint was that there was inadequate court review provided for the Board's decisions. Proposed bills in this area ranged from changing the size of the Board to removing its unfair labor practice jurisdiction.

(2) *Representation problems:* There was much criticism of the Board's determination of appropriate bargaining units, and there were various proposals to amend the majority-rule concept of Section 9(a). Much of this controversy was directly attributable to the craft-unit question arising out of the disputes between the AFL and the CIO.

(3) *The scope and procedures of collective bargaining:* Of particular concern was the growing union practice of bargaining for the closed shop. Some of the proposals would have placed unions under the antitrust laws.

(4) *Union or employee unfair labor practices:* The one-sided nature of employer unfair labor practices also became an issue.

---

[30]H.R. 4908, 79th Cong., 2d Sess. (1946).
[31]Millis & Brown, *supra* note 5 at 333.

(5) *Stricter controls of unions and disputes:* Other proposals were offered to place restrictions on certain types of concerted activities, to place stricter legal obligations and responsibilities on unions and employers, and to provide better methods of dispute settlement.

The large number of such bills introduced in Congress in the first 12 years of the Wagner Act reflected the increasing pressure to amend the law.[32] Although no proposal was ultimately successful, except the extraordinary Smith-Connally Act, the problem areas were being explored and the foundation was being laid for legislative action in 1947.

---

[32] Developments on the state level also reflected a growing mood of disillusionment with major portions of the Wagner Act. Although a few states had passed legislation after 1937 modeled after the Wagner Act, an overall trend of restrictive legislation was established in the late forties.

By 1947, only three states still had legislation modeled after the Wagner Act. See Millis & Brown, *supra* note 5 at 316-32.

CHAPTER 3

THE TAFT-HARTLEY CHANGES

I. INDUSTRIAL UNREST AND CONGRESSIONAL RESPONSE

A. Union Growth

While pre-1947 attempts to revise the Wagner Act had not met with tangible success, such efforts did make an important contribution to the political atmosphere in 1947. When the Eightieth Congress convened in January, it was apparent that the status quo was not immune. Between 1935 and 1947 unions had flourished in the climate provided by the Norris-LaGuardia Act[1] and the Wagner Act.[2] Union membership had expanded from three to 15 million.[3] In some industries, such as coal mining, construction, railroading, and trucking, four fifths of the employees were working under collective bargaining agreements.[4] Under governmental policy prevailing during World War II, union leaders had assumed important and prestigious positions and were often consulted by the Administration in an obvious attempt to maintain internal industrial peace. This growing image of union power led one commentator to conclude in 1947 that the labor movement in the United States was the "largest, the most powerful, and the most aggressive that the world has ever seen; and the strongest unions . . . are the most powerful private economic organizations in the country."[5] Moreover, organized labor was not at all hesitant to exercise this burgeoning power to obtain the benefits it wanted.

Perhaps the most notorious example of the exercise of this power occurred during the Second World War when the United

---

[1]47 Stat 70 (1932), 29 USC §§101-115 (1964).
[2]*See* Chapter 2 *supra.*
[3]A. Cox & D. Bok, LABOR LAW CASES AND MATERIALS 130 (6th ed., 1965).
[4]*Id.*
[5]S. Slichter, THE CHALLENGE OF INDUSTRIAL RELATIONS 154 (1947).

Mine Workers under John L. Lewis conducted two prolonged and crippling strikes in which the coal miners returned to work only after the government had made substantial concessions.[6] And following the war, in 1946 a wave of strikes developed, shutting down steel mills, seaports, automobile assembly plants, and many other industries which played vital roles in the American economy.[7]

B. A Republican Congress

1. Response to President Truman's Proposals. The disorderly state of industrial relations and resulting public indignation toward union strike activity created important issues for the mid-term political campaign of 1946, when the elections established Republican majorities in both houses of Congress for the first time since 1930. On the first day of the new congressional session, 17 bills[8] dealing with labor relations were introduced, and by the end of the first week no fewer than 200 bills on the subject had been offered.[9] Additional labor bills continued to pour in during the next few weeks; added momentum was provided by President Truman's State of the Union Message, in which he proposed a limited revision of the nation's labor laws. His proposals included: (1) prevention of jurisdictional disputes, (2) prohibition of certain secondary boycotts, (3) establishment of machinery to help solve disputes arising under existing collective bargaining agreements, and (4) creation of a temporary commission to investigate the entire field of labor-management relations.[10]

When the hearings opened in the House and Senate, however, it soon became obvious that Congress had stronger legislation in mind than the President had proposed. The Senate and House committee hearings on the numerous bills did much to marshal support for statutory revision. The emphasis in the House hearings was an investigation of abuse by labor of its power; the emphasis in the Senate hearings was on the accu-

---

[6]Cox & Bok, *supra* note 3 at 130.

[7]*See* Reilly, *The Legislative History of the Taft-Hartley Act*, 29 GEO. WASH. L. REV. 285, 288 (1960).

[8]Perhaps the most outspoken advocate of change was Senator Joseph Ball of Minnesota, who had presented four bills, including Senate Bill 360, which was to become the skeleton for Title I of the Taft-Hartley Act, the title which amended the basic Wagner Act. *See* Reilly, *supra* note 7 at 289-91.

[9]*See* H. Millis & E. Brown, FROM THE WAGNER ACT TO TAFT-HARTLEY 363 (1950).

[10]*Id.* at 364.

mulation of testimony from all sides on the merits and demerits of the proposed reforms. Although major labor legislation was by no means a foregone conclusion in January, as the session progressed it became increasingly clear that such legislation was likely.

2. Problem Areas. Attention focused upon several problem areas that had come to prominence during the war and in the immediate postwar period. These were spotlighted by the hearings: (1) the secondary boycott, which had proved to be a potent tool in the hands of some unions, injuring third parties as well as the immediate parties to the labor dispute, (2) closed- and union-shop agreements, which in many instances had led to abuse and certainly contributed to labor's political and economic strength, (3) strikes and picketing, which had often turned into violence when unions were unable to achieve their goals by peaceful means, (4) corruption, which had appeared in some unions, although it was not as conspicuous during the 1940s as it later became during the 1957 McClellan Committee investigation, and (5) frequent jurisdictional disputes between unions in the construction industry, which halted many large projects for long periods as unions bickered about the rights of different employees to various job assignments.[11]

The committee hearings were extensive. Opinions differed as to their objectivity, although it was generally conceded that the Senate hearings were conducted fairly.[12] Senator Taft noted that no bill with which he had ever been concerned had ever "been considered in more detail and more thoroughly studied."[13] But as to the House proceedings, Professors Millis and Brown concluded that they "did not do credit to that body in terms of adequate and relevant analysis of the important issues

---

[11]*See* H. REP. NO. 245 on H.R. 3020, 80th Cong., 1st Sess. (1947), 1 LEGISLATIVE HISTORY OF THE LMRA 292-354; S. REP. NO. 105 on S. 1126, 80th Cong., 1st Sess. (1947), 1 LEGISLATIVE HISTORY OF THE LMRA 407-62.

[12]Senator Morse, who opposed the majority bill, stated that "the bill represents a fine example of committee work in which men devoted to the public welfare did their best to resolve their differences on a basis of fair compromise." 93 CONG. REC. 3786 (April 17, 1947); *see also* 1 LEGISLATIVE HISTORY OF THE LMRA 1000.

[13]93 CONG. REC. 3786-3787 (April 17, 1947); *see also* 1 LEGISLATIVE HISTORY OF THE LMRA 1001.

[14]Millis & Brown, *supra* note 9 at 374. The authors commented on the minority charge, that the bill was "one-sided" and that the "wishes of employers expressed during the hearings had been given full satisfaction while labor appeals were ignored" by noting that labor representatives had failed to propose any suggested legislation of their own and would not admit that there were any abuses which would stand legislative treatment. *Id.* at 372.

presented,"[14] and even the Senate debate, in their view, "did not match the difficulty of the subject or the needs of the times."[15]

3. Differences Between Senate and House Bills. The Senate and House each passed a version of a labor reform bill, with the House bill being broader in scope and more restrictive on unions. The Conference Committee was faced with the following provisions in the House bill which differed substantially from the Senate version:

(1) The NLRB was abolished, and a new board to hear cases and an agency to prosecute cases were created.

(2) A long and detailed list of concerted activities by unions were declared unlawful, and unions were placed under the antitrust laws.

(3) Employers were permitted to seek injunctions against unions' unlawful concerted activities.

(4) Economic strikes were permitted only after an employee vote of approval and after notice and a "cooling-off" period.

(5) Mass picketing was made unlawful.

(6) Employer payments to joint health and welfare funds were outlawed.

(7) Industry-wide bargaining was severely limited.

(8) Detailed regulation of internal union activity was provided.

(9) Strikes by government employees were banned.

(10) Political contributions or expenditures in national elections were banned.[16]

On the following points, the two bills were similar though not identical:

(1) Certain union unfair labor practices were specified.

(2) "Free speech" rights were extended to employers.

(3) The closed shop was outlawed.

(4) Involuntary checkoff was prohibited.

---

[15]*Id.* at 381.
[16]*Id.* at 383.

(5) Supervisors were removed from coverage of the NLRA.

(6) Bargaining rights were denied to unions having Communist officers.

(7) The government was empowered to seek injunctions in "national emergency" disputes.

(8) An independent agency for mediation and conciliation was established outside the Department of Labor.

(9) Provision was made for damage suits in federal district courts for violation of collective bargaining agreements and for certain unlawful concerted activities.[17]

C. Presidential Veto

When the Conference Committee had completed its work, the resulting bill reflected the fact that the Senate Taft bill had served as the model for the final draft.[18] The conference report was passed by the House 320 to 79 and by the Senate 54 to 17. However, President Truman vetoed the bill, stating that, in his view:

> The bill taken as a whole would reverse the basic direction of our national labor policy, inject the Government into private economic affairs on an unprecedented scale, and conflict with important principles of our democratic society. Its provisions would cause more strikes, not fewer. It would contribute neither to industrial peace nor to economic stability and progress. It would be a dangerous stride in the direction of a totally managed economy. It contains seeds of discord which would plague this Nation for years to come.[19]

Congress was willing to risk the test of history.[20] The veto was overridden by a vote of 68 to 25 in the Senate and 331 to 83 in the House, and the bill became law on August 22, 1947.

---

[17]*Id.*

[18]S. 1126, 80th Cong., 1st Sess. (1947). The only two major provisions on which the Senate yielded were the sections dealing with strikes by government employees and political contributions by unions.

[19]President's Message on Veto of Taft-Hartley Bill (June 20, 1947), 20 LRRM 22 (1947).

[20]According to Gerard Reilly, who served as special counsel to the Senate Labor Committee and assisted in the drafting of the bill, President Truman, in his veto message, "relied upon a staff memorandum of the N.L.R.B. attacking the conference bill in the same extreme and irrational terms that characterized the C.I.O. literature on the subject. . . . Senator Taft . . . on the networks that same evening was able to make an effective rebuttal." Reilly, *supra* note 7 at 300. *But see* Millis & Brown, *supra* note 9 at 389-90, regarding the President's study of the legislation and the preparation of the veto message.

II. THE NEW AMENDMENTS

The new statute, named the Labor Management Relations Act of 1947, shifted the emphasis of federal labor law. From an attitude of federal protection for the rights of employees to organize into unions and to engage in concerted economic activity and collective bargaining, the emphasis shifted to a more balanced[21] statutory scheme that added restrictions on unions and also guaranteed certain freedoms of speech and conduct to employers and individual employees.[22]

A. Employee Rights

The change was reflected in the amended Section 1 "Findings and Policy" and in the amended Section 7 "Rights of Employees." Whereas Section 1 in the Wagner Act spoke of "denial by some employers of the right of employees to organize . . ." and "inequality of bargaining power between employees . . . and employers . . . ," the amended Section 1 was directed equally at labor organizations:

> [C]ertain practices by some labor organizations . . . have the intent or the necessary effect of burdening or obstructing commerce . . . through strikes . . . or concerted activities. . . . The elimination of such practices is a necessary condition to the assurance of the rights herein guaranteed.

It should be noted, however, that Congress left unchanged the original commitment in the final paragraph of Section 1, which declares the policy of the United States to be that of

> encouraging the process and procedure of collective bargaining and . . . protecting the exercise of full freedom of association, self-organization, and designation of representatives of their own choosing. . . .

The amended Section 7 gave employees the right to *refrain* from engaging in activities protected in the original Section 7:[23]

> [Employees] . . . shall also have the right to refrain from any or all such activities except to the extent that such right may be affected

---

[21]Organized labor contended that the new statute was overbalanced in favor of employers and dubbed the legislation a "slave labor" law. Millis & Brown, *supra* note 9 at 389. *See* notes 47-48 and accompanying text *infra*.

[22]The entire Labor Management Relations Act contains five titles, but only Title I is treated here because the scope of this book is limited to the National Labor Relations Act, which Title I amended.

[23]*See* Chapter 6 *infra* at notes 3-4 for a detailed comparison of the old §7 and the amended version.

by an agreement requiring membership in a labor organization as a condition of employment as authorized in section 8(a)(3).

B. Structural Changes in Board Administration

Some of the earlier criticisms of the Wagner Act had been directed at the procedure and structure of the NLRB itself.[24] Several changes were designed to meet those criticisms. Section 3(a) increased the size of the Board from three to five members. Section 3(d) separated the office of General Counsel from the Board proper. The General Counsel was given supervision over the attorneys employed by the Board and over the officers and employees in the regional offices. He was also given final authority over investigating charges, issuing complaints, and prosecuting them before the Board. The function of adjudication was thus separated from investigation and prosecution.[25]

C. Union Unfair Labor Practices

Section 8(b), which creates six union unfair labor practices, was added in its entirety. Section 8(b)(1) forbids restraint or coercion of employees "in the exercise of the rights guaranteed in Section 7."[26] Section 8(b)(2) makes it an unfair labor practice for a union "to cause . . . an employer to discriminate against an employee in violation of subsection (a)(3). . . ."[27] Section 8(b)(3) places an affirmative duty on employee representatives to bargain collectively with their employer.[28]

Sections 8(b)(4)(A), (B), and (C) outlaw various secondary boycotts.[29] Section 8(b)(4)(D) makes it an unfair labor practice for a union to force or require assignment of work in a jurisdictional dispute.[30]

Section 8(b)(5) forbids a union to charge excessive or discriminatory initiation fees.[31] Section 8(b)(6) is directed at the practice

---

[24]*See* Chapter 2 *supra.*
[25]*See* Chapter 32 *infra.*
[26]*See* Chapter 6 *infra.*
[27]*See* Chapter 7 *infra.* The "closed shop" was made unlawful, but a "Union Shop" was allowed in those states where it was lawful under state law. *See* §8(a)(3) *proviso* and §14(b) and Chapter 29 *infra.*
[28]*See* Chapter 13-18 *infra.*
[29]*See* Chapter 25 *infra.*
[30]*See* Chapter 27 *infra.*
[31]*See* Chapter 29 *infra.*

of "featherbedding," i.e., causing or attempting to cause an employer to pay for services not performed.[32]

D. "Free Speech" Proviso

Section 8(c), the "free speech" proviso, was added as a guarantee for both employers and unions:

> The expressing of any views, argument, or opinion, or the dissemination thereof, whether in written, graphic, or visual form, shall not constitute or be evidence of an unfair labor practice under any of the provisions of this Act, if such expression contains no threat of reprisal or force or promise of benefit.

E. Collective Bargaining Duties

Section 8(d) sets out in rudimentary form and duties of the parties in collective bargaining:

> To bargain collectively is the performance of the mutual obligation of the employer and the representative of the employees to meet at reasonable times and confer in good faith with respect to wages, hours, and other terms and conditions of employment . . . [but] . . . such obligation does not compel either party to agree to a proposal or require the making of a concession.[33]

Section 8(d) also provides that either party to a collective bargaining contract desiring termination or modification of the contract must (1) serve a 60-day written notice prior to the expiration date of the contract, (2) offer to meet and confer, (3) notify the Federal Mediation and Conciliation Service (and any comparable state mediation agency) within 30 days, and (4) continue all the terms of the agreement in full force and effect,

> without resorting to strike or lockout . . . for a period of sixty days after such notice is given or until the expiration date of such contract, whichever occurs later. . . . Any employee who engages in a strike within the sixty-day period specified in this subsection shall lose his status as an employee . . . for the purposes of sections 8, 9, and 10. . . .[34]

---

[32]See Chapter 27 infra.
[33]See Chapter 13 infra.
[34]See Chapters 13 and 21 infra.

F. Representation Under Section 9

Section 9 also made important changes. Section 9(a) gives individual employees the right to present grievances to their employer "and to have such grievances adjusted, without the intervention of the bargaining representative, as long as the adjustment is not inconsistent with the . . . collective bargaining contract" and if the "bargaining representative has been given an opportunity to be present. . . ."[35]

Section 9(b) provides that the Board shall not: (1) combine professional and nonprofessional employees in the same unit unless a majority of the professional employees vote for inclusion; (2) decide that any craft unit is inappropriate on the ground that a different unit has been established by a prior Board determination, unless a majority in the proposed craft-unit vote against separate representation; or (3) include plant guards in a unit with other employees.[36]

Section 9(c) made changes in the area of representation questions. It gives the employer the right to file a representation petition and employees the right to file a petition to decertify a union. It forbids the Board to treat unaffiliated unions in a manner different from affiliated unions. Section 9(c)(3) was also added:

No election shall be directed in any bargaining unit . . . within which, in the preceding twelve-month period, a valid election shall have been held. Employees on strike . . . not entitled to reinstatement shall not be eligible to vote. . . . In any election where none of the choices . . . receives a majority, a run-off shall be conducted . . . between the two choices receiving the largest and second largest number of valid votes. . . .[37]

Section 9(e) established a procedure whereby 30 percent of the employees in a bargaining unit could request an election to rescind a union security agreement.[38]

G. Regulation of Internal Union Affairs

Section 9(f) was directed at regulating internal affairs of unions and required any union that desired coverage or protection

---

[35]See Chapter 28 *infra.*
[36]See Chapter 11 *infra.*
[37]See Chapter 10 *infra.*
[38]See Chapter 29 *infra.*

under the Act to file with the Secretary of Labor copies of its constitution and bylaws and a report showing:

(1) The name of the organization and its principal place of business.

(2) The name and title of, and compensation paid to, any officer or agent who was paid more than $5,000 in the preceding year.

(3) The manner in which these officers were selected.

(4) Initiation fees for new members.

(5) Dues of regular members.

(6) A detailed statement of the procedure followed with respect to qualifications for membership, election of officers and stewards, calling of meetings, levying of assessments, imposition of fines, authorization of bargaining demands, ratification of contract terms, authorization for strikes, authorization for disbursement of union funds, audit of union financial transactions, participation in insurance or other benefit plans, and grounds for expulsion of members.

Also required was a report showing union receipts and their sources, total union assets and liabilities, and a list of disbursements made and their purposes.

Section 9(g) provided that any union failing to meet the foregoing filing requirements would not be certified under the Act and no complaint would be issued on a charge filed by it. Section 9(h) provided for the filing of non-Communist affidavits. No benefits of the Act would be accorded to any labor organization whose officers had not submitted affidavits within the preceding 12 months showing that they were free from Communist Party affiliation or belief.[39]

H. Procedural Changes

Section 10(a) gives the Board authority to cede jurisdiction to state agencies in certain cases, even though the dispute might affect commerce, where the applicable state law is consistent

---

[39]§§ 9(f), (g), and (h) were repealed by the Landrum-Griffin Act in 1959. *See* Chapter 4 *infra*.

with the NLRA.[40] Section 10(b) provides that no complaint may issue where the unfair labor practice occurred more than six months prior to the filing of the charge.[41]

Section 10(e) provides that "findings of the Board with respect to questions of fact if supported by substantial evidence on the record considered as a whole shall be conclusive."[42]

I. Injunctions

Section 10(j), the "discretionary injunction" section, was added. It provides that when the Board has issued a complaint charging that any person has engaged or is engaged in an unfair labor practice, it may petition a district court for appropriate temporary relief or restraining order as the court deems "just and proper."[43] Section 10(k) relates to Section 8(b)(4)(D). It requires the Board to hear and determine cases involving jurisdictional strikes unless the parties are able to show within 10 days that they have settled the dispute themselves.[44] Section 10(1), the "mandatory injunction" section, requires the Board to give priority over all other cases to any charge of an unfair labor practice under Sections 8(b)(4)(A), (B), and (C)—the secondary boycott provisions. If there are reasonable grounds for believing the charge to be true, the Board officer or regional attorney is required to petition a district court for injunctive relief pending Board determination.[45]

J. "Right to Work" Laws

Finally, Section 14(b) was added to give state "right to work" laws precedence over the new union-shop proviso in Section 8(a)(3):

> Nothing in this Act shall be construed as authorizing the execution or application of agreements requiring membership in a labor organization as a condition of employment in any State or Territory where such . . . is prohibited. . . .[46]

---

[40]See Chapters 30 and 31 infra.
[41]See Chapter 32 infra.
[42]See Chapter 34 infra at notes 62-82.
[43]See Chapters 32 and 33 infra.
[44]See Chapter 27 infra.
[45]See Chapters 25 and 33 infra. With respect to §8(b)(4)(D) jurisdictional dispute cases, "where appropriate," §10(1) injunctions are also made available (but are not mandatory). See Chapter 27 infra.
[46]See Chapter 29 infra.

III. THE REACTION

A. Labor Response

American labor policy had undergone its second sweeping revision in 12 years. The initial response of organized labor to passage of the Taft-Hartley Act was to publicize its opposition to what it called the "slave labor law." It was the objective of labor leaders of all unions to work steadfastly for repeal.[47] This response was not surprising, for it was consistent with the position that organized labor had taken throughout the legislative proceedings. In the face of some recognized shortcomings within the labor movement, and even in the light of President Truman's limited call for labor legislation, the unions had decided to oppose any and all revision of the Wagner Act. In adopting this intransigent position, labor virtually destroyed any chance that it might have had of exerting significant influence on the final outcome of Taft-Hartley. The result was a statute on which union views had no measurable impact. Consequently, labor's critics were able to exert the most influential pressures on the 1947 legislation. As Professors Archibald Cox and Derek Bok explain:

> [T]he Taft-Hartley Act was the product of diverse forces—the offspring, a critic might say, of an unhappy union between the opponents of all collective bargaining and the critics of the unions' abuses of power. The former group was probably the more influential of the two in writing the Taft-Hartley amendments, for organized labor's unfortunate decision to oppose all legislation left its sympathetic critics in a dilemma.[48]

Union leadership continued to hold to this "all or nothing at all" attitude in the period immediately following passage of the Act. Its aim was not to amend but to repeal. The first manifestation of this approach was seen in 1948, when union leaders—erroneously assessing the upset victory of President Truman—thought the time had come to wipe Taft-Hartley off the books. In the words of one commentator, labor viewed the election as a "popular mandate" to "return to the good old days of the Wagner Act."[49] Leaders of both the AFL and the CIO publicly

---

[47]A. McAdams, POWER AND POLITICS IN LABOR LEGISLATION 29 (1964).
[48]Cox & Bok, *supra* note 3 at 133.
[49]Aaron, *Amending the Taft-Hartley Act: A Decade of Frustration*, 11 INDUS. & LABOR REL. REV. 327, 329 (1958).

urged Congress to follow a "two-package approach" toward labor legislation: It should immediately repeal Taft-Hartley and restore the status quo of the Wagner Act; only then should it consider the Administration's proposed amendments.[50]

B. Congressional Response

The House response was to pass a bill which substantially reenacted Taft-Hartley. In the Senate, a substitute bill sponsored by Senator Taft was passed in place of an Administration bill. At this point, the Administration chose to drop the fight, and Taft-Hartley was left on the books unchanged. The tactics of organized labor had been proved unrealistic:

> Their "all or nothing" demands seemed arrogant and unreasonable, especially when contrasted with the deceptively conciliatory proposals of Taft to discuss and, if need be, amend or eliminate any provision of the existing law that was demonstrably unworkable or prejudicial to labor's legitimate interests. Whatever slight hope there might have been for popular support of substantial revision of Taft-Hartley was shattered by the unions' intransigent position.[51]

C. Stalemate Years

The years 1949 to 1952 were marked by a general stalemate in attempts to revise Taft-Hartley. This was a period of intense internal rivalry within the labor movement. Individual unions embarked on a program of pursuing their individual interests, opposing any suggestions from rival unions which might threaten their own positions.[52]

In the early 1950s both management and labor began developing programs of proposed legislation to amend the National Labor Relations Act. Management groups had two primary goals: to close "loopholes" in Section 8(b)(4), which still permitted certain types of secondary activities (such as "hot cargo" agreements and "roving picketing") and to establish strict regulations for organizational picketing. As they had done in 1937, management interests set up an informal organization, known as the Secondary Boycott Committee, to further these goals. Its first

---

[50]*Id.*
[51]*Id.* at 330.
[52]McAdams, *supra* note 47 at 32.

move was to undertake a broad program aimed at educating the business community, the public, and Congress. Two subcommittees were formed, one concentrating on drafting legislation and presenting it to Congress, and the other providing materials aimed at the general public.[53] In contrast to labor, management was able to put aside other differences and present a generally united front on matters pertaining to labor legislation.[54]

Certain labor unions did develop specific proposals that they wished to see enacted. For example, the building and construction trades desired a provision allowing "prehire" agreements. Since the employers in the building industry depend heavily on transient labor, each union wanted to be allowed to negotiate a contract with a contractor before the union's status as a representative had been certified by the time-consuming process of an NLRB election, or even before the workers were hired for the job. Such an arrangement was an unfair labor practice under Taft-Hartley.

Although both management and labor groups had in mind definite amendments to the NLRA during the early 1950s, neither side was able to generate much support for its proposals. It was not until 1957 that the issue of labor legislation again came to the forefront.

---

[53]*Id.* at 68-69.
[54]*Id.* at 71.

CHAPTER 4

THE LANDRUM-GRIFFIN CHANGES

I. THE IMPETUS OF LEGISLATIVE INVESTIGATION

The attention of the nation was focused once again on labor problems in 1957 when the Senate Committee on Improper Activities in Labor-Management Relations, chaired by Senator McClellan (D—Ark), opened hearings to investigate alleged wrongdoings in the labor-management field.[1] As the hearings progressed, they gradually began to center on corruption in several strong unions. Testimony indicated that certain high officials within these unions were engaged in misconduct "ranging from embezzlement to illicit secret profits."[2] Much public feeling was aroused by the disclosures, and one commentator concluded that the activity of the committee "was clearly the motivating force in bringing about the passage of legislation in 1959."[3]

The public clamor and legislative interest in corrective labor legislation were directed primarily at achieving internal union democracy, a subject not theretofore effectively covered by the national labor laws.[4] At the same time, the labor unions attempted to turn congressional attention to amending the Taft-Hartley Act.

---

[1]See A. McAdams, POWER AND POLITICS IN LABOR LEGISLATION 36–40 (1964), for a discussion of the political make-up of the McClellan Committee. See also THE LABOR REFORM LAW (Washington: BNA Books, 1959).

[2]A. Cox, LAW AND THE NATIONAL LABOR POLICY 18 (1960).

[3]McAdams, supra note 1 at 39.

[4]As Professor Benjamin Aaron pointed out, "[T]he Labor Management Relations (Taft-Hartley) Act of 1947 included only a few provisions purporting to regulate the conduct of union government." Aaron, The Labor-Management Reporting and Disclosure Act of 1959, 73 HARV. L. REV. 851 (1960). During passage of Taft-Hartley a campaign had begun to strengthen, through federal legislation, internal union democracy. It was "formally launched by the American Civil Liberties Union, which submitted a Trade Union Democracy bill to the Congress during the 1947 hearings on new labor legislation." Id. See Chapter 3 supra. See also Aaron & Komaroff, Statutory Regulation of Internal Union Affairs—II, 44 ILL. L. REV. 631, 636-72 (1949).

In 1958 Congress made its first unsuccessful response to the McClellan Committee disclosures when the Senate passed the bipartisan Kennedy-Ives bill[5] by a vote of 88-to-1. This bill had five titles directed at abuses that had been spotlighted by the McClellan Committee and a sixth title containing limited amendments to the Labor Management Relations Act of 1947. The sixth title had been added as a "sweetener" for certain unions in return for their support of the bill.[6] The union strategy was to oppose any labor legislation that did not also include several desired amendments to the 1947 Act.

Despite its overwhelming passage in the Senate, the bill had received only lukewarm backing of most of the senators, and it was doomed to failure in the House. The sweeteners had not succeeded in stimulating enthusiastic labor support for the bill. The AFL-CIO ostensibly supported it, but George Meany's comment, "God save us from our friends,"[7] reflected labor's true attitude.

II. THE POLITICAL CLIMATE

The national elections in the fall of 1958 had a misleading effect on efforts to pass labor legislation in 1959. The Republican party, attempting to capitalize on the public resentment raised by the McClellan disclosures, chose to make "right to work" laws a major issue in a number of states.[8] Fearing widespread enactment of new right-to-work legislation, organized labor threw all the opposition it could muster into these campaigns. As a result, all the right-to-work laws but one were defeated and 70 percent of the AFL-CIO-supported candidates for Congress won.[9] The Republican response bordered on despair, and "union bosses" were generally credited with the Democratic sweep.[10] Conversely, the Democrats were elated; however, the Democratic leadership was convinced that it was necessary to pass a labor reform bill, plus certain amendments to the Taft-Hartley Act, in order to demonstrate the "responsibility" of the Democratic party in the area of union regula-

---

[5]S. 3974, 85th Cong., 2d Sess. (1958).
[6]McAdams, *supra* note 1 at 45.
[7]*Id.* at 46.
[8]*Id.* at 2.
[9]*Id.* at 48.
[10]N.Y. Times, Dec. 1958, at 1, col. 1.

tion.[11] A combination of factors—McClellan Committee publicity, confidence given labor by the success of the 1958 elections, Democratic determination to pass a bill, and public endorsement of legislation by President Eisenhower—resulted in passage of the Landrum-Griffin Act, a statute which many have considered to be less favorable to labor than the political climate of 1958 would have indicated.[12]

III. SENATE ACTION

Early in the 1959 session, Senator John F. Kennedy found himself uncomfortably situated in his relations with organized labor. The Democratic leadership in Congress had concluded that the Kennedy-Ives bill had failed in the House in 1958 because of the Title VI sweeteners added to garner union support. They therefore wanted to pursue a two-package approach by splitting the reform measures and the amendments to the 1947 Act into separate bills. They intended first to secure passage of a reform measure, then proceed with the amendments.[13] Influential labor leaders, however, made it known to Kennedy that they would not support any reform bill that did not also contain the sweeteners. Labor's refusal to compromise proved a major tactical error. The labor demand for Taft-Hartley amendments had opened a Pandora's box, and now labor was unable to control the cumulative response of a national demand for more restrictive Taft-Hartley amendments.

Acceding to union wishes, Senator Kennedy introduced the Kennedy-Ervin bill.[14] It was closely modeled upon the 1958 bill and, like its predecessor, contained the sweeteners.[15] Other bills, including the McClellan bill[16] and the Administration bill,[17] also were introduced.

---

[11]McAdams, *supra* note 1 at 9.
[12]For treatment of the legislative background of the Landrum-Griffin Act, *see* THE LABOR REFORM LAW, *supra* note 1; LEGISLATIVE HISTORY OF THE LABOR-MANAGEMENT REPORTING AND DISCLOSURE ACT OF 1959 (GPO, 1959).
[13]McAdams, *supra* note 1 at 49.
[14]S. 505, 86th Cong., 1st Sess. (1959) (drafted in major part by Professor Archibald Cox and union attorney Arthur Goldberg).
[15]The sweeteners were found in S. 505, Title VI, which amended the 1947 Act. They included §603(a) (authorizing prehire agreements in the building and construction industry), §604 (amending §9(c)(3) to permit voting by economic strikers), and §605 (restricting the definition of "supervisor" in §2(11)).
[16]S. 1137, 86th Cong., 1st Sess. (1959) (containing no Taft-Hartley amendments).
[17]S. 748, 86th Cong., 1st Sess. (1959) (sponsored by Senator Goldwater and containing revisions to Taft-Hartley desired by both labor and management).

When the Labor Subcommittee, chaired by Senator Kennedy, began its hearings, it became apparent that management would not support a bill that included sweeteners only for labor and not for management.[18] Organized employers thus demanded further statutory restrictions on union activities, especially picketing and boycotts.[19] Nevertheless, the Administration bill, which contained the desired management sweeteners, was defeated in subcommittee; and the Kennedy-Ervin bill, after referral to the full committee, was reported out with no management sweeteners.[20]

Senators McClellan and Ervin asked Senator Kennedy to drop the Title VI sweeteners in return for full support of the reform measures and aid in defeating any amendments offered from the floor that were unfavorable to labor. The labor leadership, again misreading the temper of Congress, refused to support the bill without the Title VI provisions.[21] As a result, Senator McClellan introduced a floor amendment which became known as the McClellan "Bill of Rights of Members of Labor Organizations."[22] This amendment provided for more extensive regulation of internal union affairs than did the Kennedy bill. Following an impassioned speech by Senator McClellan, the amendment passed by the slim margin of 47 to 46.[23]

After the passage of the McClellan amendment, several other amendments which had previously been expected to meet with rejection, also were passed, further changing the complexion of the original bill. Added were provisions dealing with economic strikers, "hot cargo" agreements, the "no man's land" jurisdictional question, and organizational picketing. After some modification of the Bill of Rights section, the bill (now with seven titles)[24] was passed and sent to the House.

IV. STRUGGLE IN THE HOUSE

During the interim before House consideration of the Senate bill, the AFL-CIO developed a strategy that it would follow in

---

[18]*Hearings on Labor-Management Reform Legislation Before the Subcomm. on Labor of the Senate Comm. on Labor and Public Welfare*, 86th Cong., 1st Sess. 145-48 (1959).

[19]*See* Aaron, *supra* note 4 at 1088.

[20]S. 1555, 86th Cong., 1st Sess. (1959).

[21]McAdams, *supra* note 1 at 87-88.

[22]105 CONG. REC. 5810 (daily ed., Apr. 22, 1959).

[23]*Id.* at 5827.

[24]McClellan's Bill of Rights amendment became Title I of the seven titles of S. 1555.

the House. It was decided that no further support would be given to the Kennedy bill because of distaste for the Title I Bill of Rights section and the Title VII provisions dealing with hot-cargo agreements and organizational picketing.[25] However, at the same time labor intended to continue to press for its desirable Title VII provisions amending Taft-Hartley.

When hearings began in the House Labor Committee, the AFL-CIO felt it had enough votes to bottle up the Kennedy bill in committee. Again, labor miscalculated its strength. The House was under the same pressure to pass a bill as the Senate had been. When it finally became obvious that a bill was, indeed, emerging from committee, union leaders adopted the strategy of supporting a straight reform bill without any amendments to the LMRA.[26] But this concession had come too late. The Administration and many influential congressmen were now pressing for the restrictive amendments dealing with hot-cargo agreements, secondary boycotts, and organizational picketing. Title VII remained intact. After several weeks of wrangling, the committee reported out the Elliott bill,[27] which was, nevertheless, more favorable to labor than the Senate bill.[28]

Once the Elliott bill had been reported out of committee, other bills were introduced. The most important were the Shelley[29] and the Landrum-Griffin bills.[30] The Shelley bill was substantially the same as the Elliott bill except that it deleted the Title VII provisions offensive to labor. The Landrum-Griffin proposals were also substantially identical to the Elliott bill but included stringent provisions in Title VII relating to hot-cargo agreements, secondary boycotts, and recognitional and organizational picketing. The AFL-CIO supported the Shelley bill, though it obviously stood no chance of passing.[31]

Once the Landrum-Griffin bill had been unveiled, management groups throughout the country launched a massive cam-

---

[25]McAdams, *supra* note 1 at 123.
[26]*Id.* at 148. This was the approach originally suggested by the Democratic leadership.
[27]H.R. 8342, 86th Cong., 1st Sess. (1959).
[28]Levitan, *Union Lobbyists' Contributions to Tough Labor Legislation*, 10 LAB. L.J. 675, 678 (1959).
[29]H.R. 8490, 86th Cong., 1st Sess. (1959).
[30]H.R. 8400, 8401, 86th Cong., 1st Sess. (1959).
[31]*See* Levitan, *supra* note 28 at 678.

paign of support for it. The campaign reached its peak when President Eisenhower appeared on national television and radio to plead for public support for the measure.[32] After his address, Congress was deluged with mail supporting the bill. Backers of the moderate Elliott bill, primarily the House Democratic leadership, were left in a precarious position: Labor supported the Shelley bill, but widespread public support was growing for the Landrum-Griffin bill. When debate began in the House, the Landrum-Griffin bill was substituted for the committee's Elliott bill,[33] and the Landrum-Griffin bill passed by a vote of 303 to 125.[34] The House then requested that a House-Senate conference committee be appointed to resolve the differences between it and the Senate bill.

V. RECONCILING TITLE VII

The conference committee had little trouble reconciling the first six titles of the Senate and House bills and came to agreement on these provisions in a little more than three days.[35] The real struggle was to come over the Title VII provisions.

An examination of the pertinent Title VII provisions of the two bills illustrates the major differences that had to be resolved by the committee.

A. A Jurisdictional Problem: "No Man's Land"

The first major discrepancy in the two bills concerned the "no-man's-land" question. The Senate bill provided that state agencies but *not* courts could assert jurisdiction over cases that

---

[32]McAdams, *supra* note 1 at 193-98.

[33]In commenting on the procedures employed in the House in adopting the LMRDA, Goldberg and Meiklejohn concluded:

"It is, of course, unusual for either body of Congress to adopt a bill on the floor without prior consideration by the appropriate committee. This is true of nearly all legislation, let alone legislation of the importance and far-reaching effect of that here involved.

"Yet, the Landrum-Griffin Bill was adopted by the House in precisely this unorthodox manner. The House Education and Labor Committee . . . reported out the Elliott Bill. Although the Landrum-Griffin Bill was substantially different from the Elliott Bill in major respects, it was substituted for this bill directly on the House floor and adopted without referral to the Labor Committee for study and calm consideration." Goldberg & Meiklejohn, *Title VII: Taft-Hartley Amendments, with Emphasis on the Legislative History*, 54 NW. U.L. REV. 747, 780 (1960).

[34]105 CONG. REC. 14540-14541 (daily ed., Aug. 14, 1959).

[35]McAdams, *supra* note 1 at 249-51.

the NLRB had declined to accept.[36] The Senate version further provided that when the state agencies took such jurisdiction, they had to apply federal law and enforcement and appeal would be through the federal courts. The Landrum-Griffin bill provided that state agencies *and* courts could take jurisdiction over cases that the NLRB had declined to handle. The Board was empowered to decline jurisdiction "over any labor dispute involving any class or category of employers, where, in the opinion of the Board, the effect of such labor dispute on commerce is not sufficiently substantial to warrant the exercise of its jurisdiction."[37] The House bill made no mention of which law was to be applied in such cases.

When the conference committee met, a modified version of the Landrum-Griffin "no-man's-land" provision was accepted. The Board was forbidden to decline jurisdiction of those disputes that were within its jurisdictional standards on August 1, 1959.

B. The "Hot-Cargo" Provision

A second amendment to Taft-Hartley dealt with "hot-cargo" agreements. The Senate bill made it an unfair labor practice to make a hot-cargo agreement with a *common carrier*. The House bill made it an unfair labor practice to make a hot-cargo agreement with *any employer*. The House bill also made it an unfair labor practice for a union to induce individuals employed by any person to refuse to handle goods in order to force any person to cease doing business with another person. The House

---

[36]This provision, Section 701 of Title VII, was originally a product of the McClellan Committee. This committee had recommended that states assume jurisdiction over those labor disputes that the Board refused to hear. SENATE SELECT COMM. ON IMPROPER ACTIVITIES IN THE LABOR AND MANAGEMENT FIELD, INTERIM REPORT, S. DOC. NO. 1417, 85th Cong., 2d Sess. 453 (1958) (41 LRRM 54). During the First Session of the 86th Congress, the Senate Labor Committee had included in the Kennedy-Ervin bill a proposal that the Board be required to assert jurisdiction over all disputes arising under the National Labor Relations Act. Goldberg & Meiklejohn, *supra* note 33. This proposal was rejected by the Senate, and thus the Senate bill provided that state agencies but not courts could assert jurisdiction over such cases. *See* discussion of Guss v. Utah L.R.B., 353 US 1, 39 LRRM 2567 (1957), and the jurisdictional "no man's land" which precipitated this legislative drive, Chapters 30 and 31 *infra*.

[37]S. 1555, as passed by the House of Representatives Aug. 14, 1959, 86th Cong., 1st Sess. §701. The House version of §701 was also modified to provide for a procedural change amending §3(b) of the Act and empowering the Board to refer representation cases to its regional directors for a final determination, subject to the Board's review. *See* Goldberg & Meiklejohn, *supra* note 33 at 750.

bill further made it unlawful for a union to "threaten" any person to force any person to cease doing business with another.[38]

C. Restrictions on Organizational and Recognitional Picketing

There were differences in the two bills concerning organizational and recognitional picketing.[39] The Senate bill provided that organizational picketing was an unfair labor practice if the employer had recognized another union, or if a valid representation election had been held in the preceding nine months without the picketing union being certified as the bargaining representative. The Senate version also provided that an employer unfair labor practice was a defense to a charge of unlawful picketing.

The House version provided that such picketing was an unfair labor practice if

(1) another union had been recognized by the employer or,

(2) a valid election had been held in the preceding 12 months without the picketing union being certified or,

(3) the union could not show "sufficient interest" on the part of the employees or,

(4) the picketing had continued for 30 days without the filing of an election petition.

The House bill had no provision making an employer unfair labor practice a defense to the charge of unlawful picketing.

D. Prehire Agreements

The Senate bill permitted prehire agreements in the construction industry requiring union membership after seven days' employment. Landrum-Griffin allowed such agreements only where there had been a prior history of collective bargaining and left the time limit for union membership at 30 days.[40]

---

[38]*See* Chapter 26 *infra*.

[39]These provisions were to be the most bitterly opposed provisions in the Act. Organized labor asserted such provisions were designed to undermine legitimate labor activities rather than smoke out "racketeers." Business and management groups argued that the provisions were necessary to cope with the corrupt and improper activities within the unions. Goldberg & Meiklejohn, *supra* note 33 at 762. *See* Chapter 23 *infra*.

[40]*See* Chapters 13 and 29 *infra*.

E. Voting Rights for Economic Strikers

The Senate bill provided that economic strikers could vote subject to regulations prescribed by the NLRB. The House bill contained no provisions at all on this subject.[41]

VI. The Completed Version

A. The Changes

The final bill hammered out by the conference committee made several important changes in the NLRA:

1. Recognitional and Organizational Picketing. Section 8(b)(7) was added to deal with the issue of recognitional or organizational picketing.[42] Such picketing was made unlawful if

(a) another union had been recognized and a question of representation could not be raised or,

(b) a valid election had been held within the preceding 12 months or,

(c) the picketing continued without the filing of an election petition within a reasonable time, not to exceed 30 days.

Expedited investigations are required under this provision, and when a petition is filed under (c) an election must be directed forthwith without regard to the 30-percent showing of interest. A proviso to (c) permits truthful "publicity" picketing not having the effect of inducing individuals employed by other persons "not to pick up, deliver or transport any goods or not to perform any services."

2. Secondary-Boycott Changes. Section 8(b)(4) was amended to tighten up "loopholes" in the secondary-boycott provisions of Taft-Hartley.[43] Taft-Hartley had made it an unfair labor practice for a union to "engage in, or to induce or encourage the employees of any employer to engage in, a strike or a concerted refusal in the course of their employment" for the proscribed objects enumerated in 8(b)(4). This provision had been

---

[41]*See* Chapters 10 and 21 *infra.*
[42]*See* Chapter 23 *infra.*
[43]*See* Chapter 25 *infra.*

interpreted not to extend to direct pressure on neutral employers.[44] The section was amended to read that "threatening, coercing or restraining any person" for the proscribed objects constitutes an unfair labor practice.

A proviso to Section 8(b)(4) exempts from the secondary-boycott ban the publication of a labor dispute (other than by picketing) for the purpose of truthfully advising the public that a primary dispute exists with an employer and that the employer's products are being distributed by another employer. The proviso further states, however, that such publicity shall not result in inducing any individual employed by any person other than the primary employer to refuse to pick up, deliver, or transport any goods or to fail to perform any services at the establishment of the employer engaged in such distribution.

3. "Employer" and "Employee" Redefined. The definitions of "employer" and "employee" were amended to include "any individual employed by any person."[45] Under the old definitions, agricultural laborers, family employees, employees covered by the Railway Labor Act, government employees, supervisors, and independent contractors had not been included.[46] Taft-Hartley had banned the inducement or encouragement of employees engaged in a *concerted* refusal to perform a service. To prohibit appeals to individual employees or neutral employers, the Landrum-Griffin amendment deleted the word "concerted."

4. Hot-Cargo Restrictions. Section 8(e), dealing with the hot-cargo issue,[47] was added in full. This amendment made it an unfair labor practice "for any labor organization and any employer to enter into any contract or agreement, express or implied, whereby such employer ceases or refrains . . . from handling . . . any of the products of any other employer. . . ." Thus, if any such agreement is made, it is unenforceable. Exempted from this provision are such agreements in the construction industry (if the work is to be performed at the site) and in the apparel and clothing industry.

---

[44]*See* discussion of the 1959 amendments in Chapter 25 *infra* and discussion of "person" in Chapter 30 *infra*.
[45]§8(b)(4)(i).
[46]*See* Chapter 30 *infra*.
[47]*See* Chapter 26 *infra*.

5. Prehire Agreements. Section 8(f) was added to permit the execution of prehire agreements in the building and construction industry.[48]

6. Voting Rights for Economic Strikers. Taft-Hartley had provided in Section 9(c)(3) that "[e]mployees on strike who are not entitled to reinstatement shall not be eligible to vote."[49] This provision was interpreted to mean that a replaced economic striker was ineligible to vote. It was amended to read as follows:

> Employees engaged in an economic strike who are not entitled to reinstatement shall be eligible to vote under such regulations as the Board shall find are consistent with the purposes and provisions of this Act in any election conducted within twelve months after the commencement of the strike.

7. Delegation of Board Authority Authorized. Section 3(b) was amended to change certain internal operations of the Board. The Board was empowered to delegate to regional directors its Section 9 powers of determining the appropriate bargaining unit, of investigating and providing for hearings, and of determining whether questions of representation exist.[50]

8. Taft-Hartley Provisions Repealed. Finally, Sections 9(f), (g), and (h) of the Taft-Hartley Act were repealed by Section 201(d) of the LMRDA.[51]

B. Enactment

The bill containing the Title VII amendments to the NLRA was signed into law by President Eisenhower on September 14, 1959. The national labor policy had undergone another important and, in this case, unexpected change. The change was the culmination of campaigns launched by both labor and management groups in 1947 to amend the Taft-Hartley Act. As long as the political strength of these two groups remained balanced, no effort to amend that Act had been successful. The equilibrium was upset in 1959 by two factors: (1) the McClellan Committee and its attendant publicity and (2) labor's unwillingness

---

[48]*See* Chapters 13 and 29 *infra.*
[49]*See* Chapters 10 and 32 *infra.*
[50]*See* Chapter 32 *infra.*
[51]*See* note 4 *supra.* Titles I through VI of the LMRDA pertain to internal union affairs and are outside the scope of the present work.

to support any legislation unless its demands for Taft-Hartley changes were met.[52] Once the drive for Taft-Hartley amendments had been launched, labor was unable to control its course. The outcome for organized labor was a bitter lesson in political expediency.

---

[52]*See* Aaron, *supra* note 4; Levitan, *supra* note 28.

CHAPTER 5

THE POST-LANDRUM-GRIFFIN PERIOD

Perhaps the most significant historical fact about the 24 years that have ensued since passage of the Landrum-Griffin amendments is that the Act has remained essentially unchanged. There have been minor amendments, however, and these comprise the principal subject matter of this chapter.

I. JURISDICTION OVER UNITED STATES POSTAL SERVICE

Without formally amending the National Labor Relations Act, Congress in 1970 incorporated the provisions of that Act, with certain modifications, into the Postal Reorganization Act of 1970 (PRA)[1] and thereby granted enforceable collective bargaining rights to rank-and-file postal employees.[2] Extension of the Act to this large group of federal sector employees was the first time this heretofore exclusively private sector statute was given application to public employees. In Section 1208(b) of the PRA,[3] Congress also incorporated the language of Section 301 of the

---

[1] 84 Stat 720, 39 USC §101 *et seq.* (1970).

[2] *See* U.S. Postal Serv., 208 NLRB 948, 85 LRRM 1212 (1974); Postal Employees v. Klassen, 369 F Supp 747, 85 LRRM 2609 (D DC, 1974), *aff'd*, 514 F2d 189, 85 LRRM 2558 (CA DC, 1975), *cert. denied*, 423 US 1037 (1975) (exclusive jurisdiction to investigate unfair labor practice charges and to issue unfair labor practice complaints vested in Board). Excluded from collective bargaining rights under the PRA are (1) any management official or supervisor and (2) any employee engaged in personnel work in other than a purely nonconfidential clerical capacity. 39 USC §1202.

[3] In the administration of its postal jurisdiction, the Board has applied "private sector" criteria in many situations. *E.g.,* U.S. Postal Serv., 208 NLRB 145, 90 LRRM 1212 (1974) (processing of grievances by a minority union); U.S. Postal Serv., 221 NLRB 735, 90 LRRM 1679 (1975) (application of deferral policies to grievance-arbitration procedures); *see also* Malone v. U.S. Postal Serv., 526 F2d 1099, 90 LRRM 3287 (CA 6, 1975) (employees may not bypass the collective bargaining representative in grievance-arbitration proceedings). *Accord*, 39 USC §1208(b). *But see* U.S. Postal Serv., 208 NLRB 948, 85 LRRM 1212 (1974) (determination of appropriate bargaining units); Chapter 11 *infra* at notes 326-47.

LMRA. Accordingly, the body of law developed under Section 301 has been held to be pertinent to the interpretation of Section 1208.[4]

II. SECTION 302 AMENDMENTS AND ADDITIONAL BARGAINING SUBJECTS

Although not amendments to the National Labor Relations Act itself, three amendments to Section 302(c)[5] of the Taft-Hartley Act (LMRA) have broadened the scope of matters which may be negotiated under the Act. Each amendment relates to the purposes for which employers may contribute funds to joint employer-union managed trust funds without being in violation of statutory prohibitions relating to employer contributions.[6]

The first amendment, adopted in 1969, allows contributions to trust funds for (1) scholarships for the benefit of employees, their families, and dependents for study at educational institutions, and (2) child care centers for preschool and school-age dependents of employees.[7] The amendment provides, however, that no labor organization or employer may be required to bargain over the establishment of any such trust fund and that refusal to do so will not constitute an unfair labor practice. The subject is thus statutorily determined to be a permissive rather than a mandatory subject of bargaining.[8]

The second amendment,[9] enacted in 1973, permits payments to trust funds established for the purpose of defraying the costs of legal services for employees, their families, and dependents for legal counsel or a legal-service plan of their choice. The use of such legal services is precluded (1) in matters involving the specific employer and union which have negotiated the plan, (2) in matters arising under the National Labor Relations Act and the Labor Management Relations Act, and (3) in any proceeding in which a labor organization would be precluded from defraying the cost of legal services under the Labor-Management Reporting and Disclosure Landrum-Griffin Act.

---

[4]Postal Workers v. U.S. Postal Serv., 356 F Supp 1, 83 LRRM 3032 (ED Tex, 1972); Laborers Local 317 v. Post Office Mailhandlers, 100 LRRM 2949 (D Ala, 1979). *See generally* Chapter 19 *infra.*
[5]29 USC §186(c) (1973).
[6]§302(a), 29 USC §186(a) (1973).
[7]29 USC §186(c)(7) (1973).
[8]*See generally* Chapter 16.
[9]87 Stat 314, 29 USC §186(c)(8) (1973).

In 1978 Section 302(c) was again amended to authorize employer contributions to a plant, area, or industrywide labor-management committee.[10] Employer payments are permissible if the committee is established for one or more of the purposes prescribed by the Labor Management Cooperation Act of 1978.[11] These purposes, set forth in Section 6(b) of that Act,[12] are the following: (1) to improve communication between representatives of labor and management; (2) to provide workers and employers with opportunities to study and explore new and innovative joint approaches to achieving organizational effectiveness; (3) to assist workers and employers in solving problems of mutual concern not susceptible to resolution within the collective bargaining process; (4) to study and explore ways of eliminating potential problems which reduce the competitiveness and inhibit the economic development of the plant, area, or industry; (5) to enhance the involvement of workers in making decisions that affect their working lives; (6) to expand and improve working relationships between workers and managers; and (7) to encourage free collective bargaining by establishing continuing mechanisms for communication between employers and their employees through federal assistance to the formation and operation of labor-management committees.[13]

The content of collective bargaining was also affected by the Health Maintenance Organization Act of 1973 ("HMO Act"),[14] which was enacted to foster the development of health maintenance organizations (HMOs). HMOs are organizations formed to provide a broad range of basic and supplemental health services to their members. Under the HMO Act, covered

---

[10]92 Stat 2021, 29 USC §186(c)(8) (1978).

[11]29 USC §173(e), 175a. The Labor Management Cooperation Act of 1978 authorizes and directs the Federal Mediation and Conciliation Service to encourage and support the establishment and operation of joint labor-management activities conducted by plant, area, and industrywide committees designed to improve labor-management relationships—including improving communications with respect to subjects of mutual interest and concern, job security, and organizational effectiveness—enhancing economic development or involving workers in decisions affecting their jobs.

[12] §6(b), Pub. L. No. 95-524, 92 Stat 2020, 29 USC §175a (1978). The amendment to §302(c) states that employer payments are permitted to be made to labor-management committees established for one or more of the purposes set forth in "Section 5(b)" of the Labor Management Cooperation Act of 1978. The compiler's note following 29 USCA §186 states that this reference to §5(b) "probably means Section 6(b) of Pub. L. No. 95-524. . . ."

[13]*Cf.* Chapter 8 *infra* at notes 13-41.

[14]87 Stat 914 *et seq.*, 42 USC §300e *et seq.* (1973).

employers[15] must include in any health benefit plan offered to their employees the option of membership in a qualified HMO.[16] The HMO Act provides that employers are not required to pay more for health benefits under the HMO Act than is required by prevailing collective bargaining agreements.[17]

III. HEALTH CARE INSTITUTION AMENDMENTS

Prior to 1974, although the Board had asserted jurisdiction over proprietary hospitals and nursing homes which otherwise met its jurisdictional standards for institutions of those types, it was precluded by statute from asserting jurisdiction over nonprofit hospitals.[18] In 1974 the Act was amended to eliminate the exclusion of nonprofit hospitals and to create a new category of employer, denominated "health care institution," which was broadly defined to include "any hospital, convalescent hospital, health maintenance organization, health clinic, nursing home, extended care facility, or other institution devoted to the care of sick, infirm or aged person(s)."[19]

Related amendments designed to meet what was felt to be the special problems of health care institutions were also adopted. Section 8(d) of the Act defines the duty to bargain collectively and sets forth certain procedures the bargaining parties must exhaust before terminating or modifying their agreements. That section was amended to provide more stringent notice require-

---

[15]Any employer who is required to pay minimum wages in any calendar quarter under the Fair Labor Standards Act and who also employs in that quarter an average number of not less than 25 employees. 42 USC §300e-9 (1973).

[16]An employer's obligation to offer his employees the HMO option does not arise, however, unless a qualified HMO has requested inclusion in the employer's health benefits plan. 42 CFR §110.802(a)(2)(ii) (1976).

[17]42 USC §300e-9(c) (1976). Regulations issued by the Department of Health, Education and Welfare (now the Department of Health and Human Services) in 1975 provided that the employer's offer of the HMO option to his employees "shall be carried out consistently with the obligations imposed on such employer . . . under the National Labor Relations Act and the Railway Labor Act. . . ." 40 CFR §110.808. In 1976 Congress adopted this interpretation by providing that an employer must first offer the HMO option to the bargaining agent, and thereafter to its employees on an individual basis only if the option is accepted by the collective bargaining agent. 90 Stat 1950, 42 USC §300e-9(a)(1) (1976). In 1978, Congress also added a provision requiring employers, upon the consent of the employee, to arrange for the deduction of HMO membership payments from the employee's salary. 92 Stat 2135, 2140, 42 USC §300e-9(c) (1978).

[18]§2(2) had read: "The term 'employer' . . . shall not include . . . any corporation or association operating a hospital, if no part of the net earnings inures to the benefit of any private shareholder or individual." 49 Stat 449, 29 USC §152(2) (1947).

[19]88 Stat 395, 29 USC §152(14) (1974). *See* Chapter 30 *infra* at notes 61-80.

ments in the health care industry than are prescribed for other industries.[20] A new Section 8(g) was added, setting forth special notice requirements to be met before a union may strike or picket at a health care institution;[21] Section 8(d) was modified regarding the loss of employee status of those striking in violation of the notice requirements of Sections 8(d) and 8(g); and the Board was specifically admonished to give due consideration to avoid proliferation of bargaining units in the industry.[22]

IV. RELIGIOUS CONSCIENTIOUS OBJECTORS EXEMPTED FROM UNION SECURITY COVERAGE

In the closing days of the Carter Administration, the Congress passed and the President signed a religious conscientious objector amendment to the union security requirements of the Act.[23] The amendment expands Section 19, which had previously applied only to employees of health care institutions, to exempt all employees belonging to a "bona fide religion, body, or sect which historically has held conscientious objections to joining or financially supporting labor organizations" from compulsory union membership. However, such employees may be required, through a collective bargaining agreement, to contribute a sum equal to dues and initiation fees to a nonreligious charity. The provision also requires such employees to reimburse the union bargaining agent for the cost of representation in a grievance or arbitration procedure.[24]

V. UNSUCCESSFUL EFFORTS TO AMEND THE BASIC ACT

As indicated by the sparsity of the above changes, legislative stability has been the prevailing rule in the development of the Act since 1959. This is not to say that there have not been many proposals to amend the Act. Numerous bills have been proposed, most never emerging from committee. But until the latter half of the 1970s, no major effort to amend the Act in any

---

[20] 88 Stat 395, 396, 29 USC §158(d) (1974).
[21] *See* Chapters 13 and 21 *infra* at notes 723-33 and 50-53 respectively.
[22] S. REP. No. 93-766, 93rd Cong., 2d Sess., *reprinted in* [1974] U.S. CODE CONG. & AD. NEWS 3950. *See* Chapter 11 *infra* at notes 125-253.
[23] Pub. L. No. 96-593, 94 Stat. 3452 (1980). *See* LRX 3768.
[24] *See* Chapter 29 *infra* at notes 28-29 and 392-96.

fundamental manner was attempted. In the latter half of the 1970s, however, unions and their political allies made three all-out efforts, two of which came within a hair's breadth of success.

The first, which almost succeeded, involved an attempt by the construction unions to change the law regarding "common-situs" picketing at construction sites,[25] to make picketing of the whole site legal whenever a union had a dispute with a contractor or subcontractor at the site. A bill to that effect, introduced in 1975,[26] was passed by both the House and the Senate[27] only to be vetoed by President Ford.[28] The Senate overrode the veto, but the House did not.[29] Following the election of President Carter in 1977, a second effort was made.[30] This time, however, the bill was defeated in the House, never reaching the Senate.[31]

Undeterred by these two defeats, and with hopes buoyed by the accession of President Carter to the Executive Office, an effort to achieve major changes in the statute was again made. In July 1977, a far-reaching bill, supported by the President, was introduced in the House. That bill, entitled the Labor Law Reform Bill,[32] proposed to streamline the procedures of the Board and provide more effective means of enforcement. This was to be achieved primarily by the following devices: speeding up schedules for conducting union representation elections and processing complaints; substituting rule making for most hearings in representation cases; providing for mandatory Section 10(l) injunctions in discharge cases; making Board orders self-enforcing; and stiffening penalties for employers who oppose union organizing by illegal means, by requiring awards of double back pay to employees fired for union activities and by barring flagrant labor law violators from receiving government

---

[25]See generally Chapter 25 for a discussion of secondary strikes and picketing.
[26]H.R. 5900, 94th Cong., 1st Sess., 121 CONG. REC. 10012 (1975).
[27]Id. at 24844 (House passage); id. at 37462 (Senate passage); id. at 40067 (House agreement to Conference Committee Report); id at 40553 (Senate agreement to Conference Committee Report).
[28]Id. at 42015.
[29]The House neither overrode nor sustained the veto. Instead, it committed the bill to Committee. H.R. 5900, 94th Cong., 2nd Sess., 122 CONG. REC. 145 (1976).
[30]H.R. 4250, 95th Cong., 1st Sess., 123 CONG. REC. H1657 (daily ed. March 2, 1977).
[31]House Roll Call Vote No. 98, H.R. 4250, 95th Cong., 1st Sess., March 23, 1977, 123 CONG. REC. 8713 (1977).
[32]H.R. 8410, 95th Cong., 1st Sess., 123 CONG. REC. H10714 (daily ed. July 19, 1977). A companion bill was introduced in the Senate on the same day. S. 1883, 95th Cong., 1st Sess., 123 CONG. REC. S12266 (daily ed. July 19, 1977).

contracts.[33] On October 6, 1977, the bill passed the House by a vote of 257 to 163.[34]

The Senate did not act on the legislation in 1977. Its Human Resources Committee instead held hearings on a companion bill, and in January 1978, reported out its version by a 13-to-2 vote. The Senate bill, in addition to what was provided in the House version, provided for expansion of the membership of the National Labor Relations Board to seven members, gave "equal access" to union organizers to the work place under certain circumstances, reduced election time limits, and provided for a make-whole remedy when an employer was responsible for an unreasonable delay in negotiations.[35]

A five-week Senate filibuster blocked congressional approval of the legislation. After six unsuccessful attempts at invoking cloture, on June 22, 1978, the bill was recommitted to the Senate Human Resources Committee,[36] a move which was tantamount to killing the bill. There the bill languished and died.[37]

By the end of 1979, the nation and the Congress, beset by many other problems both foreign and domestic, had turned attention elsewhere. Prospects for major changes in the Act in the near future are deemed unlikely.[38]

---

[33]*See* 1977 CQ Almanac 144-46, 95th Cong., 1st Sess. (1977).

[34]H.R. 8410, 95th Cong., 1st Sess., 123 Cong. Rec. H10714 (daily ed. October 6, 1977). *See* note 33 *supra*.

[35]*See* 1978 CQ Almanac 285, 95th Cong., 2nd Sess. (1978).

[36]S. 1883, 95th Cong., 2nd Sess., 124 Cong. Rec. S9411 (daily ed. June 22, 1978).

[37]Following recommittal, the Senate Human Resources Labor Subcommittee held hearings and drafted a "barebones" bill which eliminated certain controversial provisions of earlier proposals, but that bill was never reported out of the Subcommittee.

[38]In November 1979, the House by a vote of 227 to 167 unexpectedly failed to approve a bill (H.R. 2222) that would have amended the Act by extending coverage to hospital interns and residents and thereby would have overturned the 1976 NLRB ruling in *Cedars-Sinai Medical Center*, 223 NLRB 251 (1976). H.R. 2222, 96th Cong., 1st Sess., 125 Cong. Rec. H11295 (daily ed. November 28, 1979). *See* Chapter 30 *infra* at notes 296-301.

PART II

PROTECTED EMPLOYEE ACTIVITY

CHAPTER 6

INTERFERENCE WITH PROTECTED RIGHTS

I. OVERVIEW

A. Introduction

In regulating organizational activities, the Board's primary concern is to protect the statutory rights of employees, but in doing so it must also balance those rights against the rights of the employer and, to a lesser extent, those of the union.[1] The

---

[1]For scholarly comment on many of the topics in this chapter, *see* J. Getman, S. Goldberg & J. Herman, UNION REPRESENTATION ELECTIONS: LAW AND REALITY (1976); R. Williams, P. Janus & K. Huhn, NLRB REGULATION OF ELECTION CONDUCT (1974); Truesdale, *From General Shoe to General Knit: A Return to Hollywood Ceramics*, 30 LAB. L. J. 67 (1979); Hudson & Werther, *Section 8(c) and Free Speech*, 28 LAB. L. J. 608 (1977); King, *Pre-Election Conduct—Expanding Rights and Some New and Renewed Perspectives*, 2 IND. L. J. 185 (1977); Wellington, *Union Fines and Worker Rights*, 85 YALE L. J. 1022 (1976); Barksdale, *Employer Speech During Union Organizational Campaigns*, 46 MISS. L. J. 401 (1975); Cantor, *Dissident Worker Action, After The Emporium*, 29 RUTGERS L. REV. 35 (1975); Fanning, *Union Solicitation and Distribution of Literature on the Job—Balancing the Rights of Employers and Employees*, 9 GA. L. REV. 367 (1975); Helm, *Union Waiver of Initiation Fees During the Organizational Campaign*, 63 KY. L. J. 841 (1975); Field, *Representation Elections, Films, and Free Speech*, 25 LAB. L. J. 217 (1974); Millian, *Disciplinary Developments Under §8 (b)(1)(A) of the National Labor Relations Act*, 20 LOYOLA L. REV. 245 (1974); Craver, *The Boeing Decision: A Blow to Federalism, Individual Rights and Stare Decises*, 122 U. PA. L. REV. 556 (1974); Zimny, *Access of Union Organizers to "Private" Property*, 25 LAB. L. J. 618 (1974); Jarvis, *Organizational Campaigns: Private Rights v. Public Rights*, NYU TWENTY-SIXTH ANNUAL CONFERENCE ON LABOR 3 (1973); Johannesen, *Disciplinary Fines as Interference with Protected Rights: Section 8 (b) (1) (A)*, 24 LAB. L. J. 268 (1973); Seham, *Limitations Upon and Directions of a Union's Right to Discipline Its Members*, NYU TWENTY-FIFTH ANNUAL CONFERENCE ON LABOR 191 (1973); Swift, *NLRB Overkill: Predictions of Plant Relocation and Closure and Employer Free Speech*, 8 GA. L. REV. 77 (1973); Shaffer, *Some Gray Areas in Employer Free Speech*, 6 CREIGHTON L. REV. 39 (1972); Dereshinsky, *The Solicitation and Distribution Rules of the NLRB*, 40 U. CIN. L. REV. 417 (1971); Coleman, *Union Discipline Under 8 (b) (1) (A) of the National Labor Relations Act: The Emergence of a New Trilogy*, 45 ST. JOHN'S L. REV. 219 (1970); Lubin & Schlossberg, *Union Fines and Union Discipline Under the National Labor Relations Act*, NYU TWENTY-THIRD CONFERENCE ON LABOR 207 (1971); Bok, *The Regulation of Campaign Tactics in Representation Elections Under the National Labor Relations Act*, 78 HARV. L. REV. 38 (1964); Christensen, *Free Speech Propaganda and the National Labor Relations Act*, 38 NYU L. REV. 213 (1963); Aaron, *Employer Free Speech: The Search for Policy*, in PUBLIC POLICY AND COLLECTIVE BARGAINING 28 (Shister, Aaron, & Summers, eds., 1962); Pokempner, *Employer Free Speech Under the National Labor Relations Act*, 25 MD. L. REV. 111 (1965); Koretz,

various sections of the Act bearing on organizational activities and their contextual background, along with some of the Board's preelection rules, will be examined in this chapter; and their application and interrelation will be discussed in relation to particular kinds of conduct. Additional material on preelection rules and conduct, particularly conduct which might violate "laboratory conditions" without the commission of unfair labor practices, is treated elsewhere.[2]

B. Section 7—Rights of Employees

1. To Form, Join, or Assist Labor Organizations. Since its inception in 1935, the Act has had as its primary concern the rights of employees, both individually and collectively:

> It is hereby declared to be the policy of the United States . . . [to protect] the exercise by workers of full freedom of association, self-organization, and designation of representatives of their own choosing, for the purpose of negotiating the terms and conditions of their employment or other mutual aid or protection.[3]

Section 7 was fashioned to implement this policy. The 1935 statute provided that the rights of employees shall include the rights to "self-organization, to form, join, or assist labor organizations" and to engage in "other concerted activities for the purpose of collective bargaining or other mutual aid or protection." The Act made it an unfair labor practice for an employer "to interfere with, restrain or coerce employees" in the exercise of those guaranteed rights.

2. To Refrain From Such Activities. In 1947 the protection of Section 7 was expanded by the Taft-Hartley Act. In Section 8(b)(1)(A) employees were guaranteed the right "to refrain from any and all of such activities," and, to protect this right, further amendments made it an unfair labor practice for a union to restrain or coerce employees in the exercise of their Section 7 rights. The amendments were rooted in the statute's amended

---

Employer Interference With Union Organization Versus Employer Free Speech, 29 GEO. WASH. L. REV. 399 (1960); Fairweather, *What Can Employers Do in Election Campaigns*, NYU SEVENTEENTH ANNUAL CONFERENCE ON LABOR 183 (1964); Brown, *Free Speech in NLRB Representation Proceedings*, 50 LRRM 72 (1962); Fields, *Free Speech Under the Taft-Hartley Act*, 11 LAB. L. J. 967 (1963); Platt, *Rules on Free Speech Under Taft-Hartley Act*, 55 LRRM 105 (1964).
[2]Chapter 9 *infra*.
[3]§1.

declaration of policy "to protect the rights of individual employees in their relations with labor organizations . . . ."[4]

3. Other Concerted Activities.[5] The protection extended to employees by Section 7 is not limited to the right to join or assist labor organizations or to refrain from such activities; it also includes activity engaged in for "other mutual aid or protection," and it has been invoked to protect concerted employee activity unrelated to union organization.[6] Interference, restraint, or coercion in the exercise of these additional rights is an unfair labor practice under Section 8(a)(1); discrimination against engaging in such concerted activities may also result in a violation of Section 8(a)(3).

The ambit of Section 7 is extremely broad, though certain limits have been defined. Employee activity, to be protected, must be of a "concerted" nature, but even a conversation, "although it involves only a speaker and a listener," may constitute concerted activity if it has some relation to group action in the interests of employees.[7] An individual employee's action, even though pursued singly, to enforce the terms of a collective bargaining agreement or to question some aspect of employ-

---

[4]§1(b), Short Title and Declaration of Policy, Labor-Management Relations Act of 1947, Pub. L. No. 101, 80th Cong., 1st. Sess.; 29 USC §141 *et seq.* (1976). *See* Chapter 3 *supra.*

[5]For detailed treatment of this subject, *see* Part III *infra.*

[6]*E.g.,* Redwing Carriers, Inc., 137 NLRB 1545, 50 LRRM 1440 (1962), *aff'd sub nom.,* Teamsters Local 79 v. NLRB, 325 F2d 1011, 54 LRRM 2707 (CA DC, 1963), *cert. denied,* 377 US 905, 55 LRRM 3023 (1964) (refusing, in the course of employment, to cross a picket line located at another employer's place of business). Brown & Root, Inc. v. NLRB, 634 F2d 816, 106 LRRM 2391 (CA 5, 1981) (refusal to work in the face of dangerous working conditions); Wheeling-Pittsburgh Steel Corp. v. NLRB, 618 F2d 1009, 104 LRRM 2054 (CA 3, 1980) (expressing concern for safety of fellow employees and refusal to work in the face of dangerous working conditions); Jim Causley Pontiac v. NLRB, 620 F2d 122, 104 LRRM 2190 (CA 6, 1980), *on remand,* 253 NLRB 695, 105 LRRM 1683 (1980) (discussing excessive paint fumes in work area with fellow employees and filing of complaint with state public health department); Walls Mfg. Co. v. NLRB, 321 F2d 753, 53 LRRM 2428 (CA DC, 1963), *cert. denied,* 375 US 923, 54 LRRM 2596 (1963) (writing a letter complaining of sanitary conditions on behalf of fellow employees); Salt River Valley Water Users' Ass'n v. NLRB, 206 F2d 325, 32 LRRM 2598 (CA 9, 1953) (circulating a petition to authorize an individual to collect wages allegedly due under the Fair Labor Standards Act); *see also* Lewittes Furn. Enterprises, 244 NLRB 810, 102 LRRM 1266 (1979) (nonunion employees banding together and requesting wage increase).

[7]*Compare* Supreme Optical Co. v. NLRB, 628 F2d 1262, 105 LRRM 3022 (CA 6, 1980); Owens-Corning Fiberglas Corp. v. NLRB, 407 F2d 1357, 70 LRRM 3065 (CA 4, 1969); Interboro Contractors, Inc., 157 NLRB 1295, 61 LRRM 1537 (1966), *enforced,* 388 F2d 495, 67 LRRM 2083 (CA 2, 1967); Mushroom Transp. Co. v. NLRB, 330 F2d 683, 56 LRRM 2034 (CA 3, 1964); Self Cycle & Marine Distributor Co., Inc., 237 NLRB 75, 98 LRRM 1517 (1978), *with* Pelton Casteel, Inc. v. NLRB, 627 F2d 23, 105 LRRM 2124 (CA 7, 1980), *denying enforcement to* 246 NLRB 310 (public venting of a personal grievance is not a concerted activity); Kohls v. NLRB, 629 F2d 173, 104 LRRM 3049 (CA DC,

ment policy governing a group of unorganized employees has also been deemed "concerted" activity by the Board as long as the individual's efforts are directed at goals shared by other employees.[8]

Activity for "mutual aid and protection" has been construed to embrace expressions of "common cause," including common cause with workers employed elsewhere.[9] Furthermore, employees do not lose their protection under the "mutual aid and protection" clause "when they seek to improve terms and conditions of employment or otherwise improve their lot as employees through channels outside the immediate employee-employer relationship."[10] The protective umbrella of Section 7, however, will be removed from concerted activity which is violent, unlawful, in breach of contract, or "indefensibly disloyal."[11]

Illustrative of some of the efforts which have been made to stretch the limits of Section 7 was the decision in *Packinghouse Workers (Farmers' Cooperative),*[12] in which Judge Skelly Wright,

---

1980) (individual protest against work assignment is not a concerted activity); Krispy Kreme Doughnut Corp. v. NLRB, 635 F2d 304, 105 LRRM 3407 (CA 4, 1980) (discharge of an individual for refusing to forgo workmen's compensation claim is not interference with a protected "concerted" activity); NLRB v. Adams Delivery Serv., Inc., 623 F2d 96, 104 LRRM 3093 (CA 9, 1980) (individual "griping" about disputed overtime pay is not a concerted activity); Puerto Rico Food Prods. Corp. v. NLRB, 619 F2d 153, 104 LRRM 2304 (CA 1, 1980) (employee protest over a change in supervisory personnel held not protected); Air Surrey Corp. v. NLRB, 601 F2d 256, 102 LRRM 2599 (CA 6, 1979) (employee seeking information about amount of funds in employer's payroll checking account held not protected because employer was unaware that employee was acting in concert); G & W Elec. Specialty Co. v. NLRB, 360 F2d 873, 62 LRRM 2085 (CA 7, 1966); National Wax Co., 251 NLRB 1064, 105 LRRM 1371 (1980) (individual's pursuit of personal merit pay increase held not a concerted activity); Jewel Companies, Inc., 245 NLRB 1356, 102 LRRM 1510 (1979) (activities in attempting to establish or affect management of a credit union held not protected).

[8]*See* cases cited in note 7 *supra.*

[9]*See* General Elec. Co., 169 NLRB 1101, 67 LRRM 1326 (1968); NLRB v. Peter Cailler Kohler Swiss Chocolate Co., 130 F2d 503, 10 LRRM 852 (CA 2, 1942); Fort Wayne Corrugated Paper Co. v. NLRB, 111 F2d 869, 6 LRRM 888 (CA 7, 1940); Washington State Serv. Employees, 188 NLRB 957, 76 LRRM 1467 (1971); Yellow Cab, Inc., 210 NLRB 568, 86 LRRM 1145 (1974).

[10]Eastex, Inc. v. NLRB, 437 US 556, 565, 98 LRRM 2717, 2720 (1978); NLRB v. Washington Aluminum Co., 370 US 9, 50 LRRM 2235 (1962); NLRB v. Electrical Workers (IBEW) Local 1229, 346 US 464, 33 LRRM 2183 (1953); *see* notes 391-414 *infra* and accompanying text.

[11]*See* notes 483-513 *infra* and accompanying text.

[12]416 F2d 1126, 70 LRRM 2489 (CA DC, 1969), *cert. denied,* 396 US 903, 72 LRRM 2658 (1969), *on remand,* 194 NLRB 85, 78 LRRM 1465 (1971). The court remanded the case to the Board for a factual determination as to whether the employer maintained a racially discriminatory policy. The court was of the opinion that an employer's invidious discrimination on account of race or national origin sets up an unjustified clash of interests between groups of workers which tends to reduce the likelihood and effectiveness of their working in concert to achieve legitimate statutory goals, and, further-

writing for the District of Columbia Circuit, held that racial discrimination by an employer violates Section 8(a)(1) because it interferes with or restrains employees in the exercise of their right to act concertedly for their own aid or protection. In *Jubilee Manufacturing Co.*,[13] however, the Board disagreed with that legal conclusion and held that race, color, religion, sex, or national origin discrimination can be violative of Section 8(a)(1) only where

> there has been the necessary direct relationship between the alleged discrimination and our traditional and primary functions of fostering collective bargaining, protecting employees' rights to act concertedly, and conducting elections in which the employees have the opportunity to cast their ballots for or against a union in an atmosphere conducive to the sober and informed exercise of the franchise.[14]

Thus, for conduct to be protected, it must be directly related to objectives embodied in the National Labor Relations Act.

C. Employer Interference With Section 7 Rights: Section 8(a)(1)

The mandate of Section 8(a)(1) is the broadest of the subdivisions of Section 8(a). Violations of Section 8(a)(1) are regarded as either *derivative* or *independent*.

1. Derivative Violations. The Board has noted since its earliest days that "a violation by an employer of any of the four subdivisions of Section 8, other than subdivision one, is also a violation of subdivision one."[15] Derivative 8(a)(1) violations are therefore treated elsewhere in this work in connection with the primary unfair labor practices to which they are attached.

2. Independent Violations. Some acts infringe upon Section 8(a)(1) only and are not incidental to the violation of any other subdivision of Section 8. Acts constituting general interference

---

more, racial discrimination creates in its victims an apathy or docility which inhibits them from asserting their rights. In the court's view, the confluence of these factors deters the exercise of §7 rights and thus violates §8 (a) (1). On remand, the Board ruled that the evidence did not support a finding that the employer maintained a policy and practice of invidious discrimination against employees on account of race or national origin. *But cf.* Chapter 28 *infra* regarding the duty of fair representation in the context of racial discrimination by unions.

[13]202 NLRB 272, 82 LRRM 1482 (1973), *aff'd sub nom.* Steelworkers v. NLRB, 504 F2d 271, 87 LRRM 3168 (CA DC, 1974). *See also* notes 363-64 *infra*.

[14]202 NLRB at 273.

[15]1938 NLRB ANN. REP. 52 (1939).

with Section 7 rights, but not specifically prohibited by other subdivisions of Section 8(a), fall within this category and are treated in this chapter.

3. Motive Not an Essential Element of Section 8(a)(1) Violations.

Motive, in the NLRB's view, is not the critical element of a Section 8(a)(1) violation. The Board's "well settled" test has been that

> interference, restraint, and coercion under Section 8(a)(1) of the Act does not turn on the employer's motive or on whether the coercion succeeded or failed. The test is whether the employer engaged in conduct which, it may reasonably be said, tends to interfere with the free exercise of employee rights under the Act.[16]

The view of the Supreme Court has been generally supportive but not nearly so clear.[17] In *Burnup & Sims*[18] the Court upheld the Board's position in the context of a good-faith discharge of employees engaged in protected activity. The employer's good-faith but mistaken belief as to the employee's conduct was held not to be a defense to the resultant interference with the employees' Section 7 rights. Justice Harlan wrote in a separate opinion, however, that only in a "rare situation" might the Board ignore motive. But a year later Justice Harlan asserted in his opinion for the Court in *Darlington*[19] that "a violation of Section 8(a)(1) alone . . . presupposes an act which is unlawful even absent a discriminatory motive."[20] Justice Harlan's citations of *Republic Aviation Corp.*[21] and *Nutone*[22] in this connection bolster the conclusion that motive is not an essential element, but this seemingly clear picture has been somewhat blurred by succeeding cases.

---

[16]American Freightways Co., 124 NLRB 146, 147, 44 LRRM 1302 (1959); *see also* NLRB v. Illinois Tool Works, 153 F2d 811, 17 LRRM 841 (CA 7, 1946); Roadway Express, Inc., 250 NLRB 393, 104 LRRM 1349 (1980); Cooper Thermometer Co., 154 NLRB 502, 503 n.2, 59 LRRM 1767 (1965).

[17]For a detailed analysis of this problem, *see* Christensen & Svanoe, *Motive and Intent in the Commission of Unfair Labor Practices: The Supreme Court and the Fictive Formality,* 77 YALE L. J. 1269 (1968); and Oberer, *The Scienter Factor in Sections 8 (a) (1) and (3) of the Labor Act: Of Balancing Hostile Motive, Dogs and Tails,* 52 CORNELL L. Q. 491 (1967).

[18]NLRB v. Burnup & Sims, Inc., 379 US 21, 57 LRRM 2385 (1964).

[19]Textile Workers v. Darlington Mfg. Co., 380 US 263, 58 LRRM 2657 (1965). See Chapter 7 *infra* at notes 238-42.

[20]380 US at 269.

[21]Republic Aviation Corp. v. NLRB, 324 US 793, 16 LRRM 620 (1945). *See* notes 95-98 and 141 *infra* and accompanying text.

[22]NLRB v. Steelworkers (Nutone, Inc.), 357 US 357, 42 LRRM 2324 (1958).

In the context of the later lockout cases, the Court, in *Brown*[23] and *American Ship Building*,[24] placed great emphasis upon motive in finding no violation of Section 8(a)(1). The Court referred to the distinction it had drawn in *Erie Resistor*[25] between acts that are so "inherently discriminatory" or "destructive" of employee rights that the employer may be held to have foreseen the unlawful consequences, and those that are not inherently discriminatory or destructive. Since the Court in *Brown* and *American Shipbuilding* viewed the employers' acts as neither "inherently discriminatory" nor *per se* unlawful, the lack of a hostile motive appeared to be determinative.[26]

After the Court's 1967 decisions in *Fleetwood Trailer*[27] and *Great Dane*,[28] a clear evaluation still remained elusive. Those cases involved rights of striking employees and were decided in the context of Section 8(a)(3) violations. Presence or absence of unlawful motivation was not relied upon by the Court in upholding the finding of a Section 8(a)(3) violation. A *fortiorari*, scienter would not seem to be essential in Section 8(a)(1) cases.

Despite the Board's finding of Section 8(a)(1) and (3) violations in *Burnup & Sims*,[29] the Court rested its decision solely on Section 8(a)(1). Conversely, the Court's decision in *Darlington* was grounded solely upon Section 8(a)(3), whereas the Board had also found a violation of Section 8(a)(1). The extent to which a Section 8(a)(1) violation overlaps a Section 8(a)(3) violation may be relevant. One commentator[30] has suggested that in overlapping situations it may make sense to engraft a hostile-motive requirement but that this should not normally be done in the

[23]NLRB v. Brown, 380 US 278, 58 LRRM 2663 (1965). *See* Chapter 7 *infra* at note 231 and Chapter 22 *infra* at notes 91-124.

[24]American Ship Bldg. Co. v. NLRB, 380 US 300, 58 LRRM 2672 (1965). *See* Chapter 7 *infra* at notes 226-30 and Chapter 22 *infra* at notes 58-90.

[25]NLRB v. Erie Resistor Corp., 373 US 221, 53 LRRM 2121, 2124 (1963). *See* Chapter 7 at notes 85-91.

[26]These decisions appeared to manifest the Court's renewed emphasis upon motive when viewed in the light of its earlier opinion in NLRB v. Exchange Parts, 375 US 405, 55 LRRM 2098 (1964). In that case a basic §8 (a) (1) violation stemming from preelection wage increases was made dependent upon lawful motive. Earlier, in Garment Workers (Bernhard-Altmann Texas Corp.) v. NLRB, 366 US 731, 739, 48 LRRM 2251 (1961), the Court stated that "[w]e find nothing in the statutory language prescribing scienter as an element of the unfair labor practices [8 (a) (1) and (2)] here involved."

[27]NLRB v. Fleetwood Trailer Co., 389 US 375, 66 LRRM 2737 (1967). *See* Chapter 21 *infra* at note 86.

[28]NLRB v. Great Dane Trailers, Inc., 388 US 26, 65 LRRM 2465 (1967). *See* Chapter 7 *infra* at note 92.

[29]*Supra* note 18.

[30]*See* Oberer, *supra* note 17 at 516.

case of independent Section 8(a)(1) violations. He further suggests a rough "rule of thumb" that motive should be "presumptively irrelevant" in cases of independent Section 8(a)(1) violations and "presumptively relevant" in Section 8(a)(3) violations.[31]

D. Union Restraint and Coercion—Section 8(b)(1)(A)

Section 8(b)(1)(A) is concerned with the rights of individual employees in their relations with labor organizations.[32] This provision makes it an unfair labor practice for a union to "restrain or coerce employees in the exercise of the rights guaranteed in Section 7: Provided, that this paragraph shall not impair the right of a labor organization to prescribe its own rules with respect to the acquisition or retention of membership therein . . . ."

1. Not a Derivative Counterpart of Section 8(a)(1). Although Section 8(b)(1)(A) may be thought of generally as a counterpart of Section 8(a)(1), the Board from the outset has taken the position that "Congress did not intend that Section 8(b)(1)(A) be given the broad application accorded Section 8(a)(1)."[33] Thus, in *National Maritime Union*,[34] its earliest decision under the provision, the Board concluded that violations of other parts of Section 8(b) did not give rise to derivative violations of Section 8(b)(1)(A):

> Nothing in this legislative history indicates that a union which refuses to bargain is to be considered as having per se "restrained" or "coerced" employees in the exercise of their rights guaranteed in Section 7 . . . . Nor is there any suggestion in the legislative history of Section 8(b)(1)(A) that "coercion" and "restraint" may be found to flow automatically from a union's violation of Section 8(b)(2) . . . .[35]

This relatively narrow scope of Section 8(b)(1)(A) was given specific approval by the Supreme Court in *Curtis Brothers*.[36] The

---

[31]*Id. See* generally Chapter 7 *infra* for a discussion of discrimination under §§8(a)(3).
[32]For detailed treatment of §8(b)(1)(A) *see* notes 514-81 *infra* and accompanying text.
[33]1949 NLRB ANN. REP. 81 (1950).
[34]National Maritime Union, 78 NLRB 971, 22 LRRM 1289 (1948), *enforced*, 175 F2d 686, 24 LRRM 2268 (CA 2, 1949), *cert. denied*, 338 US 954, 25 LRRM 2395 (1950).
[35]78 NLRB at 985.
[36]NLRB v. Drivers Local 639 (Curtis Bros., Inc.), 362 US 274, 45 LRRM 2975 (1960). *See* Chapter 23 *infra* at notes 4-9.

Court cited with approval the Board's decision in *National Maritime Union*[37] that

Section 8(b)(1)(A) is a grant of power to the Board limited to authority to proceed against union tactics involving violence, intimidation, and reprisal or threats thereof—conduct involving more than the general pressures upon persons employed by the affected employers implicit in economic strikes.[38]

2. Nature of the Violation. Violence or threats of violence constitute coercion and restraint within the meaning of Section 8(b)(1)(A). Thus, threatening an employee with bodily harm may constitute an unfair labor practice. Restraint and coercion may also be found in cases where nonviolent physical force is used to prevent employees from exercising their Section 7 rights, e.g., mass picketing by a union preventing employees from gaining entrance to the employer's premises.[39]

Although the Act literally proscribes only restraint and coercion of "employees" in Section 8(b)(1)(A), violent conduct directed at nonemployees has been held violative of the section when it is substantially certain that employees will hear about it[40] or when the violence is committed in their presence.[41]

Resort to the Board is not the exclusive remedy for such conduct. States, under their criminal laws, may punish violence that constitutes an unfair labor practice[42] or enjoin it.[43] State courts may also grant compensatory and punitive damages in common-law tort actions involving intimidation or violence.[44]

---

[37]78 NLRB 971, 22 LRRM 1289 (1948), *enforced,* 175 F2d 686, 24 LRRM 2268 (CA 2, 1949).

[38]362 US at 290. *See* Chapter 28 *infra* for treatment of §8(b)(1)(A) conduct that constitutes a breach of a union's duty of fair representation.

[39]*E.g.,* Mid-States Metal Prods., Inc., 156 NLRB 872, 61 LRRM 1159 (1966), *enforced,* 403 F2d 702, 69 LRRM 2656 (CA 5, 1968); Longshoremen and Warehousemen Local 6 (Sunset Line & Twine Co.), 79 NLRB 1487, 23 LRRM 1001 (1948).

[40]Brooklyn Spring Corp., 113 NLRB 815, 36 LRRM 1372 (1955), *enforced,* 233 F2d 539, 38 LRRM 2134 (CA 2, 1956).

[41]Retail, Wholesale & Dept. Store Union (B. Brown Associates, Inc.), 157 NLRB 615, 61 LRRM 1382 (1966), *enforced,* 375 F2d 745, 64 LRRM 2750 (CA 2, 1967); Retail, Wholesale & Dep't Store Union (I. Posner, Inc.), 133 NLRB 1555, 49 LRRM 1066 (1961). Threats of *future* picket line violence made during an election campaign have not, however, been held to violate §8(b)(1)(A) or to constitute grounds for setting aside an election. Hickory Springs Mfg. Co. (Teamsters Local 373), 239 NLRB 641, 99 LRRM 1715 (1978).

[42]Automobile Workers (Kohler Co.) v. Wisconsin Employment Relations Bd., 351 US 266, 38 LRRM 2165 (1956). *See generally* Chapter 31 *infra* for discussion of federal preemption and its exceptions.

[43]Automobile Workers, *supra* note 42.

[44]*See* Construction Workers v. Laburnum Constr. Corp., 347 US 656, 34 LRRM 2229 (1954). *See also* Automobile Workers v. Russell, 356 US 634, 42 LRRM 2142 (1958).

The bulk of the cases concerning violations of Section 8(b)(1)(A) do not involve violence; they most often concern threats of loss of employment, improper use of union discipline, or discriminatory or other improper conduct practiced by a union in violation of its duty of fair representation or its obligations under hiring-hall or union-shop procedures. These cases are treated in detail elsewhere.[45]

3. Motive Not an Essential Element of Section 8(b)(1)(A) Violations. The Board does not require evidence of unlawful intent to support a finding of violation of 8(b)(1)(A).[46] As in the case of Section 8(a)(1), however, there is some uncertainty on this point in the courts.[47]

E. "Freedom of Speech"—Section 8(c) in General

The enactment of Section 8(c) in the Taft-Hartley amendments resulted from a line of early Board decisions severely limiting an employer's freedom of speech.[48] The Board had been insisting that the employer maintain strict impartiality in matters pertaining to unions, holding that statements concerning unionism constituted interference with Section 7 rights of employees.[49] However, in 1941, the Supreme Court, in *NLRB v. Virginia Electric & Power Co.*,[50] held that employers had a constitutional right to express opinions that were noncoercive in nature. The Board thereafter developed a less restrictive approach toward employer speeches but otherwise continued to limit employer expression.[51] Prior to the passage of Taft-Hartley, there was some indication that the Board had changed

---

[45]*See* Part IV *infra; also* Chapters 28 and 29 *infra.*

[46]Garment Workers (Bernhard-Altmann Tex. Corp.) v. NLRB, *supra* note 26; Painters Local 798 (Master Painters Ass'n), 212 NLRB 615, 86 LRRM 1728 (1974), *enforced,* 91 LRRM 2924 (CA 7, 1976). The Board has, however, ruled that evidence of legitimate motivation will exonerate a union from a §8(b)(1)(A) violation. Ashley, Hickham-Uhr Co., 210 NLRB 32, 86 LRRM 1024 (1974).

[47]*E.g.,* NLRB v. Teamsters Local 294 (August Bohl Contracting Co., Inc.), 470 F2d 57, 81 LRRM 2920 (CA 2, 1972).

[48]*See* commentary, *supra* note 1.

[49]*E.g.,* Schult Trailers, Inc., 28 NLRB 975, 7 LRRM 162 (1941); Ford Motor Co., 23 NLRB 732, 6 LRRM 310 (1940); Southern Colo. Power Co., 13 NLRB 699, 4 LRRM 341 (1939), *enforced,* 111 F2d 539, 6 LRRM 1011 (CA 10, 1940).

[50]NLRB v. Virginia Elec. & Power Co., 314 US 469, 9 LRRM 405 (1941). *See also* NLRB v. American Tube Bending Co., 134 F2d 993, 12 LRRM 615 (CA 2, 1943), *cert. denied,* 320 US 768, 13 LRRM 850 (1943).

[51]*See, e.g.,* Monumental Life Ins., 69 NLRB 247, 18 LRRM 1206 (1946) (holding speech coercive where coupled with other unfair labor practices); Clark Bros. Co., 70 NLRB 802, 18 LRRM 1360 (1946), *enforced,* 163 F2d 373, 20 LRRM 2436 (CA 2, 1947) (speech during working time on plant premises held to be unfair labor practice).

its position and was according more latitude to employer speeches;[52] the shift, however, came too late to prevent passage of Section 8(c). As stated in the Senate Report:[53] "The committee believes these [Board] decisions to be too restrictive and . . . provides that if, under all the circumstances, there is neither an express or [sic] implied threat of reprisal, force, or offer of benefit, the Board shall not predicate any finding of unfair labor practice upon the statement." The House version was more restrictive: "[A] statement may not be used against the person making it unless it, standing alone, is unfair within the express terms of Section 7 and 8 of the amended act."[54]

The final version of Section 8(c) as passed by Congress was the House version, with only minor changes:

> The expressing of any views, argument, or opinion, or the dissemination thereof, whether in written, printed, graphic, or visual form, shall not constitute or be evidence of an unfair labor practice under any of the provisions of this Act, if such expression contains no threat of reprisal or force or promise of benefit.[55]

This language, according to the Supreme Court's decision in *NLRB* v. *Gissel Packing Co.*,[56] "merely implements the First Amendment," but the Court also made clear that the protections afforded to speech by Section 8(c) are not absolute. "Any assessment of the precise scope of employer expression," the Court noted, "must be made in the context of its labor relations setting. Thus, an employer's rights cannot outweigh the equal rights of the employees to associate freely, as those rights are embodied in §7 and protected by §8(a)(1) and the proviso to §8(c)."[57] The evaluation of employer speech under this standard thus requires, according to the Court, an approach markedly different from the tolerance for "robust debate"[58] required by the First Amendment in the context of political elections. "What is basically at stake" in an NLRB election, the Court concluded, "is the establishment of a nonpermanent, limited relationship between the

---

[52]*See* Herzog, *Words and Acts: Free Speech and the NLRB*, 18 LRRM 147 (1946).

[53]S. REP. NO. 105 on S. 1126, 1 LEGISLATIVE HISTORY OF THE LABOR MANAGEMENT RELATIONS ACT 1947, 429-30 (1948).

[54]H. R. REP. NO. 345 on H. R. 3020, 1 LEGISLATIVE HISTORY OF THE LABOR MANAGEMENT RELATIONS ACT 1947, 299, 324.

[55]§8(c). *See* H. R. REP. NO. 510, 80th Cong. 1st Sess. 15 (1947).

[56]395 US 575, 71 LRRM 2481 (1969). §8(c). *See* note 208 *infra*.

[57]395 US at 617.

[58]*See* New York Times Co. v. Sullivan, 376 US 254 (1964). *Cf.* Linn v. Plant Guards Union, 383 US 53, 61 LRRM 2345 (1966), discussed in Chapter 31 *infra* at notes 176-87.

employee and his union agent, not the election of legislators or the enactment of legislation whereby that relationship is ultimately defined and where the independent voter may be freer to listen more objectively and employers as a class freer to talk."[59]

Following passage of Section 8(c), the Board engaged in a continuing effort to balance the right of free speech and the prohibition of interference, restraint, or coercion of employees in their exercise of Section 7 rights.[60] The character of threats or promises found unlawful spans the range of human expression. A sampling of one year's decisions discloses Board condemnation of

> threatened loss of employment, threatened closing of plant or going out of business, threatened moving of plant to new location, threatened unfavorable reply concerning credit rating, threatened loss or reduction in pay or overtime, threatened loss of promotion, and threatened violence.[61]

During the same year the Board found unlawful, promises

> to "take care" of employees who voted against the union, to give paid holidays, to assist in securing Air Force approval for additional benefit, to grant raises if the pay scale rose in the area, or to "get a raise next week" for the employee who affirmed he was on the employer's side.[62]

1. Threat or Prophecy? The most troublesome element in employer-speech cases has been that of distinguishing between illegal threats and legitimate prophecies. The Supreme Court's opinion in *Gissel* provided a guideline for evaluating employer speech by declaring that any balancing of the employer rights of free speech and the rights of employees to be free from coercion, restraint, and interference "must take into account the economic dependence of the employees on their employers, and the necessary tendency of the former, because of that relationship, to pick up intended implications of the latter that might be more readily dismissed by a more disinterested ear."[63] In distinguishing "threats" from "predictions" in the context of employer statements about plant closings, the Court indicated that

---

[59]NLRB v. Gissel Packing Co., *supra* note 56 at 617-18.
[60]*See* Koretz, *supra* note 1, and Bok, *supra* note 1.
[61]1962 NLRB ANN. REP. 89 (1963).
[62]*Id.*
[63]*Supra* note 56 at 617.

[a] prediction must be carefully phrased on the basis of objective fact to convey an employer's belief as to demonstrably probable consequences beyond his control . . . . If there is an implication that an employer may or may not take action solely on his own initiative for reasons unrelated to economic necessities and known only to him, the statement is no longer a reasonable prediction based on available facts but a threat of retaliation based on misrepresentation and coercion, and as such without the protection of the First Amendment.[64]

Because the employer has control over the employment relationship and knows it best, the Court concluded that the employer "can easily make his views known without engaging in brinkmanship . . . . At least he can avoid conscious overstatements he has reason to believe will mislead his employees."[65]

---

[64]*Supra* note 56 at 618.

[65]*Supra* note 56 at 620. The Seventh Circuit, prior to *Gissel,* had announced a rule of caution, stating that "one who engages in 'brinkmanship' may easily overstep and tumble into the brink." Wausau Steel Corp. v. NLRB, 377 F2d 369, 372, 65 LRRM 2001 (CA 7, 1967). The following cases and discussion provide additional background setting for the Supreme Court's *Gissel* decision:

The seeds of the Court's distinction between "threats" and "predictions" could be found in earlier Board and court decisions, but the line of demarcation was less than rigid. For example, in 1953 the Board stated that a "prophecy that unionization might ultimately lead to loss of employment is not coercive where there is no threat that the employer will use its economic power to make its prophecy come true." Chicopee Mfg. Co., 107 NLRB 106, 107, 33 LRRM 1064 (1953).

The Sixth Circuit, in a detailed attempt at clarification prior to *Gissel,* held that no violation would have occurred had an employer's remarks "been limited to a prediction of economic problems if the union came in." But a violation resulted when the employer went on to advert "to the probability that if the company did not choose to meet the excessive union demands and a strike resulted, the company might decide to move the operation elsewhere or to shut it down." The court held that such a statement went further than "predicting the economic result which would necessarily follow from the advent of the union, over which the employer had no control, in that it involved possible action on the part of the company to close down the plant rather than meet the union's demands." Surprenant Mfg. Co. v. NLRB, 341 F2d 756, 58 LRRM 2484 (CA 6, 1964). (*Surprenant* was cited in *Gissel* for the proposition that predictions must be made in terms of demonstrable economic consequences.)

Similarly, the District of Columbia Circuit found unprotected by §8 (c) an employer's remark that he could not say "whether the plant would move or not, but he would say two of [its] biggest customers . . . wouldn't do business with a union company [and also] that possibly [the plant] would be cut down to three or four days in operation a week . . . ." Electrical Workers (IUE) (NECO Elec. Prod. Corp.) v. NLRB, 289 F2d 757, 46 LRRM 2534 (CA DC, 1960). The same court, however, differed with the Board's finding that the following "serious harm" notice violated §8(a)(1):

"Our sincere belief is that if the Union were to get in here it would not work to your benefit but would in the long run itself operate to your serious harm. It is our intention to oppose the Union and by every proper means to prevent it from coming into this operation."

Although the Board had found this statement to be a veiled threat of reprisal, the court concluded that absent supporting evidence in the surrounding circumstances the statement alone was not violative of the Act. Clothing Workers (Hamburg Shirt Corp.) v. NLRB, 365 F2d 898, 63 LRRM 2581 (CA DC, 1966). For similar results, *see* Wellington Mill Div. v. NLRB, 330 F2d 579, 55 LRRM 2914 (CA 4, 1964), *cert. denied,* 379 US 882, 57 LRRM 2277 (1964).

In distinguishing between *threat* and *prophecy*, the Board and the courts have long been concerned with the effect to be given circumstances surrounding employer speech. *Virginia Electric*,[66] a pre-Section 8(c) case, suggested that the "totality of conduct" be considered so the Board might "look at what the Company has said, as well as what it has done."[67] Decisions during the Eisenhower Administration, after the passage of Section 8(c), "tended to view each contested statement in isolation from other comments or conduct of the employer."[68] During the 1960s, the Board began placing greater emphasis on surrounding conduct so that the existence of a violation turned not upon the express words used but upon their meaning in the context in which they were uttered.[69] The Board continued to emphasize surrounding conduct and circumstances during the 1970s.[70]

2. The Outer Limit of Employer Speech. The outer limit of employer speech may be viewed in two ways: Speech that is coercive under Section 8(a)(1) is not protected by Section 8(c). Speech that is protected under Section 8(c) is not violative of Section 8(a)(1). The outer limit may vary depending upon which viewpoint is emphasized. A Ninth Circuit case in 1967 illustrates the significance of the approach selected. In *NLRB* v. *TRW-Semiconducters, Inc.*,[71] the Board had found that a series of electioneering communications amounted to a violation of Section 8(a)(1). It did not specifically refer to Section 8(c). On review, the court held that the "broad language of Section 8(a)(1) is not the test of whether election propaganda violates the Act." Rather, it "must first be found that it contains a threat of force or reprisal or promise of benefit." Finding none, the court declared that Section 8(c) determined the outer limit,[72] whereas the trial examiner, relying on the Supreme Court's decision in *Exchange Parts*,[73]

---

[66]314 US 469, 9 LRRM 405 (1941).

[67]314 US at 478; *see* NLRB v. Eastern Oil Co., 340 F2d 607, 58 LRRM 2255 (CA 1, 1965), *cert. denied*, 381 US 951, 59 LRRM 2432 (1965); *see also* International Harvester Co., 258 NLRB No. 155, 108 LRRM 1180 (1981).

[68]Christensen, *supra* note 1 at 258.

[69]*See* Lord Baltimore Press, 142 NLRB 328, 53 LRRM 1019 (1963); Lake Catherine Footwear, Inc., 133 NLRB 443, 48 LRRM 1683 (1961); *see also* Dal-Tex Optical Co., 137 NLRB 1782, 50 LRRM 1489 (1962).

[70]According to some commentators, however, the Board often produced inconsistent results when deciding whether the same words amounted to a threat or prediction. *See* Getman, Goldberg, & Herman, *supra* note 1 at 21.

[71]385 F2d 753, 66 LRRM 2707 (CA 9, 1967), *denying enforcement to* 159 NLRB 415, 62 LRRM 1469 (1966).

[72]385 F2d at 758.

[73]NLRB v. Exchange Parts, *supra* note 26. *See* note 242 *infra* and accompanying text.

had considered the surrounding circumstances in which the statements were made and also their impact upon the employees. The Ninth Circuit indicated that whatever the impact and intent of the propaganda, they did not deprive the employer of the protection of Section 8(c).[74]

In direct contrast to the Ninth Circuit's approach was that of the First Circuit in the 1968 *Sinclair* case,[75] which case later formed the basis of the *Gissel* ruling.[76] There it was contended that since each of a series of statements was lawful in itself, the statements in combination could not be considered unlawful.[77] In upholding the order, the First Circuit stated that in considering coercive effect, the test must include the totality of the circumstances; and whether language is coercive in its effect is for the Board to resolve on the basis of its specialized experience. On review of *Sinclair* (as part of its *Gissel*[78]decision), the Supreme Court affirmed the approach taken by the Board and the First Circuit, holding that any assessment of the precise scope of employer expression must be made in the context of its setting and should also take into account the economic dependence of the employees on their employers.

---

[74]Unless *Exchange Parts* can be considered simply as a clear promise-of-benefit case, it may be difficult to determine the importance of the impact and intent elements in the case, since both formed the basis of the Supreme Court's decision. The hallmark of the Court's opinion lies in its dramatic comparison of the preelection increase to "the fist inside the velvet glove." Because the opinion was cast in terms of §8(a)(1), it may be that the Court was not ignoring §8(c) but was simply looking inside the "velvet glove." *See* notes 242-43 *infra* and accompanying text.

[75]Sinclair Co., 164 NLRB 261, 65 LRRM 1087 (1967), *enforced*, 397 F2d 157, 68 LRRM 2720 (CA 1, 1968), *aff'd sub nom.* NLRB v. Gissel Packing Co., *supra* note 56. *See* Chapter 12 *infra* for the portion of the *Gissel* opinion concerning union recognition without an election; *see also* note 208 *infra*.

[76]*Supra* notes 56-59.

[77]*Id. Compare* American Greetings Corp., 146 NLRB 1440, 56 LRRM 1064 (1964), in which a similar pattern with similar content was held not to interfere with free choice in the election, *with* the split opinions of the Seventh Circuit in Wausau Steel Corp. v. NLRB, *supra* note 65, *and* the Second Circuit in NLRB v. Golub Corp., 388 F2d 921, 66 LRRM 2769 (CA 2, 1967). The *Golub* case is especially noteworthy because of both the exhaustive majority opinion and Judge Hays' caustic dissent, in which he pointed up the difficulty inherent in judicial attempts to identify threatening language, and thereby foretold the later teaching of *Gissel*. Judge Hays charged:

"The majority opinion demonstrates once more the inescapable truth that United States Circuit Judges safely ensconced in their chambers do not feel threatened by what employers tell their employees. An employer can dress up his threats in the language of prediction ('You will lose your job' rather than 'I will fire you') and fool judges. He doesn't fool his employees; they know perfectly clearly what he means." 388 F2d at 929.

[78]*Supra* note 75. *See* further discussion at notes 207-208 *infra*.

II. ORGANIZATIONAL AND PREELECTION ACTIVITY

A. In General: Relation of Unfair Labor Practices to "Laboratory Conditions" Required for Elections

Violations of the Board's restrictions on preelection activity may take one of two forms. (1) Some violations may comprise unfair labor practices—these generally take the form of independent 8(a)(1) conduct. (2) Other violations may breach preelection rules or "laboratory conditions" without contravening any statutory unfair labor practice provisions. In cases of the former type case, the Board is authorized to find unfair labor practices and to remedy them by appropriate means,[79] including setting aside the result of the election,[80] ordering a new election,[81] and, in extreme cases, issuing a bargaining order without an election.[82] In the latter type case, the Board's sanctions are limited to setting aside the results of the election and rerunning the election at an appropriate time.[83] The legal distinction between the two types of conduct is important, although from the pragmatic standpoint of what actually happens during an election campaign the difference relates primarily to the remedial sanctions which will be available.

The distinction between the two types of conduct provides the basis for separating the material relating to preelection conduct in this treatise. The material on preelection conduct contained in this chapter relates primarily to unfair labor practices, whereas Chapter 9 relates primarily to violations of laboratory conditions and to preelection rules that do not comprise unfair labor practices. To ascertain the full range of do's and don'ts applicable to union elections, related portions of both chapters must be read together.

The protection of Section 8(c) literally applies only to unfair labor practice cases. The Board has made extensive use of this distinction in regulating elections. In its 1948 *General Shoe Corp.*[84] decision it defined the "laboratory conditions" required for the conduct of elections under Section 9:

---

[79]*See* Chapter 33 *infra.*
[80]*See* Chapter 10 *infra.*
[81]*Id.*
[82]*See* Chapter 12 *infra.*
[83]*See* Chapter 33 *infra* at notes 8-13.
[84]77 NLRB 124, 21 LRRM 1337 (1948).

[T]he criteria applied . . . in a representation proceeding . . . need not necessarily be identical to those employed in testing whether an unfair labor practice was committed . . . . In election proceedings, it is the Board's function to provide a laboratory in which an experiment may be conducted, under conditions as nearly ideal as possible, to determine the uninhibited desires of the employees . . . .[85]

Under this doctrine, fault is not an issue. When conduct affecting the election drops below acceptable standards, the requisite "laboratory conditions" are not present and the experiment must be conducted again.

During the period of the Eisenhower Board the *General Shoe* doctrine was eclipsed in favor of Section 8(c) as the outer limit in election cases.[86] In some instances, Section 8(c) was applied more restrictively in employer unfair labor practice cases than were the Board's rules for employer conduct during an election campaign.[87] With the advent of new Board Members in 1961, the criterion applied to employer speeches was changed radically. In *Dal-Tex Optical Co.*[88] the Board announced a *per se* rule applicable to unfair labor practices committed during election campaigns:

Conduct violative of Section 8(a)(1) is, a *fortiori,* conduct which interferes with the exercise of a free and untrammeled choice in an election. This is so because the test of conduct which may interfere with the "laboratory conditions" for an election is considerably more restrictive than the test of conduct which amounts to interference, restraint, or coercion which violates Section 8(a)(1).

During the 1970s, the Board qualified its *Dal-Tex* approach; it is now no longer regarded as a *per se* requirement that an election be automatically set aside whenever Section 8(a)(1) conduct has occurred during the preelection period. The Board has ruled that *de minimis* employer misconduct affecting the results of an election, even though amounting to an unfair labor

---

[85]77 NLRB at 127. As to how realistic this objective is, *see* Bok, *supra* note 1, at 45-47; Getman, Goldberg, & Herman, *supra* note 1.

[86]*See* National Furniture Co., 119 NLRB 1, 40 LRRM 1442 (1957); Lux Clock Mfg. Co., 113 NLRB 1194, 36 LRRM 1432 (1955); Esquire, Inc., 107 NLRB 1238, 33 LRRM 1367 (1954); American Laundry Mach. Co., 107 NLRB 511, 33 LRRM 1181 (1953).

[87]Wirtz, *The New National Labor Relations Board; Herein of "Employer Persuasion,"* 49 Nw. U. L. REV. 594 (1954).

[88]137 NLRB 1782, 50 LRRM 1489 (1962). The Board expressly overruled the cases cited in note 86 *supra.*

practice, will not be grounds for setting an election aside.[89] Accordingly, in evaluating the impact of misconduct to determine whether it is *de minimus,* "the Board [now] takes into consideration the number of violations, their severity, the extent of dissemination and other relevant factors."[90] Section 8(a)(1) "violations as to which it is virtually impossible to conclude that they would have affected the results of the election" do not require that it be set aside.[91]

B. Unlawful Employer Conduct

1. Employer's Restrictions on Union and Employee Activity on Employer's Property. Although the primary objective of organizing is to obtain bargaining rights, an organizing campaign is not normally initiated with the ultimate administrative or judicial forum clearly in view. But, because of the structure of this treatise, the preelection conduct discussed here will be conduct involving alleged unfair labor practices.[92]

Access or nonaccess to employees is frequently a threshold concern in an organizing campaign. The Board and the courts have therefore long been engaged in "working out an adjustment between the undisputed right of self-organization assured to employees . . . and the equally undisputed right of employers to maintain discipline in their establishments."[93] Because "reasonable men can and do differ in striking this adjustment,"[94] strong reliance has been placed on presumptions to facilitate the decision-making process.

a. Basic Presumptions. In its early landmark decision in *Republic Aviation,*[95] the Supreme Court adopted the presumption that the enforcement and promulgation of a rule prohibiting union solicitation by employees outside working time, although on company property, "is an unreasonable impediment to self-organization and therefore discriminatory in the absence of

---

[89]Caron Int'l, Inc., 246 NLRB 1120, 103 LRRM 1066 (1979); Super Thrift Mkts., 233 NLRB 409, 96 LRRM 1523 (1977); *see also* Coca Cola Bottling Co. Consol., 232 NLRB 717, 96 LRRM 1289 (1977).
[90]Caron Int'l, Inc., *supra* note 89 at 1067.
[91]Super Thrift Mkts., *supra* note 89 at 1523. *Accord,* Custom Trim Prods., 255 NLRB 787, 107 LRRM 1198 (1981).
[92]Material concerning conduct which does not violate the Act but which is sufficient to set aside an election may be found in Chapter 9 *infra.*
[93]Republic Aviation Corp. v. NLRB, *supra* note 21 at 797-98.
[94]Stoddard-Quirk Mfg. Co., 138 NLRB 615, 616 n.2, 51 LRRM 1110 (1962).
[95]324 US 793, 16 LRRM 620 (1945). *See generally* Dereshinsky, *The Solicitation and Distribution Rules of the NLRB,* 40 U. CIN. L. REV. 417 (1971).

evidence that special circumstances make the rule necessary" for maintaining "production and discipline."[96] The genesis of this presumption was the Board's 1943 decision in *Peyton Packing Co.*, where the Board formulated the corollary presumption that the promulgation and enforcement of a no-solicitation rule for working hours "must be presumed to be valid in the absence of evidence that it was adopted for a discriminatory purpose." The Board's rationale was that "working time is for work," but the time outside working hours "is an employee's time to use as he wishes without unreasonable restraint although the employee is on company property."[97] In 1981, in *T.R.W., Inc.*[98] the Board clarified the presumption, holding that rules "prohibiting employees from engaging in solicitation during 'work time' or 'working time,' without further clarification, are, like rules prohibiting such activity during 'working hours,' presumptively unlawful." It noted, however, that employers could overcome this presumption of illegality by incorporating in the rule itself a clear statement that the rule does not apply to break periods, mealtimes, or other specified nonwork periods of the day.

b. Rights of Employees Over Nonemployees. A distinction is made between rules of law applicable to employees and those applicable to nonemployees, i.e., union organizers; and "the distinction is one of substance."[99] Consequently, in *Babcock & Wilcox*[100] the Supreme Court held that an employer may prohibit the distribution of union literature by nonemployee union organizers if (1) "reasonable efforts . . . through other available channels of communication will enable it to reach the employees,"

---

[96]324 US at 803 n.10, *citing* Peyton Packing Co., 49 NLRB 828, 843-44, 12 LRRM 183 (1943), *enforced,* 142 F2d 1009, 14 LRRM 792 (CA 5, 1944), *cert. denied,* 323 US 730, 15 LRRM 973 (1944). For application of the "special circumstances" exception in the context of structured large group meetings in a lunchroom with potential for disturbance and disruption, *see* National Vendors v. NLRB, 630 F2d 1265, 105 LRRM 2281 (CA 8, 1980). In American Cast Iron Pipe Co. v. NLRB, 600 F2d 132, 101 LRRM 2522 (CA 8, 1979), the court held that rules barring written or verbal "false, vicious, or malicious" statements about the company on or off company property were overly broad, reasoning that the company would only be justified in prohibiting "maliciously false or disloyal" statements under the special circumstances exception; *see also* Great Lakes Steel v. NLRB, 625 F2d 131, 104 LRRM 3156 (CA 6, 1980); Wheeling-Pittsburgh Steel Corp., 244 NLRB No. 166, 102 LRRM 1386 (1979).
[97]*Supra* note 96 at 843-44.
[98]257 NLRB No. 47, 107 LRRM 1481 (1981), *overruling* Essex Int'l, Inc., 211 NLRB 749, 86 LRRM 1411 (1974).
[99]NLRB v. Babcock & Wilcox, 351 US 105, 113, 38 LRRM 2001 (1956).
[100]*Id.*

and (2) the employer does not discriminate against the union by allowing distribution of items by other nonemployees.[101]

The Court also took cognizance of the location of the plant and the residences of the employees, noting that if employees lived beyond the reach of reasonable union efforts to reach them, the employer's property must be made available.[102] Special problems of communication obviously exist in company towns, lumber camps, and remote petroleum reserve exploration camps, such as those in Alaska.[103] The 1968 decision of the Board in *Solo Cup Co.*[104] concerning industrial parks, however, suggested that this special problem of nonaccessibility may not be confined to isolated work camps and company towns. As discussed by the Supreme Court in *Logan Valley Plaza*[105] earlier in 1968, the privately owned shopping center was viewed as the functional equivalent of a "normal municipal business district" to which the public had unrestricted access for purposes of constitutionally protected freedom of expression under the First Amendment. In the circumstances of *Solo Cup,* the Board analogized to *Logan Valley*[106] and found the barring of organizers from private property to be a violation of the Act; the Seventh Circuit, however, reversed that decision.[107]

Ultimately, the Supreme Court, in *Central Hardware,*[108] declined to extend the "quasi-public" doctrine of *Logan Valley* beyond the

---

[101]The Board's position, that in applying the *Babcock & Wilcox* principle the employer bears the burden of demonstrating that alternative channels of communication are available to the union, was rejected in Sabine Towing & Transp. Co. v. NLRB, 599 F2d 663, 101 LRRM 2956 (CA 5, 1979); the court held that the union bears the affirmative obligation of showing that no other reasonable means exist for communicating its organizational message. *See also* Belcher Towing Co. v. NLRB, 614 F2d 88, 103 LRRM 2939 (CA 5, 1980). For an example of the distinction between rules applicable to employees and union organizers, *see* G. C. Murphy Co., 171 NLRB 370, 68 LRRM 1108 (1968), *enforced,* 422 F2d 685, 71 LRRM 2397 (CA DC, 1969). *See also infra* at notes 180-81.

[102]NLRB v. Babcock & Wilcox, *supra* note 99.

[103]*See* NLRB v. Stowe Spinning Co., 366 US 226, 23 LRRM 2371 (1949); NLRB v. Lake Superior Lumber Corp., 167 F2d 147, 21 LRRM 2707 (CA 6, 1948); Husky Oil NPR Operations, Inc., 245 NLRB No. 68, 102 LRRM 1450 (1979), *enforced,* 669 F2d 643, 109 LRRM 2548 (CA 10, 1982). *See also* note 179 *infra.*

[104]172 NLRB 1110, 68 LRRM 1385 (1968), *rev'd and modified,* 422 F2d 1149, 73 LRRM 2789 (CA 7, 1970).

[105]Food Employees Local 590 v. Logan Valley Plaza, Inc., 391 US 308, 68 LRRM 2209 (1968). *See* note 181 *infra* and Chapter 21 *infra* at notes 20-34.

[106]The Board had found that almost 99% of the employees drove into work from dispersed outlying areas, and distribution immediately outside the park was prohibitive for reasons of safety. Also, the employer had refused to furnish a list of employee names and addresses.

[107]Shortly before *Logan Valley,* the Board, with approval of the Second Circuit, ordered a resort hotel to permit union organizers on its premises for purposes of solicitation. Many of the employees lived on the hotel premises. NLRB v. S. & H. Grossinger's, Inc., 372 F2d 26, 30, 64 LRRM 2295 (CA 2, 1967), *enforcing in part* 156 NLRB 233, 61 LRRM 1025 (1965). *See* note 166 *infra.*

[108]Central Hardware Co. v. NLRB, 407 US 539, 80 LRRM 2769 (1972). *See* Chapter 21 *infra* at notes 23-26 and note 183 *infra* in this chapter.

facts of that case. Moreover, in *Hudgens* v. *NLRB*,[109] the Court, in an effective reversal of *Logan Valley*, announced that only the balancing standards established in *Babcock & Wilcox* would govern in determining the access rights of nonemployee union organizers to private shopping center property open to the public; however, the case was remanded to the Board for application of statutory standards.[110]

c. No-Solicitation and No-Distribution Rules Generally. An adjustment has been struck for oral solicitation, which is different from that applicable to distribution of literature. Distribution has been regarded as posing special problems: Littering may be involved and different techniques may be required because of location and opportunity for effectively communicating the message. In striking the appropriate balance, the "development of the law regarding oral solicitation has been attended with less travail than that regarding the distribution of literature."[111]

As previously noted, *Republic Aviation* spoke specifically to the problem of solicitation. The Board has maintained the position that oral solicitation by employees may be prohibited only during working time.[112] But distribution by employees may be prohibited both during working time and in working areas.[113] The Board, with Second Circuit approval, has invalidated a prohibition of distribution which extends beyond working areas and into nonworking areas,[114] but this position has not been accepted in two other circuits.[115]

Solicitation of authorization cards is treated in the category of oral solicitation.[116]

---

[109]424 US 507, 91 LRRM 2489 (1976). *See infra* at notes 110 and 181.
[110]*See* Scott Hudgens, 230 NLRB 414, 95 LRRM 1351 (1977), *on remand from* Hudgens v. NLRB, *supra* note 109, *reaff'g*, 192 NLRB 671, 77 LRRM 1872 (1971). *See* notes 181-90 *infra* and accompanying text.
[111]Stoddard-Quirk Mfg. Co., *supra* note 94. *See* Bok, *supra* note 1 at 93.
[112]*See also* Stoddard-Quirk Mfg. Co., *supra* note 94; Paceco, Div. of Fruehauf Corp. v. NLRB, 601 F2d 180, 102 LRRM 2146 (CA 5, 1979); Keystone Resources, Inc. v. NLRB, 597 F2d 1041, 101 LRRM 2784 (CA 5, 1979), *on remand*, 245 NLRB No. 72, 102 LRRM 1320 (1979).
[113]Stoddard-Quirk Mfg. Co., *supra* note 94. In the absence of a no-solicitation rule, an employer may not seize union literature placed on workers' desks prior to the start of working hours. F. W. Woolworth Co. v. NLRB, 530 F2d 1245, 92 LRRM 2240 (CA 2, 1976), *cert. denied*, 429 US 1023, 93 LRRM 3019 (1976).
[114]United Aircraft Corp., 139 NLRB 39, 51 LRRM 1259 (1962), *enforced*, 324 F2d 128, 54 LRRM 2492 (CA 2, 1963), *cert. denied*, 376 US 951, 55 LRRM 2769 (1964).
[115]Republic Aluminum Co. v. NLRB, 374 F2d 183, 64 LRRM 2447 (CA 5, 1967); NLRB v. Rockwell Mfg. Co., 271 F2d 109, 44 LRRM 3004 (CA 3, 1959). *See also* Times Publishing Co. v. NLRB, 605 F2d 847, 102 LRRM 2710 (CA 5, 1979). *See* Chapter 19 *infra* at note 222 regarding no-solicitation clauses in collective bargaining contracts.
[116]Stoddard-Quirk Mfg. Co., *supra* note 94 at 619 n.5; *see also* Rose Co., 154 NLRB 228, 229 n.1, 59 LRRM 1738 (1965).

(1) Presumptions of validity. As previously noted, to be presumptively valid, a rule prohibiting union solicitation must incorporate a clear statement of its scope and limitations. Although the language used to frame no-solicitation rules has been far from uniform, even a rule which is carefully tailored to achieve the presumption of validity may be violative if it is promulgated or enforced in a discriminatory manner.[117]

(2) Facial validity of rule. No-solicitation rules drawn so broadly as to encompass nonworking time are presumptively unlawful.[118] An exception to this presumption is made for retail department stores, which may prohibit employee solicitation on the selling floor even during nonworking time because of the nature of their business.[119]

Another exception to the basic presumption has been created for health care facilities. The Board's general approach for these establishments has been to permit a health care facility to ban employee solicitation as well as distribution in "immediate patient care areas," such as operating rooms, patients' rooms, and patients' lounges, and to require the health care institution to carry the burden of justifying any greater restrictions as being necessary to avoid disruption of patient care or disturbance of patients. This approach was endorsed by the Supreme Court in *Beth Israel Hospital*[120] and in *Baptist Hospital* .

---

[117]Head Div., AMF, Inc. v. NLRB, 593 F2d 972, 100 LRRM 3035 (CA 10, 1979). *See also* note 130 *infra*.

[118]For an exhaustive collection of such cases, *see* Gould, *The Question of Union Activity on Company Property*, 18 VAND. L. REV. 73, 75-76 n.10 (1964); *see also* Fanning, *Union Solicitation and Distribution of Literature on the Job—Balancing the Rights of Employers and Employees*, 9 GA. L. REV. 367 (1975); Dereshinsky, *The Solicitation and Distribution Rules of the NLRB*, 40 U. CIN. L. REV. 417 (1971). In T.R.W., Inc., *supra* note 98, the Board held that rules prohibiting solicitation during "work time" or "working time" are presumptively invalid, the same as rules prohibiting such conduct during "working hours," overruling the contrary holding in Essex Int'l, Inc., 211 NLRB 749, 86 LRRM 1411 (1974), where the Board, distinguishing between "working time" and "working hours," held that a rule which was applied to ban distribution during "working time" was lawful. See *infra* at notes 128-29.

[119]Goldblatt Bros., 77 NLRB 1262, 22 LRRM 1153 (1958); Meier & Frank Co., 89 NLRB 1016, 26 LRRM 1081 (1950); Marshall Field & Co., 34 NLRB 1, 8 LRRM 325 (1941), *enforced*, 129 F2d 169, 10 LRRM 753 (CA 7, 1942), *aff'd*, 318 US 253, 12 LRRM 519 (1943); *see also* Marriott Corp., 223 NLRB 978, 92 LRRM 1028 (1976); McDonald's Corp., 205 NLRB 404, 84 LRRM 1316 (1973); Maxam Buffalo, Inc., 139 NLRB 1040, 51 LRRM 1459 (1962). In Times Publishing Co. v. NLRB, *supra* note 115, it was determined that the lobby of a building which housed the newspaper publisher employer's offices, although a work area, was not sufficiently like the selling areas of a retail establishment to be entitled to the retail department-store exception. *See also* notes 162-65 and accompanying text.

[120]Beth Israel Hosp. v. NLRB, 437 US 483, 98 LRRM 2727 (1978). The Court upheld the Board's ruling that it was unlawful for the hospital to prohibit solicitation and distribution of literature in its cafeteria, which was operated primarily for employees

The Court and the Board have disagreed, however, as to which parts of a health care institution are "immediate patient care areas." In *Baptist Hospital*[121] the Court determined, contrary to the Board, that corridors and sitting rooms on floors of a hospital housing either patients' rooms or operating and therapy rooms were "immediate patient use areas" where solicitation could be banned; but it agreed with the Board that solicitation in the cafeteria, gift shop, and lobbies on the first floor of the hospital could not be lawfully prohibited where there was no showing by the hospital that the needs of essential patient care would be adversely affected.[122] In *Beth Israel Hospital* the Court had admonished the Board that it " '[bears] a heavy continuing responsibility to review its policies concerning organizational activities in various parts of hospitals.' "[123] In *Baptist Hospital* the Court observed that "the experience to date raises serious doubts as to whether the Board's interpretation of its present presumption adequately takes into account the medical practices and

---

and infrequently used by patients or their families. *See also* Eastern Me. Medical Center, 253 NLRB 224, 105 LRRM 1665 (1980) (rule banning solicitation in second floor waiting room lobby held unlawful); Los Angeles New Hosp., 244 NLRB 960, 102 LRRM 1189 (1979) (ban on solicitation and distribution in employee break area adjacent to an operating room held unlawful); Vassar Bros. Hosp., 243 NLRB 1142, 102 LRRM 1024 (1979) (ban on solicitation in corridor adjacent to employee cafeteria held unlawful). In NLRB v. Baylor Medical Center, 439 US 9, 99 LRRM 2953 (1978), the Supreme Court, *per curiam*, vacated a D. C. Circuit decision, 578 F2d 351, 97 LRRM 2669 (CA DC, 1978), holding that a hospital's rule banning solicitation in its cafeteria did not violate §8(a)(1) and remanded the issue for reconsideration in light of *Beth Israel*. The Court left intact the lower court's holding that union solicitation could be barred in the hospital's corridors, noting that *Beth Israel* had not considered this issue. On remand, the Board reaffirmed its prior holding that the rule prohibiting solicitation in the cafeteria violated §8(a)(1) because the employer had not established that the total ban on solicitation by employees in the cafeteria was necessary to fulfill its mission as a health care facility. Baylor Univ. Medical Center, 247 NLRB 1323, 103 LRRM 1311 (1980), *enforcement denied*, 662 F2d 56, 108 LRRM 2041 (CA DC, 1981). *See also* Albert Einstein Medical Center, 245 NLRB No. 26, 102 LRRM 1508 (1979).

[121]NLRB v. Baptist Hosp., Inc., 442 US 773, 101 LRRM 2556 (1979). *See also* NLRB v. National Jewish Hosp., 593 F2d 911, 99 LRRM 3141 (CA 10, 1978), *vacated*, 443 US 903, 101 LRRM 2628 (1979) (hospital could not demonstrate distribution of union literature in cafeteria affected patient care); NLRB v. St. Joseph's Hosp., 587 F2d 1060, 99 LRRM 3404 (CA 10, 1978); Medical Center Hosp., 244 NLRB 742, 102 LRRM 1105 (1979) (hospital could not prohibit solicitation and distribution in walkways and driveways leading to front entrance of hospital when conducted at times designed to coincide with periods in which a majority of employees arrive or leave hospital); NLRB v. Presbyterian Medical Center, 586 F2d 165, 99 LRRM 3137 (CA 10, 1978) (hospital could not prohibit distribution of union literature outside the hospital building).

[122]101 LRRM at 2561. The Board, on remand for a determination of the outstanding issues remaining after the Supreme Court's decision, determined that the hospital also violated §8(a)(1) by prohibiting solicitation in the snack bar adjacent to the cafeteria and in locker rooms on the hospital's first floor. Baptist Hosp., Inc., 246 NLRB 149, 102 LRRM 1418 (1979).

[123]437 US at 508.

methods of treatment incident to the delivery of patient care services in a modern hospital."[124]

The wording of a no-solicitation rule may be significant. In a number of cases the employer's rule was susceptible to differing interpretations. For example, a rule in a retail establishment prohibiting solicitation "on store premises during working hours by any persons" was held invalid because it could be read as prohibiting employee activity in nonselling areas during employees' nonworking time.[125] Also deemed ambiguous and invalid was a rule prohibiting unauthorized solicitation "except such solicitation during the employees' nonworking time as is protected by the National Labor Relation Act"; likewise invalid was the prohibition of unauthorized distribution of literature "except such distribution during nonworking time in nonworking areas as is protected by the National Labor Relations Act."[126] A rule prohibiting solicitation or distribution in a "working area" may be subject to varying interpretation depending on the circumstances of its application.[127] The Board's position regarding ambiguous rules is aptly summed up in the Second Circuit's declaration that "the risk of ambiguity must be held against the promulgator of the rule rather than the employees who are supposed to abide by it."[128] Clarifications of ambiguous rules or narrowing interpretations of overly broad rules must be effec-

---

[124]101 LRRM at 2562. See also NLRB Gen. Counsel Guidelines for Handling No-Solicitation, No-Distribution Rules in Health-Care Facilities, Memorandum 79-76 (October 5, 1979).

[125]G. C. Murphy, supra note 101. See T.R.W., Inc., supra note 98. See also Lyman Steel Co., 249 NLRB 296, 104 LRRM 1323 (1980). Prohibitions phrased in terms of "company time" have also been ruled ambiguous and invalid. See Birmingham Iron Co. v. NLRB, 615 F2d 661, 104 LRRM 2132 (CA 5, 1980) (prohibition on solicitation "at any time" ruled unlawful); Paceco, Div. of Fruehauf Corp. v. NLRB, supra note 112; General Motors, Frigidaire Div., 240 NLRB 168, 100 LRRM 1283 (1979). See also Pepsi Cola Bottlers of Miami, Inc., 155 NLRB 527, 60 LRRM 1357 (1965), where a prohibition against solicitation "on the job" was held valid on its face.

[126]Westinghouse Elec. Corp., 240 NLRB 905, 100 LRRM 1391, aff'd, 612 F2d 1072, 103 LRRM 2171 (CA 8, 1979); McDonnell Douglas Corp., 240 NLRB 794, 100 LRRM 1483 (1979); Chrysler Corp., 227 NLRB 1256, 95 LRRM 1448 (1977), enforcement denied, 595 F2d 364, 101 LRRM 2837 (CA 6, 1979). See also Baldor Elec. Co., 245 NLRB 614, 102 LRRM 1261 (1979) (rule prohibiting solicitation in working areas without company approval held invalid).

[127]Thermo Elec. Co., 222 NLRB 358, 91 LRRM 1310 (1976), enforced, 94 LRRM 2947 (CA 3, 1977), defined work areas as including space near a time clock and permitted enforcement of a no-solicitation rule there. See also Times Publishing Co. v. NLRB, supra note 115 (lobby of a building housing employer's business offices held to be a "work area").

[128]NLRB v. Miller Charles & Co., 341 F2d 870, 874, 58 LRRM 2507 (CA 2, 1965). See also James F. Stanford, Inc., 249 NLRB 623, 104 LRRM 1449 (1980); G. C. Murphy Co., supra note 101; Fashion Fair, Inc., 163 NLRB 97, 64 LRRM 1318 (1967). See T.R.W., Inc., supra at notes 98 and 118.

tively communicated to an employer's work force before the Board will conclude that the impact of facially illegal rules has been eliminated.[129]

(3) Unlawful promulgation or enforcement. A rule presumptively valid on its face is also presumptively valid as to its promulgation and enforcement. But these presumptions can be rebutted by evidence establishing a discriminatory purpose in the adoption or application of the rule.[130] A significant development in Board law involved the nature of the evidence that would serve to rebut the presumption of validity and establish the illegality of a rule valid on its face. In *Star-Brite Industries,*[131] a 1960 decision, a rule presumptively valid because it referred only to "working time" was challenged on the ground that it had been promulgated shortly after a union organizing campaign had begun, and it applied only to union activities. The Board found that the limitation and timing of the rule did not establish a discriminatory purpose because it would be "an anomaly" to permit an employer to adopt a rule yet "hold that he may not do so when the occasion for its use arises."[132] As to the actual enforcement of the rule by interrogation and warning of two employees, the Board found no evidence that the rule had been unfairly applied.

In 1964 *Star-Brite* was overruled,[133] signalling a change in the "nature of evidence required to establish a discriminatory motive in adopting and/or enforcing a no-solicitation rule."[134] Since then, careful consideration has been given to the extent to which the promulgation of a rule coincided with the ebb and flow of union activity. Discriminatory enforcement to stifle employee criticism of union leadership or of management action may also rebut the presumptive validity of a rule.[135]

---

[129]Chicago Magnesium Castings Co., 240 NLRB 400, 100 LRRM 1267 (1979), *aff'd,* 612 F2d 1028, 103 LRRM 2241 (CA 7, 1980); Essex Int'l, Inc., *supra* note 118. *But see* American Safety Equipment Corp. v. NLRB, 643 F2d 693, 106 LRRM 2836 (CA 10, 1981).

[130]Head Div., AMF, Inc., 228 NLRB 1406, 95 LRRM 1027 (1977), *enforced,* 593 F2d 972, 100 LRRM 3035 (CA 10, 1979); Top Security Patrol, Inc., 226 NLRB 46, 93 LRRM 1280 (1976); Walton Mfg. Co., 126 NLRB 697, 45 LRRM 1370 (1960), *enforced,* 289 F2d 177, 47 LRRM 2794 (CA 5, 1961).

[131]127 NLRB 1008, 1010, 56 LRRM 1139 (1960).

[132]*Id.* at 1011.

[133]Wm. H. Block Co., 150 NLRB 341, 57 LRRM 1531 (1964).

[134]*Id.* at 343 n.6. In overruling *Star Brite,* the Board specifically stated that it would have found a violation on the facts of *Star Brite.*

[135]NLRB v. Transcon Lines, 599 F2d 719, 101 LRRM 3031 (CA 5, 1979); American Hosp. Ass'n, 230 NLRB 54, 95 LRRM 1266 (1977), *enforced,* 84 LC §10826 (CA 7, 1978); United Parcel Serv., Inc., 230 NLRB 1147, 95 LRRM 1520 (1977); Dreis & Krump Mfg. Co. v. NLRB, 544 F2d 320, 93 LRRM 2739 (CA 7, 1976).

A *prima facie* case rebutting the presumption of validity has been established by the following:[136] (1) promulgation at the time of "intensive union activity" and application in the first instance to a known union adherent; (2) the permission for solicitations of other kinds during working time; (3) a pattern of conduct hostile to organizational efforts and found violative of Sections 8(a)(1) and (3).[137]

d. *Implementation of Rules: Timing as an Element of Legality.* The timing of implementation of a no-solicitation or no-distribution rule remains an important consideration in assessing its validity.[138] Timing the implementation of an otherwise lawful rule to coincide with union organizational activity does not automatically result in illegality where "the surrounding context is devoid of unlawful activity."[139] Strict enforcement of an existing rule, or promulgation of a new one during a union organizing campaign, has been regarded as evidence of illegal conduct, unless a showing is made that an objectively observable decline in productivity was caused by solicitation or by the campaign.[140]

e. *Union Buttons and Insignia.* In the *Republic Aviation*[141] case, the Supreme Court upheld, as a protected activity, the right of employees to wear union buttons while at work. This general rule also encompasses the right to wear other emblems, such as badges and T-shirts, demonstrating union support.[142] But again, this right must be balanced against the right of the employer to

---

[136]State Chem. Co., 166 NLRB 455, 65 LRRM 1612 (1967).

[137]Friendly Ice Cream Corp., 254 NLRB 1206, 106 LRRM 1300 (1981); Uniflite, Inc., 233 NLRB 1108, 97 LRRM 1115 (1977); Rose Co., *supra* note 116. *But see* Serv-Air, Inc., 161 NLRB 382, 63 LRRM 1270 (1966), *rev'd on that point,* 395 F2d 557, 67 LRRM 2337 (CA 10, 1968), *cert. denied,* 393 US 840, 69 LRRM 2435 (1968).

[138]*See* Ward Mfg., Inc., 152 NLRB 1270, 59 LRRM 1325 (1965), where the rule was promulgated one day after the first union meeting; *see also* Elmendorf & Fort Richardson Barber Concessions, 247 NLRB 667, 103 LRRM 1236 (1980); Sardis Luggage Co., 170 NLRB 1649, 70 LRRM 1230 (1968); State Chem. Co., *supra* note 136; Pepsi Cola Bottlers of Miami, Inc., *supra* note 125.

[139]NLRB v. Roney Plaza Apts., 597 F2d 1046, 101 LRRM 2794 (CA 5, 1979); F. P. Adams Co., 166 NLRB 967, 968, 65 LRRM 1695 (1967).

[140]*See* note 139 *supra;* Bankers Club, Inc., 218 NLRB 22, 89 LRRM 1812 (1975); North Am. Rockwell Corp., 195 NLRB 1046, 79 LRRM 1593 (1972).

[141]*Supra* note 21. *See also* Han-Dee Pak, Inc., 249 NLRB 725, 104 LRRM 1009 (1980); Dixie Mach. Rebuilders, Inc., 248 NLRB 881, 104 LRRM 1094 (1980); Carbonex Coal Co., 248 NLRB 779, 104 LRRM 1009 (1980); Permanent Label, 248 NLRB 118, 103 LRRM 1513 (1980); Regal Tube Co., 245 NLRB No. 124, 102 LRRM 1531 (1979); Pepsi-Cola Bottling Co., 242 NLRB 265, 101 LRRM 1141 (1979); Laredo Packing Co., 241 NLRB 184, 100 LRRM 1573 (1979); Dependable Lists, Inc., 239 NLRB 1304, 100 LRRM 1148 (1979).

[142]Publishers Printing Co., Inc., 246 NLRB 206, 102 LRRM 1628 (1979); De Vilbiss Co., 102 NLRB 1317, 31 LRRM 1374 (1953).

manage its business in an orderly fashion. The adjustment has resulted in the promulgation of a rule prohibiting the wearing of union emblems only where the prohibition is necessary because of "special circumstances," such as maintenance of production and discipline,[143] safety,[144] preventing alienation of customers,[145] or a possible adverse effect on patients in a health care institution.[146] Thus, for example, where friction and animosity exist between groups of employees because of a strike, prohibition of union insignias may prove to be a legitimate precaution against discord and violence.[147]

A rule based on "special circumstances" must be narrowly drawn to restrict the wearing of union insignia only in areas or under circumstances which justify the rule.[148] Enforcement of a valid rule prohibiting the wearing of certain objects, including union insignia, is unlawful if it is applied strictly to union insignia while other breaches of the rule are permitted.[149]

Although the wearing of union insignia may not be prohibited absent special circumstances, in order to qualify beyond the reach of reasonable employer rules, the prohibited insignia must

---

[143]Standard Fittings Co., 133 NLRB 928, 48 LRRM 1808 (1964); Floridan Hotel of Tampa, Inc., 137 NLRB 1484, 50 LRRM 1433 (1962), enforced as modified, 318 F2d 545, 53 LRRM 2420 (CA 2, 1963); Fabric-Tek, Inc. v. NLRB, 352 F2d 577, 60 LRRM 2376 (CA 8, 1965). See also May Dep't Stores Co., 174 NLRB 770, 70 LRRM 1307 (1969). The fact that an employer maintains a dress code does not alone justify prohibitions on wearing union insignia. Woonsocket Health Centre, 245 NLRB 652, 102 LRRM 1494 (1979); Motor Inn of Perrysburg, Inc., 243 NLRB 280, 101 LRRM 1526 (1979).
[144]Fluid Packaging Co., Inc., 247 NLRB 1469, 103 LRRM 1415 (1980); Andrews Wire Corp., 189 NLRB 108, 76 LRRM 1568 (1971).
[145]Rooney's at the Mart, 247 NLRB 1004, 103 LRRM 1291 (1980). See also Davison-Paxon Co. v. NLRB, 462 F2d 364, 80 LRRM 2673 (CA 5, 1972); NLRB v. Harrah's Club, 337 F2d 177, 57 LRRM 2198 (CA 9, 1964). Buttons which are not provocative and which do not serve to alienate customers, particularly when worn by employees not in contact with the public, may not be prohibited. Floridan Hotel of Tampa, Inc., supra note 143.
[146]George J. London Memorial Hosp., 238 NLRB 704, 99 LRRM 1680 (1978).
[147]United Aircraft Corp., 134 NLRB 1632, 49 LRRM 1384 (1961) (involving pins worn by employees who had not crossed the picket line during a bitter strike); Caterpillar Tractor Co. v. NLRB, 230 F2d 357, 37 LRRM 2619 (CA 7, 1956) (involving "scab buttons"); Boeing Airplane Co. v. NLRB, 217 F2d 369, 34 LRRM 2821 (CA 9, 1954) (involving rival unions in a violent strike). The Board's citation of all three cases for the same proposition in Floridan Hotel of Tampa, Inc., supra note 143 at 1486 n.6, may indicate an adoption of the Seventh and Ninth Circuit decisions consistent with United Aircraft.
[148]George J. London Memorial Hosp., supra note 146, where a psychiatric hospital's rule prohibiting the wearing of insignia other than of a professional nature was ruled unlawfully broad because it was not restricted to patient care areas.
[149]Nestle Co., 248 NLRB 732, 103 LRRM 1567 (1980). See also Pay 'n Save Corp., 247 NLRB 1346, 103 LRRM 1334 (1980), enforced, 641 F2d 697, 106 LRRM 3040 (CA 9, 1981); C. Markus Hardware, Inc., 243 NLRB 903, 102 LRRM 1353 (1979); St. Joseph's Hosp., 225 NLRB 348, 93 LRRM 1179 (1976).

be sufficiently identified with employee union sympathies. For example, the mere wearing of flowers unaccompanied by any legend by some of the 5,000 employees in a large department store was judged not to have this effect.[150]

Employer-supplied campaign badges are not treated the same as union insignia. They may constitute unlawful[151] interference or grounds for setting aside an election, [152] for the employer's supplying of badges may, depending on the circumstances, place employees in the position of declaring themselves as if they had been interrogated.[153]

f. "Captive Audience" Speeches, Conferences, and Interviews. When the employer makes a "captive audience speech" while using a no-solicitation/no-distribution rule to deny a union an opportunity to reply under similar conditions, the consequences may be complex. Prior to the advent of Section 8(c), the Board adopted a rule of absolute prohibition of captive-audience speeches.[154] In 1948 this rule was repudiated as inconsistent with Section 8(c).[155] Nonetheless, the Board attempted to control captive-audience speeches to some degree by formulating its *Bonwit-Teller*[156] doctrine of equal opportunity. That doctrine held that captive-audience speeches by the employer, when coupled with a no-solicitation rule, constituted a discriminatory application of the rule. The Board sought to avoid conflict with Section 8(c) by emphasizing the employer's refusal to permit a reply under similar conditions, rather than its delivery of a noncoercive speech. Two years later, in 1953, a reconstituted Board panel (during the Eisenhower Administration) rejected the equal-opportunity doctrine. In *Livingston Shirt Corp.*[157] the Board held

---

[150]Gimbel Bros., 147 NLRB 500, 505, 56 LRRM 1287 (1964). *See also* Pillowtex Corp., 234 NLRB 560, 97 LRRM 1369 (1978).

[151]Kurz-Kasch, Inc., 239 NLRB 1044, 100 LRRM 1118 (1978).

[152]Chas. V. Weise Co., 133 NLRB 765, 48 LRRM 1709 (1961). *See also* note 276 *infra* and accompanying text. The Board, however, refused to set aside an election where: the employer merely made buttons available to employees by placing them in a central location; there was no supervisory involvement in the distribution process; employees were told that wearing buttons was strictly voluntary; there was no independent coercive conduct. Black Dot, Inc., 239 NLRB 929, 100 LRRM 1051 (1978).

[153]Chas V. Weise Co., *supra* note 152. *See* discussion of unlawful interrogation *infra* at notes 267-308.

[154]Clark Bros., *supra* note 51. For a general discussion of captive-audience speeches, *see* Note, *NLRB Regulation of Employer's Pre-Election Captive Audience Speeches*, 65 Mich. L. Rev. 1236 (1967).

[155]Babcock & Wilcox Co., 77 NLRB 577, 578, 22 LRRM 1057 (1948).

[156]Bonwit-Teller, Inc., 96 NLRB 608, 28 LRRM 1547 (1951), *modified,* 104 NLRB 497, 32 LRRM 1102 (1953).

[157]Livingston Shirt Co., 107 NLRB 400, 33 LRRM 1156 (1953).

that "an employer does not commit an unfair labor practice if he makes a preelection speech on company time and premises to his employees and denies the union's request for an opportunity to reply."[158] Supreme Court dicta in *Nu Tone*[159] seemingly approved this rule, at least where the union has other means to carry its message to the employees.

Decided with *Livingston Shirt* was *Peerless Plywood*,[160] which formulated the still-current "24-hour rule" prohibiting both unions and employers from delivering captive-audience speeches to massed groups of employees within 24 hours of an election.[161] Conflict with Section 8(c) was avoided because an infringement of the rule is not deemed an unfair labor practice but merely a basis for setting aside the election.

In 1962, another reconstituted Board (during the Kennedy Administration), in *May Department Stores*,[162] distinguished *Livingston Shirt* on the ground that the *Livingston* no-solicitation rule was presumptively valid and inapplicable to nonworking hours. But use of a broad, privileged no-solicitation rule, coupled with anti-union speeches, was deemed to create "a glaring 'imbalance in opportunities for organizational communication' " within the *Nu Tone* doctrine, thus violating Section 8(a)(1). The Sixth Circuit, however, refused enforcement, charging that the Board had failed to give adequate consideration to various other means of communication available to the union.[163] But

---

[158]*Id.* at 409.

[159]NLRB v. Steelworkers (Nutone, Inc.), *supra* note 22.

[160]Peerless Plywood Co., 107 NLRB 427, 33 LRRM 1151 (1953). *See* Chapter 9 *infra* at note 27.

[161]The "24-hour rule" is not violated when campaign literature is distributed within 24 hours of an election as long as a captive audience speech is not delivered during that period. General Time Corp., 195 NLRB 343, 79 LRRM 1340 (1972); Moody Nursing Home, 251 NLRB 147, 105 LRRM 1126 (1980). The rule was violated, however, when a captive audience speech extended into the 24-hour period prior to the election, where the evidence showed that the employer acted in deliberate disregard of *Peerless Plywood.* Rodac Corp., 231 NLRB 261, 95 LRRM 1608 (1977). *See also* McDowell Energy Corp., 224 NLRB 1462, 92 LRRM 1573 (1976) (rule not violated when undetermined number of employees voluntarily remained in conversation with employer representatives for an additional 15 to 30 minutes immediately after the conclusion of a captive-audience speech which concluded one minute before commencement of the 24-hour preelection period); Shop Rite Foods, 195 NLRB 133, 79 LRRM 1231 (1972) (rule not violated where the employer made captive-audience speeches to employees in a unit comprised of 26 retail stores, where some speeches occurred within 24 hours of the time the election was to start at other stores but none of the employees spoken to were scheduled to vote within 24 hours of the employer's speech).

[162]May Dep't Stores Co., 136 NLRB 797, 49 LRRM 1862 (1962), *enforcement denied,* 316 F2d 797, 53 LRRM 2172 (CA 6, 1963).

[163]*Id.*

the Board adhered to its position and in *Montgomery Ward & Co.*[164] found a violation where an unlawful no-solicitation rule, which banned union solicitation in nonworking areas during nonworking time, prevented a response to anti-union speeches to massed employees during working time. The Board found the speeches coercive and unprotected by Section 8(c); and, when coupled with a no-solicitation rule, they created a "glaring imbalance" in organizational communication. This time the Sixth Circuit enforced the Board's order, distinguishing its *May* decision on the ground that the no-solicitation rule in *May* had been valid and the speeches noncoercive.[165]

In *S. & H. Grossinger's, Inc.*[166] the Board conditioned validity of an employer's continual anti-union speeches during working time upon the granting of a similar opportunity to the union. Since many of the employees lived on the premises of the resort hotel involved, meaningful outside communication was blocked. The Second Circuit held that an equal-opportunity requirement could be imposed only when the employer is enforcing its no-solicitation rule; but because it also upheld the Board's invalidation of the employer's rule excluding union organizers from the employer's property,[167] the court found there was no need to order the employer to provide the union with an equal opportunity to address the employees.[168]

In *General Electric Co.*[169] the employer made speeches on company time to massed employees who were informed that attendance was not mandatory. The union was denied equal time. In a petition to set aside the election, the union urged the Board to overrule *Livingston Shirt* and reactivate and extend *Bonwit-Teller* as a substantive rule of preelection conduct. The Board refused, preferring to postpone any reconsideration of current Board doctrine in the area of plant access until after it had the benefit of experience with the rule adopted in *Excelsior Underwear, Inc.*[170] To date the Board has not reassessed its rule on union access to employer facilities.

---

[164]Montgomery Ward & Co., 145 NLRB 846, 55 LRRM 1063 (1964), *enforced as modified*, 339 F2d 889, 58 LRRM 2115 (CA 6, 1965).
[165]Montgomery Ward & Co. v. NLRB, *supra* note 164.
[166]S. & H. Grossinger's, Inc. *supra* note 107.
[167]NLRB v. S. & H. Grossinger's, Inc., *supra* note 107.
[168]*Id. See also* NLRB v. H. W. Elson Bottling Co., 379 F2d 223, 65 LRRM 2673 (CA 6, 1967).
[169]156 NLRB 1247, 61 LRRM 1222 (1966).
[170]156 NLRB 1236, 61 LRRM 1217 (1966), holding that parties to a pending election may have access to a list of the names and addresses of all employees eligible to vote;

Captive-audience speeches involving noncoercive anti-union remarks to small groups of employees in private areas of a workplace have been subject to different Board policies over the years. In 1974, in *NVF Co., Hartwell Div.*,[171] the Board rejected application of its *Peoples Drug Stores*[172] rule, that the making of such remarks in a small group setting is *per se* objectionable preelection conduct. Instead, it adopted a "facts and circumstances" approach to determine the objectionability of captive-audience speeches in such a setting. The Board there held that, where approximately 95 percent of the employees in the voting unit had been interviewed in the general manager's office in groups of five or six for the purpose of asking them to vote against the union and where there was no showing of any coercive or intemperate statements, there was no improper interference with the election.[173] The Board has refused to expand *Peerless Plywood* to include anti-union statements made by management representatives to individual employees at their respective work stations within 24 hours of the election.[174] But dispatching supervisors or other management personnel to interview employees in their homes constitutes sufficient grounds for setting aside an election, regardless of whether the actual remarks made by employer representatives in such interviews are coercive in character.[175]

---

the *Excelsior* rule, though not the means of its promulgation, was approved by the Supreme Court in NLRB v. Wyman-Gordon Co., 394 US 759, 70 LRRM 3345 (1969). *See* Chapter 10 *infra* at notes 239-52 and Chapter 32 *infra* at notes 197-218. *See also* Bok, *supra* note 1. Establishment of the *Bonwit-Teller* doctrine as a preelection rule of conduct would theoretically not conflict with decisions such as *Babcock & Wilcox*, since there would be no §8(a)(1) finding; the rule would thus stand on the same footing as the rule in *Peerless Plywood*.

One of the provisions of the Labor Law Reform Bill which failed of enactment in 1978 would have required the Board to develop rules and regulations involving equal access by unions to employer premises whenever an employer delivered a captive-audience speech. *See* H. R. 8410, 95th Cong., 1st Sess. (1977); S. 2467, 95th Cong., 1st Sess. (1977). *See* Chapter 5 *supra*.

[171]210 NLRB 663, 86 LRRM 1200 (1974).

[172]119 NLRB 634, 41 LRRM 1141 (1957).

[173]The Board majority overruled *Peoples Drug* and its progeny to the extent they were inconsistent with its holding. Members Fanning and Jenkins, in dissent, stated that the criteria advanced by the majority varied only imperceptibly from those long applied in *Peoples Drug. Id.*

[174]Associated Milk Producers, 237 NLRB 879, 99 LRRM 1212 (1978). The Board also refused in this case to find that a "captive audience" speech had been delivered where a management representative had informally made anti-union statements to three employees as a group within the 24-hour period. *See also* Electro-Wire Prods., 242 NLRB 960, 101 LRRM 1271 (1979); Amwood Homes, 243 NLRB 1006, 101 LRRM 1565 (1979).

[175]Peoria Plastic Co., 117 NLRB 545, 39 LRRM 1281 (1957); The Hurley Co., 130 NLRB 282, 47 LRRM 1293 (1961).

g. No-Access Rules. In defining the right of off-duty employees to enter or remain on plant premises for purposes of engaging in union activities, the Board balances employee self-organizational rights against the employer's interest in its property and productivity, and considers whether an alternative means of communication is available to the labor organization and employees it seeks to represent.

In *GTE Lenkurt, Inc.*,[176] a nondiscriminatory rule prohibiting off-duty employees from entering or remaining on the plant premises for *any* purpose was found valid. The Board reasoned that the status of an off-duty employee is more nearly analogous to that of a nonemployee, in that both are invitees or trespassers to the same extent and thus neither is entitled more than the other to admission to the premises. An off-duty employee, it was noted, might still engage in union solicitation during non-working time within the employer's premises while on-the-clock.

The Board has emphasized, however, that *GTE Lenkurt* is to be narrowly construed and confined to its precise facts. The Board clarified its position in *Tri-County Medical Center*,[177] where it declared that a rule denying off-duty employees access to the employer's premises is presumptively valid only if (1) it limits access solely with respect to the interior of the plant and other working areas; (2) it is clearly disseminated to all employees; and (3) it applies to off-duty employees seeking access to the plant for any purpose and not just to those employees engaged in union activity. Additionally, a rule which denies off-duty employees entry to parking lots, gates, and other outside non-working areas will be invalid unless justified by business reasons.[178]

---

[176]204 NLRB 921, 83 LRRM 1684 (1973).

[177]222 NLRB 1089, 91 LRRM 1323 (1976).

[178]For application of this rule in varying contexts, *see* NLRB v. Roney Plaza Apts., *supra* note 139; Stein Seal Co. v. NLRB, 605 F2d 703, 102 LRRM 2297 (CA 3, 1979); NLRB v. Presbyterian Medical Center, 586 F2d 165, 99 LRRM 3137 (CA 10, 1978); Northeastern Univ., 235 NLRB 858, 98 LRRM 1347 (1978), *enforced in part*, 601 F2d 1208, 101 LRRM 2767 (CA 1, 1979); Sparks Nugget, Inc., 230 NLRB 275, 95 LRRM 1298 (1977); East Bay Newspapers, Inc., 228 NLRB 692, 96 LRRM 1019 (1977); Carda Hotels, Inc., d/b/a Holiday Hotel & Casino, 228 NLRB 926, 94 LRRM 1702 (1977), *enforced*, 604 F2d 605, 102 LRRM 2484 (CA 9, 1979); East Bay Newspapers, Inc., 225 NLRB 1148, 93 LRRM 1102 (1976); Continental Bus Sys., 229 NLRB 1262, 95 LRRM 1307 (1971). *See also* Pioneer Finishing Corp., 247 NLRB 1299, 103 LRRM 1332 (1980); St. Anne's Hosp., 245 NLRB 1009, 102 LRRM 1527 (1979); Southern Fla. Hotel & Motel Ass'n, 245 NLRB 561, 102 LRRM 1578 (1979); St. Vincent Hosp., 244 NLRB 331, 102 LRRM 1177 (1979); Campbell Chain Co., 237 NLRB 420, 99 LRRM 1478 (1978); Harvey's Wagon Wheel, Inc., 236 NLRB 1670, 98 LRRM 1501 (1978); United Parcel Serv., 234 NLRB 223, 97 LRRM 1212 (1978).

Although no-access rules applicable to nonemployees were analyzed in accordance with the general principles contained in *Babcock & Wilcox*,[179] enforcement of a no-access rule against a nonemployee union organizer distributing literature on the employer's parking lot, and causing his arrest for trespassing, was ruled unlawful by the Board where the employer had permitted other nonemployees, such as food and news vendors, to enter and use the parking lot for nonunion purposes.[180]

h. Prohibiting Protected Activity on Private Property Open to Public. In its 1968 *Logan Valley* decision,[181] the Supreme Court ruled that property rights must yield to a union's constitutionally protected right to picket and handbill on a privately owned shopping center parking lot. Such private property, the Court said, had taken on a "quasi-public" character.[182] In *Central Hardware*,[183] however, the Court refused to extend the "quasi-public" doctrine to nonemployee solicitation on retail store customer parking lots, noting that every retail and service establishment in the United States was open to the public and thus could be deemed to be "quasi-public."[184] Subsequently, in *Hudgens* v. *NLRB*,[185] the Supreme Court effectively overruled *Logan Valley* and rejected application of constitutional principles to disputes over nonemployee access to private property normally open to the public. The Court held that in deciding whether prohibitions

---

[179]NLRB v. Babcock & Wilcox, *supra* note 99 and accompanying text. *See, e.g.,* Rochester Gen. Hosp., 234 NLRB 253, 97 LRRM 1410 (1978) (rule forbidding nonemployees access to hospital property lawful as applied to union representatives distributing literature in employer's parking lot because other channels of communication were available). *See also* Belcher Towing Co. v. NLRB, *supra* note 101; Sabine Towing & Transp. Co., *supra* note 101 (refusal to enforce Board orders invalidating rules prohibiting access of nonemployees to employer vessels). For application of *Babcock & Wilcox* principles to rules barring union business agents from access to construction job sites, *see* Villa Avila, 253 NLRB 76, 105 LRRM 1499 (1980) (refusal of access violated §8 (a)(1)); Blanchard Constr. Co., 234 NLRB 1035, 97 LRRM 1389 (1979) (refusal of access held not unlawful).

[180]Chrysler Corp., 232 NLRB 466, 96 LRRM 1382 (1977). *See also* Hutzler Bros. Co., 241 NLRB 914, 101 LRRM 1062 (1979), *enforcement denied,* 630 F2d 1012, 105 LRRM 2473 (CA 4, 1980) (Board conclusion, that alternative communication channels available to the union were either too costly or impractical to be effective, lacked substantial record-evidence support; rule barring nonemployee organizers from retail store parking lot held valid); Schlegal Okla., Inc., 250 NLRB 20, 104 LRRM 1323 (1980).

[181]Food Employees Local 590 v. Logan Valley Plaza, Inc., *supra* note 105.

[182]*See* Chapter 21 *infra* at notes 20-26 for further discussion of the constitutional aspects of *Logan Valley*.

[183]Central Hardware Co. v. NLRB, *supra* note 108. *See* Chapter 21 *infra* at notes 183-84.

[184]The Court applied the standard established in NLRB v. Babcock & Wilcox, *supra* note 99.

[185]Hudgens v. NLRB, *supra* note 109. *See* Chapter 21 *infra* at notes 185-90.

on nonemployee access to private, "quasi-public" property were reasonable, only the balancing standards under the Act, as established in *Babcock & Wilcox*,[186] would govern.

In applying the *Babcock & Wilcox* standards to activity carried out on private property open to the public, the Board on remand of *Hudgens*[187] reached results similar to those produced under the Supreme Court's *Logan Valley* decision but without relying on the discredited constitutional underpinnings of that decision. Thus, picketing on shopping mall property in support of an economic strike against a warehouse of one of the retail stores leasing premises on the mall was deemed protected activity. The Board said that the distinction between economic activities and the organizational activities in *Babcock & Wilcox* might "require a different application of the accommodation principle because of the different purposes sought to be served."[188] It ruled, nevertheless, that the mall owner's threat to arrest the picketers violated Section 8(a)(1) because the message sought to be conveyed by the picketing would have been too greatly diluted if the picketers had been forced to use alternative channels of communication and because

> safety considerations, the likelihood of enmeshing neutral employers, and the fact that many people become members of the pickets' intended audience on impulse all weigh against requiring the pickets to remove to public property, or even to the sidewalks surrounding the mall.[189]

In reaching that conclusion, the Board held that Section 8(a)(1) had been violated even though the property rights impinged upon were those of the shopping mall owner rather than those of the employer against whom the union activity was directed. It relied on the facts that the mall owner was protecting its own interests and acting as the retail store owner's agent in policing the mall and removing picketers.[190]

---

[186]NLRB v. Babcock & Wilcox, *supra* note 99.

[187]Scott Hudgens, *supra* note 110. *See also* note 190 *infra*.

[188]*Supra* note 110 at 416.

[189]*Id.* at 417.

[190]*But see* Giant Foods Mkts., Inc. v. NLRB, 633 F2d 18, 105 LRRM 2916 (CA 6, 1980). Finding an absence of substantial evidence as to whether alternative channels of communication were available to the union, and as to whether neutral employers were "enmeshed" in the union's dispute by its "area standards" picketing in a shopping center, the Sixth Circuit refused enforcement and remanded the Board's order; the Board had determined that a peaceful demand, by the employer store owner (against whom the union was picketing on shopping center property) and by another store owner conducting business there, that pickets leave the shopping center property was held to violate §8(a)(1). 241 NLRB 727, 100 LRRM 1598 (1979). However, in Seattle-First Nat'l

i. Effect of Contractual Waiver of Right to Solicit or Distribute. Provisions in collective bargaining agreements may expressly or impliedly contain overly broad or invalid rules prohibiting solicitation and distribution, purporting thereby to waive employee Section 7 rights. Over the years, Board decisions on the legal effect of such a waiver have been inconsistent. The Board's initial position was that unions could not use collectively bargained clauses to waive distribution and solicitation rights of employees who were seeking to criticize or to oppose the union's leadership, but later it expanded its interpretation of Section 7 to strike down contract provisions restricting the rights of employees seeking to support the union as well.[191]

The 1974 Supreme Court *Magnavox* decision[192] resolved a split among the circuits and the Board. It held that employee Section 7 rights to solicit and to distribute literature advocating support of or opposition to an incumbent union may not be contractually waived in the absence of production considerations that may make special restrictions necessary. "The place of work is a place uniquely appropriate for dissemination of views concerning the bargaining representative and the various options open to the employees," the Court said, and "[s]o long as the distribution is by employees to employees and so long as the in-plant solicitation is on nonworking time, banning of that solicitation might seriously dilute §7 rights."[193] The Court's decision did not, however, specifically deal with the Board's position that a union may lawfully waive any right employees might have to distribute union "institutional literature."[194]

Bank, 243 NLRB 898, 101 LRRM 1537 (1979), *enforcement denied in part and remanded,* 651 F2d 1272, 105 LRRM 3411 (CA 9, 1980), a demand by the owner of a bank building that union representatives who were handbilling on the forty-sixth floor of the building near the premises of a restaurant with which the union was engaged in a labor dispute leave the building or be arrested was held to violate §8(a)(1) (the Ninth Circuit remanded for revision of the order to ensure that the number of union representatives on the floor and their behavior be properly restricted.) *See also* Meijer, Inc., NLRB Gen. Counsel Advice Memo., Case No. 7-CA-16237, 101 LRRM 1529 (1979), for discussion of *Hudgens* principles in context of stranger picketing on shopping center property. *Cf.* Edward J. DeBartolo Corp. v. NLRB, 662 F2d 264, 108 LRRM 2729 (CA 4, 1981), Chapter 24 *infra,* note 24.

[191] *See* Magnavox Co., 195 NLRB 265, 79 LRRM 1283 (1972), *enforcement denied,* 474 F2d 1269, 82 LRRM 2852 (CA 6, 1973), *rev'd,* 415 US 322, 85 LRRM 2475 (1974); Gale Prods. Div. of Outboard Marine Corp., 142 NLRB 1246, 53 LRRM 1242 (1963), *enforcement denied,* 337 F2d 390, 57 LRRM 2164 (CA 7, 1964).

[192] NLRB v. Magnavox Co., 415 US 322, 85 LRRM 2475 (1974).

[193] *Id.* at 325.

[194] *Id.* at 329. The Board has subsequently ruled that whatever right an employee has to post union literature on a bulletin board may be lawfully waived by a restriction in a collective bargaining agreement. General Motors Corp., Frigidaire Div., *supra* note 125. *See also* Special Mach. & Eng'r Inc., 247 NLRB 884, 103 LRRM 1209 (1980).

The Board has applied the *Magnavox* decision in a wide variety of situations, most of which have involved enforcement of contractual restrictions on solicitation and distribution of matters critical of the incumbent union.[195]

j. Prohibiting Distribution of Political Materials. Guidance as to the rights of employees to distribute material of a "political" nature on company property was provided by the Supreme Court in *Eastex, Inc.* v. *NLRB.*[196] The Court adopted the Board's ruling that a company violated Section 8(a)(1) by prohibiting distribution of a newsletter which urged employees to write their legislators to oppose incorporation of the state "right-to-work" statute into a revised state constitution, criticized a Presidential veto of an increase in the federal minimum wage, and urged employees to register to vote to "defeat our enemies and elect our friends." The subject matter of the newsletter, in the Court's judgment, "bears such a relation to employees' interests as to come within the guarantee"[197] of Section 7 and "fairly is characterized as concerted activity for the 'mutual aid or protection' "[198] of the employer's employees and of employees generally. The Court stopped short, however, of adopting a general rule governing every in-plant distribution of "political" literature, noting that "[t]here may well be types of conduct or speech that are so purely political or so remotely connected to the concerns of employees as employees as to be beyond the protection of [Section 7]."[199] The Court specifically confined its holding in *Eastex* to its precise facts, leaving development of more general policy to case-by-case consideration.

---

[195]*E.g.* Ford Motor Co., 233 NLRB 698, 96 LRRM 1513 (1977); General Motors Corp., 211 NLRB 986, 87 LRRM 1167 (1974), *enforced in relevant part,* 512 F2d 447, 89 LRRM 2431 (CA 6, 1975). *See* Chapter 19 *infra* at notes 221-22 for a discussion of cases involving the Board's application of *Magnavox* to contract provisions limiting unit employees' rights to distribute literature. *See also* note 200 *infra* and accompanying text.
[196]437 US 556, 98 LRRM 2717 (1978).
[197]*Id.* at 569. *See also* Hesse Corp., 244 NLRB 985, 102 LRRM 1340 (1979) (ban on employees' wearing of stickers protesting "right to work" laws held illegal).
[198]*Supra* note 196 at 570.
[199]*Supra* note 196 at 570 n.20. *See* Firestone Steel Prods. Co., 244 NLRB 826, 102 LRRM 1172 (1979) (employer lawfully prohibited distribution of literature supporting candidates in a statewide election for supreme court justice, governor, and United States Senator); Ford Motor Co., 221 NLRB 663, 666, 90 LRRM 1731 (1975), *enforced,* 546 F2d 418, 93 LRRM 2570 (CA 3, 1976) (distributing a "purely political tract" calling for independent workers' party and workers' government on employer's premises held unprotected even though "the election of any political candidate may have an ultimate effect on employment conditions").

Another frequent application of Board rules on solicitation and distribution of a "political" nature is found in cases where the Board has ruled that distribution of nonorganizational literature complaining about an incumbent union's leadership or bargaining position may be prohibited only in accordance with the principles of *Republic Aviation*.[200]

2. Specific Conduct Violative of Section 8(a)(1). A wide assortment of traditional and imaginative techniques have been employed either to frustrate or to further union organizational efforts. Usually these have been utilized during election campaigns and have been evaluated by the Board in terms of election interference. In some instances, however, they have been employed at other stages of employer-employee relationships and have been evaluated in the broader context of interference with Section 7 rights. In the discussion that follows, various techniques are considered in terms of their legality or illegality, regardless of setting.

a. Threats and Loss of Benefits. Election campaigns and anti-union activity generally have sometimes been marked by loss of benefits and by threats, both express and implied. The discontinuance of benefits, such as coffee breaks and discount privileges on employee purchases,[201] represents objectionable reprisal. Exclusion of unionized employees from an employee stock plan is another example of a Section 8(a)(1) violation.[202] Direct threats to close a plant[203] or to discharge union adherents[204] as a means of combating an organizational drive constitute interference.

---

[200]*Supra* notes 95-98. Texaco, Inc. v. NLRB, 462 F2d 812, 80 LRRM 2283 (CA 3, 1972), *cert. denied*, 409 US 1008, 81 LRRM 2672 (1972); NLRB v. Transcon Lines, 599 F2d 719, 101 LRRM 3031 (CA 5, 1979); Local 5163, Steelworkers (Charles A. Bizzaro), 248 NLRB 943, 103 LRRM 1516 (1980); Chicago Magnesium Castings Co., 240 NLRB 400, 100 LRRM 1267 (1979); The Singer Co., 220 NLRB 1179, 90 LRRM 1433 (1975); General Motors Corp., 212 NLRB 133, 86 LRRM 1543 (1974), *enforced as modified*, 512 F2d 447, 89 LRRM 2431 (CA 6, 1975); McDonnell Douglas Corp., 210 NLRB 280, 86 LRRM 1164 (1974); Samsonite Corp., 206 NLRB 343, 84 LRRM 1369 (1973). *See also* note 195 *supra*.

[201]Davis Wholesale Co., Inc., 165 NLRB 271, 65 LRRM 1494 (1967), *enforced*, 413 F2d 407, 70 LRRM 3436 (CA DC, 1969); Buddy Schoellkopf Prods., Inc., 164 NLRB 660, 65 LRRM 1231 (1967), *enforced*, 410 F2d 82, 71 LRRM 2089 (CA 5, 1969).

[202]Bendix-Westinghouse Automatic Air Brake Co., 185 NLRB 375, 75 LRRM 1079 (1970), *enforced*, 443 F2d 106, 77 LRRM 2368 (CA 6, 1971). *But see* Goodyear Tire & Rubber Co. v. NLRB, 413 F2d 158, 71 LRRM 2977 (CA 6, 1979).

[203]*Cf.* Textile Workers v. Darlington Mfg. Co., *supra* note 19 at 274 n.20, where the Court distinguished a termination of a business from the unjustifiable threat to do so. *See* Chapter 7 *infra* at notes 238-55. *See also* Nebraska Bulk Transp., Inc., 240 NLRB 135, 100 LRRM 1340 (1979), *modified*, 608 F2d 311, 104 LRRM 2384 (CA 8, 1979).

[204]NLRB v. Neuhoff Bros., Packers, 375 F2d 372, 64 LRRM 2673 (CA 5, 1967), where Judge Brown provides a lively discussion on flagrant election campaign violations. *See*

More troublesome are implied threats. Certain campaign themes have become familiar in the election arena. Employers seeking to inform employees of unfavorable consequences of unionization may develop their themes in a number of written or oral messages. The trend of Board decisions has been to evaluate the messages, not in isolation from each other but in their "total context."[205] If the overall effect of the messages creates an atmosphere of fear by portraying the selection of a bargaining agent as "futile" and the "economic hazards" as "inevitable," free choice may be rendered impossible.[206] The conveyance of a "clear message" to employees "that it was futile for them to select [the union] as their bargaining representative for the purpose of improving their conditions of employment, and that selection . . . could only bring strikes, violence and loss of jobs" has been held unlawful interference and cause for invalidation of an election.[207]

As part of its opinion in *Gissel,* the Supreme Court established the following guidelines to test preelection predictions:

> [A]n employer is free to communicate to his employees any of his general views about unionism or any of his specific views about a particular union, so long as the communications do not contain a "threat of reprisal or force or promise of benefit." He may even make a prediction as to the precise effects he believes unionization will have on his company. In such a case, however, the prediction must be carefully phrased on the basis of objective fact to convey an employer's belief as to demonstrably probable consequences beyond his control or to convey a management decision already arrived at to close the plant in case of unionization. . . . If there is any implication that an employer may or may not take action solely on his own initiative for reasons unrelated to economic necessities and known only to him, the statement is no longer a reasonable prediction based on available facts but a threat of retaliation based on misrepresentation

---

also Donald E. Hernly, Inc., 240 NLRB 840, 100 LRRM 1368 (1979), *enforcement denied,* 613 F2d 457, 103 LRRM 2347 (CA 2, 1980).

[205]Madison Kipp Co., 240 NLRB 879, 100 LRRM 1381 (1979); Arch Beverage Corp., 140 NLRB 1385, 52 LRRM 1251 (1963); *see* notes 71-78 *supra* and accompanying text; *see also* Kleeb, *Taft-Hartley Rules During Union Organizing Campaigns,* 55 LRRM 115, 117 (1964), *and* Bok, *supra* note 1.

[206]Oak Mfg. Co., 141 NLRB 1323, 52 LRRM 1502 (1963); Storkline Corp., 142 NLRB 875, 53 LRRM 1160 (1963).

[207]Garry Mfg. Co., 242 NLRB 539, 101 LRRM 1197 (1979), *enforced in part,* 630 F2d 934, 105 LRRM 2113 (CA 3, 1980); General Dynamics Corp., 250 NLRB No. 96, 104 LRRM 1438 (1980); General Indus. Elec. Co., 146 NLRB 1139, 1141, 56 LRRM 1015 (1964).

and coercion, and as such without the protection of the First Amendment. We therefore agree with the court below that "conveyance of the employer's belief, even though sincere, that unionization will or may result in the closing of the plant is not a statement of fact unless, which is most improbable, the eventuality of closing is capable of proof." . . . [A]n employer is free only to tell "what he reasonably believes will be the likely economic consequences of unionization that are outside his control," and not "threats of economic reprisal to be taken solely on his own volition."[208]

(1) Futility. That it would be futile to select a bargaining agent has been conveyed, for example, by an explanation that the employer's wage policies would continue to be determined unilaterally, "union or no union."[209] A sense of futility was imported in blunter terms when an employer indicated that it would abide by its present policies "even if Jesus Christ were representing" the employees.[210] But ordinarily conveyance of a sense of futility may not be sufficient to set aside an election unless the employer has stated "either expressly, or by clear implication that it would not bargain in good faith with a union even if it were selected by the employees."[211] An employer's warning, for example, that "he could make negotiations last a year and therefore another election would be necessary" was ground for setting aside an election.[212] But not all promises of "future litigation" will be treated in the same manner, particularly if the surrounding circumstances are devoid of coercive conduct.[213]

---

[208]NLRB v. Gissel Packing Co., *supra* note 56 at 618-19. The court cited Textile Workers v. Darlington Mfg. Co., *supra* note 19 and NLRB v. River Togs, Inc., 382 F2d 198, 202, 65 LRRM 2987 (CA 2, 1967).

[209]The Trane Co., 137 NLRB 1506, 50 LRRM 1434 (1962). *See also* American Telecommunications Corp., Electromechanical Div., 249 NLRB 1135, 104 LRRM 1282 (1980) ("uniform benefits" regardless of existence of union representation at any of employer plants held to be unlawful statement).

[210]Metropolitan Life Ins. Co., 142 NLRB 929, 53 LRRM 1187 (1963).

[211]American Greetings Corp., *supra* note 77 at 1445 n.4. *See* American Telecommunications Corp., *supra* note 209; Dal-Tex Optical Co., 137 NLRB 1782, 1783, 50 LRRM 1489 (1962) (statement by the employer that the election process "will not mean a thing if the union wins" because the employer would take a "couple of years" to litigate it). *See also* Fry Foods, Inc., 241 NLRB 76, 100 LRRM 1513 (1979), *enforced,* 609 F2d 267, 102 LRRM 2894 (CA 6, 1979) (employer stated that he would not bargain with the union even if the union won the election and "four years" would be needed to get a union into the plant). For other decisions suggesting that a sense of futility may be conveyed in the absence of express employer statements indicating it would not bargain in good faith, *see* North Am. Car Corp., 253 NLRB 958, 106 LRRM 1036 (1980); Piezo Technology, Inc., 254 NLRB 999, 106 LRRM 1276 (1980); Pacific Tel. Co., 256 NLRB 449, 107 LRRM 1269 (1981).

[212]Wall Colmonoy Corp., 173 NLRB 40, 69 LRRM 1205 (1968).

[213]W. T. Grant Co., 147 NLRB 420, 56 LRRM 1231 (1964).

(2) Inevitability. Depicting strikes, violence, and loss of jobs as the inevitable consequence of unionization, can be ground for setting aside an election.[214] The tactic of showing the classic propaganda film "And Women Must Weep," which purported to depict violence during a 1956 strike at Potter-Brumfield Co. and emphasized enactments of picket line vandalism, telephone threats, a house bombing, and a night gunfire attack on a dissenting worker's home, frequently resulted in findings of unfair labor practices and objectionable election conduct.[215] But the Board's 1974 *Litho Press* decision overruled prior inconsistent decisions and held that presenting the movie was not violative of the Act.[216]

Stressing the likelihood of strikes is not necessarily improper if it is germane to the strike record and claims of job security of the union in issue and is not simply raised as a "straw man" to create unwarranted fear.[217] Depending on their context, employer statements as to the possibility of strikes have been found to be "rhetoric" or "opinion" and, as such, permissible campaign techniques.[218] Similarly, the lawfulness of predicting loss of customer patronage and resulting employment reductions depends on whether the loss is portrayed as an inevitable or as a possible result of unionizing.[219]

(3) Assessing campaign phrases. The Board's attempt to assess an employer's statements in the context of its pattern of conduct

---

[214]Louis Gallet, Inc., 247 NLRB No. 13, 103 LRRM 1125 (1980); Storkline Corp., *supra* note 206.

[215]*E.g.,* Storkline Corp., *supra* note 206 (employer's warning that economic injury would befall employees, intensified by showing the film "And Women Must Weep," held to have created an impression of "unreasoning fear" that impaired free choice). A filmed rebuttal entitled "Anatomy of a Lie" has frequently been used by unions as a counteraction to the employer's use of "And Women Must Weep."

[216]Litho Press, 211 NLRB 1014, 86 LRRM 1471 (1974), *enforced,* 512 F2d 73, 89 LRRM 2171 (CA 5, 1975) (the Board held that showing "And Women Must Weep" was not violative of the Act regardless of the circumstances of the campaign). *See also* Sab Harmon Indus., Inc., 252 NLRB No. 132, 105 LRRM 1353 (1980) (showing the movie "The Springfield Gun" held unobjectionable on the basis of *Litho Press*).

[217]Morristown Foam & Fibre Corp., 211 NLRB 52, 86 LRRM 1420 (1974); Universal Elec. Co., 156 NLRB 1101, 61 LRRM 1189 (1966); Coors Porcelain Co., 158 NLRB 1108, 62 LRRM 1158 (1966); American Greetings Corp., *supra* note 77.

[218]*See, e.g.,* NLRB v. Eastern Smelting Corp., 598 F2d 666, 101 LRRM 2328 (CA 4, 1979); TRW-United Greenfield Div., 245 NLRB 978, 102 LRRM 1520 (1979), *enforced,* 637 F2d 410, 106 LRRM 2768 (CA 5, 1981).

[219]*Compare* Haynes Stellite Co., 136 NLRB 95, 49 LRRM 1711 (1962), *enforcement denied sub nom.* Union Carbide Corp. v. NLRB, 310 F2d 844, 52 LRRM 2001 (CA 6, 1962), *and* R. D. Cole Mfg. Co., 133 NLRB 1455, 49 LRRM 1033 (1961), *with* Freeman Mfg. Co., 148 NLRB 577, 57 LRRM 1047 (1964). *See also* Jasta Mfg. Co., 246 NLRB 48, 102 LRRM 1610 (1979); First Data Resources, Inc., 241 NLRB 713, 100 LRRM 1587 (1979).

is illustrated in its treatment of recurrent phrases used in election campaigns. Whether or not a phrase is legally objectionable will depend upon the reading of the statement as a whole and any "evidence of accompanying unfair labor practices which might reasonably color an employee's view of the statement."[220]

Assessments are difficult and unanimity not always attainable, as the Board conceded in a divided opinion:

> Realizing full well that in all cases such as this one, where one must attempt to fathom the meaning of another's words and assess the impress of such words on employees, reasonable men may differ, we differ with our colleague.[221]

The following are examples of frequently employed campaign phrases which the Board has assessed.

(a) "Serious harm." Statements to the effect that "[i]f this union were to get in here, it would not work to your benefit but to your serious harm" are evaluated by the Board under the standard of Greensboro Hosiery Mills, Inc.:

> We have not ordinarily found such notices to be illegal in and of themselves, for the bare words, in the absence of conduct or other circumstances supplying a particular connotation, can be given a noncoercive and nonthreatening meaning.[222]

---

[220]Compare Trent Tube Co., 147 NLRB 538, 56 LRRM 1251 (1964), with Marsh Supermarkets, Inc., 140 NLRB 899, 52 LRRM 1134 (1963), enforced, 327 F2d 109, 55 LRRM 2017 (CA 7, 1963), cert. denied, 377 US 944, 56 LRRM 2288 (1964), and Astronautics Corp., 164 NLRB 623, 624 n.2, 65 LRRM 1161 (1967).

[221]Allied Egry Business Sys., Inc., 169 NLRB 514, 67 LRRM 1195 (1968).

[222]162 NLRB 1275, 1276, 64 LRRM 1164 (1967), enforced in part, 398 F2d 414, 68 LRRM 2702 (CA 4, 1968); Ohmite Mfg. Co., Subsidiary of N. Am. Philips Co., 217 NLRB 435, 89 LRRM 1530 (1975), enforced, 557 F2d 577, 95 LRRM 2766 (CA 7, 1979). "Serious harm" notices and statements were found to violate §8 (a) (1) in Holly Farms Poultry Indus., Inc., 194 NLRB 952, 79 LRRM 1127 (1972), enforced in part, 470 F2d 983, 82 LRRM 2110 (CA 4, 1972); Serv-Air, Inc., supra note 137. Compare NLRB v. Greensboro Hosiery Mills, Inc., 398 F2d 414, 68 LRRM 2702 (CA 4, 1968), and Suprenant Mfg. Co. v. NLRB, supra note 65 (no violation) with J. P. Stevens & Co. v. NLRB, 380 F2d 292, 65 LRRM 2829 (CA 2, 1967), cert. denied, 389 US 1005, 66 LRRM 2728 (1967), and Serv-Air, Inc. v. NLRB, 395 F2d 557, 67 LRRM 2337 (CA 10, 1968), cert. denied, 393 US 840, 69 LRRM 2435 (1968). See also Dillingham Marine & Mfg. Co., 239 NLRB 904, 100 LRRM 1109 (1978), enforced, 610 F2d 319, 103 LRRM 2430 (CA 5, 1980) (statement that signing union cards "would follow employees for the rest of their lives" held a violation); J. P. Stevens & Co., 245 NLRB 198, 102 LRRM 1437 (1979) (violation when employees told that identity of card signers would "become public knowledge" and that signing cards would have "serious consequences"). But in Howard Johnson Co., 242 NLRB 386, 101 LRRM 1165 (1979), employer's statement that a union "would only make things more difficult for us all" was held not to be the equivalent of a "serious harm" message.

(b) Predictions of adverse consequences of unionization. When an employer makes factual statements concerning the possible adverse results of unionization, and when the overall context is not colored by violations of the Act, the Board, following the guidelines established in *Gissel*,[223] has not found threats or objectionable conduct. For example, telling employees that merit increases and sick-leave pay would be governed by contract if the union won the election and might also be eliminated by that contract, has been held not threatening.[224] On the other hand, informing employees that voting in favor of union representation would "change" the employer-employee relationship and would require activity to be conducted "strictly by the book," or would require rules to be more "strictly enforced," may be unlawful if not based on objective fact or if made in the context of other unlawful conduct.[225]

Reference to the adverse economic impact unionization might have on the company, such as "bringing a union into our plant at this time could be the straw that broke the camel's back," may or may not be objectionable depending on whether the employer is in fact experiencing substantial economic hardships unrelated to union activity.[226]

---

[223]NLRB v. Gissel Packing Co., *supra* note 56.

[224]Federal-Mogul Corp., 232 NLRB 1200, 96 LRRM 1397 (1977); Wesco Elec. Co., 232 NLRB 479, 96 LRRM 1560 (1977); *see also* General Tel. Directory Co., 233 NLRB 422, 96 LRRM 1549 (1977), *enforcement denied*, 602 F2d 912, 102 LRRM 2487 (CA 9, 1979) (telling employees that a union victory would make a previously promised pay raise "negotiable" held lawful by the court of appeals).

[225]Moody Chip Corp., 243 NLRB 265, 101 LRRM 1496 (1979) (violation); Tipton Elec. Co., 242 NLRB 202, 101 LRRM 1154 (1979), *enforced*, 621 F2d 890, 104 LRRM 2073 (CA 8, 1980) (violation); Jamaica Towing, Inc., 236 NLRB 1700, 98 LRRM 1495 (1978), *enforced*, 602 F2d 1100, 101 LRRM 3011 (CA 2, 1979) (violation); Fidelity Tel. Co., 236 NLRB 166, 98 LRRM 1210 (1978) (no violation); Chatfield-Anderson Co., 236 NLRB 50, 98 LRRM 1190 (1978) (violation); Island Holidays, Ltd., 208 NLRB 966, 85 LRRM 1225 (1974) (no violation); Garden City Fan & Blower Co., 196 NLRB 777, 80 LRRM 1113 (1972) (no violation).

[226]Chrysler Airtemp S. C., Inc., 224 NLRB 427, 92 LRRM 1636 (1976) (no violation); NLRB v. Four Winds Indus., 530 F2d 75, 91 LRRM 2460 (CA 9, 1976) (violation); Honeywell, Inc., 225 NLRB 617, 92 LRRM 1426 (1976) (statement that new marketing approaches involving recall of 10 or more employees and designed to improve company's economic recovery would be hindered by labor organization held objectionable); Rospatch Corp., 193 NLRB 772, 78 LRRM 1360 (1971) (no violation where employer in preelection statement told employees that if union won election, it would result in considerable legal expense that would reduce profits and employer's contributions to existing profit-sharing plan). *See also* NLRB v. Intertherm, 596 F2d 267, 100 LRRM 3016 (CA 8, 1979) (statement that employer had previously closed plants or moved them elsewhere when a union would not agree to the company's position held to be a statement of the employer's opinion as to the consequences of unionization protected by §8(c)).

Telling employees that wage increases would not be given if a union prevailed in organizing[227] or that work opportunities would suffer or not be as plentiful as in nonunion plants,[228] however, have been held to be unlawful coercion.

(c) Statements regarding plant closing. Employer statements regarding plant closing which might result from unionization are also evaluated within the "total context" in which they appear, in accordance with the standards established by the Supreme Court's *Gissel* decision.[229] Such statements have most often not been found to be predictions "based on objective fact," but coercive threats instead.[230]

(d) Signing authorization cards can be "fatal." In its *Mount Ida Footwear Co.*[231] decision, a Board majority concluded that the employer did not violate Section 8(a)(1) when its president told its assembled employees not to sign "any cards" because "they can be fatal to a business." In the Board's view, the employer's statements "merely expressed respondent's position that the employees would be better served . . . by rejecting the union." The use of the word "fatal" was not deemed a threat to plant closure but rather "was a reference to the possibility that unionization could lead to difficulties if the union were to strike to obtain unreasonable demands."[232]

---

[227]Cotton Producers Ass'n, 188 NLRB 772, 76 LRRM 1411 (1971); American Telecommunications Corp., Electromechanical Div., *supra* note 209.
[228]General Elec. Co., 215 NLRB 520, 87 LRRM 1673 (1974); Media Mailers, Inc., 191 NLRB 251, 77 LRRM 1393 (1971). *See also* Birdsall Constr. Co., 198 NLRB 163, 80 LRRM 1580 (1972), *enforced,* 487 F2d 288, 84 LRRM 2801 (CA 5, 1973) (preelection statement that if company had to operate under increased cost of union it might make more economic sense to do so at different location where company would not have added cost of transporting goods found not to be coercive).
[229]*Supra* note 56.
[230]Nebraska Bulk Transp. v. NLRB, 608 F2d 311, 104 LRRM 2384 (CA 8, 1979); Patsy Bee, Inc., 249 NLRB 976, 104 LRRM 1285 (1980); Anderson Cottonwood Concrete Prods., 246 NLRB 1090, 103 LRRM 1077 (1979); Continental Kitchen Corp., 246 NLRB 611, 102 LRRM 1659 (1979); American Spring Wire Corp., 237 NLRB 1551, 99 LRRM 1127 (1978); El Rancho Mkt., 235 NLRB 468, 98 LRRM 1153 (1978); Paoli Chair Co., 231 NLRB 539, 96 LRRM 1115 (1977); Hanover House Indus., 233 NLRB 164, 96 LRRM 1463 (1977); Willow Mfg. Co., 232 NLRB 344, 96 LRRM 1272 (1977); Florida-Texas Freight, Inc., 230 NLRB 952, 95 LRRM 1426 (1977); Yellow Cab Co., 229 NLRB 643, 95 LRRM 1124 (1977); W. A. Kruger Co., 224 NLRB 1066, 93 LRRM 1129 (1976); Hedstrom Co., 223 NLRB 1409, 92 LRRM 1297 (1976), *enforced in relevant part,* 558 F2d 1137, 95 LRRM 3069 (CA 3, 1977); May Dep't Stores Co., 211 NLRB 150, 86 LRRM 1423 (1974), *enforced,* 514 F2d 894, 90 LRRM 2844 (CA DC, 1975).
[231]217 NLRB 1011, 89 LRRM 1169 (1975). Members Fanning and Jenkins dissented.
[232]The majority supported this analysis of the employer's remarks by observing that, in a later speech to the employees, the employer's president said "we are here to stay." Members Fanning and Jenkins dissented sharply, viewing the employer's entire remarks

(e) "Bargaining will start from scratch." "Bargaining from scratch" or "bargaining begins with a clean table" campaign messages may imply that existing benefits may be diminished or discontinued if the employer is forced to negotiate with the union, for the duty to bargain ordinarily forecloses unilateral changes, and bargaining begins with existing wages and conditions.[233] But, depending on the context, such phrases might simply be a reminder that the selection of a union will not automatically produce any improved benefits. "Bargaining from scratch" statements have been held both not to have interfered and to have interfered with a representation election, the difference in result depending upon the "totality of circumstances" in which the message was conveyed.[234] Moreover, employer statement that a possible consequence of collective bargaining will be a loss of benefits was not deemed unlawful when made in response to union claims that employees could "only gain and . . . get better things from collective bargaining."[235]

(4) Orders, instructions, or directions vs. views, arguments, or opinions. The Board distinguishes between an employer's "instructions" or "directions" not to sign authorization cards, or engage in other union activity, and the expression of an employer's "views" or "opinions" advising against the signing of such cards or requesting a "no" vote in a Board election. The former are unlawful; the latter lawful. The statement *"Do not sign* if you want to continue to speak for yourself" was held to be an unlaw-

---

"as a management directive to employees not to sign cards for the union unless they wished to subject themselves to dire consequences . . . . " 217 NLRB at 1014, 89 LRRM at 1172.

[233]*See* Chapter 13 *infra* at notes 68-90.

[234]*Finding objectionable conduct:* TRW-United Greenfield Div., *supra* note 218; Taylor Dunn Mfg. Co., 252 NLRB 799, 105 LRRM 1548 (1980); BRK Elec., 248 NLRB 1275, 104 LRRM 1039 (1980); Centre Eng'r, Inc., 246 NLRB 632, 102 LRRM 1660 (1979); Dominican Santa Cruz Hosp., 242 NLRB 1107, 101 LRRM 1303 (1979); Madison Kipp Co., *supra* note 205; Plastronics, Inc., 233 NLRB 155, 96 LRRM 1422 (1977); Coach & Equip. Sales Corp., 228 NLRB 440, 94 LRRM 1391 (1977); North Elec. Co., 225 NLRB 1114, 93 LRRM 1203 (1976), *enforced,* 588 F2d 213, 100 LRRM 3004 (CA 6, 1978); Saunders Leasing Sys., Inc., 204 NLRB 448, 83 LRRM 1626 (1973), *enforced in relevant part,* 497 F2d 453, 86 LRRM 2345 (CA 8, 1974); Cargill, Inc., Nutrena Mills Div., 172 NLRB 183, 69 LRRM 1293 (1968). *Finding no objectionable conduct:* Donn Prods., Inc. v. NLRB, 613 F2d 162, 103 LRRM 2338 (CA 6, 1980); NLRB v. Interstate Eng'r, 583 F2d 1087, 99 LRRM 3245 (CA 9, 1978); Checker Motors Corp., 232 NLRB 1077, 96 LRRM 1386 (1977); Campbell Soup Co., 225 NLRB 222, 93 LRRM 1046 (1976); Computer Peripherals, Inc., 215 NLRB 293, 88 LRRM 1027 (1974); Wagner Indus. Prods. Co., 170 NLRB 1413, 67 LRRM 1581 (1968).

[235]Ludwig Motor Corp., 222 NLRB 635, 91 LRRM 1199 (1976).

ful direction."[236] The statement "Refuse to sign any authorization cards and avoid a lot of unnecessary turmoil" was held to be within the protection of Section 8(c).[237]

Statements characterizing union supporters as "clowns" or as a "bunch of Communists out to destroy business" have also been viewed as permissible opinion.[238] However, directing employees to report on the union activities of others, or informing them that they would not have a "good future" with the company if they continued to hand out union cards, have been held to constitute illegal coercion.[239]

b. Promises and Grants of Benefits. Organizational campaigns have been waged with promises of benefits as well as threats. But "interference is no less interference because it is accomplished through allurement rather than coercion."[240] The promise or grant of benefits to stifle, or in some circumstances to further, an organizational campaign may be unlawful interference even though no strings are explicitly attached. As the Supreme Court said in *Medo Photo Supply:*[241] "The action of employees with respect to the choice of their bargaining agents may be induced by favors bestowed by the employer as well as by his threats or domination." In *Exchange Parts*[242] the Court explained the impact of a grant of benefit:

---

[236]Colony Printing & Labeling, Inc., 249 NLRB 223, 104 LRRM 1108 (1980), *enforced,* 651 F2d 502, 107 LRRM 3049 (CA 7, 1981). Emphasis in original. Airporter Inn Hotel, 215 NLRB 824, 88 LRRM 1032 (1974), *overruling* Trojan Battery Co., 207 NLRB 425, 84 LRRM 1619 (1973).

[237]*Accord,* Lundy Packing Co. v. NLRB, 549 LRRM 300, 94 LRRM 2512 (CA 4), *cert. denied,* 434 US 818, 96 LRRM 2512 (1977). *See also* L. S. Ayres & Co. v. NLRB, 551 F2d 586, 94 LRRM 3210 (CA 4, 1977); Building Leasing Corp., 239 NLRB 13, 99 LRRM 1543 (1978); Star Kist Samoa, Inc., 237 NLRB 238, 98 LRRM 1558 (1978); Leggett & Platt, Inc., 230 NLRB 463, 95 LRRM 1348 (1977); Hobart Corp., 228 NLRB 907, 96 LRRM 1039 (1977), *enforced,* 600 F2d 593 (CA 6, 1979).

[238]Carrom Div., Affiliated Hosp. Prods., Inc., 245 NLRB 703, 102 LRRM 1462 (1979); R. J. Reynolds Tobacco Co., 240 NLRB 620, 100 LRRM 1350 (1979) *Cf.,* Producers Rice Mill, Inc., 222 NLRB 875, 91 LRRM 1414 (1976); *see also* Fayette Cotton Mill, 245 NLRB 428, 102 LRRM 1485 (1979). For circumstances in which the protection of §8(c) was unavailing, *see* Colony Printing & Labeling, Inc., *supra* note 236.

[239]Colony Printing & Labeling, Inc., *supra* note 236; J. H. Block & Co., 247 NLRB 262, 103 LRRM 1150 (1980); Crown Zellerbach Corp., 225 NLRB 911, 93 LRRM 1030 (1976).

[240]NLRB v. Crown Can Co., 138 F2d 263, 267, 13 LRRM 568 (CA 8, 1943), *cert. denied,* 321 US 769, 13 LRRM 850 (1944), *citing* Western Cartridge Co. v. NLRB, 134 F2d 240, 244, 12 LRRM 541 (1943), *cert. denied,* 320 US 746, 13 LRRM 851 (1943). *See also* NLRB v. General Tel. Directory Co., 602 F2d 912, 102 LRRM 2487 (CA 9, 1980) (statement that wage increases had been "budgeted" ruled vague and innocuous and not an unlawful promise).

[241]Medo Photo Supply Corp. v. NLRB, 321 US 678, 686, 14 LRRM 581 (1944).

[242]NLRB v. Exchange Parts Co., 375 US 405, 55 LRRM 2098 (1964).

The danger inherent in well-timed increases and benefits is the suggestion of a fist inside a velvet glove. The employees are not likely to miss the inference that the source of benefits now conferred is also the source from which future benefits must flow and which may dry up if it is not obliged.[243]

The infringement may stem from timing and impact. The fact that the benefits are not conditioned upon voting against the union is not controlling if the purpose is one of "impinging upon . . . freedom of choice for or against unionization, and is reasonably calculated to have that effect."[244]

The Board does not automatically find that grants of employment benefits during an organizing campaign to be unlawful, but it presumes that such action will be objectionable "unless the Employer establishes that the timing of the action was governed by factors other than the pendency of the election."[245]

(1) Employer inducements. In some cases, the employer's action is clearly unlawful. An offer of money accompanied by an urging to vote a particular way will be treated as interference.[246] A bribe to work against the union will have the same result.[247] In cases not so clearly drawn, the Board has condemned increases where they (1) were given in the context of repeated references to the union;[248] (2) were made effective just before an election;[249] (3) conformed to an earlier request made by one of the union

---

[243]*Id.* at 409. Shortly before the election, the employer sent the employees a letter announcing certain new employee benefits—a birthday holiday, a more favorable system for holiday overtime, and a more favorable vacation schedule. The employer asserted that the policy behind the benefits had been established earlier, but the first general announcement was contained in the preelection letter. *See also* Honolulu Sporting Goods Co., 239 NLRB 1277, 100 LRRM 1172 (1979). For a critique of this analysis, *see* Bok, *supra* note 1 at 113.

[244]*Supra* note 242 at 409. In an early case, the Supreme Court said: "There could be no more obvious way of interfering with these rights of employees than by grants of wage increases upon the understanding that they would leave the union in return." Medo Photo Supply Corp. v. NLRB, *supra* note 241 at 686.

[245]American Sunroof Corp., 248 NLRB 748, 104 LRRM 1157 (1980); Honolulu Sporting Goods Co., *supra* note 243; Micro Measurements, 233 NLRB 76, 96 LRRM 1402 (1977). *See also* Drug Fair-Community Drug Co., 162 NLRB 843, 64 LRRM 1079 (1967); Champion Pneumatic Mach. Co., 152 NLRB 300, 306, 59 LRRM 1089 (1965); International Shoe Co., 123 NLRB 682, 43 LRRM 1520 (1959). *See also* Simpson Elec. Co. v. NLRB, 654 F2d 15, 107 LRRM 3197 (CA 7, 1981), *denying enforcement to* 249 NLRB 1481, 104 LRRM 1187 (1980).

[246]Coca Cola Bottling Co., 132 NLRB 481, 48 LRRM 1370 (1961).

[247]Wesselman's Enterprises, Inc., 248 NLRB 1017, 104 LRRM 1069 (1980).

[248]NLRB v. Colonial Haven Nursing Home, Inc., 542 F2d 691, 93 LRRM 2241 (CA 7, 1976); Allegheny Mining Corp., 167 NLRB 81, 65 LRRM 1751 (1967), *enforced*, 406 F2d 1330, 70 LRRM 2880 (CA 4, 1969).

[249]NLRB v. Exchange Parts Co., *supra* note 242. *See also* Frito-Lay, Inc. v. NLRB, 585 F2d 62, 99 LRRM 2658 (CA 3, 1978); NLRB v. Tommy's Spanish Foods, Inc., 463 F2d 116, 80 LRRM 3039 (CA 9, 1972); World Wide Press, Inc., 242 NLRB 346, 101 LRRM 1205 (1979); D'Youville Manor Nursing Home, 217 NLRB 173, 89 LRRM 1060 (1975), *enforced*, 526 F2d 3, 90 LRRM 3100 (CA 1, 1975).

rivals in an organizing campaign;[250] (4) were announced before an election when they could reasonably have been delayed until afterward;[251] (5) were sprung on the employees in a manner calculated to influence the employees' choice;[252] (6) were given to employees in fulfillment of illegal promises of benefits made by the employer during the campaign;[253] or (7) were granted to women employees after the union had filed a petition for an election, even though the increase ended a company practice in violation of the Equal Pay Act.[254]

Making effective improvements decided upon prior to the advent of a union may present a dilemma for an employer, since failure to proceed may appear to be a reprisal. A factor that will weigh heavily with the Board is whether the employer had previously told the employees of its decision to make the improvements.[255] Other important factors are (1) whether the benefit increase during the campaign is consistent with an established past practice of announcing changes in employment terms at the same time every year; (2) whether there is an absence of unjustified or excessive benefit improvements compared with past practice;[256] (3) whether the benefit changes apply to other employer facilities or to employees not involved in the organizing campaign;[257] and (4) whether the benefit improvements

<hr/>

[250]Seneca Plastics, Inc., 149 NLRB 320, 57 LRRM 1314 (1964).
[251]NLRB v. Arrow Elastic Corp., 573 F2d 702, 98 LRRM 2004 (CA 1, 1978) (enforcing Board decision that an employer violated §8 (a) (1) when two days before an election it announced a pension plan for the employees which it did not become legally committed to provide until seven months after the election); International Shoe, *supra* note 245. *See also* Coronet Instructional Media, Div. of Esquire, Inc., 250 NLRB 940, 104 LRRM 1470 (1980); American Sunroof Corp., *supra* note 245 (no violation); Faith Garment Co., Div. of Dunhall Pharmaceutical, Inc., 246 NLRB 299, 102 LRRM 1515 (1979) (violation).
[252]NLRB v. Rich's of Plymouth, Inc., 578 F2d 880, 98 LRRM 2684, 2687 (CA 1, 1978).
[253]Tipton Elec. Co., *supra* note 225.
[254]Rupp Indus., Inc., 217 NLRB 385, 88 LRRM 1603 (1975).
[255]Crown Tar & Chem. Works, Inc. v. NLRB, 365 F2d 588, 63 LRRM 2067 (CA 10, 1966). *See also* Louisiana Plastics, Inc., 173 NLRB 1427, 70 LRRM 1019 (1968). In *Exchange Parts, supra* note 242, the employer vainly asserted that the "policy" behind the announcement of benefits had been established earlier, but in Litton Dental Prods. v. NLRB, 543 F2d 1085, 93 LRRM 2714 (CA 4, 1976), the employer prevailed on that point.
[256]In Automated Prods., Inc., 242 NLRB 424, 101 LRRM 1208 (1979), although the employer gave a larger wage increase than was its past practice, no violation was found since (1) the employer was undergoing a period of rapid expansion; (2) the purpose of the increase was to improve the employer's hiring prospects; (3) the change in the wage structure had been previously announced; and (4) the timing of the increase was accelerated due to bookkeeping problems.
[257]Town & Country Supermarkets, Inc., 244 NLRB 303, 102 LRRM 1275 (1979); Tiffin Div. of Hayes-Albion Corp., 237 NLRB 20, 99 LRRM 1020 (1978); Centralia Fireside Health, Inc., 233 NLRB 139, 96 LRRM 1471 (1977); Villa Sancta Anna Home,

were essential to remain competitive with other employers in the same industry regarding the attraction and retention of a stable work force.[258]

(2) Withholding benefits during an election campaign. Promising a benefit solely for the purpose of withholding its actual grant, although assertedly to avoid the commission of an unfair labor practice, has been characterized as the "carrot on the stick" and held to be interference.[259] The Board's general rule is that an employer's legal duty during a preelection campaign period is to proceed with the granting of benefits which would otherwise have been granted to employees in the normal course of the employer's business, just as it would have done had the union not been on the scene.[260] The Second[261] and Fifth[262] Circuits, however, have flatly disagreed with Board applications of this rule; the First Circuit has identified the following factors supporting determinations that Section 8(a)(1) has been violated by withholding benefits during a union organizing campaign: "[1] if the increase was promised by the employer prior to the union's appearance; [2] if it normally would be granted as part of a

---

228 NLRB 571, 94 LRRM 1449 (1977); Micro Measurements, *supra* note 245; Medline Indus., Inc., 218 NLRB 1404, 89 LRRM 1829 (1975); Essex Int'l, Inc., 216 NLRB 575, 88 LRRM 1346 (1975). *See also* Delchamps, Inc. v. NLRB, 588 F2d 476, 100 LRRM 2555 (CA 5, 1979), *denying enforcement to* 234 NLRB 262, 97 LRRM 1363 (1978).

[258]Delchamps, Inc. v. NLRB, *supra* note 257; NLRB v. Gotham Indus., Inc., 406 F2d 1306, 70 LRRM 2289 (CA 1, 1969); Town & Country Supermarkets, Inc., *supra* note 257; Schulte's IGA Foodliner, 241 NLRB 855, 101 LRRM 1048 (1979); Automated Prods., Inc., *supra* note 256; Poultry Packers, Inc., 237 NLRB 250, 99 LRRM 1027 (1978).

[259]Goodyear Tire & Rubber Co., 170 NLRB 539, 67 LRRM 1555 (1968), *enforced as modified*, 413 F2d 158, 71 LRRM 2977 (CA 6, 1969); Cadillac Overall Supply Co., 148 NLRB 1133, 1136, 57 LRRM 1136 (1964); Interstate Smelting & Ref. Co., 148 NLRB 219, 221, 56 LRRM 1489 (1964). In Staco, Inc., 244 NLRB No. 49, 102 LRRM 1223 (1979), after the employer illegally denied an employee a $50 loan, the employer's vice president personally gave the employee a $20 loan. Reversing the administrative law judge's characterization of this transaction as a "stick and carrot approach," the Board held that this loan was a lawful "spontaneous act of personal generosity" by the vice president, even though the initial denial of the loan was unlawful.

[260]*See, e.g.,* American Telecommunications Corp., Electromechanical Div., *supra* note 209 (emphasizing that Board applies this rule not only to preelection period, but also to period subsequent to the election but before certification and to period after certification has issued). Sourdough Sales, Inc., 246 NLRB 106, 102 LRRM 1633 (1979); Travis Meat & Seafood Co., 237 NLRB 213, 98 LRRM 1574 (1978); Signal Knitting Mills, Inc., 237 NLRB 360, 98 LRRM 1580 (1978); *see also* Sargent-Welch Scientific Co., 208 NLRB 811, 85 LRRM 1563 (1974), where the withholding of accrued vacation and holiday benefits in an otherwise legal lockout was found to violate §§8(a)(1) and 8(a)(5).

[261]Newberry Co. v. NLRB, 442 F2d 897, 77 LRRM 2097 (CA 2, 1971).

[262]NLRB v. Big Three Indus. Gas & Equip. Co., 441 F2d 774, 77 LRRM 2120 (CA 5, 1971).

schedule of increases established by the employer's past practice; or [3] if the employer attempts to blame the union for the withholding."[263] Illegality occurs (according to the First Circuit) "only if the employer is found to be manipulating benefits in order to influence his employees' decision during the union's organizing campaign."[264]

Where an employer declares that benefits granted to its other (unorganized) employees will be withheld from a group of employees being organized, on the ground that the benefits may be subject to further negotiations, the Board may find a violation; but this type of statement is allowable "[i]n a context of good faith bargaining and absent other proof of unlawful motive."[265] Thus, an attempt by the employer's declaration to disparage the union by placing the onus on it for the withholding of benefits will be deemed a violation of Section 8(a)(1).[266]

c. Interrogation and Polling. With the advent of a union campaign, employers may be tempted to learn about the campaign by questioning individual employees.[267] Interrogation as to union sympathy and affiliation has been held violative "because of its natural tendency to instill in the minds of employees fear of

---

[263]NLRB v. Otis Hosp., 545 F2d 252, 254-55, 93 LRRM 2778 (CA 1, 1976) (enforcing Board order finding §8(a)(1) violation); *see also* NLRB v. Marine World USA, 611 F2d 1274, 103 LRRM 2272 (CA 9, 1980), *remanded,* 251 NLRB No. 161, 105 LRRM 1158 (1980); Convalescent Home, Inc., 585 F2d 79, 99 LRRM 2985 (CA 3, 1978); G. C. Murphy Co. v. NLRB, 550 F2d 1004, 94 LRRM 3040 (CA 4, 1977) (enforcing Board order finding §8(a)(1) violation in employer's cancelling planned wage increases and annual wage review procedure during union organizing campaign, where union had notified employer that unfair labor practice charges would not be filed if wage increases were granted).

[264]545 F2d at 255. *See also* Marine World USA, *supra* note 263.

[265]Shell Oil Co., 77 NLRB 1306, 22 LRRM 1158 (1948); Chevron Oil Co., Standard Oil Co. of Tex. Div., 182 NLRB 445, 74 LRRM 1323 (1970); McGraw-Edison Co., 172 NLRB 1604, 69 LRRM 1023 (1968), *enforced,* 419 F2d 67, 72 LRRM 2918 (CA 8, 1969).

[266]American Telecommunications Corp., Electromechanical Div., *supra* note 209; J. P. Stevens & Co., Inc., 239 NLRB 738, 100 LRRM 1052 (1978); Baker Brush Co., 233 NLRB 561, 96 LRRM 1566 (1977); Florida Steel Corp., 220 NLRB 1201, 90 LRRM 1329 (1975).

[267]*See* Kleeb, *Taft-Hartley Rules During Union Organizing Campaigns,* 55 LRRM 114, 115 (1964), where an employer's temptation was pictured as follows:

"When an employer learns that an organizational campaign is going on among his employees, human nature being what it is, he's just bursting with curiosity to know whether any of his employees have joined, if there have been union meetings, who has attended them, and what was said? How better can he find out than to ask his employees? There would be no problem for the employer or the Board if it could be established that such interrogation was purely motivated. Unfortunately for this point of view, experience has shown that in many cases such questioning is followed by reprisals against union adherents."

For general commentary on the principles discussed in this section, *see* Craver, *The Inquisitorial Process in Private Employment,* 63 CORNELL L. REV. 1 (1977).

discrimination on the basis of the information the employer has obtained."[268] Employers "cannot discriminate against union adherents without first ascertaining who they are."[269] Questioning employees as to their union sympathies is not treated as an expression of views or opinions within the meaning of Section 8(c) because the "purpose of an inquiry is not to express views but to ascertain those of the persons questioned."[270] The prohibition against interrogation also extends to laid-off employees or discharged union adherents when they have an expectation of reemployment.[271]

The Board originally viewed all interrogation by an employer as unlawful *per se*.[272] In response to judicial disapproval, the *per se* test was abandoned and a more permissive test formulated.[273] In 1954, the Board held in *Blue Flash*[274] that it would find interrogation unlawful only when it was coercive in the light of surrounding circumstances, adding that "the time, place, personnel involved, information sought and . . . the employer's known preference must be considered."[275] Preelection distribution of "Vote No" buttons to unit employees by a supervisor, for example, constituted illegal interrogation since the offer of the button by the supervisor and the acceptance or refusal by the employee required the employee to make an observable choice in the presence of the supervisor.[276]

(1) Polling. Blue Flash involved the validity of a poll conducted by the employer to determine the extent of the employees' support for the union. The Board found the poll lawful on the basis of its application of the following guidelines: (1) that the

---

[268]NLRB v. West Coast Casket Co., 205 F2d 902, 904, 32 LRRM 2353 (CA 9, 1953).
[269]Cannon Elec. Co., 151 NLRB 1465, 58 LRRM 1629 (1965).
[270]Struksnes Constr. Co., 165 NLRB 1062, 65 LRRM 1385 (1967). *See also* NLRB v. Lorben Corp., 345 F2d 346, 59 LRRM 2184 (CA 2, 1965).
[271]H. C. Nutting Co., 219 NLRB 224, 90 LRRM 1125 (1975), *enforced*, 535 F2d 357, 92 LRRM 3648 (CA 6, 1976); Chesterfield Chrome Co., 203 NLRB 36, 82 LRRM 1764 (1973).
[272]Standard-Coosa-Thatcher Co., 85 NLRB 1358, 24 LRRM 1575 (1949).
[273]Struksnes Constr. Co., *supra* note 270. *See* discussion in NLRB v. Lorben Corp., 345 F2d 346, 59 LRRM 2184 (CA 2, 1965).
[274]Blue Flash Express, Inc., 109 NLRB 591, 34 LRRM 1384 (1954).
[275]*Id.* as quoted in Struksnes Constr. Co., *supra* note 270.
[276]Kurz-Kasch, Inc., *supra* note 151; Pillowtex Corp., 234 NLRB 560, 97 LRRM 1369 (1978); York Div., Borg-Warner, 229 NLRB 1149, 95 LRRM 1283 (1977); Kellwood Co., 206 NLRB 665, 84 LRRM 1573 (1973); Bancroft Mfg. Co., 189 NLRB 619, 77 LRRM 1366 (1971); Beiser Aviation Corp., 135 NLRB 399, 49 LRRM 1508 (1962); *see also* Sterling Faucet Co., 203 NLRB 1031, 83 LRRM 1530 (1973) (employer's having "made available" buttons with company insignia held not objectionable conduct where there was no evidence that employees had been required to wear them); *see* notes 152 and 153 *supra* and accompanying text.

employer's sole purpose was to ascertain whether the union demanding recognition actually represented a majority of the employees, (2) that the employees were so informed, (3) that assurances against reprisal were given, and (4) that the questioning occurred in a background free from employer hostility to union organization.[277]

The Board encountered judicial opposition in applying the *Blue Flash* rule because of disagreement by the circuit courts as to the proper weight to be given the circumstances surrounding the interrogation.[278] The Second Circuit, for example, held in *Bourne* v. *NLRB*[279] that interrogation which is not threatening in itself will not be an unfair labor practice unless it "meets certain fairly severe standards."[280] In setting aside the Board finding of unlawful polling, that Circuit based its holding on five criteria: (1) background of employer hostility, (2) the identity of the interrogator (i.e., how high he is in the employer hierarchy), (3) the place of the interrogation, (4) the method used, and (5) the truthfulness of the employee's response.

The use of differing criteria by the circuits and the Board in applying the *Blue Flash* rule created "considerable uncertainty in this area of labor-management relations."[281] The Board finally concluded that the rule did not operate to discourage intimidation of employees by employer polls.[282] Therefore, pursuant to a suggestion by the District of Columbia Circuit that it "come to grips with this constantly recurring problem,"[283] the Board in *Struksnes Construction Co., Inc.*,[284] revised the *Blue Flash* criteria as follows:

Absent unusual circumstances, the polling of employees by an employer will be violative of Section 8(a)(1) of the Act unless the following safeguards are observed: (1) the purpose of the poll is to

---

[277]Struksnes Constr. Co., *supra* note 270.

[278]*Id.* at n.10.

[279]332 F2d 47, 56 LRRM 2241 (CA 2, 1964), *enforcing as modified* 144 NLRB 805, 54 LRRM 1158 (1963).

[280]*Id.* at 48.

[281]Struksnes Constr. Co., *supra* note 270 at 1063.

[282]*Id.*

[283]Operating Eng'rs Local 49 v. NLRB, 353 F2d 852, 856, 60 LRRM 2353 (CA DC, 1965).

[284]*Supra* note 270. *See also* Tom Wood Pontiac, Inc., 179 NLRB 581, 72 LRRM 1494 (1969), *enforced,* 447 F2d 383, 77 LRRM 2968 (CA 7, 1971); Wm. Walters, Inc., a/k/a Computronics, Inc., 179 NLRB 709, 72 LRRM 1504 (1969), *enforced,* 76 LRRM 2815 (CA 7, 1971).

determine the truth of a union's claim of majority, (2) this purpose is communicated to the employees, (3) assurances against reprisal are given, (4) the employees are polled by secret ballot, and (5) the employer has not engaged in unfair labor practices or otherwise created a coercive atmosphere.[285]

The new element in the revision was the requirement that polls be conducted by secret ballot. The Board cautioned against the use of polls while a petition for a Board election is pending, because it would not "serve any legitimate interest of the employer that would not be better served by the forthcoming Board election."[286] The *Struksnes* decision, however, did not provide any specific ground rules for conducting a secret ballot.[287]

Polls designed to elicit union sympathies indirectly, rather than by bald inquiry into an individual's preference for a particular union, have also run afoul of Section 8(a)(1). A poll of employees about their choice for department supervisor, for example, conducted after the union filed a representation petition, violated Section 8(a)(1) because employees had not been allowed to participate in the choice of a supervisor previously, and the poll was viewed as inducing employees to withdraw support from the union.[288] Similarly, a poll on the issue of whether temporary employees should be permitted to vote in the upcoming representation election violated Section 8(a)(1) because only the union favored inclusion of temporary employees; the poll was therefore viewed as a mean of revealing union sympathies.[289]

The Board, however, recognized the right of an employer in the health care industry to submit questionnaires to its employees seeking to elicit a response on intent to report for work, after the employer had received from the union the 10-day notice of intent to strike required by Section 8(g) of the Act.[290]

---

[285]165 NLRB at 1063.

[286]*Id.* See also Fontana Bros., 169 NLRB 368, 67 LRRM 1210 (1968).

[287]*See* Oleson's Food Stores, 167 NLRB 543, 66 LRRM 1108 (1967), where the ballots were privately counted by the employer in the absence of any observers.

[288]Paoli Chair Co., 213 NLRB 909, 87 LRRM 1363 (1974).

[289]Clothing Workers v. NLRB (AMF, Inc.), 564 F2d 434, 95 LRRM 2821 (CA DC, 1977). *See also* W. A. Shaeffer Pen Co. v. NLRB, 486 F2d 180, 84 LRRM 2456 (CA 8, 1973) (poll, in absence of *Struksnes* safeguards, inquiring into whether job applicants would cross a picket line in the event of strike, and conducted by employer facing strike deadline, ruled coercive); Burns Int'l Security Serv., Inc., 225 NLRB 271, 92 LRRM 1439 (1976), *enforcement denied*, 567 F2d 945, 97 LRRM 2350 (CA 10, 1977).

[290]*See* Chapter 21 *infra* at notes 50-52.

Approval, however, was conditioned on the employer's clear conveyance to the employees that the purpose of the questionnaire was to assist in planning for staff requirements in the event of a strike, and that it inform the employees that they were free to make their own decisions and assure them that no reprisals would be taken.[291]

Not all preelection polls designed to elicit union sympathies conducted in the absence of *Struksnes* safeguards violate Section 8(a)(1). The Board has dispensed with the *Struksnes* requirements where (1) employees have volunteered their sentiments to the employer, and the employer seeks to verify those previously announced preferences; (2) other safeguards are present at the time of the poll, such as the presence of union representatives when the poll is taken or a clearly manifested solidarity of the employees is demonstrated.[292]

Conducting a voluntary poll of employees to determine whether they desire continued representation by a union violates Section 8(a)(2), if conducted to procure the defeat of the union at a time when the employer had insufficient objective evidence to support a reasonable doubt of the union's continued majority status.[293]

(2) Individual or isolated questioning. The *Struksnes* case was concerned specifically with systematic polling.[294] The criteria to be applied in determining the validity of interrogation by means other than polling are not altogether clear,[295] although appli-

---

[291]Preterm, Inc., 240 NLRB 654, 100 LRRM 1344 (1979). The Board did rule illegal the employer's individual questioning of 11 employees in this case, and stressed that the safeguards outlined in Johnnie's Poultry Co., 146 NLRB 770, 55 LRRM 1403 (1964), *enforcement denied*, 334 F2d 617, 59 LRRM 2117 (CA 8, 1965), and Struksnes Constr. Co., *supra* note 270, still regulate the manner of a health care employer's interrogation. *See* Commercial Management, Inc., 233 NLRB 665, 97 LRRM 1247 (1977). *See also* notes 309-12 *infra* and accompanying text.

[292]Bushnell's Kitchens, Inc., 222 NLRB 110, 91 LRRM 1113 (1976); *see also* Jerome J. Jacomet, 222 NLRB 899, 91 LRRM 1370 (1976) (questioning found noncoercive where employees requested a meeting at which an employee spokesman informed the employer that they did not want to join the union, and the employer then inquired, "Nobody wants to join the union?"—to which all nodded "Yes").

[293]Jackson Sportwear Corp., 211 NLRB 891, 87 LRRM 1254 (1974). *See generally* Chapter 12 *infra* at notes 229-60, 368, and 409.

[294]*See* R.M.E., Inc., 171 NLRB 213 n.1, 68 LRRM 1459 (1968). *See also* Dresser Indus., Inc., 231 NLRB 591, 96 LRRM 1329 (1977), *modified*, 580 F2d 169, 99 LRRM 2634 (CA 9, 1978); Super Thrift Mkts., Inc., 233 NLRB 409, 96 LRRM 1523 (1977).

[295]*See* Bok, note 1 *supra* at 107, and *compare* West Tex. Equip. Co., 142 NLRB 1358, 53 LRRM 1249 (1963), *with* Zayre Corp., 154 NLRB 1372, 60 LRRM 1222 (1965), where the trial examiner noted that tests applicable to systematic polling do not necessarily apply to other types of interrogation but considered the Second Circuit's test an outer

cation of the Second Circuit's *Bourne*[296] tests has gained some judicial acceptance.[297] Where interrogation is sufficiently isolated and occurs in an atmosphere free of coercive conduct, an election will not be set aside;[298] nor will a remedial order issue in an unfair labor practice case.[299] On the other hand, interrogation accompanied by threats has been held to interfere with an election even though only one percent of the employees were threatened.[300] Generally, the Board has used the approach it adopted in *Blue Flash,* of evaluating interrogation in the light of all the surrounding circumstances, including the time, place, personnel involved, and known position of the employer.[301] Where the employer seeks to force an employee to disclose his union sentiments without communicating a valid purpose and an assurance against reprisal, questioning will typically be held coercive.[302] The Board has even held that questioning of open and well-known union adherents as to their union sympathies is inherently coercive, notwithstanding that it occurs in an atmosphere free from threats or fear of reprisal.[303] Questioning which places an employee in the position of acting as an informer regarding the union activities of his fellow employees is likewise unlawful.[304] On the other hand, where the inquiry is "innocu-

---

limit in finding a violation. *See also* Gruber's Food Center, Inc., 159 NLRB 629, 62 LRRM 1271 (1966); Charlotte Union Bus Station, Inc., 135 NLRB 228, 49 LRRM 1461 (1962).

[296]*Supra* notes 279-80 and accompanying text.

[297]*See* NLRB v. Intertherm, Inc., *supra* note 226; NLRB v. Roney Plaza Apartments, *supra* note 139; Donald E. Hernly, Inc., *supra* note 204.

[298]West Tex. Equip. Co., *supra* note 295; Alley Constr. Co., Inc., 210 NLRB 999, 86 LRRM 1316 (1974).

[299]Dieckbrader Express, Inc., 168 NLRB 867, 67 LRRM 1081 (1967).

[300]Huntsville Mfg. Co., 211 NLRB 54, 86 LRRM 1587 (1974), *enforcement denied*, 514 F2d 723, 89 LRRM 2592 (CA 5, 1972) (union lost election by large majority); Dresser Indus., Inc., *supra* note 294 (union lost election by one vote); Super Thrift Mkts., Inc., 233 NLRB 409, 96 LRRM 1523 (1977).

[301]*See* Bok, *supra* note 1 at 107; Gruber's Food Center, Inc., *supra* note 295.

[302]NLRB v. Solboro Knitting Mills, Inc., 572 F2d 936, 97 LRRM 3047 (CA 2, 1978), *cert. denied*, 439 US 864, 99 LRRM 2601 (1978); Teamsters Local 633 (Bulk Haulers, Inc.) v. NLRB, 509 F2d 490, 88 LRRM 2072 (CA DC, 1974); Monroe Mfg. Co., 200 NLRB 62, 82 LRRM 1042 (1972); Mississippi Extended Care Center, Inc., 202 NLRB 1065, 82 LRRM 1738 (1973), *enforced*, 496 F2d 862, 86 LRRM 3120 (CA 6, 1974); Charlotte Union Bus Station, Inc., *supra* note 295.

[303]PPG Indus., Inc., 251 NLRB 1146, 105 LRRM 1434 (1980); *see also* Anaconda Co., 241 NLRB 1091, 101 LRRM 1070 (1979); Paceco, Div. of Fruehauf Corp., 237 NLRB 399 (1978), *reversed*, 601 F2d 180, 102 LRRM 2146 (CA 5, 1979), *on remand*, 247 NLRB 1405, 103 LRRM 1327 (1980); ITT Automotive Elec. Prods. Div., 231 NLRB 878, 96 LRRM 1134 (1977). For the Board's earlier contrary position, *see* Stumpf Motor Co., Inc., 208 NLRB 431, 85 LRRM 1113 (1974); B.F. Goodrich Footwear Co., 201 NLRB 353, 82 LRRM 1262 (1973).

[304] Hanover Concrete Co., 241 NLRB 936, 101 LRRM 1016 (1979); Abex Corp., 162 NLRB 328, 64 LRRM 1004 (1966). This rule has been held applicable to an employer's interrogation of a supervisor to determine which employees had union sympathies.

ous,"[305] is part of a normal response to a conversation initiated by an employee,[306] or is conducted in a joking atmosphere where employees do not feel compelled to answer,[307] it does not rise to the level of coercion.

Interrogation of supervisors can sometimes be unlawful. For example, administration of a polygraph examination to a supervisor for the purpose of determining whether the supervisor had engaged in pro-union activities may violate Section 8(a)(1) if the questions posed have the "natural and inevitable tendency" of causing the supervisor to report on the union activities of rank-and-file employees.[308]

(3) Preparation of defense for trial of unfair labor practice case. Despite the "inherent danger of coercion,"[309] an employer may exercise a limited privilege of interrogating employees in the "investigation of facts concerning issues raised in a complaint"[310] where this is necessary to the preparation of his defense for the pending trial.[311] To minimize the coercive impact and to strike a balance between conflicting interests, the Board in *Johnnie's Poultry*[312] enunciated a number of safeguards: (1) The purpose of the questioning must be communicated to the employee. (2) An assurance of no reprisal must be given. (3) The employee's participation must be obtained on a voluntary basis. (4) The

---

Dependable Lists, Inc., *supra* note 141; *see also* Burns Elec. Security Serv., Inc., 245 NLRB No. 96, 102 LRRM 1553 (1979) ("who is filing these ridiculous unfair labor practice charges"); Pelton Casteel, Inc., *supra* note 7.

[305]Sandy's Stores, Inc., 163 NLRB 728, 65 LRRM 1034 (1967), *enforcement denied on other grounds*, 398 F2d 268, 68 LRRM 2800 (CA 1, 1968); Madison Kipp Co., *supra* note 205; Pelton Casteel, Inc., *supra* note 7.

[306]Phillips-Van Heusen Corp., 165 NLRB 1, 65 LRRM 1355 (1967).

[307]NLRB v. Scott & Fetzer Co., 570 F2d 742, 97 LRRM 2881 (CA 8, 1978). For extensive discussion of the factual setting in which interrogations are evaluated, *see* the trial examiner's decision in Campbell Soup Co., 170 NLRB 1547, 68 LRRM 1036 (1968).

[308]St. Anthony's Center, 227 NLRB 1777, 95 LRRM 1099 (1977). Member Walther dissented on the ground that the questions dealt solely with the supervisor's participation in union meetings and the election campaign; he noted that the supervisor's actual responses did not relate to the union activities of nonsupervisory employees; *see also* note 344 *infra* and accompanying text. For other applications of NLRA concepts to administration of polygraph examinations, *see* Craver, *supra* note 267 at 30-33; Fixtures Mfg. Corp., 251 NLRB No. 107, 105 LRRM 1208 (1980).

[309]Johnnie's Poultry Co., *supra* note 291.

[310]*Id.*

[311]*Id.* The Eighth Circuit's denial of enforcement did not express disagreement with the standards but held that the factual determinations were "not supported by substantial evidence." 344 F2d at 619. The Board's standards and application were upheld in other circuits. *See* Automobile Workers (Preston Prods. Co.) v. NLRB, 392 F2d 801, 66 LRRM 2548 (CA DC, 1967), *cert. denied*, 392 US 906, 68 LRRM 2408 (1968); NRLB v. Neuhoff Bros. Packers, Inc., *supra* note 204; Montgomery Ward & Co. v. NLRB, 377 F2d 452, 65 LRRM 2285 (CA 6, 1967).

[312]Johnnie's Poultry Co., *supra* note 291.

questioning must take place in an atmosphere free from union animus. (5) The questioning itself must not be coercive in nature. (6) The questions must be relevant to the issues involved in the complaint. (7) The employee's subjective state of mind must not be probed. (8) The questions must not "otherwise interfere with the statutory rights of employees."

When the employer or its attorney fails to follow these safeguards in employee interviews in preparation for an unfair labor practice hearing, the Board has been quick to find that Section 8(a)(1) has been violated.[313] It is the Board's position that "[c]ompliance with all the *Johnnie's Poultry* safeguards is the minimum required"[314] to dissipate the potential of coercion and that "failure to adhere strictly to the rules set forth in *Johnnie's Poultry* constitutes a per se violation of §8(a)(1)."[315]

The courts, by and large, have considered the *Johnnie's Poultry* standards relevant in determining whether questioning of employees is coercive, but they have declined to apply the rules in a *per se* fashion.[316] The Second Circuit applies a "totality of the circumstances" test to determine coercion.[317]

A trend toward extending the *Johnnie's Poultry* safeguards to other types of employer questioning seems to be developing.

---

[313]*See, e.g.,* A&R Transp., Inc., 237 NLRB 1084, 99 LRRM 1108 (1978), *enforced in part,* 601 F2d 311, 101 LRRM 2856 (CA 7, 1979); Answerphone, Inc., 236 NLRB 931, 98 LRRM 1385 (1978); Jack August Enterprises, Inc., 232 NLRB 881, 97 LRRM 1560 (1977), *enforced,* 583 F2d 575, 99 LRRM 2582 (CA 1, 1978); Mr. F's Beef & Bourbon, 212 NLRB 462, 87 LRRM 1601 (1974), *enforced,* 96 LRRM 2107 (CA 6, 1975); Tamper, Inc., 207 NLRB 907, 85 LRRM 1375 (1973), *enforced in part,* 522 F2d 781, 89 LRRM 3034 (CA 4, 1975); Hedison Mfg. Co., 260 NLRB No. 137, 109 LRRM 1258 (1982).

[314]Roadway Express, Inc., 239 NLRB 653, 100 LRRM 1046 (1978) (no assurances given to employee that no reprisals would be taken as a result of the interview; the Board held that §8(a)(1) was violated even though the employer's good faith was not questioned).

[315]A&R Transp. Inc. v. NLRB, *supra* note 313 (court found that interview was not coercive and denied enforcement of that portion of the order dealing with coercive interrogation). Limitations on this *per se* approach are suggested in two cases. Lammert Indus., Inc., 229 NLRB 895, 96 LRRM 1557 (1977), *enforced,* 578 F2d 1223, 98 LRRM 2992 (CA 7, 1978) (Board found that attorney made it clear that no reprisals would be taken against employee being interviewed, even though the word "reprisals" was not used); Salina Concrete Prods., Inc., 218 NLRB 496, 89 LRRM 1734 (1975) (Board found no §8(a)(1) violation even though company attorney did not use the word "voluntary" in telling employees that they were not compelled to participate).

[316]*See* NLRB v. Neuhoff Bros. Packers, Inc., *supra* note 204; Montgomery Ward & Co. v. NLRB, *supra* note 311; A&R Transport, Inc., *supra* note 313. The D.C. Circuit has also applied the *Johnnie's Poultry* interrogation safeguards, but it is not clear whether it has adopted a *per se* approach. *See* Automobile Workers (Preston Prods. Co.) v. NLRB, *supra* note 311.

[317]Retired Persons Pharmacy v. NLRB, 519 F2d 486, 89 LRRM 2879 (CA 2, 1975).

Although the Board has not clarified what role *Johnnie's Poultry* standards play in employer interrogation of employees in preparation for arbitration hearings[318] or in investigatory interviews of employees about plant rule violations,[319] it has required that those safeguards be followed by a health care institution when it interrogates employees as to their strike intentions after receipt of notice of an impending strike required by Section 8(g) of the Act.[320]

d. Surveillance. Since the earliest days of the Act, surveillance of employees by an employer, whether with supervisors, rank-and-file employees, or outsiders, has consistently been held to violate Section 8(a)(1).[321] The Board has successfully maintained that surveillance is unlawful regardless of whether the employees have knowledge of the surveillance.[322] For example, under this principle the surreptitious electronic surveillance of a union organizer's motel room by two management employees was ruled unlawful.[323]

---

[318]*Compare* Pacific Southwest Airlines, Inc., 242 NLRB No. 151, 101 LRRM 1366 (1979) (Board agreed with administrative law judge that the *Johnnie's Poultry* safeguards are not relevant to prearbitration interviews) *with* Cook Paint & Varnish Co., 246 NLRB 104, 102 LRRM 1680 (1979), *enforcement denied and remanded,* 648 F2d 712, 106 LRRM 3016 (CA DC, 1981) (administrative law judge applied *Johnnie's Poultry* safeguards to prearbitration interviews; Board affirmed administrative law judge's finding of illegal interrogation but made no mention of the *Johnnie's Poultry* rationale; the D.C. Court of Appeals refused to enforce a *per se* rule that prearbitration questioning of employees about merits of a grievance violates §8(a)(1) and remanded for further proceedings as to whether a union steward is entitled to different treatment than other employees generally with respect to prearbitration interviews and questioning under threat of discipline for noncooperation).
[319]*See* Levingston Shipbuilding Co., 249 NLRB 1, 104 LRRM 1058 (1980) (administrative law judge found that the *Johnnie's Poultry* safeguards apply to the interrogation of employees about possible plant rule violations; Board did not specifically embrace ALJ's reasoning).
[320]Preterm, Inc., *supra* note 291; Commercial Management, Inc., 233 NLRB 665, 97 LRRM 1247 (1977). In both cases the Board held that a health care institution has the right to inquire about the strike intentions of its employees after receiving a §8(g) notice of intent to strike by the union, in order to ascertain the number of replacements needed, but that the *Johnnie's Poultry* safeguards must be applied to prevent the inquiries from being coercive. *See* Chapter 21 *infra* at notes 50-52.
[321]Consolidated Edison Co. v. NLRB, 305 US 197, 3 LRRM 645 (1938). In Elder-Beerman Stores Corp. V. NLRB, 415 F2d 1375, 72 LRRM 2510 (CA 6, 1969), *cert. denied,* 397 US 1009, 73 LRRM 2849 (1970), an employer violated §8(a)(1) by instructing a supervisor to engage in surveillance of employees' union activity and by discharging him for failure to comply. The conduct was deemed unlawful regardless of whether the employees had knowledge of the instruction or the reason for the discharge. *See also* Belcher Towing Co. v. NLRB, *supra* note 101. For general commentary on the principles discussed in this section, *see* Craver, *supra* note 267.
[322]NLRB v. Grower-Shipper Vegetable Ass'n, 122 F2d 368, 8 LRRM 891 (CA 9, 1941); Bethlehem Steel Co. v. NLRB, 120 F2d 641, 8 LRRM 962 (CA DC, 1941).
[323]NLRB v. J.P. Stevens & Co., 563 F2d 8, 96 LRRM 2150 (CA 2, 1977), *cert. denied,* 434 US 1064, 97 LRRM 2747 (1978). The employer's subsequent disclaimer "disapproving" surveillance and announcing suspension of the management personnel did

The law is equally clear that an employer violates Section 8(a)(1) if he creates the impression among employees that he is engaged in surveillance,[324] for by thus highlighting his "anxiety" concerning union activities he tends to inhibit an employee's future union activities.[325] The Board has also found a Section 8(a)(1) violation in surveillance of union activities by supervisors who were motivated solely by their own curiosity and who were subsequently forbidden by the employer to continue such surveillance;[326] but it has not condemned activity by supervisors which was limited to observance of union organizers handbilling in an employer's parking lot[327] or limited to attendance at a union meeting at the specific request of the union.[328] An employer violates the Act, however, if he encourages employees to engage in surveillance of union activities.[329]

---

not absolve it of culpability. The court ruled that in light of J.P. Stevens' anti-union history, it should at the very least have assured employees that it would ignore any information obtained by the surveillance.

[324]In NLRB v. Simplex Time Recorder Co., 401 F2d 547, 69 LRRM 2465 (CA 1, 1968), because of the unusually broad, and perhaps vague, conduct forbidden by a cease-and-desist order directed against creating the "impression" of surveillance, the First Circuit added a limitation to the Board's order. It enforced an order which it interpreted as meaning "willful conduct and a justifiable impression." *See*, finding an impression of surveillance: NLRB v. Rybold Heater Co., 408 F2d 888, 70 LRRM 3159 (CA 6, 1969); Dillingham Marine & Mfg. Co., *supra* note 222; Hamilton Avnet Elec., 240 NLRB 781, 100 LRRM 1502 (1979); Keystone Pretzel Bakery, Inc., 242 NLRB No. 77, 101 LRRM 1214 (1979). J.P. Stevens & Co., 244 NLRB 407, 102 LRRM 1039 (1979); J.P. Stevens & Co., 245 NLRB 198, 102 LRRM 1437 (1979). *See*, finding no impression of surveillance: NLRB v. Pilgrim Food, Inc., 591 F2d 110, 100 LRRM 2494 (CA 1, 1978); Checker, Inc., 247 NLRB 835, 103 LRRM 1111 (1980); Tartan Marine Co., 247 NLRB 646, 103 LRRM 1247 (1980). *See also* Tipton Elec. Co., *supra* note 225.

[325]NLRB v. Prince Macaroni Mfg. Co., 329 F2d 803, 55 LRRM 2852 (CA 1, 1964); Hendrix Mfg. Co. v. NLRB, 321 F2d 100, 53 LRRM 2831 (CA 5, 1963). In CBS Records Div., 223 NLRB 709, 91 LRRM 1564 (1976), the Board ruled that the employer's focusing of a closed circuit camera on a building used for a union headquarters during an organizing campaign violated §8(a)(1) even though no actual surveillance was ever conducted. However, because the incident had taken place more than three months prior to the date of the election and was observed by only two employees, the Board ruled that the employer's conduct was insufficient to require setting aside the election.

[326]Intertype Co. v. NLRB, 371 F2d 787, 64 LRRM 2257 (CA 4, 1967). *See also* NLRB v. J.P. Stevens & Co., *supra* note 323.

[327]Porta Sys. Corp., 238 NLRB 192, 99 LRRM 1251 (1978). *See also* J.J. Newberry Co., 249 NLRB 991, 104 LRRM 1244 (1980); Tampo Mfg. Co., 245 NLRB 791, 102 LRRM 1336 (1979); Comar Glass Co., 244 NLRB 379, 102 LRRM 1237 (1979); Chemtronics, Inc., 236 NLRB 178, 98 LRRM 1559 (1978).

[328]Osco Drug, Inc., 237 NLRB 231, 99 LRRM 1150 (1978). *See also* Nice-Pak Prods., 248 NLRB 1278, 104 LRRM 1127 (1980). In Crown Cork & Seal Co., Inc., 254 NLRB 1340, 106 LRRM 1270 (1981), note-taking by employer's plant personnel manager while engaging in otherwise lawful observation of union activity was held to violate §8(a)(1).

[329]NLRB v. National Garment Co., 614 F2d 623, 104 LRRM 2069 (CA 8, 1980); Saginaw Furniture Shops, Inc. v. NLRB, 343 F2d 515, 58 LRRM 2417 (CA 7, 1965); NLRB v. Saxe-Glassman Shoe Corp., 201 F2d 238, 31 LRRM 2271 (CA 1, 1953).

Destruction of property or the appearance of quality control problems may provide legitimate business justification for increasing surveillance of employees. Under such circumstances, a violation was not found even though the increased surveillance coincided with a union organizing campaign.[330]

(1) Photographing concerted activity. The right of an employer to photograph employees engaged in concerted activity hinges on the legality of the employees' conduct being photographed. Hence, where company personnel had photographed employees on a picket line immediately after the beginning of a strike, where there had been no arrests or disturbances and no reason to anticipate striker misconduct, the Board held that the "picture taking was calculated to create and did create an impression of management surveillance of protected and peaceful activity carrying with it the implicit threat of possible future retaliation."[331] On the other hand, photographing union organizers distributing handbills was held lawful where the organizers at times had been on the employer's property and the purpose of the picture taking was to establish that the organizers had been trespassing or engaging in other illegal activity.[332]

e. Soliciting or Remedying Employee Grievances. The Board distinguishes between "solicitation" of employee grievances and "promises to remedy" solicited grievances in determining whether an employer's invitation to employees to make known their complaints during an organizing campaign is permissible. Thus, where an employer committed no independent acts of interference during a preelection period and had said specifically and repeatedly that it could make "no promises" to remedy complaints, the statements did not interfere with an election. Nor was coercion found in the holding of 10 preelection meetings

---

[330]Liberty Nursing Homes, 245 NLRB 1194, 102 LRRM 1517 (1979); Lebanon Apparel Corp., 243 NLRB 1024, 102 LRRM 1022 (1979); *see also* Pacific Intermountain Express, 250 NLRB 1451, 104 LRRM 1532 (1980); American Ship Building Co., 240 NLRB 1, 100 LRRM 1269 (1979).

[331]Larand Leisurelies, Inc., 213 NLRB 197, 197 n.1, 87 LRRM 1129 (1974), *enforced,* 523 F2d 814, 90 LRRM 2631 (CA 6, 1975). *See also* Love's Barbecue Restaurant, 245 NLRB 78, 102 LRRM 1546 (1979); Faith Garment Co., 246 NLRB 299, 102 LRRM 1515 (1979); Local 19, Hotel & Restaurant Employees, 240 NLRB 240, 100 LRRM 1354 (1979).

[332]Berton Kirshner, Inc., 209 NLRB 1081, 85 LRRM 1548 (1974), *enforced,* 523 F2d 1046, 90 LRRM 2958 (CA 9, 1975). The Board's decision relied heavily on the fact that subsequent handbilling by the union occurred without incident and no photographs of this later occasion were taken.

at which grievances and complaints were solicited.[333] But employers have been found guilty of interference when, subsequent to the filing of the petition for an election, they sought to solicit and remedy, or promise to remedy, grievances.[334]

Although an employer who has had a past practice and policy of soliciting employee grievances may continue the practice during an organizational campaign, an employer may not rely upon past practice to justify solicitation of employee grievances if the manner or method of solicitation is significantly altered.[335]

 f. *Employer's Responsibility for Third-Party Conduct.* Objectionable third-party conduct during an organizational campaign may be a basis for setting aside an election regardless of employer complicity.[336] But where the employer is charged with an unfair labor practice, rather than with objectionable preelection conduct, considerations of agency are more significant. An election may be set aside without a showing of fault by the employer,[337] but coercive conduct must be attributable to an employer before an unfair labor practice will be found.[338] For example, in a small,

---

[333]Tiffin Div. of Hayes-Albion Corp., 237 NLRB 20, 99 LRRM 1020 (1978); Montgomery Ward & Co., 225 NLRB 112, 93 LRRM 1077 (1976); Uarco, Inc., 216 NLRB 1, 88 LRRM 1103 (1974). *But see* Raley's, Inc., 236 NLRB 971, 98 LRRM 1381 (1978) (mere recitation by employer of a "no promises" position upon the initiation of an "open door" policy did not discharge duty to refrain from intimating that grievances would nonetheless be remedied).

[334]El Rancho Market, 235 NLRB 468, 98 LRRM 1153 (1978); NLRB v. Broyhill Co., 514 F2d 655, 89 LRRM 2203 (CA 8, 1975); Lasco Indus., Inc., 217 NLRB 527, 89 LRRM 1058 (1975). The Board has disapproved of employer solicitations of employee grievances by telephone "hot lines," Garry Mfg. Co., *supra* note 207, or "attitude surveys," St. Joseph's Hosp., 247 NLRB 869, 103 LRRM 1315 (1980), where the employer actions carried an implied promise to remedy grievances. *But see* Reliable Mfg. Corp., 240 NLRB 90, 100 LRRM 1350 (1979). *But see* Leland Stanford Jr. Univ. & Stanford Univ. Hosp., 240 NLRB 1138, 100 LRRM 1391 (1979), where the Board held that the employer's solicitation of grievances through an attitude survey was conducted for legitimate business reasons and not designed in response to or in opposition to the union's organizing efforts.

[335]Carbonneau Indus., Inc., 228 NLRB 597, 94 LRRM 1502 (1977). The objectionable conduct by the employer included the following: (1) replacing an old suggestion box with a new one in a more convenient location; (2) failing to limit questions at employee meetings initiated by the employer to subjects other than employee grievances; and (3) distributing paper and pencils to employees at group meetings and asking them to submit questions. The Board also found that the employer had interfered with the election by posting employee suggestions with employer responses such as "checking into," "done," "finished," or "forthcoming," and by otherwise indicating that certain grievances would be corrected.

[336]*See* Chapter 9 *infra* at notes 105-114.

[337]Al Long, Inc., 173 NLRB 447, 69 LRRM 1366 (1968).

[338]Dean Indus., Inc., 162 NLRB 1078, 64 LRRM 1193 (1967); *see also* Hyster Co. v. NLRB, 480 F2d 1081, 83 LRRM 2801 (CA 5, 1973), *enforcing in part* 198 NLRB 192, 80 LRRM 1603 (1972) (agency relationship); Cagle's, Inc., 234 NLRB 1148, 98 LRRM 1117 (1978), *enforced in part,* 588 F2d 943, 100 LRRM 2590 (CA 5, 1979) (agency relationship found in part because employer failed to disavow actions of third party);

nonindustrial community where the employer actively influenced community opinion against the union, it was held responsible for third-party distribution of a leaflet containing a threat that union representation would result in plant closure. Although the employer distributed a letter stating that it was not responsible for the activities of the anti-union individuals, it did not refute the contents of the threatening leaflet; accordingly the employer violated Section 8(a)(1).[339]

g. *Employer Violence.* Although no longer a common subject of litigation, the Board is still occasionally confronted with the need to discourage violence and to mitigate its effects. Its decisions in representation cases have gone beyond the prohibition of direct threats against employees.[340] The Board will set aside an election where there is an "atmosphere" of violence or threats of violence, since this may destroy requisite laboratory conditions and impair a free choice by employees;[341] but where an unfair labor practice is charged, a showing that the perpetrator is an agent of the employer must be made.[342]

Employer violence also need not be aimed directly at employees to be unlawful. Physical assaults upon union organizers and condonation of assaults by employees through failure to discipline have been held unlawful.[343]

h. *Discipline and Discharge of Supervisors.* Supervisors are excluded from the Act's coverage[344] and are not *per se* accorded protection thereunder from discharge or other discipline for engaging in union or concerted activity. Thus, when an employer has disciplined or discharged a supervisor out of a legitimate

---

Star Kist Samoa, Inc., *supra* note 237 (employer encouragement and failure to disavow); Panama-Williams, Inc., 226 NLRB 315, 93 LRRM 1286 (1976) (no agency relationship); Salant Corp. d/b/a Carrizo Mfg. Co., Inc., 214 NLRB 171, 88 LRRM 1314 (1974) (same).
[339]Star Kist Samoa, Inc., *supra* note 237.
[340]*E.g.*, Casino Operations, Inc., 169 NLRB 328, 67 LRRM 1177 (1968); Vera Ladies Belt & Novelty Corp., 156 NLRB 291, 61 LRRM 1066 (1965), involving picket-line violence. *See also* Teamsters Local 563 (Fox Valley Material Suppliers Ass'n), 176 NLRB 386, 71 LRRM 1231 (1969), *enforced,* 76 LRRM 3002 (CA 7, 1971), *cert. denied,* 404 US 912, 78 LRRM 2585 (1971); Mine Workers (Weirton Constr. Co.), 174 NLRB 344, 70 LRRM 1217 (1968); Steelworkers Local 586 (Inspiration Consol. Copper Co.) 174 NLRB 189, 70 LRRM 1123 (1968). *See* Chapter 9 *infra* at notes 115-26.
[341]Al Long, Inc., *supra* note 337.
[342]*See* Gabriel Co., 137 NLRB 1252, 50 LRRM 1369 (1962).
[343]Lipman Bros., Inc., 147 NLRB 1342, 56 LRRM 1420 (1964), *enforced,* 355 F2d 15, 61 LRRM 2193 (CA 1, 1966); Browning Indus., Inc., 142 NLRB 1397, 53 LRRM 1266 (1963).
[344]§2(11). *See, e.g.*, Long Beach Youth Center, Inc., 230 NLRB 648, 95 LRRM 1451 (1977); Sibilio's Golden Grill, Inc., 227 NLRB 1688, 94 LRRM 1439 (1977).

desire to assure the loyalty of its management personnel and its action was "reasonably adapted" to that end, the Board finds such conduct permissible even if an incidental effect may be that employees will fear the same fate will befall them for engaging in protected activity.[345]

In certain circumstances, however, the discipline or discharge of a supervisor may violate Section 8(a)(1). Thus, an employer may not discipline or discharge a supervisor for having given testimony adverse to an employer's interests,[346] for refusing to commit unfair labor practices,[347] or for failing to prevent unionization.[348]

The Board has redefined the circumstances in which it will find unlawful the discharge of a supervisor where the discharge allegedly interferes with employees' Section 7 rights. The Board had held that where an employee engages in a "widespread pattern of misconduct" against employees and supervisors alike, "the evidence may be sufficient to warrant a finding that the employer's conduct as a whole, including the action taken against its supervisors, was motivated by a desire to discourage union activities among its employees in general"[349] and therefore even the action taken against supervisors violates employees' Section 7 rights. In a 1982 decision the Board overruled the line of cases

---

[345] Stop & Go Foods, Inc., 246 NLRB 1076, 103 LRRM 1046 (1979).

[346] Rohr Indus., Inc., 220 NLRB 1029, 90 LRRM 1541 (1975); Ebasco Servs., Inc., 181 NLRB 768, 73 LRRM 1518 (1970); Leas & McVitty, Inc., 155 NLRB 389, 60 LRRM 1333 (1965), enforcement denied, 384 F2d 165, 66 LRRM 2353 (CA 4, 1967); Oil City Brass Works, 147 NLRB 627, 56 LRRM 1262 (1964), enforced, 357 F2d 466, 61 LRRM 2318 (CA 5, 1966); Dal-Tex Optical Co., Inc., 131 NLRB 715, 48 LRRM 1143 (1961), enforced, 310 F2d 58, 51 LRRM 2608 (CA 5, 1962); Modern Linen & Laundry Serv., Inc., 116 NLRB 1974, 39 LRRM 1126 (1956); Better Monkey Grip Co., 115 NLRB 1170, 38 LRRM 1025 (1956), enforced, 243 F2d 836, 40 LRRM 2027 (CA 5, 1957), cert. denied, 355 US 864, 41 LRRM 2007 (1957).

[347] Miami Coca Cola Bottling Co., 140 NLRB 1359, 52 LRRM 1242 (1963), enforced in part, 341 F2d 524, 58 LRRM 2458 (CA 5, 1965); General Eng'r, Inc., 131 NLRB 648, 48 LRRM 1105 (1961), enforced in part, 311 F2d 570, 52 LRRM 2277 (CA 9, 1962); Jackson Tile Mfg. Co., 122 NLRB 764, 43 LRRM 1195 (1958), enforced, 272 F2d 181, 45 LRRM 2239 (CA 5, 1959); Inter-City Advertising Co. Inc., 89 NLRB 1103, 26 LRRM 1065 (1950), enforced as modified, 190 F2d 420, 28 LRRM 2321 (CA 4, 1951), cert. denied, 342 US 908, 29 LRRM 2285 (1952); Vail Mfg. Co., 61 NLRB 181, 16 LRRM 85 (1945), enforced, 158 F2d 664, 19 LRRM 2177 (CA 7, 1947), cert. denied, 331 US 835, 20 LRRM 2185 (1947).

[348] Talladega Cotton Factory, Inc., 106 NLRB 295, 32 LRRM 1479 (1953), enforced, 213 F2d 309, 34 LRRM 2196 (CA 5, 1954).

[349] Brothers Three Cabinets, 248 NLRB 828, 829, 103 LRRM 1506 (1980). See also Nevis Indus., Inc., 246 NLRB No. 167, 103 LRRM 1035 (1979), enforcement denied, 647 F2d 905, 107 LRRM 2890 (CA 5, 1981); Downslope Indus., Inc., 246 NLRB No. 132, 103 LRRM 1041 (1979). But cf. Sheraton Puerto Rico Corp. v. NLRB, 651 F2d 49, 107 LRRM 2735 (CA 1, 1981).

which had held that an employer violates Section 8(a)(1) by discharging a supervisor as part of "a pattern of conduct aimed at coercing employees in the exercise of their Section 7 rights."[350]

3. Other Unlawful Employer Interference. a. *The Legality of "Strikebreaker" Bonuses or Benefits.* Differentiations between strikers and nonstrikers in the provision of bonuses or other benefits are viewed with disfavor by the Board. They have been justified only on a showing of legitimate business consideration as basis for the disparate treatment.[351] For example, the Board's decision in *Aero-Motive Manufacturing Co.,*[352] overruling a series of prior cases, announced that an employer had violated Section 8(a)(1) by paying a $100 bonus to employees who worked during an economic strike, while denying the bonus to strikers, even though the bonus was not announced or paid until after the strike had ended. The opinion held that regardless of the employer's motives, its action interfered with the employees' right to strike by effectively conveying the message that nonstrikers had received special benefits which had been denied to strikers. The Board adopted a similar principle under Section 8(a)(3) when it ruled that an employer's failure to pay accrued vacation benefits to strikers, while paying them to nonstrikers, was illegal, notwithstanding the employer's contention that the striking employees were not on the active payroll on the vacation eligibility date.[353] Changes in work-scheduling practices during

---

[350]Parker-Robb Chevrolet, Inc., 262 NLRB No. 58, 110 LRRM 1289 (1982). *See* Chapter 30 *infra* at notes 181-86.

[351]*See, e.g.,* NLRB v. Moore Business Forms, Inc., 574 F2d 835, 98 LRRM 2773 (CA 5, 1978), *enforcing in part* 224 NLRB 393, 93 LRRM 1437 (1976); Westinghouse Elec. Corp., 237 NLRB 1209, 99 LRRM 1184 (1978), *enforced as modified*, 603 F2d 610, 101 LRRM 2870 (CA 7, 1979); Swedish Hosp. Medical Center, 232 NLRB 16, 97 LRRM 1173 (1977).

[352]195 NLRB 790, 79 LRRM 1496 (1972), *enforced*, 475 F2d 27, 82 LRRM 3052 (CA 6, 1973). *See also* S&W Motor Lines, Inc., 236 NLRB 938, 98 LRRM 1488 (1978); Portland Williamette Co., 212 NLRB 272, 86 LRRM 1677 (1974), *enforcement denied*, 534 F2d 1331, 92 LRRM 2113 (CA 9, 1976) (retroactive pay to nonstrikers held unlawful).

[353]Elmac Corp., 225 NLRB 1188, 93 LRRM 1285 (1976). In NLRB v. Electro Vector, Inc., 539 F2d 35, 93 LRRM 2021 (CA 9, 1976), *cert. denied*, 434 US 821, 96 LRRM 2512 (1977), however, the Ninth Circuit denied enforcement of a Board decision holding that an employer violated the Act by denying a year-end bonus to employees who had been on strike on the dates that eligibility for the bonus payment was to be determined. The court held that the bonus, which had been given for only two years, was a gift rather than wages, and that as a consequence there was no employer discrimination with respect to wages, hours, or working conditions. *See* Chapter 7 at notes 122-23. *See also* NLRB v. Rubatex Corp., 601 F2d 147, 101 LRRM 2660 (CA 4, 1979), *cert. denied*, 444 US 928 (1979); Portland Williamette Co. v. NLRB, *supra* note 352; Bartlett-Collins Co., 230 NLRB 144, 96 LRRM 1581 (1977), where distribution of free work gloves to nonstrikers was held to constitute a unilateral change in working conditions in violation of §8(a)(5).

a strike, which were continued in effect after the strike to the advantage of nonstriking employees, have also been ruled in violation of Section 8(a)(1).[354]

Legitimate business considerations justifying disparate treatment of strikers and nonstrikers have been found when the nonstrikers themselves requested the work scheduling arrangements, which resulted in their higher earnings relative to striking employees, in order to protect themselves and their equipment from retaliation by strikers.[355]

b. Requests for Employee Statements to NLRB. The Board follows essentially a *per se* rule in holding that an employer's request for copies of employee statements given a Board agent in connection with unfair labor practice proceedings violates Section 8(a)(1). The Board reasons that such a request in most circumstances "would naturally inhibit its employee's desire to cooperate with the Board's investigative efforts and deter others from so cooperating."[356] The Second Circuit, however, rejected a "*per se*" rule that all requests for copies of employee statements provided the Board are inherently disruptive of employee rights. It opted instead for a more flexible approach under which the propriety of requests for statements of this type is to be determined in light of the "voluntary nature of the compliance and the employer's need for the information."[357]

In applying its rule, however, the Board did not regard inquiries by an employer, who sought to determine whether employees had submitted statements to Board agents, as unlawful conduct where the employees' answers were voluntary and the inquiry was being legitimately used in the preparation of a defense in a consolidated unfair labor practice and representation case.[358]

---

[354]Moore Business Forms, Inc., *supra* note 351; Mercy-Memorial Hosp., 231 NLRB 1108, 96 LRRM 1239 (1977).
[355]Pilot Freight Carriers, Inc., 223 NLRB 286, 92 LRRM 1246 (1976).
[356]Martin A. Gleason, 215 NLRB 340, 88 LRRM 1344 (1975), *enforcement denied*, 534 F2d 466, 91 LRRM 2682 (CA 2, 1976); John Dory Boat Works, Inc., 229 NLRB 844, 96 LRRM 1079 (1977); S.E. Nichols Marcy Corp., 229 NLRB 75, 95 LRRM 1110 (1977); S&M Grocers, Inc., 236 NLRB 1594, 98 LRRM 1471 (1978); Answerphone, Inc., *supra* note 313. *See also* NLRB v. Maxwell, 637 F2d 698, 106 LRRM 2387 (CA 9, 1981), *enforcing* 241 NLRB 264, 101 LRRM 1012 (1979) (employer failure to give assurances of no reprisals evokes modified *per se* rule).
[357]NLRB v. Martin A. Gleason, Inc., 534 F2d 466, 91 LRRM 2682, 2694 (CA 2, 1976). *See also* Robertshaw Controls Co. v. NLRB, 483 F2d 762, 84 LRRM 2156 (CA 4, 1973) (Fourth Circuit refused to enforce a Board order finding a §8(a)(1) violation where the employer requested the employees to give it copies of statements given to Board agent).
[358]Osco Drug, Inc., *supra* note 328.

c. Employer Conduct Relating to Authorization Cards. The Board also applies a *per se* rule in holding that employer encouragement and assistance to employees in withdrawing authorization cards is a violation of Section 8(a)(1); but this approach has been rejected by the Second Circuit, which declared that the propriety of soliciting employees to revoke their union support must be assessed in the light of all the facts in the case.[359] If the employer's assistance is deemed "too minimal," however, even the Board's *per se* rule does not require that a violation of Section 8(a)(1) be found.[360]

d. Suits and Threats of Suits Against Employees. The Board distinguishes between employer suits against employees and employer threats to sue. It applies a general rule that the "filing of a civil suit, as opposed to the threat to file a civil suit, does not constitute an unfair labor practice."[361] However, it has departed from a literal application of this rule where the employer's lawsuit was brought to pursue an unlawful purpose, such as to penalize an employee for filing unfair labor practice charges or otherwise seeking access to the Board or other governmental agencies.[362]

e. Discrimination Based on Race or Sex. In *Jubilee Manufacturing Co.*[363] the Board held that employer discrimination based on race, color, religion, sex, or national origin, standing alone, is

---

[359]NLRB v. Monroe Tube Co., 545 F2d 1320, 94 LRRM 2020 (CA 2, 1976); *see also* L'Eggs Prods., Inc., 236 NLRB 354, 99 LRRM 1304 (1978); Woodland Supermarket, 237 NLRB 1481, 99 LRRM 1113 (1978); Jarva, Inc., 235 NLRB 1047, 98 LRRM 1302 (1978); International Mfg. Co., 238 NLRB 1361, 99 LRRM 1328 (1978) (employer requests to workers to solicit withdrawal letters from co-workers or to reconsider the signing of authorization cards held to be a violation of §§8(a)(1)).

[360]Poly Ultra Plastics, Inc., 231 NLRB 787, 96 LRRM 1147 (1977) (employer did not initiate, sponsor, or assist in the circulation of a withdrawal petition but only gave assistance to the employees in its phrasing).

[361]S.E. Nichols Marcy Corp., *supra* note 356 at 75; United Aircraft Corp., 192 NLRB 382, 77 LRRM 1785 (1971), *enforced in part*, 534 F2d 422, 90 LRRM 2272 (CA 2, 1975), *cert. denied*, 429 US 825, 92 LRRM 2501 (1976); Frank Fisceglia, 203 NLRB 265, 83 LRRM 1066 (1973), *enforcement denied*, 498 F2d 43, 86 LRRM 2541 (CA 3, 1974); Clyde Taylor Co., 127 NLRB 103, 45 LRRM 1514 (1960). The Board's reasoning is that it "should accommodate its enforcement of the Act to the right of all persons to litigate their claims in court rather than condemn the exercise of such right as an unfair labor practice." Clyde Taylor Co., *supra* at 109.

[362]Power Sys., Inc., 239 NLRB 445, 99 LRRM 1652 (1978), *enforcement denied*, 601 F2d 936, 101 LRRM 2978 (CA 7, 1979); George A. Angle, 242 NLRB 744, 101 LRRM 1209 (1979); United Credit Bureau of Am., Inc., 242 NLRB 921, 101 LRRM 1277 (1979), *enforced*, 643 F2d 1017, 106 LRRM 2751 (CA 4, 1981); *see also* Food & Commercial Workers Dist. Union 227, 247 NLRB 195, 103 LRRM 1140 (1980).

[363]202 NLRB 272, 82 LRRM 1482 (1973), *aff'd sub nom.* Steelworkers v. NLRB, 504 F2d 271, 87 LRRM 3168 (CA DC, 1974). *But see* Packinghouse Workers v. NLRB, 416 F2d 1126, 70 LRRM 2489 (CA DC, 1969), *cert. denied*, 396 US 903, 72 LRRM 2658 (1969).

not inherently destructive of employee rights under Section 7; before a violation of the Act will be found, there must be evidence of a nexus between the alleged discriminatory conduct and interference with the exercise of employee rights to act in concert.[364]

III. OTHER CONCERTED ACTIVITY

It is usual to associate protected concerted activity under the Act with union activity. In most cases such an association is accurate. But Section 7 broadly protects "concerted" activity, not merely union activity. Thus, concerted activity which is not specifically union oriented may also be involved in Section 8(a)(1) conduct. The latter type conduct is the principal subject of this part of the chapter. Additionally, this part covers certain other forms of concerted employee activity which, though union oriented, may not be directly related to organizational activity.

A. Protected Concerted Activity: In General

1. Individual vs. Concerted Activity: The *Interboro* Rule. Under the Act, employee concerted activities fall into three categories—those prohibited by Section 8, those protected by Section 7, and those which are neither prohibited nor protected—often referred to as unprotected activities. Protected concerted activities primarily involve activities pursued by employees in a peaceful manner in the exercise of their Section 7 rights. Illustrative of this category are certain peaceful economic strikes, sympathy strikes,[365] and other conduct such as dissident activity in resistance or opposition to the union's leadership.[366] Many other examples of protected conduct will also be discussed in the material below. Unprotected concerted activities may include activities that are "unlawful, violent, in breach of contract," or indefensibly disloyal.[367] Concerted activity may

---

[364]*See* Chapter 7 *infra* at notes 311-22.

[365]Russell Sportswear Corp., 197 NLRB 1116, 80 LRRM 1495 (1972) (sympathy strike to protest employer's unfair labor practice at another plant); General Tire & Rubber Co., 190 NLRB 227, 77 LRRM 1215 (1971) (refusal of nonunit employee to cross picket line and work during strike).

[366]Red Cab, Inc., 194 NLRB 279, 78 LRRM 1699 (1971).

[367]NLRB v. Washington Aluminum Co., 370 US 9, 17, 50 LRRM 2235, 2239 (1962). *See* NLRB v. Electrical Workers Local 1229, 346 US 464, 33 LRRM 2183 (1953) (disloyalty); Southern S.S. Co. v. NLRB, 316 US 31, 10 LRRM 544 (1942) (unlawful activity); NLRB v. Fansteel Metallurgical Corp., 306 US 240, 4 LRRM 515 (1939) (violence); NLRB v. Sands Mfg. Co., 306 US 332, 4 LRRM 530 (1939) (breach of contract); *see* Chapter 7 *infra* for detailed treatment of employment discrimination relating to union

occur either with or without union involvement, participation, or membership.[368]

To be protected under Section 7, employee activity must be both "concerted" in nature and pursued for the purpose of either collective bargaining or other "mutual aid and protection." These statutory prerequisites have been broadly construed by the Board and the courts to expand the ambit of employee protection.[369] Thus, the concert requirement of Section 7 has not been literally construed to provide protection solely to employee activity involving group action directly. For example, an individual protagonist will be deemed to have engaged in "concerted activities" if a group of employees designates him to act on their behalf.[370] In determining whether activity by a single employee is concerted, the Board will look to the purpose and effect of the employee's actions. The Board has repeatedly ruled that individual activity involving attempts to enforce the provisions of an existing collective bargaining agreement is concerted activity;[371] individual action taken to implement a collective bargaining agreement is "but an extension of the concerted activity that gave rise to the Agreement."[372] Such activity is deemed concerted, regardless of whether the employee's understanding of the contract is correct.[373] Under

---

activity. *See also* Gregory, *Unprotected Activity and The NLRA*, 39 VA. L. REV. 421 (1953); Note, *Unprotected Activity Under The National Labor Relations Act*, 3 UTAH L. REV. 358 (1953).

[368]*See, e.g.,* NLRB v. Washington Aluminum Co., *supra* note 367 (walkout to protest extreme cold in shop); Walls Mfg. Co. v. NLRB, 321 F2d 753, 53 LRRM 2428 (CA DC, 1963), *enforcing* 137 NLRB 1317, 50 LRRM 1376 (1962), *cert. denied*, 375 US 923, 54 LRRM 2576 (1963) (writing a letter complaining of unsanitary conditions); Salt River Valley Water Users' Ass'n v. NLRB, 206 F2d 325, 32 LRRM 2598 (CA 9, 1953) (circulating a petition to authorize an individual to collect wages allegedly due under the Fair Labor Standards Act).

[369]*See* NLRB v. Washington Aluminum Co., *supra* note 367 and discussion at notes 410-12 *infra*. For a treatment of the historical development of the concept of concerted activity, *see* Note, *The Requirement of "Concerted" Action Under The NLRA*, 53 COLUM. L. REV. 514 (1953); Comment, *Constructive Concerted Activity and Individual Rights: The Northern Metal-Interboro Split*, 121 U. PA. L. REV. 152 (1972); Cox, *The Right To Engage in Concerted Activities*, 26 IND. L.J. 319 (1951).

[370]*See* Fotomat Corp., 207 NLRB 461, 463, 84 LRRM 1487 (1973), *enforced*, 497 F2d 901, 87 LRRM 2256 (CA 6, 1974); Pacific Electricord Co., 153 NLRB 521, 59 LRRM 1507 (1965), *enforced*, 361 F2d 310, 63 LRRM 2064 (CA 9, 1966).

[371]Interboro Contractors, Inc., 157 NLRB 1295, 61 LRRM 1537 (1966), *enforced*, 388 F2d 495, 67 LRRM 2083 (CA 2, 1967); B&M Excavating, Inc., 155 NLRB 1152, 60 LRRM 1466 (1965); Bunney Bros. Constr. Co., 139 NLRB 1516, 51 LRRM 1532 (1962); Alleluia Cushion Co., Inc., 221 NLRB 999, 91 LRRM 1131 (1975); Roadway Express, Inc., 217 NLRB 278, 88 LRRM 1503 (1975), *enforced per curiam*, 532 F2d 751, 91 LRRM 2239 (CA 4, 1976); G. W. Wilson, 240 NLRB 333, 100 LRRM 1276 (1979).

[372]Bunney Bros. Constr. Co., *supra* note 371.

[373]Interboro Contractors, Inc., *supra* note 371.

the Board's *Interboro*[374] rule, a single employee's effort to enforce provisions of a collective bargaining agreement is protected by Section 7, even in the absence of a showing of similar interest by his fellow employees.

In *Interboro*, two brothers complained that they had been discharged for making complaints concerning working conditions covered by the collective bargaining agreement. The two employees filed individual unfair labor practice charges, and a consolidated complaint alleging violations of Sections 8(a)(1) and (3) issued. The trial examiner concluded they had been discharged because of their failure to give a day's work for a day's pay. But even if they had been discharged for making complaints, in the trial examiner's view the discharges would still not have been unlawful because the complaints themselves were not for "legitimate union or concerted aims or purposes"; in fact one of the brothers had voiced the complaint for his "own selfish benefit and aggrandizement." A Board panel majority disagreed, concluding that the complaints, which were the basis for the discharges, were protected concerted activity. Even if made by a single employee acting alone, the complaints constituted protected activity since "they were made in the attempt to enforce the provisions of the existing collective bargaining agreement."[375] Complaints made for such purposes, the Board explained, "are grievances within the framework of the contract that affect the rights of all employees in the unit, and thus constitute concerted activity which is protected by Section 7 of the Act."[376]

The Second Circuit enforced the Board's *Interboro* order, indicating at least limited approval of the rule that individual employee activity involving attempts to enforce a labor agreement represents protected concerted activity, notwithstanding the absence

---

[374]Interboro Contractors, Inc., *supra* note 371. *But cf.* Eggo Frozen Foods, 209 NLRB 647, 85 LRRM 1410 (1974), *enforced sub nom.* Griffin v. NLRB, 503 F2d 1401, 87 LRRM 3276 (CA 5, 1974), where simultaneous conduct by five employees was found not to be protected concerted activity, there being no evidence of coordinated effort to protest the employer's action.

[375]157 NLRB at 1295.

[376]*Id.* In support of its conclusion in this regard, the Board cited its earlier decision in Morrison-Knudsen Co., 149 NLRB 1577, 57 LRRM 1400 (1964); New York Trap Rock Corp., 148 NLRB 374, 56 LRRM 1526 (1964); Bunney Bros. Constr. Co., 139 NLRB 1516, 51 LRRM 1532. The Board noted in *Interboro* that appraisal of the merits of employee complaints either by the employer or by the Board "'is irrelevant to the question of whether employees are engaging in protected concerted activity.'" 157 NLRB at 1295 n.7, *quoting* Mushroom Transp. Co., 142 NLRB 1150, 53 LRRM 1206 (1963), *rev'd on other grounds*, 330 F2d 683, 56 LRRM 2034 (CA 3, 1964).

of overt interest on the part of fellow employees.[377] The Third, Fifth, and Sixth Circuits have expressly disavowed the *Interboro* rule[378] on the theory that the pursuit of personal, as opposed to group, goals is not "concerted" activity and is thus unprotected. The Ninth Circuit has indicated that it does not "disagree in principle with the rule stated by the Second Circuit" in *Interboro*.[379]

Despite disapproval by some of the circuits, the Board has continued to apply the *Interboro* doctrine. In *Roadway Express, Inc.*,[380] for example, the Board held that an employer violated Section 8(a)(1) when it discharged a truck driver who had refused to drive equipment he claimed was unsafe. In the Board's view, the driver was engaged in "concerted" activity even though he acted alone, since the "nature of his complaint [had] significance and relevance under the contract to the interests of all of respondent's employees whose employment is governed under the contract."[381] The Board's decision was enforced *per curiam* by the Fifth Circuit.

---

[377]NLRB v. Interboro Contractors, Inc., *supra* note 371. The Second Circuit later qualified its approval of the Board's *Interboro* rule to the extent that attempts by employees to enforce their understanding of a collective bargaining agreement is concerted activity only "if the employees have a reasonable basis for believing that their understanding of the terms was the understanding that had been agreed upon." NLRB v. John Langenbacher Co., 398 F2d 459, 463, 68 LRRM 3842 (CA 2, 1968), *cert. denied*, 393 US 1049, 70 LRRM 2249 (1969).

[378]NLRB v. Buddies Supermarkets, Inc., 481 F2d 714, 83 LRRM 2625 (CA 5, 1979); NLRB v. Northern Metal Co., 440 F2d 881, 76 LRRM 2958 (CA 3, 1971). *But see* Anchortank, Inc. v. NLRB, 618 F2d 1153, 1160-61, 104 LRRM 2689 (CA 5, 1980). Although the District of Columbia Circuit, in Kohls v. NLRB, 629 F2d 173, 104 LRRM 3049 (CA DC, 1980), expressed "serious doubts" about the validity of the *Interboro* doctrine, which creates the legal fiction of "*constructive* concerted activity," it nevertheless found it unnecessary in the case before it to resolve the issue.

[379]NLRB v. C & I Air Conditioning, Inc., 486 F2d 977, 978, 84 LRRM 2625 (CA 9, 1973), *denying enforcement to* 193 NLRB 911, 78 LRRM 1417 (1971); *see also* Ethan Allen, Inc. v. NLRB, 513 F2d 706, 89 LRRM 2013 (CA 1, 1975); NLRB v. Ben Pekin Corp., 452 F2d 205, 78 LRRM 2429 (CA 7, 1971). The Eighth Circuit refused "to pass on the validity of the *Interboro* rule" in NLRB v. Dawson Cabinet Co., 566 F2d 1079, 1083, 97 LRRM 2075 (CA 8, 1977), *denying enforcement to* 228 NLRB 290, 96 LRRM 1373 (1977); *but see* NLRB v. Selwyn Shoe Mfg. Corp., 428 F2d 217, 221, 74 LRRM 2474 (CA 8, 1970).

[380]217 NLRB 278, 88 LRRM 1503 (1975).

[381]217 NLRB at 279. Other Board decisions applying *Interboro* including, *e.g.*, Colonial Stores, Inc., 248 NLRB 1187, 104 LRRM 1025 (1980); Industrial Steel Stampings, Inc., 238 NLRB 357, 99 LRRM 1638 (1978); KQED, Inc., 238 NLRB 1, 99 LRRM 1168 (1978); King Soopers, Inc., 222 NLRB 1011, 91 LRRM 1292 (1976); Aro, Inc., 227 NLRB 243, 94 LRRM 1010 (1976), *enforcement denied*, 596 F2d 713, 101 LRRM 2153 (CA 6, 1979). In NLRB v. Adams Delivery Serv., 623 F2d 96, 104 LRRM 3093 (CA 9, 1980), the Ninth Circuit saw no need to apply *Interboro* since the employee had enlisted the aid of his union to enforce a contractually guaranteed right. The court stressed that the employee's right to consult with his union is protected activity without reference to the legal fiction of *Interboro*.

2. Individual vs. Concerted Activity: *Alleluia Cushion Co.*
Until 1975, the Board applied *Interboro* essentially to situations
where there was a collective bargaining agreement in existence,
and an individual employee's action to enforce the agreement
was viewed as merely an extension of the initial concerted activity that had culminated in the collective bargaining agreement.
In the Board's 1975 decision in *Alleluia Cushion Co.,*[382] however,
the *Interboro* rule was extended for the first time to cover situations where there was no collective bargaining agreement in
effect and where the employee making the protest was not
represented by a collective bargaining agent.

In *Alleluia,* a nonunion employer had discharged an employee
for writing a letter to the California Occupational Safety and
Health Administration complaining about certain alleged safety
problems. The administrative law judge held that the activity of
the employee was unprotected, since at no time prior to complaining to the company or sending the letter had he discussed
the safety problem with other employees, nor had he solicited
their support or requested their assistance in the preparation
of the letter. The Board reversed. While it conceded that the
employee had acted alone and in the "absence of any outward
manifestation of support for his efforts" by his fellow employees,
the Board said that he was nonetheless engaged in protected
concerted activity. The Board reasoned that "consent of action
emanates from the mere assertion" of statutory rights declared
in California's occupational safety and health laws and that, "in
the absence of any evidence that fellow employees disavow such
representation," there was an "implied consent."[383] Such activity
was therefore deemed concerted.

The rationale of *Alleluia Cushion Co.* has been applied to other
situations where, in the absence of a collective bargaining agreement, individual employees have resorted to administrative
agencies or complained to their employer about working conditions. Thus, in *Triangle Tool & Engineering Co.,*[384] the Board
found a Section 8(a)(1) violation where an employee had been
disciplined for making a complaint to the federal Wage and
Hour Division regarding a claimed overtime payment. The con-

---

[382]221 NLRB 999, 91 LRRM 1131 (1975).
[383]*Id.* at 1000.
[384]226 NLRB 1354, 94 LRRM 1108 (1976).

cert requirement of Section 7 was found satisfied even though the employee had acted alone, with no labor agreement in effect.[385]

While *Alleluia Cushion Co.* was not reviewed directly by a court of appeals, the decision's extension of the *Interboro* rule to non-union and noncollective bargaining situations has been rejected in other cases by the Fourth, Fifth, Eighth, and Ninth Circuits.[386]

For example, the Fourth Circuit, in *Krispy Kreme Doughnut Corp. v. NLRB*,[387] refused to enforce a Board order predicated on the discharge of an employee because of his "expressed intention to file a workmen's compensation claim" instead of seeking reimbursement under a group insurance policy. The Board sought court approval for its contention: that an individual employee is engaged in concerted activity whenever he acts in a matter which arises out of the employment relationship and which may be of common interest to other employees, since it is reasonable to presume that other employees, if they had known of the complaint, would have joined in. The court rejected this notion of "presumed 'concerted activity,'" noting that its adoption would have the unwarranted effect of reversing the accepted trial procedure in such cases by permitting the Board

---

[385]The rationale of *Alleluia Cushion Co.* was also applied in Hitchiner Mfg. Co., 238 NLRB 1253, 99 LRRM 1645 (1978) (employee letter to employer complaining about supervisor's abusive conduct); Bighorn Beverage, 236 NLRB 736, 98 LRRM 1396 (1978), *vacated in pertinent part*, 614 F2d 1238, 103 LRRM 3008, 3011 (CA 9, 1980) (complaint made about safety conditions at state agency); Air Surrey Co., 229 NLRB 1064, 95 LRRM 1212 (1977), *enforcement denied*, 601 F2d 256, 102 LRRM 2599 (CA 6, 1979) (employee inquiry at employer's bank to determine whether employer had sufficient funds to meet upcoming payroll); Dawson Cabinet Co., *supra* note 379 (employee seeking to vindicate rights under Title VII of the Civil Rights Act of 1964 refused to work on machine unless paid the same rate as the men who were doing same work); Ambulance Serv. of New Bedford, Inc., 229 NLRB 106, 95 LRRM 1239 (1977) (employee filed criminal charges against his employer because of "bouncing" paychecks); P&L Cedar Prods., 224 NLRB 244, 93 LRRM 1341 (1976) (employee complained to employer of alleged safety violations).

[386]Krispy Kreme Doughnut Corp. v. NLRB, 635 F2d 304, 105 LRRM 3407 (CA 4, 1980); NLRB v. Bighorn Beverage Co., *supra* note 385; NLRB v. Dawson Cabinet Co., *supra* note 379; NLRB v. Buddie Supermarkets, Inc., *supra* note 378. The First Circuit distinguished *Alleluia Cushion Co.* in NLRB v. Wilson Freight Co., 604 F2d 712, 102 LRRM 2269 (CA 1, 1979), on the ground that the case before it involved a union steward filing various unauthorized complaints with government agencies against the employer in defiance of contract limitations on his powers. The Sixth Circuit refused to rely on the *Alleluia Cushion* doctrine in Jim Causley Pontiac v. NLRB, 620 F2d 122, 104 LRRM 2190 (CA 6, 1980), enforcing the Board's order instead with other rationales. The Board itself apparently distinguished *Alleluia Cushion Co.* in Tabernacle Community Hosp. & Health Center, 233 NLRB 1425, 97 LRRM 1102 (1977), where a nonunit employee was discharged after she sent a letter of protest to her employer about her departmental transfer. Her activity was deemed unprotected since it was purely personal and no other workers were involved or would have benefited had she been successful in her protest.

[387]*Supra* note 386.

to rely on a presumption (based on a mere "theoretical assumption") to satisfy its burden of proving the jurisdictional predicate of "concerted activity." This would thereby force the respondent to rebut the presumption before the General Counsel would be required to go forward with any proof on the issue of the concerted nature of the activity.[388] In the absence of proof that a single employee's action intended or contemplated group activity or that the employee was in fact acting on behalf of or as a representative of other employees, his action at most, the court stated, can be said to have been "for the benefit of other employees only in a theoretical sense."[389] That the employee's activity may be directed at working conditions which affect all employees would not, in the court's view, satisfy the jurisdictional prerequisite of proving "concerted activity."

3. Employee Activity for "Other Mutual Aid or Protection." Concerted activity, to be protected, must satisfy the Section 7 requirement that it be for the purpose of collective bargaining or for "other mutual aid protection."[390] The Supreme Court in *Eastex, Inc.* v. *NLRB*[391] recognized that Congress intended in the "mutual aid and protection" clause to extend and broaden the ambit of protected employee activity beyond concerted activities associated with grievance settlement, collective bargaining, and self-organization. The reach of Section 7 encompasses concerted activities of employees "in support of employees of employers other than their own."[392] It also extends to employee efforts "to improve terms and conditions of employment or otherwise improve their lot as employees through channels out-

---

[388]*Id.* at 3410-11.

[389]In stating this principle, the court relied on the Third Circuit's opinion in Mushroom Transp. Co. v. NLRB, 330 F2d 683, 688, 56 LRRM 2034 (CA 3, 1964), which concluded that in order for a single employee's activity to be deemed concerted, it must appear at the very least that "it was engaged in with the object of initiating or inducing or preparing for group action or that it had some relation to group action in the interest of the employees." Proof of a shared concern among employees, without more, is insufficient to convert an employee's "personal gripes" into "protected concerted activity." *See also* Pelton Casteel, Inc. v. NLRB, 627 F2d 23, 105 LRRM 2124 (CA 7, 1980); Indiana Gear Works v. NLRB, 371 F2d 273, 64 LRRM 2253 (CA 7, 1967). The Board does not deem picketing by an individual employee for his sole benefit to be concerted activity. Arco Insulations, Inc., 247 NLRB No. 81, 103 LRRM 1198 (1980).

[390]The words "concerted activities" in §7 are "limited in meaning by the words with which they are associated." Joanna Cotton Mills Co. v. NLRB, 176 F2d 749, 24 LRRM 2416 (CA 4, 1949). Thus, protection of concerted activities under §7 is "expressly limited" to activities pursued for the specific purposes stated therein. *Id.* at 752.

[391]437 US 556, 565, 98 LRRM 2717, 2720 (1978). *See* note 475 *infra* and accompanying text.

[392]*Id.* at 565, 98 LRRM at 2720, *citing* Phelps Dodge Corp. v. NLRB, 313 US 177, 191-92, 8 LRRM 439 (1941). *See, e.g.*, Redwing Carriers, Inc., 137 NLRB 1545, 1546-47, 50 LRRM 1449 (1962), *enforced sub nom.* Teamsters Local 79 v. NLRB, 325 F2d

side the immediate employee-employer relationship."[393] Thus, protection is afforded employees when they seek to improve working conditions through "resort to administrative and judicial forums" and through "appeals to legislators to protect their interests as employees."[394]

Although the Court in *Eastex* indicated that "some concerted activity bears a less immediate relationship to employees' interests as employees than other such activity," and "at some point the relationship becomes so attentuated" that an activity cannot fairly be viewed as within the meaning of "mutual aid and protection," it emphasized that the task of delineating the boundaries of the "mutual aid and protection" clause was for the Board to perform in the first instance.[395]

In *Kaiser Engineers*[396] the Board broadly construed the clause to protect a group of engineers who wrote a series of letters to

---

1011, 54 LRRM 2707 (1963), *cert. denied,* 377 US 905, 55 LRRM 3023 (1964) (right to honor picket line of another employer's employees); NLRB v. J.G. Boswell Co., 136 F2d 585, 595, 12 LRRM 776 (CA 9, 1943) (right to express sympathy for striking employees of another employer); NLRB v. Peter Cailler Kohler Swiss Chocolate Co., 130 F2d 503, 10 LRRM 852 (CA 2, 1942) (right to publish support for a cooperative association of dairy farmers which had called a milk strike); Fort Wayne Corrugated Paper Co. v. NLRB, 111 F2d 869, 874 (CA 7, 1940) (right to assist in organizing another employer's employees); Yellow Cab, Inc., 210 NLRB 568, 569, 86 LRRM 1145 (1974) (right to distribute literature in support of another employer's employees); Washington State Serv. Employees, 188 NLRB 957, 959, 76 LRRM 1467 (1971) (right to demonstrate in support of another employer's employees); General Elec. Co., 169 NLRB 155, 67 LRRM 1326 (1968) (right to solicit funds for benefit of agricultural laborers employed elsewhere).

[393]Eastex, Inc. v. NLRB, *supra* note 391 at 565, 98 LRRM at 2720 (1978). The employee activity which the employer sought to prohibit was the distribution of a union newsletter on company property in nonworking areas during nonworking time. The newsletter, among other things, urged employees to oppose inclusion of a right-to-work provision in the state constitution and criticized a presidential veto of an increase in the federal minimum wage.

[394]*Id. See, e.g.,* Kaiser Eng'rs v. NLRB, 528 F2d 1370, 92 LRRM 3153 (CA 9, 1976), *enforcing* 213 NLRB 752, 87 LRRM 1447 (1975); Altex Ready Mixed Concrete Corp. v. NLRB, 542 F2d 295, 297, 93 LRRM 2940 (CA 5, 1976), *enforcing* 223 NLRB 696, 91 LRRM 1591 (1976); Walls Mfg. Co., *supra* note 368; Socony Mobil Oil Co., 153 NLRB 1244, 59 LRRM 1619 (1965), *enforced,* 357 F2d 662 (CA 2, 1966); Triangle Tool & Eng'r, Inc., *supra* note 384; King Soopers, Inc., *supra* note 381; Alleluia Cushion Co., *supra* note 382; Wray Elec. Contracting, Inc., 210 NLRB 757, 86 LRRM 1589 (1974).

[395]*Supra* note 391 at 567, 98 LRRM at 2721. The "mutual aid and protection" clause has also been broadly construed by the Board, but with only limited approval by the courts, to encompass certain employee protests over changes in supervisory personnel. Puerto Rico Food Prods. Corp. v. NLRB, 619 F2d 153, 104 LRRM 2304 (CA 1, 1980); Abilities & Goodwill, Inc. v. NLRB, 612 F2d 6, 103 LRRM 2029 (CA 1, 1979); NLRB v. Okla-Inn, 488 F2d 498, 503, 84 LRRM 2585 (CA 10, 1973); American Art Clay Co. v. NLRB, 328 F2d 88, 55 LRRM 2502 (CA 7, 1964); Dobbs Houses, Inc. v. NLRB, 325 F2d 531, 538-39, 54 LRRM 2726 (CA 5, 1963); NLRB v. Guernsey-Muskingum Elec. Coop., Inc., 285 F2d 8, 47 LRRM 2260 (CA 6, 1960); NLRB v. Phoenix Mutual Life Ins. Co., 167 F2d 983, 22 LRRM 2089 (CA 7, 1948), *cert. denied,* 335 US 845, 22 LRRM 2590 (1948); Bide-A-Wee Home Ass'n, 248 NLRB 853, 104 LRRM 1036 (1980).

[396]*Supra* note 394.

several legislators in which they opposed any relaxation of immigration laws which would allow the importation into the United States of foreign-educated engineers. The position which these engineers espoused was contrary to that of their employer, who was heavily engaged in overseas engineering projects. When the employer learned of the letters, it constructively discharged the principal author. Although the employees' activity did not concern a matter over which his employer had any control and, indeed, was outside the confines of the employment relationship, the Board held, with approval of the Ninth Circuit, that it was protected concerted activity for the purpose of mutual aid and protection.[397]

4. Protected Activity vs. Employer Control. The reach of Section 7 has posed difficult questions involving the balancing of an employee's right to engage in concerted activities against the employer's right to maintain order and control in the plant. The Board in one case held that an employee who gave a pro-union speech at the plant with company permission could not be discharged for refusing to lower his voice when ordered to do so several times by his supervisor, since the employee's conduct was not shown to have had a demonstrably disturbing effect upon plant business and operations.[398] The employer's right to maintain discipline in the plant, however, was adjudged the overriding consideration in a Board decision upholding the employer's right to discharge 22 employees who disrupted a meeting which had been planned by the employer for presentation of anti-union views on the eve of an election.[399]

---

[397]In enforcing the Board's order, the Ninth Circuit concluded that "the concerted activity of employees, lobbying legislators regarding changes in national policy which affect their job security, can be action taken for 'mutual aid or protection' within the meaning of §7." *Id.* at 1385.

[398]Farah Mfg. Co., 202 NLRB 666, 82 LRRM 1623 (1973). *See* Bob Henry Dodge, Inc., 203 NLRB 78, 83 LRRM 1077 (1973) (employee's defiance in grievance procedure protected since his words did not go beyond permissible bounds of free speech and open discussion contemplated by the Act); Prescott Indus. Prods. Co., 205 NLRB 51, 83 LRRM 1500 (1973), *enforcement denied*, 500 F2d 6, 86 LRRM 2963 (CA 8, 1974) (employee insistence in questioning his employer following the latter's anti-union "24-hour" speech held protected by Board, but court of appeals disagreed, stating that a deliberate defiance of the employer in front of assembled employees is not protected); F.W. Woolworth Co., 251 NLRB 1111, 105 LRRM 1374 (1980) (employee asking question at captive-audience meeting before election held protected notwithstanding company policy against such questions); AMC Air Conditioning Co., 232 NLRB 283, 97 LRRM 1146 (1977) (discharge of employee for creating commotion in plant held unlawful where commotion was generated by employer's suppression of employee's speech during lunch period).

[399]J.P. Stevens & Co., 219 NLRB 850, 89 LRRM 1814 (1975), *enforced*, 547 F2d 792, 93 LRRM 2262 (CA 4, 1976). *See* Clark Equip. Co., 250 NLRB 1333, 105 LRRM 1071 (1980) (5-day suspension upheld for union adherent who called employer's official a

The difficulty in balancing employer and employee rights in this area is illustrated by Board decisions involving employee protests that take the form of sit-in demonstrations conducted after the end of the employees' shift. In *Overhead Door Corp.*[400] a Board panel majority found a violation in the employer's discharge of employees who engaged in a sit-in after the end of their shift. A different result, however, was reached in *Peck, Inc.*,[401] a subsequent case by the same panel, where the Board upheld the discharge of employees for refusing to leave the plant and engaging in a sit-in, preventing the employer from closing the plant. The immediacy of the situation which the employees were protesting in *Overhead Door*, in contrast to the absence of "any necessary immediacy of action" in the protestor's conduct in *Peck, Inc.*,[402] was the distinguishing factor.[403]

5. Effect of Exclusive Union Representation. In *Emporium Capwell*[404] the Supreme Court ruled that concerted activities by union-represented employees may be denied the protection of Section 7, to which they might otherwise be entitled, where the activity is in derogation of the union's statutory role as exclusive representative of all employees in the bargaining unit.

The employees involved had claimed that their department-store employer was discriminating against them by his failure to give qualified black employees assignments and promotions.

"bastard" at meeting at which official attempted to persuade employees they did not need the union). *But see* Howell Metal Co., 243 NLRB 1136, 102 LRRM 1031 (1979) (employee's profanity at meeting was merely "animal exuberance" of the moment and not a part of a scheme to disrupt meeting; employee's conduct held protected).

[400]220 NLRB 431, 90 LRRM 1257 (1975), *enforcement denied in part*, 540 F2d 878, 93 LRRM 2147 (CA 7, 1976). *See* notes 484-87 *infra* and accompanying text.

[401]226 NLRB 1174, 93 LRRM 1434 (1976). *See* notes 488-90 *infra* and accompanying text.

[402]The immediacy of the situation and the fact that the employee's stoppage of work and refusal to leave the premises was precipitated by the employer's unfair labor practices were the bases for the Board's finding of protected concerted activity in *Meilman Food Indus.*, 234 NLRB 698, 97 LRRM 1372 (1978).

[403]Employee demonstrations and meetings to discuss employee concerns about working conditions were deemed protected activity, despite employer contentions that they were disruptive or disorderly, where the employees' activity did not interfere with or impair production. *See also* Empire Steel Mfg. Co., 234 NLRB 530, 97 LRRM 1304 (1978) (employee meeting during lunch period ran 15 minutes into scheduled work period, but production was not impaired); Chrysler Corp., 228 NLRB 486, 94 LRRM 1508 (1977) (demonstration during break time did not interfere with production). *See also* AMC Air Conditioning Co., *supra* note 398 (commotion in plant itself during working time held protected since it flowed from the employer's unlawful suppression of employee's speech during lunchtime).

[404]Emporium Capwell Co. v. Western Addition Community Organization, 420 US 50, 88 LRRM 2660 (1975), *rev'g sub nom.* Western Addition Community Organization v. NLRB, 485 F2d 917, 83 LRRM 2738 (CA DC, 1974), *rev'g sub nom.* The Emporium, 192 NLRB 173, 77 LRRM 1669 (1971).

Spurning the union's invocation of the grievance-arbitration procedure, they sought to circumvent their elected bargaining representative and deal directly with the employer. They picketed the employer's premises to protest alleged racial discrimination and distributed handbills urging a consumer boycott. Reversing the lower court and affirming the Board, the Supreme Court upheld the ensuing discharges, concluding that the principle of majority rule and exclusivity expressed in Section 9(a) of the Act mandated that minority employees not bypass their collective bargaining agent and the available grievance procedure. The Court reasoned that to permit subgroups within the bargaining unit to enforce their conflicting demands would be counterproductive, for it would dissipate the union's collective strength for combating discrimination, pit one minority group against another, and create a situation where the "probability of strife and deadlock is high" and the "likelihood of making headway against discriminatory practices would be minimal."[405]

In *Dreis & Krump Manufacturing Co.* v. *NLRB*[406] the Board and Seventh Circuit, distinguishing *Emporium Capwell*, held that the employer violated Section 8(a)(3) when it discharged an employee who had distributed fliers derogatory of the employer's supervisors. Unlike the protesting employees in *Emporium Capwell*, the employee in *Dreis & Krump* had filed a grievance under the established grievance procedure and was pursuing it.[407] In con-

---

[405]420 US at 68. For a discussion of *Emporium Capwell* and the relationship between national policy under §7 of the NLRA and Title VII of the Civil Rights Act of 1964, *see* Lopatka, *Protection Under the National Labor Relations Act and Title VII of the Civil Rights Act for Employees Who Protest Discrimination in Private Employment*, 50 N.Y.U. L. REV. 1179, 1187-95 (1975). *See generally* 1973-1974 *Annual Survey of Labor Relations Law*, 15 B.C. IND. & COM. L. REV. 1105, 1198-1203 (1974); 87 HARV. L. REV. 656 (1974); Meltzer, *The National Labor Relations Act and Racial Discrimination: The More Remedies, the Better?*, 42 U. CHI. L. REV. 1, 26-38 (1975); Note, *Racial Discrimination in Employment and the Remedy of Self-Help: An Unwarranted Addition*, 15 WM. & MARY L. REV. 615 (1974); Lynd, *The Right to Engage in Concerted Activity After Union Recognition: A Study of Legislative History*, 50 IND. L. J. 720 (1975); 25 DE PAUL L. REV. 179 (1976).

[406]544 F2d 320, 93 LRRM 2739 (CA 7, 1976). *See* Chapter 21 *infra* at note 160.

[407]Also distinguishing *Emporium Capwell*, the Sixth Circuit, in Richardson Paint Co. v. NLRB, 574 F2d 1195, 1205-1207, 98 LRRM 2951 (CA 5, 1978), refused to uphold the discharge of an employee who merely circulated a petition during nonwork time concerning the layoff of fellow members of his work crew, since nothing in the employee's activity "would undermine the Union's status as the bargaining representative or pose any serious threat to stable relations." And the Board majority in Armco Steel Corp., 232 NLRB 696, 96 LRRM 1325 (1977), distinguished *Emporium Capwell* on the ground that the employee circulating the petition was requesting that the employer and union renegotiate their agreement and was not seeking to bypass the union and bargain directly with the employer.

trast, the First Circuit in a later case applied the principles of *Emporium Capwell* to various employee complaints which had been raised in opposition to positions taken by the union itself. That court declared that such conduct, "being contrary to the principle of exclusive representation," would "not seem entitled to the protection of §7."[408]

B. Protected Concerted Activity: Specific Conduct

1. Work Stoppages. A primary strike may be protected or unprotected concerted activity, depending upon the circumstances. Where the strike is protected concerted activity, discipline or discharge of the strikers will usually violate Section 8(a)(1). Conversely, where the primary strike is not protected concerted activity, discharging or disciplining the strikers ordinarily does not violate Section 8(a)(1).[409]

In *NLRB* v. *Washington Aluminum Co.*,[410] the Supreme Court enforced a Board order reinstating with back pay seven employees discharged for walking off their jobs without permission when they claimed it was too cold to work in the shop. The Fourth Circuit had refused to enforce the Board's order[411] because the workers (who were unorganized) had left without affording the company an opportunity to avoid the work stoppage by presenting a specific demand to remedy the objectionable condition. Reversing, the Supreme Court saw the language of Section 7 as "broad enough to protect concerted activities whether they take place before, after, or at the same time . . . a demand is made."[412]

While legally striking employees are entitled to enlist the support of the public for their cause, "they may not elicit that support by force, trickery or guile, nor may they deliberately inflict on the employer economic harm unnecessary to the legitimate concerted activities."[413] When strikers stray over these

---

[408]NLRB v. Wilson Freight Co., *supra* note 386 at 725 n.17, 102 LRRM at 2278 n.17.
[409]*See generally* Chapter 21 *infra* at notes 104-57.
[410]*Supra* note 367.
[411]128 NLRB 643, 46 LRRM 1385 (1960), *enforcement denied*, 291 F2d 869, 48 LRRM 2558 (CA 4, 1961).
[412]370 US at 14. *See also* Vic Tanny Int'l v. NLRB, 622 F2d 237, 104 LRRM 2395 (CA 6, 1980) (unorganized employees who walked off job to present job-related grievances held protected).
[413]Montefiore Hosp. v. NLRB, 621 F2d 510, 104 LRRM 2160, 2165 (CA 2, 1980), *citing* NLRB v. Washington Aluminum Co., *supra* note 367; NLRB v. A. Lasaponara & Sons, Inc., 541 F2d 992, 998, 93 LRRM 2314 (CA 2, 1976), *cert. denied*, 430 US 914, 94 LRRM 2798 (1977).

boundaries, they will be deemed to forfeit the Act's coverage of their otherwise protected activity.[414]

2. Honoring Picket Lines. In the absence of a contractual or other waiver, employees who refuse to cross another union's lawful picket line are generally engaging in protected activity and may not be discharged unless the discharge is "justified by legitimate business considerations of an overriding nature."[415]

The right to cross picket lines may be waived by the employee's collective bargaining representative by negotiation of no-strike provisions or picket line clauses. But such waivers must be expressed in "clear and unmistakable language."[416]

3. Filing or Processing of Grievances. The discharge or discipline of employees for filing or processing grievances, whether pursuant to a formal contractual grievance procedure or informally in the absence of such a procedure, is generally held to be a violation of Section 8(a)(1).[417]

The absence of a collective bargaining agreement does not nullify the right of employees to present grievances. Thus, in *Keokuk Gas Serv. Co. v. NLRB*,[418] the Eighth Circuit enforced a Board ruling that an employee's pursuit of a grievance in the absence of a collective bargaining agreement constituted protected concerted activity. The employee had been suspended but was later asked to return to work; when he stated that he intended to pursue the grievance, the employer withdrew the offer. The court of appeals held that if the resolution of the

---

[414]Montefiore Hosp. v. NLRB, 104 LRRM at 2166 (deceptive appeals to public by picketing doctors to turn persons away from using clinic operated by struck employer held unprotected). For general treatment of unprotected concerted activity, *see infra* at notes 483-513.

[415]Cooper Thermometer, 154 NLRB 502, 59 LRRM 1767 (1965). *See generally* Chapter 21 *infra* at notes 161-75.

[416]Gary-Hobart Water Co., 210 NLRB 742, 86 LRRM 1210 (1974), *enforced*, 511 F2d 284, 88 LRRM 2830 (CA 7), *cert. denied*, 423 US 925, 90 LRRM 2921 (1975); Keller Crescent Co., 217 NLRB 685, 89 LRRM 1201 (1975), *enforcement denied*, 538 F2d 1291, 92 LRRM 3591 (CA 7, 1976). *But see* Amcar Div. v. NLRB, 641 F2d 561, 106 LRRM 2518 (CA 8, 1981), *denying enforcement to* 247 NLRB 1056, 103 LRRM 1303 (1980). *See* Chapter 21 *infra* at notes 176-80.

[417]John Sexton & Co., 217 NLRB 80, 88 LRRM 1502 (1975); Ernst Steel Corp., 212 NLRB 78, 87 LRRM 1508 (1974); Southwestern Bell Tel. Co., 212 NLRB 43, 87 LRRM 1446 (1974); Wray Elec. Contracting Co., *supra* note 394. *But see* discussion of the *Interboro* rule and its extension in *Alleluia Cushion Co.*, *supra* notes 374-89, indicating that some courts of appeals do not agree with the Board that a single employee's efforts to enforce a collective bargaining agreement or, in the absence of such an agreement, to pursue a grievance against his employer, satisfies the concert requirement of §7.

[418]580 F2d 328, 98 LRRM 3332 (CA 8, 1978), *enforcing* 233 NLRB 496, 97 LRRM 1278 (1977).

grievance would benefit all employees the right to present it was not restricted by the absence of a collective agreement.[419]

Assembling employees to present grievances,[420] filing of grievances by employees in a manner which bypasses the union,[421] grieving under a collective bargaining agreement by probationary employees,[422] and filing of numerous grievances[423] have all been viewed by the Board as concerted activity protected by Section 7.[424]

The Board has also held that union stewards and employees, when filing and processing grievances, are protected by the Act even if they " 'exceed the bounds of contract language, unless the excess is extraordinarily obnoxious, wholly unjustified, and departs from the res gestae of the grievance procedure.' "[425] While there is a line beyond which a grievant or a union steward may not go with impunity in pursuit of protected activities, the protections of the Act are not lost merely because their concerted activities " 'exceed the bounds of lawful conduct in a moment of animal exuberance or in a manner not motivated by improper motives. . . .' "[426]

4. Employee Insistence on Union Representation: The *Weingarten* Rule. In its 1975 companion decisions in *NLRB* v. *Weingarten, Inc.,*[427] and *Garment Workers* v. *Quality Manufacturing Co.,*[428] the Supreme Court, in agreement with the Board, ruled

---

[419]*See* Columbia Univ., 236 NLRB 793, 98 LRRM 1353 (1978).

[420]Shell Oil Co. v. NLRB, 561 F2d 1196, 96 LRRM 2789 (CA 5, 1977), *enforcing* 226 NLRB 1193, 93 LRRM 1512 (1976).

[421]Crown Wrecking Co., 222 NLRB 958, 91 LRRM 1319 (1976).

[422]Seven-Up Bottling Co. of Detroit, 223 NLRB 911, 92 LRRM 1001 (1976); R&S Steel Corp., 222 NLRB 69, 91 LRRM 1137 (1976).

[423]Ad Art, Inc., 238 NLRB 1124, 99 LRRM 1626 (1978), *enforced,* 645 F2d 669, 106 LRRM 2010 (CA 9, 1980).

[424]For discussion of other protected activity arising out of the presentation of grievances, *see* May Dep't Stores Co. v. NLRB, 555 F2d 1338, 95 LRRM 2657 (CA 6, 1977), *enforcing* 220 NLRB 1096, 90 LRRM 1444 (1975); High Performance Tube, Inc., 251 NLRB 1362, 105 LRRM 1145 (1980); Pacific Coast Utilities Serv., Inc., 238 NLRB 599, 99 LRRM 1619 (1978); Greyhound Taxi Co., 234 NLRB 865, 97 LRRM 1385 (1978); Clara Barton Terrace Convalescent Center, 225 NLRB 1028, 92 LRRM 1621 (1976).

[425]Union Fork & Hoe Co., 241 NLRB 907, 101 LRRM 1014 (1979), (the steward had walked out with a grievant's time sheet during a discussion of the grievance with a supervisor) *quoting* Clara Barton Terrace Convalescent Center, *supra* note 424.

[426]Union Fork & Hoe Co., *supra* note 425 at 1015, *quoting* Prescott Indus. Prods. Co., 205 NLRB 51, 51-52, 83 LRRM 1500 (1973). *See* U.S. Postal Serv., 250 NLRB 1220, 105 LRRM 1014 (1980).

[427]420 US 251, 88 LRRM 2689 (1975).

[428]420 US 276, 88 LRRM 2698 (1975).

that employee insistence upon union representation at an employer's investigatory interview, which the employee reasonably believes might result in disciplinary action against him, is protected concerted activity. Accordingly, the disciplining or discharging of an employee for refusal to cooperate in such an investigatory interview without union representation is a violation of Section 8(a)(1).[429]

In its discussion of the source, "contours," and "limits" of the *Weingarten* rule, the Supreme Court explained that (1) the right to union representation "inheres in §7's guarantee of the right of employees to act in concert for mutual aid and protection";[430] (2) the right arises "only in situations where the employee requests representation";[431] (3) the employee's right to request representation as a condition to participation in the interview "is limited to situations where the employee reasonably believes the investigation will result in disciplinary action";[432] (4) exercise of the right may not interfere with "legitimate employer prerogatives"; (5) the employer may carry on his inquiry without interviewing the employee, thus leaving to the employee "the choice between having an interview unaccompanied by his representative, or having no interview and foregoing any benefits that might be derived from one";[433] and (6) the employer has no duty to bargain with any union representative who may be permitted to attend the investigatory interview.[434]

While it may be clear that the rule of *Weingarten* is inapplicable to "such run-of-the-mill shop-floor conversations as, for exam-

---

[429]*See generally* Note, *Union Pressure in Disciplinary Meetings*, 41 U. CHI. L. REV. 329 (1974); 12 HOUS. L. REV. 1179 (1975); 7 U. TOL. L. REV. 298 (1976); Note, 6 SETON HALL L. REV. 514 (1975); 14 DUQ. L. REV. 257 (1969). A threat of severe discipline if an employee exercised his right to union representation during an investigatory interview was also deemed a violation of §8(a)(1) under the *Weingarten* rule. Southwestern Bell Tel. Co., 227 NLRB 1223, 94 LRRM 1305 (1977).

[430]*Supra* note 427 at 256-57.

[431]*Id* at 257. *See* Kohl's Food Co., 249 NLRB 75, 104 LRRM 1063 (1980); Lennox Indus., Inc., 244 NLRB No. 88, 102 LRRM 1298 (1979).

[432]*Supra* note 427 at 257-58.

[433]*Id.* at 258-59.

[434]*Id.* at 259-60. Although the employer has no duty to bargain with the union representative, the representative must be accorded an opportunity to speak, for the rule contemplates meaningful representation. In Southwestern Bell Tel. Co., 251 NLRB 612, 105 LRRM 1246 (1980), the employer had demanded that the union steward remain silent during the interview—conduct which the Board found unlawful: "It is clear from the Supreme Court's decision that the role of the statutory representative at the investigative interview is to provide 'assistance' and 'counsel' to the employee being interrogated." 105 LRRM at 1247. *See also* Texaco, 252 NLRB 606, 105 LRRM 1239 (1980).

ple, the giving of instructions or training or needed corrections of work techniques,"[435] the Board and the courts have had difficulty in determining under what circumstances a reasonable basis exists for believing that the investigatory interview will result in disciplinary action.[436] In this regard, the Supreme Court stated that the inquiry must be based on "objective standards"[437] and upon a reasonable evaluation of "all the circumstances," not upon the subjective reaction of the employee.

The "contours and limits" of *Weingarten* are still in the process of being shaped by both the Board and the courts.* In *Certified Grocers of California, Ltd.*[438] a Board-panel majority found *Weingarten* applicable not only to investigatory interviews but also to noninvestigatory interviews about which a reasonable basis exists for believing disciplinary action will result. The employee was required to meet with the plant manager without union representation. Prior to the meeting, management had agreed to give the employee a disciplinary layoff for low production, although the notice of warning and layoff was not signed or presented to the employee until after the meeting had begun. The Ninth Circuit denied enforcement of the Board's order,[439] concluding that *Weingarten* was not controlling since the purpose of the meeting was " 'to deliver the warning notice,' not to investigate." Although the notice was unsigned prior to the meeting, it was nevertheless final, and the meeting was called merely to inform

---

[435]*Supra* note 427 at 257-58, *quoting* Quality Mfg. Co., 195 NLRB 197, 199, 79 LRRM 1269, 1271 (1972). *See* General Elec. Co., 240 NLRB 479, 100 LRRM 1248 (1979).

[436]AAA Equip. Serv. Co., 238 NLRB 390, 99 LRRM 1252 (1978), *enforcement denied*, 598 F2d 1142, 101 LRRM 2381 (CA 8, 1979); Spartan Stores, Inc., 235 NLRB 522, 100 LRRM 1181 (1978), *enforcement denied*, 628 F2d 953, 105 LRRM 2293 (CA 6, 1980); Mt. Vernon Tanker Co. v. NLRB, 218 NLRB 1423, 89 LRRM 1793 (1975), *enforcement denied*, 549 F2d 571, 94 LRRM 3054 (CA 9, 1977). The Board and Ninth Circuit, however, have agreed that employer counseling sessions deemed by management to be a "preliminary step to the imposition of discipline," fall within the ambit of the *Weingarten* rule. Alfred M. Lewis, Inc. v. NLRB, 587 F2d 403, 410, 99 LRRM 2841 (CA 9, 1978), *enforcing in part* 229 NLRB 757, 95 LRRM 1216 (1977). But counseling sessions for absenteeism conducted under management assurances that the sessions were not disciplinary meetings and would not be recorded in the employees' personnel files were deemed by the Board to be unprotected by the *Weingarten* rule. Amoco Chem. Corp., 237 NLRB 394, 99 LRRM 1017 (1978). *See also* Newton Sheet Metal, Inc. v. NLRB, 598 F2d 478, 101 LRRM 2422 (CA 8, 1979); Good Hope Refiners v. NLRB, 620 F2d 57, 104 LRRM 2883 (CA 5, 1979).

[437]*Supra* note 427 at 257 n.5. *See* Alfred M. Lewis, Inc. v. NLRB, *supra* note 436.

*[**Editor's Note:** In August 1982, the Board extended *Weingarten* rights to unorganized employees, holding that "the rationale enunciated in Weingarten compels the conclusion that unrepresented employees are entitled to the presence of a coworker at an investigatory interview." Materials Research Corp., 262 NLRB No. 122, 110 LRRM 1401, 1405 (1982). *See* note 462 *infra*.]

[438]227 NLRB 1211, 94 LRRM 1279 (1977).

[439]587 F2d 449, 100 LRRM 3029 (CA 9, 1978).

the employee of the disciplinary action; it was not "to elicit damaging facts" to support the action or "to hear [the employee's] side of the story with a view toward withholding discipline."[440] The Board, in its pre-*Weingarten* decision in *Mobil Oil Corp.*,[441] had recognized the distinction between investigative interviews and disciplinary interviews, finding that the presence of the union would not be required in the latter if the disciplinary actions "are made without a prior discussion or consultation with the affected employee."[442]

In the aftermath of the Ninth Circuit's opinion, the Board reexamined its earlier decision in *Certified Grocers*.[443] In *Baton Rouge Water Works Co.*,[444] a bare majority of the full Board concluded that *Certified Grocers* "was wrongly decided on the facts" and overruled it to the extent that it read *Weingarten* as requiring union representation, when requested, at an interview called merely to inform an employee of disciplinary action. The majority concluded that under *Weingarten* an employee has "no Section 7 right to the presence of his union representative at a meeting with his employer held solely for the purpose of informing the employee of, and acting upon, a previously made disciplinary decision."[445] The full panoply of *Weingarten* protections might become applicable even at a disciplinary interview, however, if the employer engages in any conduct "beyond merely informing the employee of a previously made disciplinary decision."[446] Thus, according to the lead opinion in the case, the right to union representation will attach where the employer's conduct goes beyond this purpose, and either (1) seeks facts or evidence in support of the disciplinary action, (2) attempts to have the employee "admit his alleged wrongdoing or to sign a

---

[440]The Ninth Circuit has followed this view in other cases, that a purpose of the interview must be to investigate in order for *Weingarten* to apply. Alfred M. Lewis, Inc. v. NLRB, *supra* note 436; Mt. Vernon Tanker Co. v. NLRB, *supra* note 436. *See also* NLRB v. Columbia Univ., 541 F2d 922, 93 LRRM 2085 (CA 2, 1976), *denying enforcement to and remanding* 217 NLRB 1080, 89 LRRM 1218 (1975). In U.S. Postal Service, 252 NLRB 61, 105 LRRM 1202 (1980), the Board held that employees were not entitled to union representation during "fitness for duty" medical examinations administered by physicians.

[441]196 NLRB 1052, 80 LRRM 1188 (1972).

[442]*Supra* note 441 at 1052 n.3. *See* U.S. Postal Serv., 237 NLRB 1104, 99 LRRM 1179 (1978).

[443]*Supra* note 438.

[444]246 NLRB 995, 103 LRRM 1056 (1979). The lead opinion was joined in by Members Jenkins and Truesdale; Member Murphy authored a concurring opinion, and Chairman Fanning and Member Penello wrote separate dissenting opinions.

[445]*Id.* at 1058. This holding was cited with approval by the court in Anchortank, Inc. v. NLRB, *supra* note 378.

[446]*Id.* at 1058.

statement to that effect," or (3) seeks to have the employee "sign statements relating to such [other] matters as workmen's compensation . . . ."[447] But the opinion observed that the fact that the employer, after informing the employee of the discipline, "engaged in a conversation at the employee's behest or instigation concerning the reasons for the previously determined discipline will not, alone, convert the meeting" to one to which *Weingarten* would apply.[448]

The issue of when *Weingarten* rights attach and mature was addressed by the full Board in *Roadway Express, Inc.*[449] There the majority[450] observed that once an employee makes a valid request for union representation, the employer is permitted one of three options:[451] (1) grant the request; (2) dispense with or discontinue the interview;[452] or (3) offer the employee the choice of continuing the interview unaccompanied by a union representative or of having no interview at all and thereby dispensing with any benefits which the interview might have conferred on him.[453] The employer, however, may not continue the interview without granting the requested union representation unless the employee "voluntarily agrees to remain unrepresented *after* having been presented by the employer with the choices" just described or "is otherwise made aware of these choices."[454]

An employee's *Weingarten* rights, as interpreted by the majority opinion in *Roadway Express,* "matures at the commencement of the interview; be it on the production floor or in the super-

---

[447]*Id.* at 1058. *See* Texaco, 251 NLRB 633, 105 LRRM 1243 (1980); Louisiana Council No. 17, State, County & Municipal Employees, 250 NLRB 880, 104 LRRM 1485 (1980).
[448]*Id.* at 1058. Applying the principles announced by the majority, the Board (3 to 2) concluded in *Baton Rouge* that the interview was merely to announce the company's previously made decision to discharge the employee, and the protracted discussion of her performance that ensued was engaged in solely at the instigation of the employee. Accordingly, she was not entitled to representation under the Act. *Baton Rouge* was subsequently followed by the Board in Airco, Inc., 249 NLRB 524, 104 LRRM 1153 (1980); Great W. Coca Cola Bottling Co., 251 NLRB 860, 105 LRRM 1191 (1980); Pacific Tel. & Tel., 246 NLRB 1007, 103 LRRM 1070 (1979).
[449]246 NLRB 1127, 103 LRRM 1050 (1979).
[450]Members Penello, Murphy, and Truesdale.
[451]103 LRRM at 1052-53. These options had been discussed by the Board in its earlier decision in U.S. Postal Serv., 241 NLRB 141, 100 LRRM 1520 (1979). *See* Amoco Oil Co., 238 NLRB 551, 99 LRRM 1250, 1251 (1978).
[452]The employer, when faced with a request for union representation, may dispense with the interview and inform the employee of any previously determined disciplinary decision. Amoco Oil Co., *supra* note 451; Chrysler Corp., 241 NLRB 1050, 101 LRRM 1020 (1979).
[453]*See* Meharry Medical College, 236 NLRB 1396, 99 LRRM 1002 (1978).
[454]U.S. Postal Serv., *supra* note 451 at 142 (emphasis in original); Penn Dixie Steel Corp., 253 NLRB 91, 105 LRRM 1470 (1980).

visor's office."[455] Should an employer, however, merely request the employee to leave the production area and proceed to an office or some other location where further discussion is contemplated, then the employee "acts at his or her peril if he or she declines to do so";[456] in such a case the employee is not privileged to ignore the employer's directions.

In *Climax Molybdenum Co.* the Board was once again called upon to define the boundaries of the *Weingarten* rule. It extended the *Weingarten* rationale to provide both the employee subject to the investigatory interview and his union representative the right to insist on preinterview consultation among themselves on company time.[457] The Tenth Circuit, however, disapproved this expansion of *Weingarten* and ruled that only the employee, not his union representative, is entitled to request the presence of a representative at the interview.[458] In the court's view, the employer is under no obligation to accord the employee "with consultation with his union representative on company time if the interview date otherwise provides the employee adequate opportunity to consult with union representatives on his own time prior to the interview."[459]

Weingarten does not require an employer to postpone an interview because the specific union representative the employee requests is absent, so long as another union representative is available at the time set for the interview. Nor is the employer obliged to suggest or secure alternative representation for the

---

[455]*Supra* note 449 at 1052.

[456]*Id.* However, an employee may be so privileged where it is clear that the employer intends solely to discuss the merits of the matter which might result in discipline *and* will not permit a *Weingarten* representative to be present; an employee need not attend an illegal interview. Roadway Express, *supra* note 449, 103 LRRM at 1051 n.4, *discussing* Glomac Plastics, Inc., 234 NLRB 1309, 97 LRRM 1441 (1977), *enforced,* 600 F2d 3, 101 LRRM 2456 (CA 2, 1978). *See* Super Valu Xenia, 236 NLRB 1581, 99 LRRM 1028 (1978), discussed at 103 LRRM at 1053 n.15. In the absence of such circumstances, an employee may not refuse to report to a supervisor's office as directed even in the absence at the moment of a *Weingarten* representative, since such a pre-interview meeting, according to the Board in *Roadway,* might result in the employer (1) "agreeing to stay the interview" until a union representative is available; (2) "discontinuing the interview permanently"; or (3) offering the employee "the choice of continuing the interview unaccompanied by a *Weingarten* representative or having no interview at all." *Supra* note 449. *See* Spartan Stores, Inc. v. NLRB, *supra* note 436 (refusal to follow directions of employer and the established procedure for summoning union representative); General Elec. Co., 240 NLRB 479, 100 LRRM 1248 (1979).

[457]Amax, Inc., Climax Molybdenum Co. Div., 227 NLRB 1189, 94 LRRM 1177 (1977).

[458]584 F2d 360, 99 LRRM 2471 (CA 10, 1978). *See also* Appalachian Power Co., 253 NLRB 931, 106 LRRM 1041 (1980).

[459]584 F2d at 365.

employee.[460] Indeed, an employee's failure to request available representation may render his request for representation invalid.[461]

An employer's unlawful refusal to recognize or bargain with a majority union cannot be used as a means for denying employees their *Weingarten* rights.[462] And, as the Fifth Circuit noted in *Anchortank*,[463] after a union wins a representation election, even while challenges to the election are pending, an employee is entitled to union representation under the *Weingarten* rule.

The Board's policy on *remedies* for violation of the *Weingarten* rule was spelled out in *Kraft Foods, Inc.*:[464]

> Initially, we determine whether the General Counsel has made a prima facie showing that a make-whole remedy such as reinstatement, backpay, and expungement of all disciplinary records is warranted. The General Counsel can make this showing by proving that respondent conducted an investigatory interview in violation of *Weingarten* and that the employee whose rights were violated was subsequently disciplined for the conduct which was the subject of the unlawful interview.
>
> In the face of such a showing, the burden shifts to the respondent. Thus, in order to negate the prima facie showing of the appropriateness of a make-whole remedy, the respondent must demonstrate that its decision to discipline the employee in question was not based on information obtained at the unlawful interview. Where the respondent meets its burden, a make-whole remedy will

---

[460]Roadway Express, Inc., *supra* note 449; Coca-Cola Bottling Co., 227 NLRB 1276, 94 LRRM 1200 (1977); Pacific Gas & Elec. Co., 253 NLRB No. 154, 106 LRRM 1077 (1981).

[461]U.S. Postal Serv., *supra* note 451. The alternative *Weingarten* representative requested, however, need not be a union official. NLRB v. Illinois Bell Tel. Co., 674 F2d 618, 109 LRRM 3244 (CA 7, 1982), *granting in part and denying in part enforcement to* 251 NLRB 932, 105 LRRM 1236 (1980); Good Samaritan Nursing Home, Inc., 250 NLRB No. 30, 104 LRRM 1390 (1980); Crown Zellerbach, Inc., 239 NLRB 1124, 100 LRRM 1092 (1978). The request must come from the employee; the Board held in Appalachian Power Co., 253 NLRB No. 135, 106 LRRM 1041 (1980), that the right could not be invoked by the employee's union steward.

[462]Glomac Plastics, Inc., *supra* note 456. The Board also expressed the view, albeit in dicta, that *Weingarten* rights are to be enjoyed by all employees, whether or not they are represented by a union. In *NLRB v. Columbia Univ.*, 541 F2d 922, 931, 93 LRRM 2085 (CA 2, 1976), the Second Circuit, also in dictum, suggested approval of the principle that *Weingarten* rights are applicable "in unionized or in non-unionized firms." *See also* Brown & Connolly, Inc., 237 NLRB 271, 98 LRRM 1572 (1978), *enforced,* 593 F2d 1373, 100 LRRM 3072 (CA 1, 1979); Anchortank, Inc. v. NLRB, *supra* note 378; Good Samaritan Nursing Home, Inc., *supra* note 461; PPG Indus., Inc., 251 NLRB 1146, 105 LRRM 1434 (1980). [*See* **Editor's Note,** p. 151 *supra.*]

[463]Anchortank, Inc., *supra* note 378.

[464]Kraft Foods, Inc., 251 NLRB 598, 105 LRRM 1233 (1980). *See also* Coyne Cylinder Co., 251 NLRB No. 198, 105 LRRM 1270 (1980); Consolidated Food Co., 253 NLRB No. 4, 105 LRRM 1407 (1980); NLRB v. Potter Signal Co., 600 F2d 120, 101 LRRM 2378 (CA 8, 1979); NLRB v. Illinois Bell Tel. Co., *supra* note 461.

not be ordered. Instead, we will provide our traditional cease-and-desist order in remedy of the 8(a)(1) violation.[465]

5. Safety-Related Protests. Cases involving alleged unsafe working conditions have raised questions concerning the scope of protected concerted activity. Employee conduct and protests involving safety strikes, refusals to accept job assignments claimed unsafe, filing of complaints at government occupational safety and health agencies, and complaining to the employer about job safety conditions have been held protected under Section 7.[466] But lack of any great or immediate danger may render an employee's refusal to work to protest safety conditions unprotected.[467]

Concerted refusal to work because of unsafe working conditions may be protected even in the face of a no-strike agreement. Thus, in *Combustion Engineering, Inc.,*[468] the Board held that a

---

[465]105 LRRM at 1233.

[466]*See* Wheeling-Pittsburgh Steel Corp. v. NLRB, 618 F2d 1009, 104 LRRM 2054, 2059-61 (CA 3, 1980) (refusing to work under contract clause granting right not to work under unsafe conditions held protected); Jim Causely Pontiac v. NLRB, *supra* note 386 (filing complaint with state public health department); Roadway Express, Inc., *supra* note 380 (refusal to drive tractor-trailer vehicle that employee claimed was unsafe held protected even though another employee drove same equipment without incident); Union Boiler Co., 213 NLRB 818, 87 LRRM 1268 (1974), *enforced,* 530 F2d 970, 90 LRRM 3057 (CA 4, 1975) (refusal to perform work, claiming it unsafe, held protected even though work was finished under same conditions by other employees without an accident); Wray Elec. Contracting, Inc., *supra* note 394 (filing OSHA complaint held protected); C & I Air Conditioning, Inc., *supra* note 379 (individual employee complaint about job safety held protected by Board but enforcement denied on ground that activity was not concerted; *see supra* at notes 365-403; Leslie Metal Arts Co., 208 NLRB 323, 85 LRRM 1314 (1974), *enforced,* 509 F2d 811, 88 LRRM 2437 (CA 6, 1975) (refusal to work, protesting failure of supervisor to protect employees from aggressions of other workers, held protected). *See also* Bighorn Beverage, *supra* note 385; Kiechler Mfg. Co., 238 NLRB 398, 99 LRRM 1578 (1978); Anheuser-Busch, Inc., 239 NLRB 207, 99 LRRM 1548 (1978); Alleluia Cushion Co., *supra* note 382; Fry Roofing Co., 237 NLRB 1005, 99 LRRM 1544 (1978); Modern Carpet Indus., Inc., 236 NLRB 1014, 98 LRRM 1426 (1978), *enforced,* 611 F2d 811, 103 LRRM 2167 (CA 10, 1979); Empire Steel Mfg. Co., 234 NLRB 530, 97 LRRM 1304 (1978); The Tappan Co., 228 NLRB 1389, 95 LRRM 1035 (1977), *enforced,* 607 F2d 764 (CA 6, 1979); P & L Cedar Prods., 224 NLRB 244, 93 LRRM 1341 (1976). Where, however, an employee protest concerning the presence of containers of cumbustible material at the job site went to the extreme of closing the entrance to the employer's operation, the Board sustained the discharge of three employees on the ground that such serious misconduct was unprotected by the NLRA. Mal Landfill Corp., 210 NLRB 167, 86 LRRM 1304 (1974). And where an employee admitted he had been looking out only for himself, his refusal to drive a truck was held not to be "concerted." Comet Fast Freight, 262 NLRB No. 40, 110 LRRM 1321 (1982).

[467]In Economy Tank Line, 99 LRRM 1198 (1978), the General Counsel in an advice memorandum stated that in order for employee activity to be protected, both the object of the activity and the manner in which it is carried out must be protected. The lack of any great or immediate danger to the employee in this case left his refusal to perform the work unprotected. Similarly, a refusal to operate certain equipment to protest safety hazards was held unprotected by the Board where the refusal continued after the equipment had been repaired and the hazards eliminated. Pyro Mining Co., 230 NLRB 782, 96 LRRM 1175 (1977).

[468]224 NLRB 542, 93 LRRM 1049 (1976).

concerted walkout of employees from a job site was not prohibited by a contractual no-strike provision, since the presence of two belligerent, partly inebriated intruders on the site created an "abnormally ·dangerous" condition within the meaning of Section 502 of the LMRA.[469] Since the employer had not provided adequate protection, the discharges for engaging in the work stoppage constituted a violation of the Act.[470]

6. Protests Relating to Employment Discrimination. Conduct protesting alleged discrimination in employment on racial and other grounds protected by antidiscrimination legislation has been held entitled to Section 7 protection. Thus, in *King Snoopers, Inc.,*[471] the Board concluded that a Spanish-American employee who acted alone in filing charges with a state fair employment practices agency and the federal Equal Employment Opportunity Commission was engaged in protected concerted activity.[472]

The protection of Section 7 may be denied, however, where employee protests against employment discrimination are in derogation of the collective bargaining representative's role as exclusive representation of all of the employees in the bargaining unit.[473] Permitting protests which take this form would be counterproductive, in the view of the Supreme Court, since they would dissipate the union's collective strength for combating

---

[469]§502 provides:
"Nothing in this Act shall be construed to require an individual employee to render labor or service without his consent, nor shall anything in this Act be construed to make the quitting of his labor by an individual employee an illegal act; nor shall any court issue any process to compel the performance by an individual employee of such labor or service, without his consent; nor shall the quitting of labor by an employee or employees in good faith because of abnormally dangerous conditions for work at the place of employment of such employee or employees be deemed a strike under this Act."

[470]In Gateway Coal Co. v. Mine Workers, 414 US 368, 85 LRRM 2049 (1974), the Supreme Court recognized that §502 provides an exception to the general rule that strikes in violation of no-strike provisions are unprotected, but characterized the exception as a "limited" one which must be supported by "ascertainable, objective evidence." *See* Chapter 19 *infra* at notes 106-107. *Cf.* Whirlpool Corp. v. Marshall, 445 US 1, 8 OSHC 1001 (1980), approving an Occupational Safety and Health regulation, 29 CFR §1977 12(b), which protects an employee's right to refuse work because of reasonable apprehension of death or serious injury.

[471]*Supra* note 381.

[472]Other cases treating employee complaints in the area of employment discrimination as protected conduct include Frank Briscoe, Inc. v. NLRB, 637 F2d 946, 106 LRRM 2155 (CA 3, 1981); Flynn Paving Co., 236 NLRB 721, 98 LRRM 1344 (1978); Dawson Cabinet Co., *supra* note 379. *See generally* Chapter 7 *infra* at notes 308-22 and authorities cited in note 405 *supra*.

[473]Emporium Capwell Co. v. Western Additional Community Organization, *supra* note 404 and text accompanying notes 404-405.

discrimination, making the "likelihood of making headway against discriminatory practices . . . minimal."[474]

7. Appeals to Agencies and Filing of Court Actions. The Supreme Court in *Eastex, Inc.* v. *NLRB*[475] construed the "mutual aid and protection" clause of Section 7 as extending protection to concerted activities by employees "to improve terms and conditions of employment or otherwise improve their lot as employees through channels outside the immediate employee-employer relationship."[476] Thus, protection is afforded employees when they seek to improve working conditions through "resort to administrative and judicial forums" and through "appeals to legislators to protect their interests as employees."[477]

Employee appeals and complaints lodged with governmental agencies and officials in the areas of occupational safety,[478] employment discrimination,[479] and labor standards[480] have been held to constitute protected concerted activities. Resort to a judicial forum by employees to further their interests as employees have similarly been afforded protection of Section 7. Thus, the filing of a labor-related lawsuit by a group of employees against their employer seeking actual and punitive damages is treated as protected activity, unless prompted by malice or bad faith.[481] If the lawsuit is filed in good faith, "the fact that it may have been groundless or that it was later dismissed on the pleadings would not in itself make the activity unprotected. . . ."[482]

---

[474]*Id.* at 68.
[475]*Supra* note 391 at 565.
[476]*Id.*
[477]*Id. See also* cases cited in note 394 *supra.*
[478]*E.g.,* The Tappan Co., *supra* note 466; Kiechler Mfg. Co., *supra* note 466; Alleluia Cushion Co., *supra* note 382; Wray Elec. Contracting, Inc., *supra* note 394.
[479]*E.g.,* Flynn Paving Co., *supra* note 472; The Massachusetts Women's Hosp., 227 NLRB 1289, 95 LRRM 1616 (1977); King Soopers, Inc., *supra* note 381. *See* notes 471-74 *supra* and accompanying text.
[480]Self Cycle & Marine Distributor Co., 237 NLRB 75, 98 LRRM 1517 (1978); Apollo Tire Co., 236 NLRB 1627, 99 LRRM 1138 (1978), *enforced,* 604 F2d 1180, 102 LRRM 2043 (CA 9, 1979); Triangle Tool & Eng'r, Inc., *supra* note 384; Brooklawn Nursing Home, Inc., 233 NLRB 267, 92 LRRM 1107 (1976). *But see* Krispy Kreme Doughnut Corp. v. NLRB, *supra* note 386.
[481]Trinity Trucking & Materials Corp., 221 NLRB 364, 90 LRRM 1499, 1500 (1975), *supplemented,* 227 NLRB 792, 94 LRRM 1223 (1977), *enforced,* 96 LRRM 3413 (CA 7, 1977) (not officially published).
[482]221 NLRB at 365. Ambulance Serv. of New Bedford, Inc., *supra* note 385 (filing of criminal charges against employer for issuing paycheck backed with insufficient funds held protected); All Brite Window Cleaning & Maintenance Serv., Inc., 235 NLRB 596, 98 LRRM 1297 (1978) (employee activity in retaining attorney in order to obtain back pay owed under collective bargaining agreement ruled protected). *See also* Kaiser Eng'rs v. NLRB, *supra* note 394, where the Ninth Circuit upheld a Board decision that the

C. Unprotected Concerted Activities

1. Sit-Down Strikes. The so-called sit-down strike, in which the strikers remain on the employer's premises during the strike, taking possession of the property and excluding others from entry, is a method of striking which the Supreme Court, shortly after passage of the Wagner Act, condemned as unprotected conduct because of the trespass on private property which the conduct entailed.[483] Employees engaging in sit-down strikes have thus historically been deprived of the protections of the Act and have been subject to discharge by their employer.

As the Board and the courts expanded the scope of protected concerted activity, however, they also reduced and limited the types of activities which may be deemed unprotected; thus, in two decisions issued in the mid-1970s previously noted, a Board panel majority read the Supreme Court's condemnation of sit-down strikes narrowly, indicating that sit-down strike activities under certain circumstances may be deemed protected:

In *Overhead Door Corp.*,[484] five employees, after being informed that their shift was to be abbreviated, engaged in a "work-in" after the scheduled hour of plant closing in defiance of employer and police directives to leave the premises. Ultimately, the protesting employees were removed from the plant under police arrest. A Board panel majority found the employee conduct protected, but the Seventh Circuit refused to enforce this aspect of the Board's decision.[485] Quoting the dissenting Board Member, the court described the "result reached by the [Board] majority and the proposition of law for which it stands" as "wholly repugnant to the purposes of the Act."[486] The court noted that the fact that other avenues of protest were open to the employees in the form of a grievance procedure "shifts the

---

lobbying efforts of a group of engineers in opposition to changes in national immigration policy concerning importation of alien engineers was "for mutual aid or protection" and that the constructive discharge of the engineer principally responsible for the lobbying effort was therefore violative of the Act; *see* discussion at notes 396-97 *supra*.

[483]Apex Hosiery Co. v. Leader, 310 US 469, 6 LRRM 647 (1940); NLRB v. Fansteel Metallurgical Corp., *supra* note 367; *See* Cone Mills Corp. v. NLRB, 413 F2d 445, 71 LRRM 2916 (CA 4, 1969). For commentary supportive of the sit-down strike concept, *see* Green, *The Case for the Sit-Down Strike*, 90 NEW REPUBLIC 199 (1937).

[484]*Supra* note 400.

[485]*Id.*

[486]*Id.* at 885.

locus of the accommodation between employees' rights and private property rights in favor of the employer."[487]

In *Peck, Inc.*,[488] however, the same Board majority[489] found a sit-down strike to be unprotected conduct, but they nevertheless continued their affirmation of the holding and reasoning of *Overhead Door*. In *Peck*, a group of employees had remained on the employer's premises after the end of the shift, "to prove a point" to their supervisor who had refused to allow them to leave early in the face of an impending snowstorm. The majority opinion distinguished the contrary result in *Overhead Door* because the protest in that case concerned a meritorious complaint, whereas in *Peck* the sole purpose was to "punish" the supervisor; also, the employees in *Overhead Door* were protesting "an immediate situation," whereas in *Peck* the sit-down was not "predicated on any necessary immediacy of action."[490]

2. Other Unprotected Activity. The concept of "disloyalty" has been used to deny the protection of Section 7 to certain concerted activities. The leading case on the point is the Supreme Court's *Jefferson Standard Broadcasting*[491] decision. A technicians' union had a collective bargaining dispute with a television station. While remaining on the job, but during their off hours, some of the technicians distributed handbills severely criticizing the quality of programming, suggesting that the city was being treated as "second class." The handbills made no reference to the union, collective bargaining, or the current labor dispute. The Court ruled that the employer had cause for discharging the employees who had distributed the handbills, for while employees continue at work they owe a duty not to disparage the product or services of their employer or to hamper his sales.[492] This duty may persist even during a strike, since strikers intend to return to work and have certain rights to reinstate-

---

[487]*Id.*

[488]*Supra* note 401.

[489]Members Fanning and Jenkins. Member Penello, the dissenting member in *Overhead Door*, concurred in the result but rejected the majority's analysis.

[490]*See* Meilman Food Indus., *supra* note 402, where the immediacy of the situation and the fact that the employee's work stoppage and refusal to leave the plant had been prompted by employer unfair labor practices were factors relied upon by the Board in finding the employees' activity protected. For further discussion of sit-down strikes, *see* Chapter 21 *infra* at notes 104-107.

[491]NLRB (Jefferson Standard Broadcasting Co.) v. Electrical Workers (IBEW) Local 1229, *supra* note 367.

[492]*See* Boeing Airplane Co. v. NLRB, 238 F2d 188, 38 LRRM 2276 (CA 9, 1956); Hoover Co. v. NLRB, 190 F2d 380, 28 LRRM 2353 (CA 6, 1951).

ment.[493] The Court stated that "there is no more elemental cause for discharge of an employee than disloyalty to his employer . . . ."[494]

In cases presenting the issue of whether particular employee conduct is sufficiently "disloyal" to remove it from the protection of Section 7, the Board has progressively narrowed the area of unprotected activity. The courts have not always agreed. These "disloyalty" cases have involved (a) breach of confidentiality, (b) false allegations or affidavits concerning the employer, and (c) disparagement of the employer's business activities.

a. Breach of Confidentiality. Employees who divulge salary information to one another in violation of their employer's rule requiring that salaries be treated as confidential are deemed to be engaged in protected activity.[495] Section 7 has similarly been invoked to protect an employee whose discussions with fellow employees disclosed computations relating to wage increases.[496]

In *Bell Federal Savings & Loan Ass'n,* [497] however, the Board refused to find protected a switchboard operator's disclosure to the union of the number of times the company president had talked with the company's labor counsel, even though the operator had never been instructed that her work was confidential. The employer, in the Board's view, had the right to expect an operator not to reveal information about telephone calls. The Board distinguished this type of information from information such as addresses of employees on time cards, which employees would have a right to use for organizational purposes.

---

[493]*See* Patterson-Sargent Co., 115 NLRB 1627, 38 LRRM 1134 (1956).

[494]*Supra* note 367 at 472. *But cf. infra* at notes 504-13.

[495]Jeannette Corp., 217 NLRB 653, 89 LRRM 1224 (1975), *enforced,* 532 F2d 916, 91 LRRM 2968 (CA 3, 1976). *See also* Blue Cross-Blue Shield of Ala., 225 NLRB 1217, 93 LRRM 1281 (1976) (rule barring employees from discussing their salaries with other employees held to be violative of the Act). In Texas Instruments, Inc., 236 NLRB 68, 98 LRRM 1299 (1978), *modified and remanded,* 599 F2d 1067, 102 LRRM 2292 (CA 1, 1979), the Board had concluded that the employer violated §§8(a)(1) and (3) when it discharged employees during a union organizing drive for publishing confidential industry wage information in disregard of the employer's internal security regulations. The First Circuit modified and remanded the decision. On remand, the Board reaffirmed its earlier order. 247 NLRB 253, 103 LRRM 1144 (1980). On review, the First Circuit reversed the Board and upheld the discharges on the ground that the confidential information disclosure was unprotected activity. "While the NLRA protects against retaliation on account of union activities, it does not license activists to violate valid company rules with impunity." Texas Instruments, Inc. v. NLRB, 637 F2d 822, 106 LRRM 2137, 2144 (CA 1, 1981).

[496]NLRB v. Sencore, Inc., 558 F2d 433, 95 LRRM 2865 (CA 8, 1977), *enforcing* 223 NLRB 113, 91 LRRM 1451 (1976).

[497]214 NLRB 75, 87 LRRM 1415 (1974).

In *Knuth Brothers, Inc.*[498] the Board and the Seventh Circuit disagreed on whether an employee's avowed purpose of aiding a union organizational campaign was sufficient, under the circumstances, to protect him from the effects of his disclosure of confidential information to the employer's customers. Since the information was sensitive and might have jeopardized some customer relationships, the court found that the employee had "acted in reckless disregard of his employer's business interests, and that revealing the information "was an act of disloyalty" which constituted cause for discharge.[499]

In *NLRB* v. *Circle Bindery, Inc.*[500] an employee disclosed to a union that his employer's nonunion bindery was preparing a booklet which carried the union label, in violation of a licensing agreement between the union and a unionized printing firm. The fact that the employer would lose business because of that action did not render the conduct unprotected. The Board reasoned that in acting to protect the integrity of the union label the employee was engaging in protected conduct, because it served to promote employment of union members under union conditions. The First Circuit agreed.

b. False Allegations or Affidavits Concerning the Employer. It has long been the rule that employees do not forfeit the protection of the Act by making false or inaccurate allegations concerning their employer in connection with appeals or complaints to government agencies, provided the allegations are not "deliberately or maliciously" false.[501] But in *Altex Ready Mix Concrete Corp.* v. *NLRB*[502] the Board, with Fifth Circuit approval, may have extended the rule. Two employees had signed false affi-

---

[498]218 NLRB 869, 89 LRRM 1422 (1975), *enforcement denied*, 537 F2d 950, 92 LRRM 3275 (CA 7, 1976). *See* Comment, *NLRB v. Knuth Brothers: The Boundaries of Unprotected "Disloyalty" When a Non-Striking Employee's Section 7 Concerted Activity Threatens Employee-Customer Relations*, 125 U. PA. L. REV. 1339 (1977).

[499]537 F2d at 956. Similarly, a union activist's efforts to obtain a restricted list of employees and their telephone numbers were considered grounds for discharge by the Fifth Circuit, also in disagreement with the Board. NLRB v. Florida Steel Corp., 544 F2d 896, 94 LRRM 2237 (CA 5, 1977). In Buddies Super Mkts., 223 NLRB 950, 92 LRRM 1008 (1976), *enforcement denied*, 550 F2d 39, 95 LRRM 2108 (CA 5, 1977), the Board and courts were in disagreement in still another case involving confidential information. There the court refused to enforce a Board decision which held that a supervisor who had revealed confidential information that his employer was "building a case" against an employee because of the latter's earlier union affiliation was engaging in protected activity for which he could not be lawfully discharged.

[500]536 F2d 447, 92 LRRM 2689 (CA 1, 1976).

[501]Walls Mfg. Co., *supra* note 368.

[502]Altex Ready Mix Concrete Corp. v. NLRB, *supra* note 394.

davits which were filed in support of the union's lawsuit. Both subsequently admitted that they knew the affidavits were inaccurate, but claimed they had not read or understood them. Their conduct was deemed protected activity, and their discharge for making the false affidavits was accordingly ruled unlawful.[503]

   c. *Disparagement of the Employer or Its Business Activities.* Employee conduct disparaging management officials or the employer's business may be protected concerted activity if the remarks or conduct relate to employee interests or working conditions and are not egregious in nature. In *Community Hospital of Roanoke Valley, Inc.,*[504] the Fourth Circuit, in a divided opinion, agreed with the Board's finding that a nurse's statement on a television broadcast protesting wages and staffing conditions at the hospital at which she was employed were protected, notwithstanding the hospital's contention that the statements were disparaging and disloyal. The Board concluded that the statements were distinguishable from those found unprotected in the *Jefferson Standard* case,[505] because they were "directly related to protected concerted activity in progress."[506]

   The Board's general approach, which was followed in *Community Hospital,* is that an employee may properly engage in communications with a third party in an effort to obtain the third party's assistance "in circumstances where the communication [is] related to a legitimate, ongoing labor dispute between the employees and their employer, and where the communication [does] not constitute a disparagement or vilification of the employer's product or its reputation."[507] But care must be taken

---

[503]*See also* Big Three Indus. Gas & Equip. Co., 212 NLRB 800, 87 LRRM 1543 (1974), *enforced,* 512 F2d 1404, 93 LRRM 2842 (CA 5, 1975) (discharge of employee for giving "inaccurate" testimony at NLRB hearing held unlawful where employee did not "knowingly and willfully testify falsely").

[504]220 NLRB 217, 90 LRRM 1449 (1975), *enforced,* 538 F2d 607, 92 LRRM 3158 (CA 4, 1976).

[505]*Supra* at notes 367 and 491-94.

[506]*See also* Great Lakes Steel, Div., 236 NLRB 1033, 98 LRRM 1551 (1978) (publication of leaflet seeking improvement of employer's medical and ambulance policy held protected); Automobile Club of Mich., 231 NLRB 1179, 96 LRRM 1267 (1977), *enforced,* 610 F2d 438, 104 LRRM 2632 (CA 6, 1979) (issuance of press release describing lawsuit employees had filed against employer held protected); Springfield Library & Museum, 239 NLRB 1623, 99 LRRM 1380 (1978); Firestone Tire & Rubber Co., 238 NLRB 1323, 99 LRRM 1429 (1978).

[507]Allied Aviation Serv. Co. of N.J., Inc., 248 NLRB 229, 103 LRRM 1454, 1455 (1980). *See* Greyhound Lines, 251 NLRB 1638, 105 LRRM 1232 (1980); Automobile Club of Mich. v. NLRB, *supra* note 506.

to distinguish between public disparagement of an employer's products or services and the mere "airing of what may be highly sensitive issues."[508] In *Allied Aviation Service Co. of New Jersey*[509] two letters sent by employees to airline customers concerning safety issues, while raising "sensitive" and "delicate" issues, did not rise, in the Board's view, "to the level of public disparagement necessary to deprive otherwise protected activities of the protections of the Act."[510] Regarding the effectiveness and timeliness of the employee communication, the Board in *Allied Aviation* declared:

> [I]n deciding cases of this sort, it is not the Board's function to appraise the potential effectiveness of the tactics utilized by employees in their disputes with management. At what point the employees determine that third-party assistance will be of more benefit than private talks with their employer is a tactical decision. Thus, if the communication is related to the dispute, the employee sending the communication is equally protected whether such a step is taken early on in the dispute, or at a later date after all internal avenues have been exhausted.[511]

Illustrative of excessive employee conduct which the Board found unprotected were the actions in the following two cases: In *American Arbitration Association*[512] the Board ruled that, although the sending of letters and a questionnaire to the employer's clients concerning the employer's dress code was concerted activity, the sarcastic and denigrating tone of the letters removed the aura of protection and subjected the employee to discharge. And in *Giant Open Air Market*[513] a discharge was ruled proper where the employee, a waitress and union activist, had engaged in divisive conduct which irritated and alienated customers and had spread rumors of thievery and illicit affairs among the employees.

---

[508]103 LRRM at 1456. "[A]bsent a malicious motive, [an employee's] right to appeal to the public is not dependent on the sensitivity of [the employer] to his choice of forum." Richboro Community Mental Health Council, Inc., 242 NLRB 1267, 101 LRRM 1319, 1320 (1979).

[509]*Supra* note 507.

[510]103 LRRM at 1456.

[511]*Id.*

[512]233 NLRB 71, 96 LRRM 1431 (1977).

[513]231 NLRB 945, 96 LRRM 1227 (1977).

IV. Union Restraint and Coercion

A. Section 8(b)(1)(A): Restraint and Coercion of Employees

Section 8(b)(1)(A) is concerned with the rights of individual employees in their relations with labor organizations. Pursuant to the dictates of this section, it is an unfair labor practice for a union to "restrain or coerce employees in the exercise of the rights guaranteed in Section 7." Under Section 7 employees are guaranteed both the right to engage in concerted activities and the "right to refrain from any or all such activities . . . ." However, the proviso to Section 8(b)(1)(A) states that the Section "shall not impair the right of a labor organization to prescribe its own rules with respect to the acquisition or retention of membership therein . . . ."[514]

1. Not A Derivative Counterpart of Section 8(a)(1). As previously noted,[515] while Section 8(b)(1)(A) may appear to be a counterpart of Section 8(a)(1), it has always been the Board's position that Section 8(b)(1)(A) was not intended to have the same broad application as Section 8(a)(1).[516] In its earlier *National Maritime*[517] decision, the Board and the Second Circuit concluded that violations of other provisions of Section 8(b) do not give rise to derivative violations of Section 8(b)(1)(A). The Supreme Court, in *Curtis Brothers*,[518] approved the Board's decision in *National Maritime Union* and noted that Section 8(b)(1)(A) only provides limited authority relating to "union tactics involving violence, intimidation, and reprisals or threats thereof."[519]

This important distinction between Sections 8(a)(1) and 8(b)(1) was reiterated by the Board in 1980 in a dismissal of a complaint against a union for interfering with the dissemination of information by an employee. The Board stated:

> The cases relied on by the Administrative Law Judge, although similar, differ critically in the material fact that they involved employee

---

[514]For detailed treatment of the closely related §8(b)(2), which prohibits a union from causing or attempting to cause an employer to discriminate in violation of §8(a)(3), *see* Chapter 7 *infra*.

[515]*Supra* at note 33.

[516]*See* note 33 *supra*.

[517]National Maritime Union, *supra* note 34.

[518]NLRB v. Drivers Local 639, *supra* note 36. *See* Chapter 23 at notes 4-9.

[519]362 US at 290.

action and an employer respondent and thus a different section of the Act. Section 8(a)(1) makes it an unfair labor practice for an employer to interfere with, restrain, or coerce employees in the exercise of the rights guaranteed in Section 7. Section 8(b)(1)(A), however, makes it an unfair labor practice for a labor organization to restrain or coerce employees in the exercise of Section 7 rights.[520]

Although union unfair labor practices involving provisions other than Section 8(b)(1)(A) generally do not automatically result in derivative violations of Section 8(b)(1)(A), an exception typically occurs when the unfair labor practice is a violation of Section 8(b)(2). Thus, in superseniority,[521] hiring hall,[522] and unfair representation cases,[523] a finding of violation of Section 8(b)(2) will usually be accompanied by a finding of violation of Section 8(b)(1)(A). These cases are treated elsewhere in connection with the specific subject areas in which they occur.[524] Another type of Section 8(b)(1)(A) conduct which is also treated elsewhere concerns the actions of minority unions when involved in employer violations of Section 8(a)(2); for example, a union which is a party to a "sweetheart" contract will be guilty of violating Section 8(b)(1)(A). Such cases are treated in the chapter on employer domination of and assistance to labor organizations.[525]

2. Fines and Discipline of Union Members. A union may fine or discipline a member so long as the fine or discipline is not imposed for the exercise of rights protected under Section 7. If the discipline does infringe upon employee Section 7 rights, the imposition violates Section 8(b)(1)(A). On the other hand, Congress did intend for discipline to remain essentially an internal union matter by virtue of the proviso to Section 8(b)(1)(A), that the Section "shall not impair the right of a labor organization to prescribe its own rules with respect to the acquisition or retention of membership therein . . . ."[526] This proviso has been

---

[520]Teamsters Local 515 (Roadway Express, Inc.), 248 NLRB 83, 103 LRRM 1318 (1980).
[521]See Chapter 7 *infra* at notes 323-27 and 375-86.
[522]See Chapter 29 *infra* at notes 219-304.
[523]See Chapter 28.
[524]See respectively the chapters referred to in notes 521, 522, and 523 *supra*.
[525]See Chapter 8 *infra* at notes 9-12 and 182-92.
[526]The argument has been advanced that "indeed within the National Labor Relations Act itself an inherent contradiction between the Union's rights and the union member's rights exists." Meyerhofer, *The Inherent Conflict between Sections 7 and 8(b)(1)(A) of the National Labor Relations Act,* 1978 WISC. L. REV. 859 (1978).

interpreted broadly by both the Board and the courts in cases where only union membership is at stake. Consequently, expulsion alone is not restraint or coercion under Section 8(b)(1)(A).[527] Similarly, subject to the exceptions noted below, unions may suspend membership[528] and impose fines for breaches of internal union rules without restraining or coercing employees within the meaning of the Act. The Supreme Court held in *NLRB* v. *Allis-Chalmers Manufacturing Co.*[529] that a union may seek enforcement in state court of such fines in cases where the employee enjoys "full membership" in the union. "Full membership" is to be distinguished from the mere tender of periodic dues and initiation fees for the purpose of compliance with a union security clause.[530]

In 1969 the Supreme Court decided *Scofield* v. *NLRB*,[531] substantially clarifying the status of union fines under the Act. The union in question had promulgated a rule designed to discourage piecework operations from exceeding a stipulated production ceiling. The rule resulted in the imposition of fines upon members who demanded full payment when they exceeded the production ceiling. The Board found no violation of Section 8(b)(1)(A), and the Seventh Circuit affirmed. The Supreme Court agreed, listing four requirements for lawful imposition of union fines under the Act:

> §8(b)(1)(A) leaves a union free to enforce [1] a properly adopted rule which [2] reflects a legitimate union interest, [3] impairs no policy which Congress has imbedded in the labor laws, and [4] is reasonably enforced against union members who are free to leave the union and escape the rule.[532]

In *NLRB* v. *Glaziers & Glassworkers Local 1621*,[533] however, the Board held that a union fine upon its members impairs the national labor policy against secondary pressure applied to neutral employers, where the fine is imposed for working in the employ of a neutral subcontractor behind a picket line. The

---

[527]American Newspaper Publishers Ass'n v. NLRB, 193 F2d 782, 29 LRRM 2230 (CA 7, 1951), *enforcing* 86 NLRB 951, 25 LRRM 1002 (1949).

[528]NLRB Gen. Counsel Ad. Rul. F-862, 44 LRRM 1113 (1959).

[529]NLRB v. Allis Chalmers Mfg. Co., 388 US 175, 65 LRRM 2449 (1967).

[530]388 US 175, 197, 65 LRRM 2449 (1967). For a discussion of some of the implications of this distinction, *see* Hanley, *Labor Law Decisions of the Supreme Court, 1966-67 Term,* LABOR RELATIONS YEARBOOK—1967 at 131 (1968). *See also* Chapter 29 *infra* at notes 30-39.

[531]Scofield v. NLRB, 394 US 423, 70 LRRM 3015 (1969).

[532]394 US at 430.

[533]NLRB v. Glaziers & Glassworkers Local 1621, 632 F2d 89, 105 LRRM 2905 (CA 9, 1980). For discussion of secondary boycotts generally, *see* Chapter 25 *infra*.

Ninth Circuit affirmed, noting that the union's disciplinary rule would institutionalize an imaginary picket line at neutral gates which, if crossed, would result in union discipline and thus encourage members to withhold their service from neutral employers.

a. *Impact of Discipline on Employee Relationship.* Application of Section 8(b)(1)(A) to the enforcement of union rules requires a dual approach. The use of external enforcement of a union rule, i.e., attempting to affect a member's employment status, is proscribed by Section 8(b)(1)(A). On the other hand, a union rule is ordinarily legally enforceable against a member by internal means, i.e., by expulsion or fine. Union discipline of members may not adversely affect an employee's employment status and may not otherwise further illegal objectives. A union thus violates Section 8(b)(1)(A) by causing an employer to reduce the seniority[534] or attempting to cause the discharge[535] of an employee. Even under a valid union security clause a union has an affirmative duty to specifically inform an employee of his obligations and to afford him a reasonable opportunity to satisfy them before seeking his discharge.[536]

b. *The Effect of Resignation on Legality of Discipline.* The Supreme Court has made clear that a union may not fine employees who are no longer union members.[537] According to the Court, "when there is a lawful dissolution of a union-member relationship the union has no more control over the former member than it has over the man on the street."[538]

In *Granite State*[539] the Court upheld the Board's determination that a union violated Section 8(b)(1)(A) by fining members who

---

[534]Automobile Workers (Pitt Processing Co.), 208 NLRB 736, 85 LRRM 1185 (1974), *supplemented,* 217 NLRB 320, 89 LRRM 1031 (1975); Red Ball Motor Freight, Inc., 157 NLRB 1237, 61 LRRM 1522 (1966), *enforced,* 379 F2d 137, 65 LRRM 2309 (CA DC, 1967).

[535]Communications Workers Local 1104 v. NLRB (New York Tel. Co.), 520 F2d 411, 89 LRRM 3028 (CA 2, 1975), *enforcing* 211 NLRB 114, 87 LRRM 1253 (1974), *cert. denied,* 423 US 1051, 91 LRRM 2099 (1976). *See also* Communications Workers Local 1127 & 1125 (New York Tel. Co.), 208 NLRB 258, 85 LRRM 1102 (1974).

[536]Teamsters Local 572 (Ralph's Grocery), 247 NLRB 934, 103 LRRM 1268 (1980). *See also* NLRB v. Teamsters Local 291, 633 F2d 1295, 105 LRRM 3458 (CA 9, 1980). *See generally* Chapter 29 *infra* and also Chapter 7 *infra* at notes 387-417.

[537]NLRB v. Textile Workers Local 1029, Granite State Joint Bd., 409 US 213, 81 LRRM 2853 (1972); Booster Lodge 405, Machinists v. NLRB, 412 US 84, 83 LRRM 2189 (1973).

[538]Textile Workers, *supra* note 537 at 217.

[539]*Supra* note 537. *See also* Graphic Arts Union, 250 NLRB 850, 105 LRRM 1073 (1980) (where the Board held a union violated §8(b)(1)(A) by threatening to fine former

had engaged in strikebreaking activities *after* they had resigned from the union. Giving "little weight" to the fact that the resigning members had voted in favor of the strike, the Court concluded that "the vitality of Section 7 requires that the member be free to refrain in November from the actions he endorsed in May and that his Section 7 rights are not lost by a union's plea for solidarity or by its pressures for conformity and submission to its regime."

Consistent with this rationale, and notwithstanding a union constitutional provision prohibiting member involvement in strikebreaking activity, the Court also found a violation where a union sought enforcement of fines imposed upon strikebreaking members who had resigned from the union.[540] But certain discipline, other than fines, may be allowable even though the "strikebreaker" has resigned from the union. The First Circuit denied enforcement of a Board order finding illegal a union's imposition of a five-year suspension from membership of members who had resigned from the union during a strike and subsequently engaged in strikebreaking activity.[541] The Court distinguished *Granite State,* concluding that a union may "bar membership to employees who have engaged in strikebreaking after having resigned from the union," which it contrasted with imposing and seeking judicial enforcement of fines. In a similar case in which former members were expelled from a union for crossing picket lines following their effective resignation from the union, the Board held such discipline to be privileged by the Section 8(b)(1) proviso.[542]

Because the legality of union fines imposed against "strikebreakers" often depends upon whether the member involved has effectively resigned from the union,[543] the validity of internal union restrictions upon a member's right to resign may be critical. To maintain union solidarity, unions have employed provisions in union constitutions and bylaws and have also used independent contracts with union members purporting to limit a member's right of resignation. But the Supreme Court declared

members for conduct occurring after the former members had effectively resigned from the unions).

[540]Booster Lodge 405, Machinists v. NLRB, *supra* note 537.

[541]NLRB v. Machinists Dist. Lodges 99 & 2139 (General Elec. Co.), 489 F2d 769, 85 LRRM 2145 (CA 1, 1974), *denying enforcement to* 194 NLRB 938, 79 LRRM 1208 (1972).

[542]Pattern Makers (Lietzau Pattern Co.), 199 NLRB 96, 81 LRRM 1177 (1972).

[543]*See* note 537 *supra. See also* NLRB v. Oil Workers Local 6-578, 619 F2d 708, 103 LRRM 2895 (1980).

in the *Scofield* case[544] that a union is free to enforce a disciplinary rule under Section 8(b)(1) only if the rule reflects a legitimate union interest, impairs no federal labor policy, and is reasonably enforced against members who are free to resign from the union to escape the rule. *Scofield* thus seemed to shift the balancing of the union's need for solidarity and the individual's right of free association in favor of the individual, so that any restraint on union resignation would need to contain some form of escape option. This shift is apparent in the cases which follow.

The Board considered whether a union may impose fines for crossing a union's picket line against nonunion employees and employees who had resigned their union membership, notwithstanding that both groups had executed written agreements to honor any strike and picket line established by the union.[545] The Board found a violation based on the fact that there was no provision in the agreements which would have allowed employees to escape the agreement or refrain from engaging in strike activity.[546] According to the Board, the absence of such a provision made the employees involuntary members; it characterized the agreement as nothing more than a "sham and subterfuge" to allow the union to retain control over employees who decided to return to work.

Although the Supreme Court specifically left open the question of whether a union's constitution could legally restrict an employee's right to resign,[547] the Board has held that any restriction on resignation must provide a meaningful period for the exercise of the right to refrain from union activity.[548] In the Board's view, union fines violate Section 8(b)(1)(A) when a union's restrictions on member resignations "prohibit . . . all resignations at all times for the purpose of performing non-union work . . . ." Such fines are deemed an attempt by the union to "impede forever the Section 7 rights to refrain from union activity."[549]*

---

[544]*Supra* note 531.
[545]Sheet Metal Workers Local 29 (Metal-Fab, Inc.), 222 NLRB 1156, 91 LRRM 1390 (1976).
[546]*Id.* at 1160.
[547]*See* notes 531 and 537 *supra.*
[548]Electrical Workers (IUE) Local 444 (Sperry Rand Corp.), 235 NLRB 98, 103, 98 LRRM 1526 (1978). *See also* Machinists Local 1327 (Dalmo Victor), 231 NLRB 719, 96 LRRM 1160 (1977), *enforcement denied and remanded,* 609 F2d 1219, 102 LRRM 2583 (CA 9, 1979). [*See* **Editor's Note** *infra.*]
[549]Carpenters Local 1233 (Polk Constr. Co.), 231 NLRB 756, 96 LRRM 1193 (1977).
*[**Editor's Note:** In September 1982 the Board issued its decision on remand of *Dalmo Victor,* holding a provision in a union's constitution prohibiting resignation from membership during a strike or within 14 days preceding the commencement of a strike an unreasonable restriction on the right to resign union membership. 263 NLRB No. 141, 111 LRRM 1115 (1982).]

In order for a restriction on resignations to be effective, the method of resignation must be phrased in clear and unambiguous terms[550] and must provide a meaningful way to resign. A constitutional restriction limiting resignation to the last ten (10) days of the calendar year followed by a 60-day waiting period was held to be too restrictive, for in effect it denied to union members a voluntary method of severing union membership.[551] Similarly, the Board held that a provision in a union constitution prohibiting a member from resigning unless he left the trade was too restrictive.[552]

c. Discipline for Refusal to Engage in Unlawful or Unprotected Activity. Discipline for refusal by union members to engage in unlawful or unprotected activity pursued by a union violates Section 8(b)(1)(A). Although, as a general proposition, a union is free to discipline a member by internal means without violation of the Act,[553] such sanctions are subject to a basic exception: "[I]f the [union] rule invades or frustrates any overriding policy of the labor laws the rule may not be enforced, even by fine or expulsion, without violating Section 8(b)(1)(A)."[554] Thus, a union violates Section 8(b)(1)(A) when it levies a fine in furtherance of unlawful secondary boycott activity[555] or of strike action taken in the face of a valid no-strike clause.[556]

A union fine which invades or frustrates an overriding policy of the labor laws may also be held violative of Section 8(b)(1)(A), even though it is not imposed in furtherance of unlawful union activity.[557] Thus the Board held that a union violated the Act by

---

[550]Broadcast Employees Local 531, 245 NLRB 638, 102 LRRM 1250 (1979) (where union constitution, which provided that any member may at any time request resignation and that resignation shall become effective at the end of 60 days in the event no action is taken by the union, was held vague and unenforceable).

[551]Automobile Workers Local 647 (General Elec. Co.), 197 NLRB 608, 80 LRRM 1411 (1972); Automobile Workers Local 1384 (Ex-Cell-O Corp.), 219 NLRB 729, 90 LRRM 1152 (1975).

[552]Sheet Metal Workers Local 170 (Able Sheet Metal Prods., Inc.), 225 NLRB 1178, 93 LRRM 1071 (1976).

[553]Although the NLRA may not be applicable to such discipline, the Labor Management Reporting and Disclosure Act of 1959 (Landrum-Griffin Act), 29 USC §§401-531 (1970), particularly Title I thereof, does provide extensive regulation of union disciplinary procedures.

[554]Scofield v. NLRB, *supra* note 531 at 429; Theatrical Stage Employees (RKO Gen., Inc.), 223 NLRB 959, 92 LRRM 1031, 1032 (1976).

[555]Carpenter's Dist. Council Local 362 (Pace Constr. Co.), 222 NLRB 613, 91 LRRM 1205 (1976); Longshoremen & Warehousemen Local 30 (U.S. Borax & Chem. Corp.), 223 NLRB 1257, 92 LRRM 1282 (1976).

[556]Building & Constr. Trades Council (Roy C. Anderson, Jr., Inc.), 222 NLRB 649, 91 LRRM 1215 (1976), *enforced,* 542 F2d 573, 93 LRRM 2943 (CA 5, 1976).

[557]Theatrical Stage Employees, *supra* note 554 (where union continued to discipline members after a federal court issued an injunction enjoining sister union's picketing).

fining members for refusing to honor a lawful picket line established by a sister union, where the union's collective bargaining agreement contained a valid no-strike clause.[558] A union also violated Section 8(b)(1)(A) when it brought charges against members who refused to participate in conduct which the Board subsequently found to be unlawful.[559]

The legality of union discipline may turn on the Board's interpretation of contractual language. For example, it held that a union did not violate Section 8(b)(1)(A) by fining two of its members for refusing to participate in a sympathy strike,[560] because in the Board's view the union had not waived the employee's right to engage in a sympathy strike by virtue of the no-strike provision in the collective agreement. Accordingly, the fines did not unlawfully tend to compel a breach of that agreement.

d. Discipline for Intra-Union Activity. A similar principle has been applied to discipline for wholly internal activity. Although Section 8(b)(1)(A) "leaves a union free to enforce a properly adopted rule which reflects a legitimate union interest and impairs no policy Congress has imbedded in the labor laws," it does not permit enforcement by fine or expulsion of a rule that invades or frustrates an overriding policy of the labor laws.[561] A union may not, under the guise of enforcing internal discipline, deprive its members of the right to participate fully and freely in the internal affairs of their own union.[562] Thus, a union fine levied on a member because of his intra-union activities in opposition to incumbent union officials was held to be a violation of Section 8(b)(1)(A).[563] Fines imposed upon members who had testified on behalf of their employer, where the union was unlawfully attempting to prevent the employer from hiring a black appren-

---

[558]Local 12419, Mine Workers Dist. 50 (National Grinding Wheel Co., Inc.), 176 NLRB 628, 71 LRRM 1311 (1969). *See also* Verville v. Machinists, 520 F2d 615, 89 LRRM 3206 (CA 6, 1975) (sympathy strike in violation of no-strike clause in collective bargaining agreement); Communications Workers Local 1104 v. NLRB, *supra* note 535 (illegal secondary boycott). *But see* Operating Eng'rs Local 18 (Davis-McKee, Inc.), 238 NLRB 652, 99 LRRM 1307 (1978), where the Board stated that *National Grinding Wheel* had been overruled *sub silentio* by subsequent decisions. *See infra* at note 560.

[559]NLRB v. Communications Workers Local 1170 (Rochester Tel. Corp.), 474 F2d 778, 82 LRRM 2101 (CA 2, 1972), *enforcing* 194 NLRB 872, 79 LRRM 1113 (1972).

[560]Operating Eng'rs Local 18 (Davis-McKee, Inc.), *supra* note 558.

[561]*Supra* note 531.

[562]Carpenters Local 22 (Graziano Constr. Co.), 195 NLRB 1, 79 LRRM 1194 (1972).

[563]*Id. See also* Helton v. NLRB, 656 F2d 883, 107 LRRM 2819 (CA DC, 1981), *granting review to* 248 NLRB 83, 103 LRRM 1318 (1980).

[564]Painters Local 1066 (Siebenoller Paint Co.), 205 NLRB 651, 84 LRRM 1013 (1973).

tice, were likewise held unlawful.[564] On the other hand, the Board held that a union did not violate the Act by fining a member for reporting to the employer that another employee was violating a company rule;[565] even though this act may have been coercive, it was not deemed an infringement of the employee's Section 7 rights.

e. Discipline for Activity Deemed Disloyal (Including the Filing of NLRB Petitions and Charges). It is well settled that a union's attempt to fine or expel a member for filing unfair labor practice charges violates Section 8(b)(1)(A), for such action frustrates Congress' basic policy of free and uncoerced access to the Board.[566]

It was not a *per se* violation, however, for a union to expel a member based upon conduct which was proscribed by the union's international constitution but which had been revealed through his testimony in an unfair labor practice proceeding.[567] And although a union may legally *expel* a member for filing a decertification petition, it is a violation of Section 8(b)(1)(A) for a union to *fine* a member for filing such a petition, because unlike expulsion, a fine does not serve any union "defense" purpose.[568] A union also violates the Act by threatening members with intra-union charges in the event they testify against other members in an arbitration proceeding.[569] But a union does not violate the Act by maintaining provisions in its constitution requiring mem-

---

[565]Communications Workers Local 5795 (Western Elec. Co.), 192 NLRB 556, 77 LRRM 1827 (1971) (the Board stated: "It may be conceded that the Union's imposition of a $500.00 fine for an employee's report of another employee's breach of a work rule would be coercive in that it would tend to discourage her and other employees from such action in the future. The Act, however, does not simply render illegal all coercive acts of a union but only such coercive acts which infringe upon the rights of employees enumerated in Section 7").

[566]NLRB v. Marine & Shipbuilding Workers (United States Lines Co.), 391 US 418, 68 LRRM 2257 (1968); Transport Workers, 249 NLRB 1171, 104 LRRM 1304 (1980); Painters Local 1555, 241 NLRB 741, 100 LRRM 1578 (1979); Graphic Arts Local 96B (Williams Printing Co.), 235 NLRB 1153, 98 LRRM 1096 (1978); General Am. Transp. Corp., 227 NLRB 1695, 95 LRRM 1580 (1977); Theatrical Stage Employees, *supra* note 554; Teamsters Local 294 (August Bohl Contracting Co., Inc.), 193 NLRB 920, 78 LRRM 1479 (1971), *enforced,* 470 F2d 57, 81 LRRM 2920 (CA 2, 1972); Clothing Workers Local 424 (Mt. Union Mfg. Co.), 193 NLRB 390, 78 LRRM 1348 (1971).

[567]Carpenters Dist. Council (Hughes Helicopters), 224 NLRB 350, 92 LRRM 1341 (1976).

[568]NLRB v. Molders Local 125, 442 F2d 92, 77 LRRM 2067 (CA 7, 1971). *See also* Sheet Metal Workers, 254 NLRB No. 92, 106 LRRM 1137 (1981) (where the union violated §8(b)(1)(A) by filing a state court action against an employee because he had filed unfair labor practice charges against the union); Teamsters Local 165 (Goodyear Tire & Rubber Co.), 211 NLRB 707, 86 LRRM 1433 (1974) (whereas a fine of a member is a violation of §8(b)(1)(A), expulsion is not, since a union constitution may lawfully include disciplinary provisions which serve to foster its own existence).

[569]Steelworkers Local 5550 (Redfield Co.), 223 NLRB 854, 92 LRRM 1062 (1976).

bers to exhaust internal remedies before resorting to court or administrative proceedings.[570]

f. Reasonableness of Fines Imposed. The Board has refused to examine in Section 8(b)(1)(A) proceedings the reasonableness of otherwise legally imposed union fines. Such refusal was approved by the Supreme Court in *NLRB* v. *Boeing Co.*,[571] where the Court relied on legislative history that indicated Congress did not intend to regulate the internal affairs of unions through Section 8(b)(1)(A); it reasoned that inquiry by the Board into the "multiplicity of factors" bearing on the reasonableness issue would "necessarily lead the Board to a substantial involvement in strictly internal union affairs."[572] Recognizing that the reasonableness issue "must be decided upon the basis of the law of contract, voluntary associations," or other principles of law to be applied in a competent forum, the Court asserted that "State Courts will be wholly free to apply state law to such issue at the suit of either the union or the member fined."[573]

3. Violence and Threats. Violence or threats of violence constitute coercion and restraint within the meaning of Section 8(b)(1)(A). Thus, threatening an employee with bodily harm may be an unfair labor practice.[574] A violation was found where a union had coerced employees into crossing a rival union's picket line.[575] Restraint and coercion have also been found in cases where nonviolent physical force was used to prevent employees from exercising their Section 7 rights—for example, mass picketing by a union that prevented employees from gaining entrance to the employer's premises.[576]

Although the Act literally proscribes only restraint and coercion of "employees" in Section 8(b)(1)(A), violent conduct directed at nonemployees has been held violative of the section when it

---

[570]Plasterers Local 521 (McKee & Co.), 189 NLRB 553, 77 LRRM 1194 (1971) where the Board held that such a clause was not *per se* unlawful. However, the Board has also held that such clauses may not be invoked against a member for filing an NLRB charge without exhausting intra-union remedies over a discriminatory referral practice. J. Willis & Son Masonry (Bricklayers Local 18), 191 NLRB 872, 77 LRRM 1693 (1971).

[571]412 US 67, 83 LRRM 2183 (1973).

[572]*Id.* at 74.

[573]*Id. See also* note 553 *supra.*

[574]*E.g.*, Rockville Nursing Center, 193 NLRB 959, 78 LRRM 1519 (1971); Teamsters Local No. 5 v. NLRB, 406 F2d 439, 70 LRRM 2226 (1969); Chemical Workers Local 738 (Midstates Metal Prods., Inc.), 156 NLRB 872, 61 LRRM 1159 (1966).

[575]Teamsters Local 729 (Penntruck Co., Inc.), 189 NLRB 696, 76 LRRM 1753 (1971).

[576]Longshoremen & Warehousemen Local 6 (Sunset Line & Twine Co.), 79 NLRB 1487, 23 LRRM 1001 (1948).

was substantially certain that employees would hear about it[577] or when the violence was committed in their presence.[578] It is also a violation of the Act to threaten nonstrikers and supervisory personnel with physical violence.[579]

A union restrains and coerces an employee when its threats cause an employer to refrain from hiring a prospective employee. Thus Section 8(b)(1)(A) was violated when a union threatened to "take some kind of action" if a nonunion employee was hired.[580] However, a threat to recommend the international union's withholding of a union trademark if a nonmember was hired was not a basis, according to the Fifth Circuit, for the Board to find a violation of Section 8(b)(1)(A), for the threat was only to bring legal action to protest the integrity of the union's trademark.[581]

B. Sections 8(b)(1)(B) and 8(b)(4)(A): Restraint and Coercion in Selection of Employer Representatives

1. Interference With the Employer's Choice of Representatives.

Section 8(b)(1)(B) prohibits a union from interfering with an employer's choice of representatives for collective bargaining or the adjustment of grievances, and Section 8(b)(4)(A) makes it unlawful for a union to force an employer or self-employed person to join any labor or employer organization. Each party to a collective bargaining relationship has both the right to select its representatives for bargaining and the duty to deal with the chosen representative of the other party.[582]

It is a violation of Section 8(b)(1)(B) for a union to engage in a course of conduct that coerces the employer into discharging

---

[577]Furniture Workers Local 140 (Brooklyn Spring Corp.), 113 NLRB 815, 36 LRRM 1372 (1955), *enforced*, 233 F2d 539, 38 LRRM 2134 (CA 2, 1956).

[578]Retail, Wholesale & Dept. Store Union (I. Posner, Inc.), 133 NLRB 1555, 49 LRRM 1066 (1961); Retail, Wholesale & Dept. Store Union (B. Brown Assoc., Inc.), 157 NLRB 615, 61 LRRM 1382 (1966), *enforced*, 375 F2d 745, 64 LRRM 2750 (CA 2, 1967).

[579]Teamsters Local 298 (Schumacher Elec. Corp.), 236 NLRB 428, 98 LRRM 1486 (1978); Congreso de Uniones Industriales de Puerto Rico (National Packing Co.), 237 NLRB 1406, 99 LRRM 1110 (1978).

[580]Theatrical Stage Employees Local 52 (American Broadcasting Co.), 238 NLRB 19, 93 LRRM 1282 (1976), *enforced*, 593 F2d 197, 100 LRRM 2766 (CA 2, 1979).

[581]Theatrical Stage Employees Local 127 v. NLRB, 633 F2d 1195, 106 LRRM 2222 (CA 5, 1981).

[582]Under §8(b)(1)(B) it is "an unfair labor practice for a labor organization or its agent . . . to restrain or coerce . . . an employer in the selection of his representatives for the purposes of collective bargaining or the adjustments of grievances." *See* Chapters 25 and 26 *infra*. A union which threatened to strike to force multi-employer bargaining violated §§8(b)(1)(A) and 8(b)(4)(A). Mine Workers Local 1854 (Amax Coal Co.), 238 NLRB 1583, *enforced in pertinent part sub nom.* Amax, Inc. v. NLRB, 614 F2d 872, 103 LRRM 2482 (CA 3, 1980). *See also* Frito-Lay, Inc. v. Teamsters Local 137, 623 F2d 1354,

or demoting its grievance-adjustment representative, whether or not the union expressly demands such action.[583]

The Board has recognized, however, that if the presence of a particular representative in negotiations makes collective bargaining impossible or futile, then the party's right to choose its own representative may be limited and the other party may be relieved of its duty to deal with that particular representative.[584] The test is whether there is *"persuasive evidence* that the presence of the particular individual would create ill will and make good-faith bargaining impossible."[585]

The Board found no violation of Section 8(b)(1)(B) where a union picketed with the aim of forcing the employer to hire an additional third mate;[586] nor was there a violation where a union struck to force an employer to conform its contract to a multi-employer contract.[587]

2. Union Discipline of Supervisor-Members. Union discipline of a supervisor-member violates Section 8(b)(1)(B) if it has the effect of restraining or coercing the employer in the selection of his representatives for the purpose of collective bargaining or the adjustment of grievances. Restraint or coercion exists if the discipline may affect the conduct of the supervisor in the

---

104 LRRM 2931 (CA 9, 1980), *cert. denied,* 449 US 1112, 106 LRRM 2200 (1981); Longshoremen & Warehousemen (General Ore., Inc.), 126 NLRB 172, 45 LRRM 1296 (1960). *But cf.* Teamsters Local 901 (Jaime Andino Trucking), 240 NLRB 925, 100 LRRM 1377 (1979), *aff'd,* 619 F2d 147, 104 LRRM 2183 (CA 5, 1980). The Supreme Court also held, in NLRB v. Amax Coal Co., 453 US 322, 107 LRRM 2769 (1981), that employer-selected trustees under §302(c)(5) of the LMRA are not employer representatives under §8(b)(1)(B).

[583]Automobile Workers Local 259 (Atherton Cadillac, Inc.) v. NLRB, 556 F2d 558, 95 LRRM 3011 (CA 2, 1977), *enforcing* 225 NLRB 421, 92 LRRM 1417 (1976); ITO Corp., 246 NLRB 810, 102 LRRM 1682 (1979); Longshoremen & Warehousemen Local 10 (Pacific Maritime Ass'n), 254 NLRB 540, 106 LRRM 1342 (1981); Union Independiente de Empleados de Servicios Legales de Puerto Rico, 249 NLRB 1044, 104 LRRM 1433 (1980); Teamsters Local 610 (Bianco Mfg. Co.) v. NLRB, 100 NLRB 3123 (1979).

[584]Fitzsimons Mfg. Co., 251 NLRB 375, 105 LRRM 1083 (1980).

[585]KDEN Broadcasting Co., subsidiary of North Am. Broadcasting Co., 225 NLRB 25, 35, 93 LRRM 1022 (1976) (emphasis in original). *See also* Teamsters Local 70 (Kockos Bros., Inc.), 183 NLRB 1330, 80 LRRM 2464 (CA 9, 1972).

[586]Masters, Mates & Pilots (Newport Tankers Corp.), 233 NLRB 245, 96 LRRM 1498 (1977) ("because the employer retained absolute control in its selection of bargaining representatives").

[587]New York Typographical Union Local 6 (Clark & Fritts), 236 NLRB 317, 98 LRRM 1279 (1978) (since the employer had signed a memorandum agreement which bound it to future contracts negotiated by the union and the multi-employer association). *See generally* Chapter 11 at notes 348-416.

performance of his grievance adjusting or collective bargaining duties.

In 1968, in *San Francisco-Oakland Mailers Union Local 18*,[588] the Board departed from its past practice of finding a violation of 8(b)(1)(B) only if the conduct clearly fits the statutory language. In that case, three union-member foremen were expelled from the union for assigning bargaining-unit work allegedly in violation of the collective agreement. Despite the absence of union pressure or coercion aimed at securing the replacement of the foremen, the Board held that by seeking to influence the manner in which the foremen interpreted the contract, the union had violated Section 8(b)(1)(B).

The Board thus extended Section 8(b)(1)(B) from its original concept that it only protected employers in the selection of their collective bargaining representatives[589] to include protection of the manner in which an employer's collective bargaining representative performs his duties. The Board declared that "[i]n enacting Section 8(b)(1)(B) Congress sought to prevent union interference with an employer's control over its own representatives."[590]

The Board has found violations of Section 8(b)(1)(B) where a union fined and suspended a supervisor-member for assigning another member to unpleasant tasks and for allegedly breaching a contractual provision relating to overtime work,[591] where a union went on strike to coerce the employer into signing an interim agreement designating a certain multi-employer organization as its bargaining representative,[592] and where a union refused to recognize the employer's selection of a nonmember as an assistant foreman.[593]

---

[588] 172 NLRB 2173, 69 LRRM 1157 (1968).

[589] In the course of the Senate's consideration of §8(b)(1)(B), Senator Ellender stated: "[Q]uite a few unions forced employers to change foremen. They have been taking it upon themselves to say that management should not appoint any representative who is too strict with the membership of the union. This amendment seeks to prescribe a remedy in order to prevent such interferences." 93 CONG. REC. 4266 (1947); LEGISLATIVE HISTORY OF THE LMRA 1077. *See* Teamsters Local 986 (Tak-Teak, Inc.), 145 NLRB 1511, 55 LRRM 1205 (1964); Los Angeles Cloak Joint Bd., Garment Workers (Helen Rose Co., Inc.), 127 NLRB 1543, 46 LRRM 1235 (1960).

[590] *Supra* note 588 at 2173.

[591] Local 333, United Marine Div., Longshoremen (Morania Oil Tankers, Inc.), 233 NLRB 387, 96 LRRM 1609 (1977).

[592] Retail Clerks Local 770 (Fine's Food Co.), 228 NLRB 1166, 95 LRRM 1062 (1977).

[593] New York Typographical Union Local 6 (The N.Y. News, Inc.), 237 NLRB 1241, 99 LRRM 1111 (1978).

In *Florida Power & Light Co.*[594] the Supreme Court held that a union does not violate Section 8(b)(1)(B) by disciplining its supervisor-members for performing rank-and-file bargaining-unit work during a lawful strike. Reviewing applicable legislative history, the Court found the conclusion

> inescapable that a union's discipline of one of its members who is a supervisory employee can constitute a violation of Section 8(b)(1)(B) only when that discipline may adversely affect the supervisor's conduct in performing the duties of, and acting in his capacity as, grievance adjuster or collective bargainer on behalf of the employer.[595]

The Court rejected the Board's argument that the statutory language encompasses "any situation in which the union's actions are likely to deprive the employer of the undivided loyalty of his supervisory employees."[596] In the Court's view, the "divided loyalty" problem was not addressed by Congress through Section 8(b)(1)(B) but, rather, through other provisions in the Act which permit the employer to refuse to hire union members as supervisors, to discharge supervisors because of union activities or membership, and to refuse to engage in collective bargaining with them.

Florida Power had the effect of overruling the "reservoir doctrine,"[597] under which all supervisory employees had been considered potential grievance adjusters, so that union discipline of any of them could be deemed a restriction on the employer in his choice of future representatives for collective bargaining or grievance adjustment.[598]

Subsequently, the Board directed its attention to the question of whether the union's discipline could adversely affect the supervisor's conduct in performing his grievance-adjustment or collective bargaining duties on behalf of the employer. This approach resulted in the Board's limiting the application of *Florida Power* only to supervisors who perform rank-and-file

---

[594]Florida Power & Light Co. v. Electrical Workers (IBEW), 417 US 790, 86 LRRM 2689 (1974). *See* Grissom, *Union Discipline of Supervisor Members under Section 8(b)(1)(B) of the National Labor Relations Act: Drawing The Line After Florida Power,* 27 ALA. L. REV. 575 (1975); Abraham, *Changing Interpretation of NLRB Section 8(b)(1)(B)—Union Discipline of Supervisors in the Aftermath of Florida Power and Light,* 10 JOHN MARHSALL J. OF PRACTICE & PROCEDURE 117 (1976).

[595]417 US at 804.

[596]*Id.* at 806.

[597]Erie Newspaper Guild Local 187, 489 F2d 416, 420, 84 LRRM 2896 (CA 3, 1973).

[598]NLRB v. Rochester Musicians Ass'n Local 66, 514 F2d 988, 89 LRRM 2193 (CA 2, 1975), where the Second Circuit noted that "Florida Power effectively undermined [the doctrine's] conceptual basis." *Id.* at 992.

work during a strike.[599] The Board held that it is an unfair practice under Section 8(b)(1)(B) for a union to discipline a supervisor-member for crossing a picket line to perform his regular functions during a strike if his regular duties include the adjustment of grievances.[600] This holding rested on the Board's conclusion that such discipline imposed on the supervisor would have a "carry-over" effect and would influence the supervisor in the performance of his adjustment functions after the strike, thereby interfering with and coercing the employer in the choice of his grievance representative.[601]

Although the Board restricted the application of *Florida Power* to supervisors performing rank-and-file work during a strike, the Federal Courts were divided over the application of *Florida Power* to supervisors who were fined for exercising both supervisory and rank-and-file work or the performance of only supervisory work during a strike.[602] The Supreme Court addressed this issue in *American Broadcasting Companies, Inc. v. Writers Guild.*[603]

In *Writers Guild,* the union had argued that it is never an unfair labor practice for a union to discipline a supervisor-member for working during a strike, regardless of the type of

---

[599]New York Typographical Union Local 6 (Triangle Publications, Inc.), 216 NLRB 896, 88 LRRM 1384 (1975).

[600]Chicago Typographical Union Local 16 (Hammond Publishers, Inc.), 216 NLRB 903, 88 LRRM 1378 (1975), *enforced,* 539 F2d 242, 98 LRRM 2740 (1976).

[601]Longshoremen & Warehousemen Local 6 (Associated Food Stores, Inc.), 220 NLRB 809, 90 LRRM 1363 (1975); Carpenters, 218 NLRB 1063, 89 LRRM 1477 (1975), *enforced,* 523 F2d 47, 91 LRRM 2961 (CA 7, 1976).

[602]*Compare* American Broadcasting Co., Inc. v. NLRB, 547 F2d 159, 93 LRRM 2958 (CA 2, 1976), *denying enforcement to* 217 NLRB 957, 89 LRRM 1221 (1975) (the Second Circuit denied enforcement of a Board order finding a §8(b)(1)(B) violation where the union fined and disciplined supervisor-members who had crossed a picket line and performed only managerial working during a strike); NLRB v. Rochester Musicians Ass'n Local 66, 514 F2d 988, 89 LRRM 2193 (CA 2, 1975) (the Second Circuit held that a fine of a supervisor engaged only in supervisory work and not in grievance adjustment or collective bargaining was not a violation of §8(b)(1)(B)); *with* Typographical Union Local 16 v. NLRB (Hammond Publishers, Inc.), 539 F2d 242 (CA DC, 1976), *enforcing* 216 NLRB 903, 88 LRRM 1378 (1975) (the D.C. Circuit affirmed the Board's finding that the union violated §8(b)(1)(B) by fining and expelling two supervisor-members who had crossed the union picket line during a strike and performed only a minimal amount of rank-and-file work in addition to their supervisory duties, which included grievance adjustment); Carpenters Wis. Dist. Council v. NLRB (Skippy Enterprises, Inc.), 523 F2d 47, 91 LRRM 2961 (CA 7, 1976), *enforcing* 218 NLRB 1063, 89 LRRM 1477 (1975) (the Seventh Circuit enforced the Board's finding of §8(b)(1)(B) violation where the union fined a supervisor-member and subsequently instituted legal action against him to collect the fine; the supervisor had spent 30% of his time performing rank-and-file work before the strike, and that amount did not increase after the strike began).

[603]437 US 411, 98 LRRM 2705 (1978), *rev'g* 547 F2d 159, 93 LRRM 2958 (CA 2, 1976).

work he may perform behind the picket line. The Supreme Court disagreed; in a five-to-four decision reversing the Second Circuit, the Court reasoned that discipline of a supervisor may have a "carry over" effect on his capacity as a grievance adjuster or collective bargainer. In such situations, therefore, the employer would be restrained and coerced in his selection of those representatives. The Court stated that the Board correctly understood *Florida Power* to mean the following:

> In ruling upon a §8(b)(1)(B) charge growing out of union discipline of a supervisory member who elects to work during a strike, it may—indeed it must—inquire whether the sanction may adversely affect the supervisor's performance of his collective bargaining or grievance adjustment tasks and thereby coerce or restrain the employer contrary to §8(b)(1)(B).[604]

In *Columbia Typographical Union Local 101*[605] the Board was confronted with the issue of whether a union violated Section 8(b)(1)(B) by disciplining supervisor-members who had crossed a picket line to work during a lawful strike in order to perform regular supervisory duties as well as a more than minimal amount of rank-and-file work. The Board stated:

> In these situations, to determine whether or not Section 8(b)(1)(B) has been violated, the only relevant inquiry is what did the supervisor-member do during the employer-union dispute. When a supervisor-member has performed a more than minimal amount of rank-and-file work during the period of the employer-union dispute, subsequent union discipline for performing such work cannot give rise to a violation of Section 8(b)(1)(B).[606]

3. Other Section 8(b)(1)(B) Developments. The Board has also found a Section 8(b)(1)(B) violation where a union had bargained to impasse over the inclusion of an interest-arbitration clause in its contract and threatened to strike to compel its inclusion.[607] The Second Circuit Court of Appeals enforced the Board's order, holding that the Board was warranted in finding that the union violated Section 8(b)(1)(B) since such actions interfered with the employer's choice of representatives.[608] Similarly, an interference with the employer's choice of represen-

---

[604]*Id.* at 430.
[605]242 NLRB 1079, 101 LRRM 1312 (1979).
[606]*Id.* at 1080.
[607]Sheet Metal Workers Local 38 (Elmsford Sheet Metal Works), 231 NLRB 699, 96 LRRM 1190 (1977), *enforced*, 575 F2d 394, 98 LRRM 2147 (CA 2, 1978). *See* Chapter 18 *infra* at notes 63-70.
[608]*Supra* note 607.

tation also existed where a union, by insisting to impasse on certain nonmandatory bargaining subjects during negotiations with an employer association, was thereby attempting to force the negotiations to a deadlock; this would have required submission of the dispute to the National Joint Adjustment Board, a body upon which the employer association had no representation.[609]

A union which denied "withdrawal benefits" from its pension fund to supervisor-members who had resigned their membership in the union pursuant to employer directives was held not to have violated Section 8(b)(1)(B). The Board found no basis on which to conclude that the union rule (which denied benefits to resigning members who remain within the industry) tended to limit the number of supervisors available to employers so as to restrain or coerce them in the selection of their representatives.[610]

The Ninth Circuit has held that a union did not violate Section 8(b)(1)(B) when it disciplined one of its members for working for a nonunion employer in violation of union bylaws, even though the member was also the bargaining representative of the employer, since the union neither represented nor demonstrated an intent to represent that employer's employees. The Court indicated the outcome would have been different had there been evidence that the union's actual purpose in enforcing its bylaws was to interfere with the employer's selection of its bargaining representative.[611]

The Board has held that a union does not violate Section 8(b)(1)(B) when it fines a supervisor-member for donating his labor to an employer, i.e., by performing bargaining-unit work before punching in on the time clock, since the fine was directed solely at the supervisor's "off the clock" performance of the bargaining-unit work.[612]

---

[609]Sheet Metal Workers Local 59 (Employer's Ass'n of Roofers), 227 NLRB 520, 94 LRRM 1602 (1976).
[610]Graphic Arts Union (The Tribune Co.), 226 NLRB 379, 93 LRRM 1257 (1976).
[611]NLRB v. Electrical Workers (IBEW) Local 73 (Chewehah Contractors, Inc.), 106 LRRM 2020 (1980), *denying enforcement to* 231 NLRB 809, 97 LRRM 1026 (1977).
[612]Teamsters Local 296, 250 NLRB No. 126, 104 LRRM 1459 (1980).

CHAPTER 7

DISCRIMINATION IN EMPLOYMENT

I. INTRODUCTION: STATUTORY PROVISIONS

The most frequently filed unfair labor practice charges are those which allege discrimination in employment.[1] This chapter addresses the general problem of employment discrimination relating to union activity.[2] Discrimination as it specifically relates to strikes,[3] lockouts,[4] union security agreements,[5] and a union's duty of fair representation[6] will be treated in detail in subsequent chapters.

A. Discrimination as an Unfair Labor Practice

Discrimination for certain specified reasons is expressly prohibited by three provisions of the National Labor Relations Act.

---

[1]1978 NLRB ANN. REP. 9 (1979).

[2]For scholarly comment on the subject of discrimination under the Act, see the following: Samoff, *NLRB Priority and Injunctions for Discriminatory Discharges*, 31 LAB. L. J. 54 (1980); Moss, *Plant Removal—Labor Law Issues*, 54 CAL. S. B. J. 42 (1979); Kaplan & Yates, *Plant Relocation: Management Solution to Labor Problems*, 34 MO. B. J. 416 (1978); Jennings & Wolters, *Discharge Cases Reconsidered*, 31 ARB. J. 164 (1976); Beaird & Player, *Whither The Nixon Board?*, 7 GA. L. REV. 607 (1973); Swift, *Plant Relocation: Catching Up With the Runaway Shop*, 14 B. C. IND. & COMM. L. REV. 1135 (1973); Bernhardt, *Lockouts: An Analysis of Board and Court Decisions Since Brown and American Ship*, 57 CORNELL L. Q. 211 (1972); Shieber, *Section 8(a)(3) of the National Labor Relations Act; A Rationale: Part I Discrimination*, 29 LA. L. REV. 46 (1968); Shieber & Moore, *Section 8(a)(3) of the National Labor Relations Act: A Rationale—Part II, Encouragement or Discouragement of Membership in any Labor Organization and the Significance of Employer Motive*, 33 LA. L. REV. 1 (1972); Christensen & Svanoe, *Motive and Intent in the Commission of Unfair Labor Practices: The Supreme Court and the Fictive Formality*, 77 YALE L. J. 1269 (1968); Cox, *The Right to Engage in Concerted Activities*, 26 IND. L. J. 319 (1951); Getman, *Section 8(a)(3) of the NLRA and the Effort to Insulate Free Employee Choice*, 32 U. CHI. L. REV. 735 (1965); Getman, *The Protection of Economic Pressure by Section 7 of the National Labor Relations Act*, 115 U. PA. L. REV. 1195 (1967); Janofsky, *New Concepts in Interference and Discrimination Under the NLRA: The Legacy of American Ship Building and Great Dane Trailers*, 70 COLUM. L. REV. 81 (1970); Oberer, *The Scienter Factor in Section 8(a)(1) and (3) of the Labor Act: Of Balancing, Hostile Motive, Dogs and Tails*, 52 CORNELL L. Q. 491 (1967); Schatzki, *Some Observations and Suggestions Concerning a Misnomer—"Protected" Concerted Activities*, 47 TEX. L. REV. 378 (1969).

[3]*See* Chapter 21 *infra.*
[4]*See* Chapter 22 *infra.*
[5]*See* Chapter 29 *infra.*
[6]*See* Chapter 28 *infra.*

Under *Section 8(a)(3)* of the Act[7] it is unlawful for an employer "by discrimination in regard to hire or tenure of employment to encourage or discourage membership in any labor organization." The foregoing provision does not, however, proscribe all types of employment discrimination. As the Supreme Court has stated, Section 8(a)(3) does not "outlaw discrimination in employment as such; only such discrimination as encourages or discourages membership in a labor organization is proscribed."[8] The statutory ban against such discrimination is qualified by two provisos. The first proviso *permits* an employer and a labor organization to enter into a union-shop agreement if the labor organization involved represents the employer's employees and the employees have not voted to prohibit a union-shop agreement in an election held within one year prior to the date of such agreement.[9] The second proviso, however, *prohibits* an employer from discriminating against an employee for nonmembership in a labor organization if the employer "has reasonable grounds for believing . . . that membership was not available to the employee on the same terms and conditions generally applicable to other members," or if he "has reasonable grounds for believing that membership was denied or terminated for reasons other than failure . . . to tender the periodic dues and initiation fees uniformly required as a condition of acquiring or retaining membership."[10]

Discrimination by unions is prohibited by *Section 8(b)(2)*.[11] That provision makes it an unfair labor practice for a labor organization or its agents "to cause or attempt to cause an employer to discriminate against an employee in violation of subsection (a)(3) or to discriminate against an employee with respect to whom membership in such organization has been denied or terminated on some grounds other than failure to tender the periodic dues and initiation fees uniformly required as a condition of acquiring or retaining membership."

---

[7]With the passage of the Taft-Hartley amendments in 1947, §8(3) of the Wagner Act, 49 Stat. 452 (1935), became §8(a)(3) of the Labor Management Relations Act of 1947, 29 USC §158(a)(3) (1970).

[8]Radio Officers Union v. NLRB, 347 US 17, 43, 33 LRRM 2417 (1954).

[9]This "first" proviso modifies an original Wagner Act provision which permitted a closed shop. Union-shop agreements are unlawful in "right to work" states by virtue of §14(b) of the Act, which provides that an agreement requiring membership in a labor organization as a condition of employment may be prohibited by state or territorial law. *See generally* Chapter 29 *infra*.

[10]The "second" proviso was enacted in 1947. *See* Chapter 29 *infra*.

[11]§8(b)(2) was enacted in 1947.

The third prohibition against employment discrimination is contained in *Section 8(a)(4)*. Section 8(a)(4), enacted as Section 8(4) with the passage of the Wagner Act in 1935, makes it unlawful for an employer "to discharge or otherwise discriminate against an employee because he has filed charges or given testimony under this Act." Although Section 8(b) of the Act does not specifically address the subject of union discrimination for filing charges or testifying in NLRB proceedings, reprisals by labor organizations for such conduct violate Section 8(b)(1)(A).[12] Thus, a union violates Section 8(b)(1)(A) if it expels, fines, or otherwise disciplines a member or officer,[13] refuses to process a grievance,[14] refuses to refer an individual for employment opportunities,[15] or threatens him with physical harm[16] because he has filed charges or given testimony under the Act.[17]

II. EMPLOYER DISCRIMINATION

A. Persons Within the Protection of Section 8(a)(3)

The protection of Section 8(a)(3) extends to applicants for employment as well as to individuals who are already employed.

---

[12]This section of the Act makes it unlawful for a labor organization "to restrain or coerce employees in the exercise of the rights guaranteed" by §7 of the Act. *See* Chapter 6 *supra*.

[13]NLRB v. Marine & Shipbuilding Workers, 391 US 418, 68 LRRM 2257 (1968); NLRB v. Teamsters Local 294 (August Bohl Contracting Co.), 470 F2d 57, 81 LRRM 2920 (CA 2, 1972); NLRB v. Local 825, Operating Eng'rs, 420 F2d 961, 73 LRRM 2413 (CA 3, 1970); Sheet Metal Workers Local 204 (Majestic Co.), 246 NLRB 318, 102 LRRM 1503 (1979). *Cf.* NLRB v. Boilermakers (General Am. Transp. Corp.), 581 F2d 473, 99 LRRM 2855 (CA 5, 1978) (a union did not violate §8(b)(1)(A) when it removed a steward from office because of his failure to pursue his discharge grievance under the collective bargaining agreement before filing unfair labor practice charges).

[14]NLRB v. Teamsters Local 703 (Dominick's Finer Foods), 81 LRRM 2488 (CA 7, 1972), *enforcing* 188 NLRB 873, 76 LRRM 1607 (1971); Selwyn Shoe Mfg. Corp., 172 NLRB 674, 68 LRRM 1417, *modified on other grounds*, 428 F2d 217, 74 LRRM 2474 (CA 8, 1970); Graphic Arts Union Local 96B (Williams Printing Co.), 235 NLRB 1153, 98 LRRM 1096 (1978); Penn Industries, Inc., 233 NLRB 928, 97 LRRM 1299 (1977); Packers & Driver's (Guy's Foods, Inc.), 188 NLRB 608, 76 LRRM 1380 (1971).

[15]Painters Local 1555 (Alaska Constructors, Inc.), 241 NLRB 741, 100 LRRM 1578 (1979); Plumbers Local 195 (Stone & Webster Eng'r Corp.), 240 NLRB 504, 100 LRRM 1460 (1979); Laborers Local 663 (Robert A. Treuner Constr. Co.), 205 NLRB 455, 84 LRRM 1314 (1973); Iron Workers Local 577 (Tri-State Steel Erectors, Inc.), 199 NLRB 37, 81 LRRM 1275 (1972).

[16]NLRB v. Union Nacional de Trabajadores, 540 F2d 1, 92 LRRM 3425 (CA 1, 1976), *enforcing* 219 NLRB 429, 89 LRRM 1746 (1975); Local 3, Electrical Workers (IBEW) (Welsbach Elec. Corp.), 236 NLRB 503, 99 LRRM 1271 (1978); Teamsters Local 705 (Assoc. Trans., Inc.), 209 NLRB 292, 86 LRRM 1119 (1974).

[17]*See* Chapter 6 *supra* at notes 566-70.

In the landmark case of *Phelps Dodge Corp.* v. *NLRB*,[18] the Supreme Court ruled that an employer violated Section 8(a)(3) by refusing to hire job applicants who were union members. Thereafter, relying on the broad definition of "employee" contained in Section 2(3), the Board frequently stated that the Act protects "members of the working class generally."[19] Thus, the protection of Section 8(a)(3) extends to employees who are not union members,[20] to foreign nationals,[21] and even to professional organizers who obtain employment solely for the purpose of organizing the employer's work force.[22] Also protected by Section 8(a)(3) are employees who are discriminated against because of the union activities of their relatives.[23]

As a general rule, supervisors,[24] certain confidential employees,[25] and managerial employees[26] are not protected by the Act and may be discharged with impunity for their union activity or

---

[18]313 US 177, 8 LRRM 439 (1941). *Accord,* Consolidated Freightways Corp., 242 NLRB 770, 101 LRRM 1454 (1979); Mack Trucks, Inc., 242 NLRB 651, 101 LRRM 1249 (1979); Alexander Dawson, Inc. v. NLRB, 586 F2d 1300, 99 LRRM 3105 (CA 9, 1978); McCain Foods, Inc., 236 NLRB 447, 98 LRRM 1345 (1978); A. S. Abell Co., 234 NLRB 802, 97 LRRM 1383 (1978); Pate Mfg. Co., 197 NLRB 793, 80 LRRM 1846 (1972); Atlantic Maintenance Co. v. NLRB, 305 F2d 604, 50 LRRM 2494 (CA 3, 1962).

[19]*E.g.*, Giant Food Mkts., Inc., 241 NLRB 727, 100 LRRM 1598, 1599 n.5 (1979); Little Rock Crate & Basket Co., 227 NLRB 1406, 94 LRRM 1385 (1977); Oak Apparel, Inc., 218 NLRB 701, 89 LRRM 1381 (1975); Briggs Mfg. Co., 75 NLRB 569, 21 LRRM 1056 (1947).

[20]NLRB v. Electrical Workers (IBEW) Local 322, 597 F2d 1326, 101 LRRM 2157 (CA 10, 1979); Narragansett Restaurant Corp., 243 NLRB 125, 101 LRRM 1579 (1979); Schorr Stern Food Corp., 227 NLRB 1650, 94 LRRM 1331 (1977).

[21]Sure-Tan, Inc., 234 NLRB 1187, 97 LRRM 1439 (1978); Amay's Bakery & Noodle Co., 227 NLRB 214, 94 LRRM 1165 (1976); Handling Equip. Corp., 209 NLRB 64, 85 LRRM 1603 (1974).

[22]Anthony Forest Prod. Co., 231 NLRB 976, 97 LRRM 1014 (1977); Oak Apparel, Inc., *supra* note 19.

[23]Mission Valley Mills, 225 NLRB 442, 93 LRRM 1227 (1976).

[24]NLRB v. Adam & Eve Cosmetics, Inc., 567 F2d 723, 97 LRRM 2173 (CA 7, 1977); Times Herald Printing Co., 252 NLRB 278, 105 LRRM 1428 (1980); Stop & Go Foods, Inc., 246 NLRB 1076, 103 LRRM 1046 (1979); Cory Coffee Serv., 242 NLRB 601, 101 LRRM 1246 (1979); Montgomery Ward & Co., 234 NLRB 13, 97 LRRM 1093 (1978); H. B. Zachry Co., 233 NLRB 1143, 97 LRRM 1298 (1977); Fair Lady, Inc., 211 NLRB 189, 87 LRRM 1027 (1974); Shop-Rite Foods, Inc., 205 NLRB 1076, 84 LRRM 1122 (1973); Hook Drugs, 191 NLRB 189, 77 LRRM 1445 (1971); Sears, Roebuck & Co., 127 NLRB 582, 46 LRRM 1055 (1960). *See* Chapter 30 *infra* at notes 154-86.

[25]NLRB v. Hendricks County Rural Elec. Membership Corp., 454 US 170, 108 LRRM 3105 (1981), *rev'g* 627 F2d 766, 104 LRRM 3158 (CA 7, 1980), *denying enforcement to* 247 NLRB 498, 103 LRRM 1129 (1980), *supplementing* 236 NLRB 1616, 98 LRRM 1526 (1978); NLRB v. Wheeling Elec. Co., 444 F2d 783, 77 LRRM 2561 (CA 4, 1971), *denying enforcement to* 182 NLRB 218, 76 LRRM 1553 (1970). *See* Chapter 30 *infra* at notes 204-13 for discussion of *Hendricks* and NLRB coverage regarding confidential employees.

[26]NLRB v. North Ark. Elec. Coop., Inc., 446 F2d 602, 77 LRRM 3114 (CA 8, 1971), *denying enforcement to* 185 NLRB 550, 75 LRRM 1068 (1970), *supplementing* 168 NLRB 921, 67 LRRM 1193 (1967). *See* NLRB v. Bell Aerospace, 416 US 267, 85 LRRM 2945 (1974), and Chapter 30 *infra* at notes 187-203.

for their failure to lawfully assist an employer in his efforts to combat a union-organizing drive.[27] However, an employer violates Section 8(a)(1) if it discharges a supervisor or exempt employee for refusing to commit unfair labor practices[28] or for testifying against the employer in NLRB proceedings.[29] An employer also violates the section if the discharge is an integral part of an overall plan to discourage employees from engaging in protected activity.[30]

Applicants for supervisory positions are generally not entitled to the protection of the Act.[31] However, the Board has held that an employer cannot refuse to promote currently employed persons to supervisory positions because of their union activities or sympathy.[32]

B. Purpose of the Discrimination

As stated previously, within the context of this chapter not all discrimination is unlawful under Section 8(a)(3). In *Radio Officers Union* v. *NLRB*[33] the Supreme Court explained:

The language of §8(a)(3) is not ambiguous. The unfair labor practice

---

[27]Western Sample Book & Printing Co., 209 NLRB 384, 86 LRRM 1171 (1974). *Cf.* P. R. Mallory Co., 175 NLRB 308, 70 LRRM 1574 (1969); Florida Builders, Inc., 111 NLRB 786, 35 LRRM 1575 (1955).

[28]Belcher Towing Co. v. NLRB, 614 F2d 88, 103 LRRM 2939 (CA 5, 1980), *enforcing in part* 238 NLRB 446, 99 LRRM 1566 (1978); Gerry's Cash Mkts., Inc. v. NLRB, 602 F2d 1021, 101 LRRM 3116 (CA 1, 1979), *enforcing* 238 NLRB 1141, 99 LRRM 1617 (1978); Russell Stover Candies, Inc. v. NLRB, 551 F2d 204, 94 LRRM 3036 (CA 8, 1977), *enforcing* 223 NLRB 592, 92 LRRM 1240 (1976); NLRB v. Thermo-Rite Mfg. Co., 406 F2d 1033, 70 LRRM 2344 (CA 6, 1969); *but cf.* Florida Steel Corp. v. NLRB, 551 F2d 306, 94 LRRM 2589 (CA 4, 1977) (dismissal of a supervisor for failing to carry out anti-union directions did not violate §8(a)(1) where it was not shown that employees had knowledge of the reason for the discharge); Budget Marketing, Inc., 241 NLRB 1108, 101 LRRM 1068 (1979); Buddie's Super Mkts., 223 NLRB 950, 92 LRRM 1008 (1976), *enforcement denied*, 550 F2d 39, 95 LRRM 2108 (CA 5, 1977); General Nutrition Center, 221 NLRB 850, 90 LRRM 1736 (1975).

[29]NLRB v. Carter Lumber, Inc., 507 F2d 1262, 88 LRRM 2975 (CA 6, 1974); NLRB v. Schill Steel Prods., Inc., 480 F2d 586, 83 LRRM 2386 (CA 5, 1973); King Radio Corp. v. NLRB, 398 F2d 14, 68 LRRM 2821 (CA 10, 1968); Oil City Brass Works v. NLRB, 357 F2d 466, 61 LRRM 2318 (CA 5, 1966); Hi-Craft Clothing Co., 251 NLRB 1310, 105 LRRM 1356 (1980).

[30]Empire Gas, 254 NLRB 626, 106 LRRM 1163 (1981); Fairview Nursing Home, 202 NLRB 318, 82 LRRM 1566 (1973), *enforced*, 486 F2d 1400, 84 LRRM 3010 (CA 5, 1973); Nevis Indus., Inc., 246 NLRB 1053, 103 LRRM 1035 (1979); Downslope Indus., Inc., 246 NLRB 948, 103 LRRM 1041 (1979); Production Stamping, Inc., 239 NLRB 1183, 100 LRRM 1141 (1979); East Belden Corp., 239 NLRB 776, 100 LRRM 1077 (1978).

[31]R & R Theatre Co., 238 NLRB 352, 99 LRRM 1531 (1978); Pacific Am. Shipowners Ass'n, 98 NLRB 582, 29 LRRM 1376 (1952).

[32]St. Anne's Hosp., 245 NLRB 1009, 102 LRRM 1527 (1979); Little Lake Indus., Inc., 233 NLRB 1049, 97 LRRM 1101 (1977).

[33]*Supra* note 8.

is for an employer to encourage or discourage membership by means of discrimination. Thus this section does not outlaw all encouragement or discouragement of membership in labor organizations: only such as is accomplished by discrimination is prohibited. Nor does this action outlaw discrimination in employment as such; only such discrimination as encourages or discourages membership in a labor organization is proscribed.[34]

Thus, in most cases, the employer's reason for discriminating will determine whether he has committed an unfair labor practice. If the discrimination is motivated by an anti-union purpose[35] and has the foreseeable effect of either encouraging or discouraging union membership, it violates Section 8(a)(3).[36]

A showing of actual encouragement or discouragement, however, is unnecessary. The Board is authorized to draw reasonable inferences from the evidence presented. If the employer's action could naturally and foreseeably have an adverse effect on employee rights, either presently or in the future, the Board may infer encouragement or discouragement of union membership.[37]

Proving a specific anti-union purpose is also unnecessary where the employer's conduct is found to be "inherently destructive" of Section 7 rights.[38] In such cases, the Board and the courts will not require an affirmative showing of the employer's unlawful motive. Rather, they will presume the unlawful motive to exist, even when the employer introduces evidence of a legitimate business purpose. In *Radio Officers*, the Supreme Court explained:

> [S]pecific evidence of intent to encourage or discourage is not an indispensable element of proof of violation of Section 8(a)(3) . . . . [A]n employer's protestation that he did not intend to encourage or discourage must be unavailing where a natural consequence of his action was such encouragement or discouragement. Concluding that encouragement or discouragement will result, it is presumed that

---

[34]*Id.* at 42-43.
[35]The Board and the courts have differed whether a violation of §8(a)(3) can be established where it is proved that union animus is only one of several motivating factors leading to the discrimination. *See* discussion at notes 46-65 *infra*.
[36]Retail Clerks Local 770 (Carl A. Palmer), 208 NLRB 356, 85 LRRM 1082 (1974).
[37]Radio Officers Union v. NLRB, *supra* note 8 at 48-52. *See* Republic Aviation Corp. v. NLRB, 324 US 793, 16 LRRM 620 (1945).
[38]*See* discussion of conduct which carries its own indicia of intent to discriminate at notes 84-156 *infra*.

he intended such consequence. In such circumstances intent to encourage is sufficiently established . . . .[39]

On the other hand, where the conduct in issue has only a "comparatively slight" adverse effect on employee rights and the employer has come forward with evidence of legitimate and substantial business ends, anti-union motivation must be proved in order to sustain a Section 8(a)(3) violation.[40]

Although the statute literally prohibits only discrimination "to encourage or discourage [union] membership," the courts have long maintained that Congress intended Section 8(a)(3) to protect more than "bare membership" and have long held that discrimination generally designed to encourage or discourage union activities or support is unlawful.[41] The term "membership" thus refers to all types of indicia of union support.

1. Conduct Requiring Proof of Union Animus. The great majority of Section 8(a)(3) cases do not involve conduct claimed to be "inherently destructive of employees rights." Most cases involving claims of unlawful discrimination arise out of employer decisions concerning whom to hire and fire, and what terms and conditions of employment to offer. Such conduct does not violate Section 8(a)(3) so long as it is motivated by legitimate and substantial business reasons and not by a desire to penalize or reward employees for union activity or the lack of it. In cases of this type, the employer's motive is determinative.[42]

If the unlawful purpose is not present or cannot be implied as a matter of law, "discrimination" does not violate the Act,

---

[39]347 US at 44-45; cf. NLRB v. Burnup & Sims, Inc., 379 US 21, 57 LRRM 2385 (1964); Chapter 6 supra at notes 16-31.

[40]NLRB v. Great Dane Trailers, Inc., 388 US 26, 65 LRRM 2465 (1967). See discussion at notes 92-97 infra.

[41]Radio Officers Union v. NLRB, supra note 8. Cf. Lunsford v. City of Bryan, 297 SW2d 115, 39 LRRM 2306 (Tex. S Ct, 1957).

[42]NLRB v. Jones & Laughlin Steel Corp., 301 US 1, 1 LRRM 703 (1937); Laidlaw Corp., 171 NLRB 1366, 68 LRRM 1252 (1968), enforced, 414 F2d 99, 71 LRRM 3054 (CA 7, 1969), cert. denied, 397 US 920, 73 LRRM 2537 (1970); Wellington Mill Div. v. NLRB, 330 F2d 579, 55 LRRM 2914 (CA 4, 1964), cert. denied, 379 US 882, 57 LRRM 2276 (1964), denying enforcement to 141 NLRB 819, 52 LRRM 1445 (1963); Edward G. Budd Mfg. Co. v. NLRB, 138 F2d 86, 13 LRRM 512 (CA 3, 1943). But cf. NLRB v. Burnup & Sims, Inc., supra note 39. In discharge and discipline cases, the Board is expressly prohibited by §10(c) of the Act from issuing orders of reinstatement or back pay where an employee has been "suspended or discharged for cause"; implicit in the notion of "cause" is that it motivated the disciplinary action. See notes 159-69 infra and accompanying text.

even if the employer's conduct is deemed unjustified or unfair.[43] Where a prohibited motive is found, it is not controlling that the employer may have been mistaken in determining whether the individual was engaged in protected activity or was a union supporter,[44] or that the employee was discriminated against solely to mask the discriminatory discharge of others.[45]

Since only discriminatory conduct which is motivated by union animus[46] violates Section 8(a)(3), establishing the employer's unlawful motivation is a precondition to finding a violation of Section 8(a)(3). An employer has the right to take disciplinary action for good cause related to the maintenance of order and efficiency in his plant.[47] Section 10(c) recognizes this right by prohibiting Board orders of reinstatement and back-pay orders where the employee was "suspended or discharged for cause." Implicit in the notion of "cause" is that the "cause" motivated (or at least was the primary reason for) the disciplinary action. Where the employer's conduct is challenged, the issue becomes: What is the employer's real motive for the action taken?[48] The burden of proof on this issue is on the General Counsel.[49]

The various circuits have been divided on the issue of the "quantum of animus" necessary to find a violation of Section 8(a)(3).[50] The First Circuit has required that the discriminatory

---

[43]Indeed, an employer may discharge for poor cause or no cause, and there is no violation of §8(a)(3) unless the employer's purpose is to encourage or discourage union membership. Associated Press v. NLRB, 301 US 103, 1 LRRM 732 (1937); NLRB v. McGahey, 233 F2d 406, 38 LRRM 2142 (CA 5, 1956); Indiana Metal Prods. v. NLRB, 202 F2d 613, 31 LRRM 2490 (CA 7, 1953); NLRB v. Montgomery Ward, 157 F2d 486, 19 LRRM 2008 (CA 8, 1946); NLRB v. Condenser Corp., 128 F2d 67, 10 LRRM 483 (CA 3, 1942); Borkin Packing Co., 208 NLRB 280, 85 LRRM 1062 (1974). *See also* NLRB v. Buddie's Super Mkts., Inc., *supra* note 28.

[44]Link Belt Co., 311 US 584, 7 LRRM 297 (1941); Pleasant View Rest Home, 194 NLRB 426, 78 LRRM 1683 (1971).

[45]Howard Johnson Co., 209 NLRB 1122, 86 LRRM 1148 (1974).

[46]*See* notes 35-36 *supra. But see infra* at notes 84-156.

[47]*See* notes 42-43 *supra.*

[48]*E.g.*, Laidlaw Corp., *supra* note 42; Wellington Mill Div. v. NLRB, *supra* note 42; Edward G. Budd Mfg. Co. v. NLRB, *supra* note 42.

[49]*See generally* discussion of unfair labor practice procedures in Chapter 32 *infra. See also* discussion of burden of proof at notes 61-66 *infra.*

[50]*See, e.g.*, NLRB v. Montgomery Ward & Co., 554 F2d 996, 1002, 95 LRRM 2433 (CA 10, 1977) ("partially motivated"); Neptune Water Meter Co. v. NLRB, 551 F2d 568, 570, 94 LRRM 2513 (CA 4, 1977) (no discharge "except for"); Oil Workers v. NLRB, 547 F2d 575, 590, 92 LRRM 3059 (CA DC, 1976), *cert. denied*, 431 US 966, 95 LRRM 2642 (1977) ("motivated in any part"); NLRB v. Townhouse TV & Appliance Corp., 531 F2d 826, 828, 91 LRRM 2636 (CA 7, 1976) ("motivated at least in part"); NLRB v. Gentithes, 463 F2d 557, 560, 80 LRRM 3057 (CA 3, 1972) ("substantial or motivating cause"); NLRB v. Fibers Int'l Corp., 439 F2d 1311, 76 LRRM 2798 (CA 1,

motive be the primary, or controlling, factor promoting the employer's conduct.[51] In one case, the First Circuit cautioned that the Board must both articulate and apply that court's standard and "find affirmatively that the discharge would not have occurred but for the improper reason."[52] Similarly, the Ninth Circuit has required that the improper motive be dominant and the "moving cause" of the employer's conduct:[53] "The test is whether the business reason or the protected union activity is the moving cause behind the discharge";[54] stated conversely, "[w]here a party has two motives, one permissible and the other impermissible, the better rule is . . . that the improper motive must be shown to have been the dominant one."[55]

The Fifth Circuit, however, has upheld a Board finding of a Section 8(a)(3) violation where the force of the anti-union motive was "reasonably equal" to the lawful motive asserted in defense by an employer.[56] Other circuits have simply required a showing that the employer's decision was "partly" motivated by union animus[57] or merely "a factor" in the employer's decision.[58] But

---

1971) ("dominant motive"); NLRB v. Gladding Keystone Corp., 435 F2d 129, 131, 76 LRRM 2099 (CA 2, 1970) ("partially motivated"); Frosty Morn Meats, Inc. v. NLRB, 296 F2d 617, 621, 49 LRRM 2159 (CA 5, 1961) ("moving cause"). See note 167 infra.
[51]NLRB v. South Shore Hosp., 571 F2d 677, 97 LRRM 3004 (CA 1, 1978); Hubbard Regional Hosp. v. NLRB, 579 F2d 1251, 98 LRRM 2891 (CA 1, 1978); NLRB v. Rich's of Plymouth, Inc., 578 F2d 880, 98 LRRM 2684 (CA 5, 1978), denying enforcement in relevant part to 232 NLRB 621, 96 LRRM 1345 (1977); Coletti's Furniture, Inc. v. NLRB, 550 F2d 1292, 94 LRRM 3071 (CA 1, 1977), enforcing per curiam 224 NLRB 1547, 92 LRRM 1585 (1976); NLRB v. Circle Bindery, Inc., 536 F2d 447, 92 LRRM 2689 (CA 1, 1976).
[52]Coletti's Furniture, Inc. v. NLRB, supra note 51.
[53]Stephenson v. NLRB, 614 F2d 1210, 103 LRRM 2238 (CA 9, 1980); Polynesian Cultural Center, Inc. v. NLRB, 582 F2d 467, 99 LRRM 3416 (CA 9, 1978).
[54]NLRB v. West Coast Casket Co., 469 F2d 871, 874, 81 LRRM 2857 (CA 9, 1972), quoting NLRB v. Ayer Lar Sanitarium, 436 F2d 45, 76 LRRM 2224 (CA 9, 1970); accord, NLRB v. Miller Redwood Co., 407 F2d 1366, 70 LRRM 2868 (CA 9, 1969); Signal Oil & Gas Co. v. NLRB, 390 F2d 338, 67 LRRM 2708 (CA 9, 1968); NLRB v. Security Plating Co., 356 F2d 725, 61 LRRM 2437 (CA 9, 1966); Mead v. Retail Clerks Local 839, 523 F2d 1371, 90 LRRM 2769 (CA 9, 1975). But see NLRB v. Central Press, 527 F2d 1156, 91 LRRM 2236 (CA 9, 1975).
[55]Famet, Inc. v. NLRB, 490 F2d 293, 296, 85 LRRM 2223 (CA 9, 1973), quoting NLRB v. Lowell Sun Publishing Co., 320 F2d 835, 842, 53 LRRM 2480 (CA 1, 1963) (Aldridge, J., concurring). See generally Comment, Employer Discrimination Under Section 8(a)(3), 5 TOL. L. REV. 722, 765 (1974).
[56]NLRB v. Aero Corp., 581 F2d 511, 99 LRRM 2800 (CA 5, 1978), enforcing 233 NLRB 401, 96 LRRM 1539 (1977).
[57]See, e.g., Edgewood Nursing Center, Inc. v. NLRB, 581 F2d 363, 99 LRRM 2036 (CA 3, 1978); NLRB v. Gogin, 575 F2d 596, 98 LRRM 2250 (CA 7, 1978).
[58]E.g., Neptune Water Meter Co. v. NLRB, supra note 50. In M.S.P. Indus., Inc. v. NLRB, 568 F2d 166, 97 LRRM 2403 (CA 10, 1977), enforcing in part 222 NLRB 220, 91 LRRM 1379 (1976), the Tenth Circuit upheld the Board's finding of a §8(a)(3) violation even though the employer submitted sufficient proof to warrant a finding that its action may have been justified. The court found that a showing of economic justifi-

CH. 7 DISCRIMINATION IN EMPLOYMENT 191

the Fourth Circuit refused to enforce the Board's finding of a Section 8(a)(3) violation where, in the court's view, the Board's finding of anti-union motivation was based on "mere suspicion and conjecture."[59] An employer's threats to discharge, or its actual discharge of, employees because of their union activities are classic examples of discrimination in which both the Board and the courts will find sufficient union animus to establish a violation of Section 8(a)(3).[60]

The Board, in its 1980 decision in *Wright Line, Inc.*,[61] attempted to eliminate this uncertainty among the courts of appeals and between the courts of appeals and the Board regarding an appropriate analysis for examining causality in cases alleging unlawful discrimination. The Board there adopted, in essence, an analysis akin to that used by the Supreme Court in *Mt. Healthy City School District Board of Education* v. *Doyle*,[62] a case involving a discharge motivated in part by constitutionally protected activity. Under the Board's analysis, the General Counsel must initially establish a prima facie case that protected conduct was a motivating factor in an employer's decision. The burden then shifts to the employer to demonstrate, as an affirmative defense, that the decision would have been the same even in the absence of protected conduct.[63] It is this shifting of the burden to the employer which distinguishes the Board's *Mt. Healthy-Wright Line* test from the "dominant motive" analysis previously applied by some circuit courts.[64] Although the burden shifts, the shift does not undermine the established principle that the General

cation was not conclusive and upheld the Board's finding that the layoffs were motivated at least in part by an unlawful purpose.

[59]Firestone Tire & Rubber Co. v. NLRB, 539 F2d 1335, 1339, 93 LRRM 2625 (CA 4, 1976).

[60]Bandag, Inc. v. NLRB, 583 F2d 765, 99 LRRM 3226 (CA 5, 1978), *enforcing in part* 228 NLRB 1045, 96 LRRM 1094 (1977); Florsheim Shoe Store Co. v. NLRB, 565 F2d 1240, 96 LRRM 3273 (CA 2), *enforcing in part* 227 NLRB 1153, 95 LRRM 1030 (1977); NLRB v. McClure Assocs., Inc., 556 F2d 725, 95 LRRM 2801 (CA 4, 1977); NLRB v. Fremont Mfg. Co., 558 F2d 889, 95 LRRM 3095 (CA 8, 1977); R. J. Lallier Trucking v. NLRB, 558 F2d 1322, 95 LRRM 3101 (CA 8, 1977); NLRB v. Florida Tile Co., 557 F2d 576, 95 LRRM 3009 (CA 6, 1977).

[61]251 NLRB 1083, 105 LRRM 1169 (1980), *enforced*, 662 F2d 899, 108 LRRM 2513 (CA 1, 1981), *cert. denied*, 455 US 989, 109 LRRM 2779 (1982). *See* discussion at notes 511-23 *infra*. *See also* discussion at notes 159-69 *infra*.

[62]429 US 274 (1977). *See also* Village of Arlington Heights v. Metropolitan Housing Dev. Corp., 429 US 252 (1977).

[63]Wright Line, Inc., note 61. *See also* Herman Bros., Inc., 252 NLRB 848, 105 LRRM 1374 (1980); United Parcel Serv., 252 NLRB 1015, 105 LRRM 1484 (1980); Valley Cabinet & Mfg., Inc., 253 NLRB 98, 105 LRRM 1467 (1980); Weather Tamer, Inc., 253 NLRB 293, 105 LRRM 1569 (1980).

[64]*See infra* at notes 511-23 for judicial reaction to the *Wright-Line* analysis.

Counsel must still establish an unfair labor practice by a preponderance of the evidence.[65]

While noting that the two types of Section 8(a)(3) cases, *pretext* and *mixed motive,* are analytically different, the Board in *Wright Line* concluded that the *Mt. Healthy* test was readily applicable to both. It would appear, however, that this test is not appropriate in cases where a Section 8(a)(3) violation does not turn on motive, as in conduct "inherently destructive of important employee rights."[66] In such cases a violation is established even if there is no improper motive or even if there is a business justification for the employer's conduct.

Where a violation of Section 8(a)(3) is charged, the question of whether the employer in fact changed the employee's tenure or terms or conditions of employment is rarely if ever disputed. What is most often in contention is whether by its actions the employer intended to encourage or discourage union membership. Also, despite a showing of a prima facie case of discriminatory intent, an employer may avoid Section 8(a)(3) liability by proving that the motive underlying the discriminatory act was not attended by "discriminatory considerations."[67]

If the employer has expressed himself in connection with his action, direct proof of intent may thus be available. However, Section 8(c) protects an employer's right of free speech as follows:

> [T]he expressing of any views, argument, or opinion or the dissemination thereof, whether in written, printed, graphic, or visual form, shall not constitute or be evidence of an unfair labor practice under

---

[65]Wright Line, *supra* note 61. [*See* **Editor's Note** *infra*, p. 266.]

[66]NLRB v. Great Dane Trailers, *supra* note 40 at 34.

[67]Continental Chem. Co., 232 NLRB 705, 96 LRRM 1327 (1977), where an employee who engaged in organizational activities was warned and placed on probation by his employer in violation of §8(a)(3) and then was discharged immediately after the union sought recognition; the Board concluded that the employer successfully rebutted the General Counsel's *prima facie* case by presenting evidence that the ultimate discharge was motivated by lawful considerations (employer had received substantial customer complaints and threats of termination of business because of the employee's behavior). *See* NLRB v. Collier, 553 F2d 425, 95 LRRM 2615 (CA 5, 1977), *denying enforcement to* 223 NLRB 1492, 92 LRRM 1280 (1976); NLRB v. Grease Co., 567 F2d 531, 94 LRRM 3197 (CA 2, 1977), *denying enforcement to* Theatre Now, Inc., 221 NLRB 1110, 91 LRRM 1031 (1975); Mueller Brass Co. v. NLRB, 544 F2d 815, 94 LRRM 2225 (CA 5, 1977), *denying enforcement to* 220 NLRB 1127, 90 LRRM 1530 (1975). *See also* Burns Int'l Sec. Servs., Inc., 234 NLRB 373, 97 LRRM 1319 (1978) (dismissal of security guards for sleeping); Mosher Steel Co. v. NLRB, 568 F2d 436, 98 LRRM 2010 (CA 5, 1978), *enforcing in part* 226 NLRB 1163, 94 LRRM 1317 (1977) (discharge and discipline of strikers who had engaged in serious misconduct during strike).

any of the provisions of this Act, if such expression contains no threat of reprisal or force or promise of benefit.

Accordingly, anti-union statements which do not include threats of reprisal, force, or promises of benefit cannot be determinative on this issue,[68] and the focal point of the inquiry remains: What was the real reason for the discharge?[69]

In determining whether the conduct in question is unlawfully motivated, the Board will rely on circumstantial as well as direct evidence to infer discriminatory motivation on the part of an employer. It will consider circumstantial evidence such as the following: (1) a delay in the discharge after knowledge of the offense;[70] (2) a departure from established procedures for discharge;[71] (3) failure to warn the employee prior to discharge;[72] (4) failure to tell the employee the reason for the discharge at the time of discharge;[73] (5) changes in position in explaining the reason for the discharge;[74] and (6) the timing of the discharge (e.g., discharge immediately after the employer gains knowledge of the employee's union activity).[75] The Board may prop-

---

[68]Indiana Metal Prods. Corp. v. NLRB, *supra* note 43; Pittsburgh S.S. Co. v. NLRB, 180 F2d 731, 25 LRRM 2428 (CA 6, 1950), *aff'd*, 340 US 498, 27 LRRM 2382 (1951). Such statements may be admissible to show background or union animus, however. *See* Chapter 6 *supra* for discussion of §8(c) in relation to independent §8(a)(1) cases.

[69]W. T. Grant Co., 210 NLRB 622, 86 LRRM 1365 (1974) (anti-union comments prior to discharge); United Cement Co., 209 NLRB 1137, 86 LRRM 1237 (1974) (comments regarding discharge after discharge); Radiadores Paragon de Puerto Rico, Inc., 206 NLRB 918, 84 LRRM 1591 (1973), *enforced*, 509 F2d 1160, 87 LRRM 3274 (CA 1, 1974) (default judgment in earlier Board case); Mademoiselle Shoppe, Inc., 199 NLRB 983, 82 LRRM 1022 (1972) (comments prior to discharge and other unfair labor practices committed on day of discharge).

[70]Merchants Truck Line, Inc. v. NLRB, 577 F2d 1011, 99 LRRM 2143 (CA 5, 1978), *enforcing* 232 NLRB 676, 96 LRRM 1318 (1977); National Grange Mut. Ins. Co., 207 NLRB 431, 84 LRRM 1656 (1973); Commonwealth Foods, Inc., 203 NLRB 891, 83 LRRM 1214 (1973), *enforcement denied in part and remanded*, 506 F2d 1065, 87 LRRM 2609 (CA 4, 1974); Montgomery Ward & Co., 197 NLRB 519, 80 LRRM 1778 (1972).

[71]Richmond Refining Co., 212 NLRB 16, 87 LRRM 1255 (1974); D. H. Baldwin Co., 207 NLRB 25, 84 LRRM 1502 (1973), *enforced*, 505 F2d 736, 90 LRRM 2891 (CA 8, 1974); Ostby & Barton Co., 202 NLRB 199, 82 LRRM 1605 (1973). *Accord,* Westinghouse Learning Corp., 211 NLRB 19, 86 LRRM 1709 (1974).

[72]Great Atl. & Pac. Tea Co., 210 NLRB 593, 86 LRRM 1444 (1974); Coble Dairy Prods. Coop., Inc., 205 NLRB 160, 84 LRRM 1094 (1973); National Food Serv., 196 NLRB 295, 80 LRRM 1017 (1972).

[73]Forest Park Ambulance Serv., 206 NLRB 550, 84 LRRM 1506 (1973); Alamo Express, Inc., 200 NLRB 178, 82 LRRM 1148 (1972), *enforced*, 489 F2d 1311, 85 LRRM 2768 (CA 5, 1974).

[74]Coca-Cola Bottling Co., 232 NLRB 794, 97 LRRM 1290 (1977); J. R. Townsend Lincoln-Mercury, 202 NLRB 71, 82 LRRM 1793 (1973); Holiday Inn, 198 NLRB 410, 80 LRRM 1697 (1972), *enforced*, 488 F2d 498, 84 LRRM 2585 (CA 10, 1973); Goodyear Tire & Rubber Co., 197 NLRB 666, 80 LRRM 1701 (1972).

[75]Marx-Haas Clothing Co., 211 NLRB 350, 87 LRRM 1054 (1974); Shivvers Corp., 213 NLRB 102, 87 LRRM 1753 (1974); Howard Johnson Co., *supra* note 45; D. M. Rotary Press, Inc., 208 NLRB 366, 85 LRRM 1477 (1974), *enforced*, 524 F2d 1342, 91

erly use evidence from a prior unfair labor practice proceeding as evidence of present union animus where other supporting evidence exists.[76] And while an employer's prior unfair labor practice may be relevant, such evidence is insufficient standing alone to support a finding of violation.[77]

An essential element in proving the existence of unlawful union animus in most cases is proof that the employer had knowledge of the affected employee's union allegiance or activities when the action was taken.[78] Thus, an employer's discipline of a union adherent does not violate Section 8(a)(3) where there is no evidence that the employer was aware of either the union's or the employee's organizational activities.[79]

Under certain circumstances, however, the Board will apply its so-called *small plant doctrine* to establish the requisite employer knowledge.[80] The employer's knowledge of union activities is thus inferred where such activities are conducted at a small plant

---

LRRM 2240 (CA 6, 1975); Uniroyal, Inc., 197 NLRB 1034, 80 LRRM 1694 (1972); Atlantic Marine, 193 NLRB 1003, 78 LRRM 1460 (1971).

[76]Tama Meat Packing Corp. v. NLRB, 575 F2d 661, 98 LRRM 2339 (CA 8, 1978), *enforcing as modified* 230 NLRB 116, 96 LRRM 1148 (1977), *cert. denied*, 439 US 1069, 100 LRRM 2268 (1979).

[77]In certain circumstances, the Board will consider anti-union conduct by the employer found in prior Board decisions. J. P. Stevens & Co., 245 NLRB 198, 102 LRRM 1437 (1979), *enforced*, 638 F2d 676, 106 LRRM 2145 (CA 4, 1980); Southwest Janitorial & Maintenance Corp., 209 NLRB 402, 85 LRRM 1590 (1974) (prior cases involving predecessor and successor employer); Dollar Gen. Corp., 204 NLRB 601, 83 LRRM 1713 (1973). *See* G & S Metal Prod. Co., 199 NLRB 705, 81 LRRM 1587 (1972), *enforced*, 489 F2d 441, 85 LRRM 2047 (CA 6, 1973) (prior Board case too remote in time and circumstances to establish element of union animus); Southwest Chevrolet Corp., 194 NLRB 975, 79 LRRM 1156 (1972), *enforced*, 82 LRRM 2620 (CA 7, 1972) (unlawful motivation cannot be established by conduct prior to settlement agreement containing nonadmission clause). The Board may properly use evidence from a prior unfair labor practice proceeding as evidence of present union animus where other supporting evidence exists. Tama Meat Packing Corp. v. NLRB, *supra* note 76. However, while the employer's prior unfair labor practice may be relevant, Kenworth Trucks, Inc., 236 NLRB 1299, 99 LRRM 1211 (1978), evidence of past union animus by itself is not sufficient to support a finding of a violation. Sioux Quality Packers v. NLRB, 581 F2d 153, 98 LRRM 3128 (CA 8, 1978), *denying enforcement to* 232 NLRB 1166, 96 LRRM 1372 (1977). A past history of amicable relations with a union does not necessarily disprove evidence of present discriminatory intent and motivation with regard to the discriminatee. Awrey Bakeries, 197 NLRB 705, 80 LRRM 1480 (1972).

[78]*See* Leyendecker Paving, Inc., 247 NLRB 28, 103 LRRM 1107 (1980). *See* discussion at notes 184-96 *infra*.

[79]Fry Roofing Co., 237 NLRB 1005, 99 LRRM 1544 (1978). Prior knowledge must be present even when there is proof of union animus. A to Z Portion Meats, Inc. v. NLRB, 643 F2d 390, 106 LRRM 2844 (CA 6, 1981).

[80]Coral Gables Convalescent Home, Inc., 234 NLRB 1198, 97 LRRM 1435 (1978), *enforced*, 85 LC §11200 (CA 5, 1979). *See* Reinauer Fuel Transp. Corp., 251 NLRB 1573, 105 LRRM 1355 (1980); Permanent Label Corp., 248 NLRB 118, 103 LRRM 1513 (1980); Webco Bodies, Inc., 237 NLRB 1213, 99 LRRM 1135 (1978). *See* discussion at notes 193-96 *infra*.

and are carried on in such a manner or at such times that it may be presumed that the employer must have noticed them.

The Section 8(a)(3) prohibition against discrimination that encourages or discourages membership in a union also includes discouraging participation in protected concerted activities, a violation of Section 8(a)(1).[81] However, discrimination alone does not establish violation of Section 8(a)(3), for it must also be found that the employer was motivated by one of the proscribed objects.[82]

A dismissal may violate Section 8(a)(3) even though the dismissed employee is not a union adherent. When an employer discharges nonunion supporters together with union adherents in an effort to disguise its unlawful intent, the discharge of both groups violates Section 8(a)(3).[83]

2. Conduct Inherently Destructive of Section 7 Rights. While Section 8(a)(3) violations normally turn "on whether the discriminatory conduct was motivated by an anti-union purpose,"[84] the Supreme Court in *NLRB* v. *Erie Resistor Corp.*[85] identified a class of employer conduct where the requisite unlawful intent "is founded upon the inherently discriminatory or destructive nature of the conduct itself."[86] In such instances, the employer is held

> to intend the very consequences which foreseeably and inescapably flow from his actions . . . [because] his conduct *does* speak for itself— it *is* discriminatory and it *does* discourage union membership, and whatever the claimed overriding justification may be, it carries with it unavoidable consequences which the employer not only foresaw but must have intended.[87]

Recognizing that employer conduct often presents a complex of motives, some lawful and some unlawful, the Court upheld the Board's admittedly delicate task of balancing one motive against another in finding violations of the Act, even in the face

---

[81]NLRB v. Erie Resistor Corp., 373 US 221, 53 LRRM 2121 (1963). *See* discussion at notes 85-91 *infra*.

[82]Radio Officers Union v. NLRB, *supra* note 8; NLRB v. Great Dane Trailers, Inc., *supra* note 40. Encouraging or discouraging union membership without discrimination is not unlawful. Nu-Car Carriers, Inc., 187 NLRB 850, 76 LRRM 1159 (1971).

[83]Howard Johnson Co., *supra* note 45.

[84]NLRB v. Great Dane Trailers, *supra* note 40.

[85]Erie Resistor Corp., *supra* note 81.

[86]*Id.* at 223. *See also* NLRB v. Brown, 380 US 278, 58 LRRM 2663 (1965) (employer's right to lock out and hire replacements during a "whipsaw" strike).

[87]373 US at 228. (Emphasis in original.)

of business exigencies, by "weighing the interest of employees in concerted activity against the interest of the employer in operating his business in a particular manner . . . ."[88] The balance was to be achieved in light of the policy of the Act—the effect upon employee rights was to be weighed against the business ends to be served by the employer's conduct.

In *Erie Resistor* the employer had granted superseniority to striker-replacements and to strikers who returned to work. This action was held to involve "conduct which carried its own indicia of intent and which is barred by the Act unless saved from illegality by an overriding business purpose justifying the invasion of union rights."[89] Turning to the employer's alleged business justification, the Court said it would not disturb "the Board's considered judgment that the Act and its underlying policy require . . . giving more weight to the harm wrought by superseniority than to the interest of the employer in operating its plant during the strike by utilizing this particular means of attracting replacements."[90] The operative policy at work was the concern expressed in the federal labor laws for the protection of the integrity of the strike weapon, "which in great measure

---

[88]*Id.* at 223. The courts have consistently rejected the argument that conduct otherwise discriminatory is *automatically* excused upon a showing of business exigency motivation. While the Court in *Erie Resistor* upheld the Board's balancing of conflicts in interests, the Court has admonished the Board for assessing the relative bargaining strength or economic power of the parties. *See* NLRB v. Insurance Agents, 361 US 477, 45 LRRM 2705 (1960); American Ship Bldg. Co. v. NLRB, 380 US 300, 58 LRRM 2672 (1965).

[89]373 US at 231. This conclusion was based on an analysis of the superseniority plan, which had the following characteristics: (1) The tenure of all strikers was affected, whereas permanent replacement under the doctrine of NLRB v. Mackay Radio & Tel. Co., 304 US 333, 2 LRRM 610 (1938), affects only those strikers who were actually replaced. (2) Superseniority operated to the detriment of participants in the strike, while benefitting individual strikers who returned to work. (3) The offer of superseniority was a crippling blow to the strike effort. (4) Future collective bargaining would be made difficult because the bargaining unit was divided between those who stayed with the union and those who returned to work before the strike ended. *See* A.P.A. Transp. Corp., 239 NLRB 1407, 100 LRRM 1165 (1979) (broad superseniority for union stewards); Teamsters Local 20 (Preston Trucking Co.) v. NLRB, 610 F2d 991, 102 LRRM 3080 (CA DC, 1979), *enforcing* 236 NLRB 464, 98 LRRM 1248 (1978) (steward superseniority "for all purposes").

[90]373 US at 232. The court distinguished and thereby refused to extend its holding in NLRB v. Mackay Radio & Tel. Co., *supra* note 89, where it stated that an employer may operate its plant during a strike and at its conclusion need not discharge those who worked during the strike in order to make way for returning strikers, because the employer's interest in carrying on its business must be deemed to outweigh the damage to concerted activities caused by permanently replacing strikers. The obvious point of departure between the *Erie Resistor* and *Mackay Radio* decisions lies in the "far greater encroachment resulting from super-seniority in addition to permanent replacement," for superseniority affects all strikers, whether replaced or not, and has a powerful impact on the strike itself.

implements and supports the principles of the collective bargaining system."[91]

NLRB v. *Great Dane Trailers*[92] established the basic rules concerning the burden of proving the presence or absence of discriminatory purpose under Section 8(a)(3). The Court declared that no proof of anti-union motivation need be advanced and that a violation could be found "if it can reasonably be concluded that the employer's discriminatory conduct was 'inherently destructive' of important employee rights"[93] despite evidence of business motivation. However, where the discriminatory conduct has a "comparatively slight" effect on employee rights, an employer's evidence of "legitimate and substantial business justifications for the conduct" will shift the burden of proof to the General Counsel to show anti-union motivation.[94] Consequently, to the extent that business justifications and legitimate employer objectives are a part of the Board's analysis in determining whether discriminatory conduct is "inherently destructive," the employer always has the burden of proof as to these elements, in either "inherently destructive" or "comparatively

---

[91]373 US at 234.

[92]*Supra* note 40.

[93]388 US at 34. The Court cited Radio Officers Union v. NLRB, *supra* note 8. While an economic strike was in progress, the employer in *Great Dane* denied strikers vacation benefits, which the union contended had accrued under the expired collective bargaining contract. Shortly thereafter, the employer paid vacation benefits to employees who were working during the strike. The Board found a violation of §§8(a)(1) and 8(a)(3). The Fifth Circuit denied enforcement. 363 F2d 130, 62 LRRM 2456 (CA 5, 1966), *denying enforcement to* 150 NLRB 438, 58 LRRM 1097 (1964). The Supreme Court reversed and enforced the Board's order. In *Radio Officers* the employer's conduct consisted of its acquiescence to a union's demand to remove an employee who had obtained his job without first going through the union. *See* notes 351-53 *infra*.

[94]388 US at 34. In *Great Dane* the Court upheld the Board's finding of a violation because the General Counsel had proved the existence of "discriminatory conduct carrying a potential for adverse effect upon employee rights," and the employer offered no evidence of proper motivation. Hence, the Court never decided whether "[t]he act of paying accrued benefits to one group of employees while announcing the extinction of the same benefits for another group of employees who are distinguishable only by their participation in protected concerted activity" was inherently destructive or had a comparatively slight effect on employee rights. *See* NLRB v. Borden, Inc., 600 F2d 313, 101 LRRM 2727 (CA 1, 1979) (*Great Dane* did not decide the question whether such conduct was inherently destructive). *See also* NLRB v. Great Atl. & Pac. Tea Co., 409 F2d 296, 70 LRRM 3246 (CA 5, 1969). *Compare* Service Employees Local 250 v. NLRB, 600 F2d 930, 101 LRRM 2004 (CA DC, 1979) (*Great Dane* interpreted as holding that termination of the benefits was inherently destructive conduct), *with* Wallace Metal Prods., Inc., 244 NLRB 41, 102 LRRM 1233 (1979); Westinghouse Elec. Corp., 237 NLRB 1209, 99 LRRM 1184 (1978), *enforced*, 603 F2d 610, 101 LRRM 2870 (CA 7, 1979); Borden, Inc., 235 NLRB 982, 98 LRRM 1098 (1978); Local 155, Molders v. NLRB, 442 F2d 742, 76 LRRM 2133 (CA DC, 1970) (which cases concluded that an employer's refusal to pay striking employees accrued vacation pay is inherently destructive of employee §7 rights).

slight" situations. The nature of the effect of discriminatory conduct on employee rights, as measured in the light of the Act's policies, will determine the weight to be accorded such evidence in Board-conducted unfair labor practice proceedings.[95]

The Supreme Court has expressed no clear standards to define what conduct is "inherently destructive" or "comparatively slight," what constitutes "legitimate and substantial business justification," or how that is to be determined.[96] In *Great Dane* and *NLRB v. Fleetwood Trailers Co.*,[97] the Court sustained Board decisions finding violations of Section 8(a)(3) where the employer failed to offer any proof on the question of legitimate and substantial business justification for otherwise unlawful discriminatory conduct, and in *Erie Resistor* the Court had reiterated its holding in *Mackay*[98] that an employer may permanently replace economic strikers in order to continue operations during a strike and need not discharge such replacements at the strike's conclusion unless anti-union motivation could be proved. In *NLRB v. Brown*,[99] the Court held that the use of a lockout and temporary replacements in response to a whipsaw strike against another member of a multi-employer bargaining group had a "comparatively slight" tendency to discourage union membership and was reasonably adapted to achieve legitimate business ends or to deal with

---

[95]In Earringhouse Imports, 227 NLRB 1107, 94 LRRM 1494 (1977), *enforcement denied sub nom.*, Service Employees Local 250 v. NLRB, *supra* note 94. The Board extended the burden-of-proof rules of *Great Dane* to alleged violations of §8(a)(4). In that case, the employer had terminated a number of its employees who had violated an express order of the employer and had left the plant to attend an NLRB representation hearing. In reversing the Board, the District of Columbia Circuit refused to extend the *Great Dane* rules to alleged violations of §8(a)(4) and held that the employer was not obliged to come forward with legitimate and substantial business justifications for its actions; instead, the burden of proof remained with the General Counsel to prove a violation of §8(a)(4). *See* note 464 *infra*.

[96]The Court did not state whether the Board was empowered to rule on the sufficiency of the "legitimate and substantial justification" proffered by an employer, thereby leaving open the question whether in comparatively slight cases the Board could balance the harm versus the alleged justification in order to find a violation of §8(a)(3). *Compare* Portland Williamette Co. v. NLRB, 534 F2d 1331, 92 LRRM 2113 (CA 9, 1976), *rehearing denied*, 534 F2d 1333, 92 LRRM 3196, *denying enforcement to* 212 NLRB 272, 86 LRRM 1667 (1974), *with* NLRB v. Knuth Bros., 584 F2d 813, 99 LRRM 2784 (CA 7, 1978), *enforcing* 229 NLRB 1204, 95 LRRM 1229 (1977). *See infra* at note 153.

[97]389 US 375, 66 LRRM 2737 (1967). *See* Chapter 21 *infra* at note 86 and *infra* this chapter at note 118.

[98]*Supra* note 89.

[99]*Supra* note 86. The court characterized inherently destructive conduct as that which is demonstrably so destructive of employee rights and so devoid of significant service as a legitimate business end that it cannot be tolerated consistently with the Act.

business exigencies, thus requiring independent evidence of improper motivation.

In *American Ship Building Co. v. NLRB*,[100] a companion case to *Brown*, the Court stated that "there are some practices which are inherently so prejudicial to union interests and so devoid of significant economic justification . . . that the employer's conduct carries with it an inference of unlawful intention so compelling that it is justifiable to disbelieve the employer's protestations of innocent purpose." Nevertheless, the employer's use of a lockout for the sole purpose of bringing economic pressure to bear in support of its legitimate bargaining position was deemed lawful.[101]

The "phrase 'inherently destructive' is thus not easily susceptible of precise definition,"[102] and appellate decisions upholding violations under this standard are relatively rare.[103] One court has stated:

> Those cases finding an employer's conduct inherently destructive, bearing their own indicia of intent, are cases involving conduct with far reaching effects which would hinder future bargaining, or conduct which discriminates solely upon the basis of participation in strikes or union activity. Examples of inherently destructive activity are permanent discharge for participation in union activities, granting super-seniority to strikebreakers, and other actions creating visible and continuing obstacles to the future exercise of employee rights.[104]

---

[100]*Supra* note 88. *See* discussion at notes 225-30 *infra*.

[101]*Id.* The Court appeared to refine the limits of inherently destructive conduct in holding that the use of the lockout does not carry with it any necessary implication that the employer acted to discourage union membership or otherwise discriminate against union members as such. *See* Radio Officers Union v. NLRB, *supra* note 8; *see also* Georgia Pac., So. Div., NLRB Gen. Counsel Advice Memo., 5-CA-11747, 104 LRRM 1167 (1980). Thus, a no-distribution rule that could be applied to unprotected as well as protected activity did not necessarily imply that its application was to discourage union membership and, therefore, it was not inherently destructive of employee rights. Texas Instruments, Inc. v. NLRB, 599 F2d 1067, 102 LRRM 2292 (CA 1, 1979), *denying enforcement to* 236 NLRB 68, 98 LRRM 1299 (1978).

[102]Inter-Collegiate Press v. NLRB, 486 F2d 837, 84 LRRM 2562 (CA 8, 1973), *aff'g* 199 NLRB 177, 81 LRRM 1508 (1972), *cert. denied sub nom.* Bookbinders Local 60 v. NLRB, 416 US 938, 85 LRRM 2924 (1974). *See* note 99 *supra*.

[103]*E.g.*, Loomis Courier Serv., Inc. v. NLRB, 595 F2d 491, 101 LRRM 2450 (CA 9, 1979), *denying enforcement to* 235 NLRB 534, 98 LRRM 1083 (1978).

[104]Portland Williamette Co. v. NLRB, *supra* note 96 at 1334 (citing *Inter-Collegiate Press*, *supra* note 102). *See* Loomis Courier Serv., *supra* note 103 at 495 ("'actions creating visible and continuing obstacles to the future exercise of employee rights' are inherently destructive"). *See also* NLRB v. Lantz, 607 F2d 290, 102 LRRM 2789 (CA 9, 1979), *enforcing* 235 NLRB 994, 100 LRRM 1223 (1978) (permanent discharge for seeking union assistance to enforce labor contract is inherently destructive).

The Board, however, has more readily found specific employer conduct to be "inherently destructive" of Section 7 rights than have the courts, and reversals have been frequent.[105] For example, in *Portland Williamette Co. v. NLRB*,[106] the Ninth Circuit held that the Board was not warranted in finding that the employer violated Section 8(a)(3) by implementing, during an economic strike, a wage proposal giving retroactive increases for time worked during a specified period before the strike only to those employees on the payroll on a specified later date.[107] The following cases describe the on-going dialogue between the Board and the circuits:

In *Loomis Courier Service, Inc.*,[108] the Board found that the conduct of the employer in terminating all branch employees during negotiations for a collective bargaining agreement was inherently destructive of employee rights. The Ninth Circuit again denied enforcement, characterizing the employer's con-

---

[105]Even prior to *Great Dane*, at least two circuit courts of appeals had refused to adopt the Board's view that particular employer conduct was so destructive of employee rights as to require no proof of anti-union motivation even though the employer offered economic and business justification for its conduct. Quality Castings Co. v. NLRB, 325 F2d 36, 54 LRRM 2674 (CA 6, 1963), *denying enforcement to* 139 NLRB 928, 51 LRRM 1422 (1962) (failure to make profit-sharing payments to 64 former employees who had engaged in a prolonged strike); Pittsburgh-Des Moines Steel Co. v. NLRB, 284 F2d 74, 47 LRRM 2135 (CA 9, 1960), *denying enforcement to* 124 NLRB 855, 44 LRRM 1518 (1959) (failure to grant a Christmas bonus to employees who had engaged in an economic strike).

[106]*Supra* note 96.

[107]Of the 162 employees who had originally gone out on strike, 107 had returned before the crucial date, four or five returned after the crucial date, a single employee continued to picket, and the rest were not heard from again. The strikers who returned to work after the crucial date did not receive the retroactive pay; neither did the strike replacements; nor did new employees actively employed on the crucial date who had not worked the specified period before the strike. Those who had worked during the prestrike period and were on the payroll on the crucial date received the retroactive pay. The Ninth Circuit found, contrary to the Board, that the employer's conduct was not inherently destructive of the employees' right to strike and that, while the conduct had a "comparatively slight" effect on such rights, the employer had a legitimate business purpose for its actions. The court reasoned that the proposal when originally made was not intended to provide a cutoff date for abandonment of the strike, that the employer had a right to insist upon its credibility by not awarding increases to those who did not return to work by that date, and that the conduct could have no continuing adverse consequences like the granting of superseniority. The Board and the court agreed that the employer had neither foreseen nor intended anti-union consequences from its actions.

[108]*Supra* note 103. *Compare* Los Angeles Marine Hardware Co. v. NLRB, 602 F2d 1302, 102 LRRM 2498 (CA 9, 1979), *enforcing* 235 NLRB 720, 98 LRRM 1571 (1978) (termination and refusal to transfer employee when, during contract term, employer transferred operations in part from one division to another, is inherently destructive conduct, and employer's desire to escape financial burden of voluntarily executed contract is insufficient business justification), *with* Ingersoll Rand Co., 247 NLRB 801, 103 LRRM 1224 (1980) (refusal to transfer unit employees while transferring nonunit employees to additional new location is not inherently destructive).

duct as economically motivated and not inherently destructive of employee rights.

In *Indiana & Michigan Electric Co.*[109] the Board found that the employer's differentiation between union officers and rank-and-file employees in meting out discipline for participating in an illegal strike was conduct inherently destructive of employee rights. In denying enforcement, the Seventh Circuit concluded that such conduct "could not reasonably be considered inherently destructive of important employee rights."[110]

In *Wilson Freight Co.*[111] the Board found that an employer's enforcement of a contract provision limiting the authority of union stewards and leaving to the employer the disciplining of stewards who engage in interruptions violative of the collective bargaining agreement was "inherently destructive." The First Circuit disagreed, holding that there was nothing inherently destructive about a collective bargaining provision requiring stewards to act through established channels rather than unilaterally. The court further stated that it was not inherently destructive for the employer to criticize a steward acting in violation of such a provision.[112]

In *Texas Instruments, Inc.* v. *NLRB*[113] the Board had contended that discharging employees for distributing organizational leaflets in violation of a rule prohibiting such conduct was "inherently destructive." Again the First Circuit disagreed, stating that if the rule was otherwise valid, "[i]t would be straining to conclude that enforcing the rule revealed an inherent intent to interfere with employee rights simply because the employees' violation occurred during the carrying on of protected activity."[114]

Likewise, in *Borden, Inc.*,[115] the Board held that the withhold-

---

[109]237 NLRB 226, 99 LRRM 1111 (1978), *enforcement denied*, 599 F2d 227, 101 LRRM 2475 (CA 7, 1979). *Compare* Midwest Precision Castings Co., 244 NLRB 597, 102 LRRM 1074 (1979).

[110]599 F2d 227, 232, 101 LRRM 2475 (CA 7, 1979). *Accord*, Gould Corp. v. NLRB, 612 F2d 728, 103 LRRM 2207 (CA 3, 1979) *denying enforcement to* 237 NLRB 881, 99 LRRM 1059 (1978).

[111]234 NLRB 844, 97 LRRM 1412 (1978).

[112]604 F2d 712, 102 LRRM 2269 (CA 1, 1979), *denying enforcement to* 234 NLRB 844, 97 LRRM 1412 (1978).

[113]*Supra* note 101.

[114]599 F2d at 1072.

[115]*Supra* note 94. *See also* Jacques Syl Knitwear, Inc., 247 NLRB 1525, 103 LRRM 1358 (1980); Cedarcrest, Inc., 246 NLRB 870, 102 LRRM 1692 (1979); Wallace Metal Prods., Inc., *supra* note 94; Conval-Penn, Inc., 244 NLRB 970, 102 LRRM 1229 (1979).

ing of accrued vacation benefits from striking employees was conduct inherently destructive of employee rights. The First Circuit disagreed, pointing out that this case involved a delay in vacation benefits as opposed to a refusal to pay vacation benefits.[116] The court vacated the Board's order and remanded the case for consideration of the employer's business reasons for its conduct. Accepting the court's ruling, that deferral of the vacation pay was "comparatively slight" conduct, as the law of the case, the Board on remand held the employer's alleged justification not supported by the evidence.[117] The Board noted, however, that an employer's preclusion of employees from working while simultaneously receiving vacation pay was, if proved, a legitimate and substantial business justification for refusing to grant vacation pay in lieu of vacation time.

In other cases, the Board and the courts have found and focused upon an absence of evidence of any legitimate and substantial business justification for the employer's action. Such focus renders it unnecessary to decide whether the action was either "inherently destructive" or "comparatively slight" in its effect on employee rights, for in either case the conduct would be unlawful. Thus, in *Laidlaw Corp.*,[118] the Board held that the employer's failure to adequately justify permanently severing its relationship with permanently replaced economic strikers— or, more specifically, its failure to justify bypassing those strikers when they had unconditionally applied for reinstatement to positions later vacated—violated Section 8(a)(3). The Board described the employer's action as "inherently destructive," but

---

[116]*Supra* note 94. *But see* NLRB v. Westinghouse Elec. Corp., 603 F2d 610, 101 LRRM 2870 (CA 7, 1979) (deferral of vacation pay is inherently destructive).

[117]Borden, Inc., 248 NLRB 387, 60, 103 LRRM 1421 (1980).

[118]*Supra* note 42. *See* Chapter 21 *infra* at notes 87-103. *See also* Arrow Indus., Inc., 245 NLRB 1376, 102 LRRM 1525 (1979); NLRB v. Fleetwood Trailers Co., *supra* note 97, on which the Board relied in *Laidlaw*. In *Fleetwood*, jobs were not available to economic strikers on the date of their applications for reinstatement. Two months later jobs became available when full production was resumed, but the employer hired new employees instead of qualified strikers, which was held to be a violation of §8(a)(3). As in *Great Dane*, *supra* note 40, the Supreme Court in *Fleetwood* did not have to decide whether the conduct involved was "inherently destructive" of employee rights, because the rights of the employees were affected to some extent by the employer's actions and the employer failed to introduce any evidence of a legitimate business objective, thus eliminating the requirement of showing union animus. *See also* discussion at notes 282-86 *infra*. *But see* Atlantic Creosoting Co., 242 NLRB 192, 101 LRRM 1144 (1979) (where employer eliminated a position during strike, General Counsel must prove anti-union intent); NLRB v. Wells Fargo Armored Serv. Corp., 597 F2d 7, 101 LRRM 2209 (CA 1, 1979), *denying enforcement to* 237 NLRB 605, 99 LRRM 1069 (1978) (failure to rehire four strikers according to seniority for new positions created after strike, while hiring less senior strikers, held not to be inherently destructive).

only by way of explaining the legal significance of its failure to prove any legitimate and substantial justification. In enforcing the Board's order, the Seventh Circuit similarly avoided that difficult question which *Great Dane Trailers* and a showing of adequate business justification would have rendered it necessary to decide.[119] The following additional cases further demonstrate the tendency of the circuits to avoid characterizing the severity of the employer's conduct:

In *Allied Industrial Workers Local 289* v. *NLRB*[120] the employer conditioned payment of accrued vacation compensation on cessation of an economic strike. The District of Columbia Circuit enforced the Board's prior holding that the employer had thereby violated Section 8(a)(3). In doing so, the court focused upon the absence of proof of any business justification and found it "unnecessary . . . to tread the uneasy path between 'inherently destructive' and 'comparatively slight' discrimination."[121]

In *Electro Vector, Inc.*,[122] the Board held that the employer violated the Act by conditioning payment of a bonus on the employees' active payroll status on the last day of the fiscal year and on the date of payment of the bonus, thus denying the bonus to employees who were on strike on both dates. Such actions were held to be inherently destructive of the employees' right to strike because the striking employees had earned a part of the bonus and there was no special business significance to the requirement that the strikers actually be at work on the two dates.

The Ninth Circuit denied enforcement, but avoided the question of whether or not the withholding of the bonus was "inherently destructive" by noting that the bonus was not a term or condition of employment but was rather in the nature of a "gift."[123]

---

[119]*Supra* note 40. *See infra* at note 280.
[120]476 F2d 868, 82 LRRM 2225 (CA DC, 1973), *enforcing as modified* 192 NLRB 290, 77 LRRM 1889 (1971).
[121]*Id.* at 878.
[122]220 NLRB 445, 90 LRRM 1241 (1975).
[123]Electro Vector, Inc. v. NLRB, 539 F2d 35, 93 LRRM 2021 (CA 9, 1976), *cert. denied,* 434 US 821, 96 LRRM 2512 (1977); *cf.* Sun Oil Co., 245 NLRB No. 11, 102 LRRM 1238 (1979) (refusal to grant severance pay not inherently destructive). *But cf.* Peyton Packing Co., Inc., 129 NLRB 1275, 47 LRRM 1170 (1961) (withholding of bonus as punishment for selecting union in election violated §8(a)(1).

In *Johns-Manville Products Corp.*[124] the employer locked out its employees in response to their widespread sabotage of its machines during collective bargaining negotiations. The employer thereafter hired permanent replacements. The Board found that although the lockout was lawful, the hiring of permanent replacements in such circumstances was inherently destructive of employee rights. The Fifth Circuit denied enforcement, but bypassed the question of whether such conduct was "inherently destructive" by holding that the employees' acts of sabotage amounted to an in-plant strike for which the hiring of permanent replacements was lawful.[125]

In *B. G. Costich & Sons, Inc.* v. *NLRB*[126] the Second Circuit also held it did not have to decide the "inherently destructive/comparatively slight" issue, since there was no tendency in the first instance to discourage or encourage union membership when employer-members of an association, the party to a labor contract, made contributions to a union pension fund on behalf of casual employees who were union members but made no contribution for casuals who were not union members.

Similarly, in *A. S. Abell Co.*,[127] the Board held that an employer's refusal to hire referred employees who were members of a striking local union, because unidentified members of that local purportedly engaged in violence and property damage at the location of another employer, constituted inherently destructive conduct. The Fourth Circuit denied enforcement but did not discuss whether the conduct in question was inherently destructive or only comparatively slight in its effect on employee rights. Nevertheless, the court treated the conduct as if its effect was comparatively slight, for it gave controlling weight to the employer's asserted business justification for its conduct.[128]

Although lockouts are treated in detail below and also in another chapter,[129] the effect of a lockout under the *Great Dane*

---

[124]223 NLRB 1317, 92 LRRM 1103 (1976), *enforcement denied,* 557 F2d 1126, 96 LRRM 2010 (CA 5, 1977). For detailed discussion of this case, *see* Chapter 22 *infra* at notes 132-37.

[125]557 F2d 1126, 1134 n.17, 96 LRRM 2010 (CA 5, 1977), *cert. denied,* 436 US 956, 98 LRRM 2617 (1978).

[126]613 F2d 450, 103 LRRM 2263 (CA 2, 1980), *denying enforcement to* 243 NLRB 79, 101 LRRM 1616 (1979).

[127]234 NLRB 802, 97 LRRM 1383 (1978).

[128]598 F2d 876, 101 LRRM 2417 (CA 4, 1979).

[129]Chapter 22 *infra,* particularly at notes 43-124, and this chapter at notes 213-34 *infra.*

test commands special attention here, especially regarding the use of temporary replacements. In the *Buffalo Linen*,[130] *Brown*,[131] and *American Ship*[132] cases, the Supreme Court expressly approved various employer uses of the lockout.

In *Evening News Ass'n*[133] the Board held, and the Sixth Circuit agreed, that two employers bargaining with the same union may lock out pursuant to a mutual-aid agreement. The Board concluded that such an action had a "bargaining purpose" and hence was not inherently destructive of employee rights. Similarly, in *Weyerhaeuser Co.*,[134] the Board held that the Act permitted an employer to lock out to support its bargaining position; and in *Darling & Co.*[135] it upheld an employer's lockout, imposed prior to impasse in negotiations, intended to force a more favorable and expeditious settlement.

In *Inland Trucking Co.*[136] and *Johns-Manville Products Corp.*,[137] however, the Board found that a lockout coupled with the use of temporary replacements was inherently destructive of Section 7 rights. In the former case, the Seventh Circuit enforced the Board's order; in the latter, the Fifth Circuit avoided deciding the issue.[138]

Subsequently, in *Ottawa Silica Co.*[139] and other cases[140] the Board limited *Inland Trucking* virtually to its facts, upholding in several instances a lockout and use of temporary replacements on the basis of proof of legitimate and substantial business justifications. But where an employer shut down its branch office and discharged its employees during contract negotiations while

---

[130]NLRB v. Teamsters Local 449 (Buffalo Linen Supply Co.), 353 US 87, 39 LRRM 2603 (1957).
[131]*Supra* note 86.
[132]*Supra* note 88.
[133]166 NLRB 219, 65 LRRM 1425 (1967), *enforced sub nom.* Teamsters Local 372 v. NLRB, 404 F2d 1159, 70 LRRM 2061 (CA 6, 1968), *cert. denied*, 395 US 923, 71 LRRM 2294 (1969).
[134]166 NLRB 299, 65 LRRM 1428 (1967).
[135]171 NLRB 801, 68 LRRM 1133 (1968), *enforced sub nom.* Lane v. NLRB, 418 F2d 1208, 72 LRRM 2439 (CA DC, 1969).
[136]179 NLRB 350, 72 LRRM 1486 (1969), *enforced*, 440 F2d 562, 76 LRRM 2929 (CA 7), *cert. denied*, 404 US 858, 78 LRRM 2465 (1971).
[137]*Supra* note 124.
[138]*Supra* notes 124 and 136.
[139]197 NLRB 449, 80 LRRM 1404 (1972), *enforced*, 482 F2d 945, 84 LRRM 2300 (CA 6, 1973), *cert. denied sub nom.* Teamsters Local 283 v. NLRB, 415 US 916, 85 LRRM 2465 (1974).
[140]*E.g., Inter-Collegiate Press, supra* note 102.

continuing to service its same customers at a different location, the Board found such conduct to be inherently destructive of employee rights and therefore violative of Section 8(a)(3).[141] Such conduct was contrasted with a situation where the employer had laid off employees during contract negotiations because it could show business exigencies and apprehension of a strike.[142]

Other instances of employer conduct which the Board has found to be inherently destructive of employees' rights include the following: (1) failure to recall any former union-represented employees at the time of resuming operations after an economic layoff;[143] (2) discharge of an employee because he had not been referred by the union's hiring hall;[144] (3) refusal to rehire an employee because he had previously served as union steward;[145] (4) refusal to honor strikers' unconditional offers to return to work where one of the objects of the strike was to obtain recognition of their union;[146] (5) requiring strikers to execute reinstatement request forms containing acknowledgments that they must renew requests within six months;[147] (6) conditioning of an individual's employment status on whether he continues to file repetitive grievances;[148] (7) discharge of a union steward who asserted his intent to be an active representative for employees;[149] (8) treating strikers who returned to work as new employees for health insurance purposes and assigning returning stri-

---

[141]Loomis Courier Serv., Inc., *supra* note 103. *See* Ethyl Corp., 231 NLRB 431, 97 LRRM 1465 (1977) (conduct tantamount to a runaway shop is "inherently destructive" conduct).

[142]Laclede Gas Co., 187 NLRB 243, 75 LRRM 1483 (1970).

[143]Rushton & Mercier Woodworking Co., 203 NLRB 123, 83 LRRM 1070 (1973), *enforced*, 86 LRRM 2151 (CA 1, 1974) (unpublished opinion).

[144]Austin & Wolfe Refrig., Air Conditioning & Heating, Inc., 202 NLRB 135, 82 LRRM 1521 (1973).

[145]Northeast Constructors, 198 NLRB 846, 81 LRRM 1140 (1972).

[146]The Barnsider, Inc., 195 NLRB 754, 79 LRRM 1587 (1972).

[147]Penn Corp., 239 NLRB 45, 99 LRRM 1661 (1978), *enforced*, 630 F2d 561, 102 LRRM 2753 (CA 8, 1979). *Cf.* Atlantic Creosoting Co., *supra* note 118.

[148]Hyster Co., 195 NLRB 84, 79 LRRM 1407 (1972), *enforced*, 83 LRRM 2091 (CA 7, 1973).

[149]Pittsburgh Press Co., 234 NLRB 408, 97 LRRM 1371 (1978). *See* Consumers Power Co., 245 NLRB 183, 102 LRRM 1500 (1979) (inherently destructive to discipline steward for administering grievance provisions of labor contract). *But cf.* NLRB v. Wilson Freight Co., *supra* note 112 (contractual clause limiting steward to act through established channels rather than unilaterally is permissible); Western Exterminator Co. v. NLRB, 565 F2d 1114, 1117, 97 LRRM 2187 (CA 9, 1977), *enforcing in part* 223 NLRB 1270, 92 LRRM 1161 (1976) (finding the *Great Dane* analysis "inappropriate" in reviewing "an isolated discharge of a single employee").

kers to less desirable shifts;[150] (9) terminating and refusing to reinstate a group of employees after unlawfully relocating a business during the term of a collective bargaining agreement.[151]

On the other hand, "discrimination based on race, color, religion, sex or national origin, standing alone, . . . is not 'inherently destructive' of employees' Section 7 rights."[152]

In a 1977 decision the Board, in *Knuth Bros., Inc.*,[153] avoided a *Great Dane* analysis where the employer refused vacation pay to replaced strikers under an established rule that accrued vacation benefits were payable only to persons on the "active payroll" on a given day. There was no basis for finding a Section 8(a)(3) violation, because there was no showing of unlawful motivation and other nonstriking terminated employees were treated in the same manner. However, the denial of benefits to strikers was a consequence of their protected activity, and the practice was therefore violative of Section 8(a)(1) as a "clear threat of economic loss to employees for engaging in protected concerted activities."[154] On appeal, the Seventh Circuit affirmed, noting that the *Great Dane* standards applicable in Section 8(a)(3) cases should apply to Section 8(a)(1) cases, since "employer conduct having the effect of disrupting Section 7 rights should not be

---

[150]Moore Business Forms, Inc., 224 NLRB 393, 93 LRRM 1437 (1976), *enforced in relevant part*, 574 F2d 835, 98 LRRM 2773 (CA 5, 1978). *See* Providence Medical Center, 243 NLRB 714, 102 LRRM 1099 (1979) (failure to reinstate strikers to substantial equivalent of prestrike jobs); Kansas City Power & Light Co., 244 NLRB 620, 102 LRRM 1177 (1979); MCC Pacific Valves, 244 NLRB 931, 102 LRRM 1183 (1979). *Cf.* Atlas Metal Parts Co., 252 NLRB 205, 105 LRRM 1582 (1980) (employer unlawfully refused to assign returning striker to second shift).

[151]Los Angeles Marine Hardware Co., *supra* note 108; *see also* Crawford Container Inc., 234 NLRB 851, 97 LRRM 1338 (1978). *Cf.* Ingersoll Rand Co., *supra* note 108, where the Board found that after lawfully relocating certain bargaining-unit work for economic reasons, an employer was not required to automatically transfer unit employees to the new location simply because it had transferred nonunit employees. The Board rejected the claim that offering to transfer, and in fact transferring, most nonunit employees without requiring them to apply for jobs, while refusing to do the same for unit employees, was inherently destructive of their §7 rights. *See also* discussion of plant closings and runaway shops at notes 235-70.

[152]Jubilee Mfg. Co., 202 NLRB 272, 82 LRRM 1482 (1973), *aff'd sub nom.* Steelworkers v. NLRB, 504 F2d 271, 87 LRRM 3168 (CA DC, 1974). *See* Chapter 6 *supra* at note 363. However, the exercise of rights under federal equal employment opportunity law is treated as protected concerted activity. Frank Briscoe v. NLRB, 637 F2d 946, 106 LRRM 2155 (CA 3, 1981).

[153]*Supra* note 96.

[154]229 NLRB at 1205.

permitted without a substantial business justification."[155] The employer's asserted business justification defense was rejected.[156]

C. Specific Conduct

1. Discharges for Union Activity. Discharge because of an employee's membership in or activities on behalf of a labor organization violates Section 8(a)(3).[157] Again, the keystone of proving a violation is determination of unlawful motive.[158]

a. Elements of an Unlawful Discharge. The essential elements of finding that a discharge violates Section 8(a)(3) are "a knowledge on the part of the employer that the employee is engaged in union activity and the actual discharge of the employee because of this activity."[159] Generally the fact of discharge will be undisputed,[160] thus leaving motivation and employer knowledge as the issues most often litigated.[161]

In establishing that a discharge violates Section 8(a)(3), the General Counsel has the initial "burden of showing that the employer had knowledge of the union activity."[162] If this burden

---

[155]584 F2d at 816. *See* NLRB v. Albion Corp., 593 F2d 936, 100 LRRM 2818 (CA 10, 1979). *Cf.* NLRB v. Teamsters Local 443 (Connecticut Limousine Serv.), 600 F2d 411, 101 LRRM 2622 (CA 2, 1979) (*Great Dane* analysis in §8(b)(2) case). *But cf.* Service Employees Local 250 v. NLRB, *supra* note 95 (*Great Dane* analysis not applicable to §8(a)(4)). The cases relied upon by the Seventh Circuit were: NLRB v. Jemco, Inc., 465 F2d 1148, 1152 n.7, 81 LRRM 2019 (CA 6, 1972), *cert. denied,* 409 US 1109, 82 LRRM 2139 (1973); Tex Tan Welhausen Co. v. NLRB, 419 F2d 1265, 1271, 72 LRRM 2885 (CA 5, 1969), *vacated on other grounds,* 397 US 819, 74 LRRM 2064, *modified on other grounds,* 434 F2d 405, 75 LRRM 2554 (CA 5, 1970), *cert. denied,* 402 US 983, 77 LRRM 2242 (1971); Allied Indus. Workers Local 289 v. NLRB, *supra* note 120. *See also* Loomis Courier Serv., Inc. v. NLRB, *supra* note 103.

[156]*See* note 96 *supra. Cf.* NLRB v. William S. Carroll, Inc., 578 F2d 1, 98 LRRM 2848 (CA 1, 1978), *denying enforcement to* 232 NLRB 1131, 97 LRRM 1037 (1977).

[157]Ogle Protection Serv., 149 NLRB 545, 57 LRRM 1337 (1964), *enforcement granted in part and denied in part,* 375 F2d 497, 64 LRRM 2792 (CA 6), *cert. denied,* 389 US 843, 66 LRRM 2308 (1967).

[158]Hambre Hombre Enterprises, Inc. v. NLRB, 581 F2d 204, 99 LRRM 2541 (CA 9, 1978).

[159]Wheeling-Pittsburgh Steel Corp. v. NLRB, 618 F2d 1009, 104 LRRM 2054 (CA 3, 1980); Sterling Aluminum Co. v. NLRB, 391 F2d 713, 67 LRRM 2686 (CA 8, 1968). In proving unlawful motive, the General Counsel must prove that the employer possessed union animus. See discussion *supra* at notes 42-83.

[160]*But see* discussion of constructive discharge at notes 170-82 *infra* for situations where the issue of discharge is disputed.

[161]The crucial determination is that of motivation. *See* NLRB v. Doug Neal Mgmt. Co., 620 F2d 1133, 104 LRRM 2045 (CA 6, 1980), *denying enforcement to* 226 NLRB 985, 94 LRRM 1254 (1976); NLRB v. Armcor Indus., 535 F2d 239, 92 LRRM 2374 (CA 3, 1976).

[162]Stone & Webster Eng'r. Corp. v. NLRB, 536 F2d 461, 92 LRRM 2904 (CA 1, 1976); *accord,* American Mfg. Assocs., Inc. v. NLRB, 594 F2d 30, 100 LRRM 2871 (CA 4, 1979); NLRB v. Computed Time Corp., 587 F2d 790, 100 LRRM 2532 (CA 5, 1979);

is satisfied, the General Counsel must then demonstrate that a discriminatory motive or unlawful intent existed.[163] Thus, "[a]bsent a showing of anti-union motivation, an employer may discharge an employee for a good reason, a bad reason, or no reason at all without running afoul of the labor laws."[164] The difficult cases arise when the employer, after the General Counsel has demonstrated that one of the motives was improper, asserts a proper business reason for the discharge. While previously the Board applied an "in part" causation test in dual-motivation cases,[165] it has now adopted *Wright-Line* two-part analysis under which the employer will prevail if the discharge would have occurred even in the absence of protected conduct.[166] In the past, from circuit to circuit and even from case to case, the actual burden imposed on the employer ranged from the "in part" test at one extreme to the "dominant motive"

Delchamps, Inc. v. NLRB, 585 F2d 91, 99 LRRM 3086 (CA 5, 1978); Independent Gravel Co. v. NLRB, 566 F2d 1091, 97 LRRM 2212 (CA 8, 1977); NLRB v. Electro Mart, 523 F2d 410, 90 LRRM 2678 (CA 9, 1975); Bayliner Marine Corp., 215 NLRB 12, 87 LRRM 1450 (1974), *petition for review dismissed sub nom.* Brook v. NLRB, 538 F2d 260, 92 LRRM 3420 (CA 9, 1976). *See* notes 185-96 *infra* for a discussion of factors which constitute circumstantial evidence of employer knowledge.

[163]NLRB v. Consolidated Diesel Elec. Co., 469 F2d 1016, 81 LRRM 2709 (CA 4, 1972); *accord,* NLRB v. Appletree Chevrolet, Inc., 608 F2d 988, 103 LRRM 2066 (CA 4, 1979); Florida Steel Corp. v. NLRB, 587 F2d 735, 100 LRRM 2451 (CA 5, 1979); District 65, Distributive Workers v. NLRB, 593 F2d 1155, 99 LRRM 2640 (CA DC, 1978); NLRB v. Pilgrim Foods, Inc., 591 F2d 110, 100 LRRM 2494 (CA 1, 1978); Sioux Quality Packers v. NLRB, *supra* note 77; Hambre Hombre Enterprises, Inc. v. NLRB, *supra* note 158; NLRB v. Cement Transp., Inc., 490 F2d 1024, 85 LRRM 2292 (CA 6), *cert. denied,* 419 US 8281, 87 LRRM 2397 (1974); Portable Elec. Tools, Inc. v. NLRB, 309 F2d 423, 51 LRRM 2330 (CA 7, 1962); NLRB v. Tepper, 297 F2d 280, 49 LRRM 2258 (CA 10, 1961). Proof of discriminatory intent is normally required to support a violation of §8(a)(3); however, "when an employer practice is inherently destructive of employee rights and is not justified by the service of important business ends, no specific evidence of intent to discourage union membership is necessary to establish a violation of §8(a)(3)." NLRB v. Brown, *supra* note 86. *See also* NLRB v. Lantz, *supra* note 104. While it has been recognized that "[t]he discharge of a large number of employees, including some union leaders, during a union organizing campaign would appear to be 'inherently destructive of employee interests' thus placing the burden on the Company of explaining away or justifying its action," NLRB v. Midwest Hanger Co., 474 F2d 1155, 82 LRRM 2693 (CA 8), *cert. denied,* 414 US 823, 84 LRRM 2421 (1973), such an analysis is apparently inappropriate "in reviewing an isolated discharge of a single employee." Western Exterminator Co. v. NLRB, *supra* note 149 at 1117.

[164]Clothing Workers v. NLRB, 564 F2d 434, 440, 95 LRRM 2821 (CA DC, 1977); *accord,* Stephenson v. NLRB, 614 F2d 1210, 103 LRRM 2238 (CA 9, 1980); Syncro Corp. v. NLRB, 597 F2d 922, 101 LRRM 2790 (CA 5, 1979); NLRB v. Knuth Bros., 537 F2d 950, 92 LRRM 3275 (CA 7, 1976); S. W. Noggle Co. v. NLRB, 478 F2d 1144, 83 LRRM 2225 (CA 8, 1973); Cannady v. NLRB, 466 F2d 583, 80 LRRM 3425 (CA 10, 1972); NLRB v. Bangor Plastics, Inc., 392 F2d 772, 67 LRRM 2987 (CA 6, 1967); Bayliner Marine Corp., *supra* note 162.

[165]*See* notes 50-60 *supra* and accompanying text.

[166]Wright Line, *supra* note 61; Herman Brothers, Inc., 252 NLRB 848, 105 LRRM 1374 (1980); United Parcel Serv., 252 NLRB 901, 105 LRRM 1484 (1980). For a discussion of initial circuit court reaction to the *Wright-Line* analysis, *see infra* at notes 511-23.

test at the other extreme.[167] It remains clear, however, that the General Counsel's burden will not be met solely by proof of union animus[168] or by proof that the discharge gave "the employer satisfaction because of the employee's union activities."[169]

b. *Constructive Discharge.* Obviously, an employee cannot claim to be a victim of discriminatory discharge unless he has been discharged. Thus, in most situations, an employee who voluntarily quits cannot contend that the separation was a discriminatory discharge in violation of Section 8(a)(3). In many cases, however, such employees have subsequently been found by the Board and the courts to have been "constructively discharged." In the *Crystal Princeton*[170] case, the Board defined "constructive discharge" as follows:

> There are two elements which must be proven to establish a "constructive discharge." First, the burden imposed upon the employee must cause, and be intended to cause, a change in his working conditions so difficult or unpleasant as to force him to resign. Second, it must be shown that those burdens were imposed because of the employee's union activities.[171]

---

[167]Chicago Magnesium Castings Co. v. NLRB, 612 F2d 1028, 103 LRRM 2241 (CA 7, 1980) ("partially motivated"); Florida Steel Corp. v. NLRB, 587 F2d 735, 742, 100 LRRM 2451 (CA 5, 1979) ("motivating" cause); NLRB v. Aero Corp., 581 F2d 511, 514-15, 99 LRRM 2800 (CA 5, 1978) ("reasonably equal"); Edgewood Nursing Center, Inc. v. NLRB, 581 F2d 363, 368, 99 LRRM 2036 (CA 3, 1978) ("partly motivated"); P.S.C. Resources, Inc. v. NLRB, 576 F2d 380, 383, 98 LRRM 2432 (CA 1, 1978) ("but for"); M.S.P. Indus., Inc. v. NLRB, 568 F2d 166, 174, 97 LRRM 2403 (CA 10, 1977) ("motivating in whole or part"); Western Exterminator Co. v. NLRB, 565 F2d 1114, 1118, 97 LRRM 2187 (CA 9, 1977) ("moving cause" or "dominant" motive); Allen v. NLRB, 561 F2d 976, 982, 95 LRRM 3158 (CA DC, 1977) ("partially motivated"); Neptune Water Meter Co. v. NLRB, *supra* note 50 ("only a factor"); Trustees of Boston Univ. v. NLRB, 548 F2d 391, 393, 94 LRRM 2500 (CA 1, 1977) ("real reason"); Northern Petrochem. Co. v. NLRB, 469 F2d 352, 355, 81 LRRM 2739 (CA 8, 1972) ("motivating basis" of refusal to hire); NLRB v. Gentithes, *supra* note 50 ("substantial or motivating cause"); NLRB v. Ayer Lar Sanitarium, 436 F2d 45, 50, 76 LRRM 2224 (CA 9, 1970) ("partially motivated," "moving cause," or "but for"); NLRB v. Swan Super Cleaners, Inc., 384 F2d 609, 614, 66 LRRM 2385 (CA 6, 1967) ("some part" discriminatory); J. P. Stevens & Co. v. NLRB, 380 F2d 292, 300, 65 LRRM 2829 (CA 2), *cert. denied,* 389 US 1005, 66 LRRM 2728 (1967) ("motivated only in part"); Wonder State Mfg. Co. v. NLRB, 331 F2d 737, 740, 55 LRRM 2814 (CA 6, 1964) ("real reason"). *See also* note 50 *supra.*

[168]*E.g.,* Delco-Remy Div., GM Corp. v. NLRB, 596 F2d 1295, 101 LRRM 2740 (CA 5, 1979); Florida Steel Corp. v. NLRB, *supra* note 167; Midwest Regional Joint Bd., Clothing Workers v. NLRB, 564 F2d 434, 440, 95 LRRM 2821 (CA DC, 1977); NLRB v. Bangor Plastics, Inc., 392 F2d 772, 777, 67 LRRM 2987 (CA 6, 1967).

[169]NLRB v. Fibers Int'l. Corp., *supra* note 50; NLRB v. Wilson Freight Co., *supra* note 111; NLRB v. Lowell Sun Publishing Co., 320 F2d 835, 842, 53 LRRM 2480 (CA 1, 1963) (concurring opinion).

[170]Crystal Princeton Ref. Co., 222 NLRB 1068, 91 LRRM 1302 (1976).

[171]*Id.* at 1069. *Accord,* Cartwright Hardware Co. v. NLRB, 600 F2d 268, 101 LRRM 2652 (CA 10, 1979), *denying enforcement in part to* 229 NLRB 781, 95 LRRM 1262 (1977); J. P. Stevens & Co. v. NLRB, 461 F2d 490, 80 LRRM 2609 (CA 4, 1972), and cases cited therein at 494.

The above criteria were satisfied when the employee had suffered a cut in pay,[172] had been assigned more onerous working conditions,[173] or had been transferred to a less desirable job.[174] Constructive discharge may also be found when an employee receives numerous warnings,[175] is denied a pay increase,[176] or is threatened with physical harm.[177] Employees who refuse to return to work after a strike to avoid unlawful discipline,[178] who quit in the face of employer harassment for union activity,[179] or who quit as a result of reduction in work hours[180] have also been found to have been constructively discharged.

Constructive discharge may also occur when the employer unlawfully withdraws recognition of the union and imposes unlawful terms and conditions of employment on its employees.[181] For proof in determining whether the employee was

---

[172]222 NLRB at 494-95. *See also* NLRB v. Tricor Prods., Inc., 636 F2d 266, 105 LRRM 3271 (CA 10, 1980); B. N. Beard Co., 248 NLRB 198, 103 LRRM 1560 (1980); Central Dispatch, Inc., 229 NLRB 979, 96 LRRM 1483 (1977).

[173]*Compare* East Bay Properties, 232 NLRB 670, 96 LRRM 1342 (1977), and Pre-Cast Mfg. Co., 200 NLRB 135, 82 LRRM 1325 (1972), *with* Monon Trailer, Inc., 217 NLRB 257, 89 LRRM 1280 (1975), Gerbes Super Mkt., Inc., 217 NLRB 394, 89 LRRM 1160 (1975), *and* NLRB v. J. W. Mortell Co., 440 F2d 455, 76 LRRM 2489 (CA 7, 1971).

[174]Production Plated Plastics, 247 NLRB 595, 103 LRRM 1228 (1980). *See* Production Stamping, Inc., 239 NLRB 1183, 100 LRRM 1141 (1979); Dumas Bros. Mfg., 205 NLRB 919, 84 LRRM 1411 (1973), *enforced*, 495 F2d 1371, 87 LRRM 2127 (CA 5, 1974); Razco, Inc., 231 NLRB 660, 97 LRRM 1561 (1977). *See also* Sullivan Transfer Co., 248 NLRB 909, 103 LRRM 1369 (1980) (reduction in work hours constituting constructive discharge); Coating Prods., 251 NLRB 1271, 105 LRRM 1399 (1980); Maywood, Inc., 251 NLRB 979, 105 LRRM 1577 (1980). *But see* Dillingham Marine & Mfg. Co., 239 NLRB 904, 100 LRRM 1109 (1978) (refusal to allow employee to change shifts not constructive discharge); KDEN Broadcasting Co., Subsidiary, North Am. Broadcasting Co., 225 NLRB 25, 93 LRRM 1022 (1976) (change in employee hours not constructive discharge); Coliseum Hosp., Inc., 202 NLRB 927, 82 LRRM 1802 (1973) (reduction in employee hours not constructive discharge); H.A. Kuhle Co., 205 NLRB 88, 84 LRRM 1147 (1973) (assigning additional duties not constructive discharge).

[175]*Compare* W. T. Grant Co., 195 NLRB 1000, 79 LRRM 1670 (1972), *with* P. E. Van Pelt, Inc., 238 NLRB 794, 99 LRRM 1576 (1978), *and* Central Casket Co., 225 NLRB 362, 92 LRRM 1547 (1976).

[176]*Compare* Mallory Capacitor Co., 169 NLRB 42, 67 LRRM 1122, *enforced*, 400 F2d 956, 69 LRRM 2448 (CA 7, 1968), *with* Tahoe Mgmt. & Leasing Co., 222 NLRB 394, 91 LRRM 1212 (1976), *and* Western Boot & Shoe, Inc., 205 NLRB 999, 84 LRRM 1140 (1973).

[177]Mishan & Sons, 242 NLRB No. 147, 101 LRRM 1344 (1979); S & K Elec., Inc., 226 NLRB 442, 93 LRRM 1303 (1976).

[178]Charge Card Ass'n, 247 NLRB 835, 103 LRRM 1298 (1980).

[179]Galax Apparel Corp., 247 NLRB 159, 103 LRRM 1143 (1980).

[180]Sullivan Transfer Co., *supra* note 174.

[181]*Compare* Crawford Door Sales Co., 226 NLRB 1144, 94 LRRM 1393 (1976), *and* Marquis Elevator Co., 217 NLRB 461, 89 LRRM 1520 (1975), *with* Cartwright Hardware Co. v. NLRB, *supra* note 171 (denying enforcement to Board order on this issue). *See also* Western Pacific Roofing Corp., 244 NLRB 501, 102 LRRM 1220 (1979); Superior Sprinkler, Inc., 227 NLRB 204, 94 LRRM 1253 (1976), for a detailed analysis of the law on this issue.

constructively discharged, the Board often relies upon employer statements made during[182] or subsequent to[183] termination.

c. Knowledge of Employee's Union Activity. In most cases, in order to prove that a particular discharge was discriminatorily motivated, it must be established that the employer had knowledge prior to the discharge of the discharged employee's union activities.[184] Both the Board and the courts recognize that a finding of knowledge can be based upon inferences drawn from circumstantial evidence; however, such inference must not be entirely speculative or improbable.[185] Knowledge is often inferred when the discharged employee has engaged in overt union activities, such as soliciting signatures on union authorization cards,[186]

---

[182]*Compare* Pre-Cast Mfg. Co., *supra* note 173, *with* Hoke Janitorial Serv., 213 NLRB 783, 87 LRRM 1754 (1974). *See also* Smyth Mfg. Co., 247 NLRB 1139, 103 LRRM 1432 (1980).

[183]*Compare* Sycor, Inc., 223 NLRB 1091, 92 LRRM 1188 (1976), *with* Breuer Elec. Mfg. Co., 184 NLRB 190, 76 LRRM 1429 (1970).

[184]Tri-State Truck Serv. v. NLRB, 616 F2d 65, 103 LRRM 2640 (CA 3, 1980); *see* notes 78-80 *supra*. In one limited situation, however, the employee who is discharged need not be the one whose union activity the employer sought to discourage. It is unlawful under §8(a)(3) for an employer to discharge "a nonunion employee to 'cover up' and confer an aura of plausibility upon his alleged 'economic justification' for the simultaneous discharge of an unwanted union activist . . . since such a discharge . . . interferes with, restrains, and coerces all of the employees in the exercise of rights under Section 7 of the Act." Jack August Enterprises, Inc., 232 NLRB 881, 900, 97 LRRM 1560 (1977), *enforced*, 583 F2d 575, 99 LRRM 2582 (CA 1, 1978); *accord*, NLRB v. Dorn's Transp. Corp., 405 F2d 706, 70 LRRM 2295 (CA 2, 1969); NLRB v. Ambrose Distrib. Co., 358 F2d 319, 61 LRRM 2575 (CA 9, 1966); NLRB v. Superex Drugs, Inc., 341 F2d 747, 58 LRRM 2455 (CA 6, 1965); NLRB v. Williams Lumber Co., 195 F2d 669, 29 LRRM 2633 (CA 4, 1952); Looney Sheet Metal Constr. Co., 160 NLRB 1635, 63 LRRM 1211 (1966); *cf.* Majestic Molded Prods., Inc., 330 F2d 603, 606, 55 LRRM 2816 (CA 2, 1964) (mass layoff constitutes §8(a)(3) violation when significant unlawful motive exists "even if some white sheep suffer along with the black"). *See also* Dillingham Marine & Mfg. Co. v. NLRB, 610 F2d 319, 103 LRRM 2430 (CA 5, 1980), where it was held not necessary to show specific knowledge of union activity of each individual employee.

[185]NLRB v. Fort Vancouver Plywood Co., 604 F2d 596, 102 LRRM 2232 (CA 9, 1979), *cert. denied*, 103 LRRM 2668 (1980) (knowledge found); Delchamps, Inc. v. NLRB, *supra* note 162 (no knowledge found); Teamsters Local 633 v. NLRB, 509 F2d 490, 88 LRRM 2072 (CA DC, 1974) (knowledge found); NLRB v. Armitage Sand & Gravel, Inc., 495 F2d 759, 86 LRRM 2245 (CA 6, 1974) (no knowledge found); Famet, Inc. v. NLRB, *supra* note 55 (knowledge found); NLRB v. Long Island Airport Limousine Serv. Corp., 468 F2d 292, 81 LRRM 2445 (CA 2, 1972) (knowledge found); Von Solbrig Hosp., Inc., 465 F2d 173, 80 LRRM 3079 (CA 7, 1972) (knowledge found); General Mercantile & Hardware Co. v. NLRB, 461 F2d 952, 80 LRRM 2622 (CA 8, 1972) (no knowledge found); NLRB v. Gentithes, *supra* note 50 (knowledge found); Winn-Dixie Stores, Inc. v. NLRB, 448 F2d 8, 78 LRRM 2375 (CA 4, 1971) (no knowledge found); Morgan Precision Parts v. NLRB, 444 F2d 1210, 77 LRRM 2870 (CA 5, 1971) (knowledge found); Texas Aluminum Co. v. NLRB, 435 F2d 917, 76 LRRM 2151 (CA 5, 1970) (knowledge found).

[186]Lizdale Knitting Mills, Inc., 211 NLRB 966, 86 LRRM 1465 (1974), *enforced*, 523 F2d 978, 90 LRRM 3341 (CA 2, 1975); Successful Creations, Inc., 202 NLRB 242, 82 LRRM 1505 (1973).

wearing union buttons or other insignia,[187] or participating in a strike.[188] Knowledge has also been inferred where the discharged employee was the instigator of the union activity[189] or where the employer learned of the employee's union activities through interrogation[190] or surveillance.[191] If the General Counsel fails to demonstrate that the employer had knowledge of the discharged employee's union activities, no violation will be found.[192]

As previously noted, the Board often infers employer knowledge of employee union activities from the small size of the employer's plant or operation.[193] However, in *Hadley Manufacturing Corp.*, the NLRB stated that "the mere fact that

[the employer's] plant is of a small size, does not permit a finding that [the employer] had knowledge of the union activities of specific employees, absent supporting evidence that the union activities were carried on in such a manner, or at times that in the normal course of events, [the employer] must have noticed them.[194]

Thus, where the discharged employee engages in no union activity on the employer's premises, regardless of the size of the plant, the Board will usually not infer that the employer possesses knowledge of the discharged employee's union activities.[195] While the courts have accepted the *small plant doctrine*,

---

[187]Coca-Cola Bottling Co. Consol., 226 NLRB 894, 93 LRRM 1383 (1976); Wintex Knitting Mills, Inc., 216 NLRB 1058, 88 LRRM 1566 (1975); Ramada Inns, Inc., 201 NLRB 431, 82 LRRM 1253 (1973).
[188]Hembree v. Georgia Power Co., 637 F2d 423, 106 LRRM 2535 (CA 5, 1981); J. P. Stevens & Co., 247 NLRB 420, 103 LRRM 1187 (1980); Transportation Enterprises, Inc., 240 NLRB 555, 100 LRRM 1330 (1979).
[189]International Baking Co., 245 NLRB 220, 102 LRRM 1277 (1979); Nebraska Bulk Transp., Inc., 240 NLRB 135, 100 LRRM 1340 (1979); Summer Hill Nursing Home, 222 NLRB 433, 91 LRRM 1316 (1976).
[190]Springfield Dodge, Inc., 218 NLRB 1429, 89 LRRM 1736 (1975); Pyro Mining Co., 204 NLRB 607, 83 LRRM 1709 (1973).
[191]Florida Steel Corp., 214 NLRB 264, 88 LRRM 1263 (1974), *enforced in pertinent part*, 551 F2d 306, 94 LRRM 2589 (CA 4, 1977).
[192]Kantor Pepsi-Cola Bottling Co., 248 NLRB 99, 103 LRRM 1388 (1980); Leyendecker Paving, Inc., *supra* note 78; Proler Int'l Corp., 242 NLRB 676, 101 LRRM 1274 (1979); Siltec Corp., 217 NLRB 282, 89 LRRM 1514 (1975); Bayliner Marine Corp., *supra* note 162; Steel-Tex Mfg. Corp., 206 NLRB 461, 84 LRRM 1384 (1973).
[193]Permanent Label Corp., *supra* note 80; Nebraska Bulk Transp., Inc., *supra* note 189; Wiese Plow Welding Co., 123 NLRB 616, 43 LRRM 1495 (1959). *See supra* at note 80.
[194]108 NLRB 1641, 1659, 34 LRRM 1246 (1954). *See also* Coral Gables Convalescent Home, Inc., *supra* note 80; Friendly Mkts., Inc., 224 NLRB 967, 92 LRRM 1584 (1976).
[195]Mantac Corp., 231 NLRB 858, 97 LRRM 1017 (1977); Picker Corp., 222 NLRB 296, 91 LRRM 1315 (1976). *But see* K & B Mounting, Inc., 248 NLRB 570, 103 LRRM 1541 (1980); B. N. Beard Co., *supra* note 172 (small plant doctrine inappropriate where employees successfully kept union activity secret). *See supra* at note 80.

they have disagreed on its application in various factual situations.[196]

d. Pretext. In defending against allegations of discriminatory discharge, employers often assert facially nondiscriminatory reasons for the termination. Such a claim may be rebutted with proof that the alleged justification is *pretextual* and that the real reason is the employer's union animus.[197]

(1) Timing. When an employee is discharged shortly after engaging in union activity, the Board often infers that the employer's asserted justifications are pretexts and that the discharge was discriminatorily motivated.[198] The courts agree that timing is an important factor in assessing motivation.[199] Nevertheless, the timing of a discharge is only one factor; while it may make a discharge "suspicious," the discharge may be held lawful if other factors indicate that it was properly motivated.[200] Fur-

---

[196]Webco Bodies, Inc. v. NLRB, 595 F2d 451, 101 LRRM 2041 (CA 8, 1979); Teamsters Local 633 v. NLRB, *supra* note 185; Famet, Inc. v. NLRB, *supra* note 55; Hackett Precision Co. v. NLRB, 459 F2d 463, 79 LRRM 3025 (CA 6, 1972); NLRB v. Sutherland Lumber Co., 452 F2d 67, 78 LRRM 2772 (CA 7, 1971); NLRB v. Meinholdt Mfg., Inc., 451 F2d 737, 78 LRRM 2892 (CA 10, 1971); NLRB v. Century Broadcasting Corp., 419 F2d 771, 72 LRRM 2905 (CA 8, 1969); NLRB v. Mid States Sportswear, Inc., 412 F2d 537, 71 LRRM 2370 (CA 5, 1969); NLRB v. Pembek Oil Corp., 404 F2d 105, 69 LRRM 2811 (CA 2, 1968); Dubin-Haskell Lining Corp. v. NLRB, 375 F2d 568, 64 LRRM 2757 (CA 4, 1967), *cert. denied*, 393 US 824, 69 LRRM 2434 (1968); NLRB v. Joseph Antell, Inc., 358 F2d 880, 62 LRRM 2014 (CA 1, 1966); NLRB v. Dove Coal Co., 369 F2d 849, 63 LRRM 2561 (CA 4, 1966).

[197]*See* discussion of burden of proof at note 49 *supra*. *See also* Appletree Chevrolet, Inc., *supra* note 163, where the Court reversed the Board because the Board failed to "find and identify 'an affirmative and persuasive reason why the employer rejected the good cause and chose a bad one.'"

[198]Atlanta Blue Prints & Graphics Co., 244 NLRB 634, 102 LRRM 1242 (1979); Haddon House, 242 NLRB 1057, 101 LRRM 1294 (1979); Big "G" Corp., 223 NLRB 1349, 92 LRRM 1127 (1976); Weather-Shield Corp., 222 NLRB 1171, 91 LRRM 1478 (1976); M Restaurants, Inc., 221 NLRB 264, 90 LRRM 1494 (1975).

[199]Jim Causley Pontiac v. NLRB, 620 F2d 122, 104 LRRM 2190, 2193 (CA 6, 1980); NLRB v. Warren L. Rose Castings, Inc., 587 F2d 1005, 100 LRRM 2303 (CA 9, 1978); NLRB v. Florida Tile Co., *supra* note 60; NLRB v. Fremont Mfg. Co., *supra* note 60; NLRB v. Stark, 525 F2d 422, 90 LRRM 3076 (CA 2, 1975), *cert. denied*, 424 US 967, 91 LRRM 2749 (1976); NLRB v. Ri-Del Tool Mfg. Co., 486 F2d 1406, 84 LRRM 2630 (CA 7, 1973); NLRB v. Armstrong Circuit, Inc., 462 F2d 355, 80 LRRM 2897 (CA 6, 1972); NLRB v. Treasure Lake, Inc., 453 F2d 202, 79 LRRM 2085 (CA 3, 1971); NLRB v. Central Power & Light Co., 425 F2d 1318, 74 LRRM 2269 (CA 5, 1970); Retail Clerks Local 880 v. NLRB, 419 F2d 329, 71 LRRM 2935 (CA DC, 1969); NLRB v. Automotive Controls Corp., 406 F2d 221, 70 LRRM 2309 (CA 10, 1969); NLRB v. Virginia Metalcrafters, Inc., 387 F2d 379, 67 LRRM 2139 (CA 4, 1967); NLRB v. Somerville Buick, Inc., 194 F2d 56, 29 LRRM 2379 (CA 1, 1952).

[200]Liberty Mutual Ins. Co. v. NLRB, 592 F2d 595, 100 LRRM 2660 (CA 1, 1979); NLRB v. South Shore Hosp., *supra* note 51; Penasquitos Village, Inc. v. NLRB, 565 F2d 1074, 97 LRRM 2244 (CA 9, 1977); General Mercantile & Hardware Co. v. NLRB, *supra* note 185; Amyx Indus., Inc. v. NLRB, 457 F2d 904, 79 LRRM 2930 (CA 8, 1972); Thermo King Corp., 247 NLRB 296, 103 LRRM 1204 (1980); Triana Indus., 245

thermore, when the discharge occurs long after the employee has engaged in union activity, such passage of time has been relied upon to establish that the discharge was nondiscriminatorily motivated.[201]

(2) Other factors. One justification for discharge commonly asserted by employers is dissatisfaction with the employee's work. If, however, there is evidence that the employer gave the employee a recent wage increase, a promotion, or a good evaluation, the Board and the courts will often find the alleged dissatisfaction to be a pretext.[202] On the other hand, when an employee is discharged for a single significant incident rather than for a negative evaluation of his overall work performance, the fact that he received an increase for satisfactory or meritorious work performance may have little impact on the employer's motive for the discharge.[203]

A variety of factors have been relied upon to determine whether an asserted justification is in reality a pretext.[204] Thus "[a] failure to investigate the incidents upon which the employer relied as grounds for discharge may reflect an employer's discriminatory

---

NLRB 1258, 102 LRRM 1323 (1979); Salvo Golden Foods, Inc., 238 NLRB 683, 99 LRRM 1616 (1978); Lassel Jr. College, 230 NLRB 1076, 95 LRRM 1601 (1977); Kings Terrace Nursing Home, 229 NLRB 1180, 95 LRRM 1602 (1977); Philo Lumber Co., 229 NLRB 210, 95 LRRM 1315 (1977); Group One Broadcasting Co., West, 222 NLRB 993, 91 LRRM 1345 (1976).

[201]Maine Medical Center, 248 NLRB 707, 104 LRRM 1031 (1980). NLRB v. Florida Medical Center, Inc., 576 F2d 666, 98 LRRM 3144 (CA 5, 1978); NLRB v. Consolidated Diesel Elec. Co., *supra* note 163; Maine Medical Center, *supra* this note; Rockland-Bamberg Print Works, Inc., 231 NLRB 305, 96 LRRM 1237 (1977); Metzger Mach. & Eng'r Co., 209 NLRB 905, 86 LRRM 1299 (1973); Murray Ohio Mfg. Co., 207 NLRB 481, 84 LRRM 1498 (1973); Civic Center Sports, Inc., 206 NLRB 428, 84 LRRM 1637 (1973).

[202]*E.g.*, NLRB v. Jack August Enterprises, Inc., *supra* note 184; Florida Steel Corp. v. NLRB, 529 F2d 1225, 92 LRRM 2040 (CA 5, 1976); NLRB v. Ri-Del Tool Mfg. Co., *supra* note 199; NLRB v. Evans Packing Co., 463 F2d 193, 80 LRRM 2810 (CA 6, 1972); NLRB v. George T. Roberts & Sons, Inc., 451 F2d 941, 78 LRRM 2874 (CA 2, 1971); Sweeney & Co. v. NLRB, 437 F2d 1127, 76 LRRM 2321 (CA 5, 1971), *modifying on other grounds* 176 NLRB 208, 71 LRRM 1197 (1969); NLRB v. Coast Delivery Serv., Inc., 437 F2d 264, 76 LRRM 2450 (CA 9, 1971); NLRB v. S.E. Nichols-Dover, Inc., 414 F2d 561, 71 LRRM 3149 (CA 3, 1969); Meat Cutters Local 347 v. NLRB, 413 F2d 407, 71 LRRM 3004 (CA DC, 1969); Ames Ready-Mix Concrete, Inc. v. NLRB, 411 F2d 1159, 71 LRRM 2411 (CA 8, 1969); NLRB v. Winn-Dixie Greenville, Inc., 379 F2d 958, 65 LRRM 2742 (CA 4), *cert. denied*, 389 US 952, 66 LRRM 2507 (1967); NLRB v. Lively Serv. Co., 290 F2d 205, 48 LRRM 2023 (CA 10, 1961). *But see* NLRB v. Consolidated Diesel Elec. Co., *supra* note 163; J. P. Stevens, *supra* note 188; Green Giant Co., 223 NLRB 377, 91 LRRM 1468 (1976).

[203]Concrete Technology, Inc., 224 NLRB 961, 965, 93 LRRM 1282 (1976); *see also* Berbigilia, Inc. v. NLRB, 602 F2d 839, 101 LRRM 3139 (CA 8, 1979).

[204]NLRB v. Gogin, 575 F2d 596, 98 LRRM 2250 (CA 7, 1978); *see also* KBM Elec., Inc., 218 NLRB 1352, 89 LRRM 1728 (1975), for discussion of many of the factors considered by the Board in assessing pretext.

motive."[205] Discharges undertaken without prior warnings as to
the seriousness of the conduct are also suspect.[206] Similarly,
changes in the employer's reasons, assertion of inconsistent or
false reasons, or failure to inform the employee of the reason
for the discharge may be significant factors in finding the
employer's actual motive to be discriminatory.[207] The converse
is also true: The presence of specific warnings for specific conduct may suggest that a subsequent discharge based upon similar conduct is not discriminatorily motivated.[208]

The existence of good reasons for a discharge may not always
justify the discharge. Discriminatory motive will often be inferred
when the employer has long tolerated similar conduct or has
condoned conduct upon which the discharge is based.[209] The

---

[205]W. W. Grainger, Inc. v. NLRB, 582 F2d 1118, 99 LRRM 2375 (CA 7, 1978); *accord*,
Marsden Elec. Co., 226 NLRB 1097, 94 LRRM 1176 (1976), *enforced*, 586 F2d 8, 100
LRRM 2314 (CA 6, 1978); NLRB v. Ayer Lar Sanitarium, *supra* note 54; NLRB v.
Aerovox Corp., 435 F2d 1208, 76 LRRM 2042 (CA 4, 1970); Clark Manor Nursing
Home, 254 NLRB 455, 106 LRRM 1231 (1981); Levingston Shipbuilding Co., 249
NLRB No. 1, 104 LRRM 1058 (1980); Tendico, Inc., 232 NLRB 735, 97 LRRM 1107
(1977).
[206]*E.g.*, NLRB v. Warren L. Rose Casting, Inc., *supra* note 199; Sweeney & Co. v.
NLRB, *supra* note 202; NLRB v. Midtown Serv. Co., 425 F2d 665, 73 LRRM 2634 (CA
2, 1970); NLRB v. Glenn Berry Mfrs., Inc., 422 F2d 748, 73 LRRM 2301 (CA 10, 1970);
NLRB v. Kay Elec., Inc., 410 F2d 499, 71 LRRM 2106 (CA 8, 1969); NLRB v. Virginia
Metalcrafters, Inc., *supra* note 199; NLRB v. Challenge-Cook Bros., 374 F2d 147, 64
LRRM 2481 (CA 6, 1967); Lockwoven Co., 245 NLRB 1362, 102 LRRM 1533 (1979);
Akron Gen. Medical Center, 232 NLRB 920, 97 LRRM 1510 (1977); River Manor
Health Related Facility, 224 NLRB 227, 93 LRRM 1069 (1976), *enforced*, 95 LRRM 3011
(CA 2, 1977) (unpublished); Chart House, Inc., 223 NLRB 100, 92 LRRM 1155 (1976).
But see Penasquitos Village, Inc. v. NLRB, *supra* note 200 (absence of prior warnings
not sufficient to establish discriminatory motive). Also, the absence of warnings may not
be significant if the offense is so serious that immediate discharge is warranted. Edgewood Nursing Center v. NLRB, *supra* note 57.
[207]NLRB v. Warren L. Rose Castings, Inc., *supra* note 199; A. J. Krajewski Mfg. Co.
v. NLRB, 413 F2d 673, 71 LRRM 2954 (CA 1, 1969); NLRB v. Mid States Sportswear,
Inc., *supra* note 196; Sterling Aluminum Co. v. NLRB, *supra* note 159; NLRB v. Milco,
Inc., 388 F2d 133, 67 LRRM 2202 (CA 2, 1968); NLRB v. Richard W. Kaase Co., 346
F2d 24, 59 LRRM 2290 (CA 6, 1965); Hercules Bumpers, 248 NLRB 1047, 104 LRRM
1056 (1980); St. Anne's Hosp., 245 NLRB 1009, 102 LRRM 1527 (1979); Martin Luther
King, Sr., Nursing Center, 231 NLRB 15, 95 LRRM 1563 (1977); Big "G" Corp., *supra*
note 198. *Cf.* NLRB v. Henriksen, Inc., 481 F2d 1156, 83 LRRM 2774 (CA 5, 1973)
(failure to give reason for discharge not significant when employee is aware of reason).
[208]Butler-Johnson Corp. v. NLRB, 608 F2d 1303, 102 LRRM 3029 (CA 9, 1979);
NLRB v. Midwest Hanger Co., *supra* note 163; NLRB v. Speed Queen, 469 F2d 189,
81 LRRM 2742 (CA 8, 1972); Winn-Dixie Stores, Inc. v. NLRB, *supra* note 185; NLRB
v. Newman-Green, Inc., 401 F2d 1, 69 LRRM 2129 (CA 7, 1968); Teledyne, Inc., 246
NLRB 766, 103 LRRM 1011 (1979); Rockland-Bamberg Print Works, Inc., *supra* note
201; Loomis Armored Car Serv., Inc., 227 NLRB 256, 94 LRRM 1108 (1976); Hydra-
Tool Co., 222 NLRB 1113, 91 LRRM 1479 (1976). *Cf.* Florida Steel Corp., 223 NLRB
174, 92 LRRM 1004 (1976) (discriminatory motive found when prior warnings unrelated to conduct upon which discharge based).
[209]NLRB v. Broyhill Co., 514 F2d 655, 89 LRRM 2203 (CA 8, 1975); NLRB v.
Princeton Inn Co., 424 F2d 264, 73 LRRM 3002 (CA 3, 1970); NLRB v. Beverage-Air

Board and the courts have also found asserted nondiscriminatory reasons pretextual when the reasons are applied disparately.[210] Conversely, evidence that the conduct in question has been dealt with on a consistent basis may rebut charges of pretext[211] even where the employer was shown to be anxious to terminate the employee.[212]

2. Lockouts. The subject of lockouts is treated extensively elsewhere,[213] but inasmuch as Section 8(a)(3) questions are raised in many types of lockouts, certain leading and illustrative cases are also discussed here. It is clear "that there are circumstances in which employers may lawfully resort to the lockout as an economic weapon."[214] But it is equally clear that an employer violates Section 8(a)(3) if the lockout is purposely used to discourage union membership, and in such cases the Board will order back pay for all employees for the period of the lockout.[215] The purpose, or motive, behind the lockout is therefore the

---

Co., 402 F2d 411, 69 LRRM 2369 (CA 4, 1968); NLRB v. Challenge-Cook Bros., *supra* note 206; NLRB v. Elias Bros. Big Boy, 325 F2d 360, 54 LRRM 2733 (CA 6, 1963); McCauley Assocs., 248 NLRB 346, 103 LRRM 1439 (1980); Penn Indus., Inc., 233 NLRB 928, 97 LRRM 1299 (1977); Han-Dee Pak, Inc., 232 NLRB 454, 97 LRRM 1054 (1977); Byrd's Terrazzo & Tile Co., 227 NLRB 866, 94 LRRM 1412 (1977); Sibilio's Golden Grill, Inc., 227 NLRB 1688, 94 LRRM 1439 (1977), *enforced*, 99 LRRM 2633 (CA 3, 1978). The classic case on this point is Edward G. Budd Mfg. Co. v. NLRB, 138 F2d 86, 13 LRRM 512, 564 (CA 3, 1943). *But cf.* NLRB v. Threads, Inc., 308 F2d 1, 2, 51 LRRM 2074 (CA 4, 1962) (no violation where the "prior misconduct . . . was tolerated under circumstances which negate any idea that the employer was searching for some false reasons to discharge the employee on account of his union activities").

[210]NLRB v. Inland Empire Meat Co., 611 F2d 1235, 103 LRRM 2746 (CA 9, 1979); Head Division, AMF, Inc. v. NLRB, 593 F2d 972, 100 LRRM 3035 (CA 10, 1979); D'Youville Manor Nursing Home v. NLRB, 526 F2d 3, 90 LRRM 3100 (CA 1, 1975); NLRB v. Long Island Airport Limousine Serv. Corp., *supra* note 185; NLRB v. Shepherd Laundries Co., 440 F2d 856, 76 LRRM 3080 (CA 5, 1971); NLRB v. Aerovox Corp., *supra* note 205; Electrical Workers (IUE) v. NLRB, 418 F2d 1191, 71 LRRM 2991 (CA DC, 1969); NLRB v. S. E. Nichols Dover, Inc., *supra* note 202; NLRB v. Lone Star Textiles, Inc., 386 F2d 535, 67 LRRM 2221 (CA 5, 1967); Aeronco Mfg. Co. v. NLRB, 385 F2d 724, 66 LRRM 2574 (CA 9, 1967); NLRB v. American Casting Serv., Inc., 365 F2d 168, 62 LRRM 2539 (CA 7, 1966); A. P. Green Fire Brick Co. v. NLRB, 326 F2d 910, 55 LRRM 2236 (CA 8, 1964); Ferland Mgmt. Co., 233 NLRB 467, 97 LRRM 1530 (1977); Tendico, Inc., *supra* note 205; Mikami Bros., 188 NLRB 522, 76 LRRM 1425 (1971).

[211]Firestone Tire & Rubber Co. v. NLRB, *supra* note 59; NLRB v. Whitfield Pickle Co., 374 F2d 576, 64 LRRM 2656 (CA 5, 1967); Frank Briscoe, Inc., 247 NLRB 13, 103 LRRM 1110 (1980). Rockland-Bamberg Print Works, Inc., *supra* note 201; Clear Lake Hosp., 223 NLRB 1, 91 LRRM 1450 (1976).

[212]Nacker Packing Co. v. NLRB, 615 F2d 456, 103 LRRM 2634 (CA 7, 1980); Petroleum Transp. Co., 236 NLRB 254, 98 LRRM 1484 (1978).

[213]*See* Chapter 22 *infra. See also* notes 129-42 *supra* and accompanying text.

[214]NLRB v. Teamsters Local 449 (Buffalo Linen Supply Co.), *supra* note 130 at 39. *See* American Ship Building Co. v. NLRB, *supra* note 88.

[215]*See, e.g.,* Loomis Courier Serv., Inc. v. NLRB, *supra* note 103; Shelly & Anderson Furniture Mfg. Co. v. NLRB, 497 F2d 1200, 86 LRRM 2619 (CA 9, 1974); NLRB v. Savoy Laundry, Inc., 327 F2d 370, 55 LRRM 2285 (CA 2, 1964); NLRB v. Somerset Shoe Co., 111 F2d 681, 6 LRRM 709 (CA 1, 1940).

critical factor in determining whether the lockout violates the Act. Ordinarily, "to find a violation of Section 8(a)(3), the Board must find that the employer acted for a proscribed purpose."[216]

Legal lockouts are often characterized as either defensive or offensive in nature. The defensive lockout was traditionally used to protect employers' legitimate business interests which might be jeopardized by union activity. For example, in *NLRB* v. *Teamsters Local 449 (Buffalo Linen)*,[217] the union engaged in a whipsaw strike against a multi-employer bargaining unit. As a defense, the nonstruck employers temporarily locked out their employees. The Board found the lockout to be "defensive and privileged in nature, rather than retaliatory and [thus] lawful."[218] The Second Circuit reversed,[219] but the Supreme Court sustained the Board, concluding that "the preservation of the integrity of the multi-employer bargaining unit"[220] provided justification for the lockout. The Court further concluded that the Act's protection for employees "is not so absolute as to deny self-help by employers when legitimate interests of employees and employers collide."[221]

The Board has also held that in circumstances where union activity would cause inordinate harm, a defensive lockout is in the legitimate interest of the employer and is lawful. Thus, an employer could shut down an entire plant in response to "quickie" strikes in certain departments[222] or lock out employees in response to a threatened sitdown strike.[223] Where a strike would have stranded many customers' unassembled automobiles in a shop, the Board found the lockout lawful.[224] More difficult to determine was the question of whether a threatened strike would in fact cause such inordinate harm as to justify a defensive lockout. The Supreme Court's subsequent approval of the broader offensive lockout in *American Ship Building Co.* v. *NLRB*,[225] however, largely mooted this issue.[226]

---

[216]American Ship Bldg. Co. v. NLRB, *supra* note 88.
[217]*Supra* note 130.
[218]*Id.* at 91.
[219]231 F2d 110, 37 LRRM 2546 (CA 2, 1956).
[220]353 US at 93.
[221]*Id.*
[222]International Shoe Co., 93 NLRB 907, 27 LRRM 1504 (1951).
[223]Link Belt Co., 26 NLRB 227, 6 LRRM 565 (1940).
[224]Betts Cadillac Olds., Inc., 96 NLRB 268, 28 LRRM 1509 (1951).
[225]American Ship Bldg. Co. v. NLRB, *supra* note 88.
[226]In Darling & Co., *supra* note 135, the Board recognized that the distinction between offensive and defensive strikes had become largely "obliterated."

In *American Ship Building,* the employer, whose business was largely concentrated in the winter months, locked out its employees during the course of contract negotiations after impasse had been reached. The purpose of the lockout was to bring about a favorable contract settlement. A new contract was subsequently signed, and all employees were recalled to work. The Board rejected the trial examiner's conclusion that the layoff was justified as a defensive lockout and held that it violated Section 8(a)(3).[227] The Court of Appeals for the District of Columbia agreed.[228] But the Supreme Court reversed, observing that after impasse has been reached an employer does not commit an unfair labor practice by locking out employees "for the sole purpose of bringing economic pressure to bear in support of his legitimate bargaining position."[229] The Court noted that the union did not have the exclusive right to time the cessation of work; consequently, the employer had not preempted the union's right to strike under Section 13. The Court further observed that the employer's action was not designed to frustrate collective bargaining and that evidence of specific discrimination against union members had not been shown. In the absence of unlawful intent, "[t]he purpose and effect of the lockout was only to bring pressure upon the union to modify its demands," and the "arguable possibility that someone . . . [might] feel himself discouraged in his membership" did not establish a violation of Section 8(a)(3).[230]

Replacement of locked-out workers may be unlawful even when the lockout itself is not. In *NLRB v. Brown,*[231] the Supreme Court held that an employer who locks out employees in response to a whipsaw strike may hire temporary replacements. The

---

[227]142 NLRB 1362, 53 LRRM 1245 (1963).

[228]331 F2d 839, 55 LRRM 2913 (CA DC, 1964).

[229]380 US 300, 318, 58 LRRM 2672 (1965); *cf.* Movers & Warehousemen Ass'n v. NLRB, 550 F2d 962, 94 LRRM 2795 (CA 4, 1977), *cert. denied,* 434 US 826, 96 LRRM 2513 (1977), where it was found to be lawful to lock out employees after impasse in support of a nonmandatory subject of bargaining. For detailed discussion of *American Ship Bldg., see* Chapter 22 *infra* at notes 58-90.

[230]380 US at 312, 313. While such lockouts are deemed not to violate the Act, they may violate a "no strike/no lockout" clause of a collective bargaining agreement. Acme Mkts., Inc. v. Bakery & Confectionery Workers Local 6, 613 F2d 485, 103 LRRM 2394 (CA 3, 1980).

[231]380 US 278, 58 LRRM 2663 (1965); *see also* NLRB v. Martin A. Gleason, Inc., 534 F2d 466, 92 LRRM 2446 (CA 2, 1976), where the Court approved the employer's hiring of locked-out employees who resigned from the union as replacements provided the employer did not induce the resignation. For detailed discussion of *Brown, see* Chapter 22 *supra* at notes 91-114.

Court declared that since the use of temporary replacements was "reasonably adapted to achieve business ends" and "the tendency to discourage union membership [was] comparatively slight," there must be independent evidence of an improper motivation before an employer's replacement of locked-out employees violates the Act. However, *permanent* replacement of locked-out workers may be so inherently destructive of employee rights that independent evidence of motive is unnecessary to establish an unfair labor practice.[232] At least two Board members have taken the position that an employer decision to replace locked-out employees because of a bargaining impasse is inherently destructive of employee interests.[233]

A significant number of lockout cases have involved employer assertion of some legitimate business reason, other than union considerations, for a temporary layoff or plant closure, for example a claim that the shutdown was necessitated by lack of work. But absent evidence to sustain such a claim, the Board has often found the shutdown to have been caused by anti-union considerations.[234]

3. Plant Shutdowns and "Runaway Shops." Employer decisions concerning the closing or relocation of all or part of its operations "are so peculiarly matters of management prerogative that they would never constitute violations of Section 8(a)(1), whether or not they involved sound business judgement, unless they also violated Section 8(a)(3)."[235] Permanent shutting down of a business, where the employer intends to resume operations after he has achieved his end,[236] is to be distinguished from a

---

[232]B.N. Beard Co., *supra* note 172; Johns-Manville Prods., *supra* note 124.

[233]Members Fanning and Jenkins, *id.;* Inter-Collegiate Press, *supra* note 102; Ottawa Silica Co., *supra* note 139. *See generally* Inland Trucking Co., *supra* note 136.

[234]*See, e.g.,* Bedford Cut Stone Co., 235 NLRB 629, 98 LRRM 1003 (1978), where the Board based the finding that the shutdown was discriminatory in its timing and on the employer's substantial union animus, thereby placing the burden on the employer to show the shutdown was economically motivated. Prineville Stud Co., 227 NLRB 1845, 94 LRRM 1332 (1977); Lloyd Wood Coal Co., 230 NLRB 234, 96 LRRM 1200 (1977). *But see* Elliot River Tours, 246 NLRB 935, 103 LRRM 1095 (1979). *See generally supra* at notes 124-42.

[235]Textile Workers v. Darlington Mfg. Co., 380 US 263, 269, 58 LRRM 2657 (1965). *See* note 252 *infra*. While *Darlington* dealt only with closures, "runaway shops" are also subject to examination under §8(a)(3). *See infra* at notes 256-70. For treatment of the bargaining obligation relating to termination of operations at an organized establishment, *see* Chapter 17 *infra* at notes 267-374.

[236]Once the Board determines that a closing is permanent and that no unfair labor practice has been committed, it must dismiss the complaint; it cannot retain jurisdiction to examine the legal implications which would ensue if the plant in question subsequently resumes operations. Bruce Duncan Co. v. NLRB, 590 F2d 1304, 101 LRRM 2033 (CA 4, 1979).

lockout, and also from a "runaway shop," where the employer "transfer[s] its work to another plant or open[s] a new plant in another locality to replace its closed plant."[237] Depending on how the employer's actions are categorized, different legal principles will govern.

   a. Complete Closings. In the *Darlington*[238] case the Supreme Court ruled that an employer, even though motivated solely by vindictiveness toward a union, may close down its entire business without committing an unfair labor practice. As the Court explained:

> A proposition that a single businessman cannot choose to go out of business if he wants would represent such a startling innovation that it should not be entertained without the clearest manifestation of legislative intent or unequivocal judicial precedent so construing the Labor Act.[239]

Under the *Darlington* rule, a complete closing is not an unfair labor practice because the employer can reap no future benefit from its act. "[The closing] may be motivated more by spite against the union than by business reasons, but it is not the type of discrimination which is prohibited by the Act."[240] The Court reasoned that the employer's personal satisfaction "or the mere possibility that other employers will follow his example are surely too remote to be considered dangers at which the labor statutes were aimed."[241]

   The Board and the courts have seldom found an employer's change in operations to be a *complete* closing under the Supreme Court's *Darlington* decision. A closing will be considered complete only if the employer undertakes a "complete liquidation of [its] business."[242]

---

[237]Textile Workers v. Darlington Mfg. Co., *supra* note 235 at 273.
[238]*Id.*
[239]380 US at 270. However, "the Board has consistently found that an employer has an obligation to bargain about decisions involving subcontracting, plant removal and partial closure." Brooks-Scanlon, Inc., 246 NLRB 476, 102 LRRM 1606, 1607 (1979), but in that case the Board dismissed a §8(a)(5) complaint because the decision was based on economic factors so compelling that bargaining could not alter them, *citing* Central Rufina, 161 NLRB 696, 63 LRRM 1318 (1966). *See generally* Chapter 17 at notes 330-74.
[240]380 US at 272.
[241]*Id.* at 273.
[242]NLRB v. Fort Vancouver Plywood Co., *supra* note 185, where the majority of the employees were stockholders in the company. When union organizing efforts began, management fired all nonstockholder employees. The Board and the Ninth Circuit rejected the employer's argument that its actions were equivalent to a complete closing. *See also* National Family Opinion, 246 NLRB 521, 102 LRRM 1641 (1979).

b. Partial Closings. Because "a discriminatory partial closing may have repercussions on what remains of the business,"[243] the Supreme Court in *Darlington* specified that different standards apply to the legality of closings which are less than complete. The Court declared the controlling principles as follows:

[A] partial closing is an unfair labor practice under 8(a)(3) if motivated by a purpose to *chill unionism* in any of the remaining plants of the single employer and if the employer may reasonably have foreseen that such closing will likely have the effect.

. . .

. . . If the persons exercising control over a plant being closed for anti-union reasons (1) have an interest in another business, whether or not affiliated with or engaged in the same line of commercial activity as the closed plant, of sufficient substantiality to give promise of their reaping a benefit from the discouragement of unionization in that business; (2) act to close their plant with the purpose of producing such a result; and (3) occupy a relationship to the other business which makes it realistically foreseeable that its employees will fear that such business will also be closed down if they persist in organizational activities, we think that an unfair labor practice has been made out.[244]

Direct evidence of requisite motive and effect is seldom available. While circumstantial evidence is admissible, it "must produce more than a mere suspicion."[245] Board cases have focused on factors which permit legitimate inferences. The decision in *Bruce Duncan Co.*[246] summarized those factors:

Generally, the Board in determining whether or not the proscribed "chilling" motivation and its reasonably foreseeable effect can be inferred considers the presence or absence of several factors including, *inter alia,* contemporaneous union activity at the employer's remaining facilities,[247] geographic proximity of the employer's facilities to the closed operation,[248] the likelihood that employees will learn of the circumstances surrounding the employer's unlawful conduct through employee interchange or contact,[249] and, of course,

---

[243]380 US at 275.
[244]*Id.* at 275-76. (emphasis added). *See also* Jasta Mfg. Co., 246 NLRB 48, 102 LRRM 1610 (1979).
[245]Joint Indus. Bd., 238 NLRB 1398, 1401, 99 LRRM 1455 (1978).
[246]Bruce Duncan Co., 233 NLRB 1243, 97 LRRM 1027 (1977), *modified on other grounds, supra* note 236.
[247]*E.g.,* Morrison Cafeterias Consol., Inc., 177 NLRB 591, 71 LRRM 1449 (1969), *modified on other grounds,* 431 F2d 254, 74 LRRM 3048 (CA 8, 1970); Sweeney & Co., *supra* note 202; Motor Repair, Inc., 168 NLRB 1082, 67 LRRM 1051 (1968); A.C. Rochat Co., 163 NLRB 421, 64 LRRM 1321 (1967).
[248]*E.g.,* George Lithograph Co., 204 NLRB 431, 431, 83 LRRM 1402 (1973); Morrison Cafeterias, *supra* note 247.
[249]Motor Repair, Inc., *supra* note 247 at 1083.

representations made by the employer's officials and supervisors to other employees.[250]

Proof of legitimate economic reasons for closing can negate inferences of a chilling purpose.[251] On the other hand, the Board has held that proof that the partial closing was accomplished for anti-union reasons will not "*ipso facto* establish" the necessary purpose to chill unionism in the remaining parts of the business; but such a showing may "indicate a disposition toward [a chilling purpose] and be sufficient to support a logical inference."[252] In such cases there must be a specific showing of purpose; the Board may not simply rely on evidence that warrants an inference that the effect of closing one plant was to discourage union activity in another. The evidence must support the inference that the plant was closed for the purpose of discouraging union activity in the other plant.[253] "It is . . . clear that the ambiguous act of closing a plant following the election of a union is not, absent an inquiry into the employer's motive, inherently discriminatory."[254]

However, in establishing the requisite effect, the General Counsel need not demonstrate that the remaining employees were *actually* "chilled" in their union activities; it need only be shown that a chilling effect was reasonably foreseeable.[255]

c. *"Runaway Shops."* It is generally accepted that when an employer changes or discontinues its business operations "in order to avoid obligations imposed upon it by the National Labor Relations Act"[256] a violation of Section 8(a)(3) has occurred.

---

[250]Midland-Ross Corp. v. NLRB, 617 F2d 977, 103 LRRM 2908 (CA 3, 1980), *cert. denied,* 447 US 871, 105 LRRM 2657 (1980). *E.g.,* George Lithograph Co., *supra* note 248; Motor Repair, Inc., *supra* note 247.

[251]*E.g.,* Joint Indus. Bd., *supra* note 245; C & T Mfg. Co., 233 NLRB 1430, 97 LRRM 1140 (1977); Food Fair Stores, Inc., 229 NLRB 730, 95 LRRM 1157 (1977); Tectura, Inc., 221 NLRB 1193, 91 LRRM 1079 (1975); South San Francisco Scavenger Co., 215 NLRB 694, 88 LRRM 1113 (1974); Thompson Transp. Co., 165 NLRB 746, 65 LRRM 1370 (1967), *modified on other grounds,* 406 F2d 698, 70 LRRM 2418 (CA 10, 1969).

[252]George Lithograph Co., *supra* note 248 at 431; *accord,* Darlington Mfg. Co., 165 NLRB 1074, 1083, 65 LRRM 1391 (1967), *following remand, supra* note 235, *enforced,* 397 F2d 760, 68 LRRM 2356 (CA 4,1968), *cert. denied,* 393 US 1023, 70 LRRM 2225 (1969).

[253]Motor Repair, Inc., *supra* note 247.

[254]Textile Workers v. Darlington Mfg. Co., *supra* note 235.

[255]George Lithograph Co., *supra* note 248.

[256]NLRB v. Rapid Bindery, Inc., 293 F2d 170, 174, 48 LRRM 2658 (CA 2, 1961); *accord,* Schieber Millinery Co., 26 NLRB 937, 7 LRRM 18, *enforced in pertinent part,* 116 F2d 281, 7 LRRM 658 (CA 8, 1940).

"The law does not permit an employer to flee the bargaining agent because of hostility to it . . . ."[257]

Although the "runaway shop" appears in different forms, it always involves a transfer of work.[258] The work may be transferred to another plant,[259] to other employees within the same plant,[260] or to an alter-ego corporation.[261] The work may even be subcontracted out to another company.[262]

Most of these Section 8(a)(3) cases turn on employer motivation in changing operations. The justification most commonly asserted is economic necessity.[263] In passing on an employer's asserted justification, "the crucial factor is not whether the business reasons cited . . . were good or bad, but whether they were

---

[257]Local 57, Garment Workers (Garwin Corp.) v. NLRB, 153 NLRB 664, 59 LRRM 1405 (1965), modified, 374 F2d 295, 64 LRRM 2159 (CA DC), cert. denied, 387 US 942, 65 LRRM 2441 (1967).

[258]See Frito-Lay, Inc. v. NLRB, 585 F2d 62, 99 LRRM 2658 (CA 3, 1978). Although a "runaway shop" often involves, as an initial step, a closing of all or part of an employer's operations at one location, it is not subject to plant-closure analysis. Because a "runaway shop" involves discriminatory employer action for the purpose of obtaining some benefit in the future from the new employees, it is analyzed under the standards generally applicable to §8(a)(3) cases. Cf. Textile Workers v. Darlington Mfg. Co., supra note 235. Thus, "there must be both discrimination and a resulting discouragement of union membership . . . . [A] finding of violation . . . will normally turn on the employer's motivation." American Ship Bldg. Co. v. NLRB, supra note 88.

[259]E.g., Royal Norton Mfg. Co., 189 NLRB 489, 77 LRRM 1022 (1971); Roman Cleanser Co., 188 NLRB 931, 76 LRRM 1446 (1971) (no discriminatory motive); Les Schwab Tire Centers, Inc., 172 NLRB 164, 69 LRRM 1290 (1968).

[260]Howmet Corp., 197 NLRB 471, 80 LRRM 1555 (1972), enforced, 495 F2d 1375, 86 LRRM 2572 (CA 7, 1974).

[261]E.g., NLRB v. Big Bear Supermarkets, 640 F2d 924, 103 LRRM 3120 (CA 9,1980); H. S. Brooks Elec., Inc., 233 NLRB 889, 97 LRRM 1083 (1977); Remke Cent. Div., Inc., 227 NLRB 1969, 95 LRRM 1113 (1977); James K. Sterritt, Inc., 215 NLRB 769, 88 LRRM 1355 (1974), enforced, 538 F2d 310, 93 LRRM 2336 (CA 2, 1975). "Runaway shops" can also constitute violation of §8(a)(5). See, e.g., Davis v. NLRB, 617 F2d 1264, 103 LRRM 2965 (CA 7, 1980); Triumph Curing Center, Inc., 222 NLRB 627, 91 LRRM 1313 (1976), enforced, 571 F2d 462, 98 LRRM 2047 (CA 9, 1978).

[262]Hood Indus., 248 NLRB 597, 103 LRRM 1540 (1980); Brown-Dunkin Co., 125 NLRB 1379, 45 LRRM 1256 (1959), enforced, 287 F2d 17, 47 LRRM 2551 (CA 10, 1961).

[263]E.g., Great Chinese Am. Sewing Co. v. NLRB, 578 F2d 251, 99 LRRM 2347 (CA 9, 1978); NLRB v. Townhouse TV & Appliances, Inc., supra note 50; NLRB v. Roberts & Sons, Inc., supra note 202; Garment Workers v. NLRB, 463 F2d 907, 80 LRRM 2716 (CA DC, 1972) (accepting employer's economic reasons); Local 57, Garment Workers (Garwin Corp.) v. NLRB, supra note 257 (rejecting employer's economic reasons); NLRB v. Preston Feed Corp., 309 F2d 346, 51 LRRM 2362 (CA 4, 1962) (initial decision economically justified but immediate decision due to union animus); NLRB v. Rapid Bindery, supra note 256 (accepting employer's economic reasons); NLRB v. Adkins Transfer Co., 226 F2d 324, 36 LRRM 2709 (CA 6, 1955) (accepting employer's economic reasons); Mount Hope Finishing Co. v. NLRB, 211 F2d 365, 33 LRRM 2742 (CA 4, 1954) (accepting employer's economic reasons); Atlantic Coast News Co., 197 NLRB 392, 80 LRRM 1415 (1972) (accepting employer's economic reasons); Royal Norton Mfg. Co., supra note 259 (rejecting employer's economic reasons); Roman Cleanser Co., supra note 259 (accepting employer's economic reasons).

honestly invoked and were in fact the cause of the change."[264] The "causal nexus between the claimed economic considerations and the move" will be important in determining whether the economic considerations were honestly invoked.[265]

"[T]he fact that the employer may have legitimate economic reasons for the transfer or liquidation does not absolve him of his conduct if violation of his employees' statutory rights was also a motivating reason."[266] An employer may, however, consider "his relationship with his plant's union as only one part of the broad economic picture he must survey when he is faced with determining the desirability of making changes in his operation."[267]

Historically, plant relocations have been considered unlawful only if discriminatorily motivated. More recently, however, the Board has begun to find certain operational changes inherently destructive of employee rights and thus unlawful without regard to motive.[268]

In *Brown Co.*[269] a divided Board held that an employer's partial relocation of operations was "inherently destructive of employee interests" and thus unlawful. The employer, a manufacturer of concrete products, operated two integrated divisions. One of the divisions (Livingston-Graham) operated under a contract with Local 420, while the other division (Tri-City) operated under a contract with Locals 467 and 871. The employer subsequently learned that by operating under "for hire" contracts with the union it could lower its wage rates. Accordingly, it notified Local 420 of its intention to set up a third division and to transfer both the employees and the work of Local 420 to the new company if Local 420 would agree to a "for hire" contract. Local 420, however, refused this offer. The employer then signed

---

[264]NLRB v. Savoy Laundry, Inc., *supra* note 215 at 371.
[265]Local 57, Garment Workers v. NLRB, *supra* note 257.
[266]C-F Air Freight, Inc., 247 NLRB 403, 103 LRRM 1156 (1980); Garwin Corp., *supra* note 257; *accord*, Garment Workers v. NLRB, *supra* note 263; Allied Mills, Inc., 218 NLRB 281, 89 LRRM 1891 (1975), *enforced sub nom.* Grain Millers Local 110, 543 F2d 417, 93 LRRM 2842 (CA DC, 1976).
[267]NLRB v. Rapid Bindery, Inc., *supra* note 256; *accord*, NLRB v. New England Web, Inc., 309 F2d 696, 51 LRRM 2426 (CA 1, 1962); Mays Foods, Inc. v. NLRB, 292 F2d 317, 48 LRRM 2715 (CA 7, 1961); NLRB v. Lassing, 284 F2d 781, 47 LRRM 2277 (CA 6, 1960); NLRB v. Adkins Transfer Co., *supra* note 263.
[268]*See* NLRB v. Industrial Insulation Co., 615 F2d 1289, 103 LRRM 2614 (CA 10, 1980); Ethyl Corp., *supra* note 141, 231 NLRB 431, 97 LRRM 1465 (1977); Rushton & Mercier Woodworking Co., Inc., *supra* note 143.
[269]243 NLRB 769, 101 LRRM 1608 (1979).

a "for hire" agreement with Locals 467 and 871, set up the new company, and transferred the work at Livingston-Graham to the new company. The incumbent employees were not allowed to transfer to the new company and some were laid off. Responding to unfair labor practice charges, the company argued that it had bargained over the matter and that under its contract it had a right to make the change for economic reasons. Rejecting these arguments, the Board stated:

> It matters not whether Respondent's transfer of its trucks was a result of union animus, nor that it first bargained with the Union and attempted to get it to sign a new agreement. It is obvious that Respondent's actions were 'inherently destructive of employee interests" and that the employees lost the jobs to which they were entitled as a result of Respondent's efforts to escape its economic obligations under the contract.[270]

4. Replacement and Reinstatement of Economic Strikers. The history of the relationship between employers and their economic strikers is the balancing of two basic considerations:[271] first, that employees should not so fear a retaliatory denial of the opportunity to work as to render illusory their right to strike for better wages, hours, and working conditions; second, that an employer should remain free to continue operating its business even in the face of an economic strike.

The Supreme Court foreshadowed much of this history when it decided *NLRB* v. *Mackay Radio & Telegraph Co.*[272] In *Mackay*, the employer had offered permanent employment to those who had replaced its economic strikers. Five replacements accepted the offer. As a result, at the conclusion of the strike the employer refused to reinstate five strikers immediately. It had agreed only that their applications "would be considered in connection with any vacancy that might thereafter occur." The Board held that the employer had violated what were then Sections 8(1) and 8(3), not by refusing to reinstate the five strikers immediately, but by selecting those most active in union affairs for, at best, delayed reinstatement.

---

[270]*Id.* Members Penello and Murphy dissented, finding nothing inherently unlawful in the employer's conduct.
[271]*See generally* Chapter 21 *infra* at notes 83-103.
[272]*Supra* note 89.

The Supreme Court agreed that refusing immediately to reinstate the five strikers was not in itself a violation of Section 8(3). The Court conceded that "the [economic] strikers remained employs [sic] for the purpose of the Act and were protected against the unfair labor practices denounced by it."[273] However, the Court also declared that employers can lawfully "replace . . . striking employees with others in an effort to carry on the business" and that employers need "not . . . discharge those hired to fill the places of strikers, upon the election of the latter to resume their employment, in order to create places for them."[274] The Court reasoned that while discharging or otherwise discriminating against economic strikers violates the Act, offering and providing permanent employment to those who will replace economic strikers does not amount to discharging or otherwise discriminating against those strikers. But the Court agreed that offering delayed reinstatement (at best) to those who had been most active in union affairs violated the Act.[275]

After *Mackay,* the Board and the appellate courts expressly held that discharging economic strikers violates the Act.[276]

For many years following *Mackay* the Board maintained, with the approval of the courts, that employers owed their permanently replaced economic strikers only a duty to consider fairly their applications for reinstatement.[277] "Permanently replaced economic strikers merely have the right not to be penalized for their concerted activity, and are not entitled to preferential status in hiring."[278] It followed that employers were under "no

[273]*Id.* at 345.
[274]*Id.* at 345-46.
[275]The Court stated:
"[T]he respondent was not bound to displace men hired to take the strikers' places in order to provide positions for them. It might have refused reinstatement on the grounds of skill or ability but the Board found that it did not do so. It might have resorted to any one of a number of methods of determining which of its striking employees would have to wait because five men had taken permanent positions during the strike but it found that the preparation and use of the list, and the action taken by respondent, was with the purpose to discriminate against those most active in the union. There is evidence to support these findings." *Id.* at 347.
[276]*E.g.,* NLRB v. International Van Lines, 409 US 48, 81 LRRM 2595 (1972); NLRB v. United States Cold Storage Corp., 203 F2d 924, 32 LRRM 2024 (CA 5), *cert. denied,* 346 US 818, 32 LRRM 2750 (1953).
[277]*E.g.,* Bartlett-Collins Co., 110 NLRB 395, 35 LRRM 1006 (1954), *aff'd sub nom.* Flint Glass Workers v. NLRB, 230 F2d 212, 37 LRRM 2409 (CA DC), *cert. denied,* 351 US 988, 38 LRRM 2238 (1956); Brown & Root, Inc., 132 NLRB 486, 48 LRRM 1391 (1961), *enforced,* 311 F2d 447, 52 LRRM 2115 (CA 8, 1963); Atlas Storage Div., 112 NLRB 1175, 36 LRRM 1171 (1955), *enforced,* 233 F2d 233, 38 LRRM 2095 (CA 7, 1956).
[278]Bartlett-Collins Co., *supra* note 277 at 397.

obligation to seek out or prefer the strikers for vacancies which occurred after their application."[279]

In 1967, however, the Supreme Court issued two decisions, both previously noted, which compelled the Board to reconsider its position. In *Great Dane Trailers*[280] the Court declared that even employer conduct that has only a "comparatively slight" impact on the rights of employees violates Section 8(a)(3) unless the employer can evidence "legitimate and substantial business justifications."[281] Later, in *Fleetwood Trailer*,[282] the Court explained that refusing to reinstate economic strikers, if not immediately upon their application for reinstatement, then at least at some later point when vacancies occur, has an adverse impact on the rights of employees. The Court concluded:

> If and when a job for which the striker is qualified becomes available, he is entitled to an offer of reinstatement. The right can be defeated only if the employer can show "legitimate and substantial business justifications."[283]

Recognizing the implications of *Fleetwood,* the Board revised its interpretation of *Mackay* and expanded the reinstatement rights of permanently replaced economic strikers. Thus, in *Laidlaw Corp.*,[284] it held that

> economic strikers who unconditionally apply for reinstatement at a time when their positions are filled by permanent replacements: (1) remain employees; (2) are entitled to full reinstatement upon the departure of replacements unless they have in the meantime acquired regular and substantially equivalent employment or the employer can sustain his burden of proof that the failure to offer full reinstatement was for legitimate and substantial business reasons.[285]

The "substantially equivalent employment" exception to the general rule was derived from Section 2(3) of the Act, which includes in the definition of "employee" a person "who has not

---

[279]Laidlaw Corp., *supra* note 42 at 1369 (explaining the holding of *Brown & Root, supra* note 277).

[280]NLRB v. Great Dane Trailers, *supra* note 40.

[281]388 US at 65.

[282]NLRB v. Fleetwood Trailer Co., *supra* note 97.

[283]*Id.* at 381. The employer refused to reinstate economic strikers upon the conclusion of their strike because a drop in production had accompanied the strike, and the employer could not yet resume full production. Later, when full production could resume, the employer bypassed strikers and offered such vacancies as occurred to applicants who had never before worked for the employer. This violated §8(a)(3).

[284]*Supra* note 42.

[285]*Id.* at 1369-70.

obtained any other regular and substantially equivalent employment."

The basic *Laidlaw* rule remains the law, although the Board has refined its application in several cases.[286]

In *Brooks Research & Manufacturing, Inc.*,[287] the Board refused to place a time limit on the duration of the reinstatement rights of economic strikers, noting that there were various procedures by which the employer could "cope" with the burden of maintaining, indefinitely, a preferential recall list.[288] The Board has recognized, however, that reinstatement rights may be limited by a strike-settlement agreement negotiated between the employer and the union.[289]

Where an employer fails to rehire economic strikers and cannot prove that permanent replacements have been hired or that there exists a legitimate and substantial business justification for the failure to rehire, reinstatement with back pay from the date of a striker's unconditional offer to return to work is the appro-

---

[286]*E.g.*, Zapex Corp., 235 NLRB 1236, 98 LRRM 1241 (1978); Bralco Metals, Inc., 227 NLRB 973, 94 LRRM 1368 (1977). But striking employees who engage in unprotected activity by picketing in violation of §8(b)(7)(B) are not entitled to reinstatement upon their unconditional application for reinstatement. Claremont Polychem. Corp., 196 NLRB 613, 80 LRRM 1130 (1972) (Member Fanning dissented from the opinion of Chairman Miller and Member Kennedy); *see also* Castle-Pierce Printing Co., Inc., 251 NLRB 1293, 105 LRRM 1567 (1980); NLRB v. Colonial Haven Nursing Homes, 542 F2d 691, 93 LRRM 2241 (CA 7, 1976), *rehearing denied*, 542 F2d 707, 93 LRRM 2596 (CA 7, 1976). For additional discussion of *Laidlaw* developments, *see* Chapter 21 *infra* at notes 91-103.

[287]202 NLRB 634, 82 LRRM 1599 (1973).

[288]For cases dealing with the issue of who is a permanent replacement, *see* Cyr Bottle Gas Co., 204 NLRB 527, 83 LRRM 1505 (1973), *enforced*, 497 F2d 900, 87 LRRM 2253 (CA 6, 1974); Covington Furniture Mfg. Co., 212 NLRB 214, 87 LRRM 1505 (1974), *enforced*, 514 F2d 995, 89 LRRM 3024 (CA 6, 1975); H & F Binch Co., 188 NLRB 721, 76 LRRM 1735 (1971), *enforcement denied in relevant part*, 456 F2d 357, 79 LRRM 2692 (CA 2, 1972). Cases dealing with the issue of which striker has been replaced include Pillows of Cal., 207 NLRB 369, 84 LRRM 1446 (1973) and Pleasant View Rest Home, *supra* note 44. Reinstatement to a job for which the striker is not qualified and for which the striker receives no training, followed by the striker's discharge for not meeting production quotas on the job, violates §8(a)(3). Elsing Mfg. Co., 209 NLRB 1089, 86 LRRM 1267 (1974); NLRB v. Penn Corp., *supra* note 147 (appellate court affirmed Board's holding that employer violated 8(a)(3) when it requested permanently replaced economic strikers to execute reinstatement-request form containing requirement that strikers must renew their request for reinstatement within six months or be removed automatically from the recall list); *see also* American Mach. Corp. v. NLRB, 424 F2d 1321, 73 LRRM 2977 (CA 5, 1970); Pease Co., 251 NLRB No. 80, 105 LRRM 1314 (1980).

[289]United Aircraft Corp., 192 NLRB 382, 77 LRRM 1785 (1971), *aff'd in part sub nom.* Machinists Lodges 743 & 1746, 534 F2d 422, 90 LRRM 2272 (CA 2, 1975), *cert. denied*, 429 US 825 (1976); NLRB v. Penn Corp., *supra* note 147. *See* discussion at notes 91-92 in Chapter 21 *infra*.

priate remedy.[290] But before liability inures to an employer, an economic striker desiring reinstatement, or the union on his behalf, must make an unconditional offer to return to work, unless it would be futile to do so.[291] The offer must be specific. A union's request for reinstatement for strikers to "their old jobs or the maximum employment opportunity which the law allows" has been held not to be sufficiently specific to include job vacancies at a new plant opened by the employer just prior to the strike.[292] But an offer to return to work made by a union was held to be "unconditional" despite the fact that its members continued to picket the employer's main entrance.[293]

An employer's offer of reinstatement to economic strikers will not toll a back-pay award if the offer does not provide the strikers a reasonable amount of time to consider the offer. Thus, a demand for an immediate acceptance was held not to constitute a valid offer.[294] And an employer's offer of reinstatement conditioned upon a no-strike commitment was not deemed a valid offer.[295]

Also, if an employer discriminates against selected strikers in connection with reinstatement, back pay accrues from the date on which each striker would have been reinstated had the strikers been taken back in order of seniority, rather than from the date on which the employer began hiring new employees.[296]

When an employer's actions convert an economic strike into an unfair labor practice strike,[297] prolonging the strike, strikers become entitled to immediate reinstatement, and the employer's

---

[290]NLRB v. Acme Wire Works, Inc., 582 F2d 153, 98 LRRM 3163 (CA 2, 1978); Automatic Plastic Molding Co., 234 NLRB 681, 97 LRRM 1326 (1978).

[291]Moore Business Forms, Inc., *supra* note 150; Swearingen Aviation Corp. v. NLRB, 568 F2d 458, 97 LRRM 2972 (CA 5, 1978); Vorpal Galleries, 227 NLRB 446, 94 LRRM 1553 (1976).

[292]Bryan Infants Wear Co., 235 NLRB 1305, 98 LRRM 1140 (1978).

[293]NLRB v. W. C. McQuaide, Inc., 552 F2d 519, 94 LRRM 2950 (CA 3, 1977), *enforcing in part* 220 NLRB 593, 90 LRRM 1345 (1975).

[294]NLRB v. Murray Prods., Inc., 584 F2d 934, 99 LRRM 3269 (CA 9, 1978), *enforcing* 228 NLRB 268, 94 LRRM 1723 (1977).

[295]Lindy's Food Center, 232 NLRB 1001, 96 LRRM 1386 (1977). However, in Roberts Oldsmobile, Inc., 252 NLRB 192, 105 LRRM 1532 (1980), the Board held that the employer did not violate the Act by proposing that the union withdraw unfair labor practice charges in connection with reinstatement of economic strikers.

[296]NLRB v. Fire Alert Co., 566 F2d 696, 96 LRRM 3381 (CA 10, 1977), *enforcing* 223 NLRB 129, 92 LRRM 1002 (1976).

[297]*See* Chapter 21 *infra* at notes 68-82.

back-pay liability commences upon their unconditional offer to return to work.[298]

An employer is not required to offer reinstatement to economic strikers who have been guilty of serious misconduct during a strike.[299] But isolated minor incidents and threats, such as egg throwing and verbal intimidation unaccompanied by physical violence, are not considered by the Board to be conduct of a sufficiently serious nature to permit an employer to deny reinstatement.[300] However, various circuit courts have disagreed with the Board as to the type of misconduct that justifies denial of reinstatement.[301]

5. Discharge or Discipline of Union Stewards for Strikes in Breach of Contract.

In *Precision Castings Co.*[302] the Board held that an employer violated Section 8(a)(3) by singling out and suspending union stewards who assertedly failed to abide by their contractual responsibility to take reasonable steps to end an unauthorized work stoppage. Although an employer has the power to discipline its employees, it cannot selectively do so on the basis of the employees' union activities.[303] A divided board subsequently reaffirmed the rationale of *Precision Castings*,[304] but the Third Circuit reversed.[305] The Board's reasoning was also rejected by the Seventh Circuit, which held that in disciplining employees "the employer was entitled to take into account the

---

[298]NLRB v. Acme Wire Works, Inc., *supra* note 290; National Fresh Fruit & Vegetable Co. v. NLRB, 565 F2d 1331, 97 LRRM 2427 (CA 5, 1978); National Car Rental Sys., Inc., 237 NLRB 172, 99 LRRM 1027 (1978); Automatic Plastic Molding Co., *supra* note 290. *See also* Mastro Plastics Corp. v. NLRB, 350 US 270, 37 LRRM 2587 (1956).

[299]Advance Indus. Div. v. NLRB, 540 F2d 878, 93 LRRM 2147 (CA 7, 1976), *denying enforcement in part to* 220 NLRB 431, 90 LRRM 1257 (1975); Jerr-Dan Corp., 237 NLRB 302, 98 LRRM 1569 (1978). *See also* Claremont Polychem. Corp., *supra* note 286 (Member Fanning dissented from the opinion of Chairman Miller and Member Kennedy). Striking employees who engage in picketing in violation of 8(b)(7) are not entitled to reinstatement upon their unconditional application. *See* Chapter 21 *infra* at notes 117-26. *Cf.* Chapter 21 *infra* at notes 72-74. For general treatment of §8(b)(7) *see* Chapter 23 *infra*.

[300]Harowe Servo Controls, Inc., 250 NLRB 958, 105 LRRM 1147 (1980); MP Indus., Inc., 227 NLRB 1709, 94 LRRM 1608 (1977).

[301]Associated Grocers v. NLRB, 562 F2d 1333, 96 LRRM 2630 (CA 1, 1977), *denying enforcement to* 227 NLRB 1200, 95 LRRM 1031 (1977); NLRB v. W. C. McQuaide, Inc., *supra* note 293; NLRB v. Moore Business Forms, Inc., *supra* note 150. *See also* Cabot & Jarin, *The Third Circuit's New Standard for Strike Misconduct Discharges: NLRB v. W. C. McQuaide, Inc.*, 23 VILL. L. REV. 645 (1978).

[302]233 NLRB 183, 96 LRRM 1540 (1977). *Accord,* Consolidation Coal Co., 263 NLRB No. 188, 111 LRRM 1205 (1982).

[303]*Id.* at 183.

[304]Gould Corp., *supra* note 110. Following the resignation of Member Murphy, the Board split evenly on the issue. *See* Rogate, 246 NLRB 898, 103 LRRM 1085 (1979).

[305]Gould Corp. v. NLRB, *supra* note 110.

union officials' greater responsibility and hence greater fault . . . ."[306] Even under the *Precision Castings* rationale, however, an exception is recognized where the union official takes a leadership role in the illegal strike. In that situation the Board holds that the official may justifiably receive a harsher penalty.[307]*

6. Other Types of Conduct. *a. Employer Discrimination Under Union Security Provisions.*

Faced with a union demand to discharge an employee, an employer must inquire into the circumstances behind the demand if the employer "is aware of facts that would lead him to believe that the discharge may be for an improper purpose."[308] The employer's obligation to investigate the demand depends on the facts known to the employer, the degree of doubt they raise, the burden the inquiry would impose, and the likelihood that an investigation would lead to a prompt resolution of the employer's doubts.[309] No employee may be discharged under a union security agreement, however, unless the employee has been put on notice of the obligation alleged to be owed to the union.[310]

b. Employer Discrimination on the Basis of Race or Sex. In *Jubilee Manufacturing Co.*[311] the Board held that discrimination based on race, color, religion, sex, or national origin, standing alone, is not a violation of the Act, absent "actual evidence, as opposed to speculation, of a nexus between the alleged discriminatory conduct and the interference with, or restraint of, employees in the exercise of those rights protected by the Act."[312] The *Jubilee* decision rejected the rationale advanced by the District of

---

[306]Indiana & Mich. Elec. Co. v. NLRB, 599 F2d 227, 101 LRRM 2475 (CA 7, 1979), *denying enforcement to* 237 NLRB 226, 99 LRRM 1111 (1978). For a detailed treatment of this issue, *see* Chapter 21 *infra* at note 157.
*[*See* **Editor's Note** Chapter 21 *infra*, p. 1025.]
[307]Atkinson Co., 251 NLRB 277, 105 LRRM 1108 (1980); Chrysler Corp., 232 NLRB 466, 96 LRRM 1382 (1977); J. P. Wetherby Constr. Corp., 182 NLRB 690, 76 LRRM 1879 (1970).
[308]Macaulay Foundry Co. v. NLRB, 553 F2d 1198, 95 LRRM 2581 (CA 9, 1977), *enforcing* 223 NLRB 815, 92 LRRM 1279 (1976), holding that the company violated §8(a)(3) when it refused to investigate an absent employee's claim that his dues could be paid upon his return to work.
[309]*Id.; see also* NLRB v. Zoe Chem. Co., 406 F2d 574, 70 LRRM 2276 (CA 2, 1969), *denying enforcement to* 160 NLRB 1001, 63 LRRM 1052 (1966).
[310]Teamsters Local 162 v. NLRB, 568 F2d 665, 97 LRRM 2917 (CA 9, 1978). However, an employer does not violate the Act merely because the union has failed to adequately inform an employee of dues delinquency. Valley Cabinet & Mfg., Inc., 253 NLRB 98, 105 LRRM 1467 (1980). *See generally* Chapter 29 *infra.*
[311]*Supra* note 152. *See* Chapter 6 *supra* at notes 12-14.
[312]202 NLRB at 272.

Columbia Circuit in *Packinghouse Workers* v. *NLRB*,[313] which held that racial discrimination violates Section 8(a)(1) because it creates a conflict of interests among the workers, thereby reducing the likelihood of concerted action and creating a docility among employees.

The Board has found employer discrimination on the basis of race or sex to be a violation of Section 8 (a)(3), however, where the employer acquiesces in the maintenance and enforcement of discriminatory seniority lists[314] or hiring-hall arrangements.[315] But in *J. S. Alberici Construction Co.*,[316] a case involving a conflict between a hiring-hall provision and a Title VII consent decree, the Board found that Section 8(a)(3) had not been violated although the referral system was discriminatory. The hiring-hall agreement permitted the employer to request up to half of its work force by name. When the employer made such a request, the union refused to comply, stating that the hiring-hall agreement was superseded by a Title VII consent decree whereby the union was required to change its existing hiring procedures and to refer job applicants on a first-come, first-served basis. The employer was not a party to the consent decree. Thereafter, the employer contacted the employees directly and hired them without following the contractual procedures. The Board held that the employer's conduct did not violate Section 8(a)(3), since the union's conduct required the employer to choose between either accepting employees from a first-come, first-served referral system to which it had not agreed, or hiring employees directly without using the referral process. The Board concluded that any inherent effect of encouraging or discouraging union membership resulting from the employer's direct hiring was due to the union's "unilateral repudiation of the contract's hiring hall provisions."[317]

Employees are considered engaged in concerted activity, however, when they protest their employer's discriminatory practices, provided they do not thereby bypass an applicable collec-

---

[313]416 F2d 1126, 70 LRRM 2489 (CA DC), *cert. denied,* 396 US 903, 72 LRRM 2658 (1969). In Emporium Capwell Co. v. Western Addition Community Organization, 420 US 50, 88 LRRM 2660 (1975), the Supreme Court explicitly left open the question whether the right to be free of racial discrimination has an independent source in the NLRA, *citing Packinghouse Workers.*
[314]Olympic S. S. Co., 233 NLRB 1178, 97 LRRM 1276 (1977).
[315]Pacific Maritime Ass'n, 209 NLRB 519, 85 LRRM 1389 (1974).
[316]231 NLRB 1030, 96 LRRM 1205 (1977). Member Jenkins dissented.
[317]*Id.* at 1032.

tive bargaining agreement. Thus, the Board has held that employers violate Section 8(a)(1) when they discharge employees for filing charges with federal or state agencies alleging discrimination,[318] for attempting to change discriminatory hiring practices,[319] and for attempting to secure racially integrated working conditions.[320] But *Emporium Capwell Co. v. Western Addition Community Organization*[321] stands as an important caveat. The Supreme Court there held that employees lose the protection of the Act when they bypass the grievance procedure and attempt to eliminate racially discriminatory employment practices on their own.[322]

c. Superseniority. To assure continuity of function and maximum use of a union steward's skill and experience, unions often bargain for and attain superseniority for stewards in a collective bargaining agreement. Collective bargaining provisions granting superseniority to union officers in matters relating to layoff and recall have been upheld where the officer's responsibilities "bear a direct relationship to the effect and efficient representation of unit employees."[323] But under the rule of *Dairylea Cooperative, Inc.,*[324] contractual provisions that give superseniority to union stewards regarding benefits other than layoff and recall are held to be presumptively unlawful, and the party which asserts the legality of such a provision has the burden of demonstrating substantial and legitimate business justification.[325] The *Dairylea* rule has been interpreted to include a pre-

---

[318]King Soopers, Inc., 222 NLRB 1011, 91 LRRM 1292 (1976), where the collective bargaining agreement contained a no-discrimination clause; Advance Carbon Prods., Inc., 198 NLRB 741, 81 LRRM 1418 (1972). *See* Frank Briscoe v. NLRB, *supra* note 152. *See* Chapter 6 *supra* at notes 471-74.

[319]Mason & Hanger-Silas Mason Co., 179 NLRB 434, 72 LRRM 1372 (1969), *enforcement denied on other grounds*, 449 F2d 425, 78 LRRM 2487 (CA 8, 1971).

[320]Tanner Motor Livery, Ltd., 148 NLRB 1402, 57 LRRM 1170 (1964), *remanded*, 349 F2d 1, 59 LRRM 2784 (CA 9, 1965), *original decision aff'd*, 166 NLRB 551, 65 LRRM 1502 (1967), *remanded*, 419 F2d 216, 72 LRRM 2866 (CA 9, 1969).

[321]*Supra* note 313.

[322]*See* Chapter 6 *supra* at notes 404-405.

[323]Allied Indus. Workers Local 148 (Allen Group, Inc.), 236 NLRB 1368, 1370, 98 LRRM 1574 (1978); Electrical Workers (UE) Local 623 (Limpco Mfg. Inc.), 230 NLRB 406, 95 LRRM 1343 (1977), *enforced sub nom.* D'Amico v. NLRB, 582 F2d 820, 99 LRRM 2350 (CA 3, 1978); Otis Elevator Co., 231 NLRB 1128, 96 LRRM 1108 (1977); Expedient Servs., Inc., *infra* note 326.

[324]219 NLRB 656, 89 LRRM 1737 (1975), *enforced sub nom.* NLRB v. Teamsters Local 338, 531 F2d 1162, 91 LRRM 2929 (CA 2, 1976); *see* note 381 *infra; see also* NLRB v. Auto Warehousers, Inc., 571 F2d 860, 98 LRRM 2238 (CA 5, 1978), *denying enforcement to* 227 NLRB 628, 94 LRRM 1445 (1976); W. R. Grace Co., 230 NLRB 259, 95 LRRM 1441 (1977); Teamsters Local 633 (Interstate Motor Freight Sys.), 230 NLRB 81, 96 LRRM 1096 (1977); Preston Trucking Co., 236 NLRB 464, 98 LRRM 1248 (1978); Connecticut Limousine Serv., Inc., 235 NLRB 1350, 98 LRRM 1299 (1978).

[325]*See* notes 381-86 *infra* and accompanying text.

sumption of validity for contractual provisions giving union stewards the right to bump laterally to avoid demotion.[326] But where an employee need not be a union member to be selected steward, the Board has indicated that a superseniority preference may not be improper.[327]

D. Discrimination for Participation in Concerted Activities

Although most of the cases involving discrimination against employees by employers arise under Section 8(a)(3), there are also discrimination cases which arise under Section 8(a)(1) alone. The latter concern discrimination against employees on account of their participation in protected concerted activity, which is not necessarily union activity. Thus, employees who are not union members or who are not engaged in union activity *per se* are subject to this protection, for Section 7 guarantees that employees "shall have the right . . . to engage in . . . concerted activities for the purpose of collective bargaining or *other mutual aid or protection.*"[328] Interference with such a right by an employer violates Section 8(a)(1). This area of the law is here noted because many of the cases involve employment discrimination, but such cases are primarily treated elsewhere[329] because they are intertwined with general 8(a)(1) conduct, which may occur without any element of discrimination and even without actual deprivation of employment or terms or conditions of employment.

III. UNION INDUCEMENT OF EMPLOYER TO DISCRIMINATE

A. Typical Section 8(b)(2) Violations

Under Section 8(b)(2) it is an unfair labor practice for a union "to cause or attempt to cause" an employer to discriminate in violation of Section 8(a)(3). This statutory standard is qualita-

---

[326]Theatrical Stage Employees Local 780 (McGregor-Werner, Inc.), 227 NLRB 558, 94 LRRM 1230 (1976); Expedient Serv., Inc., 231 NLRB 938, 96 LRRM 1436 (1977); Parker-Hannifin Corp., 231 NLRB 884, 96 LRRM 1130 (1977); Hospital Serv. Plan, 227 NLRB 585, 94 LRRM 1381 (1977).
[327]Theatrical Stage Employees Local 780 (McGregor-Werner, Inc.), *supra* note 326.
[328]Emphasis added.
[329]*See* Chapter 6 *supra* at notes 365-513.

tively different from the "restrain or coerce" language of Sections 8(a)(1) and 8(b)(1). A wide range of union conduct may be found to "cause" or "attempt to cause" an employer to discriminate.

Examples of such unlawful conduct include, when motivated by a Section 8(b)(2) purpose, threatened or real strikes, violence, or advice to an employer that he will incur the union's favor or disfavor unless certain action is taken with respect to an employee.[330] But unlawful conduct may also exist where an inducing communication is courteous or even precatory, just as it may be rude and demanding.[331] In fact, one case involved a tearful threat by a local union officer to resign her job unless the employer discharged another employee who had been critical of her leadership.[332] Section 8(b)(2), however, applies only to union conduct. Thus, the cases sometimes turn on whether a union official is merely conveying the attitude of member-employees or passing on the desire of the union itself.[333] Resolution will often depend on traditional questions of agency and ratification.

The Board and the courts have uniformly held that determining whether someone acts as an agent under this statute requires applying common-law principles of agency.[334] As one court noted, "Senator Taft, the life-force behind the bill as

---

[330]Mullett v. NLRB, 571 F2d 1292, 97 LRRM 2976 (CA 4, 1978), *denying enforcement to* 228 NLRB 216, 94 LRRM 1428 (1977); Laborers Local 341 v. NLRB, 564 F2d 834, 97 LRRM 2287 (CA 9, 1977), *enforcing* 223 NLRB 917, 92 LRRM 1112 (1976); Teamsters Local 5 v. NLRB, 389 F2d 757, 67 LRRM 2410 (CA 5, 1968); Carpenters Local 1554 (Bruchard Designs, Inc.), 238 NLRB 1683, 99 LRRM 1295 (1978); Iron Workers Local 426 (Brown Bros., Inc.), 238 NLRB 4, 99 LRRM 1194 (1978); Painters Local 829, 234 NLRB 562, 97 LRRM 1388 (1978); Operating Eng'rs Local 825 (Major Constr. Co.), 227 NLRB 1055, 95 LRRM 1544 (1977). Fruin-Colnon Corp., 227 NLRB 59, 94 LRRM 1186 (1976), *enforced,* 571 F2d 1017, 97 LRRM 2845 (CA 8, 1978); Automobile Workers (Pitt Processing Co.), 217 NLRB 320, 89 LRRM 1031 (1975); Stuart Wilson, Inc. (Teamsters Local 212), 200 NLRB 519, 82 LRRM 1165 (1972); Rust Eng'r Co. (Sheet Metal Workers Local 51), 183 NLRB 649, 74 LRRM 1655 (1970), *enforced,* 445 F2d 172, 77 LRRM 2885 (CA 6, 1971); Operating Eng'rs Local 9 (Schmidt Constr., Inc.), 147 NLRB 393, 56 LRRM 1225 (1964).
[331]NLRB v. Jarka Corp., 198 F2d 618, 621, 30 LRRM 2537 (CA 3, 1952). *See also* NLRB v. St. Joe Paper Co., 319 F2d 819, 53 LRRM 2633 (CA 2, 1963).
[332]Textile Workers Local 1362 (International Packings Corp.), 221 NLRB 479, 91 LRRM 1032 (1975).
[333]*Compare* Sheet Metal Workers Local 67 (George Williams Sheet Metal Co.), 201 NLRB 1050, 82 LRRM 1617 (1973), *with* Laborers Local 341 v. NLRB, *supra* note 330.
[334]*E.g.,* NLRB v. Plasterers Local 90, 606 F2d 189, 102 LRRM 2482 (CA 7, 1979), *enforcing* 236 NLRB 329, 98 LRRM 1263 (1978); Laborers Local 341 v. NLRB, *supra* note 330; NLRB v. Electrical Workers (IBEW) Local 3, 467 F2d 1158, 81 LRRM 2483 (CA 2, 1972), *enforcing* 193 NLRB 758, 78 LRRM 1431 (1971).

enacted, repeatedly remarked on the floor of the Senate that common law rules of agency were to govern the question of who acted for whom for purposes of determining culpability under the Act."[335]

In enforcing the Act, the Board and the courts have both invoked the principle that one may imply as well as express the authority necessary to create an agency relationship. For example, in *NLRB* v. *Plasterers Local 90*[336] the Seventh Circuit held that a union could impliedly authorize the wife of a business representative to add the names of union members to a union referral list, and that the Board could therefore hold the union liable for the wife's failure to add the name of a particular member. The business representative maintained the referral list in his home, and the representative's wife, who would often answer the referral phone, would often add names to the list. The court explained:

> [T]he Board may base a finding of an agency relationship on evidence that an individual ". . . was acting with the knowledge and acquiescence of the Union and that he had implied authority to do what he did."[337]

As Section 2(13) of the Act appears to mandate, the decisions have also held unions liable for acts within only the *apparent* authority of their agents. Section 2(13) provides: "In determining whether any person [acted] as an 'agent' . . . , the question of whether the specific acts performed were actually authorized or subsequently ratified shall not be controlling." Accordingly, in *NLRB* v. *Teamsters Local 815 (Montauk Iron & Steel Corp.)*,[338] after concluding that a union had surrounded a shop steward with the indicia of authority to order a work stoppage, the Second Circuit affirmed a Board ruling that the union was liable for the steward's ordering of an otherwise unlawful work stoppage.[339] The court stated that "in this field as elsewhere, a prin-

---

[335]NLRB v. Longshoremen & Warehousemen Local 10, 283 F2d 558, 563, 46 LRRM 3141 (CA 9, 1960).
[336]*Supra* note 334.
[337]606 F2d at 189.
[338]290 F2d 99, 48 LRRM 2065 (CA 2, 1961).
[339]The court explained that
"[w]hen Floyd declared there might be a work stoppage and the men in fact stopped working, inferably as a result of his direction, the latter lay within the area where the union had invested Floyd with a least apparent authority. The Board was amply justified in finding that the evidence belied the contention that Floyd was a mere conduit of employee sentiment." *Id.* at 104.

cipal may be held responsible for the acts of an agent whom it has placed in such a position that persons dealing with the agent reasonably believe the acts to be authorized . . . ."[340] But even as the court held the union liable for the conduct of the shop steward, it also recognized that the union is not responsible for his every act simply by virtue of his position. "If he acts only as an individual rather than within the authority the union has conferred, the union is absolved."[341] Recognizing this *mere conduit* principle, the Board, in *Sheet Metal Workers Local 67 (Williams Sheet Metal Co.),*[342] held that a union did not violate Section 8(b)(2) by merely conveying to an employer the attitudes of its members, even though the union's doing so caused the employer to discharge a particular employee.

Predicting when the Board or a court will apply the "mere conduit" concept is difficult. In *Laborers Local 341* v. *NLRB*[343] the Ninth Circuit affirmed a Board ruling that a union violated Section 8(b)(2) when its shop steward informed an employer that the crew on the job site had voted to stop work unless the employer discharged a foreman whom the union had dispatched, even though the shop steward had not participated in the vote and had expressly advised the employer that he intended only to relate the crew's sentiments. The court maintained that the employer could have reasonably inferred that the union had authorized the threat to stop working.

The courts have upheld union liability for the excesses of their agents on at least two theories. In *NLRB* v. *Electrical Workers (IBEW) Local 3*[344] the Second Circuit held that a union was liable for a foreman's enforcing of a secondary boycott even though the foreman had misrepresented his authority to speak for the union. The foreman purported to be a shop steward although he was not. The court found liability because the foreman's exceeding of his *actual* authority had not affected his *apparent* authority to speak for the union.[345] On the other hand, in *NLRB*

---

[340]*Id.* at 103.
[341]*Id.* at 104.
[342]*Supra* note 333.
[343]*Supra* note 330.
[344]*Supra* note 334.
[345]As the court noted, "[t]he union placed Fedar in a position of authority in which as foreman he also acted as steward. That he may have exceeded his authority in claiming to be steward does not affect his apparent authority when he acted as such." 467 F2d at 1160.

v. *Longshoremen & Warehousemen Local 10*[346] the Ninth Circuit relied on an entirely different principle, that a union was broadly liable for its steward's action, in this instance the refusal to allow a member to work notwithstanding that he held a proper dispatch slip. (The member had earlier sued the union.) The Ninth Circuit explained:

> [T]he present situation is not unlike that of an employee who is authorized to cut down designated trees belonging to his employer and who with zeal to increase the employer's profits fells timber belonging to a third party. . . . The Local authorized its stewards to safeguard advantages secured by the union at the bargaining table, yet the stewards exercised their power to achieve advantages to which the union was not entitled. Having created the stewards' power, the Local must take the responsibility if it was wrongly used.[347]

The most typical violations of Section 8(b)(2) involve a union which is seeking the discharge of a nonmember[348] or of a member who has incurred the disfavor of the union's leadership.[349] The discharge of a nonmember directly encourages union membership, while the discharge of the member who has incurred the leader's personal and political disfavor does so indirectly, for it teaches others to be "good" or subservient members and provides an example of union power beyond what the law per-

---

[346]*Supra* note 335.

[347]*Id.* at 564.

[348]Mullett v. NLRB, *supra* note 330; United Nuclear Corp. v. NLRB, 340 F2d 133, 58 LRRM 2211 (CA 1, 1965); NLRB v. Laborers Local 341, *supra* note 330; Local 454, Food & Commercial Workers (Central Soya), 245 NLRB 1295, 102 LRRM 1533 (1979); Detroit Typographical Union No. 18 (Sportgraphics, Inc.), 244 NLRB 1149, 102 LRRM 1337 (1979); Hickmott Foods, Inc., 242 NLRB 1357, 101 LRRM 1342 (1979); Crouse Nuclear Energy Servs., Inc., 240 NLRB 390, 100 LRRM 1422 (1979); Carpenters Local 1554 (Bruchard Designs, Inc.), *supra* note 330; Ornamental Iron Workers Local 426 (Brown Bros., Inc.), *supra* note 330; Painters Local 829, *supra* note 330; Electrical Workers (IBEW) Local 112 (Ajax Elec. Co.), 231 NLRB 162, 95 LRRM 1571 (1977); Operating Eng'rs Local 825 (Major Constr. Co.), *supra* note 330; Plumbers Local 58 (Heyse Sheet Metal), 187 NLRB 152, 76 LRRM 1192 (1970); Operating Eng'rs Local 9 (Schmidt Constr., Inc.), 147 NLRB 393, 56 LRRM 1225 (1964).

[349]Fruin-Colnon Corp. v. NLRB, *supra* note 330; Rust Eng'r Co. v. NLRB, *supra* note 330; Lummus Co. v. NLRB, 339 F2d 728, 56 LRRM 2425 (CA DC, 1964); NLRB v. Longshoremen & Warehousemen Local 10, *supra* note 335; Operating Eng'rs Local 106 (Green Island Contracting Co.), 243 NLRB 551, 101 LRRM 1596 (1979); Steelworkers Local 8061 (Arrowhead Eng'r Corp.), 233 NLRB 858, 97 LRRM 1012 (1977); Teamsters Local 282 (Explo, Inc.), 229 NLRB 347, 95 LRRM 1202 (1977); Carpenters Local 2205 (Groves-Granite), 229 NLRB 56, 96 LRRM 1146 (1977); Daniel Constr. Co., 227 NLRB 72, 94 LRRM 1547 (1976); Upper Manhattan Medical Group, 225 NLRB 153, 92 LRRM 1585 (1976) (discharge for nonpayment of dues held pretextual); Textile Workers Local 1362 (International Packings Corp.), *supra* note 332; Teamsters Local 860 (Admiral Corp.), 195 NLRB 68, 79 LRRM 1244 (1972); Electrical Workers (IBEW) Local 71 (Wagner-Smith Co.), 187 NLRB 899, 76 LRRM 1854 (1971).

mits.[350] It has long been established that a violation may be found where the result has been to encourage allegiance or obedience to union leadership or even more active participation in internal union affairs.

The Supreme Court gave early direction to the broad implications of the language of Section 8(b)(2) in *Radio Officers Union v. NLRB*.[351] It held that union inducement of an employer to discharge a union member for reasons other than failure to pay union dues or fees authorized by the union-shop proviso to Section 8(a)(3) violated Section 8(b)(2). The Court noted that it had previously held that the terms "discrimination" and "membership in any labor organization" included "discrimination to discourage participation in union activities as well as to discourage adhesion to union membership.[352] The Court stressed that

[t]he policy of the Act is to insulate employees' job rights from their organizational rights. Thus §§8(a)(3) and 8(b)(2) were designed to allow employees to freely exercise their right to join unions, be good, bad, or indifferent members, or abstain from joining any union without imperiling their livelihood.[353]

Thus, aside from dismissals pursuant to valid union-shop agreements, "[n]o other discrimination aimed at encouraging employees to join, retain membership, or stay in good standing in a union is condoned."[354]

Discrimination under Section 8(b)(2) does not always involve a discharge. The discrimination might also take the form of layoff, transfer, demotion, or simply a loss of pay.[355]

It is even possible that the questioned action, if taken by the employer alone, would not be a violation of Section 8(a)(3). However, if the action was induced by the union for wrongful

---

[350]Radio Officers Union v. NLRB, *supra* note 8.
[351]*Id.*
[352]The Court cited Associated Press v. NLRB, 301 US 103, 1 LRRM 732 (1937), 347 US at 40 n.39.
[353]347 US at 40.
[354]347 US at 41-42.
[355]*See, e.g.,* Steelworkers (DuVal Corp.), 243 NLRB 1157, 101 LRRM 1593 (1979); Maui Surf Hotel, 235 NLRB 957, 98 LRRM 1001 (1978) (a Board majority found that the union violated 8(b)(2) when it insisted that the employer pressure its employees to cease work and forfeit one hour's pay in order to attend a union meeting held on the employer's premises).

reasons, a violation of Sections 8(a)(3) and (b)(2) will be found.[356] Thus, where an employer may have been within its rights in discharging a particular employee, a violation nevertheless exists if the action was induced by the union for an improper reason. Under the rationale of *Radio Officers*, this result obtains because the other employees will perceive the union's exercise of power and will; accordingly, they may be encouraged to become more active members, or, perhaps, merely to become members. The Board will therefore presume that union activity is encouraged where a union causes a discharge.[357] Likewise, where the employer has in fact delegated to a union the authority to discharge or lay off employees, a wrongful exercise of that authority will result in Section 8(b)(2) liability against the union and a Section 8(a)(3) finding against the employer.[358]

To violate Section 8(b)(2), it is not necessary that a union act with the precise motive of encouraging union membership. A union will be held responsible for the foreseeable consequences of its actions, and if the consequence is encouragement of union membership or obedience of its members, a violation will be found.[359]

When a union or its leadership causes or attempts to cause an employer to take action with respect to an employee for a reason that is arbitrary, invidious, or in bad faith, it breaches its duty of fair representation and Section 8(b)(2) is violated.[360] An example of this type of violation is found where a layoff is required and a union leader seeks to protect the job of a relative or friend at the expense of some other members with greater seniority.[361] Similarly, Section 8(b)(2) prohibits a union from acting arbitrarily to further the desires of a majority or the internal political aspirations of a union officer.[362] Likewise, classifications by union hiring halls based on race or sex have been held prohibited by

---

[356]Carpenters Local 2205 (Groves-Granite), *supra* note 349.

[357]Operating Eng'rs Local 18, 204 NLRB 681, 83 LRRM 1455 (1973), *enforcement denied*, 496 F2d 1308, 86 LRRM 2672 (CA 6, 1974).

[358]Fruin-Colnon Corp. v. NLRB, *supra* note 330.

[359]*See, e.g.,* NLRB v. St. Joe Paper Co., *supra* note 331.

[360]Fruin-Colnon Corp. v. NLRB, *supra* note 330; Laborers Local 341 v. NLRB, *supra* note 330; Barton Brands, Ltd. v. NLRB, 529 F2d 793, 91 LRRM 2241 (CA 7, 1976); Olympic S. S. Co., *supra* note 314; Teamsters Local 282 (Explo, Inc.), *supra* note 349. For detailed discussion of the duty of fair representation, *see* Chapter 28 *infra*.

[361]Teamsters Local 282 (Explo, Inc.), *supra* note 349; Fruin-Colnon Corp. v. NLRB, *supra* note 330 ("I can't lay my uncle off because he owes money to the bank and I am on his note").

[362]Barton Brands, Ltd. v. NLRB, *supra* note 360.

Section 8(b)(2).[363] The rationale of these cases is that a union, when it acts arbitrarily or invidiously, demonstrates that employees must curry its favor to avoid unfavorable treatment at the hands of the employer.

In 1962, in *Miranda Fuel Co.*,[364] the Board held that a breach of the union's duty to properly represent bargaining-unit employees amounted to a violation of Sections 8(b)(2) and 8(b)(1)(A), thereby bringing the doctrine of fair representation under NLRB jurisdiction. Accordingly, Section 8(b)(1)(A) prohibits a union "when acting in a statutory representative capacity, from taking action against any employee upon considerations or classifications which are irrelevant, invidious or unfair."[365] This obligation is based on the right afforded employees by Section 7 "to bargain collectively through representatives of their own choosing" and on the grant of exclusive representation provided to unions by Section 9(a).

Violations of Section 8(b)(2) have also been found where a union causes the discharge of an employee under an unlawful union security agreement[366] or improperly secures an employee's discharge under an otherwise lawful agreement.[367]

A violation will not be found, however, where the union is not the cause of the employer's action.[368] Thus, where a union official merely advised an employer that individual members would strike or quit unless a particular nonunion employee was discharged, no violation was found.[369] However, both the Board and the courts have found violations where there was evidence of union involvement in or ratification of such a threat.[370]

Likewise, the Board has not found a violation where a union has attempted to cause one employer to cease doing business with another, even when the action is aimed at the nonunion

---

[363]*See, e.g.,* Olympic Steamship Co., *supra* note 314.
[364]140 NLRB 181, 51 LRRM 1584 (1962), *enforcement denied,* 326 F2d 172, 54 LRRM 2715 (CA 2, 1963). *See* Chapter 28 *infra* at notes 105-108.
[365]*Id.* at 185.
[366]*See, e.g.,* Carpenters Local 1554 (Bruchard Designs, Inc.), *supra* note 330. A full discussion of this line of cases will be found in Chapter 29 *infra.*
[367]Upper Manhattan Medical Group, *supra* note 349. Problems relating to union security agreements are discussed at notes 388-417 *infra.*
[368]Great Plains Beef Co., 241 NLRB 948, 101 LRRM 1128 (1979).
[369]*See, e.g.,* Sheet Metal Workers Local 67 (George Williams Sheet Metal Co.), *supra* note 333.
[370]Mullett v. NLRB, *supra* note 330; Operating Eng'rs Local 9 (Schmidt Constr., Inc.), *supra* note 330.

employees of the second employer. The Board's rationale in those cases was that Section 8(a)(3) does not protect employers; their remedy would lie under Section 8(b)(4).[371]

All union encouragement is not unlawful. A union which is effective may, by that very fact, lawfully encourage union activity or membership. As the Supreme Court has stated,

> the union is a service agency that probably encourages membership whenever it does its job well. But . . . the only encouragement or discouragement of union membership banned by the Act is that which is "accomplished by discrimination."[372]

Unions are allowed a wide range of reasonableness in representing their membership as a whole.[373] Thus, when there is a legitimate business action that results in disparate treatment of employees, a Section 8(b)(2) violation will not be found.[374]

B. Violations Relating to Seniority Provisions

In addition to the problem posed by a union's attempt to have a disfavored employee divested of seniority, several other problem areas relate to seniority provisions in collective bargaining agreements.

One type of problem arises when an employer either acquires or merges with another company and there is a reduction in the number of employees because of the consolidated operation. It has been held that a union does not violate Section 8(b)(2) if, prior to the effectuation of the merger, it concludes an agreement calling for the preservation of seniority of the represented employees, with the concomitant result that the unrepresented employees in the other company are placed at the bottom of the list. Since seniority is defined by contract, the unrepresented employees have no conflicting contractual rights. Moreover, when the agreement in question is concluded prior to the con-

---

[371]Mine Workers Welfare & Retirement Fund Trustees, 201 NLRB 368, 82 LRRM 1276 (1973); Malbaff Landscape Constr., 172 NLRB 128, 68 LRRM 1288 (1968). *See* Chapter 25 *infra.*
[372]Local 357, Teamsters v. NLRB, 365 US 667, 675-76, 47 LRRM 2906 (1961). *See* Chapter 29 at notes 221-25 and *infra* this chapter at note 419.
[373]*E.g., see* Ford Motor Co. v. Huffman, 345 US 330, 31 LRRM 2548 (1953), discussed at notes 266-279 in Chapter 28 *infra.*
[374]Painters Dist. 2 (Paint, Inc.), 239 NLRB 1378, 100 LRRM 1152 (1979).

solidation, there is no duty on the part of the union to negotiate on behalf of the other employees.[375]

As discussed in another chapter, although a union has a duty to represent fairly all bargaining unit employees, the interests of some will inevitably have to give way to the interests of others; the Act permits unions a "wide range of reasonableness"[376] in dealing with questions of seniority.[377] In making decisions affecting seniority, however, a union is held to a fair representation standard; thus it may not act arbitrarily, invidiously, or in bad faith. For example, in *Barton Brands, Ltd.* v. *NLRB*[378] the Seventh Circuit remanded a case to the Board for consideration of whether the "endtailing" of one group of employees amounted to a violation when it appeared that it had been done invidiously and arbitrarily. After a merger of two companies, the union had negotiated a "dovetailing" of seniority, with employees of both companies keeping their seniority on a merged list. But when layoffs appeared imminent, the larger group of employees, spurred on by one person with internal union ambitions, pressed for a new agreement placing the other group at the bottom of the list and replacing the "dovetailing" with an "endtailing" agreement. The Board held that since the union was motivated by the internal political ambitions of one person, Section 8(b)(2) was violated.[379] The Seventh Circuit disagreed, holding that the conduct of that one individual was not attributable to the union. The court concluded, however, that the Board's finding of a violation could stand if, on remand, it was found that the decision to "endtail" the smaller group was made arbitrarily or to placate the wishes of the majority at the expense of the minority.

On remand, the Board found a violation on the ground that the union had merely sought to placate the desires of the majority.[380]

---

[375]Schick v. NLRB, 409 F2d 395, 70 LRRM 3249 (CA 7, 1969); NLRB v. Whiting Milk Corp., 342 F2d 8, 58 LRRM 2471 (CA 1, 1965).
[376]Ford Motor Co. v. Huffman, *supra* note 373. *See* Chapter 28 *infra* for detailed treatment of the duty of fair representation.
[377]Brown & Williamson Tobacco Co., 227 NLRB 2005, 94 LRRM 1337 (1977) (agreement between employer and union that employees transferring out of bargaining unit could retain seniority by continuing to pay dues to union held not unlawful). *See also* Colorado Transfer & Storage, Inc. (Teamsters Local 17), 198 NLRB 252, 80 LRRM 1682 (1972).
[378]*Supra* note 360.
[379]213 NLRB 640, 87 LRRM 1231 (1974).
[380]228 NLRB 889, 95 LRRM 1357 (1977).

A second area of concern relating to seniority involves agreements calling for "superseniority" for employees who hold union office. In *Dairylea Cooperative, Inc.*,[381] the Board held that while contractual provisions granting superseniority to union stewards with respect to layoff and recall were lawful, more expansive clauses granting superseniority to stewards for all purposes, including job-bidding preference, were a violation of Section 8(b)(2).[382] Superseniority clauses are thus to be permitted only to the extent that they are necessary to the collective bargaining process.

Where superseniority for stewards is limited to layoffs, the Board has sustained the provisions, finding a legitimate purpose in the retention of an official to process grievances. That purpose was held sufficient to outweigh the obvious tendency of such provisions to encourage union membership, i.e., to encourage one to become an "active" union member in order to achieve a steward's position and its superseniority emoluments. Originally the Board limited its approval of superseniority only to stewards, and only for layoffs and recalls. Later, however, it approved the extension of superseniority for purposes of layoff and recall to union officials other than stewards.[383] Indeed, this occurred even where the written description of the officer's duties appeared to have little or no relationship to the collective bargaining process; the Board reasoned that it did not desire to "second guess" the union regarding which officers were actually necessary "in effectively representing the unit."[384]

Where superseniority has been extended to permit lateral bumping by a steward, the Board has found no violation, even

---

[381]*Supra* note 324.

[382]*See also* A.P.A. Transp. Corp., *supra* note 89; Connecticut Limousine Serv., Inc., *supra* note 324; Allied Supermarkets, Inc. (Teamsters Local 337), 233 NLRB 535, 96 LRRM 1600 (1977); Teamsters Local 823 (Campbell "66" Express, Inc.), 232 NLRB 851, 97 LRRM 1191 (1977). A seniority clause giving a union the right to veto the discharge of a union steward is presumptively illegal. Perma-Line Corp. v. Painters Local 230, 639 F2d 890, 106 LRRM 2483 (CA 2, 1981).

[383]Allied Indus. Workers Local 148 (Allen Group, Inc.), *supra* note 323; American Can Co. (Steelworkers Local 5490), 235 NLRB 704, 98 LRRM 1012 (1978); Otis Elevator Co., *supra* note 323; Electrical Workers (UE) Local 623 (Limpco Mfg., Inc.), *supra* note 323. Superseniority may also be given to employees who perform several functions that further the collective bargaining interests of the bargaining unit. D'Amico v. NLRB, *supra* note 323. "[C]redible proof that the individual in question was officially assigned duties which helped to implement the collective bargaining agreement in a meaningful way" is required. *Id.* at 825.

[384]American Can Co., *supra* note 383. The Third Circuit would place the burden on the union to demonstrate the need for superseniority for a union official other than a steward. D'Amico v. NLRB, *supra* note 323.

though the steward could have also used his seniority to bump downward.[385] The Board's rationale was that the use of super-seniority was necessary to protect the steward from the threat of future layoff. Even though the rule in *Dairylea* cloaks super-seniority clauses extending benefits beyond layoff and recall preference with presumptive invalidity, it does not purport to make them invalid *per se*. The legality of the parties' inclusion of the clause in the contract depends upon the existence of an adequate justification at the time of execution.[386]

C. Violations Relating to Union Security Provisions

Pursuant to the union-shop proviso to Section 8(a)(3), a union may lawfully cause the discharge of an employee working under a union-or agency-shop agreement if the employee fails to tender the union's regular dues and initiation fees.[387]

In *NLRB* v. *General Motors*[388] the Supreme Court held that the term "membership" as used in Section 8(b)(3) embodies only a financial obligation limited to the payment of fees and dues.

Because union security under Section 8(a)(3) is limited to payment of fees and dues, a union violates Section 8(b)(2) when it causes the discharge of an employee for failing or refusing to pay fines levied by the union.[389] Similarly, the Board has held that a union cannot procure the transfer or discharge of former members who continue to tender dues but refuse to pay a "reinstatement fee" where the union's constitution provides for a reinstatement fee only where dues are delinquent. The Board viewed the fee in question as "unlawful" and thus not within Section 8(a)(3) exception.[390] And according to the First Circuit, a union violates Section 8(b)(2) when it causes nonmembers to

---

[385]Expedient Serv., Inc., *supra* note 326; Parker-Hannifin Corp., *supra* note 326; Hospital Serv. Plan, *supra* note 326; Theatrical Stage Employees Local 780, *supra* note 326.
[386]NLRB v. Auto Warehousers, Inc., 571 F2d 860, 98 LRRM 2238 (CA 5, 1978).
[387]For detailed treatment of union security, *see* Chapter 29 *infra*.
[388]373 US 734, 53 LRRM 2313 (1963).
[389]Laborers Local 721, 246 NLRB 691, 102 LRRM 1656 (1979); Pittsburgh Press Co., 241 NLRB 666, 100 LRRM 1542 (1979).
[390]Automobile Workers Local 1756, 240 NLRB 281, 100 LRRM 1208 (1979). But failure of a member to pay a *valid* reinstatement fee entitles the union to cause his discharge. *See infra* at note 403.

be replaced for failure to pay an alleged hiring-hall fee where the union in fact was operating not an exclusive hiring hall but a referral system for members only. The Court reasoned that the fee would have been legitimate if an exclusive hiring hall had existed, but "the union could not charge the fee if it did not in fact operate the service."[391]

Even as to dues and legitimate fees, there are limits to a union's legal ability to enforce union security provisions. For example, where a union advised a former member who had resigned during a strike that it would accept his tender of a sum equal to union dues only if he rescinded his resignation, and it thereafter caused his discharge, the Act was violated; the Board reasoned that since Section 8(a)(3) requires nothing more than payment of initiation fees and dues, the union acted unlawfully in compelling active membership as a condition of employment.[392]

Similarly, a discharge for dues delinquency has been held unlawful under the following conditions: (1) where payment was sought only after an employee whose dues delinquency was longstanding had made statements critical of the union;[393] (2) where the delinquency was for a period when the employee was outside the bargaining unit;[394] (3) where the delinquency resulted from the employee's tendering his dues on his first payday after his return to work following sick leave, after he had been informed that he could wait until the "next" payday;[395] and (4) where an employee tendered his dues in cash rather

---

[391]Frattaroli v. NLRB, 590 F2d 15, 100 LRRM 2296, 2298 n.4 (CA 1, 1978). *See generally* Chapter 29 for discussion of union hiring halls; also discussion *infra* at notes 418-52.

[392]Hershey Foods Corp., 207 NLRB 897, 85 LRRM 1004 (1973), *enforced,* 513 F2d 1083, 89 LRRM 2126 (CA 9, 1975). *Accord,* Service Employees Local 680, 232 NLRB 326, 97 LRRM 1186 (1977); Communications Workers Local 1104, 211 NLRB 114, 87 LRRM 1253 (1974), *enforced,* 520 F2d 411, 89 LRRM 3028 (CA 2, 1975).

[393]Pueblo Int'l, Inc., 229 NLRB 770, 95 LRRM 1203 (1977).

[394]Hotel & Restaurant Employees Local 2, 240 NLRB 757, 100 LRRM 1324 (1979); Carpenters (Ridge Homes, Div. of Evans Prods. Co.), 224 NLRB 1144, 92 LRRM 1587 (1976).

[395]Macaulay Foundry Co. (Molders Local 164), *supra* note 308. *See also* Telephone Workers (Bell of Pennsylvania), 226 NLRB 427, 93 LRRM 1289 (1976) (Board quoted with approval from its prior decision in Simmons Co., 150 NLRB 709, 58 LRRM 1148 (1964), in which it held "that an employee may not be required to pay back dues for a period when membership was not validly required as a condition of employment"); Sheet Metal Workers, 254 NLRB 773, 106 LRRM 1137 (1981) (union violated §8(b)(2) by causing discharge of employee who remitted delinquent dues in accordance with extension of time granted by union).

than by check, money order, or check-off authorization as demanded by the union.[396] The Board has also found that a union operating under a contractual union security agreement violated Section 8(b)(5)[397] when it increased its initiation fee from two weeks' pay to four weeks' pay; the increase was found to be excessive and deliberately calculated to cause the employer to hire unemployed members whose initiation fees had been paid, rather than hire persons who were not members.[398]

The Eighth Circuit[399] enforced a Board order holding that a union operating under an agency-shop agreement violated Section 8(b)(2) when it caused the discharge of a nonmember employee who was late in paying service fees. Under the union's constitution, union members were afforded a 90-day grace period for dues payments, whereas nonmembers were allowed only a 10-day grace period in which to pay their service fees. The court said that "[r]egardless whether the Union may treat its members more favorably than nonmembers, it may not cause the employer to do so."[400] Similarly, a union may not selectively invoke dues delinquency in order to procure the discharge of dissidents while overlooking equivalent delinquency by supporters.[401]

The Board has held that the obligation to pay dues under a union security clause accrues from the date of the execution of the collective bargaining agreement and not from the date to which the agreement was made retroactive.[402] But it was not a violation where the union caused the discharge of an employee

---

[396]AMF, Inc., 247 NLRB 231, 103 LRRM 1122 (1980).

[397]For discussion of check-off authorizations, see Chapter 29 infra at notes 305-306.

[398]Theatrical Stage Employees Local 841, 225 NLRB 994, 93 LRRM 1072 (1976); see also Television & Radio Broadcasting Studio Employees Local 804, 135 NLRB 632, 49 LRRM 1541 (1962). Board compared challenged initiation fee with initiation fees prevailing for sister locals in the industry and rejected the union's contention that the increase was designed to improve union's financial condition.

[399]Hospital & Nursing Home Employees Local 113, 228 NLRB 1500, 96 LRRM 1422, enforced, 567 F2d 831, 97 LRRM 2160 (CA 8, 1977).

[400]Supra note 399 at 832.

[401]District 1199, Retail, Wholesale & Dep't Store Union (Upper Manhattan Medical Group), supra note 349; Jersey Shore Medical Center-Fitkin Hosp. (Jersey Nurses Economic Sec. Organization), 225 NLRB 1191, 93 LRRM 1133 (1976).

[402]Typographical Union Local 53 (Plain Dealer Publishing Co.), 225 NLRB 1281, 93 LRRM 1151 (1976); Teamsters Local 25 (Tech Weld Corp.), 220 NLRB 76, 90 LRRM 1193 (1975); Namm's, Inc., 102 NLRB 466, 31 LRRM 1328 (1953). The wording of the dues check-off card may in some cases be dispositive. See Carpenters (Campbell Indus.), 243 NLRB 147, 101 LRRM 1394 (1979); Frito-Lay, Inc., 243 NLRB 137, 101 LRRM 1390 (1979).

whose tender of back dues was rejected because, following his suspension from membership, he had failed to pay the reinstatement fee required by the union's bylaws.[403] A member's failure to pay previously levied fines or assessments, however, does not justify refusal of tendered dues; and a resulting attempt to have the employee denied employment or discharged is unlawful.[404]

While the Board has not set any particular time limitations on when a union must act to enforce a union security provision, the failure to give members "reasonable" notice of delinquency and adequate opportunity to make payment may result in a finding of violation.[405] The Board has adhered strictly to the rule that a union may not cause the discharge of a member until it has fulfilled its fiduciary duty to him, such as "informing the member of the amount owed, the method used to compute that amount, when such payments are to be made, and that discharge will result from failure to pay."[406] It is the union's duty to fulfill this duty, notwithstanding a member's own voluntary efforts to ascertain the same information. A member's inquiries as to his dues obligations do not lessen the union's affirmative obligation to provide the member with the necessary information and opportunity to pay.[407] Under this rationale, the Board has held that, where the union has failed to give the requisite notice, it is not necessary "to establish a causal connection" between that failure to give notice and the member's nonpayment in order to find a violation.[408]

The Board has held that for valid application, a union-shop agreement must be in effect "at the moment" the union requests an employee's discharge for nonpayment of dues. In *Machinists District 15 (Burroughs Corp.)*[409] the union was held to have violated

---

[403]John J. Roche & Co., Inc., 231 NLRB 1082, 96 LRRM 1281 (1977), *enforced sub nom.* Larkins v. NLRB, 596 F2d 240, 101 LRRM 2018 (CA 7, 1979).

[404]Painters Local 1627 (Johnson's Plastering Co.), 233 NLRB 820, 97 LRRM 1010 (1977); Longshoremen & Warehousemen Local 13 (Pacific Maritime Ass'n), 228 NLRB 1383, 96 LRRM 1450 (1977), *enforced,* 581 F2d 1321, 99 LRRM 2435 (CA 9, 1978), *cert. denied,* 440 US 935, 100 LRRM 2687 (1979).

[405]*See* Teamsters Local 122 (Busch & Co.), 203 NLRB 1041, 83 LRRM 1235 (1973), *enforced,* 509 F2d 1160, 87 LRRM 3274 (CA 1, 1974); Valley Cabinet & Mfg., *supra* note 310; Food & Commercial Workers Local 1445 (Gallahue's Supermarkets), 247 NLRB 1031, 103 LRRM 1267 (1980); Teamsters Local 572 (Ralph's Grocery), 247 NLRB 934, 103 LRRM 1268 (1980).

[406]Distillery Workers Local 38, 242 NLRB 370, 101 LRRM 1150, 1151 (1979).

[407]Teamsters Local 572, *supra* note 405.

[408]Teamsters Local 150, 242 NLRB 454, 101 LRRM 1175 (1979).

[409]231 NLRB 602, 96 LRRM 1625 (1977).

the Act by requesting an employee's discharge after the authority to maintain a union security clause had been revoked in a deauthorization election, even though the employee's dues obligation arose while the agreement was in effect. But mere *filing* of a deauthorization petition will not relieve employees of their obligations under an existing union-shop agreement. In *King Electrical Manufacturing*[410] a deauthorization petition was filed one week after the effective date of the contract containing a union security clause. The election on the petition was scheduled for a date following the 31-day period in which the employees were required to join the union. When the employer refused to honor the requested discharge of employees who had failed to join during that period, the union filed Section 8(a)(5) charges, thereby blocking the election. The employer was found to have violated Section 8(a)(5) by refusing to comply with the clause. The Board said that a union security clause is enforceable until an affirmative deauthorization vote has actually been cast.

In *Platt Electric Supply*[411] the Board found no violation where the employer had rejected a union's request that it discharge strike replacements who had failed to tender union dues and initiation fees required by a union security contract. Following a strike and the replacement of strikers, the union sent letters to the strike replacements "in care of" the employer, advising them of their obligation to tender union dues and initiation fees; but the employer failed to forward the letters to the strike replacements. The Board held that because a union seeking to enforce a union security provision must inform the employee of his membership obligations before it can legally request his discharge, the employer was under no obligation to discharge the replacements. But it also held that the employer's failure to forward the letters was "inextricably involved" with the employer's unlawful repudiation of the union security contract; it therefore ordered the employer to forward any subsequent communications from the union regarding the union security obligation to the replacements and to offer reinstatement to the strikers if replacements failed to fulfill their union security obligations.

---

[410]229 NLRB 615, 96 LRRM 1370 (1977).
[411]224 NLRB 1477, 92 LRRM 1389 (1976), *enforced sub nom.* Teamsters Local 162 v. NLRB, 568 F2d 665, 97 LRRM 2917 (CA 9, 1978).

In *H. C. Macaulay Foundry Co. v. NLRB*[412] the union caused termination of an employee it mistakenly assumed was working but who, in fact, was on sick leave. The Ninth Circuit enforced the Board's order finding that the union violated Section 8(b)(2) because its letter advising the employee of his delinquency was ambiguous with respect to the date on which payment was required; the employer was found to have violated Section 8(a)(3) by acceding to the union's discharge request without inquiry.[413]

In *St. Luke's Hospital Center*[414] the Board found Section 8(b)(2) and 8(a)(3) violations when, pursuant to a union's demands, the employer threatened hospital employees with discharge because of their failure to join the union or to pay initiation fees and dues as required by the agreement. Finding that the employees were professional employees, the Board consequently refused to recognize the validity of a state-conducted election and certification where the state board had included both professional and nonprofessional employees in the same unit without determining whether a majority of the professional employees had voted to be included.[415] The Board held that the state board's determination was repugnant to Section (9)(b)(1); it therefore refused to defer to an arbitrator's finding that the union security provision of the collective agreement was applicable to the professional employees.

As a general rule, the Board requires that supervisors returning to the bargaining unit be treated as "new" employees for union security purposes.[416] In *A. O. Smith Corp.*[417] that rule was qualified, and a distinction was made for cases in which the line between "supervisor" and "employee" was not clearly drawn. The Board found that where individuals are often shuttled back and forth between unit and supervisory functions, the proper test is "whether there is a reasonable expectancy that when an individual becomes a supervisor he may soon return to the unit." Finding that there was such an expectancy in the instant case, the Board rejected the General Counsel's argument that the

---

[412]*Supra* note 308.
[413]*See also* Food & Commercial Workers Local 1445 (Gallahue's Supermarkets), *supra* note 405; Forsyth Hardwood Co., 243 NLRB 1039, 102 LRRM 1019 (1979).
[414]221 NLRB 1314, 91 LRRM 1150 (1976).
[415]*See* Chapter 11 *infra* at notes 43-56.
[416]Electrical Workers (IBEW) Local 329 (Illinois Bell Tel. Co.), 200 NLRB 1050, 82 LRRM 1077 (1972), *enforced*, 499 F2d 56, 86 LRRM 2826 (CA 7, 1974).
[417]227 NLRB 854, 94 LRRM 1115 (1977).

individual involved had accrued no dues obligation for a 29-day period between supervisory assignments during which he had worked in the unit. Thus, neither the employer nor the union violated the Act by denying the supervisor the right to return to the unit because of his expulsion for nonpayment of dues for the period in question. The Board distinguished *Illinois Bell Telephone Co.* because there the evidence did not suggest frequent movement of unit members to and from supervisory positions.

D. Violations Relating to Hiring Halls

Hiring-hall arrangements are another source of discrimination violations under Sections 8(a)(3) and 8(b)(2).[418] *Teamsters Local 357* v. *NLRB*[419] is the leading case in which a hiring-hall agreement was drawn into question under these provisions. The employer, a trucking association, had entered into a hiring-hall agreement with the union under which casual employees were dispatched from hiring halls on the basis of seniority in the trucking industry. Seniority began with a minimum of three months' service, "irrespective of whether such employee is or is not a member of the Union." The union procured the discharge of a union member because he had obtained employment without being dispatched by the union. Reversing the Board[420] and the District of Columbia Circuit,[421] which had held that the hiring-hall agreement in question was unlawful and that the member's discharge was in violation of Sections 8(a)(3) and 8(b)(2), the Supreme Court held that discrimination could not be inferred from the face of the agreement, for it had specifically prohibited discrimination against casual employees because of union membership or nonmembership.[422]

While a hiring-hall agreement may be nondiscriminatory on its face, its administration may be otherwise.[423] Thus, the courts

---

[418]For detailed discussion of hiring halls, *see generally* Chapter 29 *infra*.
[419]*Supra* note 372 and accompanying text. *See also* Chapter 29 *infra* at note 220.
[420]121 NLRB 1629, 43 LRRM 1029 (1958).
[421]275 F2d 646, 45 LRRM 2752 (CA DC, 1960).
[422]*See* Chapter 29 *infra* at notes 221-23.
[423]*E.g.,* NLRB v. Local 269, Electrical Workers (IBEW), 357 F2d 51, 61 LRRM 2371 (CA 3, 1966); Lummus Co. v. NLRB, *supra* note 349; NLRB v. Houston Maritime Ass'n, 337 F2d 333, 57 LRRM 2170 (CA 5, 1964); NLRB v. Southern Stevedoring & Contracting Co., 332 F2d 1017, 56 LRRM 2507 (CA 5, 1964); Cargo Handlers, 159 NLRB 321,

and the Board have found violations in the following situations: (1) where unions have refused to refer nonmember applicants,[424] or union applicants who were not members of the union which operated the hiring hall,[425] or applicants who were not employed in a union shop;[426] (2) where unions have refused referral in retaliation for an applicant's criticism of the union;[427] (3) where a nonmember allegedly usurped union members' prerogatives by instigating a work slowdown;[428] and (4) where an applicant filed unfair labor practice charges against the union or refused to pay internal union fines[429] or was otherwise disenchanted with the union.[430] Similarly, the Board and the Ninth Circuit found a violation where a union, operating an exclusive hiring hall pursuant to a collective bargaining agreement, made referrals in disregard of that agreement. The court concluded that this "backdooring" had a "natural consequence" of encouraging union membership and was therefore discriminatory.[431] Likewise, an employer violated the Act by unilaterally instituting a hiring procedure by which it employed only·union members dispatched by the union.[432]

---

62 LRRM 1228 (1966); Local 742, Carpenters (J. L. Simmons Co.), 157 NLRB 451, 61 LRRM 1370 (1966). *See also* Summers, *A Summary Evaluation of the Taft-Hartley Act,* 11 IND. & LAB. REL. REV. 405, 409-10 (1958).

[424]NLRB v. Electrical Workers (IBEW) Local 322, 597 F2d 1326, 101 LRRM 2157 (CA 10, 1979), *enforcing* 223 NLRB 925, 92 LRRM 1220 (1976); Carpenters Local 1089 (E. F. Hargett & Co.), 233 NLRB 275, 96 LRRM 1508 (1977); Operating Eng'rs Local 18 (S. J. Groves & Sons Co.), 227 NLRB 1477, 94 LRRM 1336 (1977); Elevator Constructors Local 16 (Westinghouse Elevator Co.), 229 NLRB 439, 95 LRRM 1191 (1977); Plumbers Local 630, 222 NLRB 524, 91 LRRM 1224 (1976); Carpenters, 222 NLRB 551, 91 LRRM 1178 (1976).

[425]Sachs Elec. Co., 248 NLRB No. 92, 104 LRRM 1070 (1980).

[426]New York Typographical Union Local 6 (Royal Composing Room, Inc.), 242 NLRB 378, 101 LRRM 1148 (1979), *enforcement denied in pertinent part,* 632 F2d 171, 105 LRRM 2529 (CA 2, 1980).

[427]Laborers Local 300 (Memorial Park Dev. Ass'n), 235 NLRB 334, 98 LRRM 1599 (1978), *enforced,* 613 F2d 203, 103 LRRM 2292 (CA 9, 1980); Carpenters Local 1914 (W&H Conveyer Systems, Inc.), 250 NLRB 1426, 105 LRRM 1116 (1980); Iron Workers Local 75 (Tyler Reinforcing), 232 NLRB 1194, 96 LRRM 1377 (1977); Operating Eng'rs Local 138 (Building Contractors Ass'n, Inc.), 233 NLRB 267, 96 LRRM 1564 (1977); Laborers Local 525, 223 NLRB 939, 92 LRRM 1160 (1976).

[428]Plumbers Local 388, 245 NLRB 1252, 102 LRRM 1531 (1979).

[429]Iron Workers Local 136 (United Exposition Serv.), 252 NLRB 394, 105 LRRM 1325 (1980); Nederland Theatrical Corp., 240 NLRB 678, 100 LRRM 1441 (1979).

[430]NLRB v. Laborers Local 300, *supra* note 427; Laborers Local 252 (Associated Gen. Contractors), 233 NLRB 1358, 97 LRRM 1128 (1977); Plumbers Local 121, 223 NLRB 1250, 92 LRRM 1185 (1976); Plumbers Local 17, 224 NLRB 1262, 92 LRRM 1599 (1976), *enforced,* 575 F2d 585, 98 LRRM 3209 (CA 6, 1978); Electrical Workers (IBEW) Local 675, 223 NLRB 1499, 92 LRRM 1207 (1976).

[431]NLRB v. Iron Workers Local 433 (Associated Gen. Contractors), 600 F2d 770, 101 LRRM 3119, 3123 (CA 9, 1979).

[432]Panscape Corp., 231 NLRB 693, 96 LRRM 1214 (1977), *enforced,* 607 F2d 198, 102 LRRM 2660 (CA 7, 1979).

In the construction industry, preference in job referrals given to residents of a particular geographic area is generally lawful.[433] Nevertheless, where only U.S. citizens, or those who had expressed an interest in becoming citizens, were eligible for union membership, it was unlawful for the union to establish a system of job referrals which gave preference to persons born in the United States and to Mexican nationals whose families reside in the United States. The union's request that an employer transfer an employee because he was not an American citizen and because his family resided in Mexico was a violation of Section 8(b)(2).[434]

Generally, it is unlawful for a union to require that preference in employment be given to employees whose names appear on an "experience" roster, when the qualifying experience necessary for placement on the roster is limited to experience obtained with employers having collective bargaining agreements with the union.[435]

Construction industry unions, however, may lawfully maintain and enforce hiring-hall provisions which give priority in job referrals based on applicants' length of service with employers who are subject to collective bargaining agreements with the union. In *Interstate Electric Co.*[436] a Board majority rejected the contention that such a provision is implicitly discriminatory

---

[433]§8(f)(4) provides that "it shall not be an unfair labor practice . . . for an employer engaged primarily in the building and construction industry to make an agreement . . . (4) . . . [that] provides for priority in opportunities for employment based upon length of service with such employer, in the industry or in the particular geographical area . . . ." *See* Local Union 8, Electrical Workers (IBEW), 221 NLRB 1131, 91 LRRM 1001 (1975); Carpenters, 194 NLRB 159, 78 LRRM 1566 (1971); Local 542, Operating Eng'rs (Ralph A. Marino), 151 NLRB 497, 58 LRRM 1444 (1965); Local Union 337, Plumbers (Townsend & Bottum, Inc.), 147 NLRB 929, 56 LRRM 1350 (1964); Bricklayers (Plaza Builders, Inc.), 134 NLRB 751, 49 LRRM 1222 (1961). *See also* Ward v. NLRB, 462 F2d 8, 80 LRRM 2748 (CA 5, 1972) (court rejected Board's finding of lawful local preference where it found, on the record, unlawful preference for union members); J. Willis & Sons Masonry (Bricklayers), 191 NLRB 872, 77 LRRM 1693 (1971) (geographical preference pretext for unlawful union preference).

[434]Manchester Terminal Corp., 196 NLRB 1186, 80 LRRM 1239 (1972).

[435]New York Typographical Union Local 6 (Royal Composing Room), *supra* note 426; Theatrical Stage Employees Local 659 (MPO-TV, Inc.), 197 NLRB 1187, 81 LRRM 1223 (1972), *enforced,* 477 F2d 450, 83 LRRM 2527 (CA DC, 1973), *cert. denied,* 414 US 1157, 85 LRRM 2227 (1974); Directors Guild (Association of Motion Picture Producers), 198 NLRB 707, 81 LRRM 1477 (1972), *enforced,* 494 F2d 692, 85 LRRM 2800 (CA 9, 1974). Board reasoned that this requirement penalized employees for having exercised statutory rights to refrain from bargaining collectively through the union in the past, while rewarding those employees who had chosen to work in the units represented by the union. *Accord,* Plumbers Local 741 (Stearns-Roger Corp.), 198 NLRB 1956, 81 LRRM 1237 (1972). *See also* Theatrical Stage Employees Local 659 (Medway Prods., Inc.), 250 NLRB 367, 105 LRRM 1079 (1980).

[436]227 NLRB 1996, 94 LRRM 1225 (1977).

because it results in rewarding applicants who are union members and in penalizing applicants with greater experience solely because the latter have worked for nonunion employers or nonsignatory employers to the union's contract. The Board relied on Section 8(f)(4), which sanctions an exclusive referral system under which priority in job referral may be "based upon length of service with such employer."[437] The term "such employer" was held to include any employer who had agreed to be bound by the union's contract with a multi-employer association, not just member employers of the association.[438] The Board has held that an employer has the burden of affirmatively demonstrating that it is qualified for an exemption under Section 8(f) in order to be entitled to the protection of *Interstate*.[439] Subsequently, in *Teamsters Local 83*,[440] a union was found in violation of the Act for enforcing hiring-hall provisions with respect to certain employers who were not "primarily engaged in the construction industry." For that determination, the Board utilized the definition of "construction" announced in another context in *Carpet Layers Local 1247*: "the provisions of labor whereby materials and constituent parts may be combined on the building site."[441] One circuit has refused to enforce a decision amended by the Board to conform to *Interstate Electric*, because it was "persuaded that *Interstate Electric* was wrongly decided" and that the Board had attempted to "rewrite" Section 8(f)(4).[442]

The Ninth Circuit has upheld the Board in finding that a union operating an exclusive hiring hall violated the Act by requiring applicants for Class B hiring-hall status to have Class A workers as sponsors, for all but an insignificant number of

---

[437]*See* Chapter 29 *infra* at notes 228-47 and Chapter 13 *infra* at notes 644-64.

[438]*See* Electrical Workers (IBEW) Local 68, 227 NLRB 1904, 94 LRRM 1229 (1977), *overruling* Nassau-Suffolk Chapter, National Elec. Contractors Ass'n, Inc., 215 NLRB 894, 88 LRRM 1226 (1974), to the extent of any inconsistency with *Interstate*, *supra* note 436.

[439]Teamsters Local 83 (Associated Gen. Contractors), 243 NLRB 328, 101 LRRM 1508 (1979). In the light of *Interstate Electric*, the Board has ordered that some of its prior decisions be amended to delete findings that unions and employers in the construction industry violated the Act solely by maintaining and enforcing agreements under which preference in referral was given to applicants who were represented by the union at prior places of employment in the industry. *E.g.*, Bechtel Power Corp., 229 NLRB 613, 96 LRRM 1105 (1977), *supplementing* 223 NLRB 925, 92 LRRM 1220 (1976), *reversed in pertinent part sub nom.* Robertson v. NLRB, 597 F2d 1331, 101 LRRM 2160 (CA 10, 1979); National Elec. Contractors Ass'n, Inc., 231 NLRB 1021, 96 LRRM 1303 (1977), *supplementing* 215 NLRB 894, 88 LRRM 1226 (1974), *supra* note 438.

[440]*Supra* note 439.

[441]156 NLRB 951, 959, 61 LRRM 1191 (1966).

[442]The Tenth Circuit, in Robertson v. NLRB, *supra* note 439 at 1333.

Class A workers were union members.[443] The Board has also held that it is unlawful for a union operating an exclusive job-referral system to refuse to permit nonmember applicants to take the journeymen's examination, thereby limiting their opportunities for job referral.[444] And a union may not require hiring-hall applicants to pay union initiation fees prior to referring them for employment.[445]

A valid hiring-hall clause may be strictly enforced, however. The Board found no violation in a union's requested discharge of employees who had not been dispatched to the employer pursuant to the parties' valid hiring agreement. The Board found that a statement by union officials to the employees that they were being replaced by union members merely indicated that they could replace them because they were hired in contravention of the hiring system.[446] Similarly, the Board found no violation in the requirement that only journeymen who had passed an examination by a duly constituted local would be referred to certain jobs.[447] And it was not unlawful for a union to enforce a hiring-hall agreement by requesting the discharge of an employee from a job that the employee obtained outside the normal hiring-hall procedure.[448]

The Board has refused, however, to extend to hiring-hall cases the benefit of its holding in *Dairylea Cooperative, Inc.*[449] Thus, in *Pattern Makers (Michigan Pattern Manufacturers Ass'n)*[450] the Board found unlawful a union practice that gave union executive committee members and former union officers priority at the top of an out-of-work list used in making referrals to new jobs. The Board distinguished its *Limpco Manufacturing,*

[443]NLRB v. Longshoremen & Warehousemen Local 13, 549 F2d 1346, 95 LRRM 2215 (CA 9, 1977), *enforcing* 210 NLRB 952, 86 LRRM 1716 (1974), *cert. denied*, 430 US 922, 96 LRRM 2747 (1977). *But see* NLRB v. New York Typographical Union Local 6, 632 F2d 171, 105 LRRM 2529 (CA 2, 1980).
[444]Electrical Workers (IBEW) Local 367, 230 NLRB 86, 96 LRRM 1182 (1977).
[445]Oil Workers Local 1-128 (Noble Constr. & Maint. Co.), 232 NLRB 271, 96 LRRM 1394 (1977).
[446]Hellenic Lines, Ltd., 228 NLRB 1, 94 LRRM 1640 (1977).
[447]Electrical Workers (IBEW) Local 592 (United Eng'r & Constr. Co.), 223 NLRB 899, 92 LRRM 1159 (1976). *See also* Electrical Workers (IBEW) Local 1701 (Dynalectric Co.), 252 NLRB 820, 105 LRRM 1647 (1980).
[448]Laborers Local 596 (Leo J. Hood Mason Contractors), 216 NLRB 820, 88 LRRM 1441 (1975).
[449]*Supra* note 324. *See also* discussion this chapter at notes 381-86 *supra*.
[450]233 NLRB 430, 96 LRRM 1544 (1977).

Inc.,[451] decision, where it had upheld the applicability of super-seniority clauses to union officers for job retention purposes, from *Pattern Makers,* where the benefit was actual preference for initial hiring, which in turn encompassed eligibility for all contract benefits. The Board also noted that the practice did not appear to bear any direct relation to furthering the effective administration of the contract on the job.

In *Teamsters Local 959,*[452] however, the Board held that a union that operated an exclusive hiring hall did not violate the Act when it insisted on dispatching its designees as union stewards in preference to other eligible employees. *Pattern Makers* was distinguished on the ground that the hiring preference there had been granted to persons who performed no steward functions at the plant. The Board also distinguished *Dairylea* (on which the administrative law judge had relied), asserting that *Dairylea* does not erect a presumption against steward preference clauses in hiring-hall agreements.

IV. Discrimination Because of Involvement With NLRB Procedures: Section 8(a)(4)

Section 8(a)(4) makes it unlawful "to discharge or otherwise to discriminate against an employee because he has filed charges or given testimony under this Act."[453] While the number of complaints filed under Section 8(a)(4) is relatively small, the cases exhibit a variety of types of discrimination,[454] and despite

---

[451]*Supra* note 323. *See also* Pattern Makers v. NLRB, 622 F2d 267, 104 LRRM 2713 (CA 6, 1980).

[452]239 NLRB 1387, 100 LRRM 1160 (1979). *Accord,* Carpenters Local 1243, 240 NLRB 1118, 100 LRRM 1384 (1979).

[453]§8(a)(4) does not apply to filing charges or testifying under legislation other than the NLRA. *See* B & M Excavating, Inc., 155 NLRB 1152, 60 LRRM 1466 (1965). Thus, a discharge in response to an employee's threat to go to "the Labor Department" did not violate that section where the employer did not understand it to be a threat to resort to the NLRB. Inked Ribbon Corp., 241 NLRB 7, 100 LRRM 1480 (1979). But employer discrimination because of non-NLRA activities may constitute inference with concerted activities (under §§7 and 8 (a)(1), or discrimination under §8(a)(3)). Salt River Valley Ass'n v. NLRB, 206 F2d 325, 32 LRRM 2598 (CA 9, 1953); Montgomery Ward & Co., 154 NLRB 1197, 60 LRRM 1110 (1965); Gibbs Corp., 131 NLRB 955, 48 LRRM 1167 (1961); Duralite Co., Inc., 128 NLRB 648, 46 LRRM 1385 (1960); Spandsco Oil & Royalty Co., 42 NLRB 942, 10 LRRM 208 (1942). *See* Frank Briscoe v. NLRB, *supra* note 152. *See also* Chapter 6 *supra* at notes 475-82.

[454]NLRB v. Globe Mfg. Co., 580 F2d 18, 99 LRRM 2062 (CA 1, 1978); C & W Super Mkts., Inc. v. NLRB, 581 F2d 618, 98 LRRM 3311 (CA 7, 1978); Electri-Flex Co. v.

the narrow scope of the language of the provision, the courts and the Board have given the section a broad interpretation. Thus, the Supreme Court held in 1972, in *NLRB* v. *Scrivener*,[455] that an employer violated Section 8(a)(4) by discharging employees who had given sworn written statements to an NLRB field examiner investigating unfair labor practice charges against the company, although the discharged employees neither filed the charges nor testified at the hearing.

Consistent with *Scrivener,* the Seventh and Eighth Circuits have enforced Board orders based on findings that the employer violated Section 8(a)(4) by discharging an employee for filing an affidavit with a Board agent investigating an unfair labor practice charge.[456] The Board has also found a violation where an employee was discharged because the employer suspected that he had filed or was about to file a charge with the Board.[457] An employer violates Section 8(a)(4) if he discharges an employee because he believes the employee has filed a charge, even though he has not in fact done so.[458] Similarly, an employer's disciplining of an employee who was scheduled to testify, but who did not actually testify, was found to violate the Act.[459] The same rationale was utilized where the Board found a violation when the employer constructively discharged an employee because she had given testimony in an unfair labor practice proceeding

---

NLRB, 570 F2d 1327, 97 LRRM 2888 (CA 7, 1978), *cert. denied,* 439 US 911, 99 LRRM 2743 (1978); NLRB v. News Syndicate Co., Inc., 272 F2d 323, 46 LRRM 2295 (CA 2, 1960), *aff'd,* 365 US 695, 47 LRRM 2916 (1961); Vogue Lingerie, Inc. v. NLRB, 280 F2d 224, 46 LRRM 2563 (CA 3, 1960); Electric Motors & Specialties, Inc., 149 NLRB 131, 57 LRRM 1258 (1964); Ritchie Mfg. Co., 147 NLRB 1257, 56 LRRM 1405 (1964), *modified,* 354 F2d 90, 61 LRRM 2013 (CA 8, 1965); East Tenn. Undergarment Co., 139 NLRB 1129, 51 LRRM 1466 (1962), *enforced,* 53 LRRM 2461 (CA 6, 1963); Beiser Aviation Corp., 135 NLRB 399, 49 LRRM 1508 (1962); Thomas J. Aycock, Jr., 135 NLRB 1357, 49 LRRM 1723 (1962); Esgro, Inc., 135 NLRB 285, 49 LRRM 1472 (1962); Brunswick-Balke-Collender Co., 131 NLRB 156, 48 LRRM 1025 (1961), *supplemented,* 135 NLRB 574, 49 LRRM 1531 (1962), *enforced,* 318 F2d 419, 53 LRRM 2430 (CA 3, 1963); Central Rigging & Contracting Corp., 129 NLRB 242, 46 LRRM 1548 (1960).
   [455]405 US 117, 79 LRRM 2787 (1972).
   [456]Sinclair Glass Co. v. NLRB, 465 F2d 209, 80 LRRM 3082 (CA 7, 1972), *enforcing* 188 NLRB 362, 76 LRRM 1289 (1971); NLRB v. King Louie Bowling Corp., 472 F2d 1192, 82 LRRM 2576 (CA 8, 1973).
   [457]First Nat'l Bank & Trust Co., 209 NLRB 95, 85 LRRM 1324 (1974); *accord,* Rock Road Trailer Parts & Sales, 204 NLRB 1136, 83 LRRM 1467 (1973). This rule applies even if the visit to the Board does not involve a grievance cognizable under the Act. General Nutrition Center, Inc., *supra* note 28.
   [458]Maple City Stamping Co., 200 NLRB 743, 82 LRRM 1059 (1972); *see* First Nat'l Bank & Trust Co., *supra* note 457; *accord,* Summit Nursing & Convalescent Home, Inc., 204 NLRB 70, 83 LRRM 1323 (1973).
   [459]Fuqua Homes (Ohio), Inc., 211 NLRB 399, 86 LRRM 1141 (1974). *Cf.* John Wanamaker, Phila., Inc., 199 NLRB 1266, 82 LRRM 1129 (1972); Nestle Co., 248 NLRB 732, 103 LRRM 1567 (1980).

involving another employer.[460] However, the First Circuit distinguished *Scrivener* in a case where an employee had telephoned the Board "to vent his spleen" after an unfair labor practice charge had been dismissed; the court held that the employer had lawfully discharged the employee because the call was not to provide information for a future or pending Board proceeding.[461]

An employer who discharged a group of employees who attended an NLRB representation hearing as mere spectators during working hours, contrary to the employer's directives, was held by the Board to have violated the Act.[462] But the District of Columbia Circuit reversed, holding that Section 8(a)(4) was not violated by the discharge of the group, for they had not been subpoenaed to attend the hearing, they had offered no substantial reasons for their attendance, and the employer had offered to excuse one employee from work in order to attend.[463]

In a more recent case, the Board held that an employer did not violate the Act by discharging employees who had attended a Board hearing as spectators, since the employees had not given advance notice to the employer of their intention and the employer believed they had deliberately vandalized a truck in order to obtain an excuse for not working.[464]

The Sixth Circuit relied on *Scrivener* in holding that an employer violated Section 8(a)(4) by discharging an employee partly because of the employee's refusal to appear voluntarily as a witness for the employer in an unfair labor practice proceeding against the employer.[465] But the Eighth Circuit ruled that *Scrivener* did not extend to a plant manager's instruction to an employee to testify truthfully in a forthcoming NLRB hearing coupled with a warning that the manager would be in the hearing room listening to the employee's testimony.[466] The court reasoned that the man-

---

[460]A-1 Janitorial Serv. Co., 222 NLRB 664, 91 LRRM 1210 (1976).

[461]NLRB v. Wilson Freight Co., *supra* note 149.

[462]Earringhouse Imports, *supra* note 95; *see also* Permanent Label Corp., *supra* note 80.

[463]*See* notes 94 and 95 *supra*.

[464]Unique Moving & Storage Co., Inc., 240 NLRB 40, 100 LRRM 1226 (1979).

[465]NLRB v. Retail Clerks Local 876, 570 F2d 586, 97 LRRM 2465 (CA 6, 1978), *cert. denied*, 439 US 819, 99 LRRM 2600 (1978).

[466]NLRB v. Saunders Leasing Sys. Co., 497 F2d 453, 86 LRRM 2345 (CA 8, 1974), *enforcing in relevant part* 204 NLRB 448, 83 LRRM 1626 (1973).

ager's admonition was neither coercive nor destructive of the employee's rights, since the employee was in any case obligated to testify truthfully.[467] Conversely, an employer clearly violates the section by discharging an employee who refuses to give false testimony in a Board proceeding.[468]

An employee who deliberately files false charges with the Board and gives false testimony is not protected by Section 8(a)(4).[469] On the other hand, the discharge of an employee for testifying untruthfully was a violation of the section where the employee did not willfully testify falsely and where the Board found that the real motivation for the discharge was the employee's union activity.[470]

An employer violated the Act when it refused to discuss an employee's work status and possible return to work (after leave for medical reasons) where there was a pending Board charge concerning the employee.[471]

Conditioning continued employment or reinstatement of an employee upon his withdrawal of Board charges also violates Section 8(a)(4).[472] The provision is likewise violated by various retaliatory acts short of discharge, for example: subjecting an employee to closer supervision and unilaterally changing sick-leave and lateness policies;[473] refusing to allow employees to work extra hours;[474] effecting a retaliatory transfer;[475] subjecting an employee to more onerous working conditions with a reduction in working hours.[476] Similarly, refusing to pay severance pay to an employee who is challenging his discharge under the

---

[467]In Skaggs Pay Less Drug Stores, 189 NLRB 249, 76 LRRM 1668 (1971), the Board held that an employer did not violate §8(a)(4) by discharging an employee where, at a recess in a Board hearing, the employee called the employer a liar and was discharged when she later repeated the accusation.

[468]J. C. Penney Co., 237 NLRB 643, 99 LRRM 1066 (1978).

[469]NLRB v. Brake Parts Co., 447 F2d 503, 77 LRRM 2695 (CA 7, 1971), *denying enforcement to* 178 NLRB 247, 74 LRRM 1068 (1969).

[470]Big Three Indus. Gas & Equip. Co., 212 NLRB 800, 87 LRRM 1543 (1974).

[471]NLRB v. Globe Mfg. Co., *supra* note 454.

[472]Maspeth Trucking Serv., Inc., 240 NLRB 1225, 100 LRRM 1482 (1979), *supplementing* 237 NLRB 1531, 99 LRRM 1574 (1978); Everage Bros. Mkt., 206 NLRB 593, 84 LRRM 1383 (1973); Amsterdam Wrecking Co., 196 NLRB 113, 79 LRRM 1648 (1972).

[473]Pinter Bros., 227 NLRB 921, 94 LRRM 1284 (1977).

[474]S. E. Nichols Marcy Corp., 229 NLRB 75, 95 LRRM 1110 (1977).

[475]Occidental Paper Corp., 227 NLRB 719, 94 LRRM 1347 (1977).

[476]Frenchy's K & T, 247 NLRB 1212, 103 LRRM 1397 (1980).

Act violates the section, even though the outcome of the litigation might include the employee's reinstatement with back pay.[477]

The Board has also held that an employer violates Section 8(a)(4) by filing a civil suit for malicious prosecution against an employee who had filed an unfair labor practice charge.[478] As a remedy for this violation, the offending employer was ordered to reimburse the employee for the cost of defending the civil suit.[479]

Anti-union history and general bias, standing alone, do not provide "causal connection" between the employee's actions and the discharge required to support a finding that an employer has violated Section 8(a)(4).[480] Thus, the Board generally lists a variety of factors when it holds that "the real reason" for an employer's action is activity protected by Section 8(a)(4) rather than violation of the employment policy which the employer alleges. Common among such factors is that the employer has disciplined or discharged an employee pursuant to a newly announced policy[481] or one that has been in existence but not previously enforced.[482] Additional factors which have supported a finding of violation are an employer's failure to investigate or to take into account an employee's explanation for his conduct,[483] an employer's "inconsistent defenses," and the overseverity of discharge as a punishment for the conduct in question.[484] Conversely, the employer has been held not to have violated Section 8(a)(4) when employees had prior notice of the employment policy,[485] when employees were treated uniformly,[486] when

---

[477]Manuel San Juan Co., 211 NLRB 812, 87 LRRM 1094 (1974).

[478]Johnson's Restaurants, 249 NLRB 155, 104 LRRM 1205 (1980); George A. Angle, 242 NLRB 744, 101 LRRM 1209 (1979); United Credit Bureau of Am., Inc., 242 NLRB 921, 101 LRRM 1277 (1979); Power Sys., Inc., 239 NLRB 445, 99 LRRM 1652 (1978), *enforcement denied*, 601 F2d 936, 101 LRRM 2978, 2981 (CA 7, 1979).

[479]*Id.* In one such case, the Seventh Circuit denied enforcement because substantial evidence did not support the Board's finding that the employer had no reasonable basis for the civil suit and filed it for an improper purpose. However, the court recognized that such suits "carry with them a potential for chilling employee complaints to the Board" and therefore "in a proper case" the Board may act against such conduct. Power Sys., Inc. v. NLRB, *supra* note 478.

[480]Florida Steel Corp. v. NLRB, 587 F2d 735, 100 LRRM 2451, 2455-56 (CA 5, 1979).

[481]Permanent Label Corp., *supra* note 80; Pepper Packing Co., 243 NLRB 215, 101 LRRM 1528 (1979); Vornado, Inc., 241 NLRB 64, 100 LRRM 1586 (1979).

[482]Staco, Inc., 244 NLRB 461, 102 LRRM 1223 (1979); Ward Prods. Corp., 243 NLRB 239, 101 LRRM 1578 (1979).

[483]Siro Security Serv., Inc., 247 NLRB 1266, 103 LRRM 1362 (1980).

[484]Mid-State Broadcasting, 248 NLRB 1206, 104 LRRM 1024 (1980).

[485]Joseph Schlitz Brewing Co., 240 NLRB 710, 100 LRRM 1323 (1979).

[486]United States Postal Serv., 235 NLRB 307, 100 LRRM 1222 (1978).

the employer acted as soon as he learned of the employee's violation of the employment policy,[487] and when the evidence showed that the activity protected by Section 8(a)(4) was not the reason for the discharge or discipline.[488]

Although Congress excluded "supervisors" from the statutory definition of "employee," the Board has held that a supervisor who files a charge alleging discrimination because of his union activity is, for purposes of processing the charge, an "employee" protected by Section 8(a)(4).[489] In the interest of protecting employee access to the Board's processes, the Board has likewise asserted jurisdiction over an employer who did not meet the Board's discretionary jurisdictional standards,[490] finding such employer in violation of Section 8(a)(4) for discharging two employees who had testified at a Board representation hearing.[491] Similarly, it held that a former employee who, after her discharge, threatened to complain to the Board, was an "employee" within the meaning of Section 8(a)(4).[492] The employer was found to have violated that section by refusing to give the employee post-termination pay previously promised, even though the promise of such pay was gratuitous and it was not shown that her discharge had been unlawful.

The Board has held that it will not defer under *Spielberg*[493] to an arbitration award involving an employee allegedly discharged for filing NLRB charges. In *Filmation Associates, Inc.,*[494] it concluded that issues involving Section 8(a)(4) are solely within the Board's province and that *Spielberg* would not be applied to cases involving alleged violations of that section of the Act.[495]

---

[487]McKesson Chem. Co., 246 NLRB 584, 102 LRRM 1629 (1979); Summitville Tile, Inc., 245 NLRB No. 111, 102 LRRM 1552 (1979).

[488]J. P. Stevens & Co., 247 NLRB 420, 103 LRRM 1187 (1980); Sonoma Community Press, 247 NLRB 979, 103 LRRM 1287 (1980); Seneca Foods Corp., 244 NLRB 558, 102 LRRM 1085 (1979).

[489]General Serv., Inc., 229 NLRB 940, 95 LRRM 1174 (1977), *enforcement denied*, (CA 5, 1978) (unpublished); Hi-Craft Clothing Co., 251 NLRB 1310, 105 LRRM 1356 (1980); Walt Disney World Co., 216 NLRB 836, 89 LRRM 1137 (1975).

[490]*See* Chapter 30 *infra.*

[491]Pickle Bill's, Inc., 224 NLRB 413, 92 LRRM 1609 (1976). However, the Board declined on jurisdictional grounds to entertain that portion of the complaint which alleged violation of §§8(a)(1) and (3). Clark & Hinojosa, 247 NLRB 710, 103 LRRM 1205 (1980).

[492]Clark & Hinojosa, *supra* note 491.

[493]Spielberg Mfg. Co., 112 NLRB 1080, 36 LRRM 1152 (1955). *See generally* Chapter 20 *infra.*

[494]227 NLRB 1721, 94 LRRM 1470 (1977).

[495]*Accord,* Narragansett Restaurant Corp., 243 NLRB 125, 101 LRRM 1579 (1979). *See generally* Chapter 20.

The First Circuit, however, citing *Spielberg*, held that the Board "exceeded its authority" in a case involving an alleged wrongful discharge when it "redecided in [the employee's] favor factual matters determined by the arbitrators that were essential to a determination of the contractual rights of [the employee], his union and his employer."[496]

V. Remedial Orders in Discrimination Cases

The Board's powers to remedy discrimination in unfair labor practices cases are set forth in Section 10(c) of the Act.[497] On finding that an unfair labor practice has been committed, the Board is empowered to issue "an order requiring such person to cease and desist from such unfair labor practice and to take such affirmative action including reinstatement of employees with or without back pay, as will effectuate the policies of this Act." The statute also provides that the Board's order "may further require such person to make reports from time to time showing the extent to which it has complied with the order." Although the 1947 amendments to the Act reiterated that "where an order directs the reinstatement of an employee, back pay may be required of the employer or the labor organization . . . responsible for the discrimination suffered," the same amendments placed a limitation on the Board's remedial power, to wit: "No order of the Board shall require the reinstatment of any individual as an employee who has been suspended or discharged, or the payment to him of any back pay, if such individual was suspended or discharged for cause."[498] Remedies in discrimination cases generally take the form of orders for reinstatement of employees who have been discharged and for back pay for loss of wages and other employment benefits. These remedial orders are treated in detail in a later chapter.[499]

---

[496]NLRB v. Wilson Freight Co., *supra* note 112. The arbitrator had found that the discharge was justified under the terms of the collective bargaining agreement. The First Circuit acknowledged that the discharge might have been an unfair labor practice even though it was contractually authorized, but it noted that "a good deal more is required . . . to support an unfair labor practice finding for wrongful discharge in the presence of an objectively established 'good' ground for discharge than where the employer's tendered good reason turns out to be weak or extraneous." *Id.* at 723.

[497]*See generally* Chapter 33 *infra.*

[498]*See* Chapter 21 *infra* at notes 72-74.

[499]*See* Chapter 33 *infra* at notes 144-74.

VI. JUDICIAL REVIEW IN DISCRIMINATION CASES

Sections 10(e) and (f)[500] of the Act provide that the "findings of the Board with respect to questions of fact if supported by substantial evidence on the record considered as a whole shall be conclusive." The foregoing language dates from the Taft-Hartley amendments and replaces Wagner Act language which made the Board's findings of fact conclusive if supported "by evidence."[501]

In *Universal Camera Corp.* v. *NLRB*[502] the Supreme Court explicated the purpose and effect of the changes in Sections 10(e) and (f), and articulated the standard of review of NLRB decisions by reviewing courts:

> Whether or not it was ever permissible for courts to determine the substantiality of evidence supporting a Labor Board decision merely on the basis of evidence which in and of itself justified it, without taking into account contradictory evidence or evidence from which conflicting inferences could be drawn, the new legislation definitely precludes such a theory of review and bars its practice. The substantiality of evidence must take into account whatever in the record fairly detracts from its weight . . . . [503]

At one time a question existed as to whether the scope of review in discrimination cases differed from the scope of review applicable to other unfair labor practices. The Fifth Circuit had taken the position that an employer's sworn testimony concerning the reason for a discharge was controlling unless the employer's testimony was impeached, or there was substantial contradiction, or circumstances raising grave doubts were inconsistent with his sworn testimony.[504] However, in *NLRB* v. *Walton Manufacturing Co.*[505] the Supreme Court ruled that the Act does not sanction a more rigorous application of the substantial-evidence test in reinstatement cases than in other cases. It emphasized that "[t]here is no place in the statutory scheme for one test of the substantiality of evidence in reinstatement cases and another

---

[500]*See* Chapter 34 *infra* at notes 61-82.

[501]Prior to amendment in 1947, §10(e) read, in pertinent part, as follows: "The findings of the Board as to the facts if supported by evidence shall be conclusive." §10(f) contained virtually identical language.

[502]340 US 474, 27 LRRM 2373 (1951).

[503]*Id.* at 487-88.

[504]NLRB v. Walton Mfg. Co., 286 F2d 16, 47 LRRM 2367 (CA 5, 1961); NLRB v. Williamson-Dickie Mfg. Co., 130 F2d 260, 10 LRRM 867 (CA 5, 1942); NLRB v. Tex-O-Kan Flour Mills, 122 F2d 433, 8 LRRM 675 (CA 5, 1941).

[505]*Supra* note 504, 369 US 404, 49 LRRM 2962 (1962), *on remand*, 322 F2d 187, 54 LRRM 2118 (CA 5, 1963).

test in other cases."[506] Citing its decisions in *NLRB* v. *Pittsburgh Steamship Co.*[507] and *Universal Camera Corp.*,[508] both decided the same day and both involving reinstatement, the Court reiterated that "[t]hey state a rule for review by Courts of Appeals in all Labor Board cases."[509] The Board is thus free to reject an employer's sworn testimony and to predicate findings of discrimination on the basis of all the evidence, both direct and circumstantial.

When an employer has a mixed motive for discriminating against an employee, one motive being lawful and the other unlawful, the circuit courts and the Board have differed over the proper test for finding a Section 8(a)(3) violation. However, as was noted previously, the Board has now abandoned its controversial "in part" test and substituted the two-stage *Wright-Line*[510] test: The General Counsel must establish a *prima facie* showing that protected conduct was a motivating factor in the employer's decision to discipline or discharge the employee; and upon satisfying that requirement, the burden of proof shifts to the employer to establish, as an affirmative defense, that the action would have been taken regardless of the protected conduct. Several circuit courts have written on the new standard, and most have approved it, though some with significant modifications.

The First Circuit, in *Statler Industries, Inc.* v. *NLRB*,[511] a pre-*Wright-Line* case, characterized the *Wright-Line* test "as a conscientious effort to reduce the confusion and discord in dealing with mixed motive cases."[512] On direct review of *Wright Line*,[513] that court enforced the Board's decision, but it altered the test by ruling that once the General Counsel has established a *prima facie* case, only a burden of production—not a burden of persuasion—shifts to the employer to show it would have taken the same action regardless of the protected activity.

---

[506]369 US at 407.

[507]340 US 498 (1951).

[508]*Supra* note 502.

[509]369 US at 407 (emphasis added). *See* discussion at notes 50-79 *supra*.

[510]*Supra* note 61. *See* Coleman, *Wright Line: A Variation on the Old Shell Game—"Now You See It, Now You Don't,"* 28 FED. BAR NEWS & J. 208 (1981); Remar, *Climbing* Mt. Healthy: *In Search of the "Wright Line" on Mixed-Motive Discharges Under Section 8 (a)(3),* 4 IND. REL. L. J. 636 (1981).

[511]644 F2d 902, 106 LRRM 2799 (CA 1, 1981), *remanding with directions* 244 NLRB No. 19, 102 LRRM 1195 (1979).

[512]*Id.* at 905.

[513]*Supra* note 61. In NLRB v. Transportation Mgmt. Corp., 674 F2d 130, 109 LRRM 3291 (CA 1, 1982), the First Circuit applied its *Statler Industries* alteration of *Wright Line* and denied enforcement of the Board's order. [*See* **Editor's Note** *infra,* p. 266.]

The Sixth Circuit applied the *Wright-Line* standard in two cases.[514] The Seventh Circuit also affirmed the standard, though it reversed the Board as to its application in *Peavey Co.* v. *NLRB*.[515]

The Eighth Circuit accepted the standard in *NLRB* v. *Fixtures Manufacturing* Corp.[516] The Ninth Circuit was explicit as to its reasons for approving the standard. In *NLRB* v. *Nevis Industries*[517]

[The *Wright-Line* rule] is consistent with the legislative history of the Act, which reveals an intent to require the employer to show that an employee was discharged for cause . . . . It is also consistent with the reality that the employer has the best access to proof of motivation . . . . The new rule strikes an acceptable balance between protection of employees' rights and preservation of employers' rights to discharge employees for valid business reasons.[518]

The Second,[519] Third,[520] and Fourth[521] Circuits have merely noted the *Wright-Line* standard without giving a clear signal as to whether the standard would be adopted. The Third Circuit, in agreement with the First Circuit,[522] has stated that the Board's *Wright-Line* standard misallocates the burden of persuasion, holding that once a *prima facie* case is established the employer has only the burden of going forward with evidence of a legitimate business reason for its action.[523]*

---

[514]NLRB v. Allen's I.G.A. Foodliner, 651 F2d 438, 107 LRRM 2596 (CA 6, 1981); NLRB v. Lloyd A. Fry Roofing Co., 651 F2d 442, 107 LRRM 2926 (CA 6, 1981). *But cf.* NLRB v. Consolidated Freightways, Inc., 651 F2d 436 (CA 6, 1981), where the Sixth Circuit cited *Wright Line*, but denied enforcement of the Board's order, stating that "the proper test in determining whether the discharge or failure to hire an employee is an unfair labor practice is whether the anti-union animus was a dominant motive. . . . . [T]he burden is upon the General Counsel to establish that in the absence of protected activities, the discharge would not have taken place." *Id.* at 437.
[515]Peavey Co. v. NLRB, 648 F2d 460, 107 LRRM 2359 (CA 7, 1981).
[516]669 F2d 547, 109 LRRM 2581 (CA 8, 1982).
[517]647 F2d 905, 107 LRRM 2890 (CA 9, 1981).
[518]*Id.* at 909.
[519]NLRB v. Charles Batchelder Co., Inc., 646 F2d 33, 106 LRRM 3050 (CA 2, 1981).
[520]NLRB v. Permanent Label Corp., 657 F2d 512, 106 LRRM 2211 (CA 3, 1981).
[521]In NLRB v. Burns Motor Freight, Inc., 635 F2d 312, 106 LRRM 2020 (CA 4, 1981), however, the Fourth Circuit said that it "need not consider whether the burden-shifting test adopted in Wright Line . . . is more appropriate . . . ." *Id.* at 315; and in NLRB v. Kiawah Island Co., 650 F2d 485, 107 LRRM 2599 (CA 4, 1981), it failed to mention *Wright Line* entirely.
[522]Behring Int'l, Inc. v. NLRB, 675 F2d 83, 109 LRRM 3265 (CA 3, 1982), *remanding* 252 NLRB 354, 105 LRRM 1452 (1980).
[523]The court stated that "[t]he shifting burden of persuasion undermines the 'but for' test and reintroduces the confusion which Wright Line purported to eliminate." 109 LRRM at 3268. The court found *Mt. Healthy, supra* note 62, inapposite because "the Board is bound by statutory limitations [§10(c)] which foreclose the issue." 109 LRRM at 3269.
*[**Editor's Note:** The conflict among the circuits and the Board regarding the *Wright-Line* allocation of burden of proof will be resolved by the Supreme Court in NLRB v. Transportation Mgmt. Corp., *supra* note 513. Certiorari was granted in November 1982.]

CHAPTER 8

EMPLOYER DOMINATION AND ASSISTANCE TO LABOR ORGANIZATIONS

I. INTRODUCTION

It is an unfair labor practice for an employer "to dominate or interfere with the formation or administration of any labor organization or contribute financial or other support to it . . . ."[1] This restriction was included in the Wagner Act as Section 8(2) and retained without change as Section 8(a)(2) of the Taft-Hartley Act.[2]

Section 8(a)(2)'s prohibition extends only to employer domination or interference with or support to a "labor organization," a term defined in Section 2(5) of the Act. Therefore, labor

---

[1]§8(a)(2). The additional language of the clause reads as follows: "*Provided*, That subject to rules and regulations made and published by the Board pursuant to section 6, an employer shall not be prohibited from permitting employees to confer with him during working hours without loss of time or pay[.]"

[2]The literature dealing with §8(a)(2) includes the following: Crager, *Company Unions Under the National Labor Relations Act*, 40 MICH. L. REV. 831 (1942); Getman, *The Midwest Piping Doctrine: An Examination of the Need for Reappraisal of Labor Board Dogma*, 31 U. CHI. L. REV. 292 (1964); Jackson, *An Alternative to Unionization and the Wholly Unorganized Shop: A Legal Basis for Sanctioning Joint Employer-Employee Committees and Increasing Employee Free Choice*, 28 SYRACUSE L. REV. 809 (1977); Kesselring & Brinker, *Contract Difficulties Under §8(a)(2)*, 31 LAB. L. J. 139 (1980); Kesselring & Brinker, *Financial and Material Support Under §8(a)(2)*, 31 LAB. L. J. 3 (1980); Kesselring & Brinker, *Discriminatory Treatment of Employees Under §8(a)(2)*, 30 LAB. L. J. 611 (1979); Kesselring & Brinker, *Employer Domination Under §8(a)(2)*, 30 LAB. L. J. 340 (1979); Murmann, *The Scanlon Plan Joint Committee and Section 8(a)(2)*, 31 LAB. L. J. 299 (1980); Sangerman, *Employee Committees: Can They Survive Under the Taft-Hartley Act?*, 24 LAB. L. J. 684 (1973); Van Dusen, *What is Employer Domination or Support?* 13 TEMP. L. Q. 63 (1938); Comment, *Discarding the Doctrine of Supervisory Domination: New Solutions to an Old Conflict of Interest*, 30 HASTINGS L. J. 763 (1979); Note, *The West German Model of Codetermination Under Section 8(a)(2) of the NLRA*, 51 IND. L. J. 795 (1976); Note, *Does Employer Implementation of Employee Production Teams Violate §8(a)(2) of the National Labor Relations Act?*, 49 IND. L. J. 516 (1974); Note, *New Standards for Domination and Support Under Section 8(a)(2)*, 82 YALE L. J. 510 (1973); Annot., 10 ALR3d 861 (1966); Annot., 100 ALR2d 1280 (1965).

267

organization status is a threshold issue in every Section 8(a)(2) case. An employer is free to support groups that are not labor organizations, such as employee recreation committees and credit unions.[3]

The primary purpose of Section 8(2) of the Wagner Act was to eradicate company unionism, a practice whereby employers would establish and control in-house labor organizations in order to prevent organization by bona fide unions.[4] The Section thus makes it unlawful for an employer to "dominate" a labor organization.[5] However, Section 8(a)(2) is not limited to cases where an employer dominates a labor organization, for it is also an unfair labor practice for an employer to "interfere with" or "contribute financial or other support to" a labor organization. Employer interference with a labor organization is conduct short of domination and often takes the form of low-level supervisors participating in a labor organization's activities.[6] The Board, with considerable disapproval from the courts of appeals, has interpreted the provision to require an employer to maintain neutrality in a situation where rival unions are competing for recognition.[7] Section 8(a)(2) also prohibits an employer from "contribut[ing] financial or other support" to a labor organization. The provision is cast in broad language which, if given its full literal meaning, would make trivial employer civility unlawful. The Board and courts therefore draw a line between prohibited employer *support* and permitted employer *cooperation*, an important line that is often difficult to perceive.[8]

It is not always easy for even the well-intentioned employer to steer clear of prohibited support or other, sometimes technical, 8(a)(2) violations. An employer may want to argue that its action was done in good faith without any intention of violating the Act. Such an argument, however, is not available in Section 8(a)(2) cases. The Supreme Court in *Garment Workers (Bernhard-*

---

[3]*E.g.*, Chicago Rawhide Mfg. Co. v. NLRB, 221 F2d 165, 35 LRRM 2665 (CA 7, 1955). The law concerning labor organization status is discussed *infra* at notes 15-41.

[4]*See, e.g.*, Remarks of Senator Wagner, *reprinted in* 1 LEGISLATIVE HISTORY OF THE NATIONAL LABOR RELATIONS ACT, 1935, at 15-16 (1949).

[5]The law concerning employer domination of labor organizations is discussed *infra* at notes 42-74.

[6]These cases are discussed *infra* at notes 75-105.

[7]This neutrality requirement, commonly referred to as the *Midwest Piping* doctrine, is discussed *infra* at notes 106-153. [*See* **Editor's Note** *infra*, p. 294.]

[8]The law regarding the distinction between employer support and employer cooperation is set forth at notes 154-81 *infra*.

Altmann Texas Corp.) v. *NLRB*[9] emphatically rejected an employer's "good faith" defense by noting that nothing in the statutory language prescribes scienter as an element of an 8(a)(2) violation.[10] The Court observed that to hold otherwise would allow a "permissibly careless" employer and union to completely frustrate employee rights.[11] In *Bernhard-Altmann* the employer was held to have violated Section 8(a)(2) by extending recognition to a labor organization at a time when the employer and the union held a good faith, although mistaken, belief that the union represented a majority of the employees. The union, for its participation, was held to have violated Section 8(b)(1)(A). Neither the employer nor the union in *Bernhard-Altmann* was able to use good faith as a defense to the unfair labor practice charges.

In *Majestic Weaving Co.*[12] the Board held invalid negotiations with a minority union and the resulting agreement conditioned upon the union's subsequently obtaining a majority of employee support. The Board held that such grant of recognition, even when conditioned upon attainment of majority status before execution, is similar to formal recognition and thus illegal.

II. LABOR ORGANIZATION STATUS

Section 2(5) of the Act defines a labor organization as

any organization of any kind, or any agency or employee representation committee or plan, in which employees participate and which exists for the purpose, in whole or in part, of dealing with employers concerning grievances, labor disputes, wages, rates of pay, hours of employment, or conditions of work.[13]

Under this broad definition, it is often difficult to determine whether employee committees,[14] or other groups of employees

---

[9]366 US 731, 48 LRRM 2251 (1961). *See infra* at notes 79 and 184.
[10]*See* Chapter 6 *supra* at notes 16-31 and Chapter 7 *supra* at notes 42-83 for discussion of scienter in relation to §8(a)(1) and §8(a)(3) conduct respectively.
[11]366 US at 739.
[12]147 NLRB 859, 56 LRRM 1330 (1964), *enforcement denied on procedural grounds,* 355 F2d 854, 61 LRRM 2132 (CA 2, 1966), *overruling its earlier decision in* Julius Resnick, Inc., 86 NLRB 38, 24 LRRM 1581 (1949). *See also* Wickes Corp., 197 NLRB 128, 80 LRRM 1458 (1972). For a discussion of a union as a party to an employer's §8(a)(2) violation, *see infra* at notes 182-92.
[13]For further discussion of the meaning of §2(5), particularly in the context of representation proceedings, *see* Chapter 30 *infra* at notes 344-67.
[14]Mattiace Indus., Inc., 239 NLRB 15, 99 LRRM 1476 (1978); Easy-Heat Wirekraft, 238 NLRB 1695, 99 LRRM 1681 (1978); Kux Mfg. Corp., 233 NLRB 317, 97 LRRM 1052 (1977); NLRB v. Fremont Mfg. Co., 558 F2d 889, 95 LRRM 3095 (CA 8, 1977),

not traditionally viewed as unions,[15] are labor organizations within the meaning of the Act.

Section 2(5) does not require labor organizations to have any formal structure. A group of individuals may comprise a labor organization even though they lack a constitution or bylaws, elected officials, formal meetings, dues, or other formal structure.[16]

The cases generally focus on two statutory prerequisites: the element of employee participation and the purpose of "dealing with employers concerning grievances, labor disputes, wages, rates of pay, hours of employment, or conditions of work."

A. Participation by "Employees"

Section 2(5) states that a labor organization is a group in which "employees participate." The Board and the courts have held that in the absence of any participation by "employees" as defined in Section 2(3) of the Act, no statutory labor organization can exist. Thus, groups comprised entirely of individuals excluded from the definition of "employees," such as agricultural laborers[17] and supervisors,[18] are not "labor organizations" within the

---

enforcing 224 NLRB 597, 92 LRRM 1508 (1976); Eastern Indus., 217 NLRB 712, 89 LRRM 1134 (1975), *enforced,* 95 LRRM 2336 (CA 3, 1976).

[15]*See, e.g.,* Elliott River Tours, Inc., 246 NLRB 935, 103 LRRM 1095 (1979) (association of white-water canoe guides held to be a labor organization); Major League Rodeo, Inc., 246 NLRB 743, 103 LRRM 1015 (1979) (league of rodeo participants and member clubs held to be a labor organization); North Am. Soccer League, 236 NLRB 1317, 98 LRRM 1445 (1978) (association of professional soccer players held to have labor organization status).

[16]*E.g.,* Columbia Transit Corp., 237 NLRB 1196, 99 LRRM 1114 (1978); Arkay Packaging, 221 NLRB 99, 90 LRRM 1728 (1975); Lane Aviation Corp., 211 NLRB 824, 86 LRRM 1518 (1974); Stow Mfg., 103 NLRB 1280, 31 LRRM 1635 (1953), *enforced,* 217 F2d 900, 35 LRRM 2210 (CA 2, 1954), *cert. denied,* 348 US 964, 35 LRRM 2612 (1955). In representation cases, the Board has held that corrupt unions, *see, e.g.,* Alto Plastics Mfg., 136 NLRB 850, 49 LRRM 1867 (1962), and unions engaging in prohibited discrimination, *see, e.g.,* American Mailing Corp., 197 NLRB 246, 80 LRRM 1294 (1972) (sex discrimination), are nevertheless labor organizations within the meaning of §2(5).

[17]Di Giorgio Fruit Corp. v. NLRB, 191 F2d 642, 28 LRRM 2195 (CA DC), *cert. denied,* 342 US 869, 29 LRRM 2022 (1951). *But see* Ojai Valley Community Hosp., 254 NLRB 1134, 106 LRRM 1278 (1981) (association composed almost exclusively of public employees is §2(5) labor organization).

[18]*See, e.g.,* Masters, Mates & Pilots v. NLRB, 539 F2d 554, 93 LRRM 2429 (CA 5, 1976); Masters, Mates & Pilots v. NLRB, 486 F2d 1271, 84 LRRM 2439 (CA DC, 1973); *cert. denied,* 416 US 956, 85 LRRM 3018 (1974); Directors Guild of Am., 198 NLRB 707, 81 LRRM 1477 (1972), *enforced,* 494 F2d 692, 85 LRRM 2800 (CA 9, 1974). However, groups composed entirely of supervisors have been held to be labor organizations under other titles of the Act. *E.g.,* District 2, Marine Eng'rs v. Amoco Oil Co., 554 F2d 774, 95 LRRM 2241 (CA 6, 1977) (Congress did not intend to exclude organizations comprised entirely of supervisors from coverage of §301 jurisdiction), and cases cited therein.

meaning of Section 2(5). However, in cases interpreting Section 2(5) in the context of Section 8(b) "labor organization" unfair labor practices, the Board and the courts have found labor organization status even where only a minority of the organization's members are employees as defined by Section 2(3) of the Act.[19] For example, in *Masters, Mates & Pilots (Chicago Calumet Stevedoring Co.)* v. *NLRB*,[20] the District of Columbia Circuit affirmed a Board determination that an 11,000-member union constituted a labor organization for purposes of Section 8(b) even though only 170 of its members were "employees" under the Act. The employee-participation requirement has not posed a significant obstacle to finding labor organization status in the context of Section 8(a)(2) charges.

B. "Dealing With" Employers

Section 2(5) limits labor organization status to an organization "which exists for the purpose, in whole or in part, of *dealing with* employers concerning grievances, labor disputes, wages, rates of pay, hours of employment, or conditions of work.[21] In its early decisions, the Board established that the "dealing with" language broadly included various types of employee committees, such as any employer-employee committees which discuss grievances or working conditions, even though they never engaged in formal collective bargaining.[22] And in 1957, in *Cabot Carbon Co.*,[23] the Board held that such an employee-committee system, one in which elected employee representatives regularly met with management to discuss matters of mutual interest, was

---

[19]*See, e.g.*, Masters, Mates & Pilots v. NLRB, *supra* note 18; Masters, Mates & Pilots, 146 NLRB 116, 55 LRRM 1265 (1964), *enforced*, 351 F2d 771, 59 LRRM 2566 (CA DC, 1965).
[20]351 F2d 771, 59 LRRM 2566 (CA DC, 1965).
[21]Emphasis added.
[22]*E.g.*, Stow Mfg., *supra* note 16 (§2(5) labor organization found where company president conducted monthly question-and-answer period at which working conditions were often discussed and which sometimes resulted in changes in working conditions); Standard Coil Prods. Co., 110 NLRB 412, 35 LRRM 1013 (1954), *modified on other grounds and enforced*, 224 F2d 465, 36 LRRM 2463 (CA 1), *cert. denied*, 350 US 902, 37 LRRM 2083 (1955) (employer-employee committee formed to "discuss" working conditions is §2(5) labor organization; Board rejects trial examiner's recommendation to modify its §2(5) decisions to allow for "necessary and proper media of communication"); General Shoe Corp., 90 NLRB 1330, 26 LRRM 1331 (1950), *enforced*, 192 F2d 504, 29 LRRM 2112 (CA 6, 1951), *cert. denied*, 343 US 904, 29 LRRM 2606 (1952); Wrought Iron Range Co., 77 NLRB 487, 22 LRRM 1050 (1948); J. W. Greer Co., 52 NLRB 1341, 13 LRRM 70 (1943); B. Z. B. Knitting Co., 28 NLRB 257, 7 LRRM 129 (1940).
[23]117 NLRB 1633, 40 LRRM 1058 (1957), *enforcement denied*, 256 F2d 281, 42 LRRM 2272 (CA 5, 1958), *rev'd and remanded*, 360 US 203, 44 LRRM 2204 (1959). For discussion of definition of labor organization, *see* Chapter 30 *infra* at notes 364-67.

a Section 2(5) labor organization because the meeting discussions dealt with grievances and working conditions. That committee system was held to be employer dominated; accordingly, the Board ordered the employer to disestablish it. The Fifth Circuit, however, denied enforcement of the Board's order, holding instead that the employee committee was not a labor organization, and, therefore, Section 8(a)(2) was inapplicable. The circuit held that "dealing with" as used in Section 2(5) embraced only activity within the usual meaning of collective bargaining. That court construed the Section 9(a) proviso,[24] which as amended by Taft-Hartley allowed employees individually to present their grievances to the employer for adjustment, as being in conflict with the Board's interpretation of "dealing with."

The Supreme Court, in reversing the Fifth Circuit's decision, held that the employee-committee system was a labor organization, agreeing with the Board that discussions relating to seniority, job classifications, holidays, vacations, and various other conditions of employment constituted "dealing with" as set forth in Section 2(5). The Court rejected the employer's argument that the committee's proposals and requests "amounted only to recommendations"[25] and that the final decision remained with the employer. The Court found this to be "true of all such 'dealings,' whether with an independent or a company administered 'labor organization.' The principal distinction lies in the unfettered power of the former to insist upon its requests."[26] After reviewing the legislative history, the Court found no indication that the broad phrase, "dealing with," should be viewed as synonymous with the more limited term, "bargaining with." The Court also disagreed with the Fifth Circuit's construction of the Section 9(a) proviso. According to the Supreme Court, the Section 9(a) proviso merely allows employees personally to present their own grievances to their employer; it does not state

---

[24]The §9(a) proviso states: "[A]ny individual employee or a group of employees shall have the right at any time to present grievances to their employer *and to have such grievances adjusted, without the intervention of the bargaining representative, as long as the adjustment is not inconsistent with the terms of a collective-bargaining contract or agreement then in effect: Provided further, That the bargaining representative has been given opportunity to be present at such adjustment.*" (Emphasis was added by Taft-Hartley amendment.) *See* Chapter 13 *infra* at notes 91-93 and Chapter 6 *supra* at notes 404-408 for discussion of the proviso to §9(a).
[25]360 US at 214.
[26]*Id.*

that an employer may form or maintain an employee committee for the purpose of dealing with the employer concerning grievances; therefore, the proviso as amended did not limit the traditional 8(a)(2) proscriptions on employer-dominated or -assisted labor organizations.

In the aftermath of *Cabot Carbon,* the Board and the courts generally continued to give a broad interpretation to the "dealing with" requirement.[27] In *Thompson Ramo Wooldridge, Inc.,*[28] an employer argued that an employee committee was not a Section 2(5) labor organization, because it merely communicated employee "views" to management and did not make recommendations; management did not negotiate, but simply made unilateral changes when it saw fit to do so. The Board rejected these arguments, holding that "presentation to management of employee 'views,' without specific recommendations as to what action is needed to accommodate those views," constitutes "dealing with" under Section 2(5).[29] In *NLRB* v. *Ampex Corp.*[30] an employer argued that an employee committee was not a labor organization because it had no formal structure, employees were selected at random to attend meetings, and all employees attended one meeting before any employees were selected to attend a second meeting; furthermore, the employer had a separate grievance procedure, and the matters discussed at committee meetings ranged widely beyond the subjects ordinarily discussed

---

[27]*See, e.g.,* Scott & Fetzer Co. (Steamway Div.), 249 NLRB 396, 104 LRRM 1289 (1980); Mattiace Indus., Inc., *supra* note 14; Alta Bates Hosp., 226 NLRB 485, 93 LRRM 1288 (1976); Rensselaer Polytechnic Inst., 219 NLRB 712, 89 LRRM 1879 (1975); Money Oldsmobile Co., 201 NLRB 155, 82 LRRM 1379 (1973); North Am. Rockwell Corp., 191 NLRB 833, 77 LRRM 1634 (1971); Utrad Corp., 185 NLRB 434, 75 LRRM 1069 (1970), *modified on other grounds and enforced,* 454 F2d 520, 79 LRRM 2080 (CA 7, 1971).

[28]132 NLRB 993, 48 LRRM 1470 (1961).

[29]*Id.* at 995. *See* Stephens Inst., 241 NLRB 454, 100 LRRM 1603 (1979), where the Board found a university faculty senate to be a labor organization. *But cf.* Northeastern Univ., 218 NLRB 247, 89 LRRM 1862 (1975), where the employer argued in a representation case that the union's petition was barred because the faculty senate was a labor organization and the faculty handbook was a collective bargaining agreement constituting a contract bar. (*See* Chapter 10 *infra* at notes 117-200 for a discussion of the contract-bar doctrine.) The Board easily rejected the contract-bar argument because the faculty handbook did not contain a termination date. Nevertheless two of the three panel members chose to address the §2(5) labor organization issue, indicating that the faculty senate was not a labor organization because "the Faculty Senate functions as advisory committees and makes recommendations (which are totally different from bargaining demands that a union would make upon an employer during contract negotiations) to the president. Accordingly, we find that the Faculty Senate does not function as a labor organization . . . ." *Id.* at 248.

[30]442 F2d 82, 77 LRRM 2072 (CA 7, 1971), *enforcing* 168 NLRB 742, 67 LRRM 1134 (1967), *cert. denied,* 404 US 939, 78 LRRM 2704 (1971).

by unions and management. The employer likened the "committee mechanism to a suggestion box, made less impersonal, and suggest[ed] that it was a channel of communication and a means of bring[ing] 'the monolithic corporation into relevant contact with its people.' "[31] While enforcing the Board's order finding the committee to be a Section 2(5) labor organization, the Seventh Circuit opined: "We might well be persuaded that this particular mechanism was not a labor organization in the ordinary sense of the term. The statutory definition, however, is very broad."[32]

In three cases decided in the late 1970s, however, the Board may have narrowed its interpretation of what "dealing with" means. In *Sparks Nugget, Inc.*,[33] a two-to-one Board panel held that a joint employee-employer grievance committee performed a "purely adjudicatory" function and therefore was not "dealing with" an employer within the meaning of Section 2(5). The grievance committee operated under rules dictated by the employer. The committee consisted of an employee representative, an employer representative, and a neutral member selected by the two representatives. According to the stated rules, the committee convened only to hear cases filed by individual employees; it did not initiate grievances, recommend changes in terms and conditions of employment, or advocate employee interests. The Board majority's opinion concluded: "[T]he Employees' Council performs a purely adjudicatory function and does not interact with management for any purpose or in any manner other than to render a final decision on the grievance. Therefore it cannot be said that the Employees' Council 'deals with' management. Rather, it appears to perform a function for management, i.e., resolving employee grievances."[34]

In *Mercy-Memorial Hospital*[35] a three-to-two Board held that a joint employee-employer grievance committee was not "dealing

---

[31]442 F2d at 84.
[32]*Id.*
[33]230 NLRB 275, 95 LRRM 1298 (1977).
[34]*Id.* at 276. This dispute occurred in the context of an overall refusal by the employer to continue recognition of a Hotel & Restaurant Employees local. The Board held the refusal to continue recognition was a §8(a)(5) violation and, accordingly, held that unilateral implementation of the grievance plan was also a §8(a)(5) violation.
[35]231 NLRB 1108, 96 LRRM 1239 (1977). Chairman Fanning and Member Jenkins wrote a strong dissent, stating: "We find no support for *Sparks Nugget* in Board precedent, *Cabot Carbon*, or the Act." *Id.* at 1108 n.2. Moreover, the dissenters believed that §2(5) status should have been found even assuming that *Sparks Nugget* was correctly decided, because the grievance committee engaged in general discussions with management, unlike the committee in *Sparks Nugget*.

with" the employer, even though the committee discussed individual employee grievances and, on occasion, engaged in dialogue with high-level management officials over various employment conditions. Thus the procedure in *Mercy-Memorial Hospital* went beyond the strict "purely adjudicatory" grievance committee in *Sparks Nugget*.[36]

In a third Board decision, *General Foods Corp.*,[37] a unanimous three-member panel, including the two *Mercy-Memorial Hospital* dissenters, adopted an administrative law judge's findings and conclusions that an employer's job enrichment program was not "dealing with" the employer pursuant to Section 2(5) and was therefore not a statutory labor organization. The job enrichment program divided the 25–30 affected employees into four teams, which in turn acted by consensus to make job assignments, schedule overtime, and, occasionally, participate in interviewing job applicants. Over a period of two years, management officials and a consultant met with the teams to discuss the program; and such discussions included at least some reference to Section 8(d) subjects,[38] such as wages, vacation schedules, and assignments of overtime. The program also included employee committees whose functions were to investigate plant safety, reevaluate job procedures and, on one occasion, draft a job description. The administrative law judge held that the team's activities involved "managerial functions [which were] flatly delegated to employees and do not involve any dealing with the employer within the meaning of Section 2(5) however expansively that term is applied . . . . These functions were just other assignments of job duties, albeit duties not normally assigned to rank-and-file personnel."[39] The ALJ characterized the meetings with the consultant as "a sophisticated training exercise" akin to "mental gymnastics," and concluded that the discussions with management officials touching on terms and conditions of employment were *de minimis*.[40] The *General Foods* decision may be significant in relation to various worker-participation pro-

---

[36]*Cf.* Center for United Labor Action, 219 NLRB 873, 90 LRRM 1004 (1975) (a 2-to-1 decision holding in §8(b)(4) context that a social action group seeking to promote unionism, the interests of women, minorities, and consumers did not exist for the purpose of dealing with employers and therefore was not a §2(5) labor organization).
[37]231 NLRB 1232, 96 LRRM 1204 (1977).
[38]*See generally* Chapter 17 *infra.*
[39]231 NLRB at 1235. *See* S & W Motor Lines, Inc., 236 NLRB 938, 98 LRRM 1488 (1978); Roytype, 199 NLRB 354, 81 LRRM 1219 (1972).
[40]231 NLRB at 1235. The ALJ also concluded that the program was not a labor organization because it functioned on a "committee of the whole" basis and not as a

grams, such as Scanlon plans, quality work circles, codetermination, and other plans that are designed to solicit worker involvement in day-to-day job activities and decision making.[41]

III. EMPLOYER DOMINATION

Section 8(a)(2) prohibits employer *domination* of a labor organization. Prohibited domination exists when the organization is directed by the employer, rather than by the employees.[42] The original intent of Section 8(a)(2) was principally to eradicate "company unions" created by employers to minimize the threat of employee representation by outside labor organizations. However, Congress did not intend to prohibit employees from freely selecting representation by a "company" or "enterprise" union, i.e., an independent union organized solely on a company-wide basis.[43]

The Board's first case under the Wagner Act involved Pennsylvania Greyhound Lines, which formed and controlled a com-

---

"group or a person which stands in an agency relationship" to other employees. *Id.* at 1234. *But see* the statutory language, "[a]ny organization of any kind, *or* any agency *or* employee representation committee *or* plan . . . ." *See also* NLRB v. Ampex Corp., *supra* note 30.

[41]*See generally Worker Alienation: Hearings on S.3916 Before the Subcommittee on Employment Manpower, and Poverty of the Senate Committee on Labor and Public Welfare*, 92d Cong., 2d Sess. (1972); D. Jenkins, JOB POWER (1973); WORKERS' CONTROL (G. Hunnius, G. D. Garson & J. Case eds. 1973); National Center for Productivity and Quality of Working Life, RECENT INITIATIVES IN LABOR-MANAGEMENT COOPERATION (1976); Jackson, *supra* note 2; Murmann, *supra* note 2; Sangerman, *supra* note 2; Shaw, *Worker Participation—American Style*, 3 EMPLOYEE RELATIONS L. J. 38 (1977); Walton, *How to Counter Alienation in the Plant*, 50 HARV. BUS. REV. (Nov.-Dec. 1972); Winpisinger, *An American Unionist Looks at Co-determination*, 2 EMPLOYEE RELATIONS L. J. 133 (1976) (Machinist president is apprehensive about worker participation plans); Note, *Does Employer Implementation of Employee Production Teams Violate §8(a)(2) of the National Labor Relations Act?*, *supra* note 2; Note, *The West German Model of Codetermination Under Section 8(a) (2) of the NLRB*, *supra* note 2; Note, *Employee Codetermination: Origins In Germany, Present Practice in Europe, and Applicability to the United States*, 47 HARV. J. OF LEGIS. 946 (1977). *Cf.* discussion of §302(c) of LMRA in Chapter 5 *supra* at notes 10-13.
Worker committees in unorganized plants have come under §8(a)(2) review almost exclusively. To the extent that such committees are the result of mature, arm's-length collective bargaining at organized plants, §8(a)(2) should not pose a serious obstacle. *See generally* Chapter 17.

[42]*E.g.*, Han-Dee Spring & Mfg. Co., 132 NLRB 1542, 48 LRRM 1566 (1961); Wahlgren Magnetics, 132 NLRB 1613, 48 LRRM 1542 (1961).

[43]"Nothing in the bill prohibits the formation of a company union, if by that term is meant an organization of workers confined by their own volition to the boundaries of a particular plant or employer. What is intended is to make such organization the free choice of the workers, and not a choice dictated by forms of interference which are weighty precisely because of the existence of the employer-employee relationship." H. R. REP. NO. 972, 74th Cong., 1st Sess. 15-16 (1935), *reprinted in* 2 NLRB, LEGISLATIVE HISTORY OF THE NATIONAL LABOR RELATIONS ACT, 1935, at 2971-72 (1949). An international comparative note: Almost all Japanese trade unions are "enterprise" unions, confined to the employees of a single employer. *See generally* Hanami, Japan, 5 INTERNATIONAL ENCYCLOPEDIA FOR LABOUR LAW AND INDUSTRIAL RELATIONS ¶¶ 188-94 (R. Blanpain ed. 1978).

pany union (The Employees Association of Pennsylvania Greyhound Lines) for the handling of employee grievances, in an effort to avoid dealing with a more militant outside organization.[44] The Board completely disestablished the company union and ordered the employer never to bargain with it again.[45] By the eve of the enactment of the Taft-Hartley amendments in 1947, Board Chairman Herzog was able to observe, in the *Detroit Edison* case,[46] that employer domination of company unions had ceased to be the problem it had been in 1935. The prohibition was nevertheless kept intact in the new Act.

The Board's basic approach to unlawful domination of labor organizations was approved by the Supreme Court in *Newport News Shipbuilding & Drydock Co. v. NLRB*.[47] The Board there ordered disestablishment of an employee committee which gave the employer the power to veto the organization's proposed actions, even though the challenged organization had prevented serious labor disputes and had employee support; and there was no evidence that the employer had actually exercised its power to control it. The Board and the Court found that the employer possessed such "control of the form and structure of an employee organization" as to deprive the employees of the "complete freedom of action guaranteed to them by the Act."[48]

While there is uniform agreement that Section 8(a)(2) was designed to facilitate employee free choice and self-organization, the Board and the Courts have wrestled with the problem of distinguishing between *cooperation* which the Act permits, and *domination*, which the Act prohibits.[49] In *Humble Oil & Refining Co. v. NLRB*[50] the Fifth Circuit noted that the Board is neither

---

[44]Pennsylvania Greyhound Lines, Inc., 1 NLRB 1, 1 LRRM 303 (1935), *enforced*, 303 US 261, 2 LRRM 599 (1938).

[45]Disestablishment of company unions is the traditional Board remedy whenever prohibited domination or control is found. *See, e.g.*, Metropolitan Alloys Corp., 233 NLRB 966, 97 LRRM 1220 (1977); Kux Mfg. Corp., *supra* note 14. *See infra* at notes 193-206.

[46]674 NLRB 267, 20 LRRM 1160 (1947).

[47]308 US 241, 5 LRRM 665 (1939).

[48]*Id.* at 249. Similarly, in NLRB v. Brown Paper Mill Co., 108 F2d 867, 5 LRRM 782 (CA 5, 1940), the employee association members testified that they were not dominated or coerced by the employer and that they desired representation by the association. Although the Board found no evidence that the employer in fact dominated the association, disestablishment was ordered because the employer had supported its formation.

[49]*See* Hertzka & Knowles v. NLRB, 503 F2d 625, 87 LRRM 2503 (CA 9, 1974), *denying enforcement to* 206 NLRB 191, 84 LRRM 1556 (1973), *cert. denied*, 423 US 875, 90 LRRM 2554 (1975).

[50]113 F2d 85, 6 LRRM 816 (CA 5, 1940).

the "guardian or ruler over the employees, but is only empowered to deliver them from restraint at the hands of the employer when it exists."[51] Concerning employees' preference for an inside committee system rather than an outside union, Judge Magruder, in *Coppus Engineering Corp.* v. *NLRB*,[52] commented that the "choice was theirs," and the Act was limited to guaranteeing them the "freedom to exercise that choice unimpeded by employer interference or coercion."[53]

A. Factors Relevant to Finding Domination

In *Spiegel Trucking Co.*[54] the Board found the following factors relevant to finding domination: (1) the relationship of the employer to the labor organization; (2) the nature of the collective bargaining negotiations between the parties; (3) what control, if any, the employer has over the union's membership; (4) whether the organization has a constitution and bylaws; (5) the nature and place of meetings of the organization; (6) whether employees are compensated for time and attendance at such meetings; and (7) whether supervisory personnel attend such meetings, and if so, their role in the organization.[55]

Generally, the Board considers a labor organization unlawfully dominated if the employer has the *potential* power to control it,[56] but reviewing courts have required evidence of *actual control.*[57] This difference in approach was illustrated by the Board's

---

[51]*Id.* at 88.

[52]240 F2d 564, 39 LRRM 2315 (CA 1, 1957).

[53]*Id.* at 573 (Magruder, C. J. concurring). Judge Magruder added: "[T]he statute does not make it the duty of the employer, nor a function of the Board to 'baby' along the employees in the direction of choosing an outside union as a bargaining representative." *Id.* at 574.

[54]225 NLRB 178, 179, 92 LRRM 1604 (1976); *accord,* Wahlgren Magnetics, *supra* note 42.

[55]In *Spiegel,* the Board declined to find unlawful domination, although the employer was the moving force in the formation of the Spiegel Trucking Company Drivers Committee, because of an absence of proof of domination after the formation of the organization.

[56]*See, e.g.,* Stephens Inst., 241 NLRB 454, 100 LRRM 1603 (1979); Janesville Prods. Div., 240 NLRB 854, 100 LRRM 1383 (1979); Northeastern Univ., 235 NLRB 858, 98 LRRM 1347 (1978), *enforcement denied,* 601 F2d 1208, 101 LRRM 2767 (CA 1, 1979); Duquesne Univ., 198 NLRB 891, 81 LRRM 1091 (1972); Tuscarora Plastics Co., 167 NLRB 1059, 66 LRRM 1229 (1967); Hydraulic Accessories Co., 165 NLRB 864, 65 LRRM 1603 (1967).

[57]As the Ninth Circuit stated in Hertzka & Knowles v. NLRB, *supra* note 49 at 630: "The sum of this is that a section 8(a)(2) finding must rest on a showing that the employees' free choice, either in type of organization or in the assertion of demands, is stifled by the degree of employer involvement at issue." *See* Federal-Mogul Corp. v. NLRB, 394 F2d 915, 918, 68 LRRM 2332 (CA 6, 1968); NLRB v. Prince Macaroni Mfg.

decision in *Northeastern University*[58] and the First Circuit's denial of enforcement.[59] The Board found the following facts evidence of domination: The university allowed meetings on company property and company time, assisted with election procedures, provided printing and secretarial services, and funded some social activities; management representatives attended some meetings of the employee organization, individual members of the organization consulted with management, and the university originally announced that it had "established" the employee organization.[60] In applying its test of requiring *actual* domination, the First Circuit commented that "allowing meetings on company property and company time, assisting with election procedures, providing for printing and secretarial services, and funding occasional social activities—does not a domination case make."[61]

The courts have recognized that the potential means for domination are always present to some degree in any employer-employee relationship;[62] however, there is no basis for a finding of a Section 8(a)(2) violation without evidence of its realization. "Words and actions which might dominate the employees in their choice of a bargaining agent do not constitute domination proscribed by the Act unless the employees are actually dominated."[63]

Courts have also held that employer cooperation which assists the employees or their bargaining representative in expressing their interests does not violate Section 8(a)(2);[64] indeed, such assistance may be needed where the bargaining representative is "a feeble instrument."[65] Several court decisions have insisted that an organization is not *per se* dominated simply because it

---

Co., 329 F2d 803, 809-12, 55 LRRM 2852 (CA 1, 1964); Coppus Eng'r Corp. v. NLRB, 240 F2d 564, 39 LRRM 2315 (CA 1, 1957); Chicago Rawhide Mfg. Co. v. NLRB, *supra* note 3 at 167-68; *but cf.* Newport News Shipbuilding & Drydock Co., *supra* note 47.

[58]*Supra* note 56.

[59]*Id.*

[60]The Board ordered disestablishment even though there was no outside labor organization seeking to represent the employees, there was no movement among the employees to seek representation by another union, and the admittedly useful services performed by the organization would go undone.

[61]601 F2d at 1214.

[62]*See, e.g.,* Chicago Rawhide Mfg. Co. v. NLRB, *supra* note 3.

[63]*Id.* at 167.

[64]*See, e.g.,* NLRB v. Northeastern Univ., *supra* note 56.

[65]Coppus Eng'r Corp. v. NLRB, *supra* note 57 at 573, *also quoted* in NLRB v. Northeastern Univ., *supra* note 61 at 1213.

has no formal membership, no dues, no mass meetings, and no written collective bargaining agreement.[66] In one case, the appellate court found insufficient evidence of actual domination where the employer had permitted meetings on company time, had controlled the length of meetings, and had advised an employee representative not to concern himself with a particular safety problem.[67] In another case, the reviewing court found insufficient proof of actual domination where the employees' organization had submitted proposed changes in its bylaws to management for approval, the organization's bylaws allowed the foreman to participate in calling departmental meetings and permitted him to submit reports of the meetings to management, and the employer had the power to change the status of employee representatives by transferring them to another department.[68]

The Board and the courts are in general agreement, however, that domination exists where the employer creates an employee committee, selects the employee representatives, requires that committee membership be on a rotating basis, and determines when meetings will be held and also presides over them.[69] The same standards apply equally to labor organizations acting as employers.[70]

The degree of supervisory involvement required to establish unlawful domination has been the subject of numerous Board

---

[66]See, e.g., NLRB v. Northeastern Univ., supra note 56; Hertzka & Knowles v. NLRB, supra note 49. The courts have held that the Act does not require approval of a purely adversarial model of labor relations. Hertzka & Knowles v. NLRB, 503 F2d at 631. For criticism of the Board's adversarial approach, see also Note, Discarding the Doctrine of Supervisory Domination: New Solutions to an Old Conflict of Interest, 30 HASTINGS L. J. 763 (1979).

[67]Federal-Mogul Corp. v. NLRB, supra note 57.

[68]Hotpoint Co. v. NLRB, 289 F2d 683, 48 LRRM 2101 (CA 7, 1961).

[69]See, e.g., Utrad Corp v. NLRB, supra note 27; NLRB v. Ampex Corp., supra note 30; NLRB v. Reed Rolled Thread Pie Co., 432 F2d 70, 75 LRRM 2344 (CA 5, 1970); S & W Motor Lines, supra note 39; STR, Inc., 221 NLRB 496, 90 LRRM 1591 (1975); Rensselaer Polytechnic Inst., supra note 27; Rupp Indus., 217 NLRB 385, 88 LRRM 1603 (1975); Versatube Corp., 203 NLRB 456, 83 LRRM 1118 (1973), enforced, 492 F2d 795, 86 LRRM 2128 (CA 6, 1974); American Mfg., 196 NLRB 248, 79 LRRM 1694 (1972). In Kux Mfg. Corp., supra note 14, the employer paid representatives for time spent in meetings, unilaterally prepared and issued minutes of the meetings, and responded favorably only to those complaints and suggestions brought by representatives which it found beneficial to its own interests. See also Liberty Mkts., Inc., 236 NLRB 1486, 99 LRRM 1163 (1978); Kurz-Kasch, Inc., 239 NLRB 1044, 100 LRRM 1118 (1978); Fremont Mfg. Co., supra note 14; Rideout Memorial Hosp., 227 NLRB 1338, 94 LRRM 1703 (1977).

[70]In Teamsters Local 688, 215 NLRB 852, 88 LRRM 1217 (1974) the labor organization-employer violated §8(a)(2) by entering into a collective bargaining agreement with itself as representative of its clerical employees.

decisions. In *Kresge Department Store*[71] the Board held that Section 14(a) of the Act, which expressly permits supervisors to join and remain union members, does not prohibit consideration of supervisor membership in unions as a factor in finding unlawful employer domination. In *Nassau & Suffolk Contractors Association*,[72] the Board found a Section 8(a)(2) violation where the employer had acquiesced in the union's placement of supervisors on the union's negotiating committee. Such acquiescence, however, was insufficient to support a finding of domination, because there was no proof that the employer was in any way responsible for placing the supervisors on the negotiating committee. The issue of supervisory involvement more frequently arises in representation cases. The Board has held that in representation cases it will consider issues of supervisory involvement where such involvement is so severe as to constitute a conflict of interest preventing the labor organization from acting in the employees' interest.[73] Issues relating to supervisory involvement are therefore considered in representation cases, even though they may also involve activity proscribed by Section 8(a)(2).

A Section 8(a)(2) "domination" violation cannot be based solely on events occurring beyond the six-month limitations period imposed by Section 10(b) of the Act. But a violation will be found where the prior conduct is sufficiently connected with conduct within the limitations period, such as where the employer retains control during the period.[74]

IV. EMPLOYER INTERFERENCE

Another unlawful means of undermining employee rights to select the bargaining representative of their choice is employer *interference* with the creation or operation of a labor organiza-

---

[71] 77 NLRB 212, 21 LRRM 1345 (1948).

[72] 118 NLRB 174, 40 LRRM 1146 (1957).

[73] *E.g.*, Sierra Vista Hosp., 241 NLRB 631, 100 LRRM 1590 (1979); *accord*, Rockford Memorial Hosp., 247 NLRB 319, 103 LRRM 1165 (1980); Farber Cancer Inst., 247 NLRB 1, 103 LRRM 1132 (1980); Healdsburg Gen. Hosp., 247 NLRB 212, 103 LRRM 1135 (1980); Exeter Hosp., 248 NLRB 292, 104 LRRM 1052 (1980); Arlington Hosp., 246 NLRB 992, 103 LRRM 1093 (1979); Baptist Hosps., 246 NLRB 170, 102 LRRM 1394 (1979); *see* Brunswick Pulp & Paper Co., 152 NLRB 973, 59 LRRM 1230 (1965); Alaska Salmon Indus., 78 NLRB 185, 22 LRRM 1190 (1948). *See also* Home Box Office, 103 LRRM 1159 (1979) (advice memorandum).

[74] *E.g.*, NLRB v. Erie Marine, Inc., 465 F2d 104, 80 LRRM 3330 (CA 3, 1972); Consolidated Flavor Corp., 238 NLRB 326, 99 LRRM 1416 (1978); *see* Local Lodge 1424, Machinists v. NLRB, 362 US 411, 45 LRRM 3212 (1960). *See* Chapter 32 *infra* at notes 116-19.

tion. Such activity goes beyond merely interfering with Section 7 rights of individual employees;[75] it is aimed instead at the labor organization as an entity.[76] A narrow and often obscure line divides actual or attempted unlawful "interference" or "assistance" from what constitutes unlawful "domination." Board and court decisions often create confusion by using the three terms indistinguishably to describe similar conduct. The difference between "domination" and "interference" or "assistance" is a matter of degree. "Domination" of a union constitutes an irreversible subjugation of the union to the employer's will; "interference" or "assistance" is less severe misconduct, so that the union is deemed capable of functioning as a union once the "interference" or "assistance" is removed.[77] For example, an employer was held to have unlawfully assisted a union in *Garment Workers* v. *NLRB (Bernhard-Altmann)*,[78] where it recognized the union as the exclusive representative of the employees at a time when it did not have a majority status. Such misconduct was unlawful assistance but not domination; there were no allegations or evidence that the employer was able to control the activities of the union, and the employer held a good-faith belief that the union had majority status. As previously noted, however, that good faith was not a defense to the Section 8(a)(2) violation.[79]

It is also well established that an employer renders unlawful 8(a)(2) assistance by recognizing and executing a collective bargaining agreement with a union at a time when the employer does not employ a substantial and representative complement of the projected work force in the relevant bargaining unit, or at a time when it is not engaged in normal operations.[80] In *Spiegel Trucking Co.*[81] the Board upheld an administrative law judge's decision that an employer's active role in the formation of an employee group was unlawful interference under Section 8(a)(2),

---

[75]*See generally* Chapter 6 *supra.*
[76]*See, e.g.*, Nassau & Suffolk Contractors Ass'n, *supra* note 72.
[77]For cases discussing the distinction between domination and interference, *see* Liquor Salesmen Local 195 v. NLRB, 452 F2d 1312, 78 LRRM 2641 (1971); NLRB v. Dennison Mfg. Co., 419 F2d 1080, 72 LRRM 2972 (CA 1, 1969); Newman-Green, Inc., 161 NLRB 1062, 63 LRRM 1405 (1966); Lunardi-Central Distrib. Co., Inc., 161 NLRB 1443, 63 LRRM 1457 (1966).
[78]*Supra* note 9.
[79]*See* notes 9-12 *supra* and accompanying text.
[80]Sheraton Great Falls Inn, 242 NLRB 1255, 101 LRRM 1381 (1979); Allied Prods. Corp., 220 NLRB 732, 735, 90 LRRM 1476 (1975).
[81]*Supra* note 54.

but reversed the ALJ's conclusion that such conduct was also unlawful domination. The Board noted that while unlawful interference as the moving force in the formation of the union had indeed occurred, "it did not automatically follow that [the employer] was guilty of unlawful domination" in the absence of proof that the employer controlled the union after its formation.[82] This was an example of employer conduct which fell short of the standard required for a finding of domination but was nevertheless unlawful under Section 8(a)(2) as proscribed interference.

While the distinction between "domination" and "interference" or "assistance" is often obscure, it nevertheless has significant implications regarding the appropriate remedy which the Board has established for each particular type of conduct.[83] The Board utilizes severe remedies when an employer's conduct constitutes illegal "domination," while less extreme remedies are used in cases of "interference" or "assistance."[84]

A. Employer Preference for a Particular Labor Organization

Section 8(a)(2) ensures that employees designate a collective bargaining representative of their own independent choice without interference by the employer, who might prefer dealing with a less aggressive or inside labor organization. It is unlawful for an employer to form or urge its employees to form an inside labor organization.[85] Thus, in *NLRB* v. *Fremont Manufacturing Co.*,[86] the Eighth Circuit upheld a Board decision that an employer had violated Section 8(a)(2) by conducting an election to select employees to serve on a newly-created "Progress Team" and to

---

[82]*Id.* at 179.

[83]*See, e.g.,* Packerland Packing Co. of Tex., 221 NLRB 1119, 91 LRRM 1062 (1975), *enforced in relevant part,* 537 F2d 1343, 93 LRRM 2128 (CA 5, 1976); Graham Ford, Inc., 218 NLRB 980, 89 LRRM 1796 (1975); Harpeth Steel, Inc., 208 NLRB 545, 85 LRRM 1174 (1974).

[84]*See infra* at notes 193-213.

[85]*E.g.,* Miller Materials Co., 244 NLRB 496, 102 LRRM 1069 (1979); G. Q. Security Parachutes, Inc., 242 NLRB 508, 101 LRRM 1247 (1979); World Wide Press, Inc., 242 NLRB 346, 101 LRRM 1205 (1979); Rideout Memorial Hosp., *supra* note 69; Doces Sixth Avenue, Inc., 225 NLRB 806, 93 LRRM 1091 (1976); Victor M. Sprys, 217 NLRB 712, 89 LRRM 1134 (1975); Sportspal, Inc., 214 NLRB 917, 88 LRRM 1533 (1974); Tappan Knitting Indus., 201 NLRB 3, 82 LRRM 1447 (1973).

[86]558 F2d 889, 95 LRRM 3095 (CA 8, 1977), *enforcing* 224 NLRB 597, 92 LRRM 1508 (1976); *accord,* Utrad Corp. v. NLRB, *supra* note 27.

present employee grievances to the employer contemporaneously with an outside union's organizational campaign. However, an employer may tell its employees that it favors an inside union, or it may even suggest that the employees form such an organization, provided it does not help them plan and organize it.[87] Similarly, employer conduct that actively benefits a preferred outside labor organization over an incumbent,[88] or prefers one of two rival outside labor organizations,[89] is violative of the Act.

Employer conduct which supports a preferred labor organization over another generally falls within the definition of unlawful "assistance."[90] For example, the Sixth Circuit, in *Schlabach Coal Co. v. NLRB*,[91] held that an employer violated the Section 8(a)(2) rights of its employees when it assisted a preferred outside labor organization, threatened to shut down if the employees supported a rival union, and discharged an employee because he supported the other union.

B. Conduct of Supervisors

Participation by an employer's supervisors in a union organizing effort has frequently been held unlawful. In representation cases, the Board has identified certain conduct by supervisors which is deemed so coercive of employee Section 7 rights as to "taint" a petitioning labor organization's showing of interest

---

[87]Missouri Heel Co., 209 NLRB 481, 85 LRRM 1442 (1974); Walker's Midstream Fuel Serv. Co., 208 NLRB 158, 85 LRRM 1065 (1974); Greyhound Airport Servs., Inc., 204 NLRB 900, 83 LRRM 1712 (1973). In Hertzka & Knowles v. NLRB, *supra* note 49, the Ninth Circuit denied enforcement to a Board order which had held that an employer violated §8(a)(2) by allowing employees to meet on company time and premises to set up an inside employee committee. The court noted that the idea for such committee originated with the employees themselves, who had given their approval to the organization in its final form.

[88]Independent Ass'n of Steel Fabricators, 231 NLRB 264, 97 LRRM 1391 (1977), *enforcement denied in part*, 582 F2d 135, 98 LRRM 3150 (CA 2, 1978); Precision Carpet, Inc., 233 NLRB 329, 92 LRRM 1333 (1976); Arkay Packaging Corp., 221 NLRB 99, 90 LRRM 1728 (1975); Freeman G. Gaffney, Inc., 205 NLRB 1012, 84 LRRM 1248 (1973); Carbona Mining Corp., 198 NLRB 293, 80 LRRM 1628 (1972); Penn Bldg. Maintenance Corp., 195 NLRB 183, 79 LRRM 1416 (1972); Columbus Janitor Serv., 191 NLRB 902, 77 LRRM 1737 (1971).

[89]Ralco Sewing Indus., Inc., 243 NLRB 438, 101 LRRM 1578 (1979); Ravenswood Elec. Corp., 232 NLRB 609, 97 LRRM 1170 (1977); Hartz Mountain Corp., 228 NLRB 492, 96 LRRM 1589 (1977); River Manor Health Related Facility, 224 NLRB 227, 93 LRRM 1069 (1976); Suburban Transit Corp., 203 NLRB 465, 83 LRRM 1588 (1973); Shreveport Packing Corp., 196 NLRB 498, 80 LRRM 1206 (1972); Northrop Corp., 187 NLRB 172, 76 LRRM 1824 (1970).

[90]*See infra* at notes 106-153.

[91]611 F2d 1161, 104 LRRM 2593 (CA 6, 1979).

among unit employees, thereby resulting in the Board's dismissal of the representation petition or the setting aside of an election won by the labor organization. In this situation, strict principles of agency are not followed, and an employer violates Section 8(a)(2) when its supervisors engage in offending conduct, whether such conduct is known, actually authorized, or subsequently ratified by the employer.[92] As the Supreme Court noted in *Machinists Lodge 35* v. *NLRB*:[93]

> The employer . . . may be held to have assisted . . . a union even though the acts of the so-called agents were not expressly authorized or might not be attributable to him on strict application of the rules of *respondeat superior*. We are dealing here not with private rights . . . nor with technical concepts pertinent to an employer's legal responsibility to third persons . . . but with a clear legislative policy to free the collective bargaining process from all taint of an employer's compulsion, domination or influence.[94]

In *Stevenson Equipment Co.*[95] the Board explained its rationale for holding that supervisory participation in the solicitation of authorization cards would be a basis for not counting these "tainted" cards either in a "showing of interest" card check or as valid objections to an election. The Board noted that supervisors' solicitation of cards (1) "might well imply to the employee that their employer favors the union"[96] or (2) may coerce employees into signing authorization cards for fear of future retaliation by supervisors who exert considerable leverage over their jobs. In the former situation, an employer's vigorous anti-union campaign subsequent to the supervisors' pro-union conduct may serve to negate the potential coercion of employees;[97] and in the latter, the employer's termination of the offending supervisor may cause employees not to fear subsequent retaliation.[98] Other Board decisions have prohibited an employer from asserting "supervisory taint" as the basis for objections to an election, where the employer knew of the offensive conduct

---

[92]*E.g.*, Local 636, Plumbers v. NLRB, 287 F2d 354, 47 LRRM 2457 (CA DC, 1961), *enforcing* 126 NLRB 1381, 45 LRRM 1482 (1960); University of Chicago Library, 205 NLRB 220, 83 LRRM 1678 (1973).

[93]311 US 72, 7 LRRM 282 (1940).

[94]*Id.* at 80.

[95]174 NLRB 865, 70 LRRM 1302 (1969).

[96]*Id.* at 866.

[97]Gary Aircraft, 220 NLRB 187, 90 LRRM 1216 (1975).

[98]Rocky Mountain Bank Note Co., 230 NLRB 922, 95 LRRM 1421 (1977), where the employer suspended the offending supervisor and later discharged him prior to the date of the representation election.

of its supervisors and had a reasonable period of time prior to the election to disavow the particular conduct but did not do so.[99]

Supervisory conduct found objectionable includes signing of authorization cards by supervisors in the presence of unit employees,[100] supervisors' solicitation of employees to sign authorization cards, and their participation at organizational meetings where such cards are signed.[101] For example, in *Packing House & Industrial Services, Inc.* v. *NLRB*,[102] the Eighth Circuit held that an employer violated Section 8(a)(2) when its agents passed out union-designation cards at the time job applications were accepted at a facility recently purchased by a successor employer.[103]

However, a low-level supervisor's solicitation of cards will generally not warrant a finding of "supervisory taint,"[104] nor will a mere statement of personal preference by a supervisor who favors the union constitute unlawful coercion of employee rights.[105]

V. THE REQUIREMENT OF EMPLOYER NEUTRALITY*

Section 8(a)(2) prohibits an employer from contributing "support" to a labor organization. However, in the absence of unlaw-

---

[99]NLRB v. Dobbs House, Inc., 613 F2d 1254, 103 LRRM 2889 (CA 5, 1980); Tac Indus., Inc., 231 NLRB 554, 96 LRRM 1443 (1977); Decatur Transfer & Storage, Inc., 178 NLRB 63, 71 LRRM 1672 (1969); Talladega Cotton Factory, Inc., 91 NLRB 470, 26 LRRM 1517 (1950).

[100]Boyer Bros., 170 NLRB 1108, 68 LRRM 1494 (1968), *enforced*, 448 F2d 555, 78 LRRM 2225 (CA 3, 1971); Boston Pet Supply, Inc., 227 NLRB 1891, 95 LRRM 1096 (1977); Glomac Plastics, Inc., 194 NLRB 406, 78 LRRM 1662 (1971); Sopps, Inc., 175 NLRB 296, 70 LRRM 1555 (1969).

[101]Lamar Elec. Membership Corp., 164 NLRB 979, 65 LRRM 1199 (1967); *contra*, Red Barn Systems, Inc., 224 NLRB 1586, 92 LRRM 1404 (1976); Independent Sprinkler & Fire Protection Co., 220 NLRB 941, 90 LRRM 1564 (1975); Yonkers Hamilton Sanitarium, Inc., 214 NLRB 668, 88 LRRM 1357 (1974); Howard Creations, Inc., 212 NLRB 179, 87 LRRM 1466 (1974); Lawrence Rigging, Inc., 202 NLRB 1094, 82 LRRM 1784 (1973); Scottex Corp., 200 NLRB 446, 82 LRRM 1287 (1972); Luby Leasing, Inc., 198 NLRB 951, 81 LRRM 1097 (1972); Tierney Elec. Mfg. Co., 192 NLRB 229, 77 LRRM 1751 (1971); Idaho Potato Foods, Inc., 188 NLRB 522, 76 LRRM 1425 (1971); Prospect Gardens, Inc., 177 NLRB 136, 72 LRRM 1173 (1969); Park Inn Hotel, Inc., 139 NLRB 669, 51 LRRM 1369 (1962).

[102]590 F2d 688, 100 LRRM 2356 (CA 8, 1978), *enforcing* 231 NLRB 735, 97 LRRM 1215 (1977).

[103]*Id.* at 694; *accord,* NLRB v. Mears Coal Co., 437 F2d 502, 76 LRRM 2081 (CA 3, 1970).

[104]Admiral Petroleum Corp., 240 NLRB 894, 100 LRRM 1373 (1979); Willett Motor Coach Co., 227 NLRB 882, 95 LRRM 1082 (1977).

[105]*See* NLRB v. San Antonio Portland Cement Co., 611 F2d 1148, 103 LRRM 2631 (CA 5, 1980), where mere presence of supervisor wearing union button at union meeting was held not to be coercive.

*[*See* **Editor's Note** *infra*, p. 294.]

ful interference, the Act does not prohibit an employer from expressing a preference for a particular union over its rival.[106] The line between employer preference and unlawful support has been the subject of numerous Board and court decisions.

A. Development of the Neutrality Requirement

In *Midwest Piping Co., Inc.*[107] the Steelworkers and Steamfitters each petitioned the Board for an election. While both petitions were pending, the employer recognized and entered into a closed-shop contract with the Steamfitters.[108] The Board held that the contract violated Section 8(a)(1). The substantive basis of the offense, however, was the violation of Section 8(a)(2): The employer's execution of the agreement "indicated its approval of the Steamfitters, accorded it unwarranted prestige, encouraged membership therein, discouraged membership in the Steelworkers, and thereby rendered unlawful assistance to the Steamfitters, which interfered with, restrained and coerced its employees in the exercise of rights guaranteed in §7 of the Act."[109] The original *Midwest Piping* doctrine thus made it an unfair labor practice for an employer to recognize one of two or more competing labor organizations after a representation question had been submitted to the Board by the filing of a petition.[110]

In 1954, the doctrine was narrowed in *William D. Gibson Co.*[111] There the union contract, covering a unit of product and maintenance employees, had expired, and the union and the employer were in negotiations for a new agreement. A rival union asserted that it represented 30 toolroom employees who had been included

---

[106]Alley Constr. Co., 210 NLRB 999, 86 LRRM 1316 (1974); Plymouth Shoe Co., 182 NLRB 1, 73 LRRM 1610 (1970).

[107]63 NLRB 1060, 17 LRRM 40 (1945). For a critical analysis of the Board's *Midwest Piping* doctrine, see Kesselring & Brinker, *Contract Difficulties Under §8(a)(2)*, *supra* note 2; Note, *New Standards for Domination and Support Under Section 8(a)(2)*, *supra* note 2.

[108]The closed shop was not illegal under the Wagner Act. *See* Chapter 29 *infra* at notes 19-20.

[109]63 NLRB at 1071.

[110]The Board has consistently condemned employer resolution of a question concerning representation while rival unions are involved in Board election proceedings. Vanella Buick Opel, 194 NLRB 744, 79 LRRM 1090 (1971), *enforced*, 475 F2d 1395, 82 LRRM 3092 (CA 3, 1973); Captive Plastics, Inc., 209 NLRB 749, 86 LRRM 1235 (1974); Mosler Safe Co., 209 NLRB 71, 85 LRRM 1392 (1974); Shreveport Packing Corp., *supra* note 89; Belleville News Democrat, Inc., 195 NLRB 431, 79 LRRM 1376 (1972).

[111]110 NLRB 660, 35 LRRM 1092 (1954); *accord*, William Penn Broadcasting Co., 93 NLRB 1104, 27 LRRM 1532 (1951) (company may *bargain* with incumbent while rival union's petition is pending).

in the 500-employee plant unit. When the employer refused the rival union's demand for recognition, the rival union petitioned the Board for an election. But while the matter was pending before the Board, the employer entered into a new contract with the incumbent union, which included the toolroom in its coverage. The rival union charged that this agreement violated *Midwest Piping*, but the Board reasoned that application of the doctrine in this situation would not aid the statutory goal of industrial stability. It therefore held that the ongoing bargaining relationship with an *incumbent* union, even though challenged by an outside union, justified an exception to *Midwest Piping*.

In 1958, in *Shea Chemical Corp.*,[112]* the Board was asked to extend *Gibson* to cover bargaining with an incumbent union. In *Shea*, the Chemical Workers Union demanded recognition, but prior to receiving that demand the company had entered into a recognition agreement with the Mine Workers. After the employer had denied the Chemical Workers' demand, the latter union petitioned for a Board election, whereupon the company and the Mine Workers entered into a collective bargaining agreement even though the Chemical Workers' petition was still pending. The Board overruled *Gibson*, holding that the employer violated the Act by entering into a collective bargaining agreement while the representation case was pending, even though the contracting union had been recognized as the bargaining representative before the intervening union filed its petition. The Board stated its new version of the *Midwest Piping* doctrine as follows:

> [U]pon presentation of a rival or conflicting claim which raises a real question concerning representation an employer may not go so far as to bargain collectively with the incumbent (or any other) union unless and until the question concerning representation has been settled by the board.[113]

But this exception was added:

> The Midwest Piping Doctrine does not apply in situations when, because of contract bar or certification year or other established reason, the rival claim does not raise a real representation question.[114]

---

[112]121 NLRB 1027, 42 LRRM 1486 (1958).
*[*See* **Editor's Note** *infra*, p. 294.]
[113]*Id.* at 1028.
[114]*Id.* In an earlier case the same year, the Board had held that an employer could not recognize one of two competing unions once "a real question concerning representation" had arisen. Novak Logging, 119 NLRB 1573, 41 LRRM 1436 (1958).

According to the Board, "a real question concerning representation" is presented when a competing union files a petition and
the Board indicates that it has administratively determined that
there is a showing of interest by taking cognizance of the case.[115]

The next important case in the development of the doctrine
was *Playskool, Inc.*[116] The company had voluntarily submitted to
a card check before a state labor department conciliator who
found that the Retail, Wholesale, and Department Store Union
(RWDSU) represented a majority of the employees; whereupon
the employer recognized RWDSU. But the rival Furniture
Workers Union had also been seeking recognition, although it
had received only 29.7 percent of the vote in a Board-conducted
election the previous year and had been unsuccessfully seeking
to organize the employer for 20 years. The Board found a
Section 8(a)(2) violation, holding that it had "never established
any numerical percentage as a condition precedent to establishing the existence of a question concerning representation" and
that the "sole requirement . . . is that the claim of the rival union
must not be clearly unsupportable and lacking in substance."[117]

In a 1975 case, *American Can Co.,*[118] where the rival union's
claim was not supportable according to the administrative law
judge, the Board found that extending recognition to a union
which apparently represented an overwhelming majority of the
employees in the unit violated Section 8(a)(2). The Board relied
on its holding in *Boys' Markets, Inc.,*[119] to the effect that it is
sufficient that the rival claim to representation is not "clearly
unsupportable or specious, or otherwise not a colorable claim,"[120]
and further declared: "An employer faced with conflicting claims
of rival unions which give rise to a real question concerning
representation may not recognize or enter into a contract with
one of these unions until the representation question has been
settled under the special procedures of the Act."[121]

---

[115]Swift & Co., 128 NLRB 732, 46 LRRM 1381 (1960).
[116]195 NLRB 560, 79 LRRM 1507 (1972), *enforcement denied*, 477 F2d 66, 82 LRRM
2916 (CA 7, 1973), *supplemented*, 205 NLRB 1009, 84 LRRM 1129 (1973).
[117]*Id.* at 560. *See* discussion *infra* at notes 122-36.
[118]218 NLRB 102, 89 LRRM 1585 (1975), *enforced*, 535 F2d 180, 92 LRRM 2251 (CA
2, 1976).
[119]156 NLRB 105, 61 LRRM 1001 (1965), *enforced sub nom.* Retail Clerks Local 770 v.
NLRB, 370 F2d 205, 64 LRRM 2155 (CA 9, 1966); *accord*, U & I, Inc., 227 NLRB 1, 94
LRRM 1064 (1976).
[120]156 NLRB at 107.
[121]218 NLRB at 103.

B. The Requirement of a Real Question Concerning Representation

The Board has never defined the amount of support required to raise a real question concerning representation.[122] In *American Bread Co.*[123] the Board found that a substantial question concerning representation had been raised by a union which possessed only one authorization card in a unit of 92 when it demanded recognition and had only eight authorization cards when the company recognized the rival union.[124]

In *Robert Hall*,[125] however, the Board found a union's claim "insufficient to compel application of the *Midwest Piping* doctrine" and "no more than a naked claim," where the union had 24 authorization cards in a unit of 153 and it had recently withdrawn its petition for a Board election but had continued to assert an interest in the employees in the appropriate unit. In *Dillon's Cos.*[126] the Board held no real question concerning representation existed where the complaining union had informed the employer of its organizing efforts but had obtained only one authorization card and had never requested recognition.

Although the Board asserts that an employer may ignore a "naked claim,"[127] whether a claim is "naked" may depend on facts ascertained after recognition and during unfair labor practice proceedings.[128]

In *Riviera Manor Nursing Home, Inc.*[129] the employer extended recognition to a rival union two weeks after the Seventh Circuit denied enforcement to the Board's bargaining order which had

---

[122]For general treatment of "question concerning representation," *see* Chapter 10 *infra* at notes 3-9.

[123]170 NLRB 85, 67 LRRM 1430 (1968), *enforcement denied*, 411 F2d 147, 71 LRRM 2243 (CA 6, 1969).

[124]*Accord*, Buck Knives, Inc., 223 NLRB 983, 92 LRRM 1017 (1976), *enforcement denied*, 549 F2d 1319, 94 LRRM 2813 (CA 9, 1977); Wintex Knitting Mill, Inc., 223 NLRB 1293, 92 LRRM 1113 (1976), *enforcement denied*, 610 F2d 430, 104 LRRM 2529 (CA 6, 1979).

[125]207 NLRB 692, 84 LRRM 1538 (1973).

[126]237 NLRB No. 114, 99 LRRM 1065 (1978).

[127]Note 159 *infra*.

[128]*See, e.g.*, Kona Surf Hotel, 201 NLRB 139, 82 LRRM 1279 (1973), where the employer was held to have unlawfully recognized and executed a contract with one union on the basis of a card check the day after another union had filed a petition. At the time of recognition, there was no way for the employer to know whether or not the petition was adequately supported.

[129]220 NLRB 124, 90 LRRM 1186 (1975), *enforcement denied*, 539 F2d 714, 93 LRRM 2019 (CA 7, 1976).

been issued in favor of another union nearly two years earlier. While the Board conceded that the presumption of majority status did not survive the court's final decision, it held that its own "considerable efforts" to enforce the bargaining order, as well as the existence of unremedied violations of Sections 8(a)(3) and (1), put the employer on notice that the first union maintained "a continuing and substantial interest" in representing the employees.[130]

The presumption of continuing majority status afforded an incumbent bargaining representative[131] may also prevent an employer from recognizing a rival union, especially if the parties are engaged in litigation concerning the existence of a bargaining agreement between them.[132] A refusal to negotiate with the incumbent union under such circumstances is not a refusal to bargain in violation of Section 8(a)(5).[133]

The Board has also applied the *Midwest Piping* doctrine where an employer grants recognition at a time when rival unions are litigating the scope of the unit in a representation proceeding.[134] Similarly, an employer must maintain neutrality at a time when the unit is in flux. For example, in *American Can*[135] the employer had opened a new manufacturing facility and hired many employees from its former plant. At the old plant the employer had recognized two separate bargaining units: a production-and-maintenance unit and a smaller unit of lithographic-production employees. At the new facility, prior to start-up of lithographic production, the employer recognized the production-and-maintenance union as the sole representative. But certain lithographic equipment and work was transferred to the new facility, and the employer expected to hire some of the old facility's lithographic workers. The Board held that such expectancy, together with communications from the union representing the lithographic employees, raised a "colorable claim," even though the employer had no obligation to transfer the union's bargaining status to the new facility.[136]

---

[130]*Id.* at 125.
[131]*See* Chapter 12 *infra* at notes 352-442.
[132]*See* Greyhound Airport Servs., Inc., 204 NLRB 900, 83 LRRM 1712 (1973); Western Commercial Transp., Inc., 201 NLRB 17, 82 LRRM 1366 (1973), *enforced*, 487 F2d 332, 84 LRRM 2814 (CA 5, 1973).
[133]Greyhound Airport Servs., Inc., *supra* note 132.
[134]Holyoke Food Mart, 191 NLRB 470, 77 LRRM 1772 (1971).
[135]*Supra* note 118.
[136]*Accord,* Newspaper Agency Corp., 201 NLRB 480, 82 LRRM 1509 (1973), *enforced sub nom.* Graphic Arts Union v. NLRB, 505 F2d 335, 86 LRRM 3234 (CA DC, 1974);

C. Exceptions

The *Midwest Piping* doctrine is inapplicable where an employer recognizes the rival receiving the most votes in an election while objections are pending, provided the objections are ultimately dismissed.[137] However, an employer who incorrectly guesses that a rival union has raised a real question concerning representation does not violate Section 8(a)(5) if he fails to bargain with the majority union.[138]

If a local union disaffiliates from its international and can demonstrate its continuing uncoerced majority status to the employer and thereafter executes an agreement as an independent union, the Board has held that a *Midwest Piping* problem does not exist, even in the face of claims by the international.[139] In *Southern Stevedoring Co., Inc.*[140] the Board held that the chartering of a new local was essentially an "intra-union affair" which did not raise a real question concerning representation.[141]

In industries where dual membership is common, the employer may not resolve a question of representation if both rivals present evidence of authorization from a majority of the employees.[142] Improper recognition of one of two rival unions will be found where recognition is based upon cards signed by employees who, prior to recognition, have signed cards for both unions.[143]

---

see also Fruehauf Trailer Co., 162 NLRB 195, 64 LRRM 1037 (1966); Twin County Transit Mix, Inc., 137 NLRB 1708, 50 LRRM 1478 (1962) (*Midwest Piping* violation where employer recognized rival union on basis of support from strikebreakers hired to replace incumbent unions' supporters who were on strike).

[137]In Taylor Forge Div., Gulf & Western Mfg. Co., 227 NLRB 696, 95 LRRM 1061 (1977), the Board held that the employer acted at its peril when it recognized one of two competing labor organizations under such circumstances, but it did not violate §8(a)(2) of the Act since it guessed correctly. *Accord,* Sundstrand Heat Transfer, Inc. v. NLRB, 538 F2d 1257, 92 LRRM 3266 (CA 7, 1976).

[138]Union Carbide, 105 NLRB 441, 32 LRRM 1276 (1953).

[139]American Cystoscope Makers, 190 NLRB 590, 77 LRRM 1399 (1971); Pall Corp., 190 NLRB 594, 77 LRRM 1397 (1971); Sinclair Mfg. Co., 178 NLRB 182, 72 LRRM 1035 (1969).

[140]230 NLRB 609, 96 LRRM 1342 (1977).

[141]*Id.* at 613. *See also* Associated Gen. Contractors of Am., Inc., 182 NLRB 224, 74 LRRM 1050 (1970); H. L. Washum, 172 NLRB 328, 68 LRRM 1535 (1968), *reversed on other grounds,* 446 F2d 210, 77 LRRM 3076 (CA 9, 1971); Climax Molybdenum Co., 146 NLRB 508, 55 LRRM 1357 (1964).

[142]*See* Epsilon Fishing Co., 198 NLRB 918, 81 LRRM 1208 (1972), *enforced sub nom.* NLRB v. Fishermen's Local 33, 483 F2d 952, 84 LRRM 2280 (CA 9, 1973).

[143]NLRB v. Hi-Temp, Inc., 503 F2d 583, 87 LRRM 2437 (CA 7, 1974). *See also* R. L. Sweet Lumber Co., 207 NLRB 529, 85 LRRM 1073 (1973), *enforced,* 515 F2d 785, 89 LRRM 2326 (CA 10, 1975); Italco Aluminum Corp. v. NLRB, 417 F2d 36, 72 LRRM 2368 (CA 9, 1969); Allied Super Mkts., Inc., 169 NLRB 927, 67 LRRM 1298 (1968).

D. The Circuit Courts' Differing Approach

The Board's *Midwest Piping* doctrine has met strong resistance from the circuit courts.[144] Most of the circuits have refused to find a violation of Section 8(a)(2) when an employer has recognized one of two competing unions which has clearly demonstrated its majority support.[145] The Board and the courts thus differ in their approach to this problem. The Board looks first to the support held by the minority union, finding a "question concerning representation" if the claim of the union is "not clearly unsupportable." The courts, on the other hand, usually examine the support held by the majority union in order to find that no question concerning representation exists, provided the union enjoys uncoerced majority status; in that event the rival is deemed to be "no genuine contender."[146] Accordingly, as expressed by the Seventh Circuit, by extending recognition to a union enjoying majority support, the employer has not rendered "unlawful assistance" or "illegal support," but "has merely obeyed the duty imposed upon him to recognize the agent which his employees have designated."[147] In determining the applicability of the *Midwest Piping* doctrine, the courts tend to ask: (1) Did the recognized union represent a majority at the time it was recognized; and (2) was the majority due to any unlawful activity on the part of the employer or recognized union?[148] The *Midwest Piping* doctrine was similarly criticized by a dissenting Board

---

[144]*E.g.*, Wintex Knitting Mill v. NLRB, 610 F2d 430, 104 LRRM 2529 (CA 6, 1979); Buck Knives, Inc. v. NLRB, 549 F2d 1319, 94 LRRM 2813 (CA 9, 1977); NLRB v. Inter-Island Resorts, Ltd., 507 F2d 411, 87 LRRM 3075 (CA 9, 1974); NLRB v. Suburban Transit Corp., 499 F2d 78, 86 LRRM 2626 (CA 3, 1974); Playskool, Inc. v. NLRB, *supra* note 116; NLRB v. Peter Paul, Inc., 467 F2d 700, 80 LRRM 3431 (CA 9, 1972); NLRB v. Modine Mfg. Co., 453 F2d 292, 79 LRRM 2109 (CA 8, 1971); Sturgeon Elec. Co. v. NLRB, 419 F2d 51, 72 LRRM 2872 (CA 10, 1969); American Bread Co. v. NLRB, 411 F2d 147, 71 LRRM 2243 (CA 6, 1969); Iowa Beef Packers, Inc. v. NLRB, 331 F2d 176, 56 LRRM 2071 (CA 8, 1964); NLRB v. John Swift Co., 277 F2d 641, 46 LRRM 2090 (CA 7, 1960); Cleaver-Brooks Mfg. Corp., 264 F2d 637, 43 LRRM 2722 (CA 7, 1959), *cert. denied*, 361 US 817, 44 LRRM 2983 (1959); Pittsburgh Valve Co. v. NLRB, 234 F2d 565, 38 LRRM 2294 (CA 4, 1956); NLRB v. Indianapolis Newspapers, 210 F2d 501, 33 LRRM 2536 (CA 7, 1954).

[145]Buck Knives, Inc. v. NLRB, *supra* note 144; NLRB v. Inter-Island Resorts, Ltd., *supra* note 144; Playskool, Inc. v. NLRB, *supra* note 116; NLRB v. Peter Paul, Inc., *supra* note 144; Modine Mfg. Co. v. NLRB, *supra* note 144; American Bread Co. v. NLRB, *supra* note 144; Iowa Beef Packers, Inc. v. NLRB, *supra* note 144; NLRB v. Indianapolis Newspapers, Inc., *supra* note 144.

[146]Playskool, Inc. v. NLRB, *supra* note 116, 477 F2d at 70 n.3.

[147]*Id.* at 70. *Accord*, NLRB v. Indianapolis Newspapers, Inc., *supra* note 144.

[148]*E.g.*, Playskool, Inc. v. NLRB, *supra* note 116; NLRB v. Indianapolis Newspapers, *supra* note 144.

member in *U & I, Inc.*[149] The Fifth Circuit, however, has accepted the Board's view.[150]

The hostility of the appellate circuits to the *Midwest Piping* doctrine has not resulted in any modification of the Board's position.* The Board stated in *Kona Surf Hotel*[151] that it would adhere to its view until the Supreme Court resolves the issue.[152] On a number of occasions, however, the Board has avoided the *Midwest Piping* issue and relied instead on other unlawful interference or assistance to find Section 8(a)(2) violations.[153]

[**Editor's Note:** In July 1982 the Board in two cases reexamined its *Midwest Piping* doctrine and ruled that (1) although an employer continued to recognize and bargain with an incumbent bargaining agent in the face of a competing claim from a rival union, such conduct did not violate the Act, and (2) it was not unlawful for an employer to recognize one of two unions competing to organize its unrepresented employees provided (a) the recognized union represents an uncoerced, unassisted majority of the employees, and (b) no valid petition for representation has been filed. *RCA Del Caribe, Inc.*, 262 NLRB No. 116, 110 LRRM 1369 (1982); *Bruckner Nursing Home*, 262 NLRB No. 115, 110 LRRM 1374 (1982). *See also* **Editor's Note** in Chapter 13 *infra*, p. 650.]

VI. SUPPORT VERSUS COOPERATION

In addition to prohibiting employer domination and interference, Section 8(a)(2) makes it unlawful for an employer to "contribute financial or other support to a labor organization." Illegal support or assistance generally takes the form of affirmative acts of tangible benefit to a labor organization which are not sufficiently serious to constitute illegal domination.[154] Because

---

[149]227 NLRB 1, 94 LRRM 1064 (1976) (Member Walther's dissenting opinion).

[150]NLRB v. Western Commercial Transp., Inc., *supra* note 132; Oil Transp. Co. v. NLRB, 440 F2d 664, 75 LRRM 2609 (CA 5, 1971); NLRB v. Signal Oil & Gas Co., 304 F2d 785, 50 LRRM 2505 (CA 5, 1962).

*[*But see* **Editor's Note** this page.]

[151]*Supra* note 128 at 142 n.12.

[152]The Board's continued strict application of the *Midwest Piping* doctrine is illustrated by Riviera Manor Nursing Home, *supra* note 129, and Associated Gen. Contractors of Calif., Inc., 220 NLRB 540, 90 LRRM 1719 (1975).

[153]*See, e.g.*, Lyndale Mfg. Corp., 238 NLRB 1281, 99 LRRM 1330 (1978); Atlas Lumber Co., 237 NLRB 823, 99 LRRM 1046 (1978); B. F. G. Gourmet Foods, Inc., 236 NLRB 489, 98 LRRM 1344 (1978); Mountaineer Shaft & Tunnel Constr. Co., 234 NLRB 929, 98 LRRM 1148 (1978).

[154]*See supra* at notes 42-74.

illegal domination under Section 8(a)(2) also often involves illegal assistance to a labor organization, the Board and courts have occasionally created confusion by using the terms indistinguishably. The characterization of certain employer conduct as unlawful assistance or illegal domination is a matter of degree; domination exists when the employer is able to exercise a strong influence over the organization. The distinction between domination and assistance is all-important, for it determines the Board's remedy.[155]

In *Coamo Knitting Mills, Inc.*[156] the Board indicated its refusal to apply a mechanistic test in assessing unlawful assistance. While noting that the employer had given his support to a union during its successful organizing drive, the Board stated:

> We have held that the use of company time and property does not, *per se*, establish unlawful support and assistance. Rather, each case must be decided on the totality of its facts . . . . We think that the use of company time for these few employees . . . is subject, under the circumstances of this case, to the application of a *de minimis* rule.[157]

The courts have also recognized a distinction between unlawful support or assistance and lawful cooperation.[158] Lawful cooperation has been described as activity "which does not have the effect of inhibiting self-organization and free collective bargaining."[159] The Board and the courts thus evaluate the totality of an employer's conduct[160] in determining whether the "natural tendency of [that] support would be to inhibit employees in their choice of a bargaining representative" and to restrict the employee group in maintaining an arm's-length relationship with their employer.[161]

---

[155]*See infra* at notes 193-213.
[156]150 NLRB 579, 58 LRRM 1116 (1964).
[157]*Id.* at 582.
[158]Hertzka & Knowles v. NLRB, *supra* note 49; Federal-Mogul Corp. v. NLRB, *supra* note 57; NLRB v. Prince Macaroni Mfg., *supra* note 57; Chicago Rawhide Mfg. v. NLRB, *supra* note 3; NLRB v. Wenyss, 212 F2d 465, 34 LRRM 2124 (CA 9, 1954).
[159]Federal-Mogul Corp. v. NLRB, *supra* note 57 at 917.
[160]District 65, Distributive Workers v. NLRB, 593 F2d 1155, 99 LRRM 2640 (CA DC, 1978), *enforcing sub nom.* Hartz Mountain Corp., 228 NLRB 49, 96 LRRM 1589 (1977); Duquesne Univ., 198 NLRB 891, 91 LRRM 1091 (1972). *See also* NLRB v. Vernitron Elec. Components, Inc., 548 F2d 24, 94 LRRM 2380 (CA 1, 1977), *enforcing* 221 NLRB 464, 90 LRRM 1497 (1975), where the court held that the use of company facilities for a union organizational meeting, "standing alone," was not unlawful support.
[161]Kaiser Foundation Hosps., Inc., 223 NLRB 322, 322, 91 LRRM 1523 (1976); *accord,* NLRB v. Keller Ladders S., Inc., 405 F2d 663, 70 LRRM 2001 (CA 5, 1968), *enforcing* 161 NLRB 21, 63 LRRM 1280 (1966).

Many types of employer conduct that may constitute evidence of unlawful domination may also be characterized as unlawful support. Unlawful financial support of a union generally exists when an employer furnishes a meeting place on its premises to a union and pays employees for time spent at such meetings[162] or during other union-related activities,[163] or provides supplies and other services of benefit to a union.[164] An employer also engages in unlawful support if it requires job applicants to sign union dues check-off cards as a condition precedent to their future employment,[165] pays membership fees or other dues to a union on behalf of its employees,[166] or gives direct financial assistance to a union or its members.[167]

In *NLRB* v. *Vernitron Electrical Components, Inc.*[168] an employer assembled its employees on its own premises for organizational meetings with union representatives; it arranged for its supervisors to personally attend those meetings and observe the signing of authorization cards; it recognized the union on that same day; and shortly thereafter it entered into a collective bargaining agreement with the union. The First Circuit upheld the Board's conclusion that such conduct represented unlawful support regardless of whether the employer actually intended to aid the union in an unlawful manner.[169]

Extending voluntary recognition to a union which represents a majority[170] of the employees in an appropriate bargaining unit

---

[162]St. Vincent's Hosp., 244 NLRB 84, 102 LRRM 1196 (1979); World Wide Press, Inc., *supra* note 85; Tuschak-Jacobson, Inc., 223 NLRB 1298, 92 LRRM 1280 (1976); Rensselaer Polytechnic Inst., *supra* note 27; Bee Line Eng'r, Inc., 217 NLRB 367, 89 LRRM 1026 (1975); Sportspal, Inc., *supra* note 85.

[163]Mountaineer Shaft & Tunnel Constr. Co., *supra* note 153; NLRB v. Vernitron Elec. Components, Inc., *supra* note 160; Rockville Nursing Center, 193 NLRB 959, 78 LRRM 1519 (1971); *accord*, Kurz-Kasch, Inc., *supra* note 69; Kux Mfg. Corp., *supra* note 14; Rideout Memorial Hosp., *supra* note 69; C. H. Heist Corp., 186 NLRB 355, 76 LRRM 1062 (1970).

[164]*See* Easy-Heat Wirekraft, *supra* note 14 (employer offered to pay union's attorneys' fees); Bee Line Eng'r, Inc., *supra* note 162. *See also* Kaiser Foundation Hosps., Inc., *supra* note 161 (employer provided the union with use of company clerical supplies and copying machines for producing its newsletter). *Contra*, S & W Motor Lines, Inc., *supra* note 39 (*de minimis* assistance); Monon Trailer, Inc., 217 NLRB 257, 89 LRRM 1280 (1975) (use of company Xerox machine held to be *de minimis* assistance and thus not unlawful).

[165]*E.g.*, Baggett Indus. Constructors Inc., 219 NLRB 171, 90 LRRM 1175 (1975).

[166]*See* Business Envelope Mfrs., Inc., 227 NLRB 280, 94 LRRM 1351 (1976); Stockton Door Co., 218 NLRB 1053, 89 LRRM 1428 (1975). *See also* Dura-Vent Corp., 235 NLRB 1300, 98 LRRM 1225 (1978).

[167]Prestige Bedding Co., 212 NLRB 690, 87 LRRM 1299 (1974) (employer offered to pay insurance premiums only for employees who were union members).

[168]*Supra* note 160.

[169]*Id.* at 27.

[170]*See* Bernhard-Altmann, *supra* note 9 and accompanying text.

is not in itself unlawful. But an employer violates Section 8(a) (2) when it recognizes an incumbent union as the representative of its employees at a new facility, in the absence of a lawful accretion, and extends coverage of an existing contract to such employees.[171] It is likewise unlawful to extend union recognition to a group of employees in an inappropriate unit.[172] Similarly, it is unlawful for an employer to recognize a labor organization prior to employment of a representative work force at a new or existing facility.[173] However, as the Board pointed out in *Hayes Coal Co.:*[174]

> A determination of premature recognition . . . cannot be predicated on whether existing jobs are temporarily unfilled by reason of quit or discharge, or on a possibility that future conditions may warrant an increase in personnel subsequent to the granting of recognition. The correct test is whether, at the time of recognition, the jobs or job classifications designated for the operation involved are filled or substantially filled and the operation is in normal or substantially normal production.[175]

Improper enforcement of union security and check-off clauses in a collective bargaining agreement may result in unlawful assistance to a labor organization.[176] It is unlawful for an employer to maintain and give effect to an illegal closed-shop provision in a collective bargaining agreement,[177] or to require union membership prior to the expiration of the 30-day grace period

---

[171]Meijer, Inc. v. NLRB, 564 F2d 737, 96 LRRM 2738 (CA 6, 1977), *enforcing* 222 NLRB 18, 91 LRRM 1153 (1976); NLRB v. Security-Columbian Banknote Co., 541 F2d 135, 93 LRRM 2049 (CA 3, 1976), *enforcing in relevant part* 215 NLRB 450, 88 LRRM 1043 (1974); NLRB v. General Cinema Corp., 526 F2d 427, 91 LRRM 2193 (CA 5, 1976), *enforcing in relevant part* 214 NLRB 1074, 87 LRRM 1563 (1974); Arco Elec., Inc., 241 NLRB 256, 100 LRRM 1541 (1979).

[172]*E.g.*, Atlas Guard Serv., 229 NLRB 698, 95 LRRM 1207 (1977) (employer recognized a union in an inappropriate two-state unit). *See also* California Gen. Linen Supply Co., 206 NLRB 203, 84 LRRM 1613 (1973); Northrop Corp., 187 NLRB 172, 76 LRRM 1824 (1970).

[173]*E.g.*, NLRB v. Cen-Vi-Ro Pipe Corp., 457 F2d 775, 79 LRRM 2895 (CA 9, 1972), *enforcing* 180 NLRB 344, 73 LRRM 1089 (1969); Sheraton Great Falls Inn, 242 NLRB No. 199, 101 LRRM 1381 (1979); Klein's Golden Manor, 214 NLRB 807, 88 LRRM 1418 (1974); Norris Indus., 214 NLRB 629, 88 LRRM 1061 (1974); Helrose Bindery, Inc., 204 NLRB 499, 83 LRRM 1388 (1973); Wockes Corp., 197 NLRB 860, 80 LRRM 1458 (1972). *See infra* at note 191.

[174]197 NLRB 1162, 80 LRRM 1501 (1972).

[175]*Id.* at 1163; *accord,* Fraser & Johnston Co., 189 NLRB 142, 77 LRRM 1036 (1971), *enforced in part,* 469 F2d 1259, 81 LRRM 2964 (CA 9, 1972); W. L. Rives Co., 136 NLRB 1050, 49 LRRM 1902 (1962), *enforced in part,* 328 F2d 464, 55 LRRM 2428 (CA 5, 1964).

[176]Enforcement of such clauses by an employer often results in the union being a party to the unlawful conduct. *See infra* at notes 185-92. *See generally* Chapter 29 *infra.*

[177]NLRB v. American Dredging Co., 276 F2d 286, 45 LRRM 2405 (CA 3, 1960), *enforcing as modified* 123 NLRB 139, 43 LRRM 1387 (1959).

provided by Section 8(a)(3) of the Act.[178] An employer violates Section 8(a)(2) when it remits dues to a union in the absence of valid authorization from the affected employee,[179] refuses to honor an otherwise valid revocation of dues checkoff by an employee,[180] or in any way solicits on behalf of the union for authorization of dues checkoff from its employees.[181]

VII. THE UNION AS A PARTY TO THE EMPLOYER'S DOMINATION, ASSISTANCE, OR SUPPORT

Various types of employer conduct violative of Section 8(a)(2) also involve illegal conduct by a labor organization prohibited by Section 8(b)(1)(A), which makes it unlawful for a labor organization or its agents to "restrain or coerce employees" in the exercise of their rights guaranteed by Section 7 of the Act.[182] A joint violation of these provisions occurs when an employer executes a contract with a labor organization representing only a minority of its employees. The union violates Section 8(b)(1)(A) by entering into such a contract, while the employer violates Section 8(a)(2) by extending exclusive recognition and conferring the contractual benefits.[183] A labor organization's "good faith" mistaken belief as to its status as a majority repre-

---

[178]E.g., NLRB v. Western Bldg. Maintenance Co., 402 F2d 775, 69 LRRM 2623 (CA 9, 1968), enforcing 162 NLRB 778, 64 LRRM 1120 (1967); NLRB v. Campbell Soup Co., 378 F2d 259, 65 LRRM 2515 (CA 9, 1967), enforcing 152 NLRB 1645, 59 LRRM 1369 (1965); Teamsters Health & Welfare Fund, 223 NLRB 814, 97 LRRM 1174 (1977).

[179]E.g., NLRB v. Jo-Jo Mgmt. Corp., 556 F2d 558, 95 LRRM 3011 (CA 2, 1977), enforcing 225 NLRB 1133, 93 LRRM 1475 (1976); Fieldston Ambulance & Med. Sys., Inc., 242 NLRB 185, 101 LRRM 1141 (1979); Brown Transp. Corp., 239 NLRB No. 91, 100 LRRM 1016 (1978); Welsbach Elec. Corp., 236 NLRB 503, 99 LRRM 1271 (1978); American Geriatric Enterprises, Inc., 235 NLRB 1532, 98 LRRM 1220 (1978); Supreme Equip. & Sys. Corp., 235 NLRB 244, 98 LRRM 1600 (1978).

[180]E.g., Trico Prods. Corp., 238 NLRB 1306, 99 LRRM 1473 (1978); Miller Brewing Co., 193 NLRB 528, 78 LRRM 1323 (1971); Nathan's Famous of Yonkers, Inc., 186 NLRB 131, 75 LRRM 1321 (1970).

[181]E.g., Tribulani's Detective Agency, Inc., 233 NLRB 1121, 97 LRRM 1169 (1977); Atlas Guard Serv., 229 NLRB 698, 95 LRRM 1207 (1977); Wackenhut Corp., 226 NLRB 1085, 94 LRRM 1328 (1976); Steak & Brew, 213 NLRB 450, 87 LRRM 1664 (1974); Luke Constr. Co., 211 NLRB 602, 87 LRRM 1087 (1974).

[182]See generally Chapter 6 supra at notes 514-81.

[183]E.g., Garment Workers v. NLRB (Bernhard-Altmann Tex. Corp.), supra note 9. See also NLRB v. Hospital Workers Local 250 (Kaiser Foundation Hosps.), 577 F2d 649, 99 LRRM 2431 (CA 9, 1978), enforcing 228 NLRB 468, 96 LRRM 1345 (1977); Carpenters Dist. Council, 238 NLRB 1683, 99 LRRM 1295 (1978); Atlas Lumber Co., supra note 153; Supreme Equip. & Sys. Corp., supra note 179; Desco Vitro-Glaze, Inc., 230 NLRB 379, 96 LRRM 1467 (1977); Atlas Guard Serv., supra note 181; Tuschak-Jacobson, Inc., supra note 162; Seaview Manor Home for Adults, 222 NLRB 596, 91 LRRM 1198 (1976); Ellery Prods. Mfg. Co., 149 NLRB 1388, 57 LRRM 1478 (1964).

sentative is not a defense to a Section 8(b)(1)(A) violation.[184] Additionally, a labor organization violates Section 8(b)(2) of the Act if the unlawful contract contains a union security clause favoring the assisted union.[185] For example, in *NLRB* v. *Retail Clerks Local 588 (Raley's, Inc.)*,[186] the Ninth Circuit affirmed the Board's finding that a union violated Sections 8(b)(1)(A) and (2) when it demanded and obtained recognition, including application of a contract with a union security clause, for a unit of employees of an entire store after another union had previously been recognized in a smaller unit consisting of a portion of the store's employees.

Similarly, a union violates the Act when it collects dues payments pursuant to an unlawful union security clause,[187] or coerces checkoff authority from employees where there is a valid union security clause.[188] The Board has also found violations of Section 8(b)(2) when an unlawfully assisted union causes the discharge of an employee who refuses to support the union,[189] when a union obtains recognition in breach of a valid preexisting Section 8(f) prehire agreement between the employer and another union,[190] or when it acquires recognition from an employer at a new facility in the absence of a lawful accretion.[191] A union

---

[184]Garment Workers v. NLRB (Bernhard-Altmann Tex. Corp.), *supra* notes 9-11 and 79.

[185]Bristol Consolidators, Inc., 239 NLRB 602, 100 LRRM 1026 (1978); Party Cookies, Inc., 237 NLRB 612, 99 LRRM 1468 (1978); Desco Vitro-Glaze, Inc., *supra* note 183; Southern Oregon Log Scaling & Grading Bureau, 223 NLRB 430, 92 LRRM 1216 (1976). *Contra,* Ramey Supermarkets, 238 NLRB No. 228, 99 LRRM 1342 (1978). *See generally* Chapter 29 *infra.*

[186]587 F2d 984, 100 LRRM 2299 (CA 9, 1978), *enforcing* 227 NLRB 670, 94 LRRM 1443 (1976).

[187]*E.g.,* McKees Rocks Foodland, 216 NLRB 968, 88 LRRM 1575 (1975); Howard Creations, Inc., 212 NLRB 179, 87 LRRM 1466 (1974); NLRB v. Fishermen's Local 33, *supra* note 142; Amalgamated Local 355 (Russell Motors, Inc.) v. NLRB, 481 F2d 996, 83 LRRM 2849 (CA 2, 1973), *enforcing and modifying* 198 NLRB 351, 80 LRRM 1757 (1972).

[188]*E.g.,* Brown Transp. Corp., *supra* note 179; NLRB v. Hope Indus., Inc., 481 F2d 1399, 83 LRRM 2701 (CA 3, 1973), *enforcing* 198 NLRB 853, 81 LRRM 1205 (1972); NLRB v. Printing Pressmen Local 527, 215 NLRB 237, 87 LRRM 1744 (1974); True Temper Corp., 217 NLRB 1120, 89 LRRM 1228 (1975). American Geriatric Enterprises, *supra* note 179.

[189]*E.g.,* Tuschak-Jacobson, Inc., *supra* note 162.

[190]Fenix & Scission, Inc., 207 NLRB 752, 85 LRRM 1380 (1973), *enforced,* 506 F2d 1404, 87 LRRM 3276 (CA 7, 1974). *See generally* Chapter 29 *infra* at notes 143-81.

[191]*E.g.,* NLRB v. Hospital Workers Local 250, *supra* note 183; Meijer, Inc., *supra* note 171; NLRB v. Hershey Foods Corp., 506 F2d 1052, 90 LRRM 2890 (CA 3, 1974), *enforcing* 208 NLRB 452, 85 LRRM 1312 (1974); Teamsters Local 814, 223 NLRB 527, 91 LRRM 1543 (1976); Laconia Shoe Co., 215 NLRB 573, 88 LRRM 1427 (1974); Teamsters Local 705, 210 NLRB 210, 86 LRRM 1011 (1974); Fenix & Scission, Inc., *supra* note 190. *See supra* at note 173.

likewise violates Section 8(b)(1)(A) when it executes a contract in contravention of the *Midwest Piping* doctrine.[192]

VIII. REMEDIES

Prior to the enactment of the Taft-Hartley amendments in 1947, the Board observed a distinction in determining the appropriate remedy for an employer's violation of Section 8(2), based on whether the benefited labor organization was an independent employee group or whether it was an organization affiliated with a national or international federation. In the former situation, the Board ordered the employer to withhold recognition forever from the benefited employee group and ordered complete disestablishment of the organization. In contrast, employer conduct benefiting a labor organization affiliated with a national or international federation was held to be only a violation of Section 8(1), and the Board would issue a cease-and-desist order directing the employer to withhold recognition from the organization only until it was certified.[193] The Board based this difference in treatment between affiliated and nonaffiliated organizations on the "belief that a labor organization affiliated with a national or international federation that was outside the ambit of the employer's control could not be permanently and completely subjugated to the will of the employer."[194] Thus it was assumed that the lesser remedy of issuance of a cease-and-desist order was sufficient to remedy the effects of employer interference and to restore employee freedom of self-organization.

The Taft-Hartley amendment of Section 10(c)[195] evidenced congressional displeasure with the foregoing distinction between affiliated and nonaffiliated labor organizations, and specifically directed the Board to utilize the same remedies irrespective of the nature of the benefited labor organization. Within several months following the enactment of the Taft-Hartley amendments, the Board, in *Carpenter Steel Co.*,[196] noted the "congres-

---

[192]*E.g.*, Southern Oregon Log Scaling & Grading Bureau, *supra* note 185; Seaview Manor Home for Adults, *supra* note 183.

[193]Carpenter Steel Co., 76 NLRB 670, 21 LRRM 1232 (1948).

[194]*Id.* at 672.

[195]Taft-Hartley added the following proviso language to §10(c):

"[I]n determining whether a complaint shall issue alleging a violation of section 8(a)(1) or section 8(a)(2), and in deciding such cases, the same regulations and rules of decision shall apply irrespective of whether or not the labor organization affected is affiliated with a labor organization national or international in scope."

[196]*Supra* note 193.

sional rejection of [its] prior view that mere affiliation with a national federation" placed a labor organization in so different a position from an unaffiliated employee group as to justify the use of different remedies.[197] It observed, however, that there was no evidence that Congress intended to abolish the remedy of disestablishment itself, but rather intended only to prohibit "discrimination in its use."[198] While abandoning its previous distinction between affiliated and unaffiliated labor organizations, the Board asserted that it would replace that distinction with a future enforcement policy under which different remedies would be ordered depending on whether the offensive employer conduct constituted unlawful domination or merely illegal interference or assistance:

> In all cases in which we find that an employer has dominated, or interfered with, or contributed support to a labor organization, or has committed any of these proscribed acts, we will find such conduct a violation of Section 8(a)(2) of the Act . . . regardless of whether the organization involved is affiliated. Where we find that an employer's unfair labor practices have been so extensive as to constitute *domination* of the organization, we shall order its disestablishment, whether or not it be affiliated. The Board believes that disestablishment is still necessary as a remedy . . . in those cases, perhaps few in number, in which the employer's control of *any* labor organization has extended to the point of actual domination. But when the Board finds that an employer's unfair labor practices were limited to interference and support and never reached the point of domination, we shall only order that recognition be withheld until certification, again without regard to whether or not the organization happens to be affiliated.[199]

As a consequence, the conclusion by the trier of fact as to whether unlawful employer conduct constitutes "domination" or "assistance" under Section 8(a)(2) is the key factor in fashioning an appropriate remedy. If disestablishment of a dominated labor organization is ordered, the employer will generally be required to cease all contact with the dominated union[200] and make a public announcement of its intent to cease bargaining with that union.[201] After disestablishment has been ordered, the employ-

---

[197]*Id.* at 672.
[198]*Id.*
[199]*Id.* at 673 (emphasis in original).
[200]*See, e.g.,* Dade Drydock Corp., 58 NLRB 833, 15 LRRM 67 (1944); Andrew Jergens Co., 43 NLRB 457, 11 LRRM 23 (1942); American Smelting & Ref. Co., 126 F2d 680, 10 LRRM 423 (1942).
[201]NLRB v. Tappan Stove Co., 174 F2d 1007, 24 LRRM 2125 (CA 6, 1949); Kansas City Power & Light Co. v. NLRB, 111 F2d 340, 6 LRRM 938 (CA 8, 1940); Remington Arms Co., 62 NLRB 611, 16 LRRM 199 (1945).

ees may then form a new union, but the employer cannot take part in its organization.[202] If the employer's support of a labor organization has undermined the majority support of a rival union and is accompanied by other unfair labor practices, the Board may issue a *Gissel* bargaining order requiring the employer to bargain with the disfavored labor organization.[203] For example, in *Kurz-Kasch, Inc.*,[204] the Board granted a *Gissel* bargaining order when the employer formed an "employee committee," dominated that organization in an attempt to forestall an outside union's organizing efforts, and also committed other substantial independent unfair labor practices to the detriment of the outside disfavored labor organization.

Disestablishment has been frequently ordered in cases of dominated company unions or employee committees,[205] even in cases where the complaint has alleged only unlawful employer assistance.[206]

Where the unlawful employer conduct falls short of domination but nevertheless constitutes unlawful assistance, the Board frequently issues a cease-and-desist order that prohibits the employer from recognizing the assisted labor organization and from giving effect to any contract between the employer and the union until the union is properly certified.[207] Although re-

---

[202]NLRB v. Continental Oil Co., 121 F2d 20, 8 LRRM 907 (CA 10, 1941); Continental Oil Co. v. NLRB, 113 F2d 473, 6 LRRM 1020 (CA 10, 1940).

[203]Professional Ambulance Serv., Inc., 232 NLRB 1141, 97 LRRM 1109 (1977); Federal Alarm, 230 NLRB 518, 96 LRRM 1141 (1977); Surface Indus., Inc., 224 NLRB 155, 93 LRRM 1074 (1976). *See also* Hirsch v. Trim Lean Meat Prods., Inc., 479 F Supp 1351, 102 LRRM 2950 (D Del, 1979), where a district court granted a §10(e) temporary injunction compelling bargaining. *See* Chapter 12 *infra* at notes 159-60.

[204]*Supra* note 69.

[205]Fry Foods, Inc., 241 NLRB 76, 100 LRRM 1513 (1979); Mattiace Indus., *supra* note 14; Interstate Eng'r, Inc., 230 NLRB 1, 96 LRRM 1135 (1977); International Signal & Control Corp., 226 NLRB 661, 93 LRRM 1384 (1976); STR, Inc., 221 NLRB 496, 90 LRRM 1591 (1975); Lowen Co., 203 NLRB 449, 83 LRRM 1147 (1973); Solmica, 199 NLRB 224, 81 LRRM 1334 (1972); Glover Packing Co., 191 NLRB 547, 77 LRRM 1695 (1971); Idaho Potato Foods, Inc., *supra* note 101.

[206]NLRB v. Fremont Mfg. Co., *supra* note 14; Kux Mfg. Corp., *supra* note 14. *But see* Kent Corp., 212 NLRB 595, 87 LRRM 1730 (1974), in which the Board refrained from ordering disestablishment where the pleadings did not allege, but the proof at the hearing established, such unlawful employer domination.

[207]*E.g.*, Presbyterian Community Hosp., 230 NLRB 599, 95 LRRM 1610 (1977); Diamond Int'l Corp., 229 NLRB 1314, 95 LRRM 1281 (1977); Hartz Mountain Corp., *supra* note 160; Roberts Elec. Co., 227 NLRB 1312, 95 LRRM 1159 (1977); Press Specialties Mfg. Co., 220 NLRB 361, 90 LRRM 1384 (1975); Colony Knitwear Corp., 217 NLRB 245, 88 LRRM 1552 (1975); McKees Rocks Foodland, *supra* note 187; Vic's Shop 'n Save, 215 NLRB 28, 88 LRRM 1478 (1974); Traub's Mkt., Inc., 205 NLRB 787, 84 LRRM 1078 (1973); Haley Bros., 201 NLRB 389, 82 LRRM 1384 (1973).

scission of a collective bargaining agreement entered into by an employer with an unlawfully assisted labor organization is the common device used to restore the parties to the *status quo ante*,[208] the Board has also ordered employers to maintain provisions in the tainted collective bargaining agreement which provide for increased wages, seniority, or other rights over and above the conditions which existed prior to the agreement.[209] A cease-and-desist order, however, is inappropriate if the union's majority status is unaffected by the employer's unlawful support,[210] or in certain instances where more narrowly drawn orders can remedy relatively minor unlawful employer assistance.[211] However, as in the case of unlawful employer domination, the Board will utilize a *Gissel* bargaining order as a remedy if the unlawful employer assistance and other employer unfair labor practices have undermined the majority support of a rival disfavored labor organization.[212]

In addition to its power to order disestablishment of a dominated labor organization, or to issue a cease-and-desist order to an employer to stop bargaining with an assisted labor organization, the Board has the discretion to order the employer to reimburse its employees for initiation fees and dues paid to a favored labor organization. This remedy is generally used only where an illegal collective bargaining agreement has actually coerced the employees into paying such dues and initiation fees. The typical situation in which reimbursement is required is where the employer and a union that does not represent an uncoerced majority of its employees have entered into a collective bargaining agreement providing for a union security clause and dues checkoff. In *Virginia Electric & Power Co. v. NLRB*[213]

---

[208]NLRB v. Hunter Outdoor Prods., Inc., 440 F2d 876, 76 LRRM 2969 (CA 1, 1971), *enforcing* 176 NLRB 449, 73 LRRM 1632 (1969).

[209]*E.g.*, Triangle Sheet Metal Works, 237 NLRB 364, 98 LRRM 1585 (1978); Eastern Indus., 217 NLRB 712, 89 LRRM 1134 (1975).

[210]True Temper Corp., *supra* note 188.

[211]*E.g.*, Jeffrey Mfg. Co., 208 NLRB 75, 85 LRRM 1336 (1974) (order merely prohibits the employer from dealing with a collective bargaining representative who was a supervisor); *see* Schwenk, Inc., 229 NLRB 640, 95 LRRM 1129 (1977); Graphic Arts Union v. NLRB, *supra* note 136; Associated Gen. Contractors of Calif., Inc., 220 NLRB 540, 90 LRRM 1719 (1975).

[212]Professional Ambulance Serv., Inc., *supra* note 203; Doces Sixth Ave., Inc., *supra* note 85; General Iron Corp., 224 NLRB 1180, 93 LRRM 1260 (1976). *Contra,* Business Envelope Mfrs., Inc., 227 NLRB 280, 94 LRRM 1351 (1976). *See* Chapter 12 *infra* for general treatment of *Gissel* and its progeny.

[213]319 US 533, 12 LRRM 739 (1943).

the Supreme Court rejected the employer's argument that a reimbursement remedy was penal in nature. The Court stated:

> To hold that the Board is without power here to order reimbursement of the amount so exacted is to hold that an employer is free to fasten firmly upon his employees the cost of maintaining an organization by which he effectively defeats the free exercise of their rights to self-organization and collective bargaining. That this may pervert the purpose of the Act is clear . . . . An order such as this, which deprives an employer of advantages accruing from a particular method of subverting the Act, is a permissible method of effectuating the statutory policy.[214]

The Board routinely requires employers to reimburse their employees for dues and other funds obtained under such circumstances.[215] However, if the labor organization is named as a respondent and found guilty of Section 8(b)(1)(A) violations as a party to an unlawful agreement, the union and employer may be held jointly and severally liable for the cost of reimbursement to the employees.[216] However, actual coercion of such payments is a condition precedent to the granting of the reimbursement remedy, and unless the employer actually coerced the employees to make such payment, the reinstatement remedy is deemed "punitive and beyond the power of the Board."[217] Thus, reimbursement will not be ordered, even if dues were obtained improperly by an employer from his employees, where the employees were subject to a lawful union security clause.[218] Similarly, the Board will not order reimbursement if there is no union security clause[219] or where circumstances show a lack of

---

[214]*Id.* at 540-41.
[215]*E.g.,* Baine Serv. Sys., Inc., 248 NLRB 563, 103 LRRM 1518 (1980); Hudson River Aggregates, Inc., 246 NLRB 192, 102 LRRM 1524 (1979); Bronxwood Home for Adults, 244 NLRB 905, 102 LRRM 1120 (1979); B. F. G. Gourmet Foods, Inc., *supra* note 153; Triangle Sheet Metal Works, *supra* note 209; Presbyterian Community Hosp., *supra* note 207; Teamsters Health & Welfare Fund, *supra* note 178. In *Dyna Corp.,* 223 NLRB 1200, 92 LRRM 1284 (1976), the Board ordered the employer to reimburse the incumbent disfavored union the amount of its dues, which the employer had withheld pursuant to its contract with that union but which it had transmitted to an outside favored union.
[216]*E.g.,* Romar Carrot Co., 228 NLRB 369, 94 LRRM 1734 (1977); Desco Vitro-Glaze, Inc., *supra* note 183; Atlas Guard Serv., *supra* note 181. In Kaiser Foundation Hosp., 228 NLRB 468, 96 LRRM 1345 (1977), the reimbursement remedy was applied to the union alone where the charge against the employer was dismissed as time-barred.
[217]Local 60, Carpenters v. NLRB, 365 US 651, 47 LRRM 2900 (1961).
[218]IBEC Housing Corp., 245 NLRB No. 165, 102 LRRM 1420 (1979); American Geriatric Enterprises, Inc., *supra* note 179.
[219]Wintex Knitting Mill, Inc., 223 NLRB 1293, 92 LRRM 1113 (1976).

actual coercion,[220] such as where employees have joined the union before a union's security clause has even become effective.[221]

Where an employee has been discharged because of failure to pay dues pursuant to a union security provision between an employer and an unlawfully recognized union, reinstatement with back pay is the standard remedy.[222] Additional "make whole" relief and special remedies may be utilized to remove advantages obtained by a favored union.[223]

---

[220]Al Pfister Truck Serv., 236 NLRB 217, 99 LRRM 1024 (1978) (reimbursement inappropriate where employees were longtime union members and were not coerced into joining the union).

[221]Unit Train Coal Sales, Inc., 234 NLRB 1265, 98 LRRM 1469 (1978); Acme Wire Works, Inc., 229 NLRB 333, 96 LRRM 1603 (1977).

[222]E.g., Southern Oregon Log Scaling & Grading Bureau, supra note 185; Captive Plastics, Inc., 209 NLRB 749, 86 LRRM 1235 (1974); Western Exterminator Co., 223 NLRB 1270, 92 LRRM 1161 (1976).

[223]See, e.g., Scottex Corp., supra note 101; Kent Corp., supra note 206; Colony Knitwear Corp., supra note 207; Teamsters Local 688, 215 NLRB 852, 88 LRRM 1217 (1974). For general treatment of NLRB orders and remedies, see Chapter 33 infra.

PART III

THE REPRESENTATION PROCESS
AND UNION RECOGNITION

CHAPTER 9

RESTRICTIONS ON PREELECTION ACTIVITY: "LABORATORY CONDITIONS"

I. INTRODUCTION

Section 7 of the National Labor Relations Act gives employees "the right to bargain collectively through representatives of their own choosing . . . ." In addition to granting the substantive right, the Act also establishes the procedure through which employees may choose a bargaining representative. As set forth in Section 9 of the Act,[1] this procedure is the representation election, which culminates in formal certification of the results by the National Labor Relations Board.

This chapter deals with preelection conduct by employers and unions which improperly interferes with the election process but which is not an unfair labor practice. Certain preelection conduct which is an unfair labor practice is *a fortiori* conduct which improperly interferes with the election process. Preelection conduct which is also an unfair labor practice is dealt with in other chapters and is outside the scope of this chapter.[2]

A. The Board's Authority Under Section 9

Section 9 vests in the Board what has been characterized as "the broad duty of providing election procedures and safeguards . . . ."[3] In particular, the Board has the authority to "police" preelection campaigns in order to assure that the parties do not

---

[1]*See generally* Chapter 10 *infra.*
[2]*See particularly* Chapter 6 *supra* dealing with unfair labor practices under §8(a)(1) and Chapter 7 *supra* dealing with unfair labor practices under §8(a)(3). Unfair labor practices under other sections of the Act may also provide a basis for setting aside an election.
[3]NLRB v. Sanitary Laundry, Inc., 441 F2d 1368, 1369, 77 LRRM 2359 (CA 10, 1971).

engage in conduct of such a nature as to prevent the employees from making a free choice in the election or force them to act contrary to their desires. Where the results of the election are the product of extraneous and coercive influence and therefore do not represent the free and uninhibited choice of the employees, the Board has the authority to set aside the results of the vote and order a new election.[4]

B. Relation to Unfair Labor Practices

Conduct disrupting the free choice of a bargaining representative may also have the effect of interfering with, restraining, or coercing employees in the exercise of their Section 7 rights. Thus, certain conduct which is the basis for overturning an election may also be the basis for finding a violation of Section 8(a)(1).[5] However, conduct which is not a violation of Section 8(a)(1) may nevertheless improperly interfere with the election process and provide a basis for setting aside an election. The Board's understanding of the relation between the two standards of conduct has undergone several changes in the course of time.

1. "Laboratory Conditions": The *General Shoe* Doctrine.
In its 1948 *General Shoe Corp.*[6] decision, the Board held that conduct which may not be so egregious as to violate Section 8(a)(1) may nevertheless provide a basis for setting aside an election:

> Conduct that creates an atmosphere which renders improbable a free choice will sometimes warrant invalidating an election, even though that conduct may not constitute an unfair labor practice. . . .
>
> . . .
>
> [T]he criteria applied . . . in a representation proceeding . . . need [not] be identical to those employed in testing whether an unfair labor practice was committed. . . .
>
> . . .
>
> In election proceedings, it is the Board's function to provide a laboratory in which an experiment may be conducted, under conditions as nearly ideal as possible, to determine the uninhibited desires of the employees.[7]

---

[4]*See* discussion of remedies at Part III *infra.*

[5]For detailed treatment of unfair labor practices under §8(a)(1), *see* Chapter 6 *supra.*

[6]77 NLRB 124, 21 LRRM 1337 (1948).

[7]*Id.* at 127. How realistic is this objective? *See* Bok, *The Regulation of Campaign Tactics in Representation Elections Under the National Labor Relations Act,* 78 HARV. L. REV. 38, 45-47; J. Getman, S. Goldberg, & J. Herman, UNION REPRESENTATION ELECTIONS: LAW AND REALITY (1976).

Thus, the "laboratory conditions" test enunciated in *General Shoe* holds the parties to a more demanding standard of conduct than the strictures of Section 8(a)(1).

It has been argued that the Board's holding in *General Shoe* is not consistent with Section 8(c) of the Act, which declares that the finding of an unfair labor practice may not be predicated on a party's communications if such communications contain "no threat of reprisal or force or promise of benefit."[8] The Board has squared its *General Shoe* holding with this section by emphasizing that Section 8(c) literally applies only to unfair labor practice cases and makes no mention of representation proceedings. Thus, under *General Shoe,* communications not containing a threat of reprisal or force or promise of benefit may provide the basis for setting aside an election even though such communications could not result in a party's being found to have violated the Act.

The "double standard" which emerged from *General Shoe* fell into disfavor during the period of the Eisenhower Board. The rule of conduct delineated in Section 8(c) was held to be the applicable standard both in questions of representation and in unfair labor practice proceedings.[9] The result was a relaxation of the regulation of preelection campaigns. Indeed, in some instances, a more demanding standard of conduct was applied in unfair labor practice cases than in representation proceedings.[10]

2. *Dal-Tex Optical:* The Resurgence of *General Shoe.* With the advent of a newly constituted Board in 1961, the criteria enunciated in *General Shoe* reemerged as the standard for judging conduct in the context of a representation proceeding. In *Dal-Tex Optical Co.* the Board stated that "[c]onduct violative of Section 8(a)(1) is, *a fortiori,* conduct which interferes with the exercise of a free and untrammeled choice in an election."[11] Thus, conduct which constitutes an unfair labor practice will almost always also violate the Board's election rules. Other improper conduct which may destroy the "laboratory condi-

---

[8]*See* Chapter 6 *supra* at notes 48-59.

[9]*See* National Furniture Co., 119 NLRB 1, 40 LRRM 1442 (1957); Lux Clock Mfg. Co., 113 NLRB 1194, 36 LRRM 1432 (1955); Esquire, Inc., 107 NLRB 1238, 33 LRRM 1367 (1954); American Laundry Mach. Co., 107 NLRB 511, 33 LRRM 1181 (1953).

[10]Wirtz, *The New National Labor Relations Board; Herein of "Employer Persuasion,"* 49 Nw. U. L. Rev. 594 (1954).

[11]137 NLRB 1782, 1786, 50 LRRM 1489 (1962). *See* Chapter 6 *supra* at notes 88-91 for discussion of the case and its application.

tions" for an election, though not an unfair labor practice, may nonetheless be the basis for setting aside an election. Such improper conduct is the subject of this chapter.[12]

C. Timing of "Laboratory Period"

In contrast to the six-month "statute of limitations" for unfair labor practices,[13] in postelection objection proceedings the Board bases its findings only upon conduct which has occurred between an established cutoff date and the election.

The establishment of an optimum cutoff date represents an attempt to balance the advantage of "eliminating from postelection consideration conduct too remote to have prevented free choice"[14] with the disadvantage of intentional delays for the purpose of strategic interference. In 1952, in the A&P case[15] the Board established the cutoff date as either (1) the execution date of a consent-election agreement, or (2) in contested cases, the issuance of a notice of hearing. Two years later, in Woolworth,[16] the Board moved the cutoff date in contested cases closer to the election, namely, to the date of issuance of the direction of election.

In 1961 the Board reconsidered the cutoff date in the light of its experience with the delegation of decisional authority in

---

[12]Getman, Goldberg, & Herman, supra note 7, analyzed and criticized the assumptions on which the Board's "laboratory conditions" standard is based. Following an empirical inquiry into voting behavior in Board elections, they recommended that the Board should cease regulating speech and, for election purposes, nearly all conduct. Considerable controversy surrounded their findings and recommendations. Some commentators objected to deregulating conduct or speech involving threats of reprisal (see Kochan, Book Review, Legal Nonsense, Empirical Examination and Policy Evaluation, 29 STAN. L. REV. 1115, 1121 (1977); Goetz & Wike, Book Review, Union Representation Elections: Law and Reality, 25 KAN. L. REV. 375, 383 (1977)); others criticized the methodology underlying the Getman study or charged that their data failed to support some of the study's conclusions (see Eames, An Analysis of the Union Voting Study From a Trade-Unionist's Point of View, 28 STAN. L. REV. 1181, 1182 (1976); Peck, Book Review, NLRB Election Law, Union Representation Elections: Law and Reality, 22 WASH. L. REV. 197, 206-208 (1977); Craver, Book Review, Union Representation Elections, Law and Reality, 22 VILL. L. REV. 891, 896-97 (1977); King, Pre-Election Conduct—Expanding Employer Rights and Some New and Renewed Perspectives, 2 IND. REL. L. J. 185, 206-13 (1977); Lopatka, Book Review, Union Representation Elections: Law and Reality, 72 NW. U. L. REV. 420, 429-30 (1977)). Neither the Board nor the courts have fully accepted the study's recommendations on deregulation of election campaigns, although for a year and a half, following its decision in Shopping Kart Food Mkts., Inc., 228 NLRB 1311, 94 LRRM 1705 (1977) (see infra at note 60), the Board partially deregulated in reliance on the study. In 1982 the Board again returned to its Shopping Kart position. See infra at note 67.
[13]§10(b).
[14]Ideal Elec. & Mfg. Co., 134 NLRB 1275, 1277, 49 LRRM 1316 (1961).
[15]Great Atl. & Pac. Tea Co., 101 NLRB 1118, 31 LRRM 1189 (1952).
[16]F. W. Woolworth Co., 109 NLRB 1446, 34 LRRM 1584 (1954).

representation cases to the regional directors.[17] Since that delegation had resulted in a decrease in the elapsed time between the filing of a petition and an election, considerations of remoteness were no longer as compelling. Thus, in *Ideal Electric,*[18] *Woolworth* was overruled and the date of filing of the petition rather than the direction of election became the cutoff date.

Left unchanged by *Ideal Electric* was the cutoff date in uncontested elections. The following year, uniformity in cutoff dates was prescribed in *Goodyear Tire.*[19] Thereafter, the filing of the petition marked the commencement of the "laboratory period" for purposes of a representation case.

There is no assurance that the "laboratory conditions" standard will remain continuously in effect during the entire period between the filing of the petition and the election. For example, if the petition is withdrawn and shortly thereafter refiled, employer conduct in the interval which otherwise might merit Board remedial action may be countenanced.[20] On the other hand, a promise of benefit made by an employer immediately after an election and before the time has elapsed for the filing of election objections may fall within the proscription of Section 8(a)(1).[21]

D. Procedural Considerations

The procedural posture in which an election campaign case arises may materially affect the criteria used in judging the lawfulness of employer communications. If preelection conduct is being ruled upon in a representation case, the criteria for judgment will be compliance with "laboratory conditions." The same conduct in an unfair labor practice proceeding will be judged by the standard of Section 8(c), which precludes the Board from finding an unfair labor practice based on a party's communications unless the communications contain threats or promises of benefit.[22]

---

[17]Ideal Elec. & Mfg. Co., *supra* note 14.
[18]*Id.* Objectionable conduct occurring on the day the petition was filed, but before the actual filing, will still be considered as ground for setting aside the election. West Tex. Equip. Co., 142 NLRB 1358, 53 LRRM 1249 (1963).
[19]Goodyear Tire & Rubber Co., 138 NLRB 453, 51 LRRM 1070 (1962).
[20]*See* Sigo Corp., 146 NLRB 1484, 56 LRRM 1078 (1964).
[21]*See* Ralph Printing & Lithographing Co., 158 NLRB 1353, 1354 n.3, 62 LRRM 1233 (1966).
[22]Dal-Tex Optical Co., *supra* note 11; *see also* Eagle-Picher Indus., Inc., 171 NLRB 293 n.1, 68 LRRM 1570 (1968). *See supra* at notes 7-10 and Chapter 6 *supra* at notes 48-78. For added treatment of objection period, *see* Chapter 10 *infra* at notes 410-11.

Where the unfair labor practice and representation cases are consolidated into one action,[23] however, the distinction breaks down. In such circumstances, the administrative law judge presumably has two standards for guidance in judging the same conduct. The possibility of these standards becoming entangled as the case moves from the administrative law judge to the Board, and possibly to the courts, is not difficult to imagine.[24]

II. GROUNDS FOR SETTING ASIDE ELECTIONS

A. Preelection Rules of Conduct

Both before and after the enactment of Taft-Hartley, the Board imposed restrictions upon the parties' preelection activities. These have included such mechanical devices as "rules"[25] prohibiting electioneering activities at the polling place,[26] prohibiting speech-making to captive audiences within 24 hours preceding the election,[27] and requiring management to provide names and addresses of all employees qualified to vote in the election.[28] These and other prospective rules, made pursuant to

---

[23]Ordinarily both the objection to the election and the unfair labor practice complaint will be consolidated for hearing before the law judge. NLRB FIELD MANUAL 11420.1. See discussion of this procedure in Freeport Marble & Tile Co., 153 NLRB 810, 59 LRRM 1561 (1965), enforced in part, 367 F2d 371, 63 LRRM 2289 (CA 1, 1966).

[24]See Eagle-Picher Indus., supra note 22. An illustration of the process of disentangling the standards appears in Sinclair Co., 164 NLRB 261, 65 LRRM 1087 (1967), enforced, 397 F2d 157, 68 LRRM 2720 (CA 1, 1968), aff'd sub nom. NLRB v. Gissel Packing Co., 395 US 575, 71 LRRM 2481 (1969), where, in the course of recommending a bargaining order, the trial examiner, citing Dal-Tex Optical, supra note 22, found employer communications to have violated §8(a)(1) and also to have interfered with the free choice in the election. The examiner recommended that, "assuming arguendo" that the employer's conduct was not held to be violative of §8(a)(1), the election nevertheless be set aside because of impairment of "laboratory conditions." Although the Board and the First Circuit affirmed the order, thus not reaching the alternative conclusion, the trial examiner's analysis is of interest.

[25]All of these rules were promulgated in adjudicated cases, rather than under the formal rule-making procedures of the Administrative Procedure Act, 5 USC §553 (1966). See Chapter 32 infra at notes 197-218 and discussion infra at notes 29-30.

[26]Alliance Ware, Inc., 92 NLRB 55, 27 LRRM 1040 (1950); Detroit Creamery Co., 60 NLRB 178, 15 LRRM 221 (1945); Kilgore Mfg. Co., 45 NLRB 468, 11 LRRM 139 (1942); cf. Higgins, Inc., 106 NLRB 845, 32 LRRM 1566 (1953); J. I. Case Co., 85 NLRB 576, 24 LRRM 1431 (1949).

[27]Peerless Plywood Co., 107 NLRB 427, 33 LRRM 1151 (1953). In Honeywell, Inc., 162 NLRB 323, 64 LRRM 1007 (1966), the prohibition on speechmaking within 24 hours preceding the election was extended to include informal "question and answer" sessions; however the Peerless Plywood rules have been held inapplicable to sound-car broadcasting so long as the broadcasts consisted not of speeches, but merely of appeals interspersed with music. Southland Cork Co., 146 NLRB 906, 55 LRRM 1426 (1964), enforced in part, 342 F2d 702, 58 LRRM 2555 (CA 4, 1965). But see U.S. Gypsum Co., 115 NLRB 734, 37 LRRM 1374 (1956). See Chapter 6 supra at notes 160-61.

[28]Excelsior Underwear, Inc., 156 NLRB 1236, 61 LRRM 1217 (1966).

the Board's power to conduct elections for certification of a bargaining agent, are mandatory rules for the conduct of elections; their violation furnishes grounds for setting aside the election without reference to whether the conduct constituted an unfair labor practice.

B. Promulgation of Rules: *Stare Decisis* vs. APA Rule-Making

There are, in theory, two ways in which the Board can promulgate the standards which regulate election campaign activities: (1) through the rule-making power granted to the Board by Section 6 of the National Labor Relations Act, and regulated by the Administrative Procedure Act,[29] or (2) by announcing a principle of general applicability in the context of a particular two-party action. In practice, the Board has regulated preelection activities through the second method only. The myriad rules governing preelection conduct have been formulated by the Board through *ad hoc* adversary litigation in much the same way as the principles of the common law have been formulated by the courts. By virtue of the doctrine of *stare decisis,* rules of conduct announced by the Board in this manner acquire a measure of permanence and may serve to direct the future actions of employers and unions.[30]

C. Employer and Union Conduct

A wide assortment of traditional and imaginative techniques have been employed either to frustrate or to further union organizational efforts. Usually these have been utilized during election campaigns and have been evaluated by the Board in terms of election interference. In some instances, however, they have been employed at other stages of employer-employee relationships and have been evaluated in the broader context of interference with Section 7 rights. The following discussion focuses upon the various techniques in the context of the representation election.[31]

---

[29]5 USC §551, *et seq.* (1966). For comment on the Board's rule-making procedures, *see* authorities cited in Chapter 32 *infra* at notes 199 and 201.

[30]*Cf.* NLRB v. Bell Aerospace Co., 416 US 267, 85 LRRM 2945 (1974).

[31]Discussion on unfair labor practices is reserved for Chapter 6. This chapter considers conduct which, though not constituting an unfair labor practice, may be grounds for setting aside an election.

1. Campaign Propaganda and Misrepresentations. During an election campaign, parties may, either intentionally or unintentionally, make statements that are factually inaccurate. Employees, relying upon such assertions, may vote in a particular way, and, as a result, the outcome of the election may be different than it would be if the employees had known the true facts. The Board for a long period was reluctant to undertake the censorship of election propaganda,[32] explicitly stating that "exaggeration, inaccuracies, half-truths, and name calling, though not condoned, will not be grounds for setting aside an election."[33] The Board's view was that "absolute precision of statement and complete honesty are not always attainable in an election campaign, nor are they expected by the employees."[34] Consequently, the Board's preference was to leave misstatements for the opposing parties to correct and for the employees to evaluate.[35] Nevertheless, it sought to balance this preference against "the right of employees to an untrammeled choice, and the right of the parties to wage a free and vigorous campaign with all the normal legitimate tools of electioneering."[36] Over the last 20 years, the manner in which the Board has struck this balance has passed through several stages.

   a. The Hollywood Ceramics *Rule.* In *Hollywood Ceramics*[37] the Board formulated its position on campaign misrepresentations in the following terms:

> [A]n election should be set aside only where there has been a misrepresentation or other similar campaign trickery, which involves a substantial departure from the truth, at a time which prevents the other party or parties from making an effective reply, so that the misrepresentation, whether deliberate or not, may reasonably be expected to have a significant impact on the election.[38]

The *Hollywood Ceramics* rule requires the Board to evaluate the truth or falsity of the parties' assertions. Not every misrepresentation, however, will result in setting aside the election.

---

[32]Cleveland Trencher Co., 130 NLRB 600, 603, 47 LRRM 1371 (1961); Merck & Co., 104 NLRB 891, 32 LRRM 1160 (1953); Gummed Prods. Co., 112 NLRB 1092, 36 LRRM 1156 (1955).
[33]Hollywood Ceramics Co., 140 NLRB 221, 224 n.6, 51 LRRM 1600 (1962).
[34]*Id.* at 223.
[35]United States Gypsum Co., 130 NLRB 901, 904, 47 LRRM 1436 (1961).
[36]Hollywood Ceramics Co., *supra* note 33. *Cf.* Linn v. United Plant Guard Workers Local 114, 383 US 53, 61 LRRM 2345 (1966).
[37]*Supra* note 33.
[38]*Id.* at 224.

The phrasing of the rule is in the conjunctive so that even a substantial misrepresentation may not upset an election if it concerned an unimportant matter and had only a *de minimis* effect. Similarly, the misrepresentation may be "so extreme so as to put employees on notice of its lack of truth," or the employees themselves may have independent knowledge permitting them to evaluate the statements.[39]

Under *Hollywood Ceramics,* if there is a fair opportunity for rebuttal, even at a late moment, an election will not be set aside.[40] But lack of a fair opportunity for rebuttal of a particular last-minute statement may not be controlling where the issue itself was injected in the campaign sufficiently in advance of the election to have provided a basis for evaluation by the employees and exploration by the parties.[41]

(1) Misleading wage and fringe-benefit data. Wages and fringe benefits prevailing or contractually obtained elsewhere in comparable companies may be presented in a way that is quite misleading yet literally true. Thus, an assertion made just prior to an election that a contract elsewhere "provides for" a stated increase without disclosing that the increase was spread over three years may be misleading but literally true, absent the representation that the increases are effective immediately.[42] Some assertions may be so misleading as to leave little or no room for literal truth or varied interpretations.[43] Since different estimates may be made as to the monetary value of fringe benefits contained in an "economic package," the Board has tolerated some "puffing."[44] In many instances, however, the circuit

---

[39]*Id.*

[40]*Id; see also* General Elec. Co., 162 NLRB 912, 64 LRRM 1104 (1967).

[41]Elmcrest Convalescent Hosp. Mgmt. Corp., 173 NLRB 38, 69 LRRM 1196 (1968). *Cf.* United States Gypsum Co., *supra* note 35, where an election was set aside because the earlier interjection of the issue did not assume a dominant role as did the later telegram.

[42]Russell-Newman Mfg. Co., 158 NLRB 1260, 62 LRRM 1195 (1966); *but see* S. S. Kresge Co., 173 NLRB 520, 69 LRRM 1382 (1968), *on remand from* Gallenkamp Stores Co., 402 F2d 525, 69 LRRM 2024 (CA 9, 1968), *denying enforcement to* 162 NLRB 498, 64 LRRM 1045 (1966).

[43]Grede Foundries, Inc., 153 NLRB 984, 59 LRRM 1552 (1965), where union handbills distributed the day before an election claimed that the "average" take-home pay under one of its contracts was $140 per week when, in fact, only two of the 350 employees received that "average."

[44]Southern Foods, Inc., 171 NLRB 922, 68 LRRM 1230 (1968). In *Hollywood Ceramics* the Board stated that messages that are "inartistically or vaguely worded and subject to different interpretations will not suffice to . . . set the election aside." *Supra* note 33 at 224.

courts have taken a more restrictive view than the Board regarding last-minute misstatements about wage rates and fringe benefits.[45]

(2) Special knowledge. Special knowledge of the assertions has occasionally been controlling. Thus, an employer's estimation as to the likelihood of a rise in union dues, based upon hearsay, will not invalidate an election.[46] The First Circuit's view of *Hollywood Ceramics* is that the test implied is not whether the speaker in fact had special knowledge, but whether listeners would believe that he had.[47] This view was applied by the Board in a subsequent case where a union misquoted an employer's speech in such a manner as to represent the employer's position, falsely, as one of support for the union. In overturning the election the Board found that the union's message "lent itself to the belief" that the employer had confided privately to the union official "what he could not express publicly."[48]

(3) Misrepresentation and trickery. Issues of misrepresentation and campaign trickery take many forms. The use of literature that conceals the true identity of the sponsor may be grounds for setting aside an election.[49] Thus, employer issuance of anti-union materials over the signature of popular employees,[50] and distribution by one union of alleged reports from rival union organizers describing employees in insulting terms, were deemed improper.[51] On the other hand, the use of pay stubs to dramatize an employer's union-dues argument is not necessarily improper. The validity of the technique depends upon the accuracy of the deduction, the timing, the manner of distribution, and the accompanying description—for example, whether a dues check-off is represented as mandatory.[52] The portrayal of strikes and

---

[45]*See* NLRB v. Bonnie Enterprises, Inc., 341 F2d 712, 58 LRRM 2395 (1965); NLRB v. Allis-Chalmers Mfg. Co., 261 F2d 613, 43 LRRM 2246 (CA 7, 1958); *see also* 3 ALR3d 889 (1965) for a comprehensive collection of cases.
[46]York Furniture Corp., 170 NLRB 1487, 67 LRRM 1606 (1968).
[47]NLRB v. A. G. Pollard Co., 393 F2d 239, 67 LRRM 2997 (CA 1, 1968).
[48]Cranbar Corp., 173 NLRB 1287, 69 LRRM 1581 (1968).
[49]Kelsey-Hayes Co., 126 NLRB 151, 45 LRRM 1290 (1960).
[50]Timken-Detroit Axle Co., 98 NLRB 790, 29 LRRM 1401 (1952), *petition to restrain enforcement dismissed,* 197 F2d 512, 30 LRRM 2328 (CA 6, 1952).
[51]Sylvania Elec. Prods., Inc., 119 NLRB 824, 828, 41 LRRM 1188 (1954).
[52]Fontaine Truck Equip. Co., Inc., 166 NLRB 576, 65 LRRM 1552 (1967); TRW, Inc., 173 NLRB 1425, 70 LRRM 1017 (1968); Crown Laundry & Dry Cleaners, Inc., 160 NLRB 746, 63 LRRM 1035 (1966); Trane Co., 137 NLRB 1506, 50 LRRM 1434 (1962); Mosler Safe Co., 129 NLRB 747, 47 LRRM 1058 (1960).

violence as the inevitable consequence of unionization can be grounds for setting aside an election.[53]

(4) Application of the Hollywood Ceramics *rule to union conduct.* The *Hollywood Ceramics* standard was applied to unions as well as to employers.[54] Two appellate cases in which the standard was applied are illustrative. Both cases involved alleged union misrepresentations concerning profit margins of employers. The Sixth Circuit denied enforcement of a Board bargaining order where a letter sent out by the union had inaccurately stated that the company made substantial profits; a second letter from the union, which did not reach the employees until after the election, disclosed that the profits were of the parent company.[55] The Eighth Circuit refused to enforce a bargaining order where a union organizer had stated that the company's profits were such that it could afford to pay an increase in wages, when in fact the company was losing money.[56]

On the other hand, the Board upheld an election where a union business representative stated that the company had "made" approximately one million dollars when, in fact, although the company had grossed that amount, its profits were substantially lower.[57] And because the misrepresentations were deemed minor, the Board upheld an election where a union had misrepresented its dues requirement for unemployed members and its authority to fine members for refusal to honor a picket line in a sympathy strike.[58]

---

[53]Louis Gallet, Inc., 247 NLRB 63, 103 LRRM 1125 (1980). Prior to the Board's 1974 decision in Litho Press, 211 NLRB 1014, 86 LRRM 1471 (1974), *enforced,* 512 F2d 73, 89 LRRM 2171 (CA 5, 1975), the film "And Women Must Weep," depicting strike violence, frequently resulted in findings of objectionable election conduct. In *Litho Press,* the Board reversed all prior precedent and held the film was not objectionable regardless of the circumstances of the campaign. *See also* Sab Harmon Indus., Inc., 252 NLRB 953, 105 LRRM 1353 (1980) (movie, "The Springfield Gun," found unobjectionable). *See* Chapter 6 *supra* at notes 215-16.

[54]Medical Ancillary Serv., Inc., 212 NLRB 582, 86 LRRM 1598 (1974); Pointe Enterprises, 216 NLRB 747, 88 LRRM 1519 (1975). Indeed, the original *Hollywood Ceramics* case involved union conduct.

[55]Argus Optics v. NLRB, 515 F2d 939, 89 LRRM 2280 (CA 6, 1975).

[56]LaCrescent Constant Care Center, Inc. v. NLRB, 510 F2d 1319, 88 LRRM 2849 (CA 8, 1975). *Accord,* Aircraft Radio Corp. v. NLRB, 519 F2d 590, 89 LRRM 3060 (CA 3, 1975).

[57]Henderson Trumbull Supply Corp., 220 NLRB 210, 90 LRRM 1477 (1975). The company offered no evidence that this statement had affected the close outcome of the election; the company's three employee witnesses all stated that it had not affected their vote because their minds had been made up at the time of the statement. Also, the business agent subsequently explained to an employee that he had been referring to total sales before expenses, and this explanation was passed on to other employees.

[58]Ebsco Subscription Serv., 221 NLRB 18, 90 LRRM 1393 (1975). The Board stated that these issues were not determinative of the election and that it was unrealistic to

b. The Overruling of Hollywood Ceramics*: The* Shopping Kart *Rule.* In 1977, in its *Shopping Kart* decision,[59] the Board reversed *Hollywood Ceramics,* deciding that it would no longer set aside an election solely because of misleading campaign statements or misrepresentations of fact. The decision was based on a conviction that employees are in a better position than the Board to judge the truth or falsity of campaign statements: "[W]e believe that Board rules in this area must be based on a view of employees as mature individuals who are capable of recognizing campaign propaganda for what it is and discounting it."[60] While indicating that it would not probe the veracity of campaign statements, the Board said that it would continue to intervene in those instances where "a party has engaged in such deceptive campaign practices as improperly involving the Board and its processes," or where forged documents were used, rendering "the voters unable to recognize the propaganda for what it is."[61]

The *Shopping Kart* rule was applied in the following situations: An employer's misrepresentation of wages and fringe benefits paid under the current union contract at other plants was held not to warrant setting an election aside.[62] Misrepresentations by a union concerning an employer's reasons for engaging in certain business transactions were held to be no basis for granting a new election.[63] However, a letter sent to employees by a union claiming that the employer had been found guilty of unfair labor practices, when in fact the employer had entered into a settlement agreement that contained a nonadmissions clause, was deemed to be a "substantial mischaracterization or misuse of a Board document" within the narrow exception to the *Shopping Kart* rule and warranted setting aside the election.[64]*

c. General Knit: *A Temporary Return to* Hollywood Ceramics. In late 1978 the Board abandoned the policy of nonintervention

---

think that employees in an election would be especially concerned with the possibility of paying monthly dues as unemployed members, or with their responsibility concerning picket duty.

[59]*Supra* note 12.

[60]*Id.* at 1313. The Board relied heavily upon an empirical study conducted by Professors Getman and Goldberg, *The Behavioral Assumptions Underlying NLRB Regulation of Campaign Misrepresentations: An Empirical Evaluation,* 28 STAN. L. REV. 263 (1976). *See* note 7 *supra.*

[61]228 NLRB at 1313.

[62]Thomas E. Gates & Sons, Inc., 229 NLRB 705, 95 LRRM 1198 (1977).

[63]Cormier Hosiery Mills, 230 NLRB 1052, 95 LRRM 1461 (1977).

[64]Formco, Inc., 233 NLRB 61, 96 LRRM 1392 (1977). [*But see* **Editor's Note** *infra.*]

*[**Editor's Note:** In late 1982, in Riveredge Hosp., 264 NLRB No. 146, 111 LRRM 1425 (1982), *supplementing* 251 NLRB 196, 105 LRRM 1028 (1980), the Board overruled

announced in *Shopping Kart* and readopted the rule that an election would be set aside where its outcome may have been affected by a substantial and material misrepresentation. Reviving the standards enunciated in *Hollywood Ceramics*, the Board wrote in *General Knit of California:*[65]

> In returning to the rule of *Hollywood Ceramics*, we are convinced that the rule better enhances employee free choice and fairness of Board elections than did *Shopping Kart*. The *Hollywood Ceramics* rule further assures the public that the Board will not tolerate substantial and material misrepresentations made in the final hours of an election campaign, and thereby gives stability to any bargaining relationship resulting from the election.[66]

Accordingly, under *General Knit* an election would be set aside when a misrepresentation or similar campaign trickery, deliberate or not, which involves a substantial departure from the truth and occurs at a time which prevents effective rebuttal by the opposition, may reasonably be expected to have a significant effect on the election.

d. Return to Shopping Kart: Hollywood Ceramics *Again Abandoned.* In August 1982 the Board once again reversed its position; it overruled *General Knit* and *Hollywood Ceramics* and returned to the standards first enunciated in *Shopping Kart*. In *Midland National Life Insurance Co.*[67] the Board majority indicated their "emphatic" belief that "Shopping Kart is the most appropriate accommodation of all the interests . . . involved, and should be given a fair chance to succeed." Thus, under *Midland National Life Insurance Co.,* elections will no longer be set aside solely because of misleading campaign statements or misrepresentations of fact. However, the Board will intervene in cases where a party has "used forged documents which render the voters unable to recognize propaganda for what it is" or where "an official Board document has been altered in such a way as to indicate an endorsement by the Board of a party to the election."

2. Misuse of the Board's Election Process. The term "misuse of the Board's election process" refers to a particular campaign technique by which one party seeks to create the impression that the Board or government favors a particular outcome in

---

Formco, Inc., *supra* note 64, holding that a party's preelection mischaracterizations of NLRB actions are to be treated the same as other misrepresentations. *See infra* at note 67.]
[65]239 NLRB 619, 99 LRRM 1687 (1978).
[66]*Id.* at 623.
[67]263 NLRB No. 24, 110 LRRM 1489 (1982). (The quotations which follow may be found in 110 LRRM 1493, 1494, and 1494 n. 25, respectively.)

the election. Even under *Shopping Kart,* where the successful party has used such a tactic, the Board will set the election aside.

a. Reproduction of Board Documents. The most frequently encountered form of misuse of the Board's election process is the distribution by one party of a facsimile of a Board document which is altered in such a way as to suggest that the Board endorses a particular choice. In *Allied Electric Products, Inc.,*[68] the Board specifically ruled that the distribution of marked copies of Board election ballots would result in the ordering of a new election:

> The reproduction of a document that purports to be a copy of the Board's official secret ballot, but which is altered for campaign purposes, necessarily, at the very least, must tend to suggest that the material appearing thereon bears the Agency's approval.[69]

Consequently, in *Building Leasing Corp.,*[70] the Board set aside an election where the employer had distributed a copy of the official ballot with a highlighted "NO" box and a statement that "your 'X' in the *NO box will mean you* do not want a union." The Board concluded that the additional comments were indistinguishable from the ballot itself and thus appeared to have the Board's approval.[71]

Some problems have arisen with the Board's definition of the scope of the *Allied Electric Products* rule. The prohibition is "not limited to exact reproductions, but is aimed at the reproduction of documents 'purportive' to be a copy of the Board's ballot."[72] However, it is not always clear whether a particular document "purports" to be a Board election ballot.

The Board has set aside an election where the employer distributed a leaflet with the company's name and symbol at the top, followed by campaign matter and a duplicate NLRB official sample ballot with an "X" marked in the "No" box over which

---

[68]109 NLRB 1270, 34 LRRM 1538 (1954).
[69]*Id.* at 1272.
[70]239 NLRB 13, 99 LRRM 1543 (1978).
[71]*See also* Regency Elecs., Inc., 200 NLRB 625, 81 LRRM 1587 (1972), *enforced,* 499 F2d 1129, 84 LRRM 2891 (CA 7, 1973); Silco, Inc., 231 NLRB 110, 95 LRRM 1516 (1977).
[72]Custom Molders of P. R., 121 NLRB 1007, 1009, 42 LRRM 1505 (1958), where deletion of the official headnote of the ballot did not prevent the Board from setting the election aside. *But see* Glidden Co., 121 NLRB 752, 42 LRRM 1429 (1958), and Paula Shoe Co., 121 NLRB 673, 42 LRRM 1419 (1958), where only portions of the ballot were reproduced as part of a handbill in such a manner as to avoid the impression of governmental endorsement.

was superimposed a red heart.[73] The ruling was subsequently upheld by the Seventh Circuit. However, in another case the Board concluded the sample ballot as marked by the employer was nothing other than what it purported to be—a campaign document prepared for use by the employer—and it was unlikely, said the Board, that the employees would be led to believe that the Board endorsed the position expressed on the document.[74]

Where the ballot does not contain any reference to the "United States Government" or the "National Labor Relations Board," the Board has indicated that the document is not within the *Allied Electric* rule since it does not mislead employees into believing that the government or the Board has endorsed a particular choice.[75]

The rule against partisan use of Board documents is not limited to ballots. Duplication of part of the Board's election notice with a partisan supplement attached to it may also result in setting aside the election.[76] However, the Board overruled employer objections in a case where, one week before the election, a union organizer had distributed to employees a reproduction of the regional director's election order with considerable underlining and a notation in the margin that "[t]he Government would not have ordered this election if it had not been for The Teamsters Union—Vote Yes."[77]

Reproduction of a complaint which seeks to invoke the support of the government by conveying the impression of actual findings of violations of federal law, as opposed to unproven allegations, is also cause for setting aside an election. In *Mallory Capacitor Co.*,[78] the Board stated:

> [W]e cannot sanction the reproduction of a Board document which is altered for campaign purposes and used under circumstances where it is reasonably calculated to mislead employees into believing that the Board has judged the Employer to have violated federal

---

[73]Regency Elecs., Inc., *supra* note 71.
[74]Associated Lerner Shops, 207 NLRB 348, 84 LRRM 1463 (1973).
[75]Stedman Wholesale Distribs., Inc., 203 NLRB 302, 83 LRRM 1055 (1973); Triangle Superdollar Mkt., 225 NLRB 403, 92 LRRM 1576 (1976).
[76]Rebmar, Inc., 173 NLRB 1434, 70 LRRM 1018 (1969).
[77]A. Brandt Co., Inc., 199 NLRB 504, 81 LRRM 1279 (1972). The Board reasoned that the underlinings and marginal note could not reasonably be construed by the employees to be a part of the regional director's decision; and, in any event, the employer had ample time to respond.
[78]161 NLRB 1510, 63 LRRM 1473 (1966).

law whereas, in truth, it has only made allegations which have yet to be proved.[79]

In *Ona Corp.*,[80] a Board panel held that the union interfered with an election by mailing employees copies of a Board complaint against the employer where the union had deleted the paragraphs concerning the time and the place of hearing, the employer's right to answer the complaint, and the effect of failing to answer allegations. The fact that the mailing stated below the regional director's name that a hearing had been set and that the employer denied the allegations of the complaint did not cure the misleading effect of the document. On the other hand, a statement in union campaign literature that issuance of a complaint against the employer shows that "there has to be merit in the case" was not deemed impermissible.[81]

b. Misrepresentation of Board Action. Misrepresentation pertaining to the Board and its processes constitutes a sufficient basis for setting aside an election. While such a misrepresentation may be incidental to reproduction of a Board document,[82] it need not be. The Board has held that a union interferes with an election when it distributes a letter which falsely reports that the employer had been guilty of unfair labor practices.[83] The Board reasoned that since only the Board could find the employer "guilty" the union's statement improperly drew the Board into the election. In several cases elections have been set aside where one of the parties mischaracterized a settlement agreement, implying that the employer had been found guilty of unfair labor practices.[84] [*But see* **Editor's Note** *supra*, p. 320.]

c. Electioneering at the Polls. In the actual conduct of the election the Board is "especially zealous in preventing instructions"[85] to voters. It has long been held that campaigning too close to the polls may be objectionable.[86] In 1968 the Board adopted the

---

[79]*Id.* at 1512.
[80]235 NLRB 595, 98 LRRM 1005 (1978).
[81]George J. London Memorial Hosp., 236 NLRB 797, 98 LRRM 1312 (1978).
[82]*E.g., Mallory Capacitor, supra* note 78.
[83]Formco, Inc., *supra* note 64. [*But see* **Editor's Note** *supra*, p. 320.]
[84]*See, e.g.,* Dubie Clark Co., Inc., 209 NLRB 217, 85 LRRM 1322 (1974); Natter Mfg. Corp., 210 NLRB 118, 86 LRRM 1091 (1974), *enforced*, 580 F2d 948, 99 LRRM 2965 (CA 10, 1978); Gulton Indus., 240 NLRB 546, 100 LRRM 1321 (1979).
[85]Claussen Baking Co., 134 NLRB 111, 112, 49 LRRM 1092 (1961).
[86]*Id.;* Continental Can Co., 80 NLRB 785, 23 LRRM 1126 (1948).

strict *Michelm*[87] rule that, "regardless of the content of the remarks exchanged," prolonged conversation by representatives of any party with prospective voters in the polling area "constitutes conduct which, in itself," will invalidate an election.[88] The Board's interpretation of this rule extends to impressions conveyed to employees during the balloting. Moreover, keeping a list of employees who have voted (aside from the official eligibility list used to check off voters as they receive their ballots) has been found to interfere with the election.[89] And an employer may not bar any individuals from entering the voting place and casting a ballot. The Board has held that anyone who presents himself or herself at the polls has the right to cast at least a challenged ballot and to assert, directly to the Board's agent,[90] his or her right to vote. Supervisory participation as an observer has also been found to interfere with an election.[91] Even the Board's own agents must avoid creating impressions that will impair the integrity and neutrality of its election procedures.[92]

3. Appeals to Racial Prejudice. Racial appeals in a preelection campaign may result in the setting aside of the election. However, injection of racial prejudice into a campaign will not necessarily constitute a valid objection, for the subject may be germane to the issues. Employees are free to allow their prejudices to affect their choice in union representation matters. But where pure racial prejudice, or fear inspired by racial conflict, is made the dominant theme of a campaign so as to reduce the

---

[87]Michelm, Inc., 170 NLRB 362, 67 LRRM 1395 (1968), emphasizing the importance of ensuring that "[t]he final minutes before an employee casts his vote should be his own, as free from interference as possible." This *Michelm rule* apparently contemplates that the Board agent conducting the balloting will specify "no electioneering" in the polling area. Star Expansion Indus. Corp., 170 NLRB 364, 67 LRRM 1400 (1968). But the rule does not apply to "conversations with prospective voters unless the voters are . . . in the polling area or in line waiting to vote." Harold W. Moore & Son, 173 NLRB 1258, 70 LRRM 1002 (1968).

[88]170 NLRB at 362.

[89]Piggly-Wiggly, 168 NLRB 792, 66 LRRM 1360 (1967), where the making of notations on a list as employees passed by to enter the employer's premises during the balloting caused the election to be set aside. Use of this technique may cause employees to infer that their names are being recorded. A.D. Juilliard & Co., 110 NLRB 2197, 2199, 35 LRRM 1401 (1954). *See also* International Stamping Co., 97 NLRB 921, 29 LRRM 1158 (1951); NLRB Form 722 instructing observers not to keep such lists; and Chapter 10 *infra* at note 323.

[90]Sabine Towing & Transp. Co., 226 NLRB 422, 93 LRRM 1277 (1976).

[91]Cooper Supply Co., 120 NLRB 1023, 42 LRRM 1094 (1958). *See Chapter* 10 *infra* at notes 316-17.

[92]Athbro Precision Eng'r Corp., 166 NLRB 966, 65 LRRM 1699 (1967). The Board's interest in protecting the integrity of the election process is also illustrated in its decision to set aside an election where the ballot box was left unsealed and unattended for only two to five minutes, without regard to what might have occurred. Austill Waxed Paper Co., 169 NLRB 1109, 67 LRRM 1366 (1968).

election to a vote on racial rather than on collective bargaining issues, there will be ground for setting aside the election.[93]

The rules for determining whether an election should be set aside on this ground were first enunciated in *Sewell Manufacturing Co.*[94] The Board there invalidated an election in two Georgia plants where the anti-union campaign was based on appeals to prejudice by excessive publicizing of an AFL-CIO donation of money to the Committee on Racial Equality for the support of freedom-ride projects in Alabama and Mississippi. The publicity, which included photographs of a white union official dancing with a black woman, was not germane to the election. In setting aside the election, the Board announced its test for application to future cases: When a party injects racial subjects into an election, it must limit comment to truthful statements of the other party's position on racial matters and must not seek to overstress or exacerbate racial feelings by irrelevant and inflammatory appeals; the party who brings racial statements into the campaign has the burden of establishing that they were both truthful and germane to the election issues.[95]

This burden was successfully sustained in *Allen Morrison Sign Co.*[96] An employer wrote a truthful letter that the international union seeking to represent the employees had given financial, moral, and official backing to desegregation activities and that one local had been placed in trusteeship when its members voted to purchase bonds to finance segregated white schools in an attempt to combat public school integration. The employer did not have the support of widespread community campaigning in this matter, as was true in some other racial appeal cases, and the letter was not the sole or central theme of the employer's campaign. The Board noted that the letter presented factual argument which the employees could consider in the light of their racial prejudices instead of substituting appeals to racial prejudice for factual argument, as in *Sewell Manufacturing Co.* The union's loss of the election was certified.

---

[93]For a review of the race issue in election campaigns, *see* Pollit, *The National Labor Relations Board and Race Hate Propaganda in Union Organization Drives,* 17 STAN. L. REV. 373 (1965); *see also* Sovern, *The National Labor Relations Act and Racial Discrimination,* 62 COLUM. L. REV. 563 (1962).

[94]138 NLRB 66, 50 LRRM 1532 (1962).

[95]*Id.*

[96]138 NLRB 73, 50 LRRM 1535 (1962); *see also* Archer Laundry Co., 150 NLRB 1427, 58 LRRM 1212 (1965); Aristocrat Linen Supply Co., 150 NLRB 1448, 58 LRRM 1216 (1965).

In *P.D. Gwaltney, Jr. & Co.,*[97] where 80 percent of the employees were black, the employer, the local press, the sheriff, and other public officials made known their anti-union sympathies. The threat of Ku Klux Klan reactivation in the event of a union victory was prominently proclaimed; two black union members who had come to the city to speak at a union meeting were frightened away before the meeting began; and the sheriff and the chief of police stationed themselves at the polling place throughout the elections. The Board held that in its "experienced judgment" such circumstances made the freedom of choice guaranteed by the Act impossible.[98]

The Board has treated appeals to the racial pride of a particular ethnic minority in a different manner from appeals to racial prejudice. Generally it has found appeals to racial pride to be germane to the issues of the campaign and not designed to inflame racial hatred, but rather to encourage self-respect and concerted efforts for betterment.[99] The Board has explained that

> [c]ampaign material of this type is directed at undoing disadvantages historically imposed . . . upon Negroes because of their race, through an appeal to collective action of the disadvantaged. . . .
>
> . . .
>
> . . . Traditionally, trade unions have sought to unify groups of employees by focusing group attention on common problems, and to further the acceptance of union spokesmen by emphasizing the extent to which the spokesmen have identified themselves with those problems. To hold that this traditional approach may not be utilized because of the ethnic composition of the work force might itself be discriminatory.[100]

In *Bancroft Manufacturing Co.,*[101] the Board, with Fifth Circuit approval, refused to set aside an election because of a union organizer's campaign remarks to employees that "if blacks did not stay together as a group and the union lost the election all the blacks would be fired," and "that seemingly the trend was . . . that the blacks were going to be laid off if they didn't stick together and try to get the plant organized to where they would have some protection . . . ." In a divided opinion, the

---

[97]74 NLRB 371, 20 LRRM 1172 (1947).
[98]*Id.* at 373.
[99]Archer Laundry Co., *supra* note 96; Aristocrat Linen Supply Co., *supra* note 96.
[100]Baltimore Luggage Co., 162 NLRB 1230, 1233-34, 64 LRRM 1145, 1146 (1967).
[101]210 NLRB 1007, 86 LRRM 1376 (1974), *enforced,* 516 F2d 436, 89 LRRM 3105 (CA 5, 1975).

Board held that in the context of three recent layoffs, in which mainly black employees had been laid off, the statements concerning the impact of future layoffs were not "appeals to racial prejudice on matters unrelated to election issues" but were "germane to the larger issue of the advantages and disadvantages of the union as a means of promoting economic security and job rights."[102]

The Fifth Circuit also agreed with the Board in *NLRB v. Sumter Plywood Corp.*[103] that the union's preelection campaign, which centered around blacks to the relative exclusion of whites, did not unduly influence the election. The union was attempting to organize a group composed predominantly of black employees. The court said that racial considerations were not at the core of the campaign, whites were not absolutely excluded, and statements such as "blacks must stick together" were merely general appeals for support of the union. Other ethnic messages were deemed by the court to be permissible "consciousness-raising" calls to ethnic pride and unity similar to the union's traditional call to economic betterment.

Not all courts have agreed with the Board's position on appeals to racial pride. The Fourth Circuit, in *NLRB v. Schapiro & Whitehouse, Inc.*,[104] refused to enforce an order requiring the employer to bargain, since the union in its preelection campaign had made appeals to the racial pride of black employees.

4. Third-Party Interference. There are situations where an employer may be responsible for third-party conduct, or for countermeasures when such conduct occurs. In several cases, outsiders, such as townspeople of the community in which a plant being organized is located, have joined in the campaign against the union in the belief, accurate or not, that unionization would cause the plant to shut down or move. This has presented special problems where the employer did not participate in, condone, or otherwise support the third-party intervention, and in fact, may not have been able to prevent it. Nonetheless, in a representation case the right to a free and untrammeled choice of bargaining representative is not diminished by the fact that

---

[102]210 NLRB at 1008.
[103]535 F2d 917, 92 LRRM 3508 (CA 5, 1976), *cert. denied*, 429 US 1092, 94 LRRM 2643 (1977).
[104]356 F2d 675, 61 LRRM 2289 (CA 4, 1966).

the campaign against the union is conducted by, or in the name of, townspeople rather than the employer.[105] This principle has been applied to intervention by a state official,[106] intervention by an outside placement service for handicapped workers,[107] and the actions of an unknown employee or group of employees.[108]

The reaction of the employer to the third-party campaign may be determinative. Adequate disavowal of objectionable outside campaigning may dissipate the impact of the objectionable features and obviate the need to set the election aside.[109]

In *Falmouth Co.*,[110] a citizens group actively campaigned to defeat the union, emphasizing and utilizing rumors of plant closure. The employer disclaimed the rumors, but the Board held the disclaimer to be insufficient and ordered a new election despite its failure to find the employer at fault in the preelection campaign. In *Utica-Herband Tool Division*[111] the employer took positive advantage of objectionable campaigning against unionization, and the Board set aside the election. In *Claymore Manufacturing Co.*, however,[112] an unequivocal disclaimer by the

---

[105]Universal Mfg. Corp., 156 NLRB 1459, 61 LRRM 1258 (1966); P.D. Gwaltney, Jr. & Co., *supra* note 97. *See also* NLRB v. General Metal Prods. Co., 410 F2d 473, 70 LRRM 3327 (CA 6, 1969), *cert. denied*, 396 US 830, 72 LRRM 2432 (1969); Cagle's Inc., 234 NLRB 1148, 98 LRRM 1117 (1978), *enforced in part*, 588 F2d 943, 100 LRRM 2590 (CA 5, 1979); Star Kist Samoa, Inc., 237 NLRB 238, 98 LRRM 1558 (1978); Claymore Mfg. Co., 146 NLRB 1400, 56 LRRM 1080 (1964); Electra Mfg. Co., 148 NLRB 494, 57 LRRM 1054 (1964); Utica-Herband Tool Div., 145 NLRB 1717, 55 LRRM 1223 (1964); Falmouth Co., 114 NLRB 896, 37 LRRM 1057 (1955).

[106]Richlands Textile, Inc., 220 NLRB 83, 90 LRRM 1391 (1975) (state legislator mailed letter to employees threatening plant closure); *see also* Columbia Tanning Corp., 238 NLRB 899, 99 LRRM 1382 (1978) (letter endorsing union mailed by state labor commissioner held to be sufficient grounds for setting election aside).

[107]Montgomery Ward & Co., 228 NLRB 750, 96 LRRM 1383 (1977). *See* note 114 *infra.*

[108]Florida-Tex. Freight, Inc., 230 NLRB 952, 95 LRRM 1426 (1977) (Board held that where unknown and unauthorized employees obtained and published secret files of the employer, which outlined a plan for closing the facility if the union won the election, the election should be set aside because a coercive atmosphere was created); *see also* Marlowe Mfg. Co., 213 NLRB 278, 87 LRRM 1133 (1974) (leaflet allegedly threatening plant closure distributed by group of unit employees, which employer did not prepare or distribute, was not grounds for setting aside election).

[109]General Metal Prods. Co., 164 NLRB 64, 65 LRRM 1002 (1967), *enforced*, 410 F2d 473, 70 LRRM 3327 (CA 6, 1969), *cert. denied*, 396 US 830, 72 LRRM 2432 (1969); Electra Mfg. Co., *supra* note 105; Claymore Mfg. Co., *supra* note 105; Utica-Herband Tool Div., *supra* note 105; Falmouth Co., *supra* note 105. *But see* Raytheon Co., 179 NLRB 678, 72 LRRM 1454 (1969), where the Board found no violation when the employer remained silent following a radio news broadcast quoting "informed sources" as predicting the closing of the plant if the union won the election.

[110]*Supra* note 105.
[111]*Supra* note 105.
[112]*Supra* note 105.

employer was sufficient to forestall remedial action by the Board. At the union's request, the employer issued a letter to employees disavowing rumors created by the community campaign and stating it would continue operations whatever the result of the election.

Where the employer is charged with an unfair labor practice, rather than with objectionable preelection conduct only, considerations of agency status are more significant. An election may be set aside without a showing of fault by a party,[113] but coercive conduct must be attributable to an employer before an unfair labor practice will be found.[114]

5. Violence and Threats. The Board will set aside an election where there is an "atmosphere" of violence or threats of violence, since this may impair a free choice by employees. It is "immaterial that fear and disorder may have been created by individual employees or non-employees and that their conduct cannot be attributed either to the employer or to the union. The significant fact is that such conditions existed and that a free election was thereby rendered impossible."[115] But zealous partisanship alone does not justify setting an election aside.[116]

The test for determining if the election should be set aside, the Board has said, is "whether the election was held with a general atmosphere among the employees of confusion, violence, and threats of violence, such as might reasonably be

---

[113]Al Long, Inc., 173 NLRB 447, 69 LRRM 1366 (1968).

[114]Dean Indus., Inc., 162 NLRB 1078, 64 LRRM 1193 (1967). *E.g.*, where a state legislator mailed letters to employees threatening plant closure, and the employer knew of the mailing and of in-plant circulation of the letter but did not repudiate the letter, the Board held that the employer's conduct constituted ratification; hence there was an unlawful threat of plant closure. Richland's, Inc., 220 NLRB 83, 90 LRRM 1391 (1975). *See also* Montgomery Ward & Co., *supra* note 107, where the employer had retained an outside placement service to aid in the placement of handicapped workers. An employee of the service was found to have unlawfully interrogated an employee by questioning her about her union involvement and warning her that such involvement would jeopardize her job. The employer was held responsible for the outside placement specialist's conduct because the specialist had performed counseling services for the employer, often on company time and premises, and because the employees were aware of the specialist's role in placing employees. *See also* Star Kist Samoa, Inc., 237 NLRB 238, 98 LRRM 1558 (1978). For unfair labor practice treatment of third-party conduct, *see* Chapter 6 *supra* at notes 336-39.

[115]Al Long, Inc., *supra* note 113 at 448, involving anonymous telephone calls threatening bodily injury, rifle shots by unknown persons, bomb threats, and massed and unruly picketing. *See* Chapter 6 *supra* at notes 337 and 341. Where an unfair labor practice is charged, a showing that the perpetrator is an agent of the employer must be made. *See* Gabriel Co., 137 NLRB 1252, 50 LRRM 1369 (1962).

[116]American Wholesalers, Inc., 218 NLRB 292, 89 LRRM 1352 (1975).

expected to generate anxiety and fear of reprisal, and to render impossible a rational uncoerced expression of choice as to bargaining representative."[117] This type of atmosphere destroys the "laboratory conditions" in which Board-conducted elections must be conducted.

The Board has held that verbal threats are sufficient to set aside an election only when they have coerced the employees into voting in a particular manner. "For conduct to warrant setting aside an election, not only must that conduct be coercive, but it must be so related to the election as to have had a probable effect on the employees' action at the polls."[118]

In *Hickory Springs Manufacturing Co.,*[119] the Board held that preelection statements adopted by union officials, which related to what actions the union would take against employees who crossed a picket line in the event of a strike and to picketing after the election, were not grounds for setting aside the election. The Board stated that inasmuch as there was no picket line then in existence, the so-called threats were thus conditioned on the union winning the election, the contract negotiations with the company failing, the union calling a strike, and some employees opting not to honor the picket line; "with these contingencies standing between the threats and their possible execution," the Board perceived "little if any likelihood of the state-

---

[117]Poinsett Lumber & Mfg. Co., 116 NLRB 1732, 39 LRRM 1083 (1956); Al Long, Inc., *supra* note 113; *but cf.* Tennessee Plastics, Inc., 215 NLRB 315, 88 LRRM 1472 (1974), *enforced,* 91 LRRM 2240 (CA 6, 1975) (employer's objection dismissed where based on union adherents' statement to an employee, as she arrived at work on election day, that if she or any other employee did not vote for the union, they would get their hair cut off); American Wholesalers, Inc., *supra* note 116 (employer's objection dismissed where "statements by pro-union supporters . . . made in a climate of no violence whatever" were considered "overzealous partisanship rather than meaningful threats"). *See also* Riverton Gen'l Hosp., 219 NLRB 1199, 90 LRRM 1190 (1975). Central Photo Co., Inc., 195 NLRB 839, 79 LRRM 1568 (1972).

[118]The Great Atl. & Pac. Tea Co., Inc., 177 NLRB 942, 71 LRRM 1554 (1969); Hickory Springs Mfg. Co., 239 NLRB 641, 99 LRRM 1715 (1978) (overruling the Board's decision in Provincial House, Inc., 209 NLRB 215, 85 LRRM 1326 (1974)), wherein the Board set aside an election because of a union representative's campaign statement to employees that "the union had ways of taking care of people who tried to cross its picket lines"). Threats of other than physical harm may also be grounds for ordering a new election. In Lyon's Restaurants, subsidiary of Consolidated Foods Co., 234 NLRB 178, 97 LRRM 1116 (1978), the Board set aside an election where employees were threatened with loss of their jobs unless they supported the union. *See also* Aire Flo Corp., 167 NLRB 679, 66 LRRM 1214 (1967); Vicker's, Inc., 152 NLRB 793, 59 LRRM 1196 (1965).

[119]*Supra* note 118.

ments having an immediate coercive impact on the employees and the election results."[120]

Isolated statements by unions or employees which have no effect on the outcome of the election are disregarded by the Board. In one instance, a threat of job loss made to an employee by a member of a union's election conference committee seven or eight days before an election was held to be too isolated and too remote in time from the date of the election to have had a coercive effect.[121] The Board also found that a union's statements threatening employees with economic reprisal if they did not support the union were too isolated to warrant setting aside an election.[122] The Board further found that it was not election interference (1) where pro-union employees made threatening statements to persuade co-workers to support the union,[123] (2) where threats were made to a co-worker by an employee who quit his job a month before the election was held,[124] (3) where union representatives made statements that persons crossing picket lines "wouldn't cross no more,"[125] and (4) where a union agent told employees that the union controls actions on the picket line but not off the line, and people who crossed the picket line had accidents attributed to "acts of God."[126]

D. Union Conduct

1. Promise or Grant of Benefits. Generally, the same standards of preelection conduct apply to both employers and unions. Conduct which will invalidate an election if committed by an employer will usually do so when committed by a union; however, this is not always the case. An employer's promise or grant of benefits violates Section 8(a)(1) and constitutes interference if made for the purpose of inducing employees to vote against the union.[127] Union promises, on the other hand, have customarily been considered part of the give-and-take of cam-

---

[120]239 NLRB at 642.
[121]E. I. du Pont de Nemours and Co., 32 LRRM 1335 (1953).
[122]Shoreline Enterprises, 37 LRRM 1048 (1955).
[123]Firestone Tire & Rubber Co., 241 NLRB 382, 100 LRRM 1612 (1979).
[124]Hamilton Label Serv., Inc., 243 NLRB No. 105, 101 LRRM 1518 (1979).
[125]Weyerhaeuser Co., 244 NLRB No. 178, 102 LRRM 1222 (1979).
[126]Loose Leaf Hardware, Inc., 246 NLRB No. 46, 102 LRRM 1551 (1979).
[127]NLRB v. Exchange Parts Co., 375 US 405, 55 LRRM 2098 (1964). *See generally* Chapter 6 *supra* at notes 240-45.

paign propaganda and not legally objectionable.[128] The Board has reasoned that the employer has it within his power to implement promises of benefits, whereas the union does not, and the employees will be aware of that distinction:

> Employees are generally able to understand that a Union cannot obtain benefits automatically by winning an election; but must seek to win them through collective bargaining. Union promises . . . are easily recognized by employees to be dependent on contingencies beyond the Union's control and do not carry with them the same degree of finality as if uttered by an employer who has it within his power to implement promises or benefits.[129]

The courts have occasionally disagreed with the Board's position on union promises of benefits. In *NLRB* v. *Madisonville Concrete Co.*,[130] the Sixth Circuit held that the Board had improperly certified a union which, prior to the representation election, promised to take care of a traffic ticket for an employee. The court based its decision on the facts that (1) the employee told other employees of the union's offer, (2) a union agent reassured the employee in the presence of other employees, (3) an attorney retained by the union appeared on behalf of the employee, and (4) the employee paid no part of the fine.

While the Board has generally been unwilling to set aside an election because a union *promised* benefits, it has ordered a new election where the union actually *granted* benefits. A gift of life insurance coverage to prospective voters was found to be "akin to an employer's grant of a wage increase in anticipation of a representation election" and therefore required that the election be set aside.[131] Such a gift is different from a waiver of initiation fees because it results in the "enhancement of the employees' economic position" and is not "merely an avoidance of possible future liability."[132]

2. Waiver of Initiation Fees. Unions have sometimes sought to win preelection support by granting employees a waiver of

---

[128]Sherrington Supermkt., Inc., 106 NLRB 666, 32 LRRM 1519 (1953). *See* El Monte Tool & Die Casting, Inc. v. NLRB, 633 F2d 160, 105 LRRM 3307 (CA 9, 1980), *enforcing* 244 NLRB 40, 102 LRRM 1139 (1979).
[129]The Smith Co., 192 NLRB 1098, 1101, 78 LRRM 1266, 1267 (1971). *See also* Acme Wire Prods. Corp., 224 NLRB 701, 92 LRRM 1482 (1976).
[130]552 F2d 168, 95 LRRM 2001 (CA 6, 1977), *denying enforcement to* 220 NLRB 668, 90 LRRM 1336 (1976).
[131]Wagner Elec. Corp., 167 NLRB 532, 66 LRRM 1073 (1967); *but see* Primco Casting Corp., 174 NLRB 244, 70 LRRM 1128 (1969).
[132]Wagner Elec. Corp., *supra* note 131 at 533.

334 THE DEVELOPING LABOR LAW CH. 9

initiation fees conditioned upon their joining the union before the election, signing an authorization card, or promising to vote in favor of the union. Such conditional waivers have troubled the Board and the courts. Prior to 1954 the Board took the position that a statement that employees would not have to pay initiation fees if they "join the union before but not after the election [is] lawful campaign propaganda."[133] Then, in *Labue Brothers*,[134] the Board held that it would set aside an election where the offer of reduced initiation fees to employees who joined the union was made contingent upon the result of the election. Thereafter, the legality of conditional waivers of initiation fees was in doubt until 1967, when the Board in *DIT-MCO*[135] returned to its pre-1954 position. The Board in that case said that the offer to waive or reduce initiation fees for those who sign authorization cards before the election is a "legitimate membership-recruiting and campaign device," since there is nothing which coerces these employees into voting in favor of the union.

The Board's position, as announced in *DIT-MCO*, met with mixed reception from the courts of appeals.[136] And finally, in *NLRB* v. *Savair Manufacturing Co.*,[137] the Board's position was rejected by the Supreme Court, which held that a union may not offer to waive initiation fees for employees who sign authorization cards before an election. The Court was persuaded that some employees signing a membership or authorization card might feel obligated to carry through on their stated intention to support the union when they vote; thus, unions should not be allowed to "buy endorsements and paint a false portrait of employee support during its election campaign."[138] "[T]he statutory policy of fair elections," declared the Court, "[does not permit endorsements], whether for or against the union, to be bought and sold in this fashion."[139] The Court noted, however,

---

[133]The DeVilbiss Co., 102 NLRB 1317, 1318 (1953).

[134]109 NLRB 1182 (1954).

[135]163 NLRB 1019, 64 LRRM 1476 (1967), *enforced*, 428 F2d 775, 74 LRRM 2664 (CA 8, 1970).

[136]*See, e.g.*, NLRB v. Gilmore Indus., Inc., 341 F2d 240, 58 LRRM 2419 (CA 6, 1965); NLRB v. Gorbea, Perez & Morrell, 328 F2d 679, 55 LRRM 2586 (CA 1, 1964); Clothing Workers v. NLRB, 345 F2d 264, 59 LRRM 2228 (CA 2, 1965).

[137]414 US 270, 84 LRRM 2929 (1973), *aff'g* 470 F2d 305, 82 LRRM 2085 (CA 6), *rev'g* 194 NLRB 298, 78 LRRM 1605 (1971). Also overruled was the Board's decision in DIT-MCO, Inc., *supra* note 135. *See* Chapter 12 *infra* at notes 309-17.

[138]414 US at 277.

[139]*Id.*

that the union's legitimate interest in overcoming employees' reluctance to pay out money before the union has done anything for them "can be preserved as well by waiver of initiation fees available not only to those who have signed up with the union before an election but also to those who join after the election."[140]

Even after *Savair,* a waiver of initiation fees does not interfere with an election absent a showing that the waiver is contingent upon preelection support, the signing of authorization cards, or a commitment to vote only for the union.[141] Consequently, the specific language used by the union in waiving initiation fees is often of critical importance. Where a union offered to waive initiation fees for "charter members" but failed to explain the term to employees, thereby leaving the impression that only those who signed before the election were "charter members," the Board set the election aside.[142] And a union's statement that no initiation fees would be paid by "anyone joining now, during this campaign" was held to be objectionable because it could have been interpreted by employees as being conditioned upon a commitment to support the union.[143]

In *Certain-Teed Products Corp.* v. *NLRB*[144] the Seventh Circuit agreed with the Board that distribution of union literature, which stated that the union "usually does not charge an initiation fee until after giving employees a certain period of time to join the union after a labor board election," was an unconditional waiver of fees for all employees after the election and was therefore permissible under *Savair.* The court also agreed that the use of the word "usually" did not confuse the employees or pressure them into signing cards prior to the election.

The Ninth Circuit, in *NLRB* v. *L. D. McFarland Co.,*[145] agreed with the Board that the union's offer to waive initiation fees for

---

[140]*Id.* at 274, n.4.

[141]Solon Mfg. Co. v. NLRB, 544 F2d 1108, 93 LRRM 2786 (CA 1, 1976); NLRB v. Sumter Plywood Corp., 535 F2d 917, 92 LRRM 3508 (CA 5, 1976), *cert. denied,* 429 US 1092, 94 LRRM 2643 (1977); Prudential Ins. Co. v. NLRB, 529 F2d 66, 91 LRRM 2422 (CA 6, 1976), *cert. denied,* 425 US 993, 92 LRRM 2582 (1976); Lake Charles Memorial Hosp., 226 NLRB 849, 93 LRRM 1420 (1976). *See also* NLRB v. Whitney Museum Am. Art, 636 F2d 19, 105 LRRM 3239 (CA 2, 1980), *enforcing* 247 NLRB 573, 10. LRRM 1176 (1980).

[142]Inland Shoe Mfg. Co., Inc., 211 NLRB 724, 86 LRRM 1498 (1974).

[143]Crane Co., 225 NLRB 657, 93 LRRM 1181 (1976).

[144]652 F2d 500, 96 LRRM 2504 (CA 7, 1977), *enforcing* 225 NLRB 971, 93 LRRM 1192 (1976).

[145]572 F2d 256, 98 LRRM 2037 (CA 9, 1978), *enforcing* 219 NLRB 575, 90 LRRM 1119 (1975).

all "members" and to waive monthly dues until an agreement
was signed did not violate *Savair*. The term "members" was held
to refer to incoming as well as existing members, and neither
waiver of initiation fees nor waiver of dues was held to be
improper because both applied regardless of whether the
employee joined before or after the election.

In addition to the difficulties involved in construing the language of the union's offer, *Savair* raises other problems of application. For example, questions may arise as to how long after
the election the waiver must continue in effect. In *Maple Shade
Nursing Home*[146] the Board found no election interference where
the union's waiver of fees was specifically limited to the period
prior to the negotiation of a collective bargaining agreement.

Questions may also arise with respect to whether the waiver
was in fact authorized by the union. Statements by members of
an in-plant organizing committee regarding waiver of initiation
fees, in contravention of the *Savair* rule, were found not to
constitute election interference because the offer had not been
authorized by the union.[147]

In *Aladdin Hotel Corp.*[148] the Board considered a union organizing policy which required prepayment of a reduced initiation
fee and one month's dues by a majority of unit employees before
the union would file an election petition. If the union lost the
election, the amounts prepaid were forfeited to the union to
defray the union's campaign expenses; if the union won the
election, the dues payments were applied to the first month's
dues after a contract was signed, and the reduced initiation fee
was open to all employees until the signing of an agreement. In
finding this organizational policy lawful, the Board majority
reasoned that a union is not obligated to seek to represent
employees, and if a majority of employees do not prepay, thus
causing the union to abandon its efforts, the employees are
denied no rights. If a majority of employees do prepay, those
who choose not to do so at the outset are not prejudiced because
they can pay the reduced initiation fee after the election. The
majority saw no objection that the union's policy might create

---

[146]223 NLRB 1475, 92 LRRM 1178 (1976).
[147]Firestone Steel Prods. Co., 235 NLRB 548, 98 LRRM 1014 (1978).
[148]229 NLRB 499, 95 LRRM 1150 (1977).

"an early—though not binding—commitment to favor the Petition."[149]

In *Jarp Corp.*[150] the Board ruled that a union's policy of refunding advance fees if it withdrew from the representation proceeding or if it was unable to negotiate a satisfactory contract, but not refunding the advance fee if it lost the election, did not amount to interference with an election.

3. Other Union Conduct. *a. Interrogation.* The Board has held that a union's polling of unit employees as to how they would vote does not warrant setting aside an election.[151] The Seventh Circuit was in agreement, holding there is "no merit in the . . . argument that, because such a poll might have been coercive if conducted by the company, it is likewise coercive when conducted by the union. The employer occupies a far different position with regard to the coercive impact of its actions upon employees than does a Union."[152]

b. Failure to Disclose Information. Is a union under an affirmative duty to disclose any information prior to an election? That question arose in *Florida Mining & Materials Corp. v. NLRB,*[153] where the Fifth Circuit was called upon to resolve, in its words, a "single extremely complex issue." On the day before the election the petitioning local union was placed under temporary trusteeship by its parent international union. Prior to the election, which the union won, the existence of the trusteeship and the reasons therefor were not made known to the public, to the company, or to the employees. The employer filed objections alleging that concealment of the trusteeship invalidated the election results. The Board opposed what, in its view, was the employer's attempt to inject an "affirmative disclosure" requirement into representation campaigns, thus creating an impossi-

---

[149]*Id.* at 500. Members Penello and Walther dissented, observing that the union admitted that one of its reasons for the dues policy was to discourage employees from just "window shopping" for a union. The dissenters viewed this as clear interference with the employees' freedom of choice in direct conflict with *Savair.*

[150]230 NLRB 660, 95 LRRM 1425 (1977) (panel of Chairman Murphy and Member Jenkins, with Member Walther in dissent).

[151]Springfield Discount, Inc., 195 NLRB 921, 79 LRRM 1542 (1972), *enforced,* 82 LRRM 2173 (CA 7, 1972). Chairman Miller concurred in the result, contending that polling by *either* party ought not to require *per se* that an election be set aside.

[152]Louis-Allis Co. v. NLRB, 463 F2d 512, 517, 80 LRRM 2864 (CA 7, 1972).

[153]481 F2d 65, 83 LRRM 2793 (CA 5, 1973), *enforcing* 198 NLRB 601, 80 LRRM 1848 (1972), *cert. denied,* 514 US 990, 85 LRRM 2711 (1974).

ble administrative burden in return for only marginal benefits. The circuit court agreed that such a rule had never before been formulated or imposed. It also noted that the union, even though under trusteeship, would still be able to function as a viable union organization and adequately represent the employees.

   c. Discrimination on the Basis of Race or Sex. While not involving an objection to union conduct during an election campaign, the Board and the courts have questioned whether a union which discriminates on the basis of race or sex should be certified. The concern was that by certifying such a union, the Board would become a partner in illegal discrimination, thereby violating the constitutional guarantee of due process and equal protection.[154]

   In *Bekins Moving & Storage Co., Inc.,*[155] the Board held, in a split decision, that it would consider an objection to a union's certification, where it was contended that the union engaged in invidious discrimination on the basis of race, alienage, or national origin (but not sex), if such objection were filed within five days of issuance of the tally of ballots. To confer the benefits of certification upon a labor organization which was shown to be engaging in a pattern and practice of invidious discrimination, the majority said, would be to run "afoul of the due process clause of the fifth amendment"; and such action on the Board's part "would clearly be anomalous in view of the federal government's express policy against such discrimination and the many laws which prohibit it."

   In *Bell & Howell Co.*[156] the Board again split, but this time denied the employer's postelection motion to disqualify the union from certification because of the union's alleged sex discrimination.

   In 1977 the Board, in *Handy Andy, Inc.,*[157] overruled *Bekins.* The majority held that an employer may no longer, prior to Board certification of the union, raise issues relating to whether

---

[154]NLRB v. Mansion House Corp., 473 F2d 471, 82 LRRM 2608 (CA 8, 1973). *See* discussion in Chapter 10 *infra* at notes 444-47, Chapter 12 *infra* at notes 343-50, and Chapter 28 *infra* at notes 123-38.
    [155]211 NLRB 138, 86 LRRM 1323 (1974). *See also* Union Carbide Corp., Case No. 13-RC-13269, 86 LRRM 1606 (1974).
    [156]213 NLRB 407, 87 LRRM 1172 (1974).
    [157]228 NLRB 447, 94 LRRM 1354 (1977).

the union engages in racial, national origin, or alienage discrimination.[158]

Subsequent to *Handy Andy*, the Board also held that an employer cannot successfully defend against a refusal-to-bargain charge based on a contention that certification was improperly granted because the certified union discriminated on the basis of sex.[159]

d. *Requirement of "Sincere Money."* May a union require employees to pay initiation fees or dues as a precondition to union participation in an election? The Fifth Circuit, in agreement with the Board, held in *Hickory Springs Manufacturing Co. v. NLRB*[160] that a union did not interfere with employee freedom of choice when it conditioned its continued support in the election process on the advance payment of "sincere money" (representing one months' dues and an initiation fee) by a majority of the employees in the unit. The court found *Savair*[161] inapplicable for the reason that "there was no vote buying [or] special concession to those who endorsed the union in the course of the election campaign . . . ." Nor did the court find "any *false* depiction of employee support . . . , since support with cash as well as words is true support indeed."[162] The court concluded that the tactic "was entirely legitimate: no duress was involved and the choice to put up the 'sincere money' or not was a free one. Indeed, it was a lesser step than another that would also have been entirely legitimate: affiliation with the union in advance of the election . . . ."[163]

III. REMEDIES

Typically, when the Board sustains a party's objections to an election it will set aside the election and direct a rerun.[164] In addition, it may order the employer to post a *Lufkin Notice* which explains to the employees why the original election was set

---

[158]For a more complete discussion of the *Handy Andy* decision, *see* Chapter 10 *infra* at notes 439-447.
[159]Bell & Howell Co., 230 NLRB 420, 95 LRRM 1333 (1977).
[160]645 F2d 506, 107 LRRM 2404, *remanding on other grounds* 247 NLRB 1208, 103 LRRM 1394 (1980).
[161]*Supra* note 137.
[162]645 F2d at 508. (Emphasis in original.)
[163]*Id.*
[164]NLRB CASE HANDLING MANUAL, Pt. 2, Representation Proceedings, ¶11436.

aside.[165] The Board will normally schedule the rerun election as soon as possible after the original election has been set aside. There are at least two circumstances, however, under which the election may be postponed: (1) where there is a concurrent unfair labor practice case pending against a party, or (2) where a party has been found guilty of unfair labor practices which must be remedied before the rerun.[166]

In limited circumstances, involving certain types of unfair labor practices, the Board has authority to remedy an employer's election interference by ordering the employer to recognize and bargain with the union in spite of the union's loss of the election. These cases are treated elsewhere.[167]

---

[165]Lufkin Rule Co., 147 NLRB 341, 56 LRRM 1212 (1964). *See also* NLRB CASE HANDLING MANUAL, Pt. 2, Representation Proceedings, ¶11452.1. The language adopted from the *Lufkin* decision is as follows:

"NOTICE TO ALL VOTERS"

"The election conducted on ＿＿＿＿＿＿＿＿was set aside because the National Labor Relations Board found that certain conduct of the (Employer) (Union) interfered with the employees' exercise of a free and reasoned choice. Therefore, a new election will be held in accordance with the terms of this notice of election. All eligible voters should understand that the National Labor Relations Act, as amended, gives them the right to cast their ballots as they see fit, and protects them in the exercise of this right, free from interference by any of the parties."

See Chapter 10 *infra* at note 433.

[166]NLRB CASE HANDLING MANUAL, Pt. 2, Representation Proceedings, ¶11452.

[167]*See* Chapter 12 *infra*.

REPRESENTATION PROCEEDINGS AND ELECTIONS

I. Questions Concerning Representation

Central to the administration of the National Labor Relations Act is the machinery that provides for determining union representation.[1] The mandate which the Act creates is contained in a single sentence:

> Representatives designated or selected for the purposes of collective bargaining by the majority of the employees in a unit appropriate for such purposes, shall be the exclusive representatives of all the employees in such unit for the purposes of collective bargaining in respect to rates of pay, wages, hours of employment or other conditions of employment . . . .[2]

The Act thus provides for union recognition and bargaining when the circumstances of *majority representation* and *appropriate bargaining unit* are present. Although the statute does not require the parties to use the formal processes of the NLRB to determine these questions,[3] it does provide administrative machinery under Section 9 to resolve questions concerning representation. A *question concerning representation* (often referred to as a QCR) exists when a labor organization or individual seeks recognition as bargaining agent and the employer declines to recognize it, thus requiring the Board to determine whether the union or individual represents a majority of the employees in an appropriate bargaining unit.

Employees, labor organizations, or employers may file representation petitions to determine whether a labor organization

---

[1] *See generally* K. McGuiness, How to Take a Case Before the National Labor Relations Board 4-216 (4th ed. BNA Books, 1976).

[2] §9(a).

[3] *See* Chapters 12 and 13 *infra*.

or individual is entitled to recognition (or to continued recognition) for purposes of collective bargaining. The Board has charged its regional directors[4] with the investigation of these petitions to decide whether "a question of representation affecting commerce exists."[5] However, the employer and the labor organization may resolve by agreement that the labor organization is in fact the choice of a majority of employees in the bargaining unit,[6] that certain employees constitute an appropriate unit,[7] and that the Act is applicable. But if the Board's processes are invoked by a representation petition, then the Board will decide whether its jurisdictional requirements are met,[8] and if so whether the bargaining unit is appropriate and whether a majority of the employees has selected a representative.

If, pursuant to a petition, the regional director holds a hearing[9] and finds that a question concerning representation exists, an election is directed and the results certified. If two or more petitions involving the same employer are pending, they may be consolidated into one hearing because of common issues. When it appears to the Board, after investigation by the regional director, that an expedited election under Section 8(b)(7)(C) is warranted, an election may be held without a prior hearing.[10] An election may also be held without a hearing on the basis of a consent agreement resolving certain issues preliminary to the election.[11]

After the hearing the regional director may transfer the record to the Board for a ruling on the petition. Normally, however, the director rules on it initially, and that decision is final subject to discretionary Board review upon timely request.[12] If, pur-

---

[4]For a discussion of the 1961 delegation of authority, *see* Chapter 32 *infra* at notes 68-70 and accompanying text.

[5]§9(c)(2).

[6]*But see* Bernhard-Altmann Texas Corp., 122 NLRB 1289, 43 LRRM 1283 (1959), *enforced sub nom.* Garment Workers v. NLRB (Bernhard-Altmann Texas Corp.), 280 F2d 616, 46 LRRM 2223 (CA DC, 1960), *aff'd*, 366 US 731, 48 LRRM 2251 (1961), discussed in Chapter 8 *supra* at notes 9 and 78-79.

[7]*See* Chapter 11 *infra*.

[8]For discussion of the Board's jurisdictional standards, *see* Chapter 30 *infra*.

[9]*See* Chapter 32 *infra* at notes 62-67 and accompanying text. *See also infra* at notes 219-31.

[10]*See* Chapter 23 *infra*.

[11]*See* Chapter 32 *infra* at notes 75-76 and accompanying text and *infra* this chapter at notes 225-27.

[12]*Id.* at notes 71-73 and accompanying text.

suant to the director's or the Board's direction, an election is held, ballots may be challenged and objections may be made to the election.[13] The postelection procedure to resolve such issues is similar in many respects to the preelection procedure: the common practice includes an investigation by the regional director without a hearing, followed by a report and recommendations to the Board, with the Board making the final determination.[14] The conclusion of the process is marked by certification of the winning union (or individual) as the exclusive bargaining representative, or merely by certification of the results if no union wins.

A. Petitions by Labor Organizations and Employees

1. Showing of Interest. A union (or individual) desiring to be certified as the collective bargaining representative files a petition (colloquially referred to as an "RC" petition) describing the bargaining unit alleged to be appropriate. Section 9(c)(1)(A) of the Act provides that the petition must be supported by a "substantial number of employees." The Board by rule defines "substantial" to mean at least 30 percent.[15] The evidence of support, which is usually in the form of signed and dated[16] authorization cards, must accompany the petition or be presented shortly thereafter, generally within 48 hours of its filing.[17] The 30-percent showing is not necessarily required of a union seeking to intervene; its interest may be otherwise shown if it seeks the same unit as the petitioner.[18] A cross-petitioning union

---

[13]*Id.* at notes 87-101 and accompanying text; *see also* Chapter 9 *supra.*

[14]*But see* NLRB v. Chelsea Clock Co., 411 F2d 189, 71 LRRM 2263 (CA 1, 1969), where the regional director was held to have improperly abdicated to the NLRB his responsibility for deciding disputes arising out of an agreement for consent election. When the employer filed objections to the election on the grounds that an alleged supervisor engaged in pro-union conduct, the regional director consolidated the representation case for hearing with the unfair labor practice case which had been filed by the same supervisor. *See also* Chapter 32 *infra* at notes 87-101.

[15]NRLB RULES AND REGULATIONS AND STATEMENTS OF PROCEDURE, SERIES 8, §101.18 (as last amended, Jan. 8, 1976) (GPO, 1976) (hereinafter referred to as Rules and Regs. and Statements of Procedure); Esso Standard Oil Co., 124 NLRB 1383, 45 LRRM 1020 (1959).

[16]A showing of interest is deemed inadequate where none of the cards is dated, Werman & Sons, Inc., 114 NLRB 629, 37 LRRM 1021 (1955), although exceptions to this rule may exist; *see* Windemuller Electric, Inc., 180 NLRB 686, 686 n. 1, 73 LRRM 1111 (1970) (validity of petition merely "questionable" where cards undated).

[17]McGuiness, *supra* note 1 at 69.

[18]1958 NLRB ANN. REP. 14 (1959). *See* NLRB FIELD MANUAL, issued by the General Counsel of the NLRB, Aug. 1, 1968 (hereinafter referred to as NLRB Field Manual),

seeking a substantially different unit from that claimed to be appropriate by the initial petitioner must comply with the 30-percent showing.[19]

Investigation of the cards includes checking them against a current payroll list of employees furnished by the employer to the regional director's agent. The agent's responsibility is to determine whether the cards are current and sufficient in number. The employer is not permitted to inspect the cards,[20] and at the hearing no litigation is permitted concerning fraud, forgery, or coercion in obtaining cards. The adequacy of petitioner's showing in general is by prehearing administrative determination of the Board, "not subject to direct or collateral attack at hearings."[21]

The Act also authorizes procedures for decertification and deauthorization petitions.[22] A decertification petition (colloquially referred to as an "RD" petition)[23] seeks certification that an incumbent union no longer has the support of the unit; a deauthorization petition (colloquially referred to as a "UD" petition)[24]

11022.3c and d: "A [full intervenor] union which seeks to intervene on the basis of a showing of designation by at least 10 percent of the employees . . . may 'block' any consent election in such unit; and it may participate fully in any hearing thereon. Cf. Corn Prods. Ref. Co., 87 NLRB 187, 25 LRRM 1085 (1949). . . . A [participating intervenor] union which seeks to intervene on a timely showing of less than 10 percent (it may be only one of two designations) in any unit may not 'block' a consent election in such unit. However, it should be accorded a place on the ballot under the terms agreed upon by the other parties. If a hearing is held it may participate fully. Union Carbide & Carbon Corp., 89 NLRB 460, 25 LRRM 1585 (1950)."

[19]NLRB Field Manual 11022.3b.

[20]The Board has successfully resisted employer efforts to gain disclosure of authorization cards under the Freedom of Information Act. 5 USC §552 (1976). See, e.g., Howard Johnson Co., Inc. v. NLRB, 618 F2d 1, 103 LRRM 2888 (CA 6, 1980); Howard Johnson Co., Inc. v. NLRB, 96 LRRM 2214 (WD NY, 1977); Committee on Masonic Homes v. NLRB, 556 F2d 214, 95 LRRM 2457 (CA 3, 1977); Pacific Molasses Co. v. NLRB, 577 F2d 1172, 99 LRRM 2048 (CA 5, 1978). However, it has been held that subpoenaed authorization cards must be disclosed to the attorneys of an employer and a union under criminal indictment on charges of conspiracy and obstruction of administrative proceedings. Irving v. DiLapi, 600 F2d 1027, 101 LRRM 2903 (CA 2, 1979). At least one court has reached a different result with respect to Board Form 4069 utilized by Board agents to report facts concerning a union's showing of interest in support of a representation proceeding. Pacific Molasses Co., supra.

[21]O. D. Jennings & Co., 68 NLRB 516, 518, 18 LRRM 1133 (1946). See also Union Mfg. Co., 123 NLRB 1633, 44 LRRM 1188 (1959) (decertification proceedings). Adequacy of showing of interest may be contested by submission of affidavits to the regional director. Globe Iron Foundry, 112 NLRB 1200, 36 LRRM 1170 (1955).

[22]§9(c)(1)(A)(ii).

[23]Rules and Regs. §102.61; Statements of Procedure §101.18. The unit for purposes of an "RD" election is coextensive with the contract unit. Arlan's Dep't Store, Inc., 131 NLRB 565, 567 n.7, 48 LRRM 1115 (1961).

[24]§9(e)(1) Rules and Regs. Subpart E; Statements of Procedure Subpart E. See Chapter 29 infra at notes 135-42 and accompanying text.

seeks rescission of the union's authority to make an existing union-shop agreement with the employer. Such petitions may be filed by an employee or group of employees or an individual or labor organization acting in their behalf, and must demonstrate that at least 30 percent of the employees in the unit support the petition.

No showing of interest is required for an expedited election under Section 8(b)(7)(C) of the Act.[25]

2. Employer Denial of Recognition. Section 9(c)(1)(A) contemplates an allegation that an employer "declines to recognize" the union representative through which the employees wish to engage in collective bargaining. However, the failure of the union to demand recognition before filing the petition is not a basis for its dismissal[26] provided the employer refuses to recognize the union at the hearing. Indeed, after a union has gained recognition from an employer without certification, it may nonetheless seek and obtain an election by petition in order to reap the statutory benefits conferred especially by the 1947 Taft-Hartley amendments upon unions that are certified by the NLRB as representatives.[27]

3. Joint Petitions. Joint petitions may be filed by two or more labor organizations that desire to act as a joint representative.[28] The employees' authorizations may be made in the individual name of any of the joint petitioners, and the cards may even be silent as to the question of joint representation.[29] If the unions are successful in the election, certification will issue in the joint names of the unions, and the employer may insist that they bargain jointly.[30]

---

[25]See Chapter 23 *infra* at notes 217-21 and accompanying text.
[26]"M" Sys., Inc., 115 NLRB 1316, 38 LRRM 1055 (1956).
[27]General Box Co., 82 NLRB 678, 23 LRRM 1589 (1949).
[28]See Mid-South Packers, Inc., 120 NLRB 495, 41 LRRM 1526 (1958). In the absence of petitioners' intention to represent the employees jointly and to bargain jointly with the employer, the Board will not allow a joint petition. *See, e.g.,* Suburban Newspaper Publications, Inc., 230 NLRB 1215, 95 LRRM 1482 (1977), where the Board declared the election a nullity and dismissed the joint petition after the posthearing investigation revealed that the unions had assured employees that the joint representation election was only a formality and that each union would continue to represent its traditional constituency.
[29]Stickless Corp., 115 NLRB 979, 37 LRRM 1466 (1956).
[30]Jackson Manor Nursing Home, 194 NLRB 892, 79 LRRM 1166 (1972); Swift & Co., 115 NLRB 752, 37 LRRM 1392 (1956).

B. Petitions by Employers[31]

1. History Under the Wagner Act. Although the original statute declared that "whenever a question affecting commerce arises concerning the representation of employees, the Board may investigate such controversy,"[32] it provided no mechanism for bringing the controversy to the Board's attention. Drawing upon the experience of other governmental agencies, the Board adopted a procedure authorizing any person or labor organization desiring investigation of a controversy concerning representation to file a petition.[33] There was no provision for employer petitions.[34]

This policy met with widespread opposition, especially as it affected an employer caught in the middle of a jurisdictional dispute.[35] The American Bar Association's Committee on Labor Employment and Social Security called for amendment of the Act.[36]

The American Federation of Labor also advocated amendment of the Act. It had charged that the Board, in acting upon union petitions, had exercised its discretion in favor of the CIO and against the AFL. To remedy this situation, it supported a bill[37] to amend Section 9(c) by making it mandatory upon the Board to investigate union petitions; the bill would also have amended Section 9(c) to provide for employer petitions. The bill was not enacted into law. The Board was opposed to it, expressing its opposition as follows:

> The reasons for not permitting employers an unlimited right of petition are first, that normally the employer has no legitimate interest in the question whether or when his employees wish to choose

---

[31]For general discussion of this subject, *see* Lewis, *Employer Petitions—New York and Federal—A Comparison,* NYU FIFTH ANNUAL CONFERENCE ON LABOR 249 (1952).

[32]§9(c), deleted in 1947.

[33]NLRB RULES AND REGS., SERIES 1, Art. III, §1 (1935).

[34]Nevertheless, it was not unusual for the regional director, at the instance of the employer, to induce the union to file a petition. Bowman, PUBLIC CONTROL OF LABOR RELATIONS 298 (1942); Rosenfarb, THE NATIONAL LABOR POLICY 303 (1940).

[35]For example, one editorial advised: "Many of those connected with the NLRB admit in private that the employer is often at the mercy of two conflicting unions, neither of which will concede that the other has the right to bargain for the workers, though neither, until it is certain it has a majority, will ask for an election." N.Y. Times, Nov. 30, 1937, at 22.

[36]25 A.B.A.J. 119, 124 (1936).

[37]S. 1000, 76th Cong., 1st Sess. (1939). For its legislative history, *see* H. Millis & E. Brown, FROM THE WAGNER ACT TO TAFT-HARTLEY 347-53 (1950).

representatives or whom they wish to choose; and second, that if an employer is given the right to demand an election at will he can, by choosing a strategic time, effectively hinder or block self-organization among his employees. The right of employees to choose their representatives when and as they wish is normally no more the affair of the employer than the right of the stockholders to choose directors is the affair of the employees.[38]

However, in response to strong public pressure, the Board in 1939 amended its rules to grant employers a limited right to petition if the petition alleged that two or more unions were making conflicting claims of representative status.[39] This right was not altered under the statute or the rules until the Taft-Hartley amendments.

2. History Under the Taft-Hartley Act. The most frequently voiced objection to employer petitions in the debate on the 1947 amendments was that they could be used to force a premature test and thereby obtain a vote rejecting the union. A further objection was based upon another amendment which would disenfranchise permanently replaced economic strikers. President Truman's veto message stressed that employer petitions could be used to obtain elections during strikes and thereby capitalize on the strikers' disenfranchisement.[40]

To meet those objections, the measure as enacted conditioned the employer's right to petition for an election upon a prior claim for recognition by a union. Accordingly, Section 9(c)(1) reads as follows:

> Whenever a petition shall have been filed . . . by an employer, alleging that one or more individuals or labor organizations have presented to him a claim to be recognized as the representative defined in Section 9(a); the Board shall investigate such petition. . . .

This amendment was designed to grant an employer the right to petition in two situations previously unavailable to it. The first involves a claim for recognition by one union only; previously an employer's right to petition was contingent upon claims for recognition by two or more unions. The second concerns an employer desire to question the current majority standing of an

---

[38]*Report of NLRB Before Sen. Comm. on Education and Labor, Hearings on National Labor Relations Act and Proposed Amendments*, 76th Cong., 1st Sess., Part 3, pp. 467, 540-43 (1939).

[39]NLRB RULES AND REGS., SERIES 2, Art. III, §§1-3 (1939).

[40]H.R. DOC. NO. 334, 93 CONG. REC. 7486 (1947). For similar criticism, *see* 93 CONG. REC. 4032, 6527 (1947) (remarks of Senators Murray and Pepper).

incumbent union; before 1947 the Board would not entertain an employer petition (now colloquially referred to as an "RM" petition) in such a situation.[41]

a. Unrecognized Unions. Section 9(c)(1)(B) specifies that an employer petition must contain an allegation that a union (or individual) has "presented to [the employer] a claim to be recognized as the representative defined in Section 9(a)." The Board considers that absent such a claim it would be without jurisdiction to proceed with its investigation.[42] The phrase "representative defined in Section 9(a)" means a labor organization (or individual) chosen by a majority of employees in a unit appropriate for collective bargaining to be the exclusive representative of all employees therein for such purposes. Mere campaigning by a union and knowledge of such campaigning by the employer are not the equivalent of a claim by the union that it represents a majority of the employees, nor do they constitute a request for exclusive bargaining rights under the Act.[43] It is not necessary, however, that a claim of majority representation be made in the exact terms of Section 9(a). It is sufficient if the union submits or requests a proposed contract.[44]

The Supreme Court has upheld the Board's position that an employer's petition for an election, though permissible, is not required. In *Linden Lumber* v. *NLRB*[45] the Court held that an employer which has not committed independent unfair labor practices does not violate Section 8(a)(5) of the Act by refusing to recognize authorization cards as evidence of a union's majority status, even though the employer fails to petition the Board for an election. The decision resolved a question which the Court had expressly reserved in *NLRB* v. *Gissel Packing Co.*[46]

---

[41]*E.g.*, Cincinnati Times-Star Co., 66 NLRB 414, 17 LRRM 340 (1946); Toledo Steel Products Co., 65 NLRB 56, 17 LRRM 211 (1945); Colonial Life Ins. Co. of America, 65 NLRB 58, 17 LRRM 195 (1945); Landis Machine Co., 65 NLRB 60, 17 LRRM 210 (1945).

[42]Herman Loewenstein, Inc., 75 NLRB 377, 21 LRRM 1032 (1947).

[43]Baldwin Co., 81 NLRB 927, 23 LRRM 1438 (1949); Electro Metallurgical Co., 72 NLRB 1396, 19 LRRM 1291 (1947).

[44]Johnson Bros. Furniture Co., 97 NLRB 246, 29 LRRM 1089 (1951); Kimel Shoe Co., 97 NLRB 127, 29 LRRM 1069 (1951). *See* Chapter 23 *infra* at notes 50-68 and accompanying text for a discussion of the nature of evidence used to show recognitional objectives.

[45]419 US 301, 87 LRRM 3236 (1974). *See* Chapter 12 *infra* at notes 230-41.

[46]395 US 575, 595, 601 n.18, 71 LRRM 2481 (1969). For a full discussion of the *Gissel* case, *see* text accompanying notes 56-84 in Chapter 12 *infra*.

b. Incumbent Unions. Section 9(c)(1)(B) is not restricted to situations where an unrecognized union claims recognition. A request by an incumbent union for renewal of its contract constitutes a "claim to be recognized" within the meaning of this section.[47] Therefore, an employer who questions a union's continuing support by a majority of the employees may file a petition for an election.

Under former Board policy it was not necessary that the employer have a reasonable basis for doubting majority status, nor was withdrawal of recognition required.[48] The reasonable, or good-faith, basis for the doubt was an issue only in the event of subsequent unfair labor practice charges alleging a refusal to bargain.[49] In *United States Gypsum Co.*[50] the Board changed that rule, thenceforth dismissing an employer petition where no "reasonable basis" was shown for questioning the status of an incumbent union. It formulated an "objective evidence" test, premising the rule in part upon its reading of the legislative history of Section 9(c)(1)(B). It asserted that the provision was designed to give relief to employers who had "reasonable grounds for believing" that the claiming union was not really the choice of the majority, for "[t]here is no indication that Congress . . . contemplated the creation of a device by which an employer acting without good-faith doubt of the union's status . . . could disrupt collective bargaining and frustrate the policy of the Act favoring stable relations."[51] The Board therefore held that,

> in petitioning the Board for an election to question the continued majority of a previously certified incumbent union, an employer, in addition to showing the union's claim for continued recognition, must demonstrate by objective considerations that it has some reasonable grounds for believing that the union has lost its majority status since its certification.[52]

In considering the sufficiency of the "objective considerations," it is not the fact of the union's majority status that is in question, but whether the employer has reasonable cause to

---

[47]Philadelphia Elec. Co., 95 NLRB 71, 28 LRRM 1296 (1951); Whitney's, 81 NLRB 75, 23 LRRM 1297 (1949).
[48]J. P. O'Neil Lumber Co., 94 NLRB 1299, 28 LRRM 1190 (1951); J. C. Penney Co., 86 NLRB 920, 25 LRRM 1039 (1949); Continental Southern Corp., 83 NLRB 668, 24 LRRM 1127 (1949).
[49]Celanese Corp. of America, 95 NLRB 664, 28 LRRM 1362 (1951).
[50]157 NLRB 652, 61 LRRM 1384 (1966).
[51]*Id.* at 656.
[52]*Id.* For a detailed discussion of this history, *see* Talent, *United States Gypsum Co.—More of the Same,* 17 LAB. L.J. 559 (1966).

believe that the union has lost its majority status.[53] Objective considerations which constitute reasonable grounds for believing that the union has lost its majority status have been found in a variety of situations. Examples include admissions by union officials that the union has lost majority support[54] and written and oral statements by union employees repudiating the union.[55] A combination of factors, such as a decline in dues checkoff authorizations, the union's inactivity in failing to monitor contract provisions or to process grievances, or to recommend employees for promotion or to safety committees, and significant turnover in the work force may serve as a basis for reasonable doubt of the union's continued majority.[56]

The Board has also decided that an employer's demonstration of the "objective considerations" is to be submitted confidentially to the regional director for administrative determination as to the *prima facie* showing. As an administrative determination, that issue would thus not be litigable at any stage of the representation proceeding.[57]

The Board has often found that no question concerning representation exists where an employer's petition requests a unit which is narrower than the unit sought by a labor organization. In *Sonic Knitting Industries, Inc.*[58] this rule was applied to dismiss an employer's petition for an election in a single-plant unit where the union historically had represented employees in a multiplant unit.

3. Disclaimer of Interest. Section 9(c)(1)(B) was designed to permit an employer to file an election petition when a union is claiming to be an exclusive representative for purposes of collective bargaining. Apparently unforeseen by the drafters of this provision was the possibility that a union, having made such a claim, might withdraw it.

---

[53]NLRB Field Manual 11042.5. *Cf.* Chapter 12 *infra* at notes 352-442 for discussion of withdrawal of recognition without an election.
[54]Lodge 1746, Machinists v. NLRB (United Aircraft Corp.), 416 F2d 809, 71 LRRM 2336 (CA DC, 1969), *cert. denied*, 396 US 1058, 73 LRRM 2278 (1970).
[55]Riverside Produce Co., 242 NLRB 615, 101 LRRM 1371 (1979); NLRB v. Gallaro Bros., 419 F2d 97, 73 LRRM 2043 (CA 2, 1969).
[56]Ingress-Plastene, Inc. v. NLRB, 430 F2d 542, 74 LRRM 2658 (CA 7, 1970); *see also* NLRB v. Massachusetts Mach. & Stamping, Inc., 578 F2d 15, 98 LRRM 2939 (CA 1, 1978).
[57]United States Gypsum Co., 161 NLRB 601, 63 LRRM 1308 (1966).
[58]228 NLRB 1319, 95 LRRM 1076 (1977).

The issue was first presented in *Ny-Lint Tool & Manufacturing Co.*[59] The union had represented the employees for several years without benefit of Board certification. In August 1947, having given notice that it would not renew the current contract, it submitted a new contract proposal covering the same employees. Thereupon, the employer expressed doubt that the union continued to represent a majority of the employees, refused to negotiate a new contract, and filed a petition. At the hearing, the union disavowed any claim to majority representation and asked that the employer's petition be dismissed. The Board did so, on the ground that since a question concerning representation no longer existed it was without jurisdiction to proceed. The Board continues to adhere to this policy, dismissing employer petitions whenever the union disclaims interest.[60]

Similarly, in the handling of a decertification petition, a disclaimer of interest by the union results in a dismissal of the petition. For example, in *Federal Shipbuilding & Drydock Co.*[61] the Board held that a union may disclaim interest even after the Board has directed that an election be held (but before the date of the election).

The failure of a union to appear at the hearing,[62] or the failure of a union to intervene,[63] will not constitute a disclaimer of interest. And a union's filing of a refusal-to-bargain charge is not deemed inconsistent with a disclaimer of interest.[64] In addition, a union may, in certain instances, disclaim interest but engage in picketing.[65] It was argued in *Hubach & Parkinson*

---

[59]77 NLRB 642, 22 LRRM 1061 (1948). Both majority and dissenting opinions observed that the situation of an incumbent contractual representative, as in this case, presents the same issue and calls for the same construction of the statute as that of an unrecognized union.

[60]*E.g.,* Josephine Furniture Co., 172 NLRB 404, 68 LRRM 1311 (1968); Coeur D'Alene Grocers Ass'n, 88 NLRB 44, 25 LRRM 1301 (1950); Murray B. Marsh Co., 79 NLRB 76, 22 LRRM 1377 (1948); Brockton Wholesale Grocery Co., 78 NLRB 663, 22 LRRM 1264 (1948); Louella Balierino, 77 NLRB 738, 22 LRRM 1076 (1948); De De Johnson, 77 NLRB 730, 22 LRRM 1076 (1948).

[61]77 NLRB 463, 22 LRRM 1034 (1948).

[62]Felton Oil Co., 78 NLRB 1033, 22 LRRM 1332 (1948).

[63]Penn Paper & Stock Co., 88 NLRB 17, 25 LRRM 1279 (1950).

[64]Franz Food Prods., Inc., 137 NLRB 340, 50 LRRM 1143 (1962).

[65]Hubach & Parkinson Motors, 88 NLRB 1202, 25 LRRM 1466 (1950). To the same effect, *see* Martino's Complete Home Furnishings, 145 NLRB 604, 55 LRRM 1003 (1963); General Paint Corp., 95 NLRB 539, 28 LRRM 1345 (1951). *See also* Tribune Publishing Co., 147 NLRB 841, 56 LRRM 1273 (1964); Smith's Hardware Co., 93 NLRB 1009, 27 LRRM 1556 (1951); Hamilton's, Ltd., 93 NLRB 1076, 27 LRRM 1538 (1951); Palace Knitwear Co., 93 NLRB 872, 27 LRRM 1481 (1951); Bur-Bee Co., 90 NLRB 9, 26 LRRM 1153 (1950). *But see* Knitgoods Workers Local 155 (Boulevard

Motors that the continued picketing demonstrated that the union's disclaimer was not made in good faith and that the union was continuing to assert its claim to be the statutory representative of the employees. The Board disagreed, stating that in order "to defeat an employer's petition or a petition for decertification, a union's disclaimer of status as exclusive bargaining representative must be clear and unequivocal,"[66] although the determination of the sufficiency of a disclaimer may involve considering not only the words used but also other conduct of the union. The Board concluded, however, that despite the resumption of picketing, the union's disclaimer had been clear and unequivocal.[67]

Not all disclaimers of interest by unions result in the dismissal of the employer's petition. Where the disclaimer is not "clear and unequivocal,"[68] or where the union's picket signs may be interpreted as expressing a continued claim to majority representation, the Board will refuse, notwithstanding the disclaimer, to dismiss the employer's petition.[69]

II. TIMELINESS OF PETITIONS

A. One-Year Rule

1. The Statutory Bar. Representation elections may not be conducted more often than once a year in any given bargaining unit or subdivision of a unit. This limitation was imposed in

---

Knitwear Corp.), 167 NLRB 763, 66 LRRM 1157 (1967) (regarding picketing in violation of §8(b)(7) after disclaimer).

[66]88 NLRB at 1204. For treatment of organizational and recognitional picketing, *see* Chapter 23 *infra*.

[67]*Id. See also* John's Valley Foods, 237 NLRB 425, 99 LRRM 1414 (1978), where the Board found insufficient evidence that a union's current informational picketing had a recognitional objective. The regional director had improperly relied on an unsupported presumption that an earlier recognitional objective continued despite a substantial hiatus in picketing which followed an injunctive order. Nor had he sufficiently considered the union's avowed informational objective and the absence of union conduct inconsistent with its disclaimer. Accordingly, the Board dismissed the employer's petition for an election.

[68]*E.g.*, Johnson Bros. Furniture Co., 97 NLRB 246, 29 LRRM 1089 (1951); Coca-Cola Bottling Co., 80 NLRB 1063, 23 LRRM 1160 (1948). *See also* McClintock Market, Inc., 244 NLRB No. 85, 102 LRRM 1141 (1979) (there had been no hiatus in picketing, no leaflets advising the public of the purpose of picketing, and the union's disclaimer of interest had followed its demand for a contract by only a few days). *See also* Ogden Enterprises, 248 NLRB 290, 103 LRRM 1395 (1980), where the Board directed an election on an employer's petition even though the union picketing the employer had disclaimed an interest in representing the employees, since its "activity prior to the disclaimer" was "tantamount" to a demand for recognition and its picketing thereafter furthered that objective.

[69]Kimel Shoe Co., 97 NLRB 127, 29 LRRM 1069 (1951).

1947 by the addition of Section 9(c)(3). In applying this rule the Board has stated that although a representation petition filed within 60 days of the anniversary date of the earlier election will be processed, the election itself will be scheduled for a date after the expiration of the one-year period. A petition filed more than 60 days before the anniversary date will be dismissed as untimely.[70] The prohibition, however, refers only to conclusive elections; the Board is not precluded from directing a rerun or runoff election within the year, or from directing a second election within the year where the first election was set aside on the basis of valid objections timely filed.[71] A deauthorization election to revoke a union's authority to execute a union security contract is not barred by any form of election other than another deauthorization election within the one-year period.[72]

In the 1949 *National Container* case,[73] the Board ruled that elections held by private or state agencies come within the 12-month bar of Section 9(c)(3). In 1950 it reversed itself,[74] but in more recent cases it has returned to the *National Container* rule. The Board's present position appears to be that elections conducted by responsible agencies which afford employees an opportunity to express their true desires and which respect the fundamentals of due process will bar NLRB elections in the same unit within the one-year period.[75]

Where no union is certified, the year begins to run from the date of the election (i.e., date of balloting).[76] The Board maintains this position even where there are postelection objections or challenges that are not resolved for several months.[77] The

---

[70]Randolph Metal Works,Inc., 147 NLRB 973, 56 LRRM 1348 (1964).
[71]NAPA New York Warehouse, Inc., 76 NLRB 840, 21 LRRM 1251 (1948).
[72]Monsanto Chem. Co., 147 NLRB 49, 56 LRRM 1136 (1964).
[73]National Container Corp., 87 NLRB 1065, 25 LRRM 1234 (1949).
[74]Punch Press Repair Corp., 89 NLRB 614, 26 LRRM 1012 (1950).
[75]West Indian Co., 129 NLRB 1203, 47 LRRM 1146 (1961); Olin Mathieson Chem. Corp., 115 NLRB 1501, 38 LRRM 1099 (1956); T-H Prods. Co., 113 NLRB 1246, 36 LRRM 1471 (1955); Interboro Chevrolet Co., 111 NLRB 783, 35 LRRM 1567 (1955). A Board majority failed to give effect to such an election in applying §8(b)(7) in Bartenders Local 58 (Fowler Hotel, Inc.), 138 NLRB 1315, 51 LRRM 1180 (1962). And more recently in NLRB v. Western Meat Packers, 350 F2d 804, 60 LRRM 2101 (CA 10, 1965), the Board was chided for refusing to honor such an election. *Compare* Monroe Coop. Oil Co., 86 NLRB 95, 24 LRRM 1591 (1949), *with* National Waste Material Corp., 93 NLRB 477, 27 LRRM 1413 (1951).
[76]Palmer Mfg. Co., 103 NLRB 336, 31 LRRM 1520 (1953); Mallinckrodt Chem. Works, 84 NLRB 291, 24 LRRM 1253 (1949). When balloting is conducted over a period of several weeks or months, the year begins at the end of the balloting period. Alaska Salmon Indus., 90 NLRB 168, 26 LRRM 1199 (1950).
[77]Bendix Corp., 179 NLRB 140, 72 LRRM 1264 (1969).

rigidity of the rule was illustrated in *NLRB* v. *Tri-ExTower Corp.*[78] An election had been held on July 22, 1975, but the union's objections to the election were not resolved until June 10, 1976, when the Board overruled the objections and certified the election results. In the meantime, on June 1, 1976, the union petitioned for another election in the same unit. The second election was held on August 17, 1976, and was won by the union. Since that election had occurred more than one year after the date of the first election, the Board rejected the employer's contention that the one-year rule was violated.

The one-year rule applies only to new elections in the same bargaining unit or in a subdivision of that unit. An election in a given unit will not preclude the holding of an election in a broader, more inclusive unit within the year.[79] Needless to say, a prior election in a larger unit will not preclude an election within a year in a smaller unit of employees who were barred from voting in the first election.[80] On the other hand, the bar applies if the smaller unit is within the scope of the broader unit in which the prior election was held.[81]

2. The Certification Year. In order to permit collective bargaining to function and to stabilize industrial relations, the Board, with the approval of the Supreme Court, adopted a rule that in the absence of unusual circumstances a certified union's majority status must be honored for one year; and a petition filed during the one-year period will ordinarily be barred. This rule subsequently was incorporated by implication in the statute.[82] In *Brooks* v. *NLRB* the Court approved the Board's requirement that an employer must recognize a union for the entire "certification year" even if it has evidence of the union's loss of majority, except in "unusual circumstances."[83] Unusual circumstances,

---

[78]595 F2d 1 (CA 9, 1979).

[79]Robertson Bros. Dep't Store, Inc., 95 NLRB 271, 28 LRRM 1335 (1951).

[80]Philadelphia Co., 84 NLRB 115, 24 LRRM 1251 (1949). *See also* Ideal Roller & Mfg. Co. v. Douds, 111 F Supp 156, 32 LRRM 2030 (SD NY, 1953).

[81]Krambo Food Stores, No. 13-RC-57 (NLRB Feb. 14, 1958); Allied Chem. & Dye Corp., No. 5-RC-1745, 1748 (NLRB Aug. 19, 1955) (not reported in Board volumes). Note that the prohibition on the holding of a representation election within a year of a previous election is not a defense to an employer's refusal to bargain with a union on the basis of authorization cards. Conren, Inc., 156 NLRB 592, 61 LRRM 1090 (1966), *enforced*, 368 F2d 173, 63 LRRM 2273 (CA 7, 1966), *cert. denied*, 386 US 974, 64 LRRM 2640 (1967). *See* Chapter 12 *infra*.

[82]§8(b)(7)(A), added in 1959.

[83]348 US 96, 35 LRRM 2158 (1954), and cases cited therein; *see also* Nick Trutanich & John Vilicich, 133 NLRB 238, 46 LRRM 1529 (1961); Rocky Mountain Phosphates, Inc., 138 NLRB 292, 51 LRRM 1019 (1962). For discussion of schism and defunctness, *see* text at notes 174-82 *infra*. *See also* Chapter 12 *infra* at notes 352-62.

according to the Court, include (1) a schism within the certified union or its defunctness and (2) radical fluctuation in the size of the bargaining unit within a short period of time.

The presumption of the union's continuing majority status during the first year of certification is almost conclusive. Even where the employer has objective evidence that the union has lost its majority status during the first year of certification, the duty to bargain must ordinarily be honored for the entire year.[84]

In *Mar-Jac Poultry Co.*[85] the Board modified the policy which the Supreme Court had approved in *Brooks* by extending the certification period beyond one year when the employer's misconduct denies the union a year's fair opportunity to bargain. For example, in the *Lamar Hotel* case[86] the Board gave the union an additional six months from the resumption of negotiations because the union had been deprived of its right to an unimpeded opportunity to bargain for six months of the certification year. In the second stage of *Mar-Jac,*[87] it appeared that the employer had indeed refused to bargain with the certified union, but subsequently it executed a settlement containing a promise to bargain. Under these circumstances the Board granted the union an additional period of an entire year, dating from the settlement agreement, for actual bargaining. It announced that it would do the same in future cases where similar factors were present. A corollary of this policy would be a denial, as untimely, of a rival petition filed in the extended period.

3. Voluntary Recognition Bar. Voluntary recognition agreements, written or oral, may also constitute a bar to an election.[88] The sufficiency of a recognition agreement depends upon the existence of a bona fide union majority at the time of

---

[84]*See* NLRB v. Pepsi-Cola Bottling Co., 613 F2d 267, 103 LRRM 2233 (CA 10, 1980). There was a change of ownership during the first year of certification. The successor employer hired 80% of the former employees, operated the business in substantially the same manner as the predecessor, and served the same customers. Even though the company may have been correct in its belief that the union no longer represented a majority of the employees, that good-faith belief was deemed irrelevant in light of the almost conclusive presumption of continuing majority status.

[85]136 NLRB 785, 49 LRRM 1854 (1962).

[86]137 NLRB 1271, 50 LRRM 1366 (1962); *see also* Interstate Brick Co., 167 NLRB 831, 66 LRRM 1160 (1967); Mid-City Foundry Co., 167 NLRB 795, 66 LRRM 1154 (1967); Cincinnati Gasket, Packing & Mfg. Co., 163 NLRB 763, 64 LRRM 1455 (1967).

[87]*Supra* note 85, *overruling* Daily Press, Inc., 112 NLRB 1434, 36 LRRM 1228 (1955), and similar inconsistent cases. *See also* J. P. Stevens Co., 239 NLRB No. 95, 100 LRRM 1052 (1978). Chicago Health & Tennis Clubs, 251 NLRB 140, 105 LRRM 1009 (1980).

[88]Dale's Super Valu, Inc., 181 NLRB 698 (1970); Keller Plastics Eastern, Inc., 157 NLRB 583, 61 LRRM 1396 (1966). In Mojave Elec. Coop., 210 NLRB 88, 86 LRRM

recognition;[89] it may be based on a card check by an impartial third party.[90] Under the Board's *Keller Plastics* rule, once a valid recognition agreement is consummated, the parties have a "reasonable time" in which to negotiate a collective bargaining agreement.[91] Construing that rule, the Board decided that a recognition agreement was not a bar when nearly five months had elapsed without consummation of a contract, and where the unit had changed from two divisions to a single division with a substantial reduction in the number of employees.[92]

The rule that a recognition agreement is an election bar for a reasonable period of time applies only to the initial organization of the employer's employees. Such an agreement does not bar a decertification election where an alleged successor employer has recognized an incumbent union as the representative of its employees, and where, at the time the decertification petition is filed, the successor employer has not accepted the collective bargaining agreement of the predecessor or executed a new agreement with the union.[93] In addition, a voluntary recognition agreement will not be a bar to an election petition where the employer is not aware at the time of recognizing one union that another union is seeking to organize its employees.[94]

A valid recognition agreement constitutes a bar only if the unit involved meets the requisite standard of appropriateness.[95] The unit need not be precisely described, however. In *Central*

1085 (1974), the Board noted that while collective bargaining agreements must be in writing in order to bar representation petitions, a recognition agreement need not be. It held, however, that oral recognition would not bar the petition of an outside union because the employer knew, at the time it orally recognized the incumbent union, that the outside union had substantial support among unit employees.

[89]Keller Plastics Eastern, Inc., *supra* note 88. *Cf.* Garment Workers (Bernhard-Altmann) v. NLRB, 366 US 731, 48 LRRM 2251 (1961), at notes 9 and 78-79 in Chapter 8 *supra*.

[90]American Ship Building Co., No. 8-RC-8037, 77 LRRM 1313 (1971) (not reported in Board volumes). The Board found that the incumbent union had made a clear and positive demonstration of employee support which satisfied the employer of its majority status. Additionally, the employer had extended recognition to the incumbent union at a time when no other organizational activity was occurring.

[91]Keller Plastics Eastern, Inc., *supra* note 88.

[92]Down River Forest Prods., Inc., 205 NLRB 14, 83 LRRM 1504 (1973).

[93]Southern Moldings, Inc., 219 NLRB 119, 89 LRRM 1623 (1975). *See* Chapter 15 *infra* for general treatment of successorship.

[94]Bridgeport Jai Alai, Inc., 227 NLRB 1519, 94 LRRM 1435 (1977).

[95]The Board has stated that nothing in the statute requires that the unit for bargaining be the "only" appropriate unit, or the ultimate unit or the most appropriate unit, but only that it be appropriate to ensure the employees in each case the fullest freedom in exercising the rights guaranteed by the Act. Morand Bros. Beverage Co., 91 NLRB 409, 26 LRRM 1501 (1950). *See* Chapter 11 *infra*.

General Hospital,[96] the Board held that the parties' recognition agreement covering "medical records employees" was not intended to establish a separate unit of those employees, which would have been inappropriate; rather, it found that the parties had merely intended the recognition agreement to add those employees to an existing unit. The resultant unit was considered "sufficiently appropriate" to render the recognition agreement a bar, since the Board permits parties "the broadest permissible latitude to mutually define the context in which collective bargaining should take place."[97]

B. Pendency of Unfair Labor Practice Charges

Generally, unless the charging party requests the Board to proceed, the Board will decline to direct an election while unfair labor practice charges which affect the unit involved in the representation proceeding are pending. The rationale is that the charges, if true, would destroy the "laboratory conditions"[98] necessary to permit employees to cast their ballots freely and without restraint or coercion. It is well established, however, that this practice is not governed by statute, apart from the exceptional expedited election under Section 8(b)(7)(C), or by rules or regulations; rather, it lies within the Board's discretion as part of its responsibility to decide whether an election will effectuate the policies of the Act.[99] This *blocking charge* rule has been held not to violate due process[100] and not to constitute an abuse of discretion by the Board.[101]

The blocking charge rule may be applied even where the charging party requests the Board to proceed, if the issues raised in the charge require resolution within the context of an unfair labor practice proceeding before the holding of an election can be deemed appropriate.[102] Normally, however, when a *request to*

---

[96]223 NLRB 110, 91 LRRM 1433 (1976).

[97]*Id.* at 112.

[98]*See generally* Chapter 9 *supra.*

[99]American Metal Prods. Co., 139 NLRB 601, 51 LRRM 1338 (1962). NLRB Field Manual 11730 sets forth the "Blocking Charge Rule" in detail.

[100]Hausley v. NLRB, 81 LRRM 2254 (ED Tenn, 1972).

[101]Gem Int'l, Inc. v. Hendrix, 80 LRRM 3302 (WD Mo, 1972). *But see* Chapter 34 *infra* at notes 153-57. The "blocking charge" practice has not been without judicial criticism. *See, e.g.,* NLRB v. Minute Maid Corp., 283 F2d 705, 47 LRRM 2072 (CA 5, 1960); NLRB v. Gebhard-Vogel Tanning Co., 389 F2d 71, 67 LRRM 2364 (CA 7, 1968).

[102]E. & R. Webb, Inc., 194 NLRB 1135, 79 LRRM 1163 (1972). The election would have been barred by the agreement between the employer and incumbent union unless the employer's recognition of the incumbent was itself unlawful and violative of §§8(a)(2)

proceed is filed the pendency of an unfair labor practice charge will not block an election. In *NLRB* v. *Tri-City Linen Supply,*[103] the Ninth Circuit held that the Board did not abuse its discretion by scheduling an election during the pendency of unfair labor practice charges against the employer where a request to proceed had been filed by the union; the court also held that the investigation of the charges by a Board agent the day before the election did not adversely affect the voters or the Board's laboratory conditions.[104]

Various exceptions have developed as a result of the Board's common practice of directing elections forthwith as a means of effectuating the policies of the Act. Factors on which the Board has relied to proceed with a representation case, despite the pendency of unfair labor practice charges, include the following: (1) the length of the time the proceeding has been pending, (2) the fact that employees in the unit have been without an election during that period, (3) the dismissal of earlier charges that were grounded upon the same basic pattern of conduct as the pending charges, (4) "eleventh hour" filing of the charges, (5) the existence of a strike, or (6) a past practice by the charging party of using the filing of charges as a tactic to delay representation proceedings.[105]

The Board has also directed an immediate election on a union's petition notwithstanding the employer's pending Section 8(e) charge against the union.[106] The charge was based on an allegedly unlawful hot-cargo contract between the union and an employer association. The Board noted that in contrast to Section 8(a) and (b) cases, a Section 8(e) charge, even if true, deals only with the terms of an agreement between an employer and a labor organization, and that such an agreement would not necessarily restrain or coerce employees or in any other way prevent the holding of a fair election. In the absence of any

---

and 8(b)(1)(A) and (2) of the Act. The Board reasoned that to make such a determination in the representation case would be contrary to established Board policy that unfair labor practice allegations are not properly litigable in a representation proceeding.

[103]579 F2d 51, 98 LRRM 2155 (CA 9, 1978), *enforcing* 226 NLRB 669, 93 LRRM 1431 (1976).

[104]*See also* Bishop v. NLRB, 502 F2d 1024, 87 LRRM 2524 (CA 5, 1974).

[105]NLRB v. Lawrence Typographical Union (Kansas Color Press), 375 F2d 643, 65 LRRM 2176 (CA 10, 1967); Kingsport Press, 146 NLRB 260, 1111, 56 LRRM 1006, 1007 (1964); Surprenant Mfg. Co., 144 NLRB 507, 54 LRRM 1097 (1963); West-Gate Sun Harbor Co., 93 NLRB 830, 27 LRRM 1474 (1951); Columbia Pictures Corp., 81 NLRB 1313, 23 LRRM 1504 (1949); Bercut Richards Packing Co., 70 NLRB 84, 18 LRRM 1336 (1946).

[106]Holt Bros., 146 NLRB 383, 55 LRRM 1310 (1964). *See* note 146 *infra.*

allegation that the union sought to influence the employees' choice of a bargaining representative, the Board will proceed with the election.

The Board has also directed an immediate election, despite pending charges, in order to hold the election within 12 months of the beginning of an economic strike so as not to disenfranchise economic strikers.[107]

C. Unlawful Employer Assistance

Even though no charge is pending, an election petition may be dismissed because of employer domination of, or assistance to, the petitioning union. As noted above, whether the requisite showing of interest has been made is ordinarily an issue for administrative determination rather than for resolution in an adversary proceeding. However, when it can be shown that authorization cards have been obtained with the help of supervisors, allegations to that effect, accompanied by supporting evidence, will be heard on collateral request to the regional director. If it is thereafter administratively determined that the cards are tainted by reason of supervisory participation, the showing of interest may be found to be impaired and the petition will be dismissed.[108] The dismissal of a petition on these grounds does not affect subsequent proceedings on a new petition, provided a new showing of interest is obtained without the assistance of supervisors.[109]

D. Fluctuating Work Force

A petition for an election among a fluctuating work force will be dismissed, without prejudice to the filing of a petition at a more appropriate time, if it appears that a representative employment complement has not yet been established or if other

---

[107]§9(c)(3) of the Act provides: Employees "engaged in an economic strike who are not entitled to reinstatment shall be eligible to vote . . . in any election conducted within twelve months after the commencement of the strike." *See* American Metal Prods. Co., 139 NLRB 601, 51 LRRM 1338 (1962). *See* notes 99-100 and accompanying text in Chapter 21 *infra*.

[108]Union Mfg. Co., 123 NLRB 1633, 44 LRRM 1188 (1959); Georgia Craft Co., 120 NLRB 806, 42 LRRM 1066 (1958). *See also* Southeastern Newspapers, Inc., 129 NLRB 311, 46 LRRM 1541 (1960); Modern Hard Chrome Serv. Co., 124 NLRB 1235, 44 LRRM 1624 (1959); Desilu Productions, Inc., 106 NLRB 179, 32 LRRM 1418 (1953); American Dist. Tel. Co., 89 NLRB 1635, 26 LRRM 1135 (1950); Alaska Salmon Indus., 78 NLRB 185, 22 LRRM 1190 (1948). *See* Chapter 8 *supra* for general treatment of employer assistance to labor organizations.

[109]Toledo Stamping & Mfg. Co., 56 NLRB 1291, 14 LRRM 192 (1944).

substantial corporate changes are occurring.[110] However, the Board will not dismiss a petition, despite the employer's anticipated expansion, if the present number of employees represents a substantial percentage of the anticipated employee complement and if they are performing nearly all of the projected job classifications. A substantial and representative segment of the ultimate projected complement of employees has been held sufficient to order an election.[111] Moreover, mere speculation[112] as to the uncertainty of future operations will not render a petition untimely.[113] A posthearing motion to reopen the record in a representation case was held appropriate, however, where an employer indicated that it had decided to make substantial corporate changes, which involved moving unit employees from their existing location, thus affecting the appropriateness of the unit.[114]

In seasonal industries, the Board usually directs that the election be held at or about the approximate seasonal peak. If the peak has already passed, the Board will generally fix the election date at or about the next seasonal peak.[115]

---

[110]K-P Hydraulics Co., 219 NLRB 138, 89 LRRM 1601 (1975); Some Indus., Inc., 204 NLRB 1142, 83 LRRM 1481 (1973); Noranda Aluminum, Inc., 186 NLRB 217, 75 LRRM 1328 (1970); Cramet, Inc., 112 NLRB 975, 36 LRRM 1138 (1955).

[111]Y & S Candies, Inc., 233 NLRB 1311, 97 LRRM 1035 (1977); Cincinnati S.I. Co., 225 NLRB 1196, 93 LRRM 1197 (1976); Hearth Craft, Inc., 222 NLRB 1304, 91 LRRM 1387 (1976); World Southern Corp., 215 NLRB 287, 87 LRRM 1633 (1974); Some Indus., Inc., supra note 110; Bell Aerospace Co., 190 NLRB 509, 77 LRRM 1278 (1971).

[112]Canterbury of Puerto Rico, Inc., 225 NLRB 309, 92 LRRM 1486 (1976); Meramec Mining Co., 134 NLRB 1675, 49 LRRM 1386 (1961); Douglas Motors Corp., 128 NLRB 307, 46 LRRM 1292 (1960); Gordon B. Irvine, 124 NLRB 217, 44 LRRM 1336 (1959); General Eng'r, 123 NLRB 586, 43 LRRM 1486 (1959); General Elec. Co., 106 NLRB 364, 32 LRRM 1465 (1953).

[113]Bekaert Steel Wire Corp., 189 NLRB 561, 76 LRRM 1698 (1971); in Gerlach Meat Co., 192 NLRB 559, 77 LRRM 1832 (1971), the employer's work force at the time of the hearing consisted of 35% of the employee complement working in 50% of the job classifications projected for the nine months following the hearing. The regional director was found to have erroneously applied a projection for a date almost two years subsequent to the hearing. The Board applied the earlier projection date and directed an election. See also Witteman Steel Mills, Inc., 253 NLRB 320, 105 LRRM 1561 (1980).

[114]Risdon Mfg. Co., 195 NLRB 579, 79 LRRM 1442 (1972). But see NLRB v. Caravelle Wood Prods., Inc., 466 F2d 675, 80 LRRM 3411 (CA 7, 1972), where, in a refusal-to-bargain case decided almost three years after an election, the Seventh Circuit rejected the employer's assertion that a new election should be held because of substantial employee turnover and the passage of time since the original election. The court distinguished an earlier holding by the Sixth Circuit in Clark's Gamble Corp. v. NLRB, 422 F2d 845, 73 LRRM 2669 (CA 6), cert. denied, 400 US 868, 75 LRRM 2416 (CA 6, 1970), on the ground that the delay of five years in the latter case from the date of the original election was occasioned primarily by Board inaction.

[115]Cleveland Cliffs Iron Co., 117 NLRB 668, 39 LRRM 1319 (1957); Bordo Prods. Co., 117 NLRB 313, 39 LRRM 1220 (1957); Dick Kelchner Excavating Co., 236 NLRB 1414, 98 LRRM 1442 (1978).

No election will be conducted where an employer ceases its operations and the employees have no reasonable expectation of employment in the near future. In *Tracinda Investment Corp.*[116] the Board dismissed a petition for a unit of stagehands where the employer had closed the stage show at a resort facility for economic reasons. The Board held, however, that should the employer open a new show in the near future, the regional director would be authorized to reinstate the petition without prejudice.

E. Contract-Bar Doctrine

In an effort to stabilize the employer-union relationship, the Board has established the *contract bar* doctrine whereby a current and valid contract will ordinarily prevent the holding of an election for a certain period of time.[117] Although now recognized by implication in Section 8(b)(7), the doctrine is discretionary, and not statutorily mandated. The formulation, application, and modification of the Board's contract-bar rules are considered committed to the Board's judgment and not subject to ordinary judicial review.[118]

1. Requisites of the Contract. In order to bar an otherwise timely petition, a contract must be reduced to writing and executed by both parties.[119] It must also be clearly identifiable as a controlling document[120] and must contain substantial terms and

---

[116]235 NLRB 1167, 98 LRRM 1089 (1978). *But see* Allegheny Pepsi-Cola Bottling Co., 222 NLRB 1298, 91 LRRM 1369 (1976).

[117]The doctrine applies only to employees covered by the terms of the agreement. Millbrook, Inc., 204 NLRB 1148, 83 LRRM 1482 (1973).

[118]Local 1545, Carpenters v. Vincent, 286 F2d 127, 47 LRRM 2304 (CA 2, 1960). *But see* NLRB v. Wyman-Gordon Co., 394 US 759, 70 LRRM 3345 (1969); Leedom v. Electrical Workers (IBEW) Local 108, 278 F2d 237, 45 LRRM 3005 (CA DC, 1960). *See* Chapter 34.

[119]The agreement need not be formally executed to constitute a bar. In Georgia Purchasing, Inc., 230 NLRB 1174, 95 LRRM 1469 (1977), the Board held that the exchange of telegrams between an employer and a union precluded a petition for a decertification election—the union telegram, when read in conjunction with the prior agreement which it incorporated by reference, charted "with adequate precision a continuing contractual relationship between the parties." 230 NLRB at 1175. The Board similarly ruled in Diversified Services, Inc., 225 NLRB 1092, 93 LRRM 1068 (1976), that an employer's signed cover letter accompanying an unsigned proposal, coupled with the union's execution of the proposal prior to the filing of the petition, created a contract bar. In Gaylord Broadcasting, 250 NLRB 198, 104 LRRM 1361 (1980), a Board majority (Member Penello dissenting) held that the parties' initials constituted sufficient signatures for contract-bar purposes. *See also* Bendix Corp., 210 NLRB 1026, 86 LRRM 1547 (1974) (informal letter of agreement signed by parties on date that petition was filed). *Cf.* Lane Constr. Corp., 222 NLRB 1224, 91 LRRM 1337 (1976).

[120]In Delta Co., 202 NLRB 921, 82 LRRM 1725 (1973), the Board was confronted with two substantially identical collective bargaining agreements between the same parties. One contained an automatic renewal clause, whereas the other did not. An

conditions of employment.[121] Ratification by the union membership is not a necessity for upholding a contract as a bar unless the contract itself requires ratification.[122] Ordinarily, the question of whether an agreement constitutes a bar is determined in a representation proceeding based on the face of the document and not upon extrinsic evidence.[123] However, in implementing its discretionary contract-bar rules the Board has developed an exception to this general principle: A bar will not be found where it appears that the alleged contract is not "one imparting sufficient stability to the bargaining relationship to justify . . . withholding a present determination of representation."[124]

2. Duration of the Contract. A contract must also have a definite duration if it is to serve as a bar to an election;[125] it will then preclude petitions by either the employer or a certified incumbent union for the entire term of the agreement.[126] Petitions by rival unions, however, are barred only for a reasonable

---

outside union filed a petition which would have been timely if the disputed renewal clause was invalid. The incumbent union relied upon the contract containing the renewal clause, while the employer argued for the contract which lacked the renewal clause. Unable to determine which contract was controlling, the Board decided there was no contract bar.

[121]*See* J. P. Sand & Gravel Co., 222 NLRB 83, 91 LRRM 1187 (1976), in which the Board declared that a contract provided neither the employees nor the employer with "guidance in governing their day-to-day relations" and did not impart "sufficient stability to the bargaining relationship" to justify a bar.

[122]Appalachian Shale Prods. Co., 121 NLRB 1160, 42 LRRM 1506 (1958) (overruling numerous earlier cases and eliminating exceptions). In Merico, Inc., 207 NLRB 101, 84 LRRM 1395 (1973), the agreement stated that "the Union Committee is unanimous for acceptance and each member is hereby pledged to recommend this agreement for ratification by the membership." The Board held that such language required ratification as a condition precedent to the agreement's validity, and accordingly did not find a contract bar.

The Board has also ruled that where a number of locals of an incumbent union negotiate a master contract which is "subject to ratification by the Local Unions," the agreement may operate as a bar if a majority of locals vote in favor of it prior to filing of a petition. Swift & Co., 213 NLRB 49, 87 LRRM 1041 (1974).

[123]Jet Pak Corp., 231 NLRB 552, 96 LRRM 112 (1977); Loree Footwear Corp., 197 NLRB 360, 80 LRRM 1339 (1972); Pine Transp., Inc., 197 NLRB 256, 80 LRRM 1334 (1972); Paragon Prods. Corp., 134 NLRB 662, 49 LRRM 1160 (1961). *But see infra* note 132 and accompanying text.

[124]Frank Hager, Inc., 230 NLRB 476, 96 LRRM 1117 (1977); Raymonds, Inc., 161 NLRB 838, 63 LRRM 1363 (1966). In order to bar a petition, a contract must embrace an appropriate unit. Appalachian Shale Prods. Co., *supra* note 122; Moveable Partitions, Inc., 175 NLRB 915, 71 LRRM 1095 (1969). *Cf.* Stur-Dee Health Prods., 248 NLRB 1100, 104 LRRM 1012 (1980), where the Board held that an agreement providing for interest arbitration is sufficiently complete, even prior to the arbitration award, on the ground that "the agreement . . . contains substantial terms and conditions of employment as well as a definite and readily ascertainable method for determining economic terms." *Id.* at 1101.

[125]Cind-R-Lite Co., 239 NLRB 1255, 100 LRRM 1138 (1979); Kroger Co., 173 NLRB 397, 69 LRRM 1333 (1968); Pacific Coast Ass'n of Pulp & Paper Mfrs., 121 NLRB 990, 42 LRRM 1477 (1958).

[126]Absorbent Cotton Co., 137 NLRB 908, 50 LRRM 1258 (1962); Montgomery Ward & Co., 137 NLRB 346, 50 LRRM 1137 (1962).

part of the term of an agreement if the agreement is of unreasonably long duration. An uncertified incumbent union may file a petition during the term of an agreement where it seeks the benefits of certification—the *General Box* doctrine.[127]

At one time, the Board applied the "substantial part of the industry" test as a measure of the reasonable period during which a contract would bar a rival union petition. This test was abandoned in the 1958 *Pacific Coast* case as "administratively burdensome,"[128] and two years was determined to be a reasonable period applicable to all industries. Then in 1962, in *General Cable Corp.*,[129] the Board discarded that rule in favor of a uniform three-year rule which is still in effect. Thus, the current rule is that contracts of a definite duration for terms up to three years bar election petitions for the entire period, and contracts for longer fixed terms operate as a bar to rival petitions for the first three years.

If, during the term of a contract, the parties agree to an amendment, or execute a new contract which contains a terminal date later than that of the existing contract, the amendment or new contract will be considered "premature"; a prematurely extended contract will not bar an election if the petition is otherwise timely.[130] This *premature extension* doctrine does not apply (1) to contracts executed during the insulated period preceding the terminal date (or first three years) of the old contract, (2) after the terminal date (or first three years) of the old contract, or (3) at a time when the existing contract would not have barred an election because of other contract-bar rules.[131]

The duration dates recited on the face of a contract are not always determinative, for the Board will look behind "inartful drafting" to establish actual contract duration in the light of bargaining history.[132]

---

[127]General Box Co., 82 NLRB 678, 23 LRRM 1589 (1949).

[128]Pacific Coast Ass'n of Pulp & Paper Mfrs., *supra* note 125 at 992. The Board's position had evolved after experience with a variety of tests. Originally, a one-year contract was thought to be reasonable in conjunction with the test of "custom in the industry." Presumptions of reasonableness would vary in accordance with industry custom. That rule, with its many problems of proof, was difficult to administer. For a discussion of this earlier development and application, *see* Cushman's Sons, Inc., 88 NLRB 121, 25 LRRM 1296 (1950); Puritan Ice Co., 74 NLRB 1311, 20 LRRM 1268 (1947); Reed Roller Bit Co., 72 NLRB 927, 19 LRRM 1227 (1947).

[129]139 NLRB 1123, 51 LRRM 1444 (1962).

[130]*See* discussion *infra* at notes 183-99 for rules concerning timeliness of petitions.

[131]Deluxe Metal Furniture Co., 121 NLRB 995, 42 LRRM 1470 (1958).

[132]Youngstown Osteopathic Hosp. Ass'n, 216 NLRB 766, 88 LRRM 1591 (1975). However, parties to a contract may be estopped from asserting that the effective dates

3. Unlawful Clauses. On several occasions the Board has modified its contract-bar rules with respect to checkoff, union security, and other key contract provisions. As with many other issues concerning contract-bar application, it has attempted to strike a balance between the interests of industrial stability and the right of employees to select bargaining representatives. The fluctuation of the balance in these priorities is manifested in the effect given certain contractual provisions.[133]

a. *Union Security.* In the 1958 *Keystone* case,[134] the Board ruled that contracts containing union security and checkoff provisions would not bar elections unless on their face they conformed to the express terms of the Act. The effect of this rule of interpretation in *Keystone* was to "require a presumption of illegality"[135] with respect to any contract containing a union security clause that did not expressly reflect the precise language of the statute. In 1961, in the *News Syndicate* case,[136] the Supreme Court cast serious doubt upon the exercise of administrative discretion based on the attachment of presumptions of illegality to provisions in collective bargaining agreements. Accordingly, in *Paragon Products Corp.*,[137] the Board, adverting to the "unsettling" of bargaining relationships engendered by the *Keystone* rules, reformulated its position as follows:

> [O]nly those contracts containing a union-security provision which is clearly unlawful on its face, or which has been found to be unlawful in an unfair labor practice proceeding, may not bar a representation petition. A clearly unlawful union-security provision for this purpose is one which by its express terms clearly and unequivocally goes beyond the limited form of union-security permitted by Section 8(a)(3) of the Act, and is therefore incapable of a lawful interpretation.[138]

As examples, unlawful provisions under this rule would include: a clause by which the employer agrees to give union members preference in hiring, layoff, or other terms of employment; a clause specifically denying new employees, or incumbent non-

---

of the agreement are other than as shown on the cover of printed copies if a petitioning union is thereby precluded from making a clear determination as to the proper time for filing its petition. Bob's Big Boy Family Restaurants, 235 NLRB 1227, 98 LRRM 1114 (1978).

[133]*See generally* Chapter 29 *infra* for treatment of checkoff and union security agreements.

[134]Keystone Coat, Apron & Towel Supply Co., 121 NLRB 880, 42 LRRM 1456 (1958).

[135]Paragon Prods. Corp., *supra* note 123 at 664.

[136]NLRB v. News Syndicate Co., 365 US 695, 47 LRRM 2916 (1961).

[137]134 NLRB 662, 49 LRRM 1160 (1961).

[138]134 NLRB at 666.

union employees, the statutory 30-day grace period; or a clause requiring the payment to the union of money other than "periodic dues and initiation fees uniformly required."[139]

In further clarification, the Board held that absent express contractual saving features, the "mere existence of a clearly unlawful union security provision in a contract will render it no bar"[140] regardless of whether it was intended to be enforced. However, two means of curing the defect were recognized: (1) inclusion of an express contractual provision clearly deferring the effectiveness of the unlawful clause or (2) elimination of the unlawful clause by properly executed rescission or amendment.[141] The Supreme Court accorded these so-called "deferral clauses" this saving virtue in two 1961 cases.[142]

b. *Checkoff.* The Board has similarly relaxed the rule governing checkoff clauses, since *Keystone* was applicable to such clauses in the same manner as to other union security provisions.[143] Currently, a checkoff clause does not affect the standing of a contract as a bar to an election unless it is unlawful on its face, or has been held unlawful in an unfair labor practice proceeding or in a court proceeding brought by the Attorney General.[144]

c. *Racial Discrimination.* A contract which discriminates between groups of employees by reason of race will not operate as a bar to an election.[145] Such discrimination is inherent in agreements that sanction groupings of employees along racial lines, and the Board has concluded that to permit its rules to be used to shield such contracts from election petitions would in effect extend governmental sanction to such discrimination.

d. *"Hot Cargo."* Although a clause may violate Section 8(e), the Board distinguishes between "hot-cargo" and unlawful union

---

[139]§8(a)(3)(B).

[140]134 NLRB at 667. For applications of the *Paragon Products* principle, *see* Sentry Investigation Corp., 198 NLRB 1074, 81 LRRM 1046 (1972); Liquid Transport, Inc., No. 7-RC-10741, 78 LRRM 1248 (1971) (not reported in Board volumes).

[141]134 NLRB at 667. For a specific application, *see* American Broadcasting Co., 134 NLRB 1458, 49 LRRM 1365 (1961); Columbia Broadcasting Sys., 134 NLRB 1466, 49 LRRM 1366 (1961).

[142]NLRB v. News Syndicate Co., 365 US 695, 47 LRRM 2916 (1961); International Typographical Union (Haverhill Gazette) v. NLRB, 365 US 705, 47 LRRM 2920 (1961).

[143]The first modification was a response to certain Department of Justice interpretations. William Wolf Bakery, Inc., 122 NLRB 630, 43 LRRM 1447 (1958). Further relaxation came in Boston Gas Co., 129 NLRB 369, 46 LRRM 1546 (1960), and 130 NLRB 1230, 47 LRRM 1429 (1961).

[144]Gary Steel Supply Co., 144 NLRB 470, 54 LRRM 1082 (1963).

[145]Pioneer Bus Co., 140 NLRB 54, 51 LRRM 1546 (1962). *See* Chapter 28 *infra* at note 138.

security provisions, holding that the hot-cargo clause does not act as a restraint upon the employees' choice of a bargaining representative. Therefore, the presence of a clause that violates Section 8(e) does not remove the contract as a bar.[146]

4. Expanding Units. Current case law concerning expanding employee complements draws its essence from the rules which the Board promulgated in its *General Extrusion*[147] opinion. The contract-bar doctrine formulated in that case establishes guidelines for determining whether an election should be directed in an expanding unit in the face of a valid contract. Decided in 1958 along with many of the landmark contract-bar cases,[148] *General Extrusion* laid down a series of rules relating to prehire agreements, relocation and consolidation, and good-faith purchasers.

a. Prehire Agreements. A contract executed before any employees have been hired, or prior to a "substantial increase" in personnel, does not bar an election. When a question of a substantial increase in personnel exists, an agreement will bar an election only if (1) "at least 30 percent of the complement employed at the time of the hearing had been employed at the time the contract was executed"[149] *and*[150] (2) "50 percent of the job classifications in existence at the time of the hearing were in existence at the time the contract was executed."[151]

---

[146]Food Haulers, Inc., 136 NLRB 394, 49 LRRM 1774 (1962), *overruling* Calorator Mfg. Corp., 129 NLRB 704, 47 LRRM 1109 (1960); American Feed Co., 129 NLRB 321, 46 LRRM 1541 (1960); Pilgrim Furniture Co., 128 NLRB 910, 46 LRRM 1427 (1960). The same policy obtains when the §8(e) question takes the form of a blocking charge of unfair labor practice. Holt Bros., *supra* note 106. For general treatment of "hot cargo" clauses, *see* Chapter 26 *infra*.

[147]121 NLRB 1165, 42 LRRM 1508 (1958).

[148]*See* Deluxe Metal Furniture Co., 121 NLRB 995, 42 LRRM 1470 (1958); Appalachian Shale Prods. Co., *supra* note 122; Hershey Chocolate Corp., 121 NLRB 901, 42 LRRM 1460 (1958); Keystone Coat, Apron & Towel Supply Co., *supra* note 134; Pacific Coast Ass'n of Pulp & Paper Mfrs., *supra* note 125.

[149]General Extrusion Co., *supra* note 147 at 1167. But the actual date of signing may not in all instances be determinative. *See* H. L. Klion, 148 NLRB 656, 660, 57 LRRM 1073 (1964).

[150]Although the conjunctive "and" is used in General Extrusion Co., *supra* note 147, it was reemphasized in West Penn Hat & Cap Corp., 165 NLRB 543, 543 n.1, 65 LRRM 1417 (1967). *See also* United Serv. Co., 227 NLRB 1469, 94 LRRM 1250 (1977).

[151]121 NLRB at 1167. A contract executed with a minority union pursuant to §8(f), although a legal contract, cannot function as a bar to a representation petition. However, if the union attained majority status prior to the execution of the agreement, the ordinary rules of contract bar will apply. Mishara Constr. Co., 171 NLRB 471, 68 LRRM 1120 (1968); Island Constr. Co., 135 NLRB 13, 49 LRRM 1417 (1962). *See* Chapter 13 *infra* at notes 644-64 and Chapter 29 *infra* at notes 143-62.

When a successor relationship is found, the objectionable "prehire" nature of the contract may be removed. Unlike an employer in a prehire situation, who is under an obligation *not* to bargain until a representative complement of employees has been hired, a successor employer is under an immediate and continuing obligation to bargain. In the successor situation, the employees have already selected a bargaining representative, whereas in a prehire situation they have not.[152]

   b. *Relocation and Consolidation.* In *General Extrusion* the Board distinguished between a "relocation of operations" and a "consolidation of two or more operations."[153] It stated that a contract would not be a bar if changes had occurred in the "*nature* as distinguished from the *size* of the operations between the execution of the contract and the filing of the petition, involving (1) a merger of two or more operations resulting in the creation of an entirely new operation with major personnel changes,"[154] *or* "(2) resumption of operations at either the same or a new

---

[152]General Elec. Co., 173 NLRB 511, 69 LRRM 1395 (1968); Western Freight Ass'n, 172 NLRB 303, 68 LRRM 1364 (1958). In Davenport Insulation, Inc., 184 NLRB 908, 74 LRRM 1726 (1970), the Board distinguished Ranch-Way, Inc., 183 NLRB 1168, 74 LRRM 1389 (1970), and reaffirmed that a successor employer was not obligated to bargain with a union that had executed a prehire §8(f) agreement with its predecessor, or to honor that agreement, in the absence of independent proof of the union's majority status. *See* Chapter 13 *infra* at notes 675-708 and Chapter 15 *infra* at notes 48-51 and 76-191.
[153]Kroger Co., 155 NLRB 546, 548, 60 LRRM 1351 (1965). The Board in *General Extrusion* did not actually use the term "consolidation," but in *Kroger* the distinction was so characterized.
[154]121 NLRB at 1167 (emphasis added). In *Kroger,* the contract bar was not upheld because of a merger of two or more operations. Plants A and B were closed and their operations transferred to plant C. Of the 69 employees at C, 42 were from A and 27 from B. The Board held that this created an entirely new operation with major personnel changes on the ground that plant C could not be regarded simply as a relocation of B to the exclusion of A. *Accord,* General Elec. Co., 170 NLRB 1272, 67 LRRM 1561 (1968), where facilities A and B merged into C and the Board found C to be an "amalgam of the two separate facilities" rather than a "relocation." Determinative factors were (1) the uncertainty of the proportion of employees transferring, (2) consolidation of different product lines, and (3) changes in supervisory personnel. *See also* Mego Corp., 223 NLRB 279, 92 LRRM 1080 (1976). *Contra,* Arrow Co., 147 NLRB 829, 56 LRRM 1303 (1964), where the Board found a "relocation" and upheld the bar where plants A and B closed and operations were transferred to C. Of 78 employees at C, 45 were from A and 5 tentatively from B. The basis of the holding was that "when the relocation . . . is complete," a "considerable portion" of the employees at A and B "will have been transferred" to C. On this basis, the decision is difficult to square with *General Extrusion* on timeliness and with *Kroger* and *General Electric* on the conclusion reached. Also puzzling was the Board's use of the term "consolidation" along with "relocation." The other ground for decision was that intervenor at C was the incumbent at both A and B. *See also* Bowman Dairy Co., 123 NLRB 707, 43 LRRM 1519 (1959), where a contract bar was upheld. *Bowman* was distinguished in *Kroger* on the ground that it simply involved plant A merging into an existing plant B, without there being a newly constructed plant C, as in *Kroger.*

location, after an indefinite period of closing, with new employees."[155]

The Board distinguishes these patterns from a "mere relocation" involving a considerable transfer of employees to another
plant without a change in the character of the jobs and the
functions of the employees. In the latter situation, the contract
will not be removed as a bar.

Following a merger of two or more corporate entities covered
by separate contracts with different unions, a resulting integration of operations may be found to be a new operation. In these
circumstances the existing bargaining agreements may be deemed
abrogated, and previously existing separate bargaining units
may no longer be considered appropriate.[156]

On the other hand, if, after merger, the previously independent companies continue as separate operating divisions of the
newly created corporate entity (absent evidence of substantial
integration and the factors of common operation discussed above),
the preexisting bargaining units, together with their collective
bargaining relationships, will remain in existence.[157]

   c. *Purchasers.* Under another *General Extrusion* rule, assumption of an operation by a good-faith purchaser who had not
bound itself to assume the contract of a predecessor would
remove the contract as a bar. This was a reaffirmance of an
earlier rule.[158] The Board later held that, absent unusual circumstances, a successor employer was bound as a matter of law
by the contract of the predecessor,[159] but the Supreme Court

---

[155]121 NLRB at 1167. For this precise fact situation, *see* Slater Sys. Md., Inc., 134
NLRB 865, 49 LRRM 1294 (1961). *See also* Sheets & Mackey, 92 NLRB 179, 27 LRRM
1087 (1950).
   [156]Massachusetts Elec. Co., 248 NLRB 155, 103 LRRM 1404 (1980); Hooker Electro-
chem. Co., 116 NLRB 1393, 38 LRRM 1482 (1965); Pacific Isle Mining Co., 118 NLRB
740, 40 LRRM 1253 (1957); Industrial Stamping & Mfg. Co., 111 NLRB 1038, 35
LRRM 1648 (1955); L. B. Spear & Co., 106 NLRB 687, 32 LRRM 1535 (1953); Greyhound Garage, Inc., 95 NLRB 902, 28 LRRM 1388 (1951). *See also* Hudson Berlind
Corp., 203 NLRB 421, 83 LRRM 1090 (1973), *enforced,* 494 F2d 1200, 86 LRRM 2008
(CA 2, 1974); General Elec. Co., 170 NLRB 1272, 67 LRRM 1561 (1968) (where this
issue was raised in an accretion text); National Carloading Corp., 167 NLRB 801, 66
LRRM 1166 (1967); Panda Terminals, Inc., 161 NLRB 1215, 63 LRRM 1419 (1966).
   [157]United Illuminating Co., No. 1-RC-6586 (1962) (not reported in Board volumes);
Consolidated Edison Co., 132 NLRB 1518, 48 LRRM 1539 (1961), *supplemented,* 134
NLRB 1137, 49 LRRM 1341 (1961); Illinois Malleable Iron Co., 120 NLRB 451, 41
LRRM 1510 (1958).
   [158]*Supra* note 147; Jolly Giant Lumber Co., 114 NLRB 413, 36 LRRM 1585 (1955).
   [159]Burns Int'l Sec. Serv., Inc., 182 NLRB 348, 74 LRRM 1098 (1970), *enforced in part,*
441 F2d 911, 77 LRRM 2081 (CA 2, 1971), *aff'd,* 406 US 272, 80 LRRM 2225 (1972).

rejected that concept, declaring that a successor does not automatically assume the predecessor's contract.[160] Thus, the *General Extrusion* rule continues to apply to a purchase situation where the contract is not assumed.

5. Accretions. An employer's acquisition or construction of an additional operation or facility after the execution of the contract frequently gives rise to a claim of accretion. One or both of the contracting parties may seek to have the additional facility "accreted." If the additional facility is found to be an accretion to the existing operation, the preexisting contract may be extended to cover employees in the new operation and thus bar an election there. The question of accretion can arise in myriad factual and procedural contexts,[161] but in most instances the Board utilizes established guidelines in making its determination.

The guidelines encompass the presence or absence of a variety of factors such as: (1) the degree of interchange among employees,[162] (2) geographical proximity,[163] (3) integration of operations, (4) integration of machinery and product lines,[164] (5) centralized administrative control,[165] (6) similarity of working conditions, skills, and functions,[166] (7) common control over labor relations,[167] (8) collective bargaining history, and (9) the

---

[160]*Id. Accord,* Howard Johnson Co. v. Detroit Executive Bd., Hotel & Restaurant Employees, 417 US 249, 86 LRRM 2449 (1974). *See* Chapter 15 *infra* at notes 61-70.

[161]Procedurally, accretion may become an issue in a number of situations in addition to the "contract bar" context in representation proceedings: (1) unit-clarification proceedings, *infra;* (2) as part of a defense to an unfair labor practice charge, Masters-Lake Success, Inc., 124 NLRB 580, 44 LRRM 1437 (1959), *enforced as modified,* 287 F2d 35, 47 LRRM 2607 (CA 2, 1967). *See also* Great Atl. & Pac. Tea Co. (Local 1407, Retail Clerks), 140 NLRB 1011, 52 LRRM 1155 (1963) (containing an exhaustive discussion of the accretion doctrine by the trial examiner). Factually, accretion can involve a prototype situation such as the opening of a new store by a retail chain, Sunset House, 167 NLRB 870, 66 LRRM 1243 (1967), *enforced,* 415 F2d 545, 72 LRRM 2283 (CA 9, 1969); or a subdivision of store units, Parkview Drugs, Inc., 138 NLRB 194, 50 LRRM 1564 (1962); or categories of employees, Horn & Hardart Co., 173 NLRB 1077, 69 LRRM 1522 (1968). It can also involve extremely complex fact situations where two unions are each seeking to accrete the facility at which the other has a contract. Panda Terminals, Inc., *supra* note 156.

[162]Dura Corp., 153 NLRB 592, 59 LRRM 1519 (1965), *enforced,* 375 F2d 707, 64 LRRM 2828 (CA 6, 1967); Buy Low Supermarket, Inc., 131 NLRB 23, 47 LRRM 1586 (1961).

[163]Sunset House, *supra* note 161; Meijer, Inc. v. NLRB, 564 F2d 737, 96 LRRM 2738 (CA 6, 1977), *enforcing* 222 NLRB 18, 91 LRRM 1153 (1976); Pay Less Drug Stores, 127 NLRB 160, 45 LRRM 1520 (1960).

[164]Beacon Photo Serv., Inc., 163 NLRB 706, 64 LRRM 1439 (1967).

[165]Masters-Lake Success, Inc., *supra* note 161.

[166]Public Serv. Co., 190 NLRB 350, 77 LRRM 1129 (1971).

[167]Buy Low Supermarket, Inc., *supra* note 162.

number of employees at the facility to be acquired as compared with the existing operation.[168] These factors determine the basic issue of whether the new[169] facility is sufficiently integrated into the existing operation to justify the application of the contract as a bar.[170] Applying these criteria, a new facility would likely be treated as an independent operation and not an accretion where (1) new employees are hired specifically for the new facility, (2) the facility is separately managed, (3) there is no interchange of employees between the new and previous operations, and (4) either the facilities are geographically distant or the operation of the new facility is autonomous despite close geographical proximity.[171]

A conflict occasionally arises where the contracting parties have negotiated an "accretion clause" that clearly covers any new operation the employer may subsequently own or operate. The Board is then confronted with the alternatives of (1) treating this issue as one of contract interpretation or (2) determining for itself, in accordance with its own guidelines, whether an accretion exists. Despite the holding of an arbitrator that a contract was intended to cover later-hired employees at new facilities, the Board has refused to find the contract a bar to a

---

[168]Panda Terminals, *supra* note 156. The Board refused to find an accretion where the new operation had four times as many employees as the old one. *See also* Renaissance Center Partnership, 239 NLRB No. 180, 100 LRRM 1121 (1979), in which a union was certified as the bargaining representative for security officers and guards employed by the employer for certain facilities. A few months later, the employer took on the responsibility of providing security for a hotel and consolidated its existing security force with that already serving the hotel. When the union sought to clarify the existing certified unit to include the hotel's security force, the employer contended that the consolidation affected the continuing representative status of the union and, therefore, an election was necessary to determine whether the hotel's security force desired union representation. The Board found that the hotel's security force was not an accretion to the certified bargaining unit and, in addition, that the certified unit was no longer appropriate. On this basis, it directed an election among all the employees in the consolidated security force. In reaching its decision, the Board relied heavily on the fact that the number of employees the union sought to add to the certified unit exceeded the number already within that unit. *See also,* United Hosps., 249 NLRB 562, 104 LRRM 1163 (1980), where the Board held that a hospital's unrepresented admitting-department employees and those of another facility with which it was in the process of merging did not constitute an accretion to a service and maintenance unit covered by a multi-employer contract, since these employees were traditionally excluded from the multi-employer unit that included such employees in only two of the association's 21 members.

[169]However, the Board's accretion guidelines may also apply to a consolidation of existing facilities. Public Serv. Co., *supra* note 166.

[170]*E.g.,* Bryan Infants Wear, 235 NLRB 1305, 98 LRRM 1140 (1978).

[171]Renaissance Center Partnership, *supra* note 168; W. C. Ducomb Co., 239 NLRB No. 134, 100 LRRM 1061 (1978); Pay Less Drug Stores, 127 NLRB 160, 45 LRRM 1520 (1960). *See also* Denver Publishing Co., 238 NLRB No. 33, 99 LRRM 1222 (1978); Illinois Bell Tel. Co., 222 NLRB 485, 91 LRRM 1274 (1976).

petition without its own independent determination that the new facilities represented an accretion to the contract unit.[172] The Board has also held that where the union seeking to apply an accretion clause in a collective agreement fails to present the employer with proof that it has acquired majority status at the new facility, the employer is not obligated to extend recognition.[173]

6. Schism, Defunctness, and Disclaimer. The Board has long held that a mere change in designation or affiliation of the contractual representative of the employees does not remove an otherwise valid and subsisting contract as a bar. However, the Board does disregard the contract when the contracting union has become defunct. It also holds the contract to be no longer a bar if a schism arises and destroys the identity of the contractual bargaining representative. The Board has been inconsistent with respect to whether disclaimer by a viable incumbent union removes a contract as a bar.[174]

a. Schism. Generally speaking, a schism occurs when a substantial number of the employees in the unit express dissatisfaction with their representation. The crosscurrent must be so compelling that (1) there is a basic intra-union conflict over fundamental policy questions and (2) employees take action which creates such confusion in the bargaining relationship that stability can be restored only by an election. To be described as a "schism" for this purpose, the conflict must pervade the local as well as the national or international level and be so disruptive as to warrant the conclusion that industrial stability would be served by affording the employees an opportunity to select a new bargaining representative. Thus far, however, the only kinds of policy splits which the Board has considered schismatic have involved issues relating to communism or corruption.[175]

---

[172]Pullman Indus., Inc., 159 NLRB 580, 62 LRRM 1273 (1966). *See also* W. C. Ducomb Co., *supra* note 171; Anheuser-Busch, Inc., 170 NLRB 46, 67 LRRM 1376 (1968); Beacon Photo Serv., *supra* note 164. *But compare* Horn & Hardart Co., *supra* note 161, *and* Westinghouse Elec. Corp., 162 NLRB 768, 64 LRRM 1082 (1967), *with* Raley's Inc., 143 NLRB 256, 53 LRRM 1347 (1963), involving interpretations of contracts regarding preexisting facilities or employee categories. Accommodation of Board action to the arbitration process is treated in detail in Chapter 20 *infra. See particularly* discussion of representation cases therein at notes 330-46.

[173]W. C. Ducomb Co., *supra* note 171. *But see* Public Serv. Co., *supra* note 166.

[174]Hershey Chocolate Corp., 121 NLRB 901, 42 LRRM 1460 (1958), and cases cited in notes 175-84 *infra. See generally* Chapter 14 *infra.*

[175]In addition to *Hershey,* Great Atl. & Pac. Tea Co., 120 NLRB 656, 42 LRRM 1022 (1958); Lawrence Leather Co., 108 NLRB 546, 34 LRRM 1022 (1954). *See also* Clayton

b. Defunctness. A contract by an employer with a union which has become defunct will not operate as a bar.[176] Generally, the Board holds a union to be defunct if it has ceased to exist as an effective labor organization and is no longer able or willing to fulfill its responsibilities in administering the contract. The Board looks to whether the union has been processing grievances, holding meetings of the members, collecting dues, and electing officers. The absence of anyone remaining in the union to discharge the representative's responsibilities would show that the union is defunct. However, procedural steps taken to disaffiliate and sever all connection with the national or international union ordinarily are not sufficient to establish defunctness.[177]

Moreover, the Board has recognized that unions may be tempted to use the claim of schism or defunctness as a means to circumvent the contract-bar doctrine. Accordingly, the Board considers the element of good faith regarding various measures which might seem to lead to such a result. Where it appeared that the real purpose of the measure was to rid the local members of what they consider to be an unfavorable contract, the Board has refused to apply the exceptions on the ground that holding the contract to be a bar would be more likely to effectuate the policies of the Act.[178] The Board has also rejected arguments that an "old" union was defunct, where it has found that the "new" union was in fact the "alter ego" or "successor" to the old union.[179]

& Lambert Mfg. Co., 128 NLRB 209, 46 LRRM 1275 (1960); Swift & Co., 145 NLRB 756, 55 LRRM 1033 (1963). *Cf.* American Seating Co., 106 NLRB 250, 32 LRRM 1439 (1953); Prudential Ins. Co., 106 NLRB 237, 32 LRRM 1448 (1953).

[176]Francis L. Bennett, 139 NLRB 1422, 51 LRRM 1518 (1962).

[177]Aircraft Turbine Serv., Inc., 173 NLRB 709, 69 LRRM 1406 (1968); Swift & Co., *supra* note 175. Polar Ware Co., 139 NLRB 1006, 51 LRRM 1462 (1962); Hebron Brick Co., 135 NLRB 245, 49 LRRM 1463 (1962); Pepsi-Cola Bottling Co., 132 NLRB 1441, 48 LRRM 1514 (1961); W. H. Nicholson & Co., 119 NLRB 1412, 41 LRRM 1319 (1958); A. O. Smith Corp., 107 NLRB 1415, 33 LRRM 1393 (1954).

[178]Schism: Allied Container Corp., 98 NLRB 580, 29 LRRM 1388 (1952); Saginaw Furniture Shops, Inc., 97 NLRB 1488, 29 LRRM 1281 (1952).

Defunctness: News-Press Publishing Co., 145 NLRB 803, 55 LRRM 1045 (1964); Hebron Brick Co., *supra* note 177.

[179]Charles Beck Mach. Corp., 107 NLRB 874, 33 LRRM 1248 (1954). *See also* Harbor Carriers v. NLRB, 306 F2d 89, 50 LRRM 2863 (CA 2, 1962), *cert. denied*, 372 US 917, 52 LRRM 2471 (1963); NLRB v. Weyerhaeuser Co., 276 F2d 865, 45 LRRM 3088 (CA 7, 1960); Carpinteria Lemon Ass'n v. NLRB, 240 F2d 554, 39 LRRM 2185 (CA 9, 1957), *enforcing* 112 NLRB 121, 35 LRRM 1724 (1955). *Cf.* Fluhrer Bakeries, 232 NLRB 212, 96 LRRM 1491 (1977); Visitainer Corp., 237 NLRB 257, 98 LRRM 1553 (1978); Arthur C. Harvey Co., 110 NLRB 338, 34 LRRM 1650 (1954). *But cf.* Cleveland Decals, Inc., 99 NLRB 745, 30 LRRM 1129 (1952).

c. Disclaimer. When a viable incumbent union disclaims its interest in continuing to represent the employees covered by a contract, the situation is different from a schism or defunctness, inasmuch as the incumbent union has experienced no internal change and is capable of administering the contract. The disclaimer might result from genuine employee rejection of the union, but it might also be a means to permit escape from an unfavorable contract by having another union replace the incumbent and attempt to negotiate a more favorable contract.[180] In either event, the stability of the bargaining relationship engendered by the existing contract is impaired. It has been difficult for the Board, in these disclaimer cases, to reconcile the competing interests of free employee choice of a representative and stability in the bargaining relationship. In the same year, it held in one case that a disclaimer does not remove a contract as a bar[181] but in another case held that it may have such an effect, absent evidence of collusion between the incumbent and intervening unions.[182]

7. Expiration of the Contract Bar: Timeliness. Most of the rules concerning the contract-bar doctrine come sharply into focus as the period of the contract bar approaches its expiration date.[183] At this juncture, three distinct procedural stages arise. In an attempt to reduce uncertainty, the Board has developed rules of timeliness as to each stage.[184]

---

[180]The new union is not bound by the existing contract. American Sunroof Corp., 243 NLRB 1128, 102 LRRM 1086 (1979); American Seating Co., 106 NLRB 250, 32 LRRM 1439 (1953).

[181]East Mfg. Corp., 242 NLRB 5, 101 LRRM 1079 (1979). The Board declared that "[t]o permit a viable contracting . . . representative . . . to disavow its lawful contractual commitments during the term of an enforceable contract, even if the disavowal stems from an awareness of employee dissatisfaction with that representative, impugns the integrity of the collective bargaining process and encourages circumvention of our contract-bar doctrine." 101 LRRM at 1081. *See also* Estate of Bella Moses, 247 NLRB 144, 103 LRRM 1081 (1980).

[182]American Sunroof Corp., *supra* note 180. The Board relied on the following considerations in finding that the disclaimer removed the contract as a bar: (1) the disclaimer was made in response to a deauthorization petition filed by an employee; (2) the disclaimer was made one and one-half months before a representation petition was filed by the other union; (3) the incumbent union took no actions inconsistent with its disclaimer; and (4) there was no evidence of collusion between the two unions. Relying on East Mfg. Corp., *supra* note 181, Member Penello registered a strong dissent.

[183]For most collective bargaining contracts, the period of the contract—three years—will be coextensive with the period of the contract bar. *See* General Cable Corp., *supra* note 129.

[184]*See* Deluxe Metal Furniture Co., 121 NLRB 995, 42 LRRM 1470 (1958),which superseded an earlier doctrine of recognizing a petition as timely filed if filed within 10 days following claim for recognition; General Elec. X-Ray Corp., 67 NLRB 997, 18 LRRM 1047 (1946). *See* notes 189-91 *infra* and accompanying text.

a. The Open Period. In order to provide employees with an opportunity for a free choice of bargaining representative at reasonable intervals, the Board has established an *open period* during which petitions may be filed. Formerly this open period extended from 150 days to 60 days prior to the terminal date,[185] i.e., the expiration date of the contract or, if the contract exceeded three years, the last day of the third year. When the election process was accelerated upon delegation to the regional directors, the Board shortened the open period so that it would extend from 90 to 60 days prior to the terminal date.[186]

b. The Insulated Period. The Board will not consider a petition to be timely if it is filed during the 60-day period preceding the terminal date. This is the *insulated period* and immediately follows the open period. It is during this period that the parties will be permitted to negotiate "free from the 'threat of overhanging rivalry and uncertainty.'"[187]

---

[185]*See* note 184 *supra.*

[186]Leonard Wholesale Meats Co., 136 NLRB 1000, 49 LRRM 1901 (1962). A petition filed before the commencement of an "open" period, however, may be entertained as to seasonal operations. *See, e.g.,* Cooperativa Azucarera Los Canos, 122 NLRB 817, 43 LRRM 1193 (1958). The Board has also held that, even though a petition is prematurely filed, it will not be dismissed if a hearing is directed, despite the prematurity of the petition, and that the Board's decision issues on or after the commencement of the open period. Royal Crown Cola Co., 150 NLRB 1624, 58 LRRM 1306 (1965). *See also* W. A. Foote Memorial Hosp., 230 NLRB 540, 96 LRRM 1099 (1977).

Because of a presidential wage-price freeze, in 1972 the Board granted a special exception to the open-period rule in several cases. Otherwise timely petitions were dismissed as untimely because the freeze had prevented intelligent bargaining during the insulated period; the Board therefore granted the bargaining parties new, uninterrupted periods of time in which to negotiate a contract. Litton Business Sys., Inc., 199 NLRB 354, 81 LRRM 1219 (1972); Dennis Chem. Co., 196 NLRB 226, 79 LRRM 1659 (1972); Hill & Sanders-Wheaton, Inc., 195 NLRB 1137, 79 LRRM 1617 (1972); West India Mfg. and Serv. Co., 195 NLRB 1135, 79 LRRM 1619 (1972).

Another exception to the usual open and insulated periods was made for health care institutions. The open period in the health care industry is 120 to 90 days prior to an agreement's terminal date or the first three years of the agreement, whichever is sooner, thereby making the insulated period 90 days. The Board adopted these modifications for the health care industry in order to accommodate its contract-bar rules to amend §8(d)(4) of the Act, requiring 90 days' notice to the other party of the proposed termination or modification of a health care collective bargaining agreement. Trinity Lutheran Hosp., 218 NLRB 199, 89 LRRM 1238 (1975). *See* Chapter 13 *infra* at notes 723-33.

[187]Deluxe Metal Furniture Co., *supra* note 184 at 1001; General Dynamics Corp., 158 NLRB 956, 62 LRRM 1132 (1966). In the health care industry, the insulated period is 90 days. *See* note 186 *supra.* In *General Dynamics,* a petition filed during the insulated period was dismissed even though it was not processed until after the terminal date. However, the freedom to negotiate afforded the parties during the insulated period does not necessarily establish a "good faith" defense for the employer against unfair labor practice charges of assistance to the incumbent union stemming from the execution of the contract during the insulated period. *See* Chapter 8 *supra* at notes 106-53. for a discussion of the *Midwest Piping* doctrine, and *compare* Hart Motor Express, Inc., 164 NLRB 382, 65 LRRM 1218 (1967) and Kenrich Petrochem., Inc., 149 NLRB 910, 57 LRRM 1395 (1964), *with* City Cab, Inc., 128 NLRB 493, 46 LRRM 1332 (1960).

In the borderline case, petitions filed on the sixtieth day preceding and including the terminal date will normally be considered untimely as falling within the insulated period, and the Board has specifically held that where a contract provides that it is in effect "until" or "to" a specific date, the date following the word "until" or "to" will not be counted in the 60-day computation.[188]

c. *Post-terminal Date*. If an employer and a union do not enter into a contract during the 60-day insulated period, the Board will entertain a petition after the terminal date, subject to new tests of timeliness.[189] Previously, under the Board's *General Electric X-Ray* doctrine,[190] a union's bare claim to representation prevented another union's subsequent contract from being a bar if the claim was succeeded within 10 days by the filing of a petition. The Board discarded this rule in *Deluxe Metal*[191] because it found that it had become a means of disrupting the stability of labor relations rather than a means of protecting the employees' free choice of representative.

In *Deluxe Metal*, the Board established the following rules:

(1) A contract executed after the expiration of a prior contract will not bar an election if a petition is filed with the Board (a) before the execution date of a contract effective immediately or retroactively, or (b) before the effective date if the contract goes into effect at some time after its execution.[192]

(2) In the borderline case, a petition filed on the day the contract is executed is not timely unless the employer has "been informed at the time of the execution that a petition has been filed."[193]

---

[188]Hemisphere Steel Prods., Inc., 131 NLRB 56, 47 LRRM 1595 (1961).
[189]For purposes of timeliness at this stage, there would be no difference between petitions filed with respect to "old" contracts and petitions filed with respect to "first" contracts.
[190]General Elec. X-Ray Corp., *supra* note 184.
[191]Deluxe Metal Furniture Co., *supra* note 184.
[192]In Weather Vane Outerwear Corp., 233 NLRB 414, 96 LRRM 1621 (1977), the Board reaffirmed the rule established in General Dyestuff Corp., 100 NLRB 72, 30 LRRM 1230 (1952), that when one petition is timely filed and a second petition is filed during the pendency of the unresolved representation question raised by the earlier one, the contract-bar doctrine will not apply to the later petition.
[193]Deluxe Metal Furniture Co., *supra* note 184 at 999. As to what constitutes being "informed" in timely fashion, *see* Portland Associated Morticians, Inc., 163 NLRB 614, 64 LRRM 1402 (1967); Rappahannock Sportswear Co., 163 NLRB 703, 64 LRRM 1417 (1967).

(3) A petition filed the day before the contract's execution will always be timely.[194]

While the Board seeks to avoid having its contract-bar rules circumvented by premature extensions of contract expiration dates, it also recognizes that there is no need to penalize the parties by attaching more stringent rules than would otherwise have been applicable to the initial contract. Thus, it noted:

> The primary purpose of the premature-extension rule is to protect petitioners in general from being faced with prematurely executed contracts at a time when the Petitioner would normally be permitted to file a petition. However, the Board's rule is not an absolute ban on premature extensions, but only subjects such extensions to the condition that if a petition is filed during the open period calculated from the expiration date of the old contract, the premature extension will not be a bar.[195]

As indicated above, petitions filed during the insulated period of the old contract remain untimely.[196] Similarly, the *premature extension* doctrine does not apply to a contract executed at a time when the existing contract would have been vulnerable because of other contract-bar rules, e.g., a contract containing a union security provision clearly unlawful on its face.[197]

Notice to modify the contract, or actual modification short of termination, will not remove the contract as a bar to an election, regardless of the scope of any such clause.[198] This has not always been the case, however. Returning to its earlier *Western Electric* rule,[199] the Board in *Deluxe Metal*[200] overturned intervening decisions which had held that the reopening destroyed the bar.

F. Clarification of Units

The Board's Rules and Regulations provide a means whereby either party to a bargaining unit, regardless of whether the unit was established by formal NLRB representation procedures,

---

[194]The cutoff date in applying these rules is midnight, even though the contract eventually executed after midnight is the result of continuous bargaining. Deluxe Metal Furniture Co., *supra* note 184.
[195]H. L. Klion, Inc., 148 NLRB 656, 660, 57 LRRM 1073 (1964).
[196]Deluxe Metal Furniture Co., *supra* note 184.
[197]St. Louis Cordage Mills, 168 NLRB 981, 67 LRRM 1017 (1967).
[198]*Id.*
[199]Western Elec. Co., 94 NLRB 54, 28 LRRM 1002 (1951). *See also* Greenville Finishing Co., 71 NLRB 436, 19 LRRM 1023 (1946).
[200]Deluxe Metal Furniture Co., *supra* note 184.

may obtain a clarification of the unit.[201] The applicable rule provides that in the absence of a question concerning representation, a labor organization or an employer may file a petition for clarification of an existing bargaining unit or a petition for amendment of certification.[202] In 1964, the Board held in the *Locomotive Firemen* case[203] that such a petition may be filed even though the Board has never passed on the appropriateness of the bargaining unit and no certification exists. In that case, the Board treated an employer's representation petition as a motion for clarification in view of (1) the parties' long bargaining history, (2) the recognition of the union as majority representative of the employees, and (3) a finding that the existing bargaining unit was not repugnant to the ACT. The earlier *Bell Telephone* decision[204] had held that, since the Board was not empowered to render declaratory judgments or advisory opinions, it did not have authority to determine the status of employees with reference to an uncertified unit.

Locomotive Firemen has been construed as holding only that, on proper motion, the Board will undertake to clarify an uncertified unit, not that any petition for an election may be treated as one for clarification. And the Board will not certify or recertify a union as an incident to clarifying a unit[205] unless an election is conducted. Whether certified or not, a definite unit must exist or the Board will dismiss the motion for clarification.[206] As stated in the applicable rule, there must be no question concerning representation.[207] Thus, clarification cannot be used as an alternative to a petition for election when the object is to add a

---

[201]Rules and Regs. §102.60(b): "A petition for clarification of an existing bargaining unit or a petition for amendment of certification, in the absence of a question concerning representation, may be filed by a labor organization or by an employer. Where applicable the same procedures set forth in section 102.60(a) above [pertinent to conventional petitions] shall be followed." *See also* Chapter 20 *infra* at notes 330-46.

[202]Rules and Regs. §102.61(d), outlines the contents of a petition for clarification. Unlike election petitions, unit-clarification petitions are not limited to the 90-to-60-day open period. *But see* Arthur C. Logan Memorial Hosp., 231 NLRB 778, 96 LRRM 1063 (1977).

[203]Locomotive Firemen & Enginemen, 145 NLRB 1521, 55 LRRM 1177 (1964).

[204]Bell Tel. Co., 118 NLRB 371, 40 LRRM 1179 (1957).

[205]Crown Zellerbach Corp., 147 NLRB 1223, 56 LRRM 1438 (1964).

[206]FWD Corp., 131 NLRB 404, 48 LRRM 1055 (1961).

[207]Rules and Regs. §102.60(b); Renaissance Center Partnership, *supra* note 168. In Southern Calif. Water Co., 241 NLRB No. 122, 100 LRRM 1583 (1979), an employer's enterprise had substantially changed by the addition of a unit of employees already represented by another certified labor organization operating under a collective bargaining agreement then in force. The Board held that under such circumstances a question of representation existed, and accordingly it dismissed the employer's petition to clarify the original unit.

classification of employees which had been deliberately omitted from the unit.[208] However, a petition for unit clarification will be entertained if there has been a proper accretion to the unit.[209] In *Western Cartridge Co.*,[210] the Board found a proper accretion because the employees in question were interchangeable with the existing unit, had a community of interest in employment conditions, performed the same duties, and worked under common supervision.

The Board has dismissed petitions for clarification or amendment where professionals were entitled to an election,[211] where a union sought to amend and transfer certifications,[212] where a union sought to substitute the name of another local for its own,[213] and where a union was attempting to effectuate a change in work assignments.[214] The clarification requested must not have been precluded by a previous Board determination,[215] but to be conclusive a previous determination must have resolved the exact question upon which clarification is sought.[216]

The Board has also refused to allow the unit-clarification procedure to be used as a device to resolve jurisdictional disputes. Local 289, Graphic Arts, 246 NLRB No. 155, 103 LRRM 1025 (1979). *See* Chapter 27 *infra.*

[208]Machinists & Aerospace Workers, 242 NLRB 44, 101 LRRM 1098 (1979); Lufkin Foundry & Mach. Co., 174 NLRB 556, 70 LRRM 1262 (1969); Dayton Power & Light Co., 137 NLRB 337, 50 LRRM 1147 (1962). In Desert Palace, Inc., 209 NLRB 950, 85 LRRM 1594 (1974), the Board dismissed a clarification petition seeking the accretion of plainclothes investigators to a unit of security officers. It rejected as irrelevant the fact that the exclusion of the plainclothes investigators at the time of the certification may have resulted from Board precedent which had since changed. The Board reasoned that, notwithstanding the existence of their job classification for several years and the negotiation of intervening contracts, the investigators had never had an opportunity to express themselves as to union representation.

[209]Boston Gas Co., 235 NLRB 1354, 98 LRRM 1146 (1978); Western Cartridge Co., 134 NLRB 67, 49 LRRM 1098 (1961). *See* discussion of accretions at notes 161-73 *supra.*

[210]134 NLRB 67, 49 LRRM 1098 (1961).

[211]Lockheed Aircraft Corp., 155 NLRB 702, 60 LRRM 1390 (1965).

[212]Monon Stone Co., 137 NLRB 761, 50 LRRM 1248 (1962).

[213]Gulf Oil Corp., 135 NLRB 184, 49 LRRM 1465 (1962).

[214]Cincinnati Gas & Elec. Co., 235 NLRB 424, 97 LRRM 1523 (1978); T.I.M.E.-D.C., Inc., 225 NLRB 1175, 93 LRRM 1270 (1976); Borg-Warner Corp., 150 NLRB 912, 58 LRRM 1168 (1965).

[215]Security Guard Serv., Inc., 154 NLRB 33, 59 LRRM 1684 (1965). *But see* Fairleigh Dickinson Univ., 227 NLRB 239, 94 LRRM 1044 (1976), where the Board clarified a unit of university professors by adding department chairpersons to the faculty unit found appropriate by the Board in a prior representation proceeding. In the earlier proceeding, the employees in question had been found to be supervisors and were excluded from voting. The Board ruled that the duties of the department chairpersons had been changed by the parties' collective bargaining agreement, so they were no longer supervisors. *But cf.* NLRB v. Yeshiva Univ., 444 US 672, 103 LRRM 2526 (1980), discussed at notes 259-73 in Chapter 11 *infra* and at notes 190-92 in Chapter 30 *infra*; College of Osteopathic Medicine & Surgery, 265 NLRB No. 37, 111 LRRM 1523 (1982), discussed in Chapter 30 *infra* note 191. *See also* note 441 *infra* this chapter.

[216]West Virginia Pulp & Paper Co., 140 NLRB 1160, 52 LRRM 1196 (1963); Boston Gas Co., 136 NLRB 219, 49 LRRM 1742 (1962).

Ultimately, the normal enforcement mechanism for a unit-clarification decision, like other decisions in representation cases,[217] will be a refusal-to-bargain unfair labor practice case. Thus, in *Libbey-Owens-Ford* v. *NLRB*,[218] following protracted litigation, the Third Circuit enforced a Board order finding the employer in violation of Section 8(a)(5) when it refused to add a single-plant unit to an existing multiplant unit pursuant to the Board's prior unit clarification order.

III. ELECTION PROCEDURES

A. Preelection Matters

A cardinal policy of the Act is to protect the exercise by employees of full freedom to express their desires on union representation. A union (or individual) becomes the sole representative for purposes of collective bargaining if "designated or selected for the purposes of collective bargaining by the majority of the employees in a unit appropriate for such purposes."[219] For a union (or individual) to become a *certified* representative, however, there must be an "election by secret ballot" conducted by the NLRB after the filing of a proper petition and a determination that a question of representation exists.[220]

Pursuant to Section 3(b) of the Act, the Board has delegated to the regional directors its above-noted powers under Section 9.[221] The election is held in the region where the representation case is pending. The regional director under whose supervision the election is conducted is responsible for its proper conduct.[222] Following long-established policy, the regional director, under ordinary circumstances, is allowed to exercise his own discretion concerning the conduct of elections.[223] He may, however, trans-

---

[217]*See* Chapter 33 *infra* at notes 17-22.
[218]495 F2d 1195, 85 LRRM 2668 (CA 3, 1974), *enforcing* 202 NLRB 29, 82 LRRM 1417 (1973), *cert. denied*, 419 US 998, 87 LRRM 2658 (1974).
[219]§9(a). *See* Chapter 12 *infra* for treatment of the process of obtaining recognition without an election.
[220]§9(c)(1). Until the Taft-Hartley amendments, the Board had (though it did not use) "wide discretion" in determining how to insure free employee choice. NLRB v. A. J. Tower Co., 329 US 324, 19 LRRM 2128 (1946); Southern Steamship Co. v. NLRB, 316 US 31, 10 LRRM 544 (1942). *See* Chapter 3 *supra* and Chapter 12 *infra*.
[221]Statements of Procedure §101.21(a). *See supra* at notes 9-14.
[222]Rules and Regs. §102.69; NLRB Field Manual 11300.
[223]V. La Rosa & Sons, 121 NLRB 671, 42 LRRM 1418 (1958); Independent Rice Mill, Inc., 111 NLRB 536, 35 LRRM 1509 (1955).

fer parts of the case to the Board for determination. The director acts through an assigned Board agent, a field attorney, or a field examiner, any of whom may hold informal preelection conferences with interested parties in an attempt to settle the details of the election.[224]

1. Types of Elections. If the parties can voluntarily resolve the details of the election, either of two types of consent election agreements may be used.[225] The two types of agreements pursuant to which a regional office may conduct an election are: (1) Agreement for Consent Election[226] (colloquially referred to as a "pure consent" agreement), providing for determination by the regional director of any dispute arising from the subsequent proceedings; and (2) Stipulation for Certification on Consent Election (colloquially referred to as a "stip" agreement), providing for a determination by the Board of any subsequent dispute.[227] In either case the parties enter into a written agreement setting forth the details of the election (i.e., time, place, etc.), which must be approved by the regional director. He rules on all requests or motions made after the execution of the agreement and conducts the election. His rulings (unless arbitrary or capricious) are final in connection with a "pure consent" election but are reviewable by the Board under a "stip" agreement. Before approval by the regional director, or before a hearing in a case where there is no agreement, any party may withdraw.

In the absence of a consent election agreement (used hereinafter to refer to both Agreements for Consent Election and Stipulations for Certification upon Consent Elections), the regional director will proceed to a hearing. If the evidence at the hearing establishes the existence of a question concerning representation (QCR) and the appropriateness of the unit, the regional director will issue a Decision and Direction of Election. In cases which are transferred to the Board, the Board may, upon a finding that a QCR exists, issue a Direction of Election.[228]

After approval, or hearing: (1) a petitioning union may withdraw prior to the election if no inconsistent action is taken (such as recognition picketing), subject to six months' prejudice

---

[224]Statements of Procedure §101.19(a)(1); NLRB Field Manual 11300.
[225]§9(c)(4).
[226]Rules and Regs. §102.62(a).
[227]*Id.* §102.62(b).
[228]*Id.* §§102.63, 102.64, 102.67.

regarding the filing of a new petition; (2) an intervening union may withdraw until administrative functions have begun (i.e., the printing of ballots or notices);[229] and (3) a petitioning employer may withdraw only if unusual and compelling reasons exist or no union party opposes the withdrawal.[230]

The usual preliminaries are modified for expedited elections conducted under Section 8(b)(7)(C): no showing of substantial interest is required if the petition is filed within 30 days of the commencement of picketing for organizational or recognitional objectives. Regional offices conduct these elections, but the usual investigatory and hearing prerequisites are omitted.[231]

2. Details of the Election. *a. Date.* An election may not be held less than 10 days after the date the regional director schedules for receipt of the required list of eligible voters and their addresses.[232] Unless a waiver of review of the direction of election is filed, the regional director normally will not schedule an election until a date more than 20 days but less than 30 days from the date of the direction of election. This is to allow the Board to rule on any request for review.[233] If an election is directed by the Board, the election may be held at any time within 30 days of the date of the direction of election.[234] The exact day on which the election is held will usually be one when it is likely that the greatest number of eligible employees will be present and able to vote.[235]

b. Time.[236] The election may be held on company time with the employer's permission; otherwise it is held on the employees'

---

[229]NLRB Field Manual 11098.1. *See* Sears, Roebuck & Co., 107 NLRB 716, 33 LRRM 1233 (1954). *See* Waumbec Dyeing & Finishing Co., 101 NLRB 1069, 31 LRRM 1185 (1952); Thiokol Chem. Corp., 114 NLRB 21, 36 LRRM 1508 (1955); American Meter Co., 89 NLRB 401, 25 LRRM 1584 (1950).

[230]NLRB Field Manual 11098.2a; Alloy Mfg. Co., 107 NLRB 1201, 33 LRRM 1352 (1954).

[231]§8(b)(7)(C). *See* Chapter 23 *infra* for treatment of organizational and recognitional picketing and expedited elections under §§8(b)(7)(C). *See also* Rules and Regs. §102.67(b), on the decision and direction of election by the regional director, and paragraph (j) on such orders by the Board; Woodco Corp., 129 NLRB 1188, 47 LRRM 1143 (1961), for a discussion of appropriate unit considerations in expedited elections.

[232]NLRB Field Manual 11302.1. *See* notes 239-52 *infra.*

[233]Statements of Procedure §101.21(d); NLRB Field Manual 11302.1.

[234]NLRB Field Manual 11302.1; K. McGuiness, *supra* note 1 at 9-4.

[235]*E.g.*, a day in the middle of the workweek or a payday. NLRB Field Manual 11302.1. However, the Ninth Circuit held that the Board did not abuse its discretion when it declined to schedule the election for payday and designated a different day when 26 employees were absent. Beck Corp. v. NLRB, 590 F2d 290, 100 LRRM 2719 (CA 9, 1978), *enforcing* 231 NLRB 907, 96 LRRM 1627 (1977).

[236]For specific rules relating to time and procedural aspects of the election, *see* NLRB Field Manual 11300-11342.

own time. The actual time or times for voting will be set so as to give all eligible employees adequate opportunity to vote, with minimum interference with the workday.

In a multishift, multiplant, or multiemployer situation, the polls may be kept open long enough to give each employee sufficient opportunity to vote, then moved or reopened later so that another shift, plant, or unit may vote.

When appropriate, such as where long distances are involved or where voters are widely scattered, voting may be conducted by mail, and the time for voting will be lengthened accordingly.[237]

   c. *Place*. The polls are to be situated for easy accessibility and convenience to the voters.[238] For this reason the election is usually held on company property, if possible.

   3. Voter List and Eligibility. *a. The* Excelsior *List*. After the direction of the election or approval of the consent election agreement, the employer will be required to prepare a list of eligible voters and their addresses, and file it with the regional director within seven days of such direction or approval. This rule was promulgated in *Excelsior Underwear, Inc.*,[239] where the Board held that the failure of an employer to provide a list of names and addresses of employees eligible to vote provides grounds, upon proper objection, for setting aside an election. The list must be filed with the regional director within seven days of the direction of election or approval of a consent election

   [237]NLRB Field Manual 11336. *See* notes 328-31 *infra* and accompanying text.
   [238]Manchester Knitted Fashions, Inc., 108 NLRB 1366, 34 LRRM 1214 (1954); NLRB Field Manual 11302.2.
   [239]156 NLRB 1236, 61 LRRM 1217 (1966). The Board determined that the early release of voters' names and addresses is necessary to a fair election. The Supreme Court directed enforcement of the Board's subpoena for an *Excelsior* list, but without concurrence of a majority in support of the reasons for enforcement. NLRB v. Wyman-Gordon Co., 394 US 759, 70 LRRM 3345 (1969). The subpoena was enforced notwithstanding that a majority of the justices, although for differing reasons, were of the opinion that the *Excelsior* requirement should have been promulgated pursuant to the formal rule-making procedures specified in the Administrative Procedure Act. 5 USC §553 (1976). Chief Justice Warren and Justices Fortas, Stewart, and White were of this opinion but nevertheless favored enforcement of the subpoena. Justices Douglas and Harlan, in separate dissenting opinions, contended that the *Excelsior* rules were invalid under the Administrative Procedure Act. Justices Black, Brennan, and Marshall contended that the rules were merely the by-product of the Board's adjudication and thus a "direct consequence of the proper exercise of its adjudicatory powers." 394 US at 773. *See* Chapter 9 *supra* at note 28, and Chapter 32 *infra* at notes 197-218.

agreement. The regional director then makes the list available to all parties.[240]

The list is designed to facilitate communication in order to insure a free and reasoned choice by the employees and to avoid the necessity of a challenge when an employee who is previously unknown to the union, but whose name is on the eligibility list, appears to vote. The names and addresses should be listed systematically (e.g., alphabetically, or by clock or card number, either as a whole or by department or unit). This list will also serve as the basis for composing the voting list.[241] The list should be checked and approved promptly by the parties in order to allow maximum time for resolving eligibility questions prior to the election, and the list should be kept up to date while the election procedures are pending.[242] If the list is not received, or if it contains names but not addresses, the director will proceed to hold the election unless requested in writing not to do so by the petitioner or an intervenor with sufficient showing of interest.[243] The *Excelsior* requirement is not dependent on a showing of the union's need for the information—the Board has held that it will not accept an employer's argument that it should not be required to furnish the list because the union already possesses all the information.[244]

Since its original decision in 1966, the Board has considered whether deviations from *Excelsior* requirements, either failure to properly list eligible voters or failure to meet time requirements, constitute grounds for setting aside an election. The Board has accepted deviations in some cases, finding that the requirements were satisfied by substantial compliance.[245]

-----

[240]NLRB Field Manual 11312.1; Blaise Parking Serv., Case No. 15-CA-3646, 65 LRRM 1707 (1967) (not reported in Board volumes).

[241]NLRB Field Manual 11312.3. See discussion *infra* at note 321.

[242]Statements of Procedure §101.19(a)(1); NLRB Field Manual 11312.4.

[243]NLRB Field Manual 11312.6. An intervenor with less than 30% cannot block the election but may file objections, and the Board may set the election aside for failure to supply the list.

[244]Gray Drug Stores, Inc., 197 NLRB 924, 80 LRRM 1449 (1972). The Board refused to admit evidence of the union's lack of need, reasoning that the list would be beneficial to the union in correcting and updating its information, and that furnishing the list would tend to reduce challenges because it would enable the union to know prior to the election the employer's position on voter eligibility.

[245]In one case a petitioning union objected to the time limits, claiming that seven days from the direction of an election was too long to wait, in view of the fact that the proceeding in issue was the third election to be conducted following the filing of its petition. The Board found this reason unpersuasive and denied the motion to reconsider

In *Pole-Lite Industries, Ltd.,*[246] the Board outlined the major factors which it takes into account when considering a union objection to an election based on untimely submission of the *Excelsior* list: (1) the number of days by which the list was overdue; (2) the number of days for which the union has had the list prior to the election; (3) the number of employees eligible to vote in the election; and (4) whether there is a showing of a lack of good faith on the part of the employer in providing the union with the required information. Previously, the Board had held that a new election was unwarranted even though a union received the *Excelsior* list only eight days before the election; the employer had furnished the regional office with the eligibility list 12 days prior to the election, and the regional director mailed the list to the union 10 days before the election, which was immediately upon receipt of the union's execution of the consent stipulation.[247] Since *Pole-Lite,* the Board has set aside an election in circumstances where, because of delays by both the Board and the postal service, the union did not receive the list until eight days before the election.[248] In another case,[249] rejecting the employer's contention that it was justified in delivering the *Excelsior* list 15 days late because it had filed a motion to set aside the consent agreement, the Board ordered a new election. It pointed out that the employer could have submitted the list while its motion was under consideration, and its failure to do so had resulted in the union being denied up to 40 percent of its election campaigning time.

Substantial compliance as to the names on the list appears to satisfy *Excelsior* requirements. The Board excused an employer's 7-percent error factor in submitting incorrect addresses and omitting names, finding that an error of that magnitude did not amount to "insubstantial compliance" with the rule.[250] Similarly,

---

the union's objection to that policy. Sabine Towing & Transp. Co., 226 NLRB 422, 93 LRRM 1277 (1976). In the same case, the Board set aside the election because alleged off-duty employees whose names did not appear on the list were prevented by the employer from asserting their right to vote to the Board agent conducting the election.
    [246]299 NLRB 196, 95 LRRM 1080 (1977).
    [247]Peerless Eagle Coal Co., 220 NLRB 357, 90 LRRM 1229 (1975).
    [248]McGraw Edison Co., 234 NLRB 630, 97 LRRM 1262 (1978).
    [249]Rockwell Int'l, 235 NLRB 1159, 98 LRRM 1077 (1978).
    [250]Kentfield Medical Hosp., 219 NLRB 174, 89 LRRM 1697 (1975); *but see* Ponce Television Corp., 192 NLRB 115, 77 LRRM 1622 (1971) (22% error factor not substantial compliance); Sonfarrel, Inc., 188 NLRB 969, 76 LRRM 1497 (1971) (omission of five names out of unit of 52 held to warrant new election).

a 13-percent error factor in the addresses of eligible voters was held to constitute neither gross negligence nor an absence of good faith warranting a new election.[251] However, a list that omitted 10 percent of the eligible voters and had incorrect addresses for 18 percent was found not to constitute substantial compliance and, therefore, provided grounds for setting aside the election.[252] In the latter case, the Board stated that omissions are more serious than inaccurate addresses and indicated that the election would have been set aside on the basis of the omissions alone.

b. Eligibility. Generally, all employees in the unit found appropriate who were employed during the payroll period immediately preceding the date of the direction of election or approval of the consent agreement, are eligible to vote provided they are still employed at the time of the election.[253] Laid-off employees who have a "reasonable expectation of re-employment" in the foreseeable future are also eligible to vote.[254] Probationary employees are eligible to vote if their duties and working conditions are substantially the same as those of regular employees and they have reasonable expectation of permanent employment.[255] Employees on sick leave or leave of absence are eligible

---

[251]Days Inns, Inc., 216 NLRB 384, 88 LRRM 1224 (1975). The Board has also held that providing a list of only surnames and first and middle initials and failing to volunteer subsequently updated addresses did not violate the Act because there was no showing that it was a "product of intent to frustrate communication or impede Board processes." St. Francis Hosp., 249 NLRB 180, 104 LRRM 1213 (1980).

[252]Chromalloy Am. Corp., 245 NLRB No. 119, 112 LRRM 1405 (1979). In Centre Eng'r, 253 NLRB 419, 105 LRRM 1637 (1980), an employer was held not to have complied with the *Excelsior* requirements when it submitted a list which was not alphabetized, nor arranged according to department or plant location, and which contained zip codes for only 25 of the 424 addresses.

[253]Columbia Pictures Corp., 61 NLRB 1030, 16 LRRM 128 (1945); Vultee Aircraft, Inc., 24 NLRB 1184, 6 LRRM 459 (1940). *But see* Carl B. King Drilling Co., 164 NLRB 419, 65 LRRM 1096 (1967); Great Lakes Pipe Line Co., 64 NLRB 1296, 17 LRRM 169 (1945); Remington Rand Corp., 50 NLRB 819, 12 LRRM 219 (1943). An employee must be actively employed on the eligibility date; and the Board has held that an employee who was hired two days before the eligibility date and took his physical on that date, but who did not actually begin work until a later date is not eligible to vote. B.L.K. Steel, Inc., 245 NLRB 1347, 102 LRRM 1532 (1980).

[254]Kustom Elec., Inc. v. NLRB, 590 F2d 817, 100 LRRM 2097 (CA 10, 1978), *enforcing* 230 NLRB 1037, 96 LRRM 1454 (1977); NLRB v. Jesse Jones Sausage Co., 309 F2d 664, 51 LRRM 2501 (CA 4, 1962); Marley Co., 131 NLRB 866, 48 LRRM 1168 (1961). *But see* Thomas Engine Corp., 196 NLRB 706, 80 LRRM 1755 (1972). The Board held that employees who had been laid off and told to find other work because the employer could not estimate the duration of the layoff were ineligible to vote, even though they were called back to work shortly after the election. *See also* Precision Tumbling Co., 252 NLRB 1014, 105 LRRM 1365 (1980).

[255]Vogue Art Ware & China Co., 129 NLRB 1253, 47 LRRM 1169 (1961); V.I.P. Radio, Inc., 128 NLRB 113, 46 LRRM 1278 (1960); Sheffield Corp., 123 NLRB 1454, 44 LRRM 1155 (1959); Beattie Mfg. Co., 77 NLRB 361, 22 LRRM 1015 (1948).

to vote if they are to be automatically restored to their duties when ready to resume work.[256] Employees who have quit or been discharged for cause before the election are generally ineligible,[257] but employees who have been discriminatorily discharged[258] are entitled to vote.

The status of employees who have given notice of termination has been clarified in several cases. Employees who have given notice of intent to quit but are still on the payroll at the time of the election are entitled to vote.[259] But in one case the Board held that an employee who had given notice of his resignation before the election and who did not work on election day was ineligible to vote even though he was on the payroll, because " 'it is well settled that in order to be eligible to vote, an individual must be employed *and working* on the established eligibility date, unless absent for one of the reasons set out in the Direction of Election.' "[260] The Board's policy in this regard is not to "fractionalize" workdays, and it has held that an employee who worked a full shift but was discharged prior to voting was an eligible voter;[261] although the Seventh Circuit denied enforcement of a bargaining order based on that vote,[262] the Board continues to adhere to this policy.[263] In addition, the Board has held that an employee who quit his employment in the middle of a payroll

---

[256]NLRB v. Atkinson Dredging Co., 329 F2d 158, 55 LRRM 2598 (CA 4, 1964), *cert. denied*, 377 US 965, 56 LRRM 2416 (1964); Helen Rose Co., 127 NLRB 1682, 46 LRRM 1242 (1960); Armour & Co., 83 NLRB 333, 24 LRRM 1062 (1949). *See also* Keeshin Charter Serv., 250 NLRB 780, 105 LRRM 1030 (1980).

[257]Rish Equip. Co., 150 NLRB 1185, 58 LRRM 1274 (1965), *enforced*, 359 F2d 391, 61 LRRM 2719 (CA 4, 1966); Gemex Corp., 117 NLRB 656, 39 LRRM 1312 (1957); Dura Steel Prods. Co., 111 NLRB 590, 35 LRRM 1522 (1955); United States Rubber Co., 86 NLRB 338, 24 LRRM 1621 (1949).

[258]Tampa Sand & Material Co., 137 NLRB 1549, 50 LRRM 1438 (1962); Sioux City Brewing Co., 85 NLRB 1164, 24 LRRM 1534 (1949); *see also* Pacific Tile & Porcelain Co., 137 NLRB 1358, 50 LRRM 1394 (1962) (voting permitted even though pending grievance or arbitration procedure over discharged employee had not been made subject of unfair labor practice charge). *See also* B.L.K. Steel, Inc., 252 NLRB 256, 105 LRRM 1495 (1980).

[259]NLRB v. General Tube Co., 331 F2d 751, 56 LRRM 2161 (CA 6, 1964); Ely & Walker, 151 NLRB 636, 58 LRRM 1513 (1965); Reidbord Bros. Co., 99 NLRB 127, 30 LRRM 1047 (1952).

[260]Roy N. Lotspeich Publishing Co., 204 NLRB 517, 83 LRRM 1380 (1973) (emphasis in original), *quoting* Ra-Rich Mfg. Corp., 120 NLRB 1444, 1447, 42 LRRM 1182 (1958).

[261]Choc-Ola Bottlers, Inc., 192 NLRB 1247, 78 LRRM 1049 (1971).

[262]Choc-Ola Bottlers, Inc. v. NLRB, 478 F2d 461, 83 LRRM 2204 (CA 7, 1973).

[263]*E.g.*, Firestone Tire & Rubber Co., 206 NLRB 614, 84 LRRM 1582 (1973), *enforced*, 503 F2d 759 (CA 10, 1974) (Board held that an employee who had been absent from work for several months, who returned to work on the election day but did no unit work before voting, was eligible to vote even though he was assigned to a probationary supervisory position after the election).

eligibility period, but was subsequently rehired and worked on the day of the election, was eligible to vote on the ground that "payroll eligibility is in fact conferred by some work during the payroll eligibility period."[264] On the other hand, an employee who had been previously retired, but was placed on leave-of-absence status prior to the election and returned to work six days after the election, was held ineligible.[265]

Seasonal, casual, or temporary employees are generally not eligible to vote unless they have a reasonable expectation of reemployment and a substantial interest in working conditions at the employer's place of business.[266] However, the Board has held that employees employed under the Comprehensive Employment and Training Act (CETA) who share a community of interest with the employer's regular employees are not ineligible as temporary employees.[267] With respect to temporary employees, the Board has held that those "who are employed on the eligibility date, and whose tenure of employment remains uncertain, are eligible to vote."[268] The Board has applied two standards to determine the eligibility of temporary employees: a reasonable expectation of further employment test[269] and a date certain test.[270] After reviewing the cases, the First Circuit has held that the date certain test is "the better and more prevalent standard."[271] Under that standard, "an employee may be fully aware that his or her employment will be short lived, but, as long as no definite termination date is known and the employee was employed on the eligibility and election dates, he or she will be eligible to vote."[272]

---

[264]Leather by Grant, Inc., 206 NLRB 961, 84 LRRM 1448 1973).
[265]Universal Paper Goods Co. v. NLRB, 638 F2d 1159, 102 LRRM 2218 (CA 9, 1979), *enforcing* 238 NLRB 1088, 99 LRRM 1579 (1978).
[266]Sentinel Printing & Publ. Co., 137 NLRB 1610, 50 LRRM 1469 (1962); S. Martinelli & Co., 99 NLRB 43, 30 LRRM 1031 (1952).
[267]Evergreen Legal Services, 246 NLRB No. 146, 103 LRRM 1028 (1979); Workshop, Inc., 246 NLRB 962, 103 LRRM 1072 (1979). *See also* Mt. Graham Hosp., 250 NLRB 433, 104 LRRM 1375 (1980); Montgomery County Opportunity Bd., 249 NLRB 880, 104 LRRM 1238 (1980).
[268]Personal Prods. Corp., 114 NLRB 959, 960, 37 LRRM 1079 (1955).
[269]*See, e.g.,* Trustees of Stevens Inst. of Technology, 222 NLRB 16, 91 LRRM 1087 (1976); Georgia-Pacific Corp., 201 NLRB 831, 82 LRRM 1355 (1973).
[270]M. J. Pirolli & Sons, Inc., 194 NLRB 241, 78 LRRM 1631 (1971), *enforced without published opinion sub nom.* NLRB v. M. J. Pirolli & Sons, 80 LRRM 3170 (CA 1), *cert. denied,* 409 US 1008, 81 LRRM 2672 (1972); Lloyd A. Fry Roofing Co., 121 NLRB 1433, 43 LRRM 1013 (1958).
[271]NLRB v. New England Lithographic Co., 589 F2d 29, 100 LRRM 2001 (CA 1, 1978).
[272]*Id.* at 34.

Regular part-time, as distinguished from casual, employees are permitted to vote.[273] Likewise, temporarily transferred employees may vote.[274] A dual-function employee who spends part of his time doing bargaining-unit work may have sufficient interest in conditions of employment in the unit to be deemed eligible to vote, even though he does not spend a majority of his time on unit work.[275] To determine the eligibility of day laborers, the Board balances the factors of length, regularity, and currency of employment.[276]

Employees engaged in an economic strike who are "not entitled to reinstatement" (i.e., who have been permanently replaced) are eligible to vote under Board regulations in any election held within 12 months of the commencement of the strike.[277] Conversely, the Board has held that replaced economic strikers who were on a recall list were not eligible to vote in a decertification election held more than 12 months after the strike began.[278] The striker retains his right to vote absent some affirmative action other than replacement (such as the acceptance of permanent employment elsewhere, elimination of his job, discharge, or denial of reinstatement for conduct rendering him unsuitable for reemployment) indicating that his employment has ended.[279] The Board has applied the same principles in determining the eligibility of replaced sympathy strikers, holding that they have the same status as the economic strikers they are supporting.[280]

---

[273]Motz Poultry Co., 244 NLRB 573, 102 LRRM 1198 (1979); Tol-Pac, Inc., 128 NLRB 1439, 46 LRRM 1485 (1960); Providence Pub. Market Co., 79 NLRB 1482, 23 LRRM 1011 (1948).

[274]Huntley-Van Buren Co., 122 NLRB 957, 43 LRRM 1228 (1959) (production employee assigned as a night watchman).

[275]NLRB v. Joclin Mfg. Co., 314 F2d 627, 52 LRRM 2415 (CA 2, 1963); Berea Publ. Co., 140 NLRB 516, 52 LRRM 1051 (1963).

[276]The most common cutoff point is to allow irregular employees, who otherwise have a community of interest with unit employees, to vote if they have worked 15 days in the calendar quarter immediately preceding the direction of election. See, e.g., Capitol Insulation Co., 233 NLRB 902, 96 LRRM 1592 (1977), citing Scoa, Inc., 140 NLRB 1379, 52 LRRM 1244 (1963). See also Avon Prods., 250 NLRB 1479, 105 LRRM 1128 (1980), where the Board held that the parties' agreement that "reserve employees" who had worked four or more hours in nine of the 13 weeks preceding the direction of election would be eligible to vote was not inconsistent with the Act.

[277]§9(c)(3). The Board's regulation has been upheld by the Ninth Circuit in Bio-Science Labs. v. NLRB, 542 F2d 505, 93 LRRM 2154 (CA 9, 1976). See Chapter 21 infra at note 99.

[278]Wahl Clipper Corp., 195 NLRB 634, 79 LRRM 1433 (1972).

[279]W. Wilton Wood, Inc., 127 NLRB 1675, 46 LRRM 1240 (1960). Cf. Laidlaw Corp., 171 NLRB 1366, 68 LRRM 1252 (1968), enforced, 414 F2d 99, 71 LRRM 3054 (CA 7, 1969), cert. denied, 397 US 920, 73 LRRM 2537 (1970). See Chapter 21 infra at note 100.

[280]Levitz Furniture Co., 248 NLRB 15, 103 LRRM 1320 (1980).

The Board has rejected an employer's argument that a pending strike caused such a substantial reduction in available work that none of the strikers could reasonably expect to be recalled in the foreseeable future and hence were ineligible to vote. The elimination of jobs as the result of a strike was not deemed justification for disenfranchisement of strikers within the 12-month period prescribed in Section 9(c)(3).[281] Statements by a striker to his new employer that he had no intention of returning to his unit job were held insufficient to prove affirmatively that the striker had abandoned all interest in returning to his unit employment.[282]

Replacements employed on a permanent basis prior to the voting eligibility cutoff date are also eligible to vote.[283] However, the Fifth Circuit enforced a Board decision holding that permanent replacements who had been hired before the eligibility date and worked on the day of the election, but did not actually report for work until one month after the eligibility cutoff date, were not entitled to vote.[284] Employees who *are* entitled to reinstatement (unfair labor practice strikers) are entitled to vote regardless of the 12-month statutory limitation.[285] Replacements for such strikers are not.[286] However, the Board has held that employees discharged prior to the representation election for striking to protest the termination of a fellow employee were not eligible to vote.[287] Since no unfair labor practice charge had been filed with respect to the discharges, and unfair labor practices cannot be adjudicated in representation proceedings, the Board presumed that the discharges were lawful.

---

[281]Globe Molded Plastics Co., 200 NLRB 377, 81 LRRM 1433 (1972).

[282]Q-T Tool Co., 199 NLRB 500, 81 LRRM 1520 (1972). Member Kennedy dissented on the ground that the presumption of eligibility does not require foreclosing *every* possibility that an employee might return to his old job.

[283]Pacific Tile & Porcelain Co., 137 NLRB 1358, 50 LRRM 1394 (1962). If the strike occurs after the direction of election, permanent replacements of economic strikers attain eligibility if they remain employees on election day. Tampa Sand & Material Co., 129 NLRB 1273, 47 LRRM 1166 (1961) (strike began after direction of election and ended before election). But if the strike is called before the direction of election, replacements enjoy no exception to the general rule specifying eligibility both at the time of direction of election and on election day. Greenspan Engraving Corp., 137 NLRB 1308, 50 LRRM 1380 (1962).

[284]NLRB v. Dalton Sheet Metal Co., 472 F2d 257, 82 LRRM 2468 (CA 5, 1973). The court distinguished Tampa Sand & Material Co., *supra* note 283, where replacements employed after the eligibility deadline but before the election were permitted to vote, on the ground that in *Tampa Sand* the union had attempted to control eligibility by its timing of the strike after the eligibility cutoff date had passed.

[285]Kellburn Mfg. Co., 45 NLRB 322, 11 LRRM 142 (1942).

[286]Larand Leisurelies, Inc., 222 NLRB 838, 91 LRRM 1305 (1976).

[287]Spray Sales & Sierra Rollers, 225 NLRB 1089, 93 LRRM 1025 (1976).

Under a principle first enunciated in *Norris-Thermador Corp.*,[288] the Board will respect a written agreement expressly providing that the same shall be final and binding as to specified questions of eligibility, unless it is contrary to the Act or Board policy. For example, the Board has upheld an eligibility agreement that included an employee who did not begin work until after the eligibility period and who would have been disqualified from voting absent the agreement.[289] The Board said that the customary basis for determining eligibility to vote is neither a requirement of the Act nor a policy of the Board, but rather a rule of administrative convenience that may be waived by a *Norris-Thermador* agreement. The Board has also upheld an employer's challenge to the ballot of an employee whom the parties had agreed to exclude from the list because he had worked on a casual basis and had recently been discharged.[290] After the election, the Board determined that the employee had been unlawfully discharged but upheld the challenge based on the agreement because the question of the employee's eligibility involved a determination of his community of interest with other employees rather than the application of a statutory exclusion. *Norris-Thermador* agreements will not, however, preclude a challenge based on a statutory exclusion, e.g., inclusion of a supervisor under the Act.[291] The Board has extended the *Norris-Thermador* rule to an unequivocal oral agreement, sustaining a challenge to a voter where there was clear evidence that the parties had in fact orally agreed to the voter's ineligibility.[292]

4. Notice of Election. When a petition is filed, the parties receive a Board poster outlining their rights. The Board urges but does not require that this notice be posted. Prior to the date of election, however, the election must be adequately publicized by the posting of official notices to inform eligible voters of the

---

[288]119 NLRB 1301, 41 LRRM 1283 (1958).
[289]Trilco City Lumber Co., 226 NLRB 289, 93 LRRM 1360 (1976).
[290]Pilgrim Foods, Inc., 234 NLRB 136, 97 LRRM 1187 (1978), *modified,* 591 F2d 110, 100 LRRM 2494 (CA 1, 1978).
[291]Esten Dyeing & Finishing Co., 219 NLRB 286, 89 LRRM 1621 (1975). In addition, the Board has refused to give effect to a *Norris-Thermador* agreement excluding certain classifications of employees who belong within the bargaining unit because "the parties are not free to agree that certain classes of employees, although admittedly in the bargaining unit, may not vote." Illinois Valley Community Hosp., 249 NLRB 410, 104 LRRM 1154 (1980).
[292]Banner Bedding, Inc., 214 NLRB 1013, 87 LRRM 1417 (1974).

election details.[293] A standard Board form,[294] which reproduces a sample ballot and outlines such details as location of polls, time of voting, and eligibility rules, is used. The notices are posted by the employer in its place of business in conspicuous places, such as on bulletin boards and timecard racks whenever possible. Notices may also be posted in other places, or the publicizing of the election may be achieved by the "use of other means considered appropriate and effective."[295]

The Board has never specified a required time prior to the election for the posting of election notices, leaving such details to the discretion of the regional director; but it has set aside elections because of late postings,[296] though the appellate courts have disagreed in at least two such cases.[297]

---

[293]NLRB Field Manual 11314.

[294]NLRB Form 707.

[295]Statements of Procedure §101.19(a)(1); NLRB Field Manual 11314.3.

[296]E.g., in Congoleum Indus., 227 NLRB 108, 93 LRRM 1503 (1976), a Board panel (Member Penello dissenting) set aside an election where notices were not posted until two days before the election, even though 97% of the eligible employees voted. The Board said that there was no excuse offered by the employer for the last-minute posting, and for the Board to ignore the employer's inaction would encourage other employers to do the same. The Board additionally pointed out that the notices contain important information with respect to employees' rights under the Act. Similarly, in Singer Co., 238 NLRB No. 229, 99 LRRM 1462 (1978), the Board set aside an election because the employer had not posted the official Board notices in the eight stores in which the election was conducted in time to allow the employees to read and adequately study them. Member Penello dissented on the ground that the official notices were posted in all but one store "at least one day prior to the election" and argued that unofficial communications by both the employer and the union, as part of the election campaign, constituted giving adequate notice to the employees. But see Printhouse Co., 246 NLRB 741, 102 LRRM 1663 (1979), where the Board did not set an election aside even though the employer posted the notice only one day in advance of the election. Similarly, in Kane Indus., 246 NLRB 738, 102 LRRM 1664 (1979), notice was held to be sufficient even though a plantwide layoff prevented voters from reading the posted notice until the day of the election. In Contractors Redi-Mix, 250 NLRB 121, 104 LRRM 1339 (1980), the Board did not set aside an election, which the union had won, where the notice had not been posted until the day before the election, since the employer was found to have contributed to the delay by failing to post the notice until three days after receiving it. In Flo-tronic Metal Mfg., 251 NLRB 1546, 105 LRRM 1144 (1980), the Board set aside an election where, as a result of a mistake by the Board's regional office, the notice of election was in English only but the unit consisted primarily of Spanish-speaking employees.

[297]In Cerlo Mfg. Corp. v. NLRB, 585 F2d 847, 99 LRRM 3054 (CA 7, 1978), the Seventh Circuit denied enforcement of the Board's bargaining order on the ground that the Board had erred in setting aside a representation election which the union had lost. The Board had set the election aside because no official notice of the election had been published. The court found that the regional director had failed to supply the employer with an official notice, and the employer had instead posted a copy of the stipulation for certification, an official Board document. In NLRB v. Kilgore Corp., 510 F2d 1165, 88 LRRM 2833 (CA 6, 1975), the Sixth Circuit refused to enforce a Board order based on an election that had been set aside because the employer had posted the notices only in inconspicuous places shortly before the election. The court relied on the fact that the employees had actually been notified of the procedures, almost 100%

THE DEVELOPING LABOR LAW   CH. 10

Adequacy of notice has also been raised with respect to employees not familiar with English. The Board will generally provide notices in other languages if requested by a party, and has set aside an election on the ground that bilingual notices requested by the employer were not provided until a few days before the election.[298] However, it has also overruled an employer's objection to the lack of bilingual notices where the employer failed to show that a substantial number of Spanish-surnamed employees could not read or understand English.[299]

5. Review of Direction of Election. The order of a regional director, setting forth findings, conclusions, and ordering or directing an election, is final.[300] However, within 10 days of service of the direction, any party may file a request for review with the Board. Such request must be a self-contained document enabling the Board to rule on the basis of its contents without recourse to the record.[301] The Board will grant a request for review only where one or more of the following "compelling reasons" exist: (1) a substantial question of law or policy is raised, and there is an absence of or departure from officially reported Board precedent; (2) the regional director's decision on a substantial factual issue is both clearly erroneous on the record and prejudicial; (3) the conduct of the hearing resulted in prejudicial error; or (4) compelling reasons exist for reconsideration of an important Board rule or policy.[302] Within seven days of the deadline for filing a request for review, any party may file a statement in opposition to the request.[303] If the request for review is granted, the parties may file briefs within seven days of the order granting review, and the Board will consider the entire record in light of the grounds relied on for review.[304]

If it appears to the regional director that the proceeding raises questions that should be decided by the Board, he may transfer the case to the Board for decision. If the case is so transferred, the parties may file with the Board the briefs previously filed

---

of them had voted, the employer had offered to postpone the election, and there was no evidence of bad faith.

[298]Thermalloy Corp., 233 NLRB 428, 96 LRRM 1505 (1977).
[299]Wicks Forest Indus., 227 NLRB 299, 94 LRRM 1029 (1976).
[300]Rules and Regs. §102.67(b). *See* §3(b) of the Act and Chapter 4 *supra* at note 50.
[301]Rules and Regs. §102.67(d).
[302]*Id.* §102.67(c).
[303]*Id.* §102.67(e).
[304]*Id.* §102.67(g).

(or due to be filed) with the regional director.[305] Immediately upon issuance of an order transferring the case or granting the request for review, the regional director may transmit the record to the Board.[306]

Further briefs or reply briefs are permitted only by special leave of the Board. The Board decides the issues referred to it (or reviews the regional director's decision), either on the record or after oral argument or following submission of briefs or further hearing. The Board then directs an election, dismisses the petition, affirms or reverses the regional director's order, or disposes of the matter in such other way as it deems appropriate.[307]

Normally, Board orders in election and certification proceedings under Section 9(c) are not directly reviewable by the courts.[308] The Supreme Court in *Leedom* v. *Kyne*[309] held that a party might, however, by proceeding against the Board members in a district court, attack an order of election and unit determination made "in excess of [the Board's] delegated powers and contrary to a specific prohibition in the Act."[310] But the Court subsequently emphasized that the *Leedom* exception is a narrow one.[311] Such decisions are more conventionally reviewable by an indirect procedure: in a refusal-to-bargain unfair labor practice proceeding in which the correctness of the certification may be put in issue.[312]

B. The Election Proper

1. Observers. Any party may be represented at the voting by observers of its own selection. In directed elections, this privilege is extended by the Board; in consent elections, the consent

---

[305]*Id.* §§102.67(h), 102.67(i).

[306]*Id.* §102.68.

[307]*Id.* §102.67(j).

[308]Custom Recovery v. NLRB, 597 F2d 1041, 101 LRRM 2784 (CA 5, 1979).

[309]358 US 184, 43 LRRM 2222 (1958), *aff'g* 249 F2d 490, 40 LRRM 2600 (CA DC, 1957), *aff'g* 148 F Supp 597, 39 LRRM 2197 (D DC, 1956).

[310]358 US at 188. The Board had included both professional and nonprofessional employees in the same unit without a vote of the professional employees, in contravention of §9(b)(1) of the Act.

[311]Boire v. Greyhound Corp., 376 US 473, 55 LRRM 2694 (1964). *See also* Goldberg, *District Court Review of NLRB Representation Proceedings*, 42 IND. L.J. 455, 487, 489 (1967); Railway Clerks v. Non-Contract Employees, 380 US 650, 59 LRRM 2051 (1965). *See* Chapter 34 *infra* at notes 122-60.

[312]*See* §9(d) of the Act and Administrative Procedure Act, 5 USC §554 cl. 6 (1976). For a general discussion of judicial review, *see* Chapter 34 *infra*.

agreement or stipulation form supplied by the Board provides for the observers, making their use a matter of right.[313] Each party appoints an equal number of observers, the number to be determined by the Board agent based on the circumstances of the election (such as number of voters, voting places, etc.). Parties may waive, expressly or by default, the opportunity to be represented by observers.[314]

The use of observers is also subject to such limitations as the regional director may prescribe, for they are to be "appropriate" representatives.[315] Board policy requires that observers be non-supervisory employees[316] and not be "persons closely identified" with the employer.[317] However, the Board has approved an election where the employer's observer was a former supervisor who temporarily occupied a nonsupervisory position on the day of the election.[318] An employee who is eligible to vote may act as an election observer and still vote.[319] Neither nonparticipating unions nor "no-union" groups are permitted to select observers.[320]

A *preelection conference* of the parties and the Board agent is usually held. At this conference, the voter eligibility list[321] is checked, the authorized observers are identified, and other election details are handled.

Observers are given their instructions[322] by the Board agent prior to the election. They check procedures at the balloting and the counting of ballots, aid in identifying voters, and generally assist the Board agent. Their most important function is that of challenging voters. For this purpose, they may keep a

---

[313]Breman Steel Co., 115 NLRB 247, 37 LRRM 1273 (1956).
[314]Rules and Regs. §102.69(a); NLRB Field Manual 11310.
[315]Rules and Regs. §102.69(a); Statements of Procedure §101.19(a)(2).
[316]NLRB Field Manual 11310; Worth Food Market Stores, Inc., 103 NLRB 259, 31 LRRM 1527 (1953). *But cf.* Soerens Motor Co., 106 NLRB 1388, 33 LRRM 1021 (1953) (presence of union secretary who was former employee of employer permitted, since (1) discharge was subject of unfair labor practice charges at time of election and (2) presence did not exert undue influence on voters).
[317]Watkins Brick Co., 107 NLRB 500, 33 LRRM 1176 (1953) (employer's vice-president, treasurer, and office manager); International Stamping Co., 97 NLRB 921, 29 LRRM 1158 (1951) (son and sister-in-law of employer's president); Peabody Eng'r Co., 95 NLRB 952, 28 LRRM 1391 (1959) (employer's attorney).
[318]Mountain States Tel. & Tel. Co., 207 NLRB 552, 84 LRRM 1483 (1973).
[319]Kroder-Reubel Co., 72 NLRB 240, 19 LRRM 1155 (1947).
[320]NLRB Field Manual 11310. *See* Chapter 9 *supra* at notes 85-92.
[321]*See* notes 239-52 *supra* and accompanying text.
[322]NLRB Form 722.

list of voters whose ballots they intend to challenge but not a list to establish who votes.[323]

2. Balloting. *a. The Ballot.* Ballots are furnished by the Board in all cases. According to established Board practice, no one but the Board agent and the voter may handle a ballot.[324] The color of the ballot for a particular group or unit will not be disclosed to the parties prior to the voting. If the regional director concludes that the voters will not be misled, a union may be permitted to use a shortened name, regardless of whether the matter was raised in the hearing. The phrasing of the question on the ballot is determined by the direction of election.[325] The ballot gives the employee a choice whether or not to be represented by the petitioner. In a craft-severance election, however, the only question is: By whom does the employee wish to be represented?[326]

b. Voting. The actual polling is always conducted and supervised by Board agents.[327] Voting is by secret ballot and takes place in voting booths, because of the necessity that the employees be furnished a place where they can vote in absolute secrecy. As the voter identifies himself, his name is checked against the eligibility list and the Board agent hands him a ballot. He marks only his choice on the ballot (any other mark may affect the validity of the ballot) and puts it directly into the ballot box provided by the Board.

c. Mail Ballots. When an election involves long distances or widely scattered votes,[328] the regional director may conduct the voting by mail, in whole or in part. Specific provision for voting by mail in the direction of election is not required.[329] Prospective voters are mailed a notice of the election and a voting "kit" containing a ballot and return envelope. The parties are given notice at least 24 hours prior to dispatching the mail ballots. The returned envelopes are treated as voters for the purpose of identification and challenge, and the mail ballots are commin-

---

[323]Milwaukee Cheese Co., 112 NLRB 1383, 36 LRRM 1225 (1955) (use of duplicate of official voting list to check off employees voting held improper); Bear Creek Orchards, 90 NLRB 286, 26 LRRM 1204 (1950).
[324]NLRB Field Manual 11306.
[325]*Id.*
[326]*See* discussion of craft severance at notes 71-94 in Chapter 11 *infra.*
[327]Statements of Procedure §101.19(a)(2).
[328]NLRB Field Manual 11336.
[329]Simplot Fertilizer Co., 107 NLRB 1211, 33 LRRM 1357 (1954).

gled with any regular ballots before counting.[330] The ballots must generally be returned by the time set for receipt of ballots, but the Board made an exception to this rule in a case where a late ballot was mailed three days before due, on the basis of a finding that it was mailed at a time when the employee could reasonably have anticipated timely receipt.[331]

d. *Defective Ballots.* Unmarked[332] or improperly marked[333] ballots are void, as are write-in ballots.[334] A ballot is invalid if identification of the voter is possible,[335] or if the voter shows his marked ballot to other voters.[336] However, a defaced ballot is valid if the voter's intent is clearly indicated and the ballot has none of the above infirmities.[337] Despite several contrary decisions by circuit courts,[338] the Board takes the position that a ballot which contains no markings on its face, but indicates clear voter intent on the reverse side, is void.[339]

3. Challenges. The Board agent or any party (through its authorized observers) has the privilege of challenging for good cause the eligibility of any person to apply for a ballot and vote in the election. The ballots of such challenged persons are segregated and impounded,[340] thus allowing the Board temporarily

---

[330]NLRB Field Manual 11336.2, 11336.3, 11336.5.

[331]Queen City Paving Co., 243 NLRB 71, 101 LRRM 1472 (1979).

[332]NLRB v. Vulcan Furniture Mfg. Corp., 214 F2d 369, 34 LRRM 2449 (CA 5, 1954), *cert. denied,* 348 US 873, 35 LRRM 2058 (1954); Q-F Wholesalers, Inc., 87 NLRB 1085, 25 LRRM 1254 (1949).

[333]Semi-Steel Casting Co. v. NLRB, 160 F2d 388, 19 LRRM 2458 (CA 8, 1947), *cert. denied,* 332 US 758, 20 LRRM 2673 (1947). *See also* San Joaquin Compress, 251 NLRB 23, 105 LRRM 1007 (1980), where the Board held random marks in addition to an "X" in the "No" box voided a ballot.

[334]Woodmark Indus., Inc., 80 NLRB 1105, 23 LRRM 1209 (1948).

[335]George K. Garrett Co., 120 NLRB 484, 41 LRRM 1519 (1958); Eagle Iron Works, 117 NLRB 1053, 39 LRRM 1379 (1957); Burlington Mills Corp., 56 NLRB 365, 14 LRRM 148 (1944). *See also* NLRB v. A. G. Parrott Co., 630 F2d 212, 105 LRRM 2035 (CA 4, 1980), involving multiple ballot errors.

[336]General Photo Prods., 242 NLRB No. 197, 101 LRRM 1352 (1979). *But cf.* Sewell Plastics, Inc., 241 NLRB No. 144, 100 LRRM 1589 (1979), where the Board refused to set aside an election in which two observers had seen how some ballots were marked as they were being deposited in the ballot box.

[337]Abtex Beverage Corp., 237 NLRB 1271, 99 LRRM 1107 (1978); Belmont Smelting & Ref. Works, Inc., 115 NLRB 1481, 38 LRRM 1104 (1956); American Cable & Radio Corp., 107 NLRB 1090, 333 LRRM 1324 (1954); General Motors Corp., 107 NLRB 1096, 33 LRRM 1318 (1954).

[338]NLRB v. Wrape Forest Indus., 596 F2d 817, 101 LRRM 2001 (CA 8, 1979); Roberts Door & Window Co. v. NLRB, 540 F2d 350, 92 LRRM 3531 (CA 8, 1976); NLRB v. Tobacco Processors, Inc., 456 F2d 248, 79 LRRM 2602 (CA 4, 1972); NLRB v. Titche-Goettinger Co., 433 F2d 1045, 75 LRRM 2561 (CA 5, 1970). NLRB v. Manhattan Corp., 620 F2d 53, 104 LRRM 2700 (CA 5, 1980).

[339]Manhattan Corp., 240 NLRB 272, 100 LRRM 1193 (1979); Staco, Inc., 234 NLRB 593, 97 LRRM 1238 (1978).

[340]Rules and Regs. §102.69(a); Statements of Procedure §101.19(a)(2).

to reserve ruling on questions of voter eligibility; but the process preserves the challenged votes in the event they are found relevant. The Board agent must challenge any voter whose name is not on the official eligibility list or any voter who the agent knows or has reason to believe is ineligible. The reason for the challenge should be stated at the time the challenge is made.[341] Anyone in a job classification specifically excluded by the direction of election will be denied a ballot unless he presents plausible reasons for voting, despite the exclusion, or there is some question as to whether he is actually within the excluded group.[342]

In *NLRB* v. *A. J. Tower Co.*,[343] the Supreme Court approved the requirement that challenges to the eligibility of voters be made "prior to the actual casting of ballots," thereby giving all uncontested votes absolute finality. The Court compared this rule with the rule in political elections that once a ballot has been cast without challenge and its identity lost, its validity can no longer be challenged, adding that the political rule is "universally recognized as consistent with democratic process."[344] It follows from this rule that the Board will not permit challenges in the guise of "objections" after the election.[345] Each voter's ballot must be challenged individually when the voter appears at the polls; a party's statement at the opening of the polls that it challenges each and every voter is not a sufficient challenge.[346]

Board agents may make challenges requested by a party. In one case, for example, an election was set aside on account of the failure of a Board agent to challenge a ballot on the union's

---

[341] NLRB Field Manual 11338.

[342] *Id.* 113385.5. In NLRB v. W. R. Grace & Co., 571 F2d 279, 98 LRRM 2001 (CA 5, 1978), the Fifth Circuit upheld a Board decision rejecting an employer's contention that the election should have been set aside because the Board agent failed to investigate the employee status of an individual who was temporarily filling a supervisory position and did not offer him an opportunity to cast a challenged ballot, which could have affected the outcome of the election.

[343] 329 US 324, 19 LRRM 2128 (1946); NLRB Field Manual 11360.

[344] 329 US at 332.

[345] Norris, Inc., 63 NLRB 502, 17 LRRM 4 (1945), *enforced*, 162 F2d 50, 20 LRRM 2304 (CA 5, 1947).

[346] Whittaker Co., 94 NLRB 1151, 28 LRRM 1150 (1951); Cities Serv. Oil Co., 87 NLRB 324, 25 LRRM 1112 (1949). *See also* Westinghouse Elec. Corp., 118 NLRB 1625, 40 LRRM 1440 (1957). The Eighth Circuit, however, has held that the Board should have set aside an election because an elderly, illiterate employee, who might have been confused by a challenge to his ballot, voted for the union contrary to his intent. In so deciding this "unusual case," the court refused to apply the general rule that considerations of ballot secrecy and election finality preclude consideration of evidence as to how an employee voted or intended to vote. Alpers Jobbing Co. v. NLRB, 547 F2d 402, 94 LRRM 2145 (CA 8, 1976).

behalf;[347] the objection was sustained because there was no union observer present during the voting, and the agent was aware of a preelection agreement between the parties that the employee would vote subject to challenge. In a subsequent case, the Board held that a Board agent had no duty to make a party's challenge, which had been noted in a preelection agreement, when that party had an observer present during the election who could have exercised the challenge but failed to do so.[348] The District of Columbia Circuit has announced the following guidelines to be applied when it is necessary for a Board agent to state challenges: (1) The Board agent must be completely impartial and show no favoritism in any manner in stating the challenge; (2) the Board agent must not state challenges except when necessitated by an unexpected occurrence; and (3) if an allegation is made that the Board agent was not completely impartial, the burden rests on the alleging party to prove partiality.[349]

A challenged vote is cast as follows: The voter is given a ballot and an envelope which identifies the voter, the reason for challenge, and the challenger. The voter then marks the ballot, puts it into the envelope, and casts the sealed envelope in the ballot box. At the time of the count, the challenged ballots are segregated. If the number of challenged ballots is sufficient to affect the outcome of the election, the validity of the challenges must be determined. The regional director or Board need rule only on what is necessary to decide the election. If the number of challenged ballots is insufficient to affect the outcome, the challenges will not be resolved. If a ballot is ruled eligible, the challenge is waived unless objection is made within three days.[350] Generally the Board will not open a challenged ballot until the individual has been determined to be eligible. But in one case, the Board refused to open and examine the challenged ballot of a discharged employee as to whom there were unfair labor practice charges pending against the employer, on the ground that the employee had not explicitly waived the secrecy of her ballot so as to allow it to be opened.[351] Nevertheless, in a case involving seven discharged employees with unfair labor practice charges pending, the Board refused to open and examine the

---

[347]Laubenstein & Portz, Inc., 226 NLRB 804, 93 LRRM 1367 (1976).
[348]Fern Laboratories, Inc., 232 NLRB 379, 97 LRRM 1315 (1977).
[349]NLRB v. Schwartz Bros., 475 F2d 926, 82 LRRM 2376 (CA DC, 1973).
[350]Rules and Regs. §102.69(h).
[351]Monarch Federal Savings & Loan, 236 NLRB 874, 98 LRRM 1348 (1978).

ballots of these voters even though they had signed affidavits waiving their rights to a secret ballot.[352] The Board has held that the premature opening of challenged ballots constitutes grounds for vacating an election, because it might create an appearance that the Board had prejudged the eligibility questions.[353] The Board's normal procedure is to hold the ballots of challenged voters in abeyance until a determination of their voting eligibility has been made.[354]

C. Standards for the Conduct of Elections

The procedures for the conduct of elections are designed to insure, insofar as possible, that the outcome reflects a free and fair choice of the voters; "it has long been established that the Board is responsible for assuring properly conducted elections. . . ."[355] The Board's goal is to conduct elections "in a laboratory under conditions as nearly ideal as possible to determine the uninhibited desires of employees" and to provide "an atmosphere conducive to sober and informed exercise of the franchise, free not only from interference, restraint or coercion violative of the Act, but also from other elements which prevent or impede a reasonable choice."[356] However, the Board has also cautioned against the application of "unrealistic standards," noting that conduct which might be determinative in a small unit election might be isolated and thus insignificant in a larger unit.[357]

---

[352]El Fenix Corp., 234 NLRB 1212, 98 LRRM 1020 (1978).
[353]D & N Delivery Corp., 201 NLRB 27, 82 LRRM 1208 (1973).
[354]El Fenix Corp., *supra* note 352.
[355]Kerona Plastics Extrusion Co., 196 NLRB 1120, 80 LRRM 1231 (1972), *citing* New York Tel. Co., 109 NLRB 788, 34 LRRM 1441 (1954).
[356]Sewell Mfg. Co., 138 NLRB 66, 50 LRRM 1532 (1962), *supplemented,* 140 NLRB 220, 51 LRRM 1611 (1962). *See generally* Chapter 9 *supra.*
[357]Newport News Shipbuilding & Dry Dock Co., 239 NLRB 82, 99 LRRM 1518 (1978). The Board overruled numerous objections from the employer and an incumbent union, holding that there were no substantial and material issues warranting a hearing. The Fourth Circuit denied enforcement of a §8(a)(5) order against the employer for refusal to bargain following the Board's certification. Newport News Shipbuilding & Dry Dock Co. v. NLRB, 594 F2d 8, 100 LRRM 2798 (CA 4, 1979). The court observed that the use of paper ballots presented special risks of vote fraud, and concluded that a hearing was necessary for the limited purpose of ascertaining whether there was a reasonable likelihood that the election was corrupted by chain voting. Because of the presence of blank ballots found in trash receptacles outside the polling area, coupled with objections suggesting that a substantial number of blank ballots had been left in voting booths, and other objections that the Board was not able to account adequately for all ballots, a hearing was ordered. Upon remand and after hearing, the Board found that logistical difficulties made it not "reasonably likely" that chain voting had occurred, and it again certified the union. Newport News Shipbuilding & Dry Dock Co., 243 NLRB 99, 102

In order to test whether an election was conducted consistent with the required safeguards, parties to an election may file objections to *conduct of the election*. Such objections should be distinguished from objections to *conduct affecting the results of the election*. The latter involve alleged misconduct by a party during the campaign leading up to an election and frequently involve behavior which constitutes an independent violation of Section 8 of the Act.[358] Objections to the conduct of an election, in contrast, may involve behavior by the Board agent, union representative, employer representatives, observers, or voters, and are as likely to involve inadvertent departures from requisite standards as deliberate attempts to influence voters. In general, the Board's standards for conduct of an election involve questions regarding the opportunity to vote, conduct in and around the polling area, protection of the ballot box, and conduct of Board agents which might be construed as, or tend to imply, partiality by the Board.

1. The Opportunity to Vote. Because a certification as exclusive representative is based on the majority of those who vote, the Board has set aside elections where eligible voters have been deprived of an opportunity to vote, either by departures from the scheduled time of the election or by being prevented from reaching the polls.[359]

For example, in several cases the Board set aside elections where there had been departures from the scheduled voting period involving either delayed opening or early closing of the polls. In one case, where a Board agent had arrived 40 minutes late, the election was set aside because the votes of those "possibly excluded" from voting may have affected the outcome, and "the ensuing votes may have been affected by the conduct of the Board agent."[360] In a case involving a 40-minute delay in the opening of the polls, the Board set aside the election even though the number of eligible voters who did not vote could not have affected the outcome; the Board agreed with the regional direc-

---

LRRM 1051 (1979). The Circuit Court enforced a bargaining order based on that certification. Newport News Shipbuilding & Dry Dock Co. v. NLRB, 602 F2d 73, 102 LRRM 2531 (CA 4, 1979).

[358]*See* Chapters 6 and 9 *supra*.

[359]In addition, as discussed *supra* at notes 293-99, the Board may set aside elections where there has been inadequate posting of notices.

[360]B & B Better Baked Foods, Inc., 208 NLRB 493, 85 LRRM 1092 (1974).

tor's finding that "the votes cast may have been affected by the conduct of the Board agent."[361] In a later case, however, the Board declined to set aside an election where the Board agent was an hour and a half late in opening the polls; the Board stated that "in order to find such conduct objectionable, we require also that the late arrival of the Board agent caused, or may have caused, eligible voters to be disenfranchised."[362] Elections have also been set aside for early closing of the polls where the number of eligible voters who did not vote was sufficient to affect the outcome.[363]

Where every reasonable opportunity should be provided to allow employees to vote, closing the polls at the scheduled time, even if employees are thereby prevented from voting, is generally not considered objectionable conduct.[364] However, if an employee is permitted to case a ballot after the polls are scheduled to be closed, the Board will usually allow the ballot to be counted,[365] although the Fourth Circuit refused to enforce a bargaining order in a case where a Board agent had permitted at least 30 employees to vote after the polls were closed and had improperly excluded at least one voter.[366]

The Board has also set aside an election where an employer refused to permit possibly eligible voters to cast a ballot.[367] Elections will normally not be set aside where voters are prevented

---

[361]Nyack Hosp., 238 NLRB No. 39, 99 LRRM 1362 (1978).

[362]Jim Kraut Chevrolet, Inc., 240 NLRB 460, 100 LRRM 1227 (1979). *See also* Jobbers Meat Packing Co., 252 NLRB 41, 105 LRRM 1184 (1980).

[363]Kerona Plastics Extrusion Co., 196 NLRB 1120, 80 LRRM 1231 (1972) (polls were closed 20 minutes early in first of two voting sessions); Repcal Brass Mfg. Co., 109 NLRB 4, 34 LRRM 1277 (1954) (polls were closed 1½ to 2 minutes early and the number of employees who had not voted was sufficient to affect the outcome). *See also* Dominguez Valley Hosp., 251 NLRB 842, 105 LRRM 1122 (1980).

[364]Bancroft Mfg. Co., 210 NLRB 1007, 86 LRRM 1376 (1974), *enforced,* 516 F2d 436, 89 LRRM 3105 (CA 5, 1975). *But see* Hanford Sentinel, Inc., 163 NLRB 1004, 64 LRRM 1482 (1967) (Board set aside an election for failure to extend the voting time because of "special circumstances," including, *inter alia,* the brief duration of the voting period, the Board agent's awareness that two employees had presented themselves to vote previously, and the fact that they sought to vote "only minutes" after the polls were closed and prior to the opening of the ballot box).

[365]Howard Johnson Co., 221 NLRB 542, 90 LRRM 1575 (1975) (Member Murphy dissented on the ground that the voters had no reasonable excuse for being late).

[366]NLRB v. Bata Shoe Co., 377 F2d 821, 65 LRRM 2318 (CA 4, 1967). The court held that the Board had abused its discretion by not setting aside the election in light of the extreme closeness of the vote (1,082-to-1,036) and the high probability that the Board agent's conduct had deterred other employees from voting.

[367]Neuhoff Bros. Packers, 154 NLRB 438, 59 LRRM 1761 (1965), *enforced,* 362 F2d 611, 62 LRRM 2380 (CA 5, 1966).

from voting for personal reasons or by circumstances outside the control of the parties.[368] However, the Board has set aside an election where an employee was prevented from voting by the need to correct an emergency situation which was found to be within the control of the employer.[369]

2. Conduct in and Around the Polling Areas. The Board has held that "the final minutes before an employee casts his vote should be his own, as free from interference as possible."[370] Accordingly, the Board prohibits prolonged conversations between parties and voters waiting to vote.[371] This practice also applies to prolonged conversations between observers and voters[372] and even applies to other conversations, regardless of whether they involve electioneering.[373] The same principle was extended to conduct in which an employer representative shook hands with employees waiting to vote.[374] In another case, union partisans wearing T-shirts displaying the words "Vote UAW" paraded back and forth in view of the voters—conduct which the Fifth Circuit, in disagreement with the Board, held to be illegal electioneering.[375] The Board set aside an election where employer officials were present near the voting area.[376] The Board has held, however, that the wearing of union insignia by the union's election observers does not constitute interference with an election,[377] even in circumstances where the employer's

---

[368]Southland Corp., 232 NLRB 631, 96 LRRM 1279 (1977); Yerges Van Liners, Inc., 162 NLRB 1259, 64 LRRM 1173 (1967); Versail Mfg., Inc., 212 NLRB 592, 86 LRRM 1603 (1974).

[369]Cal Gas Redding, Inc., 241 NLRB 290, 100 LRRM 1486 (1979). It was the employer who filed the objections. Noting that it would not normally set aside an election on the basis of the conduct of the objecting party, the Board did so here because of the special circumstance that the employer had no reason to anticipate the emergency situation.

[370]Milchem, Inc., 170 NLRB 362, 67 LRRM 1395 (1968).

[371]Id. See also Midwest Stock Exch. v. NLRB, 620 F2d 629, 104 LRRM 2243 (CA 7, 1980); Star Expansion Indus. Corp., 170 NLRB 364, 67 LRRM 1400 (1968).

[372]General Dynamics Corp., 181 NLRB 874, 73 LRRM 1535 (1970). Cf. Princeton Refinery, Inc., 244 NLRB 1, 101 LRRM 1603 (1979), where conversations between an observer and a voter, which did not involve electioneering, were found not to have interfered with an election because they were not prolonged or sustained. Similarly, when the union's observer invited employees to come in and vote, this was not deemed interference. Amalgamated Indus. Union, Local 76B (University of New Haven), 246 NLRB 727, 102 LRRM 1666 (1979).

[373]Modern Hard Chrome Serv. Co., 187 NLRB 82, 75 LRRM 1498 (1970).

[374]Volt Technical Corp., 176 NLRB 832, 71 LRRM 1608 (1969).

[375]NLRB V. Decibel Prods., Inc., 657 F2d 727, 108 LRRM 2598 (1981), denying enforcement to and remanding 248 NLRB 1337, 104 LRRM 1055 (1980).

[376]Performance Measurements Co., 148 NLRB 1657, 57 LRRM 1218, supplemented, 149 NLRB 1451, 58 LRRM 1037 (1964). But cf. Components, Inc., 197 NLRB 163, 80 LRRM 1834 (1972); Serv-Air, Inc., 183 NLRB 263, 74 LRRM 1284 (1970).

[377]Colfor, Inc., 243 NLRB 465, 101 LRRM 1495 (1979).

observers were required to remove their badges identifying them as section supervisors.[378]

3. The Integrity of the Ballots and the Ballot Box. The Board has always been concerned with the integrity of the ballots and the ballot box, and avers that it "has gone to great lengths to establish and maintain the highest standards to avoid any taint of the balloting process; and where a situation . . . casts doubt or cloud over the integrity of the ballot box itself, the practice has been, without hesitation, to set aside the election."[379] In determining whether there is a cloud on the integrity of the ballot box, all relevant facts are examined.[380] Thus the Board has set aside an election where the ballot box was left unattended for between two and five minutes,[381] though it declined to set aside an election where the Board agent had left the ballot box and the unmarked ballots in the possession of the parties' observers.[382] Similarly, where an envelope containing blank ballots had been outside the Board agent's possession for a short period and there was no evidence of anyone else in the vicinity, the Board upheld the election, noting that "it is not every conceivable possibility of irregularity which requires setting aside an election, but only reasonable possibilities."[383]

4. Conduct of Board Agents. The Board has usually sought to maintain the integrity and neutrality of its procedures by insisting on high standards of conduct from Board agents, holding that

> the commission of an act by a Board agent conducting an election which tends to destroy confidence in the Board's election process, or which would reasonably be interpreted as impugning the election standards we seek to maintain, is a sufficient basis for setting aside that election.[384]

---

[378]Firestone Textiles Co., 244 NLRB 168, 102 LRRM 1197 (1979) (employer's observers were not statutory supervisors).

[379]Austill Waxed Paper Co., 169 NLRB 1109, 67 LRRM 1366 (1968).

[380]Polymers, Inc., 174 NLRB 282, 70 LRRM 1148 (1969), *enforced,* 414 F2d 999, 71 LRRM 3107 (CA 2, 1969), *cert. denied,* 396 US 1010, 73 LRRM 2121 1970).

[381]Austill Waxed Paper Co., *supra* note 379.

[382]Benavent & Fournier, Inc., 208 NLRB 636, 85 LRRM 1143 (1974).

[383]Trico Prods. Corp., 238 NLRB 380, 99 LRRM 1265 (1978).

[384]Athbro Precision Eng'r Corp., 166 NLRB 966, 65 LRRM 1699 (1967), *vacated sub nom.* Electrical Workers (IUE) v. NLRB, 67 LRRM 2361 (CA DC, 1968), *acq. sub nom.* Athbro Precision Eng'r Corp., 171 NLRB 21, 68 LRRM 1001 (1968), *enforced,* 423 F2d 573, 73 LRRM 2355 (CA 1, 1970). *Athbro* has a curious litigation history. The Board originally set aside an election on the basis of the Board agent's misconduct. The union then obtained an injunction in federal district court forcing the Board to issue a certi-

For example, in one case the Board set aside an election where an employee, who had already voted, observed the Board agent having a drink with a union representative between sessions of an election.[385]

Not all ambiguous or arguably partial conduct requires the Board or the courts to set aside an election. Elections were not set aside where, at the beginning of a voting period, a Board agent announced that the polls were opened and the employees could, if they desired, "now vote for your union representative";[386] where, after the counting of the ballots, the Board agent told two new Board lawyers who had accompanied her to the election that they were lucky, because "[y]ou've got yourself a winner";[387] and where the Board agent told the employer's observer that he thought the union would win the election and that would do the people a lot of good.[388]

In several cases, however, the Board has been held to a more exacting standard. The Fifth Circuit refused to enforce a bargaining order based on an election where a Board agent, while traveling from one polling place to another, had stopped at a motel room of a union representative and was thus observed by a company supervisor.[389] The Sixth Circuit held that the Board erred in refusing to set aside an election won by the union where a Board agent, while conducting an investigation of unfair labor practice charges,[390] had allowed himself to be introduced to employees at a union organization meeting. The Court held that the agent, whether inadvertently or not, had allowed himself to be used in a manner which seriously affected the neutrality of the Board's procedures. On the other hand, the Ninth

---

fication, and the Board acquiesced in that decision. The employer, who had not appealed the district court decision, attempted to have the First Circuit set aside a bargaining order based on that certification, which the court refused because both the Board and the employer had failed to appeal from the district court's judgment. The court did, however, agree with the Board's position with respect to the importance of the fairness and integrity of election procedures, stating: "We cannot think that the Board any less than a court, is uninterested in maintaining, as well as fairness, the appearance of fairness. The Board's public image provides the basis for its existence. The running of an election is a small price to pay for the preservation of public respect." 423 F2d at 575.

[385]Athbro Precision Eng'r Corp., *supra* note 384.

[386]Wabash Transformer Corp., 205 NLRB 148, 83 LRRM 145 (1973), *aff'd*, 509 F2d 647, 88 LRRM 2545 (CA 8), *cert. denied*, 423 US 827, 90 LRRM 2553 (1975).

[387]Wald Sound, Inc., 203 NLRB 366, 83 LRRM 1125 (1973).

[388]NLRB v. Dobbs Houses, Inc., 435 F2d 704, 76 LRRM 2120 (CA 5, 1970).

[389]Delta Drilling Co. v. NLRB, 406 F2d 109, 70 LRRM 2272 (CA 5, 1969).

[390]Provincial House, Inc. v. NLRB, 568 F2d 8, 97 LRRM 2307 (CA 6, 1977).

Circuit upheld the Board's rejection of an employer's contention that a Board agent's investigation of unfair labor practice charges filed by the union on the day before the election had destroyed the requisite laboratory conditions.[391] The court found no evidence that the agent's actions indicated favoritism or partiality. Likewise, the First Circuit held that no substantial or material fact issues warranted a hearing based on an employee's sworn allegation that the Board agent conducting the election had attempted to influence him to vote for the union.[392] Although the court stated that the Board had erred in applying only an "impact" standard to that allegation, it sustained the Board on the ground that there was no evidence that any employee's vote had been influenced by the alleged conduct.

D. Resolution of Challenges and Objections to the Election

1. Challenges. Prior to the count of the votes the parties may wish to dispose of some challenged ballots by consent.[393] Although the Board agent may encourage such action, it should not be urged on reluctant parties.[394] If the number of challenges remaining is sufficient to affect the results of the election,[395] and if they were made before the challenged votes were cast,[396] the regional director investigates the challenges.[397] This investigation is deemed nonadversary. The regional director's investigator is responsible for obtaining all available relevant facts so that full consideration may be given to all matters elicited by the investigation, whether or not urged by, or known to, the parties.[398]

2. Objections to the Election.[399] Within five working days after the parties are furnished with the tally of ballots (the parties

---

[391]NLRB v. Tri-City Linen Supply, *supra* note 103. *See also* NLRB v. Osborn Transp., Inc., 589 F2d 1275, 100 LRRM 2787 (CA 5, 1979).
[392]NLRB v. Fenway Cambridge Motor Hotel, 601 F2d 33, 101 LRRM 2858 (CA 1, 1979).
[393]*I.e.,* by withdrawing challenges, *not* by throwing out the ballots.
[394]NLRB Field Manual 11340.3.
[395]Statements of Procedure §101.19(a)(4); NLRB Field Manual 11360.
[396]NLRB v. A. J. Tower Co., 329 US 324, 19 LRRM 2128 (1946).
[397]Rules and Regs. §102.69(c); United States Rubber Co. v. NLRB, 373 F2d 602, 64 LRRM 2393 (CA 5, 1967).
[398]NLRB Field Manual 11362; J. Weingarten, Inc., 172 NLRB 2020, 69 LRRM 1118 (1968). In 1981 the Board amended §102.69(d) of its Rules and Regulations to make it clear that the regional director should hold a hearing when objections raise "substantial and material factual issues."
[399]*See* Chapter 6 *supra* and Chapter 12 *infra.*

usually receive the tally on the day of the election), any party may file with the regional director objections to the conduct of the election or to conduct affecting the results of the election.[400] The five-day limit is not tolled by unresolved challenges of voters sufficient to affect the election. The objections must contain a short statement of reasons and a recitation of service on the other parties (as well as their counsel)[401] within the five-day limit. In certain unusual circumstances, the five-day time limit has not been strictly applied. For example, the Board has held that objections received by the regional office one day late should be treated as timely where the regional office was in a time zone ahead of the objecting party's time zone; the Board considered the objecting party's efforts to file and found them reasonably calculated to effect delivery on the last permissible day.[402]

Upon receipt of timely objections, the regional director must conduct an investigation unless the party filing the objections is unable to furnish sufficient evidence to support a *prima facie* case.[403] The Board will sustain a dismissal of objections if the objecting party does not furnish supporting evidence in a timely manner;[404] however, this may be a matter of some discretion, for the Board has found that a regional director's failure to extend the time limit to be an abuse of discretion.[405] The Fourth Circuit reversed a Board decision which rejected objections supported by specific allegations of fact and directed an investigation, holding that the regional director should have conducted an investigation as required by Board rules where the information submitted suggested that laboratory conditions could have been destroyed.[406]

---

[400]Rules and Regs. §102.69; NLRB Field Manual 11392.1 ("[T]o warrant consideration, [objections] must have been filed by the close of business on the *fifth* working day following . . . the service of the tally of ballots"). *See* NLRB Field Manual 11392.1 for procedure where the deadline is missed because of delays in the mail. *See also* Rio de Oro Uranium Mines, Inc., 119 NLRB 153, 41 LRRM 1057 (1957).

[401]Rules and Regs. §102.69(a). Failure to serve the objections may constitute grounds for their dismissal. Coach and Equip. Sales Corp., 239 NLRB 340, 100 LRRM 1063 (1978). However, substantial compliance may satisfy the service requirements. Electro-Wire Prods., Inc., 242 NLRB 960, 101 LRRM 1271 (1979).

[402]Bechtel, Inc., 218 NLRB 827, 89 LRRM 1434 (1975). *See also* Nestlé Co., 240 NLRB 1310, 100 LRRM 1463 (1979). Chromalloy Mining & Minerals v. NLRB, 620 F2d 629, 104 LRRM 2987 (CA 5, 1980).

[403]NLRB Field Manual 11392.5.

[404]Classic Courts, 246 NLRB 603, 102 LRRM 1631 (1979).

[405]Midland Nat'l Life Ins. Co., 244 NLRB 3, 102 LRRM 1156 (1979), *enforced*, 621 F2d 901, 104 LRRM 2293 (CA 8, 1980); Vintage Homes, Inc., 240 NLRB 609, 100 LRRM 1303 (1979).

[406]Electronic Components Corp. v. NLRB, 546 F2d 1088, 93 LRRM 280 (CA 4, 1976).

The Board requires that the objections include a statement of reasons.[407] But Board policy also permits a regional director to set aside an election based on conduct discovered during the investigation of objections to the election, even though the particular conduct relied on was not the subject of a specific objection.[408] The Board's rationale for this approach is that it is consistent with the trend of modern pleading practice, which tends to lessen if not eliminate technical niceties. The Sixth Circuit has agreed, rejecting an employer's argument that the election was improperly overturned because the union objections did not specify the ground upon which the election was thereafter set aside.[409] The court held the objection sufficient even though it did not refer to an antiunion speech by the employer's general manager, upon which the union had relied in successfully challenging the election, since it did not appear that the company was prejudiced or taken by surprise.

The time span of conduct subject to investigation generally begins with the filing of the petition.[410] This restriction, however, has been held not to apply in certain circumstances; for example, the Board has set aside elections based on prepetition misconduct occurring in connection with a union's effort to develop a showing of interest.[411]

3. Resolution of Challenges and Objections. If the election was held under a direction of election and it appears to the regional director that substantial and material factual issues exist which can be resolved only after a hearing, a hearing must be held on such issues; otherwise the holding of a hearing is within the regional director's discretion.[412] Whether or not a hearing is held, as to a directed election the regional director may (1) issue

---

[407]Rules and Regs. §102.69(a).

[408]Seneca Foods Corp., 244 NLRB 558, 102 LRRM 1085 (1979); Midland Nat'l Life Ins. Co., *supra* note 405; Siskin Steel & Supply Co., 240 NLRB 177, 100 LRRM 1263 (1979); Dayton Tire & Rubber Co., 234 NLRB 504, 97 LRRM 1308 (1978); American Safety Equip. Corp., 234 NLRB 501, 97 LRRM 1305 (1978). *See also* Moody Nursing Home, Inc., 251 NLRB 147, 105 LRRM 1126 (1980).

[409]NLRB v. Leslie Metal Arts Co., 530 F2d 720, 92 LRRM 2428 (CA 6, 1976).

[410]Jerome J. Jacomet, 222 NLRB 899, 91 LRRM 1370 (1976); Ideal Elec. & Mfg. Co., 134 NLRB 1275, 49 LRRM 1316 (1961). *See* Chapter 9 *supra* at notes 13-21.

[411]Consolidated Foods Co., 234 NLRB 178, 97 LRRM 1116 (1978); Gibson's Discount Center, 214 NLRB 221, 87 LRRM 1291 (1974).

[412]Rules and Regs. §102.69(c); Home Town Foods, Inc. v. NLRB, 379 F2d 241, 65 LRRM 2681 (CA 5, 1967) (holding that if there are substantial and material issues of fact, employer must be given opportunity for a hearing to establish his charges).

a report on the objections and/or challenges, specifically recommend a disposition, and forward the report to the Board; or
(2) issue a supplemental decision appropriately disposing of the
objections and challenges. If the regional director issues a report
to the Board, the parties have a right to file exceptions with the
Board within 10 days. If he issues a supplemental decision, the
parties may seek Board review. As in the case of orders directing
elections, review is limited to four categories, namely:
(1) departure from reported Board precedent involving a substantial question of law or policy, (2) clear and prejudicial error
on the record regarding a substantial issue of fact, (3) prejudicial
error in the conduct of the hearing, and (4) compelling reasons
to reconsider an important Board rule or policy.[413]

In a "pure consent" election the foregoing procedure is not
applicable because the regional director's decision is virtually
final on all issues, without even a discretionary appeal. In rare
situations, however, the Board may consider a motion to set
aside the regional director's decision as being arbitrary or capricious.[414]

In a "stipulated" election the Board, rather than the regional
director, makes final determinations of challenges and objections. The regional director prepares a report on the investigation, serves it on the parties, and forwards it to the Board.
But if he orders a hearing, he may omit making the report.[415]
When the regional director forwards a report to the Board, the
parties have a right to file exceptions within 10 days. Such
exceptions may be accompanied by briefs and may be opposed
by an answering brief from any other party within 17 days of
the regional director's report. If no exceptions are filed, the
Board may decide the case on the record or otherwise dispose
of it.[416] If the election was held pursuant to a stipulation agreement, and the exceptions filed to the Board's decision do not
appear to raise substantial and material issues, the Board may
decide the case forthwith. But if the exceptions do appear to
raise such issues, the Board may order a further hearing and a
report, in which case the parties would again have the right to

---

[413]Rules and Regs. §§102.67(c), 102.69(c); but where objections raise substantial and
material issues, a hearing should be held. §102. *See* Chapter 32 *infra* at note 96.
[414]*Id.* §102.62(a).
[415]*Id.* §102.69(c).
[416]*Id.*

file (within 10 days) exceptions to the report, which the Board will then consider on their merits.[417]

If the objections to the election are overruled, a certification will be issued, provided there are no problems pending due to unresolved challenges. If the objections are found to have merit, the election will be set aside and a new election conducted.[418] A decision of the Board sustaining objections, setting aside an election, and ordering a new vote, is not directly reviewable in the courts.[419]

E. Runoff and Rerun Elections

A prerequisite to the holding of a *runoff election* is that none of the three or more choices that appeared on the ballot in the original election has received a majority of the valid votes cast. For example, in an election involving 18 eligible voters, union *A* receives seven votes, "neither" receives six votes, and union *B* receives five votes—this would be considered an inconclusive election; the regional director would then conduct a runoff election between the choices on the ballot that received the highest and the next highest number of votes, i.e., union *A* and "neither."[420] There can be no runoff of an election in which there are only two choices,[421] so there can be no runoff of a runoff election.[422] The runoff election is held as soon as possible after the original election, but not while objections are pending or still timely.[423] A timely objection to a runoff election will be considered only insofar as it relates to circumstances occurring subsequent to the original election.[424] Those eligible to vote are those who were eligible at the time of the original election.[425] However, the Board did make one exception to its general eligibility rule: Where there was a long lapse of time between the elections, with substantial employee turnover,[426] a current

---

[417]*Id.* §102.69(e).
[418]Statements of Procedure §101.19(a)(4).
[419]Bonwit Teller, Inc. v. NLRB, 197 F2d 640, 30 LRRM 2305 (CA 2, 1952). *See generally* Chapter 34 *infra.*
[420]NLRB Field Manual 11350.1.
[421]This would include a craft severance election where there were only two choices on the ballot. *Id.*
[422]*Id.* 11350.5.
[423]*Id.* 11350.3.
[424]*Id.*
[425]Thus the list can only change "downward." *Id.* 11350.5.
[426]Interlake S.S. Co., 178 NLRB 128, 72 LRRM 1008 (1969).

eligibility date was used in order to provide a more representative vote. But in a subsequent case, the Board declined to make an exception where 13 months had elapsed since the original election and the record failed to demonstrate substantial employee turnover.[427]

A runoff election may not be appropriate where voters in the original election are faced with answering two questions by a single vote. In one such *Globe election* case,[428] a single vote was taken among powerhouse employees to ascertain whether they preferred a separate unit and, if so, which union, if any, they desired to represent them. The election was conclusive concerning the preference of the employees for a separate unit, but no union on the ballot received a majority. The Board rejected the employer's contention that a second election should be deemed a runoff election with the ballot limited to the two choices in the original election that received the highest vote. Instead, the Board deemed its investigation concerning representation incomplete, and ordered a second election, since one union had not sought to represent the separate unit in the original election.

A *rerun election* is an exception to the runoff procedure (which is premised on the emergence of the top two nonmajority choices). On occasion, two of the nonmajority choices may receive the same number of votes, while the third choice may receive a higher vote but still less than a majority. In that event, the election is considered a *nullity* and is rerun.[429] A runoff may result from a rerun,[430] but a second nullity will cause a dismissal of the petition.[431] For rerun purposes, the payroll period determining eligibility is a "recent" one set by the regional director or the Board.[432]

Rerun elections will also be conducted pursuant to an order setting aside the original election because of violations of "laboratory conditions." When the first election has been set aside on account of employer or union interference, the notice of

---

[427]Lane Aviation Corp., 221 NLRB 898, 91 LRRM 1012 (1975).

[428]B. P. Alaska, Inc., 234 NLRB 125, 98 LRRM 1060 (1978); *see* Sohio Petroleum Corp. v. NLRB, 625 F2d 223, 104 LRRM 2804 (CA 9, 1980). *See also* discussion of *Globe election doctrine* at notes 29-33 in Chapter 11 *infra*.

[429]NLRB Field Manual 11350.1.

[430]*Id.* 11456.

[431]*Id.* 11350.1.

[432]*Id.* 11452.

election may include a paragraph explaining why the election is being rerun.[433]

A further exception to the runoff procedure occurs when all eligible votes have been cast, two or more choices have received an equal number of votes, the other choice has received no votes, and there are no challenges; e.g., of 16 valid votes, union A receives none, union B receives eight, and "neither" receives eight.[434] In that situation, the election will not be rerun and there will be no certification of representative; the regional director will merely certify the results of the election.

F. Certification and Revocation

When there are no timely filed objections and the voting is determinative, the regional director issues a certification of the results of the election and, where appropriate, a certification of representative. This certification has the same force and effect as if issued directly by the Board, and the proceeding is thereby closed.[435] If no union receives more than half the votes, the results of the election will be certified, showing that the union or unions are not the choice of the majority of the employees.

A union that receives a majority of the valid votes cast will be certified as the representative of the employees in the unit for purposes of collective bargaining. Thus, a union cannot be certified on the basis of a tie vote.[436] The Board may refuse certification if the legality of any stage in the representation proceeding is properly called into question,[437] or if the labor organization would be precluded from representing the employees because of supervisory domination or control, or as a result of a conflict of interest.[438]

The Board has consistently held that certifications are subject to reconsideration and that it may police its certifications by

---

[433]*Id.* 11452.1, incorporating the device adopted by the Board in *Lufkin Rule Co.*, 147 NLRB 341, 56 LRRM 1212 (1964) (notice to employees in the second election included a statement that the first election was set aside because of employer interference and that the Act gives employees the right to cast ballots as they see fit and protects them in the exercise of that right).
[434]*Id.* 11350.2.
[435]Rules and Regs. §102.69(b).
[436]John W. Thomas Co., 111 NLRB 226, 36 LRRM 1444 (1955).
[437]Worthington Pump & Mach. Corp., 99 NLRB 189, 30 LRRM 1052 (1952).
[438]*See* Sierra Vista Hosp., Inc., 241 NLRB No. 107, 100 LRRM 1590 (1979).

amendment, clarification, or even revocation.[439] In *Hughes Tool Co.*,[440] for example, the Board rescinded a certification where the certified unions had executed racially discriminatory contracts and had administered them in a manner that tended to perpetuate racial discrimination in employment. A certification may also be revoked where the certified union has exhibited a pattern of coercion or violence.[441]

The Board has extended comity to a certification issued pursuant to an election conducted by a responsible state agency, where the state agency's election procedures conformed to due process and effectuated the policies of the Act.[442] However, the Third Circuit Court of Appeals denied enforcement to a bargaining order based on the extension of comity, on the basis of its finding that the state-certified unit was inappropriate under the Act.[443]

In *Handy Andy, Inc.*,[444] the Board held that a representation proceeding is an inappropriate forum in which to adjudicate employer allegations of invidious racial, national origin, or alienage discrimination by a union. Previously, under its *Bekins*[445] rule, the Board had taken the position that issues of racial discrimination could be considered prior to certification should the union prevail in a pending election. Even under that prior rule, however, the Board held that sex discrimination would not constitute grounds for setting aside an election.[446] After *Handy Andy*, the appropriate vehicle for considering allegations of invidious discrimination is an unfair labor practice proceeding.[447]

---

[439]*See* K. McGuiness, *supra* note 1 at §10-31 *et seq;* Rules and Regs. §§102.60(b), 102.61(d), 102.61(e).

[440]147 NLRB 1573, 56 LRRM 1289 (1964). *See* Chapter 28 *infra* at note 109.

[441]Union Nacional de Trabajadores (Carborundum Co. of Puerto Rico), 219 NLRB 862, 90 LRRM 1023 (1975), *enforced,* 540 F2d 1, 92 LRRM 3425 (1976), *cert. denied,* 429 US 1039, 94 LRRM 2201 (1977). *See also* College of Osteopathic Medicine & Surgery, *supra* note 215, where union's certification of faculty unit was revoked after Board reclassified all faculty members as managerial employees, leaving no covered employees in unit.

[442]Doctors Osteopathic Hosp., 242 NLRB 447, 101 LRRM 1192 (1979); Allegheny Gen. Hosp., 230 NLRB 954, 96 LRRM 1022 (1977).

[443]Memorial Hosp. of Roxborough v. NLRB, 545 F2d 351, 93 LRRM 2571 (CA 3, 1976), *denying enforcement to* 220 NLRB 402, 90 LRRM 1369 (1975).

[444]228 NLRB 447, 94 LRRM 1354 (1977).

[445]Bekins Moving & Storage Co., 211 NLRB 138, 86 LRRM 1323 (1974).

[446]Bell & Howell Co., 213 NLRB 407, 87 LRRM 1172 (1974).

[447]*See also* Bell & Howell Co., 230 NLRB 420, 95 LRRM 1333 (1977), *enforced,* 598 F2d 136, 100 LRRM 2192 (CA DC, 1979). For further discussion of issues relating to allegations of union discrimination on the basis of race or sex, *see* Chapter 28 *infra.*

CHAPTER 11

APPROPRIATE BARGAINING UNITS

I. BACKGROUND

The bargaining unit is the formal arena of employee organizational efforts and the framework of mutual bargaining duties at the base of the entire collective bargaining process. Section 9(a) of the National Labor Relations Act provides that

> [r]epresentatives designated or selected for the purpose of collective bargaining by the majority of the employees in *a unit appropriate for such purposes,* shall be the exclusive representative of all the employees in such units . . . .[1]

The scope and composition of the bargaining unit is often a subject of dispute between union and employer and between contending unions, since this decision can determine whether the union is entitled to representative status. A union which may have organized a sufficient number of employees within a small unit may not be able to establish its majority in a larger unit. Similarly, the scope and composition of the bargaining unit may determine which of two contending unions gains representative status.

In the absence of an agreement between the parties,[2] the Board may be called upon to determine whether a petitioned-for unit of employees is an "appropriate unit" for collective bargaining. In a simple case, the issue may be whether a plant-wide unit or a separate unit of production and maintenance employees is appropriate. In more complex cases, for example, the Board may face such questions as the following: (1) Is a single-plant unit appropriate, but not a multiplant unit? (2) Do

---

[1]Emphasis added. For literature relating to bargaining units, *see* bibliographical references cited at pertinent places in this chapter.

[2]NLRB v. J.J. Collins' Sons, Inc., 332 F2d 523, 56 LRRM 2375 (CA 7, 1964). For discussion of consent election agreements, *see* Chapter 10 *supra* at notes 11 and 225-27 and Chapter 32 *infra* at notes 59-61.

413

carpenters qualify as a craft for a separate unit? (3) Is a particular department so distinct that it should be regarded as an appropriate unit?

In resolving the unit issue, "the Board's primary concern is to group together only employees who have substantial mutual interests in wages, hours, and other conditions of employment."[3] Stated in another fashion, the Board determines whether the employees share a similar *community of interests*. In approaching any unit question, it should be noted at the outset that the Board construes the statutory language to mean that the Board need not determine "the *only* appropriate unit, or the *ultimate* unit, or the *most* appropriate unit: the Act requires only that the unit be 'appropriate.' "[4]

The Board has found the "appropriate bargaining unit" concept elusive, and has not employed the discretion conferred by the Act to establish hard-and-fast rules defining units for all cases. Instead, it makes bargaining-unit determinations by use of a number of tests, including (1) extent and type of union organization of the employees; (2) bargaining history in the industry, as well as with respect to the parties before the Board; (3) similarity of duties, skills, interests, and working conditions of the employees; (4) organizational structure of the company; and (5) the desires of the employees.

In the original Wagner Act, Congress imposed on the Board the duty of determining whether a proposed or existing unit was appropriate as the employees' bargaining unit. Because of the wide differences in forms of employee organizations, the complexities of modern industry, and other variables, it was virtually impossible for Congress to include strict rules and limitations on Board actions in making unit determinations. Therefore, by use of the discretionary term "appropriate" and the inclusion of the broad standard, "in order to assure to employees the fullest freedom in exercising the rights guaranteed by this Act,"[5] Congress delegated to the Board wide latitude

---

[3]1950 NLRB ANN. REP. 39 (1951).
[4]Morand Bros. Beverage Co., 91 NLRB 409, 418, 26 LRRM 1501 (1950), *enforced*, 190 F2d 576, 28 LRRM 2364 (CA 7, 1951) (emphasis in original); *accord*, Florida Steel Corp., 222 NLRB 546, 91 LRRM 1189 (1976); Capital Bakers, Inc., 168 NLRB 904, 66 LRRM 1385 (1967); Federal Elec. Corp., 157 NLRB 1130, 61 LRRM 1500 (1966); F.W. Woolworth Co., 144 NLRB 307, 54 LRRM 1043 (1963).
[5]§9(b).

to determine appropriate bargaining units.[6] When the National Labor Relations Act was amended in 1947, Congress reenacted the same basic language for general unit determination;[7] however, it also imposed some specific limitations, as follows:

(1) Professional employees may not be included in a unit with other employees unless a majority of the professionals vote for inclusion in that unit.[8]

(2) The Board may not decide that any craft unit is inappropriate on the ground that prior Board determinations established a different unit.[9]

(3) Guards may not be included in a unit with other employees, and any organization representing guards may not be affiliated with any organization that admits other employees to membership.[10]

(4) The extent of union organization shall not be controlling in determining whether a unit is appropriate.[11]

Outside the area of these restrictions, the Board still has extremely broad discretion in determining appropriate bargaining units under the statutory polestar of "assur[ing] employees the fullest freedom in exercising the rights guaranteed by this Act."[12]

---

[6]In NLRB v. Hearst Publications, Inc., 322 US 111, 134, 14 LRRM 614 (1944), a case under the Wagner Act, the Supreme Court noted the Board's broad discretion in unit determination as follows:
"Wide variations in the forms of employee self-organization and the complexities of modern industrial organization make difficult the use of inflexible rules as the test of an appropriate unit. Congress was informed of the need for flexibility in shaping the unit to the particular case and accordingly gave the Board wide discretion in the matter."
[7]§9(b).
[8]§9(b)(1).
[9]§9(b)(2).
[10]§9(b)(3).
[11]§9(c)(5).
[12]§9(b). NLRB v. Mercy Hosps., 589 F2d 968, 98 LRRM 2800 (CA 9, 1978); Stephens Produce Co. v. NLRB, 515 F2d 1373, 89 LRRM 2311 (CA 8, 1975) (Board unit determination should not be set aside unless "arbitrary" or "capricious").
For a general discussion of the Board's overall approach to unit determinations, see Kaminsky, Overview of the Law, and the Basic Manufacturing Unit, in Appropriate Units for Collective Bargaining 1 (P. Nash & G. Blake eds. 1979); Hall, The Appropriate Bargaining Unit: Striking a Balance Between Stable Labor Relations and Employee Free Choice, 18 W. Reserve L. Rev. 479 (1967).
The statutory provisions and procedures for determination of bargaining units under the NLRB may be contrasted with those of the Railway Labor Act, 45 USC §§151-88 (1974), under which the National Mediation Board (NMB) has the duty of deciding in what craft or class the election and bargaining shall take place. Railway Labor Act §2 (Ninth), 45 USC §152 (Ninth) (1976). The NMB does not have as wide a discretion to

II. GENERAL FACTORS IN UNIT DETERMINATIONS

A. Community of Interest Among Employees

In resolving the unit issue, "the Board's primary concern is to group together only employees who have substantial mutual interests in wages, hours, and other conditions of employment."[13] Stated in another fashion, the Board determines whether the employees share a similar community of interests.

Community of interest is the fundamental factor in bargaining-unit determination involving previously unrepresented employees and also in units where an attempt is being made to sever groups of already represented employees from larger bargaining units.[14] In *Kalamazoo Paper Box Corp.*,[15] a unit-severance case, the Board enumerated the factors to be considered in determining community of interest apart from other employees:

[A] difference in method of wages or compensation; different hours of work; different employment benefits; separate supervision; the degree of dissimilar qualifications, training and skills; differences in job functions and amount of working time spent away from the employment or plant situs . . . . ; the infrequency or lack of contact with other employees; lack of integration with the work functions of other employees or interchange with them; and the history of bargaining.[16]

---

structure bargaining units, although its determinations of craft or class are not subject to judicial review. Railway Clerks v. Association for the Benefit of Non-Contract Employees (United Airlines, Inc.), 380 US 650, 59 LRRM 2051 (1965); Switchman's Union v. National Mediation Bd., 320 US 297, 13 LRRM 616 (1943); *see* Comment, *Procedure and Judicial Review under Section 2, Ninth of the Railway Labor Act,* 32 J. AIR L. & COMM. 249 (1966); A.R. Weber, THE STRUCTURE OF COLLECTIVE BARGAINING 228 (1961); *see generally* Eischen, *Representation Disputes and Their Resolution in the Railroad and Airline Industries,* in THE RAILWAY LABOR ACT AT FIFTY: COLLECTIVE BARGAINING IN THE RAILROAD AND AIRLINE INDUSTRIES 23-70 (C.M. Rehmus ed. 1977). Judicial review of NLRB unit determinations is discussed in Chapter 34 *infra.* For a comparison of procedures under the RLA and the NLRA, *see* Morris, *Procedural Reform in Labor Law—A Preliminary Paper,* 35 J. AIR L. & COMM. 537 (1969).
    [13] 1950 NLRB ANN. REP. 39 (1951). *See* Grooms, *The NLRB and Determination of the Appropriate Unit: Need for a Workable Standard,* 6 WM. & MARY L. REV. 13 (1965).
    [14] In bargaining-unit severance cases, the group of employees seeking a separate bargaining unit must not only show that they share a community of interest among themselves; they must also meet several other Board criteria for severance, as discussed at notes 71-100 *infra.*
    [15] 136 NLRB 134, 49 LRRM 1715 (1962). *Cf.* Olincraft, Inc., 179 NLRB 414, 72 LRRM 1337 (1969) (refusing to sever truck drivers from a production and maintenance unit because of similarity of employee duties and interests).
    [16] 136 NLRB at 137. While the *Kalamazoo* case dealt specifically with severance of truck drivers from a production unit, the principles announced in that case have been given general application in cases involving unit severance and in cases involving previously unrepresented employees. *See* NLRB v. Campbell Sons' Corp., 407 F2d 969, 70 LRRM

Community of interest affects the appropriateness of multi-employer units as well as single-employer units, plantwide units as well as multiplant units, and craft units as well as departmental units.

The Act itself suggests the possible appropriateness of aggregating employees by "employer unit, craft unit, plant unit, or sub-division thereof."[17] And the Board has asserted the presumptive appropriateness of the single-location unit.[18] On the other hand, the specific amendments of 1947 attach special significance to the community of skills among professionals and craftsmen, and to the security needs of the employer regarding plant guards.[19]

Thus, the Board's basic function in determining the appropriateness of a potential bargaining unit is to decide whether or not the employees share a sufficient "community of interest" and to group together for purposes of collective bargaining employees who share a common interest in wages, hours, and other conditions of employment. Although the Board has attempted to define community of interest in cases such as *Kalamazoo Paper Box Corp.*, community of interest is not susceptible to precise definition or to mechanical application. As illustrated by the cases discussed throughout this chapter, the ultimate determination frequently depends on detailed factual analysis on a case-by-case basis, rather than on the simple application of well-settled rules of law.

B. Extent of Union Organization

The scope of the union's organizing campaign, i.e., the groups of employees on which the union has focused its organizing efforts, may play a significant role in the Board's decision as to what constitutes an appropriate unit. This factor is now treated separately in the Act[20] and is referred to as *extent of organization*.

Prior to 1947, the Board found extent of organization to be an especially significant factor in determining appropriateness

---

2886 (CA 4, 1969). For application of the principle to unit clarification, *see* Kennecott Copper Corp., 176 NLRB 96, 71 LRRM 1188 (1969).

[17]§9(b).

[18]Frisch's Big Boy Ill-Mar, Inc., 147 NLRB 551, 56 LRRM 1246 (1964). For an argument challenging the Board's position, *see* Siegel, *Problems and Procedures in the NLRB Election Process*, in LABOR LAW DEVELOPMENTS 1968 (Fourteenth Annual Institute on Labor Law, Southwestern Legal Foundation) 29, 43 (1969).

[19]*See* notes 8-10 *supra* and accompanying text.

[20]§9(c)(5).

of a unit on the theory that it is often desirable to render collective bargaining a reasonably early possibility for the employees involved, lest prolonged delay expose these organized employees to the temptation of striking to obtain recognition.[21] The weight given this factor by the Board aroused considerable criticism.[22]

The critics of the Board persuaded Congress in 1947 to enact Section 9(c)(5), which provides that

> [i]n determining whether a unit is appropriate . . . the extent to which the employees have organized shall not be controlling.

Thus, a unit based solely or essentially on extent of organization is inappropriate.[23] However, the Board may give weight to the extent of organization in finding a unit appropriate, provided there are other substantial factors present on which to base the unit determination.[24] Accordingly,

> [i]t is not the Board's policy to compel labor organizations to represent the most comprehensive grouping; nor is it the Board's function to compel all employees to be represented or unrepresented at the same time or to require that a labor organization represent employees it does not wish to represent unless an appropriate unit does not otherwise exist.[25]

So long as the Board gives less than controlling weight to the extent of organization, its unit determination does not contravene the statute.[26] It may even treat extent of organization as a determinative factor which tilts the balance in favor of a particular unit and still comply with the statutory command that extent of organization not be a controlling factor.[27] Problems

[21]1947 NLRB ANN. REP. 21 (1948).
[22]See dissent by Member Reynolds in Garden State Hosiery Co., 74 NLRB 318, 20 LRRM 1149 (1947), claiming that the Board's application of the doctrine permitted "gerrymandering" by the petitioning union so as to establish a unit in which it could win an election.
[23]John A. Sundwall & Co., 149 NLRB 1022, 57 LRRM 1435 (1964); Quality Food Mkts., Inc., 126 NLRB 349, 45 LRRM 1316 (1960).
[24]Beck Corp. v. NLRB, 590 F2d 290, 100 LRRM 2719 (CA 9, 1978); NLRB v. Morganton Full Fashioned Hosiery Co., 241 F2d 913, 39 LRRM 2493 (CA 4, 1957); NLRB v. Smythe, 212 F2d 664, 34 LRRM 2108 (CA 5, 1954); Mosler Safe Co., 188 NLRB 650, 651, 76 LRRM 1524 (1971); Overnite Transp. Co., 141 NLRB 384, 52 LRRM 1361 (1963), enforced as modified, 327 F2d 36, 55 LRRM 2126 (CA 4, 1963); Waldensian Hosiery Mills, 83 NLRB 742, 24 LRRM 1129 (1949).
[25]Ballentine Packing Co., 132 NLRB 923, 925, 48 LRRM 1451 (1961).
[26]NLRB v. Metropolitan Life Ins. Co., 380 US 438, 58 LRRM 2721 (1965); NLRB v. Salant & Salant, 171 F2d 292, 23 LRRM 2265 (CA 6, 1948) (per curiam); Dixie Belle Mills, Inc., 139 NLRB 629, 631 n.7, 51 LRRM 1344 (1962).
[27]NLRB v. Southern Metal Serv., 606 F2d 512, 102 LRRM 2907 (CA 5, 1979), enforcing 236 NLRB 827, 98 LRRM 1489 (1978). See also Allied Stores of New York, Inc., 150

may arise, however, where the Board rules on extent of organization but fails to indicate precisely the weight which it is given.[28]

C. Desires of the Employees—the *Globe* Doctrine

The effectiveness of the collective bargaining process depends in large part on the coherence of the employees in the unit.[29] Where there are two or more equally appropriate units, the desires of the employees oftentimes become the critical factor. When such a situation arises, the Board's *Globe* doctrine[30] comes into play, and an election is held to determine the employees' desires on the unit issue. The doctrine is derived from *Globe Machine & Stamping Co.*[31] In a typical *Globe* situation, craft employees

> are afforded the opportunity to indicate that they prefer to be established as a separate bargaining unit, apart from a broader industrial unit in which they would otherwise be included, by voting for the craft union that seeks to represent them separately, as against the industrial union that desires to represent them as part of the broader unit. But in such an election, a majority of the employees in the craft group will sometimes vote for the "no-union" choice, or for an industrial union which fails to win a majority in the balance of the industrial unit for which it desires to bargain.[32]

NLRB 799, 807, 58 LRRM 1081 (1965), where the Board stated that the petitioner's motive in seeking a particular unit is immaterial as long as the Board does not give controlling weight to extent of organization.

[28]*See* Metropolitan Life Ins. Co. v. NLRB, 330 F2d 62, 55 LRRM 2930 (CA 6, 1964), *vacated and remanded*, 380 US 525, 59 LRRM 2063 (1965). On statewide units, *see* Central Power & Light Co., 195 NLRB 743, 79 LRRM 1489 (1972); Local 1327, Retail Clerks v. NLRB, 414 F2d 1194, 71 LRRM 2721 (CA DC, 1969).

[29]The idea of the coherence of the employees has been especially important in craft and departmental severance questions, and the *Globe* doctrine has special impact in these areas. *See infra* in this chapter at notes 71-100. For determining whether separate multiplant units should be merged into a single-employer unit, *see* Libbey-Owens-Ford Glass Co., 169 NLRB 126, 67 LRRM 1096 (1968). On the necessity of a self-determination election to determine a petition for addition of classifications in existence at the time of certification, *see* National Cash Register Co., 170 NLRB 1022, 67 LRRM 1541 (1968), *enforcement denied*, 415 F2d 1012, 72 LRRM 2051 (CA 5, 1969). Before such a self-determination election is held, the Board must determine what units would be appropriate. Pacific Southwest Airlines v. NLRB, 587 F2d 1032, 100 LRRM 2566 (CA 9, 1978), *denying enforcement to* 227 NLRB 1578, 94 LRRM 1704 (1977).

[30]3 NLRB 294, 1-A LRRM 122 (1937). The doctrine was upheld in NLRB v. Underwood Mach. Co., 179 F2d 118, 25 LRRM 2195 (CA 1, 1949). The *Globe* procedure received Supreme Court approval in Pittsburgh Plate Glass Co. v. NLRB, 313 US 146, 8 LRRM 425 (1941).

[31]*Supra* note 30.

[32]1949 NLRB Ann. Rep. 33 n.26 (1950); *see also* Western Condensing Co., 85 NLRB 981, 24 LRRM 1506 (1949).

The *Globe* procedure involves using two or more ballots in the same election (or holding two or more elections simultaneously among the different groups). To illustrate: The employees in the smaller group—ordinarily but not necessarily a craft group—vote separately to indicate whether they desire representation by (1) the union seeking to represent them in the smaller (craft) unit or (2) the union seeking to represent all of the employees in a broader (e.g., production and maintenance) unit. If a majority of the smaller group selects its own representation, its choice of unions will be certified for the smaller unit, and the representation of the remaining employees in the broader "industrial" unit will be dependent upon the "industrial" union's polling a majority in a unit which excludes the smaller group. If the "industrial" union polls a majority among both groups, its certification will cover both groups of employees.

A *Globe*-type election may also be ordered where only one union is seeking representation and the Board finds either (1) a larger all-inclusive unit or (2) a smaller unit of a group within the larger unit to be appropriate for purposes of collective bargaining. That was the situation in *Underwood Machinery Co.*,[33] where the Board found that the decisive factor was the wishes of the smaller group of employees. Accordingly, it ordered separate elections among the two employee groups and awaited the results of the elections before determining the appropriate unit or units. It declared that if the union secured a majority of the votes cast by the larger (production) group only, it would find that the larger (production) group, excluding the smaller group (erection and maintenance department), constituted the appropriate unit; but if, in addition, a majority of the smaller group also selected the union, the smaller group would be included in the same bargaining unit.

D. Bargaining History

The Board is reluctant to disturb longstanding bargaining units, whether established by agreement or by certification, when bargaining in those units has been successful. Bargaining history is therefore an important factor in unit determination.[34]

---

[33]59 NLRB 42, 15 LRRM 109 (1944).
[34]Tool Craftsmen v. Leedom, 276 F2d 514, 45 LRRM 2826 (CA DC), *cert. denied*, 364 US 815, 46 LRRM 3080 (1960); Buffalo Broadcasting Co., 242 NLRB 1105, 101 LRRM 1306 (1979); Gulf Oil Corp., 4 NLRB 133, 1-A LRRM 270 (1937). *But cf.* NLRB v.

Nevertheless, although bargaining history is customarily accorded great weight, it is not given such weight where the history runs counter to well-established Board policy,[35] where the history resulted from a consent election,[36] where the history was "checkered," brief, or ineffective,[37] where there have been changes in the bargaining unit,[38] or where the unit does not conform reasonably well to other standards of appropriateness.[39]

E. Employer's Organizational Structure

Generally, an employer is vitally interested in having the collective bargaining unit coincide with its organizational or administrative structure. Similarity of working conditions among employees, lines of supervision, and degree of functional integration[40] in the employer's operations are important factors in unit determinations, and these factors are given considerable weight in the Board's unit determinations.[41] Moreover, changes in an employer's organizational structure may require the alteration of established bargaining units.[42]

III. TYPES OF UNITS

A. Unit Classifications Required by the Act

Section 9(b) of the Act places certain statutory limitations on

---

Porter County Farm Bureau Co-op. Ass'n, 314 F2d 133, 52 LRRM 2485 (CA 7, 1963), *denying enforcement to* 133 NLRB 1019, 48 LRRM 1760 (1961) (bargaining history, not predicated on a Board certification, is not controlling as to what constitutes an appropriate bargaining unit). *See also* Puerto Rico Marine Mgmt., Inc., 242 NLRB No. 31, 101 LRRM 1134 (1979), where bargaining history was determinative because it was the only evidence adduced regarding the unit issue.

[35]Manufacturing Woodworkers Ass'n of Greater N.Y., Inc., 194 NLRB 1122, 79 LRRM 1214 (1972); Land Title Guar. & Trust Co., 194 NLRB 148, 78 LRRM 1500 (1971).

[36]A.L. Mechling Barge Lines, Inc., 192 NLRB 1118, 78 LRRM 1119 (1971); Mid-West Abrasive Co., 145 NLRB 1665, 55 LRRM 1209 (1964); Macy's San Francisco, 120 NLRB 69, 41 LRRM 1433 (1958).

[37]Duke Power Co., 191 NLRB 308, 77 LRRM 1417 (1971); Western Elec. Co., 98 NLRB 1018, 29 LRRM 1463 (1952).

[38]Pacific Northwest Bell Tel. Co., 253 NLRB 795, 106 LRRM 1006 (1980); Plymouth Shoe Co., 185 NLRB 732, 75 LRRM 1169 (1970); General Elec. Co., 185 NLRB 13, 74 LRRM 1710 (1970).

[39]Crown Zellerbach Corp., 246 NLRB 202, 102 LRRM 1434 (1979).

[40]Kaiser Aluminum & Chem. Corp., 177 NLRB 682, 71 LRRM 1422 (1969); Minnesota Mining & Mfg. Co., 129 NLRB 789, 47 LRRM 1061 (1960). *See* J. Ray McDermott & Co., Inc., 240 NLRB 864, 100 LRRM 1401 (1979).

[41]Central Greyhound Lines, 88 NLRB 13, 25 LRRM 1273 (1950); Douglas Aircraft Co., 49 NLRB 819, 12 LRRM 212 (1943).

[42]Frito-Lay, Inc., 177 NLRB 820, 71 LRRM 1442 (1969); Mahoning Mining Co., 61 NLRB 792, 16 LRRM 110 (1945).

the Board with respect to its unit determinations for at least two specific classes of employees: professional employees and guards.

1. Professionals. Prior to passage of the Taft-Hartley Act, the Board treated professional employees in the same fashion as other employees. Evidencing a concern that professionals were different from other employees and that their legitimate interests could be submerged if they were grouped with other employees, Congress provided in Section 9(b)(1) that a unit including both professionals and other employees was inappropriate "unless a majority of such professional employees vote for inclusion in such unit."[43]

The right to a separate election cannot be limited "to a single opportunity in the course of their employment for a particular employer."[44] Professional employees are entitled to a separate election even though they may have on a prior occasion voted in favor of inclusion in the larger unit with nonprofessionals.[45]

The holding of a separate election is mandatory even when the number of nonprofessionals seems insignificant. In *Leedom v. Kyne,*[46] the Supreme Court held that the failure of the Board to afford 233 professionals an opportunity to vote on whether they wished to be included in a unit with nine nonprofessionals violated the plain command of the statute.

The Board has interpreted Section 9(b)(1) as being applicable "only in situations where a representation election is sought in

---

[43]§2(12), also added by Taft-Hartley, defines "professional" employee as "(a) any employee engaged in work (i) predominantly intellectual and varied in character as opposed to routine mental, manual, mechanical, or physical work; (ii) involving the consistent exercise of discretion and judgment in its performance; (iii) of such a character that the output produced or the result accomplished cannot be standardized in relation to a given period of time; (iv) requiring knowledge of an advanced type in a field of science or learning customarily acquired by a prolonged course of specialized intellectual instruction and study in an institution of higher learning or a hospital, as distinguished from a general academic education or from an apprenticeship or from training in the performance of routine mental, manual, or physical processes; or (b) any employee, who (i) has completed the courses of specialized intellectual instruction and study described in clause (iv) of paragraph (a), and (ii) is performing related work under the supervision of a professional person to qualify himself to become a professional employee as defined in paragraph (a)." *Compare* Ryan Aeronautical Co., 132 NLRB 1160, 48 LRRM 1502 (1961), *with* Starrett Bros. & Eken, Inc., 77 NLRB 275, 22 LRRM 1003 (1948).
   Depending on their job duties, however, professionals may be exempted from the NLRA's coverage as supervisors or managerial employees. NLRB v. Yeshiva Univ., 444 US 672, 103 LRRM 2526 (1980). *See* discussion of this case *infra* at notes 259-73. *See also* discussion of managerial employees in Chapter 30 *infra* at notes 187-203.
   [44]Westinghouse Elec. Corp., 116 NLRB 1545, 1547, 39 LRRM 1039 (1956).
   [45]*Id.*
   [46]358 US 184, 43 LRRM 2222 (1958). *See* the discussion of this case in Chapter 34 *infra* at notes 128-31.

a unit including professional employees among others."[47] Applying this rule, the Board dismissed a petition to decertify a professional segment of a larger unit.[48] Where a union enters into a contract covering a professional and nonprofessional unit without first having an election, there is no violation of the law.[49] The Board holds that such a unit is appropriate on an historical basis and that an election is mandatory only when the Board establishes the unit.

Since enactment of the health care amendments to the Act, cases involving units of professional employees have appeared with increasing frequency.[50] Likewise, representation developments concerning colleges and universities have produced an increase in cases relating to academic professionals.[51]

In other areas, the Board has, on a case-by-case basis, applied the statutory definition of a "professional" to the particular jobs in dispute to determine whether or not "professional" criteria are present.[52] Under Section 2(12), the controlling factor is generally the work required of the job, rather than the individual employee's qualifications.[53] However, Section 2(12) also allows for examination of an individual's personal qualifications.[54]

Although cast in general terms, Section 2(12) contains concrete criteria which must be met before the Board will find professional status. For example, in *Express-News Corp.*,[55] the Board concluded that "journalists" (reporters, staff writers, columnists, copy editors, editorial writers and a cartoonist) were

---

[47]Westinghouse Elec. Corp., 115 NLRB 530, 542, 37 LRRM 1341 (1956).

[48]*Id.* The proper method to achieve separation is thus through a representation proceeding, not through decertification.

[49]Retail Clerks Local 324, 144 NLRB 1247, 54 LRRM 1226 (1963), where the Board stated: "We find nothing in Section 9(b)(1) or in its legislative history to suggest that Congress intended . . . to invalidate as inappropriate a historically established contract unit simply because of a joinder of professional and nonprofessional employees." *Id.* at 1252.

[50]Developments concerning health care professionals are discussed *infra* at notes 138-76.

[51]*See infra* at notes 274-313.

[52]For a comprehensive listing of such cases by specific professions, *see* Annot., 40 ALR Fed. 25 (1978).

[53]*See, e.g.,* Ohio State Legal Serv. Ass'n, 239 NLRB 594, 100 LRRM 1001 (1978); Willet Motor Coach Co., 227 NLRB 882, 95 LRRM 1082 (1977); Aeronca, Inc., 221 NLRB 326, 90 LRRM 1709 (1975); Chesapeake & Potomac Tel. Co., 192 NLRB 483, 77 LRRM 1807 (1971).

[54]*See, e.g.,* Catholic Bishop of Chicago, 235 NLRB 776, 98 LRRM 1037 (1978), in which the Board found teachers and social workers to be professionals based on the individuals' educational background and experience.

[55]223 NLRB 627, 91 LRRM 1489 (1976).

nonprofessionals because they did not have a "prolonged course of specialized intellectual instruction and study in an institution of higher learning . . . as distinguished from a general academic education" as required by Section 2(12)(a)(iv). According to the Board majority, most "journalists" had a general college education but lacked specialized education in the field of journalism or communications.[56]

2. Guards. Section 9(b)(3), which was added by the Taft-Hartley Act, prevents the Board from including in a unit "any individual employed as a guard to enforce against employees and other persons rules to protect property of the employer or to protect the safety of persons on the employer's premises." That provision also prevents the Board from certifying any labor organization as the representative of a guard unit "if such organization admits to membership or is affiliated directly or indirectly with an organization which admits to membership employees other than guards."[57]

The intent of Congress in enacting Section 9(b)(3) was "to insure to an employer that during strikes or labor unrest among his other employees he would have a core of plant-protection employees who would enforce the employer's rules for the protection of his property and persons thereon without being confronted with a division of loyalty between the employer and dissatisfied fellow union members."[58]

In situations where employees perform the duties of guards in addition to other duties, the Board will find guard status only if the guard function is an essential part of the employees' duties.[59] Thus, for example, the Board has held that firemen

---

[56]*See also* Binghamton Press Co., 226 NLRB 808, 93 LRRM 1355 (1976), where a majority of the Board followed the strict construction approach of *Express-News*.

[57]The Board has said that "mutual sympathy, common purpose, and assistance between a guard union and a nonguard union is not, without more, indicative of indirect affiliation within the meaning of Section 9(b)." Bonded Armored Carrier, Inc., 195 NLRB 346, 346, 79 LRRM 1317 (1972); *see* International Harvester Co., 145 NLRB 1747, 55 LRRM 1227 (1964) (certification revoked where union representing guards used nonguard union as its negotiator, allowed nonguard union to participate in internal union affairs, and received substantial financial aid from nonguard union).

[58]McDonnell Aircraft Corp., 109 NLRB 967, 969, 34 LRRM 1489 (1954) ("Senator Taft . . . stated that Section 9(b)(3) of the Act was inserted because the conferees were impressed with the reasoning of the Court of Appeals for the Sixth Circuit in *NLRB* v. *Jones & Laughlin Steel Corp.*, 154 F2d 932, 17 LRRM 982, deciding that guards could not be represented by the same union as represented the production and maintenance employees at their plant because otherwise they would be confronted with conflicting loyalties during periods of industrial unrest and strikes." *Id.* at 969 n.3.).

[59]For a detailed summary of decisions concerning guard status, *see* Annot., 45 ALR Fed. 428 (1979).

are guards where "an essential part of their duties and responsibilities is the enforcement of the employer's other plant protection rules and regulations."[60] Likewise, plainclothesmen who investigate traffic accidents and, on occasion, theft are considered guards, even though they lack the authority to restrain or arrest other employees.[61] On the other hand, persons who are called "guards" and "watchmen" but who lack responsibility for the enforcement of the employer's rules are not subject to the statutory exclusion from bargaining units.[62] Thus, servicemen of alarm systems are not guards within the meaning of Section 9(b)(3) because they do not enforce the employer's rules against employees, search for intruders, or restrain persons from entering the employer's premises.[63] On two occasions, the Board has held that employees engaged in traffic control were part of the production process and were not guards within the meaning of the Act.[64]

The Board, with court approval, also applies Section 9(b)(3) to guard-services employees who act as guards for other employers.[65] In applying this rule, the Board has extended guard status to armored-car company employees whose job consists of transporting other employers' money and valuables.[66]

---

[60]Chance Vought Aircraft, Inc., 110 NLRB 1342, 1346, 35 LRRM 1338 (1954); see also United Technologies Corp., 245 NLRB No. 118, 102 LRRM 1328 (1979).

[61]Burns Security Sys., Inc., 188 NLRB 222, 76 LRRM 1267 (1971) (plainclothesmen included in unit with uniformed guards who perform full range of police functions). See also Desert Palace, Inc., 209 NLRB 950, 85 LRRM 1594 (1974) (union unsuccessfully sought unit clarification to include plainclothes investigators in a unit of uniformed guards).

[62]Shattuck School, 189 NLRB 886, 77 LRRM 1164 (1971); Container Research Corp., 188 NLRB 586, 76 LRRM 1369 (1971). See also Lion Country Safari, Inc., 246 NLRB 156, 102 LRRM 1419 (1979) (nursery attendants not guards because primary function is animal care; reporting rule infractions only incidental). But see Wackenhut Corp., 196 NLRB 278, 79 LRRM 1673 (1972), where the Board excluded as "guards" employees who possessed and exercised responsibility to observe and report infractions of the employer's rules, despite the fact that they lacked power to compel compliance with such rules.

[63]Wells Fargo Alarm Serv. v. NLRB, 533 F2d 121, 92 LRRM 2009 (CA 3, 1976), enforcing 218 NLRB 68, 89 LRRM 1368 (1975).

[64]Deluxe Gen., Inc., 241 NLRB 229, 100 LRRM 1478 (1979) (movie company whistlemen and flagmen who regulate the flow of traffic during filming); City of Boston Cab Ass'n, 177 NLRB 64, 71 LRRM 1370 (1969) (taxicab "starters" who monitor the flow of taxicabs at airport and report drivers who violate taxicabs rules).

[65]E.g., Brink's, Inc., 226 NLRB 1182, 94 LRRM 1022 (1976). The Board initially held that §9(b)(3) applied only to an employer's own plant-protection employees. Brink's, Inc., 77 NLRB 1182, 22 LRRM 1133 (1948). However, in Armored Motor Serv. Co., 106 NLRB 1139, 32 LRRM 1628 (1953), the Board overruled the earlier Brink's decision, expressly adopting the Third Circuit's reasoning in NLRB v. American Dist. Tel. Co., 205 F2d 86, 32 LRRM 2210 (CA 3, 1953).

[66]E.g., Brink's, Inc., 226 NLRB 1182, 94 LRRM 1022 (1976) (couriers who deliver nonnegotiable instruments and bank correspondence in vans held "guards" under the

Guards who have been temporarily assigned out of a guard unit are analogous to employees on temporary layoff and, as such, are eligible to vote in a guard-unit election.[67]

As with professional employees, an employer and a union may voluntarily establish a unit which includes guards with other employees, since only units established by the Board fall within the statutory prohibition.[68] However, the Board will order a severence election where guards petition to sever themselves from a unit that includes nonguards, even though the larger unit had a history of successful collective bargaining.[69] Moreover, the Board will conduct a decertification election for guards, even though they do not comprise a separate bargaining unit, but rather are part of a longstanding unit of guards and nonguards.[70]

B. Unit Classifications in General

1. Craft and Departmental Units. *a. Craft Units.* Since passage of the Wagner Act in 1935, the Board has continuously been faced with the issue: Under what circumstances will separate-unit status be granted to the various crafts? In the late 1930s, the CIO was conducting massive organizing campaigns seeking predominantly plant or industrial units. The AFL, however, was organizing along craft lines, and it was often confronted with established plant or industrial units which included craft employees. Consequently, the AFL often argued that the Board should allow for craft-severance elections, enabling employees in a specific craft to obtain a separate bargaining unit.

The Board's 1939 *American Can*[71] decision was the first in a series of major craft-severance decisions issued over a span of 25 years. In *American Can* the Board held that it "is not authorized by the Act to split [an] appropriate unit thus established

---

Act; couriers included in unit with armored-car guards); Teamsters Local 639 (Dunbar Armored Express), 211 NLRB 687, 86 LRRM 1396 (1974); Armored Motor Serv. Co., *supra* note 65.
    [67]United States Steel Corp., 188 NLRB 309, 76 LRRM 1266 (1971).
    [68]NLRB v. J.J. Collins' Sons, Inc., 332 F2d 523, 56 LRRM 2375 (CA 7, 1964).
    [69]Los Angeles Bonaventure Hotel, 235 NLRB 96, 97 LRRM 1453 (1978). *See* discussion of bargaining history as factor in unit determinations at notes 34-39 *supra*.
    [70]Fisher-New Center Co., 170 NLRB 909, 67 LRRM 1502 (1968).
    [71]American Can Co., 13 NLRB 1252, 4 LRRM 392 (1939).

by collective bargaining . . . . To permit such small groups to break up an appropriate unit . . . would make stability and responsibility in collective bargaining impossible."[72] The effect of this approach was to deny craft severance once the craft was included in a broader industrial unit.

In later cases, however, the *American Can* doctrine was not rigidly applied,[73] and in its 1944 decision in *General Electric Co.*,[74] the Board modified the doctrine, declaring that severance would be permitted only if (1) the group constituted a true craft, (2) it had maintained its identity while bargaining in the more comprehensive unit, and (3) the group had protested its inclusion in the broader unit, or the broader unit had been established without its knowledge and there had been no previous consideration of the merits of a separate unit.[75]

With the intention of diminishing the restrictive effect of the *American Can* doctrine,[76] Congress included in the Taft-Hartley Act a proviso, Section 9(b)(2), to the effect that

the Board shall . . . not decide that any craft unit is inappropriate on the ground that a different unit has been established by a prior Board determination, unless a majority of the employees in the proposed craft unit vote against separate representation.

Passage of the proviso, however, failed to yield the expected effect on Board policy in craft-unit determinations. The Board retained its policy of severely limiting craft severance, though it reduced its emphasis on collective bargaining history.

Starting in 1948, the Board issued a series of decisions known collectively as the *National Tube* doctrine,[77] under which the Board focused on the integration of general production and

---

[72]*Id.* at 1256. For a discussion of the craft-severance problem, *see* Case Note, 8 B.C. IND. & COM. L. REV. 988 (1967). For definition of a craft, *see* note 78 *infra*.
[73]International Minerals & Chem. Corp., 71 NLRB 878, 19 LRRM 1059 (1946); Remington Rand, Inc., 62 NLRB 1419, 16 LRRM 274 (1945); General Elec. Co., 58 NLRB 57, 15 LRRM 33 (1944); Aluminum Co. of Am., 42 NLRB 772, 10 LRRM 202 (1942); Bendix Aviation Corp., 39 NLRB 81, 10 LRRM 4 (1942).
[74]*Supra* note 73, as discussed in Case Note, *supra* note 72, at 989-90.
[75]General Elec. Co., *supra* note 73.
[76]S. REP. NO. 105, 80th Cong., 1st Sess. 13 (1947), charged: "Since the decision in the *American Can* case (13 NLRB 1252), where the Board refused to permit craft units to be carved out from a broader bargaining unit already established, the Board, except under unusual circumstances, has virtually compelled skilled artisans to remain parts of a comprehensive plant unit."
[77]Permanente Metals Co., 89 NLRB 804, 26 LRRM 1039 (1950); Weyerhaeuser Timber Co., 87 NLRB 1076, 25 LRRM 1173 (1949); Corn Prods. Ref. Co., 80 NLRB 362, 23 LRRM 1090 (1948); National Tube Co., 76 NLRB 1199, 21 LRRM 1292 (1948).

craft operations in the industry involved and imposed a restrictive definition of what constitutes a true craft.[78] Under the *National Tube* doctrine, the Board denied craft severance and initial establishment of craft units in four industries,[79] based on the rationale that the industries were so highly integrated that to allow severance, even of a true craft, would upset the stability of labor relations in these industries contrary to the purpose of the Act.

The next major decision, in 1954, was *American Potash & Chemical Corp.*,[80] which represented an important step toward lessening the restrictions on craft severance. The Board reexamined the legislative history of the 1947 proviso and concluded that "the right of separate representation should not be denied the members of a craft group merely because they are employed in an industry which involves highly integrated production processes and in which the prevailing pattern of bargaining is industrial in character."[81] Henceforth, "a craft group will be appropriate for severance purposes in cases where a true craft group is sought and where, in addition, the union seeking to represent it is one which traditionally represents that craft."[82] Although *American Potash* rejected the *National Tube* doctrine, the Board nevertheless declared in *American Potash* that it would not allow craft severance in those industries to which the *National Tube* doctrine had been applied.

The Board's 1966 *Mallinckrodt Chemical Works*[83] decision and two related decisions[84] are the final cases in the series of major decisions on craft severance. In *Mallinckrodt* the Board sharply

---

[78]For a group to be defined as a craft, its members must possess skills requiring a substantial period of training, the group seeking severance must be homogeneous, and its members must have little or no interchange with the employees working at unskilled or semiskilled jobs. Allis-Chalmers Mfg. Co., 77 NLRB 719, 22 LRRM 1085 (1948); Caterpillar Tractor Co., 77 NLRB 457, 22 LRRM 1033 (1948); American Mfg. Co., 76 NLRB 647, 21 LRRM 1232 (1948); Lockheed Aircraft Corp., 57 NLRB 41, 14 LRRM 216 (1944).
[79]The four industries were basic steel, basic aluminum, lumbering, and wet milling.
[80]107 NLRB 1418, 33 LRRM 1380 (1954).
[81]*Id.* at 1421.
[82]*Id.* at 1422. The Board defined a true craft unit as consisting of "a distinct and homogeneous group of skilled journeymen craftsmen, working as such, together with their apprentices and/or helpers. To be a 'journeyman craftsman' an individual must have a kind and degree of skill which is normally acquired only by undergoing a substantial period of apprenticeship or comparable training." *Id.* at 1423.
[83]162 NLRB 387, 64 LRRM 1011 (1966).
[84]Holmberg, Inc., 162 NLRB 407, 64 LRRM 1025 (1966). E. I. du Pont, 162 NLRB 413, 64 LRRM 1021 (1966).

criticized the *American Potash* decision for "confining consideration solely to the interests favoring severance"[85] and for "arbitrarily [freezing] the so-called *National Tube* industries."[86] Instead, the Board declared that henceforth craft severance would be based on all the relevant factors, including, but not limited to the following:

1. Whether or not the proposed unit consists of a distinct and homogeneous group of skilled journeymen craftsmen performing the functions of their craft on a nonrepetitive basis, or of employees constituting a functionally distinct department, working in trades or occupations for which a tradition of separate representation exists.

2. The history of collective bargaining of the employees sought at the plant involved, and at other plants of the employer, with emphasis on whether the existing patterns of bargaining are productive of stability in labor relations, and whether such stability will be unduly disrupted by the destruction of the existing patterns of representation.

3. The extent to which the employees in the proposed unit have established and maintained their separate identity during the period of inclusion in a broader unit, and the extent of their participation or lack of participation in the establishment and maintenance of the existing pattern of representation and the prior opportunities, if any, afforded them to obtain separate representation.

4. The history and pattern of collective bargaining in the industry involved.

5. The degree of integration of the employer's production processes, including the extent to which the continued normal operation of the production processes is dependent upon the performance of the assigned functions of the employees in the proposed unit.

6. The qualifications of the union seeking to "carve out" a separate unit, including that union's experience in representing employees like those involved in the severance action.[87]

In *Mallinckrodt* the union had sought a unit composed of all instrument mechanics, apprentices, and helpers. There were 12 such employees out of a total of 280 production and maintenance employees, all of whom were represented in the existing bargaining unit. In dismissing the petition, the Board based its decision primarily on the facts that (1) the work of the instrument mechanics was intimately related to the production proc-

---

[85]Mallinckrodt Chem. Works, *supra* note 83 at 396.
[86]*Id.*
[87]Mallinckrodt Chem. Works, *supra* note 83. Although *Mallinckrodt* dealt with craft severance, the Board, in a companion case to *Mallinckrodt*, held that the same factors would be applied to cases involving the appropriateness of establishing craft units at unorganized employers. E. I. du Pont, *supra* note 84.

ess, (2) they had been represented as part of a production and maintenance unit for the preceding 25 years, and (3) the petitioner had not traditionally represented the craft of instrument mechanic.

Mallinckrodt remains the standard against which the Board measures craft-severance petitions. The cases[88] and the commentators[89] have indicated that the *Mallinckrodt* standard usually results in a denial of craft severance. For example, in *Dow Chemical Co.*,[90] the Board denied petitions for severance of five separate groups of craftsmen (electrical workers, pipe fitters, painters, sheet metal workers, and carpenters) where they shared substantially common working conditions and benefits with production employees, where their work was highly integrated with the employer's entire production process, and where the bargaining history favored a single overall unit.

Likewise, in *La-Z-Boy Chair Co.*,[91] a petition to sever tool and die employees from a unit of production and maintenance employees was rejected by a Board majority.[92] In applying the *Mallinckrodt* standard, the majority gave controlling weight to the successful 20-year bargaining history, the high degree of

---

[88]*See, e.g.*, La-Z-Boy Chair Co., 235 NLRB 77, 97 LRRM 1490 (1978) (discussed *infra* at note 91); Boise Cascade Corp., 238 NLRB 1022, 99 LRRM 1411 (1978) (instrument men); International Foundation, 234 NLRB 277, 97 LRRM 1144 (1978) (printing and composing employees); Bendix Corp., 227 NLRB 1534, 94 LRRM 1596 (1976) (metal platers); Beaunit Corp., 224 NLRB 1502, 92 LRRM 1458 (1976) (electrical mechanics and instrument mechanics); Firestone Tire & Rubber Co., 223 NLRB 904, 91 LRRM 1561 (1976) (attempt to sever multicraft group from general production and maintenance unit); Union Carbide Corp., 205 NLRB 794, 84 LRRM 1065 (1973) (machinists and instrument makers); E. I. du Pont, 205 NLRB 552, 84 LRRM 1036 (1973) (engineers); Dow Chemical Co., 202 NLRB 17, 82 LRRM 1594 (1973) (discussed *infra* at note 90); ASG Indus., 190 NLRB 557, 77 LRRM 1245 (1971) (electricians and powerhouse employees); Lear-Siegler, Inc., 170 NLRB 766, 67 LRRM 1522 (1968) (union petitioned for nine separate craft units); Timber Products Co., 164 NLRB 1060, 65 LRRM 1189 (1967) (maintenance electricians); North Am. Aviation, Inc., 162 NLRB 1267, 64 LRRM 1146 (1967) (welders). For cases in which craft severance has been granted, *see* Golden Gateway Center, 195 NLRB 492, 79 LRRM 1437 (1972) (maintenance painters); Mason & Hanger-Silas Mason Co., 180 NLRB 467, 73 LRRM 1010 (1969) (discussed *infra* at note 94); Buddy L Corp., 167 NLRB 808, 66 LRRM 1150 (1968) (toolroom employees).

[89]Fanning, *The Taft-Hartley Act—Twenty Years Later*, N.Y.U. TWENTIETH ANNUAL CONFERENCE ON LABOR 209 (1968); DuRoss, *Craft Severance and National Labor Policy—The Aftermath of Mallinckrodt*, 30 U. PITT. L. REV. 577 (1969). *See* Miller & Robbins, *Accretions and Craft Severance*, in APPROPRIATE UNITS FOR COLLECTIVE BARGAINING, *supra* note 12 at 98-104, and Abodeely, *NLRB Craft Severance Policies: Preeminence of the Bargaining History Factor After Mallinckrodt*, 11 B.C. IND. & COM. L. REV. 411 (1970), where the Board is criticized for relying too heavily on bargaining history in its post-*Mallinckrodt* decisions.

[90]*Supra* note 88.

[91]*Supra* note 88.

[92]Chairman Fanning and Member Murphy dissenting.

functional integration, the degree of participation by tool and die employees in contract negotiations, the overlapping of supervision, the common seniority system, and the lack of evidence that the petitioner was specially qualified to represent tool and die employees or that the incumbent union had failed to represent them adequately.

Craft severance has been granted under *Mallinckrodt* only in isolated or unusual situations.[93] For example, in *Mason & Hanger-Silas Mason Co.,*[94] the Board granted severance to a unit of approximately 44 tool and die makers, machinists, apprentices, helpers and welders who were part of a production and maintenance unit. In ruling that severance was appropriate, the Board found controlling that the employer's 6000 employees were represented by 10 different unions and the bargaining history in the production and maintenance unit was limited to a single three-year agreement, which had been preceded by a long period of separate representation. The Board concluded that granting severance would not disrupt the stability of labor relations in the plant.

The Board's reluctance to disrupt an established stable bargaining relationship will generally prevail over a claim that a separate craft unit is entitled to different representation.

b. Departmental Units. Board policy regarding departmental units has been greatly influenced by Board policy regarding craft severance.[95] In the aftermath of *Mallinckrodt,*[96] the Board has approached departmental unit issues, whether involving unit severance or unorganized employers, by examining all of the facts on a case-by-case basis without applying strict tests. Departmental unit decisions emphasize several factors, including (1) differences in skills, (2) difference in training, (3) degree of common supervision, (4) interchange with other employees, and (5) differences in types of performance ratings.[97] For exam-

---

[93] *See* cases cited in note 88 *supra.*
[94] *Supra* note 88.
[95] *See* notes 71-94 *supra* and accompanying text.
[96] *Supra* note 83. *Mallinckrodt* overruled *American Potash, supra* note 80, under which departmental units would be held appropriate only if strong evidence was presented establishing that (1) the departmental group was functionally distinct and separate and (2) the petitioner has traditionally devoted itself to serving the special interests of employees in similar departments.
[97] *See, e.g.,* Anaheim Operating, Inc. (Sheraton-Anaheim Hotel), 252 NLRB 959, 105 LRRM 1333 (1980); Stephens Produce, 214 NLRB 131, 88 LRRM 1363 (1974), *enforced,* 515 F2d 1373, 89 LRRM 2311 (CA 8, 1975) (discussed *infra* in text); Witt-Armstrong

ple, in *Stephens Produce Co.*,[98] the Board concluded that meat department employees constituted a separate and distinct unit from bakery and dairy employees, based on evidence of differences in skills, jobs, training, compensation, benefits, working conditions, degree of supervision, the interchange and contact with other employees, the nature of the unit sought by the petitioner, predominant industry practices, and prior bargaining history.[99] As part of this trend toward flexibility, separate departmental units have frequently been held appropriate in cases involving retail stores.[100] The trend indicates that departmental unit cases are more frequently decided on overall detailed factual analysis, and few hard-and-fast rules apply.

2. Plant and Employer Units. In determining whether to direct an election in a unit encompassing more than one plant, store, or office, or to limit the unit to a single facility or less than an employer-wide grouping, the Board considers a number of factors including (1) prior bargaining history, (2) centralization of management, particularly regarding labor relations, (3) extent of employee interchange, (4) degree of interdependence or autonomy of facilities, (5) differences or similarities in skills and functions of employees, and (6) geographical location of facilities in relation to each other.[101]

The Board has also developed presumptions in favor of single-plant units in various industries. The development of these presumptions was slow and in some industries required overruling previous policies. In early decisions the Board relied on

---

Equip. Co., 214 NLRB 721, 87 LRRM 1574 (1974); Juilliard School, 208 NLRB 153, 85 LRRM 1129 (1974); Cone Mills Corp., 187 NLRB 759, 76 LRRM 1179 (1971). Employee desires may, however, be determinative. Lianco Container Co., 177 NLRB 907, 71 LRRM 1483 (1969).
[98]*Supra* note 97.
[99]The Board, however, has refused to separate meat department employees from a grocery's other employees where such factors did not exist. Yaohan of Cal., 252 NLRB 309, 105 LRRM 1293 (1980); Great Day, Inc., 248 NLRB 527, 103 LRRM 1451 (1980); Ashcraft's Mkt., Inc., 246 NLRB No. 68, 102 LRRM 1592 (1979). *See also* Weber's Food Serv., Inc., 244 NLRB No. 98, 102 LRRM 1148 (1979), where the Board held that meat department employees should not be included in an overall storewide unit; furthermore, bakery and "deli" employees should not be included in an overall storewide unit since their community of interest was more closely identified with the meat department employees.
[100]*See, e.g.,* Wickes Furniture, 231 NLRB 154, 95 LRRM 1545 (1977) (selling employees); J. C. Penney Co., 196 NLRB 708, 80 LRRM 1071 (1972) (automotive service department employees); Arnold Constable Corp., 150 NLRB 788, 58 LRRM 1086 (1965) (selling, office, and restaurant employees). *But see* Beco Stores, 197 NLRB 1105, 80 LRRM 1493 (1972) (separate unit for nonselling employees held inappropriate on overall review of facts).
[101]Trustees of Columbia Univ., 222 NLRB 309, 91 LRRM 1276 (1976).

the statutory reference to "plant unit[s]" in Section 9(b), finding a presumption in favor of plant units over types of units not expressly mentioned in Section 9(b).[102] In a 1958 decision involving manufacturing operations, the Board stated that "a single plant unit is generally appropriate for collective bargaining purposes, unless such plant unit has been so effectively merged with another as to destroy its identity."[103] This presumption with regard to manufacturing units has been frequently repeated and continues to apply today.[104]

The Board also applies this presumption in favor of single "plant" units to the retail and insurance industries, although in both industries it was necessary for the Board to overrule prior policy in order to adopt the presumption. As to retail operations, prior to 1962 the Board's policy was that "absent unusual circumstances, the appropriate bargaining unit should embrace employees of all stores located within an employer's administrative division or geographic area."[105] However, in its 1962 decision in *Sav-on Drugs, Inc.*,[106] the Board rejected the administrative-division/geographic-area policy, stating:

> Reviewing our experience under that policy we believe that too frequently it has operated to impede the exercise by employees in retail chain operations of their rights to self-organization guaranteed in Section 7 of the Act. In our opinion that policy has overemphasized the administrative grouping of merchandising outlets at the expense of factors such as geographic separation of the several outlets and the local managerial autonomy of the separate outlets; and it has ignored completely as a factor the extent to which the claiming labor

---

[102]Beaumont Forging Co., 110 NLRB 2200, 35 LRRM 1410 (1954) (plant unit presumptively favored over two departmental units); Hy-Grade Food Prods. Co., 85 NLRB 841, 848, 24 LRRM 1491 (1949) (Member Murdock, concurring opinion). §9(b) expressly mentions the "employer unit, craft unit, plant unit, or subdivision thereof."

[103]Temco Aircraft Corp., 121 NLRB 1085, 1088, 42 LRRM 1538 (1958).

[104]*E.g.*, Penn Color, Inc., 249 NLRB 1117, 104 LRRM 1229 (1980); J. Ray McDermott & Co., 240 NLRB 864, 100 LRRM 1401 (1979); Hamburg Knitting Mills, 239 NLRB 1231, 100 LRRM 1237 (1979); Kendall Co., 184 NLRB 847, 74 LRRM 1623 (1970); Kent Plastics Corp., 183 NLRB 612, 74 LRRM 1312 (1970); Leslie Metal Arts Co., 167 NLRB 693, 66 LRRM 1134 (1967); National Cash Register Co., 166 NLRB 173, 65 LRRM 1441 (1967); Marks Oxygen Co., 147 NLRB 228, 56 LRRM 1187 (1964); Dixie Belle Mills, 139 NLRB 629, 51 LRRM 1344 (1962). *Cf.* Pickering & Co., 248 NLRB 772, 103 LRRM 1489 (1980) (presumptive appropriateness of a single-employer manufacturing unit was rebutted). For judicial approval of the Board's presumption favoring a single-plant unit, *see, e.g.*, NLRB v. New Enterprise Stone & Lime Co., 413 F2d 117, 71 LRRM 2802 (CA 3, 1969).

[105]Robert Hall Clothes, Inc., 118 NLRB 1096, 1098, 40 LRRM 1322 (1957); *accord, e.g.*, Father & Son Shoe Stores, Inc., 117 NLRB 1479, 40 LRRM 1032 (1957); Sparkle Mkts. Co., 113 NLRB 790, 36 LRRM 1388 (1955); Safeway Stores, Inc., 96 NLRB 998, 28 LRRM 1622 (1951).

[106]138 NLRB 1032, 51 LRRM 1152 (1962).

organization had sought to organize the employees of the retail chain. We have decided to modify this policy and to apply to retail chain operations the same unit policy which we apply to multiplant enterprises in general. Therefore, whether a proposed unit which is confined to one of two or more retail establishments making up an employer's retail chain is appropriate will be determined in the light of all the circumstances of the case.[107]

Six years following *Sav-on Drugs,* the Board noted that it had "consistently found [single store] units appropriate unless counterveiling factors were present";[108] it therefore concluded that "a single store in a retail chain, like single locations in multi-location enterprises in other industries, is *presumptively* an appropriate unit for bargaining."[109] The Board has continued to apply the presumption in retail store cases.[110]

The early cases in the insurance industry likewise favored multilocation units. In its 1944 decision in *Metropolitan Life*[111] the Board adopted a statewide unit presumption under which "in the absence of unusual circumstances, the practice of setting up units of insurance agents smaller than state-wide in scope should be avoided."[112] The Board believed that the rapid unionization of insurance agents made it clear "that provisional units less than State-wide in scope are, under ordinary circumstances, unnecessary to make collective bargaining reasonably possible

---

[107]*Id.* at 1033.
[108]Haag Drug Co., 169 NLRB 877, 877, 67 LRRM 1289 (1968) (*see* cases cited at 877 n.3; Board analyzes mixed reaction of circuit courts to post-*Sav-on* decisions, *id.* at 879).
[109]*Id.* (emphasis in original).
[110]*E.g.,* Big Y Foods, Inc., 238 NLRB 860, 99 LRRM 1366 (1978); Bud's Food Store, Inc., 236 NLRB 1203, 98 LRRM 1386 (1978); Buehler's Food Mkts., Inc., 232 NLRB 785, 96 LRRM 1322 (1977); Wickes Corp., 231 NLRB 154, 95 LRRM 1545 (1977); Pneumo Corp., 228 NLRB 1443, 95 LRRM 1018 (1977); *see* Sears, Roebuck & Co., 253 NLRB 211, 105 LRRM 1512 (1980) (decertification election ordered for single-store unit notwithstanding history of multistore bargaining).
For examples of cases where the presumption has been rebutted, *see* ITT Continental Baking Co., 231 NLRB 326, 96 LRRM 1002 (1977) (store managers lacked authority over employee relations; close geographic proximity of stores); Petrie Stores Corp., 212 NLRB 130, 86 LRRM 1509 (1974) (high degree of employee transfer; store managers lacked authority over employee relations; close geographic proximity of stores); The Pep-Boys, 172 NLRB 246, 68 LRRM 1308 (1968) ((1) geographic proximity of many stores; (2) substantial and frequent interchange of employees; (3) limited authority of each store manager; (4) close supervision exercised by district manager). For circuit court reaction to the single-store unit presumption, *see* NLRB v. Chicago Health & Tennis Clubs, Inc., 567 F2d 331, 96 LRRM 3249 (CA 7, 1977) (in consolidated cases, court reviewed history of single-store unit presumption and approved of single-store unit in one case and disapproved of single-store unit in another). *See* Schnitzler & Giovannetti, *Retail Stores,* in APPROPRIATE UNITS FOR COLLECTIVE BARGAINING, *supra* note 12 at 120-27.
[111]Metropolitan Life Ins. Co., 56 NLRB 1635, 14 LRRM 187 (1944).
[112]*Id.* at 1640.

for them if they desire it."[113] After 17 years of a not-smaller-than-statewide-unit policy, the Board in its 1961 *Quaker City Life Insurance Co.*[114] decision changed its policy, stating: "the [statewide-unit] rule was adopted *solely* in anticipation of broader organization on a companywide or statewide basis . . . [which] has not materialized, and the result of the rule has been to arrest the organizational development of insurance agents to an extent certainly never contemplated by the Act . . . . Accordingly, . . . we shall apply our normal unit principles to the cases as they arise."[115] However, the decisions under the *Quaker City* case-by-case approach lacked coherency[116] and produced conflicting circuit court decisions, with the First Circuit concluding that the Board was giving controlling weight to the extent of organization in violation of Section 9(c)(5).[117] The Supreme Court, in its 1965 *NLRB* v. *Metropolitan Life Insurance Co.*[118] decision, remanded the case to the Board because the Board had failed to articulate its reasons for finding that debit insurance agents at a district office constituted an appropriate unit; therefore the Court could not determine whether controlling weight had been given to the extent of organization. On remand, the Board reviewed its policy and the structure of the insurance industry, concluding: "[T]he district office is the insurance industry's analogue of the single manufacturing plant, or the single store of a retail chain. Accordingly, if petitioned for, we will ordinarily find a single district office to be an appropriate bargaining unit for insurance agents . . . ."[119] The Board has continued to apply this presump-

---

[113]*Id.* The Board had previously approved of "provisional units" that were less-than-statewide, relying heavily on the extent of union organization and the belief that the "provisional units" would grow into statewide units. *See* cases discussed in Washington Nat'l Ins. Co., 64 NLRB 929, 930 n.1, 17 LRRM 154 (1945), and Metropolitan Life Ins. Co., *supra* note 111 at 1640.

[114]134 NLRB 960, 49 LRRM 1281 (1961), *aff'd,* 319 F2d 690, 53 LRRM 2519 (CA 4, 1963).

[115]134 NLRB at 962.

[116]*Compare* Metropolitan Life Ins. Co. (Cleveland), 141 NLRB 1074, 52 LRRM 1451 (1963), *enforced,* 330 F2d 62, 55 LRRM 2930 (CA 6, 1964), *vacated and remanded per curiam,* 380 US 525, 59 LRRM 2063 (1965) (unit of six city offices and three suburban offices held appropriate), *with* Metropolitan Life Ins. Co. (Chicago), 144 NLRB 149, 54 LRRM 1005 (1963) (unit of city offices, excluding suburban offices, held appropriate).

[117]*Compare* NLRB v. Metropolitan Life Ins. Co. (Woonsocket, R.I.), 327 F2d 906, 55 LRRM 2444 (CA 1, 1964), *vacated and remanded,* 380 US 438, 58 LRRM 2721 (1965), *with* Metropolitan Life Ins. Co. v. NLRB (Cleveland), *supra* note 116, *and* Metropolitan Life Ins. Co. (Wilmington, Del.) v. NLRB, 328 F2d 820, 55 LRRM 2448 (CA 3, 1964), *vacated and remanded per curiam,* 380 US 523, 59 LRRM 2063 (1965).

[118]*Supra* note 117.

[119]Metropolitan Life Ins. Co. (Woonsocket, R.I.), 156 NLRB 1408, 1414-15, 61 LRRM 1249 (1966).

tion in favor of single district office units,[120] although in specific cases it has favored regional units over district office units.[121]

The Board has thus shown a general policy trend towards finding single-plant units presumptively appropriate. As will be observed in the next section, this presumption has also been applied to the health care industry, notwithstanding the congressional admonition against unit fragmentation in that industry.[122] The general policy, however, is not without exceptions, for the Board has favored systemwide units over single-location units in the public utility[123] and oceanic transport industries.[124]

C. Specialized Units

1. Health Care Institutions Unit. *a. Background.* In 1974 the Act was amended to extend coverage to nonprofit hospitals,[125] which previously were exempt from the statutory definition of "employer."[126] This legislation included a number of

---

[120]*E.g.*, Empire Mut. Ins. Co., 195 NLRB 284, 79 LRRM 1348 (1972); Equitable Life Ins. Co., 163 NLRB 154, 64 LRRM 1300 (1967), *enforced*, 395 F2d 750, 68 LRRM 2251 (CA 6, 1968), *cert. denied*, 393 US 849, 69 LRRM 2435 (1968).

[121]Farmers Ins. Group, 187 NLRB 844, 76 LRRM 1133 (1971); Allstate Ins. Co., 171 NLRB 142, 68 LRRM 1039 (1968). *See also* Wyandotte Sav. Bank, 245 NLRB No. 120, 102 LRRM 1349 (1979) (presumption in favor of single-office units applies to banking industry); Dun & Bradstreet, Inc., 240 NLRB 162, 100 LRRM 1297 (1979) (financial information services). *See generally* Uehlein & Stern, *Insurance and Banking*, in APPROPRIATE UNITS FOR COLLECTIVE BARGAINING, *supra* note 12 at 260-74.

[122]*See* discussion at notes 228-30 *infra.*

[123]*See* New Eng. Tel. & Tel. Co., 242 NLRB No. 121, 101 LRRM 1263 (1979); New Eng. Tel. & Tel. Co., 242 NLRB No. 120, 101 LRRM 1239 (1979); National Telecommunications, 215 NLRB 184, 87 LRRM 1696 (1974); National Tel. Co., 215 NLRB 176, 87 LRRM 1688 (1974); Atlantic Gas & Light Co., 158 NLRB 311, 62 LRRM 1026 (1966); Southwestern Bell Tel., 108 NLRB 1106, 34 LRRM 1146 (1954); New Eng. Tel. & Tel. Co., 90 NLRB 639, 26 LRRM 1259 (1950). In Tidewater Tel. Co., 181 NLRB 867, 867, 73 LRRM 1512 (1970), the Board noted:

"While the Board has generally considered that the optimum unit in public utilities is systemwide, it has not required that it be multi-department at all times and in all circumstances, particularly where, as here, no labor organization seeks to represent the employees on a more comprehensive basis. In such circumstances, a more limited unit, such as one coextensive with a smaller administrative subdivision, may also be appropriate."

Accord, Concord Tel. Co., 248 NLRB 253, 103 LRRM 1363 (1979); New Eng. Tel. & Tel. Co., 247 NLRB 1277, 103 LRRM 1356 (1980); Michigan Bell Tel. Co., 217 NLRB 428, 89 LRRM 1572 (1975); Michigan Bell Tel. Co., 217 NLRB 424, 89 LRRM 1574 (1975); Michigan Bell Tel. Co., 216 NLRB 806, 88 LRRM 1495 (1975); Iroquois Tel. Corp., 169 NLRB 344, 67 LRRM 1185 (1968); Michigan Wis. Pipe Line Co., 164 NLRB 359, 65 LRRM 1065 (1967).

[124]*See* Inter-Ocean S.S. Co., 107 NLRB 330, 33 LRRM 1132 (1953); Ocean Tow, Inc., 99 NLRB 480, 30 LRRM 1086 (1952). In Moore-McCormack Lines, Inc., 139 NLRB 796, 51 LRRM 1361 (1962), the Board acknowledged presumption in favor of fleetwide units, but held in favor of a smaller unit due to unusual facts.

[125]Pub. L. No. 93-360, 88 Stat 395 (1974).

[126]§2(2).

special provisions applicable to all "health care institutions,"[127] including those previously subject to the Act.[128]

Bargaining-unit determination issues in the health care industry received significant attention from Congress during consideration of the 1974 amendments.[129] During the congressional hearings leading to passage of the amendments, concern was expressed that unit fragmentation in health care institutions would increase labor disputes and adversely affect patient care.[130] Congress responded to this concern by specifically directing in the Senate and House committee reports that "[d]ue consideration should be given by the Board to preventing proliferation of bargaining units in the health care industry."[131] The reports cited with approval two preamendment health care industry decisions in which the Board had found inappropriate a unit of maintenance department employees in a nursing home[132] and a unit of X-ray technicians in a hospital.[133] The committee reports also approved the "trend toward broader units" reflected in another preamendment case, where a separate unit of technical employees had been found inappropriate.[134] However, one element of that decision was criticized—the Board's approval of a

---

[127]§2(14). *See also* Chapter 21 *infra* at notes 50-53 and Chapter 13 *infra* at notes 723-33.

[128]S. REP. NO. 93-766, 93d Cong., 2d Sess. 3 (1974).

[129]For bibliographic materials, *see* the following: Mulcahy & Rader, *Trends in Hospital Labor Relations,* 31 LAB. L. J. 100 (1980); Bumpass, Jr., *Appropriate Bargaining Units in Health Care Institutions: An Analysis of Congressional Intent and Its Implementation by the National Labor Relations Board,* 20 B. C. L. REV. 867 (1979); Farkas, *National Labor Relations Act: The Health Care Amendments,* 29 LAB. L. J. 259 (1978); Miller, *National Labor Relations Act—History and Interpretation of the Health Care Amendments,* 60 MARQ. L. REV. 921 (1977); Corbett, *Problems and Predictions From the Management Perspective,* in LABOR RELATIONS LAW PROBLEMS IN HOSPITALS AND THE HEALTH CARE INDUSTRY 246 (A. Knapp ed. 1977) [hereinafter cited as LABOR RELATIONS LAW PROBLEMS]; D'Alba, *Health Care Decisions of the National Labor Relations Board Since the 1974 Amendments to the National Labor Relations Act,* in LABOR RELATIONS LAW PROBLEMS, *supra,* at 15; Emanuel, *Hospital Bargaining Unit Decisions,* in LABOR RELATIONS LAW PROBLEMS, *supra,* at 187; Fanning, *Health Care Labor Relations: Problems and Predictions,* in LABOR RELATIONS LAW PROBLEMS, *supra,* at 237; King, *Legislative Review: Is Congressional Intent Being Realized—or Are Significant Changes Needed?,* in LABOR RELATIONS LAW PROBLEMS, *supra,* at 147; Pepe, *An Overview of the Changes and Their Significances,* in LABOR RELATIONS LAW PROBLEMS, *supra,* at 3; Fanning, *Health Care Amendments—A Matter of Perspective,* N.Y.U. TWENTY-NINTH ANNUAL CONFERENCE ON LABOR 201 (1976).

[130]*See* SUBCOMM. ON LABOR OF THE SENATE COMM. ON LABOR AND PUBLIC WELFARE, 93d Cong., 2d Sess., LEGISLATIVE HISTORY OF NONPROFIT HOSPITALS UNDER THE NATIONAL LABOR RELATIONS ACT (1974).

[131]S. REP. NO. 93-766, 93d Cong., 2d Sess. 5 (1974), and H.R. REP. NO. 93-1051, 93d Cong., 2d Sess. 7 (1974).

[132]S. REP. and H.R. REP., *supra* note 131 (citing Four Seasons Nursing Center of Joliet, 208 NLRB 403, 85 LRRM 1094 (1974)).

[133]*Id.* (citing Woodland Park Hosp., Inc., 205 NLRB 888, 84 LRRM 1075 (1973)).

[134]*Id.* (citing Extendicare of W. Va., Inc. (St. Luke's Hosp.), 203 NLRB 1232, 83 LRRM 1242 (1973)).

separate unit of licensed practical nurses—because it was inconsistent with the trend toward broader units.

The congressional debates which preceded enactment of the amendments gave added weight to the directive against unit proliferation in health care institutions. The co-sponsors of the legislation emphasized the importance of preventing unit proliferation, stressing that it would lead to jurisdictional disputes, work stoppages, wage whipsawing, and a higher cost for medical care. The Board was instructed to examine the public interest and use great caution in deciding health care unit cases.[135] Congress, nevertheless, recognized the Board's expertise in unit determinations, as evidenced by Senator Williams' statement at the time the Senate conference report was being considered: "While the [conference] committee clearly intends that the Board give due consideration to its admonition to avoid an undue proliferation of units in the health care industry, it did not intend to preclude the Board acting in the public interest from exercising its specialized experience and expert knowledge in determining appropriate bargaining units."[136]

b. Basic Unit Structure. The Board has approved eight basic units[137] for health care institutions which will be found appropriate if sought by a labor organization: (1) physicians, (2) registered nurses (RNs), (3) other professional employees, (4) technical employees, (5) business office clerical employees, (6) service and maintenance employees, (7) either maintenance department employees or stationary engineers, and (8) guards. The validity of this structure remains uncertain, for the appellate courts have generally taken a more literal view of the unit nonproliferation instructions contained in the legislative history, resulting in reversal of many Board decisions. These court decisions, as well as the Board decisions establishing the basic unit structure, are discussed in the sections which follow.

(1) Physicians, excluding interns and residents. In *Ohio Valley Hospital Ass'n*[138] the Board decided that separate units of employed

---

[135]120 CONG. REC. 12944-45, 13559, 22949 (1974) (comments of Sen. Taft and Rep. Ashbrook).

[136]120 CONG. REC. 22575 (1974).

[137]*See* discussion and cases *infra*. Other units emerge from time to time due to special circumstances. For example, a unit of chauffeur-drivers was approved in Michael Reese Hosp. & Medical Center, 242 NLRB 322, 101 LRRM 1157 (1979), largely because it was an unrepresented residual group that otherwise would have been denied representation.

[138]230 NLRB 604, 95 LRRM 1430 (1977) (Members Penello and Walther dissenting).

physicians are appropriate, and that physicians should be excluded from units of other professional employees. This was based on a conclusion that physicians share a distinct community of interests and that "[w]ithin the hospital hierarchy, physicians are the pivotal employees and all other patient care employees are subject to their professional direction."[139] The Board also expressed the "opinion [that] doctors have at least as separate a community of interest as nurses and are therefore entitled to the same treatment," i.e., a separate bargaining unit.[140]

In *Cedars-Sinai Medical Center*[141] the Board was called upon to consider the unit placement of hospital interns and residents. It declined to decide this question, however, holding instead that interns and residents should be excluded from any unit as they are primarily students and not "employees" as defined in the Act.[142]

The Board subsequently sought a federal court injunction to prevent a state labor relations board from taking jurisdiction over interns and residents, arguing that federal law preempts the regulation of labor relations involving interns and residents, even though they are not employees under the Act. The district court denied the injunction,[143] but the Second Circuit reversed, agreeing with the Board that the preemption doctrine precludes the state board from asserting jurisdiction.[144]

A *"Leedom v. Kyne"*[145] action to overrule *Cedars-Sinai* failed in district court.[146] That ruling was reversed by a panel of the

---

[139]*Id.* at 605.
[140]*Id. See* note 268 *infra* for discussion and rejection of managerial status for hospital staff physicians.
[141]223 NLRB 251, 91 LRRM 1398 (1976). *See* Chapter 30 *infra* at notes 296-301.
[142]§2(3). This position was reiterated in Kansas City Gen. Hosp., 225 NLRB 108, 93 LRRM 1362, and in numerous cases involving the status of interns and residents. *See* Samaritan Health Serv., Inc., 238 NLRB 629, 99 LRRM 1551 (1978); St. Clare's Hosp. & Health Center, 229 NLRB 1000, 95 LRRM 1180 (1977); Wayne State Univ., 226 NLRB 1062, 93 LRRM 1424 (1976); Deaconess Hosp. of Buffalo, 226 NLRB 1143, 93 LRRM 1511 (1976); Clark County Mental Health Center, 225 NLRB 780, 92 LRRM 1545 (1976); Barnes Hosp., 224 NLRB 552, 92 LRRM 1366 (1976); Buffalo Gen. Hosp., 224 NLRB 76, 92 LRRM 1197 (1976); University of Chicago Hosp. & Clinics, 223 NLRB 1032, 92 LRRM 1039 (1976); St. Christopher's Hosp. for Children, 223 NLRB 166, 91 LRRM 1417 (1976).
[143]NLRB v. Committee of Interns & Residents, 426 F Supp 438, 94 LRRM 2739 (SD NY, 1977).
[144]NLRB v. Committee of Interns & Residents, 556 F2d 810, 96 LRRM 2342 (CA 2, 1977), *cert. denied*, 435 US 904, 97 LRRM 2809 (1978). *See* Chapter 31 *infra* for discussion of federal preemption.
[145]358 US 184, 43 LRRM 2222 (1958).
[146]Physicians Nat'l House Staff Ass'n v. Murphy, 443 F Supp 806, 97 LRRM 2444 (D DC, 1978). *See* Chapter 34 *infra* at notes 122-75 for discussion of *Leedom v. Kyne*.

District of Columbia Circuit, which held that the Board's decision in *Cedars-Sinai* flouted the intent of Congress.[147] However, after a hearing *en banc*, the full court vacated the panel's opinion and affirmed the district court's decision.[148]

Legislation designed to overrule *Cedars-Sinai* was defeated in 1979.[149]

(2) Registered nurses. The Board's decision to separate registered nurses from other professionals was announced in one of its early and important post-amendment decisions, *Mercy Hospitals of Sacramento, Inc.*[150] Although the regional director had held that an all-professional unit was required by the unit nonproliferation "mandate," the Board reversed, primarily because of its perception that registered nurses had an "impressive history of exclusive representation and collective bargaining."[151] In numerous subsequent decisions, separate RN units have been found appropriate on a *per se* basis when sought by a petitioning or intervening labor organization.[152] The rationale for this *per se* approach was repeated in a 1977 decision, where the Board emphasized the "exclusionary representation pattern of registered nurses [which existed] across the country."[153] However, in a 1978 decision, *Allegheny General Hospital (II)*,[154] the Board abandoned national bargaining history as the underpinning of its rigid RN unit policy, holding instead that a separate RN unit

---

[147]Physicians Nat'l House Staff Ass'n v. Murphy, 100 LRRM 3055 (CA DC, 1979).
[148]Physicians Nat'l House Staff Ass'n v. Fanning, 642 F2d 492, 104 LRRM 2940 (CA DC, 1980), *cert. denied*, 450 US 917, 106 LRRM 2513 (1981).
[149]H.R. Res. 2222, 96th Cong., 1st Sess. (1979).
[150]217 NLRB 765, 89 LRRM 1097 (1975), *rev'd and remanded*, 589 F2d 968, 98 LRRM 2800 (CA 9, 1978), *cert. denied*, 440 US 910, 100 LRRM 2687 (1979), *decision on remand*, 244 NLRB 229, 102 LRRM 1016 (1979).
[151]*Id.* at 767.
[152]Sutter Community Hosps. of Sacramento, Inc., 227 NLRB 181, 94 LRRM 1450 (1976); Morristown-Hamblem Hosp. Ass'n, 226 NLRB 76, 93 LRRM 1166 (1976); St. Rose de Lima Hosp., Inc., 223 NLRB 1511, 92 LRRM 1181 (1976); Methodist Hosp. of Sacramento, Inc., 223 NLRB 1509, 92 LRRM 1198 (1976); Rockridge Medical Care Center, 221 NLRB 560, 90 LRRM 1721 (1975); Mason Clinic, 221 NLRB 374, 90 LRRM 1502 (1975); Valley Hosp., Ltd., 220 NLRB 1339, 90 LRRM 1411 (1975), *modified*, 221 NLRB 1239, 91 LRRM 1061 (1975); Doctor's Community Hosp. of Victor Valley, 220 NLRB 977, 90 LRRM 1341 (1975); St. Mary's Hosp., Inc., 220 NLRB 496, 90 LRRM 1316 (1975); Newton-Wellesley Hosp., 219 NLRB 699, 90 LRRM 1090 (1975); Meharry Medical College, 219 NLRB 488, 90 LRRM 1108 (1975); Kaiser Foundation Hosps., 219 NLRB 325, 89 LRRM 1763 (1975); Gnaden Huetten Memorial Hosp., Inc., 219 NLRB 235, 89 LRRM 1761 (1975); Presbyterian Medical Center, 218 NLRB 1266, 89 LRRM 1752 (1975); Bishop Randall Hosp., 217 NLRB 1129, 89 LRRM 1249 (1975).
[153]Texas Inst. for Rehabilitation & Research, 228 NLRB 578, 94 LRRM 1513 (1977).
[154]Allegheny Gen. Hosp. (II), 239 NLRB 872, 100 LRRM 1030 (1978), *enforcement denied*, 608 F2d 965, 102 LRRM 2784 (CA 3, 1979).

was justified on traditional community of interest grounds and that one relevant factor in evaluating community of interests is *area* practice and patterns of bargaining.

The Board's *per se* approval of RN units received a sharp rebuke in the 1979 Ninth Circuit decision in *NLRB* v. *St. Francis Hospital of Lynwood.*[155] There the Board had refused to allow the hospital to introduce evidence in support of an all-professional unit, holding that an RN unit was automatically appropriate. The court refused enforcement, holding that "the *per se* policy established in the Board's *Mercy* decision . . . is [in]consistent with the congressional directive that the Board give 'due consideration' to preventing undue proliferation of bargaining units in the health care industry and Congress's expressed approval of the trend towards broader units in this area."[156] The court concluded that "Congress sought to encourage the Board to find broader bargaining units in the health care industry rather than narrower ones," and that the Board's policy "contravenes that Congressional admonition by establishing an irrebuttable presumption in favor of certain units."[157] While acknowledging that a separate RN unit conceivably might be appropriate under some circumstances, the court stressed that "a demonstration, not a mere presumption, of a disparity of interests between registered nurses and other hospital employees" would be necessary to justify that decision.[158] The court also rejected the factual conclusions underlying the Board's RN unit policy. Although the decision in *Mercy Hospitals* rested primarily on a "singular history of collective bargaining" in separate RN units, the court "fail[ed] to see why the Board in *Mercy* found such a history to be either 'singular' or impressive."[159] Notwithstanding the Board's conclusion in *Mercy* that RNs have a separate community of interests, the court held that Congress intended that factor to be "subordinated to the directive against undue proliferation."[160] The correct standard, according to the court, is not whether RNs have a separate community of interests, but

---

[155]601 F2d 404, 101 LRRM 2943 (CA 9, 1979), *denying enforcement to* 232 NLRB 32, 97 LRRM 1297 (1977).
[156]*Id.* at 414.
[157]*Id.*
[158]*Id.* at 416.
[159]*Id.* at 418.
[160]*Id.* at 419.

whether a "disparity of interests" exists between RNs and other professional employees.[161]

In its next RN unit decision, *Newton-Wellesley Hospital*,[162] the Board responded to the Ninth Circuit's criticism. There the Board disavowed its *per se* RN unit policy, and acknowledged its responsibility to adhere to the unit nonproliferation directive. However, it held that the Ninth Circuit's "disparity of interests" test is merely a component of the historic community-of-interests standard; it therefore decided to continue applying the latter standard. The Board acknowledged that a separate RN unit might be inappropriate where unusual facts exist, but made it clear that a separate unit will be approved whenever the customary hospital fact pattern of RN community of interests is present. A later case illustrated the extreme nature of the facts necessary for a contrary result.[163]

The Board's rigid RN unit policy applies only when a petitioning or intervening union seeks that unit. When a petitioning union seeks a combined all-professional unit, and a separate RN unit is not sought by an intervening union, the combined unit has been held appropriate,[164] despite employer contention that an exclusive RN unit is the only appropriate unit.[165] The Board's decisions regarding RN-LPN (Licensed Practical Nurse) units are in apparent conflict, with one such petition having been granted and another such petition having been denied.[166]

The Board includes in an RN unit "on-call" RNs[167] as well as graduate nurses (graduates of an accredited nursing school who have not passed the RN licensing examination).[168] Nurse practitioners (RNs with additional education and responsibilities)

---

[161]The court added that even if the community-of-interests standard were applicable, the facts relied on by the Board in *Mercy* were "simply insufficient" to establish a separate community of interests among RNs. *Id.*

[162]250 NLRB 409, 104 LRRM 1384 (1980).

[163]Mount Airy Foundation, 253 NLRB 1003, 106 LRRM 1071 (1981) (unit of registered nurses at 80-bed psychiatric hospital held inappropriate where there were non-nurse professional "team leaders" and other professionals who shared a community of interests with the nurses).

[164]Valley Hosp., Ltd., 221 NLRB 1239, 91 LRRM 1061 (1975); *see* Family Doctor Medical Group, 226 NLRB 118, 93 LRRM 1193 (1976).

[165]Family Doctor Medical Group, *supra* note 164.

[166]*Compare* Maple Shade Nursing Home, Inc., 228 NLRB 1457, 96 LRRM 1411 (1977) (petitioned-for RN-LPN unit held appropriate), *with* Presbyterian Medical Center, 218 NLRB 1266, 89 LRRM 1752 (1975) (petitioned-for RN-LPN unit held inappropriate). Both decisions recognized that any RN-LPN unit would require majority approval by RNs, since LPNs are nonprofessionals.

[167]*See* cases cited in note 152 *supra.*

[168]Lydia E. Hall Hosp., 227 NLRB 573, 94 LRRM 1105 (1976).

are also included,[169] but physician extenders (specialized RNs with advanced training) have been separated from RNs and placed in a unit of other professional employees.[170]

(3) Other professionals. A separate unit of all professional employees except registered nurses was first approved in the lead decision of Mercy Hospitals of Sacramento, Inc.[171] There the Board reasoned that although a diversity of health care functions exists among various professional groups, their skills, interests, and working conditions are in many respects no more diverse than those of employees in a production and maintenance unit in the industrial sphere, or in an overall service and maintenance unit in the health care industry.

Since there was a petition for an RN unit in Mercy, the Board deferred for a later case whether, in the absence of such a petition, the only appropriate unit would consist of all professional employees including RNs. This question was answered in a later case, where the Board found appropriate a unit of professional employees excluding registered nurses, even though no union sought to represent the RNs.[172] When physicians are employed in a hospital they are also automatically excluded, along with the RNs, from a unit of other professionals.[173]

The Board's policy of automatically approving a unit of professional employees, excluding RNs and physicians, was reaffirmed in Allegheny General Hospital (II), where the Board restated the rationale for its basic hospital unit structure.[174]

With the exception of RNs and physicians, the Board consistently finds inappropriate separate units for individual professional classifications (such as medical laboratory technologists and pharmacists),[175] in the absence of special circumstances inherent in the nature of the particular health care institution.[176]

---

[169]Rockridge Medical Care Center, 221 NLRB 560, 90 LRRM 1721 (1975).
[170]Kaiser Foundation Health Plan of Colo. & Permanente Servs. of Colo., Inc., 230 NLRB 438, 95 LRRM 1376 (1977).
[171]Supra note 150.
[172]Dominican Santa Cruz Hosp., 218 NLRB 1211, 89 LRRM 1504 (1975).
[173]Ohio Valley Hosp. Ass'n, supra note 138.
[174]Allegheny Gen. Hosp. II, supra note 154.
[175]San Jose Hosp. & Health Center, Inc., 228 NLRB 21, 96 LRRM 1391 (1977); Sutter Community Hosps. of Sacramento, Inc., supra note 152; Methodist Hosp. of Sacramento, Inc., 223 NLRB 1509, 92 LRRM 1198 (1976); Beth Israel Hosp. & Geriatrics Center, 219 NLRB 520, 89 LRRM 1685 (1975); Dominican Santa Cruz Hosp., supra note 172.
[176]See Jack L. Williams, DDS, 219 NLRB 1045, 90 LRRM 1188 (1975) (separate unit for dentists employed by dental clinic).

(4) Technical employees. Although the congressional committee reports cite with approval a preamendment case in which the Board rejected a separate technical unit, a technical unit was nevertheless approved as part of the Board's basic unit structure in a leading health care unit decision, *Barnert Memorial Hospital Association.*[177] In another leading decision, *Newington Children's Hospital,*[178] the Board concluded that technical employees will be excluded from a service and maintenance unit whenever the petitioning union seeks to exclude them. But as in the case of professional employees, the opposite result is reached when the petitioning union seeks to combine technical employees with service and maintenance employees and the employer seeks to separate them.[179]

In *Barnert* the Board announced that it will include in a technical unit employees "whose specialized training, skills, education and job requirements establish a community of interest not shared by other service and maintenance employees."[180] The Board explained that "[t]his separate community of interest is frequently evidenced by the fact that such employees are certified, registered or licensed," but stated that certification, registration, or licensure will not be required in every case.[181]

The Board continues to adhere rigidly to a policy of separating technical employees from service and maintenance employees whenever a petitioning union seeks to establish a separate technical unit or to exclude technical employees from a service and maintenance unit.[182] This policy was reaffirmed in *Allegheny General Hospital (II)*[183] and has been enforced by the Sixth Circuit.[184] One of the lead decisions, *Mount Airy Foundation,*[185] seems to suggest an exception for small hospitals employing only a few

---

[177]217 NLRB 775, 89 LRRM 1083 (1975).
[178]217 NLRB 793, 89 LRRM 1108 (1975).
[179]Appalachian Regional Hosps., Inc., 233 NLRB 542, 96 LRRM 1528 (1977); National G. South, Inc. (Memorial Medical), 230 NLRB 976, 95 LRRM 1478 (1977).
[180]*Supra* note 177 at 776.
[181]*Id.*
[182]Middlesex Gen. Hosp., 239 NLRB 837, 100 LRRM 1025 (1978); Pontiac Osteopathic Hosp., 227 NLRB 1706, 94 LRRM 1417 (1977); Children's Hosp. of Pittsburgh, 222 NLRB 588, 91 LRRM 1440 (1976); St. Luke's Episcopal Hosp., 222 NLRB 674, 91 LRRM 1359 (1976); Taylor Hosp., 218 NLRB 1188, 89 LRRM 1506 (1975); Trinity Memorial Hosp. of Cudahy, Inc., 219 NLRB 215, 90 LRRM 1099 (1975); Sweetwater Hosp. Ass'n, 219 NLRB 803, 90 LRRM 1055 (1975); Heights Medical Center, Inc., 221 NLRB 563, 90 LRRM 1675 (1975).
[183]*Supra* note 154.
[184]NLRB v. Sweetwater Hosp. Ass'n, 604 F2d 454, 102 LRRM 2246 (CA 6, 1979).
[185]217 NLRB 802, 89 LRRM 1067 (1975).

technical employees, although it remains uncertain whether such an exception will be applied when the petitioning union opposes combining technical employees and service and maintenance employees.[186]

Pursuant to the Board's technical unit policy, licensed practical nurses or vocational nurses (LPNs or LVNs) may not be represented in a separate unit and must be included with the other technical classifications.[187] There have been several exceptions to this policy, however, primarily because of unusual facts.[188]

(5) Business office clericals. A separate unit of "business office clerical" employees was approved in *Mercy Hospitals of Sacramento, Inc.*[189] The Board drew a distinction between

> business office clerical employees, who perform mainly business-type functions, and other types of clerical employees whose work is more closely related to the function performed by personnel in the service and maintenance unit and who have, in the past, been traditionally excluded by the Board from bargaining units of business office clerical employees.[190]

The Board later defined business office clericals as

> those clerical employees who, because they perform business office functions, have minimal contact with unit employees or patients, work in geographical areas of the hospital, or perform functions, separate and apart from service and maintenance employees, and thus do not share a community of interest with the service and maintenance unit employees.[191]

The Board has continued to find appropriate a separate unit of business office clerical employees, and to exclude such employees from a service and maintenance unit when requested

---

[186]*See* Illinois Extended Care Convalescent Center, 220 NLRB 1085, 90 LRRM 1387 (1975).

[187]St. Catharine's Hosp., 217 NLRB 787, 89 LRRM 1070 (1975).

[188]Children's Hosp. of Pittsburgh, *supra* note 182 (LPNs excluded from technical unit because they did not perform technical work); Pontiac Osteopathic Hosp., *supra* note 182 (LPNs excluded from technical unit because they had prior bargaining history in separate unit); Bay Medical Center, Inc., 218 NLRB 620, 89 LRRM 1012 (1978), *enforced,* 558 F2d 1174, 100 LRRM 2213 (CA 6, 1978), *related case,* Bay Medical Center, Inc., 239 NLRB 731, 100 LRRM 1012 (1978) (same result in similar but more complicated factual setting); Pine Manor, Inc., 238 NLRB 1654, 99 LRRM 1323 (1978) (LPNs granted self-determination election to choose between separate unit or inclusion in service and maintenance unit); Maple Shade Nursing Home, Inc., *supra* note 166 (LPNs included with registered nurses).

[189]*Supra* note 150, *related decision,* Mercy Hosps. of Sacramento, Inc., 244 NLRB 229, 102 LRRM 1016 (1979); *see* Sisters of St. Joseph of Peace, 217 NLRB 797, 89 LRRM 1082 (1975); St. Catharine's Hosp., *supra* note 187.

[190]Mercy Hosps. of Sacramento, Inc., *supra* note 150 at 770.

[191]St. Luke's Episcopal Hosp., *supra* note 182 at 676.

by the petitioning union.[192] This policy was reaffirmed in *Allegheny General Hospital (II)*;[193] however, it is unclear whether it will be applied when the employer seeks to separate business office clerical employees from service and maintenance employees, and the petitioning union seeks to combine the two groups.[194]

In *Mercy Hospitals of Sacramento, Inc.*,[195] the parties stipulated to an all-clerical unit and to a service and maintenance unit, and the stipulation was approved by the regional director. But pursuant to its business office clerical doctrine, the Board set aside these stipulated units, holding that business office clericals must have a separate unit and other clericals must be included in the service and maintenance unit. Holding that the Board's refusal to accept the stipulation was arbitrary, the Ninth Circuit declined enforcement. However, the court's decision did not address the Board's fundamental policy regarding business office clerical units.

Because of the operational and functional integration in hospital organization, the Board has experienced difficulty in drawing a precise line between business office clericals and other clerical employees. In two cases, the business office clerical definition was applied to medical-records-department employees with conflicting results, although in both cases the medical-records employees appeared to work in a separate office and their basic duties were essentially the same.[196] Again with conflicting results, the definition was applied in two cases involving admitting clerks; in both cases the clerks worked in an admitting office and their functions appeared to be essentially the same.[197] In a later case, the Board found patient-admitting clerks and patient-records clerks not to be business office clericals because of their substantial patient contact; it held, rather, that they

---

[192]Sutter Community Hosp. of Sacramento, Inc., *supra* note 152; Family Doctor Medical Group, 226 NLRB 118, 93 LRRM 1193 (1976); Seton Medical Center, 221 NLRB 120, 90 LRRM 1436 (1975); Oakwood Hosp. Corp., 219 NLRB 620, 90 LRRM 1026 (1975); St. Luke's Episcopal Hosp., *supra* note 182; William W. Backus Hosp., 220 NLRB 414, 90 LRRM 1696 (1975).

[193]*Supra* note 154.

[194]In one case the Board included business office clericals in a service and maintenance unit although the employer contended that there should be two separate units, but that decision was based on "special circumstances." Appalachian Regional Hosps., Inc., *supra* note 179.

[195]*Supra* note 150.

[196]Central Gen. Hosp., 223 NLRB 110, 91 LRRM 1433 (1976); St. Luke's Episcopal Hosp., *supra* note 182.

[197]Southwest La. Hosp. Ass'n (Lake Charles Memorial Hosp.), 226 NLRB 849, 93 LRRM 1420 (1976); St. Luke's Episcopal Hosp., *supra* note 182.

should be included in a service and maintenance unit along with other nonprofessional employees.[198]

(6) Service and maintenance employees. In one of the lead health care unit decisions, *Newington Children's Hospital,*[199] the Board reiterated that "a service and maintenance unit in a service industry is the analogue to the plant-wide production and maintenance unit in the industrial sector, and as such is the classic appropriate unit."[200] It was thus deemed appropriate for the health service industry. In another lead decision, *Mount Airy Foundation,*[201] the Board refused to allow bifurcation of a service and maintenance unit into separate units of "direct" and "indirect" patient care employees. Later attempts to split the service and maintenance unit along departmental lines were also rejected,[202] although one major exception, discussed in the following section, eventually emerged. The appropriateness of the basic service and maintenance unit was reaffirmed by the Board when it reconsidered various unit structures in *Allegheny General Hospital (II).*[203]

(7) Maintenance units. Although the service and maintenance unit is considered by the Board to be a classic appropriate unit for a health care institution, an issue frequently arises whether the Board should permit either a separate maintenance department unit or a unit of stationary engineers (boiler operators). This issue first arose in one of the early health care unit cases, *Shriners Hospitals for Crippled Children,*[204] where two members of the Board held that a separate maintenance unit could never be appropriate in a health care institution because of the congressional mandate to prevent unit proliferation and that the only appropriate unit which would encompass the stationary engineers sought by the union was "a broad unit consisting of all service and maintenance employees"; a third member concurred, upholding the result but disagreeing with the rationale; and two members dissented, contending that a separate unit

---

[198]Southwest La. Hosp. Ass'n, *supra* note 197; Appalachian Reg. Hosps., Inc., *supra* note 179; National G. South, Inc., *supra* note 179.
[199]Newington Children's Hosp., 217 NLRB 793, 794, 89 LRRM 1108 (1975).
[200]*Id.* at 794.
[201]217 NLRB 802, 89 LRRM 1067 (1975).
[202]Bay Medical Center, Inc., *supra* note 188 (housekeeping unit); Mad River Community Hosp., 219 NLRB 25, 89 LRRM 1499 (1975) (unit of laboratory and X-ray departments).
[203]*Supra* note 154.
[204]217 NLRB 806, 89 LRRM 1076 (1975).

should be approved on the basis of traditional unit factors. In a companion case, the Board stated that it was not then deciding whether a unit of hospital maintenance employees should be found appropriate.[205]

In late 1975, the Board held oral argument in a series of cases dealing with the appropriateness and scope of separate maintenance units in the health care industry. In one of the lead maintenance decisions which followed *Jewish Hospital Association of Cincinnati*,[206] a three-to-two majority denied a separate unit. The Board concluded that

> hospitals are composed of a number of departments each of which, in a general sense, could be said to be made up of skilled employees performing duties which are functionally distinct. The real question is whether the distinctions between engineering department employees and the employees in other departments show such separate interests as to warrant granting engineering department employees a separate unit while not permitting skilled employees in other departments the same privilege. In the absence of any other factors which favor a separate unit, we find that they do not.[207]

However, in *St. Vincent's Hospital*,[208] the Board found a unit of four boiler operators to be appropriate. Subsequent decisions seem inconsistent, with maintenance units having been found inappropriate in most cases[209] but appropriate in some.[210] In one case the Board found a maintenance department unit inappropriate, but it approved a separate unit of stationary engineers.[211]

---

[205]Duke Univ., 217 NLRB 799, 89 LRRM 1065 (1975).

[206]223 NLRB 614, 91 LRRM 1499 (1976).

[207]*Id.* at 617.

[208]223 NLRB 638, 91 LRRM 1513 (1976).

[209]Peter Bent Brigham Hosp., 231 NLRB 929, 96 LRRM 1546 (1977); Northeastern Hosp., 230 NLRB 1042, 95 LRRM 1464 (1977); Sutter Community Hosps. of Sacramento, Inc., *supra* note 152; Paul Kimball Hosp., Inc., 224 NLRB 458, 92 LRRM 1342 (1976); Baptist Memorial Hosp., 224 NLRB 199, 92 LRRM 1223 (1976); St. Joseph Hosp., 224 NLRB 270, 92 LRRM 1209 (1976); Greater Bakersfield Memorial Hosp., 226 NLRB 971, 93 LRRM 1386 (1976); Anaheim Memorial Hosp., 227 NLRB 161, 94 LRRM 1058 (1976); Riverside Methodist Hosp., 223 NLRB 1084, 92 LRRM 1033 (1976); Jewish Hosp. Ass'n of Cincinnati, *supra* note 206; Shriner's Hosps. for Crippled Children, *supra* note 204.

[210]Allegheny Gen. Hosp. (II), *supra* note 154; McLean Hosp., 234 NLRB 424, 97 LRRM 1322 (1978); Hebrew Rehabilitation Center, 230 NLRB 255, 95 LRRM 1279 (1977); Trinity Memorial Hosp. of Cudahy, Inc., 230 NLRB 855, 95 LRRM 1414 (1977); Sinai Hosp. of Detroit, Inc., 226 NLRB 425, 93 LRRM 1269 (1976); St. Francis Hosp.-Medical Center, 223 NLRB 1451, 92 LRRM 1172 (1976); West Suburban Hosp., 224 NLRB 1349, 92 LRRM 1369 (1976); Eskaton Am. River Healthcare Center, 225 NLRB 755, 92 LRRM 1569 (1976).

[211]Mercy Center for Health Care Servs., 227 NLRB 1814, 94 LRRM 1534 (1977).

The seeming inconsistency of the Board's decision making in maintenance unit cases, and especially its reliance on traditional unit factors when maintenance units were found appropriate, has led to judicial criticism and a number of reversals.[212] The first court decision to address the maintenance unit issue directly was *St. Vincent's Hospital* v. *NLRB*,[213] where the Third Circuit refused to enforce a decision that found a unit of four boiler operators appropriate. The court explained that when the Act was extended to health care institutions, "one of the objectives was to avoid disruptions in patient care. Diagnosing fragmentation of bargaining units as a potential obstruction to that aim, congressional committees advised the National Labor Relations Board to prevent proliferation."[214] The court concluded that the Board had "failed to heed the admonition"[215] in this case. The court rejected the Board's application of traditional unit criteria, because its reading of the legislative history made it clear that

> Congress directed the Board to apply a standard in this field that was not traditional. Proliferation of units in industrial settings has not been the subject of congressional attention but fragmentation in the health care field has aroused legislative apprehension. The Board therefore should recognize that the contours of a bargaining unit in other industries do not follow the blueprint Congress desired in a hospital.[216]

The Seventh Circuit reached the same conclusion in *NLRB* v. *West Suburban Hospital*,[217] where the Board had approved a unit of maintenance department employees. The court refused enforcement, declaring that the Board's decision "violate[s] the

---

[212]Memorial Hosp. of Roxborough v. NLRB, 545 F2d 351, 93 LRRM 2571 (CA 3, 1976), *denying enforcement to* 220 NLRB 402, 90 LRRM 1369 (1975). The Third Circuit denied enforcement after the Board established a maintenance unit by granting comity to an earlier decision of a state labor relations board. Although the court did not address the merits of the maintenance unit issue, it concluded that the Board may not grant comity to a unit determination of a state board, especially in the health care industry where the Board is required to take into account the congressional directive against proliferation. The Second Circuit also refused to enforce a decision granting comity to a state board's ruling that a hospital maintenance unit was appropriate. The court's decision was based primarily on comity grounds and did not decide whether a separate maintenance unit would be appropriate. However, it described the Board's maintenance unit decisions as being in "disarray," and commented that "no one really knows how the Board would decide any case in this area of the law." Long Island College Hosp. v. NLRB, 566 F2d 833, 843-44, 96 LRRM 3119 (CA 2, 1977), *denying enforcement to* 228 NLRB 83, 94 LRRM 1438 (1977), *cert. denied*, 435 US 996, 98 LRRM 2069 (1978).
[213]567 F2d 588, 97 LRRM 2119 (CA 3, 1977).
[214]*Id.* at 589.
[215]*Id.*
[216]*Id.* at 592.
[217]570 F2d 213, 97 LRRM 2929 (CA 7, 1978).

Congressional directive that '[d]ue consideration should be given . . . to preventing proliferation of bargaining units in the health care field.' "[218] The court criticized the Board for giving "mere lip-service mention" to the congressional nonproliferation directive, and it observed that "the Board has embarked upon an erratic course in making bargaining-unit determinations. Fixing a course with guidance from the Congressional directive . . . ought to alleviate this deficiency."[219]

In response to such judicial criticism, the Board reconsidered an earlier maintenance unit decision in *Allegheny General Hospital (II)*,[220] then pending on review before the Third Circuit. In a supplemental decision after reconsideration, the Board reaffirmed its earlier decision, declaring that it "respectfully disagreed" with earlier decisions of the Third Circuit in which hospital maintenance units were found inappropriate. Not surprisingly, the Third Circuit refused enforcement, stating that it had "no intention of reappraising" its earlier decision.[221] In response to the Board's "respectful disagreement," the court noted that "the Board is not a court nor is it equal to this court in matters of statutory interpretation. Thus, a disagreement by the NLRB with a decision of this court is simply an academic exercise that possesses no authoritative effect."[222] The Seventh and Second Circuits also rejected the Board's unit approach in *Allegheny (II),* and refused enforcement of decisions in which the Board had approved a separate maintenance unit.[223]

Notwithstanding the foregoing judicial criticism, since issuance of its decision in *Allegheny (II)* the Board has routinely approved separate maintenance units when sought by a petitioning union.[224] In one case the Board overruled a decision

---

[218]*Id.* at 216.
[219]*Id.*
[220]Allegheny Gen. Hosp. (I), 230 NLRB 954, 96 LRRM 1022 (1977).
[221]Allegheny Gen. Hosp. v. NLRB, 608 F2d 965, 102 LRRM 2784 (CA 3, 1979), *denying enforcement to* 239 NLRB 872, 100 LRRM 1030 (1978).
[222]608 F2d at 970.
[223]Mary Thompson Hosp., Inc. v. NLRB, 521 F2d 858, 103 LRRM 2739 (CA 7, 1980); NLRB v. Mercy Hosp. Ass'n, 606 F2d 22, 102 LRRM 2259 (CA 2, 1979).
[224]Garden City Hosp., 244 NLRB 778, 102 LRRM 1146 (1979); Carney Hosp., 243 NLRB 826, 101 LRRM 1581 (1979); Yonkers Gen. Hosp., 243 NLRB 226, 101 LRRM 1387 (1979); Southern Baptist Hosps., Inc., 242 NLRB 1329, 101 LRRM 1330 (1979); Trinity Memorial Hosp. of Cudahy, Inc., 242 NLRB 442, 101 LRRM 1190 (1979); Faulkner Hosp., 242 NLRB 47, 101 LRRM 1095 (1979); Franciscan Sisters of Little Falls, 241 NLRB 799, 100 LRRM 1570 (1979); Southern Md. Hosp. Center, 241 NLRB 494, 100 LRRM 1508 (1979); St. Vincent Hosp. & Medical Center of Toledo, 241 NLRB 492, 100 LRRM 1526 (1979); Fresno Community Hosp., 241 NLRB 521, 100 LRRM 1528 (1979); Long Island College Hosp., 239 NLRB 1135, 100 LRRM 1085 (1978).

issued three years earlier where a maintenance-department unit had been found inappropriate.[225]

(8) Guards. Some hospitals employ "guards" as defined in Section 9(b)(3) of the Act.[226] That section, which precludes the Board from including guards and nonguards in the same unit, is fully applicable to health care institutions. The Board has held that mixed units of guards and nonguards established prior to the amendments may be separated in a unit-clarification proceeding.[227]

c. Related Issues. (1) Single-facility vs. multi-facility units. Health care institution representation disputes have also focused on the appropriateness of single-facility units, and this issue becomes increasingly important because of the trend toward the establishment of chains of hospitals, nursing homes, and other types of health care institutions. The Board has applied its general presumption in favor of single-facility units to health care institutions, stating that "there is no legislative or practical imperative for excepting health care industry operations from the general presumption in favor of single-facility units."[228] The Board will thus find single-facility units appropriate, absent a history of multi-facility bargaining or strong proof of functional integration of facilities, i.e., centralized control of labor relations, common benefits and working conditions, interchange of employees, and geographic proximity.[229] For example, in one case the Board found appropriate a single-facility nursing home unit even though "most of the [e]mployer's policies [were] centrally controlled and basically uniformly applied to the [eighty-

---

[225]Riverside Methodist Hosp., 241 NLRB 1183, 101 LRRM 1056 (1979).

[226]*See supra* at notes 57-70.

[227]Peninsula Hosp. Center & Peninsula Gen. Nursing Home Corp., 219 NLRB 139, 90 LRRM 1034 (1975). *See* Chapter 10 *supra* at notes 201-218 for treatment of unit-clarification procedures.

[228]Samaritan Health Servs., Inc., *supra* note 142 at 632. *Accord,* National G. South, Inc. (Memorial Medical), *supra* note 179 at 978 n.5 (1974) (noting that legislative concern about undue proliferation of units referred to unit composition, not unit scope).

[229]*Compare* Samaritan Health Servs., Inc., *supra* note 142 (single hospital unit appropriate), National G. South, Inc. (Memorial Medical), *supra* note 179 (single nursing home unit appropriate, *and* Saint Anthony Center, 220 NLRB 1009, 90 LRRM 1405 (1975) (single nursing home unit appropriate); *with* Saddleback Community Hosp., 223 NLRB 247, 92 LRRM 1147 (1976) (separate units for hospital and medical center inappropriate where facilities are only 400 feet apart and where there is significant employee interaction and interchange); Kaiser Foundation Health Plan of Oregon, 225 NLRB 409, 92 LRRM 1412 (1976) (single clinic unit inappropriate where employer operates nine facilities in same metropolitan area and there is regular interchange of employees), *and* Mercy Hosps. of Sacramento, Inc., *supra* note 150 (single hospital-complex unit inappropriate where other hospital is functionally integrated and only 13 miles away).

nine] various individual facilities."[230] The Board emphasized that the administrator of the single facility maintained a significant degree of control over hiring and firing of employees, oriented new employees, scheduled vacations, and was held accountable for the overall adequacy of the services rendered to the nursing home occupants.

(2) Comity to state certification. As noted in the preceding section, the Board has resolved a number of hospital unit determination cases by granting comity to the unit decisions of state labor relations boards.[231] The courts have uniformly denied enforcement of these decisions, however.[232]

(3) Prior bargaining history in the institution. Where there has been prior bargaining history in the institution, the Board generally has refused to disrupt an existing unit structure, even though it may conflict with the basic hospital unit structure.[233] However, in one case the Board declined to perpetuate "a relatively small splinter group as a bargaining unit."[234]

(4) Stipulated units. In *Otis Hospital, Inc.*[235] the Board decided to "give effect to all stipulations designating unit compositions that do not contravene the provisions or purposes of the Act or well settled Board policies," even though a stipulation is not in conformity with the Board's basic unit structure. This policy has been followed in subsequent cases.[236] As previously noted, however, in one of the lead decisions, *Mercy Hospitals of Sacramento, Inc.*,[237] the Board set aside a stipulation establishing a service and maintenance unit and an all-clerical unit, because it conflicted with the Board's policy of approving a separate unit for business office clericals and including other clericals in a service and maintenance unit. The Ninth Circuit refused enforcement.[238]

---

[230]National G. South, Inc. (Memorial Medical), *supra* note 179 at 977.

[231]*See* notes 212 and 221 *supra.*

[232]*See* notes 212 and 221 *supra.*

[233]Bay Medical Center, Inc., *supra* note 188; Kansas City College of Osteopathic Medicine, 220 NLRB 181, 90 LRRM 1189 (1975); St. Joseph Hosp. & Medical Center, 219 NLRB 892, 90 LRRM 1088 (1975); Kaiser Foundation Hosp., 219 NLRB 168, 89 LRRM 1667 (1975). *But cf.* Valley Hosp., Ltd., *supra* note 152 (Board rejected employer's argument that employees covered by existing agreements must be part of overall nonprofessional unit; however, the Board cautioned that it would not indiscriminately "place [its] imprimatur on such preexisting units." *Id.* at 1343).

[234]North Memorial Medical Center, 224 NLRB 218, 92 LRRM 1212 (1976).

[235]219 NLRB 164, 89 LRRM 1545 (1975).

[236]*See, e.g.,* Southwest Community Hosp., 219 NLRB 351, 90 LRRM 1116 (1975).

[237]*Supra* note 150.

[238]*See* note 195 *supra* and accompanying text.

(5) Decertification elections. The appropriate unit for a decertification election is the existing contractual unit, regardless of whether the unit was formed as a result of an NLRB certification or voluntary recognition.[239] This policy is also applied to the health care industry, even though the existing contractual unit may not be consistent with the basic hospital unit structure.[240]

(6) Supervisory determinations. In *Doctor's Hospital of Modesto, Inc.,*[241] decided prior to the 1974 health care amendments, the Board announced its standard for determining which professional employees at a proprietary health care institution are supervisors. It held that charge nurses who gave directions to other employees in the exercise of professional judgment, where such directions were purely incidental to the treatment of patients, were not supervisors within the meaning of Section 2(11). In contrast, head nurses who could make effective recommendations affecting the job and pay status of the employees working under them were found to be supervisors.

This approach received congressional sanction in the committee reports accompanying the amendments. The committees stated:

> [T]he Board has carefully avoided applying the definition of "supervisor" to a health care professional who gives direction to other employees in the exercise of professional judgment, which direction is incidental to the professional's treatment of patients, and thus is not the exercise of supervisory authority in the interest of the employer. The Committee expects the Board to continue evaluating the facts of each case in this manner when making its determinations.[242]

Subsequent to enactment of the amendments, the Board indicated that it would continue to follow the policy announced in *Doctor's Hospital of Modesto,* as well as traditional standards, for determining supervisory status.[243] Under this standard, an

---

[239]*See, e.g.,* Campbell Soup Co., 111 NLRB 234, 35 LRRM 1453 (1955). *See* Chapter 10 *supra* at notes 22-23.
[240]Foote Memorial Hosp., 230 NLRB 540, 96 LRRM 1099 (1977).
[241]183 NLRB 950, 76 LRRM 1784 (1970), *enforced,* 489 F2d 772, 85 LRRM 2228 (CA 9, 1973).
[242]S. REP. NO. 93-766 *supra* note 131 at 6, and H.R. REP. NO. 93-1051, *supra* note 131 at 7.
[243]Sutter Community Hosps. of Sacramento, Inc., *supra* note 152; Trustees of Noble Hosp., 218 NLRB 1441, 89 LRRM 1806 (1975); Wing Memorial Hosp. Ass'n, 217 NLRB 1015, 89 LRRM 1183 (1975); Doctors Hosp., 217 NLRB 611, 89 LRRM 1525 (1975).

employee who possesses any of the attributes enumerated in Section 2(11) will be found to be a supervisor.[244]

The Board has generally found that shift and departmental supervisors are statutory supervisors.[245] However, "head nurses" and "nursing coordinators" have been deemed to be statutory supervisors only when sufficient evidence has indicated that these nurses have the authority to effectively recommend wage increases, hire and fire employees, settle grievances and assign work.[246] "Head nurses" and "nursing coordinators" who lack this authority have been found to be employees rather than supervisors.[247] The same standards have been applied in determining supervisory status of in-service and assistant in-service education directors.[248]

In cases decided after *Doctor's Hospital of Modesto,* the Board has been reluctant to find that "charge nurses" or "team leader nurses" are statutory supervisors,[249] even when they appear to satisfy some of the attributes enumerated in Section 2(11). For example, in *McAlester General Hospital*[250] the Board refused to find that charge nurses were supervisors even though their performance evaluations of other employees were the deter-

---

[244]*See, e.g.,* Vic's Shop 'n Save, 215 NLRB 28, 88 LRRM 1478 (1974); Illinois Steel Fabricators, Inc., 197 NLRB 296, 80 LRRM 1582 (1972). *See generally* Chapter 30 *infra* at notes 154-86.

[245]Women Care, Inc., 246 NLRB 753, 103 LRRM 1109 (1979); Newton-Wellesley Hosp., *supra* note 152; Trustees of Noble Hosp., *supra* note 243; Wing Memorial Hosp. Ass'n, *supra* note 243; Doctors Hosp., *supra* note 243.

[246]A. Barton Hepburn Hosp., 238 NLRB 95, 99 LRRM 1230 (1978); Associated Hosps. of the East Bay, 237 NLRB 1473, 99 LRRM 1069 (1978); Gnaden Huetten Memorial Hosp., Inc., *supra* note 152; Presbyterian Medical Center, *supra* note 152; Bishop Randall Hosp., *supra* note 152.

[247]Misericordia Hosp. Medical Center, 246 NLRB 351, 102 LRRM 1562 (1979); Texas Institute for Rehabilitation & Research, 228 NLRB 578, 94 LRRM 1513 (1977); Sutter Community Hosps. of Sacramento, Inc., *supra* note 152; Brattleboro Memorial Hosp., 226 NLRB 1036, 94 LRRM 1129 (1976); St. Rose de Lima Hosp., Inc., *supra* note 152; Newton-Wellesley Hosp., *supra* note 152; Trustees of Noble Hosp., *supra* note 243; Wing Memorial Hosp. Ass'n, *supra* note 243; Doctors Hosp., *supra* note 243.

[248]*See, e.g.,* Woonsocket Health Center, 245 NLRB 652, 102 LRRM 1494 (1979); A. Barton Hepburn Hosp., *supra* note 246.

[249]Turtle Creek Convalescent Centers, Inc., 235 NLRB 400, 98 LRRM 1407 (1978); McAlester Hosp. Foundation, Inc. (McAlester Gen. Hosp.), 233 NLRB 589, 96 LRRM 1524 (1977); Shadecrest Health Care Center, 228 NLRB 1081, 94 LRRM 1670 (1977); Sutter Community Hosp., *supra* note 152; St. Rose de Lima Hosp., Inc., *supra* note 152; Pinecrest Convalescent Home, Inc., 222 NLRB 13, 91 LRRM 1082 (1976); Presbyterian Medical Center, *supra* note 152; Western Medical Enterprises, Inc. (Driftwood Convalescent Hosp.), 217 NLRB 1026, 89 LRRM 1493 (1975); Doctors Hosp., 217 NLRB 611, 89 LRRM 1525 (1975). *But see* Gnaden Huetten Memorial Hosp., Inc., *supra* note 152 (charge nurses who spend only 20% of their time performing staff nurse duties were found to be statutory supervisors).

[250]233 NLRB 589, 96 LRRM 1524 (1977).

minant of pay increases. Since the evaluations were in the form of multiple-choice entries regarding various criteria of employee performance, the Board majority emphasized that the point score rather than the charge nurse's *stated* recommendation was determinative of whether the employee would receive a raise, and the charge nurse did not know the point values of the specific evaluations. The Board indicated that in health care cases it would consider supervision over nonunit employees only if the alleged supervisor spends more than 50 percent of his or her time engaged in this supervisory function. Thus, a charge nurse's supervision of LVNs and other technical employees will generally not be determinative of supervisory status.

The Board has also applied the *Doctor's Hospital of Modesto* standard to LVNs and LPNs—who are considered nonprofessional employees—and has generally held that these employees are not supervisors.[251] In these cases, the Board has again emphasized an employee's participating in the interviewing of employees and making effective recommendations in the hiring and firing of employees as prerequisites to a finding that the employee is a statutory supervisor.[252]

On this issue, the Board's decisions have fared well in the courts. The courts have held that the Board has wide discretion in determining which employees are supervisors, and, inasmuch as the Board's conclusion rests on findings of fact, the court must defer to it "if the evidence is supported by substantial evidence in the record."[253]

2. Units in Colleges and Universities. *a. Background.* In 1951, in *Trustees of Columbia University*,[254] the Board declined to assert jurisdiction over private nonprofit colleges and universities. Its 1970 decision in *Cornell University*[255] reversed this longstanding policy. In arriving at the decision to assert jurisdiction over private institutions of higher learning, the Board reexamined

---

[251]*See* Pine Manor Nursing Home, 230 NLRB 320, 95 LRRM 1356 (1977), *enforced*, 578 F2d 575, 99 LRRM 2156 (CA 5, 1978); Greenpark Care Center, 231 NLRB 753, 96 LRRM 1066 (1977); Pinecrest Convalescent Home, *supra* note 249.
[252]*See, e.g.*, Greenpark Care Center, 231 NLRB 753, 96 LRRM 1066 (1977).
[253]NLRB v. St. Francis Hosp. of Lynwood, 601 F2d 404, 100 LRRM 2943 (CA 9, 1979) (assistant head nurses found not to be supervisors); Methodist Home v. NLRB, 596 F2d 1173, 101 LRRM 2139 (CA 4, 1979) (charge nurses found not to be supervisors). *Cf.* Universal Camera Corp. v. NLRB, 340 US 474, 27 LRRM 2373 (1951). *See* Chapter 34 *infra* at notes 66-82.
[254]97 NLRB 424, 29 LRRM 1098 (1951).
[255]183 NLRB 329, 74 LRRM 1269 (1970).

the legislative history of the Act with respect to nonprofit institutions and noted the rapid growth of higher education since 1951. Shortly thereafter, by formal rule-making,[256] the Board established a minimum gross annual revenue figure of $1 million for assertion of Board jurisdiction over private nonprofit educational institutions.[257]

The Board has divided college and university bargaining units into two basic groupings: (1) professional units usually centered around full-time faculty members, and (2) nonprofessional units. The composition of the professional units has been dealt with in numerous decisions, wherein the Board and the courts have attempted to adapt the principles of industrial labor relations to fit the "ivory tower" of academia. This section will discuss these decisions concerning professional units. The nonprofessional units are readily governed by general unit criteria applicable to service and manufacturing industries,[258] and therefore will not be discussed in this section.

  b. *Professional Units. (1) Composition of the units. (a) Faculty as managerial and supervisory employees*—NLRB v. Yeshiva University. The Supreme Court's 1980 decision in *NLRB* v. *Yeshiva University*[259] has had a major impact on decisions dealing with

---

[256]NLRB RULES AND REGULATIONS AND STATEMENTS OF PROCEDURE, SERIES 8 (as last amended, Jan. 8, 1976). §103.1 (GPO, 1976). For discussion of rule making by the Board, see Chapter 32 *infra* at notes 197-218.
  [257]There still remain unanswered questions concerning the Board's jurisdiction over certain types of nonprofit educational institutions. Educational institutions are sometimes quasi-public, leaving the Board with having to decide whether the institution is private, and thus covered by the Act, or public, and thus not covered by the Act. The line between public and private has not always been easy to determine. *See* Howard Univ., 224 NLRB 385, 92 LRRM 1249 (1976) (newly constituted Board reverses its earlier decision in Howard Univ., 211 NLRB 247, 86 LRRM 1389 (1974), and extends jurisdiction to Howard University despite its close relationship with the Federal Government); Temple Univ., 194 NLRB 1160, 79 LRRM 1196 (1972) (high degree of state control makes Temple University a "state related university"; the Board declines to assert its jurisdiction); *cf.* Cornell Univ., *supra* note 255 (jurisdiction extended to Cornell University, including the New York State School of Industrial and Labor Relations, a "contract" college funded by the State of New York). *See* Chapter 30 *infra* at notes 141-49 for a discussion of the Act's coverage of quasi-public employers.
  The Supreme Court's decision in NLRB v. Catholic Bishop of Chicago, 440 US 490, 100 LRRM 2913 (1979), raises questions concerning the Act's coverage of church-operated and church-affiliated colleges and universities. *See* Chapter 30 *infra* at notes 18-23 for a discussion of that case and subsequent Board decisions asserting jurisdiction over church-affiliated schools.
  [258]*See, e.g.,* Harvard College, 229 NLRB 586, 587, 95 LRRM 1390 (1977) ("[t]raditional principles for determining appropriate bargaining units [are] applic[able] to universities operating several facilities"); Tuskegee Inst., 209 NLRB 773, 86 LRRM 1082 (1974) (Board applies traditional community-of-interest factors in deciding composition of service and maintenance unit).
  [259]444 US 672, 103 LRRM 2526 (1980).

the composition of professional units at colleges and universities. Rejecting a long line of Board decisions,[260] a five-to-four Court refused to enforce a bargaining order because the bargaining unit, comprised of various full-time faculty members, included managerial employees excluded from the coverage of the Act.[261] The decision thus makes managerial status a threshold issue in representation cases involving faculty members. The decision however does not proclaim all faculty members on every campus to be managerial employees; it is therefore important to review the facts and criteria set forth in *Yeshiva* so that they may be applied on a case-by-case basis to determine whether particular faculty members have managerial status.

In *Yeshiva* the Board held appropriate a unit of faculty members, including assistant deans, department chairpersons, senior professors, associate professors, assistant professors and instructors, at 10 of the university's 13 colleges.[262] The Board rejected the employer's argument that the university faculty were managerial employees. After certification and issuance of a bargaining order, the Board sought enforcement of its order in the Second Circuit, which held that the faculty exercised managerial authority and thus were excluded from coverage of the Act.[263]

The Supreme Court's decision is premised entirely on the high degree of authority and participation in decision making which was exercised by the Yeshiva faculty. The Court summarized those factors as follows:

> The controlling consideration in this case is that the faculty of Yeshiva University exercise authority which in any other context unquestionably would be managerial. Their authority in academic matters is absolute. They decide what courses will be offered, when they will be scheduled, and to whom they will be taught. They debate and determine teaching methods, grading policies, and matriculation standards. They effectively decide which students will be admitted, retained, and graduated. On occasion their views have determined the size of the student body, the tuition to be charged, and the location of a school. When one considers the function of a university, it is difficult to imagine decisions more managerial than these. To the extent the industrial analogy applies, the faculty determines

---

[260]*See, e.g.,* Northeastern Univ., 218 NLRB 247, 89 LRRM 1862 (1975); University of Miami, 213 NLRB 634, 87 LRRM 1634 (1974).
[261]*See* Chapter 30 *infra* at notes 161 and 190-92.
[262]Yeshiva Univ., 221 NLRB 1053, 91 LRRM 1017 (1975).
[263]NLRB v. Yeshiva Univ., 582 F2d 686, 98 LRRM 3245 (1978).

within each school the product to be produced, the terms upon which it will be offered, and the customers who will be served.[264]

The Board argued that faculty members were called upon to exercise "independent professional judgment," which is different from managerial decision making. While recognizing that "[t]here may be some tension between the Act's exclusion of managerial employees and its inclusion of professionals,"[265] the Court rejected the Board's distinction between managerial decisions and decisions requiring "independent professional judgment," as inconsistent with the goal of "ensur[ing] that employees who exercise discretionary authority on behalf of the employer will not divide their loyalty between employee and union."[266] The Court described "[t]he problem of divided loyalty [as] particularly acute for a university like Yeshiva, which depends on the professional judgment of its faculty to formulate and apply crucial policies constrained only by necessarily general institutional goals."[267]

The majority opinion concluded with a footnote, indicating the limited reach of the Court's holding:

> We recognize that this is a starting point only, and that other factors not present here may enter into the analysis in other contexts. It is plain, for example, that professors may not be excluded merely because they determine the content of their own courses, evaluate their own students, and supervise their own research. There thus may be institutions of higher learning unlike Yeshiva where the faculty are entirely or predominantly nonmanagerial. There also may be faculty members at Yeshiva and like universities who properly could be included in a bargaining unit. It may be that a rational line could be drawn between tenured and untenured faculty members, depending upon how a faculty is structured and operates. But we express no opinion on these questions, for it is clear that the unit approved by the Board was far too broad.[268]

---

[264]NLRB v. Yeshiva Univ., *supra* note 259 at 686.
[265]*Id.*
[266]*Id.* at 687-88.
[267]*Id.* at 689.
[268]*Id.* at 690 n.31. In 1982 the Board issued five decisions interpreting *Yeshiva.* In Ithaca College, 261 NLRB No. 83, 110 LRRM 1059 (1982); Thiel College, 261 NLRB No. 84 (1982); and Duquesne Univ. of the Holy Ghost, 261 NLRB No. 85, 110 LRRM 1046 (1982), it dismissed representation petitions, holding that the full-time faculty members at those institutions were managerial employees because they exercised extensive control over policy in a manner similar to the *Yeshiva* faculty. In Bradford College, 260 NLRB No. 81, 110 LRRM 1055 (1982), however, it ordered an election, finding that the college president, not the faculty, ran the school. In Montefiore Hosp. & Medical Center, 261 NLRB No. 82, 110 LRRM 1048 (1982), the Board declined to extend the *Yeshiva* conception of managerial status to the health care field, finding that the medical

The Ninth Circuit distinguished *Yeshiva* in a case involving the faculty at an art institute.[269] The court rejected the employer's argument that the faculty were managerial employees, stating: "In *Yeshiva* the Court applied the managerial employee exception to a 'mature' university. The Court relied heavily on the policy making role of the faculty at such an institution. The instructors at the [art institute] hardly share such a role. They have no input into policy decisions, and do not engage in management level decision making. They simply are employees."[270]

The Supreme Court, in *Yeshiva,* did not resolve the issue of *supervisory status* of the Yeshiva faculty. The Board, in cases decided prior to the Court's *Yeshiva* decision, had refused to find that an entire faculty consisted of supervisors.[271] Instead, it found that certain faculty and administrative positions were supervisory, but only on a case-by-case basis after careful scrutiny of the particular positions.[272] Additionally, the Board has applied its "50 percent rule," under which professionals are excluded as supervisors if more than 50 percent of their time is spent supervising personnel.[273] Supervisory status will probably continue to be applied only to specific positions, rather than to a faculty as a whole, while the Board and the courts proceed with the arduous process of applying and clarifying *Yeshiva's* holding regarding managerial status.

(b)   The full-time faculty unit generally. Prior to *Yeshiva,* the basic

---

center's highly centralized structure justified ordering an election among staff doctors and dentists, including doctors with faculty appointments to the Albert Einstein College of Medicine. *See supra* at notes 138-40.

[269]Stephens Inst. v. NLRB, 620 F2d 720, 104 LRRM 2524 (CA 9, 1980).

[270]*Id.* at 727. In Ithaca College v. NLRB, 623 F2d 224, 104 LRRM 2493 (1980), the Second Circuit criticized the Board for refusing to reopen the record in a faculty unit case in light of the Second Circuit's decision in *Yeshiva.* The case was heard after the Supreme Court's affirmance of the Second Circuit's *Yeshiva* decision. The court denied enforcement of the Board's bargaining order, deciding not to remand the case for further hearings because the Board's prior refusal to address the issue of faculty status "exposed the College to needless expense and unwarranted prejudicial publicity." *Id.* at 230.

[271]*E.g.*, Northeastern Univ., *supra* note 260; University of Miami, *supra* note 260.

As to a related issue, in New York Univ. (I), 205 NLRB 4, 83 LRRM 1549 (1973), the Board held that faculty members in general are not independent contractors, stating: "Instruction is performed on the Employer's premises with its equipment; faculty may become tenured; and they receive sabbatical leave, a fixed annual salary, and Employer contributions to a retirement fund. The faculty are not subject to the entrepreneurial risks and profits normally associated with independent contractors." *Id.* at 5-6. *See* Chapter 30 *infra* at notes 227-78. for discussion of independent contractor status.

[272]*See* discussion *infra* in this chapter under separate subheadings for department chairpersons, principal investigators, administrative officials, program directors, and librarians.

[273]*E.g.*, New York Univ. (II), 221 NLRB 1148, 91 LRRM 1165 (1975).

professional unit at colleges and universities had centered around the full-time faculty, including the various levels of full-time professors and instructors. The Board's approach was to build a basic professional unit around the full-time faculty, but including other assorted professional employees according to the skills and functions which they exercise and the desires of the petitioning labor organization. For example, in an early professional unit case, *C. W. Post Center of Long Island University*,[274] the union sought a unit of all professionals engaged in teaching, including full-time professors and instructors, part-time professors and lecturers, librarians, laboratory personnel, a research associate, guidance counselors, admission counselors, and academic counselors. The employer argued initially that jurisdiction should not be applied to a university's professional employees, and later took the position that a separate unit should be established for full-time faculty. The Board found appropriate a unit of full-time professors and instructors, part-time professors and lecturers, professional librarians, and guidance counselors. The Board has continued this case-by-case structuring of faculty bargaining units, although it has also established certain rules and patterns, discussed below.

In the aftermath of *Yeshiva*, the Board is now evaluating on a case-by-case basis the decision-making authority and input of an institution's faculty in general, and the various levels of faculty positions in particular, in order to determine which faculty members, if any, are nonmanagerial.[275] The Board will thus be able to construct a basic professional unit around the nonmanagerial faculty, where such faculty exists, in much the same fashion as in its pre-*Yeshiva* decisions, although certain other professional employees could also be affected by *Yeshiva's* managerial analysis.

(c) Department chairpersons. Prior to the Supreme Court's *Yeshiva* decision, department chairpersons in some cases had been excluded from faculty units on the ground that they were "supervisors" within the meaning of Section 2(11), and in other cases they had been included in such units on the ground that they were not "supervisors." The decisions often turned on whether the department chairpersons have the power to "make

---

[274]189 NLRB 904, 77 LRRM 1001 (1971).
[275]*See* cases cited in note 268 *supra* and also College of Osteopathic Medicine & Surgery, 265 NLRB No. 37, 111 LRRM 1523 (1982), discussed in Chapter 10 *supra* note 441 and in Chapter 30 *infra* note 191.

effective recommendations as to hiring, firing or change of status" or whether such power has been "effectively diffused among the department faculty pursuant to the principle of collegiality."[276] In cases where the Board found that department chairpersons were merely a conduit for faculty recommendations regarding personnel matters, they were included in the faculty unit.[277] Alternatively, where department chairpersons had the power to make effective recommendations in personnel matters, the Board excluded them from faculty units as supervisors.[278]

In *Trustees of Boston University* v. *NLRB*[279] the First Circuit upheld the Board's ruling that department chairpersons were not supervisors and, therefore, could be included in a faculty unit. Although the chairpersons made recommendations concerning hiring, reappointment, promotion, and discipline of full-time faculty members, and these recommendations were generally followed, they were made after consulting with all of the full-time tenured faculty in the particular department. In addition, the final decision on all such matters rested with the board of trustees of the university based on the written recommendation of the president, the academic vice president, and the dean of the college involved.

In the aftermath of *Yeshiva,* the Board will need to reevaluate its department chairpersons decisions to conform with the Court's managerial employee analysis. *Yeshiva* itself was a case where the Board had held that the department chairpersons were not supervisors and were therefore included in a broad professional unit. The Court's decision in *Yeshiva* suggests that department chairpersons who exercise significant decision-making authority or participation will be excluded as managerial employees, even

---

[276]Northeastern Univ., *supra* note 260 at 251-52.

[277]Stephens College, 240 NLRB 166, 100 LRRM 1268 (1979); Yeshiva Univ., 221 NLRB 1053, 91 LRRM 1017 (1975), *enforcement denied on other grounds,* 582 F2d 686, 98 LRRM 3245 (CA 2, 1978), *aff'd on other grounds,* 444 US 672, 103 LRRM 2526 (1980); Fordham Univ. (II), 214 NLRB 971, 87 LRRM 1643 (1974); Univ. of Miami, *supra* note 260; Rosary Hill College, 202 NLRB 1137, 82 LRRM 1768 (1973); Fordham Univ. (I), 193 NLRB 134, 78 LRRM 1177 (1971); University of Detroit, 193 NLRB 566, 78 LRRM 1273 (1971); *see* Trustees of Boston Univ. v. NLRB, 575 F2d 301, 98 LRRM 2070 (CA 1, 1978), *enforcing* 228 NLRB 1008, 96 LRRM 1408 (1977).

[278]University of Vt., 223 NLRB 423, 91 LRRM 1570 (1976); New York Univ. (II), *supra* note 273; Rensselaer Polytechnic Inst., 218 NLRB 1435, 89 LRRM 1844 (1975); Syracuse Univ., 204 NLRB 641, 83 LRRM 1373 (1973); C. W. Post Center of Long Island Univ., *supra* note 274; Long Island Univ. (Brooklyn Center), 189 NLRB 909, 77 LRRM 1006 (1971).

[279]*Supra* note 277.

where the department chairpersons' recommendations are not always accepted.

(d) "Principal investigators." Principal investigators are faculty members who prepare grant proposals and administer the projects once the funds have been awarded by government or private granting agencies.[280] The status of principal investigators as supervisory or managerial employees turns on their authority over other college or university employees working on the grant proposals and projects. In *New York University (II)*[281] the Board included principal investigators in the bargaining unit, because "principal investigators do not 'supervise' employees of the University, they 'supervise' faculty only seasonally, and the work is not performed at the direction of the University."[282] Principal investigators were also included in bargaining units in another case where the grant employees whom they supervised were not university employees.[283] However, principal investigators were excluded from units in four cases where they had supervisory authority over research associates who were included in the bargaining unit.[284]

The decisions discussed above were decided prior to the Supreme Court's *Yeshiva* decision and have focused primarily on supervisory status, rather than managerial status. In future cases, it will be necessary to focus on the question of managerial status as well as supervisory status.

(e) Administrative officials. Ordinarily, administrative officials—including deans, assistant and associate deans, admissions directors, and registrars—are excluded from a faculty bargaining unit as supervisory employees.[285] In some cases, however, including *Yeshiva*, the Board has included in the faculty bargaining unit assistant or associate deans whose primary duty is to teach.[286] The Supreme Court's *Yeshiva* decision obviously impels

---

[280]Faculty often drift in and out of principal investigator status on a year-to-year basis depending upon whether they are currently working on a grant. The process of "popping in and out" of the bargaining unit, in units excluding principal investigators, has been termed in at least one Board decision as the creation of a "popcorn unit." Northeastern Univ., *supra* note 260 at 253.

[281]*Supra* note 273.

[282]*Id.* at 1155.

[283]Fordham Univ. (I), *supra* note 277. *See also* New York Univ. (I), *supra* note 271.

[284]University of Vt., *supra* note 278; Yeshiva Univ., *supra* note 277; Rensselaer Polytechnic Inst., *supra* note 278; Northeastern Univ., *supra* note 260.

[285]In most cases administrative officials such as deans are excluded by stipulation. *See, e.g.,* Syracuse Univ., *supra* note 278; University of Detroit, *supra* note 277.

[286]Yeshiva Univ., *supra* note 277; University of Miami, *supra* note 260.

a careful analysis of factors relevant to managerial and supervisory status before administrative officials are included in future bargaining units.

(f) *Program directors.* Whether individuals holding the title of "program director" are included or excluded from a faculty unit depends upon the particular functions and duties they perform. In some instances, "program directors" have been excluded from a faculty unit because they hold supervisory status.[287] In other cases, program directors have been included in faculty bargaining units.[288] The Supreme Court's *Yeshiva* decision suggests that program directors whose jobs involve substantial decision-making authority and participation, as opposed to a predominantly ministerial function, will be excluded as managerial employees.[289]

(g) *Coaches.* Athletic coaches whose academic credentials are comparable to other faculty members, and whose duties include teaching, are held to be professionals and are included in faculty units.[290] However, coaching positions that do not require advanced degrees or teaching are deemed nonprofessional and are excluded from faculty bargaining units.[291]

(h) *Visiting faculty.* The Board has excluded visiting faculty members from faculty bargaining units because they usually have no expectation of permanent employment by the institution at which they are teaching as visitors.[292] In one case, visiting faculty were excluded even though they had full-time teaching loads and were entitled to full participation in governance, including voting privileges.[293]

(i) *Members of religious orders.* The Board, in a series of decisions, has had to decide whether members of religious orders should be included in faculty units at church-operated[294] and

---

[287]*See, e.g.,* Loretto Heights College, 205 NLRB 1134, 84 LRRM 1163 (1973) (full-time and part-time program directors excluded as supervisors).

[288]*See, e.g.,* University of Miami, *supra* note 260; Adelphi Univ., 195 NLRB 639, 79 LRRM 1545 (1972).

[289]*See* discussion at notes 259-69 *supra.*

[290]Manhattan College, 195 NLRB 66, 79 LRRM 1253 (1972) (teaching duties related to extracurricular activities, not classroom teaching for college credit); Rensselaer Polytechnic Inst., *supra* note 278.

[291]University of Miami, *supra* note 260.

[292]Goddard College, 216 NLRB 457, 88 LRRM 1228 (1975); *see* Trustees of Boston Univ., 228 NLRB 1008, 96 LRRM 1408 (1977), *enforced,* 575 F2d 301, 98 LRRM 2070 (CA 1, 1978).

[293]Goddard College, *supra* note 292.

[294]*But see infra* at note 300.

church-affiliated colleges and universities. Members of religious orders have been excluded from faculty units where the religious order controlled or strongly influenced the operation of the institution and the members of the order returned a large part of their salaries to the order pursuant to spiritual vows or contractual obligations.[295] Under such circumstances, the faculty members of the order were deemed "in a sense part of the employer since the Order owns and administers the College."[296] However, faculty members of orders have been included in faculty bargaining units where the institution was operated by a different religious order,[297] and where the institution was not church operated but merely church affiliated and the faculty members' obligations to their order were significantly independent of their obligations to the institution.[298] In two cases, courts of appeals have disagreed with the Board and have held that faculty members of religious orders should have been included in faculty bargaining units where the institutions were only church affiliated, not church operated, and the faculty members of the religious order were not under any direct spiritual or contractual obligations to the institution that would have been inconsistent with collective bargaining.[299]

The decisions discussed above were decided prior to the Supreme Court's 1979 decision in *Catholic Bishop of Chicago* v. *NLRB*,[300] where the Court held that the Act's coverage impliedly excluded lay teachers and, *a fortiori*, clergy teachers at church-operated schools.[301] Therefore future Board jurisdiction in this

---

[295]Seton Hill College, 201 NLRB 1026, 82 LRRM 1434 (1973); *see* Niagara Univ. (I), 226 NLRB 918, 94 LRRM 1082 (1976), *enforcement denied*, 558 F2d 1116, 95 LRRM 3354 (CA 2, 1977); Saint Francis College, 224 NLRB 907, 92 LRRM 1551 (1976), *enforcement denied*, 562 F2d 246, 96 LRRM 2134 (CA 3, 1977).

[296]Seton Hill College, *supra* note 295 at 1027.

[297]Niagara Univ. (II), 227 NLRB 313, 94 LRRM 1001 (1976). In *Niagara Univ. (I)*, *supra* note 295, an election was conducted and a bargaining order issued for a unit excluding 18 faculty who were members of religious orders. In *Niagara Univ. (II)*, the Board, in a unit-clarification proceeding, included in the faculty unit three nuns and a priest who were not members of the religious order that operated the university. The Second Circuit subsequently denied enforcement to *Niagara Univ. (I)*, holding that all faculty members of religious orders should have been included in the faculty unit. Niagara Univ. v. NLRB, 558 F2d 1116, 95 LRRM 3354 (CA 2, 1977).

[298]D'Youville College, 225 NLRB 792, 92 LRRM 1578 (1976) (by stipulation of parties; regional director held that *Seton Hill*, *supra* note 295, required exclusion from unit despite parties' agreement to the contrary); Fordham Univ. (II), *supra* note 277 (by stipulation of parties); Fordham Univ. (I), *supra* note 277.

[299]Niagara Univ. v. NLRB, *supra* note 297; NLRB v. Saint Francis College, 562 F2d 246, 96 LRRM 2134 (CA 3, 1977).

[300]*Supra* note 257.

[301]*See* Chapter 30 *infra* at notes 18-23 for a discussion of *NLRB* v. *Catholic Bishops of Chicago*.

area will be limited to faculty at colleges and universities that are church affiliated, not church operated. Faculty members of religious orders in such institutions are more likely to have sufficient independence from the employer to be includable in faculty bargaining units.

(j) *Part-time faculty.* After the Board decided to assert jurisdiction over private higher educational institutions, it initially decided, consistent with its policy in the industrial sector, to include part-time faculty members in a unit of full-time faculty.[302] However, in a major policy change in 1973, in *New York University (I)*,[303] the Board abandoned its prior policy and decided to exclude all part-time faculty members from the faculty unit. For rationale, it stated: "We are now convinced that the differences between the full-time and part-time faculty are so substantial in most colleges and universities that we should not adhere to the principle announced in the *New Haven* case."[304] The factors it relied upon were (1) differences in compensation; (2) the lack of participation by part-time faculty in university governance; (3) the unavailability of tenure for part-time faculty; and (4) differences in working conditions. The Board's decision in *New York University* has been followed in subsequent decisions involving the issue of unit placement of part-time faculty.[305]

A variation of the *New York University (I)* rule was approved by the Seventh Circuit in *Kendall College* v. *NLRB*,[306] where the Board had included in a full-time faculty unit "pro-rata" part-time faculty members, i.e., part-time faculty whose pay and fringe benefits were on the same basis as the full-time faculty

---

[302]C. W. Post Center of Long Island Univ., *supra* note 274, which was followed in University of New Haven, 190 NLRB 478, 77 LRRM 1273 (1971), and Fordham Univ. (I), *supra* note 277. In University of Detroit, 193 NLRB 566, 78 LRRM 1273 (1971), the Board adopted a four-to-one rule, under which part-time faculty would be included in a faculty unit only if they taught at least 25% of a full-time teaching load. The "four-to-one" rule was applied in Manhattan College, *supra* note 290; Florida S. College, 196 NLRB 888, 80 LRRM 1160 (1972); Tusculum College, 199 NLRB 28, 81 LRRM 1345 (1972); and Catholic Univ., 201 NLRB 929, 82 LRRM 1385 (1973) (where formula was modified slightly for part-time law faculty due to difficulty of strict application of four-to-one rule).

[303]205 NLRB 4, 83 LRRM 1549 (1973).

[304]*Id.* at 6.

[305]NLRB v. Wentworth Inst. & Wentworth College of Technology, 515 F2d 550, 89 LRRM 2033 (CA 1, 1975); Yeshiva Univ., *supra* note 277; Goddard College, *supra* note 292; University of Miami, *supra* note 260; Point Park College, 209 NLRB 1064, 85 LRRM 1542 (1974); University of San Francisco, 207 NLRB 12, 84 LRRM 1403 (1973).

[306]570 F2d 216, 97 LRRM 2878 (CA 7, 1978).

members but proportional to their respective work schedules. Part-time "per course" faculty members, however, were excluded because they were paid a flat fee per course taught and received no fringe benefits.

In *Goddard College*[307] the petitioner sought to represent part-time faculty in a separate unit as an alternative to a unit of full-time and part-time faculty. The Board excluded part-time faculty from the faculty unit and also rejected the petitioner's alternative request, finding that the facts were insufficient to establish a community of interest among what the Board viewed as various "heterogeneous" groups of individuals whose only common identification was their part-time work for the college.

(k) Librarians. The Board has held that librarians are normally includable in a faculty bargaining unit since they "possess a sufficient community of interest to be included in the unit, as a closely allied professional group whose ultimate function, aiding and furthering the educational and scholarly goals of the University, converges with that of the faculty, though pursued through different means and in a different manner."[308]

This unit concept, however, was not applicable where the library was a distinct entity within the university community, such as in *Teachers College, Columbia University.*[309] The Board there found a separate unit of professional librarians appropriate because the librarians were not faculty members, did not share faculty prerogatives, salary scales, or fringe benefits, and had little contact or interchange with faculty members. Although the library building was centrally located on campus, the library was administratively independent from the faculty in terms of hiring, firing, discipline, promotions, and wage increases.[310]

(l) Research associates and assistants. Research associates and research assistants are normally included in a faculty unit, since

---

[307]*Supra* note 292.

[308]New York Univ. (I), *supra* note 271, at 8; *accord,* Fordham Univ. (II), *supra* note 277; C. W. Post Center of Long Island Univ., *supra* note 274. *But cf.* Northeastern Univ., *supra* note 260, where all but two of the professional librarians were excluded as supervisors, either because they exercised supervisory authority over other professional librarians or they spent more than 50% of their time supervising nonprofessional library staff and clerical workers. See Chapter 30 *infra* at note 180 for a discussion of the "50 percent rule."

[309]226 NLRB 1236, 93 LRRM 1481 (1976); *accord,* Claremont Univ. Center, 198 NLRB 811, 81 LRRM 1317 (1972) (separate unit for librarians found appropriate; librarians given option to vote for inclusion with unit of nonprofessional library staff).

[310]226 NLRB 1236, 93 LRRM 1481 (1976). The majority also noted that the petitioner did not seek an overall professional unit.

such persons usually have educational qualifications comparable to those of the faculty, have similar benefits and working conditions as faculty, and engage in some form of teaching.[311]

(m) Graduate students. Graduate students working on advanced degrees often perform teaching functions and receive financial assistance for performing such duties. Generally, however, they are directed by faculty members and do not have significant input in governance. The Board has found graduate assistants to be primarily students and lacking a community of interest with the faculty; accordingly, graduate students are normally excluded from the faculty unit.[312]

(n) Counselors. Counselors who hold advanced degrees and perform activities such as career counseling have been included in faculty units as professional employees; but absent such duties they are excluded.[313]

(2) Scope of the units. (a) Multicampus units. Universities often have more than one campus, thereby creating potential issues concerning inclusion or exclusion of multiple campuses. In one case, an institutionwide, multicampus faculty bargaining unit was found appropriate where there was (a) integration and centralization of administrative functions between campuses; (b) some campus interchange between faculty members; (c) a university senate which included representatives from all campuses; (d) similarity of wages, hours, and working conditions for faculty members at all campuses; and (e) a petitioner that was seeking a universitywide unit.[314] In two related cases, the

---

[311]University of Vt., *supra* note 278; Northeastern Univ., *supra* note 260; Rensselaer Polytechnic Inst., *supra* note 278; C. W. Post Center of Long Island Univ., *supra* note 274. *But cf.* New York Univ. (I), *supra* note 271, and Fordham Univ. (I), *supra* note 277, where research personnel were held not to be university employees.

[312]*E.g.*, Adelphi Univ., *supra* note 288; Leland Stanford Junior Univ., 214 NLRB 621, 87 LRRM 1519 (1974) (graduate students who received stipends and grants to perform research for advanced degrees held not to be employees within the meaning of §2(3) of the Act).

[313]Mount Vernon College, 228 NLRB 1237, 95 LRRM 1349 (1977) (college's academic advisor-career counselor excluded from faculty unit as a nonprofessional employee); Northeastern Univ., *supra* note 260 (career counselors included in faculty unit; academic counselors excluded); C. W. Post Center of Long Island Univ., *supra* note 274 (guidance counselors included in faculty unit; admissions and academic counselors excluded); *see* Goddard College, *supra* note 292 (counselors held to be professional employees; however, counselors who worked in psychological services office were excluded from faculty unit along with various other professionals).

[314]Fairleigh Dickinson Univ., 205 NLRB 673, 84 LRRM 1033 (1973); *cf.* Tulane Univ., 195 NLRB 329, 79 LRRM 1366 (1972) (Board rejects petitioner's request for main campus nonprofessional unit; unit must include university's three other facilities located

Board found appropriate two separate units for two of a university's three campuses where separate units had been sought by the petitioner and the employer did not object to separate units.[315]

(b) Separate units for professional and graduate school faculty. The Board has generally excluded law school faculty from overall faculty units or has ordered self-determination elections, depending upon the units sought by the petitioning unions. In *Fordham University (I)*[316] one union sought a faculty unit excluding law school faculty while another union sought a unit solely for the law school faculty. Stating that "it is clear that [a universitywide unit of professional employees] may be appropriate here,"[317] the Board nevertheless held that a separate law school faculty unit was appropriate because the law school faculty's "community of interest is not irrevocably submerged in the broader community of interest which they share with other faculty members,"[318] and no union sought to include the law school faculty in a broader unit.[319] Subsequently, in *Syracuse University*,[320] the Board ordered a self-determination election for law school faculty where one union sought a universitywide unit and another union sought a separate unit for the law school faculty. The Board gave the law school faculty a self-determination election with the added, unusual choice of voting for no representation regardless of the vote among other faculty members, because the Board believed it "must be especially watchful in guarding the rights of minority groups whose intellectual pursuits and interests differ in kind from the bulk of the faculty."[321]

---

within a 40-mile radius of the main campus); Cornell Univ., *supra* note 255 (statewide unit of nonprofessional employees held to be the only appropriate unit, even though the university operated a facility in New York City some 280 miles away from the rural upstate New York campus and a union sought a separate unit for the New York City facility).

[315]C. W. Post Center of Long Island Univ., *supra* note 274; Long Island Univ. (Brooklyn Center), *supra* note 278.

[316]*Supra* note 277, followed in University of San Francisco, *supra* note 305, and Catholic Univ., *supra* note 302.

[317]Fordham Univ. (I), *supra* note 277, at 136.

[318]*Id.* at 137.

[319]*Fordham Univ. (I)* was followed under similar circumstances in University of Miami, *supra* note 260.

[320]*Supra* note 278. *Accord,* New York Univ. (I), *supra* note 271 *(Syracuse Univ.* followed).

[321]*Supra* note 278 at 643, followed in New York Univ. (I), *supra* note 271. This separate choice of no representation is not usually given to employees in self-determination elections. *See* discussion of *Globe* doctrine at notes 30-33 *supra.*

Generally, the Board has either included or excluded other professional school faculty from overall faculty units depending on the scope of the units sought by the unions. For example, medical school faculty have been excluded in cases where unions sought overall faculty units, but excluding medical school faculty.[322] In one case the Board required that a dentistry school be included in an overall faculty unit where the school was located near a major campus, the dentistry faculty participated in university programs and governance, and no union sought a separate unit for the dentistry school.[323] In another case, an overall unit, excluding the dentistry school as well as the law and medical schools, was held appropriate where the dentistry school was located away from the campus, even though no union sought to represent dentistry school faculty.[324] In some cases, graduate school faculty have been excluded from overall faculty bargaining units because the graduate school faculty did not share a substantial community of interest with other faculty.[325]

3. Units in the United States Postal Service. *a. Background.* In 1970 Congress enacted the Postal Reorganization Act (PRA)[326] establishing the United States Postal Service as an independent establishment of the executive branch of the Federal Government.[327] Chapter 12 of the PRA,[328] effective in 1971, brought the Postal Service and its employees under the jurisdiction of the Board, and to the extent not inconsistent with the PRA, under the coverage of the National Labor Relations Act. The intent of Congress, as reflected in Chapter 12, was that labor relations in the Postal Service should be similar to the pattern in the private sector.[329]

---

[322]Trustees of Boston Univ. v. NLRB, *supra* note 277 (law and graduate dentistry faculty excluded for same reason); University of Vt., *supra* note 278; Yeshiva Univ., *supra* note 277; University of Miami, *supra* note 260 (school of marine and atmospheric science excluded on same basis).

[323]Fairleigh Dickinson Univ., *supra* note 314.

[324]Trustees of Boston Univ. v. NLRB, *supra* note 277.

[325]Goddard College, *supra* note 292 (graduate faculty and their programs located far away from campus and operated apart from campus governance structure; union sought inclusion in overall unit); University of Miami, *supra* note 260 (school of marine and atmospheric sciences located away from main campus and having substantially different educational mission; union sought overall unit excluding, *inter alia*, the marine and atmospheric sciences school).

[326]Pub. L. No. 91-375, 84 Stat 719 (1970) (codified in Title 39 USC).

[327]*See* Chapter 5 *supra* at notes 1-4.

[328]39 USC §1209(a).

[329]*See generally* Granof & Moe, *Grievance Arbitration in the U.S. Postal Service; The Postal Service View,* 29 ARB. J. 1 (1974).

Prior to the effective date of the PRA, collective bargaining between the Post Office Department and labor unions representing postal employees was governed by Executive Order,[330] pursuant to which the Post Office Department determined in 1962 that appropriate bargaining units should be national in scope and coincide with seven traditional "craft" lines.[331] At that time the seven craft groups were (1) letter carriers, (2) mailhandlers, (3) clerks, (4) special delivery messengers, (5) rural letter carriers, (6) motor vehicle employees, and (7) maintenance employees.[332] In elections held in 1962 and 1963, a majority of the employees voting in the seven national craft units selected seven national craft unions, which the Department of Labor certified as national exclusive representatives for postal employees in those units.[333] Thereafter, the Post Office Department and the seven craft unions entered into successive collective bargaining agreements.[334]

To facilitate the transition from the national craft unit bargaining pattern established in 1962 by the Department of Labor to the Board-governed method newly enacted by the PRA, Section 10(a) of the PRA provided:

> As soon as practicable after the enactment of this Act, the Postmaster General and the labor organizations which as of the effective date of this section hold national exclusive recognition rights granted by the Post Office Department, shall negotiate an agreement or agreements covering wages, hours, and working conditions of the employees represented by such labor organizations.[335]

---

[330]Exec. Order No. 10,988, 3 CFR 130 (1962); Exec. Order No. 11,491, 3 CFR 451 (1970).
[331]Kennedy, *The Postal Reorganization Act of 1970: Heading Off Future Postal Strikes?*, 59 GEO. L. J. 305 (1970).
[332]*Id.*
[333]*See generally* Postal Employees v. Klassen, 514 F2d 189, 89 LRRM 2558 (CA DC, 1975).
[334]*Id.*
[335]39 USCA §1201. §10(a) has withstood constitutional challenge. Thus, although unions other than the national craft unions protested that §10(a) denied their members equal protection of law by entrenching the national craft unions as exclusive bargaining representatives, the courts have held that the congressional grant of exclusive bargaining rights during a "transitional period" to labor organizations which had been successful in previous elections administered by the Department of Labor was a reasonable scheme to incorporate the status quo in labor representation among postal employees. Additionally, it was determined that the "transitional period" provided for in the PRA was not intended by Congress to be limited to a period of two years, but was to extend until the Board had established bargaining units and provided for the election of representatives, or until accomplishment of such other actions as might be taken by the Board defining the rights and obligations of the Postmaster General, the labor organizations representing postal employees, and their members. National Postal Union v. Blount,

Pursuant to that statutory mandate, the Postmaster General and the national craft unions have entered into successive national agreements under which the national craft unions have been recognized as the exclusive bargaining agents for postal workers.[336]

b. The Basic Unit. The congressional mandate to the Board in the comprehensive PRA legislation is to determine "in each case the unit appropriate for collective bargaining in the Postal Service."[337] While an explicit standard for determining unit appropriateness is not set forth in the PRA, the legislative history instructs the Board to apply its private sector criteria. Thus, the conference report stated:

> It is the intent of the conference committee that these provisions of the conference substitute leave to the National Labor Relations Board the judgment as to what will be the appropriate units for collective bargaining in the Postal Service on the basis of the same criteria applied by the Board in determining appropriate bargaining units in the private sector. The conference substitute deems it desirable to leave the determination of appropriate bargaining units entirely in the judgment of the NLRB rather than to predetermine such matters in any way.[338]

In 1974 the Board rendered its landmark decision concerning postal employee bargaining units.[339] The Board had consolidated for hearing six petitions filed by various unions to represent units as large as 70,000 employees (part, not all, of the New York region) and as small as 90 motor vehicle employees working at different Baltimore, Md. facilities. In dismissing all six petitions, the Board stated that "any less-than-nationwide unit which does not at least encompass all employees within a district or sectional center is too fragmented for meaningful collective bargaining."[340] In arriving at that decision, the Board reasoned as follows:

> The Employer's size, collective-bargaining history, number of employees, geographic dispersion, and centralized operational organization impose certain practical limitations on the numerical proliferation of bargaining units. It is obvious that meaningful

---

341 F Supp 370, 79 LRRM 2861 (D DC, 1972); Postal Employees v. Klassen, 369 F Supp 747, 85 LRRM 2609 (D DC, 1974), *aff'd,* 514 F2d 189 (CA DC, 1975).
   [336]Postal Employees v. Klassen, *supra* note 335.
   [337]39 USC §1202.
   [338]Conf. Rep. No. 91-1363, 91st Cong., 2d Sess. 81-82 (1970), *reprinted in* [1970] U.S. Code Cong. & Ad. News 3715.
   [339]U.S. Postal Serv., 208 NLRB 948, 85 LRRM 1212 (1974).
   [340]*Id.* at 954.

collective bargaining could not realistically occur at each of the Employer's 32,000 individual facilities. On the other hand, we are aware that certain broad horizontal or vertical divisions of employees into homogenous units with the requisite community of interests might well promote meaningful, or at least feasible, collective bargaining.[341]

Since it was not directly confronted with the issue, the Board reserved for future consideration the question of whether a unit encompassing all employees within a region, metropolitan center, metropolitan area, district, or sectional center would in fact constitute an appropriate unit.[342]

Appropriate bargaining units have been delineated by the Board, however, in several cases involving Postal Service employees engaged in duties ancillary to regular postal clerk and mail delivery operations. Thus, in one decision, employees of the Postal Service's two area supply centers, located in New Jersey and Kansas, were combined with employees of the Postal Service's 14 Mail Bag Depositories to form an appropriate bargaining unit.[343] In the same decision, the Board found appropriate a separate unit for employees at the Mail Equipment Shops in Washington, D.C.[344]

Similarly, in a subsequent decision the Board found employees at the Postal Service's six postal data centers to constitute an appropriate bargaining unit.[345] In so finding, the Board relied upon the fact that the employees at all of the data centers enjoyed similar working conditions, terms of employment, fringe benefits, and overall supervision, and that the centers represented "a highly-integrated data processing operation whose employees share a community of interest."[346]

---

[341]Id. at 953.

[342]There are five postal regions in the United States; there are metropolitan centers in the 10 largest urban concentrations of post offices; and metropolitan areas in the 21 next largest. The remaining post offices are grouped into 86 districts. There are 552 sectional centers, with 50 to 120 post offices assigned to each sectional center. Sectional centers operate across the aforementioned administrative subdivisions.

[343]U.S. Postal Serv., 200 NLRB 1143, 82 LRRM 1049 (1972). Area Supply Centers provide all types of supplies and equipment to postmasters throughout the country and to certain large mailing customers. Employees at Mail Bag Depositories receive, examine, and store mail bags and eventually ship them to locations where there is a shortage. Mail Equipment Shops manufacture mail bags and various types of clocks and keys.

[344]The Board emphasized that while Area Supply Center and Mail Bag Depository employees were operationally integrated and had common supervision, Mail Equipment Shop employees shared no such community of interest, inasmuch as Mail Equipment Shops were a separate entity as to both function and operation.

[345]U.S. Postal Serv., 210 NLRB 477, 86 LRRM 1097 (1974).

[346]Id. at 478.

In a 1977 decision, the Board found appropriate a bargaining unit consisting of the Postal Service's Research and Development Department employees.[347] In finding the petitioned-for unit appropriate, the Board emphasized that the department exercises a great degree of autonomy, has a unique function that is not duplicated at the Postal Service's headquarters or elsewhere in its system, and is relatively self-contained in a location approximately 15 miles from the Postal Service's headquarters.

D. Multi-Employer Bargaining Units

This section focuses upon the nature of the multi-employer bargaining unit: how it is formed, how the parties may enter it, and how they may withdraw from it. Once the unit is formed, the multi-employer group becomes the employer for purposes of bargaining, with the obligation under Sections 8(a)(5) and 8(d) to bargain collectively with the representative of all the employees in the unit.[348] The bargaining requirements applicable to the "multi-employer" are substantially the same as for any employer. The major differences are noted in this section.[349]

1. The Role of Multi-Employer Units in the Bargaining Process. The institution of multi-employer bargaining, i.e., bargaining between a union or unions and groups of employers, has existed in this country for over 85 years.[350] Employers first grouped together in the 1880s, forming associations of large corporations, not for the purpose of collective bargaining, but in order to achieve a coordinated counterforce to the Knights of Labor.[351] Since the establishment of the principle of collective bargaining, however, multi-employer bargaining has become, to a considerable degree, a device employed by small employers to offset the bargaining strength of powerful unions.[352] Unions

---

[347]U.S. Postal Serv., 232 NLRB 556, 97 LRRM 1062 (1977).

[348]*E.g.*, NLRB v. Strong, 393 US 357, 70 LRRM 2100 (1969).

[349]*See* Chapter 13 *infra* for a discussion of the requirements of good-faith bargaining generally, and Chapter 22 *infra*, which covers lockouts, for a discussion of the body of law relating to lockouts affecting multi-employer units.

[350]*See* F. Pierson, MULTI-EMPLOYER BARGAINING: NATURE AND SCOPE 35 (1949); Sommers, *Pressures on an Association in Collective Bargaining*, 6 IND. & LAB. REL. REV. 557 (1953).

[351]*See* S. Perlman, A HISTORY OF TRADE UNIONISM IN THE UNITED STATES 94, 194, 252 (1950); Note, 66 HARV. L. REV. 886 (1953).

[352]J. Freiden, THE TAFT-HARTLEY ACT AND MULTI-EMPLOYER BARGAINING 4-5 (1949); J. Bachman, MULTI-EMPLOYER BARGAINING 14 (1951). *See* NLRB v. Truck Drivers Local 449, 353 US 87, 94-95, 39 LRRM 2603, 2606 (1957).

nevertheless recognize a number of important advantages in multi-employer bargaining. The standardization of wage rates and working conditions within an industry is a fundamental union objective.[353] Decertification petitions, which require a 30-percent showing of interest, become increasingly less practical as the size of the unit expands.[354] Economies of scale accrue when a union must negotiate only one contract covering several employers. Finally, both weak and powerful unions can join together, thereby avoiding an employer's "divide and conquer" strategy.

Large corporations may not feel union pressures strongly enough to justify their entering an association for collective bargaining,[355] although some industries, such as basic steel and refractories, have engaged in industrywide—hence, multi-employer—bargaining for years. Such bargaining is also prevalent in industries like longshore and construction, where workers frequently change employers and hiring halls[356] are common.[357] Employers recognize that an employers' association can eliminate wage competition,[358] help to prevent whipsaw strikes,[359] and achieve certain economies of scale.

The Wagner Act did not explicitly authorize the Board to find multi-employer units appropriate, although such bargaining was not uncommon in 1935. However, in a 1938 decision, the Board, with Supreme Court approval, construed the Act to allow for multi-employer units.[360] The Board noted that Section 9(b) provided for "employer" units, that Section 2(2) defined "employer" to include any "person" acting in an employer's

---

[353]See Apex Hosiery Co. v. Leader, 310 US 469, 503, 6 LRRM 647, 657 (1940); Testimony of James A. Suffridge, President, Retail Clerks Int'l Ass'n, in GEN. SUBCOMM. ON LABOR OF THE HOUSE COMM. ON LABOR AND EDUCATION, 88th Cong., 2d Sess., MULTI-EMPLOYER ASSOCIATION BARGAINING AND ITS IMPACT ON THE COLLECTIVE BARGAINING PROCESS (Comm. Print 1965).

[354]Employees of a single employer in a multi-employer unit cannot obtain a decertification election; the petition must be filed on behalf of all employees in the unit. See, e.g., Alston Coal Co., 13 NLRB 683, 4 LRRM 337 (1939); American Consol. Co., 226 NLRB 923, 93 LRRM 1446 (1976). See generally Chapter 10 supra at notes 22-23.

[355]See Bachman, supra note 352 at 60-61.

[356]See generally Chapter 29 infra at notes 219-304.

[357]See NLRB v. Truck Drivers Local 449, supra note 352 at 94; Rains, Legal Aspects and Problems of Multi-Employer Bargaining, 34 B.U. L. REV. 159 (1954).

[358]Bachman, supra note 352 at 16-18. See also Chapter 31 infra at notes 334-418 for a discussion of the antitrust laws and variations of multi-employer bargaining.

[359]See Chapter 22 infra.

[360]Shipowners' Ass'n of the Pac. Coast, 7 NLRB 1002, 1024-25, 2 LRRM 377 (1938), review denied sub nom. AFL v. NLRB, 103 F2d 933, 4 LRRM 78 (CA DC, 1939), aff'd, 308 US 401, 5 LRRM 670 (1940); Waterfront Employers Ass'n, 71 NLRB 80, 110, 18 LRRM 1465, 1469 (1946).

interest, and that Section 2(1) defined "person" to include "associations." Therefore, the Act contemplated that an employer unit could consist of an association acting in the employer's interest, i.e., a multi-employer unit.

Prior to the passage of the Taft-Hartley Act, a substantial body of opinion viewed multi-employer bargaining as a lever for big unionism and therefore a real or potential hazard to many employees. In consequence, in the course of the Taft-Hartley debates, many proposals to limit multi-employer bargaining were introduced. Perhaps the most sweeping of those, sponsored by the National Association of Manufacturers, was one which would have prohibited unions "representing workers of two or more employers [from taking] joint wage action or engag[ing] in other monopolistic practices." The Hartley bill, passed by the House of Representatives, placed severe restrictions upon multi-employer bargaining.[361] However, none of these proposals survived in the final version of the Taft-Hartley Act.

The Taft-Hartley amendments of 1947 substituted for "any person acting in the interest of an employer" the phrase "any person acting as an agent of the employer." The Board implicitly read this amendment as detracting nothing from its authority to conduct elections in multi-employer units.[362] In *NLRB* v. *Truck Drivers Local 449*,[363] the Supreme Court reviewed the failure of legislative efforts to curb such bargaining and concluded that Congress intended the Board to "continue its established administrative practice of certifying multi-employer units."[364]

The procedures referred to as "multi-employer bargaining" include industrywide and multi-association bargaining as well as bargaining between a union and several companies associated on the side of the employer. The Board applies the same principles to all these subtypes.[365]

---

[361]§9(f)(1) of H.R. 3020, with certain provisos, declared unions representing employees of one employer ineligible to be certified as the representative of the employees of a competing employer of more than 100 workers at a facility less than 50 miles distant. LEGISLATIVE HISTORY OF THE LABOR MANAGEMENT RELATIONS ACT, 1947, at 187-88 (1948). *See, e.g.,* Wolman, *Industry-Wide Bargaining*, 1 LAB. L.J. (1949).

[362]Associated Shoe Indus. of S.E. Mass., Inc., 81 NLRB 224, 23 LRRM 1320 (1949). Dissenting Members Houston and Murdock interpreted the legislative history as expanding the Board's authority to find multi-employer units appropriate. *Id.* at 235 n.28.

[363]353 US 87, 39 LRRM 2603 (1957).

[364]353 US at 95-96.

[365]*See* Chester County Beer Distrib. Ass'n, 133 NLRB 771, 48 LRRM 1712 (1961); Morgan Linen Serv., Inc., 131 NLRB 420, 48 LRRM 1054 (1961); Mutual Rough Hat

2. Establishment of the Multi-Employer Unit: Its Consensual Nature.

Unlike other bargaining units, the multi-employer unit is *consensual*. A multi-employer association need not have a formal organizational structure; nor must the members delegate to the association the authority to execute a final and binding contract; nor must the resulting contract be signed by all members of the group. The essential criterion for the establishment of a multi-employer unit is the unequivocal manifestation by each member of the group that all be bound in collective bargaining by group, rather than by individual, action.[366] The formation of the unit must be entirely voluntary, the assent of the union having representative status also being required. The Board will not sanction the creation of such a unit over the objection of any party, union, or employer.[367]

Co., 82 NLRB 440, 24 LRRM 1641 (1949). The multi-employer unit issues discussed herein are different from the "joint employer" issue presented in such cases as Greyhound Corp. v. Boire, 205 F Supp 686, 50 LRRM 2485 (SD Fla., 1962), *aff'd*, 309 F2d 397, 51 LRRM 2509 (CA 5, 1962), *rev'd*, 376 US 473, 55 LRRM 2694 (1964). *See* Chapter 30 at notes 103-125 for a discussion of the joint-employer issue; *see also* Chapter 13 *infra* at notes 787-808 for a discussion of the "double-breasted" issue.

Multi-employer bargaining should also be distinguished from "coordinated" and "coalition" bargaining. Unions have developed a "coordinated" bargaining strategy in response to the diversification of many major corporations through mergers and acquisitions, and to coordinated or centralized bargaining by management within and among large corporations. Having organized the numerous plants of conglomerates and corporate giants in separate collective bargaining units, unions have often felt overpowered in a framework of separate negotiations, for the employer could deal first with the weaker unions and then impose the pattern settlement on the stronger unions, who could not strike successfully because production could be shifted to other plants of the same company. Through coordinated bargaining, by negotiating a series of separate contracts containing common or similar terms, unions have sought the benefits of multi-employer bargaining, but without merging into a single bargaining unit. Coordinated bargaining thus represents an intermediate position between single-employer bargaining and multi-employer bargaining. For a discussion of coordinated bargaining and a related form, "coalition" bargaining, *see* Chapter 13 *infra* at notes 734-61.

[366]Kroger Co., 148 NLRB 569, 57 LRRM 1021 (1964); York Transfer & Storage Co., 107 NLRB 139, 33 LRRM 1078 (1953); *Kroger* also illustrates that a multi-employer unit does not require the execution of a single, master agreement. It is sufficient if members of the group have bargained as a group over a period of time (17 years in this case) and, as a result of joint negotiations, have executed separate, but substantially similar, contracts with the union representing their employees. *See also* Crane Sheet Metal, Inc., 248 NLRB 75, 103 LRRM 1365 (1980); Bel-Window, 240 NLRB 1315, 100 LRRM 1464 (1979); A. B. Hirschfeld, Inc., 140 NLRB 212, 51 LRRM 1607 (1962); Rayonier, Inc., 52 NLRB 1269, 13 LRRM 91 (1943). An employer's membership in a multi-employer unit is assumed by a corporation which purchases the employer's stock. RKB Int'l Corp., 240 NLRB 1082, 100 LRRM 1426 (1979).

[367]United Fryer & Stillman, Inc., 139 NLRB 704, 51 LRRM 1385 (1962). Early in the Wagner Act period, the Board created a multi-employer unit over the objections of the employers. Shipowners' Ass'n of the Pac. Coast, *supra* note 360. In Alston Coal Co., *supra* note 354, the Board first required unanimous employer consent. The union's consent may be implied from its failure to object. Authorized Air Conditioning Co. v. NLRB, 606 F2d 899, 102 LRRM 2647 (CA 9, 1979). Forcing an employer, such as by threatening to strike, to bargain through a multi-employer association violates §§8(b)(1)(A) and 8(b)(4)(A). Mine Workers Local 1854 (Amax Coal Co.), 99 LRRM 1670 (1978). *See also* note 387 *infra* this chapter and Chapter 6 *supra* at note 582.

An employer's objective intent must be manifest either by express delegation to the association's bargaining arm or by participation in the group bargaining process.[368] But in the absence of both participation and delegation of authority, the Board will not accept, over the objection of any party, a mere showing of a custom of past adoption of terms of a multi-employer agreement.[369]

The history of collective bargaining—not only in the particular industry but with respect to particular units—is always an important consideration in determining the appropriateness of a unit. In the multi-employer context, bargaining history assumes unique significance. The absence of any history of multi-employer bargaining in a proposed multi-employer unit is usually determinative against such a unit.[370] However, there have been instances of approval of new multi-employer units in industries where such units are characteristic.[371] On the other hand, a multi-employer bargaining history of brief duration not predicated upon a Board certification does not ensure that only a multi-employer unit is appropriate.[372] Thus, when an employer with a history of individual bargaining joins a multi-employer association and adopts its contract, a rival petition for a single-employer unit will prevail if timely filed before the insulated period of the last individual contract, whether or not the multi-

---

[368]Greenhoot, Inc., 205 NLRB 250, 83 LRRM 1656 (1973); Rock Springs Retail Merchants Ass'n, 188 NLRB 261, 76 LRRM 1254 (1971); Van Eerden Co., 154 NLRB 496, 59 LRRM 1770 (1965); Kroger Co., *supra* note 366. In *Rock Springs*, for example, the Board ruled inappropriate a unit of employees of 31 members of an association, but directed an election in a unit composed of the five employer-members who had previously negotiated or signed contracts with the union and had indicated their intent to be bound by joint action.

[369]NLRB v. E-Z Davies Chevrolet, 395 F2d 191, 68 LRRM 2228 (CA 9, 1968); A. B. Hirschfeld, Inc., *supra* note 366; Colonial Cedar Co., 119 NLRB 1613, 41 LRRM 1353 (1958); West End Brewing Co., 107 NLRB 1542, 33 LRRM 1432 (1954); Pacific Metals Co., Ltd., 91 NLRB 696, 26 LRRM 1558 (1950). Associated Shoe Indus. of S.E. Mass., Inc., *supra* note 362; N.Y. Typographical Union No. 6 (Royal Composing Room), 242 NLRB No. 54, 101 LRRM 1148 (1979).

[370]Arden Farms, 117 NLRB 318, 39 LRRM 1216 (1957). Rainbo Bread Co., 92 NLRB 181, 27 LRRM 1067 (1950). *But see* Taylor Motors, Inc., 241 NLRB 711, 100 LRRM 1558 (1979).

[371]*E.g.*, Calumet Contractors Ass'n, 121 NLRB 80, 42 LRRM 1279 (1958); Western Ass'n of Eng'rs, Architects & Surveyors, 101 NLRB 64, 31 LRRM 1010 (1952). A new unit without multi-employer bargaining history is appropriate if no party seeks a single-employer unit. Broward County Launderers & Cleaners Ass'n, 125 NLRB 256, 45 LRRM 1113 (1959). *See also* Checker Cab Co., 141 NLRB 583, 52 LRRM 1357 (1963), and 153 NLRB 651, 59 LRRM 1503 (1965), *enforced*, 367 F2d 692, 63 LRRM 2243 (CA 6, 1966), *cert. denied*, 385 US 1008, 64 LRRM 2108 (1967).

[372]Miron Bldg. Prods. Co., 116 NLRB 1406, 39 LRRM 1002 (1956).

employer contract would otherwise bar a petition.[373] Bargaining history is considered qualifying even when successive agreements contain clauses held to violate the Act.[374] Individual bargaining on a limited basis, under a mutually recognized privilege to do so concomitant with group bargaining on subjects of general concern, does not negate a desire to be bound on a multiemployer basis.[375] But if either the union or an employer manifests an unequivocal intent to pursue an individual course of action, even a substantial history of multi-employer bargaining will not suffice to establish such a unit in the face of the determination to bargain individually.[376] In one case, a substantial history of multi-employer bargaining was deemed insufficient to maintain the multi-employer unit after the dissolution of the local union representing the employees and its merger with another local left no successor union with a claim to represent all employees in the multi-employer unit.[377]

The freedom of choice extended an employer under the foregoing rules is subject to a limitation which results from the freedom of association accorded employees by the Act. The Board has held that an employer "could not unilaterally and without the express or implied consent of its employees bind them to representation in a multi-employer unit" by signing a multi-employer collective bargaining agreement which granted recognition to a particular union.[378] When the employer seeks to enter the multi-employer bargaining unit, the relevant majority is that of the employees of the particular employer. However, once the multi-employer bargaining unit is established, the relevant majority is the entire unit. Thus, even if a majority of the

---

[373]Etna Equip. Co., 236 NLRB 1578, 98 LRRM 1591 (1978). The first multi-employer contract is not a bar where the employees have not ratified their inclusion in the larger unit. U.S. Pillow Corp., 136 NLRB 584, 50 LRRM 1216 (1962). See Chapter 10 supra at notes 117-200 for discussion of the contract-bar doctrine.

[374]Tom's Monarch Laundry & Dry Cleaning Co., 168 NLRB 217, 66 LRRM 1277 (1967).

[375]Kroger Co., supra note 366. The resulting multi-employer agreement may be executed in a series of individual-member agreements embodying the terms of joint bargaining (and also side agreements reached by individual bargaining). Detroit News, 119 NLRB 345, 41 LRRM 1085 (1957); Balaban & Katz, 87 NLRB 1071, 25 LRRM 1197 (1949).

[376]Donaldson Sales, Inc., 141 NLRB 1303, 1305, 52 LRRM 1500 (1963).

[377]McKesson Wine & Spirits Co., 232 NLRB 208, 96 LRRM 1465 (1977).

[378]Mohawk Business Mach. Corp., 116 NLRB 248, 249, 38 LRRM 1239, 1240 (1956); accord, Dancker & Sellew, Inc., 140 NLRB 1824, 52 LRRM 1120 (1963), enforced sub nom. NLRB v. Local 210, Teamsters, 330 F2d 46, 55 LRRM 2902 (CA 2, 1964); Pepsi-Cola Bottling Co. of Kan. City, 55 NLRB 1138, 14 LRRM 75 (1944). Cf. Douds v. Anheuser-Busch, Inc., 99 F Supp 474, 28 LRRM 2277 (D NJ, 1951); Lamson Bros., 59 NLRB 1561, 15 LRRM 209 (1945).

employees of a single employer within the multi-employer unit no longer wish to be represented by the union, "that fact would not relieve [the employer] of its obligation to bargain with the Union as to the appropriate multi-employer unit, nor justify an untimely withdrawal from such unit."[379]

3. Dissolution—Entire and Partial. By 1958, it was well established that even in the face of a long history of multi-employer bargaining, an employer could unilaterally withdraw from its association and thus reduce the size of the unit.[380] Conversely, it was equally well established that a union could not unilaterally terminate a multi-employer bargaining relationship and could not negotiate with individual members of the association, without first bargaining to impasse under the existing framework; even after such an impasse, the Board emphasized, separate negotiations did not signal the end of the multi-employer relationship.[381]

It was in 1958 that the Board first indicated that unions, as well as employers, had the right to withdraw from a multi-employer bargaining relationship. In *Retail Associates*[382] the Board conditioned either party's withdrawal upon adequate written notice given prior to the contractually established date for modification of the collective agreement or to the agreed-upon date for the commencement of multi-employer negotiations. Where actual bargaining had begun, either party could withdraw only by mutual consent[383] or under "unusual circumstances."[384] The

---

[379]Sheridan Creations, Inc., 148 NLRB 1503, 57 LRRM 1176, 1178 (1964), *enforced*, 357 F2d 245, 61 LRRM 2586 (CA 2, 1966), *cert. denied*, 385 US 1005, 64 LRRM 2108 (1967). Similarly, a decertification petition must be filed for the multi-employer unit; a petition filed on a single-employer basis will be dismissed. American Consol. Co., 226 NLRB 923, 93 LRRM 1446 (1976).

[380]McAnary & Welter. Inc., 115 NLRB 1029, 37 LRRM 1483 (1956); Johnson Optical Co., 87 NLRB 539, 25 LRRM 1135 (1949).

[381]Stouffer Corp., 101 NLRB 1331, 31 LRRM 1200 (1952); Morand Bros. Beverage Co., 91 NLRB 409, 26 LRRM 1501 (1950), *enforced*, 190 F2d 576, 28 LRRM 2364 (CA 7, 1951).

[382]120 NLRB 388, 41 LRRM 1502, 42 LRRM 1119 (1958).

[383]The essence of multi-employer bargaining is a tripartite relationship between the union, the multi-employer bargaining association, and the individual employer-members of the association. An employer who wishes to perfect an untimely withdrawal must secure the consent of both the union and the multi-employer association of which it has been a member. A union violates §8(b)(3) by executing an independent contract with a former association member where the association has not consented to the withdrawal. Conversely, an employer violates §8(a)(5) by an untimely withdrawal from the unit without the association's and the union's consent. Teamsters Local 378 (Capital Chevrolet Co.), 243 NLRB 1086, 102 LRRM 1007 (1979). In one case, consent to an employer's withdrawal was not inferred from a union's four and one-half month delay in requesting the employer to execute the association contract. Reliable Roofing Co., 246 NLRB 716, 103 LRRM 1006 (1979).

[384]Retail Assocs., Inc., *supra* note 382 at 395. *See also* Evening News Ass'n, 154 NLRB

Retail Associates rules require that notice of withdrawal be both timely and unequivocal. To be unequivocal, "the decision to withdraw must contemplate a sincere abandonment, with relative permanency, of the multi-employer unit and the embracement of a different course of bargaining on an individual employer basis."[385] Should timeliness of the notice of withdrawal turn upon the date agreed upon for the start of negotiations, the date in question relates to the actual negotiations, not to the service of a notice or demand for conference.[386] After either party gives such timely and unequivocal notice, the other party may not exert economic pressure to preserve the multi-employer relationship.[387]

Following *Retail Associates,* the Board generally limited application of the term "unusual circumstances" to cases where the withdrawing employer has faced dire economic circumstances such that "the very existence of an employer as a viable business entity has ceased or is about to cease."[388] However, the Board

---

1494, 60 LRRM 1149 (1965), *enforced sub nom.* Detroit Newspaper Publishers Ass'n v. NLRB, 372 F2d 569, 64 LRRM 2403 (CA 6, 1956); Comment, *The Status of Multiemployer Bargaining Under the National Labor Relations Act,* 1967 DUKE L.J. 558; Comment, *Withdrawal From Multi-Employer Bargaining—Reconsidering Retail Associates,* 115 U. PA. L. REV. 464 (1967).

[385]Retail Assocs., *supra* note 382 at 394.

[386]Carmichael Floor Covering Co., 155 NLRB 674, 60 LRRM 1364 (1965); Quality Limestone Prods., Inc., 153 NLRB 1009, 59 LRRM 1589 (1965); Detroit Window Cleaners (Daelyte Serv. Co.), 126 NLRB 63, 45 LRRM 1275 (1960).

[387]§8(b)(4)(A) prohibits a union from exerting pressure to force an employer "to join any labor or employer organization." Longshoremen & Warehousemen (General Ore, Inc.), 126 NLRB 172, 45 LRRM 1296 (1960). *See* Chapter 6 *supra* at note 582, note 367 *supra* this chapter and related text. §8(b)(1)(B) prohibits a union from coercing an employer in the selection of a representative for purposes of collective bargaining. *See* Chapter 6 *supra* at notes 582-612. Hotel & Restaurant Employees Local 2 (Zim's Restaurant), 240 NLRB 757, 100 LRRM 1324 (1979). §8(b)(3) prohibits a union from unilaterally attempting to enlarge a bargaining unit. Amax Coal Co. v. NLRB, 614 F2d 872, 103 LRRM 2482 (CA 3, 1980); Electrical Workers (IUE) Local 323 (Active Enterprises, Inc.), 242 NLRB 305, 101 LRRM 1179 (1979). *See* Chapter 18 *infra* at notes 47-48. §8(a)(3) prohibits an employer from locking out employees to force their union's adherence to a multi-employer unit. Great Atl. & Pac. Tea Co., 145 NLRB 361, 54 LRRM 1384 (1964), *enforced in pertinent part,* 340 F2d 690, 58 LRRM 2232 (CA 2, 1965). The employer's right to lock out to protect the integrity of the multi-employer bargaining unit from whipsaw strikes, *e.g.,* NLRB v. Truck Drivers Local 449 (Buffalo Linen), 353 US 87, 39 LRRM 2603 (1957), is discussed in Chapter 22 *infra.*

[388]Hi-Way Billboards, Inc., 206 NLRB 22, 23, 84 LRRM 1161, 1162 (1973), *enforcement denied,* 500 F2d 181, 87 LRRM 2203 (CA 5, 1974). The Board has held that an employer may withdraw from a multi-employer bargaining association after negotiations have begun: (1) where the employer is subject to extreme economic difficulties resulting in an arrangement under the bankruptcy laws, U.S. Lingerie Corp., 170 NLRB 750, 67 LRRM 1482 (1968); (2) where the employer is faced with the imminent prospect of such adverse economic conditions as would require it to close its plant, Spun-Jee Corp., 171 NLRB 557, 68 LRRM 1121 (1968); (3) and where the employer is faced with the prospect of being forced out of business for lack of qualified employees and the union refuses to assist the employer by providing employees, Atlas Elec. Serv. Co., 176 NLRB

has, in some cases, found "unusual circumstances" and allowed an employer to withdraw where the bargaining power of the association had been dissipated by a series of consensual withdrawals and the execution of separate agreements by the majority of the association's members.[389]

The Board and the courts of appeals have disagreed as to two situations. First, where a minority of the employers in an association argued that the majority had ignored their interests in negotiations, the Board found no "unusual circumstances."[390] While recognizing that mere dissatisfaction with the results of the group bargaining does not justify an untimely withdrawal, the Eighth Circuit concluded that where the multi-employer association fails to fairly represent the interests of a class of employer members, their withdrawal is justified.[391] Second, and more important, the Board has consistently held that a bargaining impasse does not constitute "unusual circumstances" justifying an employer's withdrawal from a multi-employer unit once negotiations have begun. In *Hi-Way Billboards*[392] the Board

---

827, 71 LRRM 1625 (1969). The Board refused to find "unusual circumstances": (1) where an employer asserted a good-faith doubt of the union's majority status among his own employees, Sheridan Creations, Inc., 148 NLRB 1503, 57 LRRM 1176 (1964), *enforced*, 357 F2d 245, 61 LRRM 2586 (CA 2, 1966), *cert. denied*, 385 US 1005, 64 LRRM 288 (1967); (2) where all the employer's unit employees were discharged, John J. Corbett Press, Inc., 163 NLRB 154, 64 LRRM 2108 (1967), *enforced*, 401 F2d 673, 69 LRRM 2480 (CA 2, 1968); (3) where the union executed separate agreements with individual employer-members of the association, WE Painters, Inc., 176 NLRB 964, 72 LRRM 1089 (1969); (4) where the employer had been suspended from the association for failure to pay its dues, Senco, Inc., 177 NLRB 882, 71 LRRM 1532 (1969); (5) where the employer was subjected to a strike, State Elec. Serv., Inc., 198 NLRB 592, 80 LRRM 1763 (1972), *enforced*, 477 F2d 749, 82 LRRM 3154 (CA 5, 1973), *cert. denied*, 414 US 911, 84 LRRM 2458 (1973); and (6) where the employer suffered a sharp decline in its business, Serv-All Co., 199 NLRB 1131, 81 LRRM 1495 (1972), *enforcement denied on other grounds*, 491 F2d 1273, 85 LRRM 2677 (CA 10, 1974). Dire economic circumstances will not justify withdrawal from the unit after an agreement is reached. Co-Ed Garment Co., 231 NLRB 848, 97 LRRM 1502 (1977); Arco Elec. Co. v. NLRB, 618 F2d 698, 103 LRRM 3114 (CA 10, 1980).

[389]Typographic Serv. Co., 238 NLRB 1565, 99 LRRM 1649 (1978); Connell Typesetting Co., 212 NLRB 918, 87 LRRM 1001 (1974). *But see* Tobey Fine Papers, 245 NLRB 1393, 102 LRRM 1343 (1979); Graham Paper Co., 245 NLRB 1388, 102 LRRM 1345 (1979); Butler Paper Co., 245 NLRB 1398, 102 LRRM 1347 (1979). The Board failed to find "unusual circumstances" that would allow an employer to withdraw from a multi-employer unit where the union had negotiated a series of interim agreements with more than two thirds of the employer-members of the association. Callier's Custom Kitchens, 243 NLRB 1114, 102 LRRM 1008 (1979), *enforced*, 630 F2d 595, 105 LRRM 2510 (CA 8, 1980).

[390]Siebler Heating & Air Conditioning, Inc., 219 NLRB 1124, 90 LRRM 1239 (1975).

[391]NLRB v. Siebler Heating & Air Conditioning, Inc., 563 F2d 366, 96 LRRM 2613 (CA 8, 1977), *cert. denied*, 437 US 911, 98 LRRM 2705 (1978). *See also* NLRB v. Unelko Corp., 478 F2d 1404, 83 LRRM 2447 (CA 7, 1973).

[392]206 NLRB 22, 84 LRRM 1161 (1973), *enforcement denied*, 500 F2d 181, 87 LRRM 2203 (CA 5, 1974). *Accord,* Charles D. Bonanno Linen Serv., Inc., 229 NLRB 629, 95 LRRM 1128 (1977), *reconsidered,* 243 NLRB 1093, 102 LRRM 1001 (1979), *enforced,* 630

explained that impasse was an expected part of negotiations, as to which both parties may utilize economic weapons to restart negotiations. The Board asserted that multi-employer negotiations would be destroyed if members of the unit could withdraw upon reaching impasse, since a member could avoid its bargaining obligations by intentionally creating an impasse whenever an impending agreement seemed unfavorable. Several courts of appeals rejected the Board's position,[393] for they equated a union's right to strike selectively (to obtain interim agreements with members of the multi-employer unit after reaching impasse) with an employer's unilateral right to withdraw from the bargaining unit. The courts reasoned that the union's right to strike created an imbalance of power between the union and employer members of the unit, including a potential for whipsaw strikes; this was sufficient to justify granting the employer an equivalent right of unilateral withdrawal.[394]

Following the rejection of its "impasse" position by five circuits, the Board, in *Charles D. Bonanno Linen Service, Inc.*[395] *sua sponte* reconsidered its prior decisions. While restating its *Hi-Way Billboards* rationale, it clarified its position concerning interim agreements. The Board stated that a true interim agreement establishes terms and conditions of employment for one or more employer-members pending the outcome of renewed group bargaining, and that it does not derogate the association's bar-

---

F2d 25, 105 LRRM 2477 (CA 1, 1980), *aff'd*, 454 US 404, 109 LRRM 2257 (1982) (*see infra* at note 396); Goodsell & Vocke, Inc., 223 NLRB 60, 92 LRRM 1187 (1976), *enforced*, 559 F2d 1141, 96 LRRM 2370 (CA 9, 1977); Associated Shower Door Co., 205 NLRB 677, 84 LRRM 1108 (1973), *enforced on other grounds*, 512 F2d 230, 88 LRRM 3024 (CA 9, 1975), *cert. denied*, 423 US 893, 90 LRRM 2614 (1975); Bill Cook Buick, Inc., 224 NLRB 1094, 92 LRRM 1582 (1976); Florida Fire Sprinklers, Inc., 237 NLRB 1034, 99 LRRM 1078 (1978).

[393]H & D, Inc. v. NLRB, 633 F2d 139, 105 LRRM 3070 (CA 9, 1980); NLRB v. Independent Ass'n of Steel Fabricators, 582 F2d 135, 98 LRRM 3150 (CA 2, 1978), *cert. denied*, 429 US 1130, 100 LRRM 2334 (1979); NLRB v. Beck Engraving Co., 522 F2d 475, 90 LRRM 2089 (CA 3, 1975); NLRB v. Associated Shower Door Co., 512 F2d 230, 88 LRRM 3024 (CA 9, 1975), *cert. denied*, 423 US 893, 90 LRRM 2614 (1975); NLRB v. Hi-Way Billboards, Inc., *supra* note 392; Fairmont Foods Co. v. NLRB, 471 F2d 1170, 82 LRRM 2017 (CA 8, 1972). *Contra*, NLRB v. Charles D. Bonanno Linen Serv., Inc., *supra* note 392. *See generally Effect of Negotiating Impasse on an Employer's Right to Withdraw From A Multi-Employer Bargaining Association*, 17 B.C. IND. & COM. L. REV. 525 (1976).

[394]Plumbers Local 323 (P.H.C. Mechanical Contractors), 191 NLRB 592, 77 LRRM 1769 (1971); Sangamo Constr. Co., 188 NLRB 159, 77 LRRM 1039 (1971); Morand Bros. Beverage Co., *supra* note 381; Southwestern Wholesale Grocery Co., 92 NLRB 1485, 27 LRRM 1265 (1951).

[395]*Supra* note 392; *see* Seattle Auto Glass, 246 NLRB 94, 102 LRRM 1376 (1979); Birkenwald Distrib. Co., 243 NLRB 1151, 102 LRRM 1005 (1979); Maine Mach. Works, 243 NLRB 1098, 102 LRRM 1006 (1979).

gaining authority because any resulting agreement would supersede the interim contract. Under these circumstances, all employer-members of the association maintain a vested interest in the terms of the ultimate agreement. In contrast, the multi-employer unit would be fragmented by a pseudo-interim agreement which does not conform to the union's pre-impasse proposals and is offered with variations to employer-members of the group. In this latter circumstance, employer-members with favorable interim agreements may seek to prolong the impasse in order to gain a competitive advantage. The Board concluded that true interim agreements are calculated to further the integrity of the bargaining unit by preserving the members' mutual interest in a final associationwide contract; thus, the union's right to negotiate interim agreements after impasse should not excuse an employer's untimely withdrawal from the multi-employer unit.

Acknowledging its disagreement with the other circuits, the First Circuit enforced *Bonanno*. It reasoned that the balance of economic power arguably created by the union's right to negotiate an interim agreement "should have little bearing" on whether impasse justifies withdrawal; and the union's right to negotiate interim agreements had never been contingent upon reaching impasse—a term incapable of precise definition and, therefore, an event which either party could manipulate. The court viewed the enforcement of the Board's order as promoting labor peace by preserving the stability of the multi-employer unit. Because of the divergent views of the courts of appeals, the Supreme Court granted certiorari and subsequently affirmed the First Circuit and the Board.[396]

Withdrawal from the multi-employer unit may be total or partial. A total withdrawal dissolves the entire multi-employer unit. Partial withdrawal takes different forms. An individual employer may timely withdraw as far as his own employees are concerned. Comparably, the union may elect to withdraw only as to the employees of some employers.[397] In either situation, the multi-employer unit continues as to the remaining employer-members; the union must bargain with the departing employers

---

[396]Bonanno Linen Service v. NLRB, *supra* note 392. *See* discussion of the Supreme Court's opinion in Chapter 13 *infra* at notes 567-71.
[397]*See, e.g.,* Pacific Coast Ass'n of Pulp & Paper Mfrs., 163 NLRB 892, 64 LRRM 1420 (1967).

on an individual employer basis. And after lawfully withdrawing from a multi-employer unit, the employer must negotiate with the union, for the union's majority status is presumed to continue despite the changed structure of the unit.[398]

Partial withdrawal may also involve the severance of certain crafts from the multi-employer unit. Upon a timely petition by the incumbent or an outside union, the Board will conduct a severance election among all employees in specified crafts or job classifications employed by all the employers in the unit, in effect creating a second multi-employer unit.[399] However, the Board will not conduct an election to sever specific classifications at only one of the employers in the unit[400] or where there is substantial interchange among employees in the various classifications.[401] With mutual consent, the parties may also sever classifications to create a second multi-employer unit.

4. Scope of the Multi-Employer Unit. Until 1952, the Board took the position that the appropriateness of a multi-employer unit was controlling as to all categories of employees of the employers in the unit.[402] Thus, once multi-employer bargaining was established with respect to some employees, all subsequent organization involving participating employers had to proceed on a multi-employer basis.

The Board's concern that this requirement would impede organization led to its abandonment in *Joseph E. Seagram &*

---

[398]Holiday Hotel & Casino, 228 NLRB 926, 94 LRRM 1702 (1977), *enforced*, 604 F2d 605, 102 LRRM 2484 (CA 9, 1979); Tahoe Nugget, Inc., 227 NLRB 357, 94 LRRM 1343 (1976), *enforced*, 584 F2d 293, 99 LRRM 2509 (CA 9, 1978), *cert. denied*, 442 US 921, 101 LRRM 2428 (1979); Nevada Lodge, 227 NLRB 368, 94 LRRM 1345 (1976), *enforced sub nom.* NLRB v. Tahoe Nugget, Inc., 584 F2d 2983, 99 LRRM 2509 (CA 9, 1978); Barney's Club, Inc., 227 NLRB 414, 94 LRRM 1444 (1976). The presumption was rebutted where the employer reclassified its employees to change the composition of the unit and thereby reduced the union's support in the newly defined unit. NLRB v. Sac Constr. Co., 603 F2d 1155, 102 LRRM 2513 (CA 5, 1979). *See generally* Chapter 12 *infra* at notes 352-442 and Chapter 13 *infra* at notes 675-708.

[399]Allen, Lane & Scott, 137 NLRB 223, 50 LRRM 1140 (1962); Printing Indus. of Del., 131 NLRB 1100, 48 LRRM 1196 (1961); Employing Printers of Peoria, 130 NLRB 1511, 47 LRRM 1537 (1961).

[400]Pioneer, Inc., 86 NLRB 1316, 25 LRRM 1068 (1949); Coeur d'Alene Mines Corp., 77 NLRB 570, 22 LRRM 1069 (1948); Jahn-Tyler Printing & Publishing Co., 112 NLRB 167, 35 LRRM 1730 (1955); Washington Hardware Co., 95 NLRB 1001, 28 LRRM 1406 (1951); Coca-Cola Bottling Works Co., 91 NLRB 351, 26 LRRM 1488 (1950).

[401]Packaging Corp. of Am., 146 NLRB 1620, 56 LRRM 1104 (1964); Teamsters Local 705 (Roper Corp.), 244 NLRB 522, 102 LRRM 1081 (1979). *See supra* at notes 71-94 for treatment of craft severance in general.

[402]Kenosha Auto Transp. Corp., 98 NLRB 482, 29 LRRM 1370 (1952); Columbia Pictures Corp., 84 NLRB 746, 24 LRRM 1291 (1949).

Sons.[403] Although the *Seagram* rule was enunciated in a case involving a multiplant unit of a single employer, it soon found application in multi-employer cases as well. Under the new policy, the Board has approved single-employer units of office clericals[404] and of salesmen,[405] for example, although the employer had been bargaining as to other employees in a multi-employer unit. The essential criterion for the creation of a single-employer unit is that the employee classifications sought have an "internal homogeneity and cohesiveness" permitting them to stand alone.[406]

If the unrepresented employees do not form a cohesive group, but comprise groups of miscellaneous employees having in common only the fact that they lack representation, the Board has found a unit consisting of such employees appropriate simply as a "residual" unit. But such a unit is deemed appropriate only if it includes all unrepresented employees in the multi-employer group.[407] Where multi-employer bargaining has been confined to certain craft and special interest groups, a residual multi-employer unit cannot be considered the only appropriate unit, on the basis of bargaining history, when such a unit would in effect embrace the main force of employees.[408] Should an employee classification be employed by one or more but less than all the employer-members, such classification may be represented in a unit smaller than the all-employer unit.[409]

Once a multi-employer unit is established, the employer's consent to the inclusion of other categories of employees to the unit is unnecessary. Thus, the Board placed unrepresented timekeepers in an existing multi-employer unit despite an express resolution by association members denying the association the authority to represent them with respect to such employees. The Board held that the Act's requirement that bargaining be

---

[403]101 NLRB 101, 31 LRRM 1022 (1952).

[404]Hyatt House Motel, 174 NLRB 1009, 70 LRRM 1378 (1969); Continental Baking Co., 109 NLRB 33, 34 LRRM 1298 (1954); Sovereign Prods., Inc., 107 NLRB 359, 33 LRRM 1171 (1953); Miller & Miller Motor Freight Lines, 101 NLRB 581, 31 LRRM 1118 (1952).

[405]NLRB v. E-Z Davies Chevrolet, 395 F2d 191, 68 LRRM 2228 (CA 9, 1968); Lownsbury Chevrolet Co., 101 NLRB 1752, 31 LRRM 1261 (1952).

[406]Los Angeles Statler Hilton Hotel, 129 NLRB 1349, 1351, 47 LRRM 1194 (1961) (single-employer unit denied).

[407]Los Angeles Statler Hilton Hotel, *supra* note 406; Daily Press, Inc., 110 NLRB 573, 35 LRRM 1048 (1954).

[408]Pacific Drive-In Theatres Corp., 167 NLRB 661, 66 LRRM 1119 (1967).

[409]Holiday Hotel, 134 NLRB 113, 49 LRRM 1095 (1961); Desaulniers & Co., 115 NLRB 1025, 37 LRRM 1481 (1956).

conducted in an appropriate unit must supersede the employers' choice to exclude timekeepers from the multi-employer unit, where the timekeepers shared a community of interests with the other employees who were part of the multi-employer unit.[410]

5. Multi-Level Bargaining Units. While multi-employer bargaining units are generally conducive to industrial peace and are thus favored by national policy, unions and employers recognize that associationwide solutions are not practical for all subjects of bargaining. Thus, within the framework of multi-employer bargaining, the parties may agree to bargain individually or in smaller groups on specific issues. Bargaining in the trucking industry, for example, has evolved into a master agreement dealing primarily with economic and other national issues, and 32 geographic supplements covering essentially regional matters such as seniority and local grievance procedures.[411]

Multi-level bargaining may also occur in a less developed form where one or more members of an association specifically reserve the right to bargain separately on matters peculiar to their respective plants. However, the union must consent to this limited delegation of bargaining authority to the association.[412] Such an agreement is the equivalent of a waiver during negotiations and is effective for the duration of the bargaining. If the union revokes its acquiescence during the renegotiation of the contract, the employer is obligated to negotiate the issue on a multi-employer basis.[413] Where an employer party to a multi-employer association implements local rules changes, it must bargain with the affected union on request.[414]

When a union that is party to a national or multi-employer agreement organizes a previously unrepresented facility of a covered employer, the new facility will be included in the multi-employer unit only with the parties' implicit or explicit consent.

---

[410]Steamship Trade Ass'n of Baltimore, Inc., 155 NLRB 232, 60 LRRM 1257 (1965).
[411]See, e.g., Davey v. Fitzsimmons, 413 F Supp 670, 92 LRRM 2130 (D DC, 1976).
[412]Rice Lake Creamery Co., 131 NLRB 1270, 48 LRRM 1251 (1961), enforced sub nom. Teamsters Local 662 v. NLRB, 302 F2d 908, 50 LRRM 2243 (CA DC, 1962), cert. denied, 371 US 827, 51 LRRM 2222 (1962); Kroger Co., 141 NLRB 564, 52 LRRM 1352 (1963), aff'd sub nom. Retail Clerks v. NLRB, 330 F2d 210, 55 LRRM 2212 (CA DC, 1964), cert. denied, 379 US 828, 57 LRRM 2239 (1964).
[413]Pacific Coast Ass'n of Pulp & Paper Mfrs., 133 NLRB 690, 48 LRRM 1696 (1961), enforced, 304 F2d 760, 50 LRRM 2626 (CA 9, 1962).
[414]NLRB v. Miller Brewing Co., 408 F2d 12, 70 LRRM 2907 (CA 9, 1969).

And if the new facility is included, the employer may refuse to bargain with the union as to matters covered by the master agreement, but must bargain on local issues.[415]

Another form of multilevel bargaining occurs when parties to a multi-employer agreement cannot agree upon a successor contract and they submit the unresolved issues to a panel composed of representatives of parent union and employer bodies. The Board has held that an employer does not violate the Act by referring to the panel disputed issues, including the continued application of the panel system in the next contract.[416]

---

[415]Eltra Corp., 205 NLRB 1035, 84 LRRM 1234 (1973); Radio Corp. of Am., 135 NLRB 980, 49 LRRM 1606 (1962).
[416]Mechanical Contractors Ass'n of Newburgh, 202 NLRB 1, 82 LRRM 1438 (1973). The Board has distinguished this procedure from interest arbitration. *See* Chapter 18 *infra* at notes 63-64.

CHAPTER 12

RECOGNITION AND WITHDRAWAL OF RECOGNITION WITHOUT AN ELECTION

I. INTRODUCTION

An employer may be required to recognize and bargain with a union that has not received certification by the National Labor Relations Board. This duty to recognize the representative "designated or selected for the purposes of collective bargaining by the majority of the employees in a unit appropriate for such purposes"[1] may exist independently of NLRB election procedures. An employer may also extend recognition voluntarily to a union without a Board election having been conducted. In such cases, however, the employer must act with due care in ascertaining the majority status of the demanding union, for it will have violated Section 8(a)(2) of the Act if the union does not in fact represent a majority of the employees in the unit.[2] In addition, in the limited circumstances discussed in this chapter, the Board may order an employer to bargain with a union even though a secret ballot election has not been held.

Prior to 1947, Section 9(c) of the Wagner Act authorized the Board to certify unions by using secret-ballot elections or "any other suitable method."[3] A *card check*, the most frequently invoked "other suitable method," is the procedure by which signatures

---

[1]§9(a).

[2]Garment Workers (Bernhard-Altmann Tex. Corp.) v. NLRB, 366 US 731, 48 LRRM 2251 (1961). This chapter does not treat the "sweetheart" contract and its kindred, recognition deemed unlawful under Section 8(a)(2); see Chapter 8 *supra* at notes 9, 78-79, and 182-84. Refusal of an employer to recognize a previously established bargaining agent is also treated elsewhere; see Chapter 13 *infra*.

[3]§9(c) of the Wagner Act stated: "Whenever a question affecting commerce arises concerning the representation of employees, the Board may investigate such controversy and certify to the parties, in writing, the name or names of the representatives that have been designated or selected. In any such investigation, the Board shall provide for an appropriate hearing upon due notice, either in conjunction with a proceeding under

on union authorization cards are compared with the signatures of employees on the employer's payroll. Through this procedure, it can be determined whether a majority of the employees in an appropriate unit have selected the union as their exclusive bargaining representative.[4]

The Board's use of card checks has evolved in several stages. Until 1939, the Board relied extensively upon authorization cards to determine violations of the former Section 8(5) duty to bargain and to issue certifications. In that year, in *Cudahy Packing Co.*,[5] the Board abandoned the "other suitable method" approach and began relying almost exclusively upon elections in representation cases. In 1947, a Taft-Hartley statutory amendment made the election process the *only* basis for certification.[6] In the 1950s, a shift in Board policy governing the effect of a union's participation in an election resulted in a near-total eclipse of the card check device.[7] In the mid-1960s, the Board changed its policy again and recognized the card check as a legitimate means for establishing an employer's duty to bargain. This was achieved primarily by relying on the 1949 decision in *Joy Silk Mills, Inc.*[8] Although the *Joy Silk* doctrine was accepted by the courts initially,[9] conflicts among the courts of appeals surfaced with respect

---

section 10 or otherwise, and may take a secret ballot of employees, or utilize any other suitable method to ascertain such representatives."

For a discussion of the early Board history, *see* H. Millis & E. Brown, FROM THE WAGNER ACT TO TAFT-HARTLEY, 133-34 (1950); Memorandum From Secretary of Labor Willard Wirtz to Senator Jacob Javits, in *Hearings on S.256 Before the Subcomm. of Labor of the Senate Comm. on Labor and Public Welfare*, 89th Cong., 1st Sess. 19, 20 (1965); 1937 NLRB ANN. REP. 108 (1937).

[4]Other devices, such as petitions or polls, have also been used to establish majority authorization. In San Clemente Publishing Corp., 167 NLRB 6, 65 LRRM 1726 (1967), a bargaining order was based on an unofficial poll of employees, which had been agreed upon by the union and the employer, conducted by a third person.

[5]13 NLRB 526, 4 LRRM 321 (1939). For an explanation of the Board's shift, *see* notes 15-16 *infra* and accompanying text.

[6]Since 1947, §9 no longer contains the alternative "any other suitable method."

[7]*See* note 23 *infra* and accompanying text.

[8]85 NLRB 1263, 24 LRRM 1548 (1949), *modified and enforced*, 185 F2d 732, 27 LRRM 2012 (CA DC, 1950), *cert. denied*, 341 US 914, 27 LRRM 2633 (1951). *See* notes 18-21 *infra* and accompanying text. The Board's change in policy concerning card checks was manifested by the number of references by the Board to *Joy Silk*. According to Shepard's Federal Labor Law Citations, the Board made only 94 references to *Joy Silk* in the entire period from 1950-1960; whereas in 1966 alone it referred to *Joy Silk* on 61 occasions.

[9]NLRB v. Taitel & Son, 261 F2d 1, 43 LRRM 2025 (CA 7, 1958), *cert. denied*, 359 US 944, 43 LRRM 2741 (1959); NLRB v. Wheeling Pipe Line, Inc., 229 F2d 391, 37 LRRM 2403 (CA 8, 1956); NLRB v. Pyne Molding Corp., 226 F2d 818, 37 LRRM 2007 (CA 2, 1955); NLRB v. Armco Drainage & Metal Prods., 220 F2d 573, 35 LRRM 2536 (CA 6, 1955); NLRB v. Hamilton Co., 220 F2d 492, 35 LRRM 2658 (CA 10, 1955); NLRB v. Trimfit of Cal., Inc., 211 F2d 206, 33 LRRM 2705 (CA 9, 1954); NLRB v. Epstein, 203 F2d 482, 31 LRRM 2619 (CA 3, 1953); NLRB v. Ken Rose Motors, Inc., 193 F2d 769, 29 LRRM 2343 (CA 1, 1952); NLRB v. Inter-City Advertising Co., 190 F2d 420, 28 LRRM 2321 (CA 4, 1951).

to the modified manner in which it came to be applied by the Board.[10] In its 1969 decision in *NLRB* v. *Gissel Packing Co.*,[11] the Supreme Court settled major questions concerning the Board's authority to issue bargaining orders where the union has demonstrated its majority status through authorization cards.

This chapter first focuses on the practice under the Wagner Act and traces the development and modification of the *Joy Silk* doctrine. Next, the standards that replaced the *Joy Silk* doctrine, fashioned first by the Board and then ratified by the Supreme Court in *Gissel*, are discussed.[12] Thereafter, the Supreme Court's decision in *Linden Lumber*[13] (in which the Court held that an employer, in the absence of any unfair labor practices, need not petition for an election after rejecting an offer of authorization cards) is treated. The chapter concludes with a discussion of an employer's affirmative defenses to the bargaining obligation and the conditions under which an employer may withdraw recognition from a union.

II. HISTORY

A. The Practice Under the Wagner Act

Under the original Wagner Act, a union was not required to win an NLRB election to be certified as the exclusive bargaining representative of a unit of employees. Section 9(c) of that Act provided that the Board should "take a secret ballot election or utilize any other suitable method" to determine whether a unit

---

[10]The Board's standards were rejected by the courts of appeals in NLRB v. S.S. Logan Packing Co., 386 F2d 562, 66 LRRM 2596 (CA 4, 1967); NLRB v. S. E. Nichols Co., 380 F2d 438, 65 LRRM 2655 (CA 2, 1967); Engineers & Fabricators, Inc. v. NLRB, 376 F2d 482, 64 LRRM 2849 (CA 5, 1967). They were approved in NLRB v. Dan Howard Mfg. Co., 390 F2d 304, 67 LRRM 2278 (CA 7, 1968); NLRB v. Swan Super Cleaners, Inc., 384 F2d 609, 66 LRRM 2385 (CA 6, 1967); Furrs, Inc. v. NLRB, 381 F2d 562, 64 LRRM 2422 (CA 10, 1967), and NLRB v. Southbridge Sheet Metal Works, Inc., 380 F2d 851, 65 LRRM 2916 (CA 1, 1967).

[11]395 US 575, 71 LRRM 2481 (1969). *See infra* at notes 56-84.

[12]The literature discussing these standards includes: Beeson, *Recognition Without Election*, in LABOR LAW DEVELOPMENTS—1970 (Sixteenth Annual Institute on Labor Law, Southwestern Legal Foundation) 89 (1970); Browne, *Obligation to Bargain on Basis of Card Majority*, 3 GA. L. REV. 334 (1969); Gordon, *Union Authorization Cards and the Duty to Bargain*, LABOR RELATIONS YEARBOOK—1968, 128 (1969), also in 19 LAB. L.J. 201 (1968); Lesnick, *Establishment of Bargaining Rights Without an NLRB Election*, 65 MICH. L. REV. 851 (1967); Lewis, *Gissel Packing: Was the Supreme Court Right?*, 56 A.B.A.J. 877 (1970); Sheinkman, *Recognition of Unions Through Authorization Cards*, 3 GA. L. REV. 319 (1969). *See also* Note, *NLRB v. Gissel Packing Co.: Bargaining Orders and Employee Free Choice*, 45 N.Y.U. L. REV. 318 (1970).

[13]419 US 301, 87 LRRM 3236 (1974).

of employees wanted the union to be its certified bargaining agent.[14] Although authorization cards were typically regarded as a "suitable method" of ascertaining employee desires, the Board's willingness to rely on authorization cards in the certification process waned. In 1939, in *Cudahy Packing Co.*,[15] the Board declared that "in the interest of investing . . . certifications with more certainty and prestige by basing them on free and secret elections conducted under the Board's auspices," it would no longer base them on other methods.[16] When an employer was confronted with a majority of authorization cards signed by its employees, the Board's new policy was to order an election unless it could be shown that the employer lacked a good-faith doubt of the union's majority status. This showing was often, but not always, made by evidence of the commission of unfair labor practices while representation matters were pending. These standards met with general judicial approval.[17]

B. The *Joy Silk* Period

For an employer to be ordered to bargain with a union during the Board's *Joy Silk* period, the General Counsel had the burden[18] of establishing four elements: (1) the union had to represent a majority of the employees in an appropriate unit; (2) the union had to request recognition on that basis; (3) the employer had to deny this request for recognition while lacking a good-faith doubt as to the union's majority status; and (4) the employer had to take action calculated to dissipate the union's majority status.

As the District of Columbia Circuit declared in *Joy Silk:*

> An employer may refuse recognition to a union when motivated by a good-faith doubt as to that union's majority status. . . . When, however, such refusal is due to a desire to gain time and to take action to dissipate the union's majority, the refusal is no longer

---

[14]*See* note 3 *supra.*
[15]*Supra* note 5.
[16]*Id.* at 531-32. In Joe Hearin Lumber, 66 NLRB 1276, 1283, 17 LRRM 399 (1946), the Board stated that it did "not feel . . . that a card check reflects employees' true desires with the same degree of certainty" as a secret ballot election.
[17]Medo Photo Supply Corp. v. NLRB, 321 US 678, 14 LRRM 581 (1944); NLRB v. P. Lorillard Co., 314 US 512, 9 LRRM 410 (1942); Lebanon Steel Foundry v. NLRB, 130 F2d 404, 10 LRRM 760 (CA DC), *cert. denied*, 317 US 659, 11 LRRM 839 (1942).
[18]Aaron Bros. Co., 158 NLRB 1077, 62 LRRM 1160 (1966). *See also* John P. Serpa, Inc., 155 NLRB 99, 60 LRRM 1235 (1965), *order set aside sub nom.* Retail Clerks Local 1179 v. NLRB, 376 F2d 186, 64 LRRM 2764 (CA 9, 1967); Jem Mfg., Inc., 156 NLRB 643, 61 LRRM 1074 (1966).

justifiable and constitutes a violation of the duty to bargain set forth in Section 8(a)(5) of the Act.[19]

Thus, under the *Joy Silk* doctrine, unless an employer's good-faith doubt related to the union's majority status, there was no legal justification for insistence upon an election.[20] Although an employer may have doubted in good faith that the unit proposed by the union was appropriate, if it was later found to be so, the employer had a duty to bargain notwithstanding its preference for a different unit. An employer whose refusal to bargain stemmed solely from disagreement as to the appropriate unit acted "at its peril and in violation of the Act."[21]

Although this "good-faith doubt" test was retained in name for 20 years, two factors affecting its application, and the frequency with which it was applied, changed during that period.

In 1951 the Board declared that even if a union participated in an election and lost, it could nonetheless pursue the unfair labor practice remedy of a bargaining order if the employer had unlawfully refused to recognize the union based on a pre-election card majority.[22] In 1954, in *Aiello Dairy Farms Co.*,[23] the Board reversed that position and held that if a union participated in an election after its request for recognition had been denied, it waived a bargaining-order remedy under Section 10 in favor of an election remedy under Section 9. The union would thus be confined to the election process to prove majority status. This "waiver" doctrine was followed for 10 years, and the incidence of cases arising under the *Joy Silk* doctrine drastically declined.

In 1964, in *Bernel Foam*,[24] the Board expressly overruled *Aiello* and reverted to its prior doctrine. The Board reasoned that

---

[19]Joy Silk, *supra* note 8 at 741. The Supreme Court recognized the *Joy Silk* doctrine in Mine Workers v. Arkansas Oak Flooring Co., 351 US 62, 37 LRRM 2828 (1956). *See also* Franks Bros. v. NLRB, 321 US 72, 14 LRRM 591 (1944).

[20]NLRB v. Ralph Printing & Lithographing Co., 379 F2d 687, 65 LRRM 2800 (CA 8, 1967).

[21]Tom Thumb Stores, Inc., 123 NLRB 833, 835, 44 LRRM 1005 (1959); Benson Wholesale Co., 164 NLRB 536, 65 LRRM 1278 (1967) (good-faith belief that another unit is appropriate, if erroneous, is irrelevant); *see also* NLRB v. Morris Novelty Co., 378 F2d 1000, 65 LRRM 2577 (CA 8, 1967); Oklahoma Sheraton Corp., 156 NLRB 681, 61 LRRM 1115 (1966); Southland Paint Co., 156 NLRB 22, 61 LRRM 1004 (1965); Clermont's, Inc., 154 NLRB 1397, 60 LRRM 1141 (1965).

[22]Davidson Co., 94 NLRB 142, 28 LRRM 1026 (1951).

[23]110 NLRB 1365, 35 LRRM 1235 (1954).

[24]Bernel Foam Prods. Co., 146 NLRB 1277, 56 LRRM 1039 (1964). The doctrine was approved in Southbridge Sheet Metal Works, *supra* note 10.

the so-called "choice" which the union is forced to make under *Aiello* between going to an election or filing an 8(a)(5) charge is at best a Hobson's choice. Although an election is a relatively swift and inexpensive way for the union to put the force of law behind its majority status, the procedure is highly uncertain entailing the real possibility that because of conduct by the employer no fair election will be held.

. . .

. . . Since this difficult and rather dubious "choice" is created by the employer's unlawful conduct, there is no warrant for imposing upon the union which represents the employees an irrevocable option as to the method it will pursue . . . while permitting the offending party to enjoy at the expense of public policy the fruits of such unlawful conduct.[25]

The *Bernel Foam* rule does not apply, however, unless the election is set aside on the basis of meritorious objections by the union.[26]

Another factor bearing significantly on the application of the *Joy Silk* doctrine was the conditions under which the Board found an employer's refusal to recognize a union to be lacking in good faith. *Aaron Brothers*[27] had made clear that it was the General Counsel's burden to establish the existence of the employer's lack of good-faith doubt as to the union's majority. Initially there were various ways in which the General Counsel could satisfy this burden. The Board stated that "[w]hether an employer is acting in good faith or bad faith in questioning the union's majority is a determination which must be made in light of all the relevant facts of the case, including any unlawful conduct of the employer, the sequence of events, and the time lapse between the refusal and the unlawful conduct."[28] Thus,

---

[25]Bernel Foam Prods., *supra* note 24 at 1280. This doctrine was approved by the Supreme Court in *Gissel Packing Co., supra* note 11. *See* text accompanying notes 60-76 *infra* relating to the *General Steel* case. *See also* Colson Corp. (Boilermakers) v. NLRB, 347 F2d 128, 59 LRRM 2512 (CA 8), *cert. denied*, 382 US 904, 60 LRRM 2353 (1965); Electrical Workers (IUE) v. NLRB (S.N.C. Mfg. Co.), 352 F2d 361, 59 LRRM 2232 (CA DC, 1965). *Cf.* NLRB v. Flomatic Corp., 347 F2d 74, 59 LRRM 2535 (CA 2, 1965).

[26]Irving Air Chute Co., 149 NLRB 627, 57 LRRM 1330 (1964), *enforced*, 350 F2d 176, 59 LRRM 3052 (CA 2, 1965). In Green Bay Aviation, Inc., 165 NLRB 1026, 65 LRRM 1499 (1967), the Board refused to issue a post-election bargaining order where the employer's unfair labor practices occurred prior to the filing of the petition for an election. The election may be set aside on the basis of objections filed by the employer as well as by the union. Photobell Co., 158 NLRB 738, 62 LRRM 1091 (1966).

[27]*See* Aaron Bros., note 18 *supra* and accompanying text. "Absent an affirmative showing of bad faith, an employer, presented with a majority card showing and a bargaining request, will not be held to have violated his bargaining obligation under the law simply because he refuses to rely upon cards, rather than an election, as the method for determining the union's majority." 158 NLRB at 1078.

[28]*Id.* at 1079; Converters Gravure Serv., Inc., 164 NLRB 397, 65 LRRM 1098 (1967). In NLRB v. River Togs, Inc., 382 F2d 198, 65 LRRM 2987 (CA 2, 1967), the Second

the Board considered such factors as (1) the employer's past experience in dealing with union activities;[29] (2) the employer's willingness to proceed with an expedited election;[30] (3) the timing,[31] nature, and effect of unlawful conduct;[32] and (4) the employer's disavowal of unlawful supervisory conduct[33] in making its determination regarding the employer's good-faith doubt. The Board expressly eschewed a mechanical position, that employers were "automatically precluded" from having a good-faith doubt simply because unfair labor practices had been committed, in favor of an analysis of all the facts and circumstances of the particular case.[34] For example, where there was evidence supporting the employer's doubt of majority status, the unlawful threatening of "a handful of employees in a unit of more than 250" was not a sufficient basis upon which to infer a deliberate purpose to gain time to dissipate the union's majority.[35]

While employer unfair labor practices were not always fatal to an assertion of good-faith doubt, the bad faith necessary to support a bargaining order was occasionally demonstrated by employer conduct which did not otherwise amount to an independent unfair labor practice.[36] Thus, employers were ordered

---

Circuit denied enforcement of a bargaining order, pointing out that where the evidence shows a good-faith doubt, the anti-union activities of an employer—including his unfair labor practices—are "as consistent with a desire to prevent the acquisition of a majority status as with a purpose to destroy an existing majority" (quoting Lesnick, *supra* note 12 at 855). *Accord,* Lane Drug Co. v. NLRB, 391 F2d 812, 67 LRRM 2873 (CA 6, 1968). *But see* Furr's, Inc., *supra* note 10, enforcing a bargaining order and sustaining a finding of bad faith. The court in *Furr's* accepted a violation of §8(a)(1) as strong evidence of the lack of good-faith doubt.

[29]The Walmac Co., 106 NLRB 1355, 33 LRRM 1019 (1953).
[30]Marr Knitting, Inc., 90 NLRB 479, 26 LRRM 1237 (1950).
[31]Sunset Lumber Prods., 113 NLRB 1172, 36 LRRM 1426 (1955).
[32]Beaver Mach. & Tool Co., 97 NLRB 33, 29 LRRM 1051 (1951).
[33]KTRH Broadcasting Co., 113 NLRB 125, 36 LRRM 1260 (1955).
[34]*See, e.g.,* A. L. Gilbert Co., 110 NLRB 2067, 35 LRRM 1314 (1954).
[35]Cameo Lingerie, Inc., 148 NLRB 535, 538, 57 LRRM 1044 (1964). *See also* River Togs, Inc., *supra* note 28. In Hammond & Irving, Inc., 154 NLRB 1071, 1073, 60 LRRM 1073 (1965), the Board noted that "not every act of misconduct necessarily vitiates the respondent's good faith. For, there are some situations in which the violations of the Act are not truly inconsistent with a good-faith doubt that the union represents a majority of the employees. Whether the conduct involved reflects on the good faith of the employer requires an evaluation of the facts of each case." The effect of unfair labor practices upon the employer's assertion of good-faith doubt often depended on the disposition of the reviewing court, and during this period many of the Board's refusal to bargain findings based on card majorities were reversed by appellate courts. *See, e.g.,* Engineers & Fabricators, Inc., *supra* note 10; River Togs, Inc., *supra* note 28; Peoples Serv. Drug Stores, Inc., v. NLRB, 375 F2d 551, 64 LRRM 2823 (CA 6, 1967); Indiana Rayon Corp. v. NLRB, 355 F2d 535, 61 LRRM 2311 (CA 7, 1966).
[36]Aaron Bros. Co., *supra* note 18, *citing* Snow & Sons, 134 NLRB 709, 49 LRRM 1228, *enforced,* 308 F2d 687, 51 LRRM 2199 (CA 9, 1962); Jem Mfg., Inc., *supra* note 18;

to bargain in the absence of a secret-ballot election where they (1) repudiated the results of a previously agreed-upon card check,[37] (2) withdrew from negotiations after a card check conducted by a third party had established the union's majority,[38] (3) insisted upon an election after participating in negotiations following a card check,[39] (4) questioned the union's majority after examining union membership cards and acknowledging union representation,[40] and (5) unreasonably rejected a card check that had been conducted by a third party.[41]

The foregoing illustrates that the two most significant factors in showing the absence of good faith were whether the employer "deliberately engaged in unfair labor practices in order to dissipate the union's majority and made the holding of a fair election impossible,"[42] and whether the employer, in effect, had actual independent knowledge of the union's majority.[43] Since *serious* employer unfair labor practices were interpreted as indicating a desire to gain time to undermine the union or a rejection of the principle of collective bargaining,[44] evidence of such practices was the most frequent method of establishing the lack of a

---

Dixon Ford Shoe Co., 150 NLRB 861, 58 LRRM 1160 (1965); Kellogg Mills, 147 NLRB 342, 56 LRRM 1223 (1964), *enforced*, 347 F2d 219, 59 LRRM 2340 (CA 9, 1965); Greyhound Terminal, 137 NLRB 87, 50 LRRM 1088 (1962), *enforced*, 314 F2d 43, 52 LRRM 2335 (CA 5, 1963). *See* discussion of *Gissel, infra*, indicating that the Board may no longer follow *Snow & Sons*, although the Supreme Court expressed no view on that case. *But see* Christensen & Christensen, *Gissel Packing and "Good Faith Doubt": The Gestalt of Required Recognition of Unions Under the NLRB*, 37 U. CHI. L. REV. 411 (1970). *Cf.* Wilder Mfg. Co., 185 NLRB 175, 75 LRRM 1023 (1970). For the current state of the law, see *infra* at notes 229-60.

[37]Snow & Sons, *supra* note 36. According to one commentator, later decisions, particularly Strydel, Inc., 156 NLRB 1185, 61 LRRM 1230 (1966), and Furr's, Inc., *supra* note 10, indicated that the Board was confining *Snow* to its particular facts. Lesnick, *supra* note 12 at 852-854. *But cf.* Wilder Mfg. Co., *supra* note 36, where the Board ordered an employer to bargain even though he had not committed other unfair labor practices. The employer had no basis for questioning the union's majority, which was evidenced not only by signed cards but also by the employees' striking and picketing. The Board found it significant that the employer showed no willingness to resolve the question of majority status through an election; the Board chose to base its order on this narrow ground.

[38]Kellogg Mills, *supra* note 36.

[39]Jem Mfg., Inc., *supra* note 18.

[40]Greyhound Terminal, *supra* note 36.

[41]Dixon Ford Shoe Co., *supra* note 36. However, bad faith was not to be inferred simply from the rejection of a proposal to submit the cards to an impartial determination. Strydel, Inc., *supra* note 37.

[42]Southeastern Rubber Mfg. Co., 106 NLRB 989, 32 LRRM 1590 (1953).

[43]Snow & Sons, *supra* note 36.

[44]Commission of unfair labor practices which were either too insubstantial to warrant an inference of bad faith or were not inconsistent with a good-faith doubt of majority status would not support a bargaining order. Hercules Packing Corp., 163 NLRB 264, 64 LRRM 1331, *aff'd*, 386 F2d 790, 66 LRRM 2751 (CA 2, 1967); Hammond & Irving, Inc., *supra* note 35. *See* Gordon, *supra* note 12 at 131.

good-faith doubt.[45] Applied in such a manner, the *Joy Silk* doctrine was endorsed by every circuit court of appeals.[46]

In the years following *Joy Silk,* increasing emphasis was placed on an employer's unfair labor practices in order to establish the absence of good faith in the denial of recognition based on a card majority. The General Counsel would introduce evidence of an employer's unfair labor practices and claim that (1) they dissipated the union's majority status and (2) they were in fact intended to have such a result. This evidence was intended to demonstrate the employer's awareness of the union's majority status, thereby negating the possibility of a good-faith belief that the cards were inadequate indicators of the union's majority. Such proof entailed showing a causal relationship between the employer's conduct and the union's loss of majority status.[47] Thus, no longer considering the totality of an employer's conduct, the Board stated that "the test for determining good-faith doubt of a union's majority is whether the employer has engaged in substantial unfair labor practices calculated to dissipate union support."[48] While conceding that a secret-ballot election would normally be the most reliable means of ascertaining the employees' desire for representation, the Board reasoned that if "an employer engages in unfair labor practices which make impossible the holding of a free election, the Board has no alternative but to look to signed authorization cards as the only available proof of the choice employees would have made absent the employer's unfair labor practices."[49] In *Aaron Brothers,*[50] the Board

---

[45]Joy Silk Mills, Inc., *supra* note 8; Benson Wholesale Co., 164 NLRB 536, 65 LRRM 1278 (1967); Taitel & Son, 119 NLRB 910, 41 LRRM 1230 (1957).

[46]*See* cases cited in note 9 *supra.*

[47]NLRB v. Clegg, 304 F2d 168, 50 LRRM 2524 (CA 8, 1962); Manley Transfer Co., 164 NLRB 174, 65 LRRM 1194 (1967). When an employer had engaged in conduct that warranted setting aside two successive elections, the Board's bargaining order was enforced. Borden Cabinet Corp. v. NLRB, 375 F2d 891, 64 LRRM 1206 (CA 7, 1967). Sponsorship of a rival labor organization by an employer after it had appeared to accord recognition to the union chosen by the majority warranted issuance of a bargaining order. Sturgeon Elec. Co., 166 NLRB 210, 65 LRRM 1530 (1967).

[48]National Cash Register Co., 167 NLRB 1047, 66 LRRM 1206 (1967).

[49]Bryant Chucking Grinder Co., 160 NLRB 1526, 63 LRRM 1185 (1966). In Aaron Bros., *supra* note 18, the Board defined the policy as follows: "While an employer's right to a Board election is not absolute, it has long been established Board policy that an employer may refuse to bargain and insist upon such an election as proof of a union's majority. An election by secret ballot is normally a more satisfactory means of determining employees' wishes, although authorization cards signed by a majority may also evidence their desires. Absent an affirmative showing of bad faith, an employer, presented with a majority card showing and a bargaining request, will not be held to have violated his bargaining obligation under the law simply because he refuses to rely upon cards, rather than an election, as the method for determining the union's majority." 158 NLRB at 1078. The Second Circuit, however, held that independent unfair labor

observed that the *Joy Silk* rule used the "most reliable means available"[51] to afford employees free choice in the selection of a bargaining representative. The Board reasoned that "[w]here an employer has engaged in unfair labor practices, the results of a Board-conducted election are a less reliable indication of the true desires of employees than authorization cards, whereas, in a situation free of such unlawful interference, the converse is true."[52]

Under *Aaron Brothers*, the employer's right to insist upon an election was enhanced where no unfair labor practices had been committed. The Board held that an employer would "not be subject to an 8(a)(5) violation simply because he is unable to substantiate a reasonable basis for his doubt."[53] Accordingly, an employer who committed no unfair labor practices could insist on an election even where his doubt is "founded on no more than a distrust of cards." [54]

Subsequent to its articulation, the *Joy Silk* doctrine was a subject of substantial disagreement among the courts of appeals which reviewed it, both as to the legality of the manner in which it had come to be applied and on the Board's standards governing the validity of union authorization cards generally.[55] This divergence of view provided the setting for the Supreme Court's landmark decision in *NLRB* v. *Gissel Packing Co.*[56]

C. The *Gissel* Decision

Under *Gissel*, "an employer's good-faith doubt [of a union's majority] is largely irrelevant, and the key to the issuance of a bargaining order is the commission of serious unfair labor practices that interfere with the election process and tend to preclude the holding of a fair election."[57] This change in approach may

---

practices committed by an employer did not establish that the employer lacked a good-faith doubt as to the union's majority, since the unfair practices were as consistent with a desire to prevent the union from achieving majority status as with a purpose of dissipating a majority already attained. River Togs, Inc., *supra* note 35.

[50] Aaron Bros., *supra* note 18.

[51] *Id.*

[52] *Id.*

[53] H & W Constr. Co., 161 NLRB 852, 857, 63 LRRM 1346 (1966).

[54] *Id.* at 857.

[55] *See* note 10 *supra.*

[56] 395 US 575, 71 LRRM 2481 (1969).

[57] *Id.* at 594. In Schrementi Bros., 179 NLRB 853, 72 LRRM 1481 (1969), decided after the Supreme Court's decision in *Gissel,* the Board noted that the employer's good-faith doubt in refusing to recognize a union is now "largely irrelevant." For a discussion

have been more apparent than real, for the Supreme Court noted and relied on the acknowledgement, which the Board had made during oral argument, "that it had virtually abandoned the *Joy Silk* doctrine altogether."[58] Thus, as previously indicated, long before *Gissel,* Board cases had equated substantial employer unfair labor practices with a lack of good-faith doubt of majority status. The effect of such unfair labor practices was considered the equivalent of a lack of good faith.[59]

The major principles governing the establishment of bargaining rights without an election may now be found in *Gissel.* When *Gissel* was decided, the Court consolidated four cases for decision: *Gissel Packing Co., Heck's, Inc., General Steel Products, Inc.,* and *Sinclair Co.*—the first three from the Fourth Circuit and the last from the First Circuit. In each of the Fourth Circuit cases, the union had obtained authorization cards from a majority of the employees in an appropriate bargaining unit and demanded recognition on that basis. In each instance, however, the employers had refused to extend voluntary recognition to the union on the ground that authorization cards were inherently unreliable indicators of employee desires. The ensuing anti-union campaigns engaged in by each employer gave rise to numerous unfair labor practice charges. In *Gissel* and *Heck's* the Board found unfair labor practices, including Section 8(a)(5) violations, and ordered the employers to bargain even though an election had not been held. In *General Steel* the Board set aside the election, which the union had lost, and the employer was ordered to bargain on the basis of preelection unfair labor practices. In each case the Board ruled that the union had valid authorization cards from a majority of the employees in an appropriate unit and, therefore, the employer's refusal to bargain "was motivated not by a 'good-faith' doubt of the union's majority status, but by a desire to gain time to dissipate the status."[60] On appeal, the Fourth Circuit reversed the Board's

---

of the open question of how irrelevant is "largely irrelevant," *see* Christensen & Christensen, *supra* note 36.

[58]*Supra* note 11 at 594.

[59]*See* Member Jenkins' concurring opinion in *Aaron Bros., supra* note 18, in which he said: "In my view, the proper test (and the one in fact applied by my colleagues) in such cases is whether or not the employer's refusal to accept the cards as proof of majority, and to recognize and bargain with the union, was made in bad faith, with the General Counsel having the burden of showing affirmatively the existence of bad faith. . . . [T]he concept of good-faith doubt of majority, . . . has become irrelevant to the action of cases of this type. . . ." 158 NLRB at 1081.

[60]*See Gissel, supra* note 11 at 583.

findings of refusal to bargain but affirmed the other unfair labor practice findings.[61]

The facts in *Sinclair* were similar to those in *Gissel* and *Heck's*, except that an additional issue was raised as to whether specific statements made by the employer—found by the Board to be unfair labor practices—fell outside the protection of the First Amendment of the Constitution and Section 8(c) of the Act.[62] The First Circuit upheld both the Board's findings of unfair labor practices and its order requiring the employer to recognize and bargain with the union.[63]

The Supreme Court framed the questions as follows:

"[1] [W]hether the duty to bargain can arise without a Board election under the Act; [2] whether union authorization cards, if obtained from a majority of employees without misrepresentation or coercion, are reliable enough to provide a valid, alternative route to majority status; [3] whether a bargaining order is an appropriate and authorized remedy where an employer rejects a card majority while at the same time committing unfair labor practices that tend to undermine the union's majority and make a fair election an unlikely possibility. . . ."[64]

The Court answered each question in the affirmative.

In answering the first question, the Court noted that the establishment of a bargaining obligation by means other than a Board election was an accepted principle under both the Wagner Act and the Taft-Hartley Act.[65] It emphasized that Congress had rejected a House bill[66] in 1947 which would have conditioned a Section 8(a)(5) violation upon either a Board election or current recognition of a union.[67] The Court saw nothing in Section 9(c)(1)(B), which gives employers the right to petition for elections, to suggest that Congress intended to relieve an employer of his bargaining obligation "where, without good faith, he engaged in unfair labor practices disruptive of the Board's election machinery."[68] The Court noted that, although

---

[61]General Steel Prods., Inc., 398 F2d 339, 68 LRRM 2639 (CA 4, 1968).

[62]*See* Chapter 6 *supra* at notes 56-65 for a discussion of the Supreme Court's treatment of this issue.

[63]Sinclair Co., 397 F2d 157, 68 LRRM 2720 (CA 1, 1968).

[64]*Supra* note 11 at 579. A fourth question related to free speech and §8(c) of the Act. *See* note 62 *supra*.

[65]*Citing* NLRB v. Bradford Dyeing Ass'n, 310 US 318, 339-340, 6 LRRM 684 (1940); Franks Bros., *supra* note 19; Mine Workers v. Arkansas Oak Flooring Co., *supra* note 19.

[66]§§8(1)(5) of H.R. 3020, 80th Cong., 1st Sess. (1947).

[67]*See* note 3 *supra*.

[68]*Supra* note 11 at 600.

a union had to win a secret-ballot election in order to obtain the benefits of a Board *certification*, an employer's *duty to bargain* may arise even in the absence of such an election.

In response to the second question, the Court decided that authorization cards could be reliable indicia of majority status in those situations where, due to employer unfair labor practices, "a fair election probably could not have been held, or where an election that was held was in fact set aside."[69] However, the Court expressly refused to decide whether a union could rely on authorization cards as a "freely interchangeable substitute for elections where there has been no election interference."[70]

The Court agreed with the Board that "cards, though admittedly inferior to the election process, can adequately reflect employee sentiment when that process has been impeded. . . ."[71] It thus rejected the employers' general arguments that the cards were inherently unreliable because of group pressure, that cards did not allow employees to express an informed choice, and that misrepresentation and coercion are too often present in card solicitation.

In each of the four cases before the Court, the union had used a "single-purpose" card, i.e., a card which clearly designated the union as the employees' bargaining representative and which did not state that it might also be used to obtain an election. The only case which raised an issue as to the validity of these "single purpose" cards, or the manner in which they were obtained, was *General Steel*. In that case, in reliance on and in approval of the Board's *Cumberland Shoe*[72] doctrine, the Court upheld the validity of such cards and specifically approved the Board's findings as to the manner in which they had been solicited by the union. It thus approved the following rule:

> [I]f the card itself is unambiguous (*i.e.* states on its face that the signer authorizes the union to represent the employee for collective bargaining purposes and not to seek an election), it will be counted unless it is proved that the employee was told that the card was to be used *solely* for the purpose of obtaining an election.[73]

---

[69]*Id.* at 601 n.17.
[70]*Id. See infra* at notes 229-60.
[71]*Id.* at 603.
[72]144 NLRB 1268, 54 LRRM 1233 (1963), *enforced*, 351 F2d 917, 60 LRRM 2305 (CA 6, 1965). *See* discussion *infra* at notes 285-90.
[73]*Supra* note 11 at 584 (emphasis in original).

In resolving a conflict among the circuits,[74] the Court concluded that

> employees should be bound by the clear language of what they sign unless that language is deliberately and clearly cancelled by a union adherent with words calculated to direct the signer to disregard and forget the language above his signature.[75]

The Court saw nothing inconsistent in handing an employee a card which states that the signer authorizes the union to represent him or her, while orally advising the signer that the card would probably first be used to obtain an election. The Court noted that elections are held in the vast majority of cases and Board rules require signatures from at least 30 percent of the employees before the Board will entertain a union's petition for an election.[76]

The *Gissel* Court declared that any probing of an employee's subjective motivation in signing a card would be inherently unreliable and, in this regard, noted that "employees are more likely than not, many months after a card drive and in response to questions by company counsel, to give testimony damaging to the union. . . ."[77] Therefore, the Court said that "single-purpose" cards should be invalidated not for what an employee allegedly thought, but only if the employee was actually told

---

[74]The Court reviewed the differing views of the circuits as follows: "[E]ven where the cards are unambiguous on their face, both the Second Circuit [*S. E. Nichols, supra* note 10] and the Fifth Circuit [*Engineers & Fabricators, supra* note 10] have joined the Fourth Circuit below in rejecting the Board's rule that the cards will be counted unless the solicitor's statements amounted under the circumstances to an assurance that the cards would be used only for an election. And even those circuits which have adopted the Board's approach have criticized the Board for tending too often to apply the *Cumberland* rule too mechanically, declining occasionally to uphold the Board's application of its own rule in a given case. *See, e.g.,* Southbridge Sheet Metal Works [*supra* note 10]; NLRB v. Sandy's Stores, Inc., 398 F2d 268, 68 LRRM 2800 (CA 1, 1968); Swan Super Cleaners, [*supra* note 10]; Dan Howard Mfg. [*supra* note 10]; Furrs, Inc. [*supra* note 10]; UAW [Preston Prods.] v. NLRB, 392 F2d 801, 66 LRRM 2548 (CA DC, 1967). Among those who reject the *Cumberland* rule, the Fifth Circuit agrees with the Second Circuit [*see S. E. Nichols, supra* note 10], that a card will be vitiated if an employee was left with the impression that he would be able to resolve any lingering doubts and make a final decision in an election, and further requires that the Board probe the subjective intent of each signer, an inquiry expressly avoided by *Cumberland. See* Southland Paint Co. [*supra* note 21]; Engineers & Fabricators, Inc. [*supra* note 10]. Where the cards are ambiguous on their face, the Fifth Circuit, joined by the Eighth Circuit (*see, e.g.,* NLRB v. Peterson Bros., 342 F2d 221, 58 LRRM 2570 (CA 5, 1965), and Bauer Welding & Metal Fabricators, Inc. v. NLRB, 358 F2d 766, 62 LRRM 2022 (CA 8, 1966), departs still further from the Board rule. And there is a conflict among those courts which otherwise follow the Board as to single-purpose cards (*compare* NLRB v. Lenz Co., 396 F2d 905, 908, 68 LRRM 2577 (CA 6, 1968), *with* NLRB v. C. J. Glasgow Co., 356 F2d 476, 478, 61 LRRM 2406 (CA 7, 1966))." 395 US at 604-605.

[75]*Supra* note 11 at 606.

[76]*See* Chapter 10 *supra.*

[77]*Supra* note 11 at 608.

that the sole purpose of the card was to obtain a Board election. The Court expressly declined to comment on the validity of "ambiguous, dual-purpose cards."[78]

Finally, the Court in *Gissel* delineated three categories of unfair labor practices, based on the relative severity of the violations, which it would consider in deciding whether a bargaining order would be an appropriate remedy in card-based majority cases. In the first category of cases, namely, where the employer has committed "outrageous" and "pervasive" unfair labor practices which rendered the holding of an untainted election *impossible*, the Court indicated that a bargaining order would be an appropriate remedy "without need of inquiry into majority status on the basis of cards or otherwise."[79] In the second category of cases, namely, those which were "marked by less pervasive practices which nonetheless still have the tendency to undermine majority strength and impede the election processes,"[80] a bargaining order could likewise be an appropriate remedy. This was the category into which the facts and circumstances of *Gissel* fell. The Court also identified a third category of cases in which the unfair labor practices are so minor that, "because of their minimal impact on the election machinery, [they] will not sustain a bargaining order."[81]

Noting the virtually unanimous agreement that a bargaining order was inappropriate in the third category, the Court stated that "[t]he only effect of our holding here is to approve the Board's use of the bargaining order" in cases falling into the second category.[82] In this second category, the Court wrote, a bargaining order may issue if the Board finds that the possibility of "erasing the effects" of past unfair labor practices and insuring a fair election by "traditional means" is "slight" and that the interests of the employees who had signed cards would be better protected by a bargaining order.[83] Although the Court stated that bargaining orders could issue in cases falling into the first

---

[78]*Id.* at 609. *See* notes 93 and 94 *infra* and accompanying text.
[79]*Id.* at 613.
[80]*Id.* at 614. In Gottfried v. Mayco Plastics, Inc., 615 F2d 1360, 103 LRRM 3104, 3105 (CA 6, 1980), the Sixth Circuit affirmed the district court's bargaining order pending final disposition of unfair labor practice charges before the NLRB, where the parties had stipulated that reasonable cause existed to believe that the employer's actions were in violation of the LMRA and that a bargaining order was a "just and proper relief and 10(j) is a proper remedy to preserve the status quo."
[81]*Supra* note 11 at 614-15.
[82]*Id.*
[83]*Id.*

category, notwithstanding the absence of any showing that the union had ever achieved majority status, it was not until 1981 that the Board began issuing bargaining orders in such cases.[84]

III. ELEMENTS WHICH ESTABLISH A BARGAINING OBLIGATION IN THE ABSENCE OF AN ELECTION

While *Gissel* changed the rhetoric used to describe an employer's obligation to bargain in the absence of an election, the elements needed to establish that obligation differ little from pre-*Gissel* Board practice. This is apparent if one examines the employer's conduct in pre-*Gissel* cases rather than the Board's conclusions as to an employer's lack of good-faith doubt of union majority. Inquiries into the form of the authorization card and the means by which they were solicited are also important in determining whether an obligation to bargain exists.

A. Majority Representation

The initial inquiry in these cases is whether a majority of the employees in an appropriate unit have signed authorization cards as of the date of the employer's alleged refusal to bargain.[85] This may occur either when the employer receives the demand[86] or when the employer sends a reply.[87] In *Conren, Inc.*,[88] a union was not precluded from insisting on recognition based on a card majority during the one-year period following an election even though a second election could not be held.

1. Form of Designation. The card may be a regular union membership card,[89] an application for membership,[90] a dues

---

[84]*See* notes 216-25 *infra* and accompanying text.
[85]*See* Jasta Mfg. Co., 246 NLRB 48, 102 LRRM 1610 (1979) (card of employee whose name appeared on *Excelsior* list counted as being that of a unit employee); Dadco Fashions, Inc., 243 NLRB 1193, 102 LRRM 1027 (1979) (card of employee whose name was not on payroll records during the pertinent period was not counted).
[86]Allegheny Pepsi-Cola Bottling Co. v. NLRB, 312 F2d 529, 52 LRRM 2019 (CA 3, 1962), *enforcing* 134 NLRB 388, 49 LRRM 1169 (1961).
[87]NLRB v. Burton Dixie Corp., 210 F2d 199, 33 LRRM 2483 (CA 10, 1954), *enforcing* 103 NLRB 880, 31 LRRM 1589 (1953).
[88]156 NLRB 592, 61 LRRM 1090 (1966), *enforced*, 368 F2d 173, 63 LRRM 2273 (CA 7, 1966), *cert. denied*, 386 US 974, 64 LRRM 2640 (1967). The Board held that neither the legislative history of the 12-month rule in §9(c)(3), "nor its plain terms, manifest any congressional purpose to preclude a union from obtaining recognition either without an election or within a year after an election, or within a year after an election which it did not win, if it in fact acquires majority status in an appropriate unit." 156 NLRB at 599.
[89]NLRB v. Federbrush Co., 121 F2d 954, 8 LRRM 531 (CA 2, 1941).
[90]NLRB v. Valley Broadcasting Co., 189 F2d 582, 28 LRRM 2148 (CA 6, 1951); NLRB v. Dahlstrom Metallic Door Co., 112 F2d 745, 6 LRRM 746 (CA 2, 1940).

check-off authorization,[91] or simply a card that explicitly designates the union as the signer's bargaining representative.[92] While many appellate courts disagree with the Board's practice,[93] the Board honors dual-purpose cards which both designate the union as the signer's exclusive bargaining representative and express a desire for an election.[94]

2. Name of Union. It is sufficient if union designation is indicated in only the most general terms, without identifying either a particular local or even the international union. Cards bearing the simple designation "AFL-CIO" have been held valid.[95]

3. Status of the Solicitor. Any person other than a representative of management may normally solicit an employee's signature on an authorization card. Cards that have been solicited directly by a supervisor will usually be held invalid.[96] The Board has held, however, that the mere "passing along" of a card by a supervisor does not constitute solicitation.[97]

4. Time of Execution. In order to be counted in determining a union's majority status, cards must have been signed during the union's current organizing campaign.[98] However, cards

---

[91]Lebanon Steel Foundry, *supra* note 17.

[92]NLRB v. Stow Mfg. Co., 217 F2d 900, 35 LRRM 2210 (CA 2, 1954), *cert. denied,* 348 US 964, 35 LRRM 2612 (1955).

[93]*See* Bradenburg Tel. Co., 164 NLRB 825, 65 LRRM 1183 (1967); Lenz Co., 153 NLRB 1399, 59 LRRM 1638 (1965); S.N.C. Mfg. Co., *supra* note 25. *Contra,* Dayco Corp. v. NLRB, 382 F2d 577, 656 LRRM 3092 (CA 6, 1967); S. E. Nichols Co., *supra* note 10; NLRB v. Peterson Bros., 342 F2d 221, 58 LRRM 2570 (CA 5, 1965); Swan Super Cleaners, *supra* note 10. However, in a case decided after the Supreme Court's decision in *Gissel,* the Board rejected as ambiguous certain dual-purpose cards where the top half of the card stated that its purpose was to obtain an election and the bottom half contained a reference to the signer being invited to join the union "should the union be elected" to represent him. John S. Barnes Corp., 180 NLRB 911, 73 LRRM 1215 (1970).

[94]*E.g.,* World-Wide Press, Inc., 242 NLRB 346, 101 LRRM 1205 (1979). For a general discussion of the types and purposes of union authorization cards, *see* S. Schlossberg & F. Sherman, Organizing and the Law 50-51 (rev. ed. 1971).

[95]Southbridge Sheet Metal Works, *supra* note 10. *See also* World-Wide Press, *supra* note 94 (cards valid although name and number of local union were not filled in). But if an employee executes similar cards for rival unions, neither card will be counted. International Metal Prods. Co., 104 NLRB 1076, 32 LRRM 1194 (1953). However, cards signed for two unions *will* be deemed valid where the employees understood that they authorized joint representation. Bolsa Drainage, Inc., 242 NLRB 728, 101 LRRM 1372 (1979). *See* Chapter 8 *infra* at notes 106-53 for a discussion of the *Midwest Piping* doctrine and the requirement of employer neutrality between rival unions. [*See Editor's Note* in Chapter 8 *supra,* p. 294, regarding the Board's recent retreat from the *Midwest Piping* doctrine.]

[96]Leas & McVitty, Inc., 155 NLRB 389, 60 LRRM 1333 (1965); Insular Chem. Corp., 128 NLRB 93, 46 LRRM 1268 (1960); Flint River Mills, Inc., 107 NLRB 472, 33 LRRM 1177 (1953).

[97]Engineers & Fabricators, *supra* note 10.

[98]Grand Union Co., 112 NLRB 589, 43 LRRM 1165 (1958), *enforced,* 279 F2d 83, 46 LRRM 2492 (CA 2, 1960). In Greenfield Components Corp. v. NLRB, 317 F2d 85, 53

signed more than a year prior to the union's demand for recognition may be considered "stale" and thus would not count toward the union's majority.[99]

5. Authentication. The General Counsel bears the burden of proving a card's authenticity.[100] The employees may be called as witnesses to identify their signatures. Other competent evidence, such as the testimony of a witness to the card's execution, may also be used for this purpose.[101]

6. Affirmative Defenses. There are various affirmative defenses to a bargaining obligation in the absence of a secret-ballot election which may be asserted by an employer. These are discussed in Section V of this Chapter.

B. Form of Request and Appropriate Unit

A valid bargaining request, or "demand," must be made before an employer is obligated to recognize the requesting union. The union need not explicitly state that it enjoys majority status,[102] but to be effective the request must be made when the union in fact possesses signed authorizations from a majority of the employees in an appropriate unit.[103] But this rule does not apply if the Board considers the initial demand to be a continuing one and finds that the union's deficiency in cards is overcome by the

---

LRRM 2145 (CA 1, 1963), cards signed nine months before the demand was made were counted, there having been no hiatus in the union's organizational effort. And a period exceeding two years was not too long where there was a delay in proceeding upon a petition for election. Northern Trust Co., 69 NLRB 652, 18 LRRM 1252 (1946). Undated cards have been counted where they were received by the NLRB's regional office prior to the union's demand for recognition, Curlee Clothing Co., 240 NLRB 355, 100 LRRM 1423 (1979), and where there was credible evidence as to when they were signed. World-Wide Press, Inc., *supra* note 94.

[99]Blade-Tribune Pub. Co., 161 NLRB 1512, 63 LRRM 1848 (1966); Grand Union Co., *supra* note 98. *See* Mandel Management Co., 245 NLRB No. 55, 102 LRRM 1449 (1979) (cards of former employees held invalid when shown that they were not signed on the dates indicated on the cards). *But see* NLRB v. Fort Vancouver Plywood Co., 604 F2d 596, 102 LRRM 2232 (CA 9, 1979) (cards back-dated to a point prior to employees' discharges were held valid); Axton Candy and Tobacco Co., 241 NLRB 1034, 101 LRRM 1043 (1979) (misdated cards counted towards union's majority absent evidence that they were purposely misdated and did not show union support).

[100]Dixie Cup, 156 NLRB 167, 61 LRRM 1329 (1966). However, the General Counsel is under no obligation to prove that the employees read the cards before signing. World-Wide Press, Inc., *supra* note 94; Southern Cotton Oil Crude Mill, 144 NLRB 959, 54 LRRM 1161 (1963); Franke's, Inc., 142 NLRB 551, 53 LRRM 1086 (1963).

[101]Colson Corp., *supra* note 25; NLRB v. Economy Food Center, Inc., 333 F2d 468, 56 LRRM 2263 (CA 7, 1964).

[102]Lincoln Mfg. Co., 160 NLRB 1866, 63 LRRM 1245 (1966), *enforced*, 382 F2d 411, 65 LRRM 2913 (CA 7, 1967).

[103]Decision, Inc., 166 NLRB 464, 65 LRRM 1660 (1967). For treatment of bargaining units generally, *see* Chapter 11 *supra*.

subsequent solicitation of additional cards.[104] The union's request may also be insufficient if, under all the circumstances, it is too ambiguous to apprise the employer of the contemplated unit.[105]

A request is superfluous, however, in a case where the bargaining order is designed to remedy unfair labor practices other than a refusal to bargain.[106] Thus, to effectuate the policies of the Act, the Board has issued bargaining orders where unions have obtained majority status based on cards even in the absence of a demand for recognition.[107] The Board's theory in such cases is that the employer, whether or not guilty of a refusal to bargain, has impaired the election process by committing unfair labor practices, thereby reducing the union from majority to minority status.[108] This rule applies even if the union has petitioned the Board for an election.[109]

A valid demand for recognition or bargaining need not be made in any particular form so long as it clearly indicates a

[104]Ed's Foodland of Springfield, Inc., 159 NLRB 1256, 62 LRRM 1465 (1966). *But see* Filler Prods. v. NLRB, 376 F2d 369, 65 LRRM 2029 (CA 4, 1967), denying enforcement of a bargaining order based on authorization cards where the employer had refused to read the letter containing the request and claim of majority status. The Court reasoned that the Board should have taken into account its own election regulations, which seem to require a request as a prerequisite to obtaining an election. *See* §9(c)(1)(A)(i) of the Act which states in part that "the employer *declines* to recognize their representative . . ." (emphasis added). The evidence also showed that the union never intended to rely on a card check.
[105]National Can Co. v. NLRB, 374 F2d 796, 64 LRRM 2607 (CA 7, 1967); Bryant Chucking Grinder Co., *supra* note 49.
[106]Naum Bros., Inc., 240 NLRB 311, 100 LRRM 1219 (1979); *see also* Gissel Packing Co., *supra* note 11. Compare the Second Circuit's refusal to enforce a bargaining order in the absence of a request in Flomatic Corp., *supra* note 25, with its readiness to grant enforcement where there was a request in Irving Air Chute Co., *supra* note 26. In the latter case, *Flomatic* was distinguished on the ground that the employer's unlawful acts were "only minimal" and there was no demand and refusal. The D.C. Circuit rejected the Second Circuit's reasoning in *Flomatic*, emphasizing that determining the extent of the employer's interference is within the Board's expertise. Steelworkers v. NLRB (Northwest Eng'r Co.), 376 F2d 770, 64 LRRM 2650 (CA DC, 1967), *enforcing* 148 NLRB 1136, 57 LRRM 1116 (1964) and 158 NLRB 624, 62 LRRM 1089 (1966), *cert. denied,* 389 US 932, 66 LRRM 2444 (1967). *See also* NLRB v. Gotham Shoe Mfg. Co., 359 F2d 684, 61 LRRM 2177 (CA 2, 1966). *See also* discussion *infra* at notes 224-25.
[107]*See* notes 108 and 109 *infra* and cases cited therein.
[108]Steelworkers v. NLRB (Northwest Eng'r Co.), *supra* note 106; Henry I. Siegel, Inc., 165 NLRB 493, 65 LRRM 1505 (1967); Bryant Chucking Grinder Co., *supra* note 49; American Sanitary Prods. Co. v. NLRB, 382 F2d 53, 65 LRRM 3122 (CA 10, 1967). In Wausau Steel Corp. v. NLRB, 377 F2d 369, 65 LRRM 2001 (CA 7, 1967), the Court disapproved the Board finding of refusal to bargain but nonetheless enforced the bargaining order because of other violations that destroyed the union's majority. *But see* NLRB v. Li'l Gen. Stores, Inc., 422 F2d 571, 73 LRRM 2522 (CA 5, 1970). The Fifth Circuit refused to enforce a bargaining order where there were unfair labor practices described as "extensive if not bordering on the flagrant," because the union had neither claimed a majority nor demanded recognition and there was no finding that the employer was aware of the union's majority when the petition for an election was filed.
[109]Mink-Dayton, Inc., 166 NLRB 604, 65 LRRM 1642 (1967); Tonkin Corp. of Cal., 165 NLRB 607, 65 LRRM 1521 (1967). *Cf.* Filler Prods., Inc. v. NLRB, *supra* note 104.

desire to negotiate and bargain on behalf of employees in an appropriate unit. A union's request could therefore be addressed to almost any upper level representative of management.[110] A management representative's actual lack of authority to discuss the matter does not relieve the employer of its duty to recognize the union.[111] And it has been deemed unsatisfactory simply to reply that the matter "is in the hands of an attorney."[112] Furthermore, if the union's initial request is adequate, it need not be repeated to the employer's attorney.[113]

The demand need not be stated in formal or precise terms. For example, in *Laclede Cab Co.*[114] the Board held that a union did not request recognition when its agent, asserting that he represented a discharged employee, requested that the latter be reinstated.[115] However, later that same day the union agent asked a supervisor to set a time to negotiate a collective bargaining agreement in a unit covering all employees at the facility; the Board held that the latter request constituted a valid demand for recognition and bargaining.[116]

Additionally, an employer's refusal to accept a union's letter demanding recognition will not invalidate the demand if the employer has notice of the contents of the letter.[117] In such a case, the employer was held to have "reasonably suspected" a letter to be a demand for recognition, for the employer had previously committed extensive violations of Section 8(a)(1) and the letter clearly came from the union.[118] However, where the employer marked a letter from the union "moved, left no address" and returned it unopened to the union, the Board did not infer that the employer knew the letter contained a demand for recognition.[119]

---

[110]NLRB v. Tri-City Linen Supply, 579 F2d 51, 98 LRRM 2155 (CA 9, 1978); S. E. Nichols Co., 156 NLRB 1201, 61 LRRM 1234 (1966), *enforcement denied on other grounds*, 380 F2d 438, 65 LRRM 2655 (CA 2, 1967).
[111]S. E. Nichols Co., *supra* note 110 at 1201 and 1212.
[112]*Id.*
[113]*Id.*
[114]236 NLRB 206, 98 LRRM 1426 (1978).
[115]*Id.*
[116]*Id.*
[117]Wayne Trophy Corp., 236 NLRB 299, 99 LRRM 1438 (1978), *enforced*, 595 F2d 1213, 103 LRRM 2604 (CA 3, 1979).
[118]*Id.*
[119]R & H Diesel & Trailer Serv., Inc., 238 NLRB 1432, 99 LRRM 1374 (1978).

C. Employer Unfair Labor Practices

As previously discussed, under the *Joy Silk* doctrine, if a union enjoyed majority status in an appropriate unit and made a proper demand for recognition, the employer could lawfully withhold recognition only if it entertained a good-faith doubt as to the union's majority status.[120] Under the *Gissel* test, however, good-faith doubt is largely irrelevant because the duty to bargain in the absence of an election arises only when the election process has been impeded by the employer's unfair labor practices. In *Gissel*, the Supreme Court approved what it characterized as the Board's "current practice":[121]

> When confronted by a recognition demand based on possession of cards allegedly signed by a majority of his employees, an employer need not grant recognition immediately, but may, unless he has knowledge independently of the cards that the union has a majority, decline the union's request and insist on an election, either by requesting the union to file an election petition or by filing such a petition himself under §9(c)(1)(B). If, however, the employer commits independent and substantial unfair labor practices disruptive of election conditions, the Board may withhold the election or set it aside, and issue instead a bargaining order as a remedy for the various violations. A bargaining order will not issue, of course, if the union obtained the cards through misrepresentation or coercion or if the employer's unfair labor practices are unrelated generally to the representation campaign.[122]

Thus, as discussed in detail above, the Court held that the propriety of a bargaining order varies with the extent of the employer's misconduct. Not only was a bargaining order appropriate in "exceptional cases marked by 'outrageous' and 'pervasive' unfair labor practices,"[123] it was also appropriate in a second category of "less extraordinary cases marked by less pervasive practices which nonetheless still have the tendency to undermine majority strength and impede the election processes."[124] In this second category, it is necessary to show "that at one point the union had a majority."[125] Also relevant is "the extensiveness of an employer's unfair labor practices in terms of their past effects on election conditions and the likelihood of

---

[120]Joy Silk Mills, Inc., *supra* note 8; Artcraft Hosiery Co., 78 NLRB 333, 22 LRRM 1212 (1948).
[121]*Supra* note 11 at 591.
[122]*Id.*
[123]*Id.* at 613.
[124]*Id.* at 614.
[125]*Id.*

their recurrence in the future."[126] Finally, the Court held that the Board's remedial power will not sustain bargaining orders in a third category of cases in which unfair labor practices have only a minimal impact on the election machinery. The Court rejected a *"per se* rule that the commission of any unfair labor practice will automatically result in a §8(a)(5) violation and the issuance of an order to bargain."[127]

1. Conduct Warranting a *Gissel* Bargaining Order. The Board has expressly rejected any mechanical application of *Gissel* standards governing the issuance of bargaining orders.[128] Although the Court suggested that in applying these standards the likelihood of recurrent employer misconduct should be considered, in cases decided subsequent to *Gissel* this has not been a significant concern in either the issuance or enforcement of bargaining orders, particularly where the employer's misconduct is considered "severe" in the first instance.[129] In general, bargaining orders have issued where the union has at some point attained majority status and the employer has committed unfair labor practices which, in the Board's view, rendered the holding of a fair election unlikely.[130] The following discussion illustrates the types of employer misconduct which, in light of the facts and

---

[126]*Id.* Cases illustrating the Board's application of these rules immediately following *Gissel* include the following: Marie Phillips, Inc., 178 NLRB 340, 72 LRRM 1103 (1969); Garland Knitting Mills, 178 NLRB 396, 72 LRRM 1112 (1969); Schrementi Bros., 179 NLRB 853, 72 LRRM 1481 (1969); West Side Plymouth, Inc., 180 NLRB 437, 73 LRRM 1014 (1969); Noll Motors, Inc., 180 NLRB 428, 73 LRRM 1036 (1969); Mather Co., 180 NLRB 417, 73 LRRM 1037 (1969); Blade-Tribune Publishing Co., 180 NLRB 432, 73 LRRM 1041 (1969); C & G Elec., Inc., 180 NLRB 427, 73 LRRM 1041 (1969); Lou De Young's Market Basket, Inc., 181 NLRB 35, 73 LRRM 1297 (1970), *enforced,* 430 F2d 912, 75 LRRM 2129 (CA 6, 1970); J. A. Conley Co., 181 NLRB 123, 73 LRRM 1301 (1970). In Central Soya of Canton, 180 NLRB 546, 73 LRRM 1059 (1970), the Board stressed that relatively minor unfair labor practices were not sufficient to indicate that a coercion-free rerun election could not be held; for that reason a bargaining order was not issued. In Gibson Prods. Co., 185 NLRB 362, 75 LRRM 1055 (1970), the Board held that *Gissel* "contemplated that the propriety of the bargaining order would be judged as of the time of the commission of the unfair labor practices and not in the light of subsequent events"; *see also* American Cable Sys., Inc., 179 NLRB 846, 72 LRRM 1524 (1969), where the Board ordered the employer to bargain on account of unfair labor practices which were committed in 1965 and which "undermined the Union's majority and caused an election to be a less reliable guide . . . than the signed authorization cards . . . ." On appeal, the Fifth Circuit refused to enforce the order and remanded because of the Board's failure to consider events occurring in the intervening years which could have made a free election possible. NLRB v. American Cable Sys., Inc., 427 F2d 446, 73 LRRM 2913 (CA 5, 1970).
[127]*Supra* note 11 at 615. *See* Hammond & Irving, *supra* note 35.
[128]*Supra* note 11 at 615.
[129]NLRB v. Scoler's, Inc., 466 F2d 1289, 81 LRRM 2299 (CA 2, 1972). *See also* Jamaica Towing, Inc., 602 F2d 1100, 101 LRRM 3011 (1979).
[130]*See, e.g.,* Faith Garment Co., 246 NLRB No. 44, 102 LRRM 1515 (1979); Rexart Color & Chem. Co., 246 NLRB 240, 102 LRRM 1615 (1979); Kermit Super Valu, 245 NLRB 1077, 102 LRRM 1512 (1979).

circumstances of the particular case, including the totality of the misconduct, have been held to warrant issuance of a *Gissel* bargaining order.

  a. Conduct Having a Direct Adverse Effect on the Employment Status of All Employees in the Bargaining Unit. A bargaining order has been deemed appropriate where the employer (1) closed one store in order to discourage union activity at several of its other stores that were also being organized;[131] (2) partially closed a plant;[132] (3) partially closed a plant and subcontracted other unit work;[133] (4) laid off all unit employees and transferred the work to another location;[134] (5) subcontracted all of the work of the bargaining unit;[135] and (6) unlawfully locked out employees.[136]

  Bargaining orders have also been deemed appropriate where, in the face of union activity, work rules have been enforced more stringently[137] and new, more onerous, work rules have been introduced.[138]

  b. Action Adverse to the Employment Status of Selected Employees or Employee Groups. Bargaining orders have likewise been issued in cases where the employer (1) discriminatorily disciplined, laid off, or discharged employees,[139] (2) transferred or reduced the

---

[131]Serv-U-Stores, 225 NLRB 37, 93 LRRM 1033 (1976).

[132]Great Chinese Am. Sewing Co. v. NLRB, 578 F2d 251, 99 LRRM 2347 (CA 9, 1978). *See also* Elliot River Tours, Inc., 246 NLRB 935, 103 LRRM 1095, 1096 (1979) (closing of school found to be a violation of §8(a)(5)).

[133]Great Chinese Am. Sewing Co., *supra* note 132.

[134]Case, Inc., 237 NLRB 798, 99 LRRM 1159 (1978).

[135]Townhouse TV & Appliances, Inc., 213 NLRB 716, 88 LRRM 1295 (1974), *enforcement granted in part*, 531 F2d 826, 91 LRRM 2636 (CA 7, 1976).

[136]Crockett-Bradley, Inc., 212 NLRB 435, 87 LRRM 1597 (1974), *enforced*, 523 F2d 449, 90 LRRM 3116 (CA 5, 1975).

[137]Schwab Foods, Inc., 223 NLRB 394, 92 LRRM 1285 (1976).

[138]*Id.*

[139]NLRB v. Bighorn Beverage Co., 614 F2d 1238, 103 LRRM 3008 (CA 9, 1980); Medline Indus., Inc., 233 NLRB 627, 97 LRRM 1561 (1977), *enforced in part*, 592 F2d 788, 100 LRRM 3202 (CA 7, 1979); Bandag, Inc. v. NLRB, 583 F2d 765, 99 LRRM 3226 (CA 5, 1978); Hambre Hombre Enterprises v. NLRB, 581 F2d 204, 99 LRRM 2541 (CA 9, 1978); NLRB v. Woodline, Inc., 577 F2d 463, 98 LRRM 2869 (CA 8, 1978); Multi-Medical Convalescent & Nursing Center v. NLRB, 550 F2d 974, 95 LRRM 2021 (CA 4, 1977), *cert. denied*, 434 US 835, 96 LRRM 2514 (1977); NLRB v. Montgomery Ward & Co., 554 F2d 996, 95 LRRM 2433 (CA 10, 1977); NLRB v. Pacific Southwest Airlines, 550 F2d 1148, 94 LRRM 2772 (CA 9, 1977); NLRB v. Townhouse TV & Appliances, Inc., 531 F2d 826, 91 LRRM 2636 (CA 7, 1976); NLRB v. Federated Publications (State Journal), 544 F2d 908, 93 LRRM 2877 (CA 6, 1976); NLRB v. Tahoe Vangas, 517 F2d 747, 89 LRRM 2508 (CA 9, 1975); Digital Paging Sys., 249 NLRB 127, 104 LRRM 1033 (1980); Ethan Allen, 247 NLRB 552, 103 LRRM 1251 (1980); Pay 'n Save Corp., 247 NLRB 1346, 103 LRRM 1334 (1980); Nevis Indus., Inc., 246 NLRB 1053, 103 LRRM 1035 (1979); Devon Gables Nursing Home, 237 NLRB 775, 99 LRRM 1071 (1978); Machine Tool & Gear, 237 NLRB 1109, 99 LRRM 1153 (1978); Midland-

work hours of union adherents;[140] (3) denied a vacation request because of an employee's union activities;[141] and (4) refused to reinstate strikers who made unconditional offers to return to work.[142]

c. *Threats.* For a bargaining order to be an appropriate remedy, an employer need not actually take adverse action against employees. Specifically, bargaining orders also have issued in response to employer threats (1) of reprisals or plant closure because of union activities;[143] (2) to impose more onerous working conditions;[144] (3) to withhold paychecks until employees' authorization cards are retrieved;[145] (4) to eliminate unit work,[146] the employees' pension and profit sharing plan,[147] or other fringe benefits;[148] (5) to institute a time clock procedure;[149] (6) to require employees to work harder if the plant becomes unionized;[150] (7) that violent and costly strikes would be the consequences of unionization.[151]

Ross Corp., 239 NLRB 323, 100 LRRM 1020 (1978); Chandler Motors, Inc., 236 NLRB 1565, 98 LRRM 1528 (1978); Frito-Lay, Inc., 232 NLRB 753, 96 LRRM 1335 (1977); E. H. Ltd., 227 NLRB 1107, 98 LRRM 1494 (1977); W & W Tool & Die Mfg. Co., 225 NLRB 1000, 93 LRRM 1006 (1976); Elling Halvorson, Inc., 222 NLRB 570, 91 LRRM 1179 (1976); Franklin Parish Broadcasting, Inc., 222 NLRB 1133, 91 LRRM 1474 (1976).

[140]C & W Super Mkts., Inc. v. NLRB, 581 F2d 618, 98 LRRM 3311 (CA 7, 1978); Hinky Dinky Super Mkts., Inc., 247 NLRB 1176, 103 LRRM 1314 (1980); Frederick's Foodland, Inc., 247 NLRB 284, 103 LRRM 1219 (1980); Maxi Mart, Inc., 246 NLRB 1151, 103 LRRM 1105 (1979); Kroger Co., 228 NLRB 149, 94 LRRM 1586 (1977); Occidental Paper Corp., 227 NLRB 719, 94 LRRM 1347 (1977).

[141]Pope Maintenance Corp., 228 NLRB 326, 96 LRRM 1186 (1977).

[142]Hargis Mine Supply, Inc., 225 NLRB 660, 93 LRRM 1370 (1976).

[143]Midland-Ross Corp. v. NLRB, 617 F2d 977, 103 LRRM 2908 (CA 3, 1980), *cert. denied,* 449 US 871, 105 LRRM 2657 (1980); Frito-Lay, Inc. v. NLRB, 585 F2d 62, 99 LRRM 2658 (CA 3, 1978); NLRB v. Matouk Indus., Inc., 582 F2d 125, 99 LRRM 2136 (CA 1, 1978); C & W Supermarkets, Inc. v. NLRB, *supra* note 140; Great Chinese Am. Sewing Co. v. NLRB, *supra* note 132; NLRB v. Prineville Stud Co., 578 F2d 1292, 98 LRRM 3322 (CA 9, 1978); NLRB v. Pope Maintenance Corp., 573 F2d 898, 98 LRRM 2644 (CA 5, 1978); NLRB v. Solboro Knitting Mills, Inc., 572 F2d 936, 97 LRRM 3047 (CA 2, 1978); Drug Package Co. v. NLRB, 570 F2d 1340, 97 LRRM 2851 (CA 8, 1978); Jacques Syl Knitwear, 247 NLRB 1525, 103 LRRM 1358 (1980); Wright Plastics Prods., Inc., 247 NLRB 635, 103 LRRM 1206 (1980); Ste-Mel Signs, Inc., 246 NLRB 1110, 103 LRRM 1120 (1979); Philadelphia Ambulance Serv., Inc., 238 NLRB 1070, 99 LRRM 1320 (1978); Albertson Mfg. Co., 236 NLRB 663, 98 LRRM 1402 (1978); Chatfield-Anderson Co., 236 NLRB 50, 98 LRRM 1190 (1978); Unimedia Corp., 236 NLRB 1561, 98 LRRM 1176 (1978); Hedstrom Co., 235 NLRB 1193, 98 LRRM 1105 (1978).

[144]Donovan v. NLRB, 520 F2d 1316, 89 LRRM 3127 (CA 2, 1975), *cert. denied,* 423 US 1053, 91 LRRM 2099 (1976); MPC Restaurant Corp. v. NLRB, 481 F2d 75, 83 LRRM 2769 (CA 2, 1973).

[145]Great Chinese Am. Sewing Co., *supra* note 132.

[146]NLRB v. Eagle Material Handling, Inc., 558 F2d 160, 95 LRRM 2934 (CA 3, 1977).

[147]Chatfield-Anderson Co., *supra* note 143.

[148]Drug Package Co. v. NLRB, *supra* note 143.

[149]L'Eggs Prods., 236 NLRB 354, 99 LRRM 1304 (1978).

[150]Drug Package Co. v. NLRB, *supra* note 143.

[151]NLRB v. Daybreak Lodge Nursing & Convalescent Home, 585 F2d 79, 99 LRRM 2985 (CA 3, 1978).

d. Promises. Bargaining orders likewise have issued where the employer promises or grants additional benefits in order to discourage union activity or membership.[152] Accordingly, employers who granted 20-percent pay increases to almost every employee[153] or Christmas bonuses[154] to induce employee rejection of the union were ordered to bargain with the union.

e. Actions Calculated to Undermine the Union's Status. Bargaining orders have also been issued where the employer (1) stated that selection of a union would be futile;[155] (2) stated that it would not bargain with a union;[156] (3) stated that money that could have gone to employees was spent on legal fees to fight the union;[157] (4) assisted a rival union;[158] (5) encouraged employees to form a company union;[159] (6) suggested that an employee committee be formed;[160] (7) told strikers that they might be able to arrange to return to work on more favorable terms if they met with the company without a union representative;[161] (8) offered to permit strikers to form their own union;[162] (9) solicited employees' grievances and asked employees to persuade co-workers to abandon the union;[163] and (10) solicited

---

[152]Bandag, Inc., *supra* note 139; Great Chinese Am. Sewing Co., *supra* note 132; C & W Super Mkts., *supra* note 140; Grandee Beer Dist., Inc., 247 NLRB 1280, 103 LRRM 1338 (1980); Alumbaugh Coal Corp., 247 NLRB 895, 103 LRRM 1210 (1980); Apple Tree Chevrolet, 237 NLRB 867, 99 LRRM 1505 (1978); Central Cartage, Inc., 236 NLRB 1232, 98 LRRM 1554 (1978); Hedstrom Co., 235 NLRB 1193, 98 LRRM 1105 (1978); Frito-Lay, Inc., *supra* note 139; Beasley Energy, Inc., 228 NLRB 93, 94 LRRM 1563 (1977); Drug Package Co., *supra* note 143; and Solboro Knitting Mills, *supra* note 143.

[153]Tipton Elec. Co. v. NLRB, 621 F2d 890, 104 LRRM 2073, 2080 (CA 8, 1980) (employer granting increases after election, when objections were still pending, destroyed laboratory conditions). Raley's, Inc., 236 NLRB 971, 98 LRRM 1381 (1978). *See* J. J. Newberry Co., 249 NLRB 991, 104 LRRM 1244 (1980) (grant of substantial wage increase to all employees was "sufficient to render it unlikely that a fair election could be held").

[154]Machine Tool & Gear, 237 NLRB 1109, 99 LRRM 1153 (1978).

[155]J. P. Stevens & Co., 247 NLRB 420, 103 LRRM 1187 (1980); Professional Ambulance Serv., Inc., 232 NLRB 1141, 97 LRRM 1109 (1977); Curtin Matheson Scientific, Inc., 228 NLRB 996, 94 LRRM 1742 (1977); Sparkle Mills, Inc., 227 NLRB 1981, 94 LRRM 1448 (1977); Red Barn Sys., Inc., 224 NLRB 1586, 92 LRRM 1404 (1976).

[156]*See* cases cited in note 155 *supra.*

[157]Pilot Freight Carriers, 223 NLRB 286, 92 LRRM 1246 (1976).

[158]Professional Ambulance Serv., Inc., *supra* note 155.

[159]*Id.*

[160]NLRB v. Rollins Telecasting, Inc., 494 F2d 80, 86 LRRM 2735 (CA 2, 1974); NLRB v. Hendel Mfg. Co., 483 F2d 350, 83 LRRM 2657 (CA 2, 1973); C & W Mining Co., 248 NLRB 270, 103 LRRM 1563 (1980).

[161]Merkel & Sons, 232 NLRB 140, 97 LRRM 1081 (1977). *See* Jamaica Towing, Inc., 247 NLRB 353, 103 LRRM 1161 (1980), where employer told employees that their demands would be met by dealing with management and that union representation would be of no advantage to them.

[162]Merkel & Sons, *supra* note 161.

[163]Farah Supermarkets, Inc., 228 NLRB 984, 95 LRRM 1201 (1977).

employees to repudiate signed authorization cards.[164] More-over, an employer may be ordered to bargain if it places an unreasonable condition on its willingness to bargain, for exam-ple, that it will bargain only in New York concerning employees located in Kentucky, or will bargain by mail or over the tele-phone.[165]

f. Interrogation, Surveillance, Polling, and No-Solicitation Rules. Bargaining orders are also appropriate where the employer engages in coercive interrogation, polling, or surveillance[166] of employees. For example, a bargaining order was issued where a psychologist had conducted an opinion survey which exam-ined employees' attitudes toward management.[167]

Bargaining orders have also been issued where the employer promulgated an invalid no-solicitation rule[168] or applied a lawful rule in a discriminatory manner.[169] For example, in *Medline Industries,* the Board issued a bargaining order where the employer prohibited conversations about the union and solicitation dur-ing nonworking time.[170]

g. Other Circumstances in Which Bargaining Orders Have Issued. Bargaining orders have been issued in a variety of other situa-tions. Specifically employers who ordered employees to call them "Mister,"[171] fired shots to intimidate employees,[172] or caused the

---

[164]Matouk Indus., *supra* note 143; Pope Maintenance Corp., *supra* note 143.
[165]Case, Inc., *supra* note 134.
[166]Bandag, Inc., *supra* note 139; Daybreak Lodge Nursing & Convalescent Home, Inc., 230 NLRB 800, 96 LRRM 1345 (1977), *enforced in part by* 585 F2d 79, 99 LRRM 2985 (CA 3, 1978); Frito-Lay, *supra* note 139; Great Chinese Am. Sewing Co., *supra* note 132; Prineville Stud Co., *supra* note 143; C & W Super Mkts., *supra* note 140; Broadmoor Lumber Co., 227 NLRB 1123, 95 LRRM 1117 (1977), *enforced,* 578 F2d 238, 98 LRRM 3134 (CA 9, 1978); Woodline, Inc., 231 NLRB 863, 97 LRRM 1288 (1977), *enforced,* 577 F2d 463, 98 LRRM 2869 (CA 8, 1978); Pope Maintenance, *supra* note 143; Solboro Knitting Mills, *supra* note 143; Multi-Medical Convalescent & Nursing Center, *supra* note 139; Pacific Southwest Airlines, *supra* note 139; Ann Lee Sportswear, Inc. v. NLRB, 543 F2d 739, 93 LRRM 2653 (CA 10, 1976); Crockett-Bradley, Inc., *supra* note 136; Tartan Marine Co., 247 NLRB No. 73, 103 LRRM 1247 (1980); Albert-son Mfg. Co., *supra* note 143; Boatel Alas., Inc., 236 NLRB 1458, 99 LRRM 1005 (1978); Devon Gables Nursing Home, *supra* note 139; Plastic Film Prods. Corp., 238 NLRB 135, 99 LRRM 1216 (1978); Anchorage Times Publishing Co., 237 NLRB 544, 99 LRRM 1513 (1978); International Mfg. Co., 238 NLRB 1361, 99 LRRM 1328 (1978); Freehold AMC-Jeep Corp., 230 NLRB 903, 95 LRRM 1419 (1977); Beasley Energy, *supra* note 152; Pilot Freight Carriers, *supra* note 157; Hargis Mine Supply, *supra* note 142; Red Barn Sys., *supra* note 155; Schwab Foods, *supra* note 137.
[167]Apple Tree Chevrolet, *supra* note 152.
[168]NLRB v. Tischler, 607 F2d 1104, 103 LRRM 3033 (CA 9, 1980); Bandag, Inc., *supra* note 139; Montgomery Ward & Co., *supra* note 139.
[169]Production Plating Co., 233 NLRB 116, 96 LRRM 1470 (1977).
[170]Medline Indus., *supra* note 139.
[171]Philadelphia Ambulance Serv., *supra* note 143.
[172]Hargis Mine Supply, *supra* note 142.

arrest of a relative of two union adherents[173] were ordered to bargain with the union. This result also obtained where the employer substituted a pay increase for a free lunch program which it discontinued[174] and where the employer induced employees to withdraw unfair labor practice charges against it.[175]

2. Conduct Not Warranting a *Gissel* Bargaining Order.

Conduct which in other circumstances might warrant a bargaining order will not support such an order if (1) the employer's independent unfair labor practices were not so coercive, pervasive, or extensive as to require a bargaining order to remedy their unlawful effects or (2) the application of traditional remedies would insure a fair election. Thus, in several cases the Board has refused to issue bargaining orders notwithstanding findings that the employer committed extensive and pervasive violations of Sections 8(a)(1) and (3) of the Act.[176] Bargaining orders might also be denied where the employer's unlawful conduct affects only a small number of employees in a large bargaining unit.[177]

Thus, the Board has not issued bargaining orders in some cases where the employer made threats of reprisal or granted or promised to grant benefits in response to union activity;[178] where the employer interrogated employees or suggested that

---

[173]Albertson Mfg., *supra* note 143.
[174]Elmwood Nursing Home, 238 NLRB 346, 99 LRRM 1202 (1978).
[175]Medline Indus., *supra* note 139.
[176]Cato Show Printing Co., 219 NLRB 739, 90 LRRM 1139 (1975); Rensselaer Polytechnic Inst., 219 NLRB 712, 89 LRRM 1879 (1975); Grismac Corp., 205 NLRB 1108, 84 LRRM 1256 (1973), *enforced,* 86 LRRM 2152 (CA 7, 1974); Fuqua Homes Mo., Inc., 201 NLRB 130, 82 LRRM 1142 (1973); Georgetown Dress Corp., 201 NLRB 102, 82 LRRM 1318 (1973). *See* Schultes I.G.A. Foodliner, 241 NLRB 855, 101 LRRM 1048 (1979) (bargaining order inappropriate where employer unfair labor practices were not "outrageous and pervasive").
[177]Americraft Mfg. Co., 242 NLRB 1312, 101 LRRM 1378 (1979); Dependable Lists, Inc., 239 NLRB 1304, 100 LRRM 1148 (1979); May Dep't. Stores Co., 211 NLRB 150, 86 LRRM 1423 (1974), *enforced,* 514 F2d 894, 90 LRRM 2844 (CA DC, 1975).
[178]Chef's Pantry, Inc., 247 NLRB 77, 103 LRRM 1126 (1980); Bruce Duncan Co., 233 NLRB 1243, 97 LRRM 1027 (1977); Sturgis-Newport Business Forms, 227 NLRB 1426, 94 LRRM 1611 (1977), *enforced,* 563 F2d 1252, 96 LRRM 3383 (CA 5, 1977); South Station Liquor Store, 223 NLRB 1115, 92 LRRM 1083 (1976); Walgreen Co., 221 NLRB 1096, 91 LRRM 1177 (1975); Lasco Indus., 217 NLRB 527, 89 LRRM 1058 (1975); Treadway Inn, 217 NLRB 51, 89 LRRM 1005 (1975); Franklin Park Mall, Inc., 212 NLRB 21, 87 LRRM 1255 (1974); Litho Press of San Antonio, 211 NLRB 1014, 86 LRRM 1471 (1974), *enforced,* 512 F2d 73, 89 LRRM 2171 (CA 5, 1975); Rockland Chrysler Plymouth, Inc., 209 NLRB 1045, 86 LRRM 1233 (1974); Gold Circle Dep't Stores, 207 NLRB 1005, 85 LRRM 1033 (1973); J. J. Newberry Co., 202 NLRB 420, 82 LRRM 1584 (1973); Ring Metals Co., 198 NLRB 1020, 81 LRRM 1001 (1972), *enforced,* 87 LRRM 2128 (CA DC, 1973); Claremont Polychemical Corp., 196 NLRB 613, 80 LRRM 1130 (1972); Restaurant Assoc. Indus., 194 NLRB 1066, 79 LRRM 1145 (1972).

unionization would be futile;[179] where wage and benefit increases were postponed or withheld;[180] and where the employer circumvented the union and sought to engage in individual bargaining with employees.[181]

Moreover, in specific cases, bargaining orders were not issued for the following situations: to remedy encouragement by employers of the revocation of authorizations;[182] where employees were coerced into signing cards for a rival union;[183] where the employer offered encouragement or assistance in the formation of a company union;[184] and where the employer entered into an unlawful security agreement with a rival union.[185] The same result obtained where the employer prohibited organizational activity[186] and where the employer assisted in an antiunion campaign.[187]

The Board has also declined to issue bargaining orders in some cases where the employer discriminatorily discharged employees,[188] failed to reinstate economic strikers,[189] solicited and remedied grievances,[190] or created the impression of, and engaged in, surveillance of employees' union activities.[191]

Board bargaining orders may be voided if they fail to comply with standards for enforcement developed by the courts of

---

[179]Hennessy Serv. Corp., 204 NLRB 266, 83 LRRM 1573 (1973).

[180]Ring Metals Co., *supra* note 178; Consolidated Fibers, 197 NLRB 843, 80 LRRM 1817 (1972).

[181]Rensselaer Polytechnic Inst., *supra* note 176.

[182]L.O.F. Glass, Inc., 216 NLRB 845, 88 LRRM 1654 (1975); Tennessee Shell Co., 212 NLRB 193, 86 LRRM 1704 (1974), *petition for review denied*, 515 F2d 1018, 90 LRRM 2844 (CA DC, 1972); Dakota Sand & Gravel Co., 211 NLRB 1026, 86 LRRM 1555 (1974); Consolidated Fibers, *supra* note 180.

[183]Colony Knitwear Corp., 217 NLRB 245, 88 LRRM 1552 (1975).

[184]Rensselaer Polytechnic Inst., *supra* note 176; Litho Press of San Antonio, *supra* note 178; May Dept. Stores Co., *supra* note 177.

[185]Colony Knitwear, *supra* note 183.

[186]Montgomery Ward & Co., 198 NLRB 52, 80 LRRM 1814 (1972); Grismac Corp., *supra* note 176; Litho Press of San Antonio, *supra* note 178; Cato Show Printing Co., *supra* note 176.

[187]Rensselaer Polytechnic Inst., *supra* note 176.

[188]Munro Enterprises, 210 NLRB 403, 86 LRRM 1620 (1974) (a single, unlawful discharge so long before the recognition demand as to leave a minimal impact); Beckett Aviation Corp., 218 NLRB 238, 89 LRRM 1341 (1975).

[189]Mead Corp., 211 NLRB 657, 86 LRRM 1501 (1974).

[190]Lasco Indus., *supra* note 178; White Pine, Inc., 213 NLRB 566, 87 LRRM 1386 (1974); Franklin Park Mall, Inc., 212 NLRB 21, 87 LRRM 1255 (1974); Central Diagnostic Laboratory, 206 NLRB 754, 84 LRRM 1636 (1973); Georgetown Dress, *supra* note 176; Flight Safety, Inc., 197 NLRB 223, 80 LRRM 1298 (1972).

[191]Fuqua Homes Mo., Inc., *supra* note 176; J. J. Newberry Co., *supra* note 178; Gold Circle Dept. Stores, *supra* note 178; Sands Indus., Inc., 218 NLRB 461, 89 LRRM 1730 (1975).

appeals. Thus, Board bargaining orders have gone unenforced where the Board failed to explain the nexus between the employer's unfair labor practices and the unlikelihood of holding a fair election.[192] This result has also followed where the reviewing court found no evidence to establish that the employer's unfair labor practices undermined the union's majority[193] or were sufficiently egregious to preclude the holding of a fair election.[194] And courts of appeals have refused to enforce bargaining orders on finding that the Board either failed to adequately account for prior inconsistent decisions[195] or acted arbitrarily and capriciously by determining that certain authorization cards were secured by misrepresentation while others obtained in similar circumstances were not (where the latter gave the union a majority).[196] Bargaining orders have also gone unenforced where the Board failed to afford proper weight to the changed composition of the work force[197] and where the employer, based on a good-faith doubt as to the union's continuing majority status, withdrew recognition from an incumbent union.[198]

---

[192]*E.g.*, NLRB v. General Stencils, Inc., 438 F2d 894, 76 LRRM 2288 (CA 2, 1971); Peerless, Inc. v. NLRB, 484 F2d 1108, 83 LRRM 3000 (CA 7, 1973); NLRB v. Gruber's Super Mkt., Inc., 501 F2d 697, 87 LRRM 2037 (CA 7, 1974); NLRB v. Gibson Prods. Co., 494 F2d 762, 86 LRRM 2636 (CA 5, 1974).

[193]Arbie Mineral Feed Co. v. NLRB, 438 F2d 940, 76 LRRM 2613 (CA 8, 1971); Harper & Row Publishers v. NLRB, 476 F2d 430, 83 LRRM 2199 (CA 8, 1973); NLRB v. Apple Tree Chevrolet, *supra* note 152; Rapid Mfg. Co. v. NLRB, 612 F2d 144, 103 LRRM 2162, 2166 (CA 3, 1979).

[194]Rapid Mfg., *supra* note 193; Apple Tree Chevrolet, *supra* note 152; Chatfield-Anderson, *supra* note 143; NLRB v. Pilgrim Foods, Inc., 591 F2d 110, 100 LRRM 2494 (CA 1, 1978); Shulman's, Inc. v. NLRB, 519 F2d 498, 89 LRRM 2729 (CA 4, 1975); Donn Prods., Inc. v. NLRB, 613 F2d 162, 103 LRRM 2338, 2342 (CA 6, 1980); NLRB v. East Side Shopper, Inc., 498 F2d 1334, 86 LRRM 2817 (CA 6, 1974); NLRB v. Leslie Metal Arts Co., 472 F2d 584, 82 LRRM 2002 (CA 6, 1972); Dawson Metal Prods., Inc. v. NLRB, 450 F2d 47, 78 LRRM 2674 (CA 8, 1971). *See also* NLRB v. Western Drug, 600 F2d 1324, 101 LRRM 3023 (CA 9, 1979), where enforcement was denied because the unfair labor practices were serious but not outrageous, and the Board had not found that a bargaining order would best serve the employees' interests. The court was critical of what it characterized as the Board's mechanical application of the *Gissel* criteria without affording due regard to the present context, including the impact of turnover.

[195]Midwest Stock Exch., Inc., 620 F2d 629, 104 LRRM 2243, 2247 (CA 7, 1980); Peerless, Inc., *supra* note 192; NLRB v. General Stencils, *supra* note 192.

[196]Fort Smith Outerwear, Inc. v. NLRB, 499 F2d 223, 86 LRRM 2753 (CA 8, 1974).

[197]Gruber's Super Mkt., *supra* note 192; NLRB v. Ship Shape Maintenance Co., 474 F2d 434, 81 LRRM 2865 (CA DC, 1972); Peerless, Inc., *supra* note 192.

[198]National Cash Register Co. v. NLRB, 494 F2d 189, 85 LRRM 2657 (CA 8, 1974); Automated Business Sys. v. NLRB, 497 F2d 262, 86 LRRM 2659 (CA 6, 1974). The court in *Automated* held that once the employer comes forward with sufficient evidence to cast a doubt on the union's continued majority status, the burden of proof shifts to the General Counsel to prove that on the date of withdrawal of recognition the union did in fact represent a majority. *See generally* discussion in Part VI *infra*.

D. The Bargaining Order as an Extraordinary Remedy

An employer who has committed flagrant unfair labor practices may be required to bargain with a union even though it doubts the union's majority status, and widespread unfair labor practices may warrant issuance of a bargaining order even though the employer's refusal to recognize may not independently violate Section 8(a)(5).[199] In *Steel-Fab, Inc.*[200] the Board held that "it is unnecessary to predicate the bargaining order on any 8(a)(5) violation."[201] It stated that by issuing a bargaining order to remedy "an employer's 8(a)(1) violations that have dissipated a union's majority and prevented the holding of a fair election,"[202] it was "removing from the analytical process involved in applying . . . standards [governing bargaining orders] a semantic difficulty which . . . has clouded the central issue over the years."[203]

Under *Steel-Fab,* bargaining orders not predicated upon Section 8(a)(5) violations were effective from the date of the decision only, thereby leaving unremedied earlier unilateral changes in working conditions made by an employer after the union had obtained a card majority.[204] However, this aspect of *Steel-Fab* was short-lived. After having "carefully considered and reexamined the policies and principles set forth in our decision in *Steel-Fab* and the Supreme Court's decision in *Gissel,*"[205] the Board concluded, in *Trading Port, Inc.,*[206] that "while there may be certain truths to the approaches each takes to the issuance of and legal basis for a bargaining order, we are now of the opinion that the correct approach lies somewhere in between."[207] In *Trading Port,* the Board concluded that its *Steel-Fab* holding

[199]NLRB v. Delight Bakery, Inc., 353 F2d 344, 60 LRRM 2501 (CA 6, 1965); Piasecki Aircraft Corp. v. NLRB, 280 F2d 575, 46 LRRM 2469 (CA 3, 1960), *cert. denied,* 364 US 933, 47 LRRM 2365 (1961); Kinter Bros., Inc., 167 NLRB 57, 66 LRRM 1004 (1967); Crystal Tire Co., 165 NLRB 563, 65 LRRM 1459 (1967); Better Val-U Stores of Mansfield, Inc., 161 NLRB 762, 63 LRRM 1326 (1966); 77 Operating Co. (John Hammonds), 160 NLRB 927, 63 LRRM 1057 (1966); Bishop & Malco, Inc., 159 NLRB 1159, 62 LRRM 1498 (1965). The Fourth Circuit opinions reviewed by the Supreme Court in *Gissel Packing Co., supra* note 11, 395 US at 585, conceded that one of the circumstances in which the Board could properly order an employer to bargain without an election was when "the employer's §§8(a)(1) and (3) unfair labor practices committed during the representation campaign were so extensive and pervasive that a bargaining order was the only available Board remedy irrespective of a card majority."

[200]212 NLRB 363, 86 LRRM 1474 (1974).

[201]*Id.*

[202]*Id.*

[203]*Id.* at 365.

[204]This was the subject of Member Jenkins's concurring and dissenting opinion. *Id.* at 371.

[205]Trading Port, Inc., 219 NLRB 298, 301, 89 LRRM 1565 (1975).

[206]*Supra* note 205.

[207]*Id.* at 301.

led to the unwanted result that an employer by committing serious unfair labor practices, could delay the holding of an election indefinitely (since a fair one could no longer be held), and insure himself a substantial period of time until the Board issued a remedial bargaining order, during which period he would not have to deal with a union. Since the events which "triggered" the bargaining duty occurred much earlier, i.e., at the time of the unfair labor practices, and since the employees had earlier expressed their desire for union representation, the Board's prospective bargaining order fell short of reinstating the situation as it would have been had [the employer] obeyed the law and allowed a fair election to proceed.[208]

Stressing that its "main concern in granting bargaining orders has been, and is, to correct and give redress for an employer's misconduct and to protect the employees from the effects thereof,"[209] the Board held that "an employer's obligation under a bargaining order remedy should commence as of the time the employer has embarked on a clear course of unlawful conduct or has engaged in sufficient unfair labor practices to undermine the union's majority status."[210] Read together, therefore, *Steel-Fab* and *Trading Port* stand for the proposition that a Section 8(a)(5) violation need not be present to support a bargaining order, and that a bargaining order predicated on other than Section 8(a)(5) conduct will be retroactive to the date that the employer "embarked on a clear course of unlawful conduct . . . sufficient . . . to undermine the union's majority status."[211]

Subsequent cases, however, have not established a hard-and-fast point in time to which a bargaining order will be retroactive. If the employer has committed unfair labor practices sufficient to warrant a bargaining order, and the union has not demanded recognition, the bargaining order will extend back to the point at which the union attained majority status.[212] If the bargaining order is intended to remedy only a Section 8(a)(5) violation, the Board has held that the order should be retroactive to the date

[208]*Id.*
[209]*Id.*
[210]*Id.*
[211]*Id.*
[212]Permanent Label Corp., 248 NLRB 118, 103 LRRM 1513 (1980) (order effective as of date union attained majority status); Dresser Indus., Inc., 248 NLRB 33, 103 LRRM 1473 (1980); J. P. Stevens & Co., 244 NLRB No. 82, 102 LRRM 1039 (1979); International Mfg. Co., 238 NLRB 1361, 99 LRRM 1328 (1978); Machine Tool & Gear, Inc., 237 NLRB 1109, 99 LRRM 1153 (1978); Woodland Supermarket, 237 NLRB 1481, 99 LRRM 1113 (1978); Seven-Up Bottling Co., 235 NLRB 297, 98 LRRM 1515 (1978). *See also* Lockwoven Co., 245 NLRB 1362, 102 LRRM 1533 (1979).

of the union's demand for recognition.[213] But for these rules to be applicable, the employer must already have committed the unfair labor practices which were deemed sufficient to warrant issuance of the bargaining order. Thus, if the employer first engages in unfair labor practices *after* the union has either attained majority status or demanded recognition, the bargaining order will extend back no further than the point at which the employer "embarked on a clear course of unlawful conduct."[214] Where, however, the achievement of majority status, the demand for recognition, and the commencement of the employer's unfair labor practices all occurred more than six months *prior* to the filing of the charges, the bargaining obligation is deemed retroactive to the first day of the six-month limitation period set forth in Section 10(b) of the Act.[215]

For a dozen years after *Gissel,* there was some uncertainty as to whether the Board would issue or had authority to issue a bargaining order absent a showing that the union had at some point attained majority status. Although the Supreme Court in *Gissel* indicated that where there were "outrageous" and "pervasive" unfair labor practices making a fair election impossible, a bargaining order might be appropriate "without need of inquiry into majority status on the basis of cards or otherwise,"[216] until 1981 the Board declined to issue bargaining orders absent evidence that the union at one time enjoyed majority status.[217] In *United Dairy Farmers Cooperative Association,*[218] two members of the Board asserted that the Board has the authority to issue a

---

[213]Albertson Mfg., *supra* note 143; *see* Robin Am. Corp., 245 NLRB 822, 102 LRRM 1563 (1979).

[214]Jasta Mfg. Co., *supra* note 85; Bighorn Beverage, 236 NLRB 736, 98 LRRM 1396 (1978); Chatfield-Anderson Co., *supra* note 143; Idak Convalescent Center, 238 NLRB 410, 99 LRRM 1542 (1978); L'Eggs Prods., *supra* note 149; and Michigan Prods., Inc., 236 NLRB 1143, 98 LRRM 1515 (1978).

[215]Chromalloy Mining & Minerals, 238 NLRB 688, 99 LRRM 1642 (1978).

[216]*Supra* note 11 at 613.

[217]Haddon House Food Prods., 242 NLRB 1057 (1979), *aff'd sub nom.* Teamsters Local 115 v. NLRB, 640 F2d 392, 106 LRRM 2462 (CA DC, 1981); F.W.I.L. Lundry Bros. Restaurant, 248 NLRB 415, 103 LRRM 1520, 1522 (1980); Sambo's Restaurant, Inc., 247 NLRB 777, 103 LRRM 1181 (1980); Electrical Workers (IUE) (Scott's, Inc.), 159 NLRB 1795, 62 LRRM 1543 (1966), *enforced as modified,* 383 F2d 230, 66 LRRM 2081 (CA DC, 1967), *cert. denied,* 390 US 904, 67 LRRM 2308; Fuqua Homes Mo., *supra* note 176; GTE Automatic Elec., Inc., 196 NLRB 902, 80 LRRM 1155 (1972); Loray Corp., 184 NLRB 557, 74 LRRM 1513 (1970); J. P. Stevens & Co., 157 NLRB 869, 61 LRRM 1437 (1966), *enforced as modified,* 380 F2d 292, 65 LRRM 2829 (CA 2), *cert. denied,* 389 US 1005, 66 LRRM 2728 (1967); W. H. Elson Bottling, 155 NLRB 714, 60 LRRM 1381 (1965), *enforced as modified,* 379 F2d 223, 65 LRRM 2673 (CA 6, 1967).

[218]242 NLRB 1026, 101 LRRM 1278 (1979), *aff'd and remanded for reconsideration of bargaining order issue,* 633 F2d 1054, 105 LRRM 3034 (CA 3, 1979), *on remand,* 257 NLRB No. 129 (1981).

bargaining order, notwithstanding the absence of any evidence that the union had attained majority status.[219] Two other members stated that although "the Board's remedial authority . . . may well encompass the authority to issue a bargaining order in the absence of a prior showing of majority support,"[220] they declined to issue a bargaining order where the union had at no time obtained a showing of majority support. Although these latter members noted that the employer's unfair labor practices in *United Dairy Farmers* were indeed "outrageous" and "pervasive," they decided that a bargaining order would not "effectuate the policies of the Act" where there had been no showing of majority status at any point; they chose instead to focus on the use of the Board's "remedial authority to devise remedies, including extraordinary remedies."[221] The fifth member of the Board argued that, notwithstanding the Supreme Court's dicta in *Gissel*, the Board lacked authority to issue a bargaining order where the union had never commanded majority support.[222]

On review of *United Dairy Farmers*, the Third Circuit concluded that not only did the Board have authority to issue bargaining orders absent a majority in " 'exceptional' cases marked by 'outrageous' and pervasive unfair labor practices," the failure to recognize such authority "would undermine the underlying goal of the Act to further the majority preference of all employees." The court noted that "[u]nions which would have attained a majority in a free and uncoerced election if the employer had not committed unfair labor practices would be deprived of recognition merely because of the employer's illegal conduct." The court expressed concern that "the absence of such authority might create incentives for employers to engage in illegal prophylactic action with the purpose of preventing the attainment of a card majority."[223] The court remanded the case so that the

---

[219]*Id.* at 1032 (concurring and dissenting opinion of Chairman Fanning and Member Jenkins).

[220]*Id.* at 1027 (opinion of Members Murphy and Truesdale).

[221]*Id.* at 1028. They conceded that nonbargaining extraordinary remedies might not be sufficient to eradicate totally the effects of the unfair labor practices, but they would "tend to restore an atmosphere in which employees are given a meaningful opportunity to exercise their Section 7 rights in an election." *Id.* at 1028. One such "extraordinary remedy" imposed by the Board in a different case required the employer to reimburse the union for its organizing and litigation expenses. J. P. Stevens & Co., *supra* note 155. A bargaining order, though based on a card majority, did issue in that case. For a general discussion of the Board's remedial authority, *see* Chapter 33 *infra*.

[222]*Supra* note 218 at 1038 (concurring and dissenting opinion of Member Penello).

[223]633 F2d at 1068. The Court noted that "virtually every court that has discussed the issue has stated that a bargaining order may be issued in the absence of a card majority."

Board could make the prerequisite findings as to whether the employer's unfair labor practices embodied the critical elements which would warrant issuance of a bargaining order. On remand, the Board issued a bargaining order.

Subsequently, in *Conair Corp.*,[224] the Board, acting through a three-member majority, issued a bargaining order where the employer had committed "outrageous" and "pervasive" unfair labor practices and where the union had never achieved majority status. The Board concluded that the lingering effects of the employer's "massive and unrelenting" violations foreclosed any possibility of a fair election, for such conduct could not be dissipated by either traditional or milder extraordinary remedies.[225]

Even prior to *United Dairy* and *Conair*, however, the Board did not rigidly require an actual card majority, for it approved the use of a combination of authorization cards and secret ballots cast for the union as a basis for establishing a majority in *Pinter Brothers*,[226] where the union had lost the election by a vote of 18 to 14. The administrative law judge counted six nonvoting employees who had signed cards with the 14 who had voted for

---

See NLRB v. Armcor Indus., Inc., 535 F2d 239, 92 LRRM 2374 (CA 3, 1976) and Judge Rosenn's comments therein at 244. *See also* NLRB v. Garry Mfg. Co., 630 F2d 934, 105 LRRM 2113 (CA 3, 1980); Electrical Prods. Div. v. NLRB, 617 F2d 977, 103 LRRM 2908 (CA 3, 1980); Rapid Mfg. Co. v. NLRB, 612 F2d 144, 103 LRRM 2162 (CA 3, 1979); NLRB v. Daybreak Lodge Nursing & Convalescent Home, 585 F2d 79, 99 LRRM 2985 (CA 3, 1978); Struthers-Dunn, Inc. v. NLRB, 574 F2d 796, 98 LRRM 2385 (CA 3, 1978); NLRB v. Eagle Material Handling, Inc., 558 F2d 160, 95 LRRM 2934 (CA 3, 1977); Hedstrom Co. v. NLRB, 558 F2d 1137, 95 LRRM 3069 (CA 3, 1977); J. P. Stevens Co. v. NLRB, 441 F2d 514, 76 LRRM 2817 (CA 5, 1971), *cert. denied*, 404 US 830, 78 LRRM 2464 (1971); NLRB v. Montgomery Ward & Co., 554 F2d 996, 1002, 95 LRRM 2433 (CA 10, 1977); NLRB v. S. S. Logan Packing Co., 386 F2d 562, 66 LRRM 2596 (CA 4, 1967); *but cf.* NLRB v. Roney Plaza Apartments, 597 F2d 1046, 101 LRRM 2794 (CA 5, 1979). Following remand, *supra* note 218, the Board's issuance of a bargaining order was based on the committed views of Members Fanning and Jenkins and the vote of Member Zimmerman, who recognized the appeals court's decision as binding for that case only.

[224]261 NLRB No. 178, 110 LRRM 1161 (1982), with Members Fanning, Jenkins, and Zimmerman in the majority and Chairman Van de Water and Member Hunter in dissent.

[225]The employer's conduct consisted of holding a series of meetings at which employees were threatened with plant closure, discharge, and loss of benefits if they supported the union. The employer also promised certain new benefits, solicited grievances which it implied would be remedied, interrogated employees, and created an impression of surveillance. After two employees struck to protest those unfair labor practices, the employer threatened to discharge and in fact did discharge all the strikers. It also repeated many of the former threats and engaged in new unfair labor practices, including the granting of increased benefits to nonstrikers. Following the strike it discriminated among the strikers in its reinstatement policy; and shortly before the election it committed further unfair labor practices, including threatening to move the plant to Hong Kong if the union won the election.

[226]227 NLRB 921, 94 LRRM 1284 (1977).

the union, and concluded that the union represented 20 of the 39 unit employees on the date of the election. The Board upheld the ALJ's computation, declaring that the combination of cards and ballots constituted "valid expressions of employee sentiment."[227]

In a related proceeding, the Second Circuit held that in *Gissel* cases a Board regional director may, under Section 10(j) of the Act, seek preliminary injunctive relief to require an employer to bargain pending a final determination by the Board concerning the union's status as bargaining representative.[228]

IV. BARGAINING OBLIGATION ESTABLISHED BY EMPLOYER CARD CHECKS, POLLS, AND OTHER INDEPENDENT MEANS

In *Gissel,* the Supreme Court expressly reserved decision as to the following questions:

> [W]hether, absent election interference by an employer's unfair labor practices, he may obtain an election only if he petitions for one himself; whether, if he does not, he must bargain with a card majority if the union chooses not to seek an election; and whether, in the latter situation, he is bound by the Board's ultimate determination of the card results regardless of his earlier good faith doubts, or whether he can still insist on a Union-sought election if he makes an affirmative showing of his positive reasons for believing there is a representation dispute.[229]

In *Linden Lumber,*[230] the Court answered those questions.

The union in *Linden Lumber* had demanded recognition based on a card majority. The employer refused, and, at its suggestion, the union petitioned the Board for an election. The union withdrew the petition when the employer refused to enter into a consent-election agreement or be bound by the results of an election because supervisors had improperly assisted the union's

---

[227]*Id.* at 922. Member Walther dissented, contending that since the Board had set aside the election, the tally of ballots, including those cast for the union, should also have been set aside. *Id.* at 923.

[228]Seeler v. Trading Port, Inc., 517 F2d 33, 89 LRRM 2513 (CA 2, 1975). *See also* Levine v. C & W Mining Co., 610 F2d 432, 102 LRRM 3093 (CA 6, 1979). District courts, both in the Second Circuit and elsewhere, had previously refused to grant such relief in situations involving a union's initial organizing attempts. Boire v. Pilot Freight Carriers, Inc., 86 LRRM 2976 (1974), *aff'd,* 515 F2d 1185, 89 LRRM 2908 (CA 5, 1975). Fuchs v. Steel-Fab, Inc., 356 F Supp 385, 83 LRRM 2635 (1973); Kaynard v. Lawrence Rigging, Inc., 80 LRRM 2600 (1972). For discussion of injunctions under §10(j), *see* Chapter 33 *infra* at notes 25-76.

[229]*Supra* note 11 at 601 n.18.

[230]Linden Lumber Div. v. NLRB, 419 US 301, 87 LRRM 3236 (1974).

organizing campaign. Having withdrawn its petition for an election, the union again demanded recognition and struck for recognition when the employer again refused to extend voluntary recognition. The union then filed an unfair labor practice charge alleging that Linden had unlawfully refused to bargain. There was no allegation of any other unfair labor practice.

The Board held that the employer "should not be found guilty of a violation of Section 8(a)(5) solely upon the basis of [its] refusal to accept evidence of majority status other than the results of a board election"[231] and that the employer should not be required to petition the Board for an election if it has not committed any unfair labor practices. The District of Columbia Circuit reversed, however, stating that while recognitional strikes, "ambiguous utterances of the employer," and signed cards do not necessarily constitute "convincing evidence of majority support" which would compel issuance of a bargaining order, they do give rise to "a sufficient probability of majority support as to require an employer asserting a doubt of majority status to resolve the possibility through a petition for an election . . . ."[232]

The Supreme Court observed that, in the Board's view, a union faced with an "unwilling employer" had two options: "It can file for an election; or it can press unfair labor practices against the employer under *Gissel.*"[233] Noting that the election process is typically much less time-consuming and thus more desirable "[i]n terms of getting on with the problems of inaugurating regimes of industrial peace," the Court stated that "[t]he question remains—should the burden be on the union to ask for an election or should it be the responsibility of the employer?"[234]

Stating that its problem was "not one of picking favorites but of trying to find the congressional purpose by examining the statutory and administrative interpretations that squint one way or another,"[235] a majority of the Court concluded that it could "not say that the Board's decision that the union should go forward and ask for an election on the employer's refusal to recognize the authorization cards was arbitrary and capricious

[231]Linden Lumber Div., 190 NLRB 718, 721, 77 LRRM 1305 (1971).
[232]Linden Lumber, *sub nom.* Teamsters Local 413 v. NLRB, 487 F2d 1099, 1111, 84 LRRM 2177, 2186 (CA DC, 1973).
[233]Linden Lumber, *supra* note 230 at 306.
[234]*Id.* at 307.
[235]*Id.* at 308.

or an abuse of discretion."[236] The Court commented that there was no suggestion that Congress, in enacting Section 9(c)(1)(B), "wanted to place the burden of getting a secret election on the employer."[237] Justice Douglas authored the majority opinion and Justices Stewart, White, Marshall, and Powell dissented.[238]

As a result of *Linden,* an employer who has not committed unfair labor practices cannot be required to bargain with a union absent an election, provided it does not agree to be bound by the results of some other method of ascertaining majority status.[239] Noting the Board's conclusion that the parties in *Linden* had "never voluntarily agreed upon any mutually acceptable and legally permissible means, other than a Board-conducted election, for resolving the issue of union majority status,"[240] the Court nevertheless declined comment on what result would obtain "if the employer breaches its agreement to permit majority status to be determined by means other than a Board election."[241]

Board decisional law mandates, however, that where the employer unilaterally attempts to determine majority status by means other than a Board election, for example, by interrogating or otherwise polling employees, it cannot lawfully disavow the results.[242] But in order for this latter rule to apply, the union's demand for recognition must precede the employer's inquiry into the union's majority status. The Board reached this result by reasoning that it is only *after* the union demands recognition that the employer must select the means by which it will verify a union's claim of majority status.[243] Thus, interrogations occurring before the demand for recognition, which were not completed and which therefore failed to establish a

---

[236]*Id.* at 309-10.
[237]*Id.* at 307.
[238]*Id.* at 310.
[239]*See, e.g.,* Service Employees Local 250 v. NLRB, 600 F2d 930, 101 LRRM 2004 (CA DC, 1979).
[240]*Supra* note 230 at 310 n.10.
[241]*Id.*
[242]Sullivan Elec. Co., 199 NLRB 809, 81 LRRM 1313 (1972). *Accord,* NLRB v. Gogin, 575 F2d 596, 98 LRRM 2250 (CA 7, 1978); Jerr-Dan Corp., 237 NLRB 302, 98 LRRM 1569 (1978), *enforced,* 601 F2d 575, 103 LRRM 2603 (CA 3, 1979); Idaho Pac. Steel Warehouse Co., 227 NLRB 326, 94 LRRM 1135 (1976); E. S. Merriman & Sons, 219 NLRB 972, 90 LRRM 1161 (1975) (interrogation); Rockwell Int'l Corp., 200 NLRB 1262, 90 LRRM 1481 (1975) (third-party card check); Snow & Sons, *supra* note 36; Taylor-Roe Mfg. Corp., 205 NLRB 262, 84 LRRM 1017 (1973), *enforced,* 493 F2d 1398, 86 LRRM 2152 (CA 2, 1974) ("handcount" poll); Nation-Wide Plastics Co., 197 NLRB 996, 81 LRRM 1036 (1972) (secret-ballot poll); Summersville Indus. Equip. Co., 197 NLRB 731, 80 LRRM 1664 (1972).
[243]Tennessee Shell Co., *supra* note 182.

union majority, did not waive the employer's right to a Board election to ascertain the employees' sentiments regarding the union.[244]

In *Struksnes Construction Co.*[245] the Board stated that polling employees is a violation of Section 8(a)(1) unless "1) the purpose of the poll is to determine the truth of a union's claim of majority, 2) this purpose is communicated to the employees, 3) assurances against reprisal are given, 4) the employees are polled by secret ballot, and 5) the employer has not engaged in unfair labor practices or otherwise created a coercive atmosphere."[246]

Although the necessity of adhering to the "safe harbor" of the *Struksnes* standards might be questioned in light of *Linden Lumber,*[247] those standards continue to be applied to employer polls to determine union sentiments.[248] But even a poll that failed to satisfy *Struksnes* standards was upheld by the Board where a union majority was thereby established.[249] The Board reasoned in that case that since the employees had openly indicated their union sentiments and invited the employer to verify them, the employer did not coerce them by acceding to their request.[250] Since the employer's poll merely verified what the employees had already told him, the Board found no interference.[251]

In a number of cases, the conditions under which a poll satisfying *Struksnes* standards should be allowed have been reexamined. Even where polls have been conducted with procedural

---

[244]*Id.* The Eighth Circuit has refused to enforce a bargaining order predicated upon the results of a card check where the list used to establish the union's majority included employees who were not part of the appropriate unit. Harding Glass Indus., Inc. v. NLRB, 533 F2d 1065, 92 LRRM 2147 (CA 8, 1976).

[245]165 NLRB 1062, 65 LRRM 1385 (1967). *See* Chapter 6 *supra* at notes 284-93.

[246]*Id.* at 1063. The Board further held that §8(a)(1) is violated when the poll is taken after the filing of an election petition.

[247]*Supra* note 230.

[248]Liberty Nursing Homes, Inc., 245 NLRB 1194, 102 LRRM 1517 (1979); B & L Plumbing, 243 NLRB 1016, 101 LRRM 1616 (1979); World-Wide Press, Inc., *supra* note 94; Baptist Memorial Hosp., 229 NLRB 45, 95 LRRM 1043 (1977); Burns Int'l Security Servs., 225 NLRB 271, 92 LRRM 1439 (1976), *enforcement denied,* 567 F2d 945, 97 LRRM 2350 (CA 10, 1977); B. C. Hawk Chevrolet, Inc., 226 NLRB 527, 93 LRRM 1304 (1976).

[249]Bushnell's Kitchens, 222 NLRB 110, 91 LRRM 1113 (1976). *See* Chapter 6 *supra* at note 292.

[250]*Id.*

[251]Jerome J. Jacomet, 222 NLRB 899, 91 LRRM 1370 (1976) (Members Fanning and Jenkins dissented). *See* Chapter 6 *supra* at note 292. *Cf.* Mid-Continent Refrigerated Serv. Co., 228 NLRB 917, 94 LRRM 1733 (1977) (comments of ALJ not adopted by the Board).

regularity under *Struksnes,* a poll may be deemed unlawful if its purpose is to gauge union strength rather than determine a union's claim of majority.[252] A poll will also be held unlawful if it is conducted in a coercive atmosphere.[253] Such an atmosphere was held to exist where a company service manager was present shortly before an employee vote was taken and a receptionist took notes during the meeting.[254]

One employer was ordered to bargain because it had questioned employees as to whether they had signed cards and thereafter discharged the entire proposed unit.[255] However, all inquiries into whether unit employees have signed cards are not unlawful. Where such inquiries were used to prepare the employer's defense before the Board, where participation was voluntary, and where the employer refused a demand for recognition based on cards, a questionnaire asking all employees whether they had signed cards was found lawful.[256] In another case, the Tenth Circuit, reversing the Board, held that an employer acted lawfully in acquiring employees' written opinions about the union, for the employer had received a letter from the regional director stating that it had only 48 hours in which to submit additional evidence in support of its petition.[257]

Other informal means of inquiring into a union's majority may also result in imposition of a bargaining order. Thus, an employer was deemed to have recognized a union when, after examining signed authorization cards, he stated, "You got them all."[258] The same result was reached where a union representative brought a majority of the unit's nonsupervisory employees, all wearing union buttons, into the employer's office, thereby convincing him of the union's majority.[259] The employer was

---

[252]Clothing Workers (AMF, Inc.) v. NLRB, 564 F2d 434, 95 LRRM 2821 (CA DC, 1977).

[253]NLRB v. B. C. Hawk Chevrolet, Inc., 582 F2d 591, 99 LRRM 3173 (CA 9, 1978), *enforcing* 226 NLRB 527, 93 LRRM 1304 (1976). *See also* Perko's, Inc., 236 NLRB 884, 99 LRRM 1397 (1978); Mattiace Petrochemical Co., 239 NLRB 15, 99 LRRM 1476 (1978).

[254]B. C. Hawk Chevrolet, *supra* note 253.

[255]R & H Diesel & Trailer Serv., *supra* note 119.

[256]Osco Drug, Inc., 237 NLRB 231, 99 LRRM 1150 (1978).

[257]Burns Int'l Security Servs. v. NLRB, 567 F2d 945, 97 LRRM 2350 (CA 10, 1977). *See also* NLRB v. Intertherm, Inc., 596 F2d 267, 100 LRRM 3016 (CA 8, 1979) (unlawful polling and interrogation cured by effective rescission and neutralizing statement).

[258]Jerr-Dan Corp., *supra* note 242. *See also* Brown & Connolly, Inc., 237 NLRB 271, 98 LRRM 1572 (1978), *enforced,* 593 F2d 1373, 100 LRRM 3072 (CA 1, 1979).

[259]Brown & Connolly, Inc., *supra* note 258. *See also* Lyon & Ryan Ford, 246 NLRB 1, 102 LRRM 1448 (1979).

not allowed to withdraw that expression of "recognition" one week later. The Board has consistently held that once recognition is voluntarily granted, it may not be withdrawn until a reasonable time for bargaining to take place has expired.[260]

V. AFFIRMATIVE DEFENSES TO THE BARGAINING OBLIGATION

A. Timing of the Demand

It is not necessary that a union actually possess a card majority when it demands recognition. Accordingly, where a majority of unit employees signed cards and sent them to the union, the fact that the union did not actually have the cards in its possession when the employer refused the union's demand was deemed irrelevant.[261]

In addition, the Board has invoked a "continuing demand" concept to include cards which are dated after the union's demand for recognition. In *Brown Group, Inc.*[262] the union demanded recognition by letter dated February 12. Although the union did not enjoy majority status at the time, its letter stated that the demand should be considered "continuing"; and the union did achieve majority status three days later. In issuing a *Gissel* bargaining order in response to various unfair labor practices which the employer had committed in the interim, the Board concluded that the employer had unlawfully refused to bargain as of February 15. Similarly, when a union demanded recognition on September 20 but did not attain majority status until October 1, the Board's *Gissel* bargaining order was based on the employer's refusal to bargain as of the latter date.[263] The "continuing demand" theory was also invoked in a case where the Board concluded that it would have been futile for the union to make another demand after receiving more cards, when the employer had previously ignored the union's written demand for recognition.[264]

---

[260]Jerr-Dan Corp., *supra* note 242; Brown & Connolly, *supra* note 258. *See also* Phelps Cement Prods., Inc., 257 NLRB No. 4, 107 LRRM 1474 (1981).
[261]NLRB v. Tower Records, 79 LRRM 2736 (CA 9, 1972).
[262]223 NLRB 1409, 92 LRRM 1297 (1976).
[263]Schwab Foods, Inc., 223 NLRB 394, 92 LRRM 1285 (1976).
[264]Area Disposal, Inc., 200 NLRB 350, 82 LRRM 1173 (1972). *See also* J. P. Stevens, *supra* note 212.

The "continuing demand" theory has met judicial resistance in the Third Circuit. In *Hedstrom v. NLRB*[265] that circuit disagreed with the Board's finding that the employer unlawfully refused to bargain with a union that lacked majority support at the time it demanded recognition, where the union had failed to notify the employer after it had subsequently obtained a card majority. The court rejected the concept of "continuing demand," observing that if it were adopted, the employer might be forced to violate Section 8(a)(2) by recognizing a minority union. The "continuing demand" theory would thus "force an employer to tread the fine line between 8(a)(2) and 8(a)(5)."[266]

B. Lack of Majority Status

1. In General. Lack of majority status may be a defense to the bargaining obligation. For example, in *Grismac Corp.*,[267] the union obtained signed cards from 43 of the unit's 83 employees. Two of the cards, however, were executed by employees who had been lawfully terminated prior to the union's demand for recognition. Thus, despite the employer's extensive unfair labor practices, the Board refused to issue a bargaining order because the 41 valid cards did not constitute a majority of the unit.[268]

In cases involving unlawful employer interference, majority status need not be maintained until the date of the scheduled election if the union had a valid card majority when it demanded recognition.[269] Where there has been no unlawful employer interference, however, no bargaining order will issue if the union loses its majority.[270] In cases where majority status is a prerequisite to the issuance of a bargaining order, proof of such majority status must clearly appear from the record before a bargaining order will be deemed appropriate.[271]

---

[265]558 F2d 1137, 95 LRRM 3069 (CA 3, 1977).
[266]*Id. See generally* Chapter 8 *supra.*
[267]Grismac Corp., *supra* note 176.
[268]*Id. See also* Honolulu Sporting Goods Co., Ltd., 239 NLRB 1277, 100 LRRM 1172 (1979). Other cases in which the Board has refused to issue bargaining orders absent a showing that the union had ever achieved majority status include: Triana Indus., Inc., 245 NLRB 1258, 102 LRRM 1323 (1979); Woonsocket Health Center, 245 NLRB 652, 102 LRRM 1494 (1979); Daniel Constr. Co., 244 NLRB 704, 102 LRRM 1399 (1979); Haddon House Food Prods., Inc., 242 NLRB 1057, 101 LRRM 1294 (1979); Miami Springs Properties, 245 NLRB 278, 102 LRRM 1556 (1979).
[269]Peerless, Inc., *supra* note 192.
[270]Harper & Row Publishers, *supra* note 193.
[271]Fort Smith Outerwear, *supra* note 196; Georgetown Dress Corp., *supra* note 176; Fuqua Homes Mo., *supra* note 176.

In *Business Envelope Manufacturers*[272] the Board was confronted with conflicting presumptions of majority status. The incumbent union was enjoying the presumption of continuing majority status at a time when a rival union had a card majority. Notwithstanding the employer's commission of "egregious and coercive conduct" in violation of Sections 8(a)(1) and (2), the Board refused to order the employer to bargain with the rival union.[273] It concluded that the conflicting presumptions of majority status cancelled each other; therefore a second election should be held.[274]

As noted earlier, the union's majority status need not be evidenced by signed cards alone, for in *Pinter Brothers*[275] the Board issued a bargaining order even though the union had never possessed a card majority; majority status was established by adding signed cards of nonvoters to union votes in an election that had been set aside.

In *Struthers-Dunn, Inc.*[276] the Board rejected the employer's argument that since the union lost its majority status through employee-card revocations prior to the commission of any unfair labor practices, a bargaining order could not issue. The revocations were deemed ineffective because the union had not been informed of them before it demanded recognition. However, the Third Circuit denied enforcement, finding that the revocations were effective and were not made in response to conduct by the employer that "in some way undermined union majority strength."[277] But since the first election had been set aside for valid objections, after remand the Board ordered a new election without requiring a fresh showing of interest.[278]

2. Invalid Authorization. *a. In General.* An employer may attack the validity of authorization cards on several grounds: (1) The employer may argue that the cards upon which the union relies to establish its majority status were revoked prior to the union's demand for recognition.[279] But the Board will not

---

[272]227 NLRB 280, 94 LRRM 1351 (1976).
[273]*Id.*
[274]*Id.*
[275]Pinter Bros., *supra* note 226.
[276]228 NLRB 49, 95 LRRM 1204 (1977), *enforcement denied,* 574 F2d 796, 98 LRRM 2385 (CA 3, 1978).
[277]*Id.*
[278]237 NLRB 302, 97 LRRM 1522 (1978).
[279]Reilly Tar & Chem. Corp. v. NLRB, 352 F2d 913, 60 LRRM 2437 (CA 7, 1965); J. P. Stevens Co., *supra* note 212; TMT Trailer Ferry, Inc., 152 NLRB 1495, 59 LRRM

accept this argument if the revocations are the product of the employer's unfair labor practices.[280] (2) The employer might concede that a majority of his employees had signed cards, but argue that the cards are invalid because they were obtained in reliance on solicitors' misrepresentations.[281] (3) The employer might also assert that the cards were forged.[282]

In *Englewood Lumber Co.*[283] the Board held that cards would not be counted towards a union's majority if they were signed in response to solicitors' pleas that the signatures were needed for the Board to conduct a secret-ballot election. Thus, cards bearing the bold-type inscription "I WANT AN NLRB ELECTION" were invalidated where the employees had been told that the cards were not binding.[284] Two years later, however, the Board reversed itself. In *Cumberland Shoe Corp.*[285] the Board stated that it would count cards towards a union majority even if the employees were told that they would be used to obtain an election, so long as the cards clearly designated the union as the signer's bargaining representative. Thus, cards that stated in bold type "I WANT AN ELECTION NOW" were counted towards the union's majority status. Under the *Cumberland Shoe* doctrine, if the card clearly designates the union as the signer's bargaining representative, it will be invalidated for misrepresentation only if the signer is told the card's *only* purpose is to obtain a secret-ballot election.[286] Thus, under this rule, cards

---

1353 (1965). *See also* Struthers-Dunn, *supra* note 276 (cards revoked prior to the commission of any unfair labor practices not counted towards the majority necessary to support a bargaining order).

[280]Quality Mkts., Inc., 160 NLRB 44, 62 LRRM 1582 (1966); Abrasive Salvage Co., 127 NLRB 381, 46 LRRM 1033 (1960).

[281]*See, e.g.,* NLRB v. Roney Plaza Apartments, 597 F2d 1046, 101 LRRM 2794 (CA 5, 1979); Eckerd's Mkt., Inc., 183 NLRB 337, 74 LRRM 1319 (1970); Levi Strauss & Co., 172 NLRB 732, 68 LRRM 1338 (1968), *enforced,* 441 F2d 1027, 76 LRRM 2033 (CA DC, 1970).

[282]Imco Container Co., 148 NLRB 312, 56 LRRM 1497 (1964). *See* W. B. Johnson Properties, Inc., 241 NLRB 358, 100 LRRM 1547 (1979) (card signed by solicitor on behalf of employee held invalid where employee did not give permission). *But see* J. P. Stevens, *supra* note 212 (card signed by solicitor counted as that of employee who told the solicitor, "If you want it signed, sign it yourself," where the employee subsequently gave the solicitor his telephone and post office box numbers).

[283]130 NLRB 394, 47 LRRM 1304 (1961).

[284]Morris & Assoc., Inc., 138 NLRB 1160, 51 LRRM 1183 (1962).

[285]Cumberland Shoe, *supra* note 72 and accompanying text.

[286]In the following cases, the Board found no merit in employers' contentions that the employees signed cards in reliance upon solicitors' representations that they were to be used solely to procure an election. *See, e.g.,* Pedro's Restaurant, 246 NLRB 567, 102 LRRM 1600 (1979); Motor Inn of Perrysburg, Inc., 243 NLRB 280, 101 LRRM 1526 (1979); Janesville Prods. Div., Amtel, Inc., 240 NLRB 854, 100 LRRM 1383 (1979); Midland-Ross Corp., *supra* note 139. *See also* Levi Strauss & Co., *supra* note 281; Winn-

stating "For Election Only" will not be counted.[287] As previously noted, the Supreme Court expressly approved the *Cumberland* rule in the *Gissel* case.

In applying this rule, the determinative factor is what the employee was *told*, either orally or in writing, when he or she signed the card, *not* what the employee *believed* the significance of the card to be. As previously noted, courts have agreed with the Board as to their "dim view of post-event testimony of subjective understanding."[288] Thus, although employees may believe that cards will be used only to obtain a secret-ballot election, the Board will nevertheless count them towards the union's majority unless the employees were actually *solicited* on that basis. If the card unequivocally states that the union is the signer's bargaining representative, the card will be invalidated only if the solicitor represented that the card would be used for a different, more limited purpose.[289] But even then, a misrepresentation will be disregarded if the employee clearly did not rely on it in signing the card.[290]

b. *Nature of the Card.* As the above analysis suggests, critical inquiry focuses on whether the cards are ambiguous, not whether

---

Dixie Stores, Inc., 166 NLRB 227, 65 LRRM 1637 (1967); American Cable Sys., 161 NLRB 332, 63 LRRM 1296 (1966), *enforced in part and remanded in part,* 414 F2d 661, 71 LRRM 2797 (CA 5, 1969), *on remand,* 179 NLRB 846, 72 LRRM 1524 (1969), *remanded,* 427 F2d 446, 73 LRRM 2913 (CA 5, 1970), *cert. denied,* 400 US 957, 75 LRRM 2810 (1970); Happach v. NLRB, 353 F2d 629, 60 LRRM 2489 (CA 7, 1965); Aero Corp., 149 NLRB 1283, 57 LRRM 1483 (1964), *enforced,* 363 F2d 902, 62 LRRM 2361 (CA DC), *cert. denied,* 385 US 973, 63 LRRM 2527 (1966). *But see* S. E. Nichols Co., *supra* note 10; Engineers & Fabricators, *supra* note 10.

[287]Bannon Mills, Inc., 146 NLRB 611, 55 LRRM 1370 (1964). But authorization of employees who concede in response to leading questions, on cross-examination, that they were told the cards were to be used only for an election are not thereby invalidated. American Cable Sys., *supra* note 286; General Steel Prods., Inc., 157 NLRB 636, 61 LRRM 1417 (1966). A card will not be counted if it was presented with a handbill describing the card as "only your request" for an election. NLRB Gen. Counsel Quarterly Report on Case Developments, Release No. R-1007 (April 26, 1965).

[288]NLRB v. Freeport Marble & Tile Co., 367 F2d 371, 63 LRRM 2289 (CA 1, 1966). *Cf.* Colson Corp., *supra* note 25; Winn-Dixie Stores, Inc., 341 F2d 750, 58 LRRM 2475 (CA 6, 1965), *cert. denied,* 382 US 830, 60 LRRM 2234 (1965); Joy Silk Mills, *supra* note 8.

[289]NLRB v. Gissel Packing Co., *supra* note 11. "This must be done on the basis of what the employees were told, not on the basis of their subjective state of mind when they signed the cards." Aero Corp., *supra* note 286. *Cf.* NLRB v. Sehon Stevenson & Co., 286 F2d 551, 66 LRRM 2603 (1967) (the court enforced an NLRB bargaining order where the employer's own investigation confirmed the union's claim of majority status). *See also* Keystone Pretzel Bakery, 242 NLRB 492, 101 LRRM 1214 (1979); Carlton's Mkt., 243 NLRB 837, 102 LRRM 1159 (1979). "[S]cuttlebutt" of a co-worker, who was not a union activist, that the purpose of the card was "to bring an election in the plant," did not invalidate an authorization card. J. P. Stevens, *supra* note 212.

[290]Engineers and Fabricators, *supra* note 10.

they are single-purpose or multipurpose. Thus, in *Area Disposal, Inc.*,[291] the Board counted unambiguous cards where employees had been told that the "principal purpose" of the cards was to obtain an election. In *Colonial Lincoln Mercury Sales, Inc.*[292] the Board counted unambiguous authorizations signed by employees who allegedly believed they were only for the purpose of obtaining a union meeting. In *Unarco Industries, Inc.*[293] unambiguous cards were counted where employees had been told that the union needed "so many more cards before they could go ahead and get an election."

The *Cumberland* rule has also been applied where the employees involved were unable to speak or understand English. Thus, in *Sans Souci Restaurant*,[294] cards which clearly designated the union as collective bargaining representative in English were deemed valid even when signed by Spanish-speaking employees who neither spoke nor understood English. In reaching this result, the Board found it significant that the cards had been solicited by fellow employees who could explain their meaning; also, the cards were accompanied by a pamphlet which clearly explained, in English and Spanish, the purposes to which the signed cards might be put. Similarly, in *El Rancho Market*,[295] a card printed in English but signed by a Spanish-speaking employee was deemed valid because there was no evidence either that he was "told that the card was solely for an election" or that his "command of English was so limited that he could not comprehend the meaning of the card."[296]

   c. Misrepresentations. An employer must show evidence of clearly material misrepresentations in order to invalidate unambiguous

---

[291]Area Disposal, *supra* note 264.
[292]197 NLRB 54, 80 LRRM 1842 (1972), *enforced,* 485 F2d 455, 84 LRRM 2528 (CA 5, 1973).
[293]197 NLRB 489, 80 LRRM 1621 (1972).
[294]235 NLRB 604, 98 LRRM 1134 (1978).
[295]235 NLRB 468, 98 LRRM 1153 (1978).
[296]*Id.* The ALJ in Maximum Precision Metal Prod., 236 NLRB 1417, 98 LRRM 1434 (1978), took the opposite approach. He rejected cards printed in English but signed by Spanish-speaking employees "in the absence of any other evidence" that they understood what they were signing. The Board's disposition of the case made it unnecessary to review this conclusion. *See also* Jasta Mfg. Co., *supra* note 85 (card of employee who could not read held valid where her sister, who neither read nor explained the card to her, helped her fill it out); W. B. Johnson Properties, Inc., *supra* note 282 (card of elderly employee who could neither read nor write held valid when signed by daughter with her permission). *But see* J. P. Stevens, *supra* note 212 (card of employee who, having continuing misgivings about signing a card, allowed her daughter to execute one for her held invalid upon subsequent attempt to revoke).

authorization cards. Evidence that card signers were told the cards would be used to petition for an election, to show interest in the union, and to get a representative to come to talk to employees about the union, has been held insufficient to invalidate such cards.[297] If, however, an employer can show that the employees were told that the *sole* purpose of the cards was to obtain an election, even clear and unambiguous cards will be deemed invalid for determining the union's majority status.[298] Thus, in *Bookland, Inc.,*[299] the Board invalidated a card where the employee was told that it was solicited solely to enable the union to keep in touch with the employees and it did not mean that the employee wanted a union. In reliance upon this misrepresentation, the employee signed the card without reading it.

In applying this *Cumberland* standard, cards have been held valid for the purpose of establishing majority status where employees were told that cards would be used for an election if the employer refused to recognize the union,[300] where every employee in the unit had signed a card but only one testified that solicitation was on the basis that the cards would be used solely to obtain an election,[301] and where the employee was told that "it was not binding" and that she could "have the card back at any time."[302] Cards were also deemed valid for recognitional purposes where the union agent falsely stated that "everyone else already signed" and there was testimony that the card would not have been signed but for this misrepresentation.[303] And negligent or erroneous statements concerning union welfare

---

[297]Peerless, Inc., *supra* note 192; NLRB v. WKRG-TV, Inc., 470 F2d 1302, 82 LRRM 2146 (CA 5, 1973); Bookland, Inc., 221 NLRB 35, 90 LRRM 1492 (1975).

[298]Fort Smith Outerwear, *supra* note 196; W & W Tool & Die Mfg. Co., 225 NLRB 1000, 93 LRRM 1006 (1976); Walgreen Co., 221 NLRB 1096, 91 LRRM 1177 (1975).

[299]Bookland, Inc., *supra* note 297.

[300]Jimmy Dean Meat Co., 227 NLRB 1012, 95 LRRM 1235 (1977).

[301]Randall P. Kane, Inc., 230 NLRB 355, 95 LRRM 1443 (1977); The Holding Co., 231 NLRB 383, 96 LRRM 1259 (1977).

[302]Smithtown Nursing Home, 228 NLRB 23, 94 LRRM 1699 (1977). But a card was invalidated where, in response to an employee's inquiry, the solicitor replied that a signed card was not synonymous with a binding vote for the union. J. P. Stevens, *supra* note 212.

[303]Roney Plaza Apartments, *supra* note 281. A contrary result was reached by the Fifth Circuit in Medline Indus., *supra* note 139; W. B. Johnson Properties, *supra* note 282. *But see* Kermit Super Valu, *supra* note 130, where the Board upheld the validity of cards despite allegations that, in addition to advising the employees that the union's contracts with other employers contained union-shop clauses which required all employees to join the union or risk losing their jobs, the union organizer told the employees that the store was going to be organized and that the employees had better sign the cards if they wanted to save their jobs.

534 THE DEVELOPING LABOR LAW CH. 12

benefits that allegedly induced employees to sign were not sufficient to invalidate the cards.[304]

In passing upon card validity, the fact that no employee has testified that he wished to revoke his card may be a consideration.[305] However, an employee's later attempt to withdraw his card or his regret in signing a card does not necessarily invalidate it.[306]

Cards signed by employees of a predecessor company have been deemed valid designations of the union as the bargaining representative of the successor employer's employees.[307] Similarly, the merger of other unions with the union which solicited the cards neither voids the cards nor undermines the union's majority status, especially where the employer's unfair labor practices prevented the card signers from becoming union members eligible to vote in the merger election.[308]

    d. *Coercion and Related Interference.* In *NLRB* v. *Savair Manufacturing Co.,*[309] the Supreme Court held that a union's offer to waive initiation fees for those employees who signed authorization cards prior to an election constituted election interference and grounds for setting aside the election. The Court stated that this practice "allows the union to buy endorsements and paint a false portrait of employee support during its election campaign."[310] Although the Court was primarily concerned with the coercive effect of artificially inflated union support on uncommitted employees in the preelection period, it also expressed concern about and disapproval of the use of authorization cards thus obtained as proof of majority status to support a *Gissel* bargaining order. But authorization cards obtained in response to a waiver of initiation fees that are not contingent upon support for the union and which are available to all eligible voters before and after the election are valid.[311]

---

[304]Matouk Indus., Inc., 230 NLRB 892, 96 LRRM 1013 (1977).
[305]Florsheim Shoe Store Co. v. NLRB, 565 F2d 1240, 96 LRRM 3273 (CA 2, 1977).
[306]Federal Alarm, 230 NLRB 518, 96 LRRM 1141 (1977); Emco Steel, Inc., 227 NLRB 989, 94 LRRM 1747 (1977), *enforced,* 95 LRRM 3011 (CA 2, 1977) (unpublished). *But see* J. P. Stevens, *supra* note 212.
[307]Unit Train Coal Sales, Inc., 234 NLRB 1265, 98 LRRM 1343 (1978). *See also* W. B. Johnson Properties, *supra* note 282.
[308]Goodfriend Western Corp., 232 NLRB 527, 97 LRRM 1074 (1977). *See also* Pedro's Restaurant, *supra* note 286.
[309]414 US 270, 84 LRRM 2929 (1973). For detailed discussion of *Savair, see* Chapter 9 *supra* at notes 136-50.
[310]*Id.* at 277.
[311]NLRB v. Gunton Co., 596 F2d 175, 101 LRRM 2181 (CA 6, 1979); NLRB v.

The union has the burden of clarifying ambiguities in an offer to waive initiation fees.[312] Thus, where the Board found that the union's statement that its "initiation fee would be waived for all present employees who make application for charter membership" was susceptible of various, including illegal, constructions, the offer was held unlawful.[313] Similarly, an election was set aside because the union's statement, that "there will be no initiation fee for anyone joining now during this campaign," could have been interpreted as being conditioned upon the employee's committing himself to the union before the election.[314]

Various other union campaign statements regarding initiation fees have been litigated. The Board noted that a statement that initiation fees and dues would definitely increase after the election would be objectionable.[315] However, it was not objectionable to state that fees and dues might increase, if a majority of the union membership so voted, because of litigation expenses incurred during the campaign.[316] And a statement that the union will waive retroactive dues obligations of employees who join the union prior to the election is not deemed objectionable, because it merely informs employees who join the union prior to the election that they will not be in worse condition financially than those who join after the election.[317]

e. Supervisory Interference. Supervisory involvement in a union's organizational campaign is not necessarily impermissible and is not a *per se* basis for overturning a union's card majority. However, extensive or serious supervisory interference is prohibited;

Wabash Transformer Corp., 509 F2d 647, 88 LRRM 2545 (CA 8, 1975), *cert. denied,* 423 US 827, 90 LRRM 2553 (1975); NLRB v. Con-Pac, Inc., 509 F2d 270, 88 LRRM 2977 (CA 5, 1974); NLRB v. Dunkirk Motor Inn, 524 F2d 663, 90 LRRM 2961 (CA 2, 1975); Evans Rotork, Inc., 242 NLRB No. 176, 101 LRRM 1333 (1979); Endless Mold, Inc., 210 NLRB 159, 86 LRRM 1033 (1974).

[312]Coleman Co., 212 NLRB 927, 87 LRRM 1004 (1974). *See also* GTE Lenkurt, Inc., 215 NLRB 321, 88 LRRM 1409 (1974); Inland Shoe Mfg. Co., 211 NLRB 724, 86 LRRM 1498 (1974).

[313]Coleman Co., *supra* note 312.

[314]Crane Co., 225 NLRB 657, 93 LRRM 1181 (1976). *See* Falcon Coal Co. v. NLRB, 527 F2d 570, 91 LRRM 3056 (CA 6, 1975) (election petition dismissed where cards were solicited in violation of *Savair*), and Serv-U-Stores, *supra* note 131 (cards not counted where it was not clear whether card solicitors offered to waive fees). *See also* Ralston Purina Co., 243 NLRB 165, 101 LRRM 1382 (1979), where the Board held that, despite the absence of a timely formal objection by the employer, adherence to *Savair* should be considered if the facts uncovered in a regional director's post-election investigation disclosed a possible violation.

[315]Triple A Mach. Shop, Inc., 235 NLRB 208, 97 LRRM 1551 (1978).

[316]*Id.*

[317]*Id.*

thus, cards solicited directly by supervisors from rank-and-file employees will normally be invalidated. The Board and the reviewing courts seem to have taken a pragmatic approach, whereby the totality of the supervisor's conduct is evaluated in each case.[318]

Limited supervisory involvement may be deemed insufficient to impair employee free choice. For example, cards were not invalidated where a supervisor merely signed a card himself, on his own behalf, attended union meetings, and brought a co-worker's signed card to a union representative.[319] The same result has obtained where a supervisor's union activity was limited to answering employees' questions, making authorization cards available to employees, and delivering signed cards to the union.[320]

The presence of management personnel while cards are being signed has also been considered insufficient basis for the invalidation of the cards.[321] Thus, supervisory participation in an initial union meeting did not invalidate cards signed at a later meeting which the supervisor did not attend; the supervisor's request that the employees keep his presence confidential communicated to the employees management's opposition to the union.[322] Similarly, cards signed in the presence of a supervisor were deemed valid where the card signers thought he was a rank-and-file employee.[323]

An example of supervisory conduct where the impact was sufficient to invalidate cards occurred in *Glomac Plastics, Inc.*:[324] Two supervisors solicited between 25 and 30 of the 44 cards signed in a unit of 52 employees, distributed union literature to employees, attended union meetings, and obtained employee names and addresses for the union.[325] Similarly, supervisory interference was held to taint the union's card majority where

---

[318]*See, e.g.*, Circo Resorts, Inc., 244 NLRB 880, 102 LRRM 1262 (1979); D. V. Copying & Printing, 240 NLRB 1276, 100 LRRM 1531 (1979); El Rancho Mkt., *supra* note 295.
[319]Boston Pet Supply, Inc., 227 NLRB 1891, 95 LRRM 1096 (1977). *See also* Jasta Mfg. Co., *supra* note 85.
[320]Kroger Co., *supra* note 140.
[321]Travelers Maintenance, Inc., 226 NLRB 945, 93 LRRM 1421 (1976).
[322]Red Barn Sys., *supra* note 155.
[323]American Map Co., 219 NLRB 1174, 90 LRRM 1242 (1975); Luby Leasing, Inc., 198 NLRB 951, 81 LRRM 1097 (1972), *enforced*, 486 F2d 1395, 83 LRRM 3045 (CA 2, 1973).
[324]194 NLRB 406, 78 LRRM 1662 (1971).
[325]*Id.*

the plant manager contacted the union to initiate the organizational drive, and his wife, a plant supervisor, helped arrange the initial union meeting and solicited authorization cards.[326] Recognition of a union was also set aside where a supervisor and the owner of a business solicited and assisted employees in the signing of authorization cards.[327] In *Tribulani's Detective Agency, Inc.*[328] it was unlawful for a supervisor to take employees into his office to have them sign authorization cards. However, the Board refused to set aside the employer's recognition of the union because the General Counsel failed to establish that cards so obtained were counted toward the union's card majority.[329]

A claim of supervisory taint must be timely in order to invalidate cards. Thus, in *Dayton Motels, Inc.*,[330] the Board rejected the employer's claim of supervisory interference because the employer did not initially rely on the supervisor's conduct in its doubt about the union's majority status, and it did not raise the issue until after it was time-barred under Section 10(b).

C. Change of Circumstances

Some courts have required that in order to warrant the issuance of a *Gissel* bargaining order, the Board must find that a fair election cannot be held *at the time it issues the order.*[331] In making this determination, the courts have considered such circumstances as the lapse of time between the violations and the order;[332] a significant change in employee complement;[333] subsequent picket-line misconduct by unfair labor practice strikers;[334] and a change in ownership and management.[335]

---

[326]Central Casket Co., 225 NLRB 362, 92 LRRM 1547 (1976).
[327]B.F.G. Gourmet Foods, Inc., 236 NLRB 489, 98 LRRM 1344 (1978).
[328]233 NLRB 1121, 97 LRRM 1169 (1977).
[329]*Id.*
[330]212 NLRB 553, 87 LRRM 1341 (1974), *enforced,* 525 F2d 476, 90 LRRM 3084 (CA 6, 1975).
[331]*E.g.,* NLRB v. Armcor Indus., Inc., 535 F2d 239, 92 LRRM 2375 (CA 3, 1976); Peerless, Inc., *supra* note 192. The Third Circuit has also required the Board to specifically state its reasons for issuing a bargaining order in a given case. This requirement may be met, however, by the Board's adoption of the administrative law justice's statement of reasons supporting recommendation of a bargaining order. NLRB v. Daybreak Lodge Nursing & Convalescent Home, *supra* note 151; Kenworth Trucks v. NLRB, 580 F2d 55, 99 LRRM 2157 (CA 3, 1978).
[332]NLRB v. East Side Shopper, *supra* note 194; NLRB v. Gibson Prods., *supra* note 192; May Dep't Stores Co., *supra* note 177; Munro Enterprises, *supra* note 188.
[333]NLRB v. Gruber's Super Mkt., *supra* note 192; Ship Shape Maintenance Co., *supra* note 197; NLRB v. Coca Cola Bottling Co. of San Mateo, 472 F2d 140, 82 LRRM 2088 (CA 9, 1972).
[334]Evison J. Dent, 210 NLRB 547, 86 LRRM 1357 (1974).
[335]General Steel Prods., Inc. v. NLRB, 445 F2d 1350, 77 LRRM 2801 (CA 4, 1971).

Some courts of appeals have also required that the Board detail its rationale for determining that a fair second election cannot be conducted—a requirement with which the Board has strongly disagreed. The Third Circuit has denied enforcement of bargaining orders and remanded cases to the Board for " 'a detailed analysis' of the lingering effect of the unfair labor practices and the likelihood of a fair re-run election."[336] In one such case, *Armcor Industries, Inc.*,[337] the Board stated that although it "respectfully recognizes the above-mentioned court opinion as binding upon us for the purposes of deciding this case," the validity of a bargaining order "in the present case and in all similar cases should properly rest upon [the Board's] analysis of the seriousness and pervasiveness of the unlawful conduct at the time that conduct was first presented for . . . scrutiny."[338] The Board then issued a second bargaining order, enforcement of which was again denied by the Third Circuit because of the Board's failure to evaluate effects of change in the work force.[339]

Other courts of appeals, however, have supported the Board's position. In *NLRB* v. *Pacific Southwest Airline*[340] the employer argued that the bargaining order was not an appropriate remedy because five years had elapsed since the unfair labor practice charges were first presented to the Board. Rejecting this argument, the Ninth Circuit said that the passage of time itself did not necessarily compel a new election and "the appropriate time for determination of a bargaining order relates back to the time when the case arose before the Board."[341]

---

[336]Hedstrom Co. v. NLRB, 558 F2d 1137, 95 LRRM 3069 (CA 3, 1977).

[337]227 NLRB 1543, 95 LRRM 1523 (1977), *enforcement denied*, 98 LRRM 2441 (CA 3, 1978).

[338]*Id.* at 1545. *See also* Hitchiner Mfg. Co., 243 NLRB 927, 102 LRRM 1091 (1979); Dadco Fashions, *supra* note 85. *See also* Northfield Cheese Co., 242 NLRB 1117, 101 LRRM 1539 (1979) (bargaining order granted despite the parties having entered into a collective bargaining agreement after the unfair labor practice hearing, because employer's actions indicated it was still trying to oust the union).

[339]NLRB v. Armcor Indus., *supra* note 337. The Second Circuit appears to have adopted a position similar to that of the Third Circuit in *Armcor*. NLRB v. Jamaica Towing, *supra* note 129 (where the court stated that it would decline to enforce a bargaining order absent a Board review of the facts which it deems sufficient to preclude the holding of a second election, including changes of circumstances). *But see* Glomac Plastics, *supra* note 324, where the Second Circuit enforced a Board bargaining order although six years had transpired from date of certification to the issuance of the order.

[340]Pacific Southwest Airlines, *supra* note 139.

[341]*Id.* at 1153. The Ninth Circuit may be wavering on this subject, however. In NLRB v. Western Drug, *supra* note 194, that court stated that the Board's "perfunctory conclusion [that a bargaining order should issue] . . . denied the present employees their freedom of choice without warrant," and employee turnover should be considered in

The Board has indicated its expectation that the Supreme Court must resolve the conflict among the circuits on this issue.[342]

D. Union Discrimination or Misconduct

Increased societal concern for fair employment practices prompted the Board to consider the effect of racially discriminatory union policies upon the Board's certification machinery. In *NLRB* v. *Mansion House Corp.*,[343] the Eighth Circuit in 1973 refused to enforce a *Gissel* remedy because of possible racial discrimination in union membership practices, holding that Board machinery should not be available to a union that either practiced racial discrimination or was unwilling to reform a past practice of racial discrimination. Thereafter, in *Bekins Moving & Storage Co.*,[344] a Board majority held that it would entertain as an objection to a union's certification a timely filed claim that the union engaged in invidious discrimination on the basis of race, alienage, or national origin,[345] but not sex.[346] Although *Bekins* was not an unfair labor practice case, the Board's reasoning therein was deemed applicable to *Gissel* bargaining orders.

Under the *Bekins* rule, the employer bore the burden of proving union racial discrimination as an affirmative defense to the bargaining obligation.[347] Later, in a 1977 decision, *Handy Andy, Inc.*,[348] the Board announced that it would no longer consider issues relating to union discrimination based on race, national origin, or alienage prior to certification. And in *Bell & Howell Co.*,[349] it stated that it would treat allegations of sex discrimina-

---

determining the propriety of a bargaining order. The First Circuit has also taken this approach with respect to employee turnover. NLRB v. Pilgrim Foods, Inc., 591 F2d 110, 100 LRRM 2494 (CA 1, 1978).

[342]Chandler Motors, Inc., 236 NLRB 1565, 98 LRRM 1528 (1978).

[343]473 F2d 471, 82 LRRM 2608 (CA 8, 1973). *See generally* Chapter 9 *supra* at notes 154-59 and Chapter 28 *infra* at notes 132-36.

[344]211 NLRB 138, 86 LRRM 1323 (1974).

[345]*Id.*

[346]Bell & Howell, 213 NLRB 407, 87 LRRM 1172 (1974).

[347]Williams Enterprises, Inc., 212 NLRB 880, 87 LRRM 1044 (1974), *enforced*, 519 F2d 1401, 89 LRRM 2190 (CA 4, 1975). An offer of statistical evidence that the ratio of minority members to the total union membership was less than the ratio of minorities in the general population was deemed insufficient without evidence that the deficiency was due to union policies or procedures. *Id. Cf.* Grant Furniture Plaza, 213 NLRB 410, 87 LRRM 1175 (1974). In the absence of a proven nexus between policies at the international and local levels, discriminatory policies by a local union did not necessarily taint the international, nor did discriminatory practices by the international necessarily taint each local. NLRB v. Bancroft Mfg. Co., 516 F2d 436, 89 LRRM 3105 (CA 5, 1975).

[348]228 NLRB 447, 94 LRRM 1354 (1977).

[349]Bell & Howell Co., 230 NLRB 420, 95 LRRM 1333 (1977), *enforced*, 598 F2d 136, 100 LRRM 2192 (CA DC, 1979).

tion the same way it treated allegations of other forms of invidious discrimination, i.e., through its unfair labor practice machinery. The Board thus considers a Section 8(b) unfair labor practice proceeding to be the "preferable, direct, and expeditious"[350] means of litigating the question of union discrimination.

As to the effect of aggravated union misconduct, such conduct did not warrant the withholding of an otherwise appropriate *Gissel* bargaining order in *Donovan* v. *NLRB*.[351] The Second Circuit there held that the Board is obliged to balance the respective wrongdoings of the employer and the union, and if it finds the employer to be the more guilty party, the Board should issue a bargaining order.

VI. Withdrawal of Recognition

Under the rule of *Brooks* v. *NLRB*,[352] a union enjoys an irrebuttable presumption of continuing majority status for one year after its certification. And where there has been a settlement agreement under which the employer agrees to bargain with the union, the one-year period commences as of the effective date of the agreement.[353] Where, however, the consideration for a non-Board settlement of a refusal-to-bargain charge does not include an agreement to bargain with the union, an employer may lawfully withdraw recognition in less than one year.[354] When an employer withdraws from a multi-employer unit, "the presumption of majority status flowing from the contract in the

---

[350] Handy Andy, Inc., *supra* note 348. *But see* NLRB v. Heavy Lift Serv., Inc., 607 F2d 1121, 102 LRRM 3061 (CA 5, 1979), *enforcing* 234 NLRB 1078, 98 LRRM 1177 (1978) (Fifth Circuit indicated it will not enforce a bargaining order "when the employer has proffered specific evidence sufficient to demonstrate a pattern of racially discriminatory behavior by the union which would support a finding of a definite propensity for racially unfair representation").

[351]Donovan v. NLRB, *supra* note 144.

[352]348 US 96, 35 LRRM 2158 (1954). *See* Chapter 10 *supra* at notes 82-87. *See also* Chapter 13 *infra* at notes 675-708 for detailed treatment of the effect of the presumption, or its rebuttal, in the duty to bargain. The Board has also held that the presumption of continuing majority status attaches for the duration of a collective bargaining agreement. Hence, an employer could not withdraw recognition or repudiate a collective bargaining agreement at midterm even though a lawful poll had indicated that four of the five unit employees no longer desired union representation. Precision Striping, Inc., 245 NLRB 169, 102 LRRM 1264 (1979), *enforcement denied*, 642 F2d 1144, 107 LRRM 2009 (CA 9, 1981).

[353]Straus Communications, Inc., 246 NLRB 846, 102 LRRM 1679 (1979); Pride Ref., Inc., 224 NLRB 1353, 92 LRRM 1553 (1976).

[354]NLRB v. Vantran Elec. Corp., 580 F2d 921, 99 LRRM 2207 (CA 7, 1978); Crestwood Auto Supply Co., 240 NLRB 826, 100 LRRM 1480 (1979).

multi-employer unit survives [the employer's] . . . withdrawal from that unit and carries over to the newly created single employer unit."[355]

When an employer extends voluntary recognition to a union, the presumption of majority status continues for a reasonable period of time.[356] Thus, in *Brennan's Cadillac, Inc.*,[357] after the employer had voluntarily extended recognition to the union, the parties met on eight occasions, over a three-month period, to negotiate an initial agreement. The union then struck. Shortly thereafter, three of the five unit employees wrote to the employer stating that they were withdrawing from the union and returning to work, whereupon the employer withdrew recognition. The Board held that whether a "reasonable time" has passed "turns on what transpired during [negotiations] . . . and what was accomplished therein."[358] In *Brennan's*, it concluded that the bargaining relationship had been given "a fair chance to succeed," and the employer's subsequent withdrawal of recognition was lawful.[359]

The Board and the courts have held that an employer may withdraw recognition from an incumbent union after the certification year has elapsed if it can affirmatively establish either (1) that the union no longer enjoyed majority status when recognition was withdrawn, or (2) that the employer's refusal to bargain was predicated on a reasonably grounded doubt as to the union's continued majority status, which doubt was asserted in good faith, based upon objective considerations, and raised in a context free of employer unfair labor practices.[360] Further-

---

[355]Nevada Club, Inc., 229 NLRB 1186, 96 LRRM 1466 (1977). *See also* NLRB v. Sierra Dev. Co., 604 F2d 606, 102 LRRM 2160 (CA 9, 1979). *But cf.* Western Distrib. Co. v. NLRB, 608 F2d 397, 102 LRRM 2510 (CA 10, 1979) (no presumption of continuing majority status found in merger-successorship setting).

[356]NLRB v. Sierra Dev. Co., *supra* note 355; NLRB v. Cayuga Crushed Stone, Inc., 474 F2d 1380, 82 LRRM 2951 (CA 2, 1973); Pioneer Inn Assocs., 578 F2d 835, 99 LRRM 2354 (CA 9, 1978); Capitol Temptrol Corp., 243 NLRB 575, 102 LRRM 1106 (1979); Winco Petroleum Co., 241 NLRB 1118, 101 LRRM 1100 (1979).

[357]231 NLRB 225, 96 LRRM 1004 (1977).

[358]*Id.* at 226.

[359]*Id.*

[360]NLRB v. Windham Memorial Hosp., 577 F2d 805, 99 LRRM 2242 (CA 2, 1978); Retired Persons Pharmacy v. NLRB, 519 F2d 486, 89 LRRM 2879 (CA 2, 1975); NLRB v. Dayton Motels, Inc., 474 F2d 328, 82 LRRM 2651 (CA 6, 1973); Harpeth Steel, Inc., 208 NLRB 545, 85 LRRM 1174 (1974); Restaurant Employers Bargaining Ass'n, 213 NLRB 651, 87 LRRM 1194 (1974). Upon rebuttal by the employer of the presumption of continuing majority status after expiration of the certification year, the burden shifts to the General Counsel to prove that the union represented a majority of unit employees

more, the employer must be aware of the objective facts upon which its doubt is based at the time it withdraws recognition,[361] and the Board will consider the impact of unfair labor practices on the alleged loss of majority status.[362] In applying these standards, the Board and the courts have analyzed various factors which are treated in the discussion that follows.

A. Insufficient Objective Considerations Found

This section examines the nature of the considerations relied upon by employers which, in the contexts where they arose, were deemed insufficient bases upon which to justify withdrawal of union recognition.

1. Activity or Inactivity by Employees.

Employee dissatisfaction with the union has often been held to be an inadequate basis upon which to justify withdrawal of recognition.[363] This was the result where the claim of dissatisfaction was based on oral complaints by employees,[364] even when made prior to the withdrawal of recognition.[365] Similarly, numerous employee statements to supervisors that the employees had no interest in the union have been deemed insufficient basis,[366] as have supervisory reports of employee dissatisfaction with the union.[367] In like manner, an employer poll of 300 unit employees which resulted in the receipt of 50 letters critical of the union was deemed an inadequate basis upon which to withdraw recognition.[368]

The same result has obtained where there was a lack of attendance at union meetings;[369] where there was a lack of support

---

on the day the employer withdrew recognition. Dalewood Rehabilitation Hosp., Inc. v. NLRB, 566 F2d 77, 97 LRRM 2632 (CA 9, 1977), *denying enforcement to* 224 NLRB 1618, 92 LRRM 1372 (1976); Orion Corp. v. NLRB, 515 F2d 81, 89 LRRM 2135 (CA 7, 1975).

[361]Orion Corp., *supra* note 360; Dayton Motels, Inc., *supra* note 330.

[362]NLRB v. Anvil Prods., Inc., 496 F2d 94, 86 LRRM 2822 (CA 5, 1974), *supplemental decision on remand,* 216 NLRB 158, 88 LRRM 1223 (1975); National Cash Register, *supra* note 198; Robert E. Anderson & Richard E. Anderson, 241 NLRB No. 72, 100 LRRM 1606 (1979); Warehouse Mkt., Inc., 216 NLRB 216, 88 LRRM 1145 (1975).

[363]Retired Persons Pharmacy, *supra* note 360; Felsenthal Plastics, Inc., 224 NLRB 1312, 92 LRRM 1591 (1976). *See also* Lammert Indus. Div., 229 NLRB 895, 96 LRRM 1557 (1977); Autoprod, Inc., 223 NLRB 773, 92 LRRM 1076 (1976).

[364]Burns Int'l Security Servs., *supra* note 248.

[365]NLRB v. North Am. Mfg. Co., 563 F2d 894, 96 LRRM 2635 (CA 8, 1977). *See* Grand Lodge of Ohio, 233 NLRB 143, 96 LRRM 1457 (1977).

[366]Sierra Dev. Co., 231 NLRB 22, 95 LRRM 1597 (1977); Physicians & Surgeons Community Hosp., 231 NLRB 512, 96 LRRM 1344 (1977).

[367]Dalewood Rehabilitation Hosp., Inc., *supra* note 360.

[368]Burns Int'l Security Servs., *supra* note 248.

[369]NLRB v. North Am. Mfg. Co., *supra* note 365; Grand Lodge of Ohio, *supra* note 365; Cut and Curl, Inc., 227 NLRB 1869, 94 LRRM 1332 (1977).

for a strike;[370] and where unit employees, prior to expiration of the current collective bargaining agreement, signed authorization cards of a rival union.[371] Likewise, employee resignations from the union occurring after the employer withdrew recognition were held not to justify withdrawal of recognition.[372] And where the employer received a petition signed by 12 of the 13 unit employees rejecting the union, withdrawal of recognition within the certification year was held unlawful.[373] Withdrawal of recognition was also held unlawful in a health care unit when the employer withdrew recognition from the union in response to employee repudiation of a strike, criticism by employees of the use of the strike as a bargaining tactic, and the reduction and eventual elimination of picketing.[374]

Furthermore, since union membership is not necessarily synonymous with a desire for continued representation, an employer could not justify its withdrawal of recognition by reference to union business records that established a lack of majority membership.[375] Thus, employer showing of a decline in dues checkoff authorizations[376] (even in a right-to-work state),[377] a decline in employee membership in and support of the union, and even a majority vote to withdraw a union-shop authorization[378] have

---

[370]Strange & Lindsey Beverages, Inc., 219 NLRB 1200, 90 LRRM 1236 (1975). See also NLRB v. Windham Memorial Hosp., supra note 360. But cf. Mar-Len Cabinets, Inc., 243 NLRB 523, 101 LRRM 1613 (1979) (employees resigned from the union during a strike to avoid possible union fines for crossing the picket line; the Board found that the employees did not desire the union as their bargaining representative).

[371]Triplett Corp., 234 NLRB 985, 97 LRRM 1406 (1978).

[372]Lammert Indus., supra note 363.

[373]Affordable Inns, Inc., 222 NLRB 1258, 91 LRRM 1480 (1976). See also Sacramento Clinical Laboratory, Inc., 242 NLRB 944, 101 LRRM 1266 (1979) (withdrawal of recognition based on a petition signed by 6 of 12 unit employees held unlawful where it was circulated openly and on company time and was accompanied by employer threats); Chet Monez Ford, 241 NLRB 349, 100 LRRM 1511 (1979) (withdrawn recognition unlawful where it was based on an employee disaffection petition circulated during the posting period of a Board notice resulting from several unfair labor practice discharges); NLRB v. Alterman Transp. Lines, Inc., 587 F2d 212, 100 LRRM 2269 (CA 5, 1979) (withdrawal of recognition based on disaffection petition signed by more than 80% of the unit employees, held unlawful where employer had previously engaged in bad-faith bargaining).

[374]Dalewood Rehabilitation Hosp., supra note 367. See also NLRB v. Top Mfg. Co., 594 F2d 223, 101 LRRM 2081 (CA 9, 1979).

[375]Sparks Nugget, Inc., 230 NLRB 275, 95 LRRM 1298 (1977). See also Restaurant Employers Bargaining Ass'n, supra note 360.

[376]NLRB v. North Am. Mfg. Co., supra note 365; NLRB v. Washington Manor, Inc., 519 F2d 750, 89 LRRM 3044 (CA 6, 1975); Grand Lodge of Ohio, supra note 365; Dalewood Rehabilitation Hosp., supra note 367; United Supermarkets, Inc., 214 NLRB 958, 87 LRRM 1434 (1974), petition for review denied, 90 LRRM 3344 (CA 5, 1975).

[377]North Am. Mfg. Co., 224 NLRB 1252, 93 LRRM 1191 (1976). See Wald Transfer & Storage Co., 218 NLRB 592, 89 LRRM 1346 (1975).

[378]Orion Corp., supra note 360. But see infra at note 415.

all been held inadequate objective bases upon which to justify withdrawal of union recognition.

Employers have also been held to have unlawfully withdrawn recognition from a union where there was information that a decertification petition would be filed[379] and where a decertification petition had already been filed.[380] The same result was reached where an almost unanimously supported decertification petition was filed, because the employer was unaware of it when recognition was withdrawn.[381]

2. Activity or Inactivity by the Union. Withdrawals of recognition have been held unlawful where the employer relied on a union's inactivity,[382] lack of formal organization,[383] or failure to process grievances.[384] This result was also reached where an employer relied on the infrequency of visits to the plant by union representatives[385] and the absence of bargaining for three months prior to the withdrawal of recognition.[386] Additionally, the Board found that lack of communication with the union for a 10-month period during negotiations was not a sufficient basis for withdrawal of recognition where the employer knew the union was busy negotiating contracts with other employers.[387]

Each of the following situations was likewise held to be an inadequate basis for withdrawal of recognition: (1) imposition of trusteeship by the international union;[388] (2) the union's failure to file required reports with the Department of Labor;[389] (3) the union's waiver of claims against the employer for payments that had not been made to the union's welfare funds;[390]

---

[379]Burns Int'l Security Servs., *supra* note 248.
[380]Nazareth Regional High School v. NLRB, 549 F2d 873, 94 LRRM 2897 (CA 2, 1977); Sahara-Tahoe Corp., 241 NLRB 106, 100 LRRM 1530 (1979); Columbia Bldg. Materials, Inc., 239 NLRB 1342, 100 LRRM 1182 (1979); Lammert Indus., *supra* note 363; Felsenthal Plastics, *supra* note 363; Autoprod, Inc., *supra* note 363.
[381]Lammert Indus., *supra* note 363.
[382]Triplett Corp., *supra* note 371.
[383]NLRB v. North Am. Mfg. Co., *supra* note 365. *See* Grand Lodge of Ohio, *supra* note 365.
[384]Nevada Club, *supra* note 355; Burn's Int'l Security Servs., *supra* note 368.
[385]Cut and Curl, Inc., *supra* note 369.
[386]United Supermarkets, Inc., *supra* note 376.
[387]Leatherwood Drilling Co., 209 NLRB 618, 86 LRRM 1187 (1974); Brahaney Drilling Co., 209 NLRB 624 (1974), *enforced*, 513 F2d 270, 89 LRRM 2460 (CA 5, 1975), *cert. denied*, 423 US 1016, 90 LRRM 3176 (1975).
[388]Triplett Corp., *supra* note 371; Nevada Club, *supra* note 355.
[389]Burns Int'l Security Servs., *supra* note 248.
[390]Cut and Curl, Inc., *supra* note 369.

and (4) the fact that the union had engaged in race and sex discrimination.[391]

Similarly, in withdrawing recognition from a union, employers may not lawfully rely on a union's attempts to organize employees prior to the withdrawal of recognition,[392] a union's reportedly unsuccessful recent organizing campaigns,[393] or a union's dilatory tactics which delayed an election that it ultimately lost.[394]

3. Unit Factors. It will be presumed, in the absence of evidence to the contrary, that new employees support the union in the same proportion as employees who are already in the unit or employees whom they replace.[395] Thus, employers have been held to have unlawfully withdrawn recognition when they relied on high turnover in a unit[396] or on the fact that the size of the unit had tripled.[397] This was the result even where turnover was 1700 percent annually and 50 percent between pay periods, because such high turnover was found to be inherent in the industry.[398]

Furthermore, an employer's doubt as to a union's majority status at a facility that had been included in a multiplant unit was held an inadequate basis on which to withdraw recognition.[399]

4. Miscellaneous. Withdrawal of recognition has been held unlawful where employers sought to justify it on a variety of

---

[391]R. C. Cobb, Inc., 231 NLRB 99, 95 LRRM 1576 (1977).

[392]Westinghouse Elec. Corp., 238 NLRB 763, 99 LRRM 1400 (1978).

[393]Nevada Club, Inc., *supra* note 355.

[394]Lammert Indus., *supra* note 363; Felsenthal Plastics, *supra* note 363; Autoprod, Inc., *supra* note 363.

[395]Pennco, Inc., 242 NLRB 467, 101 LRRM 1195 (1979); Dalewood Rehabilitation Hosp., *supra* note 360. *But see* Western Distrib. Co. v. NLRB, 608 F2d 397, 102 LRRM 2510 (CA 10, 1979) (presumption specifically rejected in a merger-successorship context). The Eighth Circuit has also held that this presumption does not apply to employees hired as permanent replacements for strikers. Under this reasoning, permanent replacements would not be counted towards the union's majority, and the employer would be free to withdraw recognition where all strikers have been permanently replaced. National Car Rental Sys., Inc. v. NLRB, 594 F2d 1203, 100 LRRM 2824 (CA 8, 1979).

[396]NLRB v. Washington Manor, *supra* note 376; Dalewood Rehabilitation Hosp., *supra* note 360; Wald Transfer & Storage, *supra* note 377; Leatherwood Drilling, *supra* note 387; Brahaney Drilling, *supra* note 387.

[397]See cases cited *supra* at note 366.

[398]NLRB v. Hondo Drilling Co., 525 F2d 864, 91 LRRM 2133 (CA 5, 1976), *cert. denied*, 429 US 818, 93 LRRM 2362 (1976). *See also* Sierra Dev. Co., *supra* note 366; Physicians & Surgeons Community Hosp., *supra* note 366; Burns Int'l Security Servs., *supra* note 248.

[399]Westinghouse Elec. Corp., *supra* note 392.

other factors. It was held unlawful (1) where the employer withdrew recognition because it had failed to obtain any evidence of the union's majority status when recognition had been extended voluntarily outside the Section 10(b) period,[400] (2) where the union lacked Board certification,[401] or (3) because of the closeness in time of the original election.[402] It has also been held that the employer could not lawfully rely on supervisory taint of which it was unaware at the time recognition was withdrawn.[403] And the fact that a facility is in a right-to-work state is not an adequate basis upon which to withdraw recognition.[404]

B. Sufficient Objective Considerations Found

The following discussion examines the nature of the considerations relied upon by employers which, in the contexts where they arose, were deemed sufficient to justify withdrawal of union recognition.

1. Activity or Inactivity by Employees. Employee dissatisfaction with the union and complaints that a majority do not want union representation have sometimes been held to be a sufficient basis for an employer to withdraw union recognition.[405] This dissatisfaction has been manifested in the following ways: by anti-union views expressed by many unit employees,[406] by personal and specific statements from all unit employees that they did not want the union,[407] and by expressions of several unit employees that they no longer wanted to be represented by the union.[408] The same result obtained where the dissatisfaction with the union which had been communicated to the employer was substantiated by a subsequent employer poll that revealed a majority of unit employees no longer wished union representation[409] and where the employer received a petition repudiating the union signed by 60 percent of the unit employ-

---

[400]See cases cited *supra* at note 366.
[401]*Id.*
[402]Washington Manor, Inc., *supra* note 376; Wald Transfer & Storage Co., *supra* note 377.
[403]NLRB v. Dayton Motels, Inc., *supra* note 360.
[404]Nevada Club, Inc., *supra* note 355.
[405]Dalewood Rehabilitation Hosp., *supra* note 360; Southern Wipers, Inc., 192 NLRB 816, 78 LRRM 1070 (1971).
[406]Houston Shopping News Co., 233 NLRB 105, 96 LRRM 1632 (1977).
[407]Faye Nursing Home, Inc., 215 NLRB 658, 88 LRRM 1404 (1974).
[408]Houston Shopping News, *supra* note 406.
[409]White Castle Sys., Inc., 224 NLRB 1089, 92 LRRM 1591 (1976).

ees.[410] An employer was also held justified in withdrawing union recognition based on oral criticism of the union by unit employees made over the six-month period which preceded the withdrawal of recognition.[411] And where there was evidence that a majority of the unit employees were not members of and did not support the union, withdrawal of recognition was not unlawful.[412]

In some cases, the circuit courts have disagreed with the Board as to whether particular facts justified withdrawing recognition. A sharp decrease in dues checkoff authorizations, combined with a union-shop authorization vote, was held sufficient for withdrawal of recognition from a union.[413] Similarly, a valid basis for withdrawal was found where only one fourth of all unit employees had executed checkoff authorizations[414] and the union was inactive.[415]

Employers were also held to have acted lawfully in withdrawing union recognition where only a minority of employees chose to accept employment at a new plant site;[416] where a substantial number of strikers crossed the picket line and requested reinstatement;[417] and where a substantial number of permanent replacements, who either were not interested in the union or were victims of picket line violence, were hired.[418]

The filing of a decertification petition has also been held to be an adequate basis upon which to withdraw recognition,[419] particularly where the petition is filed by union members[420] in

---

[410]Carolina Am. Textiles, Inc., 219 NLRB 457, 90 LRRM 1074 (1975). *See* NLRB v. Alvin J. Bart & Co., 598 F2d 1267, 101 LRRM 2457 (CA 2, 1979).

[411]Burns Int'l Security Servs., *supra* note 248.

[412]Houston Shopping News Co., *supra* note 406.

[413]Dalewood Rehabilitation Hosp., *supra* note 360. *Cf.* Peoples Gas Sys., Inc., 214 NLRB 944, 87 LRRM 1430 (1975), *reversed and remanded sub nom.* Teamsters Local 769 v. NLRB, 532 F2d 1385, 92 LRRM 2077 (CA DC, 1976), *rehearing in* 238 NLRB 1008, 99 LRRM 1423 (1978), *enforced in part,* 629 F2d 35, 104 LRRM 2224 (CA DC, 1980) (court found Board's bargaining order an unreasonable remedy where evidence indicated employees no longer wished union representation).

[414]Star Mfg. Co. v. NLRB, 536 F2d 1192, 92 LRRM 3179 (CA 7, 1976), *enforcing in part* 220 NLRB 582, 90 LRRM 1360 (1975).

[415]*Id.* The union inactivity included failure to appoint a steward or file valid grievances.

[416]NLRB v. Massachusetts Mach. & Stamping, Inc., 578 F2d 15, 98 LRRM 2939 (CA 1, 1978), *denying enforcement in part to* 231 NLRB 801, 96 LRRM 1187 (1977).

[417]NLRB v. Randle-Eastern Ambulance Serv., Inc., 584 F2d 720, 99 LRRM 3377 (CA 5, 1978).

[418]*Id.*

[419]Dalewood Rehabilitation Hosp., *supra* note 360.

[420]Burns Int'l Security Servs., *supra* note 248.

a timely manner, is supported by an adequate showing of interest, and occurs in a context free of employer unfair labor practices.[421] This was also the result where a letter requesting decertification of the incumbent union was sent to the Board by five of the six unit employees, and a rival union, which had obtained authorization cards from every unit employee, demanded recognition.[422]

2. Activity or Inactivity by the Union. Union inactivity has sometimes been successfully relied on by employers in withdrawing union recognition.[423] Examples of such inactivity are the following: (1) the union's failure to hold meetings for some time;[424] (2) its failure to communicate with the employer for six months;[425] general grievance inactivity,[426] such as the processing of only one substantial grievance in 20 years;[427] and the union's failure to prosecute beyond the first step the two grievances which were filed within a three-year period,[428] together with its failure to file grievances challenging the employer's nonadherence to the contract.[429]

An employer also successfully withdrew recognition where the union's bargaining committee contained no union-member shop stewards or employees.[430] This same result obtained where the union officers comprising the negotiating committee resigned and the employer was not notified of the election of new officers.[431] Employers have also successfully withdrawn recognition in response to "unusual conduct" by union representatives during negotiations,[432] and where, during negotiations, union representatives made statements inferring the union's lack of majority support.[433] And, in the context of other facts indicating loss of majority support, employers have lawfully withdrawn recogni-

---

[421]Essex Int'l, Inc., 222 NLRB 121, 91 LRRM 1413 (1976).
[422]Cadillac Mfg. Corp., 232 NLRB 586, 96 LRRM 1281 (1977).
[423]Southern Wipers, *supra* note 405.
[424]White Castle Sys., *supra* note 409.
[425]Southern Wipers, *supra* note 405.
[426]Burns Int'l Security Servs., *supra* note 248.
[427]White Castle Sys., *supra* note 409.
[428]Star Mfg. Co., *supra* note 414.
[429]*Id.*
[430]White Castle Sys., *supra* note 409.
[431]Burns Int'l Security Servs., *supra* note 248.
[432]Peoples Gas Sys., Inc., *supra* note 413 (the union's "unusual conduct" was a change in its bargaining position, including reversing its announced intention to strike by recommending, three days later, that the membership accept the employer's offer).
[433]White Castle Sys., *supra* note 409.

tion based upon a union's failure to file required reports with the Department of Labor,[434] to produce a membership list as contractually required,[435] and to appoint a shop steward during a period of more than one year.[436] This was also the case where a union representative informed the employer that "50 to 25 to 20%" of the striking employees would not return to work.[437]

3. Unit Factors. Significant employee turnover,[438] for example a turnover of 389 employees in a work force of 100,[439] has been deemed a suffficient basis for withdrawing union recognition; likewise, where there were changes in the composition of the bargaining unit[440] or where an expansion of the work force within a short period of time was anticipated.[441]

4. Contract Factors. Where a provision in the collective bargaining agreement rendered it inoperative if the plant relocated outside a specified geographic area, and the new plant was relocated, the employer was held justified in withdrawing recognition from the union.[442]

---

[434]Burns Int'l Security Servs., *supra* note 248.
[435]Star Mfg. Co., *supra* note 414.
[436]*Id.*
[437]Randle-Eastern Ambulance Serv., *supra* note 417.
[438]Burns Int'l Security Servs., *supra* note 248; Dalewood Rehabilitation Hosp., *supra* note 360; Star Mfg. Co., *supra* note 414.
[439]Southern Wipers, *supra* note 405.
[440]Peoples Gas Sys., Inc., *supra* note 413.
[441]NLRB v. Massachusetts Mach. & Stamping, Inc., *supra* note 416.
[442]*Id.* In a related situation, a district court refused to issue a §10(j) injunction compelling continued recognition where the employer had demonstrated that a large number, but not necessarily a majority, of employees had expressed discontent with the union, and where, even though union membership was a condition of employment, the union was unable, after openly soliciting the employees, to provide signed check-off forms to the employer. The court deemed it significant that no present employee had a voice in negotiating the original collective bargaining agreement, for the union had received voluntary recognition by the employer's predecessor before a substantial number of employees had been hired. Hirsch v. Pick-Mt. Laurel Corp., 436 F Supp 1342, 96 LRRM 2254 (D NJ, 1977).

Part IV

THE

COLLECTIVE BARGAINING

PROCESS

CHAPTER 13

THE DUTY TO BARGAIN

I. Introduction

A. Historical Background

There exists in the law generally, and in the field of labor relations particularly, a tendency to create catch phrases and key words to describe recurring concepts and problems. The reciprocal duty on the part of an employer and the representative of its employees to "bargain in good faith" is perhaps among the most commonly used of these shorthand terms under the National Labor Relations Act.[1] What constitutes "good faith," in terms of the employer's duty to bargain under Section 8(a)(5), or in terms of the union's duty to bargain under Section 8(b)(3), is not readily ascertainable, although hundreds of cases and exhaustive commentaries have undertaken the task.[2] The duty

---

[1]§8(d) of the National Labor Relations Act provides: "For the purposes of this section, to bargain collectively is the performance of the mutual obligation of the employer and the representative of the employees to meet at reasonable times and confer in good faith with respect to wages, hours, and other terms and conditions of employment, or the negotiation of an agreement or any question arising thereunder, and the execution of a written contract incorporating any agreement reached if requested by either party, but such obligation does not compel either party to agree to a proposal or require the making of a concession . . . ." Under §8(a)(5) it is an unfair labor practice for an employer "to refuse to bargain collectively with the representatives of his employees, subject to the provisions of section 9(a)." Under §8(b)(3), it is an unfair labor practice for a labor organization "to refuse to bargain collectively with an employer, provided it is the representative of his employees subject to the provisions of section 9(a)." See Chapter 16 *infra* at notes 1-20 for a discussion of the historical development of the statutory language.

[2]As one commentator has observed: "If one were to select the single area of our national labor law which has posed the greatest difficulties for the National Labor Relations Board, that area could be encompassed within the phrase "the duty to bargain in good faith." Cooper, *Boulwarism and the Duty to Bargain in Good Faith*, 20 RUTGERS L. REV. 653 (1966). For other commentaries, *see* the following partial listing: Abrams, *Negotiating in Anticipation of Arbitration: Some Guideposts for the Initiated*, 29 CASE W. RES. L. REV. 428 (1979); Modjeska, *Guess Who's Coming to the Bargaining Table*, 39 OHIO ST. L. J. 415 (1978); Morris, *The Role of the NLRB and the Courts in the Collective Bargaining Process: A Fresh Look at Conventional Wisdom and Unconventional Remedies*, 30 VAND. L.

to bargain in good faith is an evolving concept, rooted in statute. The Board has characterized the test of good faith as a fluctuating one, "dependent in part upon how a reasonable man might be expected to react to the bargaining attitude displayed by those across the table."[3] Such a "test," however, as the cases discussed hereinbelow will demonstrate, should not be confused with the definitional standards which the Board and the courts have developed to describe the concept.[4]

REV. 661 (1977); Murphy, *Impasse and the Duty to Bargain in Good Faith*, 39 U. PITT. L. REV. 1 (1977); Walther, *The Board's Place at the Bargaining Table*, 28 LAB. L. J. 131 (1977); *Labor Law: Unionization and Collective Bargaining* 399-495 (1976); Brooks, *Stability Versus Employee Free Choice*, 61 CORNELL L. REV. 344 (1976); Nelson & Howard, *The Duty to Bargain During the Term of an Existing Agreement*, 27 LAB. L. J. 573 (1976); Pulle, *The Private Collective Bargaining Process; A Human Dignity Approach*, 5 USFV L. REV. (1976); Kleiman, *Collective Bargaining in Perspective*, 13 DUQ. L. REV. 481 (1975); Feller, *A General Theory of the Collective Bargaining Agreement*, 61 CALIF. L. REV. 663 (1973); Note, *Mid-Term Modification of Terms and Conditions of Employment*, 72 DUKE L. J. 813 (1972); Note, *Automation and Collective Bargaining*, 84 HARV. L. REV. 1822 (1971); Note, *Coordinated-Coalition Bargaining: Theory, Legality, Practice and Economic Effects*, 55 MINN. L. REV. 599 (1971); Comment, *Coordinated Bargaining: The Unions' Attempt to Answer a Need*, 3 USF L. REV. 353 (1969); Gould, *Black Power in the Unions; The Impact Upon Collective Bargaining Relationships*, 79 YALE L. J. 46 (1969); Summers, *Collective Agreements and the Law of Contracts*, 78 YALE L. J. 525 (1969); Gross, Cullen & Hanslowe, *Good Faith in Labor Negotiations: Tests and Remedies*, 53 CORNELL L. REV. 1009 (1968); Maxwell, *The Duty to Bargain in Good Faith, Boulwarism, and a Proposal—The Ascendance of the Rule of Reasonableness*, 71 DICK. L. REV. 531 (1967); Comment, *The Status of Multi-employer Bargaining Under the National Labor Relations Act*, 67 DUKE L. J. 558 (1967); Note, *Good Faith Bargaining and the G.E. Case—The NLRB Views "Boulwarism" and Other Bargaining Practices*, 53 GEO. L. J. 1115 (1965); Note, *Boulwarism and Good Faith Collective Bargaining*, 63 MICH. L. REV. 1473 (1965); Duvin, *The Duty to Bargain: Law in Search of Policy*, 64 COLUM. L. REV. 248, 266 (1964); Fleming, *The Obligation to Bargain in Good Faith*, 16 SW. L. J. 43 (1962); Feinsinger, *The National Labor Relations Act and Collective Bargaining*, 57 MICH. L. REV. 807, 812 (1959); Cox, *The Duty to Bargain in Good Faith*, 71 HARV. L. REV. 1401 (1958); Note, *Employer's Duty to Supply Economic Data for Collective Bargaining*, 57 COLUM. L. REV. 112 (1957); Comment, *The Duty of a Labor Union to Bargain Collectively in Good Faith—An Unresolved Problem*, 25 FORDHAM L. REV. 319 (1956); *Slowdowns and Work Stoppages Not Evidence of Union's Failure to Bargain in Good Faith*, 69 HARV. L. REV. 1337 (1956); Note, *Harassment by Unions as a Refusal to Bargain Under Section 8(b)(3) of the National Labor Relations Act*, 64 YALE L. J. 766 (1955); Humphrey, *The Duty to Bargain*, 16 OHIO ST. L. J. 403, 418 (1955); Taplitz, *Refusal to Bargain*, NYU SEVENTH ANNUAL CONFERENCE ON LABOR 171 (1954); Cox, *Government Regulation of the Negotiation and Terms of Collective Bargaining Agreement*, 101 U. PA. L. REV. 1137 (1953); *Adamant Insistence on a Management Functions Clause as a Refusal to Bargain Collectively*, 52 COLUM. L. REV. 1054 (1952); *Labor Law—Collective Bargaining—Duty of an Employer to Bargain*, 36 MINN. L. REV. 109 (1951); Cox & Dunlop, *The Duty to Bargain Collectively During the Term of an Existing Agreement*, 63 HARV. L. REV. 1097 (1950); Sherman, *Employer's Obligation to Produce Data for Collective Bargaining*, 35 MINN. L. REV. 24, 32 (1950); Note, *Employer's Duty to Bargain Under the National Labor Relations Act*, 22 NOTRE DAME LAW. 95 (1946).

The Board's caseload of §§8(a)(5) and 8(b)(3) charges reflects the continuing dilemma. In fiscal year 1969 there were 3,967 charges filed against employers and 512 charges against unions alleging §8(a)(5) and §8(b)(3) violations. Ten years later, the numbers of each had risen to 8,754 and 869 respectively (although the percentage of such charges compared with total charges filed remained relatively constant). 1969 NLRB ANN. REP. 199 (1970) and 1979 NLRB ANN. REP. 268-69 (1979).

[3]Times Publishing Co., 72 NLRB 676, 682-83, 19 LRRM 1199 (1947).

[4]*See* notes 34-48 *infra* and accompanying text.

1. Origin of Concept of Collective Bargaining. Originally, most of the case law and much of the legislation in the field of labor relations were concerned with the prevention of open hostility resulting from disputes rather than the prevention of the friction between employers and employees that was the direct cause of the disputes.[5] The United States Commission Report on the Chicago Strike of 1894,[6] the Erdman Act of 1898,[7] and the Supreme Court's 1908 decision in *Adair* v. *United States,*[8] three of the earliest executive, legislative, and judicial forays into the labor relations area, were concerned primarily with the conciliation and arbitration of disputes. The Clayton Act[9] and the Norris-LaGuardia[10] Acts also dealt largely with control of concerted activity and employment disputes rather than with the prevention of disputes.

When it became apparent in 1917, however, that governmental intervention would be necessary to prevent labor disputes from interfering with war production, the establishment of the War Labor Board gave recognition to the right of workers to organize in trade unions and to bargain collectively through their chosen representatives.[11] This granting of governmental protection to collective bargaining was a step toward federal regulation to encourage settlement of conditions of employment at the bargaining table. The War Labor Board put this principle into effect in the *Western Cold Storage*[12] case by requiring that the parties "take up the differences that still exist in an earnest endeavor to reach an agreement on all points at issue."

The old National Labor Board, set up under the National Industrial Recovery Act,[13] followed the War Labor Board in announcing that it would adhere to the "incontestably sound principle that the employer is obligated by the statute to negotiate in good faith with his employees' representatives; to match

---

[5]*See generally* Chapter 1 *supra.*
[6]*See* Chapter 1 *supra* at notes 44-47.
[7]Ch. 370, 30 Stat 424 (1898) (repealed 1926). *See* Chapter 1 *supra* at notes 48-52.
[8]208 US 161 (1908). *See* Chapter 1 *supra* at notes 50-53 and 62.
[9]Ch. 323, 38 Stat 730 (1914) (current version at 15 USC §12 *et seq.*) (1976). *See* Chapter 1 *supra* at notes 54-61.
[10]Ch. 90, 47 Stat 70 (1932), 29 USC §101 *et seq.* (1976). *See* Chapter 1 *supra* at notes 72-79.
[11]National War Labor Board, Principles and Rules of Procedure 4 (1919).
[12]No. 80 (War Lab. Bd. 1919).
[13]The National Industrial Recovery Act was declared unconstitutional under the Commerce Clause, and also as an illegal delegation of legislative power, in Schechter Poultry Corp. v. United States, 295 US 495 (1935). *See* Chapter 2 *supra* at notes 2-6.

their proposals, if unacceptable, with counterproposals; and to make every reasonable effort to reach an agreement."[14] Compromise was an essential part of the statutory obligation under the National Recovery Act, and the National Labor Board decided that this statutory concept conferred a duty on employers to bargain, which was more than a bare requirement to meet and confer. The National Labor Board thus contemplated that both parties would approach negotiations with an open mind and make reasonable efforts to reach a common ground of agreement.[15]

2. The Wagner Act. Section 8(5) of the original National Labor Relations Act required that an employer "bargain collectively with the representatives of his employees." Section 9(a) stated that such bargaining should be "in respect to rates of pay, wages, hours of employment, or other conditions of employment." These two brief statements constituted the only express duties to bargain collectively that were imposed by the Wagner Act.

Section 8(5) had been deleted from the bill in the hearings on S.2926, but was restored in S.1958 at the urging of Lloyd K. Garrison, chairman of the old National Labor Board. While the legislators agreed that Section 8(5) did not compel anyone to make a contract,[16] the opinions among congressmen varied with regard to what Section 8(5) did require. For example, Senator Walsh stated that "[a]ll the bill proposed to do is escort representatives to the bargaining door, not control what goes on behind the door."[17] But Senator Wagner saw a stronger requirement: "The bill requires the parties to match unacceptable proposals and to make every effort to reach agreement."[18]

In its first effort to clarify the Act, in its *Jones & Laughlin*[19] holding, the Supreme Court stressed that the Act encourages

---

[14]Houde Eng'r Corp., 1 NLRB (old series) 35 (1935).
[15]National Lock Co., 1 NLRB (old series) 15 (1934); Hall Baking Co., 1 NLRB (old series) 83 (1934); Dresner & Son, 1 NLRB (old series) 26 (1934); Budd Mfg. Co., 1 NLRB (old series) 58 (1933).
[16]79 CONG. REC. 7571 (1935). For history of the Wagner Act *see* Chapters 1 and 2 *supra*.
[17]79 CONG. REC. 7660 (1935). *See* Chapter 16 *infra* at note 23.
[18]*Hearings on H.R. 6288,* 74th Cong., 1st Sess. 16 (1935). Senator Wagner's concept proved to be the more accurate as a prediction of how the law would actually develop.
[19]NLRB v. Jones & Laughlin Steel Corp., 301 US 1, 1 LRRM 703 (1937). For discussion of the constitutional issue in the case, *see* Chapter 30 *infra* at notes 1-11.

free opportunity for negotiation to bring about adjustments and agreements. Soon after, in *Pennsylvania Greyhound Lines*,[20] the Court emphasized the importance of union recognition in securing collective bargaining and declared that the legislative intent expressed in the NLRA was an extension of Railway Labor Act[21] principles. Finally, in the 1938 *Consolidated Edison* case,[22] the Court stated that the manifest objective of the Act in providing for collective bargaining was the contemplating of "the making of contracts with labor organizations."[23]

3. The Taft-Hartley Amendments: Present Wording of the Statutory Provisions. The basic shortcomings relative to bargaining which Congress sought to remedy in the Taft-Hartley amendments were the lack of a statutory requirement that unions must bargain (reciprocal to that of employers), and the lack of an objective standard by which the courts and the Board could determine whether a party had refused to bargain. The House of Representatives viewed a number of Board decisions as reflecting a tendency by the Board to judge the reasonableness of employers' proposals or counterproposals and the degrees of concessions an employer must make.[24] Some court decisions also tended to examine the terms of the proposals rather than the nature of the bargaining.[25] The House proposed a lengthy and detailed objective test for determining what constituted good faith in collective bargaining.[26]

---

[20]NLRB v. Pennsylvania Greyhound Lines, Inc., 303 US 261, 2 LRRM 599 (1938).

[21]44 Stat 577 (1926), 45 USC §§161-63 (1964).

[22]Consolidated Edison Co. v. NLRB, 305 US 197, 3 LRRM 645 (1938).

[23]*Id.* at 236.

[24]*See, e.g.,* J. I. Case Co., 71 NLRB 1145, 19 LRRM 1100 (1946) (refusal to consider closed shop); Burgie Vinegar Co., 71 NLRB 829, 19 LRRM 1055 (1946) (demand that union agree to reimburse employer for any damages from a strike); Jasper Blackburn Prods. Corp., 21 NLRB 1240, 6 LRRM 169 (1940) (requiring union to make itself legally responsible for contract violations); Dallas Cartage Co., 14 NLRB 411, 4 LRRM 445 (1939) (insistence on collective bargaining rather than arbitration provisions); Globe Cotton Mills, 6 NLRB 461, 2 LRRM 172 (1938), *enforced in part,* 103 F2d 91, 4 LRRM 621 (CA 5, 1939) (refusal to make counterproposals held refusal to bargain); S. L. Allen & Co., 1 NLRB 714, 1 LRRM 29 (1936) (refusal to make concessions with respect to any clause in proposed agreement held to violate duty to bargain). *See* Kuelthau, *The NLRB and the Duty to Make Concessions in Bargaining,* 18 LAB. L. J. 201, 202 (1967). The history of the Taft-Hartley Act is treated in Chapter 3 *supra.*

[25]"The fair dealing . . . must be exhibited by the parties . . . in their specific treatment of the particular subjects or items for negotiation." NLRB v. Pilling & Son Co., 119 F2d 32, 37, 8 LRRM 557 (CA 3, 1941). *See also* Texas Foundries, Inc. v. NLRB, 211 F2d 791, 33 LRRM 2883 (CA 5, 1954); Heinz Co. v. NLRB, 311 US 514, 7 LRRM 291 (1941).

[26]H.R. REP. NO. 245, 80th Cong., 1st Sess. 21 (1947).

While the proposed Senate bill, which was subsequently passed almost intact, did not prescribe a purely objective test, it had substantially that effect since it precluded the Board from determining the merits of the parties' positions.[27] The Senate's use of the word "concession" as to requirements that might not be made of the employer, rather than the word "counterproposal," was intended to meet the objection of the then-chairman of the National Labor Relations Board that eliminating any duty to make counterproposals would remove one of the readiest indicia of good or bad faith.[28] The requirements provided by Congress in Section 8(d) of the Taft-Hartley amendments, that the parties "confer in good faith," were almost identical to the requirements which had been propounded by the Supreme Court in *NLRB* v. *Jones & Laughlin Steel Corp.*[29]

Both the House and the Senate agreed that Section 8(b)(3)[30] simply promoted equality and responsibility in bargaining by making the duty to bargain mutual.[31] Such mutuality of obligation in the duty to bargain had already been considered by a few courts.[32] The provision was added to the statute as part of the Taft-Hartley amendments.

B. Elements of the Bargaining Obligation

1. The Duty to Meet, Confer, and Negotiate. The Act expressly requires the parties "to meet at reasonable times and confer in good faith with respect to . . . the negotiation of an agreement . . . ."[33] Where an employer had repeatedly declared that it would sign no written agreement, the Fourth Circuit, in *NLRB* v. *Highland Park Manufacturing Co.,*[34] declared that

> [t]he Act, it is true, does not require that the parties agree; but it does require that they negotiate in good faith *with the view of reaching an agreement if possible;* and mere discussion with the representatives of employees, with a fixed resolve on the part of the employer not

---

[27]*See* HOUSE COMM. OF CONF. REP. NO. 510, 80th Cong., 1st Sess. 34, *reprinted in* US CODE CONG. & ADM. NEWS 1135, 1140 (1947).
[28]S. REP. NO. 105, 80th Cong., 1st Sess. 24 (1947).
[29]*Supra* note 19. *See* Chapter 30 *infra* at notes 1-9.
[30]*See* note 1 *supra.*
[31]H.R. REP. NO. 245, 80th Cong., 1st Sess. 19 (1947).
[32]Globe Cotton Mills v. NLRB, *supra* note 24; NLRB v. Sands Mfg. Co., 96 F2d 721, 2 LRRM 712 (CA 6, 1938), *aff'd,* 306 US 332, 4 LRRM 530 (1939).
[33]§8(d).
[34]110 F2d 632, 6 LRRM 786 (CA 4, 1940).

to enter into any agreement with them, even as to matters as to which there is no disagreement, does not satisfy its provisions.[35]

While various decisions, such as *NLRB v. George P. Pilling & Son Co.*,[36] *NLRB v. Montgomery Ward & Co.*,[37] *NLRB v. Reed & Prince Manufacturing Co.*,[38] and *NLRB v. Boss Manufacturing Co.*,[39] have elaborated on the *Highland Park* definition, the basic requirement set forth therein remains the same: that the parties must negotiate with the view of trying to reach an agreement.[40]

2. The Good-Faith Requirement. The concept underlying the Section 8(d) mandate that the parties "bargain collectively . . . in good faith" is a difficult one. It is particularly difficult to formulate a precise definition of "good faith."

The Wagner Act had no explicit requirement that the employer bargain in good faith, only that it bargain. The Board, however, almost immediately included the additional requirement that such bargaining be done in good faith.[41] The Board's conception of this added requirement is clearly illustrated by its statement in the *Atlas Mills* decision:[42]

> [I]f the obligation of the Act is to produce more than a series of empty discussions, bargaining must mean more than mere negotiation. It must mean negotiation with a *bona fide* intent to reach an agreement if agreement is possible.[43]

When first called upon to enforce Board orders, the federal courts did not adopt the good-faith requirement as such. But they did require an employer to engage in sincere negotiations

---

[35]*Id.* at 637 (emphasis added).

[36]119 F2d 32, 8 LRRM 557 (CA 3, 1941) (requiring that good faith be exhibited in the parties' approach and attitude to negotiations as well as in their specific treatment of particular subjects, plus a common willingness to discuss their claims and demands freely and fully and, when opposed, to justify them by reason).

[37]133 F2d 676, 12 LRRM 508 (CA 9, 1943) (requiring active participation indicating a present intent to find a basis for agreement).

[38]118 F2d 874, 8 LRRM 478 (CA 1, 1941), *cert. denied*, 313 US 595, 8 LRRM 458 (1941) (allowing the Board to find refusal to bargain from the fact that employer displayed a completely closed mind without any spirit of cooperation and a complete absence of the required good faith).

[39]118 F2d 187, 8 LRRM 729 (CA 7, 1941) (requiring open and fair mind plus endeavor to overcome existing obstacles and difficulties).

[40]NLRB v. Southwestern Porcelain Steel Corp., 317 F2d 527, 53 LRRM 2307 (CA 10, 1963); NLRB v. Herman Sausage Co., 122 NLRB 168, 43 LRRM 1090 (1958), *enforced*, 275 F2d 229, 45 LRRM 2829 (CA 5, 1960); California Girl, Inc., 129 NLRB 209, 46 LRRM 1533 (1960); Majure v. NLRB, 198 F2d 735, 30 LRRM 2441 (CA 5, 1952).

[41]1937 NLRB Ann. Rep. 82, 82-85 (1937).

[42]3 NLRB 10, 1 LRRM 60 (1937).

[43]*Id.* at 21.

with an intent to settle differences and arrive at an arrangement.[44] Some cases continued to follow that view of the bargaining obligation even after Taft-Hartley had specifically added the good-faith requirement.[45] Under the original Wagner Act, the Supreme Court in NLRB v. Sands Manufacturing Co.,[46] upheld a test which did not specify good faith but did consider the sincerity of the employer's effort.[47] Two years later, in National Licorice Co. v. NLRB,[48] the Court adopted "good faith" as the standard for an employer's conduct.

3. Subjects of Bargaining. While Section 8(5) of the original Wagner Act established the employer's duty to "bargain collectively" with the employees' representative "subject to the provisions of Section 9(a)," nowhere in the original Act were the subjects of collective bargaining enumerated or defined. Section 9(a) did, however, provide that the representatives designated or selected by the employees in an appropriate unit would be the exclusive representatives "for the purposes of collective bargaining in respect to rates of pay, wages, hours of employment, or other conditions of employment . . . ." This provision was later used by the courts to determine the scope of the bargaining obligation.[49]

Three categories of bargaining subjects have evolved since 1935: mandatory, permissive, and illegal.[50] Because of the absence

---

[44]NLRB v. Biles-Coleman Lumber Co., 98 F2d 18, 2 LRRM 757 (CA 9, 1938). See also Globe Cotton Mills v. NLRB, supra note 24; Jeffery-DeWitt Insulator Co. v. NLRB, 91 F2d 134, 1 LRRM 634 (CA 4, 1937), cert. denied, 302 US 731, 2 LRRM 623 (1937).

[45]E.g., NLRB v. Shannon, 208 F2d 545, 33 LRRM 2270 (CA 9, 1953).

[46]306 US 332, 4 LRRM 530 (1939), aff'g 96 F2d 721, 2 LRRM 712 (CA 6, 1938).

[47]"The sincerity of the employer's effort is to be tested by the length of time involved in the negotiations, their frequency, and the persistence with which the employer offers opportunity for agreement." 96 F2d 721, 725, 2 LRRM 712 (CA 6, 1938).

[48]309 US 350, 6 LRRM 674 (1940). See also Heinz Co. v. NLRB, supra note 25.

[49]See generally Chapter 16 infra.

[50]For a more detailed treatment of mandatory bargaining subjects, see Chapter 17 infra. For a more detailed treatment of permissive and illegal bargaining subjects, see Chapter 18 infra. Chapter 16 infra provides a general historical perspective on all three categories. See generally, Case Comment, Duty to Bargain About Termination of Operations: Brockway Motor Trucks, Inc. v. NLRB, 92 HARV. L. REV. 768 (1979); Note, Application of the Mandatory-Permissive Dichotomy to the Duty to Bargain and Unilateral Action: A Review and Reevaluation, 15 WM. & MARY L. REV. 918 (1974); Rabin, Fibreboard and the Termination of Bargaining Unit Work: The Search for Standards in Defining the Scope of the Duty to Bargain, 71 COLUM. L. REV. 803 (1971); Schwarz, Plant Relocation or Partial Termination— The Duty to Decision-Bargain, 39 FORDHAM L. REV. 81 (1970); Comment, Union Dues Checkoff as a Subject in Labor Management Negotiations: Good Faith Bargaining and NLRB Remedies, 39 FORDHAM L. REV. 299 (1970); Sheinkman, Plant Removal Under the National Labor Relations Act: Can Bargaining Be Avoided and Should Bargaining Be Avoided, NYU SIXTEENTH ANNUAL CONFERENCE ON LABOR 81 (1963).

of a precise statutory definition of the subjects over which parties were required to bargain under the Act, it was the Board, not the Congress, which very early assumed the role of defining compulsory bargaining subjects.[51]

Interpretation of the statutory language requiring parties to "confer in good faith with respect to wages, hours, or other terms and conditions of employment" led to a distinction between *mandatory* and *permissive* subjects of bargaining. In *NLRB* v. *Wooster Division of the Borg-Warner Corp.*[52] the Supreme Court in 1958 affirmed and adopted this distinction. It observed that the duty to bargain created by Sections 8(a)(5) and 8(d) is "limited to those subjects" enumerated in those sections, "and within that area neither party is legally obligated to yield."[53] Distinguishing permissive bargaining subjects, the Court noted that "as to [such] other matters, however, each party is free to bargain or not to bargain and to agree or not to agree."[54]

Examples of *permissive* subjects of bargaining[55] include collective bargaining provisions covering supervisors[56] or agricultural labor,[57] performance bonds,[58] legal-liability clauses,[59] and internal union affairs.[60]

---

[51]In 1940 the Board held that "[p]aid holidays, vacations, and bonuses constitute an integral part of the earnings and working conditions of the employees and . . . are matters which are generally the subject of collective bargaining . . . . [I]nsistence upon treating such matters as gratuities to be granted and withdrawn at will, constitutes a refusal to bargain . . . ." Singer Mfg. Co., 24 NLRB 444, 470, 6 LRRM 405 (1940), *enforced*, 119 F2d 131, 8 LRRM 740 (CA 7, 1941), *cert. denied*, 313 US 595, 8 LRRM 458 (1941).
   Following the *Singer* case, the Board held that other integral aspects of the employment relationship were "rates of pay, wages, hours of employment or other conditions of employment" within the meaning of §9(a), and were therefore mandatory bargaining subjects. *See* Chapter 16 *infra* at notes 7-18. *See also* Cox & Dunlop, *Regulation of Collective Bargaining by the National Labor Relations Board*, 63 HARV. L. REV. 389, 397-401 (1950).
   [52]356 US 342, 42 LRRM 2034 (1958). *See generally* Chapter 16 *infra* at notes 27-35.
   [53]*Id.* at 349.
   [54]*Id.*, *citing* NLRB v. American Nat'l Ins. Co., 343 US 395, 30 LRRM 2147 (1952). For an earlier and somewhat analogous categorization, *see* Cox & Dunlop, *supra* note 51.
   [55]*See generally* Chapter 18 *infra*.
   [56]Southern Cal. Pipe Trades Dist. Council 16 (Aero Plumbing Co.), 167 NLRB 1004, 66 LRRM 1233 (1967), *enforced*, 449 F2d 668, 78 LRRM 2260 (CA 9, 1971); NLRB v. Retail Clerks (Safeway Co.), 203 F2d 165, 31 LRRM 2606 (CA 9, 1953), adjudging union in contempt for insisting on bargaining for supervisory employees in violation of a consent decree *enforcing* 96 NLRB 581, 28 LRRM 1554 (1951), *cert. denied*, 348 US 839, 34 LRRM 2898 (1954).
   [57]District 50, Mine Workers (Central Soya Co.), 142 NLRB 930, 939, 53 LRRM 1178 (1963).
   [58]Newberry Equip. Co., 135 NLRB 747, 49 LRRM 1571 (1962); NLRB v. Reeves & Sons, Inc., 47 LRRM 2480 (CA 10, 1961), *adjudicating contempt for violating* 273 F2d 710, 45 LRRM 2295 (CA 10, 1959), *cert. denied*, 366 US 914, 48 LRRM 2071 (1961); Teamsters Local 294 (Conway's Express), 87 NLRB 972, 978-79, 25 LRRM 1202, 1210 (1949), *enforced sub nom.* Rabouin v. NLRB, 195 F2d 906, 29 LRRM 2617 (CA 2, 1952); Amory

Although the law permits, but does not compel, bargaining about permissive subjects, there is another category of subjects about which the parties are forbidden to bargain. This category is traditionally referred to as *illegal* bargaining subjects.[61] Among these subjects are closed-shop provisions,[62] hiring-hall provisions that give preference to union members,[63] a "hot cargo" clause that violates Section 8(e),[64] a contract provision inconsistent with a union's duty of fair representation,[65] and contract clauses which discriminate among employees on individual bases, such as race, religion, sex, or national origin.[66]

II. *PER SE* VIOLATIONS

In determining whether an unlawful refusal to bargain has occurred, the Board and the courts usually probe the conduct of the parties for evidence of the presence or absence of subjective "good faith." However, certain types of conduct have been viewed as independent or *per se* refusals to bargain, without regard to any considerations of good or bad faith.[67] As the following cases demonstrate, such conduct generally involves an absence of bargaining, frequently selective as to subjects; thus it is the *failure to negotiate*, rather than the absence of good faith, which lies at the heart of any violation involving this type of conduct.

Garment Co., 80 NLRB 182, 23 LRRM 1081 (1948), *enforced,* 24 LRRM 2274 (CA 5, 1949); Cookeville Shirt Co. & P. M. French, 79 NLRB 667, 22 LRRM 1438 (1948). *See also* Local 164, Painters v. NLRB, 293 F2d 133, 48 LRRM 2060 (CA DC, 1961), *cert. denied,* 368 US 824, 48 LRRM 3110 (1961) (union insistence on employer performance bond).

[59]Radiator Specialty Co., 143 NLRB 350, 53 LRRM 1319 (1963), *enforced in part,* 336 F2d 495, 57 LRRM 2097 (CA 4, 1964). *See also* North Carolina Furniture, Inc., 121 NLRB 41, 42 LRRM 1271 (1958).

[60]NLRB v. Corsicana Cotton Mills, 178 F2d 344, 24 LRRM 2494 (CA 5, 1949) (*per curiam*).

[61]*See generally* Chapter 18 *infra.*

[62]Penello v. Mine Workers, 88 F Supp 935, 25 LRRM 2368 (D DC, 1950). *See* Chapter 25 *infra.*

[63]NLRB v. National Maritime Union, 175 F2d 686, 24 LRRM 2268 (CA 2, 1949), *cert. denied,* 338 US 954, 25 LRRM 2395 (1950). *See* Chapter 25 *infra.*

[64]Lithographers Local 17 (Graphic Arts Employers Ass'n), 130 NLRB 985, 47 LRRM 1374 (1961), *aff'd,* 309 F2d 31, 51 LRRM 2093 (CA 9, 1962), *cert. denied,* 372 US 943, 52 LRRM 2673 (1963). *See* Chapter 26 *infra.*

[65]Longshoremen Local 1367 (Galveston Maritime Ass'n), 148 NLRB 897, 57 LRRM 1083 (1964), *enforced,* 368 F2d 1010, 63 LRRM 2559 (CA 5, 1966), *cert. denied,* 389 US 837, 66 LRRM 2307 (1967). *See* Chapter 28 *infra.*

[66]*E.g.,* Metal Workers (Hughes Tool Co.), 147 NLRB 1573, 56 LRRM 1289 (1964). *See* Chapter 27 *infra.*

[67]During the period prior to passage of Taft-Hartley, this same category of cases existed, but the distinction did not become pronounced until the passage of the Taft-Hartley amendments added a good-faith requirement separate from the general duty-to-bargain requirement.

A. Unilateral Changes[68]

Unilateral changes by an employer during the course of a collective bargaining relationship concerning matters which are mandatory subjects of bargaining are normally regarded as *per se* refusals to bargain.[69] These actions, committed without negotiation and achieved through bypassing of the union, may sometimes support an inference of lack of good faith.[70] While such conduct has been analyzed by the Board and the circuit courts both in *per se* terms[71] and in terms based on a good-faith standard,[72] the Supreme Court did not give express recognition to the *per se* determination in this context until the 1962 case of *NLRB* v. *Katz*.[73] In *Katz* the employer's unilateral changes in conditions of employment (change in sick-leave policy, merit-wage increase policy, and general wage increase) were characterized by the Court as follows:

> A refusal to negotiate *in fact* as to any subject which is within §8(d), and about which the union seeks to negotiate, violates §8(a)(5) though the employer has every desire to reach agreement with the union upon an over-all collective agreement and earnestly and in all good faith bargains to that end.[74]

---

[68]This section treats unilateral changes as *per se* refusals to bargain. *See* discussion at notes 293-309 *infra*, this chapter, for treatment of unilateral changes as *evidence* of bad-faith bargaining. *See also* McGuckin, *Clipping the Fringes: An Employer's Duty to Bargain Prior to Unilaterally Changing Employee Benefits*, 10 USF L. REV. 175 (1975).

[69]NLRB v. Katz, 369 US 736, 50 LRRM 2177 (1962); NLRB v. American Mfg. Co., 351 F2d 74, 60 LRRM 2122 (CA 5, 1965) (granting wage increase under pressure of Interstate Commerce Commission); NLRB v. Zelrich Co., 344 F2d 1011, 59 LRRM 2225 (CA 5, 1965); NLRB v. Wonder State Mfg. Co., 344 F2d 210, 59 LRRM 2065 (CA 8, 1965), *enforcing in part, denying in part* 147 NLRB 179, 56 LRRM 1181 (1964); NLRB v. Mid-West Towel & Linen Serv., Inc., 339 F2d 958, 57 LRRM 2433 (CA 7, 1964) (all unilateral wage increases); McLean v. NLRB, 333 F2d 84, 56 LRRM 2475 (CA 6, 1964) (granting health insurance); NLRB v. Citizens Hotel Co., 326 F2d 501, 55 LRRM 2135 (CA 5, 1964) (discontinuing Christmas bonus); NLRB v. Central Ill. Pub. Serv. Co., 324 F2d 916, 54 LRRM 2586 (CA 7, 1963) (discontinuing employee discount); GTE Automatic Elec., Inc., 240 NLRB No. 30, 100 LRRM 1204 (1979). Exceptions have been made concerning impasse, necessity, and waiver; *see infra* at notes 572-643. *But cf.* Rust Craft Broadcasting, Inc., 225 NLRB 327, 92 LRRM 1576 (1976), where the Board considered the unilateral installation of time clocks to be solely within the employer's managerial discretion "which it was free to exercise" and therefore not a proper subject of bargaining. For a more detailed treatment of the subject of unilateral changes as evidence of violations of obligations created by §§8(a)(5), 8(b)(3), and 8(d) of the Act, *see* notes 293-309 *infra* and accompanying text.

[70]*See infra* this chapter at notes 293-309.

[71]NLRB v. Katz, *supra* note 69 at 738.

[72]*See, e.g.*, NLRB v. Reeves & Sons, 273 F2d 710, 713, 45 LRRM 2295 (CA 10, 1959), *enforcing* 121 NLRB 543, 42 LRRM 1555 (1958), *cert. denied*, 366 US 914, 48 LRRM 2071 (1961); NLRB v. Century Cement Mfg. Co., 208 F2d 84, 33 LRRM 2061 (CA 2, 1953).

[73]*Supra* note 69.

[74]*Supra* note 69 at 743 (emphasis in original).

Thus, a violation was found despite the absence of a finding of bad faith; indeed, where there was even a possibility of subjective good faith.

The Court in *Katz* referred to its earlier decision in *NLRB* v. *Crompton-Highland Mills*,[75] where a wage increase greater than that offered to the union was granted immediately after an impasse had developed. While that opinion was not framed in *per se* language, the absence of any other indicia of bad faith placed the decision in a *per se* context, and a number of later cases rested upon this approach,[76] some expanding it,[77] others distinguishing it.[78]

In *Katz* the Court did note, however, that certain circumstances might justify unilateral employer action;[79] and exceptions dealing with impasse,[80] necessity,[81] and waiver[82] have been developed.

The *Katz* analysis, which is confined to unilateral changes in working conditions made by employers, is not readily applicable to unions because of their relative inability to effect unilateral

---

[75]337 US 217, 24 LRRM 2088 (1949).

[76]Electri-Flex Co. v. NLRB, 570 F2d 1327, 97 LRRM 2888 (CA 7, 1978), *cert. denied,* 439 US 911, 99 LRRM 2743 (1978) (institution of a written warning system, a 60-day probationary period, and a call-in rule); Korn Indus., Inc. v. NLRB, 389 F2d 117, 67 LRRM 2148 (CA 4, 1967); NLRB v. Almeida Bus Lines, Inc., 333 F2d 129, 56 LRRM 2548 (CA 1, 1964).

[77]Taft Broadcasting Co., 185 NLRB 202, 75 LRRM 1076 (1970), *aff'd,* 441 F2d 1382, 77 LRRM 2257 (CA 8, 1971) (unilateral elimination of arbitration procedure); NLRB v. Tom Joyce Floors, Inc., 353 F2d 768, 60 LRRM 2334 (CA 9, 1965) (increased wages to strike replacements); NLRB v. Erie Resistor Corp., 373 US 221, 53 LRRM 2121 (1963) (superseniority to strike replacements).

[78]NLRB v. Southern Coach & Body Co., 336 F2d 214, 57 LRRM 2102 (CA 5, 1964) (employer may continue "automatic" increases to which it is already committed, since these are not a "change" in working conditions); NLRB v. Tex-Tan, Inc., 318 F2d 472, 53 LRRM 2298 (CA 5, 1963) (employer may make changes, but only to extent of previous offers to union, after impasse is reached); NLRB v. Superior Fireproof Door & Sash Co., 289 F2d 713, 47 LRRM 2816 (CA 2, 1961) (employer may make isolated individual wage adjustments); Armstrong Cork Co. v. NLRB, 211 F2d 843, 33 LRRM 2789 (CA 5, 1954); NLRB v. Dealers Engine Rebuilders, Inc., 199 F2d 249, 31 LRRM 2007 (CA 8, 1952); NLRB v. Landis Tool Co., 193 F2d 279, 29 LRRM 2255 (CA 3, 1952) (employer may make wage increase which union has rejected, but only after notice to and consultation with union); NLRB v. Bradley Washfountain Co., 192 F2d 144, 29 LRRM 2064 (CA 7, 1951).

[79]*Supra* note 69 at 747-48.

[80]NLRB v. Tex-Tan, Inc., *supra* note 78. *See* NLRB v. United States Sonics Corp., 312 F2d 610, 52 LRRM 2360 (CA 1, 1963). *See also* discussion of impasse *infra* this chapter at notes 538-71.

[81]*See* Duvin, *supra* note 2 at 278 n.210.

[82]Where a union is put on notice of an intended change and does not seek to bargain about it, the employer may act unilaterally. United States Lingerie Corp., 170 NLRB 750, 67 LRRM 1482 (1968). *See* discussion of waiver *infra* this chapter at notes 626-30.

changes.[83] Although the matter may be placed on the bargaining table as a union demand, normally some implementation is required by the employer in order to effect the change. Whether a union may actually compel a company to accede to its demand is usually a matter of economic power, and the possession and exercise of such power is "not at all inconsistent with the duty to bargain in good faith."[84] However, the Ninth Circuit has viewed a union's unilateral imposition of production quotas, enforced by fines upon member employees, as a refusal to bargain on a mandatory subject and thus a violation of Section 8(b)(3).[85] This represented the first application to a union of the *Katz-Fibreboard*[86] approach. However, the case has been distinguished on the ground that the union was there modifying an existing collective bargaining agreement without meeting the requirements of Section 8(d).[87]

An attempt to modify or terminate a collective bargaining agreement by means of a strike, without serving the requisite statutory notice upon federal and state mediation agencies as required by Section 8(d), is deemed an attempt to secure a unilateral change in a bargaining relationship and therefore a violation of the union's bargaining obligation.[88] And in *Chemical*

---

[83]In NLRB v. Insurance Agents Int'l Union, 361 US 477, 45 LRRM 2705 (1960), the Supreme Court expressly left open the question of whether a union's unilateral imposition of new terms and conditions is subject to the same treatment under §8(b)(3) as an employer's unilateral action. In Musicians Local 802, 164 NLRB 23, 65 LRRM 1048 (1967), *aff'd*, 395 F2d 287, 68 LRRM 2317 (CA 2, 1968), the Board distinguished the *Katz* case and declined to find a *per se* refusal to bargain where the union had amended its bylaws during negotiations to specify a higher wage scale and to establish a new welfare fund. Union members were placed under threat of union discipline for failing to observe the scales. Distinguishing *Katz*, the Second Circuit pointed out that the union could not unilaterally effect changes, but could only demand that the employer make them. 395 F2d at 290. *See also* Letter Carriers, 240 NLRB 519, 100 LRRM 1315 (1979). *But see* NLRB v. System Council T-6, 599 F2d 5, 101 LRRM 2413 (CA 1, 1979) (union violated §8(b)(3) when it unilaterally promulgated a rule prohibiting union members from accepting temporary supervisory assignments, contrary to established employer practice).
[84]NLRB v. Insurance Agents Int'l Union, *supra* note 83 at 490-91. *See infra* this chapter at notes 511-14 for further discussion of *Insurance Agents* and union conduct in collective bargaining.
[85]Associated Home Builders, Inc., 352 F2d 745, 60 LRRM 2345 (CA 9, 1965). *But see* Scofield v. NLRB, 393 F2d 49, 67 LRRM 2673 (CA 7, 1968), *aff'd*, 394 US 423, 70 LRRM 3105 (1969), where a union's enforcement of production quotas was held not to be violative of §8(b)(1). *See* Chapter 6 *supra* at notes 531-32.
[86]NLRB v. Katz, *supra* note 69; Fibreboard Paper Prods. Corp. v. NLRB, 379 US 203, 57 LRRM 2609 (1964). *See* Chapter 17 *infra* at notes 272-80.
[87]Musicians Local 802, *supra* note 83.
[88]Mine Workers (McCoy Coal Co.), 165 NLRB 592, 65 LRRM 1450 (1967); Sheet Metal Workers Local 141 (American Sign Co.), 153 NLRB 537, 59 LRRM 1512 (1965). *See* note 498 *infra*.

Workers Local 29 (Morton-Norwich Products, Inc.)[89] the Board held that by demanding the right to tape-record grievance meetings, after a 10-year history of handwritten note taking, the union was attempting to change the implied terms of the collective bargaining agreement and in effect terminate the processing of employee grievances provided for in the collective bargaining agreement.[90]

B. Bargaining Directly With Employees

The collective bargaining obligation requires "recognition that the statutory representative is the one with whom [the employer] must deal in conducting bargaining negotiations, and that it can no longer bargain directly or indirectly with the employees."[91] Just as a unilateral promulgation of a change in a mandatory subject of bargain is a *per se* violation of Section 8(a)(5) because the employer has bypassed the bargaining agent, a like change effected by the employer dealing directly with the employees rather than with the bargaining agent is also a violation.[92] Some cases, however, treat such bypassing as merely evidence of lack of good faith in the duty to bargain.[93]

C. Execution of a Written Contract

"The execution of a written contract incorporating any agreement reached" is expressly required by Section 8(d). The failure to sign a written memorandum of the agreement made has been uniformly regarded as a *per se* refusal to bargain.[94] Even prior to the enactment of Section 8(d) as part of Taft-Hartley, the

---

[89]228 NLRB 1101, 94 LRRM 1696 (1977).

[90]*Id.* at 1101.

[91]General Elec. Co., 150 NLRB 192, 194, 57 LRRM 1491 (1964), *enforced,* 418 F2d 736, 72 LRRM 2530 (CA 2, 1969), *cert. denied,* 397 US 965, 73 LRRM 2600 (1970).

[92]Medo Photo Supply Corp. v. NLRB, 321 US 678, 14 LRRM 581 (1944); Wings & Wheels, Inc., 139 NLRB 578, 51 LRRM 1341 (1962), *enforced,* 324 F2d 495, 54 LRRM 2455 (CA 3, 1963).

[93]*E.g.,* General Elec., *supra* note 91.

[94]NLRB v. Midvalley Steel Fabricators, Inc., 243 NLRB 516, 101 LRRM 1503 (1979), *order enforced as modified,* 621 F2d 49, 104 LRRM 2063 (CA 2, 1980); Procter & Gamble Mfg. Co., 248 NLRB 953, 104 LRRM 1207 (1980); Seneca Sheet Metal, 243 NLRB 1232, 102 LRRM 1055 (1979); Electra-Food Mach., 241 NLRB 1232, 101 LRRM 1083 (1979) (union accepted employer's final offer; fact that union's constitution prohibits agreed-upon open-shop clause was no defense to refusal to execute); Crimptex, Inc., 211 NLRB 855, 87 LRRM 1093 (1974); NLRB v. Big Run Coal & Clay Co., 385 F2d 788, 66 LRRM 2640 (CA 6, 1967), *enforcing* 152 NLRB 1144, 59 LRRM 1287 (1965); Lozano Enterprises v. NLRB, 327 F2d 814, 55 LRRM 2510 (CA 9, 1964) (employer signed contract, but refused to return it to union); NLRB v. Wate, Inc., 310 F2d 700,

Supreme Court in 1941, in *H. J. Heinz* v. *NLRB*,[95] viewed such failure as an independent refusal to bargain. While that decision was not specifically cast in *per se* language, it nevertheless provided the basic precedent for the *per se* doctrine. The same *per se* approach has been applied to Section 8(b)(3) in cases of union refusal to execute an agreed-upon contract.[96]

D. Meeting at Reasonable Times

Section 8(d) also requires the parties "[t]o meet at reasonable times." However, Section 8(d) does not define the term "reasonable." As an objective standard, it generally includes a minimal number of meetings.[97] Where an employer insists upon bargaining by mail or insists that the union submit all its proposals in writing despite union requests for personal meetings, an unlawful refusal to bargain results.[98]

E. Conferring

Section 8(d) also requires the parties to "confer in good faith with respect to wages, hours, and other terms and conditions of

---

51 LRRM 2701 (CA 6, 1962). This requirement is also applicable to individual employer members of multi-employer bargaining units. NLRB v. Strong, 393 US 357, 70 LRRM 2100 (1969); NLRB v. Sheridan Creations, Inc., 357 F2d 245, 61 LRRM 2586 (CA 2, 1966). Nonmembers of employer associations who, during the course of association bargaining, have agreed to be bound by the terms of the multi-employer agreement are also subject to this requirement. Buffalo Bituminous, Inc. v. NLRB, 564 F2d 267, 96 LRRM 2884 (CA 8, 1977), *enforcing* 227 NLRB 99, 94 LRRM 1398 (1977). *See* discussion of multi-employer bargaining units in Chapter 11 *supra* at notes 348-416.

[95]311 US 514, 7 LRRM 291 (1941).

[96]In NLRB v. Longshoremen (Lykes Bros. S.S. Co.), 443 F2d 218, 77 LRRM 2366 (CA 5, 1971), *enforcing* 181 NLRB 590, 76 LRRM 1700 (1970), the court found it unnecessary to determine whether the union's violation of §8(b)(3) was its refusal to reduce the final agreement to writing, or its insistence upon the nonmandatory subject of expansion of its bargaining authority beyond its own jurisdiction and its own bargaining unit. Enforcing the Board's §8(b)(3) order, the court held that, in the context presented, "the two characterizations are no more than two sides of the same coin." 443 F2d at 220. *See also* Binswanger Glass Co., 245 NLRB 253, 102 LRRM 1541 (1979); Hosp. & Health Care Employees (Dist. 1199C), 241 NLRB 270, 101 LRRM 1030 (1979); Operating Eng'rs Local 12 (Tri-County Ass'n), 168 NLRB 173, 66 LRRM 1270 (1967); Standard Oil Co., 137 NLRB 690, 50 LRRM 1238 (1962), *aff'd*, 322 F2d 40, 54 LRRM 2076 (CA 6, 1963).

[97]Carbonex Coal Co., 248 NLRB 779, 104 LRRM 1009 (1980) (2-1/2 month hiatus before scheduled hearing held unlawful); Rhodes St. Clair Buick, Inc., 242 NLRB 1320, 101 LRRM 1448 (1979) (hiatus of 2 months after union certification held unlawful); Preterm, Inc., 240 NLRB 654, 100 LRRM 1344 (1979). *See* Dunau, *supra* note 2 at 264-70. *See also* discussion on dilatory tactics *infra* at notes 261-75.

[98]*See* NLRB v. United States Cold Storage Corp., 203 F2d 924, 32 LRRM 2024 (CA 5, 1953); NLRB v. P. Lorillard Co., 117 F2d 921, 7 LRRM 475 (CA 6, 1941), *rev'd per curiam on other grounds*, 314 US 512, 9 LRRM 410 (1942). *See also* NLRB v. Yutana Barge Lines, 315 F2d 524, 52 LRRM 2750 (CA 9, 1963) (refusal to bargain with respect to

employment."[99] Although the subjective condition of "good faith" is set forth in the Act, the further requirement that the parties "confer" provides the primary basis for the *per se* determinations indicated in the *Katz* case. A refusal to bargain about a mandatory subject or an insistence to the point of impasse about a permissive subject may constitute a *per se* violation, not only because of the nature of those positions, but also because each of those activities amounts to a failure to confer in good faith.[100] On the other hand, there may be a conceptual overlap between a failure to "meet at reasonable times" and the "failure to confer"—for both may be viewed as mechanics of bargaining.[101]

F. Insisting on Nonmandatory Subjects of Bargaining

In 1958 the Supreme Court affirmed and adopted the distinction between mandatory and permissive subjects of bargaining contained in *NLRB* v. *Wooster Division of Borg-Warner Corp.*[102] The proposals at issue in *Borg-Warner* were a "recognition" clause and a "ballot" clause, both of which had been insisted upon by the employer during collective bargaining. The recognition clause disregarded the Board's certification of the local union and parent international as bargaining agent and would have given contractual recognition only to the local union. The ballot clause provided for a secret-ballot vote of all bargaining-unit employees—union as well as nonunion—on the employer's last offer in negotiations; only after exhausting this procedure would the union be free to strike. The employer maintained that both clauses were prerequisites to its reaching an agreement.

The Board found that the employer had not bargained in bad faith; but the insistence upon inclusion of both clauses in any agreements signed by the employer was held to be *per se* violative of Section 8(a)(5).[103] Agreeing with the Board's analysis, the Supreme Court declared:

> [G]ood faith does not license the employer to refuse to enter into agreements on the ground that they do not include some proposal

---

part of bargaining unit); NLRB v. American Aggregate Co., 305 F2d 559, 50 LRRM 2580 (CA 5, 1962) (ignoring requests for bargaining); Duro Fittings Co., 121 NLRB 377, 42 LRRM 1368 (1958) (refusal to sit across table and bargain in person).
[99]§8(d).
[100]NLRB v. Katz, *supra* note 69.
[101]For a critical analysis of the application of *per se* rules to this aspect of bargaining, *see* Duvin, *supra* note 2 at 271.
[102]*Supra* note 52.
[103]113 NLRB 1288, 36 LRRM 1439 (1955), *enforced,* 236 F2d 898, 38 LRRM 2660 (CA 6, 1956), *aff'd, supra* note 52.

which is not a mandatory subject of bargaining. . . . [S]uch conduct is, in substance, a refusal to bargain about the subjects that are within the scope of mandatory bargaining. This does not mean that bargaining is to be confined to the statutory subjects. Each of the two controversial clauses is lawful in itself. Each would be enforceable if agreed to by the unions. But it does not follow that, because the company may propose these clauses, it may lawfully insist upon them as a condition to any agreement.[104]

Borg-Warner thus teaches that regardless of a party's good faith in bargaining, it commits an unfair labor practice by insisting to impasse upon incorporation of permissive subject matter in the collective bargaining contract, i.e., subject matter outside the scope of "wages, hours and other terms and conditions of employment."[105]

Permissive subjects of bargaining are treated in detail elsewhere.[106] Some examples of such subjects, employer insistence upon which have resulted in findings of *per se* violations of Section 8(a)(5), include (1) clauses requiring the union to post a performance bond,[107] (2) "ballot" clauses requiring a strike vote on the employer's last offer,[108] (3) legal-liability clauses (subjecting unions to legal liability for violation of a no-strike clause, including liability for all injury or damage resulting from such violation),[109] (4) interference with internal union affairs,[110] and (5) exclusion from a bargaining unit of certain categories of employees included under the certification.[111]

Union insistence upon permissive subjects may also constitute a *per se* refusal to bargain.[112] Examples of such subjects, which

---

[104]*Supra* note 52 at 349.

[105]*See generally* Chapters 17 and 18 *infra; see also* Comment, *Subjects Included Within Management's Duty to Bargain Collectively,* 26 L.A. L. REV. 630 (1966); Goetz, *The Duty to Bargain About Changes in Operations,* 64 DUKE L. J. 1 (1964); Comment, *Employer's Duty to Bargain About Subcontracting and Other "Management" Decisions,* 64 COLUM. L. REV. 294 (1964); Fleming, *The Changing Duty to Bargain,* 14 LAB. L. J. 297 (1963).

[106]*See generally* Chapter 18 *infra.*

[107]NLRB v. American Compress Warehouse, 350 F2d 365, 59 LRRM 2739 (CA 5, 1965), *cert. denied,* 382 US 982, 61 LRRM 2147 (1966); Union Mfg. Co., 76 NLRB 322, 21 LRRM 1187 (1948), *enforced,* 179 F2d 511, 25 LRRM 2302 (CA 5, 1950); Jasper Blackburn Prods. Corp., *supra* note 24.

[108]NLRB v. Borg-Warner Corp., *supra* note 52.

[109]Radiator Specialty Co., *supra* note 59. *See also* North Carolina Furniture, Inc., *supra* note 59.

[110]NLRB v. Superior Fireproof Door & Sash Co., *supra* note 78; NLRB v. Darlington Veneer Co., 236 F2d 85, 38 LRRM 2574 (CA 4, 1956). *Cf.* Bethlehem Steel, 133 NLRB 1400, 49 LRRM 1018 (1961) (dictum indicating it would be unlawful for an employer to insist upon a clause requiring individual signatures on grievances).

[111]Preterm, Inc., *supra* note 97.

[112]NLRB v. Hod Carriers (Laborers) Local 1082 (E. L. Boggs Plastering Co.), 384 F2d 55, 66 LRRM 2333 (CA 9, 1967), *aff'd,* 78 LRRM 2260 (CA 9, 1971), *cert. denied,* 390

have led to findings of Section 8(b)(3) violations, include
(1) combination or alteration of existing bargaining units,[113]
(2) exclusion of employees included by the Board in a unit or
including additional employees,[114] (3) inclusion of supervisors
in a contract,[115] (4) inclusion of agricultural labor,[116] (5) bonds
for the payment of employees' wages and benefits,[117] (6) union
label,[118] (7) industry promotion funds,[119] and (8) interest-arbitration clauses.[120]

III. THE GOOD-FAITH REQUIREMENT

The Board and the courts recognized at an early date that
simply compelling the parties to meet was insufficient to pro-

---

US 920, 67 LRRM 2385 (1968); Bricklayers Local 3 (Associated Gen. Contractors,
Eastern Washington), 162 NLRB 476, 64 LRRM 1085 (1966), *enforced*, 405 F2d 469, 69
LRRM 2944 (CA 9, 1968); Painters Dist. Council 36 (Commercial Drywall Constructors,
Inc.), 155 NLRB 1013, 60 LRRM 1431 (1965). *See also* Southern Cal. Pipe Trades Dist.
Council 16 (Aero Plumbing Co.), *supra* note 56, where a number of nonmandatory
subjects were insisted upon. Union insistence upon hot-cargo agreements may also, in
certain circumstances, be violative. Bricklayers Local 2 (Chris. Paschen Co.), 152 NLRB
1582, 59 LRRM 1320 (1965), *enforced*, 381 F2d 381, 65 LRRM 3103 (CA 6, 1967); Sheet
Metal Workers Local 26 (Reno Employers Council), 168 NLRB 893, 67 LRRM 1130
(1967). For general treatment of permissive subjects of bargaining, *see* Chapter 18 *infra*.

[113]NLRB v. Longshoremen (Lykes Bros. S.S. Co.), *supra* note 96; Longshoremen, 118
NLRB 1481, 40 LRRM 1408 (1957), *set aside on other grounds*, 277 F2d 681, 45 LRRM
2551 (CA DC, 1960); Douds v. Longshoremen, 241 F2d 278, 39 LRRM 2388 (CA 2,
1957); Electrical Workers Local 323 (IBEW) (Active Enterprises, Inc.), 242 NLRB 305,
101 LRRM 1179 (1979).

[114]Electrical Workers Local 1049 (IBEW) (Lewis Tree Serv.), 244 NLRB 124, 102
LRRM 1166 (1979); Steere Broadcasting Corp., 158 NLRB 487, 62 LRRM 1083 (1966);
Typographical Union (Haverhill Gazette Co.), 123 NLRB 806, 823, 43 LRRM 1538
(1959), *rev'd in pertinent part*, 278 F2d 6, 46 LRRM 2132 (CA 1, 1960), *aff'd in part and
rev'd in part*, 365 US 705, 47 LRRM 2920 (1961), *without considering this issue*. *See* AFL-
CIO Joint Negotiating Comm. (Phelps Dodge Corp.), 184 NLRB 976, 74 LRRM 1705
(1970), *rev'd*, 459 F2d 374, 79 LRRM 2939 (CA 3, 1972), *cert. denied*, 409 US 1059, 81
LRRM 2893 (1972), holding unions in violation of §8(b)(3) when they demanded and
struck to obtain company-wide bargaining instead of bargaining within established
bargaining units.

[115]Southern Cal. Pipe Trades Dist. Council 16 (Aero Plumbing Co.), *supra* note 56;
NLRB v. Retail Clerks (Safeway Co.), 203 F2d 165, 31 LRRM 2606 (CA 9, 1953),
adjudging union in contempt for insisting on bargaining for supervisory employees in
violation of a consent decree *enforcing* 96 NLRB 581, 28 LRRM 1554 (1951), *cert. denied*,
348 US 839, 34 LRRM 2898 (1954).

[116]District 50, Mine Workers (Central Soya Co.), *supra* note 57.

[117]Excello Dry Wall Co., 145 NLRB 663, 55 LRRM 1015 (1963). *See also* NLRB v.
American Compress Warehouse, *supra* note 107. *Cf.* Bricklayers Local 3, 162 NLRB
476, 64 LRRM 1085 (1966) (union may not insist on penalty clause calling for reimbursement to union for dues and initiation fees lost as a result of improper subcontracting).

[118]Kit Mfg. Co., 150 NLRB 662, 671, 58 LRRM 1140 (1964), *enforced per curiam*, 365
F2d 829, 62 LRRM 2856 (CA 9, 1966).

[119]NLRB v. Sheet Metal Workers Local 38, 575 F2d 394, 98 LRRM 2147 (CA 2, 1978),
enforcing 231 NLRB 699, 96 LRRM 1190 (1977); Detroit Resilient Floor Decorators
Local 2265 (Mill Floor Covering, Inc.), 136 NLRB 769, 49 LRRM 1842 (1962), *enforced*,
317 F2d 269, 53 LRRM 2311 (CA 6, 1963).

[120]NLRB v. Sheet Metal Workers Local 38, *supra* note 119.

mote the purposes of the Act.[121] Early attempts by employers to satisfy the bargaining obligation by merely going through the motions without actually seeking to adjust differences were condemned.[122] The concept of "good faith" was brought into the law of collective bargaining as a solution to the problem of bargaining without substance.[123] In 1947 the "good faith" requirement was expressly written into Section 8(d).

A. Totality of Conduct: *General Electric* and Boulwarism

The duty to bargain in good faith is an "obligation . . . to participate actively in the deliberations so as to indicate a present intention to find a basis for agreement . . . ."[124] This implies both "an open mind and a sincere desire to reach an agreement"[125] as well as "a sincere effort . . . to reach a common ground."[126] The presence or absence of intent "must be discerned from the record."[127] Except in cases where the conduct fails to meet the minimum obligation imposed by law or constitutes an outright refusal to bargain,[128] relevant facts of a case must be studied to determine whether the employer or the union is bargaining in good or bad faith, i.e., the "totality of conduct" is the standard

---

[121]1936 NLRB ANN. REP. 85 (1936): "Collective bargaining is something more than the mere meeting of an employer with the representatives of his employees; the essential thing is rather the serious intent to adjust differences and to reach an acceptable common ground."

[122]NLRB v. Montgomery Ward & Co., *supra* note 37; Benson Produce Co., 71 NLRB 888, 19 LRRM 1060 (1946).

[123]Cox, *The Duty to Bargain in Good Faith, supra* note 2 at 1413. *See* discussion of the meaning of the good-faith bargaining requirement, *supra*, at notes 33-48. Assessing the impact of that requirement, one commentator observed: "Whether imposing a statutory duty to bargain in "good faith" could ever amount to more than a pious exhortation has been the subject of much controversy . . . . Over the years, however, there has been increasing evidence the statute has had a practical effect, including voluntary compliance by management. Thus one survey revealed that successful bargaining relationships were eventually established in 75% of the cases sampled that went through to a final Board order, and in 90% of the cases that were voluntarily adjusted after the issuance of a complaint." St. Antoine, *The Role of Law,* in U.S. INDUSTRIAL RELATIONS 1950-1980: A CRITICAL ASSESSMENT 159, 172-73 (J. Stieber, R. McKersie, & D. Mills eds. 1981). *See* P. ROSS, THE GOVERNMENT AS A SOURCE OF UNION POWER (1965), 180-230; McCulloch, *The Development of Administrative Remedies,* LABOR LAW J. 14 (April 1963). *See, e.g.,* NLRB v. Montgomery Ward & Co., *supra* note 37; Globe Cotton Mills v. NLRB, *supra* note 24.

[124]NLRB v. Montgomery Ward & Co., *supra* note 37 at 686.

[125]*Id. See* NLRB v. Truitt Mfg. Co., 351 US 149, 38 LRRM 2042 (1956).

[126]*Supra* note 37 at 686. *See* NLRB v. Herman Sausage Co., *supra* note 40.

[127]*Supra* note 91.

[128]With the important caveat that "intent" may not even be in issue if the outward conduct amounts to a *de facto* refusal to bargain. *See* NLRB v. Katz, *supra* note 69. *But cf.* NLRB v. Cascade Employers Ass'n, Inc., 296 F2d 42, 48, 49 LRRM 2049 (CA 9, 1961), where the court held that the Board had erroneously applied the *per se* rule rather than looking to the "totality of circumstances" surrounding the bargaining. *See* discussion *supra* at notes 67-120.

through which the "quality" of negotiations is tested.[129] Thus, even though some specific actions, viewed alone, might not support a charge of bad-faith bargaining, a party's overall course of conduct in negotiations may reveal a violation of the Act.[130]

In 1963 the Board decided a case that provided background for consideration of the term "Boulwarism."[131] In *Philip Carey Manufacturing Co.*[132] the Board found a Section 8(a)(5) violation because of an employer's insistence on a superseniority proposal for nonstrikers. The trial examiner found that the company had frozen its position regarding the union's arguments and proposals after 11 bargaining sessions, so that little was accomplished in the seven subsequent meetings. The Board disagreed with this aspect of the decision, noting that "the Trial Examiner placed too much stress on finality and not enough on the amount of negotiation that preceded the 'final offer.' "[133] The trial examiner had disavowed any intent to pass generally on any technique of bargaining, although he characterized the employer's bargaining as a form of "Boulwarism."[134] The Board, in turn, stated

---

[129]NLRB v. Stevenson Brick & Block Co., 160 NLRB 198, 62 LRRM 1605 (1966), *enforcement denied in pertinent part*, 393 F2d 234, 68 LRRM 2086 (CA 4, 1968); B. F. Diamond Constr. Co., 163 NLRB 161, 64 LRRM 1333 (1967), *enforced per curiam*, 410 F2d 462, 71 LRRM 2112 (CA 5, 1969), *cert. denied*, 396 US 835, 72 LRRM 2432 (1969); General Elec. Co., *supra* note 91; McCulloch Corp., 132 NLRB 201, 48 LRRM 1344 (1961). In Rhodes-Holland Chevrolet Co., 146 NLRB 1304, 1304-1305, 56 LRRM 1058 (1964), the Board stated: "In finding that Respondent violated its obligation to bargain in good faith, we, like the Trial Examiner, have not relied solely on the position taken by Respondent on substantive contract terms, a factor which, standing alone, . . . might not have provided sufficient basis for the violation found, but have considered that factor as simply one item in the totality of circumstances reflecting Respondent's bargaining frame of mind." The "totality of conduct" doctrine, generally, stems from NLRB v. Virginia Elec. & Power Co., 314 US 469, 9 LRRM 405 1941.

[130]*See, e.g.*, Continental Ins. Co. v. NLRB, 495 F2d 44, 86 LRRM 2003 (CA 2, 1974), *enforcing* 204 NLRB 1013, 83 LRRM 1406 (1973). The court relied on the employer's delaying tactics in negotiations, unreasonable bargaining demands, efforts to bypass and undermine the union, and unilateral changes in mandatory subjects of bargaining. *See also* Cagle's, Inc. v. NLRB, 588 F2d 943, 100 LRRM 2590 (CA 5, 1979); NLRB v. Pacific Grinding Wheel Co., 572 F2d 1343, 98 LRRM 2246 (CA 9, 1978); Ramona's Mexican Food Prods., Inc., 203 NLRB 663, 83 LRRM 1705 (1973), *enforced per curiam*, 531 F2d 390, 92 LRRM 2611 (CA 9, 1975); John Zink Co., 196 NLRB 942, 80 LRRM 1232 (1972), *modified*, 83 LRRM 3045 (CA 10, 1973); Pillowtex Corp., 241 NLRB 40, 100 LRRM 1546 (1979); Milgo Indus., Inc., 229 NLRB 25, 96 LRRM 1347 (1977); Byrd's Terrazzo & Tile Co., 227 NLRB 866, 94 LRRM 1412 (1977); Underwriters Adjusting Co., 214 NLRB 388, 87 LRRM 1372 (1974). *Compare* NLRB v. Advanced Business Forms Corp., 474 F2d 457, 82 LRRM 2161 (CA 2, 1973) where the court refused to find bad-faith bargaining from totality of conduct. *See also* United Engines, Inc., 222 NLRB 50, 91 LRRM 1208 (1976).

[131]For a clarification of the term "Boulwarism" *see* note 138 *infra* and text accompanying note 157 *infra*.

[132]140 NLRB 1103, 52 LRRM 1184 (1963), *enforced in part*, 331 F2d 720, 55 LRRM 2821 (CA 6, 1964), *cert. denied*, 379 US 888, 57 LRRM 2307 (1964).

[133]*Id.* at 1104.

[134]*Id.* at 1122.

that it, too, was deciding the case on the facts presented and was not passing on a bargaining procedure.[135]

About one year later, the Board had occasion to consider the implications of Boulwarism in a case involving the company that developed the concept. In late 1964, the Board rendered its extremely controversial decision in the *General Electric Co.*[136] case. Five years later the Second Circuit enforced the Board's holding.[137] The *General Electric* case vividly demonstrates a convergence between the *per se* approach and the "totality of conduct" approach to the bargaining requirement. Although the rhetoric of the various opinions in the case indicates that the totality of the employer's conduct was the basis for finding that the employer was not bargaining in good faith, the critical elements of the conduct itself, as well as the conclusion to be drawn from the totality of that conduct, amounted to an actual absence of bargaining, as the court of appeals observed. As the facts in the case will demonstrate, the employer was insisting on a negotiation procedure which avoided the bilateral aspect inherent in the statutory concept of bargaining.

"Boulwarism" is the name describing the technique which General Electric utilized in the conduct which was in issue.[138] On the basis of its own research, the company formulated a single offer that anticipated the union's demands. Some six weeks of meetings (18 sessions) and a massive publicity campaign involving virtually all media of communication preceded the presentation of the offer on August 30, 1960. The company characterized its offer as fair and firm—one which would give

---

[135]*Id.* at 1104 n.2.

[136]*Supra* note 91.

[137]*Supra* note 91.

[138]The term "Boulwarism" was not used by the Board in its opinion, although the trial examiner's report employed the term with reference to General Electric's bargaining practices. *See, e.g.,* 150 NLRB at 207. The technique of "Boulwarism" was named for Lemuel R. Boulware, a vice-president of General Electric who formulated the concept following a bitter and disastrous strike suffered by General Electric in 1946. Briefly, the concept was designed to convince its employees that the company was responsive to their needs and that the union was not needed to force the company to grant what it would voluntarily provide. This was accomplished through a massive communications program to employees, a continual research program to discover what is "best" for its employees, and a formulation of a "firm and fair" offer to the union based upon the facts it had gathered. For a full explanation of the history of the 1960 negotiations and the concept of Boulwarism, *see* Cooper, *Boulwarism and the Duty to Bargain in Good Faith,* 20 RUTGERS L. REV. 653 (1966). *See also* Gross, Cullen & Hanslowe, *Good Faith in Labor Negotiations: Tests and Remedies,* 53 CORNELL L. REV. 1009 (1968); H. R. Northrup, BOULWARISM (1964); Note, *Boulwarism: Legality and Effect,* 76 HARV. L. REV. 807 (1963).

no reason for the union to impose a strike—but it would be open and subject to change if new information showed that the original offer was not "right."[139] However, by September 9, the company had made but four changes in the offer. A contract eventually was signed on November 10, 1960.

The company was charged with Section 8(a)(1), (3), and (5) violations.[140] The Board found a failure to bargain in good faith in GE's (1) failure to furnish information requested by the union,[141] (2) attempt to bargain with locals and thereby undermine the international's position,[142] (3) presentation of its insurance proposal on a take-it-or-leave-it basis,[143] (4) overall attitude or approach as evidenced by the totality of its conduct.[144] In a split decision, the Second Circuit agreed with these rulings and enforced the Board's order in its entirety.

The importance of the *General Electric* case was underscored by the appellate court's lengthy opinion affirming the Board's action. The opinion reviewed and analyzed the complex fact situation and arrived at legal conclusions which dramatically portrayed the nature of the statutory collective bargaining process. The case describes and focuses upon the complex nature of the duty to "bargain collectively" created by Sections 8(a)(5) and 8(b)(3).[145] The duty refers to a *bilateral* procedure whereby the employer and the bargaining representative *jointly* attempt to set wages and working conditions for the employees.[146] As this case demonstrates, the Act contemplates that a *bargaining process* will occur and that the parties will negotiate in good faith. The objective that Congress hoped to achieve by this process was described by the Supreme Court in *H. K. Porter Co.*:[147]

---

[139]*Supra* note 91 at 270.

[140]Similar charges had been filed by the union in 1954 and 1958, but were dismissed. Northrup, *supra* note 138 at 60.

[141]*Supra* note 91 at 193. *See also* discussion *infra* at notes 346-510.

[142]*Supra* note 91 at 262-66.

[143]*Supra* note 91 at 269. Although the trial examiner treated this as a separate violation, the Board considered General Electric's position on the insurance proposal to be indicative of the employer's overall bad faith. *Supra* note 91 at 196.

[144]*Supra* note 91 at 193.

[145]The original declaration of policy in the Wagner Act reenacted in §1 of the Taft-Hartley Act, declared that it is "the policy of the United States to eliminate the causes of certain substantial obstructions to the free flow of commerce and to mitigate and eliminate these obstructions when they have occurred *by encouraging the practice and procedure of collective bargaining . . . .*" (emphasis added).

[146]The current chapter defines the requirements of that procedure. The subjects about which the parties must bargain, *i.e.,* "the wages, hours, and other terms and conditions of employment" of §8(d), are treated in Chapter 17 *infra*.

[147]397 US 99, 73 LRRM 2561 (1970).

The object of this Act was . . . to ensure that employers and their employees could work together to establish mutually satisfactory conditions. The basic theme of the Act was that through collective bargaining the passions, arguments, and struggles of prior years would be channeled into constructive, open discussions leading, it was hoped, to mutual agreement.[148]

Under the statutory scheme, if wages or working conditions are set unilaterally[149] or in a manner which avoids the bargaining process, such as when the employer bypasses the bargaining representative and deals directly with the employees in the setting of wages and working conditions,[150] collective bargaining has not occurred. When there is an absence of collective bargaining, good faith may be an irrelevant consideration.[151] The term *per se violation* has generally been used to describe the bypassing of the bargaining process; and *lack of good faith* has often been used to describe refusing to bargain or sham bargaining. But lack of good faith may also refer to a subjective state of mind evidenced by various types of overt conduct, as described in this chapter. *General Electric* illustrates many of the subtle requirements of this elusive "duty to bargain."

The court majority in *General Electric* reviewed in detail the long history of the negotiations. It approved the Board's findings as to specific refusals to bargain: the unilateral promulgation of an accident insurance plan and the employer's refusal to "indicate the cost of union proposals, or how much [GE] was willing to expend . . . ."[152] Relying on *Truitt*[153] and other decisions requiring disclosure of bargaining information, the court stated:

[I]f the purpose of collective bargaining is to promote the "rational exchange of facts and arguments" that will measurably increase the chance for amicable agreement, then discussions in which unsubstantiated reasons are substituted for genuine arguments should be anathema.[154]

---

[148]*Id.* at 103.
[149]NLRB v. Katz, *supra* note 69 at 743, where the Supreme Court held "that an employer's unilateral change in conditions of employment under negotiation is . . . a violation of §8(a)(5), for it is a circumvention of the duty to negotiate . . . ." *See supra* this chapter at notes 68-90.
[150]General Elec. Co., *supra* note 91.
[151]NLRB v. Katz, *supra* note 69.
[152]418 F2d at 750.
[153]NLRB v. Truitt Mfg. Co., *supra* note 125. *See* discussion at notes 348-52 *infra*.
[154]*Supra* note 91 at 750, *citing* Cox, *The Duty to Bargain in Good Faith, supra* note 2.

Concerning the employer's conduct in dealing separately with several IUE locals, the court sustained the Board's conclusion that in each instance when the employer "went behind the back of the national negotiators and offered separate peace settlements to locals"[155] it committed an unfair labor practice.

In addition to affirming the foregoing three specific unfair labor practices, the court also agreed that the employer was guilty of a refusal to bargain based on the "totality of circumstances."[156] It took note of the take-it-or-leave-it basis of the insurance proposal, that GE "occasionally took untenable and unreasonable positions and then defended them, with no apparent purposes other than to avoid yielding to the Union,"[157] and other conduct which was deemed inconsistent with a genuine desire to reach a mutual accommodation. The court observed that the employer's aim "was to deal with the union through the employees, rather than the employees through the union"[158]— the antithesis of collective bargaining.

Underlying the decisions of both the Board and the court of appeals was the view that the employer had locked itself in.[159] GE had put certain benefits in effect, according to its longstanding policy of maintaining uniformity among all its employees, and had taken the public position that there was "nothing more to come." Thus, "having created a view of the bargaining process that admitted no compromise," the court's opinion concluded that GE "was trapped by its own creation."[160] The court also emphasized what it had not held:

> We do not today hold that an employer may not communicate with his employees during negotiations. Nor are we deciding that the "best offer first" bargaining technique is forbidden. Moreover, we do not require an employer to engage in "auction bargaining," or, as the dissent seems to suggest, compel him to make concessions, "minor" or otherwise.[161]

Disagreeing with the majority's reasoning, Judge Friendly, in a concurring and dissenting opinion, warned that the holding constituted a "serious indentation of §8(c) and (d), if not, indeed,

---

[155]*Id.* at 755.
[156]*Id.* at 756.
[157]*Id.* at 758.
[158]*Id.* at 759.
[159]*See* Jaffe, *Major Developments of the Year under the National Labor Relations Act,* NYU EIGHTEENTH ANNUAL CONFERENCE ON LABOR 61, 67 (1966).
[160]*Supra* note 91 at 760.
[161]*Id.* at 762.

of the First Amendment . . . the familiar instance of a hard case producing bad law."[162]

Writing for the majority, Judge Kaufman responded by spelling out the precise analytical scope of the holding, stating:

> Our dissenting brother's peroration conjures up the dark spectre that we have taken a "portentous step" [but] paints over with a broad stroke the care we have taken to spell out the bounds of our opinion. We hold that an employer may not so combine "take-it-or-leave-it" bargaining methods with a widely publicized stance of unbending firmness that he is himself unable to alter a position once taken. It is this specific conduct that GE must avoid in order to comply with the Board's order, and not a carbon copy of every underlying event relied upon by the Board to support its findings. Such conduct, we find, constitutes a refusal to bargain "in fact . . . ." It also constitutes, as the facts of this action demonstrate, an absence of subjective good faith, for it implies that the Company can deliberately bargain and communicate as though the Union did not exist, in clear derogation of the Union's status as exclusive representative of its members under section 9(a).[163]

During the period since 1969, when the Second Circuit decided the *General Electric* case, the Board and the courts have had occasion to consider some of the elements examined in *General Electric*. They have not always agreed on what constitutes the requisite showing of "Boulwarism."

In *Finch Baking Co.* v. *NLRB*[164] the Second Circuit ruled that the employer breached its duty to bargain in good faith by informing employees of the terms of its "firm, fair" offer *prior* to the time such offer was made to the union and by thereafter notifying the employees that unless the union accepted the offer prior to the expiration of the existing contract, the offer would be made directly to the employees in the hope that they would accept it and continue on the job. The offer finally was made to the union just hours before the expiration of the old contract.[165]

---

[162]*Id.* at 774.

[163]*Id.* at 762-63. *General Electric* was distinguished in Rangaire Corp., 157 NLRB 682, 61 LRRM 1429 (1966). *See also* Stark Ceramics, Inc., 155 NLRB 1258, 60 LRRM 1487 (1965), *enforced*, 375 F2d 202, 64 LRRM 2781 (CA 6, 1967); Memorial Consultants, Inc., 153 NLRB 1, 59 LRRM 1375 (1965); *cf.* Procter & Gamble Mfg. Co., 160 NLRB 334, 62 LRRM 1617 (1966) (a noncoercive communication campaign did not demonstrate bad faith, especially since the record established the employer's good faith in seeking to reach a common ground for agreement, as evidenced by its extensive negotiations, proposals, counterproposals, and concessions).

[164]479 F2d 732, 83 LRRM 2361 (CA 2, 1973), *cert. denied*, 414 US 1032, 84 LRRM 2683 (1973), *enforcing* 199 NLRB 414, 81 LRRM 1616 (1972).

[165]Noting that such a technique seriously impaired the union's ability to function as a bargaining representative, the court further found that (1) the timing of the offer to

The Eighth Circuit, however, in *United States Gypsum Co. v. NLRB*,[166] set aside the Board's order where (1) the employer's initial and final contract proposals were essentially identical and reflected an intransigent attitude toward bargaining; (2) the employer made its final offer before bargaining could narrow the differences between the parties, and (3) the employer circulated letters among the employees denigrating the union. Even though these techniques were similar to those employed by General Electric in its 1960 negotiations, the court held that the employer had the right to refuse to make concessions during bargaining as long as it agreed to meet and discuss its proposals with the union.

In *Arnold Graphic Industries, Inc. v. NLRB*[167] the Sixth Circuit set aside that portion of a Board order holding that the employer had engaged in "take-it-or-leave-it" bargaining, agreeing with the administrative law judge that the employer had bargained further, had modified its demands, and had otherwise evidenced its good faith by taking the union's wage offer to its board of directors. In a subsequent decision, however, the Sixth Circuit enforced a Board holding that an employer "as a practical matter" had made a "take-it-or-leave-it" economic offer on 20 bargaining subjects by insisting that the entire proposal would lapse automatically five days later unless accepted by the union, and by refusing the union additional time to study the proposal.[168]

On the other hand, the Board has also held that an employer's take-it-or-leave-it position during negotiations does not constitute bad faith where the *union* refuses to compromise on any of its demands or to pursue negotiations diligently to help resolve bargaining differences.[169]

---

the union prevented any meaningful evaluation or discussion, (2) the company became so enamored with its "firm, fair" offer technique that it ignored its basic duty to allow adequate time or opportunity for discussion, and (3) the employees were assured specific increases regardless of union acceptance or rejection before the increases had even been presented to the union. The company's technique was thus not an "offer" but a "decision" completely removing the element of bargaining. According to the court, "the fountain was poisoned before it ever began to flow." *Id.* at 736.

[166]484 F2d 108, 84 LRRM 2129 (CA 8, 1973), *denying enforcement to* 200 NLRB 1098, 82 LRRM 1064 (1972).

[167]505 F2d 257, 87 LRRM 2753 (CA 6, 1974), *denying enforcement in part to* 206 NLRB 327, 84 LRRM 1343 (1973).

[168]Federal Mogul Corp., 212 NLRB 950, 87 LRRM 1105 (1974), *enforced*, 524 F2d 37, 91 LRRM 2207 (CA 6, 1975). Chairman Miller dissented on the ground that the company's time limit "was essentially a typical negotiating gambit." *Id.* at 955.

[169]Romo Paper Prods. Corp., 208 NLRB 644, 85 LRRM 1165 (1974).

Nor in the Board's view does an employer violate the Act merely by communicating with employees during bargaining while at the same time taking a hard-line bargaining posture. Accordingly, no violation was found where an employer told an assembled group of employees that it would refuse to accede to the union's demands.[170] Observing that the *General Electric* case only proscribes "a massive campaign of employee persuasion designed to undercut the bargaining representative and win support for the company's 'take-it-or-leave-it' bargain [sic] methods," the Board concluded that the employer's conduct amounted to little more than publicly taking a position on a bargaining issue and then notifying employees of that position.[171] The opinion observed that employees today are sufficiently sophisticated to appreciate such an approach.

B. Indicia of Good or Bad Faith

1. Surface Bargaining. Closely aligned with the concept which views the "totality" of the bargaining, is the notion of *surface bargaining*. In the evaluation of an employer's or a union's bargaining conduct, certain factors are relied upon to ascertain whether the parties have bargained in good or bad faith.[172] Any one of these factors, standing alone, is usually insufficient to support a refusal-to-bargain charge, but their "persuasiveness grows as the number of issues increases."[173] An inference of surface bargaining is greater, however, where it derives from conduct otherwise violative of the Act, and especially where the unlawful conduct has been viewed by the Board as a *per se* refusal to bargain.

Although an employer may be willing to meet at length and confer with the union, the Board will find a refusal to bargain in good faith if it concludes the employer is merely going through the "motions" of bargaining.[174] "Surface bargaining" has been

---

[170]Oneita Knitting Mills, Inc., 205 NLRB 500, 83 LRRM 1670 (1973).

[171]*Id.* at 500.

[172]"[T]he question of whether an employer is acting in good or bad faith at the time of the refusal is . . . one which . . . must be determined in the light of all relevant facts in the case, including any unlawful conduct of the employer, the sequence of events, and the time lapse between the refusal and the unlawful conduct." Joy Silk Mills, Inc. v. NLRB, 185 F2d 732, 742, 27 LRRM 2012, 2019 (CA DC, 1950), *cert. denied*, 341 US 914, 27 LRRM 2633 (1951). *See* Shieber, *Surface Bargaining: The Problem and a Proposed Solution*, 5 UNIV. TOL. L. REV. 656 (1974).

[173]Cox, *The Duty to Bargain in Good Faith*, *supra* note 2 at 1421.

[174]Greensboro News Co., 222 NLRB 893, 91 LRRM 1308 (1976), *enforced per curiam*, 549 F2d 308, 94 LRRM 2752 (CA 4, 1977) (union's insistence on interest-arbitration

found where an employer rejected a union's proposal, tendered its own, and did not attempt to reconcile the differences.[175] Likewise, the offering of a proposal that cannot be accepted, coupled with an inflexible attitude on major issues and no proposal of reasonable alternatives, has been condemned as violative of the good-faith obligation.[176]

In *Irvington Motors, Inc.*,[177] the employer was held to have violated the Act by engaging in surface bargaining where its offer merely reiterated existing practices and its first written

provision, coupled with advancement in the last negotiating session of a new proposal for an agreement of 12 years' duration with wage rates in excess of those sought by it in previous sessions, held evidence of surface bargaining in violation of §8(b)(3); Texas Coca Cola Bottling Co., 146 NLRB 420, 55 LRRM 1326 (1964), *enforced per curiam*, 365 F2d 321, 62 LRRM 2487 (CA 5, 1966) (employer's refusal to accept union's proposed management-rights clause even though it had suggested same clause to union, refusal to agree to arbitration clause after securing union's agreement to no-strike clause, failure to submit counterproposal on dues check-off, rejection of agreement on workweek, *inter alia*, led to conclusion that employer was merely going through the motions of negotiation without sincere desire to reach agreement); My Store, Inc., 147 NLRB 145, 56 LRRM 1176 (1964), *enforced*, 345 F2d 494, 58 LRRM 2775 (CA 7, 1965), *cert. denied*, 382 US 927, 60 LRRM 2424 (1965) (furnishing erroneous wage information to union and failing to correct it after discovering error, questioning of union's majority by raising issue covered by consent election, failure to submit counterproposal until four months after certification, and making minor agreements to give the "appearances of bargaining" considered as "evidence of Respondent's bad faith"); Tower Hosiery Mills, Inc., 81 NLRB 658, 23 LRRM 1397 (1949), *enforced*, 180 F2d 701, 25 LRRM 2509 (CA 4, 1950), *cert. denied*, 340 US 811, 26 LRRM 2611 (1950) (employer's insistence on union bond payable in event of breach of no-strike clause, and substitution of a more burdensome requirement after seven months of negotiation without modifying its requirement for an open shop, showed "lack of a sincere purpose to reach an agreement"). *See also* West Coast Casket Co., 192 NLRB 624, 78 LRRM 1026 (1971), *enforced in part*, 469 F2d 871, 81 LRRM 2857 (CA 9, 1972); Tex Tan Welhausen Co. v. NLRB, 419 F2d 1265, 72 LRRM 2885 (CA 5, 1969); Collins & Aikman Corp., 165 NLRB 678, 65 LRRM 1484 (1967), *enforced in part*, 395 F2d 277, 68 LRRM 2320 (CA 4, 1968); Southern Transport, Inc., 145 NLRB 615, 55 LRRM 1023 (1963), *enforced*, 343 F2d 558, 58 LRRM 2822 (CA 8, 1965); Atlanta Broadcasting Co., 90 NLRB 808, 26 LRRM 1287 (1950), *enforced*, 193 F2d 641, 29 LRRM 2327 (CA 5, 1952); Walter Pape, Inc., 205 NLRB 719, 84 LRRM 1055 (1973).

[175]Neon Sign Corp., 229 NLRB 861, 95 LRRM 1161 (1977), *enforcement denied*, 602 F2d 1203, 102 LRRM 2485 (CA 5, 1979) (failure of employer to move from its initial economic proposals in the face of some union movement in this area, its failure to accept the union's noneconomic proposals, and its inquiry concerning the union's position on crossing picket lines viewed as evidence of surface bargaining); A. H. Belo Corp., 170 NLRB 1558, 69 LRRM 1239 (1968), *modified*, 411 F2d 959, 71 LRRM 2437 (CA 5, 1969); General Elec. Co., *supra* note 91.

[176]NLRB v. Wright Motors, Inc., 603 F2d 604, 102 LRRM 2021 (CA 7, 1979); Brownsboro Hills Nursing Home, Inc., 244 NLRB 269, 102 LRRM 1118 (1979); K-Mart Corp., 242 NLRB 855, 101 LRRM 1406 (1979); Clear Pine Moldings, Inc., 238 NLRB 69, 99 LRRM 1221 (1978); Case, Inc., 237 NLRB 798, 99 LRRM 1159 (1978); Neon Sign Corp., *supra* note 175; San Isabel Elec. Servs., Inc., 225 NLRB 1073, 93 LRRM 1055 (1976); Yearbook House, 223 NLRB 1456, 92 LRRM 1191 (1976); Morena & Sons, Inc., 163 NLRB 1071, 65 LRRM 1054 (1967); Roy E. Hanson, Jr., Mfg., 137 NLRB 251, 50 LRRM 1134 (1962).

[177]147 NLRB 565, 56 LRRM 1257 (1964), *enforced per curiam*, 343 F2d 759, 58 LRRM 2816 (CA 3, 1965).

counterproposal was not submitted until 3-1/2 months after it had been requested.[178] An employer's (1) predetermined and inflexible position toward union security and merit increases,[179] (2) dilatory tactics and an apparent intent to reach an impasse,[180] (3) arbitrary scheduling of the day and time of a bargaining meeting,[181] (4) failure to designate an agent with sufficient authority,[182] (5) withdrawal of provisions already agreed upon,[183] and (6) injecting significant new proposals at an advanced stage in negotiations[184] have each been held to be an element which, when coupled with other factors, proves an intent to engage in "surface bargaining" rather than reach a mutually satisfactory basis for agreement.

But the mere tendering by an employer of a counterproposal which is "predictably unacceptable" is not, standing alone, sufficient to justify a finding of lack of good faith, provided the proposal does not foreclose future discussion.[185] In *NLRB v. Tomco Communications, Inc.*,[186] the Ninth Circuit disagreed with Board findings that the employer had engaged in bad-faith bargaining: The employer had insisted to impasse on a detailed management-rights clause, a broad zipper clause, a waiver-of-past-practices provision, and a no-strike provision that covered strikes over matters not covered by the employer's proposed grievance-arbitration provision; the employer's final economic offer consisted of a tendered increase of ten cents an hour to seven of the nine bargaining-unit employees and a wage review for the remaining two employees. The Board had concluded that the employer engaged in surface bargaining, and con-

---

[178]*See also* MacMillan Ring-Free Oil Co., 160 NLRB 877, 63 LRRM 1073 (1966), *enforcement denied on other grounds*, 394 F2d 26, 68 LRRM 2004 (CA 9, 1968).

[179]Duro Fittings Co., 121 NLRB 377, 42 LRRM 1368 (1958).

[180]Hilton Mobile Homes, 155 NLRB 873, 60 LRRM 1411 (1965), *modified*, 387 F2d 7, 67 LRRM 2140 (CA 8, 1967) (by implication); Wheeling Pac. Co., 151 NLRB 1192, 58 LRRM 1580 (1965). For the effect of an impasse on the bargaining obligation, *see infra* at notes 538-71.

[181]Moore Drop Forging Co., 144 NLRB 165, 54 LRRM 1024 (1963).

[182]Billups W. Petroleum Co., 169 NLRB 964, 67 LRRM 1323 (1968), *enforced per curiam*, 416 F2d 1333, 72 LRRM 2687 (CA 5, 1969); Bonham Cotton Mills, 121 NLRB 1235, 42 LRRM 1542 (1958), *enforced per curiam*, 289 F2d 903, 48 LRRM 2086 (CA 5, 1961).

[183]Valley Oil Co., 210 NLRB 370, 86 LRRM 1351 (1974).

[184]Yearbook House, *supra* note 176; Greensboro News Co., *supra* note 174.

[185]Neon Sign Corp. v. NLRB, *supra* note 175; NLRB v. Crockett-Bradley, Inc., 598 F2d 971, 101 LRRM 3040 (CA 5, 1979); NLRB v. Tomco Communications, Inc., 567 F2d 871, 97 LRRM 2660 (CA 9, 1978), *denying enforcement to* 220 NLRB 636, 90 LRRM 1321 (1975).

[186]*Supra* note 185.

demned the employer's final proposals as "terms which no self respecting union could be expected to accept," amounting to a demand that the union "abdicate virtually every right it would normally possess to represent effectively the employees involved during the contract term."[187] The Ninth Circuit concluded, however, that the case only involved "hard bargaining between two parties who were possessed of disparate economic power: a relative weak union and a relative strong company," and that the employer's use of its economic-power advantage was not inconsistent with its statutory duty to negotiate in good faith. Rejecting the Board's "self respecting union" test for good-faith negotiations, the court said that such a standard "comes perilously close to determining what the employer should give by looking at what the employees want."[188]

The Second Circuit noted in *NLRB* v. *Fitzgerald Mills Corp.*[189] that "[i]n the realities of the bargaining process, neither party expects its first proposal to be accepted."[190] And the fact that extensive negotiations fail to produce a contract does not justify an inference that the company is engaged in "surface bargaining," since the Act does not compel the parties to reach an agreement. In one Board case the parties had exchanged contract proposals, had met and discussed them, and the union negotiator had written the company a letter stating he felt that the parties were not too far apart on the issues; the Board found

---

[187]220 NLRB at 637.

[188]567 F2d at 883. *Accord*, Gulf States Mfrs. v. NLRB, 579 F2d 1298, 99 LRRM 2547 (CA 5, 1978); *but cf.*, NLRB v. Mar-Len Cabinets, Inc., 659 F2d 995, 108 LRRM 2838 (CA 9, 1981).

[189]133 NLRB 877, 48 LRRM 1745 (1961), *enforced*, 313 F2d 260, 52 LRRM 2174 (CA 2, 1963), *cert. denied*, 375 US 834, 54 LRRM 2312 (1963).

[190]*Id.* at 265. "Consideration of the negotiations themselves, rather than the proposed contracts within whose framework they were conducted, is a better guide to whether there was good faith bargaining." *Id.* at 266. This view also prevails under the Railway Labor Act. *See* Atlantic Coast Line R.R. v. Brotherhood of R.R. Trainmen, 262 F Supp 177, 64 LRRM 2177, 2182 (D DC, 1967), *rev'd on other grounds*, 383 F2d 225, 66 LRRM 2115 (CA DC, 1967). In Kohler Co., 128 NLRB 1062, 46 LRRM 1389 (1960), *enforced in part, modified and remanded in part*, 300 F2d 699, 49 LRRM 2485 (CA DC, 1962), the union had charged that the company had engaged in "surface bargaining" during prestrike negotiations by making few concessions and remaining firm on its original offer. In rejecting this charge, the Board pointed to the company's request to get to the "meat" of the contract, its regular attendance at bargaining sessions, and its exploration of alternatives and the reasonableness of arguments in support of its bargaining positions. *Id.* at 1069. The Board did find that Kohler's post-strike conduct in unilaterally increasing the wages of nonstrikers after having previously attached conditions to its offer of the same increase to the union, coupled with surveillance and discharge of strikers, constituted a §8(a)(5) violation. *Id.* at 1078. *See also* Star Expansion Indus. Corp., 164 NLRB 563, 65 LRRM 1127 (1967), *aff'd*, 409 F2d 150, 70 LRRM 2529 (CA DC, 1969).

no bad faith even though no agreement had been reached.[191] An employer's adherence to a "package" proposal during contract negotiations has been allowed in view of the employer's willingness to concede other points.[192] In addition, bargaining without concealing existing "mutual hostility,"[193] or negotiating in a "cool atmosphere,"[194] will not "dilute a finding of good faith where the totality of the party's conduct conforms to the dictates of the statute."[195] Indeed, even where an employer's conduct might have been viewed as surface bargaining, the Board has been reluctant to so hold if the union has been equally intransigent.[196]

2. Concessions, Proposals, and Demands. *a. Concessions.*

"Although . . . state of mind may occasionally be revealed by declarations, ordinarily the proof must come by inference from external conduct."[197] Thus, even though Section 8(d) does not require the making of a concession, the courts' and the Board's definitions of good faith[198] suggest that willingness to compromise is an important if not an essential ingredient.[199] The granting or withholding of concessions may be of vital importance in defending against charges of refusal to bargain in good faith. The historic language in *Reed & Prince*[200] bears this out:

> [W]hile the Board cannot force an employer to make a "concession" on any specific issue or to adopt any particular position, the employer

---

[191]Lakeland Cement Co., 130 NLRB 1365, 47 LRRM 1499 (1961). The employer committed independent §8(a)(1) violations by assisting employees in the processing of withdrawal petitions and interrogating an employee with regard to his union sympathies.
[192]Midwestern Instruments, Inc., 133 NLRB 1132, 48 LRRM 1793 (1961). But offering a union a contract on a take-it-or-leave-it basis has been consistently held to be a repudiation of collective bargaining. *See, e.g.,* NLRB v. Insurance Agents' Int'l Union, *supra* note 83; NLRB v. Truitt Mfg. Co., *supra* note 125. *See also* discussion of the *General Electric* case *supra* at notes 140-63.
[193]McCulloch Corp., *supra* note 129. *Compare* Brownsboro Hills Nursing Home, Inc., *supra* note 176.
[194]NLRB v. Almeida Bus Lines, Inc., 333 F2d 129, 731, 56 LRRM 2548 (CA 1, 1964), *setting aside* 142 NLRB 445, 53 LRRM 1055 (1963).
[195]*Id.* at 731.
[196]Unoco Apparel, Inc., 208 NLRB 601, 85 LRRM 1169 (1974), *enforced,* 508 F2d 1368, 88 LRRM 2956 (CA 5, 1975).
[197]Cox, *The Duty to Bargain in Good Faith, supra* note 2 at 1418.
[198]*See, e.g.,* NLRB v. Highland Park Mfg., 110 F2d 632, 6 LRRM 786 (CA 4, 1940), and Part I *supra* for general definitions of good faith and cases thereon.
[199]Cox, *supra* note 2 at 1414. For this reason, Professor Cox concluded "that the conventional definition of good faith bargaining as a sincere effort to reach an agreement goes beyond the statute." *Id.* at 1416. *See also* Specialty Container Corp., 171 NLRB 24, 68 LRRM 1018 (1968).
[200]NLRB v. Reed & Prince Mfg. Co., 96 NLRB 850, 28 LRRM 1608 (1951), *enforced,* 205 F2d 131, 32 LRRM 2225 (CA 1, 1953), *cert. denied,* 346 US 887, 33 LRRM 2133 (1953).

is obliged to make *some* reasonable effort in *some* direction to compose his differences with the union, if §8(a)(5) is to be read as imposing any substantial obligation at all.[201]

In *Herman Sausage Co.*[202] the Board found, as evidence of the employer's bad faith, its unwillingness "to accept or consider any contract other than its proposed contract," which, though similar to a contract previously executed by the same union, "constituted such a radical departure from the previous contract in eliminating approximately 26 existing benefits . . . as to be predictably unacceptable to the Union."[203]

Alluding to the futility of future negotiations unless the union accepts certain management proposals,[204] insistence that economic items not be discussed until all other terms are agreed upon,[205] failure to offer "concessions of value,"[206] and creating the impression that there can be no wage increase in order to assure that negotiations would founder,[207] have all been considered factors[208] pointing to bad-faith bargaining.[209] But as the

---

[201]*Id.* at 134-35.

[202]*Supra* note 40.

[203]*Id.* at 170. *See also* K-Mart Corp., *supra* note 176; Pillowtex Corp., *supra* note 130; Preterm, Inc., *supra* note 111.

[204]Howmet Corp., 197 NLRB 471, 80 LRRM 1555 (1972) (a party cannot condition its making of counterproposals upon "more realistic" offers by the other side); Lewin-Mathes Co., 126 NLRB 936, 45 LRRM 1416 (1960), *enforcement denied*, 285 F2d 329, 47 LRRM 2288 (CA 7, 1960).

[205]South Shore Hosp., 245 NLRB 848, 102 LRRM 1565 (1979); K-Mart Corp., *supra* note 176; Federal Mogul Corp., *supra* note 168; Rhodes-Holland Chevrolet Co., *supra* note 129. *See also* Vanderbilt Prods., Inc., 129 NLRB 1323, 47 LRRM 1182 (1961), *enforced per curiam*, 297 F2d 833, 49 LRRM 2286 (CA 2, 1961).

[206]NLRB v. Columbia Tribune Publishing Co., 495 F2d 1384, 86 LRRM 2078 (CA 8, 1974), *enforcing and remanding* 201 NLRB 538, 82 LRRM 1553 (1973); Collins & Aikman Corp., 165 NLRB 678, 65 LRRM 1484 (1967), *enforced in part*, 395 F2d 277, 68 LRRM 2320 (CA 4, 1968). *See also* East Texas Steel Castings Co., 154 NLRB 1080, 60 LRRM 1097 (1965).

[207]Cincinnati Cordage & Paper Co., 141 NLRB 72, 52 LRRM 1277 (1963). "For the Company to refuse at this time [the parties' last meeting and after a strike vote had been taken] to divulge that it would consider a more modest demand than had been theretofore advanced, and for it to state to the Union a position which the plant manager later admitted on the witness stand was a falsity—namely, that it could not grant *any* increase because of competition—establishes that it was not bargaining in good faith." *Id.* at 77.

[208]In Marden Mfg. Co., 106 NLRB 1335, 33 LRRM 1025 (1953), *enforced*, 217 F2d 567, 35 LRRM 2217 (CA 5, 1954), *cert. denied*, 348 US 981, 35 LRRM 2709 (1955), the Board expressly declined to "adopt a possible implication . . . in . . . the Intermediate Report that the . . . failure to make concessions to the Union with respect to wages or financial benefits was *per se* a refusal to bargain . . . rather than only 'a material factor' in assessing good faith." 106 NLRB at 1338.

[209]Other factors considered include an employer's insistence on a broad management-prerogatives clause while refusing to negotiate about a wage increase and declining to consent to arbitration. "M" System, Inc., 129 NLRB 527, 47 LRRM 1017 (1960) (the employer also violated §8(a)(5) by instituting a wage incentive plan and granting individual pay raises without consulting the union while steadfastly refusing to enter any

Board stated in *Partee Flooring Mill*,[210] "[t]he significant fact is not whether [the employer] was [in a position] to grant such concessions, but rather whether it had bargained in good faith on the subject."[211]

Granting numerous concessions may be an indication of good-faith bargaining. Although some decisions purport to look beyond the number of concessions granted or withheld,[212] others indicate that consideration is given to the quantity as well as the quality of concessions. In one case, for instance, the Fifth Circuit took note of "thirty-eight instances where [the employer] adjusted its proposals in striving to induce the Union to agree" and made "numerous concessions on substantive issues."[213] By the same token, quantitative considerations have also influenced findings of lack of good faith.[214]

Agreement on a number of major bargaining subjects may be used as evidence to overcome a refusal-to-bargain charge based on a single issue.[215] In *John S. Swift Co.*[216] a union representing only a portion of the employees at one plant sought to institute

---

agreement containing a wage increase of any size). *See also* Farmers Coop. Gin Ass'n, 161 NLRB 887, 63 LRRM 1400 (1966) (employer agreed to payroll deductions not involving the union while refusing a request for a check-off provision). In Fitzgerald Mills, *supra* note 189, the employer in contract-renewal negotiations submitted a counterproposal that was, in effect, the expiring contract. Thereafter "the Union receded from its original position and made a great many progressively lesser requests but . . . the Respondent at all times maintained an uncompromising attitude, rejecting the Union's request without explanation or discussion . . . . While an employer is not obligated to make any concession, it is required to make a reasonable effort to reach an agreement." *Id.* at 880. *See also* Alba-Waldensian, 167 NLRB 695, 66 LRRM 1445 (1967), *aff'd per curiam*, 404 F2d 1370, 69 LRRM 2882 (CA 4, 1968).
[210]Partee Flooring Mill, 107 NLRB 1177, 33 LRRM 1342 (1954).
[211]*Id.* at 1178. *But see* NLRB v. Minute Maid Corp., 283 F2d 705, 47 LRRM 2072 (CA 5, 1960), *denying enforcement to* 124 NLRB 355, 44 LRRM 1376 (1959).
[212]*See, e.g.*, Vickers, Inc., 153 NLRB 561, 59 LRRM 1516 (1965).
[213]NLRB v. General Tire & Rubber Co., 326 F2d 832, 833, 55 LRRM 2150 (CA 5, 1964), *denying enforcement to* 135 NLRB 269, 49 LRRM 1469 (1962). In Star Expansion Indus. Corp., *supra* note 190, "the company agreed to some 12 or more proposals made by the union. In subsequent negotiations, it made other concessions and offered proposals of its own on wage increases and other matters." In Dierks Forests, Inc., 148 NLRB 923, 57 LRRM 1086 (1964), "the Union [initially] presented its proposed contract, consisting of 25 articles, with a total of 61 subsections." *Id.* at 927. The employer submitted counterproposals on every issue except a no-discrimination clause, checkoff, and insurance. By the end of the negotiations, 54 of the 62 subsections that had been presented were agreed upon. *Id.* at 928.
[214]Abingdon Nursing Center, 197 NLRB 781, 80 LRRM 1470 (1972); Florida Mach. & Foundry Co., 190 NLRB 563, 77 LRRM 1272 (1971), *enforced*, 441 F2d 1005, 78 LRRM 2895 (CA DC, 1971), *cert. denied*, 409 US 846, 81 LRRM 2390 (1972).
[215]*See, e.g.*, McCourt v. California Sports, Inc., 600 F2d 1193 (CA 6, 1979); Procter & Gamble Mfg. Co., *supra* note 163.
[216]124 NLRB 394, 44 LRRM 1388 (1959), *enforced in part and denied in part*, 277 F2d 641, 46 LRRM 2090 (CA 7, 1960).

its own health and welfare plan; whereas the employer insisted upon retaining its existing company-wide plan embracing several plants. In finding that the employer had bargained in good faith with respect to the health and welfare plan, the Board noted the employer's continued willingness to discuss the issue and the fact that agreement had been reached "on virtually every major bargaining item excepting health and welfare."[217]

In the *Cummer-Graham*[218] case, where the employer would not agree to an arbitration clause but was adamant in insisting upon inclusion of a no-strike clause, the Board found a refusal to bargain in good faith, but the Fifth Circuit denied enforcement, stating that it did "not think that the Supreme Court held, or intended to hold, in *Lincoln Mills,* that a no-strike clause and an arbitration clause were so much one that a persistent demand for the one without acquiescing in the other is a refusal to bargain in good faith."[219]

As the foregoing cases demonstrate, no rule of thumb is available to measure the significance of specific concessions. Reference must usually be made to the "totality" of negotiations in order to find good or bad faith. Where a review of the record as a whole has shown no dilatory tactics or an attempt to stall efforts[220] to reach an agreement,[221] *hard bargaining* rather than unlawful bargaining has been inferred from an unyielding position by an employer on security,[222] wage offers,[223] check-off,[224]

---

[217]*Id.* at 395. However, the employer was found guilty of a §8(a)(5) violation for failing to furnish data on wages and the cost of its health and welfare plan; the finding was enforced on appeal.

[218]Cummer-Graham Co., 122 NLRB 1044, 43 LRRM 1253 (1959), *enforcement denied,* 279 F2d 757, 46 LRRM 2374 (CA 5, 1960).

[219]279 F2d at 759-60. Textile Workers v. Lincoln Mills, 353 US 448, 40 LRRM 2113 (1957). *See* Chapter 19 *infra* at notes 32-38.

[220]NLRB v. Wonder State Mfg. Co., *supra* note 69.

[221]"The fact that respondent did not accede to the Union's proposal but endeavored to secure a contract which it regarded would be compatible with its financial condition, does not of itself establish lack of good faith. The Act does not compel either party to agree to a proposal or require the making of a concession." *Id.,* 344 F2d at 217.

[222]McCulloch Corp., *supra* note 129. *But see* NLRB v. Newton-New Haven Co., 101 LRRM 2917 (D Conn, 1979), *aff'd as modified,* 506 F2d 1035, 101 LRRM 2922 (CA 2, 1979) (civil contempt for violating bargaining order); Brownsboro Hills Nursing Home, Inc., *supra* note 176; K-Mart Corp., *supra* note 176; ENDO Laboratories, Inc., 239 NLRB No. 147, 100 LRRM 1110 (1978).

[223]Neon Sign Corp. v. NLRB, *supra* note 175; Webster Outdoor Advertising Co., 170 NLRB 1395, 67 LRRM 1589 (1968); Midwestern Instruments, Inc., *supra* note 192. *But see* Orion Tool, Die & Mach. Co., 195 NLRB 1080, 79 LRRM 1636 (1972) (hard-bargaining argument rejected—no effort by company to establish that it could not afford benefits it had rejected). *See also* Longhorn Mach. Works, 205 NLRB 685, 84

management rights,[225] and arbitration and no-strike clauses discussed above. The failure of management to retreat from a rigid position has also been justified, at least partially, by the failure of the union to recede from its position or to grant concessions "for which it could reasonably expect a *quid pro quo* from the [employer]."[226]

b. *Proposals and Demands.* The Board will consider the advancement of proposals by a party as a factor in determining overall good faith.[227] The fact that a proposal is "predictably unacceptable" will not justify an inference of bad faith if the proposal does not foreclose future negotiations,[228] unless it is so harsh or patently unreasonable as to frustrate agreement.[229] Moreover, the fact that a proposal merely embodies existing practices or advances less desirable working conditions, is not, in itself, supportive of a finding of bad faith. Such fact may,

---

LRRM 1307 (1973); American Express Reservations, Inc., 209 NLRB 1105, 86 LRRM 1362 (1974).

[224]NLRB v. General Tire & Rubber Co., *supra* note 213; Cone Mills Corp., 169 NLRB 449, 67 LRRM 1241 (1968), *modified on other grounds,* 413 F2d 445, 71 LRRM 2916 (CA 4, 1969); McLane Co., 166 NLRB 1036, 65 LRRM 1729 (1967), *aff'd per curiam,* 405 F2d 483, 70 LRRM 2095 (CA 5, 1968); Raybestos-Manhattan, Inc. (General Asbestos & Rubber Div.), 168 NLRB 396, 67 LRRM 1012 (1967). *But see* Farmers Coop. Gin Ass'n, *supra* note 209. *See H. K. Porter* and discussion of checkoff at notes 240-48 *infra.*

[225]Procter & Gamble Mfg. Co., *supra* note 163.

[226]Broadway Hosp., Inc., 244 NLRB 341, 102 LRRM 1259 (1979); Memorial Consultants, Inc., 153 NLRB 1, 15, 59 LRRM 1375 (1965). *See* NLRB v. Stevenson Brick & Block Co., *supra* note 129.

[227]Hondo Drilling Co., 213 NLRB 229, 87 LRRM 1760 (1974), *aff'd,* 525 F2d 864, 91 LRRM 2133 (CA 5, 1976), *cert. denied,* 429 US 818, 93 LRRM 2362 (1976); WCUE Radio, Inc., 209 NLRB 181, 86 LRRM 1191 (1974); Reisman Bros., Inc., 165 NLRB 390, 65 LRRM 1409 (1967), *aff'd per curiam,* 401 F2d 770, 69 LRRM 2521 (CA 2, 1968); Channel Master Corp., 162 NLRB 632, 64 LRRM 1102 (1967); Anderson's, 161 NLRB 1470, 63 LRRM 1456 (1966); Procter & Gamble Mfg. Co., *supra* note 163.

[228]NLRB v. Crockett-Bradley, Inc., 598 F2d 971, 975-77, 101 LRRM 3040 (CA 5, 1979); Gulf States Mfrs. v. NLRB, 579 F2d 1298, 99 LRRM 2547 (CA 5, 1978), *rehearing en banc granted,* 598 F2d 896, 101 LRRM 2805 (CA 5, 1979), *enforcing in part, denying and remanding in part,* 230 NLRB 558, 96 LRRM 1032 (1977); NLRB v. Big Three Indus., Inc., 497 F2d 43, 86 LRRM 3031 (CA 5, 1974); NLRB v. Fitzgerald Mills, *supra* note 189; Preterm, Inc., *supra* note 97. *See* Rangaire Corp., *supra* note 163. The Ninth Circuit has stated: "We may also assume arguendo that in certain exceptional cases the extreme or bizarre character of a party's proposals may give rise to a persuasive inference that they were made only as a delaying tactic or that they should be viewed as a facade concealing an intention to avoid reaching any agreement . . . . We believe, however, that such a principle, if accepted at all, must be narrowly restricted. Otherwise, the policy supporting section 8(d)'s provision that the duty to bargain in good faith does not 'require the making of a concession' would be undermined if not more." NLRB v. MacMillan Ring-Free Oil Co., 394 F2d 26, 29, 68 LRRM 2004 (CA 9, 1968), *cert. denied,* 393 US 914, 69 LRRM 2481 (1968). *See also* Taylor Instrument Co., 169 NLRB 162, 67 LRRM 1145 (1968).

[229]NLRB v. Wright Motors, Inc., *supra* note 176; Southside Elec. Coop., Inc., 247 NLRB 705, 103 LRRM 1393 (1980) (employer proposed three-year contract with no wage increases or changes in existing benefits coupled with elimination of existing pension plan). *See* Skrl Die Casting, Inc., 245 NLRB 1041, 102 LRRM 1530 (1979);

nonetheless, be a consideration in evaluating the totality of bargaining conduct.[230] On the other hand, the withdrawal of an employer's solitary proposal which itself embodies only existing conditions[231] and the rejection or withdrawal of proposals that had previously been tentatively accepted have been considered elements of bad faith.[232]

United Contractors, Inc., 244 NLRB 72, 102 LRRM 1012 (1979); Mar-Len Cabinets, Inc., 243 NLRB 523, 101 LRRM 1613 (1979); Northfield Cheese Co., 242 NLRB 1117, 101 LRRM 1539 (1979); K-Mart Corp., *supra* note 176; Architectural Fiberglass, 165 NLRB 238, 65 LRRM 1331 (1967). *See also* NLRB v. Tower Hosiery Mills, Inc., 180 F2d 701, 25 LRRM 2509 (CA 4, 1950), *cert. denied*, 340 US 811, 26 LRRM 2611 (1950) (conditioning agreement on union acceptance of proposal requiring payment of fines and liquidated damages in event of strike); Hospitality Motor Inn, Inc., 249 NLRB 1036, 104 LRRM 1276 (1980) (the Board, while adopting the ALJ's finding of bad-faith bargaining, specifically disavowed his "no self-respecting union could agree" rationale for reaching this result.) *Cf.* Arkansas Louisiana Gas Co., 154 NLRB 878, 60 LRRM 1055 (1965) (company-proposed changes in no-strike, management-rights, arbitration-and-grievance, and insurance-and-pension provisions not so onerous or unreasonable as to bespeak bad faith); United States Gypsum Co., 94 NLRB 112, 28 LRRM 1015 (1951), *amended*, 97 NLRB 889, 29 LRRM 1171 (1951), *enforced in part, denied in part*, 206 F2d 410, 32 LRRM 2553 (CA 5, 1953), *cert. denied*, 347 US 912, 33 LRRM 2456 (1954).

[230]Existing or less favorable terms embodied in employer's proposal (more stringent requirements to qualify for holiday pay), no violation found. McCulloch Corp., *supra* note 129. *See also* Continental Bus Sys., Inc., 128 NLRB 384, 46 LRRM 1308 (1960), *enforced*, 294 F2d 264, 48 LRRM 2579 (CA DC, 1961) (employer proposed renewal of old contract); *cf.* Marathon-Clark Coop. v. NLRB, 315 F2d 269, 52 LRRM 2723 (CA DC, 1963) (across-the-board reduction in benefits). *But see* the following cases where violations were found: Southside Elec. Coop., Inc., *supra* note 229; Satilla Rural Elec. Membership Corp., 137 NLRB 387, 50 LRRM 1159 (1962), *enforced*, 322 F2d 251, 53 LRRM 2841 (CA 5, 1963) (withdrawal of proposal of conditions already in effect and failure to make counterproposal); *cf.* Houston Sheet Metal Contractors Ass'n, 147 NLRB 774, 56 LRRM 1281 (1964) (company's last offer substantially below previous contract and its own earlier offers); Irvington Motors, Inc., 147 NLRB 565, 56 LRRM 1257 (1964), *enforced per curiam*, 343 F2d 759, 58 LRRM 2816 (CA 3, 1965) (proposal to continue existing practices conditioned upon union acceptance of new wage plan offered in company); Schnell Tool & Die Corp., 144 NLRB 385, 54 LRRM 1064 (1963). *See also* Weinacker Bros., Inc., 153 NLRB 459, 59 LRRM 1542 (1965).

[231]*See* Berry Kofron Dental Laboratory, 160 NLRB 493, 62 LRRM 1643 (1966).

[232]NLRB v. Industrial Wire Prod. Corp., 455 F2d 673, 79 LRRM 2593 (CA 9, 1972), *enforcing* 177 NLRB 328, 74 LRRM 1128 (1969); San Antonio Mach. & Supply Corp. v. NLRB, 363 F2d 633, 62 LRRM 2674 (CA 5, 1966); NLRB v. Shannon, *supra* note 45; Skrl Die Casting, Inc., *supra* note 229 (employer withdrew agency-shop proposal and substituted maintenance-of-membership clause); Brownsboro Hills Nursing Home, Inc., *supra* note 176; Carpenters Local 1781, 244 NLRB 277, 102 LRRM 1150 (1979); Satilla Rural Elec. Membership Corp., *supra* note 230. *See also* NLRB v. Holmes Tuttle Broadway Ford, Inc., 465 F2d 717, 81 LRRM 2036 (CA 9, 1972), *enforcing* 186 NLRB 73, 75 LRRM 1298 (1970) (employer rejected union's unconditional acceptance of terms previously suggested by employer); Wichita Eagle & Beacon Publishing Co., 222 NLRB 742, 91 LRRM 1227 (1976) (an employer is not required to make concessions on items already agreed to, absent a showing of clear illegality in the language previously agreed to); Borden, Inc. (Dairy & Serv. Div.), 196 NLRB 1170, 80 LRRM 1240 (1972). *But see* Omaha Typographical Union v. NLRB, 545 F2d 1138, 93 LRRM 3063 (CA 8, 1976) (no inference of bad faith should be drawn from the modification of a final offer to reflect substantially changed conditions which occurred during a strike); Warehousemen & Mail Order Employees Local 743 v. NLRB, 302 F2d 865, 49 LRRM 2466 (CA DC, 1962); Wallace Metal Prods., Inc., 244 NLRB 41, 102 LRRM 1233 (1979) (employer lawfully withdrew contract proposals previously agreed to after they had been rejected by the union); Loggins Meat Co., 206 NLRB 303, 84 LRRM 1270 (1973) (panel majority

The timing of demands or proposals may also be a factor in ascertaining good faith. The injection of numerous new proposals for the first time after several months of bargaining,[233] or the submission of new issues after the parties have reached agreement[234] in order to frustrate or stall contract execution, have been found to be indications of bad faith.[235]

Specialized legal principles have evolved in response to specific types of proposals and demands:

(1) Contract duration. Proposals for contracts of excessively long or short duration may be indicia of bad faith when judged in the light of attending circumstances.[236] A proposal for a five-year contract has been considered by the Board as evidence of bad faith.[237] Proposals for contracts to be effective for very short periods, when obviously keyed to the expiration of the certification year,[238] have been similarly viewed. The bases for such holdings appear grounded on the proposition that "[w]hile the expiration date of the contract, like its substantive provisions, is a bargainable matter, a contract terminable at the will of a party, or a contract for less than a year to expire at the end of the certification year, is normally not one that will give full force and effect to the Board's certification."[239]

---

found lawful the withdrawal of two proposals after acceptance by the union); Food Serv. Corp., 202 NLRB 790, 82 LRRM 1746 (1973); Taylor Chevrolet Corp., 199 NLRB 1064, 81 LRRM 1405 (1972); Sunderland's, Inc., 194 NLRB 118, 78 LRRM 1553 (1971).
[233]MRA Associates, Inc., 245 NLRB 676, 102 LRRM 1338 (1979); Southside Elec. Coop., Inc., 243 NLRB 390, 101 LRRM 1605 (1979); Hi-Grade Materials Co., 239 NLRB 947, 100 LRRM 1113 (1978); B. F. Diamond Constr. Co., *supra* note 129; Altex Mfg. Co., 134 NLRB 614, 49 LRRM 1212 (1961), *enforced*, 307 F2d 872, 51 LRRM 2139 (CA 4, 1962).
[234]Midvalley Steel Fabricators, Inc., *supra* note 94; Cabinet Mfg. Corp., 144 NLRB 842, 54 LRRM 1144 (1963).
[235]*See* Shovel Supply Co., Inc., 162 NLRB 460, 64 LRRM 1080 (1966); New England Die Casting Co., 116 NLRB 1, 38 LRRM 1175 (1956), *enforced per curiam*, 242 F2d 759, 39 LRRM 2616 (CA 2, 1957).
[236]*See* Holmes Tuttle Broadway Ford, Inc., 186 NLRB 73, 75 LRRM 1298 (1970), *enforced*, 465 F2d 717, 81 LRRM 2036 (CA 9, 1972); Borg-Warner Corp., 128 NLRB 1035, 46 LRRM 1459 (1960).
[237]Wonder State Mfg. Co., *supra* note 69; Mooney Aircraft, Inc., 132 NLRB 1194, 48 LRRM 1499 (1961), *enforced per curiam*, 310 F2d 565, 51 LRRM 2615 (CA 5, 1962); Vanderbilt Prods., Inc., *supra* note 205.
[238]NLRB v. Strauss & Son, Inc., 536 F2d 60, 92 LRRM 3581 (CA 5, 1976); NLRB v. Hall Distrib., 341 F2d 359, 58 LRRM 2378 (CA 10, 1965), *enforcing* 144 NLRB 1285, 54 LRRM 1231 (1963); Solo Cup Co., 142 NLRB 1290, 53 LRRM 1253 (1963), *enforced*, 332 F2d 447, 56 LRRM 2383 (CA 4, 1964); NLRB v. Henry Heide, Inc., 219 F2d 46, 35 LRRM 2378 (CA 2, 1954), *cert. denied*, 349 US 952, 36 LRRM 2203 (1955).
[239]Insulating Fabricators, Inc., 144 NLRB 1325, 1329-30, 54 LRRM 1246 (1963), *enforced per curiam*, 338 F2d 1002, 57 LRRM 2606 (CA 4, 1964). Similar reasoning has been employed where the employer insisted on a one-year contract. *See, e.g.,* NLRB v. My Store, *supra* note 174. *But cf.* Grace & Hornbrook Mfg. Co., 225 NLRB 15, 92 LRRM

(2) Checkoff. The Board and the courts have long recognized that the bargaining obligation extends to a proposed checkoff clause,[240] and refusals to accede to and failure to offer counter-proposals to union demands for checkoff or other forms of union security have been treated as evidence of breach of the duty to bargain in good faith. Nevertheless, the Board did not condemn an employer's adamant stand against such a clause where it had shown willingness to discuss the issue even though such discussions proved fruitless.[241] On the other hand, if the adamant stand is merely a "device to frustrate agreement,"[242] or if it is taken despite a practice of deducting nonunion items from employees' paychecks,[243] the Board considers such conduct indicative of bad faith.[244]

In *H. K. Porter*[245] the employer objected to granting a dues checkoff solely on the ground that he was not going to give aid

---

1637 (1976), where the Board held that the employer's proposal that the contract expire on the same date as the union's certification, in two and one-half weeks, was permissible because the employer's good-faith doubt as to the union's majority status was based on objective considerations. (The board found that (1) some employees had orally expressed their dissatisfaction with the union, (2) a majority of the employees subsequently signed a petition asking for a new election, and (3) the parties had been engaged in negotiations for 10 months, during which time there had been an unsuccessful 12-week strike.) *Cf. also* Star Expansion Indus. Corp., *supra* note 190, where the Board found no bad faith in employer's insistence on a contract expiration date coinciding with termination of certification year, since contracting union had recently supplanted incumbent union in a close election and employer had reasonable cause to believe contracting union was no longer supported by majority of employees.

[240]Reed & Prince Mfg. Co., *supra* note 200; United States Gypsum Co., *supra* note 229. *See* Chapter 17 *infra* at note 187.

[241]Star Expansion Indus. Corp., *supra* note 190; McLane Co., 166 NLRB 1036, 65 LRRM 1729 (1967), *aff'd per curiam*, 405 F2d 483, 70 LRRM 2095 (CA 8, 1968); Raybestos-Manhattan, Inc. (General Asbestos & Rubber Div.), *supra* note 224. *See also* Capital Aviation, Inc. v. NLRB, 355 F2d 875, 877, 61 LRRM 2307 (CA 7, 1966), *citing* McCulloch Corp., *supra* note 129 at 211.

[242]H. K. Porter Co., 153 NLRB 1370, 1372, 59 LRRM 1462 (1965), *enforced*, 363 F2d 272, 62 LRRM 2204 (CA DC, 1966), *cert. denied*, 385 US 851, 63 LRRM 2236 (1966) (*see* notes 245-48 *infra* for further history of this case). *See also* Queen Mary Restaurants Corp. v. NLRB, 560 F2d 403, 96 LRRM 2456 (CA 9, 1977) (court and Board rejected employer's "moral principle" excuse for refusal to agree to union security and hiring-hall proposals, where both the employer and its parent corporation had previously agreed to similar language with another union); Roanoke Iron & Bridge Works, Inc., 160 NLRB 175, 62 LRRM 1464 (1966), *enforced*, 390 F2d 846, 67 LRRM 2450 (CA DC, 1967), *cert. denied*, 391 US 904, 68 LRRM 2097 (1968); Stevenson Brick & Block Co., *supra* note 129; Flowers Baking Co., 161 NLRB 1429, 63 LRRM 1462 (1966). *But cf.* American Oil Co., 164 NLRB 36, 65 LRRM 1007 (1967), *enforced*, 602 F2d 184, 101 LRRM 2981 (CA 8, 1979) (employer's intransigent position not based on desire to frustrate agreement).

[243]Farmers Coop. Gin Ass'n, *supra* note 209; H. K. Porter Co., *supra* note 242.

[244]Texton, Inc., Caroline Farms Div., 163 NLRB 854, 64 LRRM 1465 (1967), *rev'd*, 401 F2d 205, 69 LRRM 2257 (CA 4, 1968). *See also* Alba-Waldensian, Inc., *supra* note 209; General Tire & Rubber Co., *supra* note 213.

[245]*Supra* note 242. On subsequent motion to clarify the D.C. Circuit's decree, the case was remanded to the Board for consideration of whether checkoff should be granted

and comfort to the union, for in his view the collection of union dues was the "union's business."[246] The employer contended that this was merely "hard bargaining."[247] The Board found, and was sustained by the District of Columbia Circuit, that the refusal to bargain about checkoff was not done in good faith, but was done solely to frustrate the making of any collective bargaining agreement, hence was in violation of Section 8(a)(5).[248]

(3) Management rights. The landmark case on provisions dealing with management rights is the Supreme Court's decision in *NLRB v. American National Insurance Co.*[249] In that case the union had submitted a proposed agreement which, in effect, called for unlimited arbitration. In response, the company proposed a management-functions clause in which all matters pertaining to promotions, discipline, and work scheduling were to be within management's exclusive control and not subject to arbitration.[250] The parties deadlocked on the clause, but continued bargaining and reached agreement on other matters. Nonetheless, the Board found that insistence upon the management-functions clause

---

to the union as a remedy for bad-faith bargaining. The circuit court stated that §8(d) defines the limit of the duty and does not prescribe the remedy for the breach of that duty; it is within the Board's broad remedial powers to order the employer to grant a checkoff in return for reasonable union concessions or, in a proper case, for no concessions at all. United Steelworkers (H. K. Porter Co.) v. NLRB, 389 F2d 295, 66 LRRM 2761 (CA DC, 1967). On remand, the Board directed the employer to grant the checkoff provision. 172 NLRB 966, 68 LRRM 1337 (1968). The Supreme Court reversed as to remedy, holding that the Board had no authority to compel agreement as to any substantive provision in a collective bargaining contract. 397 US 99, 73 LRRM 2561 (1970). *See* Chapter 33 *infra* at notes 246-48 for further discussion of the remedial aspect of the case.

[246]*Supra* note 242, 153 NLRB at 1372.
[247]*Id.*
[248]The D.C. Circuit has also enforced a Board finding of bad faith where the sole issue was the company's refusal to grant a checkoff. The company had rejected seven alternative dues collection proposals, on the principle that no cooperation would be given in union dues collection. The Board viewed the company's history of refusing to grant checkoff in the past as a stratagem to weaken and destroy the union. The court found support for this view in the company's disavowal of any business reason for refusal to grant checkoff. The court, citing NLRB v. Katz, *supra* note 69, stated that a party may not assume an intransigent position in bad faith on a mandatory subject "even though its purpose to frustrate an agreement on that issue coincides with a willingness to reach some overall agreement." Steelworkers (Roanoke Iron & Bridge Works), *supra* note 242 at 849. The D.C. Circuit's *Roanoke* decision goes beyond its earlier *H. K. Porter* decision, *supra* note 242, where the Board had found that the employer's refusal was intended to frustrate *any* agreement. Though purporting to base its finding on subjective good faith, the reliance on *Katz* suggested a *per se* approach reminiscent of *General Elec., supra* note 127 and accompanying text.
[249]*Supra* note 54. *See also* discussion of this case in Chapter 16 *infra* at notes 24-25.
[250]The clause originally proposed read as follows: "The right to select, hire, to promote, demote, discharge, discipline, for cause, to maintain discipline and efficiency of employees, and to determine schedules of work is the sole prerogative of the Company and . . . such matters shall never be the subject of arbitration." 343 US at 397 n.2.

constituted a *per se* violation of Section 8(a)(5) without regard to considerations of good faith. The Fifth Circuit denied enforcement of the Board's holding on the management-functions clause,[251] and the Supreme Court affirmed, holding that bargaining for such a clause was neither a *per se* violation nor evidence of bad faith.

The Court reasoned that good-faith bargaining is a "two way street," and that the parties' inability to reach an agreement was due not only to the employer's unyielding position, but also to the steadfast position of the union in opposing the management-functions clause. The broader significance of the decision lies in its affirming the principle and procedure of collective bargaining as a method of resolving industrial disputes, while minimizing the role of the Board in policing the substantive character of the bargaining proposals.[252]

The Board subsequently has viewed insistence on a "broad" management-prerogative clause, one that would undermine the union's ability to adequately represent the employees, as indicia of bad faith.[253] Other related indicators that an employer is not bargaining in good faith include insistence on the union's waiving most of its rights under the Act,[254] or a demand for unilateral control of wages, hours, or terms of employment.[255]

Despite the Board's position regarding demands for broad management-rights provisions, insistence upon a management-rights clause reserving the power to assign work and to protect replacements after a strike has begun was upheld by the Seventh Circuit in *NLRB v. Lewin-Mathes Co.*[256] The court criticized the

---

[251]187 F2d 307, 27 LRRM 2405 (CA 5, 1951), *aff'd*, 343 US 395, 30 LRRM 2147 (1952).

[252]"In its general aspect, the decision appears to be an admonition to the Board to moderate its close scrutiny of the play and byplay of collective bargaining negotiations in the application of the 'good faith' standard." From address of Professor Russell A. Smith, Labor Relations Law Section of American Bar Ass'n, Aug. 24, 1953, *reprinted in part*, 32 LRRM 68, 73 (1953).

[253]Carbonex Coal Co., 248 NLRB 779, 104 LRRM 1009 (1980) (proposed management-rights clause would have required union "to waive practically all its rights"); "M" System, Inc., *supra* note 209 (employer's proposal preserved job preference, allowed termination of seniority upon discharge for just cause based on management determination, reserved final determination of grievances to management). *But cf.* Preterm, Inc., *supra* note 97.

[254]East Texas Steel Castings Co., *supra* note 206 (employer's proposal reserved, *inter alia*, right to allocate work, transfer work from unit, reduce work force, and establish and change plant rules).

[255]Dixie Corp., 105 NLRB 390, 32 LRRM 1259 (1953); Heider Mfg. Co., 91 NLRB 1185, 26 LRRM 1641 (1950). *But see* Woodworkers Local 3-10 v. NLRB, 458 F2d 852, 79 LRRM 2259 (CA DC, 1972).

[256]285 F2d 329, 47 LRRM 2288 (CA 7, 1960).

Board's finding of bad faith as passing judgment "on the reasonableness of the proposals . . . ."[257] In *Texas Industries, Inc.*,[258] the Board dismissed a complaint which was based in part on a management-rights clause that reserved, *inter alia*, the final decision in the grievance procedure as a management prerogative, where the employer had willingly negotiated and explained his proposal. Similarly, no evidence of bad faith was found where the employer had insisted upon reserving the right to grant individual merit increases[259] or to subcontract.[260]

3. Dilatory Tactics and the Obligation to Confer at Responsible Times and Intervals. The duty to bargain in good faith imposes on the parties the obligation to confer at reasonable times and intervals. Obviously, refusal to meet at all with the union would fail to satisfy the positive duty imposed on the employer.[261] Less flagrant conduct, however, such as procrastination in executing an agreement,[262] or delay in scheduling of meetings,[263] has also been found to evidence lack of good faith. Willful avoidance of meetings[264] or resorting to delaying and

---

[257]*Id.* at 332.

[258]140 NLRB 527, 52 LRRM 1054 (1963).

[259]Atlantic Research Corp., 144 NLRB 285, 54 LRRM 1049 (1963). *But see* Smyth Mfg. Co., Inc., Beacon Indus., 247 NLRB 1139, 103 LRRM 1432 (1980).

[260]Star Expansion Indus. Corp., *supra* note 190; Peerless Distrib. Co., 144 NLRB 1510, 54 LRRM 1285 (1963).

[261]NLRB v. Little Rock Downtowner, Inc., 341 F2d 1020, 58 LRRM 2510 (CA 8, 1965). Although the outright refusal to negotiate was only of five days' duration, the Tenth Circuit agreed with the Board that it nonetheless violated §8(a)(5) since it occurred at a critical time—just prior to the expiration of the contract and in the face of a threatened strike. NLRB v. Albion Corp., 593 F2d 936, 100 LRRM 2818 (CA 10, 1979).

[262]NLRB v. Ogle Protection Serv., 375 F2d 497, 64 LRRM 2792 (CA 6, 1967), *cert. denied*, 389 US 843, 66 LRRM 2308 (1967); Lozano Enterprises v. NLRB, *supra* note 94; NLRB v. Vander Wal, 316 F2d 631, 52 LRRM 2761 (CA 9, 1963); Wate, Inc., 132 NLRB 1338, 48 LRRM 1535 (1961), *enforced*, 310 F2d 700, 51 LRRM 2701 (CA 6, 1962). This duty extends to unions as well. *See, e.g.*, Ice Cream Drivers Local 717 (Ice Cream Council, Inc.), 145 NLRB 865, 55 LRRM 1059 (1964); Automobile Workers Local 453 (Maremont Automotive Prods., Inc.), 134 NLRB 1337, 49 LRRM 1357 (1961).

[263]Henry Hald High School Ass'n, 213 NLRB 463, 87 LRRM 1753 (1974) (no merit to employer's contention that bargaining sessions ought to be postponed pending court decision on government aid to parochial schools); Federal Pac. Elec. Co., 203 NLRB 571, 83 LRRM 1201 (1973), *enforced in pertinent part sub nom.* Electrical Workers (IBEW) Local 2338, 499 F2d 542, 86 LRRM 2814 (CA DC, 1974) (among other factors, the Board noted that an employee had been solicited at the same time to circulate a decertification petition). *See also* Insulating Fabricators, Inc., *supra* note 239; NLRB v. Southwestern Porcelain Steel Corp., *supra* note 40 (employer's efforts to delay scheduling of bargaining sessions was one factor in overall pattern of conduct indicating lack of good faith); Solo Cup Co., *supra* note 238; Frank E. Nash, 242 NLRB 233, 101 LRRM 1153 (1979) (two-month delay in setting initial meeting outside §10(b) period but still critical background evidence in finding §8(a)(5) violation); "M" System, Inc., *supra* note 209.

[264]Exchange Parts Co., 139 NLRB 710, 51 LRRM 1366 (1962), *enforced*, 339 F2d 829, 58 LRRM 2097 (CA 5, 1965), *petition for rehearing denied*, 341 F2d 584, 58 LRRM 2456 (CA 5, 1965).

evasive tactics[265] have likewise been considered evidence of bad faith.

The duty is a bilateral one, however, so that where it appears that both parties have been equally dilatory,[266] or where the union has broken off negotiations and made no further request for bargaining[267] or failed to request the employer to bargain,[268] the Board has refused to find bad faith on the part of the employer.

Delay in supplying requested information necessary for negotiations or for administration of the contract may also be considered a dilatory tactic.[269] Failure to supply wage information promptly,[270] or delay in furnishing the union a current list of employees, wage rates, and job classifications[271] or a pension plan,[272] has been treated as evidence of bad faith.

---

[265]Dilatory or evasive tactics are considered by the Board in assessing the totality of an employer's conduct to determine good or bad faith. Crane Co., 244 NLRB 103, 102 LRRM 1351 (1979); Rhodes St. Clair Buick, Inc., supra note 97. These tactics standing alone would not be per se violations of §8(a)(5). See, e.g., Fry Roofing Co. v. NLRB, 216 F2d 273, 35 LRRM 2009 (CA 9, 1954), amended per curiam, 220 F2d 432, 35 LRRM 2662 (CA 9, 1955); National Amusements, Inc., 155 NLRB 1200, 60 LRRM 1485 (1965); Insulating Fabricators, Inc., supra note 239; Exchange Parts Co., supra note 264 (failure to meet at reasonable times "occurring as it did in the context of a history of unfair labor practices committed by Respondents" constituted §8(a)(5) violation); Bewley Mills, 111 NLRB 830, 35 LRRM 1578 (1955) (authority of negotiator considered factor, but not sole factor, in reaching conclusion that employer did not bargain in good faith). In Architectural Fiberglass, supra note 229, the employer's insistence on using a tape recorder throughout the bargaining sessions was held to be evidence of bad faith. One member took the position that such conduct was a per se violation. See also Borg Compressed Steel Corp., 165 NLRB 394, 65 LRRM 1474 (1967) (employer representative's claimed inability to locate company president did not justify delays in scheduling bargaining session). Cf. Inter-Polymer Indus., Inc., 196 NLRB 729, 80 LRRM 1509 (1972), petition for review denied, 480 F2d 631, 83 LRRM 2735 (CA 9, 1973) (despite condemning a host of delaying and evasive tactics by the employer, the Board did not regard as indicia of bad faith the representative's (a) attempt to limit the size of the union's negotiating committee; (b) use of a stenographic reporter to record sessions; (c) canceling several scheduled meetings; and (d) imposing a four-hour limit on bargaining sessions). See Chapter 17 infra at notes 379-88.

[266]Dunn Packing Co., 143 NLRB 1149, 53 LRRM 1471 (1963). But cf. McLean v. NLRB, 333 F2d 84, 56 LRRM 2475 (CA 6, 1964), enforcing 142 NLRB 235, 53 LRRM 1021 (1963) (where the court agreed with the Board's view that the union's failure to negotiate during an eight-month period was no defense to the employer's subsequent refusal to meet and negotiate since "it seems to us that it constituted more of a violation of duty owing to its members than to McLean." 333 F2d at 88).

[267]NLRB v. Lambert, 250 F2d 801, 41 LRRM 2345 (CA 5, 1958) (dismissing contempt proceedings against employer for alleged refusal to bargain in compliance with previous court order).

[268]Lori-Ann, Inc., 137 NLRB 1099, 50 LRRM 1340 (1962).

[269]Crane Co., supra note 265; Fitzgerald Mills Corp., supra note 189.

[270]Rhodes-Holland Chevrolet Co., supra note 129; Fitzgerald Mills, supra note 189; Butcher Boy Refrigerator Door Co., 127 NLRB 1360, 46 LRRM 1192 (1960), enforced, 290 F2d 22, 48 LRRM 2058 (CA 7, 1961).

[271]International Powder Metallurgy Co., 134 NLRB 1605, 49 LRRM 1388 (1961); Gateway Luggage Mfg. Co., 122 NLRB 1584, 43 LRRM 1342 (1959).

[272]Rangaire Corp., supra note 163.

No hard-and-fast rule has evolved with regard to the number, frequency, and duration of meetings between the parties. In *Insulating Fabricators, Inc.*,[273] the Board seemed to suggest that the test, consistent with other aspects of good-faith conduct, is whether the party's subjective intent shows a willingness to reach an agreement. It has been noted that "neither the Board nor the courts have evolved, or indeed can evolve, any particular formula by which to test whether any given frequency of meetings or amount of time spent in negotiations, satisfies the statutory requirement 'to meet at reasonable times' . . . ."[274] Nonetheless, frequency of meetings is relied upon for evidence of an employer's intent.[275]

4. Inadequate Negotiators. The employer is under a duty to vest its negotiators with sufficient authority to carry on meaningful bargaining.[276] Cases finding the employer guilty of delay in failing to provide a negotiator who is qualified and readily available have expanded this duty. Thus, nonavailability of the employer's negotiator[277] or its labor counsel[278] has been held to

---

[273]*Supra* note 239.

[274]Radiator Specialty Co., *supra* note 59 at 368 (trial examiner's Report).

[275]*See, e.g.*, Rhodes St. Clair Buick, *supra* note 97 (violation found where employer postponed first meeting for two months following certification and request to bargain, agreed to meet only six times within six-month period following certification and limited length of meetings to one and one-half hours); Exchange Parts Co., *supra* note 264 (meeting average of eight hours a month over eight-month period was insufficient). *But cf.* Charles E. Honaker, 147 NLRB 1184, 56 LRRM 1371 (1964) (meeting on 11 occasions over five-month period, with meetings averaging three and one-half to four hours each, was not a failure to meet); Radiator Specialty Co., *supra* note 59 ("[T]he parties met . . . 37 times during a 10-month period. Some of these meetings . . . were at close intervals and a few meetings were lengthy. However, the great bulk of the meetings were of short duration, lasting about 2 hours, and the lags between many were considerable." 143 NLRB at 369. Nevertheless, Board's finding of bad faith was rejected on ground that evidence did not show bad faith); Texas Indus., Inc., 140 NLRB 527, 52 LRRM 1054 (1963) (meeting 11 times during four-month period was frequent enough to satisfy Act); McCulloch Corp., *supra* note 129 (employer, having met 79 times in 11 months and not having caused substantial delay, was not guilty of refusing to meet).

[276]NLRB v. Fitzgerald Mills, *supra* note 189; Valley Imported Cars, 203 NLRB 873, 83 LRRM 1477 (1973); National Amusements, Inc., *supra* note 265; Han-Dee Spring & Mfg. Co., 132 NLRB 1542, 48 LRRM 1566 (1961). In NLRB v. Alterman Transp. Lines, 587 F2d 212, 100 LRRM 2269 (CA 5, 1979), the Fifth Circuit found the employer in contempt of an earlier bargaining order, where its president sought to reject substantially all of the terms agreed to by its negotiator over a nearly two-year period under the guise of a reserved right of ratification.

[277]General Motors Acceptance Corp. v. NLRB, 476 F2d 850, 82 LRRM 3093 (CA 1, 1973), *enforcing* 196 NLRB 137, 79 LRRM 1662 (1972); Solo Cup Co., *supra* note 238 (company's vice-president and company's counsel); Allis Chalmers Mfg. Co., 106 NLRB 939, 32 LRRM 1585 (1953), *rev'd on other grounds*, 213 F2d 374, 34 LRRM 2202 (CA 7, 1954) (scheduling of negotiating sessions only at times when they would not interfere with company routine). *But cf.* Radiator Specialty Co., *supra* note 59 (enforcement denied as to failure to bargain based on unavailability of negotiator).

[278]*See, e.g.*, NLRB v. Milgo Indus., Inc., 567 F2d 540, 97 LRRM 2079 (CA 2, 1977) (court upheld a Board determination that employer impermissibly delayed negotiations

manifest bad faith,[279] as has the failure to provide a bargaining representative sufficiently knowledgeable about the company's operations and pay practices to permit fruitful, informed discussion of working conditions and employee pay.[280]

5. Imposing Conditions. The duty to bargain extends to good-faith consideration of all proper subjects for collective bargaining. Attempts to place conditions upon either bargaining or the execution of a contract are scrutinized closely by the Board to determine whether the proposed condition is so onerous or unreasonable as to indicate bad faith.[281] For example, in *Fitzgerald Mills*,[282] components of the employer's bad-faith bargaining were its demand for a union waiver of grievances which were pending under the old contract and its conditioning further bargaining upon a waiver of strikers' reinstatement rights. The Board found the latter to be tantamount to requiring abandonment of the union's pending unfair labor practice charges against the employer, a condition which the Board has frequently condemned.[283]

Conditioning further negotiations on cessation of a strike also violates the Act, since the obligation to bargain continues during a strike.[284] As the Fifth Circuit noted in *NLRB* v. *Safway Steel*

---

by making its attorney-negotiator available only 17 times in 15 months, even though the union negotiators also were responsible for a substantial portion of the delay); Franklin Equip., Inc., 194 NLRB 643, 79 LRRM 1112 (1971) ("busy lawyer" defense rejected); Insulating Fabricators, Inc., *supra* note 239 (company's labor lawyer resided in Boston, approximately 800 miles from client's plant). *See also* Skyland Hosiery Mills, Inc., 108 NLRB 1600, 34 LRRM 1254 (1954).

[279]B. F. Diamond Constr. Co., *supra* note 129; "M" System, Inc., *supra* note 209.

[280]Coronet Casuals, Inc., 207 NLRB 304, 84 LRRM 1441 (1973).

[281]*See, e.g.*, American Flagpole Equip. Co., Case No. 29-CA-1052 (no exceptions filed), 68 LRRM 1384 (1968), where an employer's reopening of negotiations was conditioned upon the union's execution of contracts with the employer's competitors. The fact that the purpose of the condition was to avoid economic disadvantage was held to be no defense to a refusal-to-bargain charge. *See also* Kroger Co., 164 NLRB 362, 65 LRRM 1089 (1967), *enforced in part, denied in part,* 401 F2d 682, 69 LRRM 2425 (CA 6, 1968); S & M Mfg. Co., 165 NLRB 663, 65 LRRM 1350 (1967) (submission of contract proposal to union conditioned upon its acceptance on same day held unlawful); Lebanon Oak Flooring Co., 167 NLRB 753, 66 LRRM 1172 (1967).

[282]*Supra* note 189.

[283]*See, e.g.*, Patrick & Co., 248 NLRB 390, 103 LRRM 1457 (1980); Palm Beach Post-Times, 151 NLRB 1030, 58 LRRM 1561 (1965); Kit Mfg. Co., 142 NLRB 957, 53 LRRM 1178 (1963), *enforced in part,* 335 F2d 166, 56 LRRM 2988 (CA 9, 1964), *cert. denied,* 380 US 910, 58 LRRM 2496 (1965); Butcher Boy Refrigerator Door Co., *supra* note 270; Lion Oil Co. v. NLRB, 245 F2d 376, 40 LRRM 2193 (CA 8, 1957); Taormina Co., 94 NLRB 884, 28 LRRM 1118 (1951), *enforced,* 207 F2d 251, 32 LRRM 2684 (CA 5, 1953).

[284]General Elec. Co., 163 NLRB 198, 64 LRRM 1312 (1967), *enforced in part, denied in part,* 400 F2d 713, 69 LRRM 2081 (CA 5, 1968); Rice Lake Creamery, 131 NLRB 1270, 48 LRRM 1251 (1961), *enforced sub nom.* General Drivers Local 662, 302 F2d 908, 50 LRRM 2243 (CA DC, 1962), *cert. denied,* 371 US 827, 51 LRRM 2222 (1962).

Scaffolds Co., "the use of economic pressure by a union does not relieve the company of the duty to bargain."[285]

Requiring agreement on certain subjects of bargaining as a prerequisite to further negotiation has been viewed as evidence of bad faith. Thus, requiring acceptance by the union of "open shop" and "freedom to discharge" provisions before the company would engage in economic discussion,[286] a refusal to negotiate unless the union signed a 120-day moratorium that required, in effect, that the union cease representing the employees for a period of four months,[287] and an employer's requirement that the union post an indemnity bond as a condition to the signing of a contract[288] all have been evidence of bad faith. Attempting to dictate the composition of the union's negotiating committee,[289] and refusing to bargain with the union unless a former employee on the union committee was removed,[290] have been similarly treated. Requiring agreement on nonmandatory subjects of bargaining as a condition to further negotiation thus falls in the same category as insisting to impasse on such subjects, which under the *Borg-Warner*[291] doctrine constitutes a refusal to bargain.[292]

6. Unilateral Changes. Unilateral action by an employer affecting its employees' wages, hours, or working conditions during bargaining is often a strong indication that it is not

---

[285]383 F2d 273, 66 LRRM 2136 (CA 5, 1967), *enforcing in part* 153 NLRB 417, 59 LRRM 1486 (1965). *See also* NLRB v. Rutter-Rex Mfg. Co., 245 F2d 594, 40 LRRM 2213 (CA 5, 1957).

[286]Vanderbilt Prods., *supra* note 205. In NLRB v. Strong Roofing & Insulating Co., 386 F2d 929, 65 LRRM 3012 (CA 9, 1967), *cert. denied,* 390 US 920, 67 LRRM 2384 (1968), the Ninth Circuit held that the Board was entitled to consider an employer's refusal to sign a contract, which occurred more than six months before the charge was filed, as background evidence of similar refusals occurring within the §10(b) period.

[287]Crusader-Lancer Corp., 144 NLRB 1309, 54 LRRM 1254 (1963). In Architectural Fiberglass-Div. of Architectural Pottery, *supra* note 229, an employer's proposal requiring both parties to waive their right to bargain during the term of the agreement, as well as the right to information pertaining to wages, hours, or other terms of employment, whether mentioned in the collective bargaining agreement or not, was viewed as a requirement that the union abandon its statutory obligation to bargain collectively as the representative of employer's employees; hence, it was basis for finding a violation of §8(a)(5).

[288]F. McKenzie Davison, 136 NLRB 742, 49 LRRM 1831 (1962), *enforced,* 318 F2d 550, 53 LRRM 2462 (CA 4, 1963).

[289]Cabinet Mfg. Corp., 140 NLRB 576, 52 LRRM 1064 (1963).

[290]Fetzer Television, Inc., 131 NLRB 821, 48 LRRM 1165 (1961), *enforced per curiam,* 299 F2d 845, 49 LRRM 2766 (CA 6, 1962). *See also* Sears, Roebuck & Co., Inc., 139 NLRB 471, 51 LRRM 1327 (1962) (refusal to meet with international union representative participating in local negotiations violated §8(a)(5)).

[291]*Supra* note 52. See also notes 55-60 and accompanying text.

[292]*See generally* Chapter 16 *infra.*

bargaining in good faith.[293] The Second Circuit has noted that a "wage increase [during bargaining] is by far the most important 'unilateral act.' "[294] That court considered such an action a deliberate attempt by the employer to deal directly with its employees and to convince them that benefits come solely from the employer. The court also noted that if the increase is contemporaneous with a strike, the "timing is particularly convincing support for the conclusion that prior negotiations were not conducted in good faith."[295] Wage increases granted to employees in excess of any previous offer to the union are normally violative of Section 8(a)(5),[296] as are unilateral increases in wage-related fringe benefits, such as holiday pay,[297] expense allowances,[298] and incentive programs.[299] Reduction or discontinuance of a wage benefit, such as a Christmas bonus, may also be indicative of a refusal to bargain.[300]

---

[293]This section discusses unilateral changes as *evidence* showing lack of good faith in the bargaining obligation. A unilateral change, however, is usually a *per se* violation and is therefore so treated at notes 69-90 *supra*, this chapter.
[294]NLRB v. Fitzgerald Mills Corp., *supra* note 189, 313 F2d at 267. *See* Trinity Valley Iron & Steel, 127 NLRB 417, 46 LRRM 1030 (1960), *enforced*, 290 F2d 47, 48 LRRM 2110 (CA 5, 1961) (granting wage increases to nonstrikers during economic strike).
[295]313 F2d at 268.
[296]Aztec Ceramics Co., 138 NLRB 1178, 51 LRRM 1226 (1962), *enforced in part, denied in part*, 320 F2d 757, 53 LRRM 2489 (CA DC, 1963); Crater Lake Mach. Co., 131 NLRB 1106, 48 LRRM 1211 (1962); Yale Upholstering Co., 127 NLRB 440, 46 LRRM 1031 (1960); Dinion Coil Co., 110 NLRB 196, 34 LRRM 1623 (1954). *Cf.* Phil-Modes, Inc., 162 NLRB 1435, 64 LRRM 1303 (1967), *enforced in part, denied in part*, 406 F2d 556, 70 LRRM 2247 (CA 5, 1969) (employer's unilateral wage increase constituted illegal change in working conditions despite fact that increases conformed with past practice, but evidence was insufficient to establish discriminatory motive in employer's changing method of wage computation). *See also* Blue Cab Co., 156 NLRB 489, 61 LRRM 1085 (1965), *enforced*, 373 F2d 661, 64 LRRM 2317 (CA DC, 1967), *cert. denied*, 389 US 836, 66 LRRM 2306 (1967).
[297]Mooney Aircraft, Inc., 138 NLRB 1331, 51 LRRM 1230 (1962).
[298]Cutter Boats, Inc., 127 NLRB 1576, 46 LRRM 1246 (1960).
[299]Phil-Modes, Inc., *supra* note 296; "M" System, Inc., *supra* note 209 (merit increases may not be unilaterally instituted).
[300]Keystone Consol. Indus., 237 NLRB 763, 99 LRRM 1036 (1978), *enforced as modified*, 606 F2d 171, 102 LRRM 2664 (CA 7, 1979) (replacement of administrator/processor of claims under the employer's self-insured major medical plan); Nello Pistoresi & Son, Inc., 203 NLRB 905, 83 LRRM 1212 (1974), *enforcement denied in relevant part*, 500 F2d 399, 86 LRRM 2736 (CA 9, 1974) (discontinuation of Christmas bonus paid to employees the previous two years); Radio Television Technical School, Inc. v. NLRB, 488 F2d 457, 84 LRRM 2794 (CA 3, 1973), *enforcing* 199 NLRB 570, 81 LRRM 1296 (1972); Century Elec. Motor Co. v. NLRB, 447 F2d 10, 78 LRRM 2042 (CA 8, 1971), *enforcing in part* 180 NLRB 1051, 73 LRRM 1307 (1970); NLRB v. McCann Steel Co., 448 F2d 277, 78 LRRM 2237 (CA 6, 1961), *enforcing in part* 184 NLRB 779, 76 LRRM 1556 (1970) (employer reduced Christmas bonus one day after union election victory); NLRB v. Zelrich Co., 344 F2d 1011, 59 LRRM 2225 (CA 5, 1965); NLRB v. Exchange Parts, *supra* note 264 (violation regardless of whether decision to make reduction was made before or after union certification); Scan Instrument Corp., 163 NLRB 284, 64 LRRM 1327 (1967), *enforced*, 394 F2d 884, 68 LRRM 2280 (CA 7, 1968) (imposing policy rider which reduced benefits to employees who received sums under other insurance policies);

There are, however, certain situations in which an employer may lawfully make unilateral changes: (1) After the lapse of the certification year, if there are reasonable grounds to believe the certified union has lost majority support.[301] But, justification for such change may require not only that the belief be reasonable, but that it be accurate.[302] (2) An employer may grant a rejected wage increase after a *bona fide* impasse has been reached,[303] but not if the impasse was caused by the employer's lack of good faith.[304] However, a unilateral change as to subject matter which was not included in the negotiations is not permissible even after impasse.[305] (3) In certain circumstances an increase may be granted even before impasse is reached.[306] For example, the continua-

---

Mooney Aircraft, Inc., *supra* note 297 (ceasing to allow employees to make up pay lost in periods of absence); Clear Pine Moldings, 238 NLRB 69, 99 LRRM 1221 (1978) (discontinuance of contributions to health and welfare fund after expiration of the contract); Gas Mach. Co., 221 NLRB 862, 90 LRRM 1730 (1975) (withholding of Christmas "gifts" employer had given to employee in each of the previous seven years). *Cf.* Federal-Mogul Corp., 209 NLRB 343, 85 LRRM 1353 (1974) (held employer violated §8(a)(5) by unilaterally imposing collective bargaining agreement covering preexisting unit on employees who had voted for inclusion in that unit, resulting in loss of benefits to new unit employees). *But see* NLRB v. Abex Corp., 543 F2d 719, 93 LRRM 2669 (CA 9, 1976), *denying enforcement to* 215 NLRB 665, 88 LRRM 1157 (1974) (in which the Board followed, but the Court distinguished, its decision in *Federal-Mogul*). *See also* Marland One-Way Clutch Co., 192 NLRB 601, 78 LRRM 1127 (1971), *enforced in part, denied in part,* 520 F2d 856, 89 LRRM 2721 (CA 7, 1975); Smith Co. of Calif., 200 NLRB 772, 82 LRRM 1269 (1972); Michigan Power Co., 192 NLRB 830, 78 LRRM 1091 (1971).

[301]McCulloch Corp., *supra* note 129; American Laundry Mach. Co., 107 NLRB 1574, 33 LRRM 1457 (1954).

[302]NLRB v. Superior Fireproof Door & Sash Co., *supra* note 78; Master Slack Corp., 230 NLRB 1054, 96 LRRM 1309 (1977) (violation found for unilateral implementation of procedure to recall unit employees to reopened plant closed for more than one year). *But cf.* Ellex Transp., Inc., 217 NLRB 750, 89 LRRM 1335 (1975) (pending decertification and deauthorization petitions provided lawful basis for unilateral institution of health, welfare, and pension programs). See Chapter 12 *supra* for detailed treatment of the requirements for withdrawal of recognition.

[303]Massey-Ferguson, Inc. v. NLRB, 78 LRRM 2289 (CA 7, 1971), *enforcing* 184 NLRB 640, 74 LRRM 1565 (1970); Continental Nut Co., 195 NLRB 841, 79 LRRM 1575 (1972); American Laundry Mach. Co., *supra* note 301. *Compare* KCW Furniture Co., Inc., 247 NLRB 541, 103 LRRM 1194 (1980). *See infra* at notes 538-71.

[304]Iron Workers Local 103 (Associated Gen. Contractors of Am.), 195 NLRB 980, 79 LRRM 1598 (1972), *enforced,* 81 LRRM 2705 (CA 7, 1972); NLRB v. Reed & Prince Mfg. Co., *supra* note 200.

[305]Caravelle Boat Co., 227 NLRB 1355, 95 LRRM 1003 (1977); Intracoastal Terminal, Inc., 125 NLRB 359, 45 LRRM 1104 (1959), *enforced as modified in other respects,* 286 F2d 954, 47 LRRM 2629 (CA 5, 1961). *But cf.* Laclede Gas Co., 173 NLRB 243, 69 LRRM 1316 (1968), *remanded,* 421 F2d 610, 73 LRRM 2364 (CA 8, 1970), discussed in Chapter 22 *infra* at notes 159-60.

[306]Wichita Eagle & Beacon Publishing Co., 222 NLRB 742, 91 LRRM 1227 (1976) (unilateral reduction in eligibility waiting period under hospitalization policy in both unit and nonunit employees lawful where union had insisted that unit members receive the same improvements in benefits as nonunit employees, backed up with unfair labor practice charge threat); AAA Motor Lines, 215 NLRB 793, 88 LRRM 1253 (1974) (union's dilatory bargaining tactics made unilateral changes permissible); Fort Smith Chair Co., 143 NLRB 514, 53 LRRM 1313 (1963), *aff'd,* 336 F2d 738, 55 LRRM 2990

tion of traditional payments or implementation of increases already promised to employees is not unlawful;[307] nor is an employer proscribed from unilaterally taking action to avoid loss of fringe benefits upon the expiration of a collective bargaining agreement.[308] (4) An employer may also put wage increases into effect for nonunit employees without incurring an obligation to make the same increase to unit employees, absent receipt of any *quid pro quo* from the union.[309]

7. Bypassing the Representative and Individual Contracts of Employment. As early as 1944 the Supreme Court, in *J. I. Case* v. *NLRB*,[310] upheld the Board's decision that an employer violates its duty to bargain by refusing to negotiate portions of a collective agreement on grounds that the unit employees were already covered by individual contracts of employment, even though such contracts had not been unfairly or unlawfully obtained. The Court's landmark opinion established that the collective bargaining contract superseded the individual employment contracts. The Court wrote:

> Individual contracts, no matter what the circumstances that justify their execution or what their terms, may not be availed of to defeat or delay . . . collective bargaining . . . ; nor may they be used to forestall bargaining or to limit or condition the terms of the collective agreement . . . . Whenever private contracts conflict with [the Board's]

(CA DC, 1964) (employer ceased bargaining and granted increases when union went on strike in violation of §8(d)(3) time limits); Betty Brooks Co., 99 NLRB 1237, 30 LRRM 1210 (1952) (union had rejected offer which new profit and loss statement showed employer capable of paying).

[307]McCulloch Corp., *supra* note 129 (contributions to profit-sharing plan); Cutter Boats, Inc., *supra* note 298 (providing free home insurance arranged before certification, but not immediately conferred due to insurance-brokerage difficulties). Isolated wage changes for a few employees during negotiations do not necessarily establish bad faith, R. C. White v. NLRB, 255 F2d 564, 42 LRRM 2001 (CA 5, 1958), but are often vulnerable to such findings. Sharkey's Tire & Rubber Co., Inc., 222 NLRB 261, 91 LRRM 1183 (1976), *enforced by consent judgment*, 542 F2d 1163, 94 LRRM 2125 (CA 1, 1976) (unilateral grant of wage increases to two employees); Insulating Fabricators, Inc., *supra* note 239 (individual merit increases for most of bargaining unit); "M" System, Inc., *supra* note 209 (individual wage adjustments in accordance with unilaterally established incentive plan).

[308]AAA Motor Lines, *supra* note 306. *But see* Mountaineer Excavating Co., Inc., 241 NLRB 414, 100 LRRM 1505 (1979) (lack of any advance notice to union evidence of bad faith).

[309]McCulloch Corp., *supra* note 129.

[310]321 US 332, 14 LRRM 501 (1944). The Court defined the collective bargaining contract as follows: "Contract in labor law is a term the implications of which must be determined from the connection in which it appears. Collective bargaining between employer and the representatives of a unit, usually a union, results in an accord as to terms which will govern hiring and work and pay in that unit." *Id.* at 334-35. *See also* Moisi & Son Trucking, Inc., 197 NLRB 198, 80 LRRM 1325 (1972) (employer seeking individual contracts after having recognized a union).

functions, they obviously must yield or the Act would be reduced to a futility.[311]

The Court then addressed the issue of individual bargaining which might result in benefits for individual employees greater than would be available under the collective bargaining agreement:

> [I]t is urged that some employers may lose by the collective agreement, that an individual workman may sometimes have, or be capable of getting, better terms than those obtainable by the group . . . . [W]e find the mere possibility that such agreements might be made no ground for holding generally that individual contracts may survive or surmount collective ones. The practice and philosophy of collective bargaining looks with suspicion on such individual advantages.[312]

Regarding the proper function of the individual contract of employment where the circumstances favor such contracts and where the bargaining agent consents, the Court said:

> Of course, where there is great variation in circumstances of employment or capacity of employees, it is possible for the collective bargain to prescribe only minimum rates or maximum hours or expressly to leave certain areas open to individual bargaining. But except as so provided, advantages to individuals may prove as disruptive to industrial peace as disadvantages.[313]

In the *Insurance Agents* case the Supreme Court stated that "the duty of management to bargain in good faith is essentially a corollary of its duty to recognize the union."[314] This obligation is said to require "at a minimum recognition that the statutory representative is the one with whom [the employer] must deal in conducting bargaining negotiations, and that it can no longer bargain directly or indirectly with the employees."[315] The statutory obligation thus imposed is to deal with the employees through the union rather than to deal with the union through the employees. Thus, attempts to bypass the representative may be considered evidence of bad faith.

---

[311]*Id.* at 337.

[312]*Id.* at 338.

[313]*Id.* Examples of individual contracts that are sanctioned and fostered by certain collective agreements are the "star" contracts common in the arts and in professional sports.

[314]NLRB v. Insurance Agents' Int'l Union, *supra* note 83 at 484-85. *See* notes 512-14 *infra* and accompanying text.

[315]General Elec., *supra* note 91. *See* notes 136-63 *supra* and accompanying text. *See also* Safeway Trails, Inc., 233 NLRB 1078, 96 LRRM 1614 (1977), *enforced,* 641 F2d 930, 102 LRRM 2328 (CA DC, 1979); Hearst Corp., 230 NLRB 216, 95 LRRM 1274 (1977), *enforced,* 590 F2d 554, 100 LRRM 2320 (CA 4, 1979) (violation of §8(a)(5) found in employer economic inducement to 13 employees to retire because of lack of available

The employer's bargaining obligation is premised upon the majority status of the union. Individual dealings with employees at a time when the union claims, but does not actually represent a majority, may not be used as evidence of bad faith.[316] But a belief that the union has lost its majority is not a ground for refusing to bargain where the majority issue is "raised by the employer in a context of illegal anti-union activities, or other conduct by the employer aimed at causing disaffection from the union" or designed to gain "time in which to undermine the union."[317]

The "injury suffered by the union,"[318] where unilateral changes in wages or other employment conditions are made without notice or consultation with the union, is "not that flowing from a breach of contract [but] 'to the union's status as a bargaining representative.' "[319] Flagrant attempts to deal directly with the employees so as to undermine a certified bargaining agent, such as offering the employees a wage increase if they will disavow the union,[320] making speeches or statements to employees demonstrating union animus,[321] or soliciting strikers to return to work[322] will be vulnerable to Board censure.[323] Likewise, grant-

---

work); NLRB v. Rude Carrier Corp., 93 LRRM 2297 (CA 4, 1976), *enforcing in part* 215 NLRB 883, 88 LRRM 1556 (1974); NLRB v. Goodyear Aerospace Corp., 497 F2d 747, 86 LRRM 2763 (CA 6, 1974), *enforcing in part* 204 NLRB 831, 83 LRRM 1461 (1973); Wings & Wheels, Inc., 139 NLRB 578, 51 LRRM 1341 (1962), *enforced,* 324 F2d 495, 54 LRRM 2455 (CA 3, 1963); Medo Photo Supply Corp. v. NLRB, 321 US 678, 14 LRRM 581 (1944); Kaiser-Permanente Med. Care Program, 248 NLRB 144, 103 LRRM 1374 (1980); General Athletics Prods. Co., 227 NLRB 1565, 95 LRRM 1130 (1977); Obie Pac., Inc., 196 NLRB 458, 80 LRRM 1169 (1972) (employer violated §8(a)(5) by soliciting employee sentiment for use against the union during negotiations); Plastics Transport, Inc., 193 NLRB 54, 78 LRRM 1185 (1971); Cal-Pacific Poultry, Inc., 163 NLRB 716, 64 LRRM 1463 (1967); Channel Master Corp., 162 NLRB 632, 64 LRRM 1102 (1967). In a real sense, bypassing the representative means failing to bargain collectively—a *per se* refusal to bargain; however, the cases also treat "bypassing" as evidence of lack of good faith in the duty to bargain.
    [316]Insular Chem. Co., 128 NLRB 93, 46 LRRM 1268 (1960).
    [317]C & C Plywood Corp., 163 NLRB 1022, 64 LRRM 1488, 1489 (1967), *quoting* Celanese Corp. of Am., 95 NLRB 664, 673, 28 LRRM 1362 (1951). *See* note 318 for subsequent history of C & C Plywood. *See also* Chapter 19 *infra* at notes 209-16.
    [318]*Id.* at 1024. *See* NLRB v. C & C Plywood, 385 US 421, 64 LRRM 2065 (1967).
    [319]*Id., quoting* Laystrom Mfg. Co., 151 NLRB 1482, 58 LRRM 1624 (1965).
    [320]Flowers Baking Co., 161 NLRB 1429, 63 LRRM 1462 (1966); Houston Sheet Metal Contractors Ass'n, 147 NLRB 774, 56 LRRM 1281 (1964); Cincinnati Cordage & Paper Co., 141 NLRB 72, 52 LRRM 1277 (1963); Walsh-Lumpkin Wholesale Drug Co., 129 NLRB 294, 46 LRRM 1535, *enforced,* 291 F2d 751, 46 LRRM 1535 (CA 8, 1960).
    [321]K-D Mfg. Co., 169 NLRB 57, 67 LRRM 1140 (1968), *enforced,* 419 F2d 467, 73 LRRM 2013 (CA 5, 1969); Colony Furniture Co., 144 NLRB 1582, 54 LRRM 1308 (1963); Solo Cup Co., *supra* note 238; Herman Sausage Co., *supra* note 40.
    [322]Chanticleer, Inc., 161 NLRB 241, 63 LRRM 1237 (1966); Crater Lake Mach. Co., 131 NLRB 1106, 48 LRRM 1211 (1961); National Furniture Mfg. Co., 130 NLRB 712, 47 LRRM 1414 (1961); Federal Dairy Co., 130 NLRB 1158, 47 LRRM 1465 (1961), *enforced,* 297 F2d 487, 49 LRRM 2214 (CA 1, 1962).
    [323]For treatment of independent §8(a)(1) conduct, *see* generally Chapter 6 *supra*.

ing general wage increases during negotiations without first consulting the union has been deemed a reflection of the employer's coercive "efforts to curtail the statutory rights of the union . . . ."[324] Where the employer's activity is viewed as having only a negligible effect on the authority of the bargaining agent, however, a violation will not be found. For example, where an employer made a direct announcement to employees inviting them to bid for a job vacancy the Board found no violation, though the matter was a subject of active discussion between the employer and the union.[325]

The Board has long followed the rule that failure by an employer to notify the majority representative and bargain with it concerning the adjustment of employee grievances and the imposition of employee discipline is a violation of Section 8(a)(5) of the Act. The representative's right not to be bypassed in such circumstances rests in the *proviso* to Section 9(a) of the Act, which declares:

> That any individual employee or a group of employees shall have the right at any time to present grievances to their employer and to have such grievances adjusted, without the intervention of the bargaining representative, as long as the adjustment is not inconsistent with the terms of a collective-bargaining contract or agreement then in effect: *Provided further,* That the bargaining representative has been given opportunity to be present at such adjustment.[326]

---

[324]Flambeau Plastics, 151 NLRB 591, 611, 58 LRRM 1470 (1965); Crestline Co., 133 NLRB 256, 48 LRRM 1623 (1961). In addition, dealing individually with employees concerning employee placement at a new plant location has been viewed by the Board as being in derogation of the union's bargaining rights. Cooper Thermometer Co., 160 NLRB 1902, 63 LRRM 1219 (1966), *enforcement denied on other grounds,* 376 F2d 684, 65 LRRM 2113 (CA 2, 1967).

[325]Union Elec. Co., 196 NLRB 830, 80 LRRM 1110 (1972). *See also* Dow Chem. Co., 215 NLRB 910, 88 LRRM 1625 (1975), *review granted, case remanded and order vacated,* Steelworkers v. NLRB, 536 F2d 550, 92 LRRM 2545 (CA 3, 1976) ("Speak Out" program for employee submission of anonymous, job-related complaints and questions to management held by Board not to bypass grievance and arbitration procedure. Court disagreed); Leland Stanford, Jr. Univ. & Stanford Univ. Hosp., 240 NLRB 1138, 100 LRRM 1391 (1979) (employer who distributed opinion survey among unionized employees did not violate Act. Board based its decision in large measure on issuance of memorandum to employees shortly after circulation of survey disclaiming any intention to deal directly with employees); Ingraham Indus., 178 NLRB 558, 72 LRRM 1245 (1969) (employer had refused to permit union representatives to attend sessions conducted by management to explain a profit-sharing plan adopted pursuant to a collective bargaining agreement).

[326]The Supreme Court explained the limited intent of the proviso in Emporium Capwell Co. v. Western Addition Community Organization, 420 US 50, 88 LRRM 2660 (1975): "The intendment of the proviso is to permit employees to present grievances and to authorize the employer to entertain them without opening itself to liability for dealing directly with employees in derogation of the duty to bargain only with the exclusive bargaining representative, a violation of §8(a)(5) . . . . The Act nowhere protects this 'right' by making it an unfair labor practice for an employer to refuse to entertain such a presentation . . . ." *Id.* at 61 n.12. *See* Chapter 6 *supra* at notes 404-408.

Thus, in *Texaco, Inc.*,[327] a 1967 case, where the employer had information that the employee had been seen leaving its premises with company property, the Board held that a union representative had the Section 9(a) right to attend the employee interview concerned with the investigation of these facts, where the probability of punishment emerging from that interview was great. The rights of the respective parties in such a situation, however, were ultimately delineated in *NLRB* v. *Weingarten, Inc.*[328] The so-called *Weingarten Rule* recognized a right, rooted in the concerted activities language of Section 7, for employees to request union presence and advice at investigatory interviews as a condition of their participation "where the employee reasonably believes the investigation will result in disciplinary action."[329] This is an employee right, deprivation of which exposes the employer to liability under Section 8(a)(1), not Section 8(a)(5), since, as the Court noted, "the employer has no duty to bargain with any union representative who may be permitted to attend the investigatory interview."[330]

8. Commission of Unfair Labor Practices. The commission of unfair labor practices during negotiations may reflect upon the good faith of the guilty party. Where an employer threatened to close the plant, promoted withdrawal from the union, reduced working hours and engaged in discriminatory layoffs during bargaining, the Board found Section 8(a)(5) violations.[331] Engaging in other unfair labor practices during the certification year may also be indicative of a course of conduct inconsistent with good faith.[332]

An employer's doubt as to a union's continued majority status may not excuse its refusal to continue negotiations if the refusal

---

[327]168 NLRB 361, 66 LRRM 1296 (1967), *enforcement denied,* 408 F2d 142, 70 LRRM 3045 (CA 5, 1970). *See also* Jacobe-Pearson Ford, 172 NLRB 594, 68 LRRM 1305 (1968); Chevron Oil Co., 168 NLRB 574, 66 LRRM 1353 (1967). While the majority representative derives its right not to be bypassed in matters involving employee discipline from §9(a), a closely related doctrine was announced by the Supreme Court in NLRB v. Weingarten, Inc., 420 US 251, 88 LRRM 2689 (1975). *See* note 328 *infra* and accompanying text.

[328]*Supra* note 327. *See* Chapter 6 *supra* at notes 427-65.

[329]*Id.* at 257.

[330]*Id.* at 259.

[331]Imperial Mach. Corp., 121 NLRB 621, 42 LRRM 1406 (1958).

[332]Borg-Warner Corp., *supra* note 236; Coachman's Inn, 147 NLRB 278, 56 LRRM 1206 (1964), *enforced,* 357 F2d 134, 61 LRRM 2445 (CA 8, 1966); Evergreen Rambler, Inc., 160 NLRB 864, 63 LRRM 1062 (1966); Berger Polishing, 147 NLRB 21, 56 LRRM 1140 (1964); Carter Mach. & Tool Co., 133 NLRB 247, 48 LRRM 1625 (1961).

is made in the context of other unlawful employer conduct.[333] If it cannot be shown with certainty how many of the employees would have withdrawn from the union in the absence of illegal conduct by the employer, a violation may be found, even though other factors might have contributed to the employees' change in attitude. This rule is premised on the propositions that doubts are to be resolved against the party whose conduct created the situation and that the union's continued majority status is to be presumed.[334] Moreover, a good-faith doubt is not one based upon employee expressions which have been encouraged, prompted, or solicited by the employer.[335] Thus, assisting employees in the preparation of decertification petitions has been deemed evidence of bad faith, since the foreseeable purpose of such assistance is to obstruct the bargaining process.[336]

The extent to which prior unfair labor practices may be relied upon as evidence of a present violation has undergone some revision by the Board. The old rule, stated in a 1951 case, *Larrance Tank Corp.*,[337] was that the Board would not consider conduct antedating a settlement agreement as evidence of a post-settlement unfair labor practice unless the party charged had (1) failed to comply with the terms of the agreement or (2) engaged in independent unfair labor practices since the settlement.[338] The old rule was modified in the 1965 *Hod Carriers* decision.[339] The Board re-examined *Larrance* and held that presettlement conduct was admissible as "background evidence" to establish the motive or object of a party in its post-settlement activities. The settlement agreement itself, however, may not be used to establish union animus.[340] But even prior to the *Larrance*

---

[333]C & C Plywood, *supra* note 317. *See generally* Chapter 12 *supra*.

[334]Movie Star, Inc., 145 NLRB 319, 54 LRRM 1387 (1963), *enforced in part, denied in part*, 361 F2d 346, 62 LRRM 2234 (CA 5, 1966).

[335]Rohlik, Inc., 145 NLRB 1236, 1243, 55 LRRM 1130 (1964).

[336]Wahoo Packing Co., 161 NLRB 174, 63 LRRM 1290 (1966); W. R. Hall Distrib., 144 NLRB 1285, 54 LRRM 1231 (1963), *enforced*, 341 F2d 359, 58 LRRM 2378 (CA 10, 1965). For treatment of decertification petitions generally, *see* Chapter 10 *supra* at notes 22-23 and Chapter 32 *infra* at note 35.

[337]94 NLRB 352, 28 LRRM 1045 (1951).

[338]In *Larrance* the trial examiner had found that the employer had not bargained in good faith after the settlement agreement and that the employer's "conduct after [the date of settlement] was of the 'same type' as its prior conduct." *Id.* at 353. This evaluation of the employer's post-settlement conduct was thus colored by the presettlement conduct, which the Board considered to be inconsistent with Board policy.

[339]Northern Cal. Dist. Council of Hod Carriers (Laborers) (Joseph's Landscaping Serv.), 154 NLRB 1384, 60 LRRM 1156 (1965), *enforced*, 389 F2d 721, 67 LRRM 2502 (CA 9, 1968).

[340]Metal Assemblies, Inc., 156 NLRB 914, 61 LRRM 1023 (1965). *Cf.* Bangor Plastics, Inc., 156 NLRB 1165, 61 LRRM 1210 (1965), *enforcement denied*, 392 F2d 772, 67 LRRM 2987 (CA 6, 1967).

modification, evidence of conduct preceding a prior finding of an unfair labor practice, as opposed to a settlement, was admitted as a factor to be considered in determining whether subsequent bargaining was in good faith.[341]

The Ninth Circuit's *NLRB* v. *MacMillan Ring-Free Oil Co.*[342] indicated some outer limits on the Board's use of "background evidence" in establishing Section 8(a)(5) violations where the Section 10(b) limitations period[343] is a factor. In *MacMillan* the Board found a refusal to bargain within the Section 10(b) period based on negotiating attitudes that were deemed substantially unchanged from the period preceding the six-month cutoff date. Denying enforcement of the Section 8(a)(5) portion of the Board's order, first the Circuit rejected the finding that an unfair labor practice had been committed within the six-month period. Turning to consideration of the sufficiency of the background evidence, i.e., evidence antedating the cutoff date, the court declared that "while . . . filing of a charge may be used to 'shed light' upon events taking place within the six-month period, the evidence of a violation drawn from within that period must be reasonably substantial in its own right" though not necessarily sufficient within itself to sustain an unfair labor practice finding.[344] Since there was no substantial evidence of violation occurring within the Section 10(b) period, in the court's view, a finding of unlawful bargaining conduct was not warranted.

IV. THE DUTY TO FURNISH INFORMATION

A. The Role of Information in the Bargaining Process—An Overview

The collective bargaining process requires that the bargaining *antagonists*—or *partners,* depending on whether one emphasizes the adversary or cooperative nature of the process—have adequate information about the immediate subjects at issue in bargaining or contract administration; otherwise, the process cannot function properly. Several key decisions have underscored the importance of the exchange of essential information in collective

---

[341]H. K. Porter Co., *supra* note 242. For discussion of settlements generally, *see* Chapter 32 *infra* at notes 128-39.
[342]*Supra* note 178.
[343]*See* Chapter 32 *infra* at notes 116-19.
[344]*Supra* note 178 at 33.

bargaining. The brief overview which follows introduces those decisions and provides the background for the discussions which follow on the nature of the duty to furnish information,[345] the occasions when the duty arises,[346] and the specific kinds of information which must be furnished.[347]

1. In Bargaining Over New Terms and Conditions.

The Supreme Court, in *NLRB v. Truitt Manufacturing Co.*,[348] held that employers have an obligation to furnish relevant information to union representatives during contract negotiations. The Court reasoned as follows:

> Good-faith bargaining necessarily requires that claims made by either bargainer should be honest claims. . . . If . . . an argument is important enough to present in the give and take of bargaining, it is important enough to require some sort of proof of its accuracy.[349]

Disclosure of relevant information is integral to the bargaining process. It encourages mutual respect between the negotiators and makes the American collective bargaining system, which so heavily relies on cooperation and open exchange, a viable approach to fashioning "a generalized code" establishing "a system of industrial self-government."[350] As the Fourth Circuit noted, unions cannot be expected to represent unit employees in an effective manner where they do not possess information which "is necessary to the proper discharge of the duties of the bargaining agent."[351] The Board's decision in *Oakland Press Co.*,[352] that unions have a like duty to furnish information to employers, follows naturally from the *Truitt* rationale.

---

[345]*See infra* at notes 367-428.

[346]*See infra* at notes 429-49.

[347]*See infra* at notes 450-510.

[348]*Supra* note 125. For a partial list of articles discussing the duty to furnish information, *see* Note, *A Union's Duty to Furnish Information to an Employer for Purposes of Collective Bargaining*, 4 U. DAYTON L. REV. 257 (1979); Note, *Psychological Aptitude Tests and the Duty to Supply Information*, 91 HARV. L. REV. 869 (1978); Morris, *The Role of the NLRB and the Courts in the Collective Bargaining Process: A Fresh Look at Conventional Wisdom and Unconventional Remedies*, *supra* note 2 at 663-67; Fanning, *The Obligation to Furnish Information During the Contract Term*, 9 GA. L. REV. 375 (1975); Bartosic & Hartley, *The Employer's Duty to Supply Information to the Union—A Study of the Interplay of Administrative and Judicial Rationalization*, 58 CORNELL L. REV. 23 (1972). *See* Annot., 2 ALR 3d 880, 905 (1965), for an exhaustive compilation of cases involving furnishing of wage information.

[349]*Supra* note 125 at 153.

[350]Steelworkers v. Warrior & Gulf Navigation Co., 363 US 574, 578, 580, 46 LRRM 2416 (1960).

[351]NLRB v. Whitin Mach. Works, 217 F2d 593, 594, 35 LRRM 2215 (CA 4, 1954), *cert. denied*, 349 US 905, 35 LRRM 2730 (1955).

[352]Detroit Newspaper Printing & Graphic Communications Local 13 (Oakland Press Co.), 233 NLRB 994, 97 LRRM 1047 (1977), *aff'd*, 598 F2d 267, 101 LRRM 2036 (CA DC, 1979). *See infra* at notes 362-66.

2. In Representation Under an Existing Collective Agreement. The second Supreme Court decision dealing with the duty to furnish information was *NLRB* v. *Acme Industrial Co.*[353] In this case the Court held that the employer's duty to furnish information, like its duty to bargain, "extends beyond the period of contract negotiations and applies to labor-management relations during the term of an agreement."[354] Thus the Supreme Court required disclosure of certain information pertaining to a grievance filed by the union.

Acme Industrial emphasized the importance of relevant information to the union in its effort to police and administer the collective bargaining agreement. It endorsed the "discovery-type standard" applied by the Board.[355] The courts and the Board, in applying *Truitt* and *Acme Industrial,* have continued to enforce this statutory obligation.[356] Indeed, it is not uncommon for collective bargaining agreements to have a provision requiring disclosure of relevant information during the contract term.[357]

3. Characterizing the Failure to Furnish Information. Is a refusal to supply requested information a *per se* violation of the duty to bargain, merely evidence of lack of good faith, or not a violation of the statute at all? The Supreme Court's majority opinion in *Truitt*[358] addressed this query but failed to supply a complete answer. It stated: "We do not hold . . . that in every case in which economic inability is raised as an argument against increased wages it automatically follows that the employees are entitled to substantiating evidence . . . . The inquiry must also be whether or not under the circumstances . . . the statutory obligation to bargain in good faith has been met."[359] And according to Justice Frankfurter's concurring opinion,[360] the Board had applied the wrong standard in ruling that the employer's failure to supply information constituted a *per se* refusal to bargain. The view that *Truitt,* properly interpreted, means that refusal to supply information is only *evidence* of bad faith, not a

---

[353]385 US 432, 64 LRRM 2069 (1967). *See infra* at notes 441-43.
[354]*Id.* at 436.
[355]*Supra* note 353 at 437. *See infra* at notes 365 and 385-88.
[356]*See* the following sections under this heading. *But cf.* Detroit Edison Co. v. NLRB, 440 US 301, 100 LRRM 2728 (1979), discussed *infra* at notes 415-17, 423, and 493.
[357]*E.g.,* United Aircraft Corp., 204 NLRB 879, 83 LRRM 1411 (1972).
[358]*Supra* note 125.
[359]*Id.* at 153.
[360]Justice Frankfurter also dissented, in that he would have remanded the case to the Board.

per se violation, has been followed in a number of circuit court decisions, though some courts have continued to apply a *per se* standard.[361]

4. The Union Duty to Supply Information. The duty to furnish information is not an obligation imposed on employers alone; a similar duty is owed by unions. This principle was established in the *Oakland Press* case.[362] Oakland Press printed a daily newspaper. The press room employees at the plant were represented by a local union which had agreed in the collective bargaining contract to an arrangement whereby it would attempt to supply the company with extra employees to handle overload work at straight-time rates. In practice, however, the union gave the assignments to regular employees, whom the company had to pay at overtime rates. The employer questioned whether the union was making a good-faith effort to find extra employees before giving overtime work to regular employees. In conjunction with negotiations for a new labor contract, the employer requested certain information from the union regarding its referral system, which the union refused to disclose; thereupon the employer filed a charge alleging a violation of Section 8(b)(3).

The Board held that "a union's duty to furnish information relevant to the bargaining process is parallel to that of an employer."[363] Reasoning that it was essential for the employer, in structuring its economic demands, to know how the referral system operated, as well as the actual availability of extra workers for overload work, the Board concluded that the information sought was relevant to the bargaining process and that therefore the union violated its statutory bargaining obligation by failing to respond to the employer's inquiries. The District of Columbia Circuit affirmed, holding that just as an employer is required to disclose information during bargaining, a union "is likewise

---

[361]*See* Woodworkers v. NLRB, 263 F2d 483, 43 LRRM 2462 (CA DC, 1959); J. I. Case Co. v. NLRB, 253 F2d 149, 41 LRRM 2679 (CA 7, 1958), *enforcing as amended* 118 NLRB 520, 40 LRRM 1208 (1957). *But see* Curtiss-Wright Corp. (Wright Aero. Div.) v. NLRB, 347 F2d 61, 59 LRRM 2433 (CA 3, 1965), *enforcing* 145 NLRB 152, 54 LRRM 1320 (1963), where the court stated that once it is established that information is relevant, it is a *per se* refusal to bargain for the employer to fail to produce the information on request.

[362]Detroit Newspaper Printing & Graphic Communications Local 13 (Oakland Press Co.), *supra* note 352.

[363]*Id.* at 996, *quoting dictum* in Tool & Die Makers Lodge No. 78 (Square D Co.), 224 NLRB 111, 92 LRRM 1202 (1976).

obliged to furnish the employer with relevant information."[364]
The court reiterated that the standard for determining relevancy was a liberal one, "much akin to that applied in discovery proceedings,"[365] and the information requested by Oakland Press fell well within this standard. In decisions handed down since *Oakland Press,* the Board has continued to require unions to turn over relevant information to employers.[366]

B. Nature of the Duty to Furnish Information

The Board has long held that, intertwined with the duty to bargain in good faith, is a duty on the part of the employer to supply the union, upon request, with sufficient information to enable it to understand and intelligently discuss the issues raised in bargaining.[367] Although the duty is reciprocal, most of the required information, by its nature, must flow from the employer to the union; hence most of the case law concerns employer recalcitrance in supplying information requested by unions, either in the bargaining process or in the administration of the collective agreement.

The employer's duty to furnish information is based upon the premise that without such information the union would be unable to perform its duties properly as bargaining agent.[368] Thus, information must be furnished to the union for purposes of representing employees in negotiations for a future contract and also for policing the administration of an existing contract.[369] The employer's refusal to supply information is as much a violation of the duty to bargain as if it had failed to meet and confer with the union in good faith.[370]

---

[364]*Supra* note 352, 598 F2d at 271.
[365]*Id. See* notes 355 *supra* and 386-88 *infra* and accompanying texts.
[366]*See infra* at notes 508-510.
[367]S. L. Allen & Co., *supra* note 24 ("Interchange of ideas, communication of facts peculiarly within the knowledge of either party [are] of the essence in the bargaining process"). *See also* Industrial Welding Co., 175 NLRB 477, 71 LRRM 1076 (1969); Oregon Coast Operators Ass'n, 113 NLRB 1338, 36 LRRM 1448 (1955), *aff'd,* 246 F2d 280; Southern Saddlery Co., 90 NLRB 1205, 26 LRRM 1322 (1950).
[368]Aluminum Ore Co. v. NLRB, 131 F2d 485, 11 LRRM 693 (CA 7, 1942).
[369]Curtiss-Wright Corp., *supra* note 361; J. I. Case Co. v. NLRB, *supra* note 361; Kroger Co., 226 NLRB 512, 93 LRRM 1315 (1976); Weber Veneer & Plywood Co., 161 NLRB 1054, 63 LRRM 1395 (1966); B. F. Goodrich Co., 89 NLRB 1151, 26 LRRM 1090 (1950); General Controls, 88 NLRB 1341, 25 LRRM 1475 (1950).
[370]Curtiss-Wright Corp., *supra* note 361. *See* Levingston Shipbuilding Co., 244 NLRB No. 18, 102 LRRM 1127 (1979).

The duty to furnish information is a statutory obligation which exists independent of any agreement between the parties;[371] however, the union's right to disclosure of relevant and necessary data can be waived by the union in a collective bargaining agreement.[372] But even where the union has made such a waiver in the agreement, the employer must still furnish information at an appropriate time when it is relevant to the negotiation of a new agreement.[373] Thus in *American Standard, Inc.*,[374] a 1973 case, the Board held that where a contract is silent on the obligation to furnish information, a request for information bearing on a possible grievance is based on a statutory, rather than contractual, right, and the Board will therefore not defer the dispute to arbitration under its *Collyer* doctrine.[375] Later in the same year, however, in *United Aircraft Corp.*,[376] where the labor contract contained a provision requiring the production of pertinent information at Step 1 of the grievance procedure, the Board held that the contract language implied a waiver of the right to have information at an earlier stage of the proceedings, and charges concerning earlier requests were therefore "clearly matters of contract interpretation" best resolved by arbitration.[377]

United Aircraft, however, may have been overruled *sub silentio*. In *International Harvester Co.*,[378] a 1979 decision, the Board affirmed, without citing *United Aircraft*, the decision of an administrative law judge holding that a provision in a collective bargaining agreement, which vested the arbitrator of a grievance with authority to order disclosure of information, did not require deferral of unfair labor practice charges alleging wrongful refusal to turn over information that would assist the union in determining whether to initiate the grievance process. Although the two cases are distinguishable on their facts, the Board's position on this deferral issue is not yet well defined.

1. Request or Demand. An employer's duty to supply the bargaining representative with information does not arise until

---

[371]American Standard, Inc., 203 NLRB 1132, 83 LRRM 1245 (1973).
[372]*See* United Aircraft Corp., 204 NLRB 879, 83 LRRM 1411 (1973), *aff'd*, 525 F2d 237, 90 LRRM 2922.
[373]McDonnell Douglas Corp., 224 LRRM 881, 93 LRRM 1280 (1976).
[374]*Supra* note 371.
[375]*Id.* at 1132. *See* Collyer Insulated Wire, 192 NLRB 837, 77 LRRM 1931 (1971), treated extensively in Chapter 20 *infra*.
[376]*Supra* note 372.
[377]*Id.* at 880.
[378]241 NLRB 600, 100 LRRM 1588 (1979).

the union makes a request or a demand that the information be furnished.[379] While the request must be made in good faith,[380] this requirement is met if at least one reason for the demand can be justified.[381]

2. Relevance or Necessity. The information demanded must be relevant to the relationship between the employer and the union in the latter's capacity as representative of the employees.[382] When the request is in general rather than specific terms, the employer has the right to determine the initial relevance of the requested information.[383] However, the Board and the courts have adopted a liberal definition of relevancy, requiring only that the information be directly related to the union's function

---

[379]NLRB v. Boston Herald-Traveler Corp., 210 F2d 134, 33 LRRM 2435 (CA 1, 1954), *enforcing* 102 NLRB 627, 31 LRRM 1337 (1953); Westinghouse Elec. Supply Co. v. NLRB, 196 F2d 1012, 30 LRRM 2169 (CA 3, 1952). *But see* Boston Herald-Traveler Corp., 110 NLRB 2097, 35 LRRM 1309 (1954), *aff'd*, 223 F2d 58, 36 LRRM 2220 (CA 1, 1955).

[380]Cases are legion in which the Board has upheld an employer refusal to turn over information because the union request or demand was deemed unreasonable. *See, e.g.,* General Elec. Co., 163 NLRB 198, 64 LRRM 1312 (1967) (the Board held *inter alia* that employer's refusal to furnish information relating to laid-off employees was not a violation of §8(a)(5) because the request was made during pendency of unfair labor practice charges complaining of the lay-off); NLRB v. Abbott Publishing Co., 331 F2d 209, 55 LRRM 2994 (CA 7, 1964) (an employer refusal to turn over its financial records for a union audit did not violate the Act, despite poverty plea response to union's demand for a wage increase, where employer offered to supply and discuss weekly profit-and-loss statements, and agreed to allow company bookkeepers who were union members to discuss the financial status of the company with union negotiators); McCulloch Corp., *supra* note 129 (employer did not breach duty when it turned over a 29-company wage-range study to the union, with a list of participating companies and job classifications, but withheld the specific wage rates paid by each of the companies because of a confidentiality agreement); Albany Garage, Inc., 126 NLRB 417, 45 LRRM 1329 (1960) (employer satisfied duty to turn over information where financial statements it supplied union had been accepted by banks doing business with the employer, by the Bureau of Internal Revenue, by the employer's stockholders, and the union had accepted the same type of information in preceding years); California Portland Cement Co., 101 NLRB 1436, 31 LRRM 1220 (1952) (employer did not violate Act where information requested was posted on plant bulletin board). *Compare* the preceding cases *with* B. F. Diamond Constr. Co., *supra* note 129 (employer presented with a general demand for wage information cannot refuse to turn over such data solely on the ground that the information is available from employees).

[381]Utica Observer-Dispatch, Inc. v. NLRB, 229 F2d 575, 37 LRRM 2441 (CA 2, 1956) (union could not obtain information solely for purpose of collecting dues, but desire of wage information for bargaining purpose as well justifies demand). *But see* Snively Groves, Inc., 109 NLRB 1394, 34 LRRM 1568 (1954) (inconsistent and confusing requests by the union relieved the employer of the obligation to furnish information).

[382]Transport of N.J., 233 NLRB 694, 97 LRRM 1204 (1977); Ellsworth Sheet Metal, Inc., 224 NLRB 1506, 92 LRRM 1590 (1976); Webster Outdoor Advertising, *supra* note 223; Midwestern Instruments, Inc., *supra* note 192; NLRB v. Item Co., 220 F2d 956, 35 LRRM 2709 (CA 5, 1955); NLRB v. Jacobs Mfg. Co., 196 F2d 680, 30 LRRM 2098 (CA 2, 1952).

[383]Food Serv. Co., 202 NLRB 790, 82 LRRM 1746 (1973) (union request for general access to employer's records).

as bargaining representative[384] and that it appear "reasonably necessary" for the performance of this function.[385] Data appropriate for disclosure "should not necessarily be limited to that which would be pertinent to a particular existing controversy."[386] As the Supreme Court pointed out in *Acme Industrial,* this is basically a "discovery-type standard."[387]

In general, requested information "must be disclosed unless it plainly appears irrelevant" in accordance with the prevailing rule in discovery procedures under "modern codes."[388] "There the information must be disclosed unless it plainly appears irrelevant."[389] According to the Board, wage and related information should be made available "without regard to its immediate relationship" to the negotiation or administration of the agreement, or to its "precise relevancy" to particular bargaining issues.[390] Subsequent execution of a contract by a union without the information does not render the information irrelevant, since the union may simply have decided that the advantages of a contract in hand would outweigh those which it might enjoy with all the information available to it.[391]

One consideration in determining relevancy and necessity is the need of the union for the information. Where a request is rendered moot by subsequent events, the employer has no statutory obligation to furnish information.[392] Such requests have no "current relevancy."[393]

---

[384]J. I. Case Co. v. NLRB, *supra* note 361; Otis Elevator Co., 170 NLRB 395, 67 LRRM 1475 (1968).

[385]NLRB v. Item Co., *supra* note 382.

[386]NLRB v. Whitin Mach. Works, *supra* note 351 at 595.

[387]NLRB v. Acme Indus. Co., *supra* note 353 at 437.

[388]NLRB v. Yawman & Erbe Mfg. Co., 187 F2d 947, 949, 27 LRRM 2524 (CA 2, 1951). The court went on to say that "[a]ny less lenient rule in labor disputes would greatly hamper the bargaining process, for it is virtually impossible to tell in advance whether the requested data will be relevant . . . ." *Id.* at 949.

[389]Teleprompter Corp. v. NLRB, 570 F2d 4, 8, 97 LRRM 2455 (CA 1, 1977), *enforcing* 227 NLRB 705, 95 LRRM 1058 (1977), *quoting* NLRB Chairman Farmer in the *Whitin* case (*see* NLRB v. Whitin Mach. Works, *supra* note 351; Boston Herald Traveler v. NLRB, *supra* note 379, 223 F2d 58, 36 LRRM 2220 (CA 1, 1955)). In *Teleprompter,* the First Circuit added a caveat: "The unqualified discovery-type rule . . . does not seem to us tailored to [the plea-of-poverty situation]. The union is entitled only to what is reasonably necessary properly to represent its members in light of the employer's triggering claim of financial inability." 570 F2d 11. *See infra* at notes 450-66.

[390]Whitin Mach. Works, 108 NLRB 1537, 34 LRRM 1251 (1954), *enforced, supra* note 351. *See* Boston Herald-Traveler Corp. v. NLRB, *supra* note 379, where the relevance of wage data was presumed. *See also* NLRB v. Fitzgerald Mills Corp., *supra* note 189.

[391]NLRB v. Fitzgerald Mills Corp., *supra* note 189; NLRB v. Yawman & Erbe Mfg. Co., *supra* note 388.

[392]Glazers Wholesale Drug Co., 211 NLRB 1063, 87 LRRM 1249 (1974).

[393]C-B Buick, Inc. v. NLRB, 506 F2d 1086, 87 LRRM 2878 (CA 3, 1974), *denying enforcement in part to* 206 NLRB 6, 84 LRRM 1173 (1973).

THE DEVELOPING LABOR LAW CH. 13

Difficult questions concerning relevance and necessity often arise when a union demands information concerning nonunit employees. In such circumstances, the bargaining representative must demonstrate the probable or potential relevance of the information to its representation of unit employees.[394] In analyzing such amorphous criteria as "relevance" and "necessity," the courts and the Board consider each case on its own unique facts; demands for information concerning nonunit employees have been both sustained[395] and rejected.[396]

Thus, in some cases the Board has held that a union has a right to wage information for nonunit personnel,[397] information regarding unit supervisors,[398] managers' and supervisors' salary rates and job descriptions,[399] the salaries of "confidential secretaries,"[400] as well as information about employees in another division not represented by the union.[401] On the other hand, the courts have rejected certain union demands: for information concerning employees not transferred into the bargaining unit,[402] for information regarding the purchase of new equipment,[403] and for personnel data on nonunion employees being trained as replacements in the event of a strike.[404]

3. Availability. Once a good-faith demand is made for relevant information, it must be made available promptly and in useful form. Even though an employer has not expressly refused to furnish the information, his failure to make diligent effort to obtain or to provide the information "reasonably" promptly may be equated with a flat refusal.[405] A long and unexplained delay

---

[394]San Diego Newspaper Guild v. NLRB, 548 F2d 863, 94 LRRM 2923 (CA 9, 1977); Adams Insulation Co., 219 NLRB 211, 89 LRRM 1699 (1975).

[395]See Goodyear Aerospace Corp., 388 F2d 673, 67 LRRM 2447 (CA 6, 1968); Curtiss-Wright Corp. (Wright Aero Div.) v. NLRB, supra note 361; California Portland Cement Co., 103 NLRB 1375, 31 LRRM 1630 (1953).

[396]Fetzer Television, Inc. v NLRB, 317 F2d 420, 53 LRRM 2224 (CA 6, 1963); NLRB v. Leland-Gifford Co., 200 F2d 620, 31 LRRM 2196 (CA 1, 1952).

[397]Brazos Elec. Power Coop., Inc., 241 NLRB 1016, 101 LRRM 1003 (1979), aff'd, 615 F2d 1100 (CA 5, 1980).

[398]Globe Stores, Inc., 227 NLRB 1251, 94 LRRM 1336 (1977); Northwest Publications, 211 NLRB 464, 86 LRRM 1345 (1974).

[399]International Harvester Co., 241 NLRB 600, 100 LRRM 1588 (1979).

[400]Greensboro News Co., 244 NLRB 689, 102 LRRM 1164 (1979).

[401]Temple-Eastex, Inc., 228 NLRB 203, 96 LRRM 1424 (1977), rev'd, 579 F2d 932, 99 LRRM 2467 (CA 5,1978). But see Binswanger Glass Co., supra note 96. See discussion infra at notes 472-75.

[402]NLRB v. Western Elec., Inc., 559 F2d 1131, 95 LRRM 3230 (CA 8, 1977).

[403]Seafarers Local 777 v. NLRB, 603 F2d 862, 99 LRRM 2903 (CA DC, 1978) (purchase of new cabs and assignment to nonunion drivers).

[404]San Diego Newspaper Guild v. NLRB, supra note 394.

[405]NLRB v. John S. Swift Co., supra note 216 (the court stated that the "Company's inaction spoke louder than its words").

in furnishing even partial information (nine months) has supported a conclusion that later bargaining was not in good faith, even though the company had expressly agreed to provide the information.[406] Although the Board finds a delay of several months to be inconsistent with good faith,[407] a short delay may be reasonable if justified.[408]

4. Manner and Form. As to the manner and form in which the information must be presented, the Board requires that it be furnished "in a manner not so burdensome or time consuming as to impede the process of bargaining," although not necessarily in the form requested by the union.[409] If the employer claims that compiling the data will be unduly burdensome, it must assert that claim at the time of the request for the information so that an arrangement can be made to lessen the burden.[410] The employer may not simply present the information in any form which it considers adequate but which is, nonetheless, unsuitable for informed consideration.[411] However, if the

---

[406]NLRB v. Fitzgerald Mills Corp. *supra* note 189 (the court also noted that the withdrawal by the union of an earlier unfair labor practice charge based on the same refusal of information did not indicate compliance or that the union was satisfied, only that the union believed the employer had begun to comply with its request). *See also* NLRB v. My Store, Inc., *supra* note 174 (employer supplied incorrect information, then failed to correct mistake "for months"); NLRB v. Feed & Supply Center, Inc., 294 F2d 650, 48 LRRM 2993 (CA 9, 1961) (six-month delay); International Powder Metallurgy Co., 134 NLRB 1605, 49 LRRM 1388 (1961) (11-month delay); Peyton Packing Co., 129 NLRB 1358, 47 LRRM 1211 (1961) (three-month delay is too long, even when data is incomplete and the persons necessary to compile the information are absent from work).

[407]Colonial Press, Inc., 204 NLRB 852, 83 LRRM 1648 (1973); Arkansas Rice Growers Coop. Ass'n, 165 NLRB 577, 65 LRRM 1567 (1967), *aff'd*, 400 F2d 565, 69 LRRM 2119 (CA 8, 1968).

[408]United Engines, Inc., 222 NLRB 50, 91 LRRM 1208 (1976) (employer did not violate the Act when it provided most of the information requested within a month of the request and two weeks before bargaining was scheduled to start); Partee Flooring Mill, 107 NLRB 1177, 33 LRRM 1342 (1954) (15-day delay not unreasonable).

[409]Old Line Life Ins. Co., 96 NLRB 499 (1951), *aff'd*, 200 F2d 52 (CA 7, 1952) (where information was being supplied regularly on a monthly basis, the employer's offer to verify accuracy of union's current list fulfilled statutory obligation); B. F. Goodrich Co., *supra* note 369 (wage data identified by employee department number rather than by name not sufficient); Cincinnati Steel Casting Co., 86 NLRB 592, 24 LRRM 1657 (1949) (oral information sufficient). *See also* NLRB v. Tex-Tan, Inc., *supra* note 78 (the data requested was considered too voluminous to compile, thus the request was overly burdensome).

[410]J. I. Case Co. v. NLRB, *supra* note 361.

[411]*Id.* at 150 (employer violated the Act when it orally presented complicated information at a single bargaining session rather than producing copies of the records in question, where the union had offered to pay copying charges); NLRB v. Otis Elevator Co., 208 F2d 176, 33 LRRM 2129 (CA 2, 1953) (contract provision specifying that certain information will be furnished to union does not preclude its obtaining other information to which it is entitled); General Elec. Co., 186 NLRB 14, 75 LRRM 1265 (1970) (employer violated §8(a)(5) when it offered the union a video tape presentation instead of allowing it to conduct an in-plant time study of the job in question).

employer presents information on its financial position in a form generally accepted in business, it will usually be considered adequate.[412] An employer may also attach conditions to the furnishing of such financial information that are reasonably related to its own business interest.[413] But where the employer allows the union free access to its records and fully cooperates with the union in answering questions, it need not furnish information in a more organized form than that in which it keeps its own records.[414]

5. Employer Defenses. A union's interest in arguably relevant information does not always predominate over other legitimate interests, as the Supreme Court pointed out in *Detroit Edison Co.* v. *NLRB*,[415] rejecting the concept of an "absolute rule"[416] relating to disclosure of information:

> A union's bare assertion that it needs information to process a grievance does not automatically oblige the employer to supply all the information in the manner requested. The duty to supply information under §8(a)(5) turns upon "the circumstances of the particular case" . . . and much the same may be said for the type of disclosure that will satisfy that duty.[417]

Employers are limited, however, as to the defenses which they may successfully invoke against a charge of refusal to bargain arising from failure to provide relevant information. Defenses based on the circumstances of specific cases—for example, defenses relating to relevancy, form, or availability—have been previously noted; and like defenses will be noted in relation to the timing of the union's request[418] and to the nature of the information requested.[419] This section concerns certain limited exceptions which might be termed "affirmative defenses."

In *NLRB* v. *Movie Star, Inc.*[420] an employer was excused from the duty to provide information where its failure to do so was

---

[412]Albany Garage, Inc., *supra* note 380 (a leading case outlining the type of documents that would constitute adequate, voluntary disclosure). *But cf.* Metlox Mfg. Co. v NLRB, 378 F2d 728, 65 LRRM 2637 (CA 9, 1967).

[413]Fruit & Vegetable Packers v. NLRB, 316 F2d 389, 52 LRRM 2537 (CA DC, 1963).

[414]NLRB v. Tex-Tan, Inc., *supra* note 78. *See also* Fafnir Bearing Co. v. NLRB, 362 F2d 716, 62 LRRM 2415 (CA 2, 1966) (even after employer makes time studies and releases results to union, union may demand access to plans and records to make its own studies to substantiate company information). *But see* NLRB v. Otis Elevator Co., *supra* note 411.

[415]*Supra* note 356. *See infra* at notes 423 and 493.

[416]*Id.* at 318.

[417]*Id.* at 314, *quoting* NLRB v. Truitt Mfg. Co., *supra* note 125 at 153.

[418]*See infra* at notes 429-49.

[419]*See infra* at notes 450-510.

[420]361 F2d 346, 62 LRRM 2234 (CA 5, 1966).

attributable to a breakdown in negotiations not caused by the employer's lack of good faith. However, employer contentions that information is confidential or privileged have been rejected,[421] as have similar contentions that the divulgence of such information violates employees' right of privacy,[422] although the latter position was upheld in relation to the results of psychological testing.[423] A few cases have pardoned an employer's refusal to furnish information on the ground that the union had waived its right to information by "clearly and unmistakably" bargaining the right away,[424] but even fewer have inferred a waiver from the union's bargaining conduct.[425] Most cases involving waiver stress that since the duty to furnish information arises under the Act, the union's right to such information can be waived only in express terms and such a waiver can never be found by implication.[426] Thus, forfeiture of the right must be by "clear and unmistakable" language and not merely by omission from the contract.[427] A general contract "zipper" provision to the effect that the agreement has settled all issues and all collective bargaining obligations for its term does not normally amount to a waiver as to information.[428]

C. When the Duty Exists

In the 1954 case of *NLRB* v. *Whitin Machine Works*[429] the Fourth Circuit concluded that it was "well settled that it is an

---

[421]Aluminum Ore Co. v. NLRB, *supra* note 368; Kroger Co., 163 NLRB 441, 64 LRRM 1364 (1967), *enforcement denied*, 399 F2d 455, 68 LRRM 2731 (CA 6, 1968); Boston Herald-Traveler Corp., *supra* note 389.

[422]Utica Observer-Dispatch, Inc. v. NLRB, *supra* note 381 (employer's notification to employees that it would furnish information if they did not object, and withholding of information only on those who did object, is refusal to bargain); NLRB v. Item Co., *supra* note 382; Northwestern Photo Engraving Co., 140 NLRB 24, 51 LRRM 1550 (1962). *But see* Webster Outdoor Advertising Co., *supra* note 223, holding that an employer did not violate the Act by refusing to supply wage data for replacements of economic strikers. The fact that the replacements had been subject to harassment and threats justified the employer's request for assurance by the union that the need was for legitimate union purposes and the data would not be used to facilitate further harassment. Furthermore, the refusal was not categorical.

[423]Detroit Edison Co. v. NLRB, *supra* note 356 and discussion at note 493 *infra*.

[424]International News Serv. Div. of Hearst Corp., 113 NLRB 1067, 36 LRRM 1454 (1955); Hughes Tool Co., 100 NLRB 208, 30 LRRM 1265 (1952).

[425]Square D Co. v. NLRB, 332 F2d 360, 56 LRRM 2147 (CA 9, 1964); Berkline Corp., 123 NLRB 685, 43 LRRM 1513 (1959).

[426]NLRB v. Perkins Mach. Co., 326 F2d 488, 55 LRRM 2204 (CA 1, 1964); Skyway Luggage Co., 117 NLRB 681, 39 LRRM 1310 (1957).

[427]Timken Roller Bearing Co. v. NLRB, 325 F2d 746, 54 LRRM 2785 (CA 6, 1963); California Portland Cement Co., 103 NLRB 1375, 31 LRRM 1630 (1953).

[428]J. I. Case Co. v. NLRB, *supra* note 361. *See* further discussion of waiver in Part VII, *infra*, this chapter.

[429]217 F2d 593, 35 LRRM 2215 (CA 4, 1954).

unfair labor practice within the meaning of section 8(a)(5) of the Act for an employer to refuse to furnish a bargaining union [such information as] is necessary to the proper discharge of the duties of the bargaining agent."[430] As previously noted, this duty to furnish to the union relevant information was given explicit approval by the Supreme Court in the *Truitt* case.[431] But *when* does the duty exist?

The duty arises as soon as the union is elected bargaining representative. The Seventh Circuit affirmed a Board decision holding that an employer acts at its peril if it refuses to provide requested information following a Board election, even though the request is made prior to certification and while objections are pending.[432]

The duty "does not terminate with the signing of the collective bargaining contract" but "continues through the life of the agreements so far as it is necessary to enable the parties to administer the contract and resolve grievances or disputes."[433] During the term of the contract, a union must be able to apprise the employees of the benefits to which they are entitled under the contract and of its readiness to enforce compliance with the agreement for their protection.[434] Since collective bargaining is a continuing process, the union not only has the duty to negotiate collective bargaining agreements, but also the statutory obligation to police and administer existing agreements;[435] thus, its right to information within the sphere of its function as

---

[430]*Id.* at 594. *See also* Sinclair Refining Co. v. NLRB, 306 F2d 569, 50 LRRM 2830 (CA 5, 1962); NLRB v. Yawman & Erbe Mfg. Co., *supra* note 388 (employer conceded that duty to provide information was incidental to its duty to bargain in good faith); Aluminum Ore Co. v. NLRB, 131 F2d 485, 487, 11 LRRM 693 (CA 7, 1942) (the court stated: "[W]e do not believe that it was the intent of Congress in this legislation that, in the collective bargaining prescribed, the union, as representative of the employees, should be deprived of the pertinent facts . . .").

[431]*Supra* note 125.

[432]Sundstrand Heat Transfer, Inc. v. NLRB, 538 F2d 1257, 92 LRRM 3266 (CA 7, 1976). *See also* East Coast Equip. Corp., 299 NLRB 825, 95 LRRM 1166 (1977), *enforced sub nom.* NLRB v. Steco Sales, Inc., 98 LRRM 2438 (CA 3, 1978) (employer who contended that certified unit was not appropriate violated Act when it denied union's request for information).

[433]Sinclair Refining Co. v. NLRB, *supra* note 430 at 570. *See also* Budde Publications, Inc., 242 NLRB 243, 101 LRRM 1140 (1979); Western Mass. Elec. Co. v. NLRB, 589 F2d 42, 100 LRRM 2315 (CA 1, 1978).

[434]*See* Prudential Ins. Co. v. NLRB, 412 F2d 77, 71 LRRM 2254 (CA 2, 1969), *cert. denied*, 396 US 928 (1969).

[435]J. I. Case Co. v. NLRB, *supra* note 361; Southwestern Bell Tel. Co., 173 NLRB 172, 69 LRRM 1251 (1968) (subcontracting cost information ordered disclosed for use in processing grievances relating to subcontracting); Twin City Lines, Inc., 170 NLRB 625, 67 LRRM 1553 (1968).

bargaining representative continues after an agreement is signed.[436]

Often the information sought by the union will be used to determine if an employer has modified or breached the terms of the collective agreement.[437] The union requires such information for the performance of its statutory duties and responsibilities, particularly when employer actions affect employees' rights under the contract.[438] The inquiry must always be whether or not, under the circumstances of the individual case, the employer has satisfied its statutory obligation.[439]

A question that has arisen in this regard is whether the right to information useful in processing grievances is limited by the scope of a particular grievance and by the grievance machinery, or whether a broader right exists under the Act.[440] In *Acme Industrial Co.*[441] the Supreme Court upheld the Board's deter-

---

[436]NLRB v. John S. Swift Co., *supra* note 216; Sheet Metal Contractors, 246 NLRB 886, 103 LRRM 1018 (1979). *See also* Hoerner-Waldorf Paper Prods. Co., 163 NLRB 772, 64 LRRM 1469 (1967), *aff'd*, 422 F2d 1258, 73 LRRM 2670 (CA 9, 1970). *See also* NLRB v. Davol, Inc., 597 F2d 782, 101 LRRM 2242 (CA 1, 1979), where the First Circuit enforced a Board order requiring an employer to disclose certain subcontracting information, even though the contract granted the employer an unlimited right to contract out work, and the union may have been attempting to capture work it had never previously performed. (*Cf.* National Woodwork Mfrs. Ass'n v. NLRB, 386 US 612, 64 LRRM 2801 (1967), Chapter 26 *infra* at notes 97-166.) The court reasoned that the information could be relevant to future contract negotiations. *But see* Safeway Stores, Inc., 240 NLRB 836, 100 LRRM 1328 (1979), where the Board refused to require the employer to furnish information regarding female supervisors on the ground that the union's role did not extend to policing promotions from out of the unit to management.
[437]Michigan Drywall Corp., 232 NLRB 120, 96 LRRM 1305 (1977). *See also* American Oil Co., 238 NLRB 294, 99 LRRM 1253 (1978), *enforced*, 602 F2d 184, 101 LRRM 2981 (CA 8, 1979); Florida Steel Corp., 235 NLRB 941, 100 LRRM 1187 (1978), *enforced as modified*, 601 F2d 125, 101 LRRM 2671 (CA 4, 1979).
[438]NLRB v. Acme Indus. Co., *supra* note 353.
[439]NLRB v. Truitt Mfg. Co., *supra* note 125.
[440]*See* Sinclair Refining Co. v. NLRB, *supra* note 430, where the Fifth Circuit stated that when a determination of the relevancy of requested information requires "determination of the critical substantive issue of the grievance itself," the Board may not adjudicate the grievance dispute "under the guise of determining relevance" any more than a court could determine the merits of the grievance under the guise of determining its arbitrability. The court went on to hold that since the employer sought earnestly to submit the disputed issue—relevance of the data—to the grievance process, the Board was foreclosed from considering the intrinsic merits of the complaint. *Compare* Sinclair Refining *with* Timken Roller Bearing Co. v. NLRB, 325 F2d 746, 54 LRRM 2785 (CA 6, 1963), where the Sixth Circuit, in upholding the union's right to similar information, relied essentially on the value of the information in the general administration of the contract. *See* Curtiss-Wright Corp., *supra* note 361, where the Third Circuit attempted to reconcile the differences between the Sinclair and Timken cases. *See also* American Oil Co., *supra* note 242; Puerto Rico Tel. Co. v. NLRB, 359 F2d 983, 62 LRRM 2069 (CA 1, 1966). Information requested by union in both cases might have assisted in disposition of grievances, hence was deemed relevant. *See* Chapter 20 *infra* at notes 178-82.
[441]NLRB v. Acme Indus. Co., *supra* note 353.

mination that a Section 8(a)(5) violation had occurred when the employer refused to furnish information which would have allowed the union to determine at the outset whether there had been a breach of the collective bargaining agreement. The circuit court had refused to enforce the order on the ground that an arbitration clause foreclosed the Board from exercising its statutory power.[442] In reversing and remanding, the Supreme Court concluded that the Board was not making a binding construction of the labor contract: "It was only acting upon the probability that the desired information was relevant, and that it would be of use to the union in carrying out its statutory duties and responsibilities."[443] The duty to bargain in good faith thus obliges the employer to furnish information enabling the union to make an informed decision about processing grievances.

The employer must also furnish information to the union in order to assist it in properly preparing for arbitration, provided the information is relevant to the grievance scheduled for arbitration.[444] With the information thus supplied, the union can make "an intelligent appraisal of the merits of the member's complaint."[445] It may decide not to take the grievance to arbitration in the first place. In the arbitral processes, however, neither party should be required "to play the game of blind man's bluff."[446] On the other hand, the union's bare assertion that it needs information to process a grievance does not automatically oblige the employer to supply all information requested by the union.[447] Likewise, in the *Square D*[448] case, where the employer was seeking information from the union for use in arbitration, the Board held that there was no statutory obligation

---

[442]Acme Indus. Co. v. NLRB, 351 F2d 258, 60 LRRM 2220 (CA 7, 1965), rev'd, 385 US 432, 64 LRRM 2069 (1967).

[443]*Id.*, 385 US at 437.

[444]Montgomery Ward & Co., 234 NLRB 588, 98 LRRM 1022 (1978); Kroger Co., *supra* note 369.

[445]P. R. Mallory & Co., 171 NLRB 457, 68 LRRM 1097, *enforced*, 411 F2d 948, 71 LRRM 2412 (CA 7, 1969).

[446]Fafnir Bearing Co., 146 NLRB 1582, 56 LRRM 1108, *enforced*, 362 F2d 716, 62 LRRM 2415 (CA 2, 1966). Unions have been allowed to conduct time studies in the employer's plant in connection with the investigation and processing of grievances. General Elec. Co. v. NLRB, 414 F2d 918, 71 LRRM 2562 (CA 4, 1969), *cert. denied*, 396 US 1005 (1970); Ingraham Indus., *supra* note 325.

[447]Detroit Edison Co. v. NLRB, *supra* note 356.

[448]Machinists Dist. 10 (Square D Co.), 224 NLRB 111, 92 LRRM 1202 (1976) (employer sought copy of a purported company document which the union representative had referred to during the grievance procedure, but would not identify, boasting that it would prove the union's case in arbitration).

on the part of either the employer or the union to turn over to the other "evidence of an undisclosed nature that the possessor of the information believes relevant and conclusive with respect to its rights in an arbitration proceeding."[449]

D. Information That Must Be Furnished

1. **Financial Information.** Financial information is relevant to negotiations in which an employer asserts financial inability to meet a union wage demand. As previously noted, the Supreme Court, in *NLRB v. Truitt Manufacturing Co.*,[450] declared that "[g]ood-faith bargaining necessarily requires that claims made by either party should be honest claims" and that if an inability-to-pay argument "is important enough to present in the give and take of bargaining, it is important enough to require some sort of proof of its accuracy."[451] The Court relied on a series of Board cases holding that if an employer "does no more than take refuge in the assertion" of poor financial condition, refusing either to prove its statement or permit independent verification, "[t]his is not collective bargaining."[452] Even before the *Truitt* decision, the Second Circuit, in *NLRB v. Jacobs Manufacturing Co.*,[453] had attempted to clarify the required degree of necessary substantiation, stating that compliance with the statute does not require that an employer produce proof that its business decision as to what it can afford to do is correct, but only that it produce whatever relevant information it has "to indicate whether it can or cannot afford"[454] to meet union demands.

Since the honesty of a claim is not in issue until it is actually made, an employer is not obligated to demonstrate that it is

---

[449]*Id.* at 112. For criticism of the Board's decision, *see* Morris, *supra* note 2 at 665-67.
[450]*Supra* note 125.
[451]*Id.* at 152. For a critical analysis of the Supreme Court's "honest claims" rules and its reliance on good-faith terminology in the *Truitt* opinion, *see* Duvin, *supra* note 2 at 282.
[452]*Supra* note 125 at 153. *See* McLean-Arkansas Lumber Co., 109 NLRB 1022, 34 LRRM 1496 (1954); Southern Saddlery Co., 90 NLRB 1205, 26 LRRM 1322 (1950); Pioneer Pearl Button Co., 1 NLRB 837, 1 LRRM 26 (1936).
[453]196 F2d 680, 30 LRRM 2098 (CA 2, 1952). *See also* NLRB v. Southland Cork Co., 342 F2d 702, 58 LRRM 2555 (CA 4, 1965).
[454]196 F2d at 684. *See also* Burns Int'l Detective Agency, 137 NLRB 1235, 50 LRRM 1367 (1962); Tennessee Chair Co., 126 NLRB 1357, 45 LRRM 1472 (1960); B. L. Montague Co., 116 NLRB 554, 38 LRRM 1289 (1956) (employer must show contracts on which it claims to have lost money). The *Truitt* case has not been construed to limit the findings of violation only to situations where the employer's claimed inability to pay relates to wage demands, since other economic benefits may be considered as important as wages. Stanley Bldg. Specialties, Inc., 166 NLRB 984, 65 LRRM 1684 (1967), *enforced*, 401 F2d 434, 69 LRRM 2196 (CA DC, 1968).

unable to raise wages unless it first claims such an inability.[455] The Board, however, with judicial support, has broadened the definition of what claims constitute a plea which will, in turn, justify a union's demand for substantiation. In the 1964 case of *Cincinnati Cordage & Paper Co.*,[456] the Board held that an employer's resistance to a union's wage demand on the ground that it could not remain competitive with comparable employers in the industry constituted a poverty plea. Notwithstanding the contention that the employer was not literally pleading "inability to pay," as in *Truitt,* the Board found *Truitt* applicable "because the employer expressed the view that the wage increases would lead to impoverishment . . . ."[457] Accordingly, the refusal to furnish data showing that it could not stay competitive was held to be unlawful.[458] Similarly, in *Taylor Foundry Co.*[459] the Board equated the employer's contention, that it could not increase its labor costs without losing its profit margin and competitive position, to a plea of inability to pay; and the Board's finding of refusal to bargain was enforced by the Fifth Circuit.[460]

In *NLRB* v. *Western Wirebound Box Co.*,[461] *Truitt* was extended even further. There the employer resisted granting wage increases because of price competition but declined a request for supporting data, insisting that he was not claiming an inability to pay, simply that price competition dictated his position. Nonetheless, he was ordered to supply the data; the Ninth Circuit specifically asserted that *Truitt* is "not confined to cases where the employer's claim is that he is unable to pay the wages

---

[455]Pine Indus. Relations Comm., Inc., 118 NLRB 1055, 40 LRRM 1315 (1957), *enforced,* 263 F2d 483, 43 LRRM 2462 (CA DC, 1959). *See also* New York Printing Pressmen v. NLRB, 538 F2d 496, 92 LRRM 3207 (CA 2, 1976); Woodworkers v. NLRB, 263 F2d 483, 43 LRRM 2462 (CA DC, 1959).

[456]141 NLRB 72, 52 LRRM 1277 (1963). For a forerunner of this decision, *see* Tennessee Coal & Iron Div., U.S. Steel Corp., 122 NLRB 1519, 43 LRRM 1325 (1959).

[457]141 NLRB at 77.

[458]But where the employer has voluntarily furnished the union with sufficient information to support a claim of inability to pay, it would be unnecessary for the Board to determine whether "inability" or "inadvisability" to pay was pleaded, since there would be no violation in any event. Albany Garage, Inc., *supra* note 380.

[459]141 NLRB 765, 52 LRRM 1407 (1963), *enforced,* 338 F2d 1003, 57 LRRM 2560 (CA 5, 1964).

[460]*See also* Goodyear Aerospace Corp., 204 NLRB 831, 83 LRRM 1461 (1973), *enforcement denied,* 497 F2d 747, 86 LRRM 2763 (CA 6, 1974); Stockton District Kidney Bean Growers, 165 NLRB 223, 65 LRRM 1300 (1967) (employer denial of access to books after saying it was in "no mood" to increase costs is tantamount to pleading inability to pay).

[461]356 F2d 88, 61 LRRM 2218 (CA 9, 1966), *enforcing* 145 NLRB 1539, 55 LRRM 1193 (1964).

demanded by the union."[462] Bargaining, the court reasoned, "is hampered and rendered ineffectual when an employer mechanically repeats his claim but makes no effort to produce substantiating data."[463]

The Board has also held that a multiplant employer who deals with separate locals at each plant location and pleads inability to meet the union's wage demands must furnish specific information concerning profitability at each plant if so requested by the union.[464] The employer does not satisfy its Section 8(a)(5) obligations by merely furnishing information concerning its lack of overall corporate profitability.[465] However, a union is not entitled to financial information for the purpose of harassing the employer, with the possible result of jeopardizing its financial position further.[466]

2. Other Information. The Board has consistently upheld the right of a union to obtain information which it needs to bargain intelligently and "to service and police the contract."[467] Since wage information is often critical to the union in fulfilling both obligations, and since employers commonly regard such information as confidential in nature, many cases have involved employer refusals to provide wage information.[468] "[A] union's

---

[462]*Id.*, 356 F2d at 90.

[463]*Id.* at 91. *See also* NLRB v. Celotex Corp., 364 F2d 552, 62 LRRM 2475 (CA 5, 1966) (the opinion is cast in terms of whether the information was "plainly irrelevant").

[464]Teleprompter Corp. v. NLRB, *supra* note 389.

[465]*Id. But see* Fruit & Vegetable Packers v. NLRB, 316 F2d 389, 52 LRRM 2537 (CA DC, 1963) (employer may attach reasonable conditions to the furnishing of financial information in its own business interest); Braswell Motor Freight Lines, Inc., 141 NLRB 1154, 52 LRRM 1467 (1963) (employer need not furnish financial information on the entire corporate chain controlled by the owners of the unit in question).

[466]NLRB v. Abbott Publishing Co., *supra* note 380. *But cf.* Metlox Mfg. Co., 153 NLRB 1388, 59 LRRM 1657 (1965), *enforced*, 378 F2d 728, 65 LRRM 2637 (CA 9, 1967), *cert. denied*, 389 US 1037, 67 LRRM 2231 (1968), holding that an employer's claimed inability to meet a union's pay demands gave the union a right to look at the salaries being paid management officials. The court of appeals upheld the NLRB's determination that the employer violated its bargaining duty by furnishing only profit and loss statements. When the employer asserted that it could not grant the union's request for wage increases or other economic benefits because of its financial plight, the union suggested that the trouble might be due to a deliberate bleeding of the assets by officers and/or controlling stockholders. The employer offered to permit an examination of its books by a certified public accountant at the expense of the union. The CPA, however, could advise the union only as to whether the employer's profit and loss statements were true. The court agreed with the NLRB that the profit and loss statements did not disclose sufficient information for the union to make a fair estimate of the employer's financial inability to pay. An order requiring redress of wrongs suffered by employees who struck over the denial of information was enforced by the court.

[467]Viewlex, Inc., 204 NLRB 1080, 83 LRRM 1634 (1973).

[468]Korn Indus. v. NLRB, 389 F2d 117, 67 LRRM 2148 (CA 4, 1967), *clarified*, 67 LRRM 2976 (CA 4, 1968); West Side Transfer, 162 NLRB 699, 64 LRRM 1098 (1967);

right to such information cannot be seriously challenged"[469]—a conclusion which was given impetus in *NLRB v. F. W. Woolworth Co.*,[470] in which the Supreme Court reversed, without argument or opinion, the Ninth Circuit's refusal to enforce a Board order requiring production of wage information. This right to information on wages, based on the statutory requirement that collective bargaining take place with respect to "wages, hours, and other terms and conditions of employment,"[471] extends to wages paid particular employees, groups of employees, and methods of computing compensation.[472] The outer limits of a union's right to wage information are difficult to determine because of the presumption of relevance applied to such information. Even disclosure of information regarding compensation of employees outside the bargaining unit has been required with increasing liberality,[473] as has information on wage rates paid at other plants maintained by the employer.[474] In certain instances, an employer may even be required to divulge information in wage rates paid by its competitors.[475]

Items of information related to "hours, and other terms and conditions of employment" have been ordered disclosed on the

---

NLRB v. Fitzgerald Mills Corp., *supra* note 189; NLRB v. John S. Swift Co., *supra* note 216; Utica Observer-Dispatch, Inc. v. NLRB, *supra* note 381; NLRB v. Whitin Mach. Works, *supra* note 390; NLRB v. Boston Herald-Traveler Corp., 210 F2d 134, 33 LRRM 2435 (CA 1, 1954); NLRB v. Yawman & Erbe Mfg. Co., *supra* note 388.

[469]Woodworkers v. NLRB, 263 F2d 483, 484, 43 LRRM 2462 (CA DC, 1959).

[470]352 US 938, 39 LRRM 2151 (1956), *rev'g* 235 F2d 319, 38 LRRM 2362 (CA 9, 1956).

[471]29 USC §158(d) (1964).

[472]Puerto Rico Tel. Co. v. NLRB, *supra* note 440; Curtiss-Wright Corp., *supra* note 361; Anaconda Am. Brass Co., 148 NLRB 474, 57 LRRM 1001 (1964).

[473]Goodyear Aerospace Corp. v. NLRB, 388 F2d 673, 67 LRRM 2447 (CA 6, 1968); Curtiss-Wright Corp., *supra* note 361; Skyland Hosiery Mills, Inc., 108 NLRB 1600, 34 LRRM 1254 (1954); California Portland Cement Co., 103 NLRB 1375, 31 LRRM 1630 (1953). *But see* Fetzer Television, Inc. v. NLRB, 317 F2d 420, 53 LRRM 2224 (CA 6, 1963); NLRB v. Leland-Gifford Co., 200 F2d 620, 31 LRRM 2196 (CA 1, 1952).

[474]Hollywood Brands, Inc., 142 NLRB 304, 53 LRRM 1012 (1963), *enforced*, 324 F2d 956, 54 LRRM 2780 (CA 5, 1963), *cert. denied*, 377 US 923, 56 LRRM 2095 (1964).

[475]General Elec. Co. v. NLRB, 466 F2d 1177, 81 LRRM 2303 (CA 6, 1972), *enforcing* 192 NLRB 68, 77 LRRM 1561 (1971). Here the Sixth Circuit enforced a series of Board orders requiring the company to provide the union with correlated wage data the company had obtained from area wage surveys taken at four of its plant locations. The company agreed generally to furnish the union with the results of the surveys, but refused to correlate the wage data with the names of the employers supplying it, arguing that it had obtained the data under assurances of confidentiality, and that employers would no longer supply it with data if it had to provide the correlated information to the union. The court held that the information requested was relevant because without it the union could not meaningfully analyze and discuss the results of the company's surveys. *But cf.* Westinghouse Elec. Supply Co. v. NLRB, 196 F2d 1012, 30 LRRM 2169 (CA 3, 1952) (employer not required to turn over wage-survey chart where union had merely requested proof of company's contention that its salary structure compared favorably with its competitors).

same basis as wage information. Insurance and pension plan information must be furnished, as well as the employer's insurance plan cost information, and employee benefits thereunder.[476] The theory supporting disclosure of this information is that the union might desire to forego such insurance in favor of increased take-home pay; therefore, information about the cost of an insurance plan is considered "necessary to effective negotiation."[477] The Board and the courts have also uniformly required disclosure of the details of a profit-sharing plan,[478] information on employee job classifications and how they are determined,[479] information about employee status and job changes,[480] time-study material, and information used in setting wage rates or incentives.[481]

---

[476]NLRB v. Borden, Inc., Borden Chem. Div., 600 F2d 313, 101 LRRM 2727 (CA 1, 1979) (employer required to furnish union insurance cost figures on a per employee per hour basis); NLRB v. Feed & Supply Center, Inc., 294 F2d 650, 48 LRRM 2993 (CA 9, 1961); NLRB v. John S. Swift Co., *supra* note 216 (health and welfare plan); Crane Co., 244 NLRB 103, 102 LRRM 1351 (1979) (pension coverage information); Industrial Welding Co., 175 NLRB 477, 71 LRRM 1076 (1969); Rangaire Corp., *supra* note 163; Skyland Hosiery Mills, Inc., *supra* note 473 (insurance coverage and portions of premiums paid by employers and employees).

[477]Sylvania Elec. Prods., Inc. v. NLRB, 358 F2d 591, 61 LRRM 2657 (CA 1, 1966); Cone Mills Corp., 169 NLRB 449, 67 LRRM 1241 (1968), *enforced in part and denied in part*, 413 F2d 445, 71 LRRM 2916 (CA 4, 1969). In Sylvania Elec. Prods. v. NLRB, 291 F2d 128, 48 LRRM 2313 (CA 1, 1961), *cert. denied*, 368 US 926, 49 LRRM 2173 (1961), the First Circuit held that the employer's cost in a noncontributory group insurance program was neither wages nor conditions of employment and that refusal to furnish cost information did not constitute a refusal to bargain, since no issue of costs arose during negotiations that would bear on the company's willingness to consider any proposal the union might make with respect to changes in the plan. The Board disagreed with the court's distinction between "costs" and "benefits" in Electric Furnace Co., 137 NLRB 1077, 50 LRRM 1322 (1962), *enforcement denied*, 327 F2d 373, 55 LRRM 2398 (CA 6, 1964); and General Elec. Co., *supra* note 91. (For a complete discussion of this case and its subsequent history, *see supra*, this chapter, at notes 136-44.) In 1965 the Board again found Sylvania had bargained in bad faith in failing to supply the requested information, 154 NLRB 1756, 60 LRRM 1178 (1965), but this time the First Circuit enforced the Board's order, 358 F2d 591, 61 LRRM 2657 (CA 1, 1966). Although holding to its 1961 opinion, the court felt that since the company had proposed changes in the plan, the union had a right to cost information so that it could weigh the company offer against an equivalent increase in take-home pay.

[478]NLRB v. Toffenetti Restaurant Co., 311 F2d 219, 51 LRRM 2601 (CA 2, 1962).

[479]Lock Joint Pipe Co., 141 NLRB 943, 52 LRRM 1410 (1963); American Sugar Refining Co., 130 NLRB 634, 47 LRRM 1361 (1961); Stanislaus Implement & Hardware Co., 101 NLRB 394, 31 LRRM 1079 (1952).

[480]NLRB v. John S. Swift Co., *supra* note 216; NLRB v. New Britain Mach. Co., 210 F2d 61, 33 LRRM 2461 (CA 2, 1954); Keller Indus., Inc., 170 NLRB 1715, 69 LRRM 1078 (1968). *But see* Pacific Tel. & Tel. Co., 246 NLRB 327, 102 LRRM 1543 (1980), where the employer was not required to disclose transfer information.

[481]In Fafnir Bearing Co., *supra* note 446, the employer was held to have violated the Act by failing to permit the union to enter the company's production facilities for the purpose of conducting time studies. *See also* Timken Roller Bearing Co. v. NLRB, 325 F2d 746, 54 LRRM 2785 (CA 6, 1963); J. I. Case Co. v. NLRB, *supra* note 361; NLRB v. Otis Elevator Co., *supra* note 411; Emeryville Research Center, 174 NLRB 114, 70 LRRM 1099 (1969), *enforcement denied*, 441 F2d 880, 77 LRRM 2043 (CA 9, 1971);

Other types of information that the Board has ordered an employer to disclose include seniority lists and data,[482] employees' ages,[483] equipment types and specifications,[484] names and addresses of customers,[485] information about vending machines and cafeteria catering services,[486] names and addresses of unit employees,[487] names and addresses of successful and unsuccess-

---

Johns-Manville Prods., 171 NLRB 451, 69 LRRM 1068 (1968); Wilson Athletic Goods Mfg. Co., 169 NLRB 621, 67 LRRM 1193 (1968). But see General Aniline & Film Corp., 124 NLRB 1217, 44 LRRM 1617 (1959) (such information must have been used in wage rates, not just for employer cost-determination purposes, in order that employer be required to furnish it).

[482]NLRB v. Gulf Atl. Warehouse Co., 291 F2d 475, 48 LRRM 2376 (CA 5, 1961); Crane Co., 244 NLRB 103, 102 LRRM 1351 (1979); Post Publishing Co., 102 NLRB 648, 31 LRRM 1336 (1953). See Oliver Corp., 162 NLRB 813, 64 LRRM 1092 (1967), where a union's request for information about the length of employment and the reasons for the discharge of employees during their probationary period was deemed relevant to future contract negotiations. Finding that an employer had engaged in an unfair labor practice by refusing to furnish the union with this data, the Board ordered that the information be provided. The dispute arose when an employee was discharged during his probationary period and the employer refused to tell the union the reason for the termination. The union then asked the employer for data on all employees discharged during their probationary period over a two-year span. The employer responded that the information was not relevant or necessary to prepare for bargaining. Disagreeing with its trial examiner, the Board held that to deny the union access to this data would significantly impair its ability to engage in meaningful bargaining concerning the terms and conditions of employment of probationary employees. In Standard Oil Co. of Calif. v. NLRB, 399 F2d 639, 69 LRRM 2014 (CA 9, 1968), the employer was required to supply the union with a mailing list of names and home addresses of all employees in the bargaining unit after the employer had mailed literature to the employees in support of its bargaining position. In Prudential Ins. Co., 412 F2d 77, 71 LRRM 2254 (CA 2, 1969), the employer was required to supply names and addresses of employees in a nationwide bargaining unit, which the union contended it needed to communicate regarding contract benefits and policing the agreement.

[483]Reed & Prince Mfg. Co., supra note 200.

[484]Oregon Coast Operators Ass'n, 113 NLRB 1338, 36 LRRM 1448 (1955), enforced, 246 F2d 280, 40 LRRM 2312 (CA 9, 1957).

[485]Custom Excavating, Inc., 228 NLRB 285, 94 LRRM 1415 (1977), enforced, 575 F2d 102, 98 LRRM 2259 (CA 7, 1978) (the Board found that the harm relating to possible employer problems with customers resulting from union contact was outweighed by the union's need to ascertain employer compliance with the terms of the collective bargaining agreement and with applicable laws).

[486]See, e.g., B. F. Goodrich Co., 221 NLRB 288, 90 LRRM 1595 (1975), where the company was found to have violated §8(a)(5) by refusing to furnish information concerning financial arrangements with a cafeteria catering service because the employer was determined to have a duty to bargain over the subcontracting of its in-plant cafeteria service. Cf. Ford Motor Co. v. NLRB, 441 US 488, 101 LRRM 2222 (1979); Chapter 16 infra at notes 47-55; and Chapter 17 infra at notes 105-10. But see NLRB v. Package Mach. Co., 457 F2d 936, 79 LRRM 2948 (CA 1, 1972), denying enforcement to 191 NLRB 268, 77 LRRM 1456 (1971), where the First Circuit reversed a Board decision requiring the company to furnish a copy of its contract with the company which supplied food items for the plant cafeteria and vending machines and a list of price increases on those items. The court held that the company's subsidy of vending concerns was not a condition of employment and that the company had no obligation to furnish the information. The rationale of this decision, however, was disapproved by the Supreme Court in the Ford Motor case supra, this note.

[487]Summer Home for the Aged, 226 NLRB 976, 93 LRRM 1489 (1976), enforcement granted in part, denied in part and remanded, 599 F2d 762, 101 LRRM 2494 (CA 6, 1979); Autoprod, Inc., 223 NLRB 773, 92 LRRM 1076 (1976); Viewlex, Inc., supra note 467.

ful job applicants,[488] information relating to benefits received by retirees under the employer's pension and insurance plans,[489] information relating to employee grievances,[490] and information pertaining to possible loss of work through a proposed leasing arrangement[491] or a layoff.[492] On the other hand, the Supreme Court, in *Detroit Edison Co. v. NLRB*,[493] upheld an employer's refusal to supply psychological aptitude test questions, answers, and individual scores. In so holding, the Court balanced the union's interest in obtaining information relevant to contract administration against the employer's interest in maintaining test security and employee confidence in the testing program.

The Board has also determined that unions are entitled to certain information in the event of a strike. Specifically, the employer must provide the names and addresses of strike replacements and update the list;[494] it must supply wage information for nonstrikers and replacements,[495] including bonuses,[496] as well as information regarding striker reinstatement and placement on a preferential hiring list.[497] The Board has also indicated that an employer must furnish to the union the names of striking employees who, according to the employer, have

---

[488]Southwestern Bell Tel., 247 NLRB 171, 103 LRRM 1127 (1980).

[489]Union Carbide Corp., 197 NLRB 717, 80 LRRM 1429 (1972), *supplementing* 187 NLRB 113, 75 LRRM 1548 (1970).

[490]ACF Indus., Inc., 231 NLRB 83, 96 LRRM 1291 (1977), *enforced*, 592 F2d 422, 100 LRRM 2710 (CA 8, 1979). There the Board held that an employer who obtained an analysis of an employee's handwriting in order to substantiate its decision to discharge the employee for falsifying sickness and accident claims, violated the Act by refusing to furnish the analysis to the union which was processing the employee's grievance. The union's right to the information was not defeated merely because it might have acquired similar information by independent investigation.

[491]Yellow Cab Co., 229 NLRB 1369, 95 LRRM 1249 (1977), *enforced in part and denied in part*, 603 F2d 862, 99 LRRM 2903 (CA DC, 1978), *petition for rehear'g denied*, 101 LRRM 2628 (CA DC, 1979).

[492]NLRB v. Production Molded Plastics, 604 F2d 451, 102 LRRM 2040 (CA 6, 1979); Florida Steel Corp. v. NLRB, 601 F2d 125, 101 LRRM 2671 (CA 4, 1979).

[493]Detroit Edison Co. v. NLRB, *supra* note 356. *See also* notes 415-17 and 423 and accompanying text. *But cf.* Equitable Gas Co., 227 NLRB 800, 95 LRRM 1088 (1977) (union entitled to disclosure of scoring method used for promotion purposes). For discussion of the duty to disclose safety and health information, *see* Chapter 17 *infra* at note 233.

[494]Georgetown Assocs., 235 NLRB 485, 98 LRRM 1162 (1978).

[495]Soule Glass & Glazing Co., 246 NLRB 792, 102 LRRM 1693 (1979).

[496]Rubatex Corp., 235 NLRB 833, 97 LRRM 1534 (1978), *enforced*, 601 F2d 147, 101 LRRM 2660 (CA 4, 1979). *But see* Crane Co., 244 NLRB 103, 102 LRRM 1351 (1979), where an employer was not required to disclose whether it intended to continue payment of benefits during a strike.

[497]Southern Florida Hotel & Motel Ass'n, 245 NLRB 561, 102 LRRM 1578 (1979); Florida Steel Corp., 242 NLRB 1333, 101 LRRM 1370 (1979); Ohio Power Co., 216 NLRB 987, 88 LRRM 1646 (1975), *enforced*, 531 F2d 1381, 92 LRRM 3049 (CA 6, 1979). *See also* Markle Mfg. Co., 239 NLRB 1142, 100 LRRM 1125 (1979).

forfeited reinstatement rights by misconduct during the strike.[498] Employers have also been required to furnish strike-related subcontracting information, including actual copies of contracts,[499] as well as information showing the total number of subcontracting man hours involved.[500] However, the Board has held that an employer did not violate the Act by refusing to provide the union with a list of employees who crossed a picket line to work during a strike, where the sole reason for the request was to enable the union to discipline members who worked.[501]

The Board has held that employers must disclose certain equal employment opportunity data. Thus, in *Westinghouse Electric Corp.*,[502] the Board ruled that the employer must furnish the following information on unit employees (but not on nonunit employees): (1) statistical data on minority group and female employees, and (2) charges and complaints filed by employees against the employer under federal and state fair employment practice laws. Such information with respect to unit employees was "presumptively relevant"; whereas, with respect to nonunit employees, the union "must ordinarily demonstrate more precisely the relevance of the data requested."[503] But the Board failed to find an employer's affirmative action plans presumptively relevant and held that copies did not have to be produced for the union unless it demonstrated relevance.[504] In *East Dayton Tool & Die Co.*[505] the employer was required to furnish data as to race and sex of job applicants, but not "subjective" reasons for not hiring more minorities and women. In both cases the Board relied upon nondiscrimination clauses contained in the collective bargaining contract.[506]

Although decisions involving employer requests for information controlled by unions are not plentiful, the decided cases

---

[498]Food Serv. Co., 202 NLRB 790, 82 LRRM 1746 (1973). In the particular circumstances of this case, however, the Board declined to find a violation because the employer subsequently informed the union that only one striker, who was identified, was ineligible to return to work.

[499]Wallace Metal Prods., Inc., 244 NLRB 41, 102 LRRM 1233 (1979).

[500]Amcar Division, ACF Indus., Inc. v. NLRB, 596 F2d 1344, 100 LRRM 3074 (CA 8, 1979). *See also* Markle Mfg. Co., 239 NLRB 1142, 100 LRRM 1125 (1979).

[501]Nordstrom, Inc., 229 NLRB 601, 96 LRRM 1092 (1977).

[502]239 NLRB 106, 99 LRRM 1482 (1978).

[503]*Id.* at 110.

[504]*Accord,* Bendix Corp., 242 NLRB 1005, 101 LRRM 1459 (1979); Kentile Floors, Inc., 242 NLRB 755, 101 LRRM 1236 (1979).

[505]239 NLRB 141, 99 LRRM 1490 (1978).

[506]*Id.* at 150.

suggest the types of information which employers may obtain: hiring hall and manning information,[507] information pertinent to union pension and welfare plans,[508] collective bargaining agreements with other employers,[509] and a list of employees on a union out-of-work list.[510]

V. ECONOMIC PRESSURE DURING BARGAINING[511]

The Supreme Court's 1960 decision in *NLRB* v. *Insurance Agents International Union*[512] affirmed the principle that economic power goes hand in hand with "reasoned discussion" in determining the outcome of collective bargaining negotiations. The Court held that the Board cannot find a lack of good-faith bargaining by a party solely because tactics designed to exert economic pressure were employed during bargaining. To exert such pressure during the period of bargaining, union members refused to solicit new business, held half-day walkouts, and refused to perform ordinary reporting duties. The Board found such action to be a *per se* violation of Section 8(b)(3) despite the union's desire to reach an agreement, but the District of Colum-

---

[507]Detroit Newspaper Printing & Graphic Communications Local 13 (Oakland Press Co.), *supra* notes 352 and 362-65.

[508]Hospital & Health Care Employees, Dist. 1199E, Div of Retail, Wholesale, & Dep't Store Union (Sinai Hosp.), 248 NLRB 631, 103 LRRM 1459 (1980); Teamsters Local 959 (Frontier Transp. Co.), 244 NLRB 19, 102 LRRM 1117 (1979).

[509]Hotel Employees Local 355 (Doral Beach Hotel), 245 NLRB 774, 102 LRRM 1410 (1979).

[510]Asbestos Workers Local 80 (W. Va. Master Insulators Ass'n), 248 NLRB 143, 103 LRRM 1370 (1980).

[511]*See generally* Carroll, *Economic Pressure in Collective Bargaining: Lockout and Permanent Replacements in the Fifth Circuit*, 10 ST. MARY'S LAW JOURNAL 179 (1978); Bernhardt, *Lockouts: An Analysis of Board and Court Decisions Since Brown and American Ships*, 57 CORNELL L. REV. 211 (1972); Pollock, *Bargaining Lockout Prior to an Impasse in Negotiations Is Not a Violation of Sections 8(a)(1) or 8(a)(3)*, 44 NOTRE DAME LAWYER 270 (1968); Note, *The Offensive Bargaining Lockout*, 52 U. VA. L. REV. 464 (1966); Comment, *Use of Lockout to Strengthen Bargaining Position After Legal Impasse Has Been Reached*, 30 ALBANY L. REV. 173 (1966).

[512]361 US 477, 45 LRRM 2705 (1960). The case involved charges against a union for violation of §8(b)(3) based upon its use of harassing tactics while collective bargaining was in progress. The employees (insurance agents) did not engage in conventional strike activities. Instead, they refused to solicit new business, refused to comply with reporting procedures, reported to work late, engaged in "sit-in-mornings," distributed union leaflets, solicited policyholders' signatures directed to the company, and engaged in other such tactics. The Court assumed, *arguendo*, that this conduct was not protected concerted activity, citing Automobile Workers v. Wisconsin Employment Relations Bd. (Briggs-Stratton), 336 US 245, 23 LRRM 2361 (1949), and NLRB v. Fansteel Metallurgical Corp., 306 US 240, 4 LRRM 515 (1939), but this did not mean that the activity constituted a refusal to bargain. (The dissent maintained that while such economic activity was not a *per se* violation, the Board should have been able to consider it as evidence of bad faith in the totality of the circumstances.) *See also* discussion in Chapter 22 *supra* at note 64.

bia Circuit denied enforcement.[513] The Supreme Court, affirming, recognized that such economic activity may be unprotected by the Act but held that the use of such pressure is not in and of itself inconsistent with the duty to bargain in good faith. The Court articulated a definition that has become a classic description of the American collective bargaining process:

> [C]ollective bargaining, under a system where the Government does not attempt to control the results of negotiations, cannot be equated with an academic collective search for truth . . . . The parties—even granting the modification of views that may come from a realization of economic interdependence—still proceed from contrary, and to a certain extent antagonistic viewpoints and concepts of self interest. The system has not reached the ideal of the philosophic notion that perfect understanding among people would lead to perfect agreement among them on values. The presence of economic weapons in reserve, and their actual exercise on occasion by the parties is part and parcel of the system . . . . [T]he truth of the matter is . . . the two factors— necessity for good-faith bargaining between parties, and the availability of economic pressure devices to each to make the other party incline to agree on one's terms—exist side by side.[514]

Overt[515] economic activity by employers during bargaining has primarily involved the use of a lockout.[516] Prior to 1965 this tactic was permitted only in limited defensive situations.[517] In 1957, for example, the Supreme Court upheld the right of members of a multi-employer bargaining unit to lock out employees in an effort to counter a union's use of a "whipsaw" strike against one of the members of the employer group.[518] In 1965, however, the Court in *American Ship Building Co.* v. *NLRB*[519]

---

[513]Insurance Agents Int'l Union v. NLRB, 260 F2d 736, 43 LRRM 2003 (CA DC, 1958). This same issue had confronted the D.C. Circuit on two prior occasions in the mid-1950s. Mine Workers (Boone County Coal Corp.) v. NLRB, 257 F2d 211, 42 LRRM 2264 (CA DC, 1958); Textile Workers (Personal Prods.) v. NLRB, 227 F2d 409, 36 LRRM 2778 (CA DC, 1955). Refusing enforcement in both instances, the court found no violation of §8(b)(3) despite harassing tactics, and took the view that Congress had not specifically limited the use of economic pressure in support of lawful demands.

[514]*Supra* note 512 at 488-89.

[515]The most common form of employer economic pressure is of course a passive response—merely refusing to give in to threatened or actual strike pressure, thus forcing or prolonging the economic consequences of impasse or strike upon the employees.

[516]For detailed treatment of lockouts, *see* Chapter 22 *infra*.

[517]*See, e.g.*, Betts Cadillac Olds, Inc., 96 NLRB 268, 28 LRRM 1509 (1951); International Shoe Co., 93 NLRB 907, 27 LRRM 1504 (1951); Duluth Bottling Ass'n, 48 NLRB 1335, 12 LRRM 151 (1943); Link-Belt Co., 26 NLRB 227, 6 LRRM 565 (1940). *See* Comment, 37 N.Y.U. L. REV. 1152 (1962).

[518]NLRB v. Truck Drivers, 353 US 87, 39 LRRM 2603 (1957). *See also* Harold, *Multiemployer Bargaining and the Whipsaw Strike: The Use of a Lockout as an Economic Weapon*, 21 BROOKLYN BARRISTER 54 (1969); Comment, 48 U. VA. L. REV. 1313 (1962).

[519]380 US 300, 58 LRRM 2672 (1965). *See* Chapter 22 *infra* at notes 27 and 58-90.

decided that an offensive lockout by an employer did not violate Sections 8(a)(1) or 8(a)(3). The Court held that a single employer, after a bargaining impasse has been reached, may temporarily shut down its plant "for the sole purpose of bringing economic pressure to bear in support of [its] legitimate bargaining position."[520] Since *American Ship Building*, the Board and the courts have adopted a tolerant view of lockouts, so long as they are not motivated by union animus.[521]

Because of the unilateral changes involved in a lockout, a question arises as to whether an impasse in bargaining must be reached as a prerequisite to a lockout conducted by a single employer. In *Darling & Co.*[522] the Board upheld a pre-impasse lockout, and was affirmed by the Court of Appeals for the District of Columbia,[523] on the basis of several factual considerations, including (1) the absence of an antiunion motive, (2) the large number of negotiating sessions occurring both before and after the lockout (there was no allegation of bad-faith bargaining), (3) the relative strength of the union, (4) the many concessions which the employer had made during negotiations, (5) the possibility of the union calling a strike at a time of its own choosing, (6) the highly seasonal nature of the employer's business, and (7) the unusual harm which would have resulted from a strike. In later decisions, the Board has followed this factual approach, permitting pre-impasse lockouts when no union

---

[520]*Id.* at 318.

[521]*See, e.g.*, Newspaper Drivers & Handlers (Detroit Newspaper Publishers Ass'n) v. NLRB, 404 F2d 1159, 70 LRRM 2061 (CA 6, 1968), *aff'g* 166 NLRB 219, 65 LRRM 1425 (1967), where an employer's lockout to support the bargaining position of another struck employer was permitted on the ground that any concessions on important issues granted by the struck employer could have impact on the nonstruck employer's ability to maintain its own bargaining position. *See also* NLRB v. Martin A. Gleason, Inc., 534 F2d 466, 91 LRRM 2682 (CA 2, 1976) (employer which lawfully locks out its employees during a "whipsaw" strike may state in response to employee inquiries that they could not return to their jobs as members of the union engaging in the whipsaw strike, so long as this was not accompanied by any solicitation or encouragement to resign from the union); Publishers Ass'n of New York City v. NLRB, 364 F2d 293, 62 LRRM 2722 (CA 2, 1966) (even where union withdraws from multi-employer unit, lockout can be utilized); Acme Mkts., Inc., 156 NLRB 1452, 61 LRRM 1281 (1966) (allowing lockout in stores not in unit); Weyerhaeuser Co., 155 NLRB 921, 60 LRRM 1428 (1965) (employers do not have to be recognized as multi-employer unit by union); Body & Tank Corp. v. NLRB, 344 F2d 330, 59 LRRM 2123 (CA 2, 1965); and NLRB v. Tonkin Corp. of Cal., 352 F2d 509, 60 LRRM 2404 (CA 9, 1965), where the courts remanded to the Board in the light of *American Ship Bldg.* *See also* Carlson Roofing Co., Inc. v. NLRB, 627 F2d 77, 105 LRRM 2145 (CA 7, 1980), and Loomis Courier Serv., Inc. v. NLRB, 595 F2d 491, 101 LRRM 2450 (CA 9, 1979) (lack of union animus). For a more detailed treatment of the subject of lockouts *see* Chapter 22 *infra*.

[522]171 NLRB 801, 68 LRRM 1133 (1968). *See also*, Comment, 44 Notre Dame Lawyer 270 (1968).

[523]Lane v. NLRB, 418 F2d 1208, 72 LRRM 2439 (CA DC, 1969).

animus exists, when the employer is acting in support of its bargaining position, and there is significant business justification for the action.[524]

One circuit court of appeals upheld an employer's lockout of its employees upon the expiration of a collective bargaining agreement, even though the lockout occurred within the 30-day notice period to the mediation services provided by Section 8(d)(3).[525] Since the union had initiated the Section 8(d)(1) notice, it was the union's sole responsibility to provide timely notice to the mediation services. Such notice in this case was not timely. By bargaining in good faith with the union, the employer fulfilled its statutory obligations and was free to resort to economic pressure in support of its position once the contract had expired.

A substantial amount of litigation arose in the 1970s over whether an employer who uses an offensive lockout as an economic weapon during bargaining may utilize replacements for locked-out employees.[526] In *NLRB* v. *Brown*,[527] decided the same day as *American Ship Building*,[528] the Court held that members of a multi-employer bargaining unit which locked out their employees in response to a "whipsaw" strike may operate with temporary replacements. The Court, however, left open the questions of whether an employer who uses the lockout as an offensive bargaining weapon may utilize temporary replacements and whether locked-out employees may be permanently replaced.

---

[524]Georgia Pacific Corp., NLRB Gen. Counsel Advice Memo., Case No. 5 CA 11747, 104 LRRM 1167 (1980); Laclede Gas Co., 187 NLRB 243, 75 LRRM 1483 (1970); Stokely-Van Camp, Inc., 186 NLRB 440, 450-51, 76 LRRM 1166 (1970). *See also* Evening News Ass'n, 166 NLRB 219, 221, 65 LRRM 1425 (1967), *aff'd*, 404 F2d 1159, 70 LRRM 2061 (CA 6, 1968), where the Board stated that *American Ship Building* "obliterated, as a matter of law, the line previously drawn by the Board between offensive and defensive lockouts."

[525]Hooker Chems. & Plastics Corp. v. NLRB, 573 F2d 965, 97 LRRM 3194 (CA 7, 1978); NLRB v. Peoria Chapter of Painting & Decorating Contractors, 500 F2d 54, 86 LRRM 2914 (CA 7, 1974). *See also* Adamson, *The Lockout Loophole*, 24 EMORY L. J. 495 (1975). For a fuller discussion of notice requirements under §8(d), *see infra* at notes 710-33.

[526]*See generally* Chapter 22 *infra* at notes 132-47.

[527]380 US 278, 58 LRRM 2663 (1965). As in *American Ship Building, supra* note 519, the Court noted the absence of union animus in the employer's actions. *See also* Musa, *Lockouts and Replacements in Bargaining—Management on the Offensive*, 9 LOYOLA OF LOS ANGELES L. REV. 67 (1975); Note, *The Offensive Bargaining Lockout*, 52 U. VA. L. REV. 464 (1966); Forkosch, *Bargaining and Economic Pressure—The New Trilogy*, 16 LAB. L. J. 323 (1965). *See* discussion in Chapter 6 *supra* at notes 16-31, on the issue of motive as an element of a §8(a)(1) violation.

[528]*Supra* note 519.

The Board initially had held that an employer violates the Act when it hires temporary replacements to continue its operations during an offensive lockout for the purpose of exerting economic pressure in support of its lawful bargaining demands.[529] In *Ottawa Silica Co.*[530] and *Inter-Collegiate Press*[531] in 1972, however, a divided Board reversed its earlier position and held that in the absence of anti-union motivation, an employer may hire or obtain from elsewhere within its organization temporary replacements for locked-out employees during an offensive lockout.[532]

A lockout over a *nonmandatory* subject of bargaining violates the Act, and the Board has held that "a lockout unlawful at its inception retains its illegal taint of illegality until it is terminated and the affected employees are made whole."[533] Thus, an employer association violated Sections 8(a)(3) and (5) when it locked out the employees during contract negotiations, when one object of the lockout was to compel the union to submit the employers' offer to ratification by a mail ballot. The retraction of this demand on the second day of the lockout did not remove the taint of illegality.[534]

In *Johns-Manville Products Corp.*[535] the Board held that an employer violated the Act by unilaterally hiring *permanent* replacements for locked-out employees "without consulting or notifying the Union of such intention," since such action "completely destroyed the bargaining unit." The Fifth Circuit, how-

---

[529]Inland Trucking Co., 179 NLRB 350, 72 LRRM 1486 (1969), *enforced,* 440 F2d 562, 76 LRRM 2929 (CA 7, 1971), *cert. denied,* 404 US 858, 78 LRRM 2465 (1971).

[530]197 NLRB 449, 80 LRRM 1404 (1972), *enforced,* 482 F2d 945, 84 LRRM 2300 (CA 6, 1973), *cert. denied,* 415 US 916, 85 LRRM 2465 (1974).

[531]199 NLRB 177, 81 LRRM 1508 (1972), *enforced,* 486 F2d 837, 84 LRRM 2562 (CA 8, 1973), *cert. denied,* 416 US 938, 85 LRRM 2924 (1974). *See also* Comment, *Use of Temporary Replacements in Bargaining Lockouts Held Legally Justified,* 4 MEMPHIS ST. U. L. REV. 629 (1974); Comment, 19 VILL. L. REV. 918 (1974).

[532]The Board has adhered to this position in subsequent cases. *See, e.g.,* Hess Oil Virgin Islands Corp., 205 NLRB 23, 83 LRRM 1529 (1973); Johns-Manville Prods. Corp., 223 NLRB 1317, 92 LRRM 1103 (1976), *rev'd on other grounds,* 557 F2d 1126, 96 LRRM 2010 (CA 5, 1977). The Seventh Circuit has indicated a willingness to acquiesce in the *Ottawa Silica* rationale. NLRB v. Wire Prods. Mfg. Corp., 484 F2d 760, 84 LRRM 2038 (CA 7, 1973). For further discussion, *see* Chapter 22 *infra* at notes 142-47.

[533]Movers & Warehousemen's Ass'n, 224 NLRB 356, 357, 92 LRRM 1236 (1976), *enforced,* 550 F2d 962, 94 LRRM 2795 (CA 4, 1977).

[534]*Id.* at 358.

[535]223 NLRB 1317, 92 LRRM 1103 (1976). *See also* Walker, *Sabotage by Unidentified Employees Held Tantamount to In-Plant Strike Allowing Permanent Replacement of Locked-Out Employees,* 52 TULANE L. REV. 878 (1978); Carroll, *supra* note 511.

ever, refused to enforce the Board's order.[536] The court found that a continuing pattern of in-plant sabotage and production disruptions by employees during the negotiations for a new agreement amounted to an "in-plant strike," thereby making permanent replacements permissible.[537] The court expressly declined to rule on the issue of whether an employer may permanently replace locked-out employees.

VI. BARGAINING IMPASSES[538]

A. Elements of Impasse

The duty to bargain does not require a party "to engage in fruitless marathon discussions at the expense of frank statement and support of his position."[539] Where there are irreconcilable differences in the parties' positions after exhaustive good-faith negotiations, the law recognizes the existence of an *impasse*.[540] Some difficulty exists in establishing the "inherently vague and fluid . . . standard" applicable to impasse reached by hard and steadfast bargaining, as distinguished from one resulting from an unlawful refusal to bargain.[541] It may be that in collective bargaining, "part of the difficulty arises from the fact that the law recognizes the possibility of the parties reaching an impasse."[542]

The existence or nonexistence of an impasse is normally put in issue when, after negotiations have been carried on for a period of time, the positions of the parties become fairly fixed and talks reach the point of stalemate. When this occurs, the employer is free to make unilateral changes in working conditions (i.e., wages, hours, etc.) consistent with its offers which the

---

[536]Johns-Manville Prods. Corp. v. NLRB, 557 F2d 1126, 96 LRRM 2010 (CA 5, 1977). *See* Chapter 22 *infra* at notes 132-37.

[537]NLRB v. Mackay Radio & Tel. Co., 304 US 333, 2 LRRM 610 (1938). For a discussion of the right of an employer to permanently replace economic strikers, *see* Chapter 21 *infra* at notes 83-103.

[538]Stewart & Engeman, *Impasse, Collective Bargaining and Action*, 39 U. CIN. L. REV. 233 (1970).

[539]NLRB v. American Nat'l Ins. Co., 343 US 395, 404, 30 LRRM 2147 (1952).

[540]Usually the more meetings, the better the chance of a finding that an impasse has arisen. Fetzer Television, Inc. v. NLRB, 317 F2d 420, 53 LRRM 2224 (CA 6, 1963). On the doctrine of impasse generally, *see* Schatzki, *The Employer's Unilateral Act—A Per Se Violation—Sometimes*, 44 TEX. L. REV. 470, 495 (1966); Comment, *Impasse in Collective Bargaining*, 44 TEX. L. REV. 769 (1966).

[541]NLRB v. Wooster Div. of Borg-Warner Corp., 356 US 342, 352, 42 LRRM 2034 (1958) (Justice Harlan concurring in part and dissenting in part). *See also* National Fresh Fruit & Vegetable Co. v. NLRB, 565 F2d 1331, 97 LRRM 2427 (CA 5, 1978).

[542]Speech of Board Member Joseph A. Jenkins, 40 LRRM 98, 105-106 (1957).

union has rejected.[543] By the very nature of the bargaining process, it is not always apparent when an impasse has been reached. Prior to making unilateral changes,[544] however, an employer must at least have reasonable cause to believe that an impasse exists.

In *Taft Broadcasting Co.*[545] the Board stated that impasse occurs "after good-faith negotiations have exhausted the prospects of concluding an agreement,"[546] and enumerated some of the considerations in making such a determination:

> Whether a bargaining impasse exists is a matter of judgment. The bargaining history, the good faith of the parties in negotiations, the length of the negotiations, the importance of the issue or issues as to which there is disagreement, the contemporaneous understanding of the parties as to the state of negotiations are all relevant factors to be considered in deciding whether an impasse in bargaining existed.[547]

The Board may also consider additional factors,[548] for the existence of an impasse is very much a question of fact.[549]

---

[543]NLRB v. Katz, 369 US 736, 50 LRRM 2177 (1962); NLRB v. Almeida Bus Lines, Inc., 333 F2d 129, 56 LRRM 2548 (CA 1, 1964); Taft Broadcasting Co., 163 NLRB 475, 64 LRRM 1386 (1967), aff'd, 395 F2d 622, 67 LRRM 3032 (CA DC, 1968); Eddie's Chop House, Inc., 165 NLRB 861, 65 LRRM 1408 (1967); American Laundry Mach. Co., 107 NLRB 1574, 33 LRRM 1457 (1954). *See also* notes 554-58 *infra* and accompanying text. An employer's right to hire replacements for strikers is based on a rationale similar to its right to make unilateral changes following impasse. If the employer were to request that it be allowed to hire replacements, the union would obviously refuse; the employer's right to keep its business operating allows it to hire replacements. NLRB v. MacKay Radio & Tel. Co., 304 US 333, 2 LRRM 610 (1938). *See* Chapter 21 *infra* at note 83.

[544]NLRB v. United States Sonics Corp., 312 F2d 610, 52 LRRM 2360 (CA 1, 1963); Cheney Cal. Lumber Co. v. NLRB, 319 F2d 375, 53 LRRM 2598 (CA 9, 1963) (a belief that talks or negotiations are deadlocked or stalemated is sufficient). *See also* NLRB v. Cambria Clay Prods., Co., 215 F2d 48, 34 LRRM 2471 (CA 6, 1954) (presence of federal mediator may indicate an impasse if agreement still cannot be reached after he is called in; since Federal Mediation and Conciliation Service has the duty to use its best efforts to bring the parties to agreement, a mediator's refusal to call any more meetings may indicate there is no chance of agreement).

[545]163 NLRB 475, 64 LRRM 1386 (1967).

[546]*Id.* at 478.

[547]*Id.*

[548]Harding Glass Indus., 248 NLRB 902, 104 LRRM 1073 (1980); Talbert Mfg., Inc., 250 NLRB No. 26, 104 LRRM 1543 (1980); Carpenter Sprinkler Corp. v. NLRB, 605 F2d 60, 102 LRRM 2199 (CA 2, 1979); Louisville Plate Glass Co., 243 NLRB 1175, 102 LRRM 1108 (1979). *See* Comment, *Impasse In Collective Bargaining, supra* note 540.

[549]*See, e.g.,* Dust-Tex Serv., Inc., 214 NLRB 398, 88 LRRM 1292 (1974) (no impasse where employer determined to change the wage structure immediately upon expiration of the contract regardless of the status of negotiations); Servis Equip. Co., 198 NLRB 266, 80 LRRM 1704 (1972) (no impasse on wages when parties only met twice and union was not given enough advance notice of employer's action to respond); Supak & Sons Mfg. Corp., 192 NLRB 1228, 78 LRRM 1289 (1971), *enforced,* 470 F2d 998, 82 LRRM 2560 (CA 4, 1973) (no impasse on wages when employer did not make its counteroffer until last regular bargaining session).

The existence of an impasse does not insulate a party from the duty to bargain, since there are numerous exceptions to the rule that an impasse suspends the duty to bargain,[550] and changed circumstances may end the suspension.[551]

B. Effect on the Bargaining Obligation

As mentioned above, when an impasse is reached, the duty to bargain is not terminated but only suspended.[552] During this suspension the employer may not take action disparaging to the collective bargaining process or amounting to a withdrawal of recognition of the union's representative status.[553]

When an impasse is reached, the employer may make unilateral changes in working conditions, but such changes must "not [be] substantially different or greater than any [offers] which the employer . . . proposed during the negotiations."[554] Thus, an employer violates Section 8(a)(5) when it gives wage increases to its employees which exceed those previously offered at the bargaining table, even if it is found that there was a continuing impasse in negotiations at the time the increases were granted.[555] Moreover, an overall bargaining impasse will not justify a unilateral change concerning a subject over which there had been no bargaining.[556] Thus, in *Manor Mining & Contracting Corp.*[557] a divided panel of the Board found that the employer had, despite the existence of an overall bargaining impasse, unilaterally granted a wage increase in violation of Section 8(a)(5). The majority based its finding of a violation on the following facts: (1) Although the certification year had already passed, there was no contention or evidence that the union had lost its

---

[550]*See* notes 559-62 *infra* and accompanying text.

[551]*See* notes 563-66 *infra* and accompanying text.

[552]NLRB v. Tex-Tan, Inc., 318 F2d 472, 53 LRRM 2298 (CA 5, 1963); Philip Carey Mfg. Co., 140 NLRB 1103, 52 LRRM 1184 (1963); Boeing Airplane Co., 80 NLRB 447, 23 LRRM 1107 (1948), *rev'd on other grounds*, 174 F2d 988, 24 LRRM 2101 (CA DC, 1949).

[553]Central Metallic Casket Co., 91 NLRB 572, 26 LRRM 1520 (1950). An employer may not insist, to impasse, on altering the existing contractual unit description. Newspaper Printing Corp. v. NLRB, 625 F2d 956, 104 LRRM 2432 (CA 10, 1980); Newport News Shipbuilding Co. v. NLRB, 602 F2d 73, 102 LRRM 2531 (CA 4, 1979). *See Borg-Warner, supra* note 52, and Chapter 16 *infra* at notes 27-35.

[554]Atlas Tack Corp., 226 NLRB 222, 227, 93 LRRM 1236 (1976), *enforced*, 559 F2d 1201, 96 LRRM 2660 (CA 1, 1977).

[555]NLRB v. Crompton-Highland Mills, Inc., 337 US 217, 24 LRRM 2088 (1949); Falcon Tank Corp., 194 NLRB 333, 78 LRRM 1587 (1971).

[556]NLRB v. Intracoastal Terminal, Inc., 286 F2d 954, 47 LRRM 2629 (CA 5, 1961).

[557]197 NLRB 1057, 80 LRRM 1535 (1972), *enforced*, 478 F2d 1399, 83 LRRM 2409 (CA 3, 1973).

majority; (2) the bargaining impasse had not occurred over the wage increase, which the employer had never offered to the union; and (3) the business needs of the employer did not excuse the bypassing of the union.[558]

The transient nature of the suspension of the duty to bargain as a result of an impasse is exemplified by other exceptions to the suspension. For example, impasse on a single issue does not suspend the obligation to bargain on other unsettled issues.[559] Further, if a party's bad-faith bargaining or unfair labor practice precludes reaching an agreement, the resulting impasse is not a valid one, and any changes the party unilaterally makes will be illegal.[560]

In *National Fresh Fruit & Vegetable Co.*[561] the employer advanced a nonmandatory subject of bargaining (the removal from the certified bargaining unit of some job classifications) during negotiations prior to impasse. The union's final position rejected the employer's entire package, which included the nonmandatory proposal. The Board held that the fact that this was one of the "unresolved points" before the parties was enough to taint the impasse, even though the overall impasse was largely due to the failure to agree on mandatory subjects. The Fifth Circuit refused to enforce the Board's decision,[562] ruling that the non-

---

[558]*See also* Atlas Tack Corp., *supra* note 554, where the employer violated the Act by, *inter alia*, unilaterally instituting a new system of rest periods when it felt the negotiations were at impasse. The new system had not been discussed during the negotiations.

[559]Patrick & Co., 248 NLRB 390, 103 LRRM 1457 (1980); Providence Medical Center, 243 NLRB 714, 102 LRRM 1099 (1979); Atlas Tack Corp., *supra* note 554; Chambers Mfg. Corp., 124 NLRB 721, 44 LRRM 1477 (1959), *enforced*, 278 F2d 715, 46 LRRM 2316 (CA 5, 1960); Pool Mfg. Co., 70 NLRB 540, 18 LRRM 1364 (1946), *remanded*, 24 LRRM 2147 (CA 5, 1949), *vacated*, 339 US 577, 26 LRRM 2127 (1950). There is a distinction, however, between generally refusing to bargain merely because of an impasse on one issue, as in *Chambers*, and the situation where the impasse on a single but critical issue precludes an agreement. *See, e.g.*, Television & Radio Artists v. NLRB, 395 F2d 622 n.13, 67 LRRM 3032 (CA DC, 1968); Taft Broadcasting Co., *supra* note 543; Dallas General Drivers v. NLRB, 355 F2d 842, 61 LRRM 2065 (CA DC, 1966); NLRB v. Intracoastal Terminal, Inc., 286 F2d 954, 47 LRRM 2629 (CA 5, 1961). In the latter situation, the employer may make "unilateral changes that are reasonably comprehended within his preimpasse proposals." Taft Broadcasting Co., *supra* note 543 at 478.

[560]NLRB v. Herman Sausage Co., 275 F2d 229, 45 LRRM 2829 (CA 5, 1960) (employer bad faith in bargaining). *See also* Neon Sign Corp., 229 NLRB 861, 95 LRRM 1161 (1977), *enforcement denied*, 602 F2d 1203, 102 LRRM 2485 (CA 5, 1979) (surface bargaining by employer); Palomar Corp. & Gateway Serv. Co., 192 NLRB 592, 78 LRRM 1030 (1971) (employer refusal to provide necessary bargaining information to the union); United Contractors, Inc., 244 NLRB 72, 102 LRRM 1012 (1979) (no impasse exists in the presence of bad-faith bargaining).

[561]227 NLRB 2014, 95 LRRM 1011 (1977).

[562]National Fresh Fruit & Vegetable Co. v. NLRB, *supra* note 541.

mandatory proposal was "a bargaining tactic" taken by the employer in response to the union's increase of its demands, and that the advancement of the subject by the employer did not "rise to the level of an impermissible insistence." Since the employer was still flexible on the subject, the court found that it did not preclude or taint the impasse.

As noted, existence of an impasse does not permanently relieve a party of its duty to bargain. In fact, a legal impasse may end suddenly; almost any changed condition or circumstance will terminate the suspension of the duty to bargain. A strike after an impasse is reached changes the bargaining atmosphere and indicates that bargaining must be resumed,[563] as do changes in the business outlook of the general industry or of the employer's specific firm,[564] or a substantial change in the bargaining position of one party.[565] Even after the certification year has passed, if changed circumstances end the impasse, the employer must bargain, unless it has reasonable grounds for believing that the union has lost its majority.[566]

On the question of whether an impasse is an unusual circumstance that will justify a member withdrawing unilaterally from a multi-employer bargaining unit, the Board[567] and the appel-

---

[563]NLRB v. United States Cold Storage Corp., 203 F2d 924, 32 LRRM 2024 (CA 5, 1953). The occurrence of a strike does not necessarily mean that negotiations prior to the strike have reached an impasse. J. H. Bonck Co., Inc., 170 NLRB 1471, 69 LRRM 1172 (1968); Neon Sign Corp. v. NLRB, *supra* note 560.

[564]Kit Mfg. Co., Inc., 138 NLRB 1290, 51 LRRM 1224 (1962), *enforced,* 319 F2d 857, 53 LRRM 3010 (CA 9, 1963) (general industry increase in production and sales, union obtaining wider membership and certification in entire industry, and employer's financial condition improved).

[565]NLRB v. Sharon Hats, Inc., 289 F2d 628, 48 LRRM 2098 (CA 5, 1961), *enforcing* 127 NLRB 947, 46 LRRM 1128 (1960) (dropping part of benefit-clause requests).

[566]Celanese Corp. of Am., 95 NLRB 664, 28 LRRM 1362 (1951). *See* discussion *infra* at notes 675-708.

[567]*See* Hi-Way Billboards, Inc., 206 NLRB 22, 84 LRRM 1161 (1973), *enforcement denied,* 500 F2d 181, 87 LRRM 2203 (CA 5, 1974). The Board held that a genuine impasse between a union and a multi-employer bargaining association does not constitute an "unusual circumstance" justifying an employer's unilateral withdrawal from the multi-employer unit. *See also* Bill Cook Buick, Inc., 224 NLRB 1094, 92 LRRM 1582 (1976); Charles D. Bonanno Linen Serv., Inc., 229 NLRB 629, 95 LRRM 1128 (1977), *aff'd by the full Board on rehearing,* 243 NLRB 1093, 102 LRRM 1001 (1979), *enforced,* 630 F2d 25, 105 LRRM 2477 (CA 1, 1980), *aff'd,* 454 U.S. 404, 109 LRRM 2257 (1982); Florida Fire Sprinklers, 237 NLRB 1034, 99 LRRM 1078 (1978); Harding Glass Indus., 248 NLRB 902, 104 LRRM 1073 (1980). At the same time it decided *Bonanno,* the Board handed down five other decisions affirming the rule that unilateral withdrawal from a multi-employer unit is not permitted merely because impasse occurs. Birkenwald Distrib. Co., 243 NLRB 1151, 102 LRRM 1005 (1979); Marine Mach. Works, Inc., 243 NLRB 1098, 102 LRRM 1006 (1979); Teamsters Local 378 (Capital Chevrolet Co.), 243 NLRB 1086, 102 LRRM 1007 (1979); Seven Motors, Ltd., 243 NLRB 1092, 102 LRRM 1008 (1979); Callier's Custom Kitchens, 243 NLRB 1114, 102 LRRM 1008 (1979).

late courts[568] were sharply divided. But the issue has now been settled by a five-to-four decision of the Supreme Court in the *Bonanno Linen Service*[569] case. The case involved a linen supply association, consisting of 10 employers, which negotiated as a multi-employer unit with the Teamsters Union. After 10 bargaining sessions, the negotiators reached agreement on a proposed contract, but it was rejected by the union membership. An impasse over method of compensation remained unresolved for seven weeks, whereupon the union initiated a selective strike against one member of the association, Bonanno. Most of the association members responded with a lockout of their drivers. The stalemate continued for several months. Bonanno hired permanent replacements for all of his striking drivers and notified the association by letter that he was withdrawing from the association with respect to negotiations because of the impasse. He gave the same notice to the union. Soon after, the lockout was ended, negotiations were resumed without Bonanno's participation, and a settlement was finally reached.

When Bonanno refused to sign the contract, the union, which had not consented to Bonanno's withdrawal from the bargaining unit, filed unfair labor practice charges. The Board found a violation of Section 8(a)(5) and ordered Bonanno to sign and implement the contract retroactively. The Board reiterated the view it had expressed in *Hi-Way Billboards*[570] that an impasse is not sufficiently destructive of multi-employer bargaining to justify a unilateral withdrawal. The Supreme Court affirmed, for "although [the Board's rule] may deny an employer a particular economic weapon, [it] does so in the interest of the proper and pre-eminent goal, maintaining the stability of the multi-employer unit."[571]

VII. Defenses and Exceptions: Waiver, Suspension, and Termination of Bargaining Rights

Under certain conditions the duty to bargain in good faith either does not arise or is obviated.

---

[568]Five circuit courts of appeals disagreed with the Board, holding that an impasse in bargaining justifies an employer's unilateral withdrawal from a multi-employer unit. NLRB v. Steel Fabricators, 582 F2d 135, 98 LRRM 3150 (CA 2, 1978); NLRB v. Beck Engraving Co., Inc., 522 F2d 475, 90 LRRM 2089 (CA 3, 1975); NLRB v. Associated Shower Door Co., Inc., 512 F2d 230, 88 LRRM 3024 (CA 9, 1975), *cert. denied*, 423 US 893, 90 LRRM 2614 (1975); Hi-Way Billboards, Inc., *supra* note 567; Fairmont Foods Co. v. NLRB, 471 F2d 1170, 82 LRRM 2017 (CA 8, 1972).
[569]*Supra* note 567.
[570]*Supra* note 567.
[571]454 US 404, 109 LRRM at 2257. *See* Chapter 11 *supra* at notes 390-96.

A. Waiver of Bargaining Rights

Among the arguments often raised in defense of unilateral changes is the contention that the charging party has waived its right to bargain about the particular subject matter. *NLRB* v. *Jacobs Manufacturing Co.*[572] stands for the general proposition that the duty to bargain continues during the term of the collective bargaining agreement. Thus, since the obligation to bargain is one which may actively continue during the term of the agreement, the issue of waiver may be raised either before or after entry into a written agreement.[573] With increasing frequency the waiver issue arises in connection with some form of unilateral employer action; for example in subcontracting, where the primary defense is likely to be that the subject matter is not a mandatory subject of collective bargaining and the secondary defense is that the union has waived whatever right it may have had to bargain.[574]

A waiver may indeed result from action or inaction by a party. A party may agree to contractual language specifically waiving its right to bargain about a particular matter,[575] or it may relinquish its right during negotiations for the collective agreement.[576] In these circumstances, established past practices of the

---

[572]196 F2d 680, 30 LRRM 2098 (CA 2, 1952). Under the Wagner Act an employer was under a duty, upon request, to bargain with the union as to terms and conditions of employment whether or not the subject had been discussed and previously embodied in a collective bargaining agreement. *See* NLRB v. Sands Mfg. Co., 306 US 332, 4 LRRM 530 (1939). The addition of §8(d) modified this obligation by expressly stating that parties to the agreement are not required "to discuss or agree to any modification of the terms and conditions . . . if such modification is to become effective before such terms and conditions can be reopened under the provisions of the contract." In *Jacobs*, 196 F2d at 684, the Second Circuit held that §8(d) does not relieve the employer of the duty to bargain "as to subjects which were neither discussed nor embodied in any of the terms and conditions of the contract." *See also* NLRB v. Niles-Bemont-Pond Co., 199 F2d 713, 31 LRRM 2057 (CA 2, 1952); Proctor Mfg. Corp., 131 NLRB 1166, 48 LRRM 1222 (1961). *See* discussion of the duty to bargain during the term of an existing agreement at notes 762-86 *infra*.

[573]The question may arise as to whether the union has waived its right to hold the employer to a binding agreement. In Tanner Motor Livery, Ltd., 160 NLRB 1669, 63 LRRM 1242 (1966), the issue arose when the employer asserted that union conduct evincing an unwillingness to accept its offer constituted a rejection allowing it to withdraw its prior proposal. In rejecting the employer's argument, the Board noted the employer's action subsequent to the purported rejection, which indicated that it did not consider the union's conduct a rejection.

[574]ACF Indus., Inc. v. NLRB, 592 F2d 422, 100 LRRM 2710 (CA 8, 1979); United States Lingerie Corp., 170 NLRB 750, 67 LRRM 1482 (1968); American Oil Co., 151 NLRB 421, 58 LRRM 1412 (1965); New York Mirror, 151 NLRB 834, 58 LRRM 1465 (1965).

[575]*See, e.g.*, Ador Corp., 150 NLRB 1658, 58 LRRM 1280 (1965).

[576]*See, e.g.*, Speidel Corp., 120 NLRB 733, 42 LRRM 1039 (1958).

parties may be persuasive evidence of a waiver.[577] In addition, the failure to protest unilateral action[578] or the failure to request bargaining despite knowledge of a contemplated unilateral change[579] may directly result in a waiver. Nonetheless, consistent with the traditional common law view of waiver, the Board and the courts have construed the waiver doctrine strictly and have been reluctant to infer a waiver.[580]

1. Waiver by Express Agreement. A party may contractually waive its right to bargain about a particular mandatory subject.[581] Where such an assertion is raised, the test applied has been whether the waiver is in "clear and unmistakable" language.[582] In this regard, a waiver is normally construed as applicable only to the specific item mentioned.[583] Conversely, a specific waiver will not embrace a more general grouping. For example, a waiver as to particular compensation for an individual employee does not necessarily constitute a waiver with respect to unilateral changes for groups of employees.[584]

---

[577]*Supra* note 576 at 741; New York Mirror, *supra* note 574; American Oil Co., *supra* note 574.

[578]Justesen's Food Stores, Inc., 160 NLRB 687, 63 LRRM 1027 (1966); Motoresearch Co., 138 NLRB 1490, 51 LRRM 1240 (1962).

[579]United States Lingerie Corp., *supra* note 574; NLRB v. Spun-Jee Corp., 385 F2d 379, 66 LRRM 2485 (*as amended*, 67 LRRM 2308) (CA 2, 1967), *decision on remand*, 171 NLRB 557, 68 LRRM 1121 (1968); Montgomery Ward & Co., 137 NLRB 418, 50 LRRM 1162 (1962). *See also* Fruehauf Trailer Co., 162 NLRB 195, 64 LRRM 1037 (1966).

[580]*See, e.g.*, New York Mirror, *supra* note 574, and cases cited therein.

[581]Ador Corp., *supra* note 575; Druwhit Metal Prods. Co., 153 NLRB 346, 59 LRRM 1359 (1965) (containing clause identical to that in *Ador*).

[582]In Norris Indus., 231 NLRB 50, 96 LRRM 1078 (1977), the employer made a contract proposal to terminate the medical group insurance of employees on medical leaves of absence. This was incorporated in a "letter of understanding" signed at the same time as the contract. Although the union may have misunderstood the scope of the proposal, the Board held that the clear language in the letter which the union signed constituted a waiver, even though the matter was not thoroughly discussed in the negotiations. On the other hand, in Elizabethtown Water Co., 234 NLRB 318, 97 LRRM 1210 (1978), the parties to a collective bargaining agreement had not discussed changes to the employee retirement plan during the negotiations, since the plan agreement expired one year later. The fact that the new collective bargaining agreement (which incorporated the plan by reference) was to "remain in full force and effect" beyond the anniversary date of the plan did not act as a waiver of the union's right to request changes in the plan when the plan agreement expired during the term of the collective agreement. *See also* Plumbers Local 669 (A-1 Fire Protection, Inc.) v. NLRB, 600 F2d 918, 101 LRRM 2014 (CA DC, 1979); Office & Professional Employees Local 425 v. NLRB, 419 F2d 314, 70 LRRM 3047 (CA DC, 1969); Leeds & Northrup Co. v. NLRB, 391 F2d 874, 67 LRRM 2793 (CA 3, 1968); NLRB v. Perkins Mach. Co., 326 F2d 488, 55 LRRM 2204 (CA 1, 1964); Timken Roller Bearing Co. v. NLRB, 325 F2d 746, 54 LRRM 2785 (CA 6, 1963), *cert. denied*, 376 US 971, 55 LRRM 2878 (1964); Consumer's Power Co., 245 NLRB 183, 102 LRRM 1500 (1979); Bunker Hill Co., 208 NLRB 27, 85 LRRM 1264 (1973), *modified*, 210 NLRB 343, 86 LRRM 1157 (1974); Conval-Ohio, Inc., 202 NLRB 85, 82 LRRM 1701 (1973).

[583]New York Mirror, *supra* note 574.

[584]C & C Plywood Corp., 148 NLRB 414, 57 LRRM 1015 (1964), *enforcement denied*, 351 F2d 224, 60 LRRM 2137 (CA 9, 1965), *rev'd and remanded*, 385 US 421, 64 LRRM 2065 (1967).

a. *"Zipper Clauses."* Prior to 1974, the Board strictly applied the rule that only "clear and unmistakable" language in the contract expressly waiving the right to negotiate over a particular subject would suffice to relieve a party of the duty to bargain. This was especially the case with broad "zipper" clauses which stated that the contract was the complete agreement between the parties on all subjects. Such clauses, standing alone, did not constitute a sufficiently clear and unmistakable waiver as to a specific bargaining item.[585]

The Board's 1974 decision in *Radioear Corp.*[586] retreated from such a rigid interpretation. The contract in question contained a broad zipper clause. During the term of the agreement, the union sought to bargain with the employer over the employer's unilateral withdrawal of a "turkey money" bonus, which was not mentioned in the contract. Two members of the Board[587] found that the union had waived the right to bargain over the bonuses, in light of the "negotiating history and other surrounding circumstances," including the fact that the union unsuccessfully had sought a maintenance-of-benefits clause during the negotiations. Rather than the waiver being solely a matter of "clear and unmistakable" language in the contract, the Board held that a contractual waiver may be apparent by "contract interpretation" encompassing relevant provisions in the contract, the bargaining history, and past practice.[588]

The Board has continued to adhere to this broader position taken in *Radioear Corp.*[589] The circuit courts, however, are split

---

[585]*See, e.g.,* Bunker Hill Co., *supra* note 582; Conval-Ohio, Inc., *supra* note 582; New York Mirror, *supra* note 574; Beacon Journal Publishing Co., 164 NLRB 734, 65 LRRM 1126 (1967), *modified,* 401 F2d 366, 69 LRRM 2232 (CA 6, 1968); Unit Drop Forge Div., Eaton, Yale & Towne, Inc., 171 NLRB 600, 68 LRRM 1129 (1968).

[586]214 NLRB 362, 87 LRRM 1330 (1974), *supplementing* 199 NLRB 1161, 81 LRRM 1402 (1972).

[587]Chairman Miller and Member Penello.

[588]Members Fanning and Jenkins dissented. In their view, Chairman Miller and Member Penello had ignored consistent and long-standing precedent which held that "catch-all contract clauses" do not constitute a waiver of a union's right to bargain as to specific terms and conditions of employment. Member Kennedy, in a concurring opinion, stated he did not believe that the arbitrator's award (which had been rendered in the case pursuant to the Board's earlier deferral to arbitration under *Collyer*) was repugnant to the purposes and policies of the Act. He would have deferred to the arbitration award and dismissed the complaint on that basis.

[589]Temple-Eastex, Inc., 228 NLRB 203, 96 LRRM 1424 (1977), *rev'd on other grounds,* 579 F2d 932, 99 LRRM 2467 (CA 5, 1978); A-1 Fire Protection, Inc., 233 NLRB 38, 96 LRRM 1440 (1977), *remanded in part,* 600 F2d 918, 101 LRRM 2014 (CA DC, 1979). A subtle shift in the Board's analyses may be occurring. *See* Pepsi-Cola Distrib. Co., 241 NLRB 869, 100 LRRM 1626 (1979); Arizona Public Serv. Co., 247 NLRB No. 54, 103 LRRM 1154 (1980). *See also* GTE Automatic Elec., Inc., 261 NLRB No. 196, 110 LRRM 1193 (1982), *supplementing* 240 NLRB 297, 100 LRRM 1204 (1979).

on the issue, with some circuits following a more flexible approach,[590] while others continue to apply other analyses.[591]

b. *"Management Rights" Clauses.* When a "management rights" clause is the source of an asserted waiver, it is normally scrutinized by the Board to ascertain whether it affords specific justification for unilateral action. Thus, in *Ador Corp.*[592] the discontinuance of a line of products and the consequent layoff of employees without notice to the union was held to be justified by a management-rights clause that gave to the employer the right to take that precise action unilaterally. The Board reasoned that in agreeing to such a clause the parties had, in effect, bargained about the manner in which such decisions were to be made during the term of the collective bargaining agreement, and had agreed that the company could take such unilateral action.[593] Similarly, where a management-rights clause afforded the employer the sole right to determine employee qualifications, the Board held that the union waived its right to bargain over the subject of physical examinations during the term of the collective agreement.[594] On the other hand, in an earlier case, the Board had refused to find a specific waiver of the right to bargain on a retirement plan despite a management-rights clause reserving exclusive control over the retirement of employees as a management prerogative.[595] Normally, a mere catchall phrase in a management-rights clause to the effect that the "Company retains the responsibility and authority of managing the Company's business,"[596] or that "all management rights

---

[590]NLRB v. Southern Materials Co., 447 F2d 15, 77 LRRM 2814 (CA 4, 1971); NLRB v. Auto Crane Co., 536 F2d 310, 92 LRRM 2363 (CA 10, 1976).

[591]Plumbers Local 669 v. NLRB, *supra* note 582. *See also* ACF Industries, Inc. v. NLRB, 592 F2d 422, 100 LRRM 2710 (CA 8, 1979): "The failure to mention a right in a bargaining agreement does not constitute a waiver of it even though there is a clause stating that the contract represents the entire agreement between the parties." *Id.* at 429. For further discussion of zipper clauses, *see infra* at notes 772-73.

[592]*Supra* note 575.

[593]*Id. See also* Druwhit Metal Prods. Co., *supra* note 581; International Shoe Co., 151 NLRB 693, 58 LRRM 1483 (1965); *but see* General Motors Corp., 149 NLRB 396, 57 LRRM 1277 (1964), *remanded,* 60 LRRM 2283 (CA DC, 1965), *on remand,* 158 NLRB 229, 62 LRRM 1009 (1966), *rev'd,* 381 F2d 265, 64 LRRM 2489 (CA DC, 1967), *cert. denied,* 389 US 857 (1967) (the District of Columbia Circuit took a more restrictive view of the waiver language than did the Board and reversed the Board's dismissal of the complaint).

[594]LeRoy Mach. Co., Inc., 147 NLRB 1431, 56 LRRM 1369 (1964).

[595]Tide Water Associated Oil Co., 85 NLRB 1096, 24 LRRM 1518 (1949).

[596]Leeds & Northrup v. NLRB, 391 F2d 874 at 877, 67 LRRM 2793 at 2795 (CA 3, 1968), *enforcing* 162 NLRB 987, 64 LRRM 1110 (1967). *See also* Tenneco Chems., Inc., 249 NLRB 1176, 104 LRRM 1347 (1980).

not given up in the contract are expressly reserved to it,"[597] or that "the exclusive functions and rights of management include, but are not restricted to the right . . . to establish or continue policies, practices or procedures," falls short of being a "clear and unmistakable" relinquishment.[598]

    c. Board Jurisdiction to Construe Collective Bargaining Agreements. The Board and the courts may differ as to whether a particular contractual provision amounts to a waiver of the union's right to bargain.[599] Their interpretation may also differ from that of an arbitrator who, for example, may be called upon to determine the effect of a management-rights clause. In undertaking these determinations, the question arises as to the extent to which the Board may enter the area of interpreting the collective bargaining agreement.[600] In *NLRB* v. *C & C Plywood*[601] the Supreme Court held that the Board had jurisdiction to interpret collective bargaining agreements to the extent necessary to determine whether the union had waived its right to bargain about a specific mandatory subject. The Court explained that the Board had not "construed a labor agreement to determine the extent of contractual rights which had been given the union by the employer," but only whether the union had waived its right to bargain.[602]

    While the Board has this limited jurisdiction to construe a labor agreement, it has nonetheless demonstrated, under the *Collyer* doctrine,[603] a willingness to defer the question of contractual waiver to an arbitrator. In *Radioear Corp.*[604] the Board deferred to an arbitrator the question of whether the zipper

---

[597]Proctor Mfg. Corp., 131 NLRB 1166, 48 LRRM 1222 (1961).

[598]In light of the Board's modification of its position on waiver in *Radioear Corp., supra* note 586, a management-rights clause might support the inference of a waiver if supported by such factors as the wording of the clause, the bargaining history of the contract (*i.e.,* proposals accepted or rejected), the degree to which the agreement is integrated, and past practice. *Supra* note 586 at 363-64; A-1 Fire Protection, Inc., *supra* note 589 at 39.

[599]*See* General Motors Corp., *supra* note 593.

[600]*See generally* Chapter 19 *infra* for discussion of Board action in relation to enforcement of collective agreements and Chapter 20 *infra* for treatment of the accommodation between Board action and the arbitration process.

[601]*Supra* note 584. *See* Chapter 19 *infra* at notes 209-16.

[602]*Supra* note 584 at 428. *See also* NLRB v. Huttig Sash & Door Co., Inc., 377 F2d 964, 65 LRRM 2431 (CA 8, 1967); Gravenslund Operating Co., 168 NLRB 513, 66 LRRM 1323 (1967) (discussing the effect of the availability of grievance and arbitration machinery in the contract and desirable procedural priorities).

[603]Collyer Insulated Wire, 192 NLRB 837, 77 LRRM 1931 (1971). For a full discussion of the *Collyer* doctrine, *see* Chapter 20 *infra*.

[604]*Supra* note 586.

clause in the collective bargaining agreement allowed the employer unilaterally to discontinue a bonus.[605] The arbitrator determined that the contract did not guarantee the continuation of the bonuses, but stated that he was without authority to decide whether the zipper clause, under the circumstances, constituted a waiver of the duty to bargain over discontinuation of the bonuses.[606] The Board held that it was within the arbitrator's power to decide the waiver issue since it was a "matter particularly suited to resolution in the forum of arbitration."[607]

2. Waiver by Bargaining History. Where a subject has been discussed in contract negotiations but has not been specifically covered in the resulting contract, a waiver will be found only where the union has "consciously yielded" its position.[608] This normally requires that the matter be "fully discussed" and "consciously explored."[609] Thus, in *TTP Corp.*,[610] a panel majority of the Board held that the absence of any provisions in a labor agreement regarding a unilaterally adopted pension plan did not constitute a waiver of the union's right to bargain over the termination of the plan, notwithstanding that (1) the unilaterally adopted plan contained express provisions reserving to the employer the right unilaterally to terminate the plan, (2) the union was fully aware of the termination provisions of the pension plan, and (3) during three successive contract negotiations the union had at no time voiced any objection to the termination provisions of the plan.[611]

---

[605]In refusing to apply automatically a "rigid rule" as to clear and unequivocal waiver, the Board stated that it was "unwilling to ignore what has taken place at the bargaining table and decide the parties' dispute on the basis of a simplistic formula . . . ." *Id.*, 199 NLRB at 1161.

[606]*Supra* note 586, 214 NLRB at 363.

[607]*Id.*

[608]New York Mirror, *supra* note 574; Proctor Mfg. Corp., *supra* note 597; Press Co., Inc., 121 NLRB 976, 42 LRRM 1493 (1958). *See* Chapter 19 *infra*.

[609]Bunker Hill Co., *supra* note 582; Press Co., Inc., *supra* note 608. Mere silence or inaction is not "conscious exploration." Litton Precision Prods., Inc., 156 NLRB 555, 61 LRRM 1096 (1966); J. C. Penney Co., 161 NLRB 69, 63 LRRM 1309 (1966). *But cf.* Berkline Corp., 123 NLRB 685, 43 LRRM 1513 (1959). Even in the absence of bargaining over an issue, waiver will not be presumed unless there is "'clear and unequivocal' evidence pointing to a 'conscious relinquishment.' " Vogt Mach. Co., 251 NLRB No. 40, 105 LRRM 1088 (1980).

[610]190 NLRB 240, 77 LRRM 1097 (1971).

[611]Chairman Miller dissented. In his view, the majority opinion did not merely stand for the proposition that "silence is not a waiver." Rather, he concluded that the majority decision was tantamount to a holding that silence had the effect of amending the pension plan to eliminate the provisions permitting the employer unilaterally to terminate it. For another case in which silence was not considered a waiver regarding an employee retirement plan, *see* Elizabethtown Water Co., *supra* note 582.

The payment of bonuses has been a frequent source of controversy because the collective bargaining agreement is often silent on this topic. The effect accorded an unsuccessful attempt by the union to incorporate this benefit into the agreement, either directly or by way of a "maintenance of benefits" clause, may turn on close factual circumstances. Where the demand is withdrawn from negotiations without "full discussion" there is a likelihood that no waiver will result.[612] This is especially true where the employer gives assurances that it has no intention of discontinuing the bonus.[613] However, where the employer specifically explains the reasons for its rejection and the union remains silent, the absence of any contractual provision may be deemed a conscious acquiescence by the union in the position which the employer took during negotiations.[614]

A waiver does not usually turn on the presence or absence of a single factor.[615] Even clear contractual language is not always determinative. In *Kennecott Copper Corp.*,[616] for example, the employer unilaterally subcontracted work, relying upon a broad and inclusive management-rights clause which the trial examiner held reserved to the employer "the right to take precisely the action it took."[617] Although the Board dismissed the complaint, it did so because of the "particular circumstances" of the case, including the facts that the employees in the appropriate unit had suffered "no significant detriment"[618] and the employer had agreed to bargain when the union protested. This rationale of lack of "significant detriment" to bargaining-unit employees, relied upon in *Kennecott,* was followed in a series of Board deci-

---

[612]Beacon Journal Publishing Co., *supra* note 585, where the union's unsuccessful attempt to obtain a Christmas bonus provision in the agreement was not found by the Board majority to be persuasive, though it was to the dissenting members.

[613]General Tel. Co., 144 NLRB 311, 54 LRRM 1055 (1963), *enforced as modified,* 337 F2d 452, 57 LRRM 2211 (CA 5, 1964).

[614]Radioear Corp., *supra* note 586; Speidel Corp., *supra* note 576, where the union dropped its demand for a "maintenance of privileges" clause and remained silent in the face of an employer's explanation that a provision in the collective agreement would make the unilateral practice contractually binding and, as such, it would be objectionable to him. *See* Tucker Steel Corp., 134 NLRB 323, 49 LRRM 1164 (1961), where the employer indicated the possibility of unilateral termination of bonuses if the union's vacation demands were met. The union's silence and the absence of a contractual provision created an estoppel. *But see* Pine Manor Nursing Home, Inc., 230 NLRB 320, 95 LRRM 1356 (1977), where no waiver was found when the union withdrew its proposal merely as a tactic to encourage movement at the bargaining table.

[615]For an examination of some of the relevant factors, *see* Radioear Corp., *supra* note 586 and accompanying text.

[616]148 NLRB 1653, 57 LRRM 1217 (1964).

[617]*Id.* at 1656.

[618]*Id.* at 1654.

sions which upheld subcontracting without prior notification to the union.[619] However, in distinguishing the *Fibreboard*[620] doctrine (which required such notification regarding certain types of subcontracting), the Board has not relied solely upon the "significant detriment" principle.[621] Rather, it has chosen to view the subcontracting in issue as consistent with established past practice, so the union had not departed from the norm. Furthermore, the union's failure to obtain a contractual restriction on subcontracting has also been viewed as persuasive.[622] While the Board has seemed reluctant to decide these cases in terms of a waiver doctrine,[623] the reasoning and the result appear to be the same.

Cases in which union acquiescence in the employer's past practice constitutes a maintenance of the status quo (e.g., an employer's continued unilateral subcontracting during the term of the agreement) may be distinguished from cases where a change in the status quo is made without consulting the union.[624] In *Leeds & Northrup*[625] the employer had unilaterally instituted a supplementary compensation plan, renewing it annually. In defending its right to alter unilaterally the formula by which benefits were computed, the employer asserted an implied waiver, relying upon the Board's subcontracting decisions. This defense was rejected by the Board and the Third Circuit on the ground that the status quo had been represented by the formula which the employer unilaterally altered; whereas in the subcontracting cases the employers had simply continued the norm of subcontracting and thus had not altered the status quo.

3. Waiver by Inaction. In the absence of a *fait accompli*, the duty to bargain arises upon request; but where an opportunity

---

[619]Westinghouse Elec. Corp. (Mansfield Plant), 150 NLRB 1574, 58 LRRM 1257 (1965); American Oil Co., 151 NLRB 421, 58 LRRM 1412 (1965); Allied Chem. Corp., 151 NLRB 718, 58 LRRM 1480 (1965), *aff'd*, 358 F2d 234, 61 LRRM 2632 (CA 4, 1966); Shell Oil Co., 149 NLRB 283, 57 LRRM 1271 (1964); Shell Chem. Co., 149 NLRB 298, 57 LRRM 1275 (1964).
[620]Fibreboard Paper Prods. Corp., 379 US 203, 57 LRRM 2609 (1964). *See* Chapter 17 *infra* at notes 268-80.
[621]*Supra* note 619.
[622]*See, e.g.*, American Oil Co., *supra* note 619.
[623]Westinghouse Elec. Corp. (Mansfield Plant), *supra* note 619.
[624]Leeds & Northrup Co. v. NLRB, 391 F2d 874, 67 LRRM 2793 (CA 3, 1968), *enforcing* 162 NLRB 987, 64 LRRM 1110 (1967).
[625]*Id.*

exists to bargain and no request is made, a waiver may result.[626] For example, if a union has been put on notice that the employer plans removal of its operations and makes no attempt to bring issues relating to plant removal to the bargaining table, it waives its rights in the matter.[627] It is not essential that the union be given formal notice of the intended unilateral change if the union does in fact know of the plans and a formal announcement would be futile,[628] but the Board is generally reluctant to give broad effect to a waiver by inaction.[629]

The interrelationship of the doctrines of waiver and futility was aptly illustrated in *U.S. Lingerie Corp.*,[630] where a demand for union cooperation because of the employer's economic condition was rejected. Despite the clear warning to the union that plant removal would otherwise be necessitated, the union remained intransigent. The subsequent failure of the employer to advise the union formally of its decision to remove and to bargain with it was therefore excused on the ground of futility, and the union's failure to request bargaining over the removal was held to be a waiver.

4. Waiver by Filing of Decertification Petition and Intervention. When bargaining-unit employees have filed a decertification petition, the Board may relieve the employer of its duty to bargain.* The origin of this defense was the Board's decision in *Teleautograph*,[631] which declared that a decertification petition supported by an adequate showing of interest should have the

---

[626]*See, e.g.*, Clarkwood Corp., 233 NLRB 1172, 97 LRRM 1034 (1977); Medicenter, Mid-South Hosp., 221 NLRB 670, 90 LRRM 1576 (1975); Coppus Eng'r Corp., 195 NLRB 595, 79 LRRM 1449 (1972); Triplex Oil Ref., 194 NLRB 500, 78 LRRM 1711 (1971). *See also* notes 574 and 579 *supra*. A "union cannot charge an employer with refusal to negotiate when it has made no attempt to bring the employer to the bargaining table." NLRB v. Alva Allen Indus., Inc., 369 F2d 310, 63 LRRM 2515 (CA 8, 1966), *citing* NLRB v. Columbian Enameling & Stamping Co., 306 US 292, 4 LRRM 524 (1939).

[627]United States Lingerie Corp., *supra* note 574. *See also* Love's Barbeque Restaurant, 245 NLRB 78, 102 LRRM 1546 (1979) (subcontracting).

[628]*See* note 627; American Bus Lines, Inc., 164 NLRB 1055, 65 LRRM 1265 (1967). *Cf.* McLoughlin Mfg. Corp., 164 NLRB 140, 65 LRRM 1025 (1967), *enforced as modified*, 463 F2d 907, 80 LRRM 2716 (CA DC, 1972); Southern Cal. Stationers, 162 NLRB 1517, 64 LRRM 1227 (1967); Dove Flocking & Screening Co., 145 NLRB 682, 55 LRRM 1013 (1963). While the union need not receive formal notice, it must receive sufficient notice of the change to give it the opportunity to make a meaningful response. *See, e.g.*, Metromedia, Inc. v. NLRB, 586 F2d 1182, 99 LRRM 2743 (CA 8, 1978); Electri-Flex Co. v. NLRB, 570 F2d 1327, 97 LRRM 2888 (CA 7, 1978); *cert. denied*, 439 US 911, 99 LRRM 2743 (1978).

[629]*See* Peerless Publications, Inc., 231 NLRB 244, 95 LRRM 1611 (1977), and cases cited therein at 258.

[630]*Supra* note 574.

*[*But see* **Editor's Note,** p. 650 *infra*.]

[631]199 NLRB 892, 81 LRRM 1337 (1972).

same effect on the employer's obligation to bargain with an incumbent union as a petition filed by a rival union. Both petitions raise a real question concerning representation, thus the rationale of *Shea Chemical Corp.*,[632] which bars bargaining with the incumbent union until the question has been resolved in a representation proceeding, is also applicable following the filing of a decertification petition.

Board members have continued to debate the merits of the *Teleautograph* decision.[633] Although the employer may refuse to bargain with an incumbent union during the pendency of a valid decertification petition, the employer may withdraw recognition only if it has a "reasonable doubt of the union's presumed majority status based upon objective considerations showing a loss of majority support."[634] Of course, the employer may not rely on a decertification petition that has been dismissed.[635]

The Board and the courts have struggled to delineate the scope of the *Teleautograph* defense. The District of Columbia Circuit has cautioned that a mere "naked showing that a decertification petition has been filed, with no indication of the number of signatures or other related matters," will not support a finding of refusal to bargain by an employer.[636] The *Teleautograph* rule does not apply "in situations where, because of contract bar, certification year, inadequate showing of interest or any other established reason, the decertification petition does not raise a real representation question."[637] Thus, a failure to bargain is not excusable when employees who signed the petition might have been compelled to do so by unlawful acts of an employer, especially if the employer's acts were aimed at persuading employees to abandon the union.[638] Nor may an employer rely on its own decertification petition to support a refusal to

---

[632]121 NLRB 1027, 42 LRRM 1486 (1958). *See also* Essex Int'l, Inc., 222 NLRB 121, 91 LRRM 1413 (1976). For detailed discussion of the *Mid-West Piping* doctrine, see Chapter 8 *supra* at notes 107-43. [*See* **Editor's Note** in Chapter 8 *supra*, p. 294.]

[633]*See, e.g.,* Lammert Indus., 229 NLRB 895, 96 LRRM 1557 (1977), *enforced,* 578 F2d 1223, 98 LRRM 2992 (CA 7, 1978).

[634]General Radiator Div., NLRB Gen. Counsel Advice Memo., Case No. 14-CA-11754-1, 100 LRRM 1083 (1978). *See generally* Chapter 12 *supra.*

[635]Westinghouse Elec. Corp., 238 NLRB 763, 99 LRRM 1400 (1978).

[636]NLRB v. Grede Foundries, Inc., 628 F2d 1, 4, 104 LRRM 2646 (CA DC, 1980).

[637]Teleautograph Corp., *supra* note 631 at 892.

[638]Warehouse Mkt., Inc., 216 NLRB 216, 88 LRRM 1145 (1975). *See also* Antonino's Restaurant, 246 NLRB 833, 103 LRRM 1013 (1979); Providence Medical Center, 243 NLRB 714, 102 LRRM 1099 (1979); Autoprod, Inc., 223 NLRB 773, 92 LRRM 1076 (1976).

bargain.[639] Knowledge by the employer of the filing of the petition may also be needed to assert the *Teleautograph* defense.[640]*

An employer may be relieved of its duty to bargain with an incumbent union when a petition is timely filed by an intervening union during the "open period."[641] If the employer's refusal to bargain is supported by a showing of interest sufficient to raise a real question of representation, the employer will be justified in refusing to bargain with the incumbent union.[642] The employer, however, "is obligated to continue to recognize and bargain with the incumbent collective-bargaining representative of his employees over the *administration* of their existing collective-bargaining agreement, despite the fact that a representation petition has been filed by a rival union."[643]

B. The Construction Industry: Section 8(f)[644]

The Labor-Management Reporting and Disclosure Act of 1959[645] added Section 8(f)[646] to the National Labor Relations

---

[639]NLRB v. Anderson, 611 F2d 1225, 103 LRRM 2103 (CA 8, 1979).

[640]Lammert Indus., 229 NLRB 895, 96 LRRM 1557 (1977) (Member Murphy, concurring), *enforced*, 578 F2d 1223, 98 LRRM 2992 (CA 7, 1978).

*[**Editor's Note:** In late 1982, in *Dresser Industries, Inc.*, 264 NLRB No. 145, 111 LRRM 1436 (1982), the Board overruled *Teleautograph Corp.*, holding that the mere filing of a decertification petition will not require or permit an employer to withdraw from bargaining or refrain from executing a contract with an incumbent union. *See also* **Editor's Note** in Chapter 8 *supra*, p. 294.]

[641]*See* Chapter 10 *supra* at notes 185-86. [*But see* **Editor's Note** in Chapter 8 *supra*, p. 294.]

[642]Greyhound Airport Serv., Inc., 204 NLRB 900, 83 LRRM 1712 (1973). *See also* Duralite Co., Inc., 132 NLRB 425, 48 LRRM 1371 (1961).

[643]St. Louis Cordage Mills, 170 NLRB 167, 67 LRRM 1378 (1968) (emphasis added); *see also* Wayne Metal Co., 246 NLRB 392, 102 LRRM 1536 (1979); Chevron Oil Co., 168 NLRB 574, 66 LRRM 1353 (1967).

[644]*See generally*, King & La Vaute, *Current Trends in Construction Industry Labor Relations, The Double Breasted Contractor and the Prehire Contract*, 29 SYRACUSE L. REV. 901 (1978).

[645]*See* Chapter 4 *supra*.

[646]§8(f) provides: "It shall not be an unfair labor practice under subsections (a) and (b) of this section for an employer engaged primarily in the building and construction industry to make an agreement covering employees engaged (or who, upon their employment, will be engaged) in the building and construction industry with a labor organization of which building and construction employees are members (not established, maintained, or assisted by any action defined in subsection (a) of this section as an unfair labor practice) because (1) the majority status of such labor organization has not been established under the provisions of §9 of the Act prior to the making of such agreement, or (2) such agreement requires as a condition of employment, membership in such labor organization after the seventh day following the beginning of such employment or the effective date of the agreement, whichever is later, or (3) such agreement requires the employer to notify such labor organization of opportunities for employment with such employer, or gives such labor organization an opportunity to refer qualified applicants for such employment, or (4) such agreement specifies minimum training or experience qualifications for employment or provides for priority in opportunities for employment based upon length of service with such employer, in the industry or in the particular geographical area: *Provided*, That nothing in this subsection shall set aside the final proviso to subsection (a)(3) of this Act; *Provided further*, That any agreement

Act. Designed to meet certain problems in the building and construction industry, the section acts as a savings clause allowing union security agreements under circumstances which would otherwise constitute unfair labor practices. Thus, an employer engaged primarily in the building and construction industry may enter into a prehire agreement requiring union membership as a condition of employment, where not prohibited by state law, notwithstanding the undetermined majority status of the union.[647] Under conventional doctrine such an employer would be guilty of an unfair labor practice by extending recognition to a minority union,[648] and any agreement executed under such circumstances would be invalid even though bargained for under the erroneous but good-faith belief that the employer was dealing with a majority union. A limited though significant departure from the traditional bargaining obligation therefore exists in the building and construction industry. Two important statutory qualifications diminish the potential impact of this section, however. First, Section 8(f) does not validate prehire agreements where the union has been established, maintained, or assisted by any action of the employer otherwise violative of Section 8(a)(2). Second, a valid prehire agreement is no bar to an election petition subsequently filed to determine the majority representative.[649]

A valid prehire agreement is also no substitute for a collective bargaining agreement between the employer and a union which has majority status. In the 1970s the Board consistently held

which would be invalid, but for clause (1) of this subsection, shall not be a bar to a petition filed pursuant to section 9(c) or 9(e)." *See* Chapter 29 *infra* at notes 143-62.

[647]Administrative Ruling SR-813, 46 LRRM 1515 (1960). The General Counsel refused to issue a complaint where a construction industry employer had complained that the minority union had coerced it into signing a contract. Although a poll of the employees showed that the majority did not wish to be represented by the union, the Act specifically allows union security agreements within the industry. The Board stated in a later decision, however, that a union security clause in a prehire agreement provides a "rebuttable presumption" of majority status. R. J. Smith Constr. Co., 191 NLRB 693, 695 n.5, 77 LRRM 1493 (1971), *rev'd and remanded sub nom.* Operating Eng'rs Local 150, 480 F2d 1186, 83 LRRM 2706 (CA DC, 1973). Thus, while it may be legal for the employer to enter into a prehire agreement containing a union security clause, the clause alone does not provide irrebuttable proof of a union's majority status should the employer choose to repudiate the agreement. The union security clause must have been enforced, and a majority of the employer's unit employees must therefore actually belong to the union. Irvin-McKelvy Co., 194 NLRB 52, 78 LRRM 1516 (1971), *aff'd in relevant part*, 475 F2d 1265, 82 LRRM 3015 (CA 3, 1973). For a discussion of employer repudiation of existing prehire agreements, *see* notes 651-64 and accompanying text *infra*.

[648]Garment Workers (Bernhard-Altmann Tex. Corp.) v. NLRB, 366 US 731, 48 LRRM 2251 (1961). *See* Chapter 8 *supra* at notes 9-12.

[649]Bear Creek Constr. Co., 135 NLRB 1285, 49 LRRM 1674 (1962). *See* Chapter 10 *supra* at notes 149-51.

that a "prehire agreement is merely a preliminary step that contemplates further action for the development of a full bargaining relationship."[650] In one case the Board held that an employer who had signed a prehire agreement with a union did not violate Section 8(a)(5) when it unilaterally repudiated the agreement during its term, because the union never obtained majority status;[651] since the union's majority may be tested under Section 8(f) at any time during the agreement, the union was not entitled to a presumption of majority status.[652]

In *NLRB* v. *Iron Workers Local 103 (Higdon Contracting Co.)*[653] the Supreme Court agreed with the Board's interpretation of Section 8(f). The employer had signed a prehire agreement with a union. Thereafter the employer formed a separate corporation to utilize nonunion labor on certain construction jobs (a "double breasted"[654] operation), and the union set up picket lines to compel the employer to apply the prehire agreement to its nonunion corporation. The employer responded by filing a Section 8(b)(7)(C)[655] charge against the union for picketing without a representation petition having been filed. The Board held that the union had indeed violated Section 8(b)(7)(C) since it never represented a majority of the employees of the nonunion corporation or of the employer itself.[656] Although the prehire agreement did not violate the Act, absent union majority status the employer was at liberty to repudiate the agreement at any time. Thus, the prehire agreement did not insulate the union from the provisions of Section 8(b)(7)(C). The District of Columbia Circuit reversed, holding that the employer's sole remedy, if it wished to annul a prehire agreement, was to request a representation election.[657]

The Supreme Court, however, reversed the circuit court and affirmed the Board.[658] The Court held that the purpose of

---

[650]Ruttman Constr. Co., 191 NLRB 701, 702, 77 LRRM 1497 (1971).

[651]R. J. Smith Constr. Co., *supra* note 647. *See also* Plott, *Pre-Hire Contracts in the Construction Industry*, 15 B. C. INDUS. & COM. L. REV. 862 (1974).

[652]R. J. Smith Constr. Co., *supra* note 647 at 694. A rebuttable presumption would be appropriate, however, if the prehire agreement contains a union security clause, which was absent in this case. *Id.* at 695 n.5. *See also* note 647 *supra*.

[653]434 US 335, 97 LRRM 2333 (1978). *See* Chapter 29 *infra* at notes 155-57.

[654]*See infra* at notes 787-808.

[655]*See generally* Chapter 23 *infra*.

[656]Iron Workers Local 103 (Higdon Contracting Co.), 216 NLRB 45, 88 LRRM 1067 (1975).

[657]Iron Workers Local 103 (Higdon Contracting Co.) v. NLRB, 535 F2d 87, 91 LRRM 2986 (CA DC, 1976).

[658]NLRB v. Iron Workers Local 103 (Higdon Contracting Co.), *supra* note 653.

Section 8(f) was to permit the *making* of prehire agreements with a minority union in the construction industry, not to enforce them:

> §8(f) itself does not purport to authorize picketing to enforce prehire agreements where the union has not achieved majority support. Neither does it expand the duty of an employer under §8(a)(5), which is to bargain with a *majority* representative, to require the employer to bargain with a union with which he has executed a prehire agreement but which has failed to win majority support in the covered unit.[659]

In sum, Section 8(f) allows a voluntary prehire agreement between an employer and a minority union, but does not mandate good-faith bargaining between the parties.[660] Since the Supreme Court's decision in *Higdon,* the courts have divided on the issue of the enforceability of prehire agreements in the absence of majority status.[661] On the other hand, if the union does represent a majority of the employees, a valid prehire agreement between a union and an employer is enforceable and triggers the duty to bargain.[662] The prehire agreement is transformed into a collective bargaining agreement when a union obtains majority status in the relevant bargaining unit.[663] For an employer hiring on a project-by-project basis, the showing of majority status at one job site does not extend to future jobs for which no employees have been hired.[664]

---

[659]*Id.* at 346. Emphasis in original.

[660]R. J. Smith Constr. Co., *supra* note 647.

[661]A number of courts have held that prehire agreements are judicially enforceable and that nonmajority status is no defense. *See* Washington Area Carpenters Welfare Fund v. Overhead Door Co. of Metropolitan Wash., 681 F2d 1, 110 LRRM 2752 (CA DC, 1982); Todd v. Jim McNeff, Inc., 667 F2d 1292, 109 LRRM 2802 (CA 9, 1982); Western-Washington Laborers-Employers Health & Sec. Trust Fund v. McDowell, 109 LRRM 3104 (CA 9, 1982); New Mexico Dist. Council of Carpenters v. Mayhew Co., 664 F2d 215, 107 LRRM 2930 (CA 10, 1981); W. C. James, Inc. v. Oil Workers, 646 F2d 1292, 107 LRRM 2226 (CA 8, 1981); Health & Welfare Plan v. Associated Wrecking Co., 638 F2d 1128, 106 LRRM 2257 (CA 8, 1980). *See also* Iron Workers Local 387 v. Southern Stress Wire Corp., 509 F Supp 1097, 108 LRRM 2982 (ND Ga, 1981); Florida Marble Polishers Health & Welfare Trust Fund v. Megahee, 102 LRRM 2740 (ND Fla, 1979).
    However, some courts have reached the opposite result. *See* Baton Rouge Bldg. & Constr. Trades Council v. E. C. Schafer Constr. Co., 657 F2d 806, 108 LRRM 2634 (CA 5, 1981); NLRB v. Haberman Constr. Co., 641 F2d 351, 106 LRRM 2998 (CA 5, 1981) (*en banc*) (dictum). *See also* Lail v. C&R Constr., Inc., No. 1-80-52 (ED Tenn, 26 Jan. 1981); Paddack v. Clark, 107 LRRM 2325 (D Ore, 1980).

[662]Irvin-McKelvy Co., *supra* note 647.

[663]Baton Rouge Bldg. & Constr. Trades Council v. E. C. Schafer Constr. Co., *supra* note 661; NLRB v. Haberman Constr. Co., *supra* note 661; Irvin-McKelvy Co., *supra* note 647.

[664]*See supra* note 663; Dee Cee Floor Covering, 232 NLRB 421, 97 LRRM 1072 (1977). *But cf.* Pacific Intercom Co., 255 NLRB 184, 106 LRRM 1289 (1981) (employer's course of unlawful conduct prevented union from maintaining majority status; employer estopped from relying on §8(f) to defend §8(a)(5) charge).

C. Suspension During Illegal or Unprotected Activity

Although the duty to bargain and recognize a union is a continuing one, certain aspects of a party's duty may be temporarily suspended when the other party is engaged in unlawful activity.[665] For example, it was held that an employer was not obligated to continue negotiations during periods during which the union endorsed illegal strike conduct,[666] including violence and vandalism, and encouraged mass demonstrations at the homes of nonstriking employees.[667] Employers have also been deemed justified in suspending negotiations when the union called a slowdown[668] or engaged in a strike in violation of a contractual no-strike pledge.[669] However, the obligation to bargain is suspended only so long as the period of the breach or unlawful action continues.[670]

The illegal or unprotected conduct, however, must be substantial, generally unprovoked, and closely related to the bargaining in question in order to support a suspension of the bargaining duty. In one case where a "handful" of strikers engaged in mass picketing, threats, assaults, and some damaging of property during a strike which had been caused by the employer's disciplinary suspension of a union activist, the employer's own extensive illegal conduct warranted issuance of a bargaining

---

[665]Carroll Contracting & Ready-Mix, Inc., 247 NLRB 890, 103 LRRM 1232 (1980). But the duty to bargain was suspended "only so long as the unlawful conduct continued." *See* note 670 *infra.*

[666]Lyman Steel Co., 249 NLRB 296, 104 LRRM 1323 (1980). The union must have been responsible for or have condoned such conduct, however.

[667]Kohler Co., 128 NLRB 1062, 46 LRRM 1389 (1960), *enforced in part and remanded in part*, 300 F2d 699, 49 LRRM 2485 (CA DC, 1962), *supplemented by* 148 NLRB 1434, 57 LRRM 1148 (1964), *enforced*, 345 F2d 748, 58 LRRM 2847 (CA DC, 1965). *See also* Johns-Manville Prods. Corp. v. NLRB, 557 F2d 1126, 96 LRRM 2010 (CA 5, 1977), *cert. denied*, 436 US 956, 98 LRRM 2617 (1978), where the court refused to enforce a Board decision finding, *inter alia*, that the employer had refused to bargain with the union. After numerous acts of in-plant vandalism and sabotage by employees, the employer locked out the employees and hired permanent replacements. The court found that the employees' conduct amounted to an "in-plant strike" and that the employer could therefore hire permanent replacements without bargaining with the union. *See* notes 535-37 *supra* and accompanying text for a fuller discussion of the case.

[668]Phelps Dodge Copper Prods. Corp., 101 NLRB 360, 31 LRRM 1072 (1952).

[669]Arundel Corp., 210 NLRB 525, 86 LRRM 1180 (1974). The Board held that an employer did not violate the Act and was under no obligation to bargain with the union while the union was engaging in an unprotected strike in violation of an oral agreement between the parties. *See also* International Shoe Corp., 152 NLRB 699, 59 LRRM 1176 (1965), *enforced*, 357 F2d 330, 61 LRRM 2559 (CA 1, 1966); Marathon Elec. Mfg. Corp., 106 NLRB 1171, 1180, 32 LRRM 1645 (1953); United Elastic Corp., 84 NLRB 768, 24 LRRM 1294 (1949).

[670]Arundel Corp., *supra* note 669; United Elastic Corp., *supra* note 669; Dorsey Trailers, Inc., 80 NLRB 478, 486, 23 LRRM 1112 (1948).

order against the employer.[671] And defamatory statements made by a union during an election campaign are not enough, in and of themselves, to relieve the employer of its duty to bargain.[672] And claims that a union[673] or an employer[674] have engaged in illegal sex or race discrimination will not support a suspension of the duty to bargain.

D. Union Loss of Majority

The Act requires the employer to recognize and bargain with the representative of the majority of its employees in an appropriate bargaining unit; thus, if a union loses its majority status, under the literal language of the statute the employer would not be required to extend recognition or to bargain. An obvious defense to the duty to bargain would therefore be the loss of majority by an incumbent union. However, there are several recognized exceptions to the literal requirement of majority status. These have been developed by both statutory provision and case law for the purpose of stabilizing industrial relations.[675] For example, a certified union must be recognized for a full year following certification, absent "unusual circumstances," even when it has lost its majority.[676] The mandatory bargaining period has also been extended following an order to bargain.[677] Another exception is the rule that majority status is presumed to continue during the term of a collective bargaining contract. This rule is

---

[671]Donovan v. NLRB, 520 F2d 1316, 89 LRRM 3127 (CA 2, 1975), *cert. denied,* 423 US 1053, 91 LRRM 2099 (1976), *enforcing* 206 NLRB 688, 85 LRRM 1227 (1973). *Cf.* Laura Modes Co., 144 NLRB 1592, 54 LRRM 1299 (1963). *See also* Evening News Publishing Co., 196 NLRB 530, 80 LRRM 1230 (1972), where the Board held that the employer could not unilaterally order its employees to cease their accepted practice of inflating their expense accounts; questions of morality and violations of tax laws, which would be raised by a continuation of the practice, did not relieve the employer of the duty to bargain on the changes. *See also* Arsham Sewing Co., 244 NLRB 918, 102 LRRM 1119 (1979).

[672]Paramount Gen. Hosp., Inc., 223 NLRB 1017, 92 LRRM 1171 (1976), *aff'd,* 554 F2d 1202, 95 LRRM 2626 (CA DC, 1977).

[673]Bell & Howell Co., 230 NLRB 420, 95 LRRM 1333 (1977), *supplementing* 220 NLRB 881, 90 LRRM 1448 (1975), *aff'd,* 598 F2d 136, 100 LRRM 2192 (CA DC, 1979). *See also* Handy Andy, Inc., 228 NLRB 447, 94 LRRM 1354 (1977).

[674]Graphic Arts Union Local 280 (James H. Barry Co.), 235 NLRB 1084, 98 LRRM 1188 (1978), *aff'd,* 596 F2d 904, 101 LRRM 2664 (CA 9, 1979).

[675]*See* discussion of the *one-year rule* and the *contract-bar doctrine* in Chapter 10 *supra* at notes 70-97 and 117-200.

[676]Brooks v. NLRB, 348 US 96, 35 LRRM 2158 (1954). In *Brooks* the Supreme Court noted that the Board had recognized "unusual circumstances" in three situations: (1) the certified union dissolves or becomes defunct, (2) a schism occurs within the certified union, and (3) existence of a radical fluctuation in the size of the bargaining unit within a short period of time. *See* Chapter 12 *supra* at notes 352-55.

[677]*See, e.g.,* Mar-Jac Poultry Co., 136 NLRB 785, 49 LRRM 1854 (1962).

applicable to contract-bar cases in Section 9 (representation) proceedings.[678]

The presumption of majority status also applies to the duty to bargain.[679] This presumption applies "to situations where the refusal to bargain is with a Board certified union or with an incumbent union which has theretofore achieved a bargaining status evidenced by a collective bargaining agreement, or, at least, by prior recognition."[680] The presumption establishes a *prima facie* requirement that the employer is obligated to bargain with the incumbent union.[681] In all of these situations, however, the prima facie case may be rebutted. As the Board outlined in *Terrell Machine Co.*:[682]

> The *prima facie* case may be rebutted if the employer affirmatively establishes either (1) that at the time of the refusal the union in fact no longer enjoyed majority representative status, or (2) that the employer's refusal was predicated on a good-faith and reasonably grounded doubt of the union's continued majority status. As to the second of these, i.e., "good faith doubt," two prerequisites for sustaining the defense are that the asserted doubt may be based on objective considerations and it must not have been advanced for the purpose of gaining time in which to undermine the union.[683]

In earlier cases the Board placed greater stress on the employer's subjective good faith "in light of the totality of all the circumstances involved."[684] In later cases, however, the Board and

---

[678]*See* United States Gypsum Co., 157 NLRB 652, 61 LRRM 1384 (1966). *See also* note 675 *supra*.

[679]*See generally* Chapter 12 *supra* at notes 353-442. But this presumption does not apply to prehire agreements in the construction industry legitimized by §8(f). *See* note 647 *supra*.

[680]Ramada Inns, Inc., 171 NLRB 1060, 1062, 68 LRRM 1209 (1968). The presumption must be based on a clear unit description in prior collective bargaining agreements or past practice as to the relevant unambiguous unit. NLRB v. West Sand & Gravel Co., 612 F2d 1326, 103 LRRM 2255 (CA 1, 1979). *See also* Glenlyn, Inc., 204 NLRB 299, 83 LRRM 1356 (1973).

[681]Terrell Mach. Co., 173 NLRB 1480, 1480-81, 70 LRRM 1049 (1969), *enforced*, 427 F2d 1088, 73 LRRM 2381 (CA 4, 1970). *See also* Pioneer Inn Assocs. v. NLRB, 578 F2d 835, 99 LRRM 2354 (CA 9, 1978).

[682]Terrell Mach. Co., *supra* note 681. *See also* Guerdon Indus., Inc., 218 NLRB 658, 89 LRRM 1389 (1975); Bartenders Ass'n of Pocatello, 213 NLRB 651, 87 LRRM 1194 (1974); Celanese Corp. of Am., 95 NLRB 664, 28 LRRM 1362 (1951).

[683]*Supra* note 681 at 1480-81. *See also* Bartenders Ass'n of Pocatello, *supra* note 682; Eastern Wash. Distrib. Co., Inc., 216 NLRB 1149, 1152 -53, 88 LRRM 1453 (1975).

[684]Celanese Corp. of Am., *supra* note 682. In the 1970s Member Kennedy soundly criticized the Board majority for too much reliance on the employer's subjective belief and not enough emphasis on the question of whether the union actually had a majority. *See, e.g.*, his dissents in Automated Business Sys., 205 NLRB 532, 539-40, 84 LRRM 1042 (1973), *enforcement denied*, 497 F2d 262, 86 LRRM 2659 (CA 6, 1974); Bartenders Ass'n of Pocatello, *supra* note 682 at 656 n.30; Wanda Petroleum, 217 NLRB 376, 89 LRRM 1042, *aff'd*, 90 LRRM 3344 (CA 5, 1975). In these same cases, he also criticized the Board's allocation of the burden of proof, arguing that an employer could rarely demonstrate sufficient "objective considerations" to satisfy the Board. *See, e.g.*, his dissent

the courts have emphasized that "good faith" primarily means that the employer's doubt be "raised in a context free of unfair labor practices."[685] The fundamental support for an employer's "reasonably based doubt" of the union's continued majority status must come from "objective considerations" put forward by the employer.[686] Though not determinative, subjective evidence of intent may be used to bolster the employer's argument that it reasonably doubted the union's continued majority.[687] If the employer does produce sufficient objective considerations to demonstrate that it had a reasonable doubt at the time it refused to bargain, the Board has held that this reasonable doubt is an absolute defense to a Section 8(a)(5) charge, even though the union may have actually possessed majority support at the time the employer withdrew recognition.[688]

Generally, proof that only a minority of the employees have authorized dues checkoffs or are members of the union is insufficient to support a reasonable doubt, since "many employees are content neither to join the union nor to give it financial

---

in Guerdon Indus., Inc., *supra* note 682 at 664. *See also* note 688 *infra* and accompanying text.

[685]Guerdon Indus., Inc., *supra* note 682 at 659, 660; Nu-Southern Dyeing & Finishing, Inc., 179 NLRB 573, 573 n.1, 72 LRRM 1410 (1969), *enforced in part,* 444 F2d 11, 77 LRRM 2425 (CA 4, 1971); NLRB v. Little Rock Downtowner, Inc., 414 F2d 1084, 1091, 72 LRRM 2044 (CA 8, 1969).

[686]Wanda Petroleum, *supra* note 684. In that case, the Board majority stated that " 'good faith' language . . . should be avoided" and that a "reasonably grounded doubt" of the union's majority status "based on objective considerations" should be the standard. Orion Corp., 210 NLRB 633, 86 LRRM 1193 (1974), *aff'd,* 515 F2d 81, 89 LRRM 2135 (CA 7, 1975); Star Mfg. Co. v. NLRB, 536 F2d 1192, 92 LRRM 3179 (CA 7, 1976); NLRB v. Vegas Vic, Inc., 546 F2d 828, 93 LRRM 3087 (CA 9, 1976); J. Ray McDermott & Co. v. NLRB, 571 F2d 850, 98 LRRM 2191 (CA 5, 1978), *cert. denied,* 439 US 893, 99 LRRM 2657 (1978). *See also* Guerdon Indus., Inc., *supra* note 682. Some courts have used the term "serious doubt" instead of "reasonable doubt." *See, e.g.,* Royal Typewriter Co. v. NLRB, 533 F2d 1030, 92 LRRM 2013, 2019 (CA 8, 1976); National Cash Register Co. v. NLRB, 494 F2d 189, 194, 85 LRRM 2657 (CA 8, 1974). The Board has stated, however, that the two terms are equivalent. Bartenders Ass'n of Pocatello, *supra* note 682. *Cf.* Printing Pressmen Local 51 (New York) v. NLRB, 575 F2d 1045, 98 LRRM 2389 (CA 2, 1978), *and* Retired Persons Pharmacy v. NLRB, 519 F2d 486, 89 LRRM 2879 (CA 2, 1975) ("good faith doubt" supported by "clear and convincing evidence").

[687]Pioneer Inn Assocs. v. NLRB, *supra* note 681; NLRB v. Windham Community Memorial Hosp., 577 F2d 805, 99 LRRM 2242 (CA 2, 1978); Orion Corp., *supra* note 686.

[688]Arkay Packaging Corp., 227 NLRB 397, 398, 94 LRRM 1197 (1976), *aff'd sub nom.* Printing Pressmen Local 51 (New York) v. NLRB, *supra* note 686; Automated Business Sys., *supra* note 684; NLRB v. Dayton Motels, Inc., 474 F2d 328, 331-32, 82 LRRM 2651 (CA 6, 1973). Some courts, however, have afforded the employer only a partial defense; once the employer establishes a reasonable and good-faith doubt, the burden shifts back to the General Counsel to prove that the union actually had majority status on the date recognition was withdrawn. If this is shown, the employer will have violated §8(a)(5). *See* Automated Business Sys., *supra* note 684; Orion Corp. v. NLRB, *supra* note 686.

support but to enjoy the benefits of its representation."[689] A pronounced trend of decreasing checkoff authorizations and union membership over a period of time, however, may lend support to an employer's doubt.[690] Other objective factors which may lend weight to an employer's claim of reasonable doubt are (1) the union's failure to police the contract, hold meetings, or elect officers;[691] (2) employee dissatisfaction with the union;[692] (3) a decertification petition filed with the Board,[693] or an informal petition circulated by the employees;[694] (4) the level of union strength in the past;[695] (5) a high rate of employee turnover;[696]

---

[689]Terrell Mach. Co. v. NLRB, *supra* note 681. *See also* NLRB v. Gulfmont Hotel Co., 362 F2d 588, 62 LRRM 2453 (CA 5, 1966); Retired Persons Pharmacy v. NLRB, *supra* note 686; Bartenders Ass'n of Pocatello, *supra* note 682; Triplett Corp., 234 NLRB 985, 97 LRRM 1406 (1978). *But see* Star Mfg. Co. v. NLRB, *supra* note 686.

[690]Peoples Gas Sys., Inc., 214 NLRB 944, 87 LRRM 1430 (1974), *rev'd and remanded sub nom.* Teamsters Local 769 v. NLRB, 532 F2d 1385, 92 LRRM 2077 (CA DC, 1976), *on remand*, 238 NLRB 1008, 99 LRRM 1423 (1978), *enforced in part*, 629 F2d 35, 104 LRRM 2224 (CA DC, 1980). Convair Div. of Gen. Dynamics Corp., 169 NLRB 131, 67 LRRM 1091 (1968).

[691]Arkay Packaging Corp., *supra* note 688; Burns Int'l Security Servs., Inc. v. NLRB, 567 F2d 945, 97 LRRM 2350 (CA 10, 1977), *denying enforcement to* 225 NLRB 271, 92 LRRM 1439 (1976); Star Mfg. Co. v. NLRB, *supra* note 686. *Cf.* United States Gypsum Co., 143 NLRB 1122, 53 LRRM 1454 (1963); Sahara-Tahoe Corp., 229 NLRB 1094, 96 LRRM 1583 (1977), *enforced*, 581 F2d 767, 99 LRRM 2837 (CA 9, 1978), *cert. denied*, 442 US 917, 101 LRRM 2428 (1979). *Cf.*, Mar-Len Cabinets, Inc., 243 NLRB 523, 101 LRRM 1613 (1979). Crossing a picket line does not necessarily indicate dissatisfaction with the union. NLRB v. Top Mfg. Co., 594 F2d 223, 101 LRRM 2081 (CA 9, 1979).

[692]Employee dissatisfaction with the union is generally not deemed indicative of withdrawal of employee support for the union as bargaining representative. *See, e.g.*, Triplett Corp., *supra* note 689; Bartenders Ass'n of Pocatello, *supra* note 682; Retired Persons Pharmacy v. NLRB, *supra* note 686. *But see* Burns Int'l Security Servs., Inc. v. NLRB, *supra* note 691. Dissatisfaction with a union should be distinguished from opposition to continued representation by a union. Crestline Memorial Hosp., 250 NLRB No. 28, 105 LRRM 1045 (1980). The employer, of course, cannot prepare letters for employees' signatures disavowing a union. Martinsburg Concrete Prods. Co., 248 NLRB 1352, 104 LRRM 1058 (1980). *See also* Riverside Produce Co., 242 NLRB 615, 101 LRRM 1371 (1979).

[693]The Board has held that the filing of a decertification or deauthorization petition is not enough by itself to support an employer's reasonable doubt of the union's majority status. *See, e.g.*, King Elec. Mfg. Co., 229 NLRB 615, 96 LRRM 1370 (1977); Allied Indus. Workers Local 289 (Seeburg Corp., Cavalier Div.) v. NLRB, 476 F2d 868, 82 LRRM 2225 (CA DC, 1973); Wabana, Inc., 146 NLRB 1162, 56 LRRM 1036 (1964). The Eighth Circuit, however, holds that a decertification petition justifies an employer's refusal to bargain with a union, provided the union's loss of majority status was not attributable to the employer's own unfair labor practices. Royal Typewriter Co. v. NLRB, *supra* note 686; National Cash Register Co. v. NLRB, *supra* note 686. *See also* Burns Int'l Security Servs., Inc. v. NLRB, *supra* note 691. An informal petition may be given little weight. Sacramento Clinical Laboratory, Inc., 242 NLRB 944, 101 LRRM 1266 (1979). *See also* discussion at notes 631-43 *supra*.

[694]Guerdon Indus., Inc., *supra* note 682; American Express Reservations, Inc., 209 NLRB 1105, 86 LRRM 1362 (1974); NLRB v. Gallaro Bros., 419 F2d 97, 73 LRRM 2043 (CA 2, 1969).

[695]NLRB v. Gallaro Bros., *supra* note 694; Royal Typewriter Co. v. NLRB, *supra* note 686.

[696]The Board takes the position that absent special circumstances, new employees are presumed to support the union in the same ratio as departing employees. Laystrom

(6) a move by the employer to a new location;[697] or (7) a poll of the employees.[698] While any one of these factors may not be sufficient to support a reasonable doubt, a combination of several or all of them may justify such a doubt.[699] Whether "objective considerations" reasonably support an employer's good-faith doubt of a union's majority status is a question of fact.[700] Often, the Board and the courts have disagreed on whether a "reasonable" doubt of a continued union majority exists.[701]

One "objective consideration" which has sparked disagreement between the Board and several circuits is the treatment of permanent replacements hired during an economic strike. In *Windham Community Memorial Hospital*[702] the Board stated that absent any "unique" circumstances, "new employees, including strike replacements, are presumed to support the union in the same ratio as those whom they have replaced."[703] The Fifth and Eighth Circuits have disagreed with the application of this rule

---

Mfg. Co., 151 NLRB 1482, 58 LRRM 1624 (1965), *enforcement denied*, 359 F2d 799, 62 LRRM 2033 (CA 7, 1966). *See also* Eastern Wash. Distrib. Co., *supra* note 683; Harpeth Steel, Inc., 208 NLRB 545, 85 LRRM 1174 (1974). The courts have been more willing than the Board to consider high employee turnover as an objective base for a reasonable doubt of a continuing union majority. *See, e.g.*, Burns Int'l Security Servs., Inc. v. NLRB, *supra* note 691; Star Mfg. Co. v. NLRB, *supra* note 686; Royal Typewriter Co. v. NLRB, *supra* note 686.

[697]NLRB v. Massachusetts Mach. & Stamping, Inc., 578 F2d 15, 98 LRRM 2939 (CA 1, 1978).

[698]Burns Int'l Security Servs., Inc. v. NLRB, *supra* note 691; Eastern Wash. Distrib. Co., *supra* note 683. Any employee poll must conform to the requirements established in Struksnes Constr. Co., 165 NLRB 1062, 65 LRRM 1385 (1967). *See* Chapter 6 *supra* at notes 284-87.

[699]*See, e.g.*, National Cash Register Co. v. NLRB, *supra* note 686; Ingress-Plastene, Inc. v. NLRB, 430 F2d 542, 546-47, 74 LRRM 2658, *modified*, 75 LRRM 2048 (CA 7, 1970); Upper Miss. Towing Corp., 246 NLRB No. 41, 102 LRRM 1536 (1979). *Cf.* Gregory's, Inc., 242 NLRB 644, 101 LRRM 1247 (1979); NLRB v. Alvin J. Bart & Co., 598 F2d 1267, 101 LRRM 2457 (CA 2, 1979).

[700]For two cases which provide excellent detailed discussions of the various factual considerations, *see* NLRB v. Tahoe Nugget, Inc., 584 F2d 293, 99 LRRM 2509 (CA 9, 1978), *cert. denied*, 444 US 887, 101 LRRM 2428 (1979) *and* Pioneer Inn Assocs. v. NLRB, *supra* note 687.

[701]*See, e.g.*, Burns Int'l Security Servs., Inc. v. NLRB, *supra* note 691; National Cash Register Co. v. NLRB, *supra* note 686; Star Mfg. Co. v. NLRB, *supra* note 686; Royal Typewriter Co. v. NLRB, *supra* note 686; NLRB v. Gallaro Bros., *supra* note 694.

[702]230 NLRB 1070, 95 LRRM 1565 (1977), *aff'd*, 577 F2d 805, 99 LRRM 2242 (CA 2, 1978).

[703]*Id.* at 1070. In Arkay Packaging Corp., *supra* note 688, the Board found that abandonment of the bargaining unit by the unions involved constituted a "unique circumstance" and justified a "limited exception" to the rule. *See* discussion of *Arkay Packaging* in *Windham, supra* note 702 at 1070. In Beacon Upholstery Co., 226 NLRB 1360, 94 LRRM 1334 (1976), the permanent replacements hired during an economic strike were not considered supporters of the union. The economic strikers had been discharged for just cause, namely the conversion of company property, and they did not retain their employee status. Since the employment status of the strike replacements depended upon the union's lack of success in the strike, the replacements could not be

to permanent displacements, however.[704] Their rationale is that permanent replacements indicate nonsupport for the union by their act of accepting employment during the strike with the realization that their continued employment depends upon the failure of the strike.[705]

As stated above, the doubt of the continuing majority status of the union must be based on objective and concrete factors, not mere intuition or supposition.[706] Moreover, evidence to support the doubt must relate directly to the bargaining unit. A change in the employer's condition which does not have significant impact on the bargaining unit will not support an employer's doubt of the union's majority status, and a subsequent refusal to bargain will violate the Act. Thus, absent special circumstances, a union is presumed to retain majority status when a successor employer takes over a going business for which the union is the bargaining representative.[707] Likewise, withdrawal from a multi-employer bargaining unit does not negate the presumption of continued union majority status.[708]

---

presumed to support the union in the same ratio as the discharged strikers. *See also* Pennco, Inc., 250 NLRB 716, 104 LRRM 1475 (1980), *supplementing* 242 NLRB 467, 101 LRRM 1195 (1979); Burlington Homes, Inc., 246 NLRB 1029, 103 LRRM 1116 (1979).

[704] NLRB v. Randle-Eastern Ambulance Serv., Inc., 584 F2d 720, 99 LRRM 3377 (CA 5, 1978); National Car Rental Sys. v. NLRB, 594 F2d 1203, 100 LRRM 2824 (CA 8, 1979).

[705] *See also* Peoples Gas Sys., Inc., *supra* note 690, where the Board refused to presume that permanent replacements would support the union in the same ratio as the strikers they had replaced three years before: "[I]t was not unreasonable for Respondent to infer that the degree of union support among these employees who had chosen to ignore a Union-sponsored picket line might well be somewhat weaker than the support offered by those who had vigorously engaged in concerted activity on behalf of Union-sponsored objectives." *See also* S & M Mfg. Co., 172 NLRB 1008, 1008-1009, 68 LRRM 1403 (1968); Titan Metal Mfg. Co., 135 NLRB 196, 49 LRRM 1466 (1962).

[706] J. Ray McDermott & Co. v. NLRB, *supra* note 686; Orion Corp. v. NLRB, *supra* note 687.

[707] *See* NLRB v. Burns Int'l Detective Agency, 406 US 272, 80 LRRM 2225 (1972); Pick-Mt. Laurel Corp. v. NLRB, 625 F2d 476, 104 LRRM 2703 (CA 3, 1980); NLRB v. Pepsi-Cola Bottling Co., 613 F2d 267, 103 LRRM 2233 (CA 10, 1980); NLRB v. Fabsteel Co., 587 F2d 689, 100 LRRM 2349 (CA 5, 1979), *cert. denied*, 442 US 943, 101 LRRM 2556 (1979); NLRB v. Middleboro Fire Apparatus, Inc., 590 F2d 4, 100 LRRM 2182 (CA 1, 1978); M & H Mach. Co., 243 NLRB 817, 102 LRRM 1038 (1979); Barrington Plaza & Tragniew, Inc., 185 NLRB 962, 75 LRRM 1226 (1970), *enforcement denied*, 470 F2d 669, 81 LRRM 2336 (CA 9, 1972). *Cf.* Western Distrib. Co. v. NLRB, 608 F2d 397, 102 LRRM 2510 (CA 10, 1979). For general treatment of the effect of change in the employing unit, *see* Chapter 15 *infra*.

[708] NLRB v. Silver Spur Casino, 623 F2d 571, 104 LRRM 3068 (CA 9, 1980); NLRB v. Roger's I.G.A., Inc., 605 F2d 1164, 103 LRRM 3126 (CA 10, 1980); NLRB v. Sierra Development Co., 604 F2d 606, 102 LRRM 2160 (CA 9, 1979); NLRB v. Carda Hotels, 604 F2d 605, 102 LRRM 2484 (CA 9, 1979); NLRB v. Tahoe Nugget, Inc., *supra* note 700; Sahara-Tahoe Corp. v. NLRB, 581 F2d 767, 99 LRRM 2837 (CA 9, 1978), *cert. denied*, 442 US 917, 101 LRRM 2428 (1979).

VIII. NOTICE TO TERMINATE OR MODIFY THE LABOR AGREEMENT

A. Notice Requirements Generally

Section 8(d), in defining the duty to bargain collectively, includes certain notice requirements which must be satisfied prior to termination or modification of a labor contract. Section 8(d)(1) requires that the party desiring termination or modification of the agreement must serve a written notice upon the other party to the contract of the proposed termination or modification 60 days prior to the expiration date of the agreement, or in the event such contract contains no expiration date, 60 days prior to the time it is proposed to make such termination or modification. Section 8(d)(3) provides that the party desiring to terminate or modify the agreement must notify the Federal Mediation and Conciliation Service (FMCS) within 30 days "after such notice of the existence of a dispute"[709] and must simultaneously notify any state or territorial agency established to mediate and conciliate disputes within the state or territory where the dispute occurred, provided no agreement has been reached by that time.[710] Section 8(d)(4) provides that the parties to the labor contract are precluded from striking or locking out for a period of 60 days (a) after the Section 8(d)(1) notice is given or (b) after the expiration date of the contract, whichever occurs later.[711]

In analyzing the interrelationship of these subsections the Board has held that failure to give the required 30-day notice to federal and state agencies under Section 8(d)(3) bars a strike or lockout. It has also held that where a union's Section 8(d)(3) notice to the FMCS is untimely filed, the parties are barred from striking or locking out until 30 days after the untimely notice is filed. In *Peoria Chapter, Painting & Decorating Contractors,*[712] the union had notified the multi-employer association more than 60 days prior to the April 30, 1972, expiration date of the labor agreement that it wished to renegotiate the agreement. How-

[709]Amax Coal Co. v. NLRB, 614 F2d 872, 103 LRRM 2482 (CA 3, 1980) (failure to provide written notice to FMCS violative of §8(b)(3), despite FMCS actual knowledge of dispute). See Chapter 21 *infra* at notes 141-46.
[710]Wilhow Corp., 240 NLRB 1109, 100 LRRM 1384 (1979) (failure to provide state agency with notice required under §8(d)(3) held violative of §8(b)(3)).
[711]*See also* discussion *infra* at notes 774-84.
[712]204 NLRB 345, 83 LRRM 1367 (1973), *enforcement denied,* 500 F2d 54, 86 LRRM 2914 (CA 7, 1974).

ever, the union did not file the Section 8(d)(3) notice with the FMCS and the appropriate state agency until April 11, 1972. Relying on the union's representation that it had filed a timely Section 8(d)(3) notice, on May 1 the association locked out the unit employees. The Board held that the lockout violated Section 8(a)(5). The Board acknowledged that under Section 8(d) the union, as the party initially desiring to modify the contract, was obligated to give the 30-day notice to federal and state mediation services. However, the Board, relied on a 1959 D.C. Circuit decision[713] for the proposition that Sections 8(d)(3) and (4) require a 30-day period between untimely notification to mediation services and a strike or lockout by the party required to give the notice. The Board held that the party not obligated to give notice under Section 8(d)(3) must also observe a 30-day moratorium following the initiating party's untimely Section 8(d)(3) notification before calling a strike or lockout. This was so, the Board said, even when the total elapsed time following receipt of notification of the initiating party's intent to modify or terminate the contract exceeds 60 days. The Seventh Circuit disagreed. In that court's view "once the non-initiating party has observed its duty to bargain collectively during the sixty-day period . . . it has fulfilled its duty under §8(d)(3) whether or not the initiating party has met its obligation under §8(d)(3) to notify state and federal mediators."[714]

In *Hooker Chemicals & Plastics Corp.*[715] the Board continued to adhere to its position that if the Section 8(d)(3) notice to the FMCS is filed late, the 60-day no-strike/no-lockout period provided by Section 8(d)(4) is extended until the 30 days of mediation contemplated by Section 8(d)(3) can take place. The Board observed that the noncontracting party may easily determine whether the initiating party has timely filed Section 8(d)(3) notices and, if it has not, can file its own notices.

---

[713]Retail Clerks Local 219 (Carroll House of Belleville, Inc.) v. NLRB, 265 F2d 814, 43 LRRM 2726 (CA DC, 1959).

[714]500 F2d at 58. The court rejected any implication that Retail Clerks Local 219 v. NLRB, *supra* note 713, extended the noninitiating party's duty to bargaining collectively beyond the 60-day "cooling off" period commencing with notice to the noninitiating party. In the *Retail Clerks* case, the D.C. Circuit had held that the initiating party (there the union) had violated §8(d)(4) by calling a strike 10 days subsequent to the giving of untimely notice to the federal and state mediators, although the strike occurred after the 60-day waiting period had passed.

[715]224 NLRB 1535, 92 LRRM 1419 (1976), *enforcement denied*, 573 F2d 965, 97 LRRM 3194 (CA 7, 1978).

In addition to the statutory notice requirements of Section 8(d), many labor agreements contain automatic renewal provisions whereby the agreement is automatically renewed (usually from year to year) unless one of the parties gives notice (usually more than 60 days) prior to the contract expiration date of its intent to renegotiate a new agreement. The language used in automatic renewal clauses varies. Whether the notice sent to the other party prevents automatic renewal will depend on the specific language used in the contract as well as the language used in the notice. Thus, the Sixth Circuit held that the term of an existing collective bargaining agreement did not expire when the union gave notice of modification, rather than notice of termination.[716] The court stated that the employer must receive clear and explicit notice of termination for the union to be relieved of its contractual obligations under the existing collective bargaining agreement.

The Board does not follow the Sixth Circuit's view. It finds a violation of Section 8(a)(5) where an employer refuses to negotiate a new contract on the ground that the prior contract was automatically renewed because the union's letter indicated a desire to modify rather than terminate the old contract.[717]

Where the Board finds that the union failed to comply with the 60-day notice provision of the contract for reopening, participation by the employer in a negotiation meeting with the union does not necessarily constitute a waiver of the contract-reopening requirement. In one case the Board found there was no waiver where the employer raised the issue of timeliness at the meeting and, in addition, asked the Board's regional office for an opinion on the question.[718]

The courts and the Board have shown some flexibility in their interpretation of automatic renewal provisions. Typically, a collective agreement requires that written notice of termination or

---

[716]Office Employees Local 42 v. Automobile Workers Local 174, 523 F2d 783, 90 LRRM 3121 (CA 6, 1975). *Cf.* Kaufman & Broad Home Sys., 607 F2d 1104, 102 LRRM 3033 (CA 5, 1979) (notice to modify prevents automatic extension of agreement). *But see* Oakland Press Co. v. NLRB, 606 F2d 689, 102 LRRM 2537 (CA 6, 1979) (notice to modify sufficient to comply with contractual requirement of notice to terminate).

[717]Associated Gen. Contractors, 190 NLRB 383, 77 LRRM 1210 (1971). *See also* KCW Furniture Co., 247 NLRB No. 79, 103 LRRM 1194 (1980) (especially if contract clause distinguishes between notice to modify and notice to terminate). *See also* Oakland Press Co. v. NLRB, *supra* note 716.

[718]Sawyer Stores, Inc., 190 NLRB 651, 77 LRRM 1434 (1971).

modification be given 60 days prior to the expiration date. In one case,[719] although the employer mailed its notice 61 days prior to contract expiration, it was not actually received by the union until 58 days prior to the expiration date. The district court, relying on the Board's decision in *United Electronics Institute*,[720] held that because the notice was delayed by conditions beyond the control of the sender (delay in mails), the expiration notice was effective to prevent automatic renewal of the contract.

In another case the Board held that timely oral notice to the employer of the union's desire to change the terms of the contract sufficed to forestall automatic renewal; accordingly, the employer's subsequent refusal to negotiate violated Section 8(a)(5).[721] The Board pointed out[722] that in the absence of a strike or lockout, this issue was purely a contractual matter and the statutory provisions of Section 8(d) had no application.

B. Notice Requirements in the Health Care Industry[723]

The National Labor Relations Act was amended in 1974 to cover employees of nonprofit hospitals.[724] The amendments established special procedures for handling labor disputes at "health care institutions." These included special time periods for filing "Section 8(d)" notices and also added a new notice requirement before health care employees would be free to strike or picket.[725]

Section 8(d)(A) requires that the party desiring to terminate or modify a bargaining agreement in the health care industry serve written notice of such intent on the other party at least 90 days before the expiration of the agreement, and give notice to the FMCS 60 days prior to the agreement's expiration date. Section 8(d)(B) specifies that in the case of initial contract nego-

---

[719]Borman Inv. Co. v. Laundry Workers Local 93, 97 LRRM 2309 (WD Mo, 1977). *See also* Louisville Plate Glass Co., 243 NLRB No. 182, 102 LRRM 1108 (1979).
[720]222 NLRB 814, 91 LRRM 1271 (1976).
[721]Jet Line Prods., Inc., 229 NLRB 322, 95 LRRM 1075 (1977).
[722]*Citing* United States Gypsum Co., 90 NLRB 964, 26 LRRM 1306 (1950).
[723]*See generally* Veron, *Labor Relations in the Health Care Field Under the 1974 Amendments to the National Labor Relations Act: An Overview and Analysis*, 70 Nw. L. Rev. 202 (1975); Feheley, *Amendments to the National Labor Relations Act: Health Care in Institutions*, 36 OHIO ST. L. J. 235 (1975).
[724]*See* Chapter 5 *supra.*
[725]*See* Chapter 21 *infra* at notes 50-53. *See also* Chapter 10, note 186.

tiations "at least 30 days' notice of the existence of a dispute" must be given to the FMCS and any state agency. Upon receiving such notice, the FMCS is required to contact the parties in an effort to achieve a settlement through mediation and conciliation.

In *Affiliated Hospital of San Francisco* v. *Searce*[726] a union representing health care employees notified the FMCS more than a month before it was required to do so under the statute. The FMCS did not, however, appoint a board of inquiry until 30 days after the last day the union could lawfully have filed its statutory notice. The district court held that the law requires that the board of inquiry be established within 30 days after notice to the FMCS is given, not 30 days after the last day the notice could have been given. The Ninth Circuit affirmed.[727]

If the parties fail to settle the dispute, the employees are not necessarily free to strike. Pursuant to Section 8(g), a union is required to give the health care institution a 10-day notice of its intent to strike or picket.

In *NLRB* v. *Electrical Workers Local No. 388 (IBEW) (Hoffman Co.)*[728] the Seventh Circuit construed the Section 8(g) 10-day notice requirement as applying only to unions directing concerted activity at the health care institution itself on behalf of employees of the institution. Thus, the court ruled, the Board was not warranted in finding that a union violated Section 8(g) when it picketed an electrical construction contractor on the premises of a hospital without first giving 10-days notice of intent to picket.

Relying on the *Hoffman* decision, the D.C. Circuit, in *Laborers Local 1057 (Mercy Hospital of Laredo)* v. *NLRB*,[729] refused to enforce a Board order, based on Section 8(g), against otherwise lawful reserved gate picketing by unions representing nonhealth care employees involved in the renovation of hospital facilities. The court held that Congress had arrived at a fair balance in limiting

---

[726]418 F Supp 711, 83 LRRM 2307 (DC Cal, 1976), *aff'd*, 583 F2d 1097, 99 LRRM 3197 (CA 9, 1978).
[727]The Fourth Circuit also holds that the language of the Act is clear in requiring the FMCS to act within 30 days after receiving notice and that nothing in the legislative history points to a contrary interpretation. Sinai Hosp. v. Searce, 561 F2d 547, 96 LRRM 2355 (CA 4, 1977).
[728]548 F2d 704, 94 LRRM 2536 (CA 7, 1977).
[729]567 F2d 1006, 96 LRRM 3160 (CA DC, 1977).

the Section 8(g) notice requirements to the employees of health care institutions to whom the Act's coverage was then being extended, and did not intend to restrict the rights already possessed by other employees.[730]

The Board has interpreted the Section 8(g) notice requirements on numerous occasions. For example, it held that the Section 8(g) 10-day notice requirement had no application to two health care employees who had engaged in a concerted work stoppage,[731] nor to a threatened, as contrasted with an actual, strike action against a health care institution.[732] The Board, however, held that a union demonstration with informational picket signs was a violation of Section 8(g), even though no work stoppage was sought by the union and no disruption occurred.[733]

IX. COALITION OR COORDINATED BARGAINING[734]

An important development attributable in some degree to the successful "divide and conquer" tactics used by some employers to gain bargaining leverage in labor negotiations is the increased use by unions of "coalition" or "coordinated" bargaining.[735] The terms "coalition" or "coordinated" bargaining are often used interchangeably, although there is a logical difference between the terms which corresponds to the intent and nature of the mutual bargaining activity. "Coordinated" bargaining connotes communication and accommodation among different bargaining agents but independent decision making in separate bargaining processes. Such activity is therefore not illegal as such. "Coalition" bargaining, on the other hand, implies a de facto merger of bargaining units, or an effort to achieve that end. Thus, to the extent such a merger is forced on a nonconsenting

---

[730]See also Beck Co., 246 NLRB No. 148, 103 LRRM 1002 (1979).

[731]Walker Methodist Residence, 227 NLRB 1630, 94 LRRM 1516 (1977); Leisure Lodge Nursing Home, 250 NLRB No. 134, 105 LRRM 1115 (1980); Villa Care, Inc., 249 NLRB 705, 104 LRRM 1275 (1980); Montefiore Hosp. & Medical Center v. NLRB, 621 F2d 510, 104 LRRM 2160 (CA 2, 1980).

[732]District 1199-E, Retail, Wholesale & Dep't Store Union (Greater Pa. Ave. Nursing Center, Inc.), 227 NLRB 132, 94 LRRM 1083 (1976).

[733]District 1199, Retail, Wholesale & Dep't Store Union (United Hosps. of Newark), 232 NLRB 443, 96 LRRM 1404 (1977).

[734]See generally Engle, Coordinated Bargaining: A Snare and a Delusion, 19 LABOR L. J. 512 (August, 1968); Goldberg, Coordinated Bargaining Tactics of Unions, 54 CORNELL L. REV. 897 (1969).

[735]See General Elec. v. NLRB, 173 NLRB 253, 69 LRRM 1305 (1968), enforced, 412 F2d 512, 71 LRRM 2418 (CA 2, 1969). See also Chapter 11 supra, note 365.

bargaining partner, a refusal to bargain, by virtue of insistence on a nonmandatory bargaining subject, results. Notwithstanding the semantic difference between the terms, popular usage has tended to blur the distinctions and to treat the terms as interchangeable.

The terms "coordinated" and "coalition" bargaining may refer to the inclusion in a bargaining committee of individuals who are not members of or connected directly with the bargaining unit. These individuals may be members of other unions with which the employer has other contractual relations.[736] They may also be members of different locals of the same parent union with whom the employer has separate agreements.[737] Such bargaining offers the participating unions the advantage of a united front, more or less, in contract negotiations.

The concept of coordinated or coalition bargaining first gained attention in 1966 when the International Union of Electrical Workers (IUE) formed a coalition with seven other members of the AFL-CIO Industrial Union Department.[738] Their avowed purpose was to evolve national goals and to adopt a "coordinated approach" to negotiations with the General Electric Company (GE). The facts in the resulting case, *McLeod v. General Electric Co.,*[739] were the following: GE representatives walked out of a meeting with the coalition committee, contending that representatives of the seven other unions who were present were not properly a part of the negotiating committee. Both IUE and GE filed unfair labor practice charges. The General Counsel found merit in the union's Section 8(a)(5) refusal-to-bargain charge against GE, but dismissed GE's Section 8(b)(1)(A) charge that IUE had violated its bargaining duty by insisting that GE deal with the coalition.[740]

---

[736]*Id. See* Minnesota Mining & Mfg. Co. v. NLRB, 173 NLRB 275, 69 LRRM 1313, *enforced,* 415 F2d 174, 72 LRRM 2129 (CA 8, 1969); American Radiator & Standard Sanitary Corp., 155 NLRB 736, 60 LRRM 1385 (1965), *enforcement denied,* 381 F2d 632, 65 LRRM 3071 (CA 6, 1967).

[737]Standard Oil Co. of Ohio, 137 NLRB 690, 50 LRRM 1238 (1962), *enforced,* 322 F2d 40, 54 LRRM 2076 (CA 6, 1963).

[738]A similar coalition was formed prior to the 1960 contract negotiations. *See* Cooper, *Boulwarism and the Duty to Bargain in Good Faith,* 20 RUTGERS L. REV. 653 at 666 n.41 (1960).

[739]McLeod v. General Elec. Co., 257 F Supp 690, 62 LRRM 2809 (SD NY, 1966), *rev'd,* 366 F2d 847, 63 LRRM 2065 (CA 2, 1966), *remanded,* 385 US 533, 64 LRRM 2129 (1967).

[740]The regional director had obtained a temporary injunction from a federal district court under §10(j) restraining the company from refusing to bargain collectively with

The Board found GE guilty of refusing to bargain because its negotiators had walked out of the meeting with the coordinated bargaining committee and had refused to deal with "outsiders."[741] The Second Circuit upheld the Board's order.[742] Addressing itself to the basic issue, "whether a union's inclusion of members of other unions on its bargaining committee justifies an employer's refusal to bargain," the court declared that the "right of employees and the corresponding right of employers . . . to choose whomever they wish to represent them in formal labor negotiations is fundamental to the statutory scheme."[743] Although it recognized that the freedom to select representatives was not absolute,[744] the court noted that the infrequency of approved exceptions emphasized the importance of the rule. The court therefore held that for the employer to prevail in its objections to outsider members of the union negotiating committee, it must sustain the burden of showing a " 'clear and present' danger to the collective bargaining process."[745] Finding no such "clear and present danger," the court held that GE was not lawfully entitled to refuse to bargain with the multi-union committee, so long as the committee sought to bargain solely on behalf of the employees who would be covered under the contract being negotiated.

Even prior to the *General Electric* case the Board had declared that an employer could not in good faith refuse to bargain with

---

the IUE negotiating committee. That court ruled that the company's failure to bargain "could not be justified by the conjectural claim that the IUE team was ineluctably bent on 'multi-union bargaining.' " 257 F Supp at 706. The Second Circuit reversed and vacated the injunction without passing on the merits, holding that "[t]he Board has not demonstrated that an injunction is necessary to preserve the status quo or to prevent any irreparable harm." 366 F2d at 850. The Supreme Court granted a stay of the Second Circuit's judgment pending certiorari proceedings, but on certiorari the Court in a *per curiam* opinion dissolved the stay and set aside the judgment with directions to remand to the district court since the employer and IUE had agreed upon a new collective bargaining contract.

[741]General Elec. Co., *supra* note 735 at 256.
[742]*Id.*, 412 F2d at 512.
[743]*Id.* at 516. *See* Prudential Ins. Co. of Am. v. NLRB, 278 F2d 181, 46 LRRM 2026 (CA 3, 1960); NLRB v. Deena Artware, Inc., 198 F2d 645, 30 LRRM 2479 (CA 5, 1952), *cert. denied*, 345 US 906, 31 LRRM 2444 (1953); Pueblo Gas & Fuel Co. v. NLRB, 118 F2d 304, 8 LRRM 902 (CA 10, 1941); Oliver Corp., 74 NLRB 483, 20 LRRM 1183 (1947).
[744]412 F2d at 517, citing, as exceptions to the general rule: NLRB v. Garment Workers (Slate Belt Apparel Contractors' Ass'n), 274 F2d 376, 45 LRRM 2626 (CA 3, 1960) ("ex-union official added to employer committee to 'put one over on the union' "); Bausch & Lomb Optical Co., 108 NLRB 1555, 34 LRRM 1222 (1954) ("union established company in direct competition with employer"); NLRB v. Kentucky Utils. Co., 182 F2d 810, 26 LRRM 2287 (CA 6, 1950) ("union negotiator had expressed great personal animosity towards employer").
[745]*Supra* note 735, 412 F2d at 517.

a union negotiating committee merely because other unions were represented on the committee. In *American Radiator & Standard Sanitary Corp.*[746] the employer was requested by all the unions representing employees at its various plants to bargain jointly. However, the employer declined to meet "with a group not legally certified as the collective bargaining representative."[747] As in *General Electric*, the employer contended that the unions had coalesced for the purpose of compelling company-wide bargaining. Relying on the Board's earlier *Standard Oil Co. of Ohio*[748] decision, enforced by the Sixth Circuit, the Board found that the employer was not relieved of the duty to meet with the duly appointed union committee, even though other unions had members on the committee, since the composition of the committee was an internal union matter over which the company has no control.

Standard Oil,[749] which involved coordinated bargaining by different locals of the same parent union, was relied upon by the courts in both the *American Radiator* and *General Electric* decisions. The Sixth Circuit's decision in *Standard Oil* confirmed that the presence on the local's bargaining committee of non-local-union members, designated "temporary representatives," did not justify the company's refusal to bargain.[750]

The Board and the courts have consistently followed the rule enunciated in the *Standard Oil*, *American Radiator*, and *General Electric* cases, regardless of whether the non-local-union committee member was a representative of a labor organization which had a contractual relationship with the employer.[751] How-

---

[746]155 NLRB 736, 60 LRRM 1385 (1965), *enforcement denied*, 381 F2d 632, 65 LRRM 3071 (CA 6, 1967) (the court agreed with the Board as to the right of the union to have outsiders present on its negotiating committee, but disagreed as to whether the employer had refused to bargain with the committee).

[747]*Id.* at 739.

[748]137 NLRB 690, 50 LRRM 1238 (1962), *enforced*, 322 F2d 40, 54 LRRM 2076 (CA 6, 1963).

[749]*Id.*

[750]"Absent any finding of bad faith or ulterior motive on the part of the Unions we conclude that it was the duty of the Company to negotiate with the bargaining committees of the Unions at the respective refinery plants even though the temporary representatives were present." 322 F2d at 44. *See also* Minnesota Mining & Mfg. Co. v. NLRB, 415 F2d 174, 72 LRRM 2129 (CA 8, 1969); Independent Drugstore Owners of Santa Clara County, 170 NLRB 1699, 69 LRRM 1031 (1968). For discussion of altering bargaining units as permissive subjects of bargaining, *see* Chapter 18 *infra* at notes 18-41.

[751]AMF, Inc., 219 NLRB 903, 90 LRRM 1271 (1975); Harley-Davidson Motor Co., 214 NLRB 433, 87 LRRM 1571 (1974); Roscoe Skipper, Inc., 106 NLRB 1238, 32 LRRM 1658 (1953), *enforced*, 213 F2d 793, 34 LRRM 2315 (CA 5, 1954); Independent Drugstore Owners of Santa Clara County, *supra* note 750.

ever, it was acknowledged even in *General Electric* that a conflict of interest could arise so as to make good-faith bargaining impractical.[752]

An example of such a conflict of interest did occur in *CBS, Inc.*, where the employer (CBS) refused to bargain with a negotiating committee that included a representative of the National Association of Broadcast Engineers and Technicians (NABET).[753] NABET had no contracts with CBS nor did it represent any employees of CBS, but it did represent employees of competitors of CBS. Since CBS planned to reveal confidential trade secrets during negotiations, it contended that the presence of NABET personnel constituted a clear and present danger to the collective bargaining process because CBS would not be able to reveal its confidential business plans under such circumstances. The Board dismissed the refusal-to-bargain charge, and the Second Circuit affirmed. The court concluded that this was a unique situation that justified an exception to the rule that employees are free to choose their own bargaining representatives.[754]

Employer opposition to coordinated or coalition bargaining has focused primarily upon the possible obliteration of "unit" determinations, particularly where separately certified unions represent distinct segments of the company's employees at various locations. A considerable burden falls upon the employer asserting such a position.[755] Employers have argued that this type of bargaining might permit a union to act as bargaining agent for a group of employees for which another union had been certified.[756] Despite a general willingness to provide employees with wide latitude in the choice of their bargaining representative, the Board and the courts have disapproved of coalition bargaining where the integrity of a certified unit would be improperly undermined. Thus, the District of Columbia Circuit upheld a Board decision that a company could legitimately

---

[752]General Elec., *supra* note 735.
[753]CBS, Inc., 226 NLRB 537, 93 LRRM 1378 (1976), *enforced,* 557 F2d 995, 95 LRRM 2996 (CA 2, 1977).
[754]*Id.* at 1000.
[755]Indiana & Mich. Elec. Co., 235 NLRB 1128, 98 LRRM 1036 (1978), *enforced,* 599 F2d 185, 101 LRRM 2470 (CA 7, 1979), *cert. denied,* 444 US 1014, 103 LRRM 2143 (1980).
[756]*See* Benetar, *Coalition Bargaining Under the NLRA,* NYU TWENTIETH ANNUAL CONFERENCE ON LABOR 219 (1968); Abramson, *Coordinated Bargaining by Unions, id.* at 231, where arguments both for and against coalition bargaining are advanced.

refuse to meet and bargain at a single time and place on the subject of pension plan benefits for 19 separate units with a union that purported to represent all 19 units.[757] That refusal was not deemed to be bad faith, even though the employer's pension plans were identical in all 19 units, because the union's demand was viewed as an attempt to consolidate the individual groups of employees without following proper Board procedures. Because bargaining-unit modifications are not mandatory bargaining subjects, the Board's decision explained:

> It is well settled that the parties to a collective-bargaining relationship may voluntarily agree—subject to any later determination of appropriateness under Section 9(b) of the Act—to the enlargement or alteration of an existing unit, or to the merger of separate units, theretofore recognized by the parties or found by the Board to be appropriate for the purposes of collective bargaining. But, in the absence of an agreement, neither party may attempt to force upon the other an enlargement, alteration or merger of an established unit or units.[758]

Similarly, the Board held that a union violated Section 8(b)(3) by insisting that identical offers be made to several bargaining units and by conditioning acceptance of an offer in any single unit upon submission of identical offers to all units.[759] In another case, however, the Fourth Circuit agreed with the Board that a union did not violate Section 8(b)(3) when it used "pooled voting procedures" with two other locals in rejecting an employer's wage offer. Since the sole purpose of pooling was to maintain common expiration dates, the integrity of the individual units was deemed to be preserved.[760] On the other hand, while "group voting, insistence on parallel contract terms for the same or commensurate job classifications, and conditional acceptance of contract proposals do not in themselves constitute illegitimate labor tactics," such tactics "can in context become part of an illegal overall pattern of conduct."[761]

---

[757]Oil Workers v. NLRB (Shell Oil Co.), 486 F2d 1266, 84 LRRM 2581 (CA DC, 1973), *denying petition for review of* 194 NLRB 988, 79 LRRM 1130 (1972).

[758]*Id.,* at 995. *But compare* AFL-CIO Joint Negotiating Comm. (Phelps Dodge Corp.) v. NLRB, 459 F2d 374, 79 LRRM 2939 (CA 3, 1972), *cert. denied,* 409 US 1059, 81 LRRM 2893 (1972), discussed in Chapter 18 *infra* at notes 29-31.

[759]Utility Workers (Ohio Power Co.), 203 NLRB 230, 83 LRRM 1099 (1973), *enforced,* 490 F2d 1383, 85 LRRM 2944 (CA 6, 1974).

[760]Lynchburg Foundry Co. v. NLRB, 80 LRRM 2415 (CA 4, 1972), *denying petition for review of* 192 NLRB 773, 78 LRRM 1021 (1971). *Cf.* Continental Nut Co., 195 NLRB 841, 79 LRRM 1575 (1972), where a union was found to have engaged in "Boulwarism."

[761]Frito-Lay, Inc. v. Teamsters Local 137, 623 F2d 1354, 104 LRRM 2931 (CA 9, 1980).

X. BARGAINING DURING THE TERM OF AN EXISTING AGREEMENT[762]

The obligation to bargain collectively is not limited to the negotiation of an agreement. In some instances bargaining can and must be carried on during the term of an existing agreement. In the words of the Supreme Court: "Collective bargaining is a continuing process involving among other things day-to-day adjustments in the contract and working rules, resolution of problems not covered by existing agreements, and protection of rights already secured by contract."[763] The continuing nature of the duty to bargain during the life of a contract was recognized in the early cases of *NLRB* v. *Sands Manufacturing Co.*[764] and *NLRB* v. *Highland Park Manufacturing Co.*[765] The Court in *Highland Park* articulated the concept that the bargaining agreement provides the "framework" within which the process of collective bargaining may be carried. Following *Highland Park,* the Sixth Circuit in *Timken Roller Bearing Co.* v. *NLRB,*[766] ruled that an employer could insist that grievances, including disputes over interpretation of the contract, must be resolved through the contractual grievance and arbitration machinery.

In *NLRB* v. *Jacobs Manufacturing Co.*[767] the Second Circuit elaborated on the scope of matters open to negotiation during the term of an existing agreement. The court held that notwith-

---

[762]*See* discussion of waiver, *supra* at notes 572-643. *See generally* Cox & Dunlop, *The Duty to Bargain Collectively During the Term of an Existing Agreement,* 63 HARV. L. REV. 1097 (1950); Seagle, *Duty of Employer to Bargain in Post-Contract Negotiations,* 51 CORNELL L. Q. 523 (1966).

[763]Conley v. Gibson, 355 US 41, 46, 41 LRRM 2089 (1957). *Accord,* NLRB v. Acme Indus. Co., 385 US 432, 64 LRRM 2069 (1967).

[764]306 US 332, 4 LRRM 530 (1939) ("the Act imposes upon the employer the further obligation to meet and bargain with his employees' representatives respecting proposed changes of an existing contract and also to discuss with them its true interpretation . . . ." *Id.* at 532). The same idea was expressed in regard to bargaining under the Railway Labor Act in Rutland Ry. Corp. v. Locomotive Eng'rs, 307 F2d 21, 50 LRRM 2535 (CA 2, 1962) ("clarification through collective bargaining of ambiguous contractual provisions is a most laudable purpose and should be encouraged rather than hampered by the Courts." *Id.* at 45 (dissenting opinion)).

[765]110 F2d 632, 6 LRRM 786 (CA 4, 1940) ("the mere fact that the collective bargaining agreement provides a framework within which the process of collective bargaining may be carried on is of incalculable value in removing the causes of industrial strife." *Id.* at 638).

[766]161 F2d 949, 20 LRRM 2204 (CA 6, 1947). *Accord,* NLRB v. Knight Morley Corp., 251 F2d 753, 41 LRRM 2242 (CA 6, 1957), *cert. denied,* 357 US 927, 42 LRRM 2307 (1958). *Cf.* Long Lake Lumber Co., 160 NLRB 1475, 63 LRRM 1160 (1966). *But see* discussion of *C & C Plywood, supra* note 601.

[767]*Supra* note 572; *see also* NLRB v. Lion Oil Co., 352 US 282, 39 LRRM 2296 (1957).

standing the language in Section 8(d) of the Act,[768] an employer is not relieved of the duty to bargain "as to subjects which were neither discussed nor embodied in any of the terms and conditions of the contract."[769] The court's decision was premised upon the general purpose of the Act to encourage peaceful resolution of industrial disputes through collective bargaining. The court left open, however, the effect on the duty to bargain, if any, of previous discussions where there was no inclusion of any terms or provisions on the matter in the contract. Some cases have indicated that such previous discussion forecloses later bargaining on the subject,[770] while others have been reluc-

---

[768]The exception provides that the duty to bargain collectively "shall not be construed as requiring either party to discuss or agree to any modification of the terms and conditions contained in a contract for a fixed period, if such modification is to become effective before such terms and conditions can be reopened under the provisions of the contract." Thus, a party may not change terms and conditions of employment governed by contract provisions during the term of the contract, absent consent of the other party. C & S Indus., Inc., 158 NLRB 454, 62 LRRM 1043 (1966). The Board has held the unilateral withdrawal of bargaining unit work during the term of a collective bargaining agreement to be proscribed by §8(d). Park-Ohio Indus., 257 NLRB No. 44, 107 LRRM 1498 (1981).

[769]Supra note 572 at 684. The union invoked a contractual wage reopener midway into the contract term. It also requested that the employer take over the entire cost of an existing group insurance plan and establish a pension plan. The employer declined to discuss anything other than wages. When the original contract was negotiated, the union had made similar proposals with respect to the insurance plan but the employer had rejected them. Instead, the parties at that time agreed to certain changes in the cost and benefits of the plan. Neither the changes nor the insurance plan itself were mentioned in the contract, and the parties had never discussed the establishment of a pension plan. In a two-to-one opinion, the Board found the refusal to discuss a pension plan a violation of §8(a)(5). On the basis of §8(d), however, no violation was found as to the refusal to discuss the insurance plan.

Members Houston and Styles, who were in the majority as to pensions but in dissent on the insurance plan, contended that for purposes of §8(d) a matter is "contained in" a contract if it has been "integrated and embodied into a writing." 94 NLRB at 1217. Since neither insurance nor pensions were mentioned in the contract, those members would have required bargaining on both. Chairman Herzog, whose vote was decisive on both issues, concluded that since pensions were neither "consciously explored" in negotiations nor embodied in the contract, bargaining was required. With regard to the insurance plan, however, Member Herzog was of the view that "rejection of the union's basic proposal, coupled in this particular instance with enhancement of the substantive benefits, constituted a part of the contemporaneous 'bargain' which the parties made when they negotiated the entire . . . contract." Id. at 1228. The Second Circuit enforced the Board order as to the pension plan because pensions were "neither discussed nor embodied" in the contract. 196 F2d 680, 684 (CA 2, 1952). The Board's decision with respect to the insurance plan was not appealed.

[770]Timken Roller Bearing Co. v. NLRB, 325 F2d 746, 54 LRRM 2785 (CA 6, 1963) (if a right or benefit for which the union desires to bargain during the term of an existing agreement is one that could be acquired only by virtue of a bargaining agreement, and the proposal for such benefit was pressed and rejected during bargaining, the failure to include such right or benefit necessarily results in failure to acquire it); United States Steel Corp. v. Nicholas, 229 F2d 396, 37 LRRM 2420 (CA 6), cert. denied, 351 US 950, 38 LRRM 2159 (1956) (if an existing policy of the employer is bargained over in negotiations and the contract is silent on a subject because of no agreement, the topic was not inadvertently overlooked but was intentionally omitted from the contract for its term).

tant to hold that one party loses a right merely by talking it over with the other.[771]

The employer may be relieved of the duty to bargain as to subjects which were neither discussed nor embodied in any of the terms and conditions of the contract if the parties to the agreement stipulate that they have resolved all proper subjects of bargaining for the duration of the contract—a "zipper" stipulation. For example, in *American League of Professional Baseball Clubs*,[772] an advisory opinion, the General Counsel concluded that the major league baseball clubs did not violate Section 8(a)(5) when they refused to bargain with the Umpires Association in light of the following "zipper" clause contained in the existing agreement:

> The parties agree that they have bargained fully with respect to all proper subjects of collective bargaining and have settled all such matters as set forth in this agreement.

Some of the subjects of bargaining in question were covered by the current contract, some had been discussed during negotiations but not agreed upon, and others had not been discussed at all during negotiations. The General Counsel concluded that the phrase "all proper subjects of collective bargaining" was intended by the parties to refer to all subjects covered by Section 8(d) of the Act. This zipper clause, therefore, encompassed all categories in question. But a zipper clause may be ineffective in certain other circumstances.[773]

Closely related to the *Jacobs Manufacturing* decision are two Supreme Court cases interpreting the modification, notification, and termination provisions of Section 8(d).[774] In *Mastro Plastics Corp. v. NLRB*[775] the Court held that the Section 8(d) time requirements apply only to economic strikes, not to strikes in protest of employer unfair labor practices. Since the purpose of an unfair labor practice strike is "not to terminate or modify the contract, but [is] designed instead to protest"[776] an employer's

---

[771]*See supra* at notes 585-91.
[772]Case No. 4-CA-9586, 99 LRRM 1724 (1978).
[773]ACF Indus. v. NLRB, 592 F2d 422, 100 LRRM 2710 (CA 8, 1979); Arizona Pub. Serv. Co., 247 NLRB No. 54, 103 LRRM 1154 (1980); Pepsi-Cola Distrib. Co., 241 NLRB 869, 100 LRRM 1626 (1979); GTE Automatic Elec., Inc., 240 NLRB 297, 100 LRRM 1204 (1979). *See generally* discussion at notes 585-91 *supra*.
[774]*See* notes 709-33 *supra* and accompanying text.
[775]350 US 270, 37 LRRM 2587 (1956). *See* Chapter 21 *infra* at notes 150-51.
[776]*Id.* at 286.

activities, the loss-of-status provisions[777] as well as the Section 8(d)(4) prohibition are inapplicable.[778] In *NLRB* v. *Lion Oil Co.*[779] the question was posed whether under a contract providing for negotiation and modification at an intermediate date during its term, the union could strike in support of modification demands after the 60-day notice period had elapsed, but prior to the terminal date of the contract. The Supreme Court noted that Congress had recognized a duty to bargain over modifications, and the contract itself contemplated such bargaining. With reasoning similar to that in the *Jacobs* case, the Court said that it would be "anomalous" for Congress to recognize such a duty and at the same time deprive the union of the strike or strike threat.[780] The Court also held that Congress meant "expiration date" to encompass both the final terminal date of the contract and any intermediate dates provided for reopening of terms of the contract.[781]

In *Local 9735, Mine Workers* v. *NLRB*[782] and *Cheney California Lumber Co.* v. *NLRB*[783] the D.C. Circuit and the Ninth Circuit expanded upon *Lion Oil* along the line of the *Jacobs Manufacturing* rule, i.e., that the Section 8(d) time limits and notice provisions do not apply to strikes during the life of the agreement whose purpose is not to modify the terms of the agreement but rather to obtain terms which the agreement has not settled or has expressly left open. The Ninth Circuit[784] has held that notice need not be given to a state agency (Arizona Industrial Commission) under Section 8(d)(3) if such agency has no funds for conciliation or mediation. Thus, the union's failure to serve notice on that state agency did not forfeit the employee status

---

[777]§8(d) reads in part: "Any employee who engages in a strike within the sixty-day period specified in this subsection shall lose his status as an employee of the employer engaged in the particular labor dispute, for the purposes of sections 8, 9 and 10 of this Act . . . ."

[778]*See* comment of Senator Ball, 93 Cong. Rec. 5014 (1947), that the provisions of §8(d) are "aimed primarily at protecting the public, as well as the employees, who have been the victims of 'quickie' strikes. I do not think that is taking away any rights of labor . . . ."

[779]352 US 282, 39 LRRM 2296 (1957).

[780]*Id.* at 290-91.

[781]Packinghouse Workers Local 3 (Wilson & Co.) v. NLRB, 210 F2d 325, 33 LRRM 2530 (CA 8, 1954), had held otherwise.

[782]258 F2d 146, 42 LRRM 2320 (CA DC, 1958).

[783]319 F2d 375, 53 LRRM 2598 (CA 9, 1963).

[784]Locomotive Firemen (Phelps-Dodge Corp.) v. NLRB, 302 F2d 198, 50 LRRM 2015 (CA 9, 1962). *But cf.* Milk, Ice Cream Drivers & Dairy Employees Local 783 (Cream Top Creamery, Inc.), 147 NLRB 264, 56 LRRM 1194 (1964).

of the strikers. The court's rationale was that a completely powerless state agency could not promote collective bargaining; therefore the statute should not be read as requiring a useless act.

Many of the Board and court decisions dealing with the bargaining obligation during the term of an existing contract involve the issue of whether the union has waived its right to bargain over a particular subject, either by virtue of a contractual provision or by reason of its prior conduct in earlier negotiations.[785]

Other cases involving bargaining during the term of an existing agreement turn on the question of whether the particular subject is or is not a mandatory subject of bargaining. In one case, for example, the Sixth Circuit, in agreement with the Board, held that not only the benefits of an employee health insurance plan, but also the designation of a particular insurance carrier, were mandatory subjects. Hence, the employer who unilaterally terminated its employee health care plan with a particular insurance carrier during the term of the labor contract was held to have violated the Act.[786]

XI. DUAL EMPLOYER OPERATIONS: THE "DOUBLE-BREASTED" ISSUE[787]

Some unionized employers, particularly in the construction industry, have established separate companies to operate on a

---

[785]It should be noted that since the Board in Collyer Insulated Wire, 192 NLRB 837, 77 LRRM 1931 (1971), adopted a prearbitration deferral doctrine, many cases involving the question of an employer's right to make a unilateral change during the term of a labor contract have been deferred to contractual grievance-arbitration procedures. See generally Chapter 20 infra.

[786]Bastian Blessing Div. of Golconda Corp. v. NLRB, 474 F2d 49, 82 LRRM 2689 (CA 6, 1973), enforcing 195 NLRB 1108, 79 LRRM 1616 (1972), supplementing 194 NLRB 609, 79 LRRM 1010 (1971). The court specifically noted, however, that in the particular case before it, it was impossible to separate the benefits from the carrier which provided them, thereby implying that the court might not order reinstatement of the benefits from an insurance carrier in all situations. See Chapter 17 infra at note 51. See also Keystone Consol. Indus. v. NLRB, 606 F2d 171, 102 LRRM 2664 (CA 7, 1979) (unilateral change of administrator of insurance plan during term of contract held violative of §8(a)(5)); Ford Motor Co. v. NLRB, 441 US 488, 101 LRRM 2222 (1979) (unilateral change in price of cafeteria food during term of agreement held to be violative of §8(a)(5)). See Chapter 17 infra for a full discussion of mandatory subjects of bargaining. See Chapter 18 infra for a full discussion of permissive and illegal subjects of bargaining.

[787]See Penfield, The Double-Breasted Operation in the Construction Industry, 27 LAB. L. J. 89 (1976); King & LaVaute, Current Trends in Construction Industry Labor Relations: The Double-Breasted Contractor and the Prehire Contract, 29 SYRACUSE L. REV. 901-40 (1978); Bornstein, Emerging Law of the "Double-Breasted" Operation in the Construction Industry, 28 LAB. L. J. 77-88 (1977). See also Chapter 30 infra at notes 99-125.

nonunion basis. This practice, often referred to as "double breasting," and union reactions to it, have given rise to developments under several sections of the Act, particularly Section 8(a)(5), but also Sections 8(b)(1), 8(b)(3), 8(b)(4), 8(e), and 301. A leading case, *South Prairie Construction Co.* v. *Operating Engineers Local 627*[788] arose under the bargaining provisions of Section 8(a)(5). The union alleged that South Prairie and Peter Kiewit Sons (both subsidiaries of the same parent company) had violated Section 8(a)(5) by refusing to apply the collective bargaining agreement between the union and Kiewit to South Prairie's employees. The Board rejected the union's contention that South Prairie and Kiewit constituted a single employer and dismissed the complaint.[789]

On the union's petition for review, the D.C. Circuit reversed and found that both companies constituted a single employer. The court relied upon criteria enunciated by the Supreme Court in *Radio Union Local 1264* v. *Broadcast Service of Mobile, Inc.*[790] Applying those criteria, the court determined that the facts evidenced "a substantial qualitative degree of integration of operations and common management—one that we are satisfied would not be found in the arms-length relationship existing among unintegrated companies."[791] It concluded that the contrary finding of the Board was not warranted by the record of the case.[792]

The Supreme Court affirmed the judgment of the D.C. Circuit on the single-employer issue, but held that the court of appeals acted improperly in deciding that employees of both

---

[788]425 US 800, 92 LRRM 2507 (1976), *aff'g in part and remanding in part* Operating Eng'rs Local 627 (Peter Kiewit Sons' Co.) v. NLRB, 518 F2d 1040, 90 LRRM 2321 (CA DC, 1975). *See* Chapter 30 *infra* at note 107.

[789]In cases decided prior to *South Prairie* arising under §8(a)(5), the Board had rejected union claims of single-employer status in connection with "double breasted" operations similar to those in *South Prairie*. Gerace Constr., Inc., 193 NLRB 645, 78 LRRM 1367 (1971), and Frank N. Smith Assocs., Inc., 194 NLRB 212, 78 LRRM 1603 (1971) (dismissing §8(a)(5) complaints). *Cf.* Carpenters' Dist. Council of Houston (Baxter Constr. Co.), 201 NLRB 23, 82 LRRM 1382 (1973) (finding a §8(b)(4) violation in picketing of neutral contractor).

[790]380 US 255, 58 LRRM 2545 (1965). *See* Chapter 30 *infra* at note 107.

[791]Operating Eng'rs Local 627 (Peter Kiewit Sons' Co.) v. NLRB, *supra* note 788 at 1047.

[792]The court of appeals held, contrary to the Board, that not all of the controlling standards bearing on the single-employer issue must be present in each case in order to find the existence of a single employer. Also, in further disagreement with the Board, the court determined that centralized control of the labor relations of both companies is not a prerequisite for finding that a single employer exists in every case.

South Prairie and Kiewit constituted an appropriate bargaining unit, an issue which the Board had not passed upon.[793] Accordingly, that part of the court of appeal's judgment which directed the Board to issue a bargaining order was remanded so that the Board could make the initial determination of the appropriate bargaining unit issue.

Upon remand, in *Kiewit Sons' Co.*,[794] the Board ruled that the employees of the two subsidiaries constituted two separate bargaining units, and accordingly dismissed the complaint. The Board found particularly relevant the separate bargaining histories (union versus nonunion), an absence of functional integration of operations, differences in the types of work and skills of employees, the extent of decentralization of management and supervision, particularly in regard to labor relations, hiring, discipline, and control of day-to-day operations, and the relatively insignificant extent of interchange and contact between the two groups of employees.

In subsequent cases, the Board has relied upon the criteria used by the circuit court in *South Prairie*. In *Western Union Corp.*[795] the Board did not find a single employer, despite evidence that (1) there was an overlap of corporate officers; (2) the financial and personnel resources for the new corporations were initially performed by the original corporation; (3) the new corporations performed the functions originally performed by the original corporation; (4) the original corporation provided service to the new corporations, and vice versa; and (5) the original corporation controlled the new corporation's budget and selection of officers and directors. The Board relied heavily on a finding that there was no common control of labor relations. Of the four key elements to a finding of a "single integrated enterprise," namely, common ownership and financial control, common management, interrelation of operations and integrated control of labor relations, the Board found that only common ownership was present.

In *United Constructors & Goodwin Construction Co.*[796] the Board refused to find that union and nonunion contractors constituted

---

[793]*See* note 788 *supra*.
[794]Kiewit Sons' Co., 231 NLRB 76, 95 LRRM 1510 (1977), *aff'd*, 595 F2d 844, 100 LRRM 2792 (CA DC, 1979).
[795]224 NLRB 274, 92 LRRM 1443 (1976), *aff'd sub. nom.* Telegraph Workers v. NLRB, 571 F2d 665, 97 LRRM 2962 (CA DC), *cert. denied*, 439 US 827, 99 LRRM 2600 (1978).
[796]233 NLRB 904, 97 LRRM 1409 (1977).

a single employer, even though the partners in the "union" firm joined with their sons to form the separate "non-union" company to operate as an open-shop contractor. The Board found significant "differences in labor relations between the two companies." It noted that, while both shared office space, office equipment, and the services of a particular individual, rent was paid for those services. There was no evidence, the Board said, that the "union" employees lost work, which they otherwise would have obtained, to the "non-union" employees.

In *Appalachian Construction, Inc.*,[797] Appalachian had a collective contract with the Boilermakers Union. A public utility contracted with Appalachian to perform certain maintenance work, which however was not performed satisfactorily; therefore the contract was cancelled. Appalachian then successfully rebid the contract, specifying that the work would be done by SE-OZ, a nonunion subsidiary of Appalachian. The Boilermakers filed an unfair labor practice charge, but the administrative law judge found that SE-OZ's failure to apply the collective bargaining agreement to its employees was not in violation of the Act in view of the Board's latest *Kiewit* holding.[798] The Board, however, reversed the ALJ, stating that it was not faced with a "double-breasted" operation, for this was not an "arms length" subcontracting arrangement. The Board emphasized that (1) daily supervision was the same under both companies, and the supervisors were on Appalachian's payroll; (2) the same person who was the president of Appalachian and the vice-president of SE-OZ was the officer responsible for both projects; (3) division of profits was determined by the officers of both companies, three out of five of whom were the same; and (4) the project was the first of its kind for SE-OZ—the only difference between Appalachian's working on the project and SE-OZ was the absence of union labor. The Board therefore found that the companies were a single integrated employer and their employees constituted a single appropriate unit; typical 8(a)(1), (3), and (5) remedies were ordered.

In *Ellsworth Sheet Metal, Inc.*,[799] the Board found two employers to constitute a single integrated employer and a single bar-

[797]235 NLRB 685, 98 LRRM 1067 (1978).
[798]*See* note 794 *supra.*
[799]235 NLRB 1273, 98 LRRM 1274 (1978), *enforced,* 603 F2d 214, 103 LRRM 2603 (CA 2, 1979).

gaining unit of employees appropriate for both employers. Ellsworth, which had a collective bargaining agreement with the Sheet Metal Workers, had established Benchmark as a nonunion company. Benchmark then engaged in the same type of operation as Ellsworth, using Ellsworth's plant and equipment, the same employees, and the same supervisors. The Board found that Benchmark's refusal to work under the collective bargaining agreement which Ellsworth had with the Sheet Metal Workers violated the Act. It specifically found a refusal to bargain in the failure of Benchmark to make payments to certain benefit funds and in its unilateral changing of wage rates without notice or consultation with the union. Make-whole remedies were ordered.

The Board has made similar findings and ordered similar remedies in several cases.[800] In *Edward J. White, Inc.*,[801] the ALJ recommended that the respondents be required to restore to a union company bargaining-unit work which had been transferred to a nonunion company. The Board reversed the ALJ as to this remedy, holding that the normal 8(a)(1), (3), and (5) remedies were sufficient to remedy the unfair labor practices committed. More extensive remedies have been ordered, however, where deemed necessary.[802]

In a different context, the Sixth Circuit has held that an employer may be compelled under Section 301 to arbitrate a double-breasted issue under its union contract.[803] The employer, having negotiated contracts with several unions, set up what the union alleged to be sham corporations to operate on a nonunion basis. When it refused to arbitrate whether the new corporations were covered by the union contracts, the unions brought suit to compel arbitration, which the Sixth Circuit granted.[804]

In another case, the union filed suit to enforce its agreement with one company against a second company which had been

---

[800]*See, e.g.*, Big Bear Supermkts., 239 NLRB 179, 100 LRRM 1067 (1978), *enforced*, 640 F2d 924, 103 LRRM 3120 (CA 9, 1980) (franchising context); Douglas Lantz, 235 NLRB 994, 100 LRRM 1223 (1978), *enforced*, 607 F2d 290, 102 LRRM 2789 (CA 9, 1979); Don Burgess Constr. Corp., 227 NLRB 765, 95 LRRM 1135 (1977), *enforced*, 596 F2d 378, 101 LRRM 2315 (CA 9, 1979); Hood Indus., Inc., 248 NLRB 597, 103 LRRM 1540 (1980); Van-Note Harvey Assocs., 247 NLRB 927, 103 LRRM 1235 (1980); Safety Elec. Corp., 239 NLRB 40, 99 LRRM 1440 (1978).
[801]237 NLRB 1020, 99 LRRM 1126 (1978).
[802]*E.g.*, Angelus Block Co., Inc., 250 NLRB 868, 105 LRRM 1141 (1980).
[803]Bricklayers Local 6 v. Heminger, Inc., 483 F2d 129, 84 LRRM 2033 (CA 6, 1973).
[804]*See generally* Steelworkers v. American Mfg. Co., 363 US 564, 46 LRRM 2414 (1960); Chapter 19 *infra* at notes 43-49.

established to operate on a nonunion basis. The district court found that the two companies were sufficiently integrated in operations to constitute a single employer and that both were bound by the terms of the collective bargaining agreement.[805]

The Board has also dealt with the double-breasted issue in other contexts. In one case, the Board dismissed Section 8(b)(4)(D) charges against a union, finding that the picketing in question did not have a jurisdictional object but arose from the union's claim to bargaining-unit work and its protest over the allegedly improper transfer of that work to a subsidiary corporation.[806] In another case, however, a union was found to have violated Sections 8(e) and 8(b)(3) by insisting on a clause that would have allowed employees it represented to refuse to operate equipment of any employer that had an interest in any nonunion firm doing construction work in the area.[807] In another case the Board held that a union's initiation of arbitration procedures in its contract with one employer to obtain an award that the contract covered the employees of the employer's nonunion subsidiary, and a subsequent threat to picket the contracting employer to enforce the arbitration award in the union's favor, did not violate Sections 8(b)(1)(A), (2), or (3).[808]

---

[805]Plumbers Local 519 v. Service Plumbing Co., 401 F Supp 1008, 90 LRRM 3217 (SD Fla, 1975). *See also* Land Equip., Inc., 248 NLRB 685, 104 LRRM 1100 (1980) (retroactive application of contracts as remedy). A union, however, may waive its right to assert the double-breasted issue. A-1 Fire Protection, 250 NLRB No. 34, 104 LRRM 1370 (1980).

[806]Plumbers Local 36 (Weinheimers, Inc.), 219 NLRB 1016, 90 LRRM 1201 (1975). The union struck the employer with which it had a contract after the employer ceased its own operations as a plumbing contractor and started up two new corporations that engaged in the same kind of work on a nonunion basis. For treatment of jurisdictional disputes generally, *see* Chapter 27 *infra*. *See also* Iron Workers Local 103 (Higdon Contracting Co., Inc.), 216 NLRB 45, 88 LRRM 1067 (1975), *rev'd*, 535 F2d 87, 91 LRRM 2986 (CA DC, 1976), *rev'd*, 434 US 335, 97 LRRM 2333 (1978), arising in a §8(b)(7)(C) context. For treatment of organizational and recognitional disputes generally, *see* Chapter 23 *infra*.

[807]Operating Eng'rs Local 542 (York County Bridge, Inc.), 216 NLRB 408, 88 LRRM 1405 (1975). The Board held that the clause violated §8(e) and was not protected by the construction industry proviso because it reached beyond the performance of work at a construction site, and the union was insisting on a nonmandatory subject for bargaining (reasoning that the clause attempted to enlarge its bargaining unit). For treatment of cases under §8(e), *see* Chapter 26 *infra*.

[808]Teamsters Local 208 (De Anza Delivery Sys., Inc.), 219 NLRB 821, 90 LRRM 1030 (1975). Even though the Board held that the two companies were separate employers, it found that no pressure was brought against the nonunion company and that the arbitration award against the company under contract with the union could not have restrained or coerced the nonunion company or its employees.

CHAPTER 14

EFFECT OF CHANGE IN BARGAINING REPRESENTATIVE

I. CONTEXT IN WHICH THE ISSUE ARISES

This chapter treats the effect of a change of representation of employees in a bargaining unit. If such change occurs when there is not a bargaining agreement in effect, or when the bargaining agreement is "open," the ordinary rules applicable to representation procedures will prevail.[1] The law discussed in this chapter relates primarily to the effect of a change in union representation upon an existing collective bargaining agreement. The focus of the discussion here is upon the question of whether such agreement binds the superseding union and the employer.

The existence of a collective agreement often constitutes a bar to an election and to the recognition of a new collective bargaining representative.[2] However, there are situations where the contract does not constitute such a bar, in which cases a change in bargaining representatives may occur during the term of an existing agreement. It is in this context that a question concerning the effect of such a change on an existing contract generally arises. More particularly, the question arises in cases (1) where the existing contract is not a bar to an election by reason of its duration,[3] (2) where there has been a schism in the bargaining representative,[4] (3) where the contracting union has

---

[1]*See* Chapter 10 *supra,* particularly the contract-bar cases at notes 117-200, *e.g.,* Avco Mfg. Corp., 106 NLRB 1104, 32 LRRM 1618 (1953); General Cable Corp., 139 NLRB 1123, 51 LRRM 1444 (1962). For consideration of the recognitional problems which are encountered when two or more unions are claiming representation in the same bargaining unit, *see* Chapter 8 *supra* at notes 106-53 and the discussion therein on the *Midwest Piping* doctrine.

[2]*See* Chapter 10 *supra* at notes 117-200.

[3]*E.g.,* American Seating Co., 106 NLRB 250, 32 LRRM 1439 (1953).

[4]*E.g.,* Purity Baking Co., 124 NLRB 159, 44 LRRM 1314 (1959); Boston Machine Works Co., 89 LRRM 59, 25 LRRM 1508 (1950). *See* Chapter 10 *supra* at notes 174-75.

become defunct[5] or disclaims interest in representing the group,[6] or (4) where another union, as a result of evolution or reorganization, inherits the powers, assets, and membership of the contracting union.[7] If a new bargaining representative displaces the prior representative, the Board may be required to determine whether the employer may refuse to bargain with the new union for a new contract that would replace the unexpired contract with the prior union.

II. RIGHTS AND OBLIGATIONS OF NEW BARGAINING REPRESENTATIVE AND EMPLOYER UNDER CONTRACT WITH PRIOR REPRESENTATIVE

A. Representation Proceedings

The Board's willingness to rule in representation cases on the effect of certification of a new bargaining representative on an unexpired collective bargaining agreement has had a checkered history. In a few early cases[8] where a rival union was seeking an election during the term of a collective bargaining contract, the Board indicated that certification of the new union would have only a limited effect. In one case, the Board stated that "it is not our intention to invalidate the contract or to disturb it in any respect . . . . The election which we shall hereinafter direct is for the purpose of determining the identity of the representative which shall administer the contract."[9] The rationale for such a rule, as later articulated by Board Member Reynolds in a dissenting opinion, was that "neither the employer nor the employee should be enabled by virtue of a proceeding before this Board

---

[5]*E.g.,* Hershey Chocolate Corp., 121 NLRB 901, 42 LRRM 1460 (1958). *Cf.* Rocky Mountain Phosphates, Inc., 138 NLRB 292, 51 LRRM 1019 (1962) (defunct union superseded by union which secured recognition with authorization cards from a majority of employees). *See* Chapter 10 *supra* at 176-79.

[6]American Sunroof Corp., 243 NLRB 1128, 102 LRRM 1086 (1979) (contracting union disclaimed interest after deauthorization petition filed; Board directed representation election on petition of different union, found unexpired contract no bar because of disclaimer and, citing *American Seating,* refused to condition possible certification on assumption of labor agreement). *See* Chapter 10 *supra* at notes 180—82.

[7]*See* Montgomery Ward & Co., 137 NLRB 346, 50 LRRM 1137 (1962); Gate City Optical Co., 175 NLRB 1059, 71 LRRM 1118 (1969). *See* Note, *Change of Status of a Party to a Collective Bargaining Agreement,* 60 YALE L. J. 1026 (1951).

[8]New England Transportation Co., 1 NLRB 130, 1 LRRM 97 (1936); Swayne & Hoyt, Ltd., 2 NLRB 282, 1 LRRM 99 (1936); *cf.* The Register & Tribune Co., 60 NLRB 360, 15 LRRM 233 (1945).

[9]The Register & Tribune Co., *supra* note 8 at 362.

to discard unilaterally any obligations incurred as a result of their collective bargaining agreement."[10] Generally, however, the Board refrained from ruling in representation cases upon the effect of the certification on the existing agreement.

In 1950, in *Boston Machine Works,*[11] the Board expressly held that it would not make a determination in a representation case as to the effect of the certification of a new representative upon an existing bargaining agreement, and overruled its earlier contrary decisions. It ordered an election in this case because of a schism in the ranks of the incumbent bargaining representative. The opinion noted, and apparently relied upon, the fact that Congress had failed to include any provision in the Act restricting the functions of a new representative, stating: "[W]e do not believe that this Board should qualify its certification of the employees' bargaining representative by imposing restrictions not to be found in any provision of the Act, and indeed, deliberately omitted therefrom."[12]

The ambiguity as to whether this meant that no restrictions were intended or that the question would be determined only in unfair labor practice proceedings has been resolved in favor of addressing the issues as they arose. It is now clear that the Board will not condition certification of a new bargaining representative upon assumption of the unexpired collective bargaining agreement. But the Board has not been reluctant to state, in directing an election, that a new bargaining representative would not be bound by the unexpired contract.[13]

B. Section 8(a)(5) Proceedings: *American Seating*

The Board squarely faced the question of the effect a certification would have upon the existing contract in a series of unfair labor practice cases.

The earliest of these was *Pacific Greyhound Lines.*[14] The Board had ordered an election, despite the existence of an unexpired

---

[10]Boston Machine Works Co., *supra* note 4 at 61 (dissenting opinion).
[11]*Id.*
[12]*Id.* at 62; *accord,* Hershey Chocolate Corp., 121 NLRB 901, 42 LRRM 1460 (1958).
[13]American Sunroof Corp., *supra* note 6, *citing American Seating. Cf.* General Dynamics Corp., 184 NLRB 553, 74 LRRM 1522 (1970) (dictum, in resolving objections that signatory union, unlike new bargaining agent, is bound by unexpired contract for remainder of its term if victorious in representation election).
[14]Pacific Greyhound, 22 NLRB 111, 6 LRRM 189 (1940). *See* Freidin, *The Board, the "Bar," and the Bargain,* 59 COLUM. L. REV. 61, 82-92 (1959); Note, *Effect of Pre-Existing Contract on New Bargaining Agent,* 54 COLUM. L. REV. 132 (1954).

contract, because the contract had been made with a union which was deemed not to be a freely chosen representative because of illegal employer action.[15] Following certification of the new representative, the employer refused to bargain with the new union. In the ensuing unfair labor practice case, the employer contended that its contract with the illegally assisted union "cannot be abrogated by employees for whose benefit it was made nor by another representative selected by a majority of the employees of the unit . . . ," a position which the Board rejected. It held that the newly selected representative could, at its option, abrogate the terms of the prior contract.

Board Member Edwin S. Smith, in a concurring opinion, expressed a different view as to the effect of a certification upon the existing agreement. He would have allowed abrogation of only those provisions of the contract which provided for recognition of the contracting union: a closed shop and administration of the contract. It was his position that provisions covering wages, hours of service, and other working conditions of the covered employees should continue in force.

The Board rendered the leading decision on this question in *American Seating Co.*[16] The pertinent facts were as follows: Two years after the execution of a three-year contract between the employer and the United Auto Workers, the Pattern Makers Union petitioned for an election in a craft unit[17] covered by the UAW contract. The NLRB ruled in the representation proceeding that the UAW contract constituted no bar to an election since three-year contracts were not customary in the industry.[18] Thereafter the Pattern Makers Union was certified as the representative of the employees in the unit. The employer, however, insisted that the UAW contract remained in effect as to all employees in the plant, although it did agree to bargain with the Pattern Makers Union in certain limited areas. In the subsequent unfair labor practice case, the employer maintained that the Pattern Makers Union, as bargaining representative of the

---

[15]Chapter 8 *supra* discusses the subject of employer assistance and domination of labor organizations under §8(a)(2) of the Act.

[16]*Supra* note 3.

[17]For a discussion of craft-severance in bargaining units, *see* Chapter 11 *supra* at notes 71-95.

[18]This case arose before the Board's ruling that three-year contracts could be a bar for the entire term regardless of custom in the industry. General Cable Corp., *supra* note 1. *See* Chapter 10 *supra* at note 129.

craft employees, was required to administer the substantive terms of the existing contract. Relying on traditional common-law principles, it contended that the employees, as principals, were bound by the contract executed on their behalf by their agent, and that a mere change in agents could not abrogate the contract. The Pattern Makers Union asserted that the certification rendered the contract inoperative as to the employees in the unit which it now represented. It urged that the unique functions of a statutory collective bargaining representative precluded a blind application of common-law agency principles to the problem.

The Board ruled that unless the collective bargaining representative was to be "emasculated" in the exercise of its functions, it must be permitted to negotiate the terms and conditions of employment. It therefore refused to "hobble" the newly certified collective bargaining representative with its predecessor's contract. The Board observed that "the rule urged by the [employer] seems hardly calculated to reduce 'industrial strife' by encouraging the 'practice and procedure of collective bargaining,' the declared purpose of the . . . Act . . . ."[19]

The Board thus adopted the general proposition that if an existing contract constitutes no bar to an election, it also is no bar to full bargaining by the new representative. The Board noted that unless the new bargaining representative had such power, "a great part of the benefit to be derived from the no-bar rule will be dissipated."[20]

Following the *American Seating* decision, the Court of Appeals for the Sixth Circuit cast some doubt upon the validity of the doctrine which the Board had promulgated in that case. In *Modine Manufacturing Co.* v. *International Association of Machinists*,[21] the court appeared to be of the view that while the union-shop and the checkoff provisions became inoperative as soon as a new bargaining representative entered the scene, the other provisions of the contract remained in effect to be administered by the newly certified union. *Modine,* however, involved a Sec-

---

[19]106 NLRB at 255.
[20]*Id.*
[21]216 F2d 326, 35 LRRM 2003 (CA 6, 1954). The court did not refer to *American Seating.* It stated that it was not ruling on "[w]hether or not the substantive provisions as to wages, hours, etc., were still binding after the certification . . . " of the successor union. 216 F2d at 329.

tion 301 suit by a decertified union against an employer for breach of contract, and the court's statements concerning the matter of administration of the contract by the newly certified union are but dicta. The only holding required was that the superseded union did not have rights under the unexpired contract. The Board subsequently reaffirmed its *American Seating* decision, holding in *Ludlow Typograph Co.*[22] that an employer was *required*, not simply *permitted*, to bargain with a new bargaining representative over rates of pay, hours, and other matters covered in the unexpired contract with the superseded union.

The Supreme Court has accepted *American Seating* as a correct statement of the law. In *NLRB* v. *Burns International Detective Agency, Inc.*[23] the Court cited the rule to support its holding that a successor employer is not bound by a collective bargaining agreement negotiated by its predecessors which it has not agreed to or assumed. The Board has rejected opportunities to dilute or question the vitality of *American Seating*.[24]

C. *American Seating* Limited

Although *American Seating* is founded firmly upon a policy of protecting the statutory rights of a new collective bargaining representative, a rigid application of the doctrine would subordinate another important policy also required by the Act. As the Board recognized in *American Seating*, industrial peace requires contractual stability, and such stability ought not to be disturbed by mere formal changes in the bargaining representative. Thus, employees can no more abrogate the terms of a contract by merely making a formal change in the structure of their union than can an employer by merely making a formal alteration in the structure of its business.[25] The problem turns upon a determination of the circumstances that will move the Board to view a change in the representative as the kind of change that should allow the new representative to bargain for a new contract.

---

[22]113 NLRB 724, 36 LRRM 1364 (1955). The Board expressly rejected any contrary inference that might have been derived from the *Modine* case.

[23]406 US 272, 80 LRRM 2225 (1972). "When the union which has signed a collective bargaining contract is decertified, the succeeding union certified by the Board is not bound by the prior contract, need not administer it and may demand negotiations for a new contract, even if the terms of the old contract have not yet expired. American Seating Co . . . ." 406 US at 285 n.8. *See* Chapter 15 *infra* at notes 41-58.

[24]*See* Consolidated Fiberglass Prods. Co., 242 NLRB 10, 101 LRRM 1089 (1979).

[25]The Board has adhered to the same doctrine in the case of employer changes. *See* Chapter 15 *infra* at notes 192-229.

Many changes in the internal structure of the union, or changes caused by transfer of responsibility from one union to another, such as by merger, consolidation, or transfer of affiliation, are not the types of changes which should affect the substantive terms of the contract. The rule of *American Seating* is therefore restricted to cases in which the noncontracting union is a new and different representative rather than a mere continuation or successor of the contracting union.

In cases involving mere successorship, as distinguished from a true change in representative, the Board imposes upon the successor all of the obligations of the predecessor. Thus, where by process of evolution or reorganization one union inherits the powers, assets, and membership of the contracting party, the successor union will not be permitted to escape the obligations of the existing contract. By the same token, an employer is obligated to bargain and honor the unexpired contract with a "successor" union.[26]

For example, the survivor of several merged or consolidated unions assumes all the obligations of its predecessors. In the *Montgomery Ward* case,[27] the certified union, Retail Clerks Local 1594, executed a five-year contract with the employer. Prior to expiration of this contract, it merged with three other locals of the same international union. No significant change in membership occurred, and the international officers who had administered each of the locals prior to the merger continued to administer the survivor, which was Local 1099. For nine months following the merger the employer checked off dues for Local 1099, and, as the Board noted, there was an "apparent understanding of both the employer and the union that the consolidated group intended to function as a continuation of the constituent unions . . . ."[28] Accordingly, the Board ruled that Local 1099 was the "successor" of Local 1594 and as such inherited the latter's contract and the benefits of its certification. Although this was a representation case, there is no reason to believe that the Board would have reached a different result in an unfair labor practice proceeding.

---

[26]*See* notes 37-42 *infra* and accompanying text.

[27]Montgomery Ward & Co., *supra* note 7. By similar reasoning, an employer was obligated to bargain with a consolidated union which resulted from the merger of a certified union with another union. The latter union succeeded to the certified union's representative status. Union Carbide & Carbon Co. v. NLRB, 224 F2d 672, 40 LRRM 2084 (CA 6, 1957), *enforcing* 116 NLRB 488, 38 LRRM 1284 (1956).

[28]Montgomery Ward & Co., *supra* note 7 at 350.

Similarly, mere changes in the name of the union will not affect the rights and duties of the parties to the collective bargaining relationship.[29]

The logic and language used by the Board in *American Seating* suggest, as its progeny make clear, that the ruling was intended to be coterminous with the no-contract-bar rules. "The same principle [succeeding union not bound by prior contract] applies when existing contract is held not to bar an election, and a new union becomes the representative of the employees previously covered by the contract."[30] Thus *American Seating* will be applied to contracts which are held not to be a bar, whether because of excessive union security, schisms, disclaimers, or other pertinent grounds recognized by the Board.[31]

The signatory union remains bound by the no-bar contract although it wins the election and is certified. If this makes the incumbent organization a "sitting duck" in an election campaign, it is "disadvantaged," the Board reasons, "only because it voluntarily chose to enter into such an agreement knowing that it would not bar an election . . . ."[32] In practical effect, the *American Seating* doctrine operates as a potent deterrent to the negotiation of agreements which do not satisfy the Board's contract-bar rules, particularly agreements for terms longer than three years.[33]

D. Right of Superseded Contracting Union

The Board and the courts have made clear that no union other than the duly recognized or certified collective bargaining

---

[29]*See* Marshall Maintenance Corp., 154 NLRB 611, 59 LRRM 1784 (1965). In Radio Corp. of America, 135 NLRB 980, 49 LRRM 1606 (1962), the Board distinguished *American Seating,* holding that a national agreement between a parent union and the employer was binding upon a local union affiliate in a newly certified local bargaining unit.

[30]American Sunroof Corp., *supra* note 6 at 1130.

[31]*Id. American Seating* applied where the unexpired contract was no bar because the union had made an arm's-length disclaimer of representational interest in the unit.

[32]General Dynamics Corp., *supra* note 13. The Board had directed an election during the term of a five-year agreement, refusing to reconsider its three-year bar rule because it allowed the petitioning union to promise a "more lucrative contract." General Dynamics Corp., 175 NLRB 1022, 71 LRRM 1113 (1969). Later, certifying the outside union, the Board overruled employer objections to campaign statements that only a victory by petitioner would "invalidate" the contract, and declined to reconsider its "long standing" *American Seating* doctrine because the objected-to campaigning was consistent with it. The Board reaffirmed the ruling that the campaign statements "accurately reflected the operation of the [*American Seating*] principle." 184 NLRB at 553.

[33]General Cable Corp., *supra* note 1.

representative retains any rights under a collective bargaining contract.[34] Even a union that is signatory to a contract, once it is decertified or otherwise loses its status as collective bargaining representative, retains no rights under that contract.[35] This feature of the collective bargaining contract underscores the *sui generis* nature of the collective agreement.[36]

III. MERGERS, CONSOLIDATIONS, AND TRANSFERS OF AFFILIATION

In cases involving union successorship, as distinguished from a true change in representative, the Board imposes upon the successor all of the obligations and rights of the predecessor union. In those cases where the successor union represents a continuation of the predecessor, an employer is obligated to bargain with the successor.

On the other hand, if there are significant changes in the actual identity of the bargaining representative, the employer is faced with a question concerning representation and thus will not be required to bargain with the new representative until a majority status is determined through Board procedures. The issue of whether the successor union is merely a continuation of the predecessor under a new name or is a different bargaining agent may arise in a Section 8(a)(5) unfair labor practice proceeding or in a representation proceeding involving efforts to amend the predecessor's certification.

When a change in bargaining representative is little more than a change in name, the employer must continue to recognize the successor bargaining representative, and both parties are bound by the unexpired collective bargaining agreement.[37]

---

[34]NLRB v. Jones & Laughlin Steel Corp., 310 US 1, 44-45, 1 LRRM 703 (1937); National Licorice Co. v. NLRB, 309 US 350, 364-65, 6 LRRM 674 (1940). Compare obligations under union contract devolving upon a successor employer, discussed in Chapter 15 *infra*.

[35]Modine Mfg. Co. v. Machinists, 216 F2d 326, 35 LRRM 2003 (CA 6, 1954) (§301 suit by decertified union to enforce collective bargaining agreement); Retail Clerks v. Montgomery Ward & Co., 316 F2d 754, 53 LRRM 2069 (CA 7, 1963) (continuation of representational status an "implied condition of the contracts").

[36]See Chapters 19 and 20 *infra* for a discussion of the nature of the collective agreement and the relation of NLRB action to arbitral and court actions enforcing such agreements.

[37]The Hamilton Tool Co., 190 NLRB 571, 77 LRRM 1257 (1971); New England Foundry Corp., 192 NLRB 785, 78 LRRM 1112 (1971); Universal Tool & Stamping Co., 182 NLRB 254, 259, 74 LRRM 1096 (1970) ("where a union is actually the continuation of another union under a different name as a result of affiliation, disaffiliation,

Similarly, the Board has upheld the employer's duty to bargain where one local merged into a larger local of the same international, and where the old local was found to have retained its identity within the new local.[38] The same rule has been applied where a division of a local union which had a contract with the employer split from that local and merged into a second local, but remained intact within the latter and retained its separate identity.[39] However, the issue of whether and to what extent the superseded union must retain autonomy within the successor union remains unsettled.[40] Further, if the predecessor union is a "functioning, viable entity, and opposes amendment," the Board will dismiss a petition to amend the certification.[41]

In cases involving merger or change of affiliation, the Board will also examine the procedural safeguards accompanying the intra-union merger or affiliation vote. Where the procedures are found to be adequate, the Board will compel the employer to recognize and bargain with the successor union.[42] An affiliation vote is viewed as "basically concerned with the organization and structure of the union and not with the representation status of employees";[43] therefore, the Board will not apply the standards of Board-conducted representation elections to affiliation votes. Rather, so long as the union conducts an affiliation vote with "adequate due process," the Board will approve the vote.[44] While the Board has not specifically defined "adequate due

---

merger, or the formation of a new organization and the predecessor union ceases to exist or unequivocally abandons its bargaining rights, its successor, in the proper case, may be entitled to the predecessor's bargaining and contractual rights").

[38]William B. Tanner, Inc., 212 NLRB 566, 86 LRRM 1613 (1974). The Sixth Circuit, however, denied enforcement of the Board's bargaining order, 517 F2d 982, 89 LRRM 2579 (CA 6, 1975).

[39]Newspapers, Inc., 210 NLRB 8, 86 LRRM 1123 (1974), enforced, 515 F2d 334, 89 LRRM 2715 (CA 5, 1975).

[40]Compare Retail Clerks Local 428 v. NLRB, 528 F2d 1225, 91 LRRM 2001 (CA 9, 1975), aff'g 211 NLRB 701, 86 LRRM 1441 (1974) (where former officers not retained and no evidence of continuing autonomy, no §8(a)(5) violation), with Quemetco, Inc., 226 NLRB 1398, 1399, 94 LRRM 1040 (1976) (although none of the former officers were retained and all monies now went to successor organization, employer violated Act by refusing to recognize successor because "it is the employees' freedom to select a bargaining representative of their choice which is of paramount importance under the Act"). See also Amoco Prod. Co. v. NLRB, 613 F2d 107, 103 LRRM 2810 (CA 5, 1980), remanding 239 NLRB 1195, 100 LRRM 1127 (1979).

[41]Missouri Beef Packers, Inc., 175 NLRB 1100, 71 LRRM 1177 (1969).

[42]Amoco Prod. Co., 220 NLRB 861, 90 LRRM 1434 (1975); American Mailers, 231 NLRB 1194, 96 LRRM 1274 (1977).

[43]Amoco Prod. Co., supra note 40. Accord, Goodfriend Western Corp., 232 NLRB 527, 97 LRRM 1074 (1977); Northern Electric Co., 165 NLRB 942, 65 LRRM 1379 (1967).

[44]Amoco Prod. Co., supra note 40, 239 NLRB at 1196.

process," it found that the standard was met where the union had provided adequate notice of the vote, an opportunity to discuss the affiliation issue, and conducted the vote by secret ballot.[45] But the Board does not require a secret ballot vote where a regional union merges with a national union and the regional union maintains its organizational structure,[46] nor does it demand these procedural standards where a national union assigns its bargaining rights to affiliated local unions.[47]

The Board's application of the "adequate due process standard" has met with a mixed response from the courts. In *Victor Comptometer Corp.*,[48] the Board held that an independent union had conducted an affiliation election with adequate procedural safeguards. Member Walther, dissenting, contended that the election had not satisfied "minimal standards of due process,"[49] noting particularly that the employees did not have an adequate opportunity to discuss and consider the question of affiliation and that the balloting was not in reality secret. The Sixth Circuit denied enforcement and adopted Member Walther's dissent.[50] The Third Circuit has refused to enforce Board orders requiring an employer to bargain with a successor union where as a result of affiliation a major change occurred in "the fulcrum of union control and representation," but without the safeguards of a Board-conducted representation election.[51] The Fifth Circuit and the Tenth Circuit, however, have enforced Board orders approving affiliation votes where the employees had an opportunity to discuss affiliation, the vote was by secret ballot, and the local union retained substantial autonomy in matters related to collective bargaining.[52]

---

[45]Providence Medical Center, 243 NLRB 714, 102 LRRM 1099 (1979). *See also* Amoco Prod. Co., *supra* note 40.

[46]Fox Memorial Hosp., 247 NLRB 356, 103 LRRM 1151 (1980); House of the Good Samaritan, 248 NLRB 539, 103 LRRM 1472 (1980).

[47]Duquesne Light Co., 248 NLRB 1271, 104 LRRM 1043 (1980).

[48]223 NLRB 1169, 92 LRRM 1097 (1976), *enforcement denied*, 587 F2d 812, 95 LRRM 3094 (CA 6, 1977).

[49]223 NLRB at 1172.

[50]The Sixth Circuit has also denied enforcement where the union did not give the employees notice of the affiliation until two days before it occurred and the voting procedures did not assure a secret ballot. NLRB v. A. W. Winchester, Inc., 588 F2d 211, 100 LRRM 2971 (CA 6, 1978).

[51]United States Steel Corp. v. NLRB, 457 F2d 660, 664, 79 LRRM 2877 (CA 3, 1972); NLRB v. Bernard Gloeckler N.E. Co., 540 F2d 197, 93 LRRM 2039 (CA 3, 1976).

[52]J. Ray McDermott & Co. v. NLRB, 571 F2d 850, 98 LRRM 2191 (CA 5, 1978); St. Vincent Hospital v. NLRB, 621 F2d 1054, 104 LRRM 2288, 2291 (CA 10, 1980) ("Failing to honor the results of the election would run flatly counter to the important policy of protecting the employees' free choice of a bargaining representative").

Board decisions have been divided on the issue of whether a local union may limit participation in an affiliation vote to union members.[53] * The most recent cases have approved the exclusion of nonmembers from affiliation votes.[54] The Board has reasoned that the exclusion of nonmembers from an affiliation vote differs little from the exclusion of nonmembers from other internal union affairs, such as strike votes and contract ratification votes.[55] However, where a union excluded a substantial number of bargaining unit employees from membership, the Board would not approve an affiliation vote that was limited to union members.[56]

As noted above, it is the current Board view that affiliation and merger are essentially internal union matters and, as in other contexts, the Board disfavors interfering in internal union affairs.[57] The rationale of its policy of demanding a lesser degree of scrutiny of the mechanics and substance of these matters was articulated as follows in *The Williamson Co.* case:[58]

> [W]e must temper our policy concerns in this area with the practical realization that the Section 9(a) representative must be free to readjust its internal organization in order to meet changing financial and contractual demands. The employees' bargaining representative has a responsibility to carry out its statutory responsibilities in the most effective way. Because of this responsibility, the bargaining representative must remain largely unfettered in its organizational quest for financial stability and aid in the negotiating process.[59]

[**Editor's Note:** In August 1982 the Board reversed its earlier decisions and ruled that an employer had lawfully refused to continue bargaining with an incumbent union affiliated with another labor organization, since only union members were permitted to vote in the affiliation election.][60]

---

[53]*Compare* Northern Electric Co., 165 NLRB 942, 65 LRRM 1379 (1967) (voting of members only approved), *with* Jasper Seating Co., 231 NLRB 1025, 96 LRRM 1195 (1977) (voting of members only not approved).
*[*See* **Editor's Note** *infra* following text at note 59.]
[54]Providence Medical Center, *supra* note 45; Amoco Prod. Co., *supra* note 40; J. Ray McDermott, *supra* note 52.
[55]Amoco Prod. Co., *supra* note 40.
[56]Ohio Poly Corp., 246 NLRB 104, 102 LRRM 1402 (1979).
[57]As an internal union decision, an affiliation vote would of course be subject to the "equal rights" and "free speech" requirements of the Labor-Management Reporting and Disclosure Act, 28 USC §411(a)(1) & (2).
[58]244 NLRB 953, 102 LRRM 1167 (1979).
[59]*Id.* at 955.
[60]Amoco Prod. Co., 262 NLRB No. 160, 110 LRRM 1419 (1982).

CHAPTER 15

EFFECT OF CHANGE IN THE EMPLOYING UNIT: SUCCESSORSHIP

I. SCOPE OF THE TOPIC

A. Factual Setting

Changes in business ownership have become increasingly common as well as varied in form. Where the seller, or prior employer, is a party to a labor agreement, has a bargaining relationship with a recently certified or recognized union, or is a respondent in an unfair labor practice proceeding, the question of the legal obligations of a potential new employer to the seller's employees, and to their representative, will inevitably arise. When these obligations are anticipated in a direct sale and purchase of a business, they may be reflected to some extent in the commercial negotiations between seller and buyer. But often such obligations are not anticipated, or the transaction effectuating the change in ownership is less direct, or more complex. And in many instances, it may also be essential to the ownership transaction to evaluate the potential legal obligations in connection with the potential legal rights of the new employer to make changes which correspond to its assessment of the needs of the business to be acquired.

This balancing of legal obligations and legal rights "across the change in ownership"[1] constitutes the development of the law

---

[1]John Wiley & Sons v. Livingston, 376 US 543, 551, 55 LRRM 2769 (1964). For a comprehensive discussion of the subject matter of this chapter, *see* the following commentary: Comment, *Successorship Clauses in Collective Bargaining Agreements,* 1979 BRIGHAM YOUNG U. L. REV. 99; Note, *Appropriate Standards of Successor Employer Obligations Under Wiley, Howard Johnson, & Burns,* 25 WAYNE L. REV. 1279 (1979); Murphy, *Successorship and the Forgotten Employee: A Suggested Approach,* NYU THIRTY-FIRST ANNUAL CONFER-

of successorship. There is no fixed definition of "successor," nor is there a uniformly accepted set of obligations which flow from the determination that, in certain circumstances, a party is a "successor."[2] Factual circumstances and procedural setting are both significant.

Procedurally, successorship issues arise in a variety of ways, but typically they are decided in Board proceedings involving alleged unfair labor practices. For the most part, these unfair labor practice cases involve an alleged violation of the new employer's duty to recognize and bargain with the representative of the employees of the former owner.[3] Less frequently, successorship issues arise in grievance-arbitration cases and/or Section 301 suits in federal court, usually pursuant to a motion by the union to compel arbitration under its contract with the former employer.[4]

B. A Summary of the Law

The body of successorship law which has developed is unusual in two major respects. First, the law is permeated to an extraor-

---

ENCE ON LABOR 75 (1978); Henry, *Is There Arbitration After Burns? The Resurrection of John Wiley & Sons*, 31 VAND. L. REV. 249 (1978); Donnelley, *Labor Union in Your Client's Business Sale or Acquisition (The Howard Johnson Case & Subsequent Precedent)*, 33 MO. B. J. 33 (1977); Comment, *Successor Management's Obligations Under Existing Collective Bargaining Agreements*, 40 MO. L. REV. 304 (1975); Note, *The Bargaining Obligations of Successor Employers*, 88 HARV. L. REV. 759 (1975); Bakaly & Bryan, *Survival of the Bargaining Agreement: The Effect of Burns*, 27 VAND. L. REV. 117 (1974); Note, *Contract Rights and the Successor Employer: The Impact of Burns Security*, 71 MICH. L. REV. 571 (1973); Benetar, *Successorship Liability Under Labor Agreements*, 1973 WIS. L. REV. 1026; Comment, *Contractual Successorship: The Impact of Burns*, 40 U. CHI. L. REV. 617 (1973); Morris & Gaus, *Successorship and the Collective Bargaining Agreement: Accommodating Wiley and Burns*, 59 VA. L. REV. 1359 (1973); Gunther, *The Supreme Court 1971 Term*, 86 HARV. L. REV. 1, 255-56 (1972); for a humorous but insightful pre-*Burns* discussion, *see* Simonoff, *How to Succeed to a Business Without Ever Contracting—or—Everything You Ever Wanted to Know About Successorships But Were Afraid (or Didn't Want) to Ask*, 23 LAB. L. J. 701 (Nov. 1972).

[2]Howard Johnson Co. v. Detroit Joint Bd., Hotel & Restaurant Employees, 417 US 249, 262 n.9, 86 LRRM 2449 (1974). In cautioning against a fixed definition of "successor," the Court characterized the normal two-step analysis (is the new employer a successor, and if so, is it obligated to bargain (or arbitrate), etc.?) as an artificial division of the question. Thus, the determination that a party is a successor does not lead to a fixed conclusion about the extent to which "successorship" obligations are applicable. However, a two-step analysis is often inescapable because if a party is not a successor, it will usually be unnecessary to consider the extent of its obligations.

[3]Successorship issues also arise in the Board's supplemental or "back pay" proceedings in which the derivative liability of a new employer for the unfair labor practices of the former employer may be litigated. *See* Chapter 32 *infra* at notes 166-67. They may also arise in a Board representation proceeding where a "contract bar" is asserted; *see* Chapter 10 *supra* at notes 158-60.

[4]*See, e.g.,* John Wiley & Sons v. Livingston, 376 US 543, 55 LRRM 2769 (1964), discussed *infra* at notes 24-32; Howard Johnson Co. v. Detroit Joint Bd., Hotel & Restaurant Employees, *supra* note 2, discussed *infra* at notes 60-69.

dinary extent by decisions of the Supreme Court itself. Second, these decisions are relatively recent. Only one of the four Supreme Court decisions, a 1964 case,[5] was rendered prior to 1972, and the potential scope of that decision has been severely narrowed. This does not suggest that the law of successorship had not emerged at all, or had been static, during the preceding or intervening years. Rather, it reflects a later synthesis of the law in which many concepts developed by the Board and the circuit courts were reformulated, affirmed, distinguished, or overturned.

The result has been that these Supreme Court decisions have been so closely scrutinized by the Board and the lower courts that the phraseology of the opinions, by advertence or inadvertence, has often become the reference point for many of the major issues which have emerged. A further result has been the visible role of the lower courts in construing these decisions. This has stemmed not merely from special procedural considerations inherent in enforcing both Section 301 actions and Board orders but from the circumstance that most successorship cases do not involve an interpretation of statutory language "but of Supreme Court pronouncements of the controlling statutory principles . . . ."[6] Thus, the lower courts have tended to take a more independent role in construing the Supreme Court's decisions than they might ordinarily adopt in reviewing Board orders, where the Board itself has construed the statutory provisions of the Act or the Board's own rules.[7]

The cores of these landmark decisions are briefly summarized as follows:

The 1964 decision in *John Wiley & Sons* v. *Livingston*[8] established, in the context of a Section 301 action, that certain con-

---

[5]John Wiley & Sons v. Livingston, *supra* note 4.
[6]Machinists (Boeing Co.) v. NLRB, 595 F2d 664, 673 n.41, 98 LRRM 2787 (CA DC, 1978), *cert. denied*, 439 US 1070, 100 LRRM 2268 (1979), where the court stated that in those circumstances "deference to the Board may ordinarily be less appropriate."
[7]This independent role has not been confined to cases in which enforcement of Board orders has been denied; *see, e.g.*, Pacific Hide & Fur Depot, Inc. v. NLRB, 553 F2d 609, 95 LRRM 2467 (CA 9, 1977); Pre-Engineered Bldg. Prods., Inc., 228 NLRB 841, 96 LRRM 1170 (1977), *enforcement denied*, 603 F2d 134, 101 LRRM 3021 (CA 10, 1979); NLRB v. Bausch & Lomb, Inc., 526 F2d 817, 90 LRRM 3217 (CA 2, 1975), *denying enforcement in part to* 214 NLRB 338, 88 LRRM 1196 (1974). It has also extended to cases in which Board orders have been enforced or affirmed; *see, e.g.*, Machinists v. NLRB, *supra* note 6; Boeing Co. v. Machinists, 504 F2d 307, 87 LRRM 2865 (CA 5, 1974), *cert. denied*, 421 US 913, 88 LRRM 3456 (1975); NLRB v. Band-Age, Inc., 534 F2d 1, 92 LRRM 2001 (CA 1, 1976).
[8]*Supra* note 4.

tractual rights under a labor agreement are not automatically extinguished by the "disappearance" of the contracting employer through merger and that the duty to arbitrate may survive and devolve upon the resultant "new" employer even though the new employer had never signed the contract nor agreed to arbitrate.

The 1972 decision in *NLRB* v. *Burns International Detective Agency, Inc.*,[9] which arose in the context of an unfair labor practice proceeding, is perhaps the centerpiece of successorship law. Many repercussions have flowed from its resolution of two major issues. First, it articulated certain fundamental criteria in determining whether a new employer has an obligation to bargain with the representative of its predecessor's employees. (These criteria have become the prerequisites for determining whether the new employer is a "successor.") Second, it held that a successor's obligation to bargain does not extend to being bound involuntarily to the substantive terms of its predecessor's labor agreement.

In 1974, in *Howard Johnson Co., Inc.* v. *Detroit Local Joint Board, Hotel & Restaurant Employees,*[10] the Supreme Court held that the criteria which the Court had established in an unfair labor practice proceeding in *Burns* for determining whether a new employer's bargaining obligation transcended a change in ownership could not be disregarded in a Section 301 action which had been instituted in federal court in reliance on *Wiley.*

Earlier that same term (in 1973), in *Golden State Bottling Co.* v. *NLRB,*[11] the Court held that the duty to remedy unfair labor practices of a predecessor may be imposed upon a successor who takes over a business with knowledge of the unfair labor practices or the pendency of unfair labor practice proceedings.

II. HISTORICAL DEVELOPMENT

A. Early Rulings

Despite the overwhelming relevance of the foregoing Supreme Court decisions, legal inquiries into a new employer's obligations

---

[9]406 US 272, 80 LRRM 2225 (1972).
[10]*Supra* note 2.
[11]414 US 168, 84 LRRM 2839 (1973). *See infra* at notes 285-331.

to a former owner's (or its representative's) employees long preceded these cases. The roots of those inquiries date at least as far back as 1939 and follow two general lines of development.

The less controversial development concerned employers found to be *alter egos* of a prior employer. As the term alter ego suggests, it refers to a situation in which the identity of the employing entities is substantially the same. Thus, the "new employer" might be "merely a disguised continuance of the old employer,"[12] or may have undergone a mere technical change, perhaps to avoid the effect of the labor laws, without any substantial change in ownership or management. In those circumstances the courts have encountered "little difficulty" in holding that the new employer "is in reality the same employer" and subject to similar obligations.[13] The practice of including in Board orders the phrase "successors and assigns" and applying the order to alter egos was upheld by the Supreme Court in 1945, in *Regal Knitwear* v. *NLRB.*[14]

As early as 1939, the Board held that, following a nominal change in corporate organization which did not materially alter the nature of the business or the employees, a successor employer was required to bargain with the employees' bargaining agent.[15] The Board continued to hold that the bargaining status of the majority representative remained unchanged when an alteration of business operations did not change the essential attributes of the employment relationship.[16]

These early rulings, however, were not confined to alter ego situations. In several cases in the 1940s, the Board held that a bona fide transferee of a business operation was bound by the certification of the bargaining agent for the unit.[17] The Board's position was that a mere change in ownership did not affect the certification of a bargaining agent in the "employing industry."[18] As early as 1953, in *Cruse Motors*, the Board drew what was to

---

[12]Southport Petroleum Co. v. NLRB, 315 US 100, 106, 9 LRRM 411 (1942).
[13]Howard Johnson, *supra* note 2 at 255.
[14]324 US 9, 15 LRRM 882 (1945).
[15]Chas. Cushman Co., 15 NLRB 90, 5 LRRM 113 (1939).
[16]Stonewall Cotton Mills, 80 NLRB 325, 23 LRRM 1085 (1948).
[17]Simmons Eng'r Co., 65 NLRB 1435, 17 LRRM 291 (1946); National Bag Co., 65 NLRB 1078, 17 LRRM 283 (1946), *enforced*, 156 F2d 679 (CA 8, 1946); Syncro Machine Co., Inc., 62 NLRB 985, 16 LRRM 230 (1945); *see also* Johnson Ready Mix Co., 142 NLRB 437, 53 LRRM 1068 (1963).
[18]*See* cases cited in note 17, *supra*.

be a prophetic distinction between contract rights and the statutory duty to bargain:

> That the Respondent may not have been bound by O'Keefe's contract with the Union—indeed that the contract may be construed as specifically rejecting such an obligation—is not controlling. Whether the Respondent was required by the statute to continue dealing with the Union as the exclusive representative of its employees is a matter of interpretation of the Act and not of the contract. Though the contract may create private rights and duties enforceable under other laws, so far as this statute is concerned, the obligation to bargain is one neither created nor alterable by private agreement.[19]

The circuit courts, prior to *Wiley*, were concerned with successorship principally in reviewing Board orders, because the permissibility of Section 301 suits to compel arbitration had not been established until 1957[20] and had not been invoked against an unconsenting successor until *Wiley*.[21] The courts upheld the concept that bargaining orders could be directed against successor employers. And in those instances where the courts refused enforcement of Board orders directed at successors, they did not reject the "employing industry" concept of continuity which the Board had adopted.[22] As in the more recent cases, continuity of the work force was a major criterion in determining whether a bargaining obligation would be imposed upon a new employer.[23]

B. *Wiley* v. *Livingston*

In *Wiley* the Supreme Court required an employer to submit to grievance arbitration pursuant to a prior employer's labor agreement even though the employer had not signed or assumed that agreement or agreed to arbitrate. The Supreme Court's holding represented a substantial departure from ordinary contract law and a commonly held view of the collective bargaining agreement. Previously, a collective agreement was viewed as

---

[19]Cruse Motors, Inc., 105 NLRB 242, 248, 32 LRRM 1285 (1953).
[20]Textile Workers v. Lincoln Mills, 353 US 448, 40 LRRM 2113 (1957). *See* Chapter 19 *infra* at notes 32-41.
[21]*Supra* note 4.
[22]*See, e.g.,* NLRB v. Lunder Shoe Corp., 211 F2d 284, 33 LRRM 2695 (CA 1, 1954); NLRB v. Auto Vent-Shade, Inc., 276 F2d 303, 45 LRRM 3010 (CA 5, 1960); NLRB v. McFarland, 306 F2d 219, 50 LRRM 2707 (CA 10, 1962); NLRB v. Alamo White Truck Serv., 273 F2d 238, 45 LRRM 2330 (CA 5, 1959); NLRB v. Aluminum Tubular Corp., 299 F2d 595, 49 LRRM 2682 (CA 2, 1962); NLRB v. Stepp's Friendly Ford, 338 F2d 833, 57 LRRM 2442 (CA 9, 1964).
[23]*See* cases cited in note 22, *supra*.

merely creating personal rights and obligations between the parties who had consented to it.[24]

This decision could have been seen as merely a logical extension of the Court's reliance on the role of arbitration as a means of effectuating the national labor policy of avoiding industrial strife, with no major implications for Board proceedings. The Court's opinion, however, was susceptible to a broader reading of the "successor's" liability because, in overcoming the primary hurdle—the contention that the new employer never consented to be bound—the Court declared that "[w]hile the principles of law governing ordinary contracts would not bind to a contract an unconsenting successor to a contracting party, a collective bargaining agreement is not an ordinary contract."[25] It added that a collective bargaining agreement "is not in any real sense the simple product of a consensual relationship."[26] The Court augmented this analytical leap by reference to specific policy considerations, leaving little doubt as to the far-reaching implications of the decision. In terms of policy, it focused upon the need to protect the employees who would not ordinarily participate in the negotiations leading to changes in ownership of businesses. In such negotiations, the interests of the employees would inevitably be incidental to business considerations, the Court stated. Therefore, said the Court, the right of owners to negotiate their own terms "must be balanced by some protections to the employees from a sudden change in the employment relationship," and the "transition . . . will . . . be eased and industrial strife avoided if employees' claims continue to be resolved by arbitration . . . ."[27]

The basic facts of *Wiley* were the following: In 1961, Interscience, for valid business reasons, was merged into a much larger publishing company, John Wiley & Sons, and Interscience ceased operating as a separate entity. At the time of the merger Wiley's employees (about 300) were not organized, but Interscience had a labor agreement with a union representing 40 of its 80 employees. That agreement did not contain a "successorship clause" purporting to bind the successors and assigns

---

[24]*See* Steelworkers v. Reliance Universal, Inc., 335 F2d 891, 56 LRRM 2721 (CA 3, 1964).
[25]John Wiley & Sons v. Livingston, *supra* note 4 at 550.
[26]*Id.*
[27]*Id.* at 549.

of Interscience,[28] and Wiley did not agree to assume the labor agreement.[29] All but a few of the Interscience employees were retained by Wiley, and they performed essentially the same work on the same products as they did before the merger.

In discussions before and after the merger, the union contended that it continued to represent the Interscience bargaining unit employees and that, after the merger, Wiley was obligated to recognize certain rights, such as severance pay, which had "vested" or "accrued" under the Interscience union contract. Wiley claimed that the labor agreement, which had expired, had terminated for all purposes. When Wiley refused the union's demand that it submit the dispute to arbitration under the Interscience agreement, the union brought a Section 301 suit in federal court to compel arbitration.

The holding on the substantive question of the obligation to arbitrate was phrased by a unanimous Court as follows:

> We hold that the disappearance by merger of a corporate employer which has entered into a collective bargaining agreement with a union does not automatically terminate all rights of the employees covered by the agreement, and that, in appropriate circumstances, present here, the successor employer may be required to arbitrate with the union under the agreement.[30]

There were several expressed limitations to this holding. First, the Court held only that the successor was obligated to arbitrate certain claims which were assertable under provisions of the predecessor's contract, and not that any such claim had merit as against Wiley.[31] Second, the Court stated that it was not holding that the duty to arbitrate survives in every case in which the ownership or corporate structure of an enterprise is changed, for the Court recognized that there could be cases where "lack of any substantial continuity of identity in the business enter-

---

[28]The absence of a "successorship" or "successors and assigns" clause that would provide that the labor agreement be binding on successors was not a deterrent to finding successorship in *Wiley*. Not even a disclaimer of such obligations was controlling. United States Gypsum Co. v. Steelworkers, 384 F2d 38, 66 LRRM 2232 (CA 5, 1967); McGuire v. Humble Oil & Ref. Co., 355 F2d 352, 61 LRRM 2410 (CA 2, 1966); Steelworkers v. Reliance Universal, Inc., *supra* note 24; Local Joint Executive Bd., Hotel & Restaurant Employees v. Joden, Inc., 262 F Supp 390, 64 LRRM 2113 (D Mass, 1966). By the same token, the presence of a "successors and assigns" clause did not establish successorship in Howard Johnson Co., *supra* note 2.

[29]The absence of such agreements was deemed immaterial by the Court.

[30]John Wiley & Sons, *supra* note 4 at 548.

[31]In the arbitration which ensued, almost all of the union's claims were rejected. Interscience Encyclopedia, Inc., 55 LA 210 (1970).

prise before and after the change [in ownership] would make a duty to arbitrate something imposed from without . . . ."[32] The Court did not attempt to define the requisites of continuity, i.e., the criteria for successorship, and it declined to express any view about bargaining obligations in an unfair labor practice proceeding. The Court merely concluded that whether rights claimed to arise under provisions of the Interscience labor contract, including some rights which the union claimed survived the expiration of that contract, were enforceable against Wiley was subject to arbitration despite Wiley's lack of consent.

1. Impact of *Wiley*: The Courts. Lower courts subsequently extended *Wiley* to changes of ownership resulting from a sale of assets. In *Wackenhut Corp.* v. *Plant Guard Workers*,[33] the Ninth Circuit held that the arbitration clause of a preexisting labor agreement "bound" a purchaser of assets who retained most of the predecessor's employees. The Third Circuit, in *Steelworkers* v. *Reliance Universal, Inc.*,[34] construed *Wiley* more narrowly than did the Ninth Circuit. Rather than hold a purchaser of assets to an unqualified duty to arbitrate, it held that the arbitrator could decide whether certain provisions in the agreement were binding upon the successor.[35]

The duty to arbitrate announced in *Wiley* was extended, in a Second Circuit decision,[36] to a case in which the new employer had retained only a small fraction of its predecessor's employees. The decision thus highlighted an issue that was not resolved until the Supreme Court's 1974 decision in *Howard Johnson*.

2. Impact of *Wiley*: The Board. The full impact of *Wiley* in shaping the Board's views did not come to fruition until 1970. In *Wiley*, the court had expressly refused to "suggest any view on the questions surrounding a certified union's claim to continued representative status following a change in ownership . . . ,"[37] i.e., the Section 8(a)(5) issue. Thus, the relevance to Board proceedings and the extent to which the Board would be

---

[32]John Wiley & Sons, *supra* note 4 at 551.
[33]332 F2d 954, 56 LRRM 2721 (CA 9, 1964).
[34]*Supra* note 24.
[35]In *Wiley*, the Court had held that procedural arbitrability is for the arbitrator to decide. *Supra* note 4 at 556-58.
[36]Monroe Sander Corp. v. Livingston, 377 F2d 6, 66 LRRM 2273 (CA 2, 1967), *aff'g* 262 F Supp 129, 63 LRRM 2273 (SD NY, 1966).
[37]*Supra* note 4 at 551.

influenced by the reasoning of *Wiley* was at first uncertain. On the one hand, the Board continued to apply its successorship doctrine with perhaps more assurance. Until 1970, however, it failed to actually hold that a successor was bound by the substantive terms of a labor agreement negotiated by its predecessor but not agreed to or assumed by the successor.[38] The Board did, however, advance one step closer to that view by adopting the position that whether or not a successor is bound by its predecessor's labor agreement, it may not institute terms different from the contractual terms without first bargaining with the representative of the predecessor's employees.[39] The Board reasoned that "[i]n this respect, the successor-employer's obligations are the same as those imposed upon employers generally during the period between collective bargaining agreements."[40]

C. The *Burns* Case

Finally, in 1970, the Board fully assimilated *Wiley* in its decision in *William J. Burns International Detective Agency, Inc.,*[41] the lead case in a series of four Board decisions,[42] in which it held that when a business changes hands, absent unusual circumstances, "the national labor policy embodied in the Act requires the successor employer to take over and honor a collective bargaining agreement negotiated on behalf of the employing enterprise by the predecessor."[43]

---

[38]Rohlik, Inc., 145 NLRB 1236, 55 LRRM 1130 (1964), where the successor was ordered to bargain, but the Board did not consider the effect of the predecessor's contract; in Fed-Mart, 165 NLRB 202, 65 LRRM 1303 (1967), bargaining was ordered, but the trial examiner's ruling binding the successor to the predecessor's contract was reversed.

[39]Valleydale Packers, Inc., 162 NLRB 1486, 64 LRRM 1212 (1967), *enforced,* 402 F2d 768, 69 LRRM 2622 (CA 5, 1968); Overnite Transp. Co., 157 NLRB 1185, 61 LRRM 1520 (1966), *enforced,* 372 F2d 765, 64 LRRM 2359 (CA 4), *cert. denied,* 389 US 838, 66 LRRM 2307 (1967); Fed-Mart, *supra* note 38; Michaud Bus Lines, Inc., 171 NLRB 193, 68 LRRM 1033 (1968).

[40]NLRB v. Burns, *supra* note 9 at 272. *See* NLRB v. Katz, 369 US 736, 50 LRRM 2177 (1962), discussed in Chapter 13 *supra* at notes 73-78.

[41]182 NLRB 348, 74 LRRM 1098 (1970).

[42]The companion cases decided with *Burns* were the following: Dura Corp., 182 NLRB 360, 74 LRRM 1104 (1970) (presenting the reverse issue, with the Board holding that the successor employer has a right to insist that the union adhere to the contract which it had signed with the predecessor employer); Travelodge Corp., 182 NLRB 370, 74 LRRM 1105 (1970) (required degree of continuity in the employing enterprise lacking, therefore no violation found); Hackney Iron & Steel Co., 182 NLRB 357, 74 LRRM 1102 (1970) (ordering assumption of the predecessor's labor contract upon remand from the court of appeals, 395 F2d 639, 68 LRRM 2065 (CA DC, 1968), for a determination of that issue).

[43]*Supra* note 41 at 350.

The case involved Burns and the Wackenhut Corporation. Both were in the business of providing plant protection and security services, and both submitted competitive bids to Lockheed Aircraft Corporation for a new contract to replace the expiring contract under which Wackenhut had been providing those services. After the contract was let out for bids, all bidders were apprised of Wackenhut's collective bargaining agreement with the United Plant Guards Union which followed a Board certification approximately four months earlier. Burns was awarded the new contract and chose to retain 27 of the 42 guards who had been employed by Wackenhut and represented by the union. In addition, Burns transferred 15 of its own employees from other facilities to Lockheed. The union demanded that Burns recognize it and honor its three-year term collective bargaining agreement with Wackenhut. Burns refused both demands, and the union filed unfair labor practice charges.

In holding that Burns was obligated to recognize and bargain with the union, the Board relied upon established precedent. In holding Burns to the substantive terms of Wackenhut's labor agreement, the Board reversed precedent with reasoning that relied upon and paralleled *Wiley*. The Board noted that in *Wiley* the Supreme Court had viewed substantive continuity in the employing industry as an essential prerequisite for the survival of a duty to arbitrate, despite a change in ownership; the Board therefore concluded that where the requisite continuity was present in an unfair labor practice proceeding, the policy considerations favoring adherence to existing labor agreements necessitated holding that Burns be bound to its predecessor's contract.

On the employee side of the equation, it was undisputed that there was a continuity in the majority of the work force. On the employer side of the equation, the Board found that the business remained essentially unchanged and that the bargaining unit remained appropriate. As for the admonition in Section 8(d) that the obligation to bargain "does not compel either party to agree to a proposal or require the making of a concession," the Board held the limitation inapplicable to a successor employer whom it viewed as one who "stands in the shoes of its predecessor."[44]

---

[44]*Id.*

A major obstacle to the enforcement of that position became apparent later in 1970, when the Supreme Court held in *H.K. Porter Co., Inc.* v. *NLRB*[45] that Section 8(d) renders the Board and lower courts powerless to compel an employer or a union to execute or agree to any substantive contractual provision. On this basis, the Second Circuit denied enforcement of that portion of the Board's order in *Burns* requiring an involuntary assumption of the collective bargaining agreement, though it granted enforcement of the bargaining order.[46] The Supreme Court affirmed the Second Circuit, unanimously on the Section 8(d) issue, and five to four on the bargaining obligation issue.

The factual vehicle which *Burns* presented (and which the Board selected) for a reversal of policy was not a typical successorship situation. The fact that the Burns relationship to Wackenhut might more aptly be described as that of a "rival" or "competitor," rather than a "successor," was a persuasive consideration, in the view of four dissenting Supreme Court justices, for holding that Burns had no obligation to bargain with the union.[47]

D. *Burns:* The Supreme Court's View

1. The Bargaining Obligation. A closely divided Supreme Court sustained the Board's holding that Burns had a duty to bargain with the United Plant Guards. It reaffirmed the view that a mere change in ownership in the employing industry is not such an "unusual circumstance" as to relieve the new employer of an obligation to bargain with its predecessor's employees. The criteria upon which it upheld the bargaining obligation were that the "bargaining unit remained unchanged and a majority of the employees hired by the new employer [were] represented by a recently certified bargaining agent . . . ."[48] On this issue, the Court majority noted that it would have been a "wholly different case" (1) if Burns' operational structure and practices had differed from Wackenhut's so that the bargaining unit was no longer appropriate, or (2) if Burns had exercised its right to assemble a work force, a majority of which, without

---

[45]397 US 99, 73 LRRM 2561 (1970). *See* Chapter 33 *infra* at notes 246-48.
[46]Burns Int'l Detective Agency, Inc. v. NLRB, 441 F2d 911, 77 LRRM 2081 (CA 2, 1971), *aff'd, supra* note 9.
[47]*Supra* note 9 at 304-305.
[48]NLRB v. Burns Int'l Detective Agency, *supra* note 9 at 281.

unlawful discrimination, did not consist of former Wackenhut employees represented by a recently certified union.[49]

The dissenters found unsupportable the Board's assumption that a majority of Burns' employees desired the United Plant Guards as their representative. They also rejected the Board's acceptance of Wackenhut's unit as necessarily appropriate for Burns. The thrust of the dissenting view, however, was that there was insufficient continuity of the enterprise on the employer's side, for the only nexus between Wackenhut and Burns was a "mere naked shifting of a group of employees from one employer to another . . . ."[50] It was pointed out that Burns, which had succeeded to the service contract only over Wackenhut's opposition, did not acquire a single asset of Wackenhut, either tangible or intangible, by negotiation or transfer. Regarding the expectations of employees that the original employer adhere to its labor agreement, the dissenters would have required that another employing entity perform the contract only when it has succeeded to some asset "by the use of which the employees might have expected the first employer to have performed his contract with them."[51]

2. The Contractual Obligation. The Court unanimously rejected the Board's position that a successor is bound to the terms of its predecessor's labor agreement, a result which seemed foreshadowed by its then recent holding in *H.K. Porter*.[52] Nonetheless, the Court distinguished *Wiley* on three separate bases. First, on the formal basis of its procedural context and factual setting, the Court noted that (1) *Wiley* arose in a Section 301 suit to compel arbitration and not in the context of an unfair labor practice case, and (2) *Wiley* was a narrow holding dealing with a merger occurring against a background of state law which provided that the surviving corporation in a merger was liable for the obligations of the disappearing corporation. (This distinction subsequently proved to be a temporary and controversial expedient.)

The second distinction invoked the same underlying factual consideration that troubled the dissenters on the bargaining obligation; namely, that Wackenhut and Burns were competi-

---

[49]*Id.* at n. 5.
[50]*Id.* at 304.
[51]*Id.* at 305.
[52]*Supra* note 45.

tors. Thus, unlike *Wiley,* "there was no merger or sale of assets, and there were no dealings whatsoever between Wackenhut and Burns."[53]

In its third distinction, the Court struck a different balance than in *Wiley* in the expression of its views concerning the mandates of federal labor policy. In acknowledging that prevention of industrial strife in favor of arbitration is an important aim, which was emphasized in *Wiley,* the Court adhered to its view in *H.K. Porter* that Congress had not intended totally to subordinate to that goal the bargaining freedom of employers and unions. While *Wiley* emphasized the possible loss of protection to employees who had no opportunity to participate in the takeover transaction, *Burns* emphasized the countervailing inequities which confronted new employers. Thus, the Court noted, a potential employer might otherwise be deterred from taking over a moribund business unless it could make essential changes. "Saddling" the new employer with all of the terms of the old labor contract might, according to the Court, make these changes impossible. Moreover, it noted that a union might be disadvantaged if it made unusual concessions to a failing predecessor employer and later found itself unable to enter into a more favorable contract with an economically strong successor employer. The Court stated:

> The Congressional policy manifested in the Act is to enable the parties to negotiate for any protection either deems appropriate but to allow the balance of bargaining advantage to be set by economic power realities. Strife is bound to occur if the concessions that must be honored do not correspond to the relative economic strength of the parties.[54]

It was thus apparent that the difference in emphasis in *Wiley* and *Burns* was so pronounced as to belie the resort to formal and narrow distinctions.

In the final portion of its opinion the Court held unanimously that Burns was not required to reimburse its employees for unilaterally changing the terms of the Wackenhut labor contract. In establishing that a new employer is ordinarily free to set initial terms and conditions of employment, the Board's pre-*Burns* rule that a new employer must bargain about such changes

---

[53]*See Burns, supra* note 9 at 286.
[54]*Id.* at 288.

was for the most part overturned.[55] A modicum of vitality was retained by the Court's hedging its position, noting that there may be instances where it is "perfectly clear" that the new employer "plans to retain" the former employees; and in that event, it would be appropriate to "consult" with the bargaining representative.[56] A further note of uncertainty was provided, however, by the caveat that in some situations it would not be clear that a successor has a duty to bargain until it has hired its "full complement" of employees.[57] The Board and lower courts have since wrestled with this issue.[58]

E. Aftermath of *Burns*

Many issues unfolded following *Burns,* but an immediate concern arose from the failure to fully reconcile the disposition of the survival of contract rights under *Wiley* with the limitation on the bargaining obligation under *Burns.*

The possibility of a dual approach to contract and bargaining obligations, based upon the distinction between Section 301 actions and unfair labor practice proceedings, remained intact for only two years. One might speculate whether its survival would have been prolonged if Section 301 actions had continued to be utilized solely for the purpose of arbitrating contractual rights of holdover employees, as in *Wiley*. In those circumstances, the emphasis upon continued "majority" status would not be as compelling as in a refusal-to-bargain context in which a continued relationship is anticipated between the new employer and the incumbent union. However, once Section 301 had been invoked to compel arbitration over the question of whether the new employer's hiring decisions were governed by the predecessor's labor agreement, the Supreme Court could easily find a conflict between *Wiley* and *Burns*.

It was inevitable that the paths of *Wiley* and *Burns* would cross, for contract rights and bargaining obligations are not readily divisible, and contracts can themselves lead to bargaining obligations, depending upon the forum chosen.[59] If, for example,

---

[55]*Id*. at 293-94. *See, e.g.,* cases cited in note 39 *supra*.
[56]*Id*. at 294-95.
[57]*Id*. at 295.
[58]*See* discussion *infra* at notes 76-90 and 177-91.
[59]*See* Christensen, *Labor Law Decisions of the United States Supreme Court—October Term, 1973—Addition, Subtraction and Conversation,* ABA LABOR RELATIONS LAW SECTION (1974 Program and Proceedings) 51, 52 (1974).

under *Wiley*, a new employer were obligated by the preexisting labor agreement to continue the employment of all of the former owner's employees, except those terminated in accordance with the discharge and layoff provisions, its status as a successor (for bargaining purposes as well) was more likely to be assured than if the new employer were free to determine the constituency of its own work force. On the other hand, if the new employer were free, under *Burns*, to decide how it would compose its own work force, its own hiring decisions would determine whether there would be the requisite continuity of the work force, and the new employer could independently affect its status as a successor. Thus, if a majority of the work force assembled were not holdovers, this fact would represent a barrier to a union seeking bargaining rights in an unfair labor practice proceeding. The union's alternative was a Section 301 action seeking to compel arbitration of those hiring decisions. It was in this setting that the *Howard Johnson*[60] case arose.

F. *Howard Johnson*

Howard Johnson purchased all of the personal property used for a restaurant and motor lodge which it had previously franchised. The predecessor establishment had employed 53 employees. The sellers retained the real property and leased it to Howard Johnson. Howard Johnson commenced operations with 45 employees, of whom only 9 were holdovers. The union commenced a Section 301 action to compel arbitration on behalf of the former employees who were not hired, with the object of obtaining an arbitration award ordering Howard Johnson to hire them. The former employer conceded that it was required to arbitrate the extent of its liability under the successorship provisions of its labor agreements, but the new employer, Howard Johnson, contested its obligation to arbitrate. The Sixth Circuit, relying upon *Wiley* rather than *Burns*, ordered Howard Johnson to arbitrate as a successor.[61]

The Sixth Circuit's rationale was that the determination of whether or not the new employer could be considered a successor ought not to depend upon the hiring decisions made by the new employer, because it would thus be in a position to deter-

---

[60]*Supra* note 2.
[61]Detroit Local Joint Executive Bd., Hotel & Restaurant Employees v. Howard Johnson Co., 482 F2d 489, 83 LRRM 2804 (CA 6, 1973).

mine by its own actions whether or not it would become a successor, i.e., if it did not retain a majority of the former employees, it would not be a successor, which the court viewed as a bootstrap operation.

Since the result would have differed under *Burns,* had the union filed a refusal-to-bargain charge, the Supreme Court chose not to straddle the two approaches. It reversed the Sixth Circuit, holding that the new employer was not obligated to arbitrate under the prevailing circumstances.

The Court first attempted to reconcile its divergent approaches by stating that the reasoning underlying *Burns* must be taken into account in any Section 301 suit because

> [i]t would be plainly inconsistent with this view [that federal common law must be fashioned from the policy of national labor laws] to say that the basic policies found controlling in an unfair labor practice context may be disregarded by the courts in a suit under §301, and thus to permit the rights enjoyed by the new employer in a successorship context to depend upon the forum in which the union presses its claim . . . .[62]

While the *Burns* rationale emerged as controlling, the Court declined to declare irreconcilable conflict between *Wiley* and *Burns,* though it acknowledged that the decisions were "to some extent inconsistent."[63] It distinguished the merger in *Wiley,* in which the former employer had completely "disappeared" and the surviving corporation had hired all the employees of the disappearing entity, from the sale of assets by the predecessor of Howard Johnson, which had remained in existence, retained substantial assets, and even conceded that it was obligated to arbitrate questions concerning its liability resulting from the change in ownership. In a significant footnote, the Court suggested the possibility that the union might have sought injunctive relief against the seller prior to sale by moving to enjoin the sale to Howard Johnson as a breach of the successorship clause in the seller's collective bargaining agreement.[64]

---

[62]*Supra* note 2 at 256.

[63]*Supra* note 2 at 254-56.

[64]Ironically, the Court referred to a lower court decision which posed a barrier to this relief in a §8(e) context. Howard Johnson Co. v. Detroit Joint Bd., *supra* note 2 at 258 n.3. This possibility, which has been referred to as a "pregnant footnote which . . . falls within the first trimester of gestation" (Christensen, *supra* note 59), would necessitate a balancing of equities as a prerequisite to the granting of injunctive relief. *See* Local 1115 Joint Bd. Nursing Home v. B & K Investments, Inc., 436 F Supp 1203, 96 LRRM 2348, (SD Fla, 1977). *See generally* Chapter 17 *infra* at notes 375-77.

Despite the Court's overt distinguishing of *Wiley,* the "heart of the controversy" was whether the *Burns* case controlled in establishing that a purchaser "had the right not to hire any of the former 'employees,' if it so desired."[65] Once the Court recognized the right of the new employer to operate with its own new work force, "majority" considerations prevailed in the Court's further conclusion that there was an insufficient continuity in the "identity of the work force across the change of ownership" to require the new employer to arbitrate.[66]

The language the Court used in referring to a "majority" became a source of controversy in subsequent decisions by the Board and lower courts.[67] Nonetheless, the reliance upon majority considerations became a relevant barometer in assessing the declining impact of *Wiley.*[68]

Reconciling *Burns* and *Howard Johnson* with *H.K. Porter,* the Tenth Circuit held in *Lone Star Steel Co.* v. *NLRB*[69] that a successorship clause applicable only to permanent disposition of assets is legal under Section 8(e) and is also a mandatory subject of bargaining.[70]

G. Golden State Bottling Co.

In 1973, a year before its *Howard Johnson* decision, the Supreme Court approved the Board's existing policy establishing the obligations of a bona fide successor to remedy the unfair labor practices of its predecessor of which it was aware at the time of acquisition.[71] The Court also took the occasion to reaffirm, as a basic policy consideration, the protection of employee interests against a sudden change in ownership (citing *Wiley*), and the considerations of majority concepts in establishing continuity (citing *Burns*).

---

[65]*Supra* note 2 at 260 and 262.

[66]*Id.* at 263.

[67]*See* discussion *infra* at notes 76-90.

[68]It would appear that *Burns* and *Howard Johnson* are destined to supplant *Wiley* as the reference point for §301 actions. *See* Service Employees Local 47 v. Cleveland Tower Hotel, Inc., 606 F2d 684, 102 LRRM 2405 (CA 6, 1979).

[69]639 F2d 545, 104 LRRM 3144 (CA 10, 1980), *aff'g sub nom.* Mine Workers, 231 NLRB 573, 96 LRRM 1083 (1977).

[70]*See* Chapter 17 *infra* at notes 375-77; *see generally* Chapter 26 *infra* for discussion of §8(e).

[71]*See* Golden State Bottling, *supra* note 11. *See* Perma Vinyl Corp., 164 NLRB 968, 65 LRRM 1168 (1967), *enforced sub nom.* U.S. Pipe & Foundry Co. v. NLRB, 398 F2d 544, 68 LRRM 2913 (CA 5, 1968).

In a potentially significant footnote, the Court pointed out that the general rule of corporate law, that the purchaser of corporate assets is ordinarily not liable for the seller's debts or liabilities unless (1) the purchaser agrees to assume the obligations, (2) the purchaser is a mere continuation of the seller, or (3) the transaction's purpose is to escape liability, is a narrower concept than the confines of the labor law doctrine of successorship:

> The refusal to adopt a mode of analysis requiring the Board to distinguish among mergers, consolidations, and purchases of assets is attributable to the fact that, so long as there is a continuity in the "employing industry," the public policies underlying the doctrine will be served by its broad application . . . .[72]

In *Howard Johnson* the Court cited that proposition with approval, but only to show that every rule has its exception and that *Wiley* constituted such an exception, because the merger there occurred against a background of state law embodying the general rule that in a merger the surviving corporation is liable for the obligations of the disappearing corporation.[73] The Board has advanced the view that where the ownership changes arise through a sale of stock, but the former corporation continues to exist, the new corporation may continue to be bound by labor contracts negotiated prior to the sale; and no issue of successorship even arises, because the employing entity has remained the same.[74] In *Clothing Workers* v. *Ratner Corp.*,[75] the Ninth Circuit, applying similar reasoning, held in a Section 301 action that a corporation remained bound by a collective bargaining agreement, though it had become a holding company and had assigned all manufacturing operations to a wholly owned subsidiary.

III. SUCCESSORSHIP AND THE BARGAINING OBLIGATION

The principle that a successor may be held to its predecessor's bargaining obligation is now well established. However, the precise definition of what constitutes a "successor" remains a point

---

[72]Golden State Bottling Co., *supra* note 11 at 182 n.5.
[73]*Supra* note 2 at 257.
[74]*See infra* at notes 192-229; Krupman & Kaplan, *The Stock Purchaser After Burns: Must He Buy the Union Contract?*, 31 LAB. L.J. 328 (1980); TKB Int'l Corp., 240 NLRB 1082, 100 LRRM 1426 (1979).
[75]602 F2d 1363, 102 LRRM 2571 (CA 9, 1979).

of continuing controversy before both the Board and the courts. The determination of successorship turns on a number of related inquiries, all focused upon the degree of continuity between the old and the new employer's business enterprise. These inquiries include (1) whether there is continuity in the work force (the "majority" issue), (2) whether there is continuity in the employing industry, (3) whether there is continuity in the appropriateness of the bargaining unit, and (4) the impact of a hiatus in operations.

A. Continuity of the Work Force: "The Concept of Majority"

The paramount criterion in determining successorship is the continuity of the work force (i.e., the "majority" issue).[76] In the years following *Burns* and *Howard Johnson,* it became increasingly evident that the concept of majority is multidimensional, i.e., "which" majority, "when," and "where." Not only may the existence of a continued "majority" turn upon the mathematical yardstick used, it may also turn upon the precise time frame in which it is measured, as well as on a consideration, where applicable, of individual employment decisions.

1. The Applicable Yardstick. Immediately following *Burns* and *Howard Johnson,* there was considerable controversy over "which" majority would be determinative, or viewed another way, which test should be used to determine majority status. This controversy stemmed from the manner in which the phraseology, or formulation, of the test in *Howard Johnson* differed from *Burns.*[77] In *Burns,* the Court stated the premise that

> where the bargaining unit remains unchanged and *a majority of the employees hired by the new employer are represented by a recently certified bargaining agent* there is little basis for faulting the Board's

---

[76]*See* Nazareth Regional High School v. NLRB, 549 F2d 873, 94 LRRM 2897 (CA 2, 1977), *enforcing in part* Roman Catholic Diocese of Brooklyn, 222 NLRB 1052, 91 LRRM 1419 (1976). In Spruce-Up Corp., 209 NLRB 194, 85 LRRM 1426 (1974), the concurring opinion, in reliance upon Goldberg, *The Labor Law Obligations of a Successor Employer,* 63 Nw U. L. Rev. 735 (1969), notes that only two cases had been discovered in over a 20-year period in which the Board had found successorship and duty to bargain where a majority of the new employer's work force was not composed of the old employees. In no Board decision since *Burns* has successorship been found absent a finding of "majority."

[77]It is uncertain whether the Court actually intended different tests or whether the apparent difference is merely a difference in phraseology.

implementation of the express mandates of §8(a)(5) and §9(a) by ordering the employer to bargain with the incumbent union.[78]

In *Howard Johnson,* on the other hand, the term "majority" was framed in terms of whether "the successor employer hires a majority of the predecessor's employees . . . ."[79]

In *Burns,* the primary reference point for determining majority status was the new employer's work force, whereas in *Howard Johnson* it was the work force of the predecessor.[80] Thus, the literal test derived from *Burns* is whether a majority of the new employer's work force consists of holdovers from the previous employer. The literal test derived from *Howard Johnson* is whether the new employer has hired a majority of the previous employer's employees.

Not surprisingly, following the decisions in *Burns* and *Howard Johnson,* members of the Board have expressed differing views of majority status. The initial differences were reflected in a series of divided decisions in which a Board majority held that the appropriate inquiry in determining whether the new employer is a successor is the percentage of the new employer's work force which was previously employed by the predecessor.[81] This view, which became unanimous, regards *Burns,* rather than *Howard Johnson,* as controlling.

One of these early divided decisions, *United Maintenance & Manufacturing Co.,*[82] aptly illustrates the difference in approach in circumstances most likely to lead to different results. There was a sharp difference in the numerical complement of the new

---

[78]*Supra* note 9 at 281 (emphasis added). Although the Court referred to a "certified" bargaining agent, this reference was not deemed to exclude recognized bargaining agents, Eklund's Sweden House Inn, Inc., 203 NLRB 413, 83 LRRM 1173 (1973), for the reference to certification was framed in terms of the presumption of continued majority stemming from a recent Board election—a presumption with which four dissenters disagreed. While the dissenters disagreed with the majority on the issue of whether Burns was a successor, they nevertheless concurred on the question of the bargaining obligations of a successor.

[79]*Supra* note 2 at 263.

[80]Significantly, the Court in neither case was required to consider the possible difference in result stemming from the failure to utilize the same terminology. In *Burns* the number of employees in the new and old employer's work force was identical, and in *Howard Johnson* neither majority test would have been met.

[81]United Maintenance & Mfg. Co., 214 NLRB 529, 87 LRRM 1469 (1974); Spruce-Up Corp., *supra* note 76. *Cf.* Boeing Co., 214 NLRB 541, 87 LRRM 1461 (1974), where the Board addressed the "clear intention" aspect rather than the work-force percentage guideline.

[82]*Supra* note 81.

employer's work force as compared with its predecessor. The new employer's work force consisted of 10 employees, of whom 7 had been employed by the predecessor. The predecessor's total unit complement had consisted of 38 employees. Hence, a majority of the new employer's employees were former employees of the predecessor. On the other hand, the new employer did not hire a majority of the predecessor's employees. The Board's majority opinion, relying on *Burns*, found that the new employer was a successor and that the new employer's work force was the yardstick against which successorship was to be measured. The majority opinion stated that "the somewhat less stringent requirement" of *Burns* was appropriate for determining representation rights, even though the Supreme Court in *Howard Johnson* had "established a more stringent test for determining contractual rights in a Section 301 proceeding."[83] The dissenting opinion viewed *Howard Johnson* as providing the applicable standard in both Section 301 suits and unfair labor practice cases.[84]

Since 1975, the Board has applied the *Burns* test of majority status without dissent;[85] and in reviewing Board orders in refusal-to-bargain cases, the courts have not questioned the application of this standard.[86] For example, the First Circuit upheld a bargaining order where 35 of the new employer's work force of 37

---

[83]*Id.* at 534 n. 15. It is not true that in all instances the application of the *Howard Johnson* test will necessarily result in a more stringent standard. For example, if the new work force is more than twice the numerical size of the old work force, under *Burns* no continuing majority would be mathematically possible, whereas it would be under *Howard Johnson*.

[84]*Id.* at 539. Although Members Fanning and Penello joined the majority opinion, they stated their separate view in a concurring opinion. In their view, *Burns* required only that "a legally significant portion of the successor's employment force consists of employees previously employed in the bargaining unit." Spruce-Up Corp., *supra* note 76 at 205. However, this position has not reemerged in subsequent decisions.

[85]*See, e.g.,* Miami Indus. Trucks, Inc., 221 NLRB 1223, 91 LRRM 1040 (1975); Bellingham Frozen Foods, 237 NLRB 1450, 99 LRRM 1270 (1978), *enforced,* 626 F2d 674, 105 LRRM 2404, (CA 9, 1980); Roman Catholic Diocese of Brooklyn (Ford Cent. Catholic High School), 236 NLRB 1, 98 LRRM 1359 (1978); Ric's Best Auto Painting, 248 NLRB 1028, 104 LRRM 1116 (1980).

[86]Machinists v. NLRB, *supra* note 6; NLRB v. Houston Distribution Servs., Inc., 573 F2d 260, 98 LRRM 2538 (CA 5, 1978), *enforcing* 227 NLRB 960, 95 LRRM 1100 (1977), *cert. denied,* 439 US 1047, 99 LRRM 3450 (1978); Pacific Hide & Fur Depot, Inc. v. NLRB, *supra* note 7; NLRB v. Band-Age, Inc., *supra* note 7; Zim's Foodliner, Inc. v. NLRB, 495 F2d 1131, 85 LRRM 3019 (CA 7, 1974), *enforcing* 201 NLRB 905, 82 LRRM 1082 (1973); NLRB v. Polytech, Inc., 469 F2d 1226, 81 LRRM 2902 (CA 8, 1972), *enforcing* 186 NLRB 984, 75 LRRM 1491 (1970). Strike replacements subject to being supplanted by unfair labor practice strikers are not counted either way. NLRB v. Fabsteel Co. of La., 587 F2d 689, 100 LRRM 2349 (CA 5, 1979), *enforcing* 231 NLRB 372, 97 LRRM 1104 (1977), *cert. denied,* 442 US 934, 101 LRRM 2556 (1979). On the other hand, employees unlawfully discharged by the predecessor appear to be counted towards the majority in determining whether the subsequent owner is liable, as a successor, for

employees were holdovers, despite the fact that the predecessor had a work force of 250 to 300 employees.[87]

While the *Burns* yardstick has now become established in measuring majority status in unfair labor practice cases, its acceptance is still doubtful in Section 301 suits to compel arbitration under a predecessor's labor agreement. At least two circuit courts have considered the precise issue. In a Section 301 suit, the Fifth Circuit, in *Boeing Co.* v. *Machinists*,[88] concluded that, as in *Howard Johnson*, the number of holdover employees should be measured against the predecessor's work force rather than the successor's:

> As a matter of principle, since the duty to arbitrate arises from an application of the contract between the predecessor employer and his organized employees, the entity whose identity is to be the reference point for judging continuity ought to be the predecessor enterprise.[89]

The court refused to compel arbitration where only 35 percent of the predecessor's employees were hired by Boeing and no tangible assets were transferred to Boeing. In *NLRB* v. *Band-Age, Inc.*, the First Circuit, in enforcing the Board's order in an unfair labor practice case, applied the *Burns* standard, but indicated its agreement with the Fifth Circuit's view that the *Howard Johnson* yardstick would be applicable in a Section 301 suit.[90]

2. The Appropriate Time for Measuring Majority Status. As evident from the developing case law, the work force of new employers at the time of takeover will frequently be fluid rather than fixed. In such circumstances, it may be inadequate to confine the measurement of majority status to the precise commercial time when the business is acquired.[91] Thus, the dimension of time has become a further significant consideration, although this issue did not fully emerge until 1977. *Pacific Hide & Fur Depot, Inc.* v. *NLRB*[92] became the reference point for further

---

the predecessor's discharges. Bell Co., 243 NLRB 977, 101 LRRM 1572 (1979), *supplementing* 225 NLRB 474, 93 LRRM 1180 (1976), *enforced in part*, 561 F2d 1264, 96 LRRM 2437 (CA 7, 1977). *See generally infra* at notes 285-331.

[87]NLRB v. Band-Age, Inc., *supra* note 7.

[88]*Supra* note 7.

[89]*Id.* at 319.

[90]*Supra* note 7.

[91]There may also be instances in which succession may be found to have occurred even prior to the date of actual purchase. In NLRB v. Ethan Allen, 544 F2d 742, 93 LRRM 2811 (CA 4, 1976), *enforcing in part* 218 NLRB 208, 89 LRRM 1780 (1975), when the sale was delayed by a bankruptcy proceeding against the seller, the new employer began operating the predecessor's plant through a leasing arrangement (with the seller's main creditor) until the sale was consummated some two months later. The seller was deemed the successor as of the time when it first took over operation of the plant.

[92]*Supra* note 7.

developments. That case raised the question of *when*, while a new employer's work force is being assembled, does the determination of majority status become fixed for purposes of determining successorship.[93]

The new employer in *Pacific Hide* commenced operations with seven employees, all of whom were holdovers. On the date the union demanded recognition, there were 10 employees, including the seven holdovers. Subsequently, a full employee complement of 19 employees was reached, of which only the original seven were holdovers. In a decision affirmed without opinion by the Board, the administrative law judge held that the critical time for measuring the union's majority status was the time the union perfected its demand for recognition and that, since there was a continuity of the majority of the work force at that point, the new employer was obligated to bargain as a successor.

The Ninth Circuit denied enforcement on the ground that the critical time for the relevant majority determination was when, under the *Burns* rationale, the "full complement" of employees had been hired. Since the majority test had not been met at the time the "full complement" was assembled, the court concluded that the new employer was not a successor. While the court noted that there was no previous case cited to it in which there was a transition from a majority to a minority of holdovers, it was careful to indicate that the precise determination of when a "full complement" had been reached can vary depending upon the factual circumstances and thus cannot be determined by a mathematical formula. According to the Ninth Circuit, the interests of the new employer, the old employees it hired, and the new employees not previously represented by the union must be balanced.

The issue in *Pacific Hide* focused upon the following dictum in *Burns*, which has been a prolific source of controversy:

> Although a successor employer is ordinarily free to set initial terms on which it will hire the employees of a predecessor, there will be instances in which it is perfectly clear that the new employer plans to retain all of the employees in the unit and in which it will be appropriate to have him initially consult with the employees' bargaining representative before he fixes terms. In other situations,

---

[93]*Id.* This issue was so closely related to the question of when the successor's duty to bargain attaches that it previously had received scant analytical treatment. *See* discussion following note 176.

however, it may not be clear until the successor employer has hired *his full complement of employees* that he has a duty to bargain with a union, since it will not be evident until then that the bargaining representative represents a majority of the employees in the unit as required by Section 9(a) of the Act . . . .[94]

In *Pacific Hide*, the Board viewed the term "full complement" as being concerned *only* with the unilateral setting of the initial terms and conditions of employment by a successor, which was not an issue in *Pacific Hide*, rather than a question of the principles governing *when* an employer becomes a successor. In the Ninth Circuit's view, the "full complement" test in *Burns* is applicable both to the determination of *whether* and *when* a new employer is a successor.

Pacific Hide highlighted two areas of controversy: (1) the problem to be anticipated when the dates of takeover, demand for recognition, and achievement of a "full complement" of employees do not coincide, and (2) the problem of determining when a "full complement" has been reached. As to the first problem, the Board has continued to adhere to the view that the critical date for measuring majority status is the same as that normally applicable to determining such status outside the context of successorship, namely, the date that the demand for bargaining is received by the employer.[95] In the Board's view, the term "full complement" is simply not applicable to this inquiry.[96] The Board's view has not, thus far, prevailed in the circuit courts. The Tenth Circuit followed the Ninth Circuit's lead in specifically rejecting the demand date as the critical date in favor of the "full complement" date.[97] The Fifth Circuit has stated its general agreement with *Pacific Hide*, but found the case before it distinguishable on the grounds that the new employer had unlawfully obstructed a continued majority by refusing to hire certain of the predecessor's employees because of anti-union bias.[98]

---

[94]*Supra* note 9 at 294 n.2 (emphasis added).
[95]Pre-Engineered Bldg. Prods., Inc., *supra* note 7; Hudson River Aggregates, Inc., 246 NLRB 192, 102 LRRM 1524 (1979); Gardena Buena Ventura, Inc., 242 NLRB 595, 101 LRRM 1248 (1979). Analytically, there may be a distinction between the significance of the date of demand outside the successorship context and the demand date within the successorship context. In the former case, it is the union's majority status which is measured; in the latter, it is the new employer's work force that is being measured to determine whether it is a successor. *See* discussion *infra* at notes 146-55.
[96]Pre-Engineered Bldg. Prods., Inc., *supra* note 7.
[97]*Id.*
[98]*See* NLRB v. Houston Distribution Servs., Inc., *supra* note 86, where the court noted that "Pacific Hide is in point except for one very important distinction. . . . [T]here was no improper refusal to hire and no improper firings." 573 F2d at 266, 267.

It is unlikely that the first issue will be easily resolved without further guidance from the Supreme Court. Indeed, the Ninth Circuit explained that while the "full complement" sentence in *Burns* was dictum, it "does not justify our disregarding what appears to be a carefully formulated standard."[99] While the Board's view has not expressly changed, there may have been a retreat from the flat statement in *Pre-Engineered Building Products, Inc.*[100] (rejected by the Tenth Circuit), that after demand for recognition "evidence of the subsequent increase in the Respondent's work force is immaterial."[101] For subsequently, in *Hudson River Aggregates, Inc.*, the Board referred to a "substantial majority" in a "representative complement" of employees as justifying its refusal to consider an increase from 30 to 40 employees to 90 employees during the six months after the demand.[102] It also acknowledged that there are difficult problems of interpretation where the post-takeover complement is initially composed mainly of predecessor employees "due to an unusual and drastic shrinkage from the unit's 'normal' size, but the eventual 'full complement' proves to consist of a majority of new hires."[103]

The second issue, ascertaining when a "full complement" has been reached, may involve a delicate balancing process. As noted by the Tenth Circuit: "It would be ludicrous to postpone defining a full complement until the successor of a small enterprise has achieved the status of a multibillion dollar international corporation."[104] At the same time, the court explained that it "could also be inappropriate to precipitately point to a full complement as existing at the moment a successor assumes operation of an essentially moribund predecessor."[105]

Thus, in ascertaining the "full complement" date, it is possible that the length of time involved will be balanced against any exigencies prevailing at the time of takeover that could predictably lead to an increased employee complement. Therefore, a showing that the employee complement during the takeover

---

[99]Pacific Hide & Fur Depot, Inc., *supra* note 7 at 612 n.2.
[100]*Supra* note 7.
[101]*Id.* at 841 n.1.
[102]*Supra* note 95. In Pre-Engineered Bldg. Prods., Inc., *supra* note 7, 603 F2d at 136, the Board's position on appeal before the Tenth Circuit referred to a balancing approach focused upon the "substantial and representative complement" that had been hired.
[103]Gardena Buena Ventura, Inc., *supra* note 95, *citing Pacific Hide.*
[104]Pre-Engineered Bldg. Prods., Inc., *supra* note 7, 603 F2d at 136.
[105]*Id.*

period was unusually or artificially low, as compared to both the normal employee complement of the predecessor as well as the numerical level reached by the new employer, could be significant.[106] And since the new employer may decide to operate, in the foreseeable future, with a smaller work force than its predecessor, it may be important to determine whether the new employer initially planned to augment its work force and whether those plans were fixed and predictable or merely speculative.[107] In attempting to strike this balance, the Tenth Circuit further contrasted the situation in which a predecessor's business is taken over in "full operation," with a case in which "the predecessor's business has essentially collapsed at the time of takeover and a successor of necessity must rebuild both production demand and work force . . . ."[108] Thus, in many cases, it may be unlikely that the full complement date can be readily pinpointed. Rather, it will, as the Ninth Circuit explained, depend upon the particular facts.[109]

3. Presumption of the Union's Continued Majority Status.

Another "majority" consideration is the question of whether the majority status of the *union* transcends the change in ownership of the business. This concerns the question of continued support for the union, as distinct from the separate question of whether the new employer is a successor.[110]

Assuming the criteria of successorship are otherwise satisfied, a successor may not escape the presumptions of continued majority status which would have been applicable to its predecessor.[111] Thus, a successor is bound to the same irrebuttable presumption of continued majority status during the year following certification as its predecessor was.[112] Similarly, the same

---

[106]*See* notes 7 and 95 *supra.*

[107]*Compare* United Maintenance & Mfg. Co., *supra* note 81, *with* Pacific Hide & Fur Depot, Inc. v. NLRB, *supra* note 7. Actually, the Board has not restricted itself to viewing the situation solely as it existed at the moment of transfer. Where other contemplated changes are imminent and certain rather than speculative, the Board has found no continuity in the employing industry. Galis Equip. Co., 194 NLRB 799, 79 LRRM 1073 (1972). *See* discussion *infra* at notes 150-61.

[108]Pre-Engineered Bldg. Prods., Inc., *supra* note 7, 603 F2d at 136.

[109]Pacific Hide & Fur Depot, Inc. v. NLRB, *supra* note 7.

[110]This distinction is demonstrated by the contrasting approaches to "majority" in *Burns* and *Howard Johnson*, discussed *supra* at notes 78-81.

[111]Ranch-Way, Inc., 203 NRLB 911, 83 LRRM 1197 (1973), *supplementing* 183 NLRB 1168, 74 LRRM 1389 (1970). *See generally* Chapter 10 *supra* at notes 82-87 and Chapter 12 *supra* at note 352.

[112]*Id. See also* Dynamic Mach. Co., 221 NLRB 1140, 91 LRRM 1054 (1975), *aff'd,* 552 F2d 1195, 94 LRRM 3217 (CA 7, 1977), *cert. denied,* 434 US 827, 96 LRRM 2513 (1977);

rebuttable presumption of continued majority status following the year of certification obtains.[113] The rebuttable presumption of continued majority status may be overcome, as in nonsuccessor situations, only by a showing of good-faith doubt based upon "objective considerations."[114]

Among those considerations which may not, standing alone, constitute a sufficient basis for good-faith doubt are (1) the failure of a majority of employees hired by the successor to authorize dues check-offs;[115] (2) the continued solicitation of authorization cards by the union;[116] (3) expressions of employee dissatisfaction with union representation occurring after a successor's unlawful refusal to bargain;[117] (4) crossing a picket line to continue working;[118] (5) a diminished work force;[119] and (6) employee turnover.[120] In *Pick-Mt. Laurel Corp.* the Board considered

---

NLRB v. Pepsi-Cola Bottling Co. of Topeka, Inc., 613 F2d 267, 103 LRRM 2233 (CA 10, 1980); Springfield Retirement Residence, 235 NLRB 884, 98 LRRM 1091 (1978). However, where the union's representation was based on a contract with the predecessor entered pursuant to §8(f), a duty to bargain will not be imposed on the successor unless there is independent proof of the union's actual majority status. Davenport Insulation, Inc., 184 NLRB 908, 74 LRRM 1726 (1970). For general discussion of the bargaining obligation in the absence of an election, *see* Chapter 12 *supra*.

[113]Roman Catholic Diocese of Brooklyn, 222 NLRB 1052, 91 LRRM 1419 (1976), *aff'd sub nom.* Nazareth Regional High School v. NLRB, 549 F2d 873, 94 LRRM 2897 (CA 2, 1977). The rebuttable presumption of continued majority status following the certification year has also been approved in other circuits: *See* NLRB v. Band-Age, Inc., *supra* note 7; Zim's Foodliner, Inc. v. NLRB, *supra* note 86; NLRB v. Fabsteel Co. of La., *supra* note 86; Valmac Indus., Inc., 237 NLRB 992, 99 LRRM 1193 (1978), *enforced*, 599 F2d 246, 101 LRRM 2389 (CA 8, 1979); Electrical Workers (IUE) (White-Westinghouse Corp.) v. NLRB, 604 F2d 689, 101 LRRM 2864 (CA DC, 1979), *enforcing* 229 NLRB 667, 96 LRRM 1078 (1977).

[114]Virginia Sportswear, 226 NLRB 1296, 94 LRRM 1411 (1976). Comment, *Successor Employer's Obligation to Bargain: Current Problems in the Presumption of a Union's Majority Status*, 8 FORDHAM URBAN L.J. 429 (1979-80). *See* discussion of "objective considerations" in Chapter 12 *supra* at notes 360-442.

[115]*See* authorities cited in note 114, *supra*.

[116]Pick-Mt. Laurel Corp., 239 NLRB 1257, 100 LRRM 1236 (1979), *enforcement denied*, 625 F2d 476, 104 LRRM 2703 (CA 3, 1980).

[117]First Food Ventures, Inc., 229 NLRB 1228, 95 LRRM 1241 (1977); Valmac Indus., Inc., *supra* note 113. *But see* Riverside Produce Co., 242 NLRB 615, 101 LRRM 1371 (1979), where the Board held that the successor employer had a good-faith doubt after four out of six unit employees told the successor they were disenchanted with the union. These conversations took place before the successor's refusal to bargain.

[118]W & W Steel Co., 232 NLRB 74, 96 LRRM 1530 (1977), *enforcement denied*, 599 F2d 934, 101 LRRM 2445 (CA 10, 1979). *See also* First Food Ventures, *supra* note 117.

[119]Dynamic Mach. Co., *supra* note 112; Middleboro Fire Apparatus, Inc., 234 NLRB 888, 97 LRRM 1384 (1978), *aff'd*, 590 F2d 4, 100 LRRM 2182 (CA 1, 1978) (reduction in unit from 100 employees to 10 employees not a sufficient basis for doubting union's majority status); NLRB v. Band-Age, Inc., *supra* notes 7 and 113; Nazareth Regional High School v. NLRB, *supra* note 76; Gardena Buena Ventura, Inc., *supra* note 95.

[120]The rationale for finding that employee turnover is an insufficient basis for doubting the union's continued majority is the *Laystrom* presumption, which establishes that new employees are presumed to support the union in the same ratio as those whom they have replaced. Laystrom Mfg. Co., 151 NLRB 1482, 58 LRRM 1624 (1965),

unlawful assistance to the union by the predecessor insufficient grounds to show good-faith doubt because the conduct preceded the Section 10(b) period, but the Third Circuit disagreed.[121]

The presumption of continued majority status may be applicable where the successor has taken over only a part of the original bargaining unit.[122] The Board has also applied the presumption where a unit had been created by a merger.[123]

4. Discriminatory Refusals to Hire Predecessor's Employees. It is well established under *Burns* and *Howard Johnson* that a new employer is free to select its own work force.[124] But it is equally clear that in exercising this freedom of selection, a new employer may not discriminatorily refuse to hire the employees of its predecessor, either because of their union membership or activities, or because of the desire to avoid having to recognize the union.[125] Where, but for the discriminatory refusal to hire,

---

enforcement denied on other grounds, 359 F2d 799, 62 LRRM 2033 (CA 7, 1966). *But see* Western Distrib. Co. v. NLRB, 608 F2d 397, 102 LRRM 2510 (CA 10, 1979), *denying enforcement to* 236 NLRB 1224, 98 LRRM 1461 (1978), where the court rejected a ratio presumption regarding nonholdover employees hired by the new employer, because the union's request to bargain followed only after the ratio had changed substantially. *Accord,* Bengal Paving Co., 245 NLRB 1271, 102 LRRM 1374 (1979). *See also* Chapter 12 *supra* at notes 352-442.

[121]*Supra* note 116. *See* Chapter 32 *infra* at notes 116-19 regarding the §10(b) statute of limitations.

[122]Fabsteel Co. of La., *supra* note 86 (presumption applied to single plant of a multiplant unit purchased by successor because majority support is presumed to be equally distributed through entire original unit); Saks & Co. d/b/a Saks Fifth Ave., 247 NRLB 1047, 103 LRRM 1241 (1980), *enforced in part,* 634 F2d 681, 105 LRRM 3274 (CA 2, 1980) (presumption applied to portion of predecessor's alteration personnel which had been the subcontractor of the successor for such work). *Contra,* W & W Steel Co. v. NLRB, *supra* note 118 (the union had been certified to represent a seven-plant unit and the successor had purchased only a single plant; the court held the successor had established a good-faith doubt based on the union's multiplant certification, and the absence of a Board election held exclusively at the successor's plant). *But see* Electrical Workers (IUE) v. NLRB, *supra* note 113 (bargaining order was enforced despite contentions of unit inappropriateness where the new employer purchased only five plants of its predecessor's 42 units).

[123]Western Distrib. Co., *supra* note 120, where the court's rejection of the presumption was focused on a number of considerations.

[124]NLRB v. Burns Int'l Detective Agency, Inc., *supra* note 9; Howard Johnson Co., *supra* note 2.

[125]Howard Johnson Co., *supra* note 2 at 262; Burns, *supra* note 9 at 280 n.5; NLRB v. Foodway of El Paso, 496 F2d 117, 86 LRRM 2809 (CA 5, 1974), *enforcing* 201 NLRB 933, 82 LRRM 1637 (1973); Sousa & Sons, Inc., 210 NLRB 982, 86 LRRM 1667 (1974). Violations were found in: Hudson River Aggregates, Inc., *supra* note 95; Love's Barbeque Restaurant No. 62, 245 NLRB 78, 102 LRRM 1546 (1979); Houston Distribution Servs., 227 NLRB 960, 95 LRRM 1100 (1977), *enforced,* 573 F2d 260, 98 LRRM 2538 (CA 5, 1978), *cert. denied,* 439 US 1047, 99 LRRM 3450 (1978); Potter's Drug Enterprises, Inc., 233 NLRB 15, 96 LRRM 1450 (1977), *enforced without opinion,* 584 F2d 980, 99 LRRM 3327 (CA 9, 1978); Mason City Dressed Beef, Inc., 231 NLRB 735, 97 LRRM

the union would have enjoyed majority status, the successor will ordinarily be subject to a bargaining order.[126]

While the successorship context adds a factual dimension, the basic problems of proof in determining whether a discriminatory motive exists remain the same as in other hiring and discharge cases under Section 8(a)(3).[127] Thus, efforts by a potential successor to discover from its predecessor the union sympathies of its employees, followed by a refusal to retain employees identified as sympathetic to the union, tend to show a discriminatory motive.[128] Individual employment decisions, when shown to be part of an overall scheme designed to insure that fewer than a majority of the new employer's work force is composed of its predecessor's employees, may also reflect union animus.[129] However, a bona fide restriction prohibiting such hiring contained in a contract with the predecessor may justify the successor's refusal to hire the predecessor's employees. But the purchaser will not be shielded from a discriminatory refusal to hire where it has been released from such contractual restriction.[130]

Factors tending to show no Section 8(a)(3) violation include the failure of a predecessor's employees to file employment applications or to attend employment interviews uniformly required of all potential employees of the new employer.[131] Where the new employer has various locations, a comparison of its hiring procedures is relevant.[132] In some instances, particularly with respect to service contractors, the absence of a discriminatory motive may be supported by a showing that the new employer has, in accordance with its customary practice, staffed

---

1215 (1977), *enforced in part sub nom.* Packing House & Indus. Servs. v. NLRB, 590 F2d 688, 100 LRRM 2356 (CA 8, 1978); Crawford Container, Inc., 234 NLRB 851, 97 LRRM 1338 (1978). The rule was extended to the discharge of a supervisor in furtherance of a plan to rid the employer's facility of all union activity. Nevis Indus., Inc., 246 NLRB 1053, 103 LRRM 1035 (1979).

[126]Hudson River Aggregates, Inc., *supra* note 95; Love's Barbeque, *supra* note 125; Houston Distribution Servs., *supra* note 125; Foodway of El Paso, 201 NLRB 933, 82 LRRM 1637 (1973), *enforced,* 496 F2d 117, 86 LRRM 2809 (CA 5, 1974); Potter's Drug Enterprises, Inc., *supra* note 125; Greengate Mall, Inc., 209 NLRB 37, 85 LRRM 1303 (1974).

[127]*See generally* Chapter 7 *supra.*

[128]*Cf.* Sousa & Sons, Inc., *supra* note 125. *But see* Big E's Foodland, 242 NLRB 963, 101 LRRM 1422 (1979).

[129]Houston Distribution Servs., *supra* note 125.

[130]Greengate Mall, Inc., *supra* note 126.

[131]*See* Houston Distribution Servs., *supra* note 125; Vantage Petroleum Corp., 247 NLRB 1492, 103 LRRM 1408 (1980).

[132]*Cf.* NLRB v. Foodway of El Paso, *supra* note 125.

its new operation with experienced personnel taken from its other locations.[133] As in other hiring and discharge cases, non-discriminatory factors such as suitability and availability for employment in the new employer's operations continue to be significant.[134] Similarly, an indication by a predecessor's employee that wage rates or terms of employment inferior to those offered by the predecessor would be unacceptable is an important consideration where the new employer initially plans to offer wage rates or other conditions which are less attractive than its predecessor's.[135]

Some uncertainty exists with respect to the application of the six-month time limitation of Section 10(b) for filing unfair labor practice charges to the matter of hiring determinations. This issue may occur where the notification to an employee, by a successor, of a decision not to rehire is made in advance of the actual takeover date. The Board has held that the six-month period runs from the date of actual takeover, whereas the Second Circuit treats the date of notification of the firm intention not to hire as the beginning of the limitations period.[136]

As noted above, the new employer may not engage in discriminatory refusals to hire and thereby contend that it is not a successor because the criteria of continued majority have not been met.[137] Nor may the new employer avoid the consequences of successorship by refusing to hire strikers found to have been unlawfully terminated by its predecessor and for whom the Board has ordered reinstatement.[138] However, unless the suc-

[133]Industrial Catering Co., 224 NLRB 972, 92 LRRM 1638 (1976); Crotona Serv. Corp., 200 NLRB 738, 82 LRRM 1110 (1972).
[134]Cf. Houston Distribution Servs., supra note 125.
[135]Vantage Petroleum Corp., supra note 131; Crotona Service Corp., supra note 133.
[136]Nazareth Regional High School v. NLRB, supra note 76. In Nazareth, the court also rejected the Board's finding that a charge filed before the notification encompassed the refusal to rehire contained in the notification.
[137]See note 125 supra.
[138]NLRB v. Fabsteel Co. of La., supra note 86. However, these factors were held not to warrant the issuance of a §10(j) injunction pending the Board's determination of these issues. Crain v. Fabsteel Co., 427 F Supp 316, 94 LRRM 2817 (WD LA, 1977). The Board had previously determined that the denial of reinstatement constituted an unfair labor practice and directed that the terminated strikers be reinstated. Mosher Steel Co., 220 NLRB 336, 90 LRRM 1459 (1975), enforced without opinion, 532 F2d 1374, 93 LRRM 2018 (CA 5, 1976). However, the facility was sold prior to compliance with the reinstatement order. The new owners hired substantially all of the employees who were on the seller's payroll as of the effective date of the sale. Those employees included replacements for the unfair labor practice strikers. The district court's refusal to issue the temporary injunction was based upon the rationale that until it was established that Fabsteel was a successor and had violated the Act, balancing of the equities militated in

cessorship criteria are otherwise clearly established, one cannot be certain that a bargaining order will be enforced as an accompaniment to the enforcement of reinstatement orders for discriminatory refusal of employment. The denial of enforcement of such a bargaining order occurred in *NLRB* v. *Tragniew, Inc.*, where the presumption of continued majority was held to have been rebutted,[139] and in *NLRB* v. *Bausch & Lomb, Inc.*, where the discriminatees were employed in a peripheral capacity in circumstances where the appropriateness of the unit was questionable.[140]

B. Continuity of Identity in the Business Enterprise or Employing Industry

The broad test for determining the existence or nonexistence of "successorship," referred to by the Supreme Court in *Howard Johnson*, is the "substantial continuity of identity in the business enterprise."[141] The Board has articulated the test as "substantial continuity of the employing industry."[142] It has stated that where a new employer "uses substantially the same facilities and work force to produce the same basic products for essentially the same customers in the same geographic area," it will be regarded as a successor.[143] But when succession is found by the Board,

---

favor of preserving the status quo, thereby not requiring the discharge of the replacements to make room for the unfair labor practice strikers. But the Board and the Fifth Circuit subsequently found Fabsteel to be a successor employer and ordered it to reinstate the unfair labor practice strikers. Fabsteel Company of La., *supra* notes 86 and 122.

[139]470 F2d 669, 81 LRRM 2336 (CA 9, 1972), *denying enforcement in part to* Barrington Plaza & Tragniew, Inc., 185 NLRB 962, 75 LRRM 1226 (1970). The administrative law judge found (1) that when the union was originally accorded recognition it had not established that it represented a majority of the unit employees, (2) that thereafter during a period of approximately four years, in which three collective bargaining agreements were negotiated, the union had never made an affirmative showing that it represented an uncoerced majority of the employees in the unit, and (3) that applications for membership cards introduced into evidence at the hearing to demonstrate majority status were tainted by evidence of coercion. 185 NLRB at 970-74. The Ninth Circuit relied on these factual findings by the administrative law judge in concluding that the presumption of majority status, on which the Board had relied, had been rebutted. 470 F2d at 674-75.

[140]*Supra* note 7.

[141]Howard Johnson, *supra* note 2.

[142]Miami Indus. Trucks, Inc., *supra* note 85. In applying this test, the Board has stated that changes effectuated by the new employer may be evaluated to determine whether they constitute "substantial and material changes" in the "employing industry." Woodrich Indus., Inc., 246 NLRB 43, 102 LRRM 1407 (1979); Gardena Buena Ventura, Inc., *supra* note 95.

[143]Valley Nitrogen Producers, Inc., 207 NLRB 208, 84 LRRM 1424 (1973). *Cf.* Radiant Fashions, Inc., 202 NLRB 938, 82 LRRM 1742 (1973).

this definition will normally be supplemented by reference to a more detailed set of criteria.

The criteria which the Board evolved prior to *Burns,* and which it has continued to articulate after *Burns,* include the following:

> Whether (1) there has been a substantial continuity of the same business operations; (2) the new employer uses the same plant; (3) the same or substantially the same work force is employed; (4) the same jobs exist under the same working conditions; (5) the same supervisors are employed; (6) the same machinery, equipment, and methods of production are used; and (7) the same product is manufactured or the same services offered.[144]

Notwithstanding its continued reference to a "totality of circumstances" in determining successorship,[145] it has been apparent, at least since *Burns,* that the threshhold criterion in determining successorship is the continuity of the work force; in no Board decision since *Burns* has a successorship been found absent a finding of "majority."[146] Moreover, once there is a finding of a continued "majority," the primacy of that criterion will ordinarily prevail over particular operational changes made by the new employer.[147] Yet, "majority" status in the work force will

---

[144]Border Steel Rolling Mills, Inc., 204 NLRB 814, 815, 83 LRRM 1606 (1973); *see also* Woodrich Indus., Inc., *supra* note 142; Miami Indus. Trucks, Inc., *supra* note 85; C.M.E., Inc., 225 NLRB 514, 92 LRRM 1634 (1976); Dynamic Mach. Co. v. NLRB, 552 F2d 1195, 94 LRRM 3217 (CA 7, 1977), *enforcing* 221 NLRB 1140, 91 LRRM 1054 (1975), *cert. denied,* 434 US 827, 96 LRRM 2513 (1977); Potter's Drug Enterprises, Inc., *supra* note 125; L.A. Beefland, Inc., 232 NLRB 1189, 96 LRRM 1481 (1977); Fabsteel Co. of La., *supra* note 86; Merchants Home Delivery Serv., Inc., 230 NLRB 1040, 95 LRRM 1357 (1977), Alcoholism Servs. of Erie County, Inc., 236 NLRB 927, 99 LRRM 1394 (1978); Valmac Indus., Inc., *supra* note 113; Mondovi Foods Corp., 235 NLRB 1080, 98 LRRM 1102 (1978); Western Distrib. Co., 236 NLRB 1224, 98 LRRM 1461 (1978), *enforcement denied,* 608 F2d 397, 102 LRRM 2510 (CA 10, 1979).

[145]C.M.E., Inc., *supra* note 144.

[146]*Supra* note 76. The Board has refrained from making express reference to the primacy of the continuity-of-work-force criterion in articulating its set of criteria, Miami Indus. Trucks, Inc., *supra* note 85; or in reviewing a finding of no successorship where a majority was lacking, Industrial Catering Co., *supra* note 133; or in basing its determination of no successorship on other criteria where the question of majority status was clouded, Woodrich Indus., *supra* note 142.

[147]Saks & Co., *supra* note 122; M & H Mach. Co., 243 NLRB 817, 102 LRRM 1038 (1979); Emerald Maintenance, Inc. v. NLRB, 464 F2d 698, 80 LRRM 2801 (CA 5, 1972); NLRB v. Zayre Corp., 424 F2d 1159, 74 LRRM 2804 (CA 5, 1970). Changes will undoubtedly accompany most takeovers; but where there is a large employee complement consisting almost exclusively of holdovers, a basic continuity of the business may be indicated—a circumstance which is likely to negate changes that might be more significant in a small work force with a slim majority of holdovers. Thus, in *Zayre,* a discount store which had been operated autonomously by a small chain was taken over and integrated into a highly centralized large chain. This and numerous internal, marketing, and policy changes raised questions of continued unit appropriateness. However, the decision turned on the large number and overwhelming percentage of holdover employees.

not, standing alone, necessarily result in a finding of successorship; for notwithstanding a continuity of employee complement, the Board has refused to find successorship where countervailing factors have destroyed the continuity of the employing industry.[148] Thus, where the continuity, other than of the work force, consisted primarily of the acquisition of a portion of the customers of a moribund company solicited in competition with other companies, the new employer's operations were viewed as constituting an entirely new and independent enterprise; and the employing industry was sufficiently fragmented to preclude a finding of successorship.[149]

While there is no single factor which will negate a finding of successorship, the Board has emphasized such combined factors as (1) a long hiatus in the resumption of operations; (2) a difference in location of the resumed operation; (3) a changeover in the supervisory hierarchy; (4) the absence of a carry-over of customers or markets supplied; and (5) a difference in the scale of the operations and the products produced, and in the methods of production.[150] These factors, in various combinations, are sometimes found in circumstances where the change in the employment relationship was not the result of a sale of the business as an ongoing enterprise, and where the employees had no reasonable basis for any expectation that their employment would be resumed at the same location.[151] The existence or nonexistence of such factors may be relevant to the employees' desires for continued representation.[152] The Board has also stated that it would not confine itself to viewing the facts solely as they existed at the time of transfer, particularly where the new employer's continuation in the same employing industry was a "temporary expedient" and a significant change in the

---

[148]See Radiant Fashions, Inc., supra note 143; Galis Equip. Co., supra note 107; Norton Precision, Inc., 199 NLRB 1003, 81 LRRM 1383 (1972); Co-Op Trucking Co., 209 NLRB 829, 86 LRRM 1242 (1974); Georgetown Stainless Mfg. Corp., 198 NLRB 234, 80 LRRM 1615 (1972); Lincoln Private Police, Inc., 189 NLRB 717, 76 LRRM 1727 (1971); Cagle's, Inc., 218 NLRB 603, 89 LRRM 1337 (1975); Atlantic Technical Servs. Corp., 202 NLRB 169, 82 LRRM 1467 (1973), enforced, 498 F2d 680, 86 LRRM 2182 (CA DC, 1974). Thus, once the "majority" prerequisite has been established, the Board's reference to its inquiry into the "totality" of circumstances becomes more meaningful.
[149]See, e.g., Co-Op Trucking, supra note 148; Lincoln Private Police, supra note 148.
[150]See, e.g., Radiant Fashions, supra note 143 (covenant not to compete); Norton Precision, Inc., supra note 148; Galis Equip. Co., supra note 107; Woodrich Indus., Inc., supra note 142.
[151]See cases cited in note 150 supra.
[152]United Maintenance & Mfg. Co., supra note 81.

nature of the operations was not only "imminent and certain," but was, in fact, effectuated.[153]

Majority considerations have also been offset by a lack of continuity in the employing industry, where the new employer takes over only a very small segment of the predecessor's bargaining unit in which the employees were previously represented solely by virtue of an accretion into a larger unit by agreement of the parties.[154] Similarly, a bare majority of a greatly reduced bargaining unit, taken over by an employer after a year's hiatus through a management agreement with a trustee in bankruptcy, was deemed insufficient to warrant a finding of successorship.[155]

C. Continuity of the Appropriate Bargaining Unit

Bargaining unit changes often accompany a takeover. Some changes may be minor, while others are pervasive. Some may stem from prior planning, while others may be the result of unintended changes in market conditions or customer acceptability. In varying degrees, these changes may affect the appropriateness of the unit.[156] And, as recognized in *Burns,* finding successorship may be dependent upon the continued appropriateness of the bargaining unit.[157]

Thus, in *Border Steel Rolling Mills, Inc.,*[158] a Board majority found no successorship where the predecessor's unit had been

---

[153]Galis Equip. Co., *supra* note 107. But where subsequent changes were not contemplated at the time, *see* Valley Nitrogen Producers, *supra* note 143. It is unclear whether and how the test of imminency applicable to operational changes will affect consideration of when a "full complement" of employees is assembled by the new employer. *See* discussion *supra* at notes 92-109.

[154]Atlantic Technical Servs. Corp., *supra* note 148. *But compare* G.T. & E. Data Servs. Corp., 194 NLRB 719, 79 LRRM 1033 (1971). *See also* Border Steel Rolling Mills, Inc., *supra* note 144, regarding significance of accretion. *But see* Band-Age, Inc., 217 NLRB 449, 89 LRRM 1522 (1976), *enforced,* 534 F2d 1, 92 LRRM 2001 (CA 1, 1975), where a comparable diminution in size of operations, although not of the magnitude of Atlantic Technical Services, did not prevent the finding of successorship where all other relevant factors supported such a finding.

[155]Cagle's, Inc., *supra* note 148; Blazer Indus., Inc., 236 NLRB 103, 99 LRRM 1046 (1978).

[156]*Cf.* NLRB v. Burns, *supra* note 9.

[157]NLRB v. Burns, *supra* note 9 at 280; for discussion of the continued appropriateness of the unit, *see* Note, *Bargaining Obligations of Successor Employers, supra* note 1; Rovins & Rosen, *Labor Law Obligations of Parties to the Sale of a Business,* 25 LAB. L.J. 231, 237-38 (1974).

[158]*Supra* note 144; *cf.* NLRB v. Security-Columbian Banknote Co., 541 F2d 135, 93 LRRM 2049 (CA 3, 1976), where the court likewise held that the new employer was not a successor because the continuity of the appropriate bargaining unit was not maintained. However, the court refused to find that the predecessor's unit was accreted into that of the succeeding employer.

integrated into a larger unit and the finding of a separate bargaining unit was no longer warranted. There, the Board held that the predecessor's unit was accreted into the succeeding employer's unit. On the other hand, where there is only a moderate expansion in the unit, accretion principles may be operative as a basis for finding a continuity in the employing industry.[159]

As noted above,[160] mere diminution in the size of the unit normally does not present a serious obstacle to a finding of successorship. When, however, the diminution represents a severance of geographic or operational facilities or a fragmentation of the employing industry, rather than merely a shrinkage of a discrete unit, the issue is more complex.

Where the new employer acquires only one of a multistore or multiplant unit, successorship will normally be established if the acquired unit is itself an appropriate unit.[161] Thus, the purchaser of one of a chain of stores may be a successor if other criteria of continuity are established.[162] Where a purchaser acquired six out of 42 separately certified units, successorship was not negated because the employees of those units were a "distinct, identifiable entity, and they shared a substantial community of interests."[163]

In situations involving service contracts, the new employer may have bid for a job at a particular location, although it may (like its predecessor) have employee complements at various other locations at which it had previously successfully bid for jobs.[164] Where the new employer takes over all of the contract work performed by its predecessor at the same location, the appropriateness of the single-unit location will ordinarily be

---

[159]*Cf.* Spruce-Up Corp., *supra* note 76, where the Board held that the addition of the eight barber shops to the existing 19-shop unit did not destroy the appropriateness of the union's certification.

[160]*Supra* notes 82-87.

[161]This may result from the presumption that a single-plant or single-store unit is appropriate, *see* Zim's Foodliner, Inc. v. NLRB, *supra* note 86. *See also* Fabsteel Co. of La., *supra* note 86. But in W & W Steel Co., *supra* note 118, the Tenth Circuit held in similar circumstances that the certified unit was no longer appropriate.

[162]Zim's Foodliner, Inc., *supra* note 86.

[163]Electrical Workers (IUE), *supra* note 113 at 696.

[164]The dissenting Justices in *Burns* focused upon the nature of service contracts, noting they were often characterized by the lack of any transaction or negotiation between the new employers and their predecessors, thus militating against the finding of successorship.

upheld, and the employing industry will be considered intact.[165] However, where the new service employer successfully solicits only a small part of the contract work, sharing services previously performed by the predecessor with other competitors at the same location, the requisite continuity may be lacking or the employing industry may be considered fragmented.[166]

Even within single locations, the recognized or certified unit of the predecessor may not encompass all of the work force, but only one or two distinct segments. Where the new employer has integrated the operations and also the employees involved, the critical question may be whether the bargaining unit remains sufficiently intact to retain its separate identity.[167] On the other hand, the omission of an employee classification from the predecessor's unit does not necessarily present a serious challenge to the continued appropriateness of the unit.[168]

D. The Effect of a Hiatus

In determining successorship, the Board has also taken into consideration the existence of a hiatus between the cessation of the predecessor's operations and the resumption of operations by the new employer. This factor, by itself, has not been regarded as controlling, but has been treated as a significant criterion in determining whether continuity in the employing industry exists.[169] In some cases, the absence of a hiatus has been considered significant.[170] In other cases, the existence of a hiatus has been deemed an indication of a lack of continuity in other respects.[171] Thus, as a factor to be considered, it is similar to bankruptcy, a condition which is often accompanied by a hiatus in operations.[172]

---

[165]NLRB v. Boston-Needham Indus. Cleaning Co., 526 F2d 74, 90 LRRM 3058 (CA 1, 1975), enforcing 216 NLRB 26, 88 LRRM 1249 (1975).

[166]Nova Servs. Co., 213 NLRB 95, 88 LRRM 1239 (1974). See also Lincoln Private Police, Inc., supra note 148; Co-Op Trucking Co., supra note 148.

[167] NLRB v. Security-Columbian Banknote Co., supra note 158.

[168]Springfield Retirement Residence, supra note 112.

[169]Industrial Catering Co., Inc., supra note 133; United Maintenance & Mfg. Co., supra note 81.

[170]Parkwood IGA, 201 NLRB 905, 909, 82 LRRM 1692 (1973), enforced sub nom. Zim's Foodliner, Inc. v. NLRB, supra note 86.

[171]See Radiant Fashions, Inc., supra note 143; Cagle's, Inc., supra note 148; Norton Precision, Inc., supra note 148; Industrial Catering Co., supra note 133.

[172]See Blazer Indus., Inc., supra note 155, where a new employer purchased the assets of a company from a receiver in bankruptcy and there was a year's hiatus in operations. No successorship was found, despite the continuity of a bare majority in the employee complement. See also Alcoholism Servs. of Erie County, supra note 144; Gladding Corp.,

Standing alone, however, a hiatus may not be determinative; even a lengthy hiatus has not prevented a finding of successorship where the same work force, after the change in employer identity, has produced the same product in the same plant.[173] A hiatus of the same duration in two separate employment contexts thus may result in contrary successorship determinations.[174] Moreover, a hiatus is not regarded as material where it resulted from a strike rather than from the former employer's decision to cease operations.[175] Likewise, the materiality of a hiatus may depend upon whether it was caused by business considerations beyond the control of the new employer.[176]

E. Determining When the Bargaining Obligation Attaches

Determining when the bargaining obligation attaches assumes that a successorship exists, i.e., that the holdover employees constitute a majority of the new work force. In such instances, the underlying question is *when* the successor employer is no longer free unilaterally to set initial terms and conditions of employment.

Burns remains the focal point for determining the ground rules. Under *Burns,* the new employer's bargaining obligation does not attach until the majority of the new employee complement is composed of the predecessor's holdover employees. Until that time, the new employer may set initial terms and conditions of employment.[177] Thereafter, on the date when it

---

192 NLRB 200, 77 LRRM 1689 (1972); Cagle's, *supra* note 148; Shopmen's Local 455 v. Kevin Steel Prods., Inc., 519 F2d 698, 89 LRRM 3133 (CA 2, 1975), arising from bankruptcy court proceedings. *Contra,* Makaha Valley, Inc., 241 NLRB 300, 101 LRRM 1040 (1979), where continued operation by the receiver in bankruptcy was not deemed a hiatus.

[173]Daneker Clock Co., Inc., 211 NLRB 719, 87 LRRM 1049 (1974), *enforced,* 516 F2d 315, 89 LRRM 2325 (CA 4, 1975) (seven-month hiatus); C.G. Conn, Ltd., 197 NLRB 442, 80 LRRM 1387 (1972), *enforced,* 474 F2d 1344, 82 LRRM 3092 (CA 5, 1973). Thus, a short hiatus where a similar continuity of other factors exists has not been a vitiating consideration. First Food Ventures, *supra* note 117; Valmac Indus., Inc. *supra* note 113; *see also* Mondovi Foods Corp., *supra* note 144, where the Board found that a hiatus of less than one week was not long enough to diminish the employees' expectation of being hired.

[174]*Compare* Pacific Aggregates, Inc., 231 NLRB 214, 96 LRRM 1340 (1977), where a two-month hiatus did not vitiate a successorship finding in a normal business purchase and sale context, *with* Industrial Catering Co., Inc., *supra* note 133 where, in a contract bid context, the new employer did not sign the service contract until a few months after the contract between the prior contractor and the owner had expired and the premises had been vacated.

[175]United Maintenance & Mfg. Co., *supra* note 81.

[176]Cagle's, *supra* note 148.

[177]The new employer would of course be free to offer terms lower or higher than those of its predecessor. Prior to its own decision in *Burns,* the Board had regarded the

may be determined that the "majority" test has been met, the successor's position is akin to that of an employer confronted with a newly selected bargaining representative.[178] At that juncture, unilateral changes in existing terms may be impermissible.[179] However, if the union fails to make a timely request to bargain, the employer may proceed with implementation of its new terms[180] unless such a request by the union would have been futile.[181]

The content of the initial terms offered at the time of hire, as contrasted to those offered or implemented after the bargaining obligation matures, may determine whether the new employer violates Section 8(a)(5) by unilaterally changing terms and conditions of employment. The test appears to be whether the unilateral changes were encompassed within the offer or initial terms set forth prior to the time the bargaining obligation ripened.[182]

The major point of controversy as to when the bargaining obligation matures has concerned the exception carved out by the Supreme Court from the general *Burns* rule for instances in which "it is perfectly clear that the new employer plans to retain

---

obligations of a successor employer in these circumstances as analogous to the obligations of an employer during the period between collective bargaining agreements. Under that approach, it would have been impermissible for the new employer upon takover to unilaterally establish substantive terms different from those of its predecessor. *See* Valleydale Packers, Inc., *supra* note 39. This view was overturned in *Burns. See* Machinists v. NLRB, *supra* note 6 at 671 n.32.

[178]Ranch-Way, Inc., *supra* note 111.

[179]A checkoff provision is regarded as being of contractual origin only, not carrying over as an "existing term" or condition of employment. *See* S-H Food Serv., Inc., 199 NLRB 95, 81 LRRM 1181 (1972), *supplementing* 183 NLRB 1216, 74 LRRM 1418 (1970), where the new employer was held not to have violated the duty to bargain when it refused to continue to comply with such a provision. However, unilateral layoff of 50% of the work force was held a refusal to bargain. M & H Mach. Co., Inc., *supra* note 147. The same was true for other changes without notice to the union, which had demanded bargaining. L.A.X. Medical Clinic, Inc., 248 NLRB 861, 104 LRRM 1092 (1980).

[180]Collinge Enterprises, Inc., 210 NLRB 52, 86 LRRM 1086 (1974); *see* Machinists v. NLRB, *supra* note 6 at 675-76, where the court noted that absent a bargaining demand, the new employer can simply institute its hiring terms as the beginning terms of employment, as was done in *Burns.* The opposite conclusion was reached where the union had not been made aware of the unilateral changes. Pinewood Care Center, Inc., 242 NLRB 816, 101 LRRM 1490 (1979).

[181]Central Am. Airways, 204 NLRB 161, 83 LRRM 1314 (1973). However, where the demand made upon the successor was confined solely to insistence that it execute a labor agreement, it was held not to constitute a proper request for bargaining so as to obligate the successor to bargain. Atlas Graphics, Inc., 227 NLRB 136, 94 LRRM 1252 (1976); East Belden Corp., 239 NLRB 776, 100 LRRM 1077 (1978).

[182]*See* S-H Food Service, *supra* note 179; NLRB v. Bachrodt Chevrolet Co., 468 F2d 963, 81 LRRM 2244 (CA 7, 1972), *enforcing in part* 186 NLRB 1035, 76 LRRM 1597 (1971); Central Am. Airways, *supra* note 181; NLRB v. Dent, 534 F2d 844, 91 LRRM 3007 (CA 9, 1976); East Belden Corp., *supra* note 181.

all of the employees in the unit."[183] The Court stated that in those instances, it will be "appropriate" for the new employer to "initially consult with the employees' bargaining representative before he fixes terms."[184] In some cases since *Burns,* the employer's plans to retain "all of the employees" have been found to be "perfectly clear." Where the offer of employment is unequivocal, or where the new employer has committed itself to hire all of the old unit employees (with no indication at the same time that they would be expected to work under new or different terms), the requirement of initial bargaining has been upheld by the Board with general Court approval.[185]

On the other hand, where the offer of employment is tentative or conditional upon acceptance of the terms offered, the exception requiring initial bargaining has not been applied. In *Spruce-Up Corp.,*[186] the lead case on conditional recruitment, the successor employer expressed a general willingness to hire all of the predecessor's employees, but at the same time indicated that

---

[183]NLRB v. Burns, *supra* note 9 at 294-95.
[184]*Id.* at 295.
[185]Howard Johnson Co., 198 NLRB 763, 80 LRRM 1769 (1972), *enforced,* 496 F2d 532, 86 LRRM 2688 (CA 9, 1974); Good Foods Mfg. & Processing Corp., 200 NLRB 623, 81 LRRM 1575 (1972), *supplementing* 195 NLRB 418, 79 LRRM 1387 (1972); Bachrodt Chevrolet Co., 205 NLRB 784, 84 LRRM 1052 (1973), *supplementing* 186 NLRB 1035, 76 LRRM 1597 (1970); The Denham Co., 206 NLRB 659, 84 LRRM 1359 (1973), *supplementing* 187 NLRB 434, 76 LRRM 1141 (1970); Spitzer Akron, Inc. v. NLRB, 540 F2d 841, 92 LRRM 3007 (CA 6, 1976), *cert. denied,* 429 US 1040, 94 LRRM 2202 (1977); Pinewood Care Center, Inc., *supra* note 180. In *Nazareth Regional High School* v. *NLRB, supra* note 76, however, the Second Circuit appeared to consider as crucial the absence of a commitment to retain existing terms rather than an announcement of new terms. The court disagreed with the Board's position, concluding that *Spruce-Up Corp., supra* note 76, cannot be limited to the narrow factual circumstance wherein the successor told the union that retention would be on new terms *at the same time* that it promised to rehire the entire unit. "The important consideration in determining whether it is perfectly clear that a successor intends to retain all the employees, is whether they have all been promised reemployment on the existing terms." *Supra* note 76 at 881. Nevertheless, the Board continues to adhere to its position that the *Burns* exception is operative where the new employer's previously announced plan to retain all predecessor employees is not qualified by any announcement that the new employer clearly intends to establish new conditions of employment. *See, e.g.,* L.A. Beefland, Inc., *supra* note 144; Joe Costa Trucking Co., 238 NLRB 1516, 99 LRRM 1719 (1978), *enforced sub nom.* NLRB v. Edjo, Inc., 631 F2d 604, 105 LRRM 3061 (CA 9, 1980); Starco Farmers Mkt., 237 NLRB 373, 98 LRRM 1587 (1978); Gardena Buena Ventura, Inc., *supra* note 95. In East Belden Corp., *supra* note 181, the same test was applied as of the time the purchaser took control (though it announced that it intended to make changes when escrow closed). In Love's Barbeque, *supra* note 125, the Board applied the same test because it was "perfectly clear" that, but for its union animus, the employer would have hired all of the predecessor's employees. *Accord,* Garrison Valley Center, Inc., 246 NLRB 700, 102 LRRM 1666 (1979).
[186]*Supra* note 76. *See also* Ranch-Way, Inc., *supra* note 111; Valley Nitrogen Producers, Inc., *supra* note 143; Machinists v. NLRB, *supra* note 6, where the court noted that the decision to retain the former employees was "inseparable" from the decision to "cling" to a scale of lower terms.

different commission rates would be paid. Since employment depended upon their willingness to accept those terms, and the possibility existed that they would not, the Board majority did not regard it as "perfectly clear" that the employer "planned to retain" all of the predecessor's employees.

Both in *Spruce-Up* and in other comparable cases,[187] the Board (by divided votes) has generally drawn the line in favor of permitting the new employer to set its initial terms and conditions of employment, on the ground that a new employer would otherwise be reluctant to comment "favorably at all upon employment prospects of old employees for fear he would thereby forfeit his right to unilaterally set initial terms . . . ."[188] The guideline formulated in *Spruce-Up*, which would permit such favorable forecasts, is that

> the caveat in *Burns*, therefore, should be restricted to circumstances in which the new employer has either actively or, by tacit inference, misled employees into believing they would all be retained without change in their wages, hours, or conditions of employment, or at least to circumstances where the new employer, unlike the Respondent here, has failed to clearly announce its intent to establish a new set of conditions prior to inviting former employees to accept employment.[189]

In *Saks & Co.*,[190] however, a divided Board panel sought to limit *Spruce-Up* by considering (as between affiliated companies, at least) immediate interviews and reference to past service credit under a pension plan sufficient to make it "perfectly clear" that the successor intended to hire all of the predecessor's employees, even though in fact it did not. The majority decision seemed to reflect only minor concern as to whether employment was con-

---

[187]United Maintenance & Mfg. Co., *supra* note 81; Anita Shops, Inc., 211 NLRB 501, 86 LRRM 1347 (1974); Boeing Co., *supra* note 81, *aff'd sub nom.* Machinists v. NLRB, *supra* note 6; Half-Century, Inc., 241 NLRB 555, 100 LRRM 1547 (1979). The most extensive discussion of the *Spruce-Up* issue is contained in Machinists v. NLRB where the union encouraged the employees of the predecessor to refuse employment at a diminished wage scale.

[188]Spruce-Up Corp., *supra* note 76 at 195. The dissenting view is that the possibility of the predecessor's employees' refusal of employment has nothing to do with the "plans" or the intent of the offering employer. The dissenting members in these cases would have found the new employer obligated to bargain "as soon as it manifests an intent to look primarily to the predecessor's unit employees to fill its work force." United Maintenance & Mfg. Co., *supra* note 81 at 536 n.21.

[189]*Supra* note 76 at 195. *See* Spitzer Akron, Inc. v. NLRB, *supra* note 185, where the court found that sufficient evidence existed to establish that the employees were misled by "tacit inference" into believing they would be retained without changes in employment conditions.

[190]*Supra* note 122.

ditioned on acceptance of different terms. The Second Circuit denied enforcement on this point.

In some cases, it may also be uncertain whether the new employer has made its hiring plans "perfectly clear" to all, or only to a specific segment, of the predecessor's work force. In one such case, the Board found, and the Ninth Circuit affirmed, that the announced intention to hire encompassed all employees; it issued a bargaining order despite the further contention that, regardless of the scope of the announced intent, many of those employees were not in fact hired, and a holdover majority did not exist.[191]

IV. Successorship and the Contractual Obligation

A. The "Alter Ego" Employer

A successor, under *Burns*,[192] is not obligated to assume and is not bound by the substantive provisions of the labor agreement of its predecessor. This proposition, however, is not applicable where the new employer is not merely a successor but is the *alter ego* of the predecessor, i.e., the former and present employer are, in reality, the same or substantially identical entity. In such a situation, the predecessor's labor contract is binding upon the new employer. In making this determination, the Board has stated that it will find an alter ego status "where the two enterprises have 'substantially identical' management, business purpose, operation, equipment, customers and supervision, as well as ownership."[193]

Although the Board has articulated a number of criteria for finding alter ego status, as in the case of successorship there is a threshold consideration to be determined. In successorship cases, it is the concept of majority; in alter ego cases, it is common ownership and control. In successorship cases, the continuity of the employee complement provides the threshold linkage between the old and the new employer. In alter ego cases, the substantial

---

[191]Bellingham Frozen Foods, Inc. v. NLRB, 626 F2d 674, 105 LRRM 2404 (CA 9, 1980), *enforcing in part* 237 NLRB 1450, 99 LRRM 1270 (1978).
[192]NLRB v. Burns, *supra* note 9.
[193]Crawford Door Sales Co., 226 NLRB 1144, 94 LRRM 1393 (1976); *see also* Marquis Printing Corp. & Mutual Lithograph Co., 213 NLRB 394, 87 LRRM 1642 (1974). *See also* Chapter 25 *infra* at notes 229-30 for discussion of §8(b)(4) implications of the *alter ego* doctrine.

identity of the employer ownership and control interests provides that threshold linkage. Thus, the fact that a new employer is not a successor does not preclude a finding that it is an alter ego.[194] Nor, of course, will a finding that the new employer is not an alter ego preclude a finding that it is a successor.[195]

The leading Board decision in the application of alter ego criteria is *Crawford Door Sales Co.*[196] There, a company that sold and installed garage doors was held to be the alter ego of a liquidated company that engaged in the same operation. Both enterprises were wholly owned by members of the same family.[197] Since there was substantially identical management, business purposes, operations, equipment, customers and supervision, alter ego status was established. Similarly, where the operations of one enterprise had been transferred to another enterprise, both of which were almost totally owned by the same individual,[198] or by the same parent company,[199] a finding of alter ego status resulted. For example, a nonunion company to which a unionized company had transferred its operations was found to be an alter ego where the same individual owned both companies.[200]

Where substantially identical ownership and control is lacking, this finding has been determinative. Thus, in *Clinton Foods, Inc.*,[201] a Board majority decided that where the only common stockholders held an 18 percent ownership in one enterprise and 30 percent in the other, the ownership was insufficient to establish alter ego status. The majority rejected the dissenting view that there need be "only some ownership link" between

---

[194]*See* Schultz Painting & Decorating Co., 202 NLRB 111, 82 LRRM 1680 (1973).

[195]Jersey Juniors, Inc., 230 NLRB 329, 95 LRRM 1283 (1977); Bell Co., Inc., *supra* note 86, where a divided Board held that the issue of successorship could be litigated on remand even though the General Counsel had relied solely on the theory of alter ego in the original hearing and a finding of alter ego had been rejected by the Seventh Circuit in NLRB v. Bell Co., Inc., 561 F2d 1264, 96 LRRM 2437 (CA 7, 1977).

[196]*Supra* note 193. For a discussion of related cases involving dual employer operations or the "double breasted" issue, *see* Chapter 13 *supra* at notes 787-808.

[197]Family relationship has been viewed by the Board as a factor in determining common ownership and control. Blake Constr. Co., Inc., 245 NLRB 630, 102 LRRM 1471 (1979); McDonald's Ready Mix Concrete & Jim's Ready Mix, 246 NLRB 152, 102 LRRM 1501 (1979); Shield-Pacific, Ltd., & W. Hawaii Concrete, Ltd., 245 NLRB 409, 102 LRRM 1497 (1979). *But see* NLRB v. Bell Co., *supra* note 195. However, such relationship is not dispositive, especially where other factors show that the transaction is at arm's length. Joe Costa Trucking Co., *supra* note 185.

[198]P.A. Hayes, Inc., 226 NLRB 230, 94 LRRM 1080 (1976).

[199]Republic Engraving & Designing Co., 236 NLRB 1150, 99 LRRM 1306 (1978).

[200]P.A. Hayes, Inc., *supra* note 198.

[201]Clinton Foods, Inc., 240 NLRB 1246, 100 LRRM 1416 (1979).

the two enterprises[202] on the ground that enterprises with only limited similarities would otherwise be treated as alter egos. The majority noted that this approach would have the "unwarranted effect of precluding a bona fide sale of a business to any new enterprise whose stockholders included one who formerly held a minor interest" in the old enterprise.[203]

Likewise, no alter ego relationship was established between two partnerships in the general construction business where the first partnership consisted of two coequal partners who later became two of seven coequal partners in the second partnership.[204] It was also persuasive that no employees worked for both partnerships at the same time, the business records consistently reflected separate identities, and neither of the two coequal partners played any part in the day-to-day operations of the second partnership.

It is particularly true of alter ego issues that "each case must turn on its own facts."[205] Certain facts, however, may not be viewed as having probative value even if they reflect relationships and practices common to both entities. Thus, even in a case where an alter ego relationship was found, the Board specifically disavowed reliance upon the fact that the two enterprises used the services of the same attorney, the same accountant, and the same bank.[206]

The question of what constitutes ownership and control has sometimes been viewed differently by the Board and the appellate court. Thus, in *NLRB v. Bell Co.*,[207] the Seventh Circuit rejected the Board's conclusion that a proprietorship was the alter ego of a corporation, even though the proprietor had formerly been the president of the corporation which had been engaged in a similar business. Noting that the cases relied upon

---

[202]*Id.* at 1246 n.2.
[203]*Id.*
[204]United Constructors & Goodwin Constr. Co., 233 NLRB 904, 97 LRRM 1409 (1977).
[205]Crawford Door Sales Co., *supra* note 193 at 1144. One example concerned a contracting business where a noncontrolling 50% interest was owned by the same person who had previously owned and controlled a liquidated business in the same field. Operationally, the owner, who handled both the "inside" office work and "outside" field operations of the predecessor, confined his role in the new business to that of "outside" operations. Because of markedly divergent labor relations and operational structures, the Board held that this did not constitute an alter ego relationship. John Fender Elec. Co., 244 NLRB 957, 102 LRRM 1398 (1979).
[206]Farmingdale Iron Works, Inc., 249 NLRB 98, 98 n.2, 104 LRRM 1210 (1980).
[207]NLRB v. Bell Co., Inc., *supra* note 195.

by the Board emphasized common ownership and control, the court concluded that the proprietor was not the prior *owner* of the corporation and there was no evidence that the prior corporate owners owned or controlled the proprietorship. As for the control over the corporation, the court was unwilling to find that the president, who served "at the pleasure of the owners" and whose "authority was subject to restrictions imposed by them,"[208] necessarily controlled the corporation.

Some factual settings, such as franchising and bankruptcies, invite a particularly close analysis. Where a franchising transaction was found to be for the purpose of ousting the union from the franchised store, the Board focused upon the retention of financial and operational control by the franchisor. It held that the two enterprises were alter egos although the franchisee (the son of an official of the franchisor) had no ownership or control of the franchisor.[209] On the other hand, in a situation where the franchise transaction was not considered a sham or a vehicle for ousting the union and where there was no common ownership or control, the Board found no alter ego relationship.[210]

Bankruptcy proceedings raise special issues[211] because trustees, receivers, and debtors-in-possession may be recognized as different "juridical" entities from the debtor under the Bankruptcy Act.[212] Moreover, even if these different "juridical" entities are found to be alter egos, they may not necessarily be bound by the predecessor's labor agreement. The obligation to assume the debtor's labor agreement is subject to the right of the new entity, in appropriate circumstances, to seek permission of the bankruptcy court to disaffirm the labor agreement.[213] However, even if the labor agreement is disaffirmed, the obligation to

---

[208]*Id.* at 1268.

[209]Big Bear Supermarkets No. 3, 239 NLRB 179, 100 LRRM 1067 (1978), *enforced*, 640 F2d 924, 103 LRRM 3120 (CA 9, 1980), *cert. denied*, 449 US 919, 105 LRRM 2809 (1980).

[210]Love's Barbeque Restaurant, *supra* note 125.

[211]*See generally* discussion of bankruptcy and the NLRA in Chapter 31 *infra* at notes 419-73.

[212]*See* Jersey Juniors, Inc., *supra* note 195, 230 NLRB at 332, *citing* Shopmen's Local 455 v. Kevin Steel Prods., Inc., *supra* note 172; and Teamsters Local 807 v. Bohack Corp., 541 F2d 312, 320, 93 LRRM 2001 (CA 2, 1976), *on remand*, 431 F Supp 646, 95 LRRM 3031 (ED NY, 1977), *aff'd*, 567 F2d 237, 97 LRRM 2275 (CA 2, 1977), *cert. denied*, 439 US 825, 99 LRRM 2600 (1978); Oxford Structures, Ltd., 245 NLRB 1180, 102 LRRM 1447 (1979).

[213]*See* cases cited *supra* note 212.

bargain may continue. In such circumstances, the alter ego's obligations are similar to those of a successor.[214]

Despite the treatment under the Bankruptcy Act, both the debtor-in-possession and the trustee in bankruptcy are normally deemed to be alter egos of debtor employers under the National Labor Relations Act.[215] However, where a trustee has transferred the assets of a declared bankrupt to a successful bidder, the bidder will not be an alter ego unless the requisite criteria are otherwise satisfied.[216] Thus, even if the bidder takes over the same operations at the same location, the absence of common ownership or control or sham transaction will militate against a finding of alter ego status.[217] However, where the original owner-operator continues in the active management and thereafter controls the receiver (e.g., causing a resale to owner-operator's family), the parties will be considered alter egos.[218] Where, however, the receiver in bankruptcy, rather than the debtor's management, operates the business in a different form with a substantially reduced work force, the Board has declined to find alter ego status.[219]

As demonstrated by the foregoing case review, an alter ego question frequently arises in the context of business changes which are alleged to have been undertaken as a subterfuge to avoid bargaining or contractual obligations under the Act. Despite the varied corporate and commercial forms in which business entities may constitute themselves, in cases of alleged subterfuge the litmus test has been whether the newly formed entity is in reality "merely a disguised continuance of the old employer."[220] As in all alter ego cases, the issue is one of substance rather than form. Cosmetic changes, which may serve some legitimate purposes under other statutes, are not determinative.[221] In *Howard Johnson*[222] the Court expressly stated that changes in corporate

---

[214]*Id.*

[215]Cagle's, Inc., *supra* note 148; Marion Simcox, 178 NLRB 516, 518, 72 LRRM 1183 (1969); *cf.* Jersey Juniors, Inc., *supra* note 195; Oxford Structure, Ltd., *supra* note 212; Makaha Valley, Inc., *supra* note 172; Airport Limousine Serv., Inc., 231 NLRB 932, 96 LRRM 1177 (1977).

[216]Jersey Juniors, Inc., *supra* note 195.

[217]*Id.*

[218]Lewis Canter, 242 NLRB 659, 101 LRRM 1226 (1979).

[219]Blazer Indus., Inc., *supra* note 155 (the form of the business was not deemed as significant as the change in supervision and management). *See also* Frank Hennigan, 236 NLRB 1517, 99 LRRM 1272 (1978).

[220]Southport Petroleum Co. v. NLRB, *supra* note 12 at 106.

[221]*See, e.g.*, Dee Cee Floor Covering, Inc., 232 NLRB 421, 97 LRRM 1072 (1977).

[222]*Supra* note 2.

forms which involve no more than a "technical change in the structure or identity of the employing entity, frequently to avoid the effect of the labor laws, without any substantial change in its ownership or management"[223] are properly disregarded and the alter ego is "subject to all the legal and contractual obligations of the predecessor."[224]

Despite the Board's acceptance of the "disguised continuance" test, its application has not been fully tested. The most obvious example of the subterfuge is where an employer goes entirely out of business for anti-union reasons and another entity in the same line of business is subsequently formed. If there is common ownership and control, the question of alter ego status is clear.[225] On the other hand, it is also well established that an employer may lawfully choose to close its entire business even if motivated by anti-union considerations.[226] Unless it is established that the individuals owning and controlling the liquidated business are sufficiently linked to any new and similar enterprise subsequently formed, alter ego criteria would not be satisfied. However, in *NLRB* v. *Bell*,[227] the Board's initial finding of alter ego status had been influenced by the union animus of the liquidating employer. The Board had viewed the relationship and transactions between the two entities as not of "arm's-length," and therefore found no complete cessation of the prior business, i.e., there was a disguised continuance.[228] But as previously noted, the Seventh Circuit rejected the Board's finding of alter ego status, based on a lack of common ownership and control. The court also acknowledged the prior employer's *Darlington*[229] right to cease business entirely despite anti-union motivations, so that it refused to apply alter ego criteria purely on the basis of an anti-union motivation.

B. The Stock Purchaser

It is well established that the obligations of an alter ego employer are more extensive than those of a successor employer, the reason being that the alter ego employer is considered to be the

---

[223]*Id.* at 259 n.5.
[224]*Id.*
[225]*See* Victor Patino, 241 NLRB 774, 100 LRRM 1616 (1979).
[226]Textile Workers v. Darlington Mfg. Co., 380 US 263, 58 LRRM 2657 (1965). *See* Chapter 7 *supra* at notes 238-44.
[227]*Supra* note 195.
[228]*Supra* note 86.
[229]*Supra* note 226.

same or substantially identical employer as the predecessor. Thus, it succeeds to, or continues to retain, the same obligations as the predecessor.

Two decisions of the Board suggest that the obligations it may seek to impose upon purchasers of stock may be analogous to the obligations of alter ego employers.[230] The Board had previously stated that the "mere change of stock ownership does not absolve a continuing corporation of responsibility under the Act."[231] However, in its 1979 decision in *TKB International Corp.*,[232] the Board, for the first time, articulated a conceptual distinction between a stock transfer transaction and a successor relationship.

In *TKB*, the Board characterized the concept of successorship, which the Supreme Court had considered in *Burns*, as one which "contemplates the substitution of one employer for another, where the predecessor employer either terminates its existence, or otherwise ceases to have any relationship to the on-going operations of the successor employer."[233] The Board stated that "once it has been found that this 'break' between the predecessor and successor has occurred," it looks to other factors to see "how wide or narrow this disjunction is,"[234] and thus determines the intent of the obligations of the successor. In contrast, according to the Board, a stock transfer differs significantly "in its genesis, from the successorship, for the stock transfer involves no break or hiatus between the two legal entities . . . ."[235] Rather, the Board contends, the stock transfer involves "the continuing existence of a legal entity, albeit under new ownership."[236] The Board thus held that membership in a multi-employer bargaining unit was "assumed by the purchasing entity, or transferee, much in the same way it assumes the debts, assets and good will of the transferor of the stock."[237]

Earlier, in its 1978 decision in *Topinka's Country House, Inc.*,[238] the Board had affirmed, without opinion, an administrative law

---

[230]TKB Int'l Corp., *supra* note 74; Topinka's Country House, Inc., 235 NLRB 72, 98 LRRM 1298 (1978).
[231]Miller Trucking Service, Inc., 176 NLRB 556, 71 LRRM 1277 (1969), *enforced in part*, 445 F2d 927, 77 LRRM 2964 (CA 10, 1971).
[232]*Supra* note 74.
[233]*Supra* note 74 at 1083 n.4.
[234]*Id.*
[235]*Id.*
[236]*Id.*
[237]*Id.* at 1085.
[238]*Supra* note 230.

judge's decision imposing alter-ego-type obligations upon a stock purchaser. The ALJ, in reliance upon "basic principles of corporate law,"[239] had held that a stock transferee is the same entity as the transferor.

Despite the similarity of imposed obligations, in neither case was there any reference to the term "alter ego." Rather, the stock transaction was treated as involving a corporate concept apart from successorship and alter ego relationships. Thus, the questions of common ownership and common management, the primary criteria of alter ego relationships, were not analyzed as they might have been in an alter ego context. Where, however, the precise issue is whether the stock transferee is an alter ego, as in the subsequent case of *Lauer's Furniture Stores, Inc.*,[240] such criteria have been determinative. In *Lauer's Furniture* the lack of any common ownership between predecessor and purchaser at the time of the sale of stock precluded a finding of an alter ego relationship.

The weight given to stock transfers in *TKB*[241] may not have been generally anticipated.[242] Subsequent to *Burns*, the Court explained in *Golden State Bottling*:

> [T]he refusal to adopt a mode of analysis requiring the Board to distinguish among mergers, consolidations, and purchases of assets is attributable to the fact that, so long as there is a continuity in the "employing industry," the public policies underlying the doctrine will be served by its broad application.[243]

Although in dicta, the Court thus minimized the form of the transaction. Previously, in its 1976 decision in *MPE, Inc.*, the Board had refused to adopt a distinction based on the form of a stock transaction.[244]

In *MPE*, the General Counsel had urged that since a sale of stock did not affect the status of the employer as an ongoing corporate entity, the *Burns* rationale regarding the limited obligations of a successor was inappropriate. Rejecting this position, the Board's approach reflected two general considerations. First, the transaction was structured in terms of a sale of stock rather

---

[239]*Id.* at 74.
[240]246 NLRB 360, 102 LRRM 1593 (1979).
[241]*Supra* note 74.
[242]*See* Krupman & Kaplan, *supra* note 74.
[243]*Supra* note 11 at 182 n.5.
[244]226 NLRB 519, 93 LRRM 1325 (1976).

than a sale of assets to preserve an essential lease. A characteristic of a stock purchase, as opposed to a purchase of assets, is the normal ability of the purchaser to retain intact essential licenses or leases. Thus, the Board expressly considered the "limited business options available to the parties to effectuate the transfer . . . ."[245] Second, the Board adopted the same type of analysis it has utilized in alter ego cases. It thus found that the case involved more than a "cosmetic" change in the structure of the enterprise, which "precludes a finding that the succeeding corporate entity is essentially but a mirror image of the predecessor."[246] These same considerations, including the necessity for purchasing stock rather than assets in order to preserve an existing lease, were also deemed significant in *Lauer's Furniture*.[247]

In *TKB*[248] the Board did not refer to *Golden State Bottling*,[249] and it discussed *MPE*[250] only in terms of whether the purchasers had been aware of the existence of the union and whether the collective bargaining agreement had expired.

The courts have not yet directly confronted this issue in a Section 8(a)(5) case. However, in a Section 301 suit, prior to the Supreme Court's *Howard Johnson* decision,[251] the Third Circuit, in *Teamsters Local 249* v. *Bill's Trucking, Inc.*,[252] held that the stock purchaser must generally assume the contract of its vendor. Subsequently, the Ninth Circuit, in *Bartenders & Culinary Workers Local 340* v. *Howard Johnson Co.*,[253] characterized *Bill's Trucking* as a minority holding to the extent that it approved the imposition of substantive terms. However, it noted that if the successor and predecessor were the same corporation, it would regard *Bill's Trucking* as correct concerning the imposition of substantive terms. But whether it would independently view a stock purchase as maintaining the requisite similarity seems unlikely in view of its subsequent decision in *NLRB* v. *Edjo, Inc.*[254] The majority expressed a reluctance, in the context of a stock pur-

---

[245]*Id.* at 521.
[246]*Id.*
[247]*Supra* note 240.
[248]*Supra* note 74.
[249]*Supra* note 11.
[250]*Supra* note 244.
[251]*Supra* note 2.
[252]493 F2d 956, 85 LRRM 2713 (CA 3, 1974).
[253]535 F2d 1160, 92 LRRM 2525 (CA 9, 1976).
[254]631 F2d 604, 105 LRRM 3061 (CA 9, 1980).

chase by one corporation of the other, to adopt a rationale advocated in a concurring opinion. The concurrence urged that the stock purchaser was a "parent" rather than a "successor" and, thus, bound to the union contract of the seller.

The question raised by *TKB* is significant in view of the criteria generally considered by purchasers in structuring the form of a purchase. Thus, the purchase might take the form of an exchange of stock rather than a sale of stock. Or such a transaction might involve questions concerning merger, a factual setting which the Court first considered in *Wiley*[255] but has never expressly resolved.

C. Adoption of Predecessor's Contract

A successor who assumes or adopts a labor contract is, of course, bound by it. While *Burns* established that a successor may not be bound to an involuntary assumption of the substantive terms of a collective bargaining agreement negotiated by its predecessor, there have been circumstances where the successor has been deemed to have adopted or assumed its predecessor's agreement.[256] Adoption (or assumption) has been found where the successor had not only applied the substantive terms of the agreement but also consulted and negotiated with the union as the bargaining agent for its employees.[257] In such circumstances, the successor's disavowal or refusal, in its purchase-sales agreement, to adopt the predecessor's labor agreement was viewed as having been abrogated.[258]

Application of the adoption theory has been predicated upon clear evidence of consent, either actual or constructive.[259] Thus, the mere continuation of economic benefits prevailing at the time of takeover will not, without more, indicate an adoption of

---

[255]*Supra* note 4.

[256]Eklund's Sweden House Inn, Inc., *supra* note 78; Stockton Door Co., 218 NLRB 1053, 89 LRRM 1428 (1975); World Evangelism, Inc., 248 NLRB 909, 104 LRRM 1096 (1980).

[257]*See* cases cited *supra* in note 256. The successor may not condition acceptance of the contract on selective enforcement of certain provisions, even though the union had acquiesced therein with the predecessor. Tasman Sea, Inc., 247 NLRB 684, 103 LRRM 1567 (1980).

[258]Eklund's Sweden House Inn, Inc., *supra* note 78.

[259]Pioneer Printers, 201 NLRB 900, 83 LRRM 1173 (1973); *see also* All State Factors, 205 NLRB 1122, 84 LRRM 1252 (1973), where the ALJ's opinion, affirmed by the Board, stated that *Burns* counsels "restraint in applying the adoption theory, absent clear and convincing evidence of consent, either actual or constructive." 205 NLRB at 1127.

the predecessor's labor agreement.[260] Thus, implementation by the successor of a wage increase provided for in the preexisting labor agreement was not deemed an assumption where the increase was also required by amendments to the minimum wage laws.[261] On the other hand, where the terms of the pre-existing labor agreement which were applied by the successor included union dues deductions and health and welfare contributions, the successor was deemed to have adopted the agreement.[262] Adoption was also found in a Section 301 suit to enforce payments to a pension fund where, among other factors, the successor assured the union it would sign the agreement, requested a moratorium on grievances, and also complied with significant contract provisions.[263]

Where a successor, by its conduct, has adopted its predecessor's labor agreement, the successor will be required, to the same extent as its predecessor, to bargain about any changes in employment practices, such as paying year-end bonuses, even though the adopted agreement is silent on that point.[264]

V. Successorship and the Contract-Bar Doctrine

Successorship and contract-bar doctrines[265] each represent an effort to balance competing policies. The successorship rules focus upon the balance between the employees' need for continuity and the new employer's need for flexibility. The contract-bar rules seek to balance the interests of stability in labor relations against the opportunity of employees to select bargaining representatives. Where the doctrines of successorship and contract bar arise in specific cases, these underlying policy considerations present an added dimension in attempting to strike the appropriate balance. In comparison with the more fully matured contract-bar rules, the contract-bar doctrine in successorship cases is still emerging from the developmental stage. Nonetheless, the decisions rendered in contract-bar cases prior to *Burns* are not dissimilar from those arising in comparable fact situa-

---

[260]*Id.*
[261]Pine Valley Div. of Ethan Allen, Inc., 218 NLRB 208, 217, 89 LRRM 1780 (1975), *enforced in part,* 544 F2d 742, 93 LRRM 2811 (CA 4, 1976).
[262]Virginia Sportswear, Inc., *supra* note 114.
[263]Teamsters Local 92 v. Strabley Bldg. Supply, Inc., 98 LRRM 3025 (ND Ohio, 1978).
[264]Pepsi Cola Distrib. Co. of Knoxville, 241 NLRB 869, 100 LRRM 1626 (1979).
[265]For a discussion of the contract-bar doctrine generally, *see* Chapter 10 *supra* at notes 117-200. *See also* discussion in Burns, *supra* note 9, 406 US at 288 n.8 and 290 n.12, in reference to contract bar in decertification situations.

tions subsequent to *Burns*, though the concepts may have become more complex.

Generally, to operate as a bar to a petition filed during its term, a contract must be in writing.[266] If the successor and the incumbent union negotiate and execute a new agreement, this requirement will normally be satisfied. In the event the successor voluntarily assumes the predecessor's preexisting labor agreement rather than entering into a new agreement, the assumption must be expressed in writing in order to operate as a bar.[267] However, where the new employer is substantially "identical" to, or an alter ego of, the prior employer, the contract between the prior employer and the incumbent union may operate as a bar to a petition from an outside union despite the failure of the new employer expressly to assume the contract. For example, where the only changes consisted of the corporate employer's becoming a subsidiary of another corporation and changing its corporate name, the contract was regarded as intact for its unexpired term.[268]

In certain instances, the policies underlying the contract-bar doctrine predominate over successorship considerations. For example, even though a successor employer enters into a written assumption of the predecessor's contract, it will not operate as a bar if it accelerates the termination date so as to reduce the designated period for filing a timely petition.[269] In contrast, successorship policies may prevail where the successor and the incumbent have entered into an agreement which has the effect of extending the expiration date beyond the term of the original agreement between the predecessor and the incumbent union.[270] In this application of its contract-bar rules, the Board has sought to harmonize and accommodate its *premature extension doctrine*[271] with its successorship policies.

Under the premature extension doctrine, a contract extended beyond its original expiration date will not bar a petition by other parties which has been timely filed in relation to the original expiration date. However, in *Ideal Chevrolet, Inc.*,[272] decided

---

[266]*See* Chapter 10 *supra* at note 119.
[267]Trans-American Video, Inc., 198 NLRB 1247, 81 LRRM 1162 (1972).
[268]M.B. Farrin Lumber Co., 117 NLRB 575, 38 LRRM 1296 (1957).
[269]Longview Terrace Co., 208 NLRB 699, 85 LRRM 1267 (1974).
[270]Ideal Chevolet, Inc., 198 NLRB 280, 80 LRRM 1599 (1972).
[271]*See* Chapter 10 *supra* at notes 130 and 195-97.
[272]*Supra* note 270.

shortly after *Burns,* the Board held that a new collective bargaining agreement entered into by the successor and the incumbent union during the unexpired term of the agreement between the predecessor and the incumbent union was a bar to a representation petition for the full term of the new agreement, even though it had been extended beyond the original expiration date of the predecessor's agreement. In refusing to invoke what otherwise would have warranted the application of its premature extension rule, the Board stated: "Were we to find that this new contract is not a bar to the petition . . . we would be discouraging the successor . . . and the incumbent union from creating a new and stable bargaining relationship."[273]

Prior to *Burns,* the Board had reached a similar result in holding that a written "extension agreement" between the successor and the incumbent union barred an otherwise timely decertification petition, where the extension agreement was regarded as a different agreement with new obligations and different starting and expiration dates.[274] In contrast, in another pre-*Burns* case, the Board had invoked its premature extension doctrine and had found no contract bar where it was the predecessor and the incumbent union who had entered into an extension agreement that was subsequently assumed in writing by the successor.[275] In still another case, the Board had also invoked its premature extension doctrine, despite the execution of a "new contract" by the new management, where the only significant change in the ownership or operation was a change in the stock ownership.[276]

Where the successor and the incumbent are permitted to "prematurely" extend a contract, contract-bar rules will nonetheless continue to be applicable to the new or extended contract. Thus, the extended agreement may not be a bar to a petition by an outside union or employees for a period in excess of three years.[277] However, a contract in excess of three years will bar a petition filed by either of the contracting parties themselves for the duration of the contract.[278]

---

[273]*Id.* at 280.
[274]Chrysler Corp., 153 NLRB 578, 59 LRRM 1529 (1965).
[275]Shop Rite Foods, Inc., 162 NLRB 1020, 64 LRRM 1123 (1956). All such cases must now be evaluated in light of *Burns, supra* note 9, and Ranch-Way, *supra* note 111.
[276]Farrin Lumber Co., *supra* note 268.
[277]*Cf.* Ideal Chevrolet, Inc., *supra* note 270. *See generally* Chapter 10 *supra* at note 129.
[278]Montgomery Ward & Co., Inc., 137 NLRB 346, 50 LRRM 1137 (1962).

When a purchaser neither assumes nor extends its predecessor's labor agreement, but commences bargaining with the incumbent union, the purchaser may be confronted with a petition from an outside union prior to the time of execution of the agreement with the incumbent. In such circumstances, the contract-bar principle of *Keller Plastics*,[279] that following lawful recognition the parties may be given a "reasonable" time in which to conclude an agreement undisturbed by challenges to the incumbent's bargaining status, will be applied to a successor.[280] Thus, the successor and the incumbent union will normally be provided with a reasonable period of time in which to conclude an agreement which may extend beyond the expiration date of the predecessor's contract.[281]

Other merger and consolidation cases illustrate additional distinctions which the Board has deemed significant: Where two companies owned by the same employer were consolidated at the location of the second company, the Board held that the labor contract at the latter location served as a bar to an election.[282] But where the merger of two separate employers resulted in a single new unit in which the former employees of both employers were intermingled, the Board held that a prior labor agreement of one of the employers did not bar an election in the single new unit since the Board viewed the merger as resulting in a new operation.[283] Likewise, the Board held that a prior contract did not bar an election where the combined operation of merged employers brought about a fivefold expansion of the number of employees employed by the predecessor whose labor agreement was in question.[284]

VI. LIABILITY OF SUCCESSOR FOR PREDECESSOR'S UNFAIR LABOR PRACTICES

A successor employer may, in many instances, become obligated to remedy unfair labor practices committed by its prede-

---

[279]157 NLRB 583, 61 LRRM 1396 (1966). *See* Chapter 10 *supra* at notes 91-92.

[280]Fed-Mart, *supra* note 38; *cf.* Glenn Spooner, 208 NLRB 891, 85 LRRM 1193 (1974), *enforced*, 76 CCH Lab. Cases ¶ 10,699 (CA 10, 1975), where the successor did not know of a recognition agreement entered into between the predecessor and the union just prior to the sale.

[281]Ideal Chevrolet, Inc., *supra* note 270.

[282]Builders Emporium, 97 NLRB 1113, 29 LRRM 1213 (1952).

[283]L.B. Spear & Co., 106 NLRB 687, 32 LRRM 1535 (1953).

[284]New Jersey Natural Gas Co., 101 NLRB 251, 31 LRRM 1048 (1952). *See also* Panda Terminals, Inc., 161 NLRB 1215, 63 LRRM 1419 (1966) (fourfold expansion); Bowman Dairy Co., 123 NLRB 707, 43 LRRM 1519 (1959) (30% of the employees in the combined unit had been employed under the contract in question).

cessor. Generally, the imposition of such an obligation and its extent will depend upon whether the successor has taken over its predecessor's operations with knowledge of pending unfair labor practice proceedings or outstanding Board orders. If it had such knowledge, joint and several liability may be imposed to remedy the unfair labor practices. This is the teaching of the Supreme Court's *Golden State Bottling* decision.[285] Where those circumstances prevail, the Board now refers to such a successor as a "*Golden State* successor," to distinguish it from a successor found to be an alter ego of the former employer.[286] An officer who is the alter ego of a corporation may even be liable for the corporation's back-pay obligation.[287]

The development of the law concerning the liability of "*Golden State* successors" has run an uneven course.[288] It was not until the Supreme Court's 1973 *Golden State Bottling* decision that the view that the Board's power to impose such obligations did not exceed its remedial powers under Section 10(c) of the Act became firmly established.[289] While the Board has uniformly followed such a policy since 1967, when it decided *Perma Vinyl*,[290] its position in prior years had been marked by a series of 180-degree turns.

Specifically, in 1944, the Board determined that a bona fide successor was not liable for the unfair labor practices of its predecessor. This position was abandoned in 1947 with the imposition of joint and several liability where the bona fide successor had knowledge of the seller's unfair labor practice at the time of purchase. In 1954, prompted by reversals in two

---

[285]Golden State Bottling Co. v. NLRB, *supra* note 11. *See generally* Du Ross, *Protecting Employee Remedial Rights Under the Perma Vinyl Doctrine*, 39 Geo. Wash. L. Rev. 1063, 1089 (1971). By analogy, a successor is also precluded from challenging the appropriateness of a bargaining unit determined in a technical §8(a)(5) proceeding where it had notice of the proceeding. North Am. Soccer League v. NLRB, 613 F2d 1379, 103 LRRM 2976 (CA 5, 1980), *enforcing* 241 NLRB 1225, 101 LRRM 1037 (1979), *cert. denied*, 449 US 899, 105 LRRM 2737 (1980).

[286]Bell Co., Inc., *supra* note 86; Victor Patino, *supra* note 225, where the new employer is an alter ego.

[287]Carpet City Mechanical Co., Inc., 244 NLRB 1031, 102 LRRM 1337 (1979).

[288]This has been unlike the development of the law concerning the liability of alter egos. Historically, the Board, even in its initial years, held with judicial support that an alter ego would be liable for the unfair labor practices of its predecessor. NLRB v. Hopwood Retinning Co., 104 F2d 302, 4 LRRM 555 (CA 2, 1939), *enforcing* 4 NLRB 922, 1A LRRM 416 (1938); Regal Knitwear Co. v. NLRB, *supra* note 14. Where such an identity of interests was found, Board orders running to "successors and assigns" of offending employers were upheld by the Supreme Court as early as the 1940s. Southport Petroleum Co., *supra* note 12; Regal Knitwear Co. v. NLRB, *supra* note 14.

[289]*Supra* note 11.

[290]*Supra* note 71.

courts of appeal, the Board, in *Symns Grocer,* returned to its 1944 position, but based upon the enunciated proposition that the Act does not authorize imposition of responsibility for remedying unfair labor practices on a person who had not engaged in the subject conduct.[291]

Overruling *Symns Grocer* in 1967, the Board held in *Perma Vinyl* that

> one who acquires and operates a business of an employer found guilty of unfair labor practices in basically unchanged form under circumstances which charge him with notice of unfair labor practice charges against his predecessor should be held responsible for remedying his predecessor's unlawful conduct.[292]

In *Perma Vinyl,* the Board ordered the purchaser to reinstate and reimburse with back pay four discharged employees. Perma Vinyl had paid back pay to the time of the sale to the purchaser, U.S. Pipe, but the issue remained as to whether and to what extent U.S. Pipe was liable for reinstatement of the discharged employees. U.S. Pipe was not an alter ego of Perma Vinyl; however, it had purchased the assets of Perma Vinyl "with knowledge of the unfair labor proceeding against that company."[293]

Recognizing that U.S. Pipe was the only employer with the power to reinstate the unlawfully discharged employees, the Board held that U.S. Pipe had the responsibility for remedying unfair labor practices attached to the business which it had bought and was continuing. The Board relied on the broad reasoning of the Supreme Court in *Wiley*[294] for fashioning this remedy, pointing to the fact that the "employee victims" of unfair labor practices were especially in need of help, for they are "without meaningful remedy when title to the employing business operation changes hands."[295]

---

[291]South Carolina Granite Co., 58 NLRB 1448, 15 LRRM 122 (1944), *enforced sub nom.* NLRB v. Blair Quarries, Inc., 152 F2d 25, 17 LRRM 683 (CA 4, 1945); Alexander Milburn Co., 78 NLRB 747, 22 LRRM 1249 (1948); Symns Grocer Co., 109 NLRB 346, 34 LRRM 1326 (1954). *See* Golden State Bottling Co. v. NLRB, *supra* note 11 at 174-75.
[292]*Supra* note 71 at 969; *see* Du Ross, *supra* note 285.
[293]*Supra* note 71 at 968. International Technical Prods. Corp., 249 NLRB 1301, 104 LRRM 1294 (1980), *supplementing* 196 NLRB 523, 80 LRRM 1222 (1972), where back-pay liability applied to a successor who had purchased assets "free and clear" in a bankruptcy proceeding (but with knowledge of the predecessor's back-pay liability).
[294]*Supra* note 4.
[295]Perma Vinyl, *supra* note 71 at 969.

In *Golden State Bottling*[296] the Supreme Court adopted the Board's position in *Perma Vinyl* as well as its reasoning. The Court held that where a purchaser with notice of a pending unfair labor practice proceeding is found to have acquired and continued the business without interruption or substantial change in operation, employee complement, or supervisory personnel, it will have joint and several liability for back pay as a consequence of its predecessor's unfair labor practices; and it will be required to offer unlawfully discharged employees immediate reinstatement to their former or substantially equivalent positions.[297]

The Court concluded that (1) the Board's discretion under Section 10(c) of the Act was broad enough to allow issuance of an order against a successor directing reinstatement with back pay;[298] (2) Rule 65(d) of the Federal Rules of Civil Procedure was not a bar to enforcement of a Board order requiring reinstatement by the successor, because a purchaser with knowledge of an unfair labor practice is in privity with the seller for purposes of the rule; (3) the Board properly balanced the "conflicting legitimate interests of the bona fide successor, the public and the affected employee" in light of the principles set forth in *Wiley*;[299] (4) the Court's holding did not conflict in any manner with its decision in *Burns*.[300] Thus, the Court highlighted the distinction between the absence of an obligation by the successor to assume the predecessor's labor agreement, and the existence of an obligation to remedy its predecessor's unfair labor practices.[301]

Finally, the Court was careful to note as a matter of due process and procedure that prior to any adjudication of its liability, the successor is entitled to notice and a hearing as to

---

[296]*Supra* note 11.

[297]For a detailed discussion of this holding in the context of a new employer's requirement to reinstate strikers who had engaged in an unfair labor practices strike against its predecessor, *see* NLRB v. Fabsteel Co. of La., *supra* note 86 at 692.

[298]§10(c) grants authority for the Board to require remedial action from "any person named in the complaint" who has engaged in "any such unfair labor practices," but also provides the Board shall have such remedial power "as will effectuate the policies of the Act."

[299]Golden State Bottling Co. v. NLRB, *supra* note 11 at 181; Wiley, *supra* note 4.

[300]Golden State Bottling Co. v. NLRB, *supra* note 11 at 182; NLRB v. Burns, *supra* note 9.

[301]Although the successor may not be required to assume the labor agreement, liability for payments to pension and health and welfare funds may be imposed where the predecessor was found to have unilaterally discontinued such payments pursuant to an unlawful withdrawal of recognition. Pacific Aggregates, Inc., *supra* note 174.

"whether it is a successor which is responsible for remedying the predecessor's unfair labor practices" and other facts relevant to the enforcement of the Board's order against it.[302] This cautionary statement was significant because wholly different parties may become involved at different stages of the proceedings, depending upon when the takeover occurs. In subsequent years procedural issues have become prevalent.

Issues concerning a successor's derivative liability may be raised and litigated for the first time at the compliance stage of an unfair labor practice proceeding in a supplementary proceeding.[303] It is not necessary for the Board to initiate a new unfair labor practice proceeding to consider this issue.[304] Nor is the Board required, where a court of appeals has already enforced its initial order, to apply to that court for permission to conduct a supplementary proceeding to determine derivative liability.[305] Since in those circumstances the courts have expressed a preference for the Board to undertake the initial determination of derivative liability, the original enforcing decree of the court will not, except in unusual circumstances, support a petition to the enforcing court to punish the parties for contempt.[306]

Frequently, where the takeover occurs after a Board order issues or after the unfair labor practice hearings have been

---

[302]Golden State Bottling Co. v. NLRB, *supra* note 11 at 180; NLRB v. East Side Shopper, Inc., 498 F2d 1334, 86 LRRM 2817 (CA 6, 1974).

[303]Coast Delivery Serv., Inc., 198 NLRB 1026, 81 LRRM 1417 (1972); *see* NLRB v. C.C.C. Assocs., Inc., 306 F2d 534, 50 LRRM 2882 (CA 2, 1962), where the derivative liability of a successor was litigated for the first time after a court enforced a Board order for back pay against the predecessor. Since supplementary proceedings are typically concerned with the extent to which back pay may be due, they are frequently designated as "back pay proceedings." *See* discussion in Chapter 32 *infra* at notes 164-67.

[304]*See* cases cited in note 303 *supra*.

[305]*Id.* Home Beneficial Life Ins. Co. v. NLRB, 172 F2d 62, 23 LRRM 2253 (CA 4, 1949); NLRB v. Royal Palm Ice Co., 201 F2d 667, 31 LRRM 2308 (CA 5, 1953); NLRB v. Bird Mach. Co., 174 F2d 404, 24 LRRM 2053 (CA 1, 1949).

[306]NLRB v. C.C.C. Assocs., *supra* note 303; NLRB v. New York Merchandise Co., 134 F2d 949, 951, 952, 12 LRRM 578 (CA 2, 1943), where it was stated that the initial enforcing decree of the court of appeals "cannot be interpreted as peremptory in the sense that it will support a proceeding to punish for contempt. Pro tanto it is interlocutory, though it is final as to any of its other provisions that require no further definition." *See* Wallace Corp. v. NLRB, 159 F2d 952, 19 LRRM 2311 (CA 4, 1947). Where, however, there is a deliberate scheme to dissipate assets or frustrate the enforcement of back-pay liability through alter ego corporations, a direct petition for contempt will be heard. *See* NLRB v. Deena Artware, 361 US 398, 45 LRRM 2697 (1960). *See also* NLRB v. Mastro Plastics Corp., 354 F2d 170, 60 LRRM 2578 (CA 2, 1965), *cert. denied*, 384 US 972, 62 LRRM 2292 (1966), which did not involve contempt but dispensed with the requirement of a separate hearing where the underlying corporate nexus was conceded and the alter ego status was indisputable following the merger of a former subsidiary.

completed, the compliance stage represents the first occasion for raising issues of derivative liability.[307] Even where there is evidence in the unfair labor practice proceeding which establishes a foundation for findings as to the relationship between the prior and the present employer, the Board will not impose derivative liability at that initial stage, unless the new employer has been named as a party and afforded a full opportunity to litigate its status in that proceeding. Otherwise, it would not have had its "day in court."[308] Instead, the Board permits its General Counsel to plead and litigate this question during the compliance stage. Thus, even though the principals of the two employers have remained the same and have testified in the underlying unfair labor practice hearing, they may still be afforded a separate day in court, particularly where they testified in their capacities as representatives of the prior employer.[309] Similarly, the Board is reluctant to grant the General Counsel's motion for summary judgment at the compliance stage, if that would deprive a new party of the opportunity to litigate its status in a hearing at that time.[310]

Although the Board has demonstrated a preference for considering issues of derivative liability at the compliance stage,[311] significant controversy has arisen in situations where a new employer was not named as a respondent in the underlying unfair labor practice proceeding despite the General Counsel's awareness of its alter ego status. In 1978 the Board held that under those circumstances, even an alter ego employer could not thereafter be held accountable in a back-pay proceeding.[312] In the following year, however, a divided Board overruled this

---

[307]Coast Delivery Serv., Inc., *supra* note 303; NLRB v. C.C.C. Assocs., Inc., *supra* note 303; Hot Bagels & Donuts of Staten Island, Inc., 244 NLRB 129, 102 LRRM 1163 (1979), *enforced*, 622 F2d 1113, 104 LRRM 2963 (CA 2, 1980).

[308]George C. Shearer Exhibitors Delivery Serv., 246 NLRB 416, 102 LRRM 1624 (1979). *See* Marine Mach. Works, Inc., 243 NLRB 1081, 101 LRRM 1576 (1979), denying the General Counsel's motion to join an alleged successor in the unfair labor practice proceeding.

[309]*See* note 308 *supra*.

[310]Dews Constr. Corp., 246 NLRB 945, 103 LRRM 1001 (1979), *supplementing* 231 NLRB 182, 95 LRRM 1574 (1977). In unusual circumstances (indisputable evidence of alter ego status and a deliberate scheme to dissipate assets or frustrate the enforcement of back-pay liability) a successor's liability was initially determined in a direct contempt proceeding. As noted above, however, absent such factors, the courts have rejected this direct procedure as inappropriate since it undermines the reviewing process and inhibits the Board's role in initially determining all undecided issues.

[311]Southeastern Envelope Co., Inc., 246 NLRB 423, 102 LRRM 1567 (1979), *supplementing* 206 NLRB 933, 84 LRRM 1577 (1973).

[312]Rose Knitting Mills, Inc., 237 NLRB 1382, 99 LRRM 1223 (1978).

position and permitted the General Counsel to litigate the question of derivative liability in a compliance proceeding even though the issue could have been pleaded and litigated in the original unfair labor practice proceeding.[313] In the compliance proceeding, the Board emphasized the finding that the employers were alter ego whose interests "are by definition identical." It therefore concluded that adequate notice had been afforded.[314]

The Board also permitted the General Counsel to litigate for the first time, in a supplementary proceeding, an employer's status as a "*Golden State* successor," even though the employer's status had already been litigated on an alter ego theory in the underlying unfair practice proceeding.[315] The Seventh Circuit, however, rejected the Board's finding that the new employer was an alter ego, but it did not consider the question of its derivative liability as a "*Golden State* successor."[316]

When the issue of derivative liability is litigated (generally at the compliance stage), the new employer may raise as defenses, as a threshold matter, that (1) it is not an alter ego or a successor;[317] (2) it did not possess the knowledge required as a "*Golden State* successor";[318] (3) it does not meet the jurisdictional standards of the Board;[319] or (4) the imposition of derivative liability is otherwise inappropriate.[320]

As to the issue of prior knowledge, the Board has placed the burden on the successor to prove lack of knowledge.[321] One obstacle to meeting that burden might be that the successor had, at the time of purchase, obtained an indemnification clause in its sale agreement regarding any obligations incurred as a result of unfair labor practice proceedings against its predecessor.[322] Where, however, there is no face-to-face relationship between the successor and the predecessor, as in a contract-bid situation, prior knowledge may not be as readily available.

---

[313]Southeastern Envelope Co., Inc., *supra* note 311, 102 LRRM at 1568.
[314]*Id.*
[315]Bell Co., Inc., *supra* note 86. The decision was by a divided Board.
[316]NLRB v. Bell Co., Inc., *supra* notes 86 and 195.
[317]Dews Constr. Corp, *supra* note 310.
[318]Mansion House Center Mgmt. Corp, 208 NLRB 684, 85 LRRM 1555 (1974).
[319]Northgate Cinema, Inc., 233 NLRB 586, 96 LRRM 1598 (1977).
[320]NLRB v. Fabsteel Co. of La., *supra* notes 86 and 297. *See* Middle E. Bakery, 243 NLRB 503, 101 LRRM 1507 (1979) (bare assertion of nonsuccessorship as a defense after failure to answer the complaint is inadequate and untimely).
[321]Mansion House Center Mgmt. Corp., *supra* note 318.
[322]Am-Del-Co., Inc., 234 NLRB 1040, 97 LRRM 1419 (1978).

A successor may also seek to show that its revenues, unlike its predecessor's, do not meet the Board's jurisdictional standards.[323] Where a full calendar year has not elapsed, the Board will assert jurisdiction on the basis of the income of the predecessor in the previous calendar years based on the projected revenue of the new employer.[324] The basis for rejecting a mutually exclusive test, such as projected revenue, is the concern that a new employer could shield itself from remedies for serious unfair labor practices by a "measured effort" to defeat Board jurisdiction.[325]

In a related context, another defense to liability may be that the purchaser's operations are based upon an independent contractor relationship, rather than the employer-employee relationship which previously existed.[326] In these circumstances, the denial of liability would be based upon the ground that the purchaser is not a successor.[327]

Derivative liability may be imposed upon a parent corporation with respect to unfair labor practices by its subsidiary in certain instances.[328] There, in the case of a bargaining violation, the test is not whether day-to-day labor relations are handled on a local level, but whether the parent corporation has the "present and apparent means" to influence the local negotiations and permits this fact to be traded upon in the local negotiations.[329]

In a collateral development, there is authority for finding that a successor may be required, in a Section 301 action, to satisfy an arbitration award arising out of a predecessor's contract, where it had knowledge of the award and expressly assumed the agreement.[330]

Not every unfair labor practice, however, will necessitate a remedial order against a "*Golden State* successor." Thus, a successor may not be required to remedy a predecessor's unlawful

---

[323]*See generally* Chapter 30 *infra* at notes 368-418.
[324]Northgate Cinema, Inc., *supra* note 319.
[325]*Id.*
[326]Merchants Home Delivery Serv., Inc., *supra* note 144.
[327]*Id.*
[328]Royal Typewriter Co. v. NLRB, 533 F2d 1030, 92 LRRM 2013 (CA 8, 1976).
[329]*Id.*
[330]Automobile Workers Local 6 v. Saga Foods, Inc., 407 F Supp 1247, 91 LRRM 2946 (ND Ill, 1976).

refusal to furnish information to the union, where the information is no longer current and the order against the predecessor suffices as a remedy.[331]

---

[331]Roman Catholic Diocese of Brooklyn, 222 NLRB 1052, 91 LRRM 1419 (1976), *affirmed sub nom.* Nazareth Regional High School v. NLRB, 549 F2d 873, 94 LRRM 2897 (CA 2, 1977). Nor will a successor to one bargaining unit be required to remedy the unfair labor practices of the predecessor in another unit in which it is not the successor. Bellingham Frozen Foods v. NLRB, *supra* note 191.

CHAPTER 16

SUBJECTS OF BARGAINING:
THEIR SIGNIFICANCE

I. Introduction

This chapter is an introduction to the law governing the subject matter of collective bargaining. The Board and the courts have divided bargaining subjects into three discrete categories: mandatory, permissive, and illegal.[1] This chapter describes generally the difference between mandatory and permissive bargaining subjects and the consequences of classifying a subject as one or the other. The development of the mandatory and permissive dichotomy is traced through a series of Supreme Court decisions that provide the foundation for analyzing questions involving the dichotomy. Chapter 17 describes in depth mandatory bargaining subjects. Chapter 18 describes in depth permissive and illegal bargaining subjects.[2]

II. Historical Background

The law concerning subjects of bargaining has evolved in Board and Supreme Court decisions, with relatively little guidance from the language of the Act or from legislative history. Section 8(5) of the Wagner Act made it an unfair labor practice for an employer "to refuse to bargain collectively with the representatives of his employees, subject to the provisions of section 9(a)." Section 9(a) of the Wagner Act provided that the employ-

---

[1]Illegal bargaining subjects are those that concern proposals in violation of federal labor law, other federal law, and state law which is not preempted by federal law. The issue of illegality is distinct from the mandatory and permissive dichotomy that forms the basis of this chapter. Therefore, the issue of illegal subjects is not discussed in this chapter, but rather is left to separate discussion as part of Chapter 18 *infra*.

[2]The nature of the duty to bargain in good faith is discussed in Chapter 13 *supra*.

ees' bargaining representative "shall be the exclusive representative of all the employees . . . for the purpose of collective bargaining in respect of *rates of pay, wages, hours of employment, or other conditions of employment*."[3] Prior to the Taft-Hartley Act of 1947, the above-quoted language was the only statutory guidance concerning subjects for collective bargaining.

In the Taft-Hartley Act, Congress added Section 8(d), which set forth several specific obligations encompassed in the duty to bargain collectively. Included were the obligation of the employer and employees' representative to "confer in good faith with respect to *wages, hours, and other terms and conditions of employment*."[4]

In the absence of definitional or restrictive statutory language, the Board, very early, assumed the role of determining what were and were not mandatory bargaining subjects. In 1940, in *Singer Manufacturing Co.*,[5] the Board held that

> [p]aid holidays, vacations, and bonuses constitute an integral part of the earnings and working conditions of the employees and . . . are matters which are generally the subject of collective bargaining . . . . [I]nsistence upon treating such matters as gratuities to be granted and withdrawn at will, constitutes a refusal to bargain . . . .[6]

Following the *Singer* case, the Board held that various integral parts of the employment relationship were embraced by Section 9(a).[7] These included such subjects as discharges,[8] pensions,[9] profit-sharing,[10] work loads and work standards,[11] insurance benefits,[12] the closed and the union shop,[13] subcontracting,[14]

---

[3]Emphasis added.

[4]Emphasis added. The "rates of pay" language of §9(a) was not included in §8d, apparently because "rates of pay" with "wages" was deemed redundant. §9(a)'s "conditions of employment" became "terms and conditions of employment" in §8(d). Taft-Hartley also added §8(b)(3), which made it an unfair labor practice for a labor organization "to refuse to bargain collectively with an employer . . . ."

[5]24 NLRB 444, 6 LRRM 405 (1940), *modified on other grounds and enforced*, 119 F2d 131, 8 LRRM 740 (CA 7, 1941).

[6]24 NLRB at 470.

[7]Cox & Dunlop, *Regulation of Collective Bargaining by the National Labor Relations Board*, 63 HARV. L. REV. 389, 397-401 (1950).

[8]NLRB v. Bachelder, 120 F2d 574, 8 LRRM 723 (CA 7, 1941).

[9]Inland Steel Co., 77 NLRB 1, 21 LRRM 1310 (1948), *enforced*, 170 F2d 247, 22 LRRM 2506 (CA 7, 1948), *cert. denied*, 336 US 960, 24 LRRM 2019 (1949).

[10]Union Mfg. Co., 76 NLRB 322, 21 LRRM 1187 (1948), *enforced*, 179 F2d 511, 25 LRRM 2302 (CA 5, 1950).

[11]Woodside Cotton Mills Co., 21 NLRB 42, 6 LRRM 68 (1940).

[12]W. W. Cross & Co., 77 NLRB 1162, 22 LRRM 1131 (1948), *enforced,* 174 F2d 875, 24 LRRM 2068 (CA 1, 1949); General Motors Corp., 81 NLRB 779, 23 LRRM 1422 (1949), *enforced,* 179 F2d 221, 25 LRRM 2281 (CA 2, 1950).

shop rules,[15] work schedules,[16] rest periods,[17] and merit increases.[18] All of these determinations were made under the original Wagner Act.

In a statement presented in 1947 to the Senate committee considering amendments to the Wagner Act, NLRB Chairman Paul Herzog asserted that the scope of collective bargaining "depends upon the industry's customs and history, the previously existing employer-employee relationship, technological problems and demands, and other factors," adding that the scope might "vary with changes in industrial structure and practice." He suggested that the job of defining the area of bargaining should be left to the Board, subject only to judicial review.[19]

Although Congress amended the Act extensively in 1947, it provided for no basic change in the legislative framework supporting the Board's definitions of the subjects of bargaining. As previously noted, the phrase "wages, hours of employment, or other conditions of employment,"[20] which the Board had construed in the context of Section 9(a), now became, with the addition of "terms" of employment, part of the definition of collective bargaining written into Section 8(d).

Despite the failure of Congress to define substantive bargaining in the Taft-Hartley amendments, the developing law of collective bargaining[21] has shown a decided pattern of change—

---

[13]Winona Textile Mills, Inc., 68 NLRB 702, 18 LRRM 1154 (1946), *enforced*, 160 F2d 201, 19 LRRM 2417 (CA 7, 1947); Andrew Jergens Co., 76 NLRB 363, 21 LRRM 1192 (1948), *enforced*, 175 F2d 130, 24 LRRM 2096 (CA 9, 1949), *cert. denied*, 338 US 827, 24 LRRM 2561 (1949); Alexander Milburn Co., 62 NLRB 482, 16 LRRM 202 (1945), *supplemented*, 78 NLRB 717, 22 LRRM 1249 (1948).
[14]Timken Roller Bearing Co., 70 NLRB 500, 18 LRRM 1370 (1946), *enforcement denied on other grounds*, 161 F2d 949, 20 LRRM 2204 (CA 6, 1947); *cf*. Emerson Elec. Mfg. Co., 13 NLRB 448, 4 LRRM 307 (1939).
[15]Timken Roller Bearing Co., *supra* note 14.
[16]Inter-City Advertising Co., 61 NLRB 1377, 1384, 16 LRRM 153 (1945), *enforcement denied on other grounds*, 154 F2d 244, 17 LRRM 916 (CA 4, 1946); Wilson & Co., 19 NLRB 990, 999, 5 LRRM 560, *enforced*, 115 F2d 759, 7 LRRM 575 (CA 8, 1940); Woodside Cotton Mills Co., 21 NLRB 42, 54-55, 6 LRRM 68 (1940).
[17]National Grinding Wheel Co., 75 NLRB 905, 21 LRRM 1095 (1948).
[18]Aluminum Ore Co. v. NLRB, 131 F2d 485, 11 LRRM 693 (CA 7, 1942), *enforcing* 39 NLRB 1286, 10 LRRM 49 (1942); NLRB v. J. H. Allison & Co., 165 F2d 766, 21 LRRM 2238 (CA 6, 1948), *cert. denied*, 335 US 814, 22 LRRM 2564 (1948), *enforcing* 70 NLRB 377, 18 LRRM 1369 (1946).
[19]*Hearings Before Senate Committee on Labor and Public Welfare on S. 55 and S. J. Res. 22*, 80th Cong., 1st Sess. 1914 (1947). For a discussion of this legislative background and the early judicial history of collective bargaining, *see* Cox & Dunlop, *supra* note 7; Smith, *The Evolution of the "Duty to Bargain" Concept in American Law*, 39 Mich. L. Rev. 1065 (1941).
[20]*See* note 4 *supra*.
[21]*See* Chapter 17 *infra*.

but change based more upon general trends in the economy than upon the predicted exercise of flexible administrative direction applied industry by industry. However, Chairman Herzog's suggestion that the task of defining the subjects of bargaining be left exclusively to the Board and to the courts has been adopted. Indeed, Justice Stewart, joined by Justices Douglas and Harlan, concurring in the 1964 *Fibreboard* decision,[22] concluded that

> [t]here was a time when one might have taken the view that the National Labor Relations Act gave the Board and the courts no power to determine the subjects about which the parties must bargain .... But too much law has been built upon a contrary assumption for this view any longer to prevail, and I question neither the power of the Court to decide this issue nor the propriety of its doing so.[23]

The Supreme Court in 1952, in its first decision on bargaining subjects, *NLRB* v. *American National Insurance Co.*,[24] reversed the Board's holding that an employer had violated Section 8(a)(5) by making a collective bargaining agreement conditioned on the inclusion of a broad management rights clause under which certain subjects, including promotion, demotion, discharge, discipline, and work schedules, would be nonarbitrable. The Board conceded that the management rights clause was not unlawful; however, it argued that insistence on such a clause was unlawful because such insistence was in derogation of the obligation to bargain over conditions of employment. The Court noted that broad management rights clauses were common in recent collective bargaining agreements, and it viewed the Board's efforts as an unwarranted interference with the collective bargaining process, stating:

> Bargaining for more flexible treatment of [conditions of employment] would be denied employers even though the result may be contrary to common collective bargaining practice in the industry. The Board was not empowered so to disrupt collective bargaining practices. On

---

[22]Fibreboard Paper Prods. Corp. v. NLRB, 379 US 203, 57 LRRM 2609 (1964). *See* Chapter 17 *infra* at notes 272-80.

[23]379 US at 219 n.2. *Contrast* the statement of Senator Walsh, Chairman of the Senate Education and Labor Committee when the Wagner Act was being passed: "The bill indicates the method and manner in which employees may organize, the method and manner of selecting their representatives or spokesmen, and leads them to the office door of their employer with the legal authority to negotiate for their fellow employees. The bill does not go beyond the office door. It leaves the discussion between the employer and the employee, and the agreements which they may or may not make, voluntary and with that sacredness and solemnity to a voluntary agreement with which both parties to an agreement should be enshrouded." 79 CONG. REC. 7659 (1935).

[24]343 US 395, 30 LRRM 2147 (1952).

the contrary, the term "bargain collectively" as used in the act has been considered to absorb and give statutory approval to the philosophy of bargaining as worked out in the labor movement in the United States.[25]

American National was the Court's last major decision on bargaining subjects prior to its holding in *NLRB* v. *Borg-Warner Corp.*,[26] the decision which established the distinction between mandatory and permissive bargaining subjects—the distinction which governs the law of bargaining subjects today.

III. BORG-WARNER; PITTSBURGH PLATE GLASS; FORD; AND FIRST NATIONAL MAINTENANCE: THE DISTINCTION BETWEEN "MANDATORY" AND "PERMISSIVE"

A. Basic Principles

The language of the statute merely directs bargaining parties to "confer in good faith with respect to wages, hours, and other terms and conditions of employment." From this, the Supreme Court has developed the distinction between *mandatory* bargaining subjects, i.e., wages, hours, and other terms and conditions of employment, and *permissive* subjects, i.e., nonmandatory subjects that are not improper bargaining subjects in that they do not conflict with federal and nonpreempted state law. As the following cases demonstrate, the Court has further refined the definition of mandatory bargaining subjects to include subjects that "vitally affect" employees, including subjects which relate directly to nonemployees, i.e., concern individuals or conditions outside the bargaining unit but which nevertheless have a substantial impact on bargaining unit employees. The Court has also declared that industry collective bargaining practices are "highly relevant" in deciding which subjects are mandatory and that Congress intended that the Board, not the courts, should have the primary responsibility for determining which subjects are mandatory. And the Court has held that a balancing test applies in cases where it is necessary to decide whether certain business decisions are mandatory bargaining subjects: The balancing is between the benefits to the collective bargaining proc-

---

[25]*Id.* at 408.
[26]356 US 342, 42 LRRM 2034 (1958).

ess and the employer's need for unencumbered decision making in certain areas affecting the employer's business.

1. *Borg-Warner*—**The Distinction.** In 1958, in *Borg-Warner Corp.*,[27] the Supreme Court adopted the analysis contained in the Board's decision, which recognized a distinction between mandatory bargaining subjects and permissive bargaining subjects. The Court reviewed Sections 8(a)(5) and 8(d),[28] and reasoned:

> Read together, these provisions establish the obligation of the employer and the representative of its employees to bargain with each other in good faith with respect to wages, hours, and other terms and conditions of employment . . . . The duty is limited to those subjects, and within that area neither party is legally obligated to yield . . . . As to other matters, however, each party is free to bargain or not to bargain, and to agree or not to agree.[29]

The employer, although bargaining in good faith concerning wages, hours, and other terms and conditions of employment, had insisted that any agreement be conditioned on inclusion of (1) a recognition clause granting recognition solely to the local union, even though the international union was the Board-certified bargaining representative, and (2) a "ballot clause" under which a strike could not be conducted over nonarbitrable issues until all bargaining unit members (union and nonunion) had voted on the company's last offer and permitting the company, if the offer was rejected, to submit a revised offer within 72 hours for a similar secret ballot. The Court concluded that the recognition clause and the ballot clause were not mandatory bargaining subjects in that they did not concern wages, hours, and other terms and conditions of employment.[30] Agreeing with the Board, the Court held that the employer's insistence on the inclusion of these nonmandatory bargaining subjects was, in

---

[27]*Id.*

[28]The same reasoning is also applicable to §8(b)(3), concerning a union's refusal to bargain. *See generally* Chapters 13 *supra* and 17 *infra.*

[29]356 US at 349.

[30]*Id.* at 356-59. The Court had little difficulty finding the recognition clause to be a nonmandatory bargaining subject, stating: "The statute requires the company to bargain with the certified representative of its employees. It is an evasion of that duty to insist that the certified agent not be a party to the collective-bargaining contract." *Id.* at 350.

The ballot-clause analysis, however, was not so easy. The Court, citing *American National Insurance Co.*, acknowledged that the employer could have insisted on a no-strike clause because such a clause "regulates the relations between the employer and the employees." *Id.* at 350. The ballot clause, however, was not viewed as a "partial 'no-strike' clause" but rather as an attempt to regulate relations "between the employees and their unions." *Id.* It was thus an attempt by "the employer, in effect, to deal with its employees rather than with their statutory representative." *Id.*

effect, a refusal to bargain over the mandatory bargaining subjects, stating:

> The company's good faith has met the requirements of the statute as to the subjects of mandatory bargaining. But that good faith does not license the employer to refuse to enter into agreements on the ground that they do not include some proposal which is not a mandatory subject of bargaining. We agree with the Board that such conduct is, in substance, a refusal to bargain about the subjects that are within the scope of mandatory bargaining. This does not mean that bargaining is to be confined to the statutory subjects. Each of the two controversial clauses is lawful in itself. Each would be enforceable if agreed to by the unions. But it does not follow that, because the company may propose these clauses, it can lawfully insist upon them as a condition to any agreement.[31]

The Court's holding in *Borg-Warner* was consistent with its holding in *American National*[32] that an employer may insist upon a broad management rights clause concerning mandatory bargaining subjects. The Court cited *American National* for the proposition that "neither party is legally obligated to yield" when negotiating with respect to wages, hours, and other terms and conditions of employment.[33]

Justice Harlan, in a dissent concurred in by three other Justices, argued that the majority's opinion was inconsistent with the Act and *American National* in that the mandatory-permissive dichotomy interferes with the "evolving character of collective bargaining agreements," gives the Board unwarranted control over substantive provisions of collective bargaining, and is an artificial device for avoiding the Board's responsibility for determining good faith on a case-by-case basis on a review of all of the facts.[34]

---

[31]*Id.* at 349.

[32]*Supra* note 24.

[33]NLRB v. Borg-Warner Corp., *supra* note 26 at 349.

[34]*Id.* at 356-59 (Justices Clark and Whittaker expressly joined in the dissent; Justice Frankfurter, in a separate opinion, stated that he "agree[d] with the views of Mr. Justice Harlan regarding the 'ballot' clause," *id.* at 351—the area in which Justice Harlan argued the inconsistency with *American National Insurance Co.*).

Justice Harlan argued that the Court in *American National Insurance Co.* had "emphasized that flexibility was an essential characteristic of the process of collective bargaining, and that whether the topics contained in the disputed clause should be allocated exclusively to management or decided jointly by management and union '. . . is an issue for determination across the bargaining table, not by the Board.' 343 U.S., at 409. It is true that the disputed [ballot] clause related to matters which concededly were 'terms and conditions of employment,' but the broad rationale of the Court's opinion undercuts an attempt to distinguish the case on any such ground. 'Congress provided expressly that the Board should not pass upon the desirability of the substantive terms of labor agreements . . . . The duty to bargain collectively is to be enforced by application

Borg-Warner teaches that a party, regardless of its good faith in bargaining, commits an unfair labor practice when it insists to impasse upon the inclusion of a permissive bargaining subject, i.e., a subject outside the scope of "wages, hours, and other terms and conditions of employment."[35]

2. ***Pittsburgh Plate Glass*—The "Vitally Affects" Test.** In a 1971 decision, *Allied Chemical & Alkali Workers Local 1* v. *Pittsburgh Plate Glass Co.*,[36] the Court was faced with the issue of whether an employer violated Section 8(a)(5) by unilaterally modifying, during the term of the contract, a health insurance plan covering retired employees. The case turned on whether the issue of benefits for already-retired employees is a mandatory bargaining subject, since unilateral changes in mandatory bargaining subjects are *per se* Section 8(a)(5) violations.[37] The Board, relying on two separate theories, held that changes in retired employees' benefits "are embraced by the bargaining obligation and that an employer's unilateral modification of them" constitutes a Section 8(a)(5) violation.[38] The Court first rejected the Board's argument that retired employees were employees within the meaning of Section 2(3) and that therefore their benefits involved terms and conditions of employment—a mandatory bargaining subject.[39] The Court then addressed the Board's second theory, to wit: Even if retirees are not Section 2(3) employees, their benefits "vitally affect" the terms and condition of employment of active employees and are therefore a mandatory bargaining subject. The Court recognized that "matters involving individuals outside the employment relationship, . . . are not wholly excluded [from being mandatory bar-

---

of the good faith bargaining standards of Section 8(d) to the facts of each case . . . .' 343 U.S., at 408-409." *Id.* at 357.

[35]The Borg-Warner decision was criticized by commentators in Wollett, *The Borg-Warner Case and the Role of the NLRB in the Bargaining Process*, NYU TWELFTH ANNUAL CONFERENCE ON LABOR 39 (1959); Note, 43 MINN. L. REV. 1225 (1959); Note, 11 STAN. L. REV. 188 (1958).

[36]404 US 157, 78 LRRM 2974 (1971).

[37]*Id.* at 183-88. (In contrast, a unilateral midcontract change relating to a permissive bargaining subject is not an unfair labor practice; the remedy for such a change is to pursue a §301 action or file a grievance under the collective bargaining agreement's grievance-arbitration procedure; if applicable.) *See* NLRB v. Katz, 369 US 736, 50 LRRM 2177 (1962), and discussion in Chapter 13 *supra* at notes 73-87.

[38]NLRB v. Allied Chem. & Alkali Workers Local 1, *supra* note 36 at 160.

[39]*Id.* at 163-76. *See* Chapter 30 *infra* at notes 304-305 for a discussion of this issue. In its discussion of §2(3), the Court held that an "established industrial practice" of collective bargaining over retirees' benefits "would not be determinative. Common practice cannot change the law and make into bargaining unit 'employees' those who are not." *Id.* at 175-76.

gaining subjects],"[40] citing *Teamsters* v. *Oliver*[41] and *Fibreboard Corp.* v. *NLRB*.[42] The Court accepted the Board's "vitally affects" test but disagreed with its conclusion that the test was met regarding retirees' benefits:

> We agree with the Board that the principle of *Oliver* and *Fibreboard* is relevant here; in each case the question is not whether the third-party concern is antagonistic to or compatible with the interests of bargaining-unit employees, but whether it vitally affects the "terms and conditions" of their employment.[43] But we disagree with the Board's assessment of the significance of a change in retirees' benefits to the "terms and conditions of employment" of active employees.[44]

The Court concluded that "[t]he benefits that active workers may reap by including retired employees under the same health insurance contract are speculative and insubstantial at best."[45] Nevertheless, *Pittsburgh Plate Glass* and its "vitally affects" test provided an avenue for expanding the scope of mandatory bargaining subjects to include issues directly relating to non-employees or other conditions, so long as a sufficient nexus with the employees' interests can be shown. The Board and the courts are currently engaged in the process of determining the impact of the "vitally affects" tests on bargaining subjects not directly related to the unit employees' terms and conditions of employment.[46]

3. *Ford Motor Co.*—The Role of the Board and Industry Bargaining Practices. The Supreme Court's 1979 decision in

---

[40]*Id.* at 178.

[41]358 US 283, 43 LRRM 2374 (1959) (federal labor law preempts state antitrust law application to collective bargaining agreement fixing truck leasing cost to lessor-drivers, a mandatory bargaining subject). *See* Chapter 17 *infra* at notes 120-21 and Chapter 31 *infra* at notes 47-51.

[42]379 US 203, 57 LRRM 2609 (1964) (decision to subcontract bargaining unit work may be a mandatory bargaining subject). *See* Chapter 17 *infra* at notes 267-80.

[43]The Court added a footnote which stated, in relevant part: "This is not to say that application of *Oliver* and *Fibreboard* turns only on the impact of the third-party matter on employee interests. Other considerations such as the effect on the employer's freedom to conduct his business, may be equally important."

[44]404 US at 179.

[45]*Id.* at 180.

[46]*See, e.g.,* Mine Workers (Lone Star Steel Co.), 231 NLRB 573, 96 LRRM 1083 (1977), *enforced in part sub nom.* Lone Star Steel Co. v. NLRB, 618 F2d 698, 104 LRRM 3144 (CA 10, 1980) ("vitally affects" test applied to (1) successorship clause requiring employer to secure successor's assumption of employer's collective bargaining agreement and (2) application of contract clause requiring employer to apply national collective bargaining agreement to any of its coal-producing facilities upon recognition or certification of the union as bargaining representative at that facility; Board found both clauses "vitally affect" employees' interests; court found successorship clause satisfies "vitally affects" test, but application of contract clause does not). *See generally,* Note, 23 STAN. L. REV. 519 (1971); Note, 49 N.C. L. REV. 575 (1971); Note, 39 U. CINN. L. REV. 573 (1970). *See also* Chapter 17 *infra* at notes 375-77.

Ford Motor Co. v. *NLRB*[47] afforded the Court an opportunity to discuss several general considerations regarding the mandatory and permissive dichotomy. At issue was whether the employer had violated Section 8(a)(5) by unilaterally approving a supplier's increase in the prices being charged at the plant cafeteria and vending machines.[48]

The Court began its analysis by declaring that the Board had primary responsibility for determining which subjects are mandatory bargaining subjects. The Court traced the legislative history of the Wagner Act of 1935 and the Taft-Hartley Act of 1947, noting congressional rejection of proposals, during the consideration of the Taft-Hartley amendments, to define and limit mandatory bargaining subjects. The Court concluded: "It is . . . evident that Congress made a conscious decision to continue its delegation to the Board of the primary responsibility of marking out the scope of the statutory language and the statutory duty to bargain."[49] The Board's decisions in this area "if reasonably defensible, . . . should not be rejected merely because the courts might prefer another view of the statute."[50] The Court, of course, recognized that there were limits on the Board's discretion in decisions concerning mandatory bargaining subjects.[51]

The Court looked closely at industry practices regarding bargaining over food services and prices and also at the history of bargaining over those subjects at the particular plant. "Although not conclusive," the Court declared, "current industrial practice is highly relevant in construing the phrase 'terms and conditions of employment.'"[52]

The employer had argued that food prices and services should not be classified as mandatory bargaining subjects because they do not "vitally affect" terms and conditions of employment within the meaning of *Pittsburgh Plate Glass* and are too trivial for mandatory bargaining subject treatment. The Court disposed

---

[47]441 US 488, 101 LRRM 2222 (1979).
[48]Ford contracted the in-plant food services to a third-party supplier. However, Ford maintained the right to review and approve the quality, quantity, and price of the food.
[49]*Id.* at 496.
[50]*Id.* at 497.
[51]Enforcement may be refused where the Board order " 'has no reasonable basis in law,' . . . [is] 'fundamentally inconsistent with the structure of the Act' and an attempt to usurp 'major policy decisions properly made by Congress' [or] . . . 'the Board was moving into a new area of regulation which Congress had not committed it to.' " *Id.*
[52]*Id.* at 501.

of the "vitally affects" argument by noting that it has no application to matters involving an employer and bargaining unit employees—it applies only to matters involving individuals or conditions outside the bargaining unit. The triviality argument was rejected by deference to the Board's determination that such subjects are not too trivial for the collective bargaining process.

The Court's decision is also noteworthy for its rejection of two possible bases on which a narrower decision might have been rendered. The decision was not limited to the particular facts of the plant in question, e.g., a short lunch break, no nearby off-premises alternatives, and a vermin problem discouraging employees from bringing their own food. The Court broadly held that "in-plant food services and prices are 'terms and conditions of employment' subject to mandatory bargaining . . . ."[53] In addition, the Court rejected Ford's argument that a bargaining order would be futile because the food services were operated by a third-party supplier. The Court reasoned that "an employer can always affect prices by initiating or altering a subsidy to the third-party supplier . . . , and will typically have the right to change suppliers at some point in the future."[54] And like other benefits administered by third parties, such as health insurance, the employer can always provide a direct subsidy to the employee.[55]

4. *First National Maintenance Corp.*—The Balancing Test.

The Court's 1981 decision in *First National Maintenance Corp.* v. *NLRB*[56] announced a balancing test regarding the duty to bargain over certain fundamental business decisions. The employer in the case operated a cleaning and maintenance business; it contracted with commercial customers to provide a labor force and supervision in return for reimbursement of its labor costs and payment of a set management fee. Because of a disagreement over a management fee, the employer cancelled its con-

---

[53]*Id.* at 504 (Justice Powell concurred in agreement with this "bright light" approach, *id.* at 503-504). The Court, however, noted that the decision does not resolve the issue of mandatory bargaining where a plant does not already have in-plant food services. *Id.* at 498 n.10.

[54]*Id.* at 503.

[55]*Id.* at 503 n.15 (*see* concurring opinion of Justice Blackmun, in which he argued that an employer who does not have control over food services and prices, due to a leasing or other similar arrangement, should not be required to bargain about food services or prices, *id.* at 504-505).

[56]452 US 666, 107 LRRM 2705 (1981). *See* Note, *Employer's Duty to Bargain With Respect to Partial Termination of Business: First National Maintenance Corp. v. NLRB,* 36 Sw. L. J. 793 (1982).

tract to provide services for a customer. However, the employer failed to bargain with the union about the decision to terminate the contract and also its effects on the 35 employees who worked under the contract. The Board held that the employer violated Section 8(a)(5) by failing to bargain as to both the decision to cancel the contract and the effects on the employees. In the Supreme Court there was no disagreement that the refusal to bargain over the effects of the decision was a *per se* violation of Section 8(a)(5). The issue before the Court was whether "an economically-motivated decision to shut down part of a business" is a mandatory bargaining subject?[57]

The Court acknowledged that the employer's decision to cancel the contract "had a direct impact on employment, since jobs were inexorably eliminated . . . ."[58] But unlike management decisions that are almost exclusively a matter of concern between employer and employees, the decision to cancel the contract, according to the Court, "had as its focus only the economic profitability of the contract with [the customer], a concern under these facts wholly apart from the employment relationship. This decision, involving a change in the scope and direction of the enterprise, is akin to the decision whether to be in business at all . . . ."[59] The Court then discussed the policies advanced by the mandatory-bargaining-subject concept and promulgated the following balancing test:

> The concept of mandatory bargaining is premised on the belief that collective discussions backed by the parties' economic weapons will result in decisions that are better for both management and labor and for society as a whole . . . . This will be true, however, only if the subject proposed for discussion is amenable to resolution through the bargaining process. Management must be free from the constraints of the bargaining process to the extent essential for the running of a profitable business . . . . [I]n view of an employer's need for unencumbered decisionmaking, bargaining over management decisions that have a substantial impact on the continued availability of employment should be required only if the benefit, for labor-management relations and the collective bargaining process, outweighs the burden placed on the conduct of the business.[60]

---

[57]107 LRRM at 2710. The union made no claim that the employer's decision to terminate the contract was based on union animus.

[58]107 LRRM at 2709.

[59]*Id.* The Court analogized to its decision in *Darlington Mfg. Co.* v. *NLRB*, 380 US 263, 58 LRRM 2657 (1965). *See* Chapter 7 *supra* at notes 237-44.

[60]107 LRRM at 2709-10. In adopting the balancing test, the Court made repeated reference to *Fibreboard Paper Products* v. *NLRB*, *supra* note 22, majority opinion and, especially, Justice Stewart's concurring opinion. *See* Chapter 17 *infra* at notes 267–374.

In the circumstances before it, the Court struck the balance in favor of the employer's interest in running a profitable business.

The Court stressed, however, that unions have significant input under their right to engage in "effects" bargaining: "[B]argaining over the effects of a decision must be conducted in a meaningful manner and at a meaningful time . . . . [The union] has some control over the effects of the decision and indirectly may ensure that the decision itself is deliberately considered."[61] The Court noted that a union also has Section 8(a)(3) protection against "partial closings motivated by anti-union animus."[62] The employer, on the other hand, "may have great need for speed, flexibility, and secrecy in meeting business opportunities and exigencies. It may face significant tax or securities consequences that hinge on confidentiality, the timing of a plant closing, or a reorganization of the corporate structure. The publicity incident to the normal process of bargaining may injure the possibility of a successful transition or increase the economic damage to the business."[63] The Court was also concerned that "[l]abeling this type of decision mandatory could afford a union a powerful tool for achieving delay, a power that might be used to thwart management's intentions unrelated to any feasible solution the union might propose."[64]

The Court observed that current industry practice supported its decision, since "provisions giving unions a right to participate in the decisionmaking process concerning alteration of the scope of an enterprise appear to be relatively rare."[65] Based on the foregoing factors, the Court concluded that

> the harm likely to be done to an employer's need to operate freely in deciding whether to shut down part of its business purely for economic reasons outweighs the incremental benefit that might be gained through the union's participation in making the decision, and we hold that the decision itself is *not* part of §8(d)'s "terms and conditions" . . . .[66]

Justice Brennan argued in dissent that the Court's balancing test "takes into account only the interests of management."[67] He criticized the Court's application of the test as being speculative,

---

[61]107 LRRM at 2711.
[62]*See* Chapter 7 *supra* at notes 243-55.
[63]107 LRRM at 2711.
[64]*Id.*
[65]*Id.* at 2712.
[66]*Id.* at 2713 (emphasis in original).
[67]*Id.* at 2714 (emphasis omitted) (Justice Marshall joined in the dissent).

noting the Second Circuit's conclusion that as a result of bargaining the union might have been able to make concessions reducing labor costs, thereby enabling the customer to increase the management fee without increasing the overall cost to the customer. He also took issue with the Court's refusal to defer to the Board's "congressionally-delegated authority and accumulated expertise."[68]

First National Maintenance will undoubtedly have a substantial impact on Board and court analysis of management decisions which are removed from the employer-employee relationship yet nevertheless impact upon that relationship. The Court's opinion expressly stated that it offered "no view as to . . . plant relocations, sales, other kinds of subcontracting, automation, etc.," and it remains to be seen how and to what extent, if any, the new balancing test will be applied by the Board and the courts to decisions involving such matters.[69]

IV. THE IMPACT OF THE MANDATORY AND PERMISSIVE DICHOTOMY

As indicated by the above cases, the dichotomy between mandatory and permissive bargaining subjects affects many aspects of the collective bargaining process. The following general principles are derived from the mandatory/permissive dichotomy:

(1) A party has a statutory obligation to bargain only with regard to mandatory bargaining subjects. Conversely, a party may refuse to bargain over a permissive bargaining subject.

(2) Bargaining to impasse over a permissive bargaining subject is a *per se* Section 8(a)(5) violation because, in effect, it is a refusal to bargain over mandatory bargaining subjects.

---

[68]*Id.* The Court's opinion acknowledged that Congress intended to give the Board power to define wages, hours, and other terms and conditions of employment and cited legislative history to that effect. *Id.* at 2709 n.14. But the Court did not spell out its grounds for not deferring to the Board's determination that the contract cancellation was a mandatory bargaining subject. *See* discussion at note 51 *supra* (standard of deference to Board's decision contained in Ford Motor Co. v. NLRB). The Court simply stated that "Congress had no expectation that the elected representative would become an equal partner in running of the business enterprise in which the union's members are employed." 107 LRRM at 2709.
[69]107 LRRM at 2713 n.22.

(3) A unilateral change of a mandatory bargaining subject usually violates Section 8(a)(5).[70] Conversely, an employer does not violate Section 8(a)(5) by unilaterally changing a permissive bargaining subject, even if the subject is covered by an existing contract.[71]

Therefore, collective bargaining strategies of both employers and unions, as well as many business decisions, critically depend on whether the subjects affected are mandatory or permissive.[72]

---

[70]*See* Chapter 13 *supra* at notes 66-90.

[71]*See Pittsburgh Plate Glass, supra* note 36. The change might constitute a breach of the collective bargaining agreement, however, in which event the remedy lies in an arbitration or court action under §301. *Id.* at 176 n.17.

[72]*See* Chapters 17 and 18 *infra* for detailed treatment of specific bargaining subjects.

CHAPTER 17

MANDATORY SUBJECTS OF BARGAINING

I. INTRODUCTION

The Act compels collective bargaining[1] with respect to mandatory subjects of bargaining. As the Supreme Court has recognized,[2] mandatory subjects of bargaining are those generally delineated in Section 9(a) as "rates of pay, wages, hours of employment, or other conditions of employment," and in Section 8(d) as "wages, hours, and other terms and conditions of employment." Congress intended, as the Court indicated, that the Board be given "the primary responsibility of marking out the scope of the statutory language and duty to bargain."[3] The scope of collective bargaining, according to the Court, could only be determined after considering prevailing industrial bargaining practices. Because of its special expertise, the Board was thus entrusted with the responsibility of evaluating the dynamics of industrial practice.[4] This chapter analyzes and catalogs those subjects which the Board and the federal courts have identified as mandatory subjects of bargaining.[5]

The language "rates of pay, wages, hours and other terms and conditions of employment" fixes not only the subjects about which an employer and a union are compelled by law to bargain, but also those subjects about which (1) the employer is barred from taking unilateral action and (2) the employee is excluded from making individual agreements with the employer, unless the union waives its right to preempt such unilateral action or

---

[1]§§8(a)(5) and 8(b)(3). For biographical materials relating to mandatory bargaining subjects, *see* references cited at pertinent places in this chapter.
[2]NLRB v. Borg-Warner Corp., 356 US 342, 42 LRRM 2034 (1958). *See* Chapter 16 *supra* for detailed treatment of this case.
[3]Ford Motor Co. v. NLRB, 441 US 488, 488, 101 LRRM 2222 (1979). *See* Chapter 16 *supra* at notes 47-55.
[4]Ford Motor Co., *supra* note 3 at 500 n.12.
[5]For treatment of the duty to bargain generally, *see* Chapter 13 *supra*.

individual bargaining.[6] A question concerning the mandatory nature of a subject can arise during the negotiation of a collective bargaining agreement or during the term of an existing agreement. In the latter situation, the Board's deferral policy[7] plays a significant role. When a party's action involves a question as to both the interpretation of a collective bargaining agreement and the legal obligations under the Act, the Board will frequently defer to the arbitration procedures contained in the parties' collective bargaining agreement.[8]

II. WAGES

The categories "rates of pay" and "wages" have been given a broad construction by the Board and the courts to cover most of the common forms of compensation for labor performed, as well as most types of agreements designed to protect standards of compensation.

A. Obvious Examples

Some mandatory subjects falling under the heading of "wages" are so obvious that little discussion is required. Basic hourly rates of pay[9] clearly constitute wages. Despite some litigation over piece rates and incentive wage plans,[10] there is no doubt that these items are mandatory subjects. Overtime pay[11] also constitutes wages. The same is true of shift differentials.[12] And

---

[6]NLRB v. Katz, 369 US 736, 50 LRRM 2177 (1962). *See* Chapter 13 *supra* at notes 68-90 and 293-309.

[7]Collyer Insulated Wire, 192 NLRB 837, 77 LRRM 1931 (1971) and related cases discussed in Chapter 20 *infra*.

[8]*See* Chapter 20 *infra* for detailed discussion of the deferral process.

[9]Gray Line, Inc., 209 NLRB 88, 85 LRRM 1328 (1974), *enforced in part and denied in part*, 512 F2d 992, 89 LRRM 2192 (CA DC, 1975); Beacon Piece Dyeing & Finishing Co., 121 NLRB 953, 42 LRRM 1489 (1958).

[10]*See* C&S Indus., Inc., 158 NLRB 454, 62 LRRM 1043 (1966); Honolulu Star Bulletin, Inc., 153 NLRB 763, 59 LRRM 1533 (1965); Staub Cleaners, Inc., 148 NLRB 278, 56 LRRM 1514 (1964); Skyway Luggage Co., 117 NLRB 681, 39 LRRM 1310 (1957); Central Metallic Casket Co., 91 NLRB 572, 26 LRRM 1520 (1950). Of course, a union may waive a right to compel bargaining over an item of wages, *e.g.*, inauguration of an incentive plan during the term of an agreement. Libby, McNeill & Libby, 65 NLRB 873, 17 LRRM 250 (1946). *See also* Lifetime Shingle Co., 203 NLRB 688, 83 LRRM 1161 (1973); Moore of Bedford, 187 NLRB 721, 76 LRRM 1182 (1971), *reversed in relevant part*, 451 F2d 406 (CA 4, 1971), *cert. denied*, 405 US 1074 (1972). However, such a waiver is not effective if the union has not been presented with the relevant facts prior to the actual implementation of a new wage incentive plan. NLRB v. Crystal Springs Shirt Corp., 637 F2d 399, 106 LRRM 2709 (CA 5, 1981), *enforcing* 245 NLRB 882, 102 LRRM 1404 (1979).

[11]*See* Braswell Motor Freight Lines, Inc., 141 NLRB 1154, 52 LRRM 1467 (1963).

[12]Smith Cabinet Mfg. Co., 147 NLRB 1506, 56 LRRM 1418 (1964); Coppus Eng'r Co., 195 NLRB 595, 79 LRRM 1449 (1972).

there is no question that paid holidays,[13] paid vacations,[14] and severance pay[15] also qualify as compensation for services performed.

B. Examples Requiring Elaboration

1. Bonuses. Whether a bonus is a mandatory subject of bargaining depends upon whether it is considered "compensation" for services rendered or a "gift." If it is the former, it is a mandatory subject, and the employer may not discontinue it unilaterally. However, if the bonus is a "gift," it is not a mandatory subject. The primary inquiry in making this determination is whether the payment of the bonus has occurred with sufficient regularity to become part of the compensation structure.

Appellate court decisions reflect the application of this inquiry in various factual contexts. The first significant court decision[16] approved the Board's holding that an employer must bargain over changes in a Christmas bonus which was in the nature of compensation. For a period of years, the employer had paid employees Christmas bonuses equivalent to a percentage of the employees' earnings. When the company installed a retirement plan, it notified the employees that the new plan would cost more than the customary bonus and consequently the amount of the bonus would be changed. The employer refused to bargain with the union concerning the new amount of the bonus. The Board held that the bonus was part of "wages" and ordered bargaining. In affirming the Board, the Second Circuit articulated the factors which contributed to its conclusion:

> Where, as here, the so-called gifts have been made over a substantial period of time and in amounts that have been based on the respective wages earned by the recipients, the Board was free to treat them as bonuses not economically different from other special kinds of remuneration like pensions, retirement plans, or group insurance,

---

[13]Singer Mfg. Co., 24 NLRB 444, 6 LRRM 405 (1940), *modified and enforced*, 119 F2d 131, 8 LRRM 740 (CA 7, 1941); Bancroft Mfg. Co., 210 NLRB 1007, 86 LRRM 1376 (1974).

[14]Note 13 *supra*; Jimmy-Richard Co., 210 NLRB 802, 86 LRRM 1591 (1974), *enforced*, 527 F2d 803, 90 LRRM 3258 (CA DC, 1975).

[15]*See* NLRB v. Adams Dairy, Inc., 137 NLRB 815, 50 LRRM 1281 (1962), *modified*, 322 F2d 553, 54 LRRM 2171 (CA 8, 1963), *vacated*, 379 US 644, 58 LRRM 2192 (1965), *on remand*, 350 F2d 108, 60 LRRM 2084 (CA 8, 1965), *cert. denied*, 382 US 1011, 61 LRRM 2192 (1966).

[16]NLRB v. Niles-Bement-Pond Co., 199 F2d 713, 31 LRRM 2057 (CA 2, 1952).

to name but a few, which have been held within the scope of the statutory bargaining requirements.[17]

In contrast, the Eighth Circuit concluded in a subsequent case that a bonus was a gift and not a mandatory subject on the basis of the following factors: (1) absence of consistency or regularity in the practice of awarding bonuses (which had been awarded during only three of the five years prior to 1962); (2) lack of uniformity in the amount of the bonus; and (3) dependence of the payment and the amount of the bonus on the financial condition of the employer.[18]

The factors set forth above have generally been determinative in characterizing a bonus as a gift or as wages.[19] In *NLRB* v. *Citizens Hotel Co.*[20] the Fifth Circuit found that a Christmas bonus constituted wages based upon the regularity with which the employer had granted such bonuses (a period of 14 years), the existence of a formalized policy for establishing eligibility, and the employer's preemployment reference to the bonus as an inducement to employment. The same court also required bargaining over Christmas bonuses in *General Telephone of Florida* v. *NLRB*.[21] There, the court rejected the company's argument that union inaction during the 35 years in which Christmas bonuses had been awarded estopped the union from asserting that the bonuses were a mandatory subject of bargaining.[22]

---

[17]*Id.* at 714.

[18]NLRB v. Wonder State Mfg. Co., 344 F2d 210, 59 LRRM 2065 (CA 8, 1965).

[19]*E.g.*, Stark Ceramics, Inc., 155 NLRB 1258, 60 LRRM 1487 (1965); NLRB v. United States Air Conditioning Corp., 336 F2d 275, 57 LRRM 2068 (CA 6, 1964); NLRB v. Citizens Hotel Co., 326 F2d 501, 55 LRRM 2135 (CA 5, 1964); NLRB v. Electric Steam Radiator Corp., 321 F2d 733, 54 LRRM 2092 (CA 6, 1963); NLRB v. Toffenetti Restaurant Co., 311 F2d 219, 51 LRRM 2601 (CA 2, 1962); American Lubricants Co., 136 NLRB 946, 49 LRRM 1888 (1962); NLRB v. Wheeling Pipe Line, Inc., 229 F2d 391, 37 LRRM 2403 (CA 8, 1956); NLRB v. Niles-Bement-Pond Co., *supra* note 16; *cf.* K-D Mfg. Co., 169 NLRB 57, 67 LRRM 1140 (1968), where the Board found that an employer violated the Act by giving Christmas gifts only to non-bargaining-unit employees.

[20]326 F2d 501, 55 LRRM 2135 (CA 5, 1964). *See also* NLRB v. Exchange Parts Co., 339 F2d 829, 58 LRRM 2097 (CA 5, 1965).

[21]337 F2d 452, 57 LRRM 2211 (CA 5, 1964).

[22]The court also rejected the employer's argument that deletion of an "existing benefits" clause from the current agreement constituted a waiver of the union's right to bargain over the question. However, the court modified the Board's remedy, since there was no finding of anti-union bias, and required the employer to bargain over only the two bonus checks that had not been paid and any future discontinuance of such bonuses. In Peyton Packing Co., 129 NLRB 1275, 47 LRRM 1170 (1961), the Board found that the bonuses were withheld to punish employees for selecting the union, and full payment to all employees in the bargaining unit was required. The sizes of the bonuses were substantial and payments amounted to as much as $1,000 per employee. *Cf.* Peyton Packing Co., 129 NLRB 1358, 47 LRRM 1211 (1961). For treatment of the

The continuing nature of the controversy concerning "gift" versus "wages" was demonstrated in the *Nello Pistoresi*[23] case, where the employer, during the course of initial contract negotiations, unilaterally discontinued a Christmas bonus that it had paid for the previous two years. A divided Board held that despite the short duration of the payments the bonus had become a bargainable matter.[24] The dissent viewed the two-year history as too short a period to justify an expectation on the part of employees that the bonuses would become part of their "wages." In denying enforcement, the Ninth Circuit agreed with the dissent, stressing the "indefinite nature of the bonuses."[25]

Where the employer bargains in good faith to impasse before discontinuing a bonus, no violation of the Act will be found.[26] The unilateral discontinuance of a bonus during the term of the contract introduces questions of waiver and of deferral to arbitration. While the Board's *Collyer*[27] principles control the deferral question, the issue of waiver may be independently significant. In *Radioear Corp.*[28] the failure of the union to obtain a "maintenance of standards" clause and the fact that the collective agreement, a first contract, contained a "zipper" clause[29] which did not mention a Christmas bonus, persuaded a divided

---

unilateral discontinuance of a bonus as a violation of §8(a)(3), *see* NLRB v. Electric Steam Radiator Corp., *supra* note 19; and for further consideration of Christmas bonuses in computation of back-pay awards, *see* NLRB v. United States Air Conditioning Corp., *supra* note 19.

[23]Nello Pistoresi & Son, Inc., 203 NLRB 905, 83 LRRM 1212 (1973), *enforcement denied in relevant part,* 500 F2d 399, 86 LRRM 2936 (CA 9, 1974).

[24]The majority relied upon its earlier holding in Wonder State Mfg. Co., 147 NLRB 179, 56 LRRM 1181 (1964), *enforcement denied in part and granted in part,* 344 F2d 210, 59 LRRM 2065 (CA 8, 1965), where a three-year history of bonus payments was viewed by the Board (though not by the Eighth Circuit) as sufficient to require bargaining concerning its discontinuance.

[25]*Supra* note 23, 500 F2d at 401. *Cf.* Marland One-Way Clutch Co., 192 NLRB 601, 78 LRRM 1127 (1971), *enforced,* 520 F2d 856, 89 LRRM 2721 (CA 7, 1975), where the Board's finding that a bonus paid regularly for 22 years constituted "wages" was upheld by the Seventh Circuit. *See also* Woonsocket Spinning Co., 252 NLRB 1170, 105 LRRM 1440 (1980); Gas Mach. Co., 221 NLRB 862, 90 LRRM 1730 (1975); Valley Oil Co., 210 NLRB 370, 86 LRRM 1351 (1974); Czas Publishing Co., 205 NLRB 958, 84 LRRM 1282 (1973); NLRB v. Progress Bulletin Publishing Co., 443 F2d 1369, 77 LRRM 3081 (CA 9, 1971).

[26]*See, e.g.,* Michigan Power Co., 192 NLRB 830, 78 LRRM 1091 (1971); Century Electric Motor Co., 192 NLRB 941, 78 LRRM 1151 (1971).

[27]*Supra* note 7. *See* Chapter 20 *infra.*

[28]214 NLRB 362, 87 LRRM 1330 (1974), *supplementing* 199 NLRB 1161, 81 LRRM 1402 (1972).

[29]*Cf.* Southern Materials Co., 198 NLRB 257, 80 LRRM 1606 (1972), where the contract's "zipper" clause was fraudulently induced by the employer who, during the negotiations, falsely denied that Christmas bonuses had been paid.

Board that the employer did not violate Section 8(a)(5) by unilaterally discontinuing a "turkey money" bonus.[30]

When a bonus is held to be wages, the Board will usually order its traditional make-whole remedy.[31] In one such case, however, the Eighth Circuit[32] partially reversed a Board determination and held that the employer's good-faith belief that it had the right to withhold bonuses precluded the award of lost bonuses to the employees. The Court relied on the fact that the employer made its proposal to discontinue bonuses during negotiations, and the union "harbored and concealed" its objections to this proposal until after the contract had been negotiated.[33]

2. Pensions. The *Inland Steel Co.*[34] decision was the first to raise the question of whether pension benefits are related to productive effort on the part of employees, and thus "wages" within the meaning of the Act. The Board held that pension benefits were "wages," stating:

> There is indeed an inseparable nexus between an employee's current compensation and his future pension benefits . . . . In substance, therefore, the respondent's monetary contribution to the pension plan constitutes an economic enhancement of the employee's money wages. . . . Realistically viewed, this type of wage enhancement or increase, no less than any other, becomes an integral part of the entire wage structure, and the character of the employee representative's interest in it, and the terms of its grant, is no different

---

[30]The Board had initially deferred to arbitration in accordance with its *Collyer* doctrine. However, after the arbitrator declined to rule on the specific issue upon which the deferral was premised, the Board reconsidered the case. *But see* Radio Tel. Technical School, Inc. v. NLRB, 488 F2d 457, 84 LRRM 2794 (CA 3, 1973), in which the Board had refused to defer to an arbitrator's finding that bonuses were a gift, notwithstanding the fact they had been paid consistently over many years; the Third Circuit enforced the resulting §8(a)(5) violation.

[31]*See, e.g.,* John Zink Co., 196 NLRB 942, 80 LRRM 1232 (1972), *enforced in part,* 83 LRRM 3045 (CA 10, 1973). That the withheld bonuses were not easily computed was not legitimate reason for denying a make-whole remedy. Southern Materials Co., *supra* note 29. *See generally* Chapter 33.

[32]Century Electric Motor Co. v. NLRB, 447 F2d 10, 78 LRRM 2042 (CA 8, 1971).

[33]For treatment of unilateral discontinuance of a bonus as a violation of §§8(a)(1) and 8(a)(3), *see* Tweel Importing Co., 219 NLRB 666, 90 LRRM 1046 (1975); Electro Vector, Inc., 220 NLRB 445, 90 LRRM 1241 (1975), *enforcement denied,* 539 F2d 35, 93 LRRM 2021 (CA 9, 1976), *cert. denied,* 434 US 821, 96 LRRM 2512 (1977).

[34]77 NLRB 1, 21 LRRM 1310, *enforced,* 170 F2d 247, 22 LRRM 2506 (CA 7, 1948), *cert. denied,* 336 US 960, 24 LRRM 2019 (1949). *See also* Pacific Coast Ass'n of Pulp & Paper Mfrs. v. NLRB, 304 F2d 760, 50 LRRM 2626 (CA 9, 1962); Note, *Proper Subjects for Collective Bargaining: Ad Hoc v. Predictive Definition,* 58 YALE L. J. 803 (1949); Note, *Pension and Retirement Matters—A Subject of Compulsory Collective Bargaining,* 43 ILL. L. REV. 713 (1948).

than in any other case where a change in the wage structure is effected.[35]

In the same decision, the Board rejected the company's contention that the term "conditions of employment" was limited to the physical conditions under which employees work and did not apply to the terms or conditions under which employment status is offered. In so doing, the Board relied on what it characterized as compelling evidence in the legislative history of the Taft-Hartley amendments that Congress recognized pension and similar welfare plans to fall within the meaning of "wages or other conditions of employment." The Board's order was upheld by the Seventh Circuit.

As with other mandatory subjects, the duty to bargain with respect to pension plans may be continuous.[36] Accordingly, unilateral effectuation of a pension plan during the term of a collective bargaining agreement which has no provision for pensions violates Section 8(a)(5). Thus, when in *Allied Mills, Inc.*,[37] the employer urged that he was relieved from such a duty to bargain by the last paragraph of Section 8(d),[38] the Board rejected the argument, declaring that Section 8(d) was intended to give stability to terms and conditions which have been embodied in a written contract, and that it has no reference to wages, hours, and other terms and conditions of employment that have not been reduced to agreement.

---

[35]77 NLRB at 4-5.

[36]*See generally* Glanzer, *Impact of ERISA on Collective Bargaining*, 52 St. JOHNS L. REV. 531 (1978); Recent Decisions, *Labor Law—Federal Preemption—Federal Labor Policy Preempts State Legislative Power to Impose Substantive Pension Obligations on an Employer Different From Those Negotiated and Contained in the Collective Bargaining Agreement*, 11 GA. L. REV. 715 (1977); Fillion & Trebilcock, *Duty to Bargain Under ERISA*, 17 WM. & MARY L. REV. 251 (1975); B. Greenberg, *ERISA and Collective Bargaining*, NYU TWENTY-EIGHTH ANNUAL CONFERENCE ON LABOR 85-97 (1975); N. A. Levin, *ERISA's Effect on Bargaining Over Pensions*, NYU TWENTY-EIGHTH ANNUAL CONFERENCE ON LABOR 67-83 (1975).

[37]82 NLRB 854, 23 LRRM 1632 (1949). *See also* Tide Water Associated Oil Co., 85 NLRB 1096, 24 LRRM 1518 (1949). *See* Jacobs Mfg. Co., 94 NLRB 1214, 28 LRRM 1162 (1951), *enforced*, 196 F2d 680, 30 LRRM 2098 (CA 2, 1952), Chapter 13 *supra* at notes 767-71 (Board held employer had duty to bargain over pensions during negotiations conducted under a wage reopener in the agreement, because the contract contained no pension provision and the subject matter had not been discussed when the previous contract was negotiated. The opposite result was reached on health and welfare because this subject had been discussed during prior negotiations). *See also* Wollett, *The Duty to Bargain Over the "Unwritten" Terms and Conditions of Employment*, 36 TEX. L. REV. 863 (1958). *Cf.* McMullans v. Kansas, Okla. & Gulf Ry., 229 F2d 50, 37 LRRM 2363 (CA 10, 1956), for treatment of retirement plan under the Railway Labor Act.

[38]§8(d) reads in relevant part:
"the duties so imposed shall not be construed as requiring either party to discuss or agree to any modification of the terms and conditions contained in a contract for a fixed period, if such modification is to become effective before such terms and conditions can be reopened under the provisions of the contract."

An employer is not obligated, however, to bargain with a union prior to modifying the existing pension and welfare benefits of retired unit employees.[39] In *Pittsburgh Plate Glass Co.*[40] the Board had held that retirees are "employees" for purposes of bargaining about retirement benefits, relying on Section 8(a)(3) cases covering applicants for employment[41] and former employees,[42] and cases under Section 302. The employer was thus found guilty of refusing to bargain about a supplementary retirement plan (prompted by enactment of Medicare legislation) and of unilaterally instituting its own plan.[43] The Supreme Court rejected the Board's reasoning that pensioners were "employees" and members of the bargaining unit so that their benefits were a "term and condition" of their employment. It also rejected the Board's alternate holding that even if pensioners were not bargaining-unit "employees," their benefits were nonetheless a mandatory subject since they "vitally" affect the "terms and conditions of employment" of active employees, principally by influencing the value of both their current and future benefits. The Court found the impact that bargaining on behalf of pensioners would have on the negotiation of retirement plans for active employees to be too speculative. While recognizing that the "classification of bargaining subjects as 'terms [and] conditions of employment' is a matter as to which the Board has special expertise," it pointed out that the legal standard to be applied is ultimately for the courts to determine. Since the matter of retired employees' benefits was not a mandatory subject, the employer did not commit an unfair labor practice by making the unilateral change in midterm.

---

[39]*See generally* Recent Cases, *Labor Law—Collective Bargaining—Retirement Benefits—Employers May Bargain Individually With Retirees Over Adjustments in Benefits*, 39 U. CIN. L. REV. 573 (1970); Note, *Labor Law-Retiree Benefits Are Not a Mandatory Subject of Bargaining—Retirees Are Not Employees—Retirees Are Not Members of the Bargaining Unit*, 20 KANS. L. REV. 801 (1972); Case Comment, *Labor Law: Retiree's Benefits—A Permissive But Not Mandatory Subject of Collective Bargaining*, 24 U. FLA. L. REV. 807 (1972).

[40]177 NLRB 911, 71 LRRM 1433 (1969), *enforcement denied*, 427 F2d 936, 74 LRRM 2425 (CA 6, 1970), *aff'd sub nom.* Allied Chem. & Alkali Workers Local 1 v. Pittsburgh Plate Glass Co., 404 US 157, 78 LRRM 2974 (1972). *See* Chapter 16 *supra* at notes 36-46.

[41]Local 872, Longshoremen, 163 NLRB 586, 64 LRRM 1467 (1967); Phelps Dodge Corp. v. NLRB, 313 US 177, 8 LRRM 439 (1941). For general treatment of employee coverage, *see* Chapter 30 *infra*.

[42]Goodman Lumber Co., 166 NLRB 304, 65 LRRM 1650 (1967); Chemrock Corp., 151 NLRB 1074, 58 LRRM 1582 (1965).

[43]For a discussion of this case and the duty to bargain about pensions generally, *see* R. Goetz, *Current Problems in Application of Federal Labor Law to Welfare and Pension Plans*, in LABOR LAW DEVELOPMENTS 1970 (Fourteenth Annual Institute on Labor Law, Southwestern Legal Foundation) 107 (1970).

Subsequent to the *Pittsburgh Glass* decision, the Board held in *Titmus Optical Co.*[44] that an employer is not relieved of the obligation to bargain with a union as the representative of its active employees about changes which will affect their benefits after retirement. The employer therefore violated Section 8(a)(5) when it unilaterally changed its life insurance plan and advised the union it would no longer pay for insurance premiums on behalf of any employees who retired after a certain date.

3. Health and Welfare, and Insurance Plans. Health and welfare insurance programs have raised a number of issues with regard to bargaining obligations. Group health insurance is clearly a mandatory subject of bargaining.[45] As the First Circuit explained:

> [T]he word "wages" in . . . the Act embraces within its meaning direct and immediate economic benefits flowing from the employment relationship . . . . So construed the word covers a group insurance program for the reason that such a program provides a financial cushion in the event of illness or injury arising outside the scope of employment at less cost than such a cushion could be obtained through contracts of insurance negotiated individually.[46]

Although the Board continues to hold that an employer's refusal to negotiate a change in insurance carriers violates Section 8(a)(5),[47] some courts have sought to analyze whether such a change actually has a substantial impact on terms and conditions of employment. In *Connecticut Light & Power Co.*[48] the Second Circuit rejected the Board's holding that the selection of a health insurance carrier was a mandatory subject of bargaining. There, the union had become dissatisfied with the insurance carrier and sought to bargain with the company over the selection of a new one. The court relied on *Pittsburgh Glass*[49] to the effect that the requirement to bargain over a subject applied only to an aspect of the employer-employee relationship

---

[44]205 NLRB 974, 84 LRRM 1245 (1973).

[45]W. W. Cross & Co. v. NLRB, 174 F2d 875, 24 LRRM 2068 (CA 1, 1949); General Motors Corp., 81 NLRB 779, 23 LRRM 1422 (1949). *See also* Standard Oil Co., 92 NLRB 227, 27 LRRM 1073 (1950), and Sylvania Elec. Prods., Inc., 127 NLRB 924, 46 LRRM 1127 (1960), where the Board found the employer's refusal to furnish data as to the premium cost of a welfare plan to be a refusal to furnish wage data. To the same effect, *see* Stowe-Woodward, Inc., 123 NLRB 287, 43 LRRM 1415 (1959).

[46]174 F2d at 878.

[47]*See, e.g.,* Master Slack Corp., 230 NLRB 1054, 96 LRRM 1309 (1977); Bancroft Mfg. Co., 210 NLRB 1007, 86 LRRM 1376 (1974) (unilateral change of carrier during pendency of objections to representation election).

[48]476 F2d 1079, 82 LRRM 3121 (CA 2, 1973).

[49]*Supra* note 40, 404 US at 179.

that "vitally affects the 'terms and conditions' of [the] employment."[50] While the benefits, coverage, and administration of a health insurance plan are proper subjects of bargaining, the court pointed out, the choice of the insurance carrier generally is not; only where the identity of the carrier vitally affects the terms and conditions of employment, or the terms of the insurance plan, would the identity of the carrier itself become a required subject of bargaining.[51]

In *Oil Workers (Kansas Refined Helium Co.) v. NLRB*,[52] the District of Columbia Circuit held that an employer must bargain over a change in insurance coverage and premiums. In holding that the employer had unlawfully made a unilateral change in insurance carriers, the court pointed to the direct impact upon employees represented by the increase in their monthly insurance premiums.

Similarly, in *Keystone Steel & Wire Division*,[53] the Board held that an employer who changed the administrator processor of its hospital, medical, and surgical insurance plan provided for in a collective bargaining contract without obtaining the union's agreement and without complying with the notice provisions of Section 8(d)(3) violated Section 8(a)(5). The Board found "specific evidence" that the change of carriers resulted in changes in administration and processing of claims as well as some alterations in coverage. However, it found no violation where no evidence was presented to indicate whether the same employer's change of administrator of its dental expense program resulted in any significant differences in the manner in which the program was administered. The Seventh Circuit accepted the Board's

---

[50]476 F2d at 1082.

[51]The court distinguished a 1973 decision of the Sixth Circuit in which the identity of the insurance carrier was held to be a mandatory subject of bargaining, since the unilateral change in carriers there adversely affected employees in three significant respects. Bastian-Blessing v. NLRB, 474 F2d 49, 82 LRRM 2689 (CA 6, 1973). There the court enforced the Board's order for the reason that it was unable upon the facts "to find a way to separate the carrier from the benefits," but it added that its conclusion was "not to be interpreted as a ruling . . . that the naming of an insurance carrier . . . in the absence of other considerations, is a mandatory subject for bargaining." 474 F2d at 54, 82 LRRM at 2692. *See also* NLRB v. Medical Manors, Inc., 497 F2d 292, 86 LRRM 2609 (CA 9, 1974), in which the Ninth Circuit, while enforcing a Board finding that the unilateral change of health insurance plans was an unfair labor practice, held the violation to be merely "a marginal violation of Section 8(a)(1)." 497 F2d at 294.

[52]547 F2d 575, 92 LRRM 3059 (CA DC, 1976), *cert. denied sub nom.* Angle v. NLRB, 431 US 966, 95 LRRM 2642 (1977).

[53]237 NLRB 763, 99 LRRM 1036 (1978), *enforced in part and remanded*, 606 F2d 171, 102 LRRM 2664 (CA 7, 1979).

holding but remanded as to the Board's order requiring the employer to reinstate the predecessor administrator at the union's request. The court directed the Board to consider a "more rational and reasonable solution,"[54] one which would be less disruptive of the employer's administration of its employee benefit program.

Decisions in this area often have also involved subsidiary questions concerning the waiver of bargaining obligations, application of the *Collyer* doctrine,[55] the duty to furnish information, and the impact of a pending decertification petition. While there are occasions where the employer's past practice and the union's acquiescence thereto will justify unilateral action,[56] there have been cases in which the Board has found unlawful an employer's unilateral discontinuance of employee benefit programs despite the employer's contentions that the union had waived its right to bargain about such termination. For example, in *T.T.P. Corp.*,[57] the Board ruled that a unilaterally established retirement income plan, which had been in effect for five years but was neither contained in the collective bargaining agreement between the employer and the union nor discussed during contract negotiations, was a mandatory subject of bargaining. The employer was held to be under a statutory duty to bargain about its decision to discontinue making contributions to the plan, despite the fact that the plan document reserved to the employer the right to terminate the plan at any time, and the union was aware of such reserved right.[58]

In *Borden, Inc.*,[59] a provision reserving to the employer the right to terminate unilaterally an insurance plan was contained in an underlying insurance document. Nonetheless, the Board held that the insurance programs (disability; accident and sickness; accidental death; group life; group hospital) had become

---

[54]606 F2d 171, 102 LRRM 2664.
[55]*Supra* note 7. *See* Chapter 20 *infra*.
[56]*See, e.g.,* A-V Corp., 209 NLRB 451, 86 LRRM 1057 (1974).
[57]190 NLRB 240, 77 LRRM 1097 (1971).
[58]Chairman Miller dissented on the grounds that the employees and the union were clearly informed that one of the provisions of the retirement-income plan was a specific and unequivocal reservation to the employer of the right to amend or terminate the plan, and that the union's failure to negotiate or even seriously propose a clarification of such provision was tacit acquiescence in the employer's right unilaterally to terminate or modify the plan. The majority of the panel rejected this reasoning because the reservation clause was not contained in a document executed by both the employer and the union.
[59]196 NLRB 1170, 80 LRRM 1240 (1972).

a "condition of employment," and there was no clear and unmistakable waiver in the contract of this subject of bargaining. Neither the management-rights clause nor the underlying insurance plan itself was regarded as a waiver. The Board noted that the right of cancellation was contained in the plan, a unilateral document to which the union was not a party. The Board also refused to defer to arbitration since the collective agreement had already expired.[60]

The Board has rejected the argument that unilateral discontinuance of sickness, life, and accident insurance is valid if such benefits are not included in the collective agreement. The Board has thus held that when such benefits have been consistently provided for years they become part of the unit's "wages, hours and conditions of employment." In such a case, the Board has refused to defer to arbitration on the ground that the benefits did not relate to any collective agreement in effect at the time of their discontinuance.[61]

In *Carpenter Sprinkler Corp.*[62] the Board ruled that an employer's substitution of its own pension and health and welfare benefits for benefits provided by an expired contract, when there is no impasse or union waiver of the right to object, violates Section 8(a)(5). But in *O'Malley Lumber Co.*,[63] the Board held that an employer lawfully discontinued monthly payments to the incumbent union's health and welfare fund where the discontinuance was subsequent to an impasse in contract negotiations over the issue of whether the employer's or the union's plan would be used.

The Board has required clear and unequivocal evidence of waiver to support a union's waiver of its right to bargain over continuation of benefits after expiration of the contract. For example, in *Triangle PWC, Inc.*,[64] the Board did find sufficient evidence of waiver of the right to bargain over the size of pension

---

[60]In refusing to defer to arbitration, the Board relied upon its decision in Hilton-Davis Chem. Co., 185 NLRB 241, 75 LRRM 1036 (1970). *But cf.* the Supreme Court's subsequent decision in Nolde Bros., Inc. v. Bakery Workers Local 358, 430 US 243, 94 LRRM 2753 (1977), regarding the duty to arbitrate after the expiration of the contract under which a grievance has arisen.
[61]*See, e.g.*, Reapp Typographic Serv., Inc., 204 NLRB 792, 83 LRRM 1604 (1973).
[62]238 NLRB 974, 99 LRRM 1356 (1978), *enforced in part and denied in part*, 605 F2d 60, 102 LRRM 2199 (CA 2, 1979).
[63]234 NLRB 1171, 98 LRRM 1166 (1978).
[64]231 NLRB 492, 96 LRRM 1629 (1977).

benefits. After negotiations for a new collective bargaining agreement had been completed, the employer refused to bargain with the union concerning pension benefit levels. The Board found no violation in the employer's refusal because the parties had agreed to bargain over pension benefits during the negotiations and had done so, albeit not extensively. During the negotiations the employer had stated that an increase in benefit levels would have to come from the total package it was offering, and the negotiations were completed without the union further pursuing the matter of pension benefit levels.[65]

In both *A.S. Abell Co.*[66] and *Hearst Corp., Baltimore News American Division*,[67] the Board held the respective employers violated Section 8(a)(5) by dealing individually and unilaterally with employees concerning pension and retirement benefits, and by paying employees these benefits in excess of the terms of the collective bargaining agreements. The employers had unilaterally increased retirement benefits to encourage employees to retire because of lack of available work.

A number of decisions concerning changes in employee benefit programs have resulted in findings of Section 8(a)(5) violations because of employers' refusals to furnish relevant and necessary information to the union upon its request. There was tacit recognition of the problem by the Supreme Court in *Katz*[68] concerning the inability of the union to know whether the employer's action is in fact a substantial departure from past practice, unless there had been negotiations with the union.[69] However, in *NLRB* v. *Milgo Industrial, Inc.*,[70] the Second Circuit considered the obligation of an employer, during negotiations with a newly certified union, to provide the union a copy of its health plan and information on the cost of its pension plan. In

---

[65]*But see* Elizabethtown Water Co., 234 NLRB 318, 97 LRRM 1210 (1978) (no waiver where parties did not specifically discuss whether negotiations on retirement plan would be carried out at same time as negotiations on new collective bargaining agreement).

[66]230 NLRB 17, 95 LRRM 1284 (1977), *enforced in part and remanded in part*, 590 F2d 554, 100 LRRM 2320 (CA 4), *supplemented*, 243 NLRB 171, 101 LRRM 1381 (1979).

[67]230 NLRB 216, 95 LRRM 1274 (1977), *enforced in part and remanded in part*, 590 F2d 554, 100 LRRM 2320 (CA 4), *supplemented*, 243 NLRB 170, 101 LRRM 1379 (1979).

[68]NLRB v. Katz, *supra* note 6.

[69]*See* Connecticut Light & Power Co., 220 NLRB 967, 90 LRRM 1307 (1975), *enforced*, 538 F2d 308, 93 LRRM 2336 (CA 2, 1976); Pic Walsh Freight Co., 216 NLRB 627, 89 LRRM 1268 (1975); L & M Carpet Contractors, Inc., 218 NLRB 802, 89 LRRM 1732 (1975).

[70]567 F2d 540, 97 LRRM 2079 (CA 2, 1977), *enforcing* 229 NLRB 25, 96 LRRM 1347 (1977).

enforcing the Board's bargaining order, the court found that the employer was not obligated to provide a copy of the health plan because it already was available from the insurer, but it affirmed the Board's holding that the employer's refusal to provide cost information on its pension plan violated Section 8(a)(5).

A number of decisions concern unilateral changes made while a decertification petition is pending. Whether an employer may unilaterally alter such benefits during this period depends upon whether or not the decertification petition justifies the employer's refusal to continue treating the union as the majority representative and therefore to cease bargaining with it.[71]

In early 1978, the Board reaffirmed its position that the subject of trust-fund payments under a current collective bargaining agreement is a mandatory subject of bargaining.[72] The Board has also held that a clause in a local agreement requiring the employer to accept preselected employer trustees as its repre-

---

[71]For example, the Board has held that an employer's unilateral extension to unit employees of health and pension plans which previously covered only nonunit employees, after the expiration of the contract and the filing of a decertification petition, was not violative of the Act. The employer had ceased making payments to the union funds and, instead, implemented coverage by its own plans. The Board held that the decertification petition raised a question concerning representation which foreclosed the employer from dealing with the union. Under these circumstances, its actions were necessary to keep its unit employees in the same relative economic position. *See generally* Chapter 12 *supra.* Ellex Transp., Inc., 217 NLRB 750, 89 LRRM 1335 (1975). *See also* Medical Manors, Inc., *supra* note 51, where the Ninth Circuit refused enforcement of a bargaining order based on unilateral changes in insurance coverage because of the pendency of a decertification petition. However, where the employer initiates or participates in the decertification activity, the pendency of a decertification petition will not be a valid basis for a unilateral discontinuance of contributions to the union's health, welfare, and pension programs. Condon Transport, Inc., 211 NLRB 297, 87 LRRM 1127 (1974). In San Luis Obispo County & Northern Santa Barbara County Restaurant & Tavern Ass'n, 196 NLRB 1082, 80 LRRM 1584 (1972), the Board held that a decertification petition was not a sufficient basis for unilaterally instituting an improved health and welfare plan. In Goodsell & Vocke, Inc., the Board held that since an employer's attempted withdrawal from an employer association was untimely and ineffective, the employer violated §8(a)(5) by unilaterally discontinuing the trust fund payments required by the association's collective bargaining agreement. 223 NLRB 60, 92 LRRM 1187 (1976), *enforced,* 559 F2d 1141, 96 LRRM 2370 (CA 9, 1977). *Accord,* Crest Beverage Co., 231 NLRB 116, 96 LRRM 1034 (1977); Vin James Plastering Co., 226 NLRB 125, 93 LRRM 1213 (1976). In Wayne's Olive Knoll Farms, Inc., 223 NLRB 260, 92 LRRM 1229 (1976), the Board held that the employer violated §8(a)(5) by unilaterally discontinuing its contributions to the pension and health and welfare plans upon the expiration of the underlying collective bargaining agreement which had established both funds.

[72]Operating Eng'rs Local 12 (Maas & Feduska, Inc.), 234 NLRB 1256, 97 LRRM 1444 (1978), *reversed sub nom.* Maas & Feduska, Inc. v. NLRB, 632 F2d 714, 102 LRRM 2185 (CA 9, 1979).

sentatives in the administration of the trust fund is a mandatory subject.[73]

4. Profit-Sharing Plans. Profit-sharing plans have been held by the Board and the courts to be a form of employee compensation and hence a mandatory subject for bargaining.[74] The Board's decision that a profit-sharing plan is a mandatory subject is consistent with its view that "wages" include almost all emoluments of value accruing to any employee by reason of the employment relationship.[75]

In *Winn-Dixie Stores, Inc.*[76] the Board refused to find a material distinction between profit-sharing plans and pension plans. The Board held that regardless of whether the plan was called a profit-sharing plan or a retirement plan plus a profit-sharing plan, the union had the right to negotiate concerning all aspects of the plan, including whether employees participating in another union-proposed retirement program would be excluded from eligibility. While recognizing that the employer's plan incorporated profit-sharing and retirement aspects, but without deciding whether an employer may refuse to bargain over exact duplication of benefits, the Fifth Circuit found sufficient differ-

---

[73]*See* Sheet Metal Workers (Central Fla. Sheetmetal Contractors Ass'n, Inc.), 234 NLRB 1238, 97 LRRM 1476 (1978).

[74]Kroger Co. v. NLRB, 401 F2d 682, 69 LRRM 2425 (CA 6, 1968); NLRB v. Black-Clawson Co., 210 F2d 523, 33 LRRM 2567 (CA 6, 1954).

[75]Kroger Co. v. NLRB, 399 F2d 455, 68 LRRM 2731 (CA 6, 1968); Dicten & Masch Mfg. Co., 129 NLRB 112, 46 LRRM 1516 (1960). *See also* Union Mfg. Co., 76 NLRB 322, 21 LRRM 1187 (1948), *enforced,* 179 F2d 511, 25 LRRM 2302 (CA 5, 1950). In accord with this view are Board decisions under §§8(a)(1) and 8(a)(3), as well as §8(a)(5). Como Plastics, Inc., 143 NLRB 151, 53 LRRM 1278 (1963). *Accord,* Ross Sand Co., 219 NLRB 915, 89 LRRM 1861 (1975). For example, during the course of an organizing campaign, an employer spokesman indicated to the employees that an existing profit-sharing plan was solely within the discretion of the employer, that the employer would not negotiate with respect to such a plan, and that the plan would be discontinued if the union won the election. This threat to refuse to bargain as to mandatory subject matter was held to be a clear threat of reprisal violative of §8(a)(1). Como Plastics, Inc., *supra.*

[76]Winn-Dixie Stores, Inc. v. NLRB, 567 F2d 1343, 97 LRRM 2866 (CA 2, 1978), *enforcing in part and denying enforcement in part to* 224 NLRB 1418, 92 LRRM 1625 (1976), *petition for rehearing and petition for rehearing en banc denied per curiam,* 575 F2d 1107, 98 LRRM 2935 (CA 5, 1978), *cert. denied sub nom.* Meat Cutters v. Winn-Dixie Stores, Inc., 439 US 985, 99 LRRM 3262 (1978). However, the court reversed the Board's holding that the employer's insistence that eligible employees forfeit their existing accounts under the employer plan also violated §8(a)(5). Since the employer was insisting only that the union accept a package proposal or else return to piecemeal negotiations, the court held that there was no violation of the employer's duty to bargain in good faith. Finally, the court refused to enforce the Board's order requiring the employer to provide extensive monetary relief for violations relating to its profit-sharing plan, noting that there was no way to identify the harm flowing to the employees as a result of those violations.

ences between the employer and the union plans to give rise to a duty on the part of the employer to bargain over coverage under both plans. Accordingly, the court affirmed the Board's holding that the employer's refusal to bargain over coverage under both plans violated the Act.

In *J.P. Stevens & Co.*[77] the Board held that an employer violated Section 8(a)(5) by unilaterally shifting the responsibilities for investing the assets of its profit-sharing plan from a corporate trustee to a committee of members of the employer's board of directors. As a profit-sharing plan is a mandatory subject of bargaining, the Board reasoned, so too is the issue of who controls the investment of the plan's assets. The Board noted that the loss of the investment expertise of the original trustee could adversely affect the plan.

5. Stock Purchase Plans. *Richfield Oil Corp.*,[78] a 1954 case, presented the Board with the issue of whether a stock purchase plan falls within the area of mandatory bargaining.[79] Participation in the plan was open to all regular employees who had completed one year of service and who were between the ages of 30 and normal retirement age. Participants contributed a fixed sum from monthly earnings to the plan, and the company made contributions on behalf of participants, ranging from 50 percent to 75 percent of an employee's payments into the plan. The monies were used by the plan's trustees to purchase Richfield common stock. Neither stock nor cash credited to an individual's account was distributable to the individual so long as he was a member of the plan. Despite the voluntary nature of the plan, the Board had no difficulty concluding that this stock purchase plan was a form of "wages" and also fell within "other conditions of employment."

The employer had argued that it would do violence to the basic policies of the Act to compel bargaining with respect to

---

[77]239 NLRB 738, 100 LRRM 1052 (1978), *enforced in part,* 623 F2d 322, 104 LRRM 2573 (CA 4, 1980).

[78]110 NLRB 356, 34 LRRM 1658 (1954), *enforced,* 231 F2d 717, 37 LRRM 2327 (CA DC), *cert. denied,* 351 US 909, 37 LRRM 2837 (1956). *See* Note, *Employee Stock Purchase Plan Is Within Scope of Compulsory Collective Bargaining,* 69 HARV. L. REV. 1511 (1956); Recent Decisions, *Employer's Refusal to Bargain Concerning Terms and Conditions of a Stock Purchase Plan Is an Unfair Labor Practice Under Section 8(a)(5) of the Taft-Hartley Act,* 43 GEO. L. J. 309 (1955).

[79]*See generally* Hutchinson, *Employee Stock Ownership Plans: A New Tool in the Collective Bargaining Inventory?,* 26 AM. U. L. REV. 536 (1977).

this subject. It contended that such bargaining (1) would require the employer to bargain about ownership and control of the company and (2) could result in the union's obtaining a seat on both sides of the bargaining table. In reply to the first contention the Board stated:

> To the extent that such compulsory bargaining infringes upon the asserted right of an employer to dispose of his property and to run his business as he sees fit, that interference . . . is not decisively distinguishable from such intrusions in management affairs as occur whenever an employer fulfills his statutory obligation to bargain collectively, as, for example, when he bargains with respect to retirement and pension plans, group health and insurance programs, merit wage-increases, and profit sharing plans, all of which, the Board and Courts have held, lie within the statutory scope of collective bargaining.[80]

With respect to the second contention, the Board noted that the bargaining representative was entitled to represent the employees who were stockholders only in their capacity as employees.

In *B.F. Goodrich Co.*,[81] after a collective bargaining agreement was executed, the employer instituted a stock purchase and savings plan for its nonunit employees. The Board held that the employer violated Section 8(a)(5) by refusing to bargain with the union concerning the participation of the unit employees in the plan. The Board rejected the employer's argument that the union had waived any rights to bargain over the issue as a result of prior negotiations. The employer had, in effect, told the union during negotiations that no stock option plan existed nor was one contemplated. However, the Board refused to require that the employer permit retroactive participation by the unit employees in the plan. Rather, it ordered the employer to bargain with the union concerning the participation of unit employees in the plan from its effective date.

An increasingly common form of allocating employee benefits is found in Employee Stock Ownership Plans (ESOPs).[82] There have been no significant case law developments concerning the bargaining obligations with respect to these plans.

---

[80]110 NLRB at 362.
[81]195 NLRB 914, 79 LRRM 1563 (1972). *Accord,* Winn-Dixie Texas, Inc., 234 NLRB 72, 98 LRRM 1343 (1978).
[82]Hutchinson, *supra* note 79.

6. Merit Wage Increases. The issue of whether an employer has a duty to bargain with respect to merit increases was first presented to the Board in *J. H. Allison & Co.*[83] The collective bargaining agreement in that case contained a scale of minimum rates. When the employer granted a series of individual wage increases, characterized as "merit increases," the union sought details in order that it might negotiate the matter. The employer refused to supply the requested information on the ground that the granting of merit increases was an exclusive managerial function and not a proper subject for bargaining. The union's request during subsequent contract negotiations to incorporate a clause on merit increases into the contract met with a similar response.

The Board held the increases to be an integral part of the wage structure and as such a mandatory subject for bargaining. In a later case[84] it held that this conclusion was not affected by the fact that it might be difficult or perhaps impossible to establish objective standards for awarding merit increases. On the other hand, where the collective agreement itself contained both a maximum and a minimum rate for each classification as well as a merit rating plan under which each employee was to be reviewed every four months, the Board held that the company had no obligation to bargain with the union before putting individual merit increases into effect.[85]

The rationale for holding merit increases to be a mandatory bargaining subject was spelled out by the Fourth Circuit in *NLRB v. Berkley Machine Works*:[86]

Merit pay where there are a number of employees means more than a gratuity or bonus paid to an occasional employee whom the company wishes to favor on account of his loyalty or efficiency. It means necessarily the formulation and application of standards; and such standards are proper subjects of collective bargaining. Collective bargaining with respect to wages might well be disrupted or become

---

[83]70 NLRB 377, 18 LRRM 1369 (1946), *enforced*, 165 F2d 766, 21 LRRM 2238 (CA 6, 1948), *cert. denied*, 335 US 814, 22 LRRM 2564 (1948). *See also* Weston & Brooker Co., 154 NLRB 747, 60 LRRM 1015 (1965); Midwestern Instruments, Inc., 133 NLRB 1132, 48 LRRM 1793 (1961); Armstrong Cork Co. v. NLRB, 211 F2d 843, 33 LRRM 2789 (CA 5, 1954); NLRB v. Dealers Engine Rebuilders, Inc., 199 F2d 249, 31 LRRM 2007 (CA 8, 1952); J. B. Cook Auto Mach. Co., 84 NLRB 688, 24 LRRM 1321 (1949).
[84]E. W. Scripps & Co., 94 NLRB 227, 28 LRRM 1033 (1951). *See also* Tide Water Associated Oil Co., *supra* note 37.
[85]General Controls Co., 88 NLRB 1341, 25 LRRM 1475 (1950).
[86]189 F2d 904, 28 LRRM 2176 (CA 4, 1951).

a mere empty form if the control over the wages of individual employees were thus removed from the bargaining area.[87]

In *White* v. *NLRB*[88] the issue was raised as to whether merit increases can be granted if such action is consistent with the past practice of the employer. During the period between union certification and commencement of initial contract negotiations, the employer unilaterally increased the pay of five of the 60 members of the bargaining unit. Each increase was made in terms of the relationship of the particular individual to his job. The Fifth Circuit held that such increases were permissible. The Board moved for rehearing on the ground that the court had erred in its holding that an employer might grant individual merit increases without negotiating with the bargaining representative. The court clarified its holding in a *per curiam* opinion:[89]

> Lest there be a misunderstanding, we state that we did not intend to and did not "thus hold." We found that these particular increases were in line with company policy to make merit increases, they had all accrued before bargaining sessions commenced, and on the record as a whole did not amount to violations of either Section 8(a)(1) or Section 8(a)(5) of the Act.[90]

The Second Circuit reached a like result.[91] It held that an increase of $5 per week to five employees plus an additional $5 per week to one of the same employees bore no resemblance to the "general increase" in rates of pay applicable to most employees which had been held to be improper in other cases.

In *NLRB* v. *Katz*,[92] the Supreme Court confirmed the prior opinions of the Board and the lower courts that, under certain conditions, merit increases are subject to mandatory bargaining. In *Katz* the merit increases had been granted, without prior notice to the union, to less than half of the employees in the bargaining unit. Concerning the effect of the employer's long-standing practice of granting discretionary merit increases, the Court observed:

> This action . . . must be viewed as tantamount to an outright refusal to negotiate . . . . Whatever might be the case as to so-called "merit

---

[87]189 F2d at 907.
[88]255 F2d 564, 42 LRRM 2001 (CA 5, 1958).
[89]White v. NLRB, 255 F2d 564, 42 LRRM 2195 (CA 5, 1958).
[90]*Id.* at 574.
[91]NLRB v. Superior Fireproof Door & Sash Co., 289 F2d 713, 47 LRRM 2816 (CA 2, 1961).
[92]*Supra* note 6.

raises" which are in fact simply automatic increases to which the employer has already committed himself, the raises here in question were in no sense automatic, but were informed by a large measure of discretion. There simply is no way in such case for a union to know whether or not there has been a substantial departure from past practice, and therefore the union may properly insist that the company negotiate as to the procedures and criteria for determining such increases.[93]

The Fifth Circuit had occasion to apply the *Katz* guidelines to define the burden on an employer who seeks to prove that wage increases during union contract negotiations do not constitute unlawful unilateral action. In *NLRB* v. *Allis-Chalmers Corp.*[94] the employer had granted increases in wages and benefits to its employees during union contract negotiations. It contended that the increases were in compliance with a periodic survey of wages and benefits and that the increases did not constitute unlawful unilateral action. However, the Fifth Circuit affirmed the Board's holding that the increases were unlawful:

The employer carries a heavy burden of proving that such adjustments of wages and benefits are purely automatic and pursuant to definite guidelines. The record reflects . . . that the increases were not automatic, in that Allis-Chalmers exercised considerable discretion in determining the timing and amount. Therefore, the union could properly demand bargaining.[95]

Therefore, as in the case of bonuses, the lawfulness of the unilateral grant or discontinuance of merit wage increases depends upon the nature of the past practices—that is, whether "automatic increases to which the employer has already committed himself" or "discretionary" increases. But this broad distinction has not resulted in a uniform application, and the permissibility of unilateral employer action in respect to merit increases has divided both the Board and the courts.

The controversy stems from the difficulty in classifying merit increases as either "automatic" or "discretionary." There may, in fact, be a combination of both features in many types of increases. For example, a program of merit increases may have varied slightly in timing and amount but nonetheless may have been granted on a semiannual basis over a period of years. They

---

[93]*Id.* at 746-47.
[94]601 F2d 870, 102 LRRM 2194 (CA 5, 1979).
[95]*Id.* at 875-76.

have thus become part of the "conditions of employment" and, like regularly granted bonuses, may justify continued employee expectations.

Broadly stated, merit increases which are in line with past practice, so that their payment may be viewed as a mere continuation of the *status quo*, may not be unilaterally discontinued.[96] Conversely, a merit increase may not be unilaterally granted where there is no identifiable or clearly established formula and the increase is almost wholly discretionary with the employer.[97]

The current Board position as to an employer's ability to grant merit increases unilaterally is found in the following language:

> An employer with a past history of a merit increase program neither may discontinue that program . . . nor may he any longer continue to unilaterally exercise his discretion with respect to such increases, once an exclusive bargaining agent is selected. . . . What is required is the maintenance of pre-existing practices, *i.e.*, the general outline of the program, however, the implementation of that program (to the extent that discretion has existed in determining the amounts or timing of the increases), becomes a matter as to which the bargaining agent is entitled to be consulted.[98]

7. Company Houses, Meals, Discounts, and Services. Generally, the rental of company-owned housing is a mandatory subject of bargaining. The Board's established rule is that employer-provided living accommodations fall within "wages" and "conditions of employment" where the accommodations are an integral part of the employment relations.[99] However, in

---

[96]*See, e.g.,* General Motors Acceptance Corp., 196 NLRB 137, 79 LRRM 1662 (1972), *enforced,* 476 F2d 850, 82 LRRM 3093 (CA 1, 1973); Allied Prods. Corp., 218 NLRB 1246, 89 LRRM 1441 (1975), *enforcement granted in part, denied in part, remanded,* 548 F2d 644, 94 LRRM 2433 (CA 6, 1977); Fourco Glass Co., 250 NLRB 953, 105 LRRM 1052 (1980).

[97]*Compare* NLRB v. Hendel Mfg. Co., 483 F2d 350, 83 LRRM 2657 (CA 2, 1973), *with* Continental Ins. Co. v. NLRB, 495 F2d 44, 86 LRRM 2003 (CA 2, 1974). *See also* NLRB v. Gray Line, Inc., *supra* note 9; Mosher Steel Co., 220 NLRB 336, 90 LRRM 1459 (1975), *enforced,* 532 F2d 1374, 93 LRRM 2018 (CA 5, 1976).

[98]Oneita Knitting Mills, Inc., 205 NLRB 500, 500 n.1, 83 LRRM 1670 (1973).

[99]*See* Elgin Standard Brick Mfg. Co., 90 NLRB 1467, 26 LRRM 1343 (1950); Hart Cotton Mills, Inc., 91 NLRB 728, 26 LRRM 1566 (1950), *enforcement denied,* 190 F2d 964, 28 LRRM 2434 (CA 4, 1951), discussed *infra* this note. The Board also decided a series of cases holding company housing to be a condition of employment within §8(a)(3), which prohibits discrimination in such matters: W. T. Carter & Brother, 90 NLRB 2020, 26 LRRM 1427 (1950); Indianapolis Wire Bound Box Co., 89 NLRB 617, 26 LRRM 1427 (1950); Indianapolis Wire Bound Box Co., 89 NLRB 617, 26 LRRM 1005 (1950); Industrial Cotton Mills Co., 50 NLRB 855, 12 LRRM 241 (1943); Abbott Worsted Mills, Inc., 36 NLRB 545, 9 LRRM 163 (1941), *enforced,* 127 F2d 438, 10 LRRM 590 (CA 1, 1942); Great W. Mushroom Co., 27 NLRB 352, 7 LRRM 72 (1940). In one case employees, though not required to live in company houses, lived in such housing because

some situations company housing may be treated as a permissive subject of bargaining. In one such case[100] the Fifth Circuit found that the evidence failed to support a conclusion that the rent charged for company houses was either wages or a condition of employment since the rental arrangement offered no substantial advantage to the employees. The court noted that other adequate housing was available with no transportation problem, that rentals for company housing were comparable to those of the community generally, and that there was no evidence that employees were required to live in the houses.[101]

Nevertheless, "conditions of employment" are not limited to the compulsory aspects of the employer-employee relationship. Predating the housing cases, the Board found company-provided meals to be a condition of employment and also wages.[102] Although the company did not expressly require that employees eat on the job, they had no realistic alternative. The Board noted that it had consistently construed "wages" broadly enough to include emoluments of value supplementary to actual wage rates that accrue to an employee from his employment relationship.[103]

Traditionally the NLRB has treated meal prices as a condition of employment. That position, while a subject of some prior controversy among the circuit courts,[104] was endorsed by the

---

other area housing was scarce. Company housing had been supplied to a part of the work force for many years at nominal rentals. The Board found that the housing represented an emolument of value in that it effected a saving of transportation expenses and accordingly ordered the employer to bargain about the amount of rent. Lehigh Portland Cement Co., 101 NLRB 529, 31 LRRM 1097 (1952). The Fourth Circuit enforced the Board's order, holding that rental of company housing is a mandatory subject of bargaining if ownership and management of the housing materially affect the conditions of employment. NLRB v. Lehigh Portland Cement Co., 205 F2d 832, 32 LRRM 2463 (CA 4, 1953). The court expanded upon an earlier decision, NLRB v. Hart Cotton Mills, Inc., *supra,* in which it had held the general subject matter of company houses to be a mandatory bargaining subject if the houses are a necessary part of the employer's enterprise or are rented at such a rate as to constitute a substantial part of an employee's pay.
    [100]NLRB v. Bemis Bros. Bag Co., 206 F2d 33, 32 LRRM 2535 (CA 5, 1953).
    [101]*Cf.* NLRB Gen. Counsel Adm. Ruling K-209, 37 LRRM 1316 (1956), where the General Counsel refused to issue a complaint on a charge that an employer informed the employees that they must purchase or vacate company houses and that the company refused to discuss the matter with the union.
    [102]Weyerhaeuser Timber Co., 87 NLRB 672, 25 LRRM 1163 (1949). *See also* Herman Sausage Co., 122 NLRB 168, 43 LRRM 1090 (1958), *enforced,* 275 F2d 229, 45 LRRM 2829 (CA 5, 1960) (unilateral discontinuance of meal allowance held a §8(a)(5) violation).
    [103]*See* Inland Steel Co., 77 NLRB 1, 21 LRRM 1310, *review denied,* 170 F2d 247, 22 LRRM 2506 (CA 7, 1948), *cert. denied,* 336 US 960, 24 LRRM 2019 (1949).
    [104]The Seventh Circuit's 1978 ruling in *Ford Motor Co.* conflicted with four previous rulings of three different courts of appeals, all of which had denied enforcement of NLRB orders requiring bargaining over in-plant food prices. NLRB v. Ladish Co., 538

Supreme Court in its 1979 ruling in *Ford Motor Co.* v. *NLRB*.[105]
The Seventh Circuit had enforced[106] the Board's order,[107] agreeing that under the facts of the case the employer was obligated to bargain about changes in employee cafeteria and vending machine prices. The Supreme Court relied less on the particular circumstances of the case, e.g., the lack of eating alternatives for employees, and more on the reasonableness of the Board's general rule requiring bargaining over in-plant food prices and services.

The Court stated: "With all due respect to the courts of appeals that have held otherwise, we conclude that the Board's consistent view that in-plant food prices and services are mandatory bargaining subjects is not an unreasonable or unprincipled construction of the statute and that it should be accepted and enforced."[108] The Court noted that the availability of food and the conditions of its consumption are of deep concern to employees, and that "one need not strain to consider them to be among those 'conditions' of employment that should be subject to the mutual duty to bargain."[109] Additionally, the Court expressed concern over the substantial disputes which can arise over the pricing of in-plant supplied foods and beverages, concluding that such disputes can properly be handled by the collective bargaining process. It noted that employers hold future, if not present leverage, over in-plant food services and prices by their ability to change suppliers or alter subsidies.[110] The Supreme Court thus rejected the case-by-case factual approach used by the circuit courts to determine whether in-plant food prices and services are mandatory subjects.

In analogous situations, the Board has found violations of the Act where the employer unilaterally decreased working hours,

---

F2d 1267, 92 LRRM 3577 (CA 7, 1976); NLRB v. Package Mach. Co., 457 F2d 936, 79 LRRM 2948 (CA 1, 1972); McCall Corp. v. NLRB, 432 F2d 187, 75 LRRM 2223 (CA 4, 1970); Westinghouse Elec. Corp. v. NLRB, 387 F2d 542, 66 LRRM 2634 (CA 4, 1967).
[105]441 US 488, 101 LRRM 2222 (1979). *See* Chapter 16 at notes 47-55 for a detailed analysis of this case.
[106]Ford Motor Co. v. NLRB, 571 F2d 993, 97 LRRM 3030 (CA 7, 1978).
[107]Ford Motor Co., 230 NLRB 716, 95 LRRM 1397 (1977).
[108]Ford Motor Co. v. NLRB, *supra* note 105 at 497.
[109]*Id.* at 498.
[110]*Cf.* Wilker Bros. Co., Inc., 236 NLRB 1371, 98 LRRM 1456 (1978), where the Board held that an employer who reduced vending machine prices in the face of an organizing campaign violated §8(a)(1).

unilaterally terminated a hot lunch program,[111] and unilaterally changed a practice of allowing employees to take coffee breaks.[112]

Free meals were also an issue where they were unilaterally granted, rather than discontinued. In *O'Land, Inc.*,[113] an employer's unilateral grant of free meals to nonstriking employees was held to violate the Act. The alleged reason for the company policy was to reduce violence on the picket line by encouraging nonstrikers to remain on the employer's premises during meal times. In the context of the employer's other unlawful unilateral actions and in the absence of notice to the employees that the free meals were a temporary measure for the purpose of protecting the nonstriking employees, the Board held that the unilateral grant of the free meals violated the Act.

Coffee benefits have been an issue in a number of Board cases. In *Chemtronics, Inc.*,[114] the Board held that an employer violated Section 8(a)(5) by unilaterally discontinuing its practices of providing employees with coffee and rolls and permitting smoking in the warehouse. On the other hand, in *Weather TEC Corp.*[115] the Board held that an employer's unilateral decision to stop providing transportation and money to purchase coffee and coffee supplies did not violate Section 8(a)(5). The Board stressed that it dismissed the allegations solely because neither action constituted a "material, substantial and a significant" change from prior practice. The Board also noted that when the union and the employer representatives discussed the change shortly after it had been implemented, the union neither requested that the change be put on the bargaining table nor that the employer revert to its prior policy.

In another case, the Board held that unilaterally discontinuing the practice of supplying free soft drinks to unit employees violated the Act. However, the Fifth Circuit concluded that such unilateral action was lawful because the employer had previously withdrawn recognition from the union in a lawful manner.[116]

---

[111]Abingdon Nursing Center, 197 NLRB 781, 80 LRRM 1470 (1972).
[112]Luby Leasing, Inc., 198 NLRB 951, 81 LRRM 1097 (1972).
[113]206 NLRB 210, 84 LRRM 1378 (1973).
[114]236 NLRB 178, 98 LRRM 1559 (1978).
[115]238 NLRB 1538, 99 LRRM 1709 (1978).
[116]Pride Refining, Inc. v. NLRB, 555 F2d 453, 95 LRRM 2958 (CA 5, 1977).

In a variety of other decisions, the Board has defined the term "benefits" to cover various emoluments of employment so that unilateral action concerning such "benefits" have violated Section 8(a)(5).[117]

8. Truck Rentals and Price Lists. In two antitrust cases, the Supreme Court has held that the concept of "wages" as a mandatory subject of bargaining embraces agreements reasonably designed to protect wage scales, although in form the agreements have dealt with "prices" (charged by bands for club dates) or "rental rates" (for leased trucks). In *Musicians* v. *Carroll*[118] the Court rejected the idea that "the distinction between mandatory and non-mandatory subjects turns on the form of the method taken to protect a wage scale."[119] *In Teamsters* v. *Oliver*[120] the Court based a federal preemption exemption from a state antitrust law upon its determination that the minimum rental to be paid by carriers to truck drivers owning their own vehicles constituted a mandatory subject of bargaining. The object of the minimum rental provision was "to protect the negotiated wage scale against the possible undermining through diminution of the owner's wages for driving which might result from a rental which did not cover his operating costs."[121]

In *Carroll* the Court found an antitrust exemption applicable to minimum price lists for orchestra leaders playing club dates, based on the fact that such minimums were deemed essential to protect the musicians' wage rates. The Court viewed the price floors, including established minimums for orchestra leaders,

---

[117]*See, e.g.*, Donn Prods., Inc., 229 NLRB 116, 95 LRRM 1033 (1977), *enforcement granted in part and denied in part*, 613 F2d 162, 103 LRRM 2338 (CA 6), *cert. denied*, 447 US 906, 104 LRRM 2552 (1980) (establishing a system to assist employees to obtain personal bank loans); Seafarers Local 777 (Yellow Cab Co.) v. NLRB, 603 F2d 862, 99 LRRM 2903 (CA DC, 1978), *enforcing in part and denying enforcement in part to* 229 NLRB 1369, 95 LRRM 1249 (1977) (drivers taking their cabs home at night); Eagle Material Handling of N.J., 224 NLRB 1529, 92 LRRM 1571 (1976), *enforced*, 558 F2d 160, 95 LRRM 2934 (CA 3, 1977) (use of company trucks to and from the plant); Florida Steel Corp., 231 NLRB 923, 96 LRRM 1173 (1977) (use of credit cards by employees and reimbursement rates for lodging and meal expenses); Master Slack Corp., 230 NLRB 1054, 96 LRRM 1309 (1977) (allowing employees to purchase employer's goods on layaway basis); Southland Paper Mills, Inc., 161 NLRB 1077, 63 LRRM 1386 (1966) (hunting privilege); Weston & Brooker Co., 154 NLRB 747, 60 LRRM 1015 (1965) (canteen at which employees had been permitted to charge purchases); NLRB v. Central Ill. Pub. Serv. Co., 324 F2d 916, 54 LRRM 2586 (CA 7, 1963) (gas discounts).
[118]Musicians v. Carroll, 391 US 99, 68 LRRM 2230 (1968).
[119]*Id.* at 110. *See* Chapter 31 *infra* at notes 362-67.
[120]Local 24, Teamsters v. Oliver, 358 US 283, 43 LRRM 2374 (1959). *See* Chapter 31 *infra* at notes 47-51.
[121]*Id.* at 293-94.

as "simply a means for coping with the job and wage competition of the leaders to protect the wage scales of musicians who respondents concede are employees on club dates, namely sidemen and subleaders."[122]

9. Effect of Wage Controls. While the federally imposed wage and price controls which existed between August 1971 and November 1973 are now history, there were several decisions during that period which reinforced the rule that "wages," even when subject to statutory control, constitute a mandatory subject of bargaining.[123]

In *National Broadcasting Co.*[124] the Board ruled that a union had not waived its right to bargain over an income savings plan merely because at the outset of negotiations the employer had stated its willingness to comply with the Carter Administration's voluntary wage guidelines. Since the employer had not stated that improvement in benefit levels and wages would have to come from the "same pie" (as defined by the 7-percent wage guidelines), the Board held that the employer had not engaged in "package bargaining." Thus the union's pursuit of certain wage terms did not operate as a waiver of its right to bargain over other benefits, such as the income savings plan.

III. HOURS

Writing in the context of an antitrust case, the Supreme Court expressed the bargaining obligation as to hours of employment as follows:

> The particular hours of the day and the particular days of the week during which employees may be required to work are subjects well within the realm of wages, hours, and other terms and conditions of employment about which employers and unions must bargain.[125]

---

[122]391 US at 109. For a general discussion of the relation of the NLRA to the antitrust laws, *see* Chapter 31 *infra*.
[123]Servis Equip. Co., 198 NLRB 266, 80 LRRM 1704 (1972); Washington Employers, Inc., 200 NLRB 825, 81 LRRM 1593 (1972); NLRB v. Big Three Indus., Inc., 497 F2d 43, 86 LRRM 3031 (CA 5, 1974). *See generally* R. W. Kopp, *Impact of the Phase II Mandatory Pay Controls on Collective Bargaining Questions*, NYU TWENTY-SIXTH ANNUAL CONFERENCE ON LABOR 111 (1973).
[124]252 NLRB 187, 105 LRRM 1304 (1980).
[125]Meat Cutters v. Jewel Tea Co., 381 US 676, 691, 59 LRRM 2376 (1965). For a discussion of the relation of mandatory subjects of bargaining to the antitrust laws, as exemplified by this case and Mine Workers v. Pennington, 381 US 657, 59 LRRM 2369 (1965) (holding that a union's agreement with multi-employers to impose certain standards relating to mandatory subjects for bargaining on employers outside the multi-

Although the Board has long held that "hours" fall within the express terms of Section 8(d) and thus are clearly a mandatory subject of bargaining, mitigating circumstances have sometimes been considered. For example, in *Massey Gin & Machine Works, Inc.,*[126] it found that the failure of the company to notify the union of a contemplated change in working hours was mitigated by an ambiguous contract provision and subsequent negotiation with the union.

As a general proposition, however, the Board has adhered to its basic position that hours, including work schedules and whether there should be Sunday work,[127] are mandatory bargaining subjects. In *Weston & Brooker Co.*[128] the Board, relying upon *Homer Gregory Co.,*[129] held the length of the workday to be a mandatory subject and that an employer's unilateral change constituted a Section 8(a)(5) violation.

In certain limited circumstances, the employer may institute changes in hours without bargaining. The Board has held that a unilateral change by an employer does not violate the Act when the change causes only minimal inconvenience to the employees.[130] In addition, an employer was able unilaterally to reduce working hours when it had previously provided the union with all the information it used in making the decision and thereafter stood ready to provide the union with explanations or additional data.[131] The Board also held that an employer

---

employers' bargaining unit would fall outside the union's exemption from the antitrust laws), *see* Chapter 31 *infra* at notes 354-61. Although hours of employment are now generally considered a mandatory subject of bargaining, this point generated some early controversy. In 1946, for example, one court, disagreeing with the Board, had held that the rearrangement of employees' working hours made "in the normal course of business" did not require prior consultation with the union. NLRB v. Inter-City Advertising Co., 154 F2d 244, 17 LRRM 916 (CA 4, 1946).

[126]78 NLRB 189, 22 LRRM 1191 (1948), *enforcement denied per curiam,* 173 F2d 758, 23 LRRM 2619 (CA 5, 1949), *cert. denied,* 338 US 910, 25 LRRM 2205 (1950).

[127]Timken Roller Bearing Co., 70 NLRB 500, 18 LRRM 1370 (1946), *enforcement denied on other grounds,* 161 F2d 949, 20 LRRM 2204 (CA 6, 1947). *See also* Camp & McInnes, Inc., 100 NLRB 524, 30 LRRM 1310 (1952); Inter-City Advertising Co., 61 NLRB 1377, 16 LRRM 153 (1945), *enforcement denied on other grounds,* 154 F2d 244, 17 LRRM 916 (CA 4, 1946); Wilson & Co., 19 NLRB 990, 5 LRRM 560 (1940), *enforced,* 115 F2d 759, 7 LRRM 575 (CA 8, 1940); Woodside Cotton Mills Co., 21 NLRB 42, 6 LRRM 68 (1940).

[128]*Supra* note 83.

[129]123 NLRB 1842, 44 LRRM 1249 (1959). The Board also cited NLRB v. Katz, *supra* note 6, as support for its decision on the unilateral aspect of the violation.

[130]Oneita Knitting Mills, Inc., *supra* note 98.

[131]Western Elec. Co., 223 NLRB 86, 92 LRRM 1189 (1976). After the employer provided the union with such information, the union subsequently made only vague and ambiguous requests for information and declined to engage in meaningful bargaining.

did not unlawfully engage in a unilateral elimination of a third work shift, where it had notified the union of its proposed change and the union failed to make any reasonable attempt to bargain over the issue.[132] And the Board has held that an employer did not violate the Act when, following expiration of the collective bargaining agreement, it unilaterally eliminated Sunday work. Noting that the management-rights clause of the expired agreement had granted to the employer the right to establish "starting times" and "shift" operations and to increase or decrease "daily or weekly working hours," the Board found that the changes were not different in degree or kind from those historically made unilaterally by the employer, and that they caused no loss of earnings or inconvenience to unit employees.[133]

In many cases, unilateral changes in hours have been found violative of Section 8(a)(5). In one such case, the District Court for the District of Columbia enjoined an employer, pursuant to Section 10(j), from unilaterally reducing the working hours of unit employees during the pendency of Board proceedings.[134] And in *Florida Steel Corp.*[135] the Board held that the employer acted unlawfully when it unilaterally scheduled a change in hours for a one-week period. In partially enforcing the Board's order, the Fourth Circuit indicated that regardless of whether the Company had acted in bad faith, its unilateral action effectively denied the union its opportunity to bargain. In *Dow Chemical Co.*[136] the Board held that an employer violated Section 8(a)(5) by unilaterally implementing a change in the work schedule of the employees in one department.

In another case, the Board held that an employer violated the Act when, in the course of contract negotiations, it unilaterally implemented a proposal which extended the workday by one-half hour. Notwithstanding the employer's contention that negotiations had reached an impasse on the issue of pensions, the Board found that the parties had not bargained to an impasse on hours and that unilateral action was therefore prohibited.[137]

---

[132]K-Mart Corp., 242 NLRB 855, 101 LRRM 1406 (1979), *enforced,* 626 F2d 704, 105 LRRM 2431 (CA 9, 1980).
[133]Winn-Dixie Stores, Inc., *supra* note 76.
[134]Humphrey v. Retired Persons Pharmacy, 84 LRRM 2599 (D DC, 1973).
[135]Florida Steel Corp., 235 NLRB 941, 100 LRRM 1187 (1978), *enforced in part,* 601 F2d 125, 101 LRRM 2671 (CA 4, 1979).
[136]244 NLRB 1060, 102 LRRM 1199 (1979).
[137]Atlas Tack Corp., 226 NLRB 222, 93 LRRM 1236 (1976), *enforced,* 559 F2d 1201, 96 LRRM 2660 (CA 1, 1977).

In *Good Hope Industries, Inc.*,[138] the Board held that unilaterally adding an "on-call" day to the four-day work week that had been worked by employees violated Section 8(a)(5). The Board reached this conclusion notwithstanding the fact that the collective bargaining agreement provided for a five-day work week, because (1) a five-day work week had not actually been in effect in several years, and (2) the employees had voted to reject the five-day work week when the employer suggested it before instituting the change.

An employer may not unilaterally change the work schedule, even advantageously to the employees, such as where the new schedule would give employees the opportunity to work on nondaylight premium pay shifts and thereby receive more money.[139]

Even with strong economic justification, an employer violates the Act if it unilaterally adds or eliminates a work shift;[140] this was even true in one case though the union, which had won a representation election, had not yet been certified.[141]

IV. OTHER TERMS AND CONDITIONS OF EMPLOYMENT

A. Obvious and Settled Examples

Numerous topics fall within the phrase "other terms and conditions of employment" as it is used in the Act, and many are now so clearly recognized to be mandatory subjects of bargaining that no discussion is required. Included among such topics are the following: provisions for a grievance procedure[142]

---

[138]230 NLRB 1132, 95 LRRM 1518 (1977).

[139]American Oil Co., 238 NLRB 294, 99 LRRM 1253 (1978), *enforced,* 602 F2d 184, 101 LRRM 2981 (CA 8, 1979).

[140]NLRB v. W. R. Grace & Co., 571 F2d 279, 98 LRRM 2001 (CA 5, 1978), *enforcing in relevant part* 230 NLRB 617, 95 LRRM 1459 (1977).

[141]Anchortank, Inc., 239 NLRB 430, 99 LRRM 1622 (1978), *enforcement granted in part and denied in part,* 618 F2d 1153, 104 LRRM 2689 (CA 5, 1980). In this case, the employer violated §8(a)(5) when, after an election but prior to certification, it unilaterally added a shift to the existing three shifts and shortened the employees working hours. The administrative law judge noted that the employer had not provided any compelling economic justification for these unilateral actions.

[142]Bethlehem Steel Co., 136 NLRB 1500, 50 LRRM 1013 (1962), *enforcement denied on other grounds,* 320 F2d 615, 53 LRRM 2878 (CA 3, 1963); Hughes Tool Co. v. NLRB, 147 F2d 69, 15 LRRM 852 (CA 5, 1945); Peerless Food Prods., Inc., 236 NLRB 161, 98 LRRM 1182 (1978); Turbodyne Corp., Gas Turbine Div., 226 NLRB 522, 93 LRRM 1379 (1976); Crown Coach Co., 155 NLRB 625, 60 LRRM 1366 (1965); *but cf.* Latrobe Steel Co., 244 NLRB 528, 102 LRRM 1175 (1979), *enforcement granted in part and denied in part,* 630 F2d 171, 105 LRRM 2393 (CA 3, 1980).

and arbitration,[143] layoffs and recalls,[144] discharge,[145] workloads,[146] vacations,[147] holidays,[148] sick leave,[149] work rules,[150] use of bulletin boards by unions,[151] change of payment from a weekly salary to an hourly rate,[152] definition of bargaining unit work,[153] performance of bargaining unit work by supervisors,[154] employee physical examinations,[155] and duration of the collective bargaining agreement.[156]

---

[143]United States Gypsum Co., 94 NLRB 112, 28 LRRM 1015 (1951); NLRB v. Montgomery Ward & Co., 133 F2d 676, 12 LRRM 508 (CA 9, 1943); NLRB v. Boss Mfg. Co., 118 F2d 187, 8 LRRM 729 (CA 7, 1941).

[144]Hilton Mobile Homes, 155 NLRB 873, 60 LRRM 1411 (1965); United States Gypsum Co., *supra* note 143. *See also* Master Slack Corp., *supra* note 117; W. R. Grace & Co., *supra* note 140; Caravelle Boat Co., 227 NLRB 1355, 95 LRRM 1003 (1977); Awrey Bakeries, Inc. v. NLRB, 217 NLRB 730, 89 LRRM 1224 (1975), *enforced*, 548 F2d 138, 94 LRRM 3152 (CA 6, 1976). *Compare* Valley Iron & Steel Co., 224 NLRB 866, 93 LRRM 1379 (1976), *with* Reliable Maintenance Sales & Serv., Inc., 225 NLRB 580, 93 LRRM 1448 (1976). *And see* L. H. & J. Coal Co., 228 NLRB 1091, 96 LRRM 1447 (1977); *and* Mount Airy Foundation, 230 NLRB 668, 96 LRRM 1202 (1977).

[145]*See* National Licorice Co. v. NLRB, 309 US 350, 6 LRRM 674 (1940); NLRB v. Bachelder, 120 F2d 574, 8 LRRM 723 (CA 7, 1941).

[146]Beacon Piece Dyeing & Finishing Co., 121 NLRB 953, 42 LRRM 1489 (1958). *See* Little Rock Downtowner, Inc., 145 NLRB 1286, 55 LRRM 1156 (1964), where employer ordered employees to stand at their stations at all times except when on breaks or relief; the Board found a violation of §8(a)(5) since there was an actual change in the work beyond "routine job directions." In Irvington Motors, Inc., 147 NLRB 565, 56 LRRM 1257 (1964), *enforced*, 343 F2d 759, 58 LRRM 2816 (CA 3, 1965), the Board held the fixing of sales quotas required bargaining; however, the unilateral setting of a requirement that salesmen make five telephone sales calls each day was not so clearly beyond a normal management function as to require notice to and consultation with the union. *Cf.* Little Rock Downtowner, Inc., 148 NLRB 717, 57 LRRM 1052 (1964), where motel maids were instructed to wash motel room windows every day; the Board held that an employer does not have an obligation to notify and consult the union with respect to matters that fall "within the normal area of detailed decisions relating to the manner in which work is to be performed."

[147]Great S. Trucking Co. v. NLRB, 127 F2d 180, 10 LRRM 571 (CA 4, 1942).

[148]NLRB v. Sharon Hats, Inc., 289 F2d 628, 48 LRRM 2098 (CA 5, 1961); Leiter Mfg. Co., 112 NLRB 843, 36 LRRM 1123 (1955); Bradley Washfountain Co. v. NLRB, 192 F2d 144, 29 LRRM 2064 (CA 7, 1951); Rockwell Register Corp., 142 NLRB 634, 53 LRRM 1113 (1963).

[149]NLRB v. Katz, *supra* note 6.

[150]NLRB v. Southern Transp., Inc., 343 F2d 558, 58 LRRM 2822 (CA 8, 1965); Tower Hosiery Mills, Inc., 81 NLRB 658, 23 LRRM 1397 (1949); Timken Roller Bearing Co., *supra* note 127.

[151]NLRB v. Proof Co., 242 F2d 560, 39 LRRM 2608 (CA 7, 1957), *cert. denied*, 355 US 831, 40 LRRM 2680 (1957).

[152]General Motors Corp., 59 NLRB 1143, 15 LRRM 170 (1944).

[153]Almeida Bus Lines, Inc., 142 NLRB 445, 53 LRRM 1055 (1963). However, a change in the description of the bargaining unit is not a mandatory subject of bargaining. Newport News Shipbuilding Co. v. NLRB, 602 F2d 73, 102 LRRM 2531 (CA 4, 1979).

[154]Crown Coach Corp., 155 NLRB 625, 60 LRRM 1366 (1965).

[155]Le Roy Mach. Co., 147 NLRB 1431, 56 LRRM 1369 (1964), where the Board held that a management-prerogatives clause constituted a union waiver of a right to require the employer to bargain about physical examinations during the term of the existing agreement. *Cf.* Wilburn v. Missouri-Ks-Tx R.R., 268 SW2d 726 (CA Tex, 1954) (physical examinations are a subject of bargaining under the Railway Labor Act).

[156]NLRB v. Yutana Barge Lines, Inc., 315 F2d 524, 52 LRRM 2750 (CA 9, 1963); United States Pipe & Foundry Co. v. NLRB, 298 F2d 873, 49 LRRM 2540 (CA 5, 1962). The question of contract retroactivity is also a mandatory subject of bargaining. Bergen

B. Examples Requiring Elaboration

Some topics of mandatory bargaining that constitute "other terms and conditions of employment" require more than a mere listing. A review of such subjects is set forth in the remainder of this chapter. Generally, any genuine and substantive change in "terms and conditions" has been deemed subject to mandatory bargaining, whether the change arose from the promulgation of new terms or from the enforcement of previously unenforced rules. However, both the courts and the Board have recognized exceptions to this rule derived from their efforts to balance employees' and employers' rights and interests. For example, changes which substantively affect only one employee have been allowed without bargaining.[157] Pertinent questions to be asked in determining whether a subject is mandatory are whether a particular subject "vitally affects"[158] the relations between an employer and employees, and whether a particular management decision will cause a significant detriment[159] to the employees. The Supreme Court has reiterated that the Board has broad discretion "in determining the mandatory subjects of bargaining."[160]

While the courts and the board are in agreement regarding some of the following areas, there are divergent views regarding the questions of subcontracting[161] and major changes in operation of a business.[162] These areas have important implications concerning future questions arising from automation and efforts designed to improve efficiency, productivity, and financial soundness.

1. Seniority, Promotions, and Transfers. Seniority, promotions, and transfers have long been recognized as mandatory

---

Point Iron Works, 79 NLRB 1133, 22 LRRM 1475 (1948). However, bargaining to require employee ratification of a contract is not. Thus, in NLRB v. Darlington Veneer Co., 236 F2d 85, 38 LRRM 2574 (CA 4, 1956), the Fourth Circuit found a violation of §8(a)(5) in an employer's insistence upon ratification of the contract by secret vote of the employees. Cf. NLRB v. Borg-Warner, supra note 2; North Country Motors, Ltd., 146 NLRB 671, 55 LRRM 1421 (1964). For further discussion of the subject of ratification, see Chapter 18 infra at notes 71-73.

[157]Foster Transformer Co., 212 NLRB 936, 87 LRRM 1010 (1974).
[158]See Ford Motor Co. v. NLRB, supra note 105, and Allied Chem. & Alkali Workers v. Pittsburgh Plate Glass Co., supra note 40.
[159]Westinghouse Elec. Corp., 150 NLRB 1574, 58 LRRM 1257 (1965).
[160]Ford Motor Co., supra note 105. See generally Chapter 16 supra.
[161]See infra at notes 267-329.
[162]See infra at notes 252-66 and 330-74.

subjects of bargaining.[163] Since seniority is so obviously a condition of employment and is a condition commonly existing under union contracts,[164] litigation questioning its mandatory status has been minimal. A few rulings should, however, be noted. Probationary periods and attendant conditions require bargaining,[165] as do promotions within a bargaining unit.[166] An employer may not unilaterally revoke preferential seniority previously granted informally to union officers and negotiators,[167] nor may it abrogate unilaterally seniority rights upon expiration of a collective agreement establishing these rights. Elimination of such an accrued benefit constitutes a change in a condition of employment.[168] Aptitude testing may not be unilaterally introduced, and bargaining about such testing is required.[169]

Unilateral changes in seniority[170] or recall policies[171] violate an employer's obligation to bargain in good faith. However, where an employer had unilaterally reclassified an employee to a lower seniority position in order to correct an inequity, the Board found no violation, because the higher position had been granted the employee on a temporary basis, the employee had been paid according to her duties, and the change reflected a long-standing company policy.[172]

---

[163]United States Gypsum Co., *supra* note 143.

[164]Ford Motor Co. v. Huffman, 345 US 330, 31 LRRM 2548 (1953). *See* Chapter 28 *infra* at notes 266-69.

[165]Oliver Corp., 162 NLRB 813, 64 LRRM 1092 (1967).

[166]Houston Chapter, Associated Gen. Contractors, 143 NLRB 409, 53 LRRM 1299 (1963), *enforced*, 349 F2d 449, 59 LRRM 3013 (CA 5, 1965), *cert. denied*, 382 US 1026, 61 LRRM 2244 (1966). The Board has held that promotion of employees to supervisory positions outside the unit is a mandatory subject when the effect is to transfer bargaining-unit work to nonunit employees. Fry Foods, Inc., 241 NLRB 76, 100 LRRM 1513 (1979), *enforced*, 609 F2d 267, 102 LRRM 2894 (CA 6, 1979).

[167]NLRB v. Proof Co., *supra* note 151. It should be noted that preferential seniority to union officers must be limited to layoff and recall. The Board has held that a preferential seniority agreement which is not so limited is presumptively unlawful. Dairylea Cooperative, Inc., 219 NLRB 656, 89 LRRM 1737 (1975). *See* Chapter 7 *supra* at notes 323-27 and 381-86. *See also* Note, *Union Steward Superseniority*, 6 N.Y.U. Rev. L. & Soc. Change 1 (1976).

[168]NLRB v. Katz, *supra* note 6; Marine & Shipbuilding Workers v. NLRB (Bethlehem Steel Co.), *supra* note 142. *See also* United States Gypsum Co., *supra* note 143.

[169]American Gilsonite Co., 121 NLRB 1514, 43 LRRM 1011 (1958), *supplemented*, 122 NLRB 1006, 43 LRRM 1242 (1959).

[170]*See, e.g.*, Longhorn Mach. Works, Inc., 205 NLRB 685, 84 LRRM 1307 (1973) (unilateral discontinuation of method of computing seniority); MCC Pac. Valves, 244 NLRB 931, 102 LRRM 1183 (1979) (unilateral termination of seniority rights of recalled economic strikers).

[171]*See, e.g.*, Grand Lodge of Free & Accepted Masons, Masonic Home, 215 NLRB 75, 88 LRRM 1294 (1974) (refusal to bargain over clause reinstating strikers). *But see* NLRB v. D. H. Farms Co., 481 F2d 830, 83 LRRM 2923 (CA 6, 1973).

[172]Foster Transformer Co., *supra* note 157.

Transfer of employees, as a general rule, is a mandatory subject of bargaining.[173] In one case, however, janitorial employees in a university hospital complex were covered by two collective bargaining agreements and belonged to two different local unions. The university laid off all the members of one local and allocated their duties to members of the other local. The laid-off employees could seek work elsewhere or be hired into lower paying jobs under the contract with the retained local. The Board found that this "transfer" of employees to what amounted to a different union was subject to mandatory bargaining.[174] The Seventh Circuit disagreed, however, reasoning that the employer was seeking only to institute a uniform higher standard for cleaning. Since the court found no union animus in the transfers but rather a legitimate business justification, it did not consider the university's failure to bargain over the transfers a violation of Section 8(a)(5).[175]

In another case, the Eighth Circuit found no violation where the transfer of workers from one cafeteria to other cafeterias was precipitated by the employer's decision to close down the one facility without notifying or bargaining with the union.[176] Although the decision to close was announced unexpectedly the day after the cafeteria's workers voted to join the union, the Court concluded that economic reasons forced the decision, and held that bargaining was mandatory only concerning the effects of the decision, not about the decision itself.[177]

2. Compulsory Retirement Age. In the *Inland Steel* case,[178] generally known for its holding that pensions are a mandatory subject for bargaining, the Board and the Seventh Circuit held that an employer must bargain with a union concerning a compulsory retirement age. The court stated:

> We are unable to differentiate between the conceded right of a Union to bargain concerning a discharge, and particularly a non-discriminatory discharge, of an employee and its right to bargain

---

[173]*Compare* Union Elec. Co., 196 NLRB 830, 80 LRRM 1110 (1972), *with* Continental Ins. Co. v. NLRB, 495 F2d 44, 86 LRRM 2003 (CA 2, 1974) (unilateral transfer of six employees). *See also* Oneita Knitting Mills, *supra* note 98.
[174]University of Chicago, 210 NLRB 190, 86 LRRM 1073 (1974).
[175]University of Chicago v. NLRB, 514 F2d 942, 89 LRRM 2113 (CA 7, 1975). *But see* Newspaper Printing Corp. v. NLRB, 625 F2d 956, 104 LRRM 2432 (CA 10, 1980).
[176]Morrison Cafeterias Consol., Inc. v. NLRB, 431 F2d 254, 74 LRRM 3048 (CA 8, 1970).
[177]*See infra* at notes 330-72.
[178]*Supra* note 34.

concerning the age at which he is compelled to retire . . . . In one instance, the cessation of employment comes perhaps suddenly and without advance notice or warning, while in the other, his employment ceases as a result of a plan announced in advance by the Company.[179]

A number of lawsuits have been brought under the Railway Labor Act[180] by employees challenging provisions in collective bargaining agreements where the union and the employer had agreed upon a compulsory retirement age. The courts have consistently held that these provisions are valid and binding since the issue of whether there should be compulsory retirement and if so, at what age, is a mandatory subject for collective bargaining.[181]

Since the enactment of the 1978 Age Discrimination In Employment Act (ADEA) amendment,[182] it has become illegal to require involuntary retirement of employees before the age of 70, with exceptions for certain employees in higher education or executive positions. Elimination of compulsory retirement provisions made illegal by ADEA would not require bargaining, but the elimination of such illegal provisions may result in or be accompanied by other changes in a retirement plan thereby giving rise to a bargaining obligation.[183]

3. Union Shop, Checkoff, Agency Shop, and Hiring Hall.

The fact that a union-shop clause is embraced by "conditions of employment" was recognized prior to *Borg-Warner*.[184] In 1949, the Ninth Circuit held that union security fell within the area of required bargaining.[185] The Third Circuit subsequently held

---

[179]*Id.* at 252.

[180]45 USC §§151-88 (1970).

[181]*See, e.g.,* Goodin v. Clinchfield R.R., 229 F2d 578, 37 LRRM 2515 (CA 6, 1956), *cert. denied,* 351 US 953, 38 LRRM 2160 (1956); McMullans v. Kan., Okla. & Gulf Ry., 129 F Supp 157, 35 LRRM 2512 (ED Okla, 1955); Lamon v. Ga. S. & Fla. Ry., 212 Ga. 63, 90 SE2d 658, 37 LRRM 2115 (SC Ga, 1955); Jones v. Martin, 37 LRRM 2839 (SD Fla, 1956). *See also* Note, *Retirees in the Collective Bargaining Process: A Critical Review of Pittsburgh Plate Glass Co. v. NLRB,* 23 Stan. L. Rev. 519 (1971).

[182]29 USC §621 *et seq.* (Supp. III 1979).

[183]*See* Smith, *Impact of the 1978 ADEA Amendments on Collective Bargaining,* Labor Relations Yearbook— 1978, at 218 (BNA, 1979). A change in the compulsory retirement age would not relieve an employer of the obligation to bargain regarding a change in the normal retirement age. Thus, if the normal retirement age were to remain at age 65, a number of issues could arise such as the pension accrual and insurance rights of employees who stay on to work after age 65. Such issues would appear to be bargainable.

[184]NLRB v. Borg-Warner Corp., *supra* note 2. *See* Chapter 16 *supra* at notes 27-35.

[185]NLRB v. Andrew Jergens Co., 175 F2d 130, 24 LRRM 2096 (CA 9, 1949), *cert. denied,* 338 US 827, 24 LRRM 2561 (1949). For a later case, *see* United States Gypsum Co., *supra* note 143. *Cf.* Vanderbilt Prods., Inc. v. NLRB, 297 F2d 833, 49 LRRM 2286 (CA 2, 1961), where the court found that insistence upon an open shop supported a finding of bad-faith bargaining.

that since a union shop is a creature of contract, Section 8(a)(5) was not violated by an employer who unilaterally ceased giving effect to union-shop and checkoff provisions of a contract upon its expiration.[186] The court's reasoning, that "[t]he right to require union membership as a condition of employment is dependent upon a contract . . ." and that a provision for "checkoff is merely a means of implementing union security . . .," is consistent with the conclusion that such topics are mandatory bargaining subjects.[187]

Under an agency-shop agreement an employee is not required to join the union, but is required to pay to the union an amount equivalent to union dues. Although the Board initially held that an agency shop was not a subject that required bargaining,[188] it later reversed itself.[189] The Sixth Circuit denied enforcement,[190] but the Supreme Court reversed,[191] reasoning that agency-shop proposals impose no burdens in addition to those imposed by

---

[186]Marine & Shipbuilding Workers v. NLRB (Bethlehem Steel Co.), *supra* note 142. A union-shop agreement derives its validity from the *proviso* of §8(a)(3). See Chapter 29 *infra*. "Checkoff" refers to a system by which an employer deducts union dues from wages upon written authorization by the employee and remits the dues directly to the union. The legality of the checkoff under federal law is governed by §302(c)(4) of the Act which allows payments from an employer to a union "with respect to money deducted from the wages of employees in payment of membership dues in a labor organization: *Provided*, that the employer has received from each employee, on whose account such deductions are made, a written assignment which shall not be irrevocable for a period of more than one year, or beyond the termination date of the applicable collective agreement, whichever occurs sooner . . . ." See Presbyterian Hosp., 241 NLRB 996, 101 LRRM 1001 (1979), where the Board held that one employer whose collective bargaining agreement contained a dues-checkoff provision violated the Act when, after a majority of its employees voted to decertify the union, it refused to remit deducted dues from the date of the election results, since the contract remained in effect until certification.

[187]320 F2d at 619, 53 LRRM at 2881. See also NLRB v. Herman Sausage Co., *supra* note 102; NLRB v. Reed & Prince Mfg. Co., 205 F2d 131, 32 LRRM 2225 (CA 1, 1953), *cert. denied*, 346 US 887, 33 LRRM 2133 (1953); and United States Gypsum Co., *supra* note 143. See also Steelworkers (H. K. Porter Co.) v. NLRB, 363 F2d 272, 62 LRRM 2204 (CA DC, 1966), *cert. denied*, 385 US 851, 63 LRRM 2236 (1966), upholding a finding of §8(a)(5) violation where the company consistently rejected the union's demand for a dues checkoff. For subsequent history of this case *see* 389 F2d 295, 66 LRRM 2761 (CA DC, 1967); 172 NLRB 966, 68 LRRM 1337, *aff'd*, H. K. Porter Co. v. NLRB, 414 F2d 1123, 71 LRRM 2207 (1969), *reversed*, 397 US 99, 73 LRRM 2561 (1970). The Supreme Court's opinion and its impact on the Board's remedial power in refusal-to-bargain cases are treated in Chapters 13 *supra* and 33 *infra*. The Court's opinion was directed at the Board's remedy, not at the basic finding of refusal to bargain about the checkoff. See grant of certiorari (397 US 102, 73 LRRM at 2562) and concurring opinion of Mr. Justice Harlan (397 US at 109-10).

[188]General Motors Corp., 130 NLRB 481, 47 LRRM 1306 (1961).
[189]General Motors Corp., 133 NLRB 451, 48 LRRM 1659 (1961).
[190]General Motors Corp. v. NLRB, 303 F2d 428, 50 LRRM 2396 (CA 6, 1962).
[191]NLRB v. General Motors Corp., 373 US 734, 53 LRRM 2313 (1963). See Chapter 29 *infra* at notes 168-71.

union-shop proposals, which are lawful and are a mandatory subject.[192]

A nondiscriminatory hiring hall operated by a union is also a mandatory subject for bargaining.[193] To the argument that a company is required to bargain only about conditions arising after the employment relationship is established and not about conditions for obtaining employment, the Board replied that "since 'employment' connotes the initial act of employing as well as the consequent state of being employed the hiring hall relates to the conditions of employment." The Board also noted that the "employees" referred to in Section 8(d) were "not limited to those individuals already working for the employer" but also included "prospective employees."[194]

4. Management Rights. The leading case involving a proposal for a broad management-rights clause is the Supreme Court's decision in *American National Insurance Co.*,[195] which held that an employer's insistence upon a broad management-rights clause covering terms and conditions of employment is not in itself a violation of Section 8(a)(5). While the Court held that the Board may not pass judgment upon the desirability of substantive terms of an agreement, it may nevertheless decide whether good-faith requirements of Section 8(d) have been met. Although determination of whether a management-rights clause is a mandatory bargaining subject depends on its contents, i.e., whether it contains nonmandatory items, more often the contents issue is only a factor in ascertaining whether the employer has bargained in good faith.[196]

---

[192]The effect of a right-to-work law which outlaws the agency shop was decided in Local 1625, Retail Clerks v. Schermerhorn, 373 US 746, 53 LRRM 2318 (1963), aff'd, 375 US 96, 54 LRRM 2612 (1963). See Chapter 29 infra for a detailed discussion of right-to-work laws.

[193]Associated Gen. Contractors, supra note 166. Accord, NLRB v. Tom Joyce Floors, Inc., 353 F2d 768, 60 LRRM 2334 (CA 9, 1965). The legality of such a hiring hall was established in Local 357, Teamsters v. NLRB, 365 US 667, 47 LRRM 2906 (1961). See discussion in Chapter 29 infra at notes 221-25. Cf. Pacific Am. Shipowners Ass'n, 90 NLRB 1099, 26 LRRM 1316 (1950), where a §8(b)(3) charge against a union striking for such a clause was dismissed.

[194]Associated Gen. Contractors, supra note 166 at 412, citing NLRB v. Borg-Warner Corp., supra note 2; Phelps Dodge Corp. v. NLRB, 313 US 177, 8 LRRM 439 (1941); Briggs Mfg. Co., 75 NLRB 569, 21 LRRM 1056 (1947); Texas Natural Gasoline Corp., 116 NLRB 405, 38 LRRM 1252 (1956).

[195]NLRB v. American Nat'l Ins. Co., 343 US 395, 30 LRRM 2147 (1952). See discussion in Chapter 16 supra at notes 24-25. For cases dealing with management-rights clauses, see Old Line Life Ins. Co. of America, 96 NLRB 499, 28 LRRM 1539 (1951); Standard Generator Serv. Co. of Mo., 90 NLRB 790, 26 LRRM 1285 (1950); Franklin Hosiery Mills, Inc., 83 NLRB 276, 24 LRRM 1047 (1949); Long Lake Lumber Co., 182 NLRB 435, 74 LRRM 1116 (1970). See also Chapter 13 supra at notes 249-52.

[196]See generally Chapter 13 supra.

In *Preterm, Inc.*[197] the Board held that a proposal of a broad management-rights clause during contract negotiations did not constitute evidence of a refusal to bargain in good faith, even though the employer submitted its proposal six months after negotiations had commenced. The clause provided that the employer's rights under the clause were not reviewable under the grievance or arbitration provisions. The Board held that the employer did not adopt an intransigent position with respect to the proposal and the proposal did not impede the negotiation process.

On the other hand, the Board has held in some cases that a rigid and inflexible insistence on a broad management-rights clause, in the context of evidence that the employer is engaged in surface bargaining with no intention of reaching agreement, is indicia of an unwillingness to bargain in good faith. For example, in *United Contractors, Inc.*,[198] it found an employer in violation of the Act where the proposed management-rights clause demanded by the employer would in effect have required the union to yield all bargaining rights on such fundamental items as establishing and enforcing work rules, scheduling of hours and assignment of duties, discipline and discharge of employees, subcontracting of work, and relocation and shutdown of operations. The Board's critical finding was that the employer had no intention of reaching an agreement, evidenced by the fact that the company insisted on a 20-percent wage reduction during the period of widespread inflation without offering any claim of economic necessity.

The courts of appeals, however, have overturned Board decisions which looked to the substantive terms of the employer's proposals in determining whether the employer had bargained in good faith. In *NLRB* v. *Tomco Communications, Inc.*,[199] for

---

[197]240 NLRB 654, 100 LRRM 1344 (1979).

[198]244 NLRB 72, 102 LRRM 1012 (1979). *See also* Dixie Corp., 105 NLRB 390, 32 LRRM 1259 (1953), distinguishing *American Nat'l Ins. Co.*, where an employer who refused to supply relevant data to the union, refused to accept the appropriate bargaining unit, and insisted on unilateral control of all subjects of bargaining as a condition precedent to agreement also was held in violation of §8(a)(5). And in Stuart Radiator Core Mfg. Co., 173 NLRB 125, 69 LRRM 1243 (1968), an employer who insisted on a detailed management-rights clause which reserved absolute unilateral control of virtually every significant term and condition of employment, coupled with a limitation of grievances and arbitration to the express terms of the contract and a waiver of bargaining, thereby manifested bad faith.

[199]567 F2d 871, 97 LRRM 2660 (CA 9, 1978) *denying enforcement to* 220 NLRB 636, 90 LRRM 1321 (1975).

example, the Ninth Circuit disagreed with Board findings of bad-faith bargaining where the employer had insisted to impasse on a detailed management-rights clause along with a broad zipper clause, a waiver-of-past-practices provision, and a no-strike provision that covered strikes over matters not covered by the employer's proposed grievance-arbitration provision.[200] The Board had condemned the employer's final proposals as "terms which no self respecting union could be expected to accept." The Ninth Circuit concluded, however, that the case only involved "hard bargaining between two parties who were possessed of disparite economic power: a relatively weak Union and a relatively strong Company," and that the employer's use of its economic-power advantage was not inconsistent with its statutory duty to negotiate in good faith.[201]

5. Plant Rules and Discipline. Generally, plant rules are considered subjects of mandatory bargaining.[202] These include rules pertaining to lunch breaks, absenteeism and tardiness,[203] dress codes,[204] parking regulations,[205] fighting,[206] working on an overtime basis,[207] and safety.[208] Moreover, if the rule affects an employee's continuation of employment, such as a warning and disciplinary system might,[209] it will be a mandatory subject

---

[200]The employer's final economic offer consisted of a proposed increase of ten cents an hour to seven of the nine bargaining-unit employees and a wage review for the remaining two employees.

[201]*But see* Vanderbilt Prods., Inc., 129 NLRB 1323, 47 LRRM 1182 (1961), *enforced,* 297 F2d 833, 49 LRRM 2286 (CA 2, 1961) (no "self-respecting union" could accept the employer's extreme demands). *See also* Chevron Oil Co., 182 NLRB 445, 74 LRRM 1323 (1970). In rejecting the Board's "self-respecting union" test for good-faith bargaining, the Ninth Circuit in Tomco Communications, Inc., *supra* note 199, said that such a standard "comes perilously close to determining what the employer should give by looking at what the employees want." 97 LRRM at 2668. *Accord,* Gulf States Mfrs. v. NLRB, 579 F2d 1298, 99 LRRM 2547 (CA 5, 1978); *but cf.* NLRB v. Mar-Len Cabinets, Inc., 659 F2d 995, 108 LRRM 2838 (CA 9, 1981).

[202]Schraffts Candy Co., 244 NLRB 581, 102 LRRM 1274 (1979); Miller Brewing Co., 166 NLRB 831, 65 LRRM 1649 (1967); Hilton Mobile Homes, 155 NLRB 873, 60 LRRM 1411 (1965).

[203]Murphy Diesel Co. v. NLRB, 454 F2d 303, 78 LRRM 2993 (CA 7, 1971); Kroehler Mfg. Co., 222 NLRB 1269, 91 LRRM 1382 (1976); Master Slack Corp., *supra* note 117; Murray Prods., Inc., 228 NLRB 268, 94 LRRM 1723 (1977).

[204]Transportation Enterprises, Inc., 240 NLRB 551, 100 LRRM 1330 (1979).

[205]Rudy's Farm Co., 245 NLRB 43, 102 LRRM 1384 (1979).

[206]National Football Players Ass'n v. NLRB, 503 F2d 12, 87 LRRM 2118 (CA 8, 1974).

[207]Colonial Press, Inc., 204 NLRB 852, 83 LRRM 1648 (1973).

[208]Boland Marine & Mfg. Co., 225 NLRB 824, 93 LRRM 1346 (1976); Pak-Mor Mfg. Co., 241 NLRB 801, 100 LRRM 1630 (1979). *See infra* at notes 231-38.

[209]In Electri-Flex Co., 228 NLRB 847, 96 LRRM 1361 (1977), *enforced as modified,* 570 F2d 1327, 97 LRRM 2888 (CA 7), *cert. denied,* 439 US 911, 99 LRRM 2743 (1978), the Board found violations of §8(a)(5) where the employer unilaterally instituted and enforced a written warning system.

regardless of the employer's legitimate reason for its promulgation.[210]

Exceptions to this general proposition have occurred in cases where the change in a plant rule had little or no impact on the employees as a group or on their working conditions.[211] In addition, at least three other situations have been treated as exceptions to the general rule.

First, in *Capital Times Co.*,[212] a Board majority found that an employer providing editorial services for a newspaper was not required to bargain before promulgating a "code of ethics," prohibiting employees from accepting gifts from outsiders occasioned by their employment, or requiring employees to disclose outside activities which might constitute conflicts of interest. The Board reasoned that such gifts were not wages since they did not flow from the employer, were not viewed as wages by the union or the employees, and were not compensation for work performed. But in the same case the Board held that a provision in the code for penalties of suspension and discharge was a mandatory subject, because it directly affected employment security.[213]

The continued vitality of this exception was called into question, however, by the District of Columbia Circuit's decision in *Newspaper Guild Local 10 (Greater Philadelphia)* v. *NLRB.*[214] In that case, the Board had adhered to the principles set forth in *Capital Times,* holding that a newspaper could unilaterally promulgate a "code of ethics" but that the imposition of a penalty for the violation of the "code" triggered a bargaining duty. The Court

---

[210]Medicenter, Mid-South Hosp., 221 NLRB 670, 90 LRRM 1576 (1975) (polygraph tests). *See also* NFL Management Council, 203 NLRB 958, 83 LRRM 1203 (1973), *remanded,* 503 F2d 12, 87 LRRM 2118 (CA 8, 1974), *supplemented,* 216 NLRB 423, 88 LRRM 1210 (1975) ("artificial turf" on playing fields was held to be a mandatory subject of bargaining).

[211]*See, e.g.,* Pacific Diesel Parts Co., 203 NLRB 820, 83 LRRM 1359 (1973); *cf.* Old Angus, Inc., 212 NLRB 539, 86 LRRM 1575 (1974), relying upon the Board's earlier decision in Steel-Fab, Inc., 212 NLRB 363, 86 LRRM 1474 (1974).

[212]223 NLRB 651, 91 LRRM 1481 (1976).

[213]Further refinement of the *Capital Times Co.* decision came in Peerless Publications, Inc. (Pottstown Mercury), 231 NLRB 244, 95 LRRM 1611 (1977). The *Peerless* employer's code of ethics not only prohibited gifts, but also prohibited employees from engaging in secondary employment if such employment would create a conflict of interest. *Cf. Capital Times, supra* note 212, where employees were only required to report secondary employment. The *Peerless* Board determined that the second employment prohibition was not a mandatory subject of bargaining. *See* note 214 *infra.*

[214]636 F2d 550, 105 LRRM 2001 (CA DC, 1980), *remanding* Peerless Publications, Inc., 231 NLRB 244, 95 LRRM 1611 (1977).

criticized the Board's approach, noting that for bargaining purposes the penalty provisions cannot easily be separated from the substantive provisions which they are designed to enforce. Accordingly, the Board was instructed to determine on remand the specific subjects in the "code of ethics" that are mandatorily bargainable.

The second exception was made in *Rust Craft Broadcasting*,[215] in which the installation of time clocks without bargaining was held not to be violative of the Act. The Board reasoned that the time clocks were merely a more dependable method of enforcing the employer's long-standing requirement that employees record their time at work, and, therefore, bargaining was not required over this procedural change.[216]

Third, in *Trading Port, Inc.*,[217] the Board held that an employee-evaluation system utilizing hourly production figures as a guide could be instituted by an employer without affording the union prior opportunity to bargain. The Board based its holding on a principle previously adopted in *Wabash Transformer Corp.*,[218] that management should be granted a substantial degree of flexibility to fashion innovations promoting a more efficient work force.

Other miscellaneous work rules affecting the working conditions of employees have been discussed in various Board decisions. Rules of thumb are often unreliable for analysis of these cases. In some the Board has found that the employer's creation or enforcement of the rule violated the Act. In others a contrary conclusion was reached.

In *Alfred M. Lewis, Inc.*[219] an employer was held to have violated Section 8(a)(5) when it unilaterally instituted both a program of supervisory counseling of employees whose productiv-

---

[215]225 NLRB 327, 92 LRRM 1576 (1976). *See also* The Bureau of Nat'l Affairs, Inc., 235 NLRB 8, 97 LRRM 1447 (1978); Moody Chip Corp., 243 NLRB 265, 101 LRRM 1496 (1979). In *Moody Chip* the former procedure of employee-kept time records was held not to be a term and condition of employment which the company was required to bargain about before installing time clocks.

[216]Nathan Littauer Hosp. Ass'n, 229 NLRB 1122, 95 LRRM 1296 (1977). *But cf.* Rust Craft Broadcasting of N.Y., Inc., 225 NLRB 327, 92 LRRM 1576 (1976), where the Board held that an employer violated the Act when it promulgated and implemented a new requirement governing the recording of time through the use of time clocks and established rules and disciplinary provisions designed to enforce the new requirement without bargaining with the union.

[217]224 NLRB 980, 92 LRRM 1606 (1976).

[218]215 NLRB 546, 88 LRRM 1511 (1974).

[219]229 NLRB 757, 95 LRRM 1216 (1977), *enforced in part,* 587 F2d 403, 99 LRRM 2841 (CA 9, 1978).

ity was not within 5 percent of accrued averages, and a procedure for disciplinary suspensions and termination of employees who failed to attain established production standards. But in *Eazor Express, Inc.*,[220] the Board allowed an employer to unilaterally send letters to employees warning them that their production was low and threatening discipline. The distinction may depend on an overall assessment of the parties' grievance and discipline system and a determination of whether the employer's unilateral action represents a material change in that system. The scope of the parties' management-rights clause may also be significant.

In *Allis-Chalmers Corp.*[221] the Board found a violation where the employer had made a unilateral decision to enforce several previously unenforced work rules, including rules that employees stay within departmental yellow lines during worktime, refrain from washing up in the restroom prior to breaks, and avoid going to the nurse's station except for serious emergencies. In contrast, in *Moody Chip Corp.*[222] the Board found that the employer did not violate the Act when it unilaterally established a uniform coffee breaktime in the plant, concluding that the uniform breaktime was necessitated by the fact that the practice of taking breaks at odd times interfered with production.

In *Womac Industries, Inc.*,[223] the employer violated Section 8(a)(5) by unilaterally requiring its employees to furnish doctors' excuses for absences due to illness.[224] In *Markle Manufacturing Co.*,[225]

---

[220]238 NLRB 1165, 99 LRRM 1478 (1978). *See* J. R. Simplot Co., 238 NLRB 374, 99 LRRM 1684 (1978), where the Board found that the employer had sufficient authority under the management-rights clause to unilaterally promulgate rules prohibiting employees from bringing radios into the plant. *See also,* Master Slack Corp., *supra* note 117 (violation of §8(a)(5) where employer changed production rates and quotas and instituted a new procedure for recalling laid-off employees; no violation where employer instructed employees to tuck in shirttails and restricted employee access to warehouse and shipping areas); Boland Marine & Mfg. Co., 228 NLRB 1304, 94 LRRM 1743 (1977) (violation of §8(a)(5) where employer instituted new pass system designed to control movement of employees within, as well as into and out of, its shipyard and to control employees' removal of personal toolboxes from shipyard). *See also* Niagara Falls Memorial Medical Center, Inc., 236 NLRB 342, 98 LRRM 1282 (1978).
[221]234 NLRB 350, 97 LRRM 1240 (1978), *enforced in part, remanded in part,* 601 F2d 870, 102 LRRM 2194 (CA 5, 1979), *enforcement stayed, remanded in part,* 608 F2d 1018, 103 LRRM 2198 (CA 5, 1979), *modified,* 252 NLRB 775, 105 LRRM 1336 (1980).
[222]*Supra* note 215.
[223]238 NLRB 43, 99 LRRM 1185 (1978).
[224]*But cf.* Brown & Connolly, Inc., 237 NLRB 271, 98 LRRM 1572 (1978), *enforced,* 593 F2d 1373, 100 LRRM 3072 (CA 1, 1979), where the Board found no violation when the employer, who suspected an employee of malingering, required him to furnish a doctor's excuse for his absence. The Board reasoned that since no other employee had been made to do so, the requirement did not constitute a rule change.
[225]239 NLRB 1353, 100 LRRM 1230 (1979).

however, where the collective bargaining agreement had been terminated by notice submitted to the employer by the union, the Board refused to hold an employer in violation of the Act when it unilaterally instituted "new" safety rules, installed a "new" absenteeism policy, and hired new employees "off the street" at rates of pay higher than unit employees received.[226]

6. Grievance Procedures and Arbitration. The subjects of grievances and proposals to establish orderly and just methods of presenting grievances are mandatory subjects for collective bargaining.[227] Arbitration clauses are specifically subject to mandatory bargaining.[228]

A proviso to Section 9(a) of the Act provides that individual employees have the right to adjust their own grievances.[229] However, the Third Circuit has held that an employer may not insist in negotiations that each grievance be signed by the employee involved since such a limitation is not within the scope of "wages, hours, and other terms and conditions of employment," hence is not a mandatory subject of bargaining.[230]

7. Safety and Health. The contention of some employers that safety regulation is a management function, not subject to negotiation, has been rejected by the Board and the courts. The Fifth Circuit stated it was "inescapable" that "workers, through their chosen representative should have the right to bargain with the

---

[226]*But* in Central Cartage, Inc., 236 NLRB 1232, 98 LRRM 1554 (1978), *enforced*, 607 F2d 1007 (CA 7, 1979), the employer was found to have violated §8(a)(5) when, in a unilateral departure from past practice, it began to issue written warnings or reprimands to employees. Similarly, in NLRB v. Amoco Chems. Corp., 529 F2d 427, 91 LRRM 2837 (CA 5, 1976), the court enforced the Board's holding that the substitution of a written reprimand disciplinary system for an informal oral warning procedure constituted a significant change in working conditions and was thus a mandatory subject.

[227]*See* NLRB v. Century Cement Mfg. Co., 208 F2d 84, 33 LRRM 2061 (CA 2, 1953); NLRB v. Independent Stave Co., 591 F2d 443, 100 LRRM 2646 (CA 8, 1979), *cert. denied*, 444 US 829, 102 LRRM 2360 (1979); Electrical Workers (UE) (Star Expansion Indus. Corp.) v. NLRB, 409 F2d 150, 70 LRRM 2529 (CA DC, 1969); Hughes Tool Co. v. NLRB, 147 F2d 69, 15 LRRM 852 (CA 5, 1945); United States Automatic Corp., 57 NLRB 124, 14 LRRM 214 (1944).

[228]*See* NLRB v. Davison, 318 F2d 550, 53 LRRM 2462 (CA 4, 1963); NLRB v. Knoxville Pub. Co., 124 F2d 875, 9 LRRM 498 (CA 6, 1942); Electrical Workers (UE) (Star Expansion Indus., Corp.) v. NLRB, 409 F2d 150, 70 LRRM 2529 (CA DC, 1969).

[229]*See* Emporium Capwell Co. v. Western Addition Community Organization, 420 US 50, 88 LRRM 2660 (1975), where the Supreme Court defined the limits of the §9(a) *proviso:* "The intendment of the proviso is to permit employees to present grievances and to authorize the employer to entertain them without opening itself to liability for dealing directly with employees with derogation of the duty to bargain only with the exclusive bargaining representative, a violation of §8(a)(5)." *Id.* at 50 n.12. *See* Chapter 6 *supra* at notes 404-407 and Chapter 28 *infra* at notes 33-34.

[230]*See* Marine & Shipbuilding Workers v. NLRB (Bethlehem Steel Co.), *supra* note 142.

Company in reference to safe work rules and practices."[231] This is also the Board's view. For example, in *Electri-Flex Co.*,[232] the employer was found to have violated the Act by unilaterally requiring employees, on pain of suspension, to wear safety glasses everywhere except in the cafeteria. In *North American Soccer League & Its Constituent Member Clubs*,[233] the Board held that the union had the right to review information concerning names of physicians and trainers utilized by the league, listing of first aid equipment, and player injury reports. In *J.P. Stevens & Co.*[234] the employer was held to have violated the Act by unilaterally deciding the type of respirator employees were to wear.

While the Board and the courts have not directly addressed what effect, if any, the 1970 Occupational Safety and Health Act[235] (OSHA) might have on Section 8(a)(5) bargaining requirements regarding safety rules, the Supreme Court has stated that "employees will in all circumstances enjoy the rights afforded them" by OSHA's guarantee that a workplace be free from recognized hazards that do or could cause death or serious physical harm.[236] In a subsequent decision involving an employee who walked off the job rather than continue working under what he considered to be seriously dangerous conditions, the Seventh Circuit said that "the OSHA legislation was intended to create a separate and general right of broad social importance existing beyond the parameters of an individual labor agreement and susceptible of full vindication only in a judicial forum."[237] The Seventh Circuit's broad language in this context, however,

---

[231]NLRB v. Gulf Power Co., 384 F2d 822, 66 LRRM 2501 (CA 5, 1967), *enforcing* 156 NLRB 622, 61 LRRM 1073 (1966). In Fibreboard Paper Prods. Corp. v. NLRB, 379 US 203, 57 LRRM 2609 (1964), the Supreme Court specifically mentioned "safety practices" as a condition of employment in defining the bargaining duty of an employer. *Fibreboard* is discussed *infra* at notes 277-80. *Cf.* Gateway Coal Co. v. Mine Workers, 414 US 368, 85 LRRM 2049 (1974). For discussion of safety-related protests as protected conduct, *see* Chapter 6 *supra* at notes 466-70.

[232]238 NLRB 713, 99 LRRM 1510 (1978), *enforced*, 104 LRRM 2612 (CA 7, 1979).

[233]245 NLRB 1301, 102 LRRM 1594 (1979). In a series of decisions issued in 1982, Minnesota Mining & Mfg. Co., 261 NLRB No. 2, 109 LRRM 1345 (1982); Colgate-Palmolive Co., 261 NLRB No. 7, 109 LRRM 1352 (1982); and Borden Chem., 261 NLRB No. 6, 109 LRRM 1358 (1982), the Board ruled that employers must bargain over union requests for the generic names of substances used or produced at the employers' plants where the unions claimed a need for such information for reasons of employee health and safety. The employers' "trade secrets" defenses were rejected.

[234]239 NLRB 738, 100 LRRM 1052 (1978), *enforced in part, modified in part*, 623 F2d 322, 104 LRRM 2573 (CA 4, 1980).

[235]29 USC §§651 *et seq.* (1976).

[236]Whirlpool Corp. v. Marshall, 445 US 1, 8 OSHC 1001 (1980).

[237]N. L. Indus., 618 F2d 1220 (CA 7, 1980).

may not represent a definitive rule on the power of other forums to consider and resolve safety claims. In *Gateway Coal Co. v. Mine Workers*,[238] for example, the Supreme Court, in a case where a union struck over an employer's decision to reinstate foremen facing criminal charges for falsifying safety records, ruled that the safety issue was arbitrable under the parties' labor agreement.

8. No-Strike and No-Lockout Clauses. No-strike and no lockout clauses are considered to be mandatory subjects of bargaining. Thus, an employer or a union may bargain for them to the point of impasse.[239] Such clauses, however, are distinguishable from a strike-ballot clause, held to be only a permissive subject of bargaining in the *Borg-Warner* case,[240] for the latter type clause relates to the union's internal affairs and the way the union chooses to implement the process of collective bargaining.

9. Work Assignments. The Board considers changes in work assignments to be a mandatory subject of bargaining, especially when the employer has a prior practice of consulting with employees about work assignments or when changes will significantly affect bargaining-unit work.

In a 1977 case, *Kendall College*,[241] the Board held that the employer violated the Act when, without notifying or bargaining with the newly certified faculty union, it changed its past practice of conferring with faculty employees before publishing class schedules for the next school term. The Board held that class schedules are encompassed within the term "hours" under Section 8(d) and that a class schedule is in effect a work schedule, which is a mandatory subject of bargaining. In reaching this result, the Board rejected the contention that determining class schedules is inherently a managerial function. However, it held that the employer had not violated Section 8(a)(5) by failing to consult with the union concerning publication of class schedules for the summer term, since there had been no such prior practice of consultation with the faculty.

---

[238]*Supra* note 231.
[239]Shell Oil Co., 77 NLRB 1306, 22 LRRM 1158 (1948); NLRB v. Boss Mfg. Co., 118 F2d 187, 8 LRRM 729 (CA 7, 1941).
[240]*Supra* note 2. *See* Chapter 16 *supra* at notes 27-35 and Chapter 18 *infra* at notes 71-73.
[241]228 NLRB 1083, 95 LRRM 1094 (1977).

In *Central Cartage, Inc.*,[242] an employer was found to have violated Section 8(a)(5) by requiring its employees to sign job descriptions. Previously, the employees' positions had been defined flexibly, and all employees were required to be able to perform all operations. In *Fry Foods, Inc.*,[243] the Board held that an employer violated Section 8(a)(5) when it reclassified certain positions as supervisory, even though the promoted employees continued to perform assembly line work included in the bargaining unit. The Board stated that while employers are free to select whom they desire to assume supervisory positions, reclassification of a bargaining-unit job to a nonunit job is a mandatory subject of bargaining where the impact of the change significantly affects bargaining-unit work.

The Board has also held that an employer's changing of work assignments for drivers from a seniority to a rotation basis without consulting with the union violates the Act.[244] Likewise, an employer was held to violate the Act when it unilaterally changed the dispatching system for its truck drivers, as those changes necessarily affected the truck drivers' rates of pay, wages, and conditions of employment.[245]

In *Charmer Industries*[246] the Board held that a group of liquor wholesalers violated Section 8(a)(5) by unilaterally promulgating new procedures for collecting payments from their c.o.d. customers. The Board found that the new collection procedures involved added time, expense, and physical danger for the salesmen.

10. No-Discrimination Provisions. Elimination of race or sex discrimination in the work force has been held by the Board to be a mandatory subject of bargaining[247] and contract provi-

---

[242]236 NLRB 1232, 98 LRRM 1554 (1978), *enforced,* 607 F2d 1007 (CA 7, 1979).
[243]241 NLRB 76, 100 LRRM 1513 (1979), *enforced,* 609 F2d 267, 102 LRRM 2894 (CA 6, 1979).
[244]Capitol Trucking, Inc., 246 NLRB 135, 102 LRRM 1481 (1979).
[245]Long Mile Rubber Co., 245 NLRB 1337, 102 LRRM 1319 (1979).
[246]Charmer Indus., 250 NLRB 293, 104 LRRM 1368 (1980).
[247]Jubilee Mfg. Co., 202 NLRB 272, 82 LRRM 1482 (1973), *aff'd sub nom.* Steelworkers v. NLRB, 504 F2d 271, 87 LRRM 3168 (CA DC, 1974). *Cf.* Alexander v. Gardner-Denver Co., 415 US 36, 7 FEP Cases 81 (1974). *See also* Emporium Capwell Co. v. Western Addition Community Organization, *supra* note 229 ("The elimination of discrimination and its vestiges is an appropriate subject of bargaining, and an employer may have no objection to incorporating into a collective bargaining agreement the substance of his obligation not to discriminate in personnel decisions . . . .").

sions prohibiting discrimination on the basis of race or sex have become commonplace in labor agreements.[248]

Race or sex discrimination may be the subject of litigation under the Act in either a duty to bargain[249] or a duty of fair representation[250] context. In *Wichita Eagle & Beacon Publishing Co.*[251] the Board held that an employer could lawfully declare an impasse with regard to a maternity leave clause that the union claimed "might not be consonant" with the Equal Employment Opportunity Commission's guidelines on discrimination, absent a showing by the union that the clause violated the law either on its face or in its application.

11. Change in Operations.[252] Assuming the parties' collective bargaining agreement is silent on the employer's right to make a particular operating change, an employer's unilateral change in operations will be subject to mandatory bargaining, but only if the change has a significant impact on the bargaining unit. For example, a company, subsequent to the commencement of a strike, discontinued the use of electric-eye inspection machines as a result of difficulty in servicing them. No employee lost his job because of the action, and the duties of only four employees were changed. The District of Columbia Circuit in *Coca Cola Bottling Works*[253] affirmed the Board's conclusion that since the

---

[248]For an example of such a provision, *see* Alexander v. Gardner-Denver Co., *supra* note 247.

[249]In Nomad Div., Skyline Corp., 240 NLRB 737, 100 LRRM 1312 (1979), *enforced*, 613 F2d 1328, 103 LRRM 3003 (CA 5, 1980), the Board found that the employer violated §8(a)(5) by conditioning its honoring of a certified union's bargaining request on the employer's receipt of certain statistical information concerning the racial, sexual, and ethnic composition of the union's membership. The Board held that allegations of racial and other types of discrimination by a union are properly cognizable under the duty of fair representation; they must thus be adjudicated under §8(b) of the Act and cannot constitute a defense to a §8(a)(5) proceeding.

[250]*See* Chapter 28 *infra*.

[251]222 NLRB 742, 91 LRRM 1227 (1976).

[252]*See generally* Morris, *The Role of the NLRB and the Courts in the Collective Bargaining Process: A Fresh Look at Conventional Wisdom and Unconventional Remedies*, 30 VAND. L. REV. 661, 667-76 (1977); Fastiff, *Changes in Business Operations: The Effects of the National Labor Relations Act and Contract Language on Employer Authority*, 14 SANTA CLARA LAWYER (now SANTA CLARA L. REV.) 281 (1974); Manson, *Technological Change and the Collective Bargaining Process*, 12 W. ONT. L. REV. 173 (1973); Recent Decisions, *Labor Law: Duty to Bargain Over Decision to Mechanize Operations*, 55 MARQ. L. REV. 179 (1972); Note, *Labor Law: Duty to Bargain Basic Business Decisions Prior to Implementation*, 1971 WISC. L. REV. 1250 (1971); Tockman, *Labor Law Considerations and Consequences of "Change" in Business Operations*, 59 ILL. B. J. 454 (1971).

[253]Retail, Wholesale & Dep't Store Union (Coca-Cola Bottling Works, Inc.) v. NLRB, 466 F2d 380, 80 LRRM 3244 (CA DC, 1972), *enforcing in part and remanding* 186 NLRB 1050, 75 LRRM 1551 (1970). *See also* Vegas Vic, Inc., 213 NLRB 841, 87 LRRM 1269 (1974).

elimination of the machines had no significant effect on the job of any worker, the company was not obligated to submit its decision to collective bargaining. The Board had held, in reliance upon *Westinghouse Electric Corp.*,[254] as follows:

> While it is now well established that an employer under an obligation to bargain with a union may violate Section 8(a)(5) by making unilateral changes affecting employees in the unit, it is also clear that those changes must have a demonstrably adverse effect on the employees in the unit. Or put another way, the changes must result in a significant detriment to employees in the unit . . . .[255]

In *Columbia Tribune Publishing*[256] the Eighth Circuit upheld the Board's ruling that the employer failed to bargain in good faith regarding a change in the type of machinery used in its business. The employer had changed from the traditional "hot-type" to a new automated process, called "cold-type," in its composing room. The new process resulted in the layoff of half the bargaining unit. The Board found that the employer had violated Section 8(a)(5) by failing to bargain in good faith concerning the change.[257]

The decision to transfer work within an employer's operations[258] may also be a mandatory subject of bargaining. And in many circumstances, the unilateral promulgation of production quotas may be a violation of the Act, even if such quota changes are characterized as "work rules."[259]

---

[254]*Supra* note 159.

[255]*Supra* note 253, 186 NLRB at 1062 (trial examiner's decision).

[256]NLRB v. Columbia Tribune Publishing Co., 495 F2d 1384, 86 LRRM 2078 (CA 8, 1974) *enforcing* 201 NLRB 538, 82 LRRM 1553 (1973). *See also* Newspaper Printing Corp. v. NLRB, 625 F2d 956, 104 LRRM 2432 (CA 10, 1980); Island Typographers, 252 NLRB 9, 105 LRRM 1455 (1980).

[257]This decision by the Eighth Circuit may be read as extending the mandatory bargaining requirements of the Supreme Court's decision in the *Fibreboard* case to encompass both automation and technological change. *See* text commencing at note 267 *infra* for a discussion of *Fibreboard*.

[258]*See* Stone & Thomas, 221 NLRB 573, 90 LRRM 1569 (1975) (unilaterally transferring work from warehouse to individual stores); North Carolina Coastal Motor Lines, Inc., 219 NLRB 1009, 90 LRRM 1114 (1975) (unilateral discontinuance of city operations and transfer to other drivers); Awrey Bakeries, Inc., *supra* note 144 (unilateral transfer of unit work and resulting lay-off). For discussion of the remedy ordered by the Board in such cases, *see* Arnold Graphic Indus., Inc., 206 NLRB 327, 84 LRRM 1343 (1973), *enforcement denied in part,* 505 F2d 257, 87 LRRM 2753 (CA 6, 1974); American Needle & Novelty Co., 206 NLRB 534, 84 LRRM 1526 (1973). *See* discussion of major business changes at notes 267-388 *infra*.

[259]*Compare* Matlock Truck Body & Trailer Corp., 217 NLRB 246, 89 LRRM 1187 (1975), *and* Fry Foods, Inc., *supra* note 243, *enforced,* 609 F2d 267, 102 LRRM 2894 (CA 6, 1979), *with* Cooper-Jarrett, Inc., 239 NLRB 840, 100 LRRM 1079 (1978), where the Board held that the employer did not violate the Act when it unilaterally changed the means by which it measured the productivity of its dock workers from a pounds-per-

In *Houston Shopping News Co.*[260] the Board held that an employer violated the Act by unilaterally offering to lease some of its equipment to its unit employees. The employer was engaged in the typesetting business and maintained both hot-type and cold-type departments. Faced with financial losses largely attributable to the hot-type department, the employer unilaterally offered to lease the hot-type equipment to the employees in that department. In finding a violation of Section 8(a)(5), the Board rejected the argument that the employer did not violate the Act because the offer was never implemented, stating that

> [t]he unfair labor practice in this case is not predicated on the employees' acceptance or rejection of Respondent's offer. Rather, the violation is premised on Respondent's failure to notify and bargain with the Union concerning a proposed change in its operations which would radically alter the status of bargaining unit employees.[261]

Member Murphy dissented on the ground that after the offer was made the union failed to protest the making of the offer and participated in the preparation of a response to the offer. The Fifth Circuit refused to enforce the decision for similar reasons, noting that the union had participated in the procedures.

In some cases the Board has found no employer violation because the union, with notice of the impending operational change has not requested bargaining. For example, in *City Hospital of East Liverpool, Ohio*,[262] the Board found evidence of union waiver of its right to bargain over the elimination of certain employment positions during the term of a collective agreement. The union had received notice of the employer's announcement of proposed changes three weeks prior to their effective date, but failed to request bargaining until approximately six weeks after their implementation. In finding that the

---

hour formula to a formula based on the number of bills of lading and pieces of merchandise handled. The Board found that the new formula did not constitute a "work standard" within the meaning of the collective bargaining agreement, but rather was simply a method of measuring production. It also noted that the new formula was not a material, substantial, or significant change from the previous method of measurement utilized by the employer. *See* text commencing at note 202 *supra* for a discussion of plant rules.

[260]223 NLRB 1133, 92 LRRM 1074 (1976), *enforcement denied,* 554 F2d 739, 95 LRRM 2801 (CA 5, 1977).

[261]*Id.* at 1134.

[262]234 NLRB 58, 97 LRRM 1125 (1978). *See* Citizens Nat'l Bank of Willmar, 245 NLRB 389, 102 LRRM 1467 (1979); Globe-Union, Inc., 222 NLRB 1081, 91 LRRM 1340 (1976).

union had waived its right to bargain, the Board relied on "[e]stablished Board precedent [which] requires a union that has notice of an employer's change in a term or condition of employment to timely request bargaining in order to preserve its right to bargain on that subject."[263]

The Board, in *Holiday Inn of Benton*,[264] held that the employer violated Section 8(a)(5) by failing to notify and bargain with the union representing the employer's waitresses with respect to both its decision to convert its restaurant into a self-service cafeteria and the effects of that decision. The Board's holding was enforced in relevant part by a divided Seventh Circuit. The court found that the restaurant conversion did not constitute an alteration of the "basic operation" within the meaning of that term as applied by the Supreme Court in its celebrated *Fibreboard decision*.[265] It noted that the cafeteria was operated in the same location during the same hours, and offered the same menu as before the change. There had been no major remodeling, nor was the food prepared differently. In the court's opinion, the only real difference between the restaurant and the cafeteria was that customers, rather than waitresses, carried the food to the tables. The court held that this difference alone was insufficient to constitute a change in the "basic operation" of the restaurant, thus precluding the employer from arguing that bargaining over the conversion would "significantly abridge" his freedom to manage the business.

In *Metromedia, Inc. v. NLRB*[266] the Eighth Circuit held that the employer violated the Act by failing to negotiate with the union which represented its newsfilm cameramen with respect to the use of portable television cameras.

12. Major Business Changes. *a. Subcontracting and Removal From the Bargaining Unit.* In 1963, the Board said that with the evolution of the relationship between employers and employees "new areas may be found which affect 'wages, hours, and other

---

[263]234 NLRB at 59.

[264]237 NLRB 1042, 99 LRRM 1235 (1978), *enforced in relevant part sub nom.* Davis v. NLRB, 617 F2d 1264, 103 LRRM 2965 (CA 7, 1980).

[265]Fibreboard Paper Prods. Corp. v. NLRB, *supra* note 231. *See* text commencing at note 267 *infra* for a discussion of *Fibreboard*.

[266]586 F2d 1182, 99 LRRM 2743 (CA 8, 1978), *enforcing in relevant part* 232 NLRB 486, 96 LRRM 1475 (1977). The employer sought unsuccessfully to defend its failure to bargain on the basis that it had recently agreed to give another union exclusive jurisdiction over the operation of its portable television cameras.

terms and conditions of employment,' and thus the list of mandatory subjects of bargaining quite properly is enlarged."[267] In *Fibreboard Paper Products Corp.* v. *NLRB*[268] the Supreme Court said that "while not determinative, it is appropriate to look to industrial bargaining practice in appraising the propriety of including a particular subject within the scope of mandatory bargaining."[269] Such observations on the expandability of the list of mandatory bargaining subjects are especially relevant to developments in the field of subcontracting and other removals of significant work from the bargaining unit.

For many years the Board held that an employer had no duty under Section 8(a)(5) to consult with the bargaining representative before deciding to subcontract part of its operation. Thus, in 1945 the Board asserted that it had never held that "an employer may not in good faith . . . change his business structure, [or] sell or contract out a portion of his operation . . . without first consulting the bargaining representative . . . ."[270] However, the Board developed a rule in subcontracting and related cases that an employer must bargain with the union about the *impact* and the *effects* of a decision to subcontract or to make other similar operational changes.[271]

As late as 1961, the Board took the position that the *decision* to subcontract was not a mandatory subject of bargaining. In its initial opinion in *Fibreboard*,[272] the Board held that an employer's decision to subcontract is not a mandatory bargaining subject because it relates to a "precondition [of employment] necessary to the establishment and continuance of the [employment] rela-

---

[267]Associated Gen. Contractors, Inc., *supra* note 166.

[268]*Supra* note 231.

[269]*Id.* at 211.

[270]Mahoning Mining Co., 61 NLRB 792, 803, 16 LRRM 110 (1945). *See also* Walter Holm & Co., 87 NLRB 1169, 25 LRRM 1270 (1949). Unfair labor practice charges in subcontracting cases often involve allegations of violation of §8(a)(3) as well as claims of violation of §8(a)(5). The present discussion is concerned with the §8(a)(5) aspect of the problem. For comprehensive treatment of §8(a)(3), *see* Chapter 7 *supra*.

[271]Shamrock Dairy, Inc., 119 NLRB 998, 41 LRRM 1216 (1957), *modified*, 124 NLRB 494, 44 LRRM 1407 (1959), *enforced*, 280 F2d 665, 46 LRRM 2433 (CA DC), *cert. denied*, 364 US 892, 47 LRRM 2095 (1960); Bickford Shoes, Inc., 109 NLRB 1346, 34 LRRM 1570 (1954); Diaper Jean Mfg. Co., 109 NLRB 1045, 34 LRRM 1504 (1954); Brown Truck & Trailer Mfg. Co., 106 NLRB 999, 32 LRRM 1580 (1953); NLRB Gen. Counsel Adm. Ruling 315, 30 LRRM 1102 (1952). *But cf.* NLRB v. Rives Co., 288 F2d 511, 47 LRRM 2766 (CA 5, 1961).

[272]Fibreboard Paper Prods. Corp., 130 NLRB 1558, 47 LRRM 1547 (1961), *supplemented*, 138 NLRB 550, 51 LRRM 1101 (1962), *enforced*, 322 F2d 411, 53 LRRM 2666 (CA DC, 1963), *aff'd*, 379 US 203, 57 LRRM 2609 (1964).

THE DEVELOPING LABOR LAW CH. 17

tionship from which conditions of employment arise."[273] The Board reasoned that an employer's bargaining obligation does not encompass the issue of whether an employment relationship exists, but, instead, covers terms and conditions of employment *after* the relationship is established. A decision to subcontract work, the Board concluded, is a basic management decision over which Congress did not intend to compel bargaining.[274]

In 1962 the Board changed its position. In *Town & Country*[275] it held that an employer violates Section 8(a)(5) if it fails to bargain over a decision to subcontract work, even if that decision is based solely on economic considerations. In that case the employer's decision to subcontract was held to be unlawfully motivated by its opposition to the union; however, the Board held that the bargaining obligation attached regardless of the employer's motivation. It was now the Board's view that

[t]he elimination of unit jobs, albeit for economic reasons, is a matter within the statutory phrase "other terms and conditions of employment" and is a mandatory subject of collective bargaining within the meaning of Section 8(a)(5) of the Act.[276]

The Board then reconsidered and reversed its original decision in *Fibreboard*. Relying on *Town & Country* and the Supreme Court's 1960 decision in *Telegraphers* v. *Chicago & North Western R.R.*,[277] the Board concluded that the employer's failure to bargain over its decision to subcontract maintenance work previously performed by bargaining-unit employees violated Section 8(a)(5) of the Act. The Board's order in the second *Fibreboard* decision was enforced by the District of Columbia Circuit,[278] and the Supreme Court affirmed.[279]

The Supreme Court held that, under the particular facts in *Fibreboard*, the decision to subcontract constituted a mandatory

---

[273]130 NLRB at 1561.
[274]*Id.*
[275]Town & Country Mfg. Co., 136 NLRB 1022, 49 LRRM 1918 (1962), *enforced*, 316 F2d 846, 53 LRRM 2054 (CA 5, 1963).
[276]136 NLRB at 1027. The Fifth Circuit enforced the Board's decision on the grounds that the company had subcontracted because of anti-union motivation in violation of §8(a)(3). *Id.*
[277]362 US 330, 45 LRRM 3104 (1960). In *Telegraphers* the Supreme Court was not dealing with the Labor Management Relations Act but rather with the Railway Labor Act. However, the Board felt that the decision of the Supreme Court made it clear that elimination of jobs in the bargaining unit for reasons that were palpably economic was still a "term or condition of employment" over which an employer must first bargain with the union—reasoning which was deemed equally applicable to both statutes.
[278]Fibreboard Paper Prods. Corp. v. NLRB, *supra* note 272.
[279]*Id.*

subject for bargaining even in the absence of anti-union motivation. The Court noted that the company's basic operation did not change as a result of the maintenance subcontract, nor was a capital investment required. Consequently, the company was obligated to bargain over the issue of whether to subcontract the work and, because of its refusal to bargain, the Board was empowered to order the resumption of the plant maintenance operations and reinstatement of the affected employees with back pay.

Although *Fibreboard* was widely heralded as a case that would resolve broad issues, the actual holding was narrow and limited. The limits of the decision were indicated by the Court:

> We are thus not expanding the scope of mandatory bargaining to hold, as we do now, that the type of "contracting out" involved in this case—the replacement of employees in the existing bargaining unit with those of an independent contractor to do the same work under similar conditions of employment—is a statutory subject of collective bargaining under §8(d). Our decision need not and does not encompass other forms of "contracting out" or "subcontracting" which arise daily in our complex economy.[280]

The Board's 1965 decision in *Westinghouse Electric Corp.*[281] provided a comprehensive interpretation of the Supreme Court's *Fibreboard* decision and announced a series of factors which the Board would use to determine whether a particular subcontracting decision necessitated bargaining. Bargaining over the decision to subcontract unit work would generally not be required

---

[280]379 US at 215. *Cf.* Local 24 Teamsters v. Oliver, 358 US 283, 43 LRRM 2374 (1959) (contract provisions imposing conditions upon contracting out and leasing of employer's trucks by employees, which governed whether drivers' wages were in fact diminished by arrangements whereby drivers' rentals supposedly covered operating costs, are mandatory subjects of bargaining). Justice Stewart, joined by Justices Douglas and Harlan, concurred in *Fibreboard* because in his view the facts simply involved the substitution of one group of workers for another to perform the same work in the same plant under the ultimate control of the same employer. He stressed that:

"This kind of subcontracting falls short of such larger entrepreneurial questions as what shall be produced, how capital shall be invested in fixed assets, or what the basic scope of the enterprise shall be. In my view, the Court's decision in this case has nothing to do with whether any aspects of those larger issues could under any circumstances be considered subjects of compulsory collective bargaining under the present law." 379 US at 225.

[281]*Supra* note 159. *Cf.* General Elec. Co., 240 NLRB 703, 100 LRRM 1510 (1979), where the Board upheld the finding of the administrative law judge that the employer had not violated §8(a)(5) in contracting out carpet cleaning utilizing a steam process, basing his ruling on *Westinghouse* criteria. However, in a concurring opinion Member Jenkins, who had participated in *Westinghouse*, said the case should have been decided on the basis of the Supreme Court's *Fibreboard* decision since the carpet cleaning fell within the category of "other forms" of subcontracting.

if (1) the subcontracting is motivated solely by economic reasons; (2) it has been customary for the employer to subcontract various kinds of work; (3) no substantial variance is shown in kind or degree from the established past practice of the employer; (4) no significant detriment results to employees in the unit; and (5) the union has had an opportunity to bargain about changes in existing subcontracting practices at general negotiating meetings.[282]

Based on the *Westinghouse* criteria, in 1965 the Board dismissed several complaints over subcontracting practices[283] without giving any precise definition of what constituted a "significant detriment" to employees. Nevertheless, the 1965 dismissals indicated that the mere fact that most of the work contracted out could have been performed by unit employees,[284] or that unit pay classifications were reduced because of lack of work,[285] or that employees were assigned to work at unskilled jobs[286] was not a sufficient basis for making subcontracting a mandatory subject of bargaining. Additionally, the Board has held that an employer has no duty to bargain over a decision to subcontract work that falls outside the scope of work normally performed by unit employees.[287]

---

[282]*See* Amcar Div. v. NLRB, 596 F2d 1344, 1349, 100 LRRM 3074, 3076 (CA 8, 1979), where the Eighth Circuit commented: "In our view the *Westinghouse* 'guidelines' substantially comport with *Fibreboard* and fairly set forth the factors which should be considered in determining whether an employer has violated the Act by contracting out of work." *See also* ACF Indus., Inc. v. NLRB, 592 F2d 422, 100 LRRM 2710 (CA 8, 1979). It may not be necessary for all of the *Westinghouse* tests to be met to avoid the obligation to bargain about the decision to subcontract. General Elec. Co., 240 NLRB 703, 100 LRRM 1510 (1979).

[283]American Oil Co., 155 NLRB 639, 60 LRRM 1369 (1965); American Oil Co., 152 NLRB 56, 59 LRRM 1007 (1965); Central Soya Co., 151 NLRB 1691, 58 LRRM 1667 (1965); Superior Coach Corp., 151 NLRB 188, 58 LRRM 1369 (1965); Fafnir Bearing Co., 151 NLRB 332, 58 LRRM 1397 (1965); American Oil Co., 151 NLRB 421, 58 LRRM 1412 (1965). *See* Note, *Mandatory Subjects of Bargaining, Operational Changes,* 17 U. FLA. L. REV. 109 (1964).

[284]Fafnir Bearing Co., *supra* note 283.

[285]American Oil Co., *supra* note 283.

[286]Superior Coach Corp., *supra* note 283.

[287]Central Soya Co., *supra* note 283. In Amcar Div., 234 NLRB 1063, 98 LRRM 1287 (1978), *enforced as modified, supra* note 282, an employer that manufactured railroad freight cars unilaterally subcontracted several kinds of work. The Board determined that bargaining over the subcontracting of the work and the rebuilding of certain presses was required under *Fibreboard,* even though bargaining-unit employees had not rebuilt such presses before, since bargaining-unit employees had performed most of the separate elements of rebuilding these presses during routine maintenance. However, the Board determined that other work was properly contracted out without notice to or bargaining with the union because the employees had not done work of a sufficiently similar kind.

The Board in its 1965 cases thus indicated that in order for contracting out to be a mandatory bargaining subject, some employees have to lose overtime, or be laid off or be transferred to lower paying jobs as a result of the contracting out of work.[288] If subcontracting caused employees to lose overtime work, the Board held that the employer had to bargain prior to subcontracting, only if the amount of lost overtime was substantial.[289] If the subcontract caused only minimum overtime loss, the Board held that there was no significant change in the employees' conditions of employment; therefore bargaining about the decision was unnecessary.[290]

In a later *Westinghouse* case[291] the Board distinguished between provable and speculative impact on employees. The union had charged that unilateral subcontracting by the employer imposed a substantial detrimental effect on the bargaining unit since employees, who were already on layoff, were not recalled. The union argued that if the subcontracting had not taken place, or had been more limited, certain of the laid-off employees might have returned to gainful employment. The Board rejected this view since there was no showing that these employees were entitled to recall under the contract, or were available or interested in returning to work. The Board said that the attempt to establish the requisite detriment rested upon sheer speculation as to the impact of the subcontracting on the individuals who were laid off. However, in another case where employees were on layoff at the time of the subcontracting, a substantial detrimental impact on the bargaining unit was found.[292] More recently,

---

[288]*See* cases cited in notes 131-140 *supra, and* Amcar Div., 231 NLRB 83, 96 LRRM 1291 (1977), *enforced,* 592 F2d 422, 100 LRRM 2710 (CA 8, 1979). However, where a company is unable to operate at all due to matters beyond its control, even a layoff does not make subcontracting a mandatory bargaining subject. Central Rufina, 161 NLRB 696, 63 LRRM 1318 (1966). *See also* Ador Corp., 150 NLRB 1658, 58 LRRM 1280 (1965). *Cf.,* Kennecott Copper Corp., 148 NLRB 1653, 57 LRRM 1217 (1964), a pre-*Fibreboard* case, holding no violation since unilateral contracting out did not involve any job losses. The D.C. Circuit may be applying a more stringent test than the Board. *See* Automobile Workers v. NLRB, 381 F2d 265, 64 LRRM 2489 (CA DC, 1967), *sub nom.* General Motors Corp. v. Automobile Workers, *cert. denied,* 389 US 857, 66 LRRM 2307 (1967), where the court reversed the Board's decision that the company had not violated the Act and held that a change in operations which caused the elimination of six jobs within the bargaining unit required mandatory bargaining.
[289]Cities Serv. Oil Co., 158 NLRB 1204, 62 LRRM 1175 (1966).
[290]General Tube Co., 151 NLRB 850, 58 LRRM 1496 (1965).
[291]Westinghouse Elec. Corp., 153 NLRB 443, 59 LRRM 1355 (1965).
[292]Amcar Div. v. NLRB, *supra* note 282. "The Board could reasonably infer from these facts that the subcontracting resulted in a loss of reasonably expected work opportunities for men [on layoff] in the bargaining unit." ACF Indus., *supra* note 282 at 1350.

the Board has held that even without layoffs a substantial detriment is suffered by the bargaining unit when unit work is removed and job classifications are permanently eliminated due to technological advancements.[293]

The Fourth Circuit, in *District 50, Mine Workers* v. *NLRB*,[294] held that an employer's duty to bargain over a subcontracting decision varies with the length of time available for implementation of the subcontract. In upholding the Board's dismissal of a refusal-to-bargain charge, the court indicated that full-scale bargaining should not be required in situations where it is necessary for the employer to implement a subcontract immediately. In such cases, according to the court, an employer may satisfy its bargaining obligation by a simple notification to the union and an opportunity for the exchange of ideas. The court explained that the union should not be permitted to stall the decision by insisting on protracted negotiations. After listening to the union's suggestions, the company should be permitted to accept or reject them as its economic judgment dictates. The court thus appeared to be redefining the nature of "impasse" to accommodate its notion of the exigencies of subcontracting decisions.[295] As the court said:

> An employer may be obligated under the compulsion of some circumstances to make subcontracting decisions without delay. Emergencies could arise that require immediate action. The employer's prerogative in this class of cases should be respected without requiring prior bargaining or even notification of the union. However, other contracting decisions may not demand immediate action, and respecting these types of decisions, there may be no practical obstacle in notification of the union, and to affording it an opportunity to be heard.[296]

Where employees have lost significant amounts of overtime or any employee has lost his job as a result of subcontracting, the Board has held that the employer had a duty to bargain

---

[293]Equitable Gas Co., 245 NLRB 260, 102 LRRM 1470 (1979).
[294]358 F2d 234, 61 LRRM 2632 (CA 4, 1966). *See also* Puerto Rico Tel. Co. v. NLRB, 359 F2d 983, 62 LRRM 2069 (CA 1, 1966) (finding no adverse impact and overruling Board determination requiring bargaining).
[295]*See* Morris, *supra* note 252 at 667-76.
[296]358 F2d at 238. *Cf.* Jersey Farms Milk Serv., Inc., 148 NLRB 1392, 57 LRRM 1166 (1964), where the Board found that unilateral subcontracting of bargaining-unit work violated the Act. The Board simply ordered the company to bargain over resumption of operations and any proposed alternatives thereto; it did not order restoration of the *status quo ante*. *See* discussion of remedies in Chapter 33 *infra*.

about the subcontracting.[297] In such circumstances, the fact that the subcontracting was economically motivated does not excuse the employer from a mandatory duty to notify and bargain about its decision with the union.[298] It remains to be seen whether the Supreme Court's 1981 decision in *First National Maintenance*[299] will affect the extent of an employer's duty to bargain about economically motivated subcontracting.

A classic example of the difficulty in applying *Fibreboard* is found in the *Adams Dairy*[300] case. Adams Dairy had been engaged in selling milk and dairy products to retail outlets through both driver-salesmen and independent contractors. The company decided to eliminate the use of driver-salesmen and consequently changed its entire distribution system to an independent contractor arrangement. It informed the union of the change and discharged all of its driver-salesmen. The Board ordered reinstatement and back pay. That decision was reversed by the Eighth Circuit.[301] On appeal, the Supreme Court remanded the case to the Eighth Circuit with instructions to reconsider the case in light of its decision in *Fibreboard*.[302] On remand, the Eighth Circuit adhered to its original decision, reasoning as follows: (1) Contrary to the situation in *Fibreboard*, the *Adams Dairy* case involved more than just the substitution of one set of employees for another, for the company had changed its basic operating procedure and had liquidated a part of its business. (2) Unlike *Fibreboard*, *Adams Dairy* involved a change in capital structure and a recoupment of capital investment. (3) Also contrary to *Fibreboard*, the work done by the independent contractors for *Adams Dairy* was not performed primarily in the Adams plant for the benefit of the dairy. And (4) in *Adams*, unlike *Fibreboard*, the decision to change to distribution by independent contractors was made at a time when the current contract still

[297]Weston & Brooker Co., 154 NLRB 747, 60 LRRM 1015 (1965), *enforced*, 373 F2d 741, 64 LRRM 2736 (CA 4, 1967).
[298]Brown Transp. Corp., 140 NLRB 954, 52 LRRM 1151 (1963), *modified as to remedy only*, 334 F2d 243, 56 LRRM 2809 (CA 5, 1964); Key Coal Co., 240 NLRB 1013, 100 LRRM 1444 (1979). *See also* Amcar Div., *supra* note 288.
[299]First National Maintenance Corp. v. NLRB, 452 US 666, 107 LRRM 2705 (1981). *See* Chapter 16 *supra* at notes 56-69. *See also infra* this chapter at notes 333-64. In *Marriott Corp.*, 264 NLRB No. 178, 111 LRRM 1354 (1982), a divided Board held that a decision to close a shrimp-processing part of a business and subcontract that operation required *Fibreboard*-type bargaining as to both the basic decision and its effects; the Board found that the shrimp-processing operation did not constitute a distinct business enterprise, and *First Nat'l Maintenance* was not deemed applicable.
[300]Adams Dairy Co., *supra* note 15.
[301]*Id.*
[302]*Id.*

had two years to run and no aura of bad faith appeared to have pervaded the employer's bargaining, as it had appeared in *Fibreboard*.[303]

The *Fibreboard* bargaining obligations have been applied to other types of "contracting out" or "subcontracting" of bargaining-unit work. It has thus been held that an employer violated the duty to bargain about the decision to sublease land requiring substantial reclamation work that resulted from coal mining.[304] Because the employer remained primarily liable on the base lease and received income from the transaction, the Board said that the sublease medium had all "the essential ingredients of basic subcontracting" and could not be regarded purely as a transfer of assets.[305]

However, where cargo containers owned by ocean vessel owners were leased to consolidators who loaded cargo into the containers at their off-pier facilities for sea shipment, thus depriving longshoremen employed by the vessel owners of performing the loading work on the piers, the Board held that such an arrangement did not constitute subcontracting.[306]

One issue that has been the subject of considerable litigation concerns the question of subcontracting during a strike. The Ninth Circuit, overruling the Board, has held that an employer need not offer to bargain with a union over the decision and effects of subcontracting bargaining-unit work during a strike.[307] Subsequently, the Board held that an employer need not bargain over subcontracting of bargaining-unit work during a strike if the facts indicate that management views the arrangement as a temporary measure adopted to continue business relationships.[308] However in *American Cyanamid Co.*[309] the Board held

---

[303]*Id. But see* Automobile Workers v. NLRB (General Motors Corp.) and discussion in note 288 *supra. See also* NLRB v. American Mfg. Co., 351 F2d 74, 60 LRRM 2122 (CA 5, 1965); Winn-Dixie Stores, Inc. v. NLRB, 361 F2d 512, 62 LRRM 2218 (CA 5), *cert. denied,* 385 US 935, 63 LRRM 2372 (1966).

[304]Key Coal Co., *supra* note 298.

[305]*Id.* 240 NLRB at 1042.

[306]Longshoremen (Consol. Express, Inc.), 221 NLRB 956, 90 LRRM 1655 (1975), *enforced,* 537 F2d 706, 92 LRRM 3260 (CA 2, 1976), *cert. denied sub nom.* New York Shipping Ass'n v. NLRB, 429 US 1041, 94 LRRM 2202 (1976), *rehearing denied sub nom.* Longshoremen v. NLRB, 430 US 911 (1977); Longshoremen (Dolphin Forwarding, Inc.,), 236 NLRB 525, 98 LRRM 1276 (1978), *enforcement denied,* 613 F2d 890, 102 LRRM 2361 (CA DC, 1979), *cert. denied,* 448 US 906, 104 LRRM 2688 (1980).

[307]Hawaii Meat Co. v. NLRB, 321 F2d 397, 53 LRRM 2872 (CA 9, 1963).

[308]Empire Terminal Warehouse Co., 151 NLRB 1359, 58 LRRM 1589 (1965), *enforced sub nom.* Local 745, Teamsters (Empire Terminal Warehouse Co.) v. NLRB, 355 F2d 842, 61 LRRM 2056 (CA DC, 1966). Other cases dealing with the right to subcontract during a strike: Shell Oil Co., 149 NLRB 283, 57 LRRM 1271 (1964); Shell Chem. Co.,

that the employer violated Section 8(a)(5) by permanently sub-contracting maintenance work and terminating maintenance employees during a strike. The employer had argued that the *Fibreboard* doctrine did not apply to strike situations, contending that the strike created an emergency which excused bargaining with respect to its decision to enter into a permanent mainte-nance subcontract. On review, the Seventh Circuit held that, while the employer during a strike could unilaterally subcon-tract its maintenance work on a temporary basis, it was illegal to do so on a permanent basis since "no harm" would have ema-nated from negotiating with the union prior to the decision to permanently subcontract.

In one case a subcontracting arrangement completed prior to the withdrawal of a strike threat to the employer, whereby the subcontractor required that it be given the river-outfitting work in issue for two annual seasons, was considered by the Board to be "an economic and business necessity" which did not require prior bargaining.[310] Thus, the temporary subcontracting which was due to the strike threat could have an extended life, since the employer's actions were forced by economic considerations rather than animus toward union representation.

The Board has also permitted subcontracting, without bar-gaining, during a hiatus between contracts, so long as the sub-contracting has been in line with past practice.[311] The Board has also ruled that when the employer had lawfully withdrawn rec-ognition from the incumbent union after expiration of the col-lective bargaining agreement, it was not a violation of Section 8(a)(5) to transfer its towing boat operations to chartering com-panies.[312]

---

149 NLRB 298, 57 LRRM 1275 (1964). *See also* Die Sinkers Lodge 50 v. Pittsburgh Forgings Co., 255 F Supp 142, 63 LRRM 2152 (WD PA, 1966), which quotes the Seventh Circuit in NLRB v. Abbott Publishing Co., 331 F2d 209, 55 LRRM 2994 (CA 7, 1964).

[309]235 NLRB 1316, 98 LRRM 1429 (1978), *enforced,* 592 F2d 356, 100 LRRM 2640 (CA 7, 1979). *See also* Alexander Linn Hosp. Ass'n, 244 NLRB 387, 102 LRRM 1252 (1979). In Markle Mfg. Co., 239 NLRB 1142, 100 LRRM 1125 (1979), *enforced in part, modified in part,* 623 F2d 1122 (CA 5, 1980), refusal by the employer during the course of a strike to furnish the union with requested information concerning its subcontracting practices violated §8(a)(5), even though NLRB had determined during the course of its investigation of unfair labor practice charges relating to the employer's subcontracting practices that such practices were consistent with past practice.

[310]Elliott River Tours, 246 NLRB 935, 103 LRRM 1095 (1979).

[311]Shell Oil Co., 149 NLRB 283, 287, 57 LRRM 1271 (1964). In a later decision involving another plant of the same employer, Shell Oil Co., 166 NLRB 1064, 65 LRRM 1713 (1967), the Board interpreted a clause in a collective bargaining contract to permit unilateral subcontracting of bargaining-unit work in accordance with past practice.

[312]Upper Miss. Towing Corp., 246 NLRB 262, 102 LRRM 1536 (1979). *See generally* Chapter 12 *supra.*

Although litigation interpreting the *Fibreboard* decision[313] continues, certain conclusions can be drawn from existing Board decisions in this area. If, for instance, the decision to subcontract involves the cessation by the employer of a particular part of its business operation where the employees are represented by a union, and the substitution of a subcontractor, that decision and its effects will necessitate bargaining.[314] Whether *First National Maintenance*[315] will cause the Board to alter this position remains to be seen.

Even where there may not be an obligation to bargain over a decision to contract out or transfer bargaining-unit work, there is a duty to bargain over the effects of such decisions. In *Walter Pape, Inc.*,[316] for example, a dairy products dealer entered into collective bargaining with a union representing its routemen, although, prior to the start of the negotiations, it had commenced arrangements to have another distributor take over that phase of its operation.[317] The Board concluded that the employer's failure to notify the union that the route termination was imminent and to bargain as to its effects constituted bad-faith bargaining violative of Section 8(a)(5). Although the employer's decision was economically motivated, and most of the drivers had found employment at higher wages, the Board ordered back pay from the date of termination until the employer commenced bargaining as to the effects of the subcontracting.

The unilateral expansion of subcontracting or the alteration in the type of work done by subcontractors can also violate the Act, depending upon the effects on the bargaining unit.[318] Thus,

---

[313]Fibreboard Paper Prods. Corp. v. NLRB, *supra* note 231.

[314]*See, e.g.*, NLRB v. Jackson Farmers, Inc., 457 F2d 516, 79 LRRM 2909 (CA 10, 1972). *See also* Empire Dental Co., 211 NLRB 860, 87 LRRM 1359 (1974), *enforced*, 538 F2d 337, 93 LRRM 2336 (CA 9, 1976). Florida-Texas Freight, Inc., 203 NLRB 509, 83 LRRM 1093 (1973), *enforced*, 489 F2d 1275, 85 LRRM 2845 (CA 6, 1974); Hijos de Ricardo Vela, Inc., 200 NLRB 379, 82 LRRM 1099 (1972); Crow, Inc., 206 NLRB 439, 84 LRRM 1550 (1973).

[315]*Supra* note 299. *See particularly Marriott Corp., supra* note 299.

[316]205 NLRB 719, 84 LRRM 1055 (1973).

[317]It is unclear whether the transaction by which the employer disposed of its route was a sale or a subcontract. The Board stated that it did not adopt and need not rule on the administrative law judge's finding that the transaction was a subcontract rather than a sale. *Id.* at 719 n.1.

[318]However, an employer does not violate §8(a)(5) by failing to negotiate a subcontracting decision with a union which represents union members only, since such a union is acting in derogation of the Act by not providing representation for the entire bargaining unit. Don Mendenhall, Inc., 194 NLRB 1109, 79 LRRM 1164 (1972).

in *Howmet Corp.*[319] an employer had historically subcontracted portions of its toolroom work. Following union certification, the employer increased the volume of subcontracted work and reassigned other duties, with the result that several employees were laid off. The employer made the decision without giving the union an opportunity to bargain about the decision or its effects. The Board held that the substantial alteration of the subcontracting "in quantity and kind" was a unilateral change in terms and conditions of employment. The employer's failure to bargain as to either the decision or its effects violated Section 8(a)(5).[320]

Even though employees are dismissed as a result of a subcontracting decision, there may be no obligation to bargain over the decision if the affected employees are not significantly injured. In *Tellepsen Petro-Chem Constructors*,[321] for example, the employer failed to notify the union of its decision to subcontract bargaining-unit work; instead, upon determining that its project was behind schedule, it dismissed eight employees and subcontracted that portion of its project. A Board majority held that this action did not violate Section 8(a)(5) since the dismissed employees were hired by the subcontractor or by other contractors under the same multi-employer agreement with the same bargaining representative. As the employees merely shifted employers with minimal impact and were protected by the agreement, there was no violation.[322]

The holding in *Central Buying Service*[323] demonstrates the Board's continuing sensitivity to the limits of the *Fibreboard* bargaining obligation. The employer in *Central Buying* was held not to have violated the Act when it failed to bargain with the union before entering into a new arrangement for an independent contractor to handle deliveries to one city. Relations with the independent contractor long antedated the union advent at the employer's

---

[319]197 NLRB 471, 80 LRRM 1555 (1972), *enforced*, 495 F2d 1375, 86 LRRM 2572 (CA 7, 1974). *See also* Torrington Constr. Co., 198 NLRB 1158, 81 LRRM 1102 (1972).

[320]For treatment of similar criteria under the Railway Labor Act, *see* Japan Air Lines Co. v. Machinists, 389 F Supp 27, 88 LRRM 2910 (SD NY, 1975), *aff'd*, 538 F2d 46, 92 LRRM 3382 (CA 2, 1976).

[321]190 NLRB 433, 77 LRRM 1235 (1971).

[322]Member Brown dissented, stating that the subcontracting was a clear departure from past practice and was thus a matter which should have required bargaining. *See* Webel Feed Mills & Pike Transit Co., 217 NLRB 815, 89 LRRM 1165 (1975) (unilateral *de minimus* subcontracting). *But see* Ohio Medical Prods., 194 NLRB 1, 78 LRRM 1488 (1971).

[323]223 NLRB 542, 92 LRRM 1145 (1976).

store, the deliveries in question constituted a small and intermittent part of the employer's business, the employer's own delivery drivers occasionally made the same deliveries, and the contracting out of the deliveries in question enabled the employer's own drivers to finish work earlier without any loss of pay. But the Board has also emphasized that legitimate economic motivation does not nullify an employer's duty to notify and bargain with the union regarding its decision to subcontract unit work as well as the effects of that decision on bargaining-unit employees.[324]

The Board has held that it is a violation of Section 8(a)(5) to insist to impasse that certain classifications be removed from a certifed bargaining unit since modification of an NLRB-certified unit is not a mandatory subject of bargaining.[325] It has also held, in *Boeing Co.*,[326] that an employer may not unilaterally transfer work from a bargaining unit represented by one union to a unit represented by another union. The Board relied on its prior decision in *University of Chicago*,[327] where it had held that an employer must obtain the union's consent to a midterm transfer of contractually established work assignments to another bargaining unit represented by a different union.[328]

---

[324]Amcar Div., *supra* note 288; Donn Prods., Inc., *supra* note 117; Seafarers Local 777 (Yellow Cab Co.), 229 NLRB 1369, 95 LRRM 1249 (1977), *modified*, 99 LRRM 2903 (CA DC, 1978), *rehearing denied*, 603 F2d 862, 101 LRRM 2628 (CA DC, 1979); Sweet Lumber Co., 227 NLRB 1084, 95 LRRM 1388 (1977); Great Chinese Am. Sewing Co., 227 NLRB 1670, 95 LRRM 1594 (1977), *enforced*, 578 F2d 251, 99 LRRM 2347 (CA 9, 1978). *See also* American President Lines, Ltd., 229 NLRB 443, 96 LRRM 1485 (1977) (no violation where union given opportunity to bargain after execution but prior to implementation of subcontract).

The applicability of the *Fibreboard* doctrine to the building and construction industry was recognized by the Board in Daniel Constr. Co., 229 NLRB 93, 95 LRRM 1442 (1977). There, the Board determined that the doctrine was applicable to a general contractor who was found to have a duty to bargain over its decision to subcontract unit work despite its prior history of subcontracting such work.

[325]*See, e.g.*, National Fresh Fruit & Vegetable Co., 227 NLRB 2014, 95 LRRM 1011 (1977), *enforcement denied*, 565 F2d 1331, 97 LRRM 2427 (CA 5, 1978). In International Harvester Co., 227 NLRB 85, 93 LRRM 1492 (1976), *enforcement granted in part and denied in part*, 618 F2d 85, 104 LRRM 3098 (CA 9, 1980), a Board majority held that the employer violated the Act when it failed to bargain with the union not only as to its decision to remove the job classification of fleet account executive from the bargaining unit and to transfer fleet account work out of the unit, but also as to the effects of such a decision on the unit employees. The Ninth Circuit disagreed as to the *decision* bargaining, but agreed as to the *effects* bargaining. *See also* Equitable Gas Co., *supra* note 293. *See* Chapter 11 *supra* for general treatment of bargaining units.

[326]230 NLRB 696, 96 LRRM 1355 (1977), *enforcement denied*, 581 F2d 793, 99 LRRM 2847 (CA 9, 1978).

[327]*Supra* notes 174-75.

[328]In *Boeing*, the Board distinguished the Seventh Circuit's opinion denying enforcement in the *University of Chicago* case, *supra* note 174, by noting that the work assigned was not identical to that being performed in each bargaining unit, there was no history

In *Seafarers Local 777* v. *NLRB*[329] the District of Columbia Circuit refused to enforce the Board's determination that taxicab companies had violated the Act by unilaterally deciding to allow their drivers to choose between leasing taxicabs or working on a commission basis. The court observed that the union had made negotiation on this issue impossible by giving a public demonstration of intransigent opposition to the leasing program, taking political action against it, and conditioning bargaining upon an illegal demand for recognition. The court also observed that *Fibreboard* and its progeny had distinguished between decisions which are primarily about the conditions of employment and thus, are mandatory subjects of bargaining, and decisions which are primarily entrepreneurial judgments about the direction of the enterprise and, thus, are not mandatory subjects. The decision at issue was, in the court's view, entrepreneurial.

b. Partial Closure, Sale of Business, or Plant Relocation. The Supreme Court has held that an employer may close its *entire* business for any reason it chooses, including an anti-union motivation. In *Textile Workers Union* v. *Darlington Manufacturing Co.*,[330] the Court recognized that a partial closing, intended "to chill unionism," could result in a violation of Section 8(a)(3), but left open the question of whether an employer must bargain about an economically motivated decision to close part of its business. In 1981 the Court answered that question in *First National Maintenance Corp.* v. *NLRB*.[331] It held that while the *effects* of such a

---

of prior transfers of such unit work, the union had always carefully policed its unit's jurisdiction, and there were no health and safety considerations allegedly involved in the transfer.

[329] *Supra* note 324.

[330] 380 US 263, 58 LRRM 2657 (1965). *See* discussion in Chapter 7, *supra* at notes 238-42. For the views of the various circuits prior to *Darlington* and *Fibreboard, see* NLRB v. Adams Dairy, Inc., 322 F2d 553, 54 LRRM 2171 (CA 8, 1963); NLRB v. New England Web, Inc., 309 F2d 696, 51 LRRM 2426 (CA 1, 1962); NLRB v. Rapid Bindery, Inc., 293 F2d 170, 48 LRRM 2658 (CA 2, 1961); NLRB v. Lassing, 284 F2d 781, 47 LRRM 2277 (CA 6, 1960); NLRB v. R. C. Mahon Co., 269 F2d 44, 44 LRRM 2479 (CA 6, 1959); NLRB v. Adkins Transfer Co., 226 F2d 324, 36 LRRM 2709 (CA 6, 1955); NLRB v. New Madrid Mfg. Co., 215 F2d 908, 34 LRRM 2844 (CA 8, 1954). *See generally:* Comment, *Labor Law-Employer's Duty to Bargain Over a Partial Closure,* 10 RUTGERS CAMDEN L. J. 737 (1979); Moss, *Plant Removal—Labor Law Issues,* 54 CALIF. S. B. J. 42 (1979); Comment, *Duty to Bargain About Termination of Operations,* 92 HARV. L. REV. 768 (1979); Morris, *supra* note 252; Bliss, *Labor Law Obligations of Parties to the Sale of a Business: Labor's Plant Closure Pains,* 24 SW. L. J. 259 (1970); Schwarz, *Plant Relocation or Partial Termination—The Duty to Decision-Bargain,* 39 FORDHAM L. REV. 81 (1970).

[331] First National Maintenance Corp. v. NLRB, *supra* note 299.

decision are subjects for mandatory bargaining,[332] the *decision* to shut down part of a business purely for economic reasons is not within Section 8(d)'s "terms and conditions of employment."

The Supreme Court's ruling in *First National Maintenance Corp.* settled the conflict among the NLRB and the circuit courts on this issue.[333] The Board's position had been that an employer must bargain about an economically motivated decision to close part of its business.[334] In *Ozark Trailers, Inc.*,[335] the Board reasoned that since the company had based its decision to partially close a plant on its claim of excessive man-hours for production and defective workmanship, and since those topics traditionally are subjects of collective bargaining, the entire matter could be submitted to bargaining just as were the labor-cost

---

[332]"There is no dispute that the union must be given a significant opportunity to bargain about these matters of job security as part of the 'effects' bargaining mandated by §8(a)(5)." *Id.* at 2711. *See also* Brockway Motor Trucks v. NLRB, 582 F2d 720, 99 LRRM 2013 (CA 3, 1978), *denying enforcement to* 230 NLRB 1002, 95 LRRM 1462 (1977).

[333]*Compare* Ozark Trailers, Inc., 161 NLRB 561, 63 LRRM 1264 (1966), *with* NLRB v. Thompson Transport Co., Inc., 165 NLRB 746, 65 LRRM 1370 (1967), *enforcement denied*, 406 F2d 698, 70 LRRM 2418 (CA 10, 1969); Brockway Motor Trucks v. NLRB, 230 NLRB 1002, 95 LRRM 1462 (1977), *enforcement denied*, 582 F2d 720, 99 LRRM 2013 (CA 3, 1978); NLRB v. Transmarine Navigation Corp., 380 F2d 933, 65 LRRM 2861 (CA 9, 1967); NLRB v. Adams Dairy, Inc., 350 F2d 108, 60 LRRM 2084 (CA 8, 1965), *cert. denied*, 382 US 1011, 61 LRRM 2192 (1966); NLRB v. Royal Plating & Polishing Co., 350 F2d 191, 60 LRRM 2033 (CA 3, 1965).

[334]*E.g.*, Thompson Transport Co., 165 NLRB 746, 65 LRRM 1370 (1967), *enforcement denied*, 406 F2d 698, 70 LRRM 2418 (CA 10, 1969); Drapery Mfg. Co., 170 NLRB 1706, 68 LRRM 1027 (1968). In Morrison Cafeterias Consol., Inc., 177 NLRB 591, 71 LRRM 1449 (1969), *reversed in part*, 431 F2d 254, 74 LRRM 3048 (CA 8, 1970), the Board sustained a §8(a)(5) charge of refusing to bargain about the decision to close, but dismissed a §8(a)(3) charge, relying on the Supreme Court's decision in NLRB v. Darlington Mfg. Co., 380 US 263, 58 LRRM 2657 (1965); the Eighth Circuit reversed as to the requirement of bargaining about the decision to close. For a discussion of *Darlington* in light of §§8(a)(1) and 8(a)(3), *see* Chapter 7 *supra* at notes 238-44. *See also* Southeastern Envelope Co., 206 NLRB 933, 84 LRRM 1577 (1973); Fraser & Johnston Co. v. NLRB, 469 F2d 1259, 81 LRRM 2964 (CA 9, 1972); Regal Aluminum, Inc., 190 NLRB 468, 77 LRRM 1303 (1971). The D. C. Circuit agreed with the Board in Garment Workers (McLoughlin Mfg. Corp.) v. NLRB, 463 F2d 907, 80 LRRM 2716 (CA DC, 1972), where the court enforced, with modifications, a Board order against an employer who had refused to bargain with the union over a decision to relocate a plant and about the effects thereof. The court distinguished the case from the decisions in Adams Dairy, *supra* note 333, and Royal Plating, *supra* note 333.

[335]161 NLRB 561, 63 LRRM 1264 (1966). *Accord*, Cooper Thermometer Co., 160 NLRB 1902, 63 LRRM 1219 (1966), *enforced in part*, 376 F2d 684, 65 LRRM 2113 (CA 2, 1967), where the Second Circuit upheld the Board's finding of a duty to bargain about transfer of employees to a new location, but refused to enforce parts of the remedy relating to back pay and reinstatement. *But see*, for distinguishable fact situations, Westinghouse Elec. Corp., 174 NLRB 636, 70 LRRM 1255 (1969), *and* Desilu Prods., Inc., 166 NLRB 1080, 65 LRRM 1727 (1967). *See also* Robertshaw Controls Co., Acro Div., 161 NLRB 103, 63 LRRM 1231 (1966) (holding that an employer had a duty to bargain over seniority rights of employees who were being transferred, along with part of the company's operations, from a union-organized plant to a new plant).

issues involved in *Fibreboard*.[336] The Board affirmed this position in its 1977 ruling in *Brockway Motor Trucks*,[337] holding that the employer violated the Act because it had not bargained over a partial shutdown decision. The Board noted that there was no showing that the employer's decision to close involved such a "significant investment or withdrawal of capital" as to "affect the scope and ultimate direction of the enterprise."[338] The Third Circuit, however, refused to enforce the order, criticizing the Board's *per se* rule on bargaining over partial closure decisions.[339]

The Fifth and Sixth Circuits adopted the Board's approach,[340] but they represented a minority position among the courts of appeals.

The Third Circuit, in *Royal Plating & Polishing Co.*,[341] concluded that nothing in *Fibreboard* required bargaining about managerial decisions "which lie at the core of entrepreneurial control," such as closing a plant to recommit and reinvest funds in the business. The Eighth Circuit, in *Royal Typewriter Co.*,[342] reaffirmed its prior decisions holding that, absent union animus, a company does not have a legal duty to bargain over the decision partially to shut down its operations for economic reasons.

The Ninth Circuit, in *Transmarine Navigation*,[343] and the Tenth Circuit, in *Thompson Transport*,[344] also repudiated the Board's

---

[336]The Board did not require that the company reopen the closed plant, but it ordered the company to pay back wages to the employees from the date of the decision to close until the date the plant was actually shut down. During this period, employees had been laid off on the basis of seniority.

[337]230 NLRB 1002, 95 LRRM 1462 (1977).

[338]GMC Truck & Coach Div., 191 NLRB 951, 77 LRRM 1537 (1971), *enforced sub nom.* Automobile Workers Local 864 v. NLRB, 470 F2d 422, 81 LRRM 2439 (CA DC, 1972). *But see* W. R. Grace & Co., 230 NLRB 617, 95 LRRM 1459 (1977) (no violation for failure to bargain over unilateral decision to close a production facility where the General Counsel conceded that the decision was motivated by legitimate business reasons, but violation of the Act was found for failure to bargain over the effects of the decision).

[339]Brockway Motor Trucks v. NLRB, 582 F2d 720, 99 LRRM 2013 (CA 3, 1978), *denying enforcement to* 230 NLRB 1002, 95 LRRM 1462 (1977).

[340]*See* NLRB v. Production Molded Plastics, 604 F2d 451, 102 LRRM 2040 (CA 6, 1979); NLRB v. Winn-Dixie Stores, Inc., 361 F2d 512, 62 LRRM 2218 (CA 5), *cert. denied,* 385 US 935, 63 LRRM 2372 (1966). The Sixth Circuit also observed, however, that Board orders involving management decisions based on economic factors should be given particularly close scrutiny in enforcement proceedings. Levine v. C & W Mining Co., 610 F2d 432, 102 LRRM 3093 (CA 6, 1979).

[341]NLRB v. Royal Plating & Polishing Co., 350 F2d 191, 60 LRRM 2033 (CA 3, 1965).

[342]209 NLRB 1006, 85 LRRM 1501 (1974), *enforced,* 533 F2d 1030, 92 LRRM 2013 (CA 8, 1976). *Cf.* Columbia Records, Div. CBS, 207 NLRB 993, 85 LRRM 1078 (1973). *See also* American Needle and Novelty Co., 206 NLRB 534, 84 LRRM 1526 (1973).

[343]NLRB v. Transmarine Navigation Corp., 380 F2d 933, 65 LRRM 2861 (CA 9, 1967).

[344]NLRB v. Thompson Transport Co., 406 F2d 698, 70 LRRM 2418 (CA 10, 1969).

position on partial closure. Where the employer had terminated his business to become a minority partner in a larger firm, the Ninth Circuit noted that "a fundamental alteration of the corporate enterprise"[345] had occurred, and "unlike *Fibreboard* it was not merely a decision to achieve economics by reducing the work force."[346]

The Board conceded that in certain partial-closure situations no duty to bargain existed, and the reviewing circuit courts agreed. This was so, for example, when, after a partial closure, the employer was no longer involved in the industry, as was the case in *General Motors*,[347] where the D.C. Circuit affirmed the Board's refusal to apply *Fibreboard* to the sale of a facility. Similarly, in *NLRB* v. *Rude Carrier Corp.*,[348] the Board and the Fourth Circuit were in agreement that bargaining was not required over the decision to discontinue a complete and discrete product line. The Board also recognized that exigent circumstances might excuse the bargaining requirement. Thus, in *Brooks-Scanlon*,[349] the Board concluded that the employer need not bargain over the decision to close an operation where that decision was predicated on economic factors so compelling that bargaining could not have altered them.

In *Brockway*,[350] however, the Third Circuit attempted to steer a middle path between the position that an employer always has a duty to bargain regarding a partial-closure decision, except where the closure constitutes a complete termination of a discrete line of business, and the position that such a decision need never be bargained so long as it is not motivated by anti-union sentiment.[351] The Second Circuit adopted this Third Circuit's

---

[345]380 F2d at 937.

[346]*Id.*

[347]Automobile Workers Local 864 (General Motors Corp.) v. NLRB, 470 F2d 422, 81 LRRM 2439 (CA DC, 1972).

[348]93 LRRM 2297 (CA 4, 1976).

[349]246 NLRB 476, 102 LRRM 1606 (1979). This rationale was applied also in Raskin Packing Co., 246 NLRB 78, 102 LRRM 1489 (1979), and M & M Transport Co., 239 NLRB 73, 100 LRRM 1076 (1978), where the need for immediate action occasioned by a lack of operating capital was held to have excused the duty to bargain over the decision to close. Financial constraints also precluded issuance of a complaint over a charged failure to bargain in Food Fair Stores, Inc., NLRB Case Nos. 4-CA-9925 and 9955, 103 LRRM 1503 (1980). In that advice opinion, the General Counsel relied, in part, on the need for immediate action by a debtor in possession upon discovery of overwhelming losses that were far worse than had been anticipated.

[350]582 F2d 720, 99 LRRM 2013 (CA 3, 1978), *denying enforcement to* 230 NLRB 1002, 95 LRRM 1462 (1977).

[351]*See* Royal Typewriter Co. v. NLRB, *supra* note 342.

compromise in deciding *NLRB* v. *First National Maintenance Corp.*,[352] which was overruled thereafter by the Supreme Court.[353]

The issue in *First National Maintenance Corp.* involved "an economically-motivated decision to shut down part of a business."[354] The employer provided housekeeping, cleaning, and maintenance services for its customers for a set management fee plus reimbursement of the costs of the labor force, which the employer hired separately for each customer. As a result of a dispute over the fee, the employer terminated its contract with one of its nursing home customers. This occurred shortly after a union had been certified as the bargaining representative of the employees assigned to the nursing home. When the employer refused to bargain over the decision to close its nursing home operation, the union filed an unfair labor practice charge. The Board ordered the employer to bargain over the decision to close as well as the effects of that decision, to pay back pay, and to offer the discharged employees equivalent employment. The Second Circuit enforced the Board's order, applying a presumption analysis, which the Supreme Court characterized as

> a *presumption* in favor of mandatory bargaining over such a decision, a presumption that is rebuttable "by showing that the purposes of the statute would not be furthered by imposition of a duty to bargain," for example, by demonstrating that "bargaining over the decision would be futile," or that the decision was due to "emergency financial circumstances" or that the "custom of the industry shown by the absence of such an obligation from typical collective bargaining agreements is not to bargain over such decisions."[355]

In reversing the Second Circuit, Justice Blackmun, writing for the majority, stated that bargaining over such decisions "should be required only if the benefit, for labor-management relations and the collective bargaining process, outweighs the burden placed on the conduct of the business."[356] The Court recognized the union's "legitimate concern over job security"[357] but noted that sufficient safeguards existed in the union's right to bargain over the *effects* of the decision and the protection against union animus afforded by Section 8(a)(3). The Court also noted that,

---

[352]627 F2d 596, 104 LRRM 2924 (CA 2, 1980).
[353]For a discussion of the impact of *First National Maintenance* on the conceptual nature of mandatory subjects of bargaining, *see* Chapter 16 *supra* at notes 56-69.
[354]First National Maintenance Corp. v. NLRB, *supra* note 299, 107 LRRM at 2710.
[355]*Id.* at 2707.
[356]*Id.* at 2710.
[357]*Id.*

if labor costs are a factor in the decision to close, "management will have an incentive to confer voluntarily with the union to seek concessions that may make continuing the business profitable."[358] Although the Court recognized many instances where unions aided employers in saving failing businesses, the Court felt it was unlikely "that requiring bargaining over the decision itself . . . will augment this flow of information and suggestions."[359] The Court de-emphasized a factor which had heavily influenced some of the circuit courts by stating that "we do not believe that the absence of 'significant investment or withdrawal of capital' . . . is crucial."[360]

Applying its analysis to the facts before it, the Court found that the balance tipped in favor of management:

> We conclude that the harm likely to be done to an employer's need to operate freely in deciding whether to shut down part of its business purely for economic reasons outweighs the incremental benefit that might be gained through the union's participation in making the decision, and we hold that the decision itself is *not* part of 8(d)'s "terms and conditions" over which Congress has mandated bargaining.[361]

The Court further supported its view with its conclusion that "Congress had no expectation that the elected union representative would become an equal partner in the running of the business enterprise in which the union's members are employed."[362]

Explicitly reserved in *First National Maintenance Corp.* were the questions of bargaining over plant relocation and sale decisions.[363] In 1966 the Board had addressed the problems of plant shutdown and plant relocation together in *Ozark Trailers,* concluding that there was "no justification for interpreting the statutory bargaining obligation so narrowly as to exclude plant removal and shutdown from its scope."[364] Later, as to sale of a business, the Board and the D.C. Circuit agreed in *General Motors*[365] that the decision was not subject to mandatory bargaining.

---

[358]*Id.* at 2711.
[359]*Id.*
[360]*Id.* at 2713.
[361]*Id.* Emphasis in original.
[362]*Id.* at 2709.
[363]*Id.* at 2713 n.22.
[364]*Supra* note 333 at 570.
[365]191 NLRB 951, 952, 77 LRRM 1537, 1539 (1971). In holding that an employer was not obligated to bargain with the union over its decision to sell a dealership facility,

Despite the new questions raised by *First National Maintenance*,[366] there will still be cases in which an employer will be ordered to bargain, if not about the decision to close or relocate a plant, then about the effects of such decision. Remedies in this area have been, and are likely to continue to be, among the most difficult that the Board must fashion. This is so because of the inevitable economic consequences of efforts to restore the status quo ante.[367] The remedy for a violation where the employer has closed without giving the union notice or an adequate opportunity to bargain has varied with the circumstances. In *Soule Glass & Glazing Co.*[368] the Board ordered the employer to reopen operations, to restore unit work, and to bargain in good faith over any proposed changes in the bargaining unit. The Board found in that case, however, that the inconvenience to the employer in reopening was "relatively slight" because it involved only some movement of trucks and supplies. In *National Family Opinion, Inc.*,[369] however, where the employer unlawfully failed to bargain over its decision to close a department, the Board did not require the reestablishment of the discontinued operation, because to do so would have required significant expense and disruption. But the Board did overrule previous decisions to hold that the employer's back-pay liability to employees terminated by reason of the discontinued operation would extend from the date of termination until the occurrence of the earliest of four conditions: (1) the parties bargain to agreement on subjects about which the employer is required to bargain, (2) the parties reach a bona fide impasse in bargaining, (3) the failure of the union to request bargaining within five days of

---

but was obligated to bargain as to the effects of that decision on the unit, the Board's majority stated:

"It appears that the Board has not dealt definitely with the specific question whether the Act imposes a duty to bargain over a decision to sell an employing enterprise. We believe, however, that this issue is controlled by the rationale the courts have generally adopted in closely related cases, that decisions such as this, in which a significant investment or withdrawal of capital will affect the scope and ultimate direction of an enterprise, are matters essentially financial and managerial in nature. They thus lie at the very core of entrepreneurial control, and are not the types of subjects which Congress intended to encompass within 'rates of pay, wages, hours of employment, or other conditions of employment.' Such managerial decisions often times require secrecy as well as the freedom to act quickly and decisively. They also involve subject areas as to which the determinative financial and operational considerations are likely to be unfamiliar to the employees and their representatives."

See also Merryweather Optical Co., 240 NLRB 1213, 100 LRRM 1412 (1979).

[366]*See* Chapter 16 *supra* at note 69.
[367]*See* Chapter 33 *infra* at notes 255-66.
[368]246 NLRB 792, 102 LRRM 1693 (1979).
[369]246 NLRB 521, 102 LRRM 1641 (1979).

the issuance of the bargaining order, or to commence negotiations within five days of the employer's notice to the union of its desire to bargain, or (4) the subsequent failure of the union to bargain in good faith. The remedy for an employer's failure to bargain over a decision to close an operation should be contrasted with the more limited remedy provided for an employer's failure to bargain solely with respect to the effects of the decision. For an effects-bargaining violation, the usual remedy is to order back pay starting five days after the date of the Board's decision and order and continuing until the occurrence of the earliest of the four conditions listed above, with a minimum of two weeks back pay.[370]

In two decisions in 1980, the Board ordered employers to resume operations at plants which had been unilaterally closed. In *Smythe Manufacturing Co.*,[371] where the employer had closed its plant and subcontracted the work to a third party without decision bargaining, the Board ordered the employer to resume operations at the closed plant and reinstate the laid-off employees with back pay. The Board justified its order on the fact that the employer's business was presently thriving and this strong remedy would not threaten its existence. The Board also reasoned that ordering resumption of discontinued operations in this case amounted simply to directing the employer to resume a course which it had initially regarded as a sound economic venture. Similarly, in *Weather Tamer*,[372] the Board ordered an employer who had unlawfully closed its plant following the union's victory in a certification election to reinstate operations. The Board held that restoring the *status quo ante* is appropriate in such situations unless the employer can show that its continued viability would be endangered by such a remedy. Here, the Board found that no heavy investment of capital would be required to restore operations, since the work had not been discontinued but was being performed at another plant.

c. Merger of Business. The First Circuit held in a case arising under the Railway Labor Act, that an employer is not required to negotiate with a union either about its decision to merge with

---

[370]National Car Rental, 252 NLRB 159, 105 LRRM 1263 (1980); *see also* the discussion in National Family Opinion, Inc., *supra* note 369 at 522 n. 5.
[371]247 NLRB 1139, 103 LRRM 1432 (1980).
[372]253 NLRB 293, 105 LRRM 1569 (1980).

another company or about the effects of the merger.[373] The court noted that the merger did not displace large numbers of workers or deprive them of benefits, the usual justifications for such bargaining.[374]

13. Successorship and Other Clauses Relating to Persons Outside the Employment Relationship. The Board has held that "successorship" clauses and "application of contract" clauses are mandatory subjects of bargaining. In *Mine Workers*[375] the "successorship" clause required the employer to secure a successor's assumption of collective bargaining agreement obligations before transfer of the business operation, and the "application of contract" clause required the employer to apply the collective bargaining agreement to employees at all of its coal properties, including those acquired after the effective date of the contract.[376] The Board found (1) the "successorship" clause would vitally affect the terms and conditions of employment for employees who remained employed at the mine after an employer transfer of ownership, and (2) the "application of contract" clause vitally affected the terms and conditions of employment by serving to protect the jobs and work standards of bargaining unit employees through the removal of economic incentives which might encourage the employer to transfer work to other mines under its control. With respect to the "successorship clause," the Tenth Circuit enforced the Board's order; but with respect

---

[373]Machinists Dist. 147 v. Northeast Airlines, Inc., 473 F2d 549, 80 LRRM 2197 (CA 1, 1972), *cert. denied*, 409 US 845, 81 LRRM 2390 (1972). For a consideration of the effect of such changes on the rights of the parties under the NLRA, *see* Chapter 15 *supra. See generally* Coughlin & de Kerckhove, *Labor Problems in Mergers and Acquisitions,* 47 WISC. B. BULL. 29 (Oct. 1974); Abodeely, *The Effect of Reorganization, Merger or Acquisition on the Appropriate Bargaining Unit,* 39 GEO. WASH. L. REV. 488 (March 1971). *See also* Monongahela Valley Hosp., Inc., 248 NLRB 69, 103 LRRM 1393 (1980).

[374]Although the case arose under the Railway Labor Act, the court analyzed cases under the NLRA and considered the impact of the Supreme Court's decision in *Fibreboard.*

[375]Mine Workers (Lone Star Steel Co.), 231 NLRB 573, 96 LRRM 1083 (1977), *enforcement granted in part, denied in part, and remanded,* 618 F2d 698, 104 LRRM 3144 (CA 10, 1980). *See also* Amax Coal Co. v. NLRB, 614 F2d 872, 103 LRRM 2482 (CA 3, 1980). *See generally* Comment, *Successorship Clauses in Collective Bargaining Agreements,* 1979 BRIGHAM YOUNG U. L. REV. 99; Comment, *Defining "Successors" and the Significance of a Successors and Assigns Clause in a Collective Bargaining Agreement,* 49 TUL. L. REV. 644 (1975); Gaus & Morris, *Successorship and the Collective Bargaining Agreement: Accommodating Wiley and Burns,* 59 VA. L. REV. 1359 (Nov. 1973); Stern, *Binding the Successor Employer to Its Predecessor's Collective Agreement Under The NLRA,* 45 TEMP. L. Q. 1 (1971).

[376]The Board cited Allied Chem. & Alkali Workers Local 1 v. Pittsburgh Plate Glass Co., *supra* note 40, as defining a mandatory subject of bargaining as one which settles "an aspect of the relationship between the employer and his employees," but also noted that the court in *Pittsburgh Plate Glass* had recognized that a matter involving individuals outside the employment relationship is a mandatory subject of bargaining *only* if it

to the "application of contract clause" it disagreed with the Board and held that it was not a mandatory subject of bargaining.[377] The court stated that the latter clause failed to satisfy each portion of the requisite two-prong test in order for a subject involving employees outside the bargaining unit to be a mandatory subject of bargaining: (1) The subject must "vitally affect" terms and conditions or job security of unit employees and (2) represent a direct frontal attack on a problem thought to threaten the basic wage structure established by the collective bargaining agreement.

The Eighth Circuit, in *Associated General Contractors*,[378] has adopted the Board's view that a "no-conflicting agreement" clause is not a mandatory subject of bargaining. The clause in question would have prevented the union from entering into any collective bargaining agreement with another employer that was more favorable in any respect, unless it offered similar favorable terms to the multi-employer bargaining association. The court reasoned that there was simply no basis to conclude that such a "no-conflicting agreement" clause would have vitally affected the wages, hours, and conditions of employment of bargaining unit employees.

14. Arrangements and Conditions for Negotiations. The Board has ruled that the parties must bargain collectively about the preliminary arrangements for negotiations in the same manner as they must bargain about substantive terms or conditions of employment. Preliminary arrangements include such matters as scheduling the time, place, length and agenda of meetings.[379] The Board has stated that "such preliminary matters are just as much a part of the process of collective bargaining as negotiation over wages, hours, etc."[380] In *Case, Inc.*,[381] the Board held that

---

"*vitally* affects the 'terms and conditions' of [bargaining-unit employees'] employment." (Emphasis supplied by the court.)

[377]Lone Star Steel Co. v. NLRB, *supra* note 375.

[378]Associated Gen. Contractors of No. Dakota v. NLRB, 637 F2d 556, 106 LRRM 2131 (CA 8, 1981), *enforcing* 245 NLRB 328, 102 LRRM 1478 (1979).

[379]*See* Ustad, *Use and Abuse of Ground Rules in Labor Negotiations*, 15 A. F.L.-C.I.O. REV. 102 (1973).

[380]General Elec. Co., 173 NLRB 253, 257, 69 LRRM 1305 (1968). The refusal of the employer to attend scheduled meetings and to deal with preliminary matters where such refusal was based on an improper objection to the composition of the union's committee constituted a violation of §8(a)(5). On review, however, the Second Circuit held that the employer "had an absolute right to refrain from preliminary meetings before the formal notice of reopening [of the contract] and it could condition its agreement to preliminary discussions . . . ." The court thus made a distinction between preliminary and formal bargaining sessions. 412 F2d 512, 521, 71 LRRM 2418 (CA 2,

an employer with facilities in Kentucky and Tennessee violated the Act by its demand that the union which represented its Kentucky employees meet with the employer in New York or, in the alternative, negotiate by telephone or mail.

The order in which issues are discussed at the bargaining table may be subjected to an increased level of scrutiny. The Board and the First Circuit have held that, absent union agreement, an employer's insistence that noneconomic issues be discussed and resolved before major economic issues are addressed violates Section 8(a)(5).[382]

The constituency of the committee representing either the employer or the union is not a mandatory subject of bargaining, because the law guarantees each party the right to choose its own representatives free of any influence from the other.[383]

The Board and the Fifth Circuit have held that the issue of remuneration of employee members of the shop committee for time spent in negotiating a collective bargaining agreement is a mandatory subject of bargaining.[384] The Board analogized the issue of payment of wages during collective bargaining to the issue of payment of wages during presentation of grievances, finding that the issue of wage payments during negotiations "vitally affect[s]" the relations between an employer and employees and "constitutes an aspect of a relationship between the employer and employees."[385] The Fifth Circuit agreed with this

---

1969). (In other respects, particularly relating to the employer's objections to the makeup of the union's bargaining committee, the Board's decision and order was affirmed.) *See* Chapter 13 *supra* at notes 734-61 for treatment of coalition and coordinated bargaining.
[381]237 NLRB 798, 99 LRRM 1159 (1978).
[382]South Shore Hosp., 245 NLRB 848, 102 LRRM 1565 (1979), *enforced,* 630 F2d 40, 105 LRRM 2640 (CA 1, 1980).
[383]General Elec. Co., *supra* note 386. For general treatment of bargaining conduct required for good-faith bargaining, *see* Chapter 13 *supra,* also note 386 *infra. See also* AMF, Inc., 219 NLRB 903, 90 LRRM 1271 (1975), where the employer refused to negotiate with a local union unless the union excluded from its negotiating team 10 representatives from a committee which had been created by the International to give assistance in contract-negotiation to its affiliated locals. The Board observed that each party to the collective bargaining process has the right to choose the members of its negotiating team and that there was no evidence presented by the employer that the presence of the individuals in question would have made good-faith bargaining impractical or that they would have sought to negotiate on behalf of employees other than those belonging to the bargaining unit represented by the local union. For detailed treatment of the requirements of §8(b)(1)(B) as to union restraint and coercion in the selection of employer representatives, *see* Chapter 6 *supra* at notes 582-612.
[384]Axelson, Inc., 234 NLRB 414, 97 LRRM 1234 (1978), *enforced,* 599 F2d 91, 101 LRRM 3007 (CA 5, 1979).
[385]234 NLRB at 415. *Cf.* Western Block Co., 229 NLRB 482, 96 LRRM 1415 (1977) (violation of §8(a)(5) where employer unilaterally promulgated policy of charging union for services of employees engaged in union business during working hours).

analogy, observing that remuneration benefited all members of the bargaining unit by encouraging the collective bargaining process, thus making it a mandatory subject.

In a 1978 decision, *Bartlett-Collins Co.*,[386] the Board overruled its prior decisions concerning stenographers at bargaining sessions and held that issues as to the presence of a stenographer during negotiations and the use of a recording device to record those negotiations are permissive rather than mandatory subjects. The Board reasoned that the question of whether a stenographer should be present during negotiations is a "threshold matter, preliminary and subordinate to substantive negotiations,"[387] and that the Board would be avoiding its statutory responsibility to foster and encourage meaningful negotiations were it to permit a party to stifle negotiations in their inception over such an issue. The Tenth Circuit enforced the Board's order, noting that any advantages from stenographic records are outweighed by the disadvantage of allowing a party to insist to impasse upon the presence of a court reporter.

In *Latrobe Steel Corp.* v. *NLRB*,[388] the Third Circuit also adopted the Board's reasoning, holding that the presence of stenographers at bargaining sessions is a permissive subject. The court's decision acknowledged that Board determinations on mandatory bargaining subjects are entitled to substantial deference where they are fully explained and reasoned and consistent with the Act.

---

[386]237 NLRB 770, 99 LRRM 1034 (1978), *enforced*, 639 F2d 652, 106 LRRM 2272 (CA 10, 1981).
[387]237 NLRB at 773.
[388]630 F2d 171, 105 LRRM 2393 (CA 3, 1980), *enforcing in part* 244 NLRB 528, 102 LRRM 1175 (1979).

CHAPTER 18

PERMISSIVE AND ILLEGAL SUBJECTS OF BARGAINING

I. INTRODUCTION

If a given subject falls within the phrase "wages, hours, and other terms and conditions of employment,"[1] it is a mandatory subject of bargaining;[2] if it falls outside that phrase, it is either a permissive subject (about which the parties may, but are not required to bargain),[3] or an illegal subject (about which the parties are forbidden to bargain).

These distinctions were recognized by the Supreme Court in 1958 in the landmark *Borg-Warner* case.[4] Since the Court's decision in that case, the Board and the courts have continued to apply and refine the distinction between mandatory and permissive subjects. Although the decisions of the Board and the courts set forth increasingly finer distinctions turning on the individual facts of each case, the legal rationale for these decisions continues to inhere in the interpretation of the statutory phrase, "wages, hours, and other terms and conditions of employment."

II. PERMISSIVE SUBJECTS OF BARGAINING

A. Early Cases

Since the issue first was raised in the early years of the Wagner Act, the Board has consistently held that there are certain sub-

---

[1] §8(d).

[2] *See generally* Chapter 16 *supra.*

[3] *See* Chapter 17 *supra.* For bibliographical references, *see* citations in pertinent notes throughout this chapter and in Chapter 17 *supra.*

[4] NLRB v. Borg-Warner Corp., 356 US 342, 42 LRRM 2034 (1958). *See* notes 43-44 *infra* and accompanying text. *See also* Chapter 16 for a detailed discussion of the case.

jects about which the parties are free to bargain even though by their nature they are not mandatory subjects of bargaining.

Among the earliest of these holdings were the cases dealing with the posting of performance bonds or surety bonds that would indemnify one party to a contract if damages resulted from a breach by the other party. The Board held that as a matter of law an employer could not insist upon a union posting such a bond as a condition precedent to the execution of an agreement.[5] In 1944 the Board held, in the *Eppinger* case,[6] that an employer could not compel a union to bargain on the question of the licensing of union agents even though Florida statutorily required such licensing.[7]

In none of these cases were the terms "voluntary" or "permissive" subjects of bargaining expressly employed. However, the reasoning which supported the holdings demonstrated that the Board was using these concepts, since in each case an employer was found guilty of a refusal to bargain because it insisted that agreement on a subject, itself not illegal, was nevertheless a condition precedent to bargaining. It was not until *Borg-Warner* that the terms were extensively used.

B. General Rules

In *Borg-Warner,* the Supreme Court made it clear that bargaining need not be confined to statutory subjects. It is lawful for either party to propose for inclusion in a collective bargaining contract any clause within the field of permissive subjects of bargaining; the parties may bargain in good faith about that clause, and, if an agreement is reached, may include it in the final contract. But the Court also made it clear that neither party is required to bargain about permissive subjects. If either party refuses to do so, there is no violation of Sections 8(a)(5) or 8(b)(3). Adamant refusal to bargain with respect to a permissive subject, or, if there has been voluntary bargaining with respect to a permissive subject, adamant refusal either to include the subject at all or to agree to a particular resolution of a voluntary subject, is not unlawful. Conversely, if as a condition precedent

---

[5]Benson Produce Co., 71 NLRB 888, 19 LRRM 1060 (1946); Scripto Mfg. Co., 36 NLRB 411, 9 LRRM 156 (1941); Interstate Steamship Co., 36 NLRB 1307, 9 LRRM 200 (1941); Jasper Blackburn Products Corp., 21 NLRB 1240, 6 LRRM 169 (1940).
[6]Eppinger & Russell Co., 56 NLRB 1259, 14 LRRM 164 (1944).
[7]*Cf.* Hill v. Florida, 325 US 538, 16 LRRM 734 (1945). *See* Chapter 31 at note 18.

to entering into a collective agreement, one party, in the face of a refusal by the other, adamantly insists upon a clause which constitutes a permissive subject, such conduct is *per se* (without regard to subjective good or bad faith) an unfair labor practice within the meaning of Sections 8(a)(5) or 8(b)(3) because "such conduct is, in substance, a refusal to bargain about the subjects that are within the scope of mandatory bargaining."[8] In addition, a party's conduct in regard to a permissive subject may be evidence of subjective good or bad faith in bargaining.[9]

Either party may bargain about a permissive topic as if it were a mandatory subject without losing the right, at any time before agreement is reached, to take a firm position that the matter shall not be included in a contract between the parties. To sustain a claim of waiver based upon a course of bargaining "would penalize a party to negotiations for endeavoring to reach agreement by consenting to bargaining upon issues as to which the Act does not require him to bargain."[10] As the Fourth Circuit stated:

> A determination that a subject which is non-mandatory at the outset may become mandatory merely because a party had exercised this freedom [to bargain or not to bargain] by not rejecting the proposal at once, or sufficiently early, might unduly discourage free bargaining on non-mandatory matters. Parties might feel compelled to reject non-mandatory proposals out of hand to avoid risking waiver of the right to reject.[11]

Applying this principle, the Supreme Court held that when a permissive subject is included in a collective bargaining agreement, that subject is not transformed into a mandatory one even for the term of that agreement.[12] It follows, that once a contract has expired a party has no obligation to bargain over a permissive subject even though one or more past contracts contained a provision dealing with that subject.[13]

---

[8]Borg-Warner, *supra* note 4 at 349.
[9]Steere Broadcasting Corp., 158 NLRB 487, 62 LRRM 1083 (1966).
[10]Kit Mfg. Co., 150 NLRB 662, 58 LRRM 1140 (1964), *enforced*, 365 F2d 829, 62 LRRM 2856 (CA 9, 1966).
[11]NLRB v. Davison, 318 F2d 550, 558, 53 LRRM 2462 (CA 4, 1963).
[12]Chemical Workers v. Pittsburgh Plate Glass Co., 404 US 157, 78 LRRM 2974 (1971). As a consequence, the Court held that unilateral midterm modification of a permissive subject that had been included in the agreement did not constitute an unfair labor practice under the Act. *See* Chapter 16 *supra* at notes 36-55.
[13]*E.g.*, Columbus Printing Pressmen, 219 NLRB 268, 89 LRRM 1553 (1975), *enforced*, 543 F2d 1161, 93 LRRM 3055 (CA 5, 1976), discussed at notes 65-66 *infra*.

It must be noted, however, that once a party does agree to a contract which includes a permissive subject, it violates Section 8(d) if it later refuses to reduce the agreement to writing,[14] and that agreement is entirely enforceable pursuant to Section 301.[15]

A party's position at the bargaining table will not be jeopardized by its putting forward a package proposal containing both mandatory and permissive items. Thus, in *Nordstrom, Inc.*[16] the employer linked a wage proposal with proposals relating to permissive subjects. The employer refused to sign a contract limited to its mandatory proposals. Dismissing the refusal-to-bargain complaint, the Board held that the union could not selectively accept portions of the employer's package offer, noting that permissive subjects may have costs which affect the employer's wage proposals. While a party may not insist to impasse upon permissive proposals, it may alter its mandatory proposals in light of the withdrawal or rejection of the permissive subjects. Thus, one party cannot conclude negotiations by agreeing only to those proposals of the other party which comprise mandatory subjects of bargaining unless "all other matters have previously, and independent of the outstanding non-mandatory subject, been agreed upon."[17]

C. A Catalog of Permissive Subjects of Bargaining

1. Definition of Bargaining Unit. Whenever bargaining takes place without a prior Board definition of unit, the parties must agree upon the unit to be covered by the contract they negotiate. "The parties cannot bargain meaningfully about wages or hours or conditions of employment unless they know the unit of bargaining."[18] Even when the Board has defined a unit, the parties are free to agree on a negotiated unit different from the certified or recognized unit. In advanced forms of collective bargaining there may be multiple bargaining units applicable to the employees in one certified unit, and one unit may include more than a single certified or recognized unit.[19] In each such instance, the

---

[14]Associated Bldg. Contractors of Evansville, Inc., 143 NLRB 678, 53 LRRM 1395 (1963), *enforced as modified,* NLRB v. Painters, 334 F2d 729, 56 LRRM 2648 (CA 7, 1964). §8(d) requires "the execution of a written contract incorporating *any* agreement . . . if requested by either party. . . ." (Emphasis added.)

[15]*See* Chapter 19 for discussion of enforcement of collective bargaining agreements.

[16]229 NLRB 601, 96 LRRM 1092 (1977).

[17]*Id.* at 602.

[18]Douds v. Longshoremen, 241 F2d 278, 39 LRRM 2388 (CA 2, 1957).

[19]Consensual bargaining patterns may assume many different forms. The actual unit for negotiations may not even coincide with the certified or recognized unit—some

combination of units may be established by voluntary agreement of the parties.[20] The Board accepts as lawful the bargaining units which the parties establish by consensual agreement.[21] Similarly, since there may be several appropriate units applicable to any group of employees,[22] parties are free to agree upon which such unit their contract will cover.

While extensive bargaining about the unit commonly occurs, scope of the unit is not a mandatory subject of bargaining. As noted by the Second Circuit:

> The statute imposes on labor and management alike a duty to bargain in good faith with respect to wages, hours and other conditions of employment. . . . This duty "does not compel either party to agree to a proposal," as Section 8(d) states, "or require the making of a concession," and the Board has no power to settle any of those questions. By way of contrast, it not only has power, but is indeed directed, to decide what is the appropriate bargaining unit in each case.[23]

Where the Board has originally fixed the unit, "it may be altered by agreement of the parties,"[24] but the party seeking to alter the unit may not insist on the alteration to the point of impasse.[25] The Board has approved the voluntary combination into one multiplant unit of several previously certified individual plant units,[26] but insistence to impasse on such a combination is unlawful.[27]

---

issues may be negotiated in local units while other issues may be negotiated in larger units. For example, it is not uncommon for the negotiating unit for pensions to be larger than the negotiating unit for seniority.

[20]*See generally* discussion of multi-employer bargaining units in Chapter 11 *supra* and discussion of multilevel bargaining units at notes 411-16 therein.

[21]Radio Corp. of America, 135 NLRB 980, 49 LRRM 1606 (1962); General Motors Corp., 120 NLRB 1215, 42 LRRM 1143 (1958); Lever Brothers Co., 96 NLRB 448, 28 LRRM 1544 (1951).

[22]*See* Chapter 11 *supra* at notes 2-4.

[23]Douds v. Longshoremen, *supra* note 18.

[24]*Id.*

[25]*See* Canterbury Gardens, 238 NLRB 864, 99 LRRM 1279 (1978); *but see* Salt River Valley Water Users' Ass'n, 204 NLRB 83, 83 LRRM 1536 (1973), *enforced,* 498 F2d 393, 86 LRRM 2873 (CA 9, 1974), where the Board found the employer violated §8(a)(5) by insisting to impasse upon excluding certain employees from the bargaining unit in the mistaken belief that they were supervisors. *See also* National Fresh Fruit & Vegetable Co., 227 NLRB 2014, 95 LRRM 1011 (1977), *enforcement denied,* 565 F2d 1331, 97 LRRM 2427 (CA 5, 1978); Retail Clerks Local 588 (Raley's), 224 NLRB 1638, 92 LRRM 1381 (1976), *enforcement denied,* 565 F2d 769, 96 LRRM 2811 (CA DC, 1977); Newport News Shipbuilding & Dry Dock Co., 236 NLRB 1637, 98 LRRM 1475 (1978); Teamsters Local 46 (Guinness-Harp Corp.), 236 NLRB 1160, 98 LRRM 1523 (1978); Newspaper Printing Corp., 232 NLRB 291, 97 LRRM 1066 (1977); Beyerl Chevrolet, Inc., 221 NLRB 710, 91 LRRM 1030 (1975).

[26]General Motors Corp., *supra* note 21; Radio Corp. of America, *supra* note 21.

[27]Young & Hay Transp. Co., 214 NLRB 252, 87 LRRM 1319 (1974), *enforced sub nom.* Teamsters Local 54 v. Young & Hay Transp. Co., 522 F2d 562, 90 LRRM 2363 (CA 8,

The distinction between mandatory and permissive subjects of bargaining with respect to the scope of the unit is often an elusive one, particularly in coordinated or coalition bargaining.[28] For example, in *AFL-CIO Joint Negotiating Committee (Phelps Dodge Corp.) v. NLRB*,[29] various unions representing a number of employee units requested bargaining through a joint committee, the aim of which was joint company-wide bargaining. When the company refused to participate, the joint negotiating committee instead engaged in separate negotiations at various locations, insisting on identical demands at each. Although the union struck in support of its uniform demands, at no time did it bargain at one location with respect to the wages or employment conditions at other locations. Overruling the Board, the Third Circuit held that even though the uniform simultaneous demands tended to support the union objective of company-wide bargaining, a permissive subject, the demands were legitimate mandatory subjects over which the unions could bargain to impasse. "The fact that a demand may have extra-unit effects does not alter its status as a mandatory subject of bargaining."[30] When, however, a union demands the merging of several units for company-wide bargaining on certain issues, it is no defense to claim that separate unit negotiations would be ineffective.[31]

As a general rule, it is an unfair labor practice for either party to insist that employees be added to or excluded from a certified unit. Thus, an employer's insistence to point of impasse upon excluding certain employees from the bargaining unit, in the

---

1975); Longshoremen, 118 NLRB 1481, 40 LRRM 1408 (1957), *set aside on other grounds*, 277 F2d 681, 45 LRRM 2551 (CA DC, 1960); Douds v. Longshoremen, 241 F2d 278, 39 LRRM 2388 (CA 2, 1957).

[28]*See* Chapter 13 *supra* at notes 734-61.

[29]459 F2d 374, 79 LRRM 2939 (CA 3, 1972), *cert. denied*, 409 US 1059, 81 LRRM 2893 (1972).

[30]*Id.* at 726. The Board had found a §8(b)(3) violation based on its conclusion that the unions never abandoned their overall objective of a company-wide labor agreement, and that their simultaneous, uniform demands at the separate locations constituted an attempt to engage in company-wide bargaining, beyond the scope of the established bargaining units, without the company's consent. AFL-CIO Joint Negotiating Comm. (Phelps Dodge Corp.), 184 NLRB 976, 74 LRRM 1705 (1970). The court noted that it would be illegal for a party to employ mandatory demands as mere stratagems to achieve a nonmandatory objective, but held that the record in the case did not support such a finding of bad faith. 470 F2d at 726.

[31]Oil Workers (Shell Oil Co.) v. NLRB, 486 F2d 1266, 84 LRRM 2581 (CA DC, 1973). The court affirmed the Board's determination (Shell Oil Co., 194 NLRB 988, 79 LRRM 1130 (1972)) that Shell did not violate §8(a)(5) by refusing the union's demand for a single negotiation of revisions to five fringe benefit plans covering 19 separate units. The court noted in passing that the 19 units together constituted only 17% of all employees covered by the five plans.

mistaken belief that they were supervisors within the meaning of Section 2(11), was held to be a violation of Section 8(a)(5).[32] Nevertheless, under the unique facts in *Newspaper Production Co. v. NLRB*,[33] the Fifth Circuit affirmed a Board order which allowed a union to bargain to impasse over the scope of the bargaining unit. There a union which represented a unit of skilled photoengravers under a contract about to expire was chosen to represent three general production workers of the same employer. While negotiations concerning the newly represented employees were pending, the photoengravers' contract expired; the union then insisted to the point of striking that the general production workers be included in a single bargaining unit with the photoengravers under one contract. In affirming the Board's conclusion that the union's conduct did not violate Section 8(b)(3), the court held that a provision in the expiring photoengravers' contract reflected the parties' intent to include the scope of the bargaining unit among the issues to be resolved at the bargaining table.[34] The court noted that the present case, unlike others, involved neither interference with the representational rights of employees affected by the unit expansion nor a jurisdictional dispute between two unions.[35]

The Second Circuit reached a contrary result in *Sperry Rand Corp. v. NLRB*.[36] There, the union attempted to represent certain of the employer's California employees who fell outside a New York bargaining unit.[37] The court characterized the union's actions as "a *sub rosa* attempt to gain the *de facto* recognition as bargaining agent" of the California employees that it had failed to achieve through an election. When the union sought enforce-

---

[32]Salt River Valley Water Users' Ass'n, *supra* note 25. It was the employer's position that the duties of certain employees had changed, making them excluded supervisors. The Board held they were not supervisors; thus the employer's insistence to impasse that they be excluded from the bargaining unit was a violation. Presumably, if the employer had been correct (that the excluded employees were supervisors) its stance would have been proper.

[33]503 F2d 821, 87 LRRM 2650 (CA 5, 1974), *enforcing* 205 NLRB 738, 84 LRRM 1186 (1973).

[34]This provision provided for inclusion under the contract of any previously unaffiliated department that chooses the union as its bargaining representative. *But see* text accompanying note 12 *supra*.

[35]The union already represented the general production workers it sought to include in the bargaining unit. Moreover, the broader unit sought would not have conflicted with the previous unit certification, and the employer conceded that it was an appropriate unit under established Board principles.

[36]492 F2d 63, 85 LRRM 2521 (CA 2, 1974), *cert. denied*, 419 US 831, 87 LRRM 2397 (1974).

[37]The union had filed a representation petition to represent those workers but subsequently lost the election.

ment of an arbitrator's award requiring the company to comply in California with wages and certain other conditions provided by the New York contract, the employer filed charges alleging a violation of Section 8(b)(3). The Board dismissed the complaint.[38] In reversing, the court concluded as a matter of law that "regardless of the Union's motive in seeking enforcement of the arbitration award, it committed an unfair labor practice because the subject of the wages and working conditions of the [California] employees was not a *permissible* subject of bargaining in the New York City unit."[39]

In distinguishing a jurisdictional dispute[40] from a question concerning the scope of the bargaining unit, the Board held that an employer properly insisted to impasse on excluding, from a unit of composing room employees, employees who typed copy for newly acquired scanner equipment.[41] The employees also worked in other departments and performed other tasks, and the Board concluded that the employer was not seeking to change the scope of the unit, even though the new scanner equipment would eliminate work previously performed by unit employees.

2. Parties to a Collective Bargaining Agreement. The only essential parties to a collective bargaining agreement are the legal employer or employers of the employees in the unit or units covered by the agreement, or the association to which the employer has delegated bargaining authority, and the certified bargaining representative or other representative of the covered employees.[42] Frequently, additional parties are named. For example: (1) the international union as well as the local, where

---

[38]Upon the company's assertion of a §8(b)(3) violation, the Board's majority held that no provision of the Act was violated when parties voluntarily agreed that the terms of their collective bargaining agreement would be minimum terms of employment for the employer's employees outside the bargaining unit if the purpose of the agreement was to protect the job security and wage structure of the employees within the unit. Electrical Workers (IUE) Local 445 (Sperry Rand Corp.), 202 NLRB 183, 82 LRRM 1491 (1973).

[39]*Supra* note 36 at 69 (emphasis added). "Generally, an employer commits the unfair labor practices of interfering with employees' §7 rights and supporting a union in violation of §8(a)(1) and (a)(2) when it imposes on employees of one unit the contract and bargaining agent of another unit." *Id.* On remand, the Board adopted the Second Circuit's finding. 216 NLRB 173, 88 LRRM 1234 (1975).

[40]For treatment of jurisdictional disputes generally, *see* Chapter 27 *infra.*

[41]World Publishing Co., 220 NLRB 1065, 90 LRRM 1566 (1975). After impasse, the employer unilaterally assigned work on the new equipment to nonunit employees. This, too, was held not to be violative of the Act.

[42]*E.g.,* a noncertified representative selected by a majority of the employees in an appropriate unit. *See* Chapter 12 *supra.*

only the local is certified; (2) the local as well as the international, where only the international is certified; (3) the employer as well as the employer association, where the unit is employer-association-wide; (4) the employer association as well as the employer. So long as the parties agree, the law will give effect to their preference; but insistence by either party, to the point of impasse or not signing an otherwise agreed-upon contract unless a given organization or individual other than a required party is added or excluded, is a *per se* refusal to bargain.

In *Borg-Warner*,[43] the employer insisted that the recognition clause name only the local union even though as the party to the contract the international union was the certified representative. The resulting impasse culminated in the Board finding a violation. The Supreme Court affirmed, holding:

> The "recognition" clause . . . does not come within the definition of mandatory bargaining. The statute requires the company to bargain with the certified representative of its employees. It is an evasion of that duty to insist that the certified agent not be a party to the collective bargaining contract. The Act does not prohibit the voluntary addition of a party, but that does not authorize the employer to exclude the certified representative from the contract.[44]

An employer may not lawfully insist, as a condition of a contract, that a labor federation be a party to a contract where a local union affiliated with that federation is the certified representative.[45] Similarly, a union is guilty of a refusal to bargain when it refuses to include the employer association where the employer is part of an established multi-employer unit represented by that association.[46]

3. Selection of Bargaining Representative. The selection of a bargaining representative is a permissive subject of bargaining. Accordingly, a union violates Section 8(b)(1)(B)[47] and Section 8(b)(3) when it insists that the employer designate an association of employers as its bargaining representative.[48] Conversely, an

---

[43]NLRB v. Borg-Warner Corp., *supra* note 4.

[44]*Id.* at 350.

[45]NLRB v. Taormina Co., 207 F2d 251, 32 LRRM 2684 (CA 5, 1953), *enforcing* 94 NLRB 884, 28 LRRM 1118 (1951); Standard Generator Co., 90 NLRB 790, 26 LRRM 1285 (1950).

[46]United Slate Workers Local 36, 172 NLRB 2248, 69 LRRM 1300 (1968). *See* note 20 *supra.*

[47]*See* Chapter 6 *supra* at notes 582-612.

[48]Mine Workers Local 1854 (Amax Coal Co.), 238 NLRB 1583, 99 LRRM 1670 (1978); Retail Clerks Local 770 (Fine's Food Co.), 228 NLRB 1166, 95 LRRM 1062 (1977); Laborers Local 264 (J. J. Dalton), 216 NLRB 40, 88 LRRM 1192 (1975).

employer violates the Act by insisting to the point of impasse that the union with which it is negotiating accept a grievance procedure that would not provide for union representation at the first step and would dictate that only an international union representative participate in subsequent steps.[49] An employer may be guilty of refusing to bargain if it refuses to meet with a union negotiating committee which includes a nonemployee.[50]

While an employer may normally insist on bargaining during working hours, the Board has held that an employer violates Section 8(a)(5) by refusing to bargain outside working hours, while at the same time refusing to give traveling members of the bargaining committee time off without pay to permit them to participate during working hours.[51] The "travelers" were members of the union negotiating committee at other units, and the Board concluded that the combined actions of the employer unlawfully interfered with the union's selection of its bargaining representatives.

4. Union Recognition Clause. A union recognition clause is not a mandatory subject of bargaining.[52] Therefore, when an employer intended to phase out a home for the aged in order to relocate elsewhere, it could not insist to impasse on the inclusion of a contract provision that would terminate union recognition upon cessation of operations at the original home.[53]

5. Performance Bonds, Indemnifications, and Legal Liability Clauses. A performance bond is consistently treated as a permissive bargaining subject.[54] In *Scripto,*[55] decided under the

---

[49]Tomco Communications, 220 NLRB 636, 90 LRRM 1321 (1975).

[50]Racine Die Casting Co., 192 NLRB 529, 77 LRRM 1818 (1971). The employer contended that language in its most recent contract with the union precluded the union from using nonemployee agents in future negotiations. Since the Board held that the contract language did not have this effect, it was able to avoid deciding whether the clause in question would be permitted under the Act or whether it would be unenforceable as repugnant to the purposes of the Act.

[51]Indiana & Michigan Elec. Co., 235 NLRB 1128, 98 LRRM 1036 (1978), reaff'g 229 NLRB 576, 95 LRRM 1122 (1977).

[52]Borg-Warner, *supra* note 4; Jewish Center for the Aged, 220 NLRB 98, 90 LRRM 1222 (1975). *Cf.* Salt River Valley Water Users' Ass'n, *supra* note 32.

[53]Jewish Center for the Aged, *supra* note 52.

[54]NLRB v. Local 264, Laborers (D & G Constr. Co.), 529 F2d 778, 91 LRRM 2209 (CA 8, 1976), *enforcing sub nom.* J.J. Dalton, 216 NLRB 40, 88 LRRM 1192 (1975); Newberry Equip. Co., 135 NLRB 747, 49 LRRM 1571 (1962); NLRB v. F.M. Reeves & Sons, Inc., 47 LRRM 2480 (CA 10, 1961), *cert. denied,* 366 US 914, 48 LRRM 2071 (1961), *adjudicating contempt for violating* 273 F2d 710, 45 LRRM 2295 (CA 10, 1959); Teamsters Local 294 (Conway's Express), 87 NLRB 972, 25 LRRM 1202 (1949), *aff'd* 195 F2d 906, 29 LRRM 2617 (CA 2, 1952); Amory Garment Co., 80 NLRB 182, 23 LRRM 1081 (1948), *enforced,* 24 LRRM 2274 (CA 5, 1949); Lathers Local 42 (Lathing

Wagner Act, the Board found that an employer violated the Act by insisting that the union furnish a bond to indemnify the employer should it be picketed by outside unions. Similarly, a demand, pursued to impasse, regarding indemnification for pressure applied to customers violates the Act.[56]

A union is guilty of a refusal to bargain if it insists to the point of impasse that the employer furnish a bond for the payment of employees' wages and benefits[57] or to secure performance of the contract.[58]

The Board held that a clause subjecting a union to liability for violation of a no-strike clause is a permissive subject of bargaining.[59] The Fourth Circuit disagreed; it held such clause to be entirely different from an indemnity requirement and therefore a mandatory subject.[60] The court viewed the clause as simply stating what the law provides. An employer violates the Act if it insists, as a condition to execution of an agreement, that the union register with a state court in order to make it amenable to any suit which might be brought thereafter by the employer.[61]

6. Administrative Expense Funds. The Board has held, with the approval of the Eighth Circuit, that a union violates Section 8(b)(3) by insisting to impasse on a contract provision which

---

Contractors Ass'n), 223 NLRB 37, 91 LRRM 1355 (1976); Cookeville Shirt Co., 79 NLRB 667, 22 LRRM 1438 (1948). Nor does the amount of the bond sought make any difference; see, e.g., Brown & Root, Inc., 86 NLRB 520, 24 LRRM 1648 (1949), modified on other grounds sub nom. NLRB v. Ozark Dam Constructors, 190 F2d 222, 28 LRRM 2246 (CA 8, 1951).

[55]Scripto Mfg. Co., 36 NLRB 411, 9 LRRM 156 (1941).

[56]Arlington Asphalt Co., 136 NLRB 742, 49 LRRM 1831 (1962), enforced, 318 F2d 550, 53 LRRM 2462 (CA 4, 1963).

[57]Excello Dry Wall Co., 145 NLRB 663, 55 LRRM 1015 (1963). See also NLRB v. American Compress Warehouse, Div. of Frost-Whited Co., Inc., 350 F2d 365, 59 LRRM 2739 (CA 5, 1965), cert. denied, 382 US 982, 61 LRRM 2147 (1966). Cf. Bricklayers Local 3, 162 NLRB 476, 64 LRRM 1085 (1966) (union may not insist on penalty clause calling for reimbursement to union for dues and initiation fees lost as a result of improper subcontracting).

[58]Local 164, Painters v. NLRB, 293 F2d 133, 48 LRRM 2060 (CA DC, 1961), cert. denied, 368 US 824, 48 LRRM 3110 (1961).

[59]Radiator Specialty Co., 143 NLRB 350, 53 LRRM 1319 (1963), enforced in part, 336 F2d 495, 57 LRRM 2097 (CA 4, 1964). See North Carolina Furniture, Inc., 121 NLRB 41, 42 LRRM 1271 (1958). See also Covington Furniture Mfg. Corp., 212 NLRB 214, 87 LRRM 1505 (1974), enforced, 514 F2d 995, 89 LRRM 3024 (CA 6, 1975), where the Board held that an employer could not insist upon union agreement to indemnify the employer against any threats, coercion, harassment, or intimidation of employees who were not union members. In Hall Tank Co., 214 NLRB 995, 88 LRRM 1208 (1974), the Board held unlawful an employer's insistence upon an indemnification clause as the quid pro quo for a grievance and arbitration provision.

[60]Radiator Specialty Co., 336 F2d 495, 57 LRRM 2097 (CA 4, 1964).

[61]Dalton Telephone Co., 82 NLRB 1001, 24 LRRM 1001 (1949), enforced, 187 F2d 811, 27 LRRM 2503 (CA 5, 1951), cert. denied, 342 US 824, 28 LRRM 2625 (1951).

would require the employer to contribute to a fund created to ensure that the employer pays for the cost of administering various employee fringe benefit funds.[62] The nexus between the means by which the administrative expenses would be paid and the ultimate provision of the fringe benefits to employees was deemed insufficient to make the fund a mandatory subject of bargaining.

7. Interest Arbitration and Bi-Level Bargaining. The Board has consistently held that those clauses by which a party contractually forgoes the right to invoke the future use of traditional economic weapons following termination of the contract are permissive and not mandatory subjects of bargaining. For instance, in *Mechanical Contractors Association of Newburgh,* [63] the parties had agreed in successive contracts that an Industrial Relations Council (IRC) composed of members selected by the international union and the employer association would resolve outstanding bargaining issues. The union objected to the perpetuation of the clause, and the administrative law judge agreed that the employer's insistence violated Section 8(a)(5). The Board, Member Fanning dissenting, distinguished the IRC clause from traditional interest-arbitration clauses for the reason that the clause merely created a bi-level bargaining system and did not represent an irretrievable surrender of economic weapons. Having found that the clause in question merely extended the bargaining process to a higher level of authority, and that no impasse had occurred, the Board found it unnecessary to decide whether the clause included nonmandatory subjects of bargaining.[64]

The Board squarely considered that issue in *Columbus Printing Pressmen,*[65] holding that an interest-arbitration clause is a permissive subject of bargaining. The Fifth Circuit agreed. The prior collective bargaining contracts, including the one in effect at the time of negotiations, had contained an interest-arbitration clause under which deadlocked bargaining issues were to be

---

[62]Local 264, Laborers (D & G Constr. Co.), *supra* note 54. *See* NLRB v. Borg-Warner, *supra* note 4.
[63]202 NLRB 1, 82 LRRM 1438 (1973).
[64]The Board found that the procedures of the IRC differed from arbitration in that (1) the IRC panel was composed of interested parties in equal number, (2) the IRC's decisions were made only after the immediate parties to the negotiations had deadlocked, (3) the IRC's decision had to be unanimous, and (4) the use of economic weapons was permissible by either side if the IRC members could not agree unanimously.
[65]219 NLRB 268, 89 LRRM 1553 (1975), *enforced*, 543 F2d 1161, 93 LRRM 3055 (CA 5, 1976). *See* Chapter 20 *infra* at notes 174-75.

resolved through tripartite arbitration. Unlike *Mechanical Contractors,* which involved an extension of the collective bargaining process prior to impasse, this case dealt with a true interest-arbitration clause upon which the union insisted to impasse, thereby violating Section 8(b)(3).[66]

Parties may voluntarily agree upon an interest-arbitration clause[67] without violating the Act, but neither party may insist to impasse on its inclusion. A party may enforce the clause in a Section 301 contract action if the previous contract continued in force during the course of negotiating modifications.[68] It is well established that a party may not use an existing interest-arbitration clause to perpetuate that clause; otherwise "a party, having once agreed to the provision, may find itself locked into that procedure for as long as the bargaining relationship endures. . . ."[69] The Fifth Circuit explained that such a result would have the effect of binding the parties to forgo use of economic weapons in support of bargaining positions.[70]

---

[66]The Board reaffirmed its position in Printing Pressmen No. 319 (Greensboro News Co.), 222 NLRB 893, 91 LRRM 1308 (1976), *enforced,* 549 F2d 308, 94 LRRM 2752 (CA 4, 1977), and Sheet Metal Workers Local 59 (Employers Ass'n of Roofers), 227 NLRB 520, 94 LRRM 1602 (1976). In Massachusetts Nurses Ass'n (Lawrence General Hospital), 225 NLRB 678, 92 LRRM 1478 (1976), *enforced,* 557 F2d 894, 95 LRRM 2852 (CA 1, 1977), this principle was applied to the health care industry. It was held that a state statute requiring arbitration of all disputes which had not been settled by collective bargaining did not require the inclusion of an interest-arbitration clause and was, in any event, preempted by the 1974 health care amendments. Finally, the Board noted that while Congress has encouraged the use of interest arbitration in the health care field, it has not permitted either party to insist on such a provision to impasse. For further discussion of the issue of preemption, *see* Chapter 31 *infra.*

[67]*See generally* Morris, *The Role of Interest Arbitration in a Collective Bargaining System,* 1 Ind. Rel. L.J. 427 (1976).

[68]Mailers Local 92 v. Chattanooga News-Free Press Co., 524 F2d 1305, 90 LRRM 3000 (CA 6, 1975). The question remains unresolved whether a lawsuit to enforce the interest-arbitration clause would be an unfair labor practice. *See* Morris, *supra* note 67 at 506-507.

[69]NLRB v. Columbus Printing Pressmen, *supra* note 65 at 1169; *see also* NLRB v. Sheet Metal Workers Local 38, 575 F2d 394, 98 LRRM 2147 (CA 2, 1978), *enforcing* Sheet Metal Workers Local 38 (Elmsford Sheet Metal Works), 231 NLRB 699, 96 LRRM 1190 (1977); Graphics Local 23 v. Newspapers, Inc., 586 F2d 19, 99 LRRM 3033 (CA 7, 1978) (where the court applied Board precedent, in the context of a §301 action to affirm a district court's refusal to compel interest arbitration to determine whether the new contract would include an interest-arbitration provision); Sheet Metal Workers Local 59 v. Employers Ass'n of Roofers, 430 F Supp 540, 95 LRRM 2149 (DC Del, 1977) (where a district court refused to enforce an arbitration award because the Board intervened, urging the court to grant the employer's motion for summary judgment); the Board in Sheet Metal Workers Local 59 (Employers Ass'n of Roofers), *supra* note 66, found the union violated §8(b)(3) by insisting upon interest arbitration.

[70]Columbus Printing Pressmen, *supra* note 65, 543 F2d at 1170. The Court further observed, "[T]here must remain opportunities for parties to readjust their relationship in response to changed economic circumstances." 543 F2d at 1170-71.

8. Internal Union Affairs. Mandatory subjects of bargaining concern relations between the employer and the employees, not between the union and the employees. An employer may request bargaining about internal union matters but may not insist to impasse over such proposals.

Thus, an employer may not insist upon a clause providing that nonunion employees shall have a right to participate in and vote at union meetings.[71] Nor may it insist upon a clause requiring a strike vote among employees before a strike occurs,[72] or upon employee ratification as a condition precedent to execution of a collective bargaining agreement.[73]

Similarly, a clause providing that the contract should become void if the percentage of employees paying their dues by checkoff dropped below 50 was held to be a permissive subject of bargaining.[74] Clauses that require the union to provide withdrawal cards to any employee who might be transferred out of the unit,[75] or which require that all shop stewards be chosen from particular classifications of employees are permissive.[76] The Board found an employer guilty of violating Section 8(a)(5) by refusing to bargain unless the certified union was qualified pursuant to pertinent state law to engage in business as a labor

---

[71]NLRB v. Corsicana Cotton Mills, 178 F2d 344, 347, 24 LRRM 2494 (CA 5, 1949).

[72]*Id. See Borg-Warner, supra* note 4, and the following cases that antedated *Borg-Warner:* Allis-Chalmers Mfg. Co. v. NLRB, 213 F2d 374, 34 LRRM 2202 (CA 7, 1954); United States Gypsum Co., 109 NLRB 1402, 34 LRRM 1595 (1954). *See also* Note, *Strike Vote Clause: Bargainable Matter?,* 44 GEO. L.J. 120 (1955).

[73]Houchens Mkt. v. NLRB, 375 F2d 208, 64 LRRM 2647 (CA 6, 1967), *enforcing* 155 NLRB 729, 60 LRRM 1384 (1965); Movers & Warehousemen's Ass'n, 224 NLRB 356, 92 LRRM 1236 (1976), *enforced,* 550 F2d 962, 94 LRRM 2795 (CA 4, 1977); Cheese Barn, Inc., 222 NLRB 418, 91 LRRM 1222 (1976), *enforced,* 558 F2d 526, 95 LRRM 3096 (CA 9, 1977); Southeastern Mich. Gas Co., 206 NLRB 60, 84 LRRM 1203 (1973). *See also* C & W Lektra Bat Co., 209 NLRB 1038, 85 LRRM 1530 (1974), *enforced,* 513 F2d 200, 89 LRRM 2766 (CA 6, 1975), in which the employer claimed that the union had specifically agreed that ratification was to be a condition precedent to signing and therefore refused to sign the contract in the absence of a ratification vote. The Board found that although ratification had been discussed at one point in the negotiations, the union had merely stated its intention to follow the general practice of seeking ratification by the members and that the question of ratification had not been part of the *quid pro quo* of the agreement. The Board said: "We are unwilling to distort words of intention into terms of agreement, particularly where the subject is unrelated to wages and terms and conditions of employment." *Id.,* 209 NLRB at 1039.

[74]NLRB v. Darlington Veneer Co., 236 F2d 85, 38 LRRM 2574 (CA 4, 1956). *Cf.* Bethlehem Steel, 133 NLRB 1400, 49 LRRM 1018 (1961) (indicating that it would be unlawful for an employer to insist upon a clause requiring individual signatures on grievances).

[75]NLRB v. Superior Fireproof Door & Sash Co., 289 F2d 713, 47 LRRM 2816 (CA 2, 1961).

[76]*Id.*

union[77] and submitted an affidavit certifying that none of its officers was affiliated with the Communist Party.[78]

Similarly, an employer violates Section 8(a)(5) when it insists to the point of impasse that a union withdraw fines previously imposed upon employees who had crossed picket lines during a strike in violation of a union rule,[79] or insists that any change in the union's constitution, bylaws, or affiliation would invalidate the contract.[80]

9. Union Label. Although unions have long contended that the union label is sufficiently related to wages, hours, and conditions of employment for it to be a mandatory subject of bargaining, the Board rejects this view and holds that it is permissive. In *Kit Mfg. Co.,*[81] the Board noted that whatever economic advantage use of the label may afford an employer, and whatever impact it may have on the salability of its product, "its relation to wages, hours or other terms or conditions of employment is at best remote and speculative."[82]

10. Industry Promotion Funds. It is established that an industry promotion fund is a permissive subject for bargaining, and a union violates Section 8(b)(3) by insisting to impasse on the adoption of a clause requiring employer contribution to such fund.

In the *Daelyte Service* case,[83] a member of a multi-employer bargaining unit refused to sign a contract that had been negotiated by its employer association and the union on the ground that the clause requiring it to contribute to a promotion fund was illegal. Subsequently, the employer filed a refusal-to-bargain charge against the union, alleging that the latter's conduct in demanding such a clause violated Section 8(b)(3). Dismissing the complaint, the Board held that the union's demand for an employer contribution to the industry fund was not unlawful; thus the acquiescence of the multi-employer group was not

---

[77]Herron Yarn Mills, Inc., 160 NLRB 629, 63 LRRM 1022 (1966). *See also* NLRB v. Dalton Telephone Co., *supra* note 61.

[78]Herron Yarn Mills, Inc., *supra* note 77.

[79]Universal Oil Products Co. v. NLRB, 445 F2d 155, 77 LRRM 2005 (CA 7, 1971); Nordstrom, Inc., 229 NLRB 601, 96 LRRM 1092 (1977).

[80]Betra Mfg. Co., 233 NLRB 1126, 97 LRRM 1005 (1977).

[81]Kit Mfg. Co., *supra* note 10.

[82]*Id.* at 662 n.1.

[83]Building Serv. Employees Local 139 (Daelyte Serv. Co.), 126 NLRB 63, 45 LRRM 1275 (1960).

unlawful. However, since the parties had mutually agreed to the clause, there was no necessity for the Board to pass on whether the subject itself was mandatory or permissive. Shortly thereafter, in the *Mill Floor* case,[84] the Board decided the issue. There, the union insisted to impasse on the following clause:

> Each employer agrees to contribute one (1¢) cent per hour for each hour worked by each Employee covered by this Agreement to [a] Promotional Fund. . . . A uniform collection machinery will be established to collect the contributions due under this section.[85]

The Board found such a fund to be a permissive subject. Therefore, because the union insisted upon inclusion of this clause to the point of impasse, it violated Section 8(b)(3). The Board considered the industry promotion fund "to be outside the employment relationship . . . ," concerned "rather with the relationship of employers to one another, or, like advertising, with the relationship of an employer to the consuming public."[86] Emphasizing the permissive nature of the subject matter, the Board stated:

> Nothing prevents an employer and a union from joining voluntarily in the mutual effort to attempt to influence their industry's course of development, provided, of course, that other legislative enactments do not prohibit such activities. To hold, however, under this Act, that one party must bargain at the behest of another on any matter which might conceivably enhance the prospects of the industry would transform bargaining over the compensation, hours, and employment conditions of employees into a debate over policy objectives.[87]

11. Employees Excluded From Coverage of the Act: Supervisors and Agricultural Labor.[88] Although the Act is not applicable to supervisors or to agricultural labor, the Board has held that the parties may bargain about such categories of employees. But a party may not insist, to the point of refusing to sign a contract applicable to employees covered by the Act, that the contract cover supervisors[89] or agricultural labor.[90]

---

[84]Carpenters Local 2265 (Mill Floor Covering, Inc.), 136 NLRB 769, 49 LRRM 1842 (1962), *enforced*, 317 F2d 269, 53 LRRM 2311 (CA 6, 1963).
[85]*Id.* at 776.
[86]*Id.* at 771.
[87]*Id. Accord,* Sheet Metal Workers Local 38 (Elmsford Sheet Metal Works), 231 NLRB 699, 96 LRRM 1190 (1977); Sheet Metal Workers Local 270 (General Sheet Metal Co.), 144 NLRB 773, 54 LRRM 1130 (1963).
[88]See Chapter 30 *infra* at notes 154-86 and 214-26 for a discussion of supervisors and agricultural laborers respectively.
[89]NLRB v. Retail Clerks Local 648 (Safeway Stores, Inc.), 203 F2d 165, 31 LRRM 2606 (CA 9, 1953), adjudging union in contempt for insisting on bargaining for supervisory employees in violation of a consent decree enforcing 96 NLRB 581, 28 LRRM

12. Settlement of Unfair Labor Practice Charges. Neither party is compelled to negotiate with the other about the settlement of unfair labor practice charges filed with the Board.[91] Thus, if a party demands that charges against it be withdrawn as a condition to negotiating,[92] or if it seeks to condition wage increases upon the withdrawal of charges against it,[93] it violates the Act. Similarly, when one party insists to impasse that the other party abandon litigation[94] or withdraw a grievance for which the union is seeking arbitration, a violation occurs.[95]

13. Transcript of Negotiations. Neither party may insist to impasse upon the presence of an official reporter during negotiations.[96] The Board had held that the presence of a reporter or the utilization of a mechanical device to record negotiations involves a threshold matter, preliminary and subordinate to

---

1554 (1951), *cert. denied,* 348 US 839 (1954); Plumbers Dist. Council 16 (Aero Plumbing Co.), 167 NLRB 1004, 66 LRRM 1233 (1967).
  [90]District 50, Mine Workers (Central Soya Co.), 142 NLRB 930, 53 LRRM 1178 (1963).
  [91]Griffin Inns, 229 NLRB 199, 95 LRRM 1072 (1977); Electrical Workers Local 1229 (IBEW) (Jefferson Standard Broadcasting Co.), 94 NLRB 1507, 28 LRRM 1215 (1951). *See also* Litton Indus. v. NLRB, 533 F2d 1030, 92 LRRM 2013 (CA 8, 1976), *enforcing* 209 NLRB 1006, 85 LRRM 1501 (1974), where the court enforced a Board order finding that an employer violated §8(a)(5) by conditioning bargaining upon withdrawal of unfair labor practice charges and upon a 60-day extension on the expiring contract. The court suggested, however, that the employer might excuse its conduct by explaining the basis for the conditions or by reasonably challenging the union's majority status at the time the conditions were imposed. *But see* Star Mfg. Co. v. NLRB, 536 F2d 1192, 92 LRRM 3179 (CA 7, 1976), *enforcing in part* 220 NLRB 582, 90 LRRM 1360 (1975), where the Seventh Court sustained the employer's good-faith doubt of the union's majority status and found that the employer's insistence upon the withdrawal of unfair labor practice charges before the commencement of bargaining did not violate the Act.
  [92]Stackpole Components Co., 232 NLRB 723, 96 LRRM 1324 (1977); Perry Publications, Inc., 151 NLRB 1030, 58 LRRM 1561 (1965); Ohio Car & Truck Leasing, Inc., 149 NLRB 1423, 58 LRRM 1008 (1964); Kit Mfg. Co., 142 NLRB 957, 53 LRRM 1178, *enforced in part,* 335 F2d 166, 56 LRRM 2988 (CA 9, 1964), *cert. denied,* 380 US 910, 58 LRRM 2496 (1965); Silby-Dolcourt Chemical Indus., Inc., 145 NLRB 1348, 55 LRRM 1160 (1964). *See also* American Stores Packing Co., 142 NLRB 711, 53 LRRM 1137 (1963); Body & Tank Corp., 144 NLRB 1414, 54 LRRM 1268 (1963); American Laundry Mach. Co., 76 NLRB 981, 21 LRRM 1275 (1948), *enforced,* 174 F2d 124, 24 LRRM 2033 (CA 6, 1949); Sussex Hats, Inc., 85 NLRB 399, 24 LRRM 1407 (1949); Burns Brick Co., 80 NLRB 389, 23 LRRM 1122 (1948). The same principle applies to a union. Iron Workers Local 600, 134 NLRB 301, 49 LRRM 1134 (1961).
  [93]Butcher Boy Refrigerator Door Co., 127 NLRB 1360, 46 LRRM 1192 (1960), *enforced,* 290 F2d 22, 48 LRRM 2058 (CA 7, 1961).
  [94]Stackpole Components Co., *supra* note 92; Peerless Food Prod., Inc., 231 NLRB 530, 96 LRRM 1048 (1977); NLRB v. Carpenters Local 964, 447 F2d 643, 78 LRRM 2167 (CA 2, 1971) (the union was found to have violated §8(b)(3) by insisting that the employer association with which it was negotiating abandon litigation concerning management of a trust fund and agree to employ as trustees of the trust fund only the employers of carpenters).
  [95]B.C. Studios, Inc., 217 NLRB 307, 89 LRRM 1126 (1975) (an employer violates §8(a)(5) by conditioning continued bargaining on the union's withdrawal from arbitration of a grievance relating to a back-pay wage claim on behalf of certain employees).
  [96]Bartlett-Collins Co., 237 NLRB 770, 99 LRRM 1034 (1978).

substantive negotiations and therefore not violative of the Act.[97] However, in *Bartlett-Collins Co.*[98] the Board reversed this rule, explaining that meaningful collective bargaining would not be encouraged if a party could stifle negotiations at their outset by insisting on the preparation of a transcript.

14. Miscellaneous. In *Western Massachusetts Electric Co.* v. *NLRB*,[99] the First Circuit, denying enforcement of a Board order, ruled that an employer did not violate the Act by refusing to furnish information relating to a decision to subcontract where the decision itself was not a mandatory subject of bargaining. Had the decision fallen in the mandatory bargaining category, then the demand for information would have been presumptively relevant.

In a class action brought by professional basketball players against the National and American Basketball Associations alleging violations of antitrust law, a federal district court held that the "reserve clause," the "player draft," and "merger" or "non-competition" agreements are permissive subjects of bargaining.[100]

Additionally, a union was held to have violated Section 8(b)(3) by conditioning its recommendation for membership ratification of an agreed-upon contract upon (1) the employer's identification of employees who would be disciplined for alleged strike misconduct and the nature of the discipline, and (2) amnesty for such misconduct. The Board reasoned that while amnesty for imposed discipline is a mandatory subject of bargaining, bargaining in the abstract is permissive. Because the company had neither selected any employee for discipline nor begun the

---

[97]Reed & Prince Mfg. Co., 96 NLRB 850, 28 LRRM 1608 (1951), *enforced on other grounds*, 205 F2d 131, 32 LRRM 2225 (CA 1, 1953), *cert. denied*, 346 US 887, 33 LRRM 2133 (1953).

[98]*Supra* note 96.

[99]573 F2d 101, 98 LRRM 2851 (CA 1, 1978), *reversing* Connecticut Light & Power Co., 229 NLRB 1032, 96 LRRM 1348 (1977). *But see* Chapter 17 *supra* at notes 267-329.

[100]Robertson v. National Basketball Ass'n, 389 F Supp 867, 88 LRRM 2787 (SD NY, 1975). Defendants argued that their activities were immune from attack because of the labor exemption to the antitrust laws. They proposed a test to determine when this exemption is available to employers which required, in part, a determination of whether the challenged practices are mandatory subjects of bargaining. However, the court held that the labor exemption is not available to these employers. In rejecting the defendants' test, it noted that even mandatory subjects might not be exempt, but went on to state that the challenged practices are not mandatory subjects of bargaining. *See* Meat Cutters Local 189 v. Jewel Tea Co., 381 US 676, 59 LRRM 2376 (1965), and discussion at notes 355-61, Chapter 31 *infra*. *See also* notes 124-25 *infra* and accompanying text.

disciplinary process, the union's conduct was deemed a violation of the Act.[101]

An instructive case with which to conclude this review of permissive subjects of bargaining is *Capital Times Co., Inc.,*[102] for it reveals a fact pattern in which the Board examined the underlying reasons for the distinction between mandatory and permissive subjects. The employer newspaper had unilaterally adopted a code of ethics and accompanying penalty provisions designed to protect the newspaper's credibility. The code prohibited employees from accepting gifts given because of their association with the newspaper unless such gifts were necessary for their duties at the newspaper. The prohibited gifts were found by the Board not to be "wages" within the meaning of Section 8(d) because (1) they did not originate with the employer, (2) neither the employees nor the union considered the gifts to be wages, (3) the gifts, unlike tips, were not provided in appreciation for past service, and (4) the gifts did not affect terms and conditions of employment since the employer regularly reimbursed employees for legitimate expenses. Accordingly, prohibiting such gifts was not a mandatory subject of bargaining. However, the unilateral institution of an accompanying warning and discharge policy was held to be a mandatory subject of bargaining. Member Fanning dissented, arguing that discipline is inextricably related to the underlying substantive rule and that both should be treated as mandatory subjects.

III. ILLEGAL SUBJECTS OF BARGAINING

A. Relationship to Duty to Bargain

Neither party may require that the other agree to contract provisions which are unlawful under the Act.[103] In 1948 the Board stated:

---

[101]Steelworkers Local 7807 (ITT Abrasive Products Co.), 224 NLRB 78, 93 LRRM 1076 (1976).

[102]223 NLRB 651, 91 LRRM 1481 (1976).

[103]Meat Cutters Local 421 (Great Atlantic & Pacific Tea Co.), 81 NLRB 1052, 23 LRRM 1464 (1949); National Maritime Union (Texas Co.), 78 NLRB 971, 22 LRRM 1289 (1948), *enforced,* 175 F2d 686, 24 LRRM 2268 (CA 2, 1949), *cert. denied,* 338 US 954, 25 LRRM 2395 (1950). *Cf.* concurring opinion of Mr. Justice Harlan in the *Borg-Warner* case, where he said that "[o]f course an employer or union cannot insist upon a clause which would be illegal under the Act's provisions." *Supra* note 4 at 360.

[W]hat the Act does not merit is the insistence, as a condition precedent to entering into a collective bargaining agreement, that the
other party to the negotiations agree to a provision or take some
action which is unlawful or inconsistent with the basic policy of the
Act. Compliance with the Act's requirement of collective bargaining
cannot be made dependent upon the acceptance of provisions in
the agreement which, by their terms or in their effectuation, are
repugnant to the Act's specific language or basic policy.[104]

Insistence upon an illegal provision thus violates the duty to
bargain. Two prominent types of clauses that violate specific
provisions of the Act are "closed shop" clauses (or other illegal
union security clauses), prohibited by Sections 8(a)(3) and
8(b)(2),[105] and "hot cargo" clauses, prohibited by Section 8(e).[106]
The relationship between illegal clauses and the duty to bargain
has been defined as follows:

Neither party may require that the other agree to contract provisions
which are unlawful. And when . . . one of the parties creates a
bargaining impasse by insisting, not in good faith, that the other
agree to an unlawful condition of employment, that party has violated
its statutory duty to bargain.[107]

Whether the mere proposal of an illegal subject is in itself an
unfair labor practice under Sections 8(a)(5) or 8(b)(3) or whether
additional evidence of bad faith is required is unanswered. Illegal subject cases generally arise in a context of other indicia of
bad faith including the insistence upon such proposals to impasse.
No decision has been found holding that the Act is violated
merely by the proposal of an illegal subject.[108] If the proposal of
an illegal subject of bargaining is a violation of Sections 8(a)(5)
or 8(b)(3) only when it is pressed to the point of impasse, the
distinction between illegal subjects and permissive subjects might
seem at first to be of little significance. The distinction lies elsewhere. Although a party may not insist on a permissive subject

---

[104]National Maritime Union (Texas Co.), *supra* note 103 at 981-82.
[105]*See generally* Chapter 29 *infra.*
[106]*See generally* Chapter 26 *infra.*
[107]Meat Cutters (Great Atlantic & Pacific Tea Co.), *supra* note 103, in which the Board
found a union's insistence upon an illegal union security clause to be a violation of
§8(b)(3) as well as §8(b)(2). *Note:* The primary emphasis in this part is upon those
decisions dealing with illegal subjects of bargaining that are not included within a specific
substantive area. For detailed discussion of decisions dealing with illegal "hiring-hall"
or "closed-shop" clauses, *see* Chapter 29 *infra;* for "hot-cargo" provisions, *see* Chapter
26, *infra;* for contractual violation of the duty of fair representation, including violations
based on race, *see* Chapter 28 *infra;* and for the effect that the inclusion of certain illegal
provisions has upon the "contract-bar" doctrine, *see* Chapter 10 *supra.*
[108]As a practical matter, it is not likely that a party receiving the illegal request would
file an unfair practice charge when the other party merely presents the illegal subject
and does not press for its inclusion in the contract.

to the point of impasse, such a subject may by mutual approval of the parties be incorporated in the agreement. But an illegal subject may not ever properly be included in the agreement.[109]

It is less clear, however, whether the Act is violated by insistence on a provision that is legal under the Act but illegal under state law. In one case,[110] the Board considered a union's insistence upon the inclusion of an agency-shop clause claimed by the company and General Counsel to be illegal under the Arizona constitution and right-to-work statutes. The General Counsel's motion for summary judgment was denied by a Board majority of four-to-one. Two members found that they could not determine the meaning of the clause with sufficient clarity to pass on its legality without an evidentiary hearing, while two other members stated that there was no authoritative state court opinion on the legality of such agency-shop agreements in Arizona.[111]

B. Examples of Illegal Subjects

Although there are few decisions defining what constitute illegal subjects of bargaining, some guidelines are available. For example, a provision for a closed shop,[112] a provision for a hiring hall giving preference to union members,[113] and a "hot cargo" clause in violation of Section 8(e)[114] are commonly recognized illegal subjects of bargaining. Additionally, a union breaches its duty to bargain in good faith under Section 8(b)(3) when it demands a contract provision that is inconsistent with the duty of fair representation owed by the union to the employees.[115] A proposal which requires separation of employees on the basis of race is an unlawful subject of bargaining.[116]

---

[109]Honolulu Star-Bulletin, Ltd., 123 NLRB 395, 43 LRRM 1449 (1959); *enforcement denied on other grounds,* 274 F2d 567, 45 LRRM 2184 (CA DC, 1959).

[110]Steelworkers Local 4102 (Capital Foundry), 199 NLRB 153, 81 LRRM 1188 (1972).

[111]One member dissented, as he was persuaded that the agency-shop clause in question violated the Arizona constitution and statutes and that insistence upon its inclusion in the contract and a strike in furtherance thereof violated §8(b)(3). *See* Chapter 29 *infra* at notes 192-218 and Chapter 31 *infra* at notes 245-58.

[112]Penello v. Mine Workers, 88 F Supp 935, 25 LRRM 2368 (D DC, 1950); Honolulu Star-Bulletin, Ltd., *supra* note 109. *See generally* Chapter 29 *infra. See* Comment, *Subjects Included Within Management's Duty to Bargain Collectively,* 26 LA. L. REV. 630 (1966).

[113]NLRB v. National Maritime Union, *supra* note 103. *See* Chapter 29 *infra* for a discussion of hiring-hall agreements.

[114]Lithographers Local 17, 130 NLRB 985, 47 LRRM 1374 (1961). *See also* Lithographers Local 78, 130 NLRB 968, 47 LRRM 1380 (1961), and Chapter 26 *infra.*

[115]Longshoremen Local 1367 (Galveston Maritime Ass'n, Inc.), 148 NLRB 897, 57 LRRM 1083 (1964). *See* Chapter 28 *infra.*

[116]Hughes Tool Co., 147 NLRB 1573, 56 LRRM 1289 (1964). *See* Chapter 28 *infra.*

If a union seeks to have its rules and regulations incorporated in an agreement with an employer, a rule or regulation requiring discrimination in favor of union members must be excluded since it would violate the Act.[117] But the rule in question must explicitly call for illegal conduct to support a finding of violation. "[I]n the absence of provisions calling explicitly for illegal conduct, the contract cannot be held illegal because it failed affirmatively to disclaim all illegal objectives."[118]

Since an employer's insistence that it have a contractual right to discharge employees for "union activity" is held to be a violation of Section 8(a)(5),[119] such a contractual clause would undoubtedly be an illegal bargaining subject. And, since an employer's grant of a 20-year seniority credit to strikers who return to work during a strike has been held to be inherently discriminatory,[120] it may be argued that such a superseniority plan is an illegal topic for bargaining.[121] As these holdings indicate, provisions of this nature are inconsistent with the underlying policies of the Act and are thus illegal.[122]

The cases that have been cited so far in this section involve questions of illegality under the NLRA or inconsistency with its underlying policies. The federal antitrust statutes[123] may also determine the illegality of certain subjects of bargaining. As the Supreme Court declared in *Mine Workers* v. *Pennington*:[124] "[A]n agreement resulting from union-employer negotiations" is not "automatically exempt from Sherman Act scrutiny simply because the negotiations involve a compulsory subject of bargaining. . . . [T]here are limits to what a union or an employer may offer or extract in the name of wages," so that antitrust laws are violated

---

[117]NLRB v. News Syndicate Co., 365 US 695, 47 LRRM 2916 (1961).

[118]*Id.* at 699-700, *citing* NLRB v. News Syndicate Co., 272 F2d 323, 46 LRRM 2295 (CA 2, 1960).

[119]Gay Paree Undergarment Co., 91 NLRB 1363, 27 LRRM 1006 (1950).

[120]NLRB v. Erie Resistor Corp., 373 US 221, 53 LRRM 2121 (1963). *See* Chapter 7 at notes 85-91.

[121]*See* Great Lakes Carbon Corp. v. NLRB, 360 F2d 19, 62 LRRM 2088 (CA 4, 1966), holding that a negotiated contract provision giving superseniority to replacements for striking employees was unlawful on its face and must be eliminated from the contract. *But cf.* Philip Carey Mfg. Co. v. NLRB, 331 F2d 720, 55 LRRM 2821 (CA 6, 1964), *cert. denied*, 379 US 888, 57 LRRM 2307 (1964).

[122]Similarly, other contractual provisions which contravene prohibitions in the statute would be illegal. For example, if an incumbent union sought a provision that would give it advantages over an outside union in soliciting or distributing literature in contravention of the underlying policies of the Act, the same reasoning could be employed to make the topic illegal for bargaining. *See* Chapters 6 and 8 *supra*.

[123]15 USC §§1-7, 12-27 (1964). *See generally* Chapter 31 *infra*.

[124]Mine Workers v. Pennington, 381 US 657, 59 LRRM 2369 (1965).

when a union agrees "with one set of employers to impose a wage scale on other bargaining units."[125]

Insistence upon a tripartite arbitration panel to resolve work jurisdiction disputes when the management representatives are neither chosen nor designated by the employer violates the Act:[126] "If the [u]nion's coercion of the [a]ssociation to accept a contract term is itself otherwise illegal—here because violative of Section 8(b)(1)(B)—insistence on that term as a condition to agreement is *ipso facto* illegal as a 'refusal to bargain collectively with an employer' in violation of Section 8(b)(3)."[127] The union's good-faith but mistaken belief that the demand was legal and hence a mandatory subject of bargaining is not a defense to a charge of refusal to bargain.[128]

An employer may nevertheless be required to bargain with a newly certified union prior to eliminating practices in which its supervisors had traditionally acquiesced, even though these practices may entail violations of law. For example, in *Evening News Publishing Co.*,[129] the company and its employees had for many years engaged in the following practices: making expense account payments in excess of expenses actually incurred; artificially increasing those payments to compensate for raises which had been denied; making overtime payments for hours not worked; and perpetuating this system so that employees were able to avoid declaring the payments on their income tax returns. In 1970 the company was purchased. Although the new management became aware of these practices, it took no steps to eliminate them until almost a year after the union had been certified. When the union protested the company's announced intention to discontinue the questionable practices, the company went through the formality of discussing the matter but at no

---

[125]*Id.* at 664-65. *See also Jewel Tea, supra* note 100. For a detailed discussion of *Pennington* and *Jewel, see* Chapter 31 *infra* at notes 354-80.

[126]Associated Gen. Contractors (Iron Workers Local 103) v. NLRB, 465 F2d 327, 80 LRRM 3157 (CA 7, 1972), *cert. denied,* 409 US 1108, 82 LRRM 2139 (1973). The court reversed the Board's finding that the union demand did not violate §8(b)(1)(B) by restraining or coercing the association "in the selection of [its] representatives for the purpose of . . . the adjustment of grievances. . . ." *Id.* at 331. The Board did not petition for certiorari and subsequently applied the law of the case, 200 NLRB 77, 81 LRRM at 1557.

[127]*Id.,* 465 F2d at 334.

[128]*Id.*

[129]196 NLRB 530, 80 LRRM 1230 (1972).

time seriously considered changing its intention.[130] The company argued, *inter alia,* that it had not been obligated to bargain over the abrogation of immoral and illegal payment practices. Rejecting the argument, the Board concluded that it would not "pass a moral judgment on a practice joined in by employer representatives as well as by the employees."[131]

An employer also violates Section 8(a)(5) by insisting to impasse that the union accede to its unlawful recognition of another union in another unit.[132] The administrative law judge's decision, affirmed by the Board, reasoned that the employer's position was antithetical to the purposes of the Act and thus, even if it were not illegal with respect to unit negotiations being conducted, it could not be so pressed by the employer.[133]

In *NLRB* v. *Longshoremen Local 13,*[134] the Ninth Circuit affirmed a Board decision that a union violated Section 8(b)(3) by insisting to impasse on a proposed hiring program giving preference or class B referrals to persons with 100 hours of longshoremen's experience and on a program requiring sponsorship for class A referrals. The court considered the proposals against the union's background of past discrimination and held that insisting to impasse on these "illegal demands" violated the Act.

A union also violated Section 8(b)(3) by insisting on the inclusion of a contract provision requiring the employer to pay an additional five cents an hour to union stewards, ostensibly for the purpose of reimbursing them for expenses incurred in administering the contract.[135] The Board majority ruled that the clause was presumptively unlawful because it conferred benefits

---

[130]Although at one point after the practices had already been discontinued, the company proposed a general monetary increase to compensate employees for their losses in exchange for the union's concession of its union security clause. *Id.* at 535.

[131]*Id.* The Board said that even if the payments were not properly reported for tax purposes, that would still not abrogate the employer's duty to negotiate with the union prior to discontinuing them.

[132]Newspaper Agency Corp., 201 NLRB 480, 82 LRRM 1509 (1973), *aff'd sub nom.* Graphic Arts Int'l v. NLRB, 505 F2d 335, 86 LRRM 3234 (CA DC, 1974).

[133]*Id.* at 493. However, the administrative law judge also held that the employer's insistence constituted a violation *vis-à-vis* the instant unit because such insistence was designed to force these employers to accept another union upon transfer to the other unit. The employer, of course, violated §§8(a)(2) when it placed the recognition clause in its collective bargaining contract with the union that it had agreed to recognize. *See also* Chapter 8 *supra.*

[134]549 F2d 1346, 95 LRRM 2215 (CA 9, 1977), *enforcing* Longshoremen & Warehousemen Local 13 (Pacific Maritime Ass'n), 210 NLRB 952, 86 LRRM 1716 (1974).

[135]Teamsters Local 20 (Seaway Food Town, Inc.), 235 NLRB 1554, 98 LRRM 1233 (1978).

exclusively on the union steward and because no evidence established the necessity for the payment.[136]

Finally, an employer violated Section 8(a)(5) by insisting on a strike settlement agreement in which it would reinstate striking employees only if the union guaranteed in writing that the employees would return to work for a specific period of time and would waive substantial legal rights of the employees.[137]

---

[136]Chairman Fanning dissented, arguing that a $100 differential barely reimburses a steward for his out-of-pocket expenses.

[137]American Cyanamid Co., 235 NLRB 1316, 98 LRRM 1429 (1978).

Part V

ARBITRATION AND THE ACT

CHAPTER 19

RELATION OF BOARD ACTION TO ENFORCEMENT OF AGREEMENTS UNDER SECTION 301

I. INTRODUCTION

The process of collective bargaining generally results in a collective bargaining contract.[1] This chapter explores the relation of Board action to the enforcement of the contract.[2] The question of accommodating Board action to the arbitration process is reserved for the following chapter.[3] The present chapter is

---

[1]"The Act contemplates the making of contracts with labor organizations. That is the manifest objective in providing for collective bargaining." Consolidated Edison v. NLRB, 305 US 197, 236, 3 LRRM 645, 656 (1938).

[2]For bibliographic materials, *see* the following: Morris, *Twenty Years of Trilogy: A Celebration*, in DECISIONAL THINKING OF ARBITRATORS AND JUDGES, Proceedings of the 33rd Annual Meeting, National Academy of Arbitrators, 331 (J. Stern & B. Dennis eds. 1980); St. Antoine, *Judicial Review of Labor Arbitration Awards: A Second Look at Enterprise Wheel and its Progeny*, 75 MICH. L. REV. 1137 (1977); Feller, *The Coming End of Arbitration's Golden Age*, in ARBITRATION—1976, Proceedings of the 29th Annual Meeting, National Academy of Arbitrators, 97 (B. Dennis & G. Somers eds. 1976); Feller, *A General Theory of the Collective Bargaining Agreement*, 61 CAL. L. REV. 663 (1973); Feldesman, *Section 301 and the National Labor Relations Act*, 30 TENN. L. REV. 16 (1962); Summers, *Collective Agreements and the Law of Contracts*, 78 YALE L. J. 525 (1969); Meltzer, *Ruminations About Ideology, Law, and Labor Arbitration*, in THE ARBITRATOR, THE NLRB, AND THE COURTS, Proceedings of the 20th Annual Meeting, National Academy of Arbitrators, 1 (D. Jones ed. 1967) (also 34 U. CHI. L. REV. 545 (1967)); Note, *Section 301(a) and the Federal Common Law of Labor Agreements*, 75 YALE L. J. 877 (1966); Note, *Labor Relations: Removal Under Section 301(a)*, 16 BAYLOR L. REV. 400 (1964); Sovern, *Section 301 and the Primary Jurisdiction of the NLRB*, 76 HARV. L. REV. 529 (1963); Comment, *The Emergent Federal Common Law of Labor Contracts: A Survey of the Law Under Section 301*, 28 U. CHI. L. REV. 707 (1961); Aaron, *On First Looking Into the Lincoln Mills Decision*, in ARBITRATION AND THE LAW, Proceedings of the 12th Annual Meeting, National Academy of Arbitrators, 1 (J. McKelvey ed. 1959); Jenkins, *The Impact of Lincoln Mills on the National Labor Relations Board*, 6 U.C.L.A. L. REV. 355 (1959); Cox, *The Legal Nature of Collective Bargaining Agreements*, 57 MICH. L. REV. 1 (1958); Dunau, *Contractual Prohibition of Unfair Labor Practices: Jurisdictional Problems*, 57 COLUM. L. REV. 52 (1957); Bunn, *Lincoln Mills and the Jurisdiction to Enforce Collective Bargaining Agreements*, 43 VA. L. REV. 1247 (1957); Feinsinger, *Enforcement of Labor Agreements—A New Era in Collective Bargaining*, 43 VA. L. REV. 1261 (1957); Wollett & Wellington, *Federalism and Breach of the Labor Agreement*, 7 STAN. L. REV. 445 (1955); Cox, *Rights Under a Labor Agreement*, 69 HARV. L. REV. 601 (1956).

[3]Contracts usually contain agreements to arbitrate. Hence, many cases in this chapter which bear upon the interpretation of contracts by the Board will also involve arbitration.

concerned with the Board's practice and jurisdiction in relation to the collective bargaining agreement. It presents the statutory source of this jurisdiction, compares it with the jurisdiction of the courts under Section 301,[4] and broadly analyzes the problems faced by the Board in interpreting a contract between an employer and a labor organization. In presenting the statutory source of Section 301 jurisdiction, however, this chapter (in Part III) treats extensively the parallel development of the law arising in Section 301 actions under collective bargaining agreements in order to supply a description of this important area of related law, even though such law does not derive directly from the provisions of the National Labor Relations Act.

II. SECTION 10(a) POWER OF THE BOARD

Under Section 10(a) of the Act, "[t]he Board is empowered . . . to prevent any person from engaging in any unfair labor practice . . . . This power shall not be affected by any other means of adjustment or prevention that has been or may be established by agreement, law, or otherwise . . . ."[5]

Prior to 1947, the same Section read: "This power shall be exclusive, and shall not be affected by any other means of adjustment . . . ." In the Taft-Hartley amendments, the exclusivity of the Board's power to remedy unfair labor practices was modified by striking the words "shall be exclusive, and" and by adding a proviso. The amended section empowers the Board to cede jurisdiction to a state or territorial agency under certain conditions,[6] but the Board has never concluded a cession agreement with a state agency.[7]

However, the cases are treated here only because of their relation to general contractual problems.
  [4]This chapter does not attempt full coverage of §301. Since this section is not part of the NLRA, it falls outside the direct scope of this treatise.
  [5]See generally Chapters 32 and 33 infra for discussion of NLRB procedures, orders, and remedies.
  [6]The proviso was drafted in response to the decision of the Supreme Court in Bethlehem Steel Co. v. New York Labor Bd., 330 US 767, 19 LRRM 2499 (1947). See S. REP. NO. 105, pt. 2, 80th Cong., 1st Sess. 26 (1947); Street, Elec. Ry. & Motor Coach Employees v. Wisconsin Employment Relations Bd., 340 US 383, 397, 27 LRRM 2385 (1951); Algoma Plywood Co. v. Wisconsin Employment Relations Bd., 336 US 301, 313, 23 LRRM 2402 (1949). The Bethlehem Steel case had left a "doubt whether a state board could act, either after a formal cession by the National Board or upon a declination of jurisdiction 'for budgetary or other reasons.'" Guss v. Utah Labor Relations Bd., 353 US 1, 8, 39 LRRM 2567 (1957). The proviso to §10(a) "is the exclusive means whereby

Under Section 10, the Board has plenary jurisdiction over the adjudication of unfair labor practices, except where it cedes jurisdiction as provided in Section 10(a) or declines jurisdiction as provided in Section 14(c). The Act does not expressly prevent the Board from resolving questions of contract interpretation when necessary to the exercise of its jurisdiction over unfair labor practice charges, and it is settled that the Board possesses such authority.[8]

III. SCOPE OF SECTION 301

A. History

1. Background. The Wagner Act of 1935[9] was directed at protecting employees' self-organization rights and, toward that goal, made unlawful employer practices that interfered with the employees' right to organize. The Wagner Act did not impose restrictions on union practices. Unions were often further insulated by the prevailing theory that they were not legal entities; thus, in many states they could not be sued directly for failure to honor their contractual obligations.[10] By the mid-1940s, the political climate had changed, and, in addition, the massive union organizing drives of the 1930s had produced ongoing collective bargaining in almost every major industry.[11]

The Taft-Hartley Act of 1947 imposed restrictions on union practices, including the Section 8(b)(3) prohibition against refusing to bargain with employers.[12] It also focused on enforcement of the collective bargaining agreement itself, for Section 301[13] was enacted to regulate suits by and against labor organizations by giving the federal courts power to enforce collective bargaining agreements.

States may be enabled to act concerning the matters which Congress has entrusted to the National Labor Relations Board." *Id.* at 9.
   [7]*See* Chapter 31 *infra* at note 261.
   [8]NLRB v. C & C Plywood Corp., 385 US 421, 64 LRRM 2065 (1967), discussed at notes 209-16 *infra*.
   [9]*See* Chapters 1 and 2 *supra*.
   [10]*See* Pullman Standard Car Mfg. v. Local 2928, Steelworkers, 152 F2d 493, 17 LRRM 624 (CA 7, 1945).
   [11]*See* Cox, *Some Aspects of the Labor Management Relations Act, 1947*, 61 HARV. L. REV. 274, 277 (1947). *See* Chapter 3 *supra*.
   [12]Cox, *supra* note 11.
   [13]61 Stat 156 (1947), 29 USC §185 (1964).

2. Legislative History. Section 301(a) of the Labor Management Relations Act provides:[14]

Suits for violation of contracts between an employer and a labor organization representing employees in an industry affecting commerce as defined in this Act, or between any such labor organizations, may be brought in any district court of the United States having jurisdiction of the parties, without respect to the amount in controversy or without regard to the citizenship of the parties.[15]

As early as 1943, Congress had considered questions of union responsibility under a collective bargaining agreement.[16] In 1946 Congress passed a bill making voluntary associations suable in the federal courts;[17] this bill was vetoed by the President.[18] In the 80th Congress, bills were introduced to make collective bargaining contracts mutually enforceable.[19] It was in this same Congress that the Taft-Hartley Act was adopted, including Section 301. This section has raised multitudinous issues of inter-

---

[14]A summary of the legislative history of §301 is given in the appendix to Justice Frankfurter's dissenting opinion in Textile Workers v. Lincoln Mills, 353 US 448, 485, 40 LRRM 2113 (1957). It is also discussed in Westinghouse Salaried Employees v. Westinghouse Elec. Corp., 348 US 437, 35 LRRM 2643 (1955) (Frankfurter, J.), and in the majority opinion of *Lincoln Mills*, 353 US 448 (1957). In spite of the foregoing judicial reliance on that legislative history, one court has described it as "extremely fragmentary." McCarroll v. Los Angeles County Dist. Council of Carpenters, 49 Cal2d 45, 58, 315 P2d 322, 329, 40 LRRM 2709 (1957). *See also* Chapter 3 *supra*.

[15]61 Stat 156 (1947), 29 USC §185 (1976). The discussion in this chapter is limited to the application of §301 to collective bargaining agreements. However, the section has also applied to contracts between labor organizations; *see, e.g.*, Plumbers Local 334 v. Plumbers, 452 US 615, 107 LRRM 2715 (1981) (international union's constitution is a contract between international and local unions); Santos v. Carpenters District Council, 547 F2d 197, 199 n.1, 94 LRRM 2244, 2245 n.1 (CA 2, 1977) (§301 applicable to Article XX of the AFL-CIO Constitution); Jensen v. Farrell Lines, Inc., 477 F Supp 335, 104 LRRM 2501, 2509 (SD NY, 1979) (same); Drywall Tapers & Pointers Local 1974 v. Plasterers Local 60, 537 F2d 669, 92 LRRM 3203 (CA 2, 1976) (§301 applicable to memorandum of understanding between two unions regarding assignment of work). Two courts have indicated that union members cannot sue under §301 for breach of a union constitution. Trail v. Teamsters, 542 F2d 961, 93 LRRM 3076 (CA 6, 1976); Hotel & Restaurant Employees Local 400 v. Svacek, 431 F2d 705, 75 LRRM 2427 (CA 9, 1970). With respect to the question whether §301 could apply to a suit by union members based on a local union charter, *see* Abrams v. Carrier Corp., 434 F2d 1234, 1247-48, 75 LRRM 2736, 2745-46 (CA 2, 1970), *cert. denied sub nom.* Steelworkers v. Abrams, 401 US 1009, 76 LRRM 2941 (1971). And *see generally* Note, *Applying the "Contracts Between Labor Organizations" Clause of Taft-Hartley Section 301: A Plea for Restraint,* 69 YALE L. J. 299 (1959). *Cf.* Retail Clerks v. Lion Dry Goods, Inc., 369 US 17, 49 LRRM 2670 (1962) (§301 also applicable to a strike-settlement agreement between an employer and a labor organization which does not represent the employer's employees).

[16]*E.g.*, H.R. 1781, 78th Cong., 1st Sess. (1943) (federal incorporations); S. 1641, 79th Cong., 1st Sess. (1945) (sanctions for contract violators); S. 1656, 79th Cong., 1st Sess. (1945) (cause of action for strikes in violation of contract); S. 55, 80th Cong., 1st Sess. (1947) (federal jurisdiction); S. 937, 80th Cong., 1st Sess. (1947) (federal labor courts).

[17]*See* S. REP. No. 1177, 79th Cong., 2d Sess., pt. 2, at 3-4, 10-14 (1946).

[18]H. R. DOC. No. 651, 79th Cong., 2d Sess. (1946).

[19]H. R. 3020, 80th Cong., 1st Sess., §302 (1947); S. 1126, 80th Cong., 1st Sess., §301 (1947).

pretation, preemption, and jurisdiction—many of which have a bearing on the Board's power to interpret a collective bargaining contract.

Congress sought in Section 301 to add stability to labor relations by providing a means to enforce agreements between unions and employers. The Senate report stated that "[s]tatutory recognition of the collective agreement as a valid, binding, and enforceable contract is a logical and necessary step. It will promote a higher degree of responsibility upon the parties to such agreements, and will thereby promote industrial peace."[20]

The Senate bill contained a proposal to make a breach of contract an unfair labor practice. This was deleted in conference on the ground that "[o]nce the parties have made a collective bargaining contract the enforcement of that contract should be left to the law and not to the National Labor Relations Board."[21]

B. Grant of Federal Substantive Law

The first major issue in litigation based on Section 301 was whether this section authorized the application of federal substantive law or whether it was simply procedural. In *Westinghouse Salaried Employees* v. *Westinghouse Electric Corp.*[22] a divided Supreme Court refused to permit a union to recover wages owed to individual employees which had allegedly been withheld in violation of a collective bargaining agreement. There was no majority opinion, although six justices in three opinions concurred that the section did not permit a union to enforce what was said to be a personal right of the employees.[23] The opinions discussed several issues which had attended prior litigation over Section 301[24] but did not resolve them. The Court's plurality opinion,

---

[20]S. REP. NO. 105, 80th Cong., 1st Sess. 17-18 (1947).

[21]H. R. CONF. REP. NO. 510, 80th Cong., 1st Sess., 42 (1947). *See* NLRB v. C & C Plywood, 148 NLRB 414, 57 LRRM 1015 (1964); *see also* Chapter 20 *infra* at notes 30-33.

[22]*Supra* note 14.

[23]348 US at 439-61 (Frankfurter, Burton & Minton, J.J.); *id.* at 461 (Warren, C.J., Clark, J.); *id.* at 464 (Reed, J.). These rights are variously characterized as "peculiar to the individual benefit which is their subject matter," *id.* at 460, "uniquely personal," *id.* at 461, and arising "from separate hiring contracts between the employer and the employee," *id.* at 464.

[24]Does §301 give to the federal courts jurisdiction to apply state law? Is such a grant of jurisdiction in conflict with Article III, §2, of the Constitution? Does §301 create a federal substantive law? Or may the federal courts apply state law under a theory of "protective jurisdiction"? For relevant cases, *see id.* at 452 nn. 25 & 26. *See also* Textile Workers v. Lincoln Mills, *supra* note 14 at 450-51 nn. 1 & 2.

written by Justice Frankfurter, concluded that the language of the statute and the legislative history indicated that the section was "a mere procedural provision"[25] which did not create any substantive federal law to govern the enforcement of collective bargaining agreements.[26] Therefore, Justice Frankfurter found it difficult to sustain the view that suits under Section 301 involved a federal question; and he also noted that such suits were not based on diversity of citizenship. Accordingly, a serious question was posed as to whether there was any constitutional basis for the exercise of jurisdiction by federal courts over suits under Section 301. To avoid that issue and the difficulties which he believed would be presented by any attempt to elaborate a "federal common law" to govern the enforcement of collective bargaining agreements, Justice Frankfurter concluded that, whether or not the applicable substantive law (federal or state) recognized a right in a union to vindicate individual causes of action, "Congress did not intend to burden the federal courts" with such suits.[27]

The concurring opinion of Chief Justice Warren and Justice Clark relied only on their view of statutory intent, concluding that Congress by Section 301 did not intend to authorize a union to enforce in a federal court the "uniquely personal right of an employee" to receive wages.[28] Justice Reed proposed that at least some federal law was applicable in Section 301 suits, but that a suit for wages arises out of a separate hiring contract and not out of the collective bargaining agreement, as would be required under Section 301.[29]

Justice Douglas' dissent stated that Congress "created federal sanctions for collective bargaining agreements, made cases and controversies concerning them justiciable questions for the federal courts, and permitted those courts to fashion from the federal statute, from state law, or from other germane sources, federal rules for the construction and interpretation of those collective bargaining agreements."[30] In addition, the dissenters

---

[25]348 US at 449.
[26]*Id.* at 459.
[27]*Id.*
[28]*Id.* at 461.
[29]*Id.* at 464.
[30]*Id.* at 465. (Black and Douglas, J.J.)

would have held that the union had standing to bring the suit.[31]

The basic constitutional question of *Westinghouse* was settled in the watershed case of *Textile Workers* v. *Lincoln Mills*.[32] The union had brought an action under Section 301 for specific enforcement of an agreement to arbitrate. The Supreme Court, in an opinion written by Justice Douglas, declared that an agreement to arbitrate is a "quid pro quo" for a no-strike agreement. Section 301 was viewed as expressing a federal policy that "federal courts should enforce these agreements . . . and that industrial peace can be best obtained only in this way."[33] The Court then held that "the substantive law to apply in suits under §301(a) is federal law, which the courts must fashion from the policy of our national labor laws."[34] It thus rejected the theory that Section 301 is not itself a source of substantive law and is merely jurisdictional.

The Court charted the course of a new common law of the collective bargaining agreement. Although some substantive law could be found in the Labor Management Relations Act, Justice Douglas noted that

> [o]ther problems will lie in the penumbra of express statutory mandates. Some will lack express statutory sanctions but will be solved by looking at the policy of the legislation and fashioning a remedy that will effectuate that policy. The range of judicial inventiveness will be determined by the nature of the problem . . . . Federal interpretation of the federal law will govern, not state law.[35]

Nevertheless, state law "if compatible with the purpose of §301, may be resorted to in order to find the rule that will best effectuate the federal policy."[36] Such state law, however, is "not . . . an independent source of private rights."[37] Since federal law was at issue, the Court found no constitutional impediment; a case arising under Section 301 is a case arising under the laws of the United States. "It is not uncommon for federal courts to fashion federal law where federal rights are concerned."[38]

---

[31]*Id.*
[32]*Supra* note 14. Two companion cases were also decided: Godall-Sanford, Inc. v. Textile Workers, 353 US 550, 40 LRRM 2118 (1957); General Elec. Co. v. Local 205, Elec. Workers (UE), 353 US 547, 40 LRRM 2119 (1957).
[33]353 US at 455.
[34]*Id.* at 456.
[35]*Id.* at 457.
[36]*Id.*
[37]*Id.*
[38]*Id.*

Although *Lincoln Mills* distinguished *Westinghouse*, it also undermined its rationale.[39] Thus it was no great surprise when in 1962, in *Smith* v. *Evening News Association*,[40] the Supreme Court finally announced the demise of *Westinghouse*. At the same time, it held that under Section 301 an individual employee, as well as a union, has a right to sue for the breach of a collective bargaining agreement.[41]

C. The *Steelworkers Trilogy*

From its inception, the new common law of the collective bargaining agreement had grievance arbitration as its centerpiece. In 1960 the Supreme Court enshrined that centerpiece in three protective decisions known as the *Steelworkers Trilogy*:[42] *American Manufacturing*,[43] *Warrior & Gulf*,[44] and *Enterprise Wheel*.[45] Justice Douglas was again the author of the Court's opinions.

In *American Manufacturing* the Court addressed the problem of judicial intervention into the merits of the grievance prior to submission to arbitration. The case involved the discharge of an employee following settlement of his worker's compensation action in which his physician had expressed the opinion that the employee's injury had rendered him permanently partially disabled. The employer relied on that opinion as the basis for refusing the grievant's reinstatement and for its own refusal to arbitrate the grievance. The district court held the employee was estopped because of his settlement in the worker's compensation action. The Sixth Circuit affirmed[46] because, in its view, the grievance was frivolous, patently baseless, and thus not subject to arbitration. The Supreme Court reversed, thereby rejecting application of the then popular *Cutler-Hammer*[47] doctrine. The court in *Cutler-Hammer* had denied arbitration when "the

---

[39]Even after *Lincoln Mills*, some courts continued to deny unions the right to sue for employee wages. *See, e.g.*, Local 2040, Machinists v. Servel, Inc., 268 F2d 692, 44 LRRM 2340 (CA 7, 1959).

[40]371 US 195, 199, 51 LRRM 2646 (1962).

[41]*But cf.* Republic Steel Corp. v. Maddox, 379 US 650, 58 LRRM 2193 (1965), requiring exhaustion of contractual grievance remedies before an action can be brought under §301. *See* Chapter 28 *infra* at notes 47-66.

[42]For comprehensive analysis of the *Steelworkers Trilogy* and discussion of its progeny, *see* Morris, *Twenty Years of Trilogy: A Celebration, supra* note 2.

[43]Steelworkers v. American Mfg. Co., 363 US 564, 46 LRRM 2414 (1960).

[44]Steelworkers v. Warrior & Gulf Navigation Co., 363 US 574, 46 LRRM 2416 (1960).

[45]Steelworkers v. Enterprise Wheel & Car Corp., 363 US 593, 46 LRRM 2423 (1960).

[46]264 F2d 624, 43 LRRM 2757 (CA 6, 1959).

[47]271 App.Div. 917, 67 NYS2d 317, *aff'd*, 297 NY 519, 74 NE2d 464, 20 LRRM 2445 (1947).

meaning of the provision of the contract sought to be arbitrated" was deemed by the court to be "beyond dispute."[48] The Supreme Court recognized that even frivolous cases could be arbitrated if the subject matter was arbitrable: "Whether the moving party is right or wrong is a question of contract interpretation for the arbitrator."[49] It was not the function of the courts to construe a collective bargaining provision that was subject to arbitration.

The second *Trilogy* case was *Warrior & Gulf*,[50] where the dispute concerned the contracting-out of maintenance work.[51] The employer relied on a provision in the collective agreement which stated that issues which were "strictly a function of management" were not arbitrable. The case thus concerned the question of *substantive arbitrability*.[52] Although the Supreme Court recognized that this was an issue to be determined by the court, it was to be determined with deference to the central role of arbitration under the collective agreement. Accordingly, the Court announced a *presumption of arbitrability:*

> [A]n order to arbitrate the particular grievance should not be denied unless it may be said with positive assurance that the arbitration clause is not susceptible of an interpretation that covers the asserted dispute. Doubts should be resolved in favor of coverage.[53]

In *Enterprise Wheel*,[54] the third *Trilogy* case, the Court addressed the issue of judicial review of the arbitrator's award. The case involved the discharge of several employees who had engaged in a work stoppage in protest of the discharge of a fellow employee. The arbitrator had found that although the work stoppage was improper, the discharges were not justified under the agreement. He therefore modified the discipline to a 10-day suspension.

The Fourth Circuit had denied enforcement of the arbitrator's remedy on the ground that the back-pay award for time subsequent to the expiration of the contract was unenforceable.

---

[48]271 App.Div. at 918.
[49]363 US at 568.
[50]*Supra* note 44.
[51]*Cf.* Fibreboard Paper Prods. Corp. v. NLRB, 379 US 203, 57 LRRM 2609 (1964); Chapter 17 *supra* at notes 268-80.
[52]*Cf.* John Wiley & Sons v. Livingston, 376 US 543, 55 LRRM 2769 (1964), where the Court ruled that the determination of *procedural arbitrability* was properly the function of the arbitrator.
[53]363 US at 582-83.
[54]*Supra* note 45.

It was the Supreme Court's view, as expressed in all the *Trilogy* opinions, that the parties had contracted for the arbitrator's judgment and the courts were not to reject that judgment merely because they disagreed with the interpretation of the arbitrator.[55] Accordingly,

> [t]he labor arbitrator's source of law is not confined to the express provisions of the contract as the industrial common law—the practices of the industry and the shop—is equally a part of the collective bargaining agreement, although not expressed in it.[56]

As the Court noted in a later case, the arbitrator was the "proctor"[57] of the parties' bargain. Consistent with that concept of the arbitrator's highly independent role, the Court in *Enterprise Wheel* approved the arbitrator's award and generally defined the limits of judicial review of an arbitrator's interpretation of the collective agreement. The respective roles of arbitrator and court were spelled out in the following language:

> [T]he arbitrator is confined to interpretation and application of the collective bargaining agreement; he does not sit to dispense his own brand of industrial justice. He may of course look for guidance from many sources, yet his award is legitimate only so long as it draws its essence from the collective agreement. When the arbitrator's words manifest an infidelity to his obligation, courts have no choice but to refuse enforcement of the award.[58]

The court expressly declined to accept a standard of review which would require an arbitrator to apply the "correct principle of law to the interpretation of the collective bargaining agreement," because

> acceptance of this view would require courts . . . to review the merits of every construction of the contract [making] meaningless the provisions that the arbitrator's decision is final . . . . It is the arbitrator's construction which was bargained for; and so far as the arbitrator's decision concerns construction of the contract, the courts have no business overruling him because their interpretation of the contract is different from his.[59]

D. Jurisdiction of the Courts: State and Federal

The jurisdiction of the courts under Section 301 was clarified in *Charles Dowd Box Co.* v. *Courtney*[60] and in *Local 174, Teamsters*

---

[55]Warrior & Gulf, *supra* note 44 at 578.
[56]*Id.* at 581-82.
[57]Alexander v. Gardner-Denver Co., 415 US 36, 53, 7 FEP Cases 81 (1974).
[58]363 US at 597.
[59]*Id.* at 598-99.
[60]368 US 502, 49 LRRM 2619 (1962).

v. *Lucas Flour Co.*[61] In the first of these cases the Court held that state courts have concurrent jurisdiction with the federal courts over suits brought under Section 301. In affirming the Supreme Judicial Court of Massachusetts, the Supreme Court held that Section 301 does not divest the state courts of jursidiction, but rather was meant to supplement state jurisdiction. Section 301 provides that suits of the kind described "may" be brought in the federal district courts, not that they must be.[62] The Court noted that "nothing in the concept of our federal system prevents state courts from enforcing rights created by federal law."[63]

In *Lucas Flour* the Court made clear, however, that federal law prevails in the substantive interpretation of labor contracts. Where local laws are incompatible with the principles of federal labor law, the former must give way to the latter.[64] In stressing the need for uniform law in cases arising under Section 301, the Court noted that "the existence of possibly conflicting legal concepts might substantially impede the parties' willingness to agree to contract terms for final arbitral or judicial resolution of disputes."[65] The Court concluded that "in enacting Section 301 Congress intended doctrines of federal labor law uniformly to prevail over inconsistent local rules."[66]

E. Jurisdiction of the Courts: Preemption

As noted, *Lincoln Mills* established the jurisdiction of the courts to enforce collective bargaining agreements. Under the doctrine of federal preemption,[67] in matters arguably subject to Section 7 or Section 8 of the Act, "the states as well as the federal courts must defer to the exclusive competence of the National Labor Relations Board."[68] Nevertheless, a series of cases decided by the Supreme Court in 1962[69] securely established that the courts have jurisdiction over suits arising under collective bargaining

---

[61]369 US 95, 49 LRRM 2717 (1962).
[62]368 US at 506.
[63]*Id.* at 507.
[64]369 US at 104.
[65]*Id.*
[66]*Id.*
[67]*See* Chapter 31 at notes 210-37 *infra* for a more detailed discussion of §301 and preemption. *See also* the discussion of preemption in fair representation cases in Chapter 28 *infra* at notes 139-59.
[68]San Diego Bldg. Trades Council v. Garmon, 359 US 236, 245, 43 LRRM 2838 (1959). *See* Chapter 31 *infra* at notes 75-86.
[69]Smith v. Evening News Ass'n, *supra* note 40; Sinclair Ref. Co. v. Atkinson, 370 US 195, 50 LRRM 2420; (1962); Local 174, Teamsters v. Lucas Flour Co., *supra* note 61; Charles Dowd Box Co. v. Courtney, *supra* note 60.

contracts by virtue of Section 301, even though the conduct involved is arguably subject to the provisions of the NLRA.[70]

In *Smith* v. *Evening News Association*,[71] the Court expressly held that "[t]he authority of the Board to deal with an unfair labor practice which also violates a collective bargaining contract is not displaced by §301, but it is not exclusive and does not destroy the jurisdiction of the courts under §301."[72] That holding was reaffirmed in 1974 in *William E. Arnold Co.* v. *Carpenters District Council.*[73]

F. Conflict or Accommodation?

1. Federal and State Courts. Since both state and federal courts have jurisdiction, "[i]t is implicit . . . that 'diversities and conflicts' may occur, no less among the courts of the . . . federal circuits, than among the courts of the several states."[74] It is the function of the Supreme Court "to resolve and accommodate such diversities"[75] under one federal law.

Lucas Flour[76] explicated the preeminence of federal law, a matter which had been considered by only a few of the state courts that had assumed jurisdiction in Section 301 suits.[77] The Court there reemphasized that "the subject matter of §301(a) 'is peculiarly one that calls for uniform law.' . . . The possibility that individual contract terms might have different meaning under state and federal law would inevitably exert a disruptive influence upon both the negotiation and administration of collective agreements."[78] In the Court's view, the existence of possibly conflicting legal concepts would impede the process of negotiating collective agreements, would stimulate and prolong

---

[70]Prior to these decisions, some courts had opted for the exclusive jurisdiction of the NLRB. *See, e.g.,* Chemical Workers v. Olin Mathieson Chem. Corp., 202 F Supp 363, 49 LRRM 2646 (SD Ill, 1962); Doll & Toy Workers v. Metal Polishers, 180 F Supp 280, 45 LRRM 2567 (SD Cal, 1960).

[71]*Supra* note 40.

[72]*Id.* at 197. The arguments in favor of the exercise of concurrent jurisdiction by the courts are thoroughly analyzed in Sovern, *Section 301 and the Primary Jurisdiction of the NLRB*, 76 HARV. L. REV. 529 (1963).

[73]417 US 12, 86 LRRM 2212 (1974) *infra* at notes 83 and 199-204. *See also* Chapter 31 *infra* at note 234.

[74]Charles Dowd Box Co. v. Courtney, *supra* note 60 at 514.

[75]*Id.*

[76]*Supra* note 61.

[77]*See, e.g.,* McCarroll v. Los Angeles County Dist. Council of Carpenters, 49 Cal2d 45, 60, 315 P2d 322, 330, 40 LRRM 2709, 2715 (1957), *cert. denied,* 355 US 932, 41 LRRM 2431 (1958); Local 774, Machinists v. Cessna Aircraft Co., 186 Kan 569, 352 P2d 420, 56 LRRM 2459 (1960).

[78]369 US at 103.

disputes, and would militate against the inclusion of arbitration provisions in a contract;[79] the area of federal labor policy is so important that "the need for a single body of federal law [is] particularly compelling."[80]

2. The Board and the Courts. The Supreme Court recognized that the exercise of concurrent jurisdiction by the Board and the courts might raise "serious problems," but it has preferred to face these problems as they occur.[81] The Board is on record to the effect that concurrent jurisdiction in this area will actually promote the purposes of the LMRA.[82] Furthermore, the Board has declined to exercise its own jurisdiction when it believes that the federal labor policy is better served by leaving the parties to other procedures.[83] As pointed out in *Charles Dowd Box*, Congress "deliberately chose to leave the enforcement of collective bargaining agreements 'to the usual process of the law.' "[84] But shortly after the Court indicated that enforcement of a contract by a court does not affect the jurisdiction of the Board to remedy unfair labor practices.[85] Thus, while the Court may assure uniformity of legal principle by reason of final review, it remains possible for the Board and a court to render contradictory decisions; it has been suggested that some inconsistency is the price to be paid to ensure prompt and efficient enforcement of contract rights.[86]

In some cases, however, the decision of one forum may, as a practical matter, determine the result in the other. An example was the decision of the Ninth Circuit in *NLRB* v. *Heyman*.[87] The employer in *Heyman* had filed a Section 301 suit seeking rescission of a labor agreement, and the district court had granted that relief.[88] Thereafter, the employer refused to make welfare

---

[79]*Id.*

[80]369 US at 104, 49 LRRM at 2721.

[81]Smith v. Evening News Ass'n, *supra* note 40 at 197-98.

[82]*Id.* at 197 n.6.

[83]*Id. See* discussion of the *Spielberg* and *Collyer* doctrines in Chapter 20 *infra*. In reaffirming the jurisdiction of the courts over §301 suits involving alleged unfair labor practices, the Supreme Court, in *William E. Arnold*, referred to the Board's policy "to refrain from exercising jurisdiction in respect of disputed conduct arguably both an unfair labor practice and a contract violation when . . . the parties have voluntarily established by contract a binding settlement procedure." *Supra* note 73 at 16 (citing, *inter alia, Collyer Insulated Wire*, 192 NLRB 837, 77 LRRM 1931 (1971)).

[84]*Supra* note 60 at 513.

[85]Smith v. Evening News Ass'n, *supra* note 40 at 197. *See also* Dunau, *supra* note 2.

[86]*See* Sovern, *supra* note 2.

[87]541 F2d 796, 92 LRRM 3603 (CA 9, 1976).

[88]The court granted rescission on the ground that the union did not represent a majority of the employees in the unit. The Supreme Court has indicated in *dictum* that

and pension fund payments required under the contract, terminated the agreement, and withdrew recognition from the union. The union filed unfair labor practice charges, and the Board held that the employer had violated Section 8(a)(5) of the Act. Noting that the Board's findings were premised on the continued existence of the contract, the Ninth Circuit refused to enforce the Board's order. The court viewed the Board proceedings as an "implicit collateral attack" on the district court's judgment of rescission, and asserted that "the Board cannot breathe new life into that which has expired by judicial decree";[89] it concluded that "[i]n the absence of a valid contract, by virtue of the district court judgment of rescission, repudiation and refusal to negotiate could not constitute unfair labor practices."[90]

By the same token, findings by the Board in unfair labor practice cases have been given effect in subsequent Section 301 suits, either as res judicata or by application of the doctrine of collateral estoppel.[91]

G. Jurisdiction of the Courts: Application of Norris-LaGuardia

1. From *Sinclair Refining* to *Boys Markets*. Section 301 cannot be read in isolation from Section 4 of the Norris-LaGuardia

---

"[a] union's majority standing is subject to litigation in a §301 suit to enforce a §8(f) contract, just as it is in a §8(a)(5) unfair labor practice proceeding, and that absent a showing that the union is the majority's chosen instrument, the contract is unenforceable." NLRB v. Iron Workers Local 103, 434 US 335, 351-52, 97 LRRM 2333 (1978). *See also* Western Washington Laborers-Employers Health & Security Trust Fund v. McDowell, 103 LRRM 2219 (WD Wash, 1979). *See also* Chapter 13 *supra* at notes 644-64 regarding §8(f) agreements.

[89]541 F2d at 799-800.

[90]*Id.* at 801. Judge Kennedy, concurring, noted that the Board had "refused to give any weight at all to the district court's decision," and stated that the court's findings should have been given "at least some collateral estoppel effect" by the Board. *Id.* at 802. In a related case, the Washington Supreme Court, sitting *en banc*, considered a suit by a welfare and pension fund which alleged that the employer owed the fund payments pursuant to the collective bargaining agreement. Trust Fund Services v. Heyman, 88 Wash2d 698, 565 P2d 805, 95 LRRM 3040 (1977). The court affirmed a judgment for the fund, refusing to be bound by the district court's rescission of the contract. *But cf.* Western Washington Laborers-Employers Health & Security Trust Fund v. McDowell, *supra* note 88.

[91]*See, e.g.,* Edward D. Sultan Co. v. Teamsters Local 427, 95 LRRM 3081 (D Hawaii, 1977). Problems of concurrent Board and court jurisdiction, and of the proper application of the doctrines of res judicata and collateral estoppel, also arise in suits under §303. *See* Chapter 25 *infra*. With respect to the separate problem of substantive conflicts between arbitration awards based on the terms of a contract and NLRB orders on the requirements of the Act, *see* Chapter 20 *infra*.

Act.[92] This section deprives the federal courts of jurisdiction to issue injunctions that would prohibit certain specified acts in connection with a labor dispute.[93] *Lincoln Mills* rejected the argument that Norris-LaGuardia withdrew from the courts jurisdiction to compel arbitration.[94] But in *Sinclair Refining Co.* v. *Atkinson*[95] the Supreme Court held that no-strike clauses in collective bargaining agreements were not specifically enforceable in the federal courts and that Section 301 had in no way diminished the force of the federal anti-injunction legislation.

The effect of the ruling in *Sinclair Refining* was made even stronger by the Supreme Court's subsequent decision in *Avco Corp.*,[96] which held that a suit brought in a state court under Section 301 to enforce a no-strike clause was removable to the

---

[92]29 USC §104 (1964). For bibliographical material *see* the following: Cantor, *Buffalo Forge and Injunctions Against Employer Breaches of Collective Bargaining Agreements*, 1980 WIS. L. REV. 247 (1980); Fried, *Injunctions Against Sympathy Strikes: In Defense of Buffalo Forge*, 54 N.Y.U. L. REV. 289 (1979); Note, *Injunctions Restraining Employers Pending Arbitration: Equity and Labor Policy*, 82 DICK. L. REV. 481 (1978); Cohen, *Strikes and Injunctions: The Buffalo Forge Case*, NYU THIRTIETH ANNUAL CONFERENCE ON LABOR 171 (1977); Lowden & Flaherty, *Sympathy Strikes, Arbitration Policy and the Enforceability of No-Strike Agreements—An Analysis of Buffalo Forge*, 45 GEO. WASH. L. REV. 633 (1977); Smith, *Supreme Court—Boys Markets Labor Injunctions and Sympathy Work Stoppages*, 44 U. CHI. L. REV. 321 (1977); Note, *Prospective Boys Markets Injunctions*, 90 HARV. L. REV. 790 (1977); Note, *Prospective Injunctions and Federal Labor Law Policy: Of Future Strikes, Arbitration, and Equity*, 52 NOTRE DAME L. REV. 790 (1976); Axelrod, *The Application of the Boys Markets Decision in the Federal Courts*, 16 B.C. IND. & COM. L. REV. 893 (1975); Comment, *Injunctions May Issue Against Labor Unions to End Strike Over Safety Disputes Despite Absence of a No-Strike Clause in Collective Bargaining Agreements*, 63 GEO. L. J. 275 (1974); Gould, *On Labor Injunctions, Unions, and the Judges: The Boys Markets Case*, 1970 SUP. CT. REV. 215 (1970); Rains, *Boys Markets Injunctions: Strict Scrutiny of the Presumption of Arbitrability*, 28 LAB. L.J. 30 (1970); Isaacson, *A Fresh Look at the Labor Injunction*, LABOR LAW DEVELOPMENTS 1970 (Seventeenth Annual Labor Law Institute, Southwestern Legal Foundation) (1970). *See also* materials cited in note 2 *supra*.

[93]The specified acts are numerous and are phrased in broad terms. Consequently the question seldom arises whether a particular act sought to be enjoined is outside the ambit of §4. That question did arise, however, in Bituminous Coal Operators Ass'n v. Mine Workers, 585 F2d 586, 99 LRRM 2612 (CA 3, 1978), where an employers' association sought an injunction enforcing an international union's alleged contractual obligation to ensure compliance by its members with the implied no-strike pledge in the collective bargaining agreement. Although the requested injunction would not by its terms have prohibited strikes or picketing, the court held §4 to be applicable, stating: "We do not hold that in a Section 301 suit an injunction would never be available to enforce a collateral, contractual undertaking not subject to arbitration, for conceivably some such contractual undertaking might not involve the activities protected by Section 4. But we do hold that where, as here, the real objective of the injunction sought is to prevent work stoppages and picketing, Section 4 applies." *Id.* at 594. Several cases have presented the question whether §4 applies to a strike called to further a union's political goals. The Supreme Court has resolved all doubts and has held that §4 applies in such cases. Jacksonville Bulk Terminals v. Longshoremen, 457 US ____, 110 LRRM 2665 (1982); *cf. also* Longshoremen v. Allied Int'l, Inc., 456 US 212, 110 LRRM 2001 (1982); Chapter 25, Part IV, *infra*.

[94]*Supra* note 14 at 457-59.

[95]*Supra* note 69.

[96]Avco Corp. v. Aero Lodge 735, Machinists, 390 US 557, 67 LRRM 2881 (1968).

federal courts. Taken together, *Sinclair Refining* and *Avco* severely limited the availability of injunctions against strikes in breach of contract. Injunction suits filed in state court could be removed to federal court, where no injunction could be issued.[97]

The decision in *Sinclair Refining* was controversial,[98] and it remained the law for only eight years. In *Boys Markets, Inc.* v. *Retail Clerks Local 770*[99] the Supreme Court reversed *Sinclair* in a five-to-two decision, holding that in certain circumstances strikes in breach of contract concerning matters which are subject to a mandatory grievance arbitration procedure may be enjoined by the federal courts.[100]

2. *Boys Markets* and Its Progeny. *a. The Prerequisites for Issuance of Injunctive Relief. (1) In general.* The *Boys Markets* majority, although asserting that Norris-LaGuardia does not bar the granting of injunctive relief in all cases, nonetheless emphasized the narrowness of its holding.[101] The Court said it was dealing only with the situation where a contract contains a "mandatory grievance adjustment or arbitration procedure." Even then, the Court stated, injunctive relief is not appropriate in every case

---

[97]Both *Sinclair* and *Avco* left unclear whether state courts could issue injunctions. *See* Avco, *supra* note 96 at 560 n.2; *cf.* Railroad Trainmen v. Jacksonville Terminal Co., 394 US 369, 382 n.18, 70 LRRM 2961 (1969). *See also* Summers, *Labor Law Decisions of the Supreme Court, 1961 Term,* in ABA LABOR RELATIONS LAW SECTION PROCEEDINGS 51, 63 (1962). For further discussion, *see infra* at notes 201-202. The Court in *Avco* reserved judgment on whether the restrictions of the Norris-LaGuardia Act are applicable when a suit brought in state court is removed to federal court. 390 US at 562 (concurring opinion).

Notwithstanding *Sinclair* and *Avco,* both state and federal courts often entered orders enforcing arbitration awards requiring the cessation of a strike. *See, e.g.,* Ruppert v. Egelhofer, 3 NY2d 576, 148 NE2d 129 (1958); New Orleans S.S. Ass'n v. Longshoremen Local 1418, 389 F2d 369, 67 LRRM 2430 (CA 5), *cert. denied,* 393 US 828, 69 LRRM 2434 (1968); Philadelphia Marine Trade Terminal Ass'n v. Longshoremen Local 1291, 365 F2d 295, 62 LRRM 2791 (CA 3, 1966), *reversed on other grounds,* 389 US 64, 66 LRRM 2433 (1967). *See generally,* M. Bernstein, PRIVATE DISPUTE SETTLEMENT 601-640 (1968); Note, *Circumventing Norris-LaGuardia with Arbitration Clauses,* 44 NOTRE DAME L. REV. 431 (1969).

[98]*See Report of Special Atkinson-Sinclair Committee,* in ABA LABOR RELATIONS LAW SECTION PROCEEDINGS 226 (1963). In that report, the neutral members of the "Special *Atkinson-Sinclair* Committee" recommended that *Sinclair* be overruled to permit injunctions against breach-of-contract strikes, but only where the dispute underlying the strike is arbitrable. *Id.* at 241-42.

[99]398 US 235, 74 LRRM 2257 (1970).

[100]Justice Black, joined by Justice White, dissented, observing that nothing had changed since 1962 except "the membership of the Court and the personal view of one Justice." Justice Stewart, the Justice to whom he referred, explained in a concurring opinion, quoting the late Justice Frankfurter, that "[w]isdom too often never comes, and so one ought not to reject it merely because it comes late." *Id.* at 255.

[101]*Id.* at 253.

"as a matter of course."[102] The Court adopted the prerequisites for injunctive relief which had been set forth in Justice Brennan's *Sinclair* dissent. Those prerequisites are as follows:

> A District Court entertaining an action under §301 may not grant injunctive relief against concerted activity unless and until it decides that the case is one in which an injunction would be appropriate despite the Norris-LaGuardia Act. When a strike is sought to be enjoined because it is over a grievance which both parties are contractually bound to arbitrate, the District Court may issue no injunctive order until it first holds that the contract *does* have the effect; and the employer should be ordered to arbitrate, as a condition of his obtaining an injunction against the strike. Beyond this, the District Court must, of course, consider whether issuance of an injunction would be warranted under ordinary principles of equity— whether breaches are occurring and will continue, or have been threatened and will be committed; whether they have caused or will cause irreparable injury to the employer; and whether the employer

---

[102]*Id.* at 253-54. In addition to §4, other sections of Norris-LaGuardia impose limitations on the issuance of injunctions which may be applicable in §301 suits brought to enforce no-strike obligations. For example, §9 [29 USC §109 (1970)], provides that "every restraining order or injunction granted in a case involving or growing out of a labor dispute shall include only a prohibition of such specific act or acts as may be expressly complained of in the . . . complaint . . . and as shall be expressly included in [the] findings of fact made and filed by the court . . . ." This section has been applied to limit the availability of broad, prospective injunctive relief in *Boys Markets* cases. See *infra* at notes 150-57. In addition, §7 [29 USC §107 (1970)], specifies several procedural and evidentiary requirements to be followed by the courts in issuing injunctions in labor disputes. The courts have generally held that the Norris-LaGuardia §7 requirements are applicable in *Boys Markets* cases consistent with the policies of §301. *See* United States Steel Corp. v. Mine Workers, 456 F2d 483, 79 LRRM 2518 (CA 3), *cert. denied*, 408 US 923, 80 LRRM 2855 (1972); Detroit Newspaper Publishers Ass'n v. Detroit Typographical Union No. 18, 471 F2d 872, 82 LRRM 2332 (CA 6, 1972), *cert. denied*, 411 US 967, 83 LRRM 2039 (1973); Celotex Corp. v. Oil Workers, 516 F2d 242, 89 LRRM 2372 (CA 3, 1975); Hoh v. Pepsico, Inc., 491 F2d 556, 85 LRRM 2517 (CA 2, 1974); United States v. Cunningham, 599 F2d 120, 126 n.12, 101 LRRM 2508 (CA 6, 1979); Hospital for Joint Diseases v. Davis, 442 F Supp 1030, 98 LRRM 2119 (SD NY, 1978). *Cf.* Associated Gen. Contractors v. Teamsters, 486 F2d 972, 975-76 n.8, 84 LRRM 2555 (CA 7, 1973). The Supreme Court has not addressed the question of the applicability of these various Norris-LaGuardia requirements in *Boys Markets* cases. In Granny Goose Foods, Inc. v. Teamsters Local 70, 415 US 423, 445 n.19, 85 LRRM 2481 (1974), the Court reserved decision on whether a temporary restraining order issued under *Boys Markets* is subject to the five-day limit contained in §7 of Norris-LaGuardia. There is a split in the circuits as to one important question in this area: whether a party's liability for injury caused by the grant of an injunction is limited to the amount it posted pursuant to the requirement of §7. *Compare* Chicago Typographical Union No. 16 v. Chicago Newspaper Publishers' Ass'n, 620 F2d 602, 605, 103 LRRM 2957, 2960 (CA 7, 1980), *and* Garment Workers v. Donnelly Garment Co., 147 F2d 246, 15 LRRM 923 (CA 8), *cert. denied*, 325 US 852, 16 LRRM 917 (1945), *with* United States Steel Corp. v. Mine Workers, *supra*.

With respect to the applicability of the *Boys Markets* concept to disputes which are subject to the Railway Labor Act, *see* Trans Int'l Airlines v. Teamsters Local 2707, 650 F2d 949, 103 LRRM 2669 (CA 9, 1980). The classic Railway Labor Act case allowing an injunction over a grievance subject to statutory arbitration was Railroad Trainmen v. Chicago River & Indiana R.R. Co., 353 US 30, 39 LRRM 2578 (1957), which the Supreme Court in Sinclair Ref. Co. v. Atkinson, *supra* note 69, had refused to follow by analogy.

will suffer more from its denial of an injunction than will the union from its issuance.[103]

These several prerequisites to injunctive relief will be treated in turn in the following sections.

(2)   The strike must be in breach of a contract. The principles enunciated in the *Sinclair* dissent and adopted by the *Boys Markets* majority emphasize that no injunction may issue against a strike unless the court first finds that the strike[104] is in breach of a no-strike clause. However, an express no-strike clause is not a prerequisite to a *Boys Markets* injunction. In *Lucas Flour*[105] the Supreme Court had held that where a dispute is arbitrable under the contract, the union ordinarily should be considered to have obligated itself not to strike over that dispute. This implied obligation served as the basis for the issuance of a *Boys Markets* injunction in *Gateway Coal Co. v. Mine Workers.*[106] The contract in *Gateway* did not contain a no-strike provision. The Supreme Court nonetheless held that absent an explicit expression of a contrary intention, an agreement to arbitrate should be construed, even in the absence of a no-strike clause, as giving rise to a no-strike obligation which is "coterminous" with the arbitration clause.[107]

The rule articulated in *Lucas Flour* and *Gateway Coal* is one of contract interpretation, and a no-strike obligation will not be implied from an arbitration clause where to do so would be inconsistent with the manifest intent of the parties.[108] In virtually

---

[103]398 US at 254 (quoting Sinclair Ref. Co. v. Atkinson, *supra* note 69, at 228) (emphasis in original).

[104]Various courts have held that there need not be a showing of an actual strike before relief may be granted. In National Rejectors Indus. v. Steelworkers, 562 F2d 1960, 96 LRRM 2120 (CA 8, 1977), *cert. denied*, 435 US 923, 97 LRRM 3040 (1978), an injunction was issued when the employer's plant was reduced to 70% of normal productivity primarily as a result of the suspension of numerous employees following a concerted refusal of employees to abide by six new work rules. *See also* Avco Corp. v. Automobile Workers Local 787, 459 F2d 968, 974, 80 LRRM 2290 (CA 3, 1972), where the court enjoined a concerted refusal to work overtime. However, an *implied* no-strike obligation will not ordinarily be construed to reach such conduct. *See* note 108 *infra*.

[105]*Supra* note 61.

[106]414 US 368, 85 LRRM 2049 (1974).

[107]*Id.* at 382.

[108]Prior to *Gateway Coal,* the Supreme Court had cautioned against linking no-strike obligations to arbitration provisions in every situation. *See* Drake Bakeries, Inc. v. Bakery Workers Local 50, 370 US 254, 261, 50 LRRM 2440 (1962). Justice Black argued in his *Lucas Flour* dissent that since employers regularly bargain for express no-strike clauses, the absence of such an express clause may indicate that the parties have considered and rejected its inclusion. 369 US at 109-10. After *Lucas Flour,* however, most courts have found that a no-strike obligation should be implied from an arbitration clause; but some courts have refused to draw such an inference where it would have been inconsistent

all cases, however, the courts have found it appropriate to infer the existence of a no-strike obligation with respect to matters which the parties are contractually bound to arbitrate.[109]

In *Carbon Fuel Co.*,[110] a damage action under Section 301, the Supreme Court held that in view of the negotiating history, where the union had reserved its right to decide what actions were appropriate to bring about the cessation of a wildcat strike, and in the absence of any proof that the union had authorized, ratified, or condoned the strike under the common-law principles of agency, an arbitration clause did not imply any obligation on the part of the union to use its "best efforts" to end the strike.[111]

Questions of interpretation have also arisen in the *Boys Markets* context with respect to certain types of express no-strike clauses. In particular, where a contract contains a broadly worded no-strike clause but specifies certain types of disputes as being exempt from the no-strike obligation, it is not always easy to determine whether the dispute sought to be enjoined is covered by the general no-strike clause or falls within one of the exemptions. In such a case, the Sixth Circuit ruled that "[w]here the union has expressly reserved its right to strike over certain issues, a *Boys Markets* injunction should not issue unless it clearly appears to the trial judge that the dispute which underlies the strike is subject to a no-strike obligation."[112]

(3) The strike must be over an arbitrable dispute. Since the object of a *Boys Markets* injunction is to aid the arbitration process, in

---

with the parties' bargaining history. *See, e.g.*, Rochester Tel. Corp. v. Communications Workers, 78 LRRM 2213 (WD NY, 1971), *rev'd on other grounds*, 456 F2d 1057, 79 LRRM 2770 (CA 2, 1972). Similarly, where the parties have bargained for an express no-strike clause narrower than the arbitration provisions, a broader no-strike obligation is not ordinarily implied. *See* NLRB v. State Elec. Serv., Inc., 477 F2d 749, 82 LRRM 3154 (CA 5), *cert. denied*, 414 US 911, 84 LRRM 2458 (1973). It has been held that an arbitration clause does not give rise to an implied "no-slowdown" obligation. Jessop Steel Co. v. Steelworkers, 428 F Supp 172, 94 LRRM 3089 (WD Pa, 1977).

[109]The Seventh Circuit found a no-strike promise in Eaton Corp. v. Machinists, 580 F2d 254, 258, 99 LRRM 2042 (CA 7, 1978), even though the contract provided that "nothing contained in this agreement is to be construed as abrogating the union's right to strike." The court relied on other contractual language requiring the exhaustion of the grievance and arbitration procedure and banning strikes pending arbitration. The court considered this unusual set of provisions to constitute an express no-strike clause notwithstanding the disclaimer.

[110]444 US 212, 102 LRRM 3017 (1979).

[111]This holding has been applied to a request for injunctive relief in Pittsburgh Steel Co. v. Steelworkers, 633 F2d 302, 307, 105 LRRM 2198 (CA 3, 1980).

[112]Waller Bros. Stone Co. v. District 23, Steelworkers, 620 F2d 132, 137, 104 LRRM 2168, 2171 (CA 6, 1980).

order to be enjoined a strike must be "over a grievance which both parties are contractually bound to arbitrate."[113] That is to say, the Supreme Court has constructed an equation: The extent to which injunctive relief will be available is equal to the extent of arbitrability under the parties' contract.

In *Boys Markets* the union had struck over a demand that supervisory employees cease performing bargaining-unit work, a dispute clearly "over" a grievance subject to the arbitration clause of the contract. By contrast, in *Buffalo Forge Co.* v. *Steelworkers*[114] the strike at issue was a sympathy strike in support of a sister union. Although the issue of whether the no-strike clause in the contract barred such sympathy strikes was subject to the grievance machinery, the strike itself "was not *over* any dispute between the Union and the employer that was even remotely subject to the arbitration provisions of the contract." Thus, "[t]he strike had neither the purpose nor the effect of denying or evading an obligation to arbitrate"[115] and therefore could not be enjoined.

The issue of whether a strike is "over" an arbitrable dispute may arise in numerous settings. For example, in *Jacksonville Bulk Terminals* v. *Longshoremen,*[116] the Supreme Court declined the invitation to overrule or modify *Buffalo Forge.* The case arose out of the ILA's boycott of cargo bound for the Soviet Union in protest of the Soviet invasion of Afghanistan. After finding the Norris-LaGuardia Act applicable to "politically motivated" work stoppages, the Court held that no *Boys Markets* injunction was available:

> *Buffalo Forge* makes it clear that a *Boys Markets* injunction pending arbitration should not issue unless the dispute underlying the work stoppage is arbitrable. The rationale of *Buffalo Forge* compels the conclusion that the Union's work stoppage, called to protest the invasion of Afghanistan by the Soviet Union, may not be enjoined pending the arbitrator's decision on whether the work stoppage violates the no-strike clause in the collective-bargaining agreement. The underlying dispute, whether viewed as an expression of the Union's "moral outrage" at Soviet military policy or as an expression of sympathy for the people of Afghanistan, is plainly not arbitrable under the collective-bargaining agreement.

---

[113]Boys Markets, *supra* note 99 at 254.
[114]428 US 397, 92 LRRM 3032 (1976). *See infra* at notes 163-64.
[115]*Id.* at 407-408. (Emphasis in original.)
[116]*Supra* note 93. *See also* Hampton Roads Shipping Ass'n v. Longshoremen, 631 F2d 282, 105 LRRM 2506 (CA 4, 1980).

The Court added:

> . . . The "underlying" disputes concerning the management-rights clause or the work-conditions clause simply did not trigger the work stoppage. To the contrary, the applicability of these clauses to the dispute, if any, was triggered by the work stoppage itself. Consideration of whether the strike intruded on the management-rights clause or was permitted by the work-conditions clause may inform the arbitrator's ultimate decision on whether the strike violates the no-strike clause. Indeed, the question whether striking over a nonarbitrable issue violates other provisions of the collective-bargaining agreement may itself be an arbitrable dispute. The fact remains, however, that the strike itself was not over an arbitrable dispute and therefore may not be enjoined pending the arbitrator's ruling on the legality of the strike under the collective bargaining agreement.[117]

The Court viewed the employer's argument as inconsistent with "the rationale of *Buffalo Forge*," namely, "the . . . Court's conclusion that, in agreeing to broad arbitration and no-strike clauses, the parties do not bargain for injunctive relief to restore the status quo pending the arbitrator's decision on the legality of the strike under the collective-bargaining agreement, without regard to what triggered the strike. Instead, they bargain only for specific enforcement of the union's promise to arbitrate the underlying grievance before resorting to a strike."[118]

Some requests for injunctions against wildcat strikes often run afoul of the requirement of arbitrability. In *Automobile Transport, Inc.* v. *Ferdnance*[119] a district court held that it lacked jurisdiction to enjoin a wildcat strike protesting the union's failure to represent properly the strikers at the bargaining table. Although the strike may have violated the no-strike clause, the arbitration provisions did not provide for interest arbitration or arbitration of internal disputes. *Complete Auto Transit, Inc.* v. *Reis*[120] also involved a wildcat strike that had not been precipitated by any dispute with the employer, but rather by differences between the union members and the union. The lower court denied injunctive relief, relying on the Supreme Court's deci-

---

[117]110 LRRM at 2672. *See* Chapter 1 *supra* at notes 72-79 for historical treatment of the Norris-LaGuardia Act and notes 162-74 *infra* this chapter regarding the applicability of that Act in sympathy strike situations.
[118]*Id.* at 2673.
[119]420 F. Supp 75, 92 LRRM 3610 (ED Mich, 1976).
[120]641 F2d 1110, 103 LRRM 2722 (CA 6, 1980), *aff'd on other grounds*, 451 US 401, 107 LRRM 2145 (1981). The Supreme Court expressly reserved decision on this issue. *Id.* at 404-405 and note 4. *See also* Jacksonville Bulk Terminals v. Longshoremen, *supra* note 93 at 2673 n.22.

sion in *Buffalo Forge*,[121] finding that the strike was not over an arbitrable dispute. Thereafter, although the union and its members settled their dispute, the strike continued over the employer's refusal to grant amnesty to the strikers. The employer again moved for injunctive relief, and the lower court again refused to issue an injunction. The Sixth Circuit reversed, finding that the work stoppage which had begun over a dispute which was not subject to arbitration had continued because of a dispute which *was* arbitrable—the amnesty issue. Accordingly, the new dispute fell within the ambit of *Boys Markets*.[122]

In determining whether a strike is over an arbitrable dispute, the Supreme Court announced in *Gateway Coal Co. v. Mine Workers*[123] that the presumption of arbitrability enunciated in *Warrior & Gulf*[124] should be applied in *Boys Markets* cases.[125]

Once it is found that the dispute is subject to an arbitration procedure, the court may not enjoin the strike unless the employer

---

[121]*Supra* note 114. *See infra* at notes 162-69.

[122]Another novel situation arose in CCSC v. Steelworkers, 436 F Supp 208, 95 LRRM 3257 (WD Pa, 1977). Various steel and iron ore companies and the Steelworkers entered into Basic Labor Agreements (BLAs) which incorporated the settlement between the Steelworkers and the employers on "national" issues. The BLAs contained mandatory arbitration and no-strike clauses. The parties also entered into an Experimental Negotiating Agreement (ENA) which provided for binding interest arbitration as the substitute for the right to strike or lockout as to all "national," but not "local," issues which the parties could not resolve at the bargaining table. The ENA did not provide for arbitration of the term "local." After agreement on the new BLAs, various locals struck, with the International's consent, allegedly over unresolved "local" issues; thereupon the employers' group sought a *Boys Markets* injunction on the theory that the arbitration provisions of the BLAs applied to these disputes, since local issues, which were not covered by the ENA, were not involved. The court denied the injunction, holding that the grievance-arbitration procedure in the BLAs was designed to resolve questions about existing rights arising out of those contracts, not questions arising out of demands for "new rights in future contracts." Hence, the strikes were not "precipitated" by issues which the union was bound to arbitrate.

[123]*Supra* note 106.

[124]*Supra* notes 44 and 53.

[125]*See also* National Rejectors Indus. v. Steelworkers, 562 F2d 1069, 96 LRRM 2120 (CA 8, 1977), *cert. denied*, 435 US 923, 97 LRRM 3040 (1978). Prior to *Gateway*, the Second Circuit had held that no injunction may issue where the union presents a "colorable claim" that the underlying dispute falls within a specific exception to the arbitration clause and the union has retained the right to strike over nonarbitrable issues. Standard Food Prods. Corp. v. Brandenburg, 436 F2d 964, 966, 76 LRRM 2367 (CA 2, 1970). *See also* Waller Bros. Stone Co. v. District 23, Steelworkers, *supra* note 112. The Fifth Circuit, in contrast, had held that a strike could be enjoined where the underlying dispute is "arguably arbitrable." Southwestern Bell Tel. Co. v. Communications Workers, 454 F2d 1333, 1336, 78 LRRM 2833 (CA 5, 1971). The Third Circuit had adopted a similar standard in Avco Corp. v. Automobile Workers Local 787, *supra* note 104.

The presumption of arbitrability in *Boys Markets* cases is important, for the choice of a standard for determining what issues are arbitrable may determine whether an injunction issues. *See* Axelrod, *The Application of the Boys Markets Decision in the Federal Courts*, 16 B.C. IND. & COM. L. REV. 893, 914-19 (1975).

is willing to arbitrate the underlying dispute.[126] In *Jacksonville Maritime Association* v. *Longshoremen*,[127] however, the Fifth Circuit rejected the union's contention that the employer must both allege and *prove* its willingness to arbitrate an admittedly arbitrable issue before an injunction could properly issue. The court stated that, while the issue was left "unsettled" by *Buffalo Forge*,[128] it would not accept such a "procedural nicety" absent a clear directive from the Supreme Court.[129] On the other hand, some district courts have held that an employer must affirmatively pursue arbitration in order to prevail in a request for injunctive relief.[130] In any event, an attempt to avoid arbitration while at the same time seeking injunctive relief would not satisfy the *Boys Markets* prerequisites.[131]

Mutuality of access to arbitration by the employer and the union is not a prerequisite to enjoining a strike. In *Eaton Corp.* v. *Machinists*[132] the Seventh Circuit rejected the union's claim that an injunction could not issue since the employer had no "obligation" to initiate a grievance and take it to arbitration. The court held that *Boys Markets* does not require that both parties have the right to initiate arbitration, but only that both parties be bound to arbitrate if the union elects to pursue that remedy.[133]

Where the arbitration obligation has expired or terminated, a *Boys Markets* injunction is inappropriate.[134] Moreover, *Boys Markets* applies only where the collective bargaining agreement

---

[126]Indeed, the court must order arbitration of the dispute prior to the issuance of the injunction. *See* discussion *infra* at notes 147-49.

[127]571 F2d 319, 98 LRRM 2184 (CA 5, 1978).

[128]*Supra* note 114.

[129]571 F2d at 324.

[130]Restaurant Associates Indus. v. Local 71, Transportation Employees, 78 LRRM 2559 (ED NY, 1971); Elevator Mfg. Ass'n of New York v. Elevator Constructors Local 1, 331 F Supp 165, 78 LRRM 2215 (SD NY, 1971).

[131]Chief Freight Lines Co. v. Teamsters Local 886, 514 F2d 572, 89 LRRM 2044, 2051 (CA 10, 1975). *But cf.* Anheuser-Busch v. Local 133, Teamsters, 477 F Supp 742, 102 LRRM 2990 (ED Mo, 1979), where the court granted an injunction to an employer despite the union's contention that the dispute had already been arbitrated and that the employer was refusing to comply with the award.

[132]580 F2d 254, 99 LRRM 2042 (CA 7, 1978).

[133]*Id.; see also* Steelworkers v. Fort Pitt Steel Casting, 598 F2d 1273, 101 LRRM 2406 (CA 3, 1979); Avco Corp. v. Automobile Workers Local 787, *supra* note 104.

[134]National Mine Serv. Co. v. Steelworkers, 385 F Supp 856, 87 LRRM 3288 (ND WV, 1974), *aff'd per curiam*, 510 F2d 966, 88 LRRM 2847 (CA 4, 1975) (contract properly terminated by union); A.S. Abell Co. v. Baltimore Typographical Union No. 12, 85 LRRM 2368 (D Md, 1974) (contract expired). It should be noted, however, that the obligation to arbitrate does not necessarily terminate with the expiration of the contract. *See* Nolde Bros. v. Local 358, Bakery Workers, 430 US 243, 94 LRRM 2753 (1977).

contains a "mandatory" grievance adjustment or arbitration procedure, i.e., one which requires that contract disputes be settled by the grievance-arbitration procedure and allows the union to invoke procedure without the employer's consent.[135] Finally, an arbitration clause, unlike a no-strike clause, must be expressly agreed upon by the parties; an arbitration clause will not be implied from other contractual commitments.[136]

(4) Irreparable injury and the balance of equities. In *Boys Markets* the Court cautioned the lower courts not to issue injunctive relief unless warranted under ordinary principles of equity, including whether the alleged contract breaches "have caused or will cause irreparable injury to the employer; and whether the employer will suffer more from the denial of an injunction than will the union from its issuance."[137] The courts have usually found irreparable injury[138] and that the equities favored the employer.[139] Often the courts have simply stated, without discussion, that the employer would suffer more from the denial of an injunction than the union would from a grant of relief.[140] In thus striking the balance in favor of the employer, however, the courts have often required the employer to take certain

---

[135]*See* Boys Markets, *supra* note 99 at 253. Courts have held that provisions requiring mutual consent for submission to arbitration cannot support a *Boys Markets* injunction, reasoning that *Boys Markets* applies only to institutionalized arbitration procedures and not to *ad hoc* arrangements. *See* Associated Gen. Contractors of Illinois v. Illinois Conference of Teamsters, 454 F2d 1324, 79 LRRM 2555 (CA 7, 1972); Womeldorf, Inc. v. Teamsters Local 220, 369 F Supp 901, 87 LRRM 2316 (WD Pa, 1974). On the other hand, the fact that a contract states that a party "may" invoke arbitration, rather than stating that it *must* do so, does not render injunctive relief unavailable. Steelworkers v. Fort Pitt Steel Casting, *supra* note 133 at 2410.

[136]*See* Lynchburg Foundry Co. v. Pattern Makers, 597 F2d 384, 101 LRRM 2047 (CA 4, 1979); Operating Eng'rs v. Trumbull Corp., 93 LRRM 2337 (SD Fla, 1976).

[137]*Supra* note 99 at 254. Earlier in its opinion the Court remarked that "an award of damages after a dispute has been settled is no substitute for an immediate halt to an illegal strike." *Id.* at 248. This statement, however, concerned whether injunctive relief should be available under any circumstances; it does not undercut the requirement that an employer must prove irreparable injury under the facts of its particular case in order to obtain an injunction. *See* Granny Goose Foods v. Teamsters, *supra* note 102 at 441-42.

[138]*See, e.g.,* Jacksonville Maritime Ass'n v. Longshoremen, *supra* note 127; General Bldg. Contractors Ass'n v. Operating Eng'rs, 371 F Supp 1130, 86 LRRM 2677 (ED Pa, 1974).

[139]*See, e.g.,* Gateway Coal Co. v. Mine Workers, *supra* note 106; Western Publishing Co. v. Graphic Arts Local 254, 552 F2d 530, 90 LRRM 2257 (CA 7, 1975), *cert. denied,* 423 US 1088, 91 LRRM 2195 (1976). On the issue of the relative equities between the employer and the union, decisions involving union efforts to obtain "status quo" injunctions, discussed *infra* at notes 179-98, are instructive.

[140]*See, e.g.,* Edward L. Nezelek, Inc. v. Teamsters Local 294, 342 F Supp 507, 80 LRRM 3459 (ND NY, 1972).

actions pending arbitration,[141] which in effect may grant the union complete or partial relief pending arbitration.[142]

There have been very few cases in which courts have completely denied injunctive relief solely on general equity grounds.[143] In one such case, *Anheuser-Busch, Inc.* v. *Teamsters Local 633*,[144] the First Circuit held that a district court abused its discretion by enjoining a strike which had been brought on by an employer's disciplining of brewery employees for wearing "tank top" shirts.[145] While the dispute over the employer's right to prohibit the wearing of such shirts was concededly an issue subject to the grievance-arbitration procedures of the contract, the First Circuit stated: "[A]n employer cannot be permitted to qualify for injunctive relief simply by responding to minor employee infractions in a way that brings serious and irreparable damage upon himself by causing a shutdown . . . ."[146] The court indicated that the real controversy was whether the employees should be allowed to wear tank-top shirts pending submission to arbitration. Viewed from this perspective, the court said that the employer's expected injury could not be deemed either irreparable or one which outweighs the loss that the union was likely to suffer through issuance of an injunction.

(5) The employer should be ordered to arbitrate. As stated in *Boys Markets*, "the employer should be ordered to arbitrate as a con-

---

[141]*E.g.*, Hanna Mining Co. v. Steelworkers, 464 F2d 565, 80 LRRM 3268 (CA 8, 1972) (per curiam).

[142]*E.g.*, Gateway Coal v. Mine Workers, *supra* note 106 (termination of two foremen who violated safety rules; district court, in issuing *Boys Markets* injunction, ordered employer to suspend the two foremen pending arbitration); Hanna Mining Co. v. Steelworkers, *supra* note 141. *Cf. infra* at notes 179-84.

[143]For example, *see* Anheuser-Busch, Inc. v. Teamsters Local 633, 511 F2d 1097, 88 LRRM 2785 (CA 1), *cert. denied*, 423 US 875, 90 LRRM 2744 (1975); North Am. Coal Corp. v. Local 2262, Mine Workers, 497 F2d 459, 86 LRRM 2339 (1974); Health Care Facilities Ass'n v. Ottley, 499 F Supp 279, 106 LRRM 2181 (SD NY, 1980) (court dissolves preliminary injunction due to employer association's inequitable conduct in engineering lockout at one facility and failing to meet obligations with regard to health plan payments; court had originally struck balance of equities in favor of employer association, relying heavily on possible injury to nursing home patients, 493 F Supp 612, 106 LRRM 2169 (SD NY, 1980)).

[144]*Supra* note 143.

[145]Sleeveless shirts which leave exposed the shoulders, arms, and underarms of the wearer.

[146]511 F2d at 1099. *Anheuser-Busch* was distinguished in an Eighth Circuit decision, where the court affirmed a district court's issuance of a *Boys Markets* injunction, stating: "[The company] did not bring about the disruption itself by insisting upon enforcement of minor work rules. The company was willing to, and did in fact suspend enforcement of its rules pending resolution of the underlying dispute through arbitration." National Rejectors Indus. v. Steelworkers, *supra* note 125 at 1077.

dition of his obtaining an injunction against [a] strike."[147] The Second Circuit, in *Teamsters Local 807* v. *Bohack Corp.,*[148] set aside a *Boys Markets* injunction because of the failure of the district court to order arbitration of the underlying dispute. The district court had relied on the fact that the employer had earlier filed for bankruptcy and was operating under the jurisdiction of the bankruptcy court. The Second Circuit ruled that a bankruptcy action does not necessarily immunize an employer from strikes, and that bankruptcy does not relax *Boys Markets* requirements.[149]

(6) Limitations on prospective relief; mootness. Ordinarily, *Boys Markets* injunctions against strikes will be granted only where the strike is occurring or is imminent. In some cases, however, employers have sought and received prospective injunctive relief, i.e., injunctions prohibiting future strikes over events that have not yet occurred. The circuit courts have reached different results in reviewing prospective injunctions; however, they have generally applied similar criteria. The Seventh Circuit[150] and the Tenth Circuit[151] have affirmed prospective injunctions in situations where there was a pattern of past strike violations deemed likely to continue if not enjoined. The First,[152] Third,[153] Fifth,[154] and Sixth[155] Circuits have reversed prospective injunc-

---

[147]*Supra* note 99 at 254; *accord,* Teamsters Local 807 v. Bohack Corp., 541 F2d 312, 93 LRRM 2001 (CA 2, 1976); Emery Air Freight Corp. v. Local 295, Teamsters, 499 F2d 586, 78 LRRM 2466 (CA 2, 1971), *cert. denied,* 405 US 1066, 79 LRRM 3092 (1972).

[148]541 F2d 312, 93 LRRM 2001 (CA 2, 1976), *cert. denied,* 439 US 825 (1978).

[149]For a discussion of the relation of bankruptcy to NLRB action, *see* Chapter 31 *infra* at notes 419-506.

[150]Old Ben Coal Co. v. Mine Workers Local 1487 (II), 500 F2d 950, 87 LRRM 2078 (CA 7, 1974). The court affirmed a broad prospective injunction prohibiting "strikes resulting from any differences or local trouble which the parties are contractually obligated to arbitrate." *Id.* at 951. The local union had engaged in 25 strikes in breach of a no-strike clause over a three-and-a-half year period. The court had previously held, in Old Ben Coal Co. v. Mine Workers Local 1487 (I), 457 F2d 162, 79 LRRM 2845 (CA 7, 1972), that such broad prospective relief was inappropriate, but it warned the union that continued strikes could result in a broad decree. When the union engaged in eight illegal strikes within seven months of *Old Ben (I),* the court decided that a broad decree was appropriate. *Accord,* Peabody Coal Co. v. Local 1670, Mine Workers, 416 F Supp 485, 93 LRRM 2532 (ED Ill, 1976) (district court applies *Old Ben (II)* and issues broad prospective injunctive relief where local union had engaged in 37 strikes over arbitrable issues during a four-and-a-half year period).

[151]C F & I Steel Corp. v. Mine Workers, 507 F2d 170, 87 LRRM 3197 (CA 10, 1974) (injunction limited to future strikes over employee discharges, employee suspensions, and work assignments—issues over which the union was shown to have had a proclivity for striking).

[152]Latas Libby's, Inc. v. Steelworkers, 609 F2d 25, 102 LRRM 2796 (CA 1, 1979).

[153]United States Steel Corp. v. Mine Workers, 534 F2d 1063, 91 LRRM 3031 (CA 3, 1976); *see* Pittsburgh Steel Co. v. Steelworkers, 633 F2d 302, 105 LRRM 2198 (CA 3, 1980); BCOA v. Mine Workers, 585 F2d 586, 99 LRRM 2612 (CA 3, 1978).

[154]United States Steel Corp. v. Mine Workers, 519 F2d 1236, 90 LRRM 2539 (CA 5, 1975).

tions where there was insufficient proof of a pattern of past violations and where the injunctions were broadly framed to encompass strikes on issues over which the union had never previously struck. The Seventh Circuit has affirmed a prospective injunction prohibiting "strikes resulting from any differences or local trouble which the parties are contractually obligated to arbitrate."[156] In direct disagreement, the Fifth Circuit had held that such a broad injunction is prohibited by Section 9 of the Norris-LaGuardia Act and violates federal labor policy.[157]

Questions of prospective injunctive relief under *Boys Markets* often arise under the rubric of mootness. In *Kentucky West Virginia Gas Co.* v. *Oil Workers Local 3-510*[158] the union gave strike notice over the discharge of an employee, alleging it was entitled to strike under the contract. The strike did not materialize, the strike notice was later withdrawn, and the underlying dispute was submitted to binding arbitration. Holding that the employer's request for injunctive relief against the threatened strike was moot, the Sixth Circuit observed: "There is no indication that the union will direct that a strike be commenced in the near future . . . . Thus, the threat of a strike over the . . . discharge is certainly not a 'continuing and brooding presence.' "[159] Although the court concluded that the case was moot regarding the strike injunction, it was not moot as to the union's contention that it had the right to strike over discharges which were arbitrable. The court therefore ordered the union to submit the no-strike clause interpretation to arbitration.[160]

In *Donovan Construction Co.* v. *Laborers Local 383*[161] the Ninth Circuit held that the entry of a permanent injunction was appro-

---

[155]Southern Ohio Coal Co. v. Mine Workers, 551 F2d 695, 94 LRRM 2609 (CA 6), *cert. denied*, 434 US 876, 96 LRRM 2512 (1977).

[156]Old Ben Coal Co. v. Mine Workers Local 1487 (II), *supra* note 150. *Cf.* Latas Libby's, Inc. v. Steelworkers, *supra* note 152 where the court stated in dictum: "[W]e do not say that repeated violations of a no-strike covenant never warrant broad prospective relief . . . ." *Id.* at 31-32.

[157]United States Steel Corp. v. Mine Workers, *supra* note 154 at 1247 n.21. The court discussed its disagreement with the Seventh Circuit's *Old Ben (II)* decision; *accord*, Drummond Co. v. District 20, Mine Workers, 598 F2d 381, 101 LRRM 2754 (CA 5, 1979) (court reaffirmed its *United States Steel Corp.* holding and reserved decision on whether a narrower prospective injunction can ever be appropriate).

[158]549 F2d 407, 94 LRRM 2652 (CA 6, 1977).

[159]*Id.* at 411.

[160]*See also* Cedar Coal Co. v. Mine Workers, 560 F2d 1153, 95 LRRM 3015 (CA 4, 1977), *cert. denied*, 434 US 1047, 97 LRRM 2441 (1978).

[161]533 F2d 481, 92 LRRM 2068 (CA 9, 1976). *See also* Jacksonville Bulk Terminals v. Longshoremen, *supra* note 93 at 2666 n.1, rejecting a mootness assertion on the grounds

priate and not moot even though the underlying jurisdictional dispute had gone to arbitration and both parties were acceding to the arbitrator's decision. The court held that a party could not moot an injunction action arising from its own misconduct simply by ceasing the challenged acts. Where a "convincing" showing is made of a reasonable apprehension of reoccurrence, an injunction operating prospectively is appropriate. At the same time, the appellate court found the district court's injunction too broad; the order should not have gone beyond enjoining any future strike similar to that which had occurred.

b. Sympathy Strikes. Following *Boys Markets,* numerous courts were faced with the issue of whether sympathy strikes were enjoinable under a *Boys Markets* rationale. The circuits were deeply divided on the issue.[162]

The Supreme Court's 1976 decision in *Buffalo Forge Co.* v. *Steelworkers*[163] held that sympathy strikes were not enjoinable under *Boys Markets* because they are not "over" issues that the striking union is obligated to arbitrate, i.e., the underlying dispute is typically between another union and the employer. The case concerned a unit of production and maintenance (P&M) employees who had refused to cross a picket line established by a unit of office and technical (O&T) employees working for the same employer. The P&M and O&T employees were represented by separate Steelworkers locals. The O&T strike had been sparked by the employer's resistance to negotiating an initial collective bargaining agreement for the O&T local. The collective bargaining agreement in effect between the employer and the striking P&M local contained broad no-strike and arbitration clauses. The parties agreed that the issue of whether the no-strike clause prohibited sympathy strikes was arbitrable. The employer, however, was seeking an injunction pending arbitration.

The Supreme Court affirmed that the case was governed by Norris-LaGuardia:

> *Boys Markets* plainly does not control this case . . . . The strike was not *over* any dispute between the Union and the employer that was even remotely subject to the arbitration provisions of the contract. The strike at issue was a sympathy strike in support of sister unions

that the issue of whether the ceased conduct violates the agreement remained and the work stoppage could resume at any time.
[162]*See* Buffalo Forge Co. v. Steelworkers, *supra* note 114 at 404 n.9.
[163]*Supra* note 114.

negotiating with the employer; neither its causes nor the issue underlying it was subject to the settlement procedures provided by the contracts between the employer and respondents. The strike had neither the purpose nor the effect of denying or evading an obligation to arbitrate or of depriving the employer of its bargain.[164]

The Court thus reinforced the equation[165] which it had constructed in *Boys Markets,* that the scope of permissible injunctive relief against strikes equals—and does not exceed—the scope of arbitrability under the collective bargaining contract.

The Court made clear that an injunction would not be appropriate simply because the sympathy strike allegedly violated the contract: "[T]he Court has never indicated that the courts may enjoin actual or threatened contract violations despite the Norris-LaGuardia Act."[166] It noted that such a rule would conflict with the congressional intent of the Taft-Hartley Act, as illustrated by Congress' specific rejection of a proposal that the Norris-LaGuardia Act's prohibition against labor-dispute injunctions be lifted to allow for federal court injunctive enforcement of collective bargaining agreements. Moreover, the courts would be called upon to resolve disputed issues of contract interpretation even though the parties had bargained for arbitral interpretation, thereby depriving the parties of the benefit of their bargain.[167] The Supreme Court refused to extend *Boys Markets* beyond its "narrow" holding, allowing for injunctive relief against strikes only where the underlying dispute is subject to a mandatory arbitration obligation.[168] Consistent with the doctrine expressed in the *Steelworkers Trilogy,* the Court thus insisted that the arbitrator—not the district court—continue to

---

[164]*Id.* at 407-408.

[165]*See supra* at note 113.

[166]*Supra* note 114 at 409.

[167]An employer might obtain injunctive relief, however, even if the underlying dispute is not arbitrable, by submitting the strike issue to arbitration and obtaining enforcement of the arbitration award, which could include injunctive relief and/or damages. *See, e.g.,* New Orleans S.S. Ass'n v. Longshoremen, 626 F2d 455, 105 LRRM 2539 (CA 5, 1980), and cases cited at note 97 *supra.* The Supreme Court in Jacksonville Bulk Terminals, *supra* note 93, expressly noted that an arbitrator's decision finding the strike to be in violation of a no-strike clause was enforceable by an injunction. The Court also noted that a damage action under §301 was available for the breach of the no-strike clause even though a *Boys Markets* injunction was not available.

[168]*Boys Markets* and *Buffalo Forge* relate only to injunctive relief; a union that strikes over an issue that is not subject to mandatory arbitration may still be held liable in monetary damages where the strike is in violation of a no-strike clause. *See, e.g.,* Iowa Beef Processors, Inc. v. Meat Cutters, 597 F2d 1138, 101 LRRM 2235 (CA 8), *cert. denied,* 444 US 84, 102 LRRM 2440 (1979) (union held liable for damages resulting from sympathy strike in breach of no-strike clause); Note, *Damage Remedies for Sympathy Strikes After Buffalo Forge,* 78 COLUM. L. REV. 1164 (1978).

be the primary interpreter of the collective bargaining agreement.

Mr. Justice Stevens, writing in dissent, noted that the no-strike promise is the *quid pro quo* for arbitration, and criticized the majority's ruling for making only a portion of the no-strike pledge "enforceable" by way of injunctive relief. He argued that a strike over a nonarbitrable issue should be enjoined pending arbitration where there was "convincing evidence that the strike is clearly within the no-strike clause."[169]

The circuit courts have developed fairly consistent criteria for determining the application of *Buffalo Forge*. Sympathy strikes will not be enjoined absent proof that the sympathy strikers have joined in the primary strike and, in effect, are seeking the same concessions on arbitrable issues sought by the primary strikers.[170] The Seventh Circuit thus refused to distinguish *Buffalo Forge*, stating "that, if the defendants' strike were simply an extension of the illegal . . . wildcat, this would be a paradigm case for a *Boys Markets* injunction. [But] the defendants were [not] adopting the grievances and goals of the [other] local as their own and thus striking 'over' a matter subject to arbitration."[171] The Fourth Circuit, however, distinguished *Buffalo Forge* and held enjoinable a strike where a union sought to compel a concession on an arbitrable issue to a sister union involving the same employer, same location, same bargaining unit, and same contract, under circumstances that would increase the union's chances of obtaining the same benefit as its sister union.[172] The union, in effect, had made the cause of the sister union "its own."[173] But in the same case the Fourth Circuit refused to distinguish *Buffalo Forge* where a union had engaged in a sympathy strike in support of a sister local's efforts to obtain a

---

[169]*Supra* note 114, 428 US at 431. He would have required the parties to submit the dispute to arbitration, and it would be up to the arbitrator to determine whether the sympathy strike actually violated the no-strike clause; meanwhile, the injunction would remain in effect.

[170]Zeigler Coal Co. v. Local 1870, Mine Workers, 566 F2d 582, 96 LRRM 3360 (CA 7, 1977), *cert. denied*, 436 US 912, 98 LRRM 2349 (1978); Cedar Coal Co. v. Mine Workers, 560 F2d 1153, 95 LRRM 3015 (CA 4, 1977), *cert. denied*, 434 US 1047, 97 LRRM 2441 (1978); Southern Ohio Coal Co. v. Mine Workers, 551 F2d 695, 94 LRRM 2609 (CA 6), *cert. denied*, 434 US 876, 96 LRRM 2512 (1977).

[171]Zeigler Coal Co. v. Local 1870, Mine Workers, *supra* note 170 at 585. This decision closely parallels the Sixth Circuit's decision in Southern Ohio Coal Co. v. Mine Workers, *supra* note 170, both as to facts and law. The Sixth Circuit stressed that the focus is whether the sympathy strike is over an arbitrable issue, not whether the primary strikers are striking over an arbitrable issue.

[172]Cedar Coal Co. v. Mine Workers, *supra* note 170.

[173]*Id.* at 1172.

concession on an arbitrable issue from another employer, since the sympathy strikers there were not seeking a concession on an arbitrable issue from their own employer. The determinative issue is thus whether the sympathy strikers are merely expressing solidarity with another group of employees or are attempting to obtain for themselves a concession on an arbitrable issue.[174]

c. *Safety Strikes.* In *Gateway Coal Co.* v. *Mine Workers*[175] the Supreme Court concluded that the " 'presumption of arbitrability' announced in the *Steelworkers* trilogy applies to safety disputes."[176] However, the Court also concluded that

> a work stoppage called solely to protect employees from immediate danger is authorized by [Section 502 of the Taft-Hartley Act] and cannot be the basis for either a damages award or a *Boys Markets* injunction . . . . [A] union seeking to justify a contractually prohibited work stoppage under Section 502 must present "ascertainable, objective evidence supporting its conclusion that an abnormally dangerous condition for work exists."[177]

Absent such evidence, *Boys Markets* is fully applicable.[178]

d. *Injunctions Against Employers to Preserve the Status Quo.* In *Locomotive Engineers* v. *Missouri-Kansas-Texas Railroad Co.* ("MKT")[179] the Supreme Court addressed the question of whether a district court may require an employer to restore the status quo as the price of obtaining a strike injunction under the Railway Labor Act.[180] The case arose after the railroad had substituted diesel locomotives for its shorter range steam locomotives and had issued a set of "General Orders" doubling the length of the railroad's runs, thereby eliminating the jobs of several employees and requiring the relocation of others. When the unions threatened to strike, the railroad submitted the dispute to the National Railroad Adjustment Board (NRAB) and sought an injunction in federal court against the strike pending decision by the Board. The district court granted the injunction,

---

[174]The line between solidarity and adoption of a grievance as one's own is not easy to determine. In the cases discussed *supra*, the Sixth and Seventh Circuits apparently required direct proof that the sympathy strikers were seeking concessions for themselves. The Fourth Circuit, however, was willing, at least in part, to infer adoption of a sister local's grievance from the close identity of the two unions.

[175]*Supra* note 106.

[176]*Id.* at 379. *See* discussion *supra* at note 53.

[177]441 US at 385-87 (quoting the dissenting opinion in the court of appeals, 466 F2d at 1162).

[178]In Gateway Coal, the district court enjoined the strike and also ordered the employer to take safety precautions pending arbitration. *See* note 142 *supra*.

[179]363 US 528, 46 LRRM 2429 (1960).

[180]Injunctions against strikes over grievance issues ("minor disputes") under the RLA had been approved by the Supreme Court as early as 1957. Railroad Trainmen v. Chicago River & Indiana R.R. Co., *supra* note 102.

but upon condition that the railroad either (1) restore the situation which existed prior to the General Orders, or (2) pay the affected employees the wages they would have received had the orders not been issued.

The Supreme Court upheld the jurisdiction of the district court to impose the conditions, stating:

> [I]f the District Court is free to exercise the typical powers of a court of equity, it has the power to impose conditions requiring maintenance of the *status quo.* Conditions of this nature traditionally may be made the price of relief when the injunctive powers of the court are invoked and the conditions are necessary to do justice between the parties.[181]

The Court rejected the employer's theory "that the conditions imposed by the District Court constituted a preliminary decision on the merits of the parties' dispute and therefore encroached upon the jurisdiction of the [NRAB]."[182] On the contrary, the Court concluded, the conditions imposed by the district court were "designed not only to promote the interests of justice, but also to preserve the jurisdiction of the [NRAB]."[183] The rationale was the following:

> The dispute out of which the judicial controversy arose does not merely concern rates of pay or job assignments, but rather involves the discharge of employees from positions long held and the dislocation of others from their homes. From the point of view of these employees, the critical point in the dispute may be when the change is made, for, by the time of the frequently long-delayed [NRAB] decision, it might well be impossible to make them whole in any realistic sense. If this be so, the action of the district judge, rather than defeating the [NRAB's] jurisdiction, would operate to *preserve* that jurisdiction by preventing injury so irreparable that a decision of the [NRAB] in the unions' favor would be but an empty victory.[184]

Although *MKT* involved the Railway Labor Act, the principles discussed in *MKT* apply as well to contracts executed under the Taft-Hartley Act which contain arbitration clauses.[185] It is thus

---

[181]363 US at 531-32.

[182]*Id.* at 532.

[183]*Id.* at 534.

[184]*Id.* (Emphasis added.) *MKT* involved conditions imposed on an employer as the price of a strike injunction. But subsequent cases have established that in certain circumstances, an injunction requiring an employer to restore the status quo pending arbitration can be entered even when no injunction against the union is sought or obtained by the employer. *See* cases cited in note 186 *infra.*

[185]*See, e.g.,* Gateway Coal Co. v. Mine Workers, 80 LRRM 2633 (WD Pa, 1971), which in due course was affirmed by the Supreme Court, *supra* note 106 at 387 (approvingly noting this feature of the injunction).

no surprise that the legacy of *Boys Markets* is not limited to strike injunctions and may also include status quo injunctions in certain arbitration cases.

The post-*Boys Markets* circuit court decisions are generally in harmony regarding the criteria for deciding upon a union's request for an injunction pending arbitration. The determinative factor is whether injunctive relief is necessary to protect the arbitration process itself. Injunctive relief may be appropriate where an employer's actions prior to an arbitrator's ruling would have the effect of undercutting the arbitrator's ability to render an effective award.[186] As the Fourth Circuit stated in *Lever Bros. Co. v. Chemical Workers Local 217:*[187]

> An injunction to preserve the *status quo* pending arbitration may be issued either against a company or against a union in an appropriate *Boys Markets* case where it is necessary to prevent conduct by the party enjoined from rendering the arbitral process a hollow formality in those instances where, as here, the arbitral award when rendered could not return the parties substantially to the *status quo ante.*[188]

The Ninth Circuit has held that a status quo injunction may also be appropriate in cases where the employer has agreed to maintain the status quo pending arbitration as a quid pro quo for the union's agreement not to strike.[189] In such cases, the

---

[186]Postal Workers v. Bolger, 621 F2d 615, 104 LRRM 2341 (CA 4, 1980); Chicago Typographical Union No. 16 v. Chicago Newspaper Publishers' Ass'n, 620 F2d 602, 103 LRRM 2957 (CA 7, 1980); Steelworkers v. Fort Pitt Steel Casting, 598 F2d 1273, 101 LRRM 2406 (CA 3, 1979) (employer enjoined, pending arbitration, from ceasing health plan payments even though contract had expired); Teamsters Local 71 v. Akers Motor Lines, Inc., 582 F2d 1336, 99 LRRM 2601 (CA 4, 1978); Lever Bros. Co. v. Chemical Workers Local 217, 554 F2d 115, 95 LRRM 2438 (CA 4, 1976); *see* Transit Union Div. 1384 v. Greyhound Lines, Inc. (II), 550 F2d 1237, 95 LRRM 2097 (CA 9), *cert. denied*, 434 US 837, 96 LRRM 2514 (1977); Bakery Drivers Local 802 v. S. B. Thomas, Inc., 99 LRRM 2253 (SD NY, 1978); *cf.* Detroit Typographical Union No. 18 v. Detroit Newspaper Publishers Ass'n, 471 F2d 872, 82 LRRM 2332 (CA 6, 1972), *cert. denied*, 411 US 967, 83 LRRM 2039 (1973) (court finds lack of irreparable harm where arbitrator could provide employees with make-whole relief).

[187]*Supra* note 186.

[188]*Id.* at 123.

[189]Transit Union Div. 1384 v. Greyhound Lines, Inc. (II), *supra* note 186. In Transit Union Div. 1384 v. Greyhound Lines, Inc. (I), 529 F2d 1073, 91 LRRM 2456 (CA 9, 1976), the court enjoined work-schedule changes pending arbitration on general equity principles. The Supreme Court, in Greyhound Lines, Inc. v. Transit Union Div. 1384, 429 US 807, 807, 93 LRRM 2362 (1976), vacated judgment and remanded the case "for further consideration in light of *Buffalo Forge.*" On remand, the Ninth Circuit held injunctive relief was inappropriate because the work-schedule changes would not frustrate and interfere with the arbitral process, and Greyhound did not commit itself to maintaining the status quo pending arbitration. *Accord*, Seattle Wash. Local Postal Workers v. Postal Service, 101 LRRM 2565 (WD Wash, 1979) (implementation of no-smoking rule enjoined where collective bargaining agreement had status quo provisions regarding working conditions).

courts would be enforcing the parties' quid pro quos—the union's no-strike obligation and the employer's status quo obligation—pending disposition of the underlying arbitrable dispute. The Seventh and Sixth Circuits, however, have held that contractual status quo obligations do not warrant injunctive relief in cases where an arbitrator himself could grant appropriate relief and effectively restore the status quo.[190]

Compelling cases for injunctions pending arbitration have included situations where the employer intended to implement a major business change that threatened to present the union and the arbitrator with a *fait accompli.* For example, injunctions have issued in favor of unions in cases where the employer intended to close a plant and move production elsewhere,[191] close down an ancillary part of its operations,[192] or liquidate assets at a time when grievances involving potential monetary liability were pending.[193] On the other hand, employers have generally prevailed in cases involving methods of operations which had been changed but where the change could be reversed if so ordered by an arbitrator and the work force would remain intact during the interim period.[194]

As in strike injunctions against unions, injunctions pending arbitration against employers are to be issued only in accordance with traditional principles of equity, including a showing of

---

[190]Chicago Typographical Union No. 16 v. Chicago Newspaper Publishers' Ass'n, *supra* note 186; Detroit Typographical Union No. 18 v. Detroit Newspaper Publishers Ass'n, *supra* note 186.

[191]Lever Bros. Co. v. Chemical Workers Union Local 217, *supra* note 186 (union relied on contract clause requiring employer to give union "due consideration" before assigning work to outside contractors); Teamsters Local 961 v. Graves Truck Line, Inc., 502 F Supp 1292, 106 LRRM 2233 (D Colo, 1980). *But cf.* Hoh v. Pepsico, Inc., 491 F2d 556, 85 LRRM 2517 (CA 2, 1974) (court refused to enjoin brewery closing where, *inter alia,* the union's contractual grievance was extremely weak, balance of equities strongly favored employer, and Norris-LaGuardia Act procedures were not followed. *See also* Local 1115 Joint Bd. Nursing Home & Hosp. Employees, Fla. Div. v. B & K Investments, Inc., 96 LRRM 2353 (SD Fla, 1977) (purchaser of nursing home enjoined from reselling home pending arbitration concerning purchaser's contractual obligations as successor).

[192]Bakery Drivers Local 802 v. S. B. Thomas, Inc., *supra* note 186 (closing down delivery of baked goods to restaurants); Koster Bakeries v. Teamsters Local 802, 97 LRRM 2807 (SD NY, 1977) (bakery enjoined pending arbitration from eliminating its bread delivery routes).

[193]Teamsters Local 71 v. Akers Motor Lines, Inc., *supra* note 186.

[194]Postal Workers v. Bolger, *supra* note 186; Chicago Typographical Union No. 16 v. Chicago Newspaper Publishers' Ass'n, *supra* note 186; Detroit Typographical Union No. 18 v. Detroit Newspaper Publishers Ass'n, *supra* note 186. In Mail Handlers v. Postal Workers, 103 LRRM 3107 (D Neb, 1978), the Postal Service was enjoined, pending arbitration, from reducing staff at a post office where the displaced employees would have to transfer, with their families, hundreds of miles away, thereby imposing a serious hardship and an obstacle to restoring the status quo should the arbitrator rule in the union's favor.

irreparable injury, that the potential harm to the employer should
an injunction issue does not clearly outweigh the potential harm
to the union should an injunction not issue, and that the union
has a reasonable likelihood of success on the merits.[195] The
element of irreparable injury is especially important in cases
where the injunction is premised on the rationale of preserving
the arbitration process, i.e., maintaining the status quo where
the employer's action threatens to present the union and the
arbitrator with a *fait accompli.*[196] The element concerning likelihood of success on the merits has been modified by some courts
so as to avoid unnecessary judicial interpretation of the contract,
in accordance with the Supreme Court's admonishments in *Buffalo Forge.*[197] According to the Fourth Circuit, "a plain-
tiff . . . need only establish that the position he will espouse in
arbitration is sufficiently sound to prevent the arbitration from
being a futile endeavor."[198]

3. Injunction Suits in State Courts. In *William E. Arnold Co.*
v. *Carpenters*[199] the Supreme Court rejected a claim that state
court jurisdiction over collective bargaining disputes should be
limited to claims for damages rather than injunctive relief. But
the Court has never resolved the question of whether a state
court is obligated to mirror the result which would obtain in the
federal courts.[200]

In *Avco Corp.* v. *Aero Lodge 735, Machinists,*[201] a pre-*Boys Markets*
decision, the Supreme Court held that Section 301 suits brought
in state courts are removable.[202] *Avco* left unanswered the ques-

---

[195]*See, e.g.,* Lever Bros. Co. v. Chemical Workers Local 217, *supra* note 186; Detroit
Typographical Union No. 18 v. Detroit Newspaper Publishers Ass'n, *supra* note 186.
  [196]*See, e.g.,* Lever Bros v. Chemical Workers Local 217, *supra* note 186.
  [197]Teamsters Local 71 v. Akers Motor Lines, Inc., *supra* note 186; Lever Bros. Co. v.
Chemical Workers Local 217, *supra* note 186; Transit Union Div. 1384 v. Greyhound
Lines, Inc. (I), *supra* note 189 (principle not affected by Supreme Court vacation and
remand or decision in *Greyhound (II)); see* Bakery Drivers Local 802 v. S. B. Thomas,
Inc., *supra* note 186. In Hoh v. Pepsico, Inc., *supra* note 191, a pre-*Buffalo Forge* case,
the Second Circuit held that the *Steelworker Trilogy* presumption of arbitrability does not
apply to the "likelihood of success on merits" test. The court cautioned trial court judges
"to exercise the sound discretion of the chancellor." *Id.* at 561. The court concluded by
noting the inequity of an injunction where the grievance "although arguably arbitrable
is plainly without merit." *Id.*
  [198]Teamsters Local 71 v. Akers Motor Lines, Inc., *supra* note 186 at 1342 (quoting, in
part, Lever Bros. Co. v. Chemical Workers Local 217, *supra* note 186 at 120).
  [199]*Supra* note 73.
  [200]The question was left open in Avco Corp. v. Aero Lodge 735, Machinists, *supra*
note 96 at 560 n.2. Since many states have their own "little Norris-LaGuardia statutes,"
this question does not frequently arise.
  [201]*Supra* note 96.
  [202]This rule was extended to removal of state administrative proceedings in Martin v.
Schwerman Trucking Co., 446 F Supp 1130, 97 LRRM 3177 (ED Wis, 1978).
  One federal court has held that a §301 suit to compel arbitration is removable even

tion of what effect removal has upon an existing state court injunction. But the answer was supplied in *Granny Goose Foods, Inc. v. Teamsters Local 70:*[203] Upon removal to a federal court, an *ex parte* temporary restraining order issued by a state court remains in force under state law, but in no event longer than the period of time provided by Rule 65(b) of the Federal Rules of Civil Procedure measured from the date of removal.[204]

IV. NLRB INTERPRETATION OF THE COLLECTIVE BARGAINING AGREEMENT

The Board's role in interpreting labor agreements has diminished since its adoption in 1971 of the prearbitral deferral policy of *Collyer Insulated Wire.*[205] However, where deferral to arbitration is not appropriate under the *Collyer* doctrine, or where the parties either have not agreed to a grievance-arbitration procedure in their contract or have declined to utilize an existing grievance-arbitration procedure, the Board has occasion to interpret the labor contract in connection with its unfair labor practice jurisdiction. The Board may also be required to construe contract provisions in other circumstances, such as determining whether a contract meets the criteria of the contract-bar doctrine. The discussion that follows deals with the Board's

---

where the collective bargaining agreement provided that neither party would seek to remove such an action. Carillo v. Hospital Employees, Local 1115, 441 F Supp 619, 96 LRRM 3196 (SD NY, 1977). The court noted that because federal law would apply even in the state court action, it would be a waste of judicial resources to remand the case to state court.

[203]*Supra* note 102.

[204]Prior to *Granny Goose,* there was uncertainty regarding how long a state court injunction or restraining order remained in effect after removal. The uncertainty was caused by the apparent conflict between 28 USC §1450 (which provides, in essence, that state court injunctions or restraining orders upon removal remain in force until dissolved by the federal court) and Rule 65(b) of the Federal Rules of Civil Procedure (which provides, in essence, that temporary restraining orders expire within 10 days unless extended). In *Granny Goose* the Supreme Court accommodated these two provisions, stating:

"We can find no indication that Congress intended §1450 as an exception to its broader, longstanding policy of restricting the duration of *ex parte* restraining orders. The underlying purpose of §1450—ensuring that no lapse in a state court temporary restraining order will occur simply by removing the case to federal court—and the policies reflected in Rule 65(b) can easily be accommodated by applying the following rule: An *ex parte* temporary restraining order issued by a state court prior to removal remains in force after removal no longer than it would have remained in effect under state law, but in no event does the order remain in force longer than the time limitations imposed by Rule 65(b) . . . ." *Id.* at 439-40.

[205]192 NLRB 837, 77 LRRM 1931 (1971). For detailed discussion of the *Collyer* deferral doctrine and its development since 1971, *see* Chapter 20 *infra.*

statutory authority to interpret labor agreements and the application of that authority.

A. Statutory Authority to Interpret Agreements

A contract violation is not of itself an unfair labor practice.[206] In early decisions, the Supreme Court recognized that the Board has jurisdiction over contract disputes to the extent necessary to resolve unfair labor practice charges.[207] With the emergence of Section 301 and the developing of a federal common law governing interpretation of collective bargaining agreements,[208] however, the Court was again faced with the issue of the Board's jurisdiction to construe a contract. The issue was presented in *NLRB* v. *C & C Plywood Corp.*[209]

The contract in that case authorized the employer " 'to pay a premium rate over and above the contractual classified wage rate to reward any particular employee for some special fitness, skill, aptitude or the like.' "[210] Relying on this provision, the employer unilaterally established an incentive pay scale. The Board found that the contract did not authorize this action and the employer therefore violated Section 8(a)(5) by its unilateral conduct.[211] The Ninth Circuit held the Board acted without jurisdiction: "[S]ince it has no jurisdiction to enforce collective bargaining agreements as such, both reason and policy dictate that adjudication of disputes, as to the scope of contractual rights and obligations, be by tribunals empowered to compel compliance with them."[212]

The Supreme Court reversed. It held that the Board did "no more than merely enforce a statutory right" and that the Board's interpretation of the agreement went no further than to determine that the union had not agreed to give up the statutory

---

[206]*E.g.*, Mine Workers v. NLRB, 257 F2d 211, 214-15, 42 LRRM 2264 (CA DC, 1958); Independent Petroleum Workers v. Esso Standard Oil Co., 235 F2d 401, 405, 38 LRRM 2307 (CA 3, 1956); NLRB v. Pennwoven, Inc., 194 F2d 521, 524, 29 LRRM 2307 (CA 3, 1952). *See* Chapter 20 *infra* at note 23.

[207]*E.g.*, J. I. Case v. NLRB, 321 US 332, 340, 14 LRRM 501 (1944); *accord,* Sbicca, Inc., 30 NLRB 60, 72, 8 LRRM 33 (1941). *See* Dunau, *Contractual Prohibition of Unfair Labor Practices: Jurisdictional Problems,* 57 COLUM. L. REV. 52, 58, 72-74 (1957). *Cf.* Carey v. Westinghouse Elec. Corp., 375 US 261, 55 LRRM 2042 (1964).

[208]*See* this chapter *supra* at notes 22-41.

[209]385 US 421, 64 LRRM 2065 (1967). *See* Chapter 20 *infra* at notes 30-33.

[210]*Id.* at 423 (quoting contract).

[211]148 NLRB 414, 57 LRRM 1015 (1964).

[212]351 F2d 224, 227-28, 60 LRRM 2137 (CA 9, 1965). The contract in question did not provide for binding arbitration.

safeguards.[213] The Court said that legislative history, precedent, and the interest of efficient administration all led to the conclusion that the Board does not exceed its jurisdiction when it construes a labor agreement where necessary to decide an unfair labor practice case.[214] The Court also noted that the contract in question did not have an arbitration clause, and therefore the Board's policy of deferring to arbitration was not involved.[215] *C & C Plywood* establishes that the Board's jurisdiction under Section 10(a) is not displaced because relief may also be available under Section 301 or because the Board must interpret the contract in order to decide the unfair labor practice issue.[216]

B. Cases Where the Board Interprets Contract Provisions

The preceding discussion has centered on the jurisdiction of the Board in cases where a contract provision is asserted as a defense to an unfair labor practice charge. There are still other ways in which issues of contract interpretation may be relevant to the Board's jurisdiction over unfair labor practices and representation proceedings. For example, a collective bargaining agreement may incorporate an affirmative statutory obligation. In such cases, the Board may resolve the question even though the decision about the unfair labor practice is *pro tanto* a resolution of the contract question. In addition, the Act makes certain contractual arrangements illegal, e.g., Section 8(a)(3) prohibits closed-shop agreements and Section 8(e) bars hot-cargo clauses. In such cases, the Board must measure the contract by the statutory standard to test its legality. Thus, issues of contract interpretation arise in many forms in the Board's exercise of its jurisdiction over unfair labor practices.

---

[213]*Supra* note 209 at 428.

[214]*Id.* at 430. The Court cited Mastro Plastics Corp. v. NLRB, 350 US 270, 37 LRRM 2587 (1956), where the Court approved the Board's construction of a no-strike clause in order to resolve §8(a)(1), (2), and (3) charges. *See* Chapter 21 *infra* at notes 81 and 151-55.

[215]The Board considers its policy of deferral to arbitration to be a matter of discretion, rather than an issue of Board jurisdiction. "There is no question that the Board is not precluded from adjudicating unfair labor practice charges even though they might have been the subject of an arbitration proceeding and award." International Harvester Co., 138 NLRB 923, 925, 51 LRRM 1155 (1962). The Supreme Court's decisions indicate general support of this position. *See* NLRB v. Acme Indus. Co., 385 US 432, 64 LRRM 2069 (1967); Carey v. Westinghouse Elec. Corp., 375 US 261, 55 LRRM 2042 (1964). *See also* text accompanying notes 81-85 *supra*. Board policy regarding deferral to the arbitral process is discussed in detail in Chapter 20 *infra*.

[216]*Accord*, NLRB v. Strong, 393 US 357, 70 LRRM 2100 (1969); NLRB v. Great Dane Trailers, Inc., 388 US 26, 30-31 n.7, 65 LRRM 2465 (1967); Carey v. Westinghouse Elec. Corp., *supra* note 207; Smith v. Evening News Ass'n, 371 US 195, 197, 51 LRRM 2646 (1962). *See also* text accompanying notes 81-85 *supra*.

The object of this discussion is to provide a broad description of various types of cases where the Board has found it appropriate to interpret and/or invalidate collective bargaining agreements or clauses. But because these same subject areas are analyzed in depth elsewhere in this treatise, no attempt is made here to present an extensive discussion of the substantive issues. It is helpful, however, in order to understand the role of the Board in contract interpretation, to identify the types of cases in which contract interpretation questions frequently reach the Board.

1. Interpretation of Lawful Contract Clauses. *a. Sections 8(a)(5) and 8(b)(3) Cases.* Questions of contract interpretation frequently arise in cases involving the duty to bargain, especially as it relates to changes in employment conditions or bargaining activity during the life of the collective bargaining agreement. Employers frequently argue that unilateral changes involving certain mandatory bargaining subjects are not Section 8(a)(5) violations because the union has waived its right to bargain over such subjects. The Board will review and interpret the contract language, often part of a management-rights clause or a "zipper" clause, to determine whether the language constitutes a clear and unmistakable waiver.[217] Likewise, an employer or a union may argue that its duty to furnish information has been waived by contract language and past practice.[218]

Under Section 8(d) a party is not obligated to engage in mid-contract discussions relative to "modification of the terms and conditions contained in a contract." The Board is therefore faced with potential contract-interpretation issues in any case where a party is being charged with an unfair labor practice for refusing to engage in discussions or negotiations during the life

---

[217]*Compare, e.g.,* Norris Indus., 231 NLRB 50, 96 LRRM 1078 (1977) (express waiver), *with* Elizabethtown Water Co., 234 NLRB 318, 97 LRRM 1210 (1978). *See* Chapter 13 *supra* at notes 585-91. As the Board noted in GTE Automatic Elec., Inc., 261 NLRB No. 196, 110 LRRM 1193 (1982), *supplementing* 240 NLRB 297, 100 LRRM 1204 (1979), a zipper clause may insulate each party to a collective bargaining contract from demands by the other during the term of the contract. The zipper clause thus acts as a "shield" against new demands not contemplated by the contract. But the clause cannot be used as a "sword," *i.e.,* such a clause will not excuse an employer who unilaterally institutes changes during the term of the contract.

[218]*See, e.g.,* Timken Roller Bearing, 138 NLRB 15, 50 LRRM 1508 (1962), *enforced,* 325 F2d 746, 54 LRRM 2785 (CA 6, 1963), *cert. denied,* 376 US 971, 55 LRRM 2878 (1964); Hekman Furniture Co., 101 NLRB 631, 31 LRRM 1116 (1952). *See generally* Chapter 13 *supra* at notes 345-510 for a discussion of the duty to furnish information.

of a collective bargaining agreement.[219] Finally, the Board may engage in contract interpretation in cases involving successorship issues.[220]

b. *Section 7 Rights.* The Board and the courts have developed a body of substantive law concerning whether and under what circumstances a union and an employer may waive employees' Section 7 rights. For example, no-strike clauses are generally held not to be unlawful interference with Section 7 rights,[221] while broad contractual restrictions on the right of employee solicitation and distribution of union literature are generally held to be unlawful interference with such rights.[222] In such cases the Board must often first construe ambiguous contract language before it can determine whether the language unlawfully interferes with employees' Section 7 rights.

c. *Section 8(a)(3) Cases.* The Board will frequently be faced with issues of contract interpretation in Section 8(a)(3) cases involving employees covered by collective bargaining agreements. The employer may argue that the employees were subject to discipline or discharge because they were engaged in conduct in violation of lawful contractual restrictions or, similarly, that the discipline or discharge was consistent with contract provisions, arbitration decisions, or past practice and therefore not motivated by union animus.[223] Sometimes unions will be made a party to such cases, being charged with Sections 8(b)(1)(A) or 8(b)(2) violations.[224]

d. *Sections 8(a)(2) and 8(b)(1) Cases.* The Board and courts have developed considerable substantive law regarding specific types of contract clauses which may be held violative of Sections 8(a)(2) and 8(b)(1). For example, cases involving superseniority and

---

[219]*See* Jacobs Mfg. Co., 94 NLRB 1214, 28 LRRM 1162 (1951), *enforced,* 196 F2d 680, 30 LRRM 2098 (CA 2, 1952). *See* Chapter 13 *supra* at notes 762-86 for a discussion of the duty to bargain during the life of an existing contract.

[220]*See generally* Chapter 15 *supra.*

[221]*See, e.g.,* Mastro Plastics Corp. v. NLRB, *supra* note 214; Dow Chem. Co. v. NLRB, 636 F2d 1352, 105 LRRM 3327 (CA 3, 1980); Arlan's Dep't Store, 133 NLRB 802, 48 LRRM 1731 (1961). *See generally* Chapter 21 *infra* at notes 147-57.

[222]*See,* NLRB v. Magnavox, 415 US 322, 85 LRRM 2475 (1974). *See generally* Chapter 6 *supra* at notes 205-209.

[223]*See, e.g.,* Mastro Plastics Corp. v. NLRB, *supra* note 214. *See generally* Chapter 7 *supra* at notes 18-329.

[224]*See generally* Chapter 7 *supra* at notes 330-374.

discrimination in favor of union members or specific unions often require the Board to construe ambiguous language.[225]

e. Work-Assignment Disputes. The parties in Section 8(b)(4)(D) work-assignment disputes will often try to support their cases by reference to contract language and past practice.[226]

f. Section 9 Proceedings. Contract issues arise in various contexts in representation cases. In representation and unit-clarification cases the Board may need to construe recognition clause language to determine the scope of existing bargaining units.[227] In cases where a contract bar is asserted, the Board will review the contract and determine whether its provisions meet the standards of the contract-bar doctrine.[228]

2. Interpretation to Determine Whether Express Statutory Prohibitions Have Been Violated. The Act specifically prohibits certain types of contractual arrangements. The Board is often faced with construing contract language in light of the statutory language and applicable case law. Union security arrangements,[229] hot-cargo clauses,[230] and featherbedding clauses[231] fit into this category.

---

[225]*See, e.g.,* Dairylea Coop., 291 NLRB 656, 89 LRRM 1737 (1975), *enforced sub nom.* NLRB v. Teamsters Local 338, 531 F2d 1162, 91 LRRM 2929 (CA 2, 1976) (superseniority clause). *See generally* Chapter 7 *supra* at notes 375-496.

[226]*See, e.g.,* NLRB v. New York Lithographers Union 1P, 600 F2d 336, 100 LRRM 3013 (CA 2, 1979); New Orleans Typographical Union No. 17 v. NLRB, 368 F2d 755, 63 LRRM 2467 (CA 5, 1966). *See generally* Chapter 27 *infra.*

[227]*See generally* Chapter 10 *supra* at notes 201-18.

[228]*See, e.g.,* Frank Hager, Inc., 230 NLRB 476, 96 LRRM 1117 (1977). *See generally* Chapter 10 *supra* at notes 117-200.

[229]*See generally* Chapter 29 *infra.*

[230]*See generally* Chapter 26 *infra.*

[231]*See generally* Chapter 27 *infra.*

CHAPTER 20

ACCOMMODATION OF BOARD ACTION
TO THE ARBITRATION PROCESS

I. INTRODUCTION AND HISTORICAL DEVELOPMENT[1]

A. Arbitration and the Courts

There can be little doubt today that in American labor law the arbitration process is the primary mechanism for resolution of disputes arising under collective bargaining agreements. As the Supreme Court has explained, the grievance-arbitration procedure is

> the very heart of the system of industrial self-government. Arbitration is the means of solving the unforeseeable by molding a system of private law for all the problems which may arise and to provide for all their solution in a way which will generally accord with the variant needs and desires of the parties. The processing of disputes through the grievance machinery is actually a vehicle by which meaning and content is given to the collective bargaining agreement.

---

[1]Literature on this subject has been extensive. Bibliographical materials include the following: Alleyne, *Arbitrators and the NLRB: The Nature of the Deferral Beast*, 4 INDUS. REL. L. J. 587 (1981); Harper, *Union Waiver of Employee Rights Under the NLRA: Part II, A Fresh Approach to Board Deferral to Arbitration*, 4 INDUS. REL. L. J. 680 (1981); Truesdale, *Is Spielberg Dead?*, NYU THIRTY-FIRST ANNUAL CONFERENCE ON LABOR 47 (1978); R. Covington, ARBITRATORS AND THE BOARD: A REVISED RELATIONSHIP (1978); Novack, *Cutting Back on Collyer: The First Step in the Right Direction*, 28 LAB. L. J. 785 (1977); Simon-Rose, *Deferral Under Collyer by the NLRB of Section 8(a)(3) Cases*, 27 LAB. L. J. 201 (1976); Teple, *NLRB Policy of Deferral to Arbitration*, 5 U. TOL. L. REV. 5 (1974); M. Trotta, ARBITRATION OF LABOR-MANAGEMENT DISPUTES 132-48 (1974); Getman, *Collyer Insulated Wire: A Case of Misplaced Modesty*, 49 IND. L. J. 57 (1973); Zimmer, *Wired for Collyer: Rationalizing NLRB and Arbitration Jurisdiction*, 48 IND. L. J. 141 (1973); Miller, *Deferral to Arbitration—Temperance or Abstinence?*, 7 GA. L. REV. 595 (1973); Nash, Wilder & Banor, *Development of the Collyer Deferral Doctrine*, 27 VAND. L. REV. 23 (1973); Murphy & Sterlacci, *Review of the National Labor Relations Board's Deferral Policy*, 42 FORDHAM L. REV. 291 (1973); Isaacson & Zifchak, *Agency Deferral to Private Arbitration of Employment Disputes*, 73 COLUM. L. REV. 1383 (1973); Johannesen & Smith, *Collyer, Open Sesame to Deferral*, 23 LAB. L. J. 723 (1972); Hilbert, *NLRB and Arbitration: The Impact of Collyer Insulated Wire*, 6 GA. L. REV. 522 (1972); Menard, *National Labor Relations Board—No Longer a Threat to the Arbitral Process?*, 23 LAB. L. J. 140 (1972); Anderson, *NLRB and Private Arbitration: Should Collyer Be Extended to Employee Discipline Cases?*, 13 B.C. INDUS.

. . . The grievance procedure is, in other words, a part of the continuous collective bargaining process.[2]

Initially there was some doubt as to whether executory agreements to arbitrate grievances under labor contracts were enforceable, because the courts generally applied the common-law rule that judicial process could not be invoked to compel compliance with an arbitration clause as to a dispute which was not in being when the agreement was executed.[3] After passage of the United States Arbitration Act of 1935,[4] some federal courts relied on that statute to specifically enforce arbitration agreements in collective bargaining contracts. It is still unclear,

---

& COM. L. REV. 1460 (1972); Schatzki, *Earliest Returns From the NLRB's New Deferral Policy in Collyer Insulated Wire*, NYU TWENTY-FIFTH ANNUAL CONFERENCE ON LABOR 97 (1972); Anderson, *Concurrent Jurisdiction—NLRB and Private Arbitration: A Pragmatic Analysis*, 12 B.C. INDUS. & COM. L. REV. 179 (1970); Peck, *Accommodation and Conflict Among Tribunals: Whatever Happened to Preemption?*, LABOR LAW DEVELOPMENTS 1969 (Fifteenth Annual Institute on Labor Law, Southwestern Legal Foundation) 121 (1969); Bond, *The Concurrence Conundrum: The Overlapping Jurisdicture of Arbitration and the National Labor Relations Board*, 42 S. CAL. L. REV. 42 (1968); Bloch, *The NLRB and Arbitration: Is the Board's Expanding Jurisdiction Justified?*, 19 LAB. I. J. 640 (1968); Brown, *The National Labor Policy, the NLRB and Arbitration*, in DEVELOPMENTS IN AMERICAN AND FOREIGN ARBITRATION (Proceedings of the Twenty-First Annual Meeting, National Academy of Arbitrators) 83 (BNA Books, 1968); Cushman, *Arbitration and the Duty to Bargain*, 1967 WISC. L. REV. 612 (1967); Rothschild, *Arbitration and the National Labor Relations Board: An Examination of Preferences and Prejudices and Their Relevance*, 28 OHIO ST. L. J. 195 (1967); Samoff, *Arbitration, Not NLRB Intervention*, 18 LAB. L. J. 602 (1967); Ordman, *Arbitration and the NLRB—A Second Look*, in THE ARBITRATOR, THE NLRB AND THE COURTS (Proceedings of the Twentieth Annual Meeting, National Academy of Arbitrators) 47 (BNA Books, 1967); Dunau, *Contractual Prohibition of Unfair Labor Practices: Jurisdictional Problems*, 57 COLUM. L. REV. 52 (1967); Seitz, *Grievance Arbitration and the National Labor Policy*, NYU EIGHTEENTH ANNUAL CONFERENCE ON LABOR 201 (1966); O'Brien, *Should the NLRB Arbitrate Labor Contract Disputes?*, 6 WASHBURN L. J. 39 (1966); Lesnick, *Arbitration as a Limit on the Discretion of Management, Union, and NLRB: The Year's Major Developments*, NYU EIGHTEENTH ANNUAL CONFERENCE ON LABOR 7 (1966); Moss, *Arbitration and the NLRB's Jurisdiction*, NYU SEVENTEENTH ANNUAL CONFERENCE ON LABOR 65 (1965); Harris, *The National Labor Relations Board and Arbitration—The Battle of Concurrent Jurisdiction*, 16 SYRACUSE L. REV. 545 (1965); McCulloch, *The Arbitration Issue in NLRB Decisions*, 19 ARB. J. 134 (1964); McCulloch, *Arbitration and/or the NLRB*, 18 ARB. J. 3 (1963); Christensen, *Arbitration, Section 301, and the National Labor Relations Act*, 37 N.Y.U. L. REV. 411 (1962); Cummings, *NLRB Jurisdiction and Labor Arbitration: "Uniformity" vs. "Industrial Peace,"* 12 LAB. L. J. 425 (1961); Levitt, *Interrelationships in the Interpretation of Collective Bargaining Agreements*, 10 LAB. L. J. 484 (1959); Samoff, *The NLRB and Arbitration: Conflicting or Compatible Currents*, 9 LAB. L. J. 689 (1958); Note, *NLRB Deferral to Arbitration Decisions*, 20 ST. LOUIS U. L. J. 20 (1976); Note, *Deference of Jurisdiction by the National Labor Relations Board and the Arbitration Clause*, 25 VAND. L. REV. 1057 (1972); Note, *New Developments in the NLRB Deference to Arbitration*, 1972 WASH. U. L. Q. 555; Note, *NLRB and Deference to Arbitration*, 77 YALE L. J. 1191 (1968); Note, *Employers' Duty to Supply Economic Data for Collective Bargaining*, 57 COLUM. L. REV. 112 (1957). *See also* bibliographical references cited in relevant footnotes throughout this chapter, particularly in footnote 70 *infra*.

[2]Steelworkers v. Warrior & Gulf Navigation Co., 363 US 574, 581, 46 LRRM 2416 (1960). *See* Chapter 19 *supra* at notes 50-53.

[3]*See, e.g.*, Red Cross Line v. Atlantic Fruit Co., 264 US 109, 125 (1924); F. Elkouri & E. Elkouri, HOW ARBITRATION WORKS, 36-37 (3d ed. 1973).

[4]9 USC §§1-14 (1976).

however, whether that Act applies to disputes under collective agreements. Section 1 of that Act, which defines its scope, specifically provides: "[N]othing herein contained shall apply to contracts of employment of seamen, railroad employees, or any other class of workers engaged in foreign or interstate commerce."[5] There is a split of authority as to whether this exclusion concerns only individual contracts of employment or is also applicable to collective bargaining contracts. The courts which have found the Federal Arbitration Act applicable to collective agreements have generally theorized that the term "contracts of employment" in Section 1 refers only to individual transactions rather than union-negotiated agreements.[6] But other courts have interpreted Section 1 to exclude coverage for labor agreements if the workers subject to the contract are in any way "engaged" in interstate commerce.[7] However, the issue of statutory coverage under the Arbitration Act became virtually moot following the Supreme Court's holding in *Textile Workers* v. *Lincoln Mills*.[8] As previously noted,[9] the Court held that Section 301[10] not only authorized federal courts to assume jurisdiction over suits for specific performance of agreements to arbitrate, but also mandated that the substantive law to be applied in such suits would be federal law, to be fashioned by the courts from the policy underlying national labor legislation. Rejecting an argument that the Norris-LaGuardia Act[11] would bar an injunction, the Court granted specific performance of an obligation to arbitrate a grievance dispute.

---

[5]9 USC §1 (1976).

[6]Electrical Workers (UE) Local 205 v. General Elec. Co., 233 F2d 85, 98, 38 LRRM 2019 (CA 1, 1956), *aff'd on other grounds*, 353 US 547, 40 LRRM 2119 (1957); *see* Machinists Local 967 v. General Elec. Co., 406 F2d 1046, 70 LRRM 2477 (CA 2, 1969); Retail, Wholesale & Dept. Store Union Local 19 v. Buckeye Cotton Oil Co., 236 F2d 776, 781, 38 LRRM 2590 (CA 6, 1956); Signal-Stat Corp. v. Electrical Workers (UE) Local 475, 235 F2d 298, 302, 38 LRRM 2378 (CA 2, 1956), *cert. denied*, 354 US 911, 40 LRRM 2200 (1957); *cf.* Erving v. Virginia Squires Basketball Club, 468 F2d 1064 (CA 2, 1972) (exclusionary clause in §1 applied only to those actually in transportation industry).

[7]These courts interpret "engaged" broadly to include workers involved in production industries as well as employees involved in transportation industries. Electrical Workers (UE) v. Miller Metal Prods., Inc., 215 F2d 221, 34 LRRM 2731 (CA 4, 1954); Pennsylvania Greyhound Lines, Inc. v. Street, Elec. Ry. & Motor Coach Employees, 193 F2d 327, 30 LRRM 2310 (CA 3, 1951); Textile Workers v. Cone Mills Corp., 166 F Supp 654, 43 LRRM 2012 (MD NC, 1958).

[8]353 US 448, 40 LRRM 2113 (1957).

[9]*See* Chapter 19 *supra* at notes 32-39.

[10]29 USC §185(a) (1976).

[11]29 USC §104 (1976).

Thereafter, in the *Steelworkers Trilogy*,[12] the Supreme Court defined the relationship between the courts' Section 301 authority and the arbitration process. These landmark cases established the following general propositions: (1) The function of the court is limited "to ascertaining whether the party seeking arbitration is making a claim which on its face is governed by the contract."[13] (2) All doubts as to the coverage of the arbitration clause should be resolved in favor of arbitration.[14] (3) An arbitrator's award, although it must draw its essence from the collective bargaining agreement, must be enforced by the courts even if the arbitrator's interpretation of the contract is ambiguous or would differ from the court's decision on the merits of the dispute.[15] The Court found support for such deference to arbitration both in legislative history[16] and in Sections 201 and 203(d) of the Labor Management Relations Act, which provide that final adjustment by a method agreed upon by the parties is the desirable method of settling grievance disputes arising from collective bargaining agreements.[17]

The courts must still make the determination as to whether the parties have agreed to arbitrate a particular issue and what issues are included in the agreement.[18] They will look to see what is embraced in the agreement to arbitrate. Since arbitration is a voluntary undertaking, parties cannot be required to arbitrate matters not included in their agreement. However, the courts have broadly interpreted arbitration clauses to include most contractual disputes.[19] Judicial development under Section

---

[12]Steelworkers v. American Mfg. Co., 363 US 564, 46 LRRM 2414 (1960); Steelworkers v. Warrior & Gulf Navigation Co., *supra* note 2; Steelworkers v. Enterprise Wheel & Car Corp., 363 US 593, 46 LRRM 2423 (1960). *See* Chapter 19 *supra* at notes 42-59.

[13]Steelworkers v. American Mfg. Co., *supra* note 12 at 568. The Court rejected the notion that a court could decide the merits of a grievance under the guise of a decision on arbitrability, and expressly disapproved of such cases, particularly Machinists v. Cutler-Hammer, Inc., 271 AD 917, 67 NYS2d 317, 19 LRRM 2232, *aff'd*, 297 NY 519, 74 NE2d 464, 20 LRRM 2445 (1947).

[14]Steelworkers v. Warrior & Gulf Navigation Co., *supra* note 2.

[15]Steelworkers v. Enterprise Wheel & Car Corp., *supra* note 12.

[16]*See* Textile Workers v. Lincoln Mills, *supra* note 8.

[17]29 USC §§171, 173(d) (1976).

[18]Nolde Bros., Inc. v. Bakery & Confectionery Workers Local 358, 430 US 243, 94 LRRM 2753 (1977); Gateway Coal Co. v. Mine Workers, 414 US 368, 85 LRRM 2049 (1974); John Wiley & Sons v. Livingston, 376 US 543, 55 LRRM 2769 (1964); Steelworkers v. Warrior & Gulf Navigation Co., *supra* note 2.

[19]For a discussion of the construction to be placed upon typical arbitration clauses, *see* F. Elkouri & E. Elkouri, *supra* note 3 at 169-80; Cox, *Reflections Upon Labor Arbitration*, 72 HARV. L. REV. 1482, 1507-10 (1959). As an example of the difficulty in narrowing the scope of arbitration, *see* Electrical Workers (IUE) v. General Elec. Co., 407 F2d 253, 70 LRRM 2082 (CA 2, 1968), *cert. denied*, 395 US 904, 71 LRRM 2254 (1969); Electrical

301 resolved most questions of conflict between arbitration and the courts in favor of the arbitral process.[20]

B. Jurisdiction of the NLRB Over Arbitral Matters

The process of achieving an accommodation between the jurisdiction of the National Labor Relations Board and grievance arbitration has been marked by both inconsistency and uncertainty. This interaction of the Board and arbitrators has primarily concerned matters of concurrent jurisdiction. Acts by an employer or a union may give rise to allegations of violations under both the labor agreement and of rights guaranteed by Sections 7, 8, or 9 of the Act. Typical examples of such overlapping claims include the following: (1) A union claim that the discipline or discharge of an employee is both a violation of the "just cause" clause in the labor contract and a violation of Sections 8(a)(1) and 8(a)(3); (2) a union claim that an employer's unilateral change in wages or working conditions not only violates provisions of the contract but also the employer's duty to bargain under Section 8(a)(5); (3) a union demand for information to process a grievance under Section 8(a)(5), where the employer refuses to supply it, based upon a contention that the union has contractually waived any right to such information.[21] In these instances, where provisions of the collective bargaining agreement and sections of the National Labor Relations Act both arguably apply, the question presented is two-fold: (1) Does the Board have power to exercise its jurisdiction under the Act when the parties by contract have provided a means to resolve all contractual disputes and, if so, (2) can the Board nevertheless withhold its jurisdiction by either honoring the award of an arbitrator who has decided the contractual dispute, or by deferring the matter to arbitration prior to an arbitral decision?

Section 10(a) of the Act establishes the Board's authority: "The Board is empowered . . . to prevent any person from engaging in any unfair labor practice . . . . *This power shall not be affected by any other means of adjustment or prevention that has been or may be established by agreement,* law or otherwise."[22] Thus, on its face, the Board's statutory authority is paramount.

Workers (IUE) v. General Elec. Co., 332 F2d 485, 56 LRRM 2289 (CA 2, 1964), *cert. denied,* 379 US 928, 57 LRRM 2608 (1964).
[20]*See* authorities cited in note 1 of Chapter 19 *supra.*
[21]*See infra* at notes 151-219.
[22]Emphasis added.

The contention that the Board may lack jurisdiction over unfair labor practices involving contract interpretation subject to arbitration is based upon legislative history, statutory language, and early federal appellate court decisions. In 1947 Congress refused to adopt an amendment to the NLRA which would have given the Board unfair labor practice jurisdiction over all breaches of collective bargaining agreements.[23] Rather, in Section 203(d) Congress declared that "the desirable method for settlement of grievance disputes arising over the application or interpretation of an existing collective-bargaining agreement" should be the method of dispute resolution agreed upon by the parties.[24] Some observers doubted that the Board had power to decide cases involving interpretation of the labor agreement. Their argument drew further support from the cases dealing with the relationship of federal courts to the arbitration process, where the Supreme Court had elevated the role of arbitration and limited the authority of the courts.[25] Nevertheless, as has been noted, the statute specifically provides that the Board's power to prevent unfair labor practices "shall not be affected by any other means of adjustment or prevention that has been or may be established by agreement, law or otherwise."[26] This oft-cited language in the Act was the basis for court and Board holdings that the Board enforces "public rights"[27] and that private contracts[28] and arbitral awards[29] cannot limit the Board's jurisdiction.

---

[23]One early version of the Senate bill contained the following provision: "§8(a) It shall be an unfair labor practice for an employer . . . (b) to violate the terms of a collective bargaining agreement or the terms of an agreement to submit a labor dispute to arbitration. . . ." §8(b)(5) would have placed a similar limit on unions. S. 1126, 80th Cong., 1st Sess., *reprinted in* 1 LEGISLATIVE HISTORY OF THE LABOR MANAGEMENT RELATIONS Act, 1947, at 109-111, 114 (1948); *see also* S. REP. No. 105, 80th Cong., 1st Sess. 20-21, 23 (1947). A similar proposal was contained in the House bill. H.R. REP. No. 245, 80th Cong., 1st Sess. 21 (1947). These sections were deleted from the bills in the House-Senate Conference. H.R. CONF. REP. No. 510, 80th Cong., 1st Sess. 42 (1947).

[24]29 USC §173(d) (1976).

[25]*E.g.,* Nolde Bros., Inc. v. Bakery & Confectionery Workers Local 358, *supra* note 18; John Wiley & Sons, Inc. v. Livingston, *supra* note 18; Steelworkers v. Enterprise Wheel & Car Corp., *supra* note 18.

[26]§10(a). *See generally* Chapter 19 *supra* at notes 42-59.

[27]*See, e.g.,* Utility Workers v. Consolidated Edison Co., 309 US 261, 6 LRRM 669 (1940); National Licorice Co. v. NLRB, 309 US 350, 6 LRRM 674 (1940).

[28]Machinists Lodge 743 v. United Aircraft Corp., 337 F2d 5, 57 LRRM 2245 (CA 2, 1964), *cert. denied,* 380 US 908, 58 LRRM 2496 (1965); NLRB v. Walt Disney Prods., 146 F2d 44, 15 LRRM 691 (CA 9, 1944), *cert. denied,* 324 US 877, 16 LRRM 918 (1945); Kelly-Springfield Tire Co., 6 NLRB 325, 2 LRRM 153 (1938), *enforced,* 94 F2d 1007, 2 LRRM 679 (CA 4, 1938); Ingram Mfg. Co., 5 NLRB 908, 2 LRRM 79 (1938).

[29]Carey v. Westinghouse Elec. Corp., 375 US 261, 55 LRRM 2042 (1964); NLRB v. Hershey Chocolate Corp., 297 F2d 286, 49 LRRM 2173 (CA 3, 1961); NLRB v. Bell Aircraft Corp., 206 F2d 235, 32 LRRM 2550 (CA 2, 1953); Zoe Chem. Co., 160 NLRB 1001, 63 LRRM 1052 (1966) (trial examiner's decision).

As to the adverse legislative history, the Supreme Court in *NLRB* v. *C & C Plywood Corp.*[30] rejected the notion that the Board lacked jurisdiction over alleged unfair labor practices solely because the dispute might also involve interpretation of terms in the collective agreement. The Court said that Congress' failure to pass the amendment to give the NLRB unfair labor practice jurisdiction over contract violations was to insure that the Board would not have a "generalized power to determine the rights of parties under all collective agreements [which] would have been a step toward governmental regulation of the terms of those agreements."[31] The Court held that in determining whether or not the employer in the case had violated its duty to bargain, the Board would not be imposing its views as to the meaning of the collective bargaining agreement; rather, it would "merely enforce a statutory right which Congress considered necessary to allow labor and management to get on with the process of reaching fair terms and conditions of employment."[32] Accordingly, the Court concluded that "the Board, in necessarily construing a labor agreement to decide this unfair labor practice case, has not exceeded the jurisdiction laid out for it by Congress."[33] The clear teaching of *C & C Plywood* was that certain acts could give rise to both an unfair labor practice under Section 8 and a violation of contract under Section 301. However, as the Court was careful to point out, the collective bargaining agreement in that case contained no arbitration clause. Thus, although the Supreme Court answered the question of whether the Board had the power to interpret a contract enforceable under Section 301, the issue remained as to whether the Board had the authority to interpret a contract that included an applicable arbitration clause.

The cases which introduced this problem, a series of circuit court decisions in the early 1960s, dealt with the right to information. In *Sinclair Refining Co.* v. *NLRB*[34] the Fifth Circuit refused to require the production of data which the union and the Board considered relevant to a demotion grievance. Relying on the *Steelworkers Trilogy*, the court said that the Board had improperly

---

[30]385 US 421, 64 LRRM 2065 (1967). *See* discussion in Chapter 19 *supra* at notes 206-16.

[31]*Id.* at 427.

[32]*Id.* at 428.

[33]*Id. See* note 42 *infra*.

[34]306 F2d 569, 50 LRRM 2830 (CA 5, 1962), *denying enforcement to* 132 NLRB 1660, 48 LRRM 1544 (1961).

adjudicated the underlying grievance under the guise of determining the relevance of the data sought.[35]

The Sixth Circuit, in *Timken Roller Bearing Co. v. NLRB*,[36] granted enforcement of a Board order to furnish information relevant to a grievance, but only because the court concluded that the issue of the duty to furnish information was not subject to arbitration under the terms of the collective bargaining agreement. In dictum, the court cited *Sinclair Refining Co.* with approval as "another example of the now established law that where a dispute or 'difference' is subject to grievance procedure and arbitration by reason of the provisions of the bargaining agreement, that procedure is *exclusive* and will be enforced."[37]

In *Square D Co. v. NLRB*[38] the Ninth Circuit refused enforcement of a Board order requiring an employer to furnish information relevant to an incentive plan grievance. The employer had argued that matters related to the incentive plan were not grievable, and, therefore, it had no obligation to furnish information. The court concluded that "[t]he answer to the dispute lies not in the provisions of the Act, for the Act does not purport to control the issue of what matters shall be subject to a contract grievance procedure. The answer lies solely in a construction of the contract—an area in which the parties themselves have agreed that the dispute shall be arbitrated."[39] The court thus recognized primary jurisdiction in the arbitral process, stating: "In the absence of an arbitrator's decision on this issue the Board *had no power* to determine that the Company committed unfair labor practices. . . ."[40]

Meanwhile, the Supreme Court had begun to address this issue of the Board's power versus the arbitral process. In its 1964 *Carey v. Westinghouse Corp.*[41] decision, the Court held that parties may resort to arbitration to resolve jurisdictional disputes even though such disputes could also be placed before the Board, under appropriate circumstances, in a Section 8(b)(4)(D) case

---

[35]The Board had in fact interpreted the contract and had decided the extent of management prerogative, concluding that the union had not waived its right to dispute the claim of lack of work.
[36]325 F2d 746, 54 LRRM 2785 (CA 6, 1963), *cert. denied,* 376 US 971, 55 LRRM 2878 (1964).
[37]*Id.* at 754 (emphasis added).
[38]332 F2d 360, 56 LRRM 2147 (CA 9, 1964).
[39]*Id.* at 365.
[40]*Id.* at 366 (emphasis added).
[41]*Supra* note 29.

or in a Section 9 unit-clarification case. In so holding, the Court noted the Board's adoption of discretionary, nonjurisdictional deference to arbitration awards. The Court acknowledged the Board's authority in such matters of concurrent jurisdiction, stating: "Should the Board disagree with the arbiter . . . , the Board's ruling would, of course, take precedence; and if the employer's action had been in accord with that ruling it would not be liable for damages under §301."[42]

In its 1967 decision in *NLRB* v. *Acme Industrial Co.*[43] the Supreme Court held that the Board has jurisdiction over cases involving the duty to furnish information relevant to grievances, even though the underlying grievances involve contract disputes subject to binding arbitration. In so holding, the Court disagreed with the approach taken by the circuit courts in *Sinclair Refining Co., Timken Roller Bearing,* and *Square D Co.*[44] The Court began its analysis by rejecting a mechanical application of the *Steelworkers Trilogy* court-versus-arbitration accommodation, saying: "The relationship of the Board to the arbitration process is of a quite different order."[45] It noted that, unlike the courts, the Board has the Section 10(a) power to prevent unfair labor practices, and this power is not affected by private means of adjustment. "Thus, to view the *Steelworkers* decisions as automatically requiring the Board in this case to defer to the primary determination of an arbitrator is to overlook important distinctions between those cases and this one."[46] However, the Court did not find it necessary to discuss the extent to which the Board could resolve disputed grievances in connection with its unfair labor practice jurisdiction. Instead, it simply observed that the Board, in ordering the employer to provide information to the union, was not deciding the merits of contract grievances—rather, it was actually aiding the arbitral process by providing a vehicle for the parties to sift out unmeritorious claims.

---

[42]*Id.* at 272. *See also infra* at notes 335-39. In its 1967 decision in NLRB v. C & C Plywood, *supra* note 30, which involved a contract that did not provide for binding arbitration, the Court held that the Board has jurisdiction to resolve disputed contractual issues to the extent necessary to reach an unfair labor practice issue.

[43]385 US 432, 64 LRRM 2069 (1967). (*C & C Plywood* and *Acme* were decided on the same day; Justice Stewart authored both opinions.) The Seventh Circuit below had adopted the reasoning of *Sinclair Refining Co., supra* note 34, and had denied enforcement of the Board's order.

[44]*See* notes 34-40 *supra.*

[45]385 US at 436 (citing Carey v. Westinghouse Corp., *supra* note 29).

[46]*Id.* at 437.

Finally, in its 1969 decision in *NLRB* v. *Strong Roofing &
Insulating Co.*,[47] the Court held that the Board, having found
that an employer violated Section 8(a)(5) by refusing to execute
a contract negotiated by its employer association, has the power
to order the employer to make payments of fringe benefits as
required by the contract. The Court rejected the argument that
an order for payment of fringe benefits could only be obtained
through the contract's grievance-arbitration procedure:

> [The Board's] authority to [remedy unfair labor practices] is not
> "affected by any other means of adjustment or prevention that has
> been or may be established by agreement, law or otherwise . . . ."
> §10(a) . . . . Hence, it has been made clear that in some circumstances
> the authority of the Board and the law of contract are overlapping,
> concurrent regimes, neither pre-empting the other. . . . [T]he Board
> may proscribe conduct which is an unfair labor practice even though
> it is also a breach of contract remediable as such by arbitration and
> in the courts. . . . It may also, if necessary to adjudicate an unfair
> labor practice, interpret and give effect to the terms of a collective
> bargaining contract.[48]

Justice Black, in concurring, would have remanded the case to
the Board to consider whether the fringe-benefit issue should
be submitted to arbitration. Justice Douglas, in a lone dissent,
argued that the fringe-benefit issue should be decided by arbitrators, not the Board, a tribunal "alien to the system envisioned
by *Lincoln Mills.*"[49]

The foregoing Supreme Court decisions support the proposition that the Board's power in unfair labor practice and representation cases is certainly not subordinate to or dependent
upon the arbitral process. Accordingly, the focus of Board and
court decisions has been upon the circumstances under which
the Board, *as a matter of discretion,* should defer to the arbitral
process.

Although the Board has unreservedly held that it has jurisdiction to determine unfair labor practices that may also be
covered under the grievance procedures of a collective bargaining agreement, it has long ruled that it may choose not to exercise that jurisdiction where it overlaps arbitral jurisdiction. In

---

[47]393 US 357, 70 LRRM 2100 (1969).
[48]*Id.* at 360-61. *Accord, e.g.,* Los Angeles Marine Hardware Co. v. NLRB, 602 F2d
1302, 102 LRRM 2498 (CA 9, 1979); Morrison-Knudsen v. NLRB, 418 F2d 203, 72
LRRM 2460 (CA 9, 1969).
[49]393 US at 366.

International Harvester Co.[50] an employee alleged that the union had violated Sections 8(b)(1)(A) and 8(b)(2) and that the employer had violated Sections 8(a)(1) and 8(a)(3) by requiring the employee's discharge for failing to pay union membership dues during the term of a valid union security agreement. An arbitrator, however, had determined the issue adversely to the employee. Although the Board deferred to the arbitrator's decision, it emphasized this caveat:

> There is no question that the Board is not precluded from adjudicating unfair labor practice charges even though they might have been the subject of an arbitration proceeding and award. Section 10(a) of the Act expressly makes this plain, and the courts have uniformly so held. However, it is equally well-established that the Board has considerable discretion to respect an arbitration award and decline to exercise its authority over alleged unfair labor practices if to do so will serve the fundamental aims of the Act.[51]

C. From *Spielberg* to *Collyer*

The Board has developed standards for exercising its discretionary authority. Its *Spielberg*[52] standards, adopted in 1955, apply to cases where an arbitral award has already been rendered. Its *Collyer*[53] standards, adopted in 1971, apply to cases where the Board defers to the arbitral machinery before an arbitral award has been rendered, subject to possible Board review of the ultimate award under *Spielberg* standards. *Spielberg* and *Collyer* have received wide acceptance by the reviewing courts.

1. The *Spielberg* Rationale. In the early days of the Act the Board was reluctant to accommodate itself to the decision of any other tribunal. Even where an arbitrator had ordered discriminatorily discharged employees to be reinstated, the Board, relying on Section 10(a), refused to recognize the award and independently examined the charged conduct to ascertain whether there had been any violation of the Act.[54] Occasionally, however, a trial examiner would honor an arbitration award

---

[50]138 NLRB 923, 51 LRRM 1155 (1962), *enforced sub nom.* Ramsey v. NLRB, 327 F2d 784, 55 LRRM 2441 (CA 7, 1964), *cert. denied,* 377 US 1003, 56 LRRM 2544 (1964).

[51]138 NLRB at 925-26; this language was cited with approval by the Supreme Court in Carey v. Westinghouse Elec. Corp., *supra* note 29 at 271.

[52]Spielberg Mfg. Co., 112 NLRB 1080, 36 LRRM 1152 (1955). *See infra* at notes 230-368.

[53]Collyer Insulated Wire, 192 NLRB 837, 77 LRRM 1931 (1971).

[54]*E.g.,* Rieke Metal Prods. Corp., 40 NLRB 867, 10 LRRM 82 (1942).

because he felt it would effectuate the policies of the Act.[55] But it was not until 1955, in *Spielberg Manufacturing Co.*,[56] that the Board set forth specific criteria for deferral to arbitration awards.

In *Spielberg* the parties had agreed, as part of a strike settlement, to arbitrate the employer's refusal to reinstate four strikers accused of picket-line misconduct. When the arbitration panel denied reinstatement, the employees filed an unfair labor practice charge. The Board decided to defer to the decision of the arbitration panel[57] and, in so doing, promulgated a three-pronged test for determining when to defer: (1) that the proceedings be fair and regular; (2) that all parties agree to be bound; and (3) that the decision not be repugnant to the purpose and policies of the Act.[58] If these criteria are met, deferral is deemed appropriate.[59]

The rationale of *Spielberg* was elucidated in *International Harvester Co.*,[60] where the Board stated:

> The Act . . . is primarily designed to promote industrial peace and stability by encouraging the practice and procedure of collective bargaining. Experience has demonstrated that collective-bargaining agreements that provide for final and binding arbitration of grievances and disputes arising thereunder, as a "substitute for industrial strife," contribute significantly to the attainment of this statutory objective. . . .
>
> . . .
>
> If complete effectuation of the Federal policy is to be achieved, . . . the Board . . . should give hospitable acceptance to the arbitral process as "part and parcel of the collective bargaining process itself," and voluntarily withhold its undoubted authority to adjudicate alleged unfair labor practice charges involving the same subject

---

[55]*E.g.*, Paramount Pictures, Inc., 79 NLRB 557, 576, 22 LRRM 1428 (1948). The trial examiner relied upon Timken Roller Bearing Co., 70 NLRB 500, 18 LRRM 1370 (1946), *enforcement denied*, 161 F2d 949, 20 LRRM 2204 (CA 6, 1947), where the Board had dismissed part of a refusal-to-bargain complaint initiated by a union that had simultaneously invoked the Board's processes and the grievance machinery in its contract and had lost the arbitral decision. The Board said in *Timken:* "It is evident that the Union has concurrently utilized two forums for the purpose of litigating the matter here in dispute. . . . [I]t would not comport with the sound exercise of our administrative discretion to permit the Union to seek redress under the Act after having initiated arbitration proceedings which, at the Union's request, resulted in a determination upon the merits." *Id.* at 501. The Board's theory in *Timken* appeared to have been that the union had made an election of remedies, rather than that the arbitrator's opinion was entitled to any weight.

[56]*Supra* note 52.

[57]The Board noted that it would not "necessarily decide the issue of alleged strike misconduct as the arbitration panel did." *Id.* at 1082.

[58]A fourth test was added later. *See infra* at notes 62 and 235-53.

[59]Spielberg Mfg. Co., *supra* note 52 at 1082. Additional standards applied by the courts are discussed *infra* at notes 377-408.

[60]*Supra* note 50.

matter, unless it clearly appears that the arbitration proceedings were tainted by fraud, collusion, unfairness, or serious procedural irregularities or that the award was clearly repugnant to the purposes and policies of the Act.[61]

Since its *Spielberg* decision the Board has added a fourth criterion: that the issue involved in the unfair labor practice case must have been presented to and considered by the arbitrator.[62]

2. The *Collyer* Rationale. In some areas of labor law, parties are required to utilize and sometimes fully exhaust grievance-arbitration machinery before being permitted to use another forum.[63] But there has never been a rigid exhaustion requirement for access to the NLRB. Prior to its 1971 *Collyer* decision, the Board usually found that failure to use an available grievance procedure was not a bar to the processing of a charge. First in *Merrimack Manufacturing Co.*[64] and then in succeeding cases,[65] the Board consistently settled disputes involving charges of discrimination. Its position was less consistent in cases involving refusal to bargain.[66] However, in its 1963 decision in *Dubo Man-*

---

[61]138 NLRB at 926-27. The Supreme Court quoted this language with approval in Carey v. Westinghouse, *supra* note 29 at 271.

[62]Raytheon Co., 140 NLRB 883, 52 LRRM 1129 (1963), *set aside on other grounds,* 326 F2d 471, 55 LRRM 2101 (CA 1, 1964). *See also* Suburban Motor Freight, Inc., 247 NLRB 146, 103 LRRM 1113 (1980). This fourth standard continues to be cited by the Board as an addition to the three *Spielberg* standards; *e.g.,* Kansas City Star Co., 236 NLRB 866, 98 LRRM 1320 (1978); United Parcel Serv., Inc., 234 NLRB 483, 97 LRRM 1403 (1978), *enforcement denied,* 104 LRRM 2612 (CA 6, 1979). *Accord,* NLRB v. General Warehouse Corp., 643 F2d 965, 106 LRRM 2729 (CA 3, 1981), *enforcing* 247 NLRB 1073, 103 LRRM 1294 (1980). Other standards for deferral suggested by various circuits are considered *infra* at notes 377-408.

[63]*See, e.g.,* Republic Steel Corp. v. Maddox, 379 US 650, 58 LRRM 2193 (1965). *See also* Drake Bakeries, Inc. v. Bakery Workers Local 50, 370 US 254, 50 LRRM 2440 (1962).

[64]31 NLRB 900, 8 LRRM 170 (1941).

[65]*See, e.g.,* Flasco Mfg. Co., 162 NLRB 611, 64 LRRM 1077 (1967); Woodlawn Farm Dairy Co., 162 NLRB 48, 63 LRRM 1495 (1966); Operating Eng'rs Local 701 (Peter Kiewit Sons' Co.), 152 NLRB 49, 59 LRRM 1009 (1965); Plumbers Local 469 (Associated Plumbing, Heating & Piping Contractors of Arizona), 149 NLRB 39, 57 LRRM 1257 (1954); Electric Motors & Specialties, Inc., 149 NLRB 131, 57 LRRM 1258 (1964); Aerodex, Inc., 149 NLRB 192, 57 LRRM 1261 (1964); National Screen Prods. Co., 147 NLRB 746, 56 LRRM 1274 (1964); Lummus Co., 142 NLRB 517, 53 LRRM 1072 (1963); Todd Shipyards Corp., 98 NLRB 814, 29 LRRM 1422 (1952); General Elec. X-Ray Corp., 76 NLRB 64, 21 LRRM 1150 (1948); Marlboro Cotton Mills, 53 NLRB 965, 13 LRRM 142 (1943); Walt Disney Prods., 48 NLRB 892, 12 LRRM 146 (1943), *enforced as modified,* 146 F2d 44, 15 LRRM 691 (CA 9, 1944), *cert. denied,* 324 US 877, 16 LRRM 918 (1945).

[66]Board Member Brown would have deferred almost every decision until a grievance had been processed. *See, e.g.,* Aetna Bearing Co., 152 NLRB 845, 59 LRRM 1258 (1965); Flintkote Co., 149 NLRB 1561, 57 LRRM 1477 (1964); Thor Power Tool Co., 148 NLRB 1379, 1382, 57 LRRM 1161 (1964), *enforced,* 351 F2d 584, 60 LRRM 2237 (CA 7, 1965).

ufacturing Corp.[67] the Board held that it would defer action pending completion of the grievance-arbitration process where the dispute was already being handled within that process.

Collyer Insulated Wire[68] marked a watershed in the accommodation of Board authority to the parties' private arbitral machinery. Although the Board had occasionally dismissed complaints in unfair labor practice cases because the issue was subject to resolution under the parties' grievance-arbitration procedures,[69] it was not until *Collyer* that a definite system of prearbitral referral was adopted. *Collyer* involved a Section 8(a)(5) charge of failure to bargain. A plurality of Chairman Miller and Member Kennedy wrote the Board's decision; Member Brown concurred, urging deferral in an even broader range of cases. Members Fanning and Jenkins, in separate opinions, strongly dissented; and they have consistently continued their opposition to the doctrine.[70]

In *Collyer* the employer contended that the union's Section 8(a)(5) charge, alleging unilateral changes in conditions of employment, should be deferred to the grievance-arbitration

---

[67]142 NLRB 431, 53 LRRM 1070 (1963) (§8(a)(3) case). The resulting arbitration award in *Dubo* was thereafter disregarded, however, since the arbitration panel had not considered the allegation of discrimination. Dubo Mfg. Corp., 148 NLRB 1114, 57 LRRM 1111 (1964), *enforced*, 353 F2d 157, 60 LRRM 2373 (CA 6, 1965). *See also infra* at note 121.

[68]*Supra* note 53.

[69]*E.g.*, Joseph Schlitz Brewing Co., 175 NLRB 141, 70 LRRM 1472 (1969). Just a few months before *Collyer*, Members Fanning, Brown, and Jenkins had adopted an administrative law judge's opinion refusing to defer §§8(a)(3) and (5) issues to existing grievance-arbitration procedures, in Curtis Mfg. Co., 189 NLRB 192, 77 LRRM 1220 (1971).

[70]*Collyer* has also been widely debated outside the Board. *See, e.g.,:* Getman, *Labor Arbitration & Dispute Resolution*, 88 YALE L. J. 916 (1979); Christensen, *Private Judges, Public Rights: The Role of Arbitration in the Enforcement of the National Labor Relations Act*, in THE FUTURE OF LABOR ARBITRATION IN AMERICA (J. Correge, V. Hughes, & M. Stone, eds.) 49 (1976); Nash, *Board Referral to Arbitration and Alexander v. Gardner-Denver: Some Preliminary Observations*, 25 LAB. L. J. 259 (1974); Teple, *Deferral to Arbitration: Implications of NLRB Policy*, 29 ARB. J. 65 (1974); Zimmer, *Wired for Collyer: Rationalizing NLRB and Arbitration Jurisdiction*, 48 IND. L. J. 141 (1973); Getman, *Collyer Insulated Wire: A Case of Misplaced Modesty*, 49 IND. L. J. 57 (1973); Belkin, *Are Arbitrators Qualified to Decide Unfair Labor Practice Cases?*, 24 LAB. L. J. 818 (1973); Schatzki, *NLRB Resolution of Contract Disputes Under Section 8(a)(5)*, 50 TEX. L. REV. 225 (1972); Johannesen & Smith, *Collyer: Open Sesame to Deferral*, 23 LAB. L. J. 723 (1972); Menard, *The NLRB—No Longer A Threat to the Arbitral Process?*, 23 LAB. L. J. 140 (1972); Atleson, *Disciplinary Discharges, Arbitration, and NLRB Deference*, 20 BUFFALO L. REV. 355 (1971); Note, *Labor Law—Arbitration—Announcement of Deferral Policy*, 17 ST. LOUIS U. L. J. 411 (1973); Note, *The NLRB's Arbitration Deferral Policy Under Collyer: The Impact of National Radio Co.*, 53 B. U. L. REV. 711 (1973); Note, *NLRB—Jurisdiction—Standards for Deferral to Arbitration Where No Award Has Been Issued*, 41 FORDHAM L. REV. 1975 (1972); Note, *Labor Law—NLRB Unfair Labor Practice Jurisdiction and Arbitration—Effect of Deferring to Arbitration Prior to Issuance of Award*, 18 WAYNE L. REV. 1191 (1972).

procedure of the parties' labor contract. The Board majority ruled that the Board should and would defer to existing grievance-arbitration procedures prior to either party's invocation of those procedures in the following circumstances: (1) Where the dispute arose "within the confines of a long and productive collective bargaining relationship," and there was no claim of "enmity by Respondent to employees' exercise of protected rights";[71] (2) where "Respondent has . . . credibly asserted its willingness to resort to arbitration under a clause providing for arbitration in a very broad range of disputes and unquestionably broad enough to embrace 'the dispute before the Board' ";[72] and (3) where the contract and its meaning lie at the center of the dispute.[73]

The Board's plurality opinion rested on broad foundations: (1) that the courts have recognized a national policy of encouraging resolution of labor disputes through the grievance-arbitration machinery; (2) that it is in keeping with the statutory policy, expressed in Section 203(d) of the LMRA to encourage the parties to resolve disputes through the "method agreed upon by the parties"; (3) and further, that "disputes such as these can better be resolved by arbitrators with special skill and experience in deciding matters arising under established bargaining relationships than by the application by this Board of a particular provision of our statute."[74]

Concluding that it would be consistent "with the fundamental objectives of federal law to require the parties here to honor their contractual obligations rather than, by casting this dispute in statutory terms, to ignore their agreed-upon procedures,"[75] the Board's opinion (by Chairman Miller and Member Kennedy) ordered the complaint dismissed. But to protect the statutory rights of the charging party, the order also retained Board jurisdiction

> solely for the purpose of entertaining an appropriate and timely motion for further consideration upon a proper showing that either (a) the dispute has not, with reasonable promptness after the issuance of this decision, either been resolved by amicable settlement in the grievance procedure or submitted promptly to arbitration, or

---

[71]Collyer Insulated Wire, *supra* note 53 at 842.
[72]*Id.*
[73]*Id.*
[74]*Id.* at 839.
[75]*Id.* at 843.

(b) the grievance or arbitration procedures have not been fair and regular or have reached a result which is repugnant to the Act.[76]

Member Brown, in concurring, supported a broader concept of deferral, emphasizing one reason in particular:

> The scope, both in function and utilization, of grievance arbitration is by itself sufficient reason to consider deferring to that process. The grievance-arbitration process is one of the most important tools of collective bargaining, and the *raison d'etre* of the National Labor Relations Act is to encourage collective bargaining.[77]

He urged that the Board should seek to determine "those situations in which the cause of industrial peace through collective bargaining will be better served by deferring to the arbitral process . . ."; however, he counseled care to avoid deferring "where the dispute is not covered by the contract and, therefore, involves the acquisition of new rights."[78] He asserted his willingness to defer in cases alleging violations of Sections 8(a)(1) and (a)(3), as well as in Section 8(a)(5) cases such as was involved in *Collyer,* a course soon to be followed by Chairman Miller and Member Kennedy.

Member Fanning argued in dissent that "[t]he majority's insistence that the parties' statutory rights cannot be adjudicated in this case except through the authority of an arbitrator verges on the practice of compulsory arbitration."[79] He indicated a willingness to defer to arbitration only in cases where there was a "minimal alleged unfair labor practice, involving the interpretation of specific contractual provisions."[80] In such cases the Board's machinery may not be necessary if the parties are in the "process of resolving their disputes in a manner sufficient to effectuate the policies of the act."[81] He also noted that arbitrators are generally "loath to intrude into the area of public rights or

---

[76]*Id.* The Board has rescinded deferral of a complaint where the dispute was not submitted to arbitration with "reasonable promptness" after the deferral decision. Typographical Union No. 101 (Washington Post Co.), 220 NLRB 1173, 90 LRRM 1523 (1975); Typographical Union No. 101 (Byron S. Adams Printing, Inc.), 219 NLRB 88, 90 LRRM 1008 (1975).

[77]*Supra* note 53 at 844.

[78]*Id.* at 845.

[79]*Id.* at 847. Chairman Miller and Member Kennedy responded that they were not compelling any party to do anything which they had not agreed to do in their labor contract. *Id.* at 847.

[80]*Supra* note 53 at 847.

[81]*Id.* at 848. Member Fanning also referred to the then existing regional office practice of delaying action on a charge where the subject of the charge is being "actively pursued" in the grievance procedure. *See* Dubo Mfg. Corp., *supra* note 67.

national labor policy."[82] He concluded that it was "inappropriate . . . to cede our jurisdiction in all cases involving arbitration to a tribunal that may, and often does, provide only a partial remedy."[83]

Member Jenkins added that the majority opinion was a "complete reversal of Board precedent" and was directly contrary to the Supreme Court's holding in *Street, Electric Railway & Motor Coach Employees* v. *Lockridge*.[84] He warned that the Board's protection would be unavailable in those situations where "unfair labor practices . . . involve in part, and perhaps distantly, the interpretation of a contract provision."[85]

At the end of 1972, in *National Radio Co.*,[86] the *Collyer* deferral policy was materially expanded to cover charges under Sections 8(a)(1) and (3). New Member Penello (who had replaced Member Brown) joined Chairman Miller and Member Kennedy to form the majority, with Members Fanning and Jenkins continuing to dissent.

The complaint in *National Radio* alleged that the employer had unilaterally imposed new conditions on union representatives with respect to reporting their movements in the plant while processing grievances on company time in violation of Section 8(a)(5), and also that the discharge of a union steward for refusal to obey the new reporting rules violated Section 8(a)(3). The administrative law judge refused to defer to a pending arbitration proceeding regarding the propriety of the discharge of the union steward because the grievance did not encompass the Section 8(a)(5) allegations; he found the employer in violation of Sections 8(a)(3) and 8(a)(5). While recognizing

---

[82]*Supra* note 53 at 849.
[83]*Id.* at 850.
[84]403 US 274, 77 LRRM 2501 (1971) (noted by Member Jenkins at 192 NLRB 855). *See* Chapter 31 *infra* at notes 83-86 and 192-93.
[85]*Supra* note 53 at 855. At footnote 23 of their opinion, Chairman Miller and Member Kennedy disagreed with Member Jenkins' conclusion; they argued that the Supreme Court in *Lockridge* contemplated that in certain cases the Board might indicate that preemption would be inappropriate; they concluded that prearbitral deferral, if subject to the preemption doctrine at all, is such a case.
[86]198 NLRB 527, 80 LRRM 1718 (1972). Member Penello had earlier joined Chairman Miller in the following definition of the scope of *Collyer*: "The Board will apply the *Collyer* rule where two basic conditions have been met: (1) the disputed issues are, in fact, issues susceptible of resolution under the operation of the grievance machinery agreed to by the parties, and (2) there is no reason for us to believe that use of that machinery by the parties could not or would not resolve such issues in a manner compatible with the purposes of the Act." Eastman Broadcasting Co., Inc., 199 NLRB 434, 437, 81 LRRM 1257 (1972).

that *Collyer* involved essentially a question of contract interpretation and that a Section 8(a)(3) allegation presents more of a statutory issue, the Board majority reversed the ALJ because "[t]he crucial determinant is . . . the reasonableness of the assumption that the arbitration procedure will resolve this dispute in a manner consistent with the standards of *Spielberg*."[87] Deferral was grounded on several factors: the vast experience of arbitrators in regularly dealing with the issue of "just cause" for discharge or discipline, the increasing case load before the Board, a recognition that the arbitration procedure is a therapeutic experience which may strengthen the relationship between the union and the employer (suggesting that Board intervention might be an unsettling force), and a belief that the union would be strongly motivated to protect the rights of employees who were engaged in activities on behalf of the union.[88] While the discharge of the union steward might have suggested union animus by the employer, the majority did not find a history of union animus such as to preclude deferral.

Predictably, Members Fanning and Jenkins strongly dissented to this extension of *Collyer* policy to discriminatory discharge cases. They stated:

> Statutory protection against discrimination on the job because of engaging in, or refraining from, Union activity is an *individual* right, unlike the Union or group right to be protected from unilateral changes in the collective bargaining agreement. Because it is granted by the statute to individuals, it cannot be reduced, altered or displaced by any agreement between the employer and the Union.[89]

They noted the Board's mandate to protect public rights, especially individual rights, and questioned the competence of arbitrators to deal with the statutory question of discrimination, because arbitrators would lack the Board's investigative and legal resources and its capabilities and expertise in handling statutory issues. They were concerned about an arbitrator finding that an employer had some cause for discipline or discharge, but without consideration of the statutory issues.[90]

---

[87]*Supra* note 86.
[88]*Id.*
[89]*Id.*
[90]They stated: "In many, and perhaps most, discharge cases, a good reason may exist for firing the employee; if so, the arbitration inquiry ends there, and the employee is out of a job. The Act, however, requires that the employee be protected against discharge for union reasons, even though there may be a different and good reason for his discharge. Consequently the Board in nearly every discriminatory discharge case exam-

The arbitrator in *National Radio*[91] held the arbitration award in abeyance while the Board considered the case. Subsequently he found that the discharge had not been motivated by union animus and was lawful.[92] Pursuant to the retention-of-jurisdiction provision in the Board's order,[93] the union filed a motion with the Board asserting that the arbitrator had failed to dispose of all of the statutory issues raised by the complaint and that he had reached a decision repugnant to the Act. A divided Board dismissed the request for further consideration.[94] Although the arbitrator had not directly ruled on the Section 8(a)(5) issue with respect to the employer's imposition of the new reporting requirement, the Board observed that the union had not initially asked the arbitrator to resolve that issue and subsequently it did not avail itself of the opportunity to expand the scope of the arbitration procedure to include the issue. Dissenting Member Fanning viewed the decision as a violation of the majority's promise to consider such issues in its retention of jurisdiction under the *Collyer* policy.[95]

When Chairman Murphy replaced Chairman Miller and Member Walther replaced Member Kennedy, the newer members refrained from expressing their views on *Collyer* policy until early 1977, at which time the reconstituted Board restricted *Collyer* to violations of Sections 8(a)(5) and 8(b)(3).[96] Previously, the Board had applied *Collyer* when prearbitral deferral request was timely raised[97] in cases alleging a wide variety of statutory

---

ines the evidence and the circumstances in order to determine whether the "good" reason was the real reason or a pretext for firing the employee." 198 NLRB at 534. *See generally* Chapter 7 *supra*.

[91]Professor Archibald Cox.

[92]National Radio Co., 60 LA 78 (1973). Arbitrator Cox found that the grievant had a duty to abide by the rule and to file a grievance.

[93]Typical of all *Collyer*-type orders. *See* note 76 *supra*.

[94]National Radio Co., 205 NLRB 1179, 84 LRRM 1105 (1973).

[95]*Id.* at 1181.

[96]General Am. Transp. Corp., 228 NLRB 808, 94 LRRM 1483 (1977) [hereinafter sometimes referred to as "GAT"]. *See infra* at notes 114-17.

[97]The Board will not defer to prospective arbitration unless the issue of deferral is raised during or before the unfair labor practice hearing. Cutten Supermkt., 220 NLRB 507, 90 LRRM 1250 (1975); Duchess Furniture, 220 NLRB 13, 90 LRRM 1160 (1975); Erie Strayer Co., 213 NLRB 344, 87 LRRM 1162 (1974); Asbestos Workers Local 22 (Rosendahl, Inc.), 212 NLRB 913, 87 LRRM 1604 (1974); Operating Eng'rs Local 9 (Fountain Sand & Gravel Co.), 210 NLRB 129, 86 LRRM 1303 (1974); Redco Constr. Corp., 206 NLRB 150, 84 LRRM 1205 (1973); Asko, Inc., 202 NLRB 330, 83 LRRM 1498 (1973); *but see* Beer Distribs. Ass'n, 196 NLRB 1150, 80 LRRM 1235 (1972) (Member Fanning, dissenting, argued that the parties had not raised deferral either at the hearing or in their briefs). *Cf.* Alameda County Ass'n for Mentally Retarded, 255 NLRB 603, 107 LRRM 1001 (1981) (respondent did not assert deferral as an affirmative defense). *See* notes 123-24 and 222 *infra*.

violations of Sections 8(a)(1),[98] 8(a)(3),[99] 8(a)(5),[100] 8(b)(1)(A),[101] 8(b)(1)(B),[102] 8(b)(2),[103] and 8(b)(3).[104] However, the Board had also refused to defer in many other types of cases. Its determination whether to defer revolved around the same factors relied upon by the Board majority to justify the deferral in *Collyer*: (1) existence of a stable collective bargaining relationship; (2) respondent's willingness to arbitrate the arbitrable issue; and (3) determination of whether the contract and its meaning are central to the dispute.[105]

3. *Collyer* in the Reviewing Courts. The appellate courts quickly approved and enforced the *Collyer* doctrine.[106] As early as 1975, the Second Circuit declared that "the validity of the

---

[98]Todd Shipyards Corp., 203 NLRB 114, 83 LRRM 1104 (1973). The General Counsel's Revised Guidelines on *Collyer* (*infra* note 220) indicate that §8(a)(2) cases may be appropriate for deferral.
[99]Bell Tel. Co., 214 NLRB 980, 87 LRRM 1542 (1974).
[100]Granite City Steel Co., 211 NLRB 880, 87 LRRM 1006 (1974); National Heat & Power Corp., 201 NLRB 1019, 82 LRRM 1436 (1973); Great Coastal Express, 196 NLRB 871, 80 LRRM 1097 (1972); Coppus Eng'r Corp., 195 NLRB 595, 79 LRRM 1449 (1972).
[101]Teamsters Local 70 (Nabisco, Inc.), 198 NLRB 552, 80 LRRM 1727 (1972), *aff'd*, 479 F2d 770, 83 LRRM 2612 (CA 2, 1973).
[102]Columbia Typographical Union No. 101 (Washington Post Co.), 207 NLRB 831, 85 LRRM 1018 (1973); Baltimore Typographical Union No. 12 (A. S. Abell Co.), 201 NLRB 120, 82 LRRM 1127 (1973); Mailers Union No. 36 (Houston Chronicle), 199 NLRB 804, 81 LRRM 1310 (1972).
[103]Newspaper Guild of Brockton (Enterprise Publishing Co.), 201 NLRB 793, 82 LRRM 1337 (1973), *aff'd*, 493 F2d 1024, 85 LRRM 2746 (CA 1, 1974).
[104]Teamsters Local 70 (Nabisco, Inc.), *supra* note 101.
[105]In Typographical Union No. 101 (Washington Post Co.), *supra* note 76, Member Penello, on the one hand, and Members Fanning and Jenkins, on the other, engaged in debate concerning the meaning of available statistics reflecting the Board's *Collyer* experience. Member Penello argued that *Collyer* has "encourage[d] unions and employers to pursue collective bargaining solutions," noting that during the period between May 1973 and April 1974 the regional offices had tentatively dismissed 511 cases under *Collyer*. Members Fanning and Jenkins contended that the Board lacked knowledge as to what final resolutions were reached in a majority of those cases. Rather than assume that collective bargaining had been fostered, they thought "it perhaps more likely that the cases were simply dropped because of lack of financial or other ability to pursue them, thus leaving unremedied whatever statutory violations may have occurred." 220 NLRB at 1175.
[106]Electrical Workers (IBEW) Local 2188 (Western Elec. Co.) v. NLRB, 494 F2d 1087, 85 LRRM 2576 (CA DC, 1974), *cert. denied*, 419 US 835, 87 LRRM 1052 (1974); Associated Press v. NLRB, 492 F2d 662, 85 LRRM 2440 (CA DC, 1974) (listing in its footnote the six courts which have given "apparent approval" to *Collyer* without directly passing on it); Provision House Workers (Urban Patman, Inc.) v. NLRB, 493 F2d 1249, 85 LRRM 2863 (CA 9, 1974), *cert. denied*, 419 US 828, 87 LRRM 2397 (1974) (deferral appropriate even though "characterization of the dispute as one involving interpretation of a contract rather than existence of a contract is not wholly free from doubt."); Nabisco, Inc. v. NLRB, *supra* note 101; T.I.M.E.-DC, Inc. v. NLRB, 504 F2d 294, 87 LRRM 2853 (CA 5, 1974); NLRB v. Railway Clerks, 498 F2d 1105 (CA 5, 1974); NLRB v. Lithographers Local 271 (United States Playing Card Co.), 495 F2d 763, 86 LRRM 2655 (CA 6, 1974); Enterprise Publishing Co. v. NLRB, 493 F2d 1024 (CA 1, 1974).

Collyer doctrine is no longer seriously in doubt."[107] The courts have also upheld the Board's refusal to defer under *Collyer*.[108]

The District of Columbia Circuit placed some limitations on its approval of *Collyer*. That court stated that deferral may not be appropriate (1) if arbitration would impose an undue financial burden on one of the parties, or (2) if it prevents an orderly exposition of the legal issue, such as where successive *ad hoc* arbitrations produce no consistent rule.[109]

The Supreme Court, in dictum in *William E. Arnold Co.* v. *Carpenters District Council*,[110] stated that the Board's *Collyer* doctrine "harmonizes" with Congress' expressed concern that voluntary dispute-resolution procedures be used to resolve labor-management disputes under a labor contract.[111]

When the Board in *National Radio*[112] expanded *Collyer* to include Section 8(a)(3) violations, the Second Circuit accepted the Board's position, agreeing that arbitration was appropriate where that process is likely to resolve the dispute between the parties.[113]

D. Contraction of *Collyer: General American Transportation* and Limitations on the Board's Deferral Policy

In 1977, in two cases decided on the same day, the Board effectively overruled the *National Radio* expansion of the *Collyer*

---

[107]Machinists Lodge 700 (United Aircraft Corp.) v. NLRB, 525 F2d 237, 239, 90 LRRM 2922 (CA 2, 1975).

[108]NLRB v. Railway Clerks (Yellow Cab. Co.), 498 F2d 1105, 86 LRRM 3199 (CA 5, 1974); NLRB v. Lithographers Local 271 (United States Playing Card Co.), *supra* note 106 (refusal to defer was not abuse of Board's discretion even though "it might have been better to defer the issues . . . to arbitration"). *See* T.I.M.E.-DC, Inc. v. NLRB, *supra* note 106 (neither *Spielberg* nor *Collyer* are applicable where grievance proceedings "are not even-handed").

[109]Electrical Workers (IBEW) Local 2188 (Western Elec. Co.) v. NLRB, *supra* note 106.

[110]417 US 12, 16, 86 LRRM 2212 (1974). *See* Chapter 19 *supra* at notes 72 and 199 and Chapter 31 *infra* at note 234.

[111]In Columbus Printing Pressmen Local 252 (R. W. Page Corp.), 219 NLRB 268, 89 LRRM 1553 (1975), *enforced*, 543 F2d 1161, 93 LRRM 3055 (CA 5, 1976), Members Kennedy and Penello described the Supreme Court's opinion in *Arnold* v. *Carpenters* as having "specifically endorsed the *Collyer* doctrine." 219 NLRB at 268-69. Member Jenkins, however, saw as "[m]ore analogous" Alexander v. Gardner-Denver Co., 415 US 36, 7 FEP 81 (1974), "a Title VII case in which the Supreme Court held that there can be no deferral of statutory rights to an arbitral tribunal. The Court's reasons in reaching this result [are] . . . fatal to the majority's position in *Collyer* type cases." 219 NLRB at 271. *Cf.* Barrentine v. Arkansas-Best Freight Sys., Inc., 24 WH 545 (CA 8, 1980), *rev'd*, 450 US 728, 24 WH 1284 (1981).

In Machinist Lodge 700 (United Aircraft Corp.) v. NLRB, *supra* note 107, the Second Circuit noted: "The Supreme Court has since added further authority to the policy by quoting favorably from the Board's reasoning in the Collyer decision in William E. Arnold Co. v. Carpenters. . . ." *Id.* at 239.

[112]*Supra* note 86.

[113]Machinist Lodge 700 (United Aircraft Corp.) v. NLRB, *supra* note 107.

doctrine, while affirming the validity of *Collyer* in its original scope.

In *General American Transportation Corp. (GAT)*[114] Chairman Murphy joined Members Fanning and Jenkins to form a majority to reverse *National Radio*. *General American* involved an allegedly discriminatory discharge in violation of Sections 8(a)(1) and (3). Members Fanning and Jenkins reasserted their disapproval of deferring the adjudication of statutory rights; Chairman Murphy, in her concurring opinion, explained that *Collyer* deferral should apply only to Sections 8(a)(5) and 8(b)(3) complaints where "the dispute is principally between the contracting parties—the employer and the union—[and] the principal issue is whether the complained-of conduct is permitted by the parties' contract."[115] She viewed such issues as "eminently suited to the arbitral process," which will ordinarily also resolve the unfair labor practice issue. Whereas in complaints under Sections 8(a)(1), 8(a)(3), 8(b)(1)(A), and 8(b)(2), she explained, the determinative issue is not whether the conduct is permitted by the contract but whether it is unlawfully motivated or interferes with employee rights protected by Section 7. She noted that the arbitrator's decision on the contractual issue is not likely to dispose of the statutory issue, "[n]or is the arbitration process suited for resolving employee complaints of discrimination under Section 7."[116] She read support for her approach in *Mastro Plastics Corp.* v. *NLRB*,[117] where the Supreme Court had stated that only after "full freedom of association" is assured can the complementary policy of effective negotiation be realized; deferring issues involving Section 7 would thus not fully protect the freedom of association.

In the second case, *Roy Robinson, Inc.*,[118] Chairman Murphy joined Members Penello and Walther, the dissenters in *General American*, to form a majority affirming the continuation of the Board's original *Collyer* policy in failure-to-bargain cases—essentially relying on the rationale contained in the original decision. In concurring, Chairman Murphy urged deferral because issues involving pure interpretation of rights and obligations under a

---

[114]*Supra* note 96.
[115]228 NLRB at 810.
[116]*Id.* at 811.
[117]350 US 270, 279-80, 37 LRRM 2587 (1956).
[118]228 NLRB 828, 94 LRRM 1471 (1977).

collective bargaining agreement are "particularly suited to the arbitral process."[119]

Shortly after these decisions, General Counsel Irving issued a policy memorandum[120] indicating that deferral was to be applied in the future only to charges of violations of Sections 8(a)(5) and 8(b)(3) which meet "the traditional *Collyer* test."

E. The Board's *Dubo* Deferral Policy

The Board's *Dubo* deferral policy results in deferral of some cases where *Collyer* alone would not. Long before *Collyer* and *National Radio,* the Board ruled in *Dubo Manufacturing Corp.*[121] that deferral of a Section 8(a)(3) allegation was appropriate pending completion of the grievance-arbitration procedure, provided the dispute had already been submitted to that procedure. In practice, continuation of the Board's *Dubo* policy moderates the impact of the Board's contraction of *Collyer* by *General American Transportation.*[122] A charging party alleging discrimination under Section 8(a)(3) who has grievance-arbitration machinery available under which to seek a remedy, can thus avoid deferral under *General American Transportation;* but, under the Board's *Dubo* policy, he can avoid deferral only at the price of forgoing his use of the grievance-arbitration machinery.[123]

---

[119]*Id.* at 831. The case involved a plant shutdown without prior notice to the union, allegedly in violation of the employer's §8(a)(5) bargaining obligation.

[120]NLRB Gen. Counsel Memo., No. 77-58 (May 25, 1977), *Regional Office Handling of Collyer Issues in Light of the Board's Decision in General American Transportation Corp.,* LABOR RELATIONS YEARBOOK—1977, 320 (BNA Books, 1978).

[121]*Supra* note 67. *See also infra* at notes 220-29.

[122]The General Counsel's memorandum following *General American Transportation, supra* note 120, states: "[T]he *GAT* decision merely broaden[s] the area of nondeferral under *Collyer.* In cases to which the *GAT* policy applies, charging parties will no longer be 'forced,' on pain of dismissal, to pursue the grievance-arbitration procedure. But even in such cases, if the charging party is in the grievance-arbitration channel and *voluntarily* elects to stay there, after having been apprised of his 'entitlement' under *GAT* to a General Counsel or Board determination, there is nothing in *GAT* that suggests that his case cannot be deferred under *Dubo* so long as he opts to continue in that channel. To the contrary, former Chairman Murphy's concurring opinion in *GAT* suggests that such deferral would be appropriate. Consequently *Dubo* will be applied to all non-*Collyer* cases, including those which are non-*Collyer* because of the *GAT* policy." *Id.* at 322.

[123]On May 14, 1979, the General Counsel issued another memorandum on the subject entitled *Procedures for Application of the Dubo Policy to Pending Charges,* NLRB Gen. Counsel Memo., No. 79-36. It emphasized that the *GAT* decision did not undermine the validity of *Dubo* referrals. Thus, while "individual" charges might no longer be subject to a *Collyer*-type deferral, they would be subject to a *Dubo* deferral "provided that the individual and the charging union are voluntarily pursuing the matter through the grievance-arbitration machinery." Where the individual and the charging union, therefore, are given the opportunity to choose between arbitration and the Board processes, and they have chosen arbitration, the case will be deferred. The memo provides, however,

In one case, however, *Youngstown Sheet & Tube Co.*,[124] the Board refused to defer under *Dubo* even though the dispute had already reached the third step of the contractual grievance procedure. It was deemed significant that the charging party had not been informed of his right to a Board determination. It was also significant to the Board that the grievance had not yet been submitted to arbitration and there was no certainty that it would be submitted.[125]

II. PREARBITRAL DEFERRAL: APPLYING THE *COLLYER* DOCTRINE

A. The Parties' Relationship

Where there is no stable collective bargaining relationship, or where the respondent's conduct indicates a rejection of collective bargaining and the organizational rights of employees, the Board will ordinarily not defer under *Collyer*.[126] However, where there is "effective dispute-solving machinery available, and if the combination of past and present alleged misconduct does not appear to be of such character as to render the use of the machinery unpromising or futile," the Board will apply its "usual deferral policies."[127] But regardless of the parties' prior collective bargaining relationship, certain conduct standing by itself

---

that there should not be a deferral where the individual and the charging union choose to drop the grievance. At that point the regional office will proceed to a merit determination. The General Counsel's revised guidelines also suggest that at three specified stages during the course of the investigation of the charge the regional office should inquire regarding respondent's willingness to arbitrate. *See also* NLRB Gen. Counsel Memo., No. 81-39 (July 17, 1981), opting in favor of deferral as to the open question of *Dubo* deferral where the individual abandons his grievance although the union continues to process it. *See* Ball Corp., 257 NLRB No. 126, 108 LRRM 1021 (1981) (Board declined to defer to contractual grievance procedure where union had processed discharge grievance through third step but decided not to proceed to arbitration or to file an unfair labor practice charge). *See also* note 228 *infra*.

[124]235 NLRB 572, 98 LRRM 1347 (1978). *See infra* at note 148.

[125]The General Counsel's 1979 memorandum, *supra* note 123, which was issued after the *Youngstown* decision, stressed that the regional offices should "fully and effectively" apprise the individual and the union of the options available and the consequences of each option. For example, if the grievance is dropped in reliance upon the Board's processes and the charge is not considered meritorious, the charging party may be left with no means of redress.

[126]Mountain States Constr. Co., 203 NLRB 1085, 83 LRRM 1208 (1973); *see* Meilman Food Indus., Inc., 234 NLRB 698, 97 LRRM 1372 (1978); AMF, Inc., 219 NLRB 903, 909, 90 LRRM 1271 (1975); Westinghouse Learning Corp., 211 NLRB 19, 86 LRRM 1709 (1974); Capital Roof & Supply Co., 217 NLRB 1004, 89 LRRM 1191 (1975). *See also* note 130 *infra*.

[127]United Aircraft Corp., 204 NLRB 879, 879, 83 LRRM 1411 (1973), *aff'd*, 525 F2d 237, 90 LRRM 2922 (CA 2, 1975); Packerland Packing Co., 216 NLRB 841, 88 LRRM 1488 (1975).

THE DEVELOPING LABOR LAW

CH. 20

may be so egregious as to prevent the Board from deferring to prospective arbitration. Thus, the Board has not deferred where the unfair labor practice charge alleges that the employer's conduct was in retaliation or reprisal for an employee's resort to the grievance procedure or otherwise "strikes at the foundation of that grievance and arbitration mechanism upon which [the Board has] relied in the formulation of [the] *Collyer* doctrine."[128] The Board has deferred to existing arbitration awards under *Spielberg*, however, rejecting claims that the employer acted in reprisal against the grievant for processing grievances.[129]

In numerous cases where it has found that the conduct of the respondent constituted a rejection of collective bargaining principles or organizational rights of employees, the Board has refused to defer.[130] Thus, where an employer interfered with the use of the grievance-arbitration procedure, prearbitral deferral was denied.[131] And if the parties at the prospective arbitration hearing will not protect or actively support the charging party's

---

[128]North Shore Publishing Co., 206 NLRB 42, 84 LRRM 1165 (1973), *quoting from* Joseph T. Ryerson & Sons, Inc., 199 NLRB 461, 467, 81 LRRM 1261 (1972). *See also* Eldorado Club, 220 NLRB 183, 90 LRRM 1373 (1975); Whirlpool Corp., 216 NLRB 183, 88 LRRM 1329 (1975); Morrison-Knudsen Co., 213 NLRB 280, 87 LRRM 1655 (1974), *enforced*, 521 F2d 1404, 90 LRRM 3074 (CA 8, 1975); Independent Stave Co., 208 NLRB 233, 85 LRRM 1394 (1974) (a separate ground for refusing to defer was the allegation in the complaint that respondent had attempted to hinder access to the Board's processes); *contra*, United States Postal Serv., 210 NLRB 560, 86 LRRM 1222 (1974).

[129]Adolph Coors Co., 208 NLRB 676, 85 LRRM 1127 (1974); Gulf States Asphalt Co., 200 NLRB 938, 82 LRRM 1008 (1972); Superior Motor Transp. Co., 200 NLRB 892, 82 LRRM 1083 (1972); Terminal Transp. Co., 185 NLRB 672, 75 LRRM 1130 (1970).

[130]Edward J. White, 237 NLRB 1020, 99 LRRM 1126 (1978) (employer's unilateral changes in working conditions and refusal to bargain); Helvetia Sugar Coop., Inc., 234 NLRB 638, 98 LRRM 1290 (1978) (refusal to bargain with certified union and unilateral change of certain terms and conditions of employment); Los Angeles Marine Hardware, 235 NLRB 720, 98 LRRM 1571 (1978), *enforced*, 602 F2d 1302, 102 LRRM 2498 (CA 9, 1979) (employer repudiated collective bargaining agreement with the union); Texaco, Inc., 233 NLRB 375, 96 LRRM 1534 (1977) (employer dealt directly with employees over change in starting times); Fairfield Nursing Home, 228 NLRB 1208, 96 LRRM 1180 (1977) (employer refused to pay wage increases and holiday benefits provided for in collective agreement); Ram Constr. Co., 228 NLRB 769, 95 LRRM 1125 (1977) (employer pressured employees to accept practice inconsistent with labor contract and retaliated against employees when they attempted to assert their contractual rights); Anaconda Co., 224 NLRB 1041, 93 LRRM 1139 (1976), *enforced*, 99 LRRM 2634 (CA 9, 1978) (employer's refusal to apply contract to employment site constituted repudiation of bargaining relationship); F. S. Willey Co., Inc., 224 NLRB 1170, 92 LRRM 1589 (1976) (employer's conditioning of employment on nonmembership in union interfered with organizational rights).

[131]St. Joseph's Hosp. (Our Lady of Providence Unit), 233 NLRB 1116, 97 LRRM 1212 (1977); United States Postal Serv., 228 NLRB 1235, 94 LRRM 1728 (1977); Nissan Motor Corp., 226 NLRB 397, 93 LRRM 1249 (1976) (employer suspended union committeeman for processing grievances); Wabash Asphalt Co., Inc., 224 NLRB 820, 93 LRRM 1254 (1976) (employer refused to hire employees referred from hiring hall because of their previous use of grievance system).

interests or, for some reason, will be hostile to the charging party or his cause, the Board will refuse to defer.[132] Similarly, it also refused to defer where the union had been decertified and therefore might not have been interested in pursuing the grievance.[133]

B. The Parties' Willingness to Arbitrate and Arbitrability

Deferral under *Collyer* is not available to parties who are unwilling to arbitrate or are unwilling to waive the procedural defense that the grievance was not timely filed.[134]

Deferral is also generally denied where the Board concludes that the issue involved is not, at least arguably, covered by the contract and its arbitration provision.[135]

Where some, though not all, of the unfair labor practice allegations can be dealt with in arbitration, the Board has indi-

---

[132]Iron Workers Local 433 (Associated Gen. Contractors of Cal., Inc.), 228 NLRB 1420, 96 LRRM 1125 (1977), *enforced*, 600 F2d 770, 101 LRRM 3119 (CA 9, 1979); Electrical Workers (IBEW) Local 367 (Gary Billcheck), 230 NLRB 86, 96 LRRM 1182 (1977), *enforced*, 578 F2d 1375, 99 LRRM 2633 (CA 3, 1978); Teamsters Local 70 (Luckey Stores, Inc.), 226 NLRB 205, 93 LRRM 1245 (1976), *enforcement modified on other grounds*, 580 F2d 1053, 99 LRRM 2634 (CA 9, 1978); Plumbers Local 725 (Power Regulator Co.), 225 NLRB 138, 93 LRRM 1045 (1976), *enforced*, 512 F2d 550, 98 LRRM 2475 (CA 5, 1978); Electrical Workers (IBEW) Local 675 (S & M Elec. Co.), 223 NLRB 1499, 92 LRRM 1207 (1976), *enforced*, 559 F2d 1208, 96 LRRM 2106 (CA 3, 1977); Western Exterminator Co., 223 NLRB 1270, 92 LRRM 1161 (1976) *enforcement denied on other grounds*, 565 F2d 1114, 97 LRRM 2187 (CA 9, 1977); Machinists Lodge 68 (West Winds, Inc.), 205 NLRB 132, 84 LRRM 1030 (1973), *vacated on other grounds sub nom.* Kling v. NLRB, 503 F2d 1044, 88 LRRM 2385 (CA 9, 1975); Pauley Paving Co., 200 NLRB 861, 82 LRRM 1005 (1972); *enforced*, 85 LRRM 2594 (CA 4, 1974); United Parcel Serv., 228 NLRB 1060, 96 LRRM 1288 (1977); Operating Eng'rs Local 18 (S. J. Groves & Sons Co.), 227 NLRB 1477, 94 LRRM 1336 (1977); Columbian Corrugated Container Corp., 226 NLRB 147, 93 LRRM 1232 (1976); Machinists Lodge 1129 (Sunbeam Corp.), 219 NLRB 1019, 90 LRRM 1040 (1975); General Motors Corp., 218 NLRB 472, 89 LRRM 1891 (1975); United States Steel Corp., 216 NLRB 874, 88 LRRM 1649 (1975); United States Postal Serv., 215 NLRB 488, 88 LRRM 1099 (1974); Standard Fruit & S.S. Co., 211 NLRB 121, 87 LRRM 1134 (1974); Seafarers (Sea-Land Serv., Inc.), 207 NLRB 958, 85 LRRM 1177 (1973); Laborers Local 207 (A & E Constr. Co.), 206 NLRB 902, 84 LRRM 1474 (1973); Fleet Carrier Corp., 201 NLRB 227, 82 LRRM 1178 (1973); Kansas Meat Packers, 198 NLRB 543, 80 LRRM 1743 (1972).

[133]Seng Co., 205 NLRB 200, 83 LRRM 1577 (1973).

[134]United States Postal Serv., 225 NLRB 220, 93 LRRM 1089 (1976); Pilot Freight Carriers, Inc., 224 NLRB 341, 92 LRRM 1338 (1976).

[135]Western Mass. Elec. Co., 228 NLRB 607, 95 LRRM 1605 (1977), *enforcement denied on other grounds*, 573 F2d 101, 98 LRRM 2851 (CA 1, 1978); Teamsters Local 70 (Luckey Stores, Inc.), *supra* note 132; Operating Eng'rs Local 400 (Hilde Constr. Co.), 225 NLRB 596, 92 LRRM 1494 (1976), *aff'd*, 561 F2d 1021, 95 LRRM 3010 (CA DC, 1977); Graphic Arts Union (S & M Rotogravure Serv.), 222 NLRB 280, 91 LRRM 1139 (1976); Raymond Int'l, Inc., 218 NLRB 202, 89 LRRM 1461 (1975); Southwestern Bell Tel. Co., 198 NLRB 569, 80 LRRM 1711 (1972), *remanded in light of arbitration award*, 86 LRRM 3247 (CA DC, 1973); Beer Distribs. Ass'n, 196 NLRB 1150, 80 LRRM 1235 (1972); Graphic Arts Local 277 (S & M Rotogravure Serv.), 219 NLRB 1053, 90 LRRM 1081 (1975); Operating Eng'rs Local 428 (Mercury Constructors, Inc.), 216 NLRB 580, 88 LRRM 1354 (1975).

cated that deferral may not be appropriate. In *Sheet Metal Workers Local 17 (George Koch Sons, Inc.)*[136] it explained its reasoning:

> Where an entire dispute can adequately be disposed of under the grievance and arbitration machinery, we are favorably inclined toward permitting the parties to do so. One of our reasons for so doing is to avoid litigating the same issues in a multiplicity of forums. But [where] we must perforce determine a part of the dispute, there is far less compelling reason for not permitting the entire dispute to be resolved in a single proceeding.[137]

Of course, should the Board find that no arbitration agreement exists, it will not defer.[138] And if the ultimate decision maker has been involved in the events giving rise to the grievance, deferral will not be allowed.[139] Deferral has also been denied where respondent's conduct limited access to the contractual grievance-arbitration procedures.[140]

Where a final and binding procedure does not exist, the Board will not defer.[141] Two cases have suggested that expiration of the labor contract can be another factor precluding deferral.[142]

Even though the final step in the grievance procedure is a bipartite panel and not conventional arbitration, the Board may nevertheless defer.[143] And a union's inability to undertake the

---

[136]199 NLRB 166, 81 LRRM 1195 (1972), *enforced,* 85 LRRM 2548 (CA 1, 1973).
[137]*Id.* at 168.
[138]Atlas Tack Corp., 226 NLRB 222, 93 LRRM 1236 (1976), *enforced,* 559 F2d 1201, 96 LRRM 2660 (CA 1, 1977).
[139]Westinghouse Elec. Corp., 206 NLRB 812, 84 LRRM 1580 (1973), *enforcement denied,* 506 F2d 668, 87 LRRM 2686 (CA 4, 1974); National Football League, 203 NLRB 958, 83 LRRM 1203 (1973), *remanded,* 503 F2d 12, 87 LRRM 2118 (CA 8, 1974).
[140]Teamsters Local 46 (Guinness-Harp Corp.), 236 NLRB 1160, 98 LRRM 1523 (1978) (dispute between employer and union over existence of collective bargaining agreement found likely to inhibit access to grievance-arbitration procedures); Edward J. White, Inc., 237 NLRB 1020, 99 LRRM 1126 (1978) (issues concerning respondent's unilateral changes and its refusal to bargain could not be resolved through existing contractual grievance procedure).
[141]Wheeler Constr. Co., 219 NLRB 541, 90 LRRM 1173 (1975); Machinists Dist. 10 (Ladish Co.), 200 NLRB 1159, 82 LRRM 1081 (1972); Tulsa-Whisenhunt Funeral Homes, 195 NLRB 106, 79 LRRM 1265 (1972) (arbitration could only be invoked by agreement of both parties); *see* Harley-Davidson Motor Co., 214 NLRB 433, 87 LRRM 1571 (1974) (suggesting deferral inappropriate where dispute arose after expiration of labor contract and no arbitration procedure existed at that time); *cf.* Columbus & S. Ohio Elec. Co., 205 NLRB 187, 83 LRRM 1558 (1973); *see* Communications Workers (Western Elec. Co.), 204 NLRB 782, 83 LRRM 1583 (1973) (Board reluctant to defer where contract did not specify means for employer to file grievance); Great Scott Supermkts., 206 NLRB 447, 84 LRRM 1563 (1973) (Board adopted *pro forma* the administrative law judge's conclusion that neither *Collyer* nor *Spielberg* permitted dismissal of a complaint without reservation of jurisdiction pending the outcome of arbitration solely because union during grievance proceedings had decided not to seek arbitration).
[142]Meilman Food Indus., Inc., *supra* note 126; Sahara Tahoe Corp., 229 NLRB 1094, 96 LRRM 1583 (1977), *enforced,* 581 F2d 767, 99 LRRM 2837 (CA 9, 1978).
[143]Teamsters Local 70 (Nabisco, Inc.), *supra* note 101.

cost of arbitration because of its financial condition does not necessarily preclude deferral where the dispute meets *Collyer* deferral prerequisites.[144]

Deferral to arbitration is only available to those who are parties to the agreement to arbitrate. Many violations of the Act (e.g., secondary boycott cases) involve persons who are not parties to the labor contract in issue. The Board will not defer to arbitration where all of the interested parties in the unfair labor practice case cannot participate in the arbitration proceeding.[145] Another example involved a nonunion company which had repudiated the union contracts of two other companies owned by the same employer. The issues arising from the repudiation and the remedies applicable to it were deemed outside the scope of the arbitrator's authority, and the Board did not defer.[146]

Deferral will also be denied if a respondent refuses unconditionally to promise to proceed to arbitration.[147] Furthermore, where the charging party had not submitted his grievance to arbitration before filing the unfair labor charge, Chairman Fanning and Members Jenkins and Murphy, in *Youngstown Sheet & Tube Co.*,[148] rejected the employer's contention that deferral was appropriate under *Dubo*.[149] The filing of the unfair labor practice charge suggested to the Board majority that the charging party was choosing the Board as the preferred forum for resolution of the dispute. In refusing to defer in another case, the Board held that a charging party's acquiescence in a court order

---

[144]Croatian Fraternal Union, 232 NLRB 1010, 97 LRRM 1209 (1977). *But see* Electrical Workers (IBEW) Local 2188 (Western Elec. Co.) v. NLRB, *supra* note 106.

[145]Masters, Mates & Pilots (Seatrain Lines, Inc.), 220 NLRB 164, 90 LRRM 1691 (1975); Fenix & Scisson, Inc., 207 NLRB 752, 85 LRRM 1380 (1973), *enforced*, 87 LRRM 3276 (CA 7, 1974) (validity of agreement under §8(f)); Machinists Dist. 10 (Ladish Co.), *supra* note 141; Boilermakers Union (Bigge Drayage Co.), 197 NLRB 281, 80 LRRM 1382 (1972) (§8(e) case).

[146]Frank Naccarato Constr. Co. & Tacoma Framing Co., 233 NLRB 1394, 97 LRRM 1060 (1977). In Consolidation Coal Co., 253 NLRB 789, 106 LRRM 1013 (1980), involving Board rejection of an employer argument that an unfair labor practice charge should have been deferred to the parties' grievance and arbitration procedure, the Board enforced an ALJ decision requiring the employer to sign a written agreement embodying the terms of an absentee policy negotiated with the union. Application of *Collyer* was refused on two separate grounds: (1) the dispute involved the fundamental existence of an agreement between the parties, as opposed to a dispute concerning the interpretation of an agreement; (2) the respondent employer had not raised the issue of deferral at any time before the filing of its exceptions to the ALJ decision. (New Member Zimmerman based his concurrence on the procedural question—failure to raise the point early enough—and expressly declined to take a position on *Collyer*.)

[147]Columbus Foundries, Inc., 229 NLRB 34, 95 LRRM 1090 (1977).

[148]*Supra* note 124.

[149]*See supra* at notes 121-25.

requiring arbitration of the underlying contract dispute could not be considered a "voluntary" submission to arbitration by the charging party, and such acquiescence would not be a factor favoring deferral.[150]

C. Whether the Dispute Centers on the Collective Bargaining Agreement

1. Matters Incidentally Related to the Collective Bargaining Agreement. *Collyer* emphasized that prearbitral deferral is appropriate where the underlying dispute before the Board centers on the interpretation or application of the collective bargaining contract.[151] As the Board stated in an early *Collyerized* case, "when . . . the alleged unfair labor practices are . . . intimately entwined with matters of contractual interpretation, it would . . . effectuate the policies of the act to remit the parties in the first instance to the procedures they have devised for determining the meaning of their agreement."[152] But notwithstanding that concept, the Board has refused to defer on certain issues which it has determined fall within the scope of its own primary jurisdiction, although they might arguably also touch upon the contractual relations between the employer and the union. One such area is the clarification of or accretion to a bargaining unit. For example, where a union has filed a grievance claiming that its collective bargaining agreement requires coverage of additional employees, the Board has generally refused deferral.[153]

One such case was *Marion Power Shovel Co.*[154] The employer had extensively reorganized operation of its plant where the employees had been represented by two different unions. After the reorganization, both unions claimed to represent certain additional employees; the employer filed a Section 9(b) unit-

---

[150]National Rejectors Indus., 234 NLRB 251, 97 LRRM 1142 (1978).
   [151]*Supra* note 53.
   [152]Teamsters Local 70 (Nabisco, Inc.), *supra* note 101. In Standard Oil Co., 254 NLRB 32, 106 LRRM 1271 (1981), the Board deferred where the employer had unilaterally offered employees free comprehensive medical examinations; the employer based its action on a contractual clause which made employee physical condition a factor in assignment of work.
   [153]Massachusetts Elec. Co., 248 NLRB 155, 103 LRRM 1404 (1980); Retail Clerks Local 588 (Raley's), 224 NLRB 1638, 92 LRRM 1381 (1976), *enforcement denied on other grounds*, 565 F2d 769, 96 LRRM 2811 (CA DC, 1977); Fort Tryon Nursing Home, 223 NLRB 769, 92 LRRM 1132 (1976); Hershey Foods Corp., 208 NLRB 452, 85 LRRM 1312, *enforced*, 90 LRRM 2890 (CA 3, 1974); Germantown Dev. Co., 207 NLRB 586, 84 LRRM 1495 (1973); Combustion Eng'r, Inc., 195 NLRB 909, 79 LRRM 1577 (1972).
   [154]230 NLRB 576, 95 LRRM 1339 (1977).

clarification petition with the Board seeking a determination that only a single bargaining unit was not appropriate. One union objected to the petition on grounds that the representation questions were properly subjects of grievances which it had filed under a current arbitration clause. Considering the matter primarily a question of unit appropriateness, the Board refused to defer to the arbitration process. It stated: "The determination of questions of representation, accretion and appropriate unit do not depend upon contract interpretation but involve the application of the statutory policy, standards, and criteria. These are matters for decision of the Board rather than an arbitrator."[155] The primary issues in such cases are not merely the contractual intent of the parties to a collective bargaining agreement; instead, they focus upon the organizational rights of employees under Section 7 and the Board's Section 9 determination of the appropriate bargaining unit.

Moreover, many unit-accretion cases involve more than one labor organization competing to include workers under their respective collective bargaining agreements.[156] If the Board were to defer such disputes to arbitration, the possibility of dual arbitration proceedings and conflicting awards would arise.[157] The Board has therefore decided that in such cases unit-clarification proceedings are more appropriate for resolution of the dispute than arbitration. All parties can fully participate in the Board proceeding, and the problems of litigation, expense, and delay arising from the enforcement of *ex parte* arbitration awards may be avoided.[158]

The Board has also refused to defer, despite *Collyer*, in cases regarding employee rights protected under Section 7 which either would not fall under provisions of a collective bargaining agreement or, in the Board's opinion, would be inadequately protected under the contract.[159] In *United States Steel Corp.*[160] the

---

[155]*Id.* at 1341-42.
[156]*See, e.g.*, Pacific Northwest Bell Tel. Co., 207 NLRB 1, 84 LRRM 1398 (1973); Crown Cork & Seal Co., 203 NLRB 171, 83 LRRM 1088 (1973).
[157]*But cf.* Carey v. Westinghouse, *supra* note 29. See also *infra* at notes 176-77.
[158]Crown Cork & Seal Co., *supra* note 156.
[159]Chrysler Corp., 242 NLRB 577, 101 LRRM 1268 (1979) (intra-union attempts by employees to convince employees not to ratify collective bargaining agreement); Potter Elec. Co., 237 NLRB 1289, 99 LRRM 1248 (1978) (discharged employees denied rights to union representation under §8(a)(1)), *enforcement modified on other grounds*, 600 F2d 120, 101 LRRM 2378 (CA 8, 1979); Youngstown Sheet & Tube Co., 235 NLRB 572, 98 LRRM 1347 (1978) (suspension for refusal to perform unsafe work violates §8(a)(1)); Iron Workers Local 433 (Associated Gen. Contractors), *supra* note 132 (union threats

employer, under its rule banning all distribution of literature anywhere on company premises, refused to allow two employees to distribute literature, a practice which the Board found to be protected under Section 7 of the Act.[161] It refused to defer to the parties' grievance-arbitration mechanism since there was no assurance that Section 7 rights of the employees were covered by the contract. Illustrative of the Board's insistence on coverage of the issue by language in the contract was this observation:

> Both the Board and the courts have consistently held that, under *Collyer*, deferral of consideration by the Board is dependent on the express language of the contract. Note that nowhere in this . . . agreement are there any provisions relating to distribution of Section 7 literature. The authority of the arbitrator is limited to those matters explicitly contained in the contract. Thus, it can be readily seen that there is no authority invested in an arbitrator to hear or decide matters not covered in the contract.[162]

Similarly, in *Joseph T. Ryerson & Sons, Inc.*,[163] the Board found that an employer had violated Section 8(a)(1) by threatening an employee-union official for his participation in the filing of a grievance. The Board refused to defer to the collective bargaining agreement because it did not appear that the threat, which was unaccompanied by any discipline or other change in the employee's employment status, could form the basis for a contractual grievance, though it was unlawful under Section 8(a)(1). Furthermore, there was no showing that an arbitrator would have any authority under the contract to remedy the company's interference with the employee's performance of grievance functions.[164]

The Board has also refused to defer to grievance arbitration the allegation that an employer interfered with the processing of unfair labor practice charges in violation of Section 8(a)(4).[165]

---

and violations of hiring-hall procedure under §§8(b)(1)(A) and 8(b)(2)); McLean Trucking Co., 231 NLRB 706, 96 LRRM 1302 (1977) (discharge of employee for seeking union representation regarding a disciplinary suspension violated §8(a)(1)).
    [160]223 NLRB 1246, 92 LRRM 1158 (1976).
    [161]*See* NLRB v. Magnavox Co., 415 US 322, 85 LRRM 2475 (1974), and Chapter 6 *supra* at notes 191-95.
    [162]223 NLRB at 1247.
    [163]199 NLRB 461, 81 LRRM 1261 (1972); *see also* Native Textiles, 246 NLRB 228, 102 LRRM 1456 (1979) (employer interferes with fundamental §7 right of employees to designate their representatives by refusing to meet with union representative for the purpose of processing grievances).
    [164]Another aspect of *Ryerson* is discussed *supra* at note 128.
    [165]M & B Contracting Corp., 245 NLRB 1215, 102 LRRM 1564 (1979); United States Postal Serv., 227 NLRB 1828, 94 LRRM 1685 (1977); Houston Chronicle Publishing Co., 227 NLRB 1829, 94 LRRM 1639 (1977) (employer threatened to sue employee

In *McKinley Transport, Ltd.*[166] an employee claimed that he had been discharged for filing unfair labor practice charges. The Board noted that questions concerning alleged interference with access to its processes were "solely within the Board's province to decide."[167] Because it was the Board's duty to maintain free access and prohibit interference with its processes, the Board found that such allegations could "not . . . be delegated to the parties or exclusively subject to collective bargaining."[168]

The Board has also refused prearbitral deferral where the issue concerns more a question of law—i.e., an interpretation of statutory rights or duties under the Act—than a matter of contractual interpretation, or where there would be some doubt as to whether the arbitrator could or would consider the statutory issue.[169] In *Atlas Tack Corp.*[170] the Board found that an employer's alleged unilateral change of working conditions could not be deferred to a grievance procedure since the propriety of the employer's action turned on whether an impasse had occurred during negotiations, and there was no arbitration procedure in effect covering that period.

Similarly, in *Ernst Construction Division*,[171] an employer sought to defer to arbitration its action in laying off an employee. The employee, who had previously been reinstated in an earlier NLRB case, had filed both a grievance and an unfair labor practice over the layoff. Although the arbitrator could have interpreted the contractual issues, the Board found deferral inappropriate because the arbitrator would not be able to determine whether the company had abided by the Board's prior order. Compliance with a previous Board order was deemed "a matter clearly inappropriate for determination by an arbitrator."[172]

---

and union for expenses incurred when employee filed an unfair labor practice charge instead of utilizing contractual grievance process); Diversified Indus., 208 NLRB 223, 85 LRRM 1394 (1974).

[166]219 NLRB 1148, 90 LRRM 1195 (1975).

[167]*Id.* at 1151.

[168]*Id.*

[169]In United States Postal Serv., 239 NLRB 97, 99 LRRM 1515 (1978), the employer moved for a summary judgment asserting that a postal employee's §§8(a)(1) and 8(a)(3) charges involving claims of employment discrimination should be deferred to administrative procedures of the Civil Service Commission, based on the Board's policy in *Dubo, supra* note 67. The Board overruled the motion and ordered a hearing on the substantive issues.

[170]226 NLRB 222, 93 LRRM 1236 (1976), *enforced,* 559 F2d 1201, 96 LRRM 2660 (CA 1, 1977).

[171]217 NLRB 1069, 89 LRRM 1233 (1975).

[172]*Id.*

946 The Developing Labor Law Ch. 20

The need for legal interpretation of the Act has also been the basis for refusal to defer where the issues involved definition of mandatory subjects of bargaining[173] or have involved the contest of two rival unions to represent employees. In *Columbus Printing Pressmen*[174] a union had insisted during negotiations on the inclusion of an interest-arbitration clause which had existed in the previous collective bargaining agreement. It also demanded, under the interest-arbitration obligation contained in the prior contract, that the company arbitrate the inclusion of the clause in the new agreement. The Board refused deferral because the issue did not concern the meaning of a term in the contract. It focused instead upon whether a proposed clause of the new agreement concerning interest arbitration was a mandatory subject of bargaining under the Act, and if the clause was not a mandatory subject whether the union had bargained to impasse on the matter in violation of Section 8(b)(3). "The questions presented are therefore not ones of contract interpretation but of statutory obligation. They are legal questions concerning the . . . Act which are within the special competence of the Board rather than of an arbitrator."[175]

In rival union situations two or more unions will typically claim to represent the employees of an employer under existing contractual provisions.[176] In such cases the Board finds arbitration inappropriate because one union is attacking the validity of another labor organization's contract with the employer.[177] The Board considers such issues to be difficult, if not impossible, for an arbitrator to resolve to finality, for they may require that an arbitrator declare invalid the very contract from which his authority is derived. And more important, a rival union will lack standing to attack the propriety of another union's contract under the latter's grievance-arbitration procedure. In such cases, the Board generally exercises its authority to determine whether a collective bargaining agreement is valid, thus insuring unifor-

---

[173]See generally Chapters 16 and 17 supra.
[174]Columbus Printing Pressmen (R. W. Page Corp.), 219 NLRB 268, 89 LRRM 1553 (1975). See Chapter 18 supra at notes 65-67. See also Anaconda Co., supra note 130; Electrical Workers (IUE) Local 742 (Randall Bearings, Inc.), 213 NLRB 824, 87 LRRM 1272 (1974), enforced, 519 F2d 815, 90 LRRM 2747 (CA 6, 1975); Communications Workers (Western Elec. Co.), 204 NLRB 782, 83 LRRM 1583 (1973).
[175]219 NLRB at 270.
[176]E.g., Fenix & Scisson Co., Inc., supra note 145; Scottex Corp., 200 NLRB 446, 82 LRRM 1287 (1972).
[177]But cf., under the Railway Labor Act, Transportation-Communication Employees v. Union Pac. R.R. Co., 385 US 157, 1032, 63 LRRM 2481 (1966).

mity of interpretation despite the contention that the underlying dispute is arbitrable.

Section 8(a)(5) cases involving alleged refusals by an employer to furnish information demanded by a union for use in a grievance proceeding have also been considered exceptions to the *Collyer* deferral doctrine.[178] The reason for the exception, as the Supreme Court held in *NLRB* v. *Acme Industrial Co.*,[179] is that the obligation to provide such information is derived from statutory duties independent of the labor contract. In one case, however, the Board determined that there was specific language in the collective agreement concerning the obligation to furnish information, and that such procedure provided a "quick and fair means" to resolve the dispute, and deferred to the arbitral process notwithstanding *Acme*.[180] But where a contract is silent on the subject or does not contain a clear and effective waiver of the union's right to information, the Board does not defer.[181] The Board views deferral in "duty to furnish information" cases as inappropriate for the additional reason that such refusal to furnish relevant information constitutes interference with the very grievance procedure to which the employer is attempting to defer.[182]

Finally, even where there is language in the contract upon which the dispute may be centered, the nature of the conduct involved in the dispute, or the language of the contract itself, may affect the Board's decision on whether to defer.[183] Where the contract language on its face is illegal,[184] or where it may

---

[178]NLRB v. Davol, Inc., 101 LRRM 2242 (CA 1, 1979); St. Joseph's Hosp., 233 NLRB 1116, 97 LRRM 1212 (1977); A. O. Smith Corp., 223 NLRB 838, 92 LRRM 1160 (1976); Worcester Polytechnic Inst., 213 NLRB 306, 87 LRRM 1616 (1974).

[179]*Supra* note 43. *See* Chapter 13 *supra* at notes 346-510.

[180]United Aircraft Corp., *supra* note 127.

[181]American Standard, Inc., 203 NLRB 1132, 83 LRRM 1245 (1973); *see also* Worcester Polytechnic Inst., *supra* note 178.

[182]St. Joseph's Hosp., *supra* note 131; A. O. Smith Corp., *supra* note 178.

[183]There are cases where the Board has refused to defer because, at least in part, there was no language in the contract upon which the underlying dispute could be resolved. Keystone Steel & Wire, 217 NLRB 995, 89 LRRM 1192 (1975); Longshoremen & Warehousemen Local 6 (Associated Food Stores), 210 NLRB 666, 86 LRRM 1534 (1973), *enforced*, 90 LRRM 1363 (CA 5, 1974); Bio-Science Laboratories, 209 NLRB 796, 85 LRRM 1568 (1974); Lithographers Local 271 (United States Playing Card Co.), 204 NLRB 418, 83 LRRM 1459 (1973), *enforced*, 495 F2d 763, 86 LRRM 2655 (CA 6, 1974); *see* Teamsters Local 85 (Tyler Bros. Drayage Co.), 206 NLRB 500, 84 LRRM 1641 (1973).

[184]Electrical Workers (IBEW) Local 901 (Ernest P. Breaux Elec. Co.), 220 NLRB 1236, 90 LRRM 1439 (1975) (§8(b)(1)(B)) case where contract reserved right of union to discipline members, including supervisors); Operating Eng'rs Local 701 (Associated Gen. Contractors), 216 NLRB 233, 88 LRRM 1243 (1975), *enforced*, 578 F2d 841, 99 LRRM 2333 (CA 9, 1978) (a §8(e) case).

compel the arbitrator to reach a result inconsistent with the policy of the Act, the Board does not defer.[185] In one case the Board declined to defer to arbitration where the respondent's argument construing the contract language to justify its conduct was deemed "patently erroneous."[186] Where the Board has considered the contract language unambiguous and, therefore, that the special competence of an arbitrator is not needed to interpret the contract,[187] or where violation of the contract has seemed so clear to the Board that there could be no contrary interpretation by an arbitrator,[188] the Board has decided the case. And where the respondent's conduct, in the Board's view, did not create even a *prima facie* case of breach of either the contract or the Act, the Board has refused to defer.[189]

2. Discharge and Discipline Cases. Undoubtedly the most controversial and inconsistent application of the Board's deferral principle has concerned actions taken against an employee who allegedly violates Sections 8(a)(3) or 8(b)(2)[190] and at the same time allegedly violates a "just cause" provision in a collective bargaining agreement. The Board's initial decision to defer in such cases, announced in *National Radio Co.*,[191] and its subsequent refusal to defer, announced in *General American Transportation*,[192] are discussed above.[193] As *GAT*[194] and *Roy Robinson Chevrolet*[195] demonstrate, the Board has remained sharply divided over basic policy regarding prearbitral deferral. As to contractual disputes between employers and unions, the Board generally continues to defer.[196] However, as to alleged violations of the Act concerning individuals, the Board continues to refuse to withhold its process pending settlement of the contractual grievances.[197]

---

[185]*See* Masters, Mates & Pilots (Seatrain Lines, Inc.), 220 NLRB 164, 90 LRRM 1691 (1975) (submitting clause that violates §8(e) to arbitrator for enforcement may compound violation of Act); Operating Eng'rs Local 701 (Associated Gen. Contractors), *supra* note 184.

[186]Harley-Davidson Motor Co., *supra* note 141.

[187]Oak Cliff-Golman Baking Co., 202 NLRB 614, 82 LRRM 1688 (1973).

[188]Struthers Wells Corp., 245 NLRB 1170, 102 LRRM 1484 (1979); Meilman Food Indus., *supra* note 126.

[189]National Football League, *supra* note 139.

[190]29 USC §§158(a)(3), (b)(2) (1976).

[191]*Supra* note 86.

[192]*Supra* note 96.

[193]*Supra* at notes 112-17.

[194]*Id.*

[195]*Supra* note 118.

[196]*See, e.g.*, Croatian Fraternal Union, *supra* note 144.

[197]*E.g.*, Jones Dairy Farm, 245 NLRB 1109, 102 LRRM 1475 (1979) (employer violated §8(a)(3) and §8(a)(1) by discharging and threatening union steward who was engaged

Not surprisingly, the delineation between deferring cases to the arbitral process under Sections 8(a)(5) and 8(b)(3) and refusing to defer under Sections 8(a)(1), 8(a)(3), 8(b)(1)(A), and 8(b)(2) has not always been clearly defined. Many cases involve issues of both employee discrimination and refusal to bargain. For example, in *Northeast Oklahoma City Manufacturing Co.*[198] the employer allegedly violated Section 8(a)(5) by failing timely to pay contractual bonuses under a collective bargaining agreement. It was further alleged that the employer later violated Sections 8(a)(3) and (1) when it discharged 12 employees who struck over the failure to make the timely payments. The administrative law judge would have deferred the case to arbitration, for he saw the underlying issue as whether the employer had violated the contract and, if so, whether the breach was material. But the Board reversed the ALJ's decision to defer. In its view the alleged delinquencies in bonus payments involved both private contractual rights under Section 8(a)(5) and "also the quite separate rights of employees to engage in conduct ostensibly coming within the protection of Section 7 of the Act . . . ."[199] Accordingly, said the Board, where the violation of a respondent's duty to bargain is "inextricably related" to violations of employees' Section 7 rights, deferral is improper.[200]

Another reason proffered by the Board for its refusal to defer in cases involving allegations of both failure to bargain and denial of employees' rights under Section 7 is that in cases alleging both types of violations it would unduly fragmentize

---

in concerted protected activity of pursuing plant safety claims and other work-related claims); New York Typographical Union Local 6 (New York News, Inc.), 237 NLRB 1241, 99 LRRM 1111 (1978) (union violated §8(b)(1)(B) notwithstanding provisions of collective bargaining agreement requiring foreman to belong to union when employer appointed nonunion foreman and union instructed members not to carry out foreman's order while grievance was pending); Teamsters Local 46 (Port Distrib. Corp.), 236 NLRB 1175, 98 LRRM 1519 (1978); Teamsters Local 46 (Guinness-Harp Corp.), *supra* note 140 (Board refused to defer where union violated §8(b)(2) by claiming that casual employees who by past practice had been excluded from a union security agreement were covered by the contractual clause); Loomis Courier Serv., Inc., 235 NLRB 534, 98 LRRM 1083 (1978), *enforcement denied as to other grounds*, 595 F2d 491, 101 LRRM 2450 (CA 9, 1979) (employer lockout in violation of §§8(a)(3), (1)).
    [198]230 NLRB 135, 95 LRRM 1276 (1977).
    [199]*Id.* at 135.
    [200]*See also* National Rejectors Indus., 234 NLRB 251, 97 LRRM 1142, 1143-44 (1978); Meilman Food Indus., *supra* note 126. However, Member Murphy stated in one case that simply because an unfair labor practice complaint contains allegation of interference with employees' basic §7 rights, she would not automatically refuse deferral—that it would take more than "a merely derivative or 'make weight' allegation . . . to avoid deferral." C & H Tire Serv., 230 NLRB 1173, 95 LRRM 1521 (1977).

the proceeding to defer only the alleged violation of the duty to bargain.[201]

3. Matters Involving the Contract: Unilateral Action. Prior to the Board's decision in *Collyer*,[202] there was some question whether an offer to arbitrate conduct that amounted to unilateral action would be an adequate defense to a refusal-to-bargain charge. Some commentators suggested that "[d]uring the term of a collective bargaining agreement an offer to follow the contract grievance procedure satisfies any duty to bargain collectively with respect to a matter to which the contract grievance procedure may apply."[203] Under that approach, if an employer should appeal to contractual arbitration in response to a protest concerning its unilateral act, the Board would look not to the whole contract but only to the meaning of the arbitration clause. Its function, similar to that of the courts,[204] would be to determine "arbitrability." Beyond that, it would abstain from interfering in the parties' contractual relationship. Although the relation of the Board to the arbitral process is different in several important respects from that of the courts,[205] in the situation of unilateral action the Board would recognize that the parties have bargained for arbitration and that the arbitral procedure is "continued bargaining." Thus, the Board would avoid deciding the merits of the dispute under the guise of determining arbitrability. Such an approach would be similar to that of the Supreme Court in *Steelworkers* v. *American Manufacturing Co.*,[206] where the Court, in construing Section 301 of the LMRA, rejected the contention that if a court could first find that the meaning of the contract was beyond dispute, it could conclude that there was nothing to arbitrate.[207]

---

[201]Meilman Food Indus., *supra* note 126; Texaco, Inc., *supra* note 130.

[202]*Supra* note 53.

[203]Cox & Dunlop, *The Duty to Bargain Collectively During the Term of an Existing Agreement*, 63 HARV. L. REV. 1097, 1101 (1950); *see also* Hanley, *The NLRB and the Arbitration Process: Conflict or Accommodation?*, LABOR LAW DEVELOPMENTS 1968 (Fourteenth Annual Institute on Labor Law, Southwestern Legal Foundation) 151 (1968); Peck, *Accommodation and Conflict Among Tribunals: Whatever Happened to Preemption?*, *supra* note 1; Note, *The NLRB and Deference to Arbitration*, 77 YALE L. J. 1191, 1210-18 (1968).

[204]*See generally* Chapter 19 *supra* at notes 42-52.

[205]*See* NLRB v. Acme Indus. Co., *supra* note 43; Carey v. Westinghouse, *supra* note 29.

[206]363 US 564, 46 LRRM 2414 (1960). *See* Chapter 19 *supra* at notes 46-49.

[207]"[T]he agreement is to submit all grievances to arbitration, not merely those that a court may deem to be meritorious." *Id.* at 567.

Support for this abstention position stems from some of the Board's early decisions, such as *McDonnell Aircraft Corp.*[208] The contract there spelled out job specifications, provided for a grievance procedure, and set out a management-rights clause. When the employer unilaterally assigned certain employees to clerical work which was being performed by others, the union filed a grievance. The contractual procedure was followed through the third step; but instead of going to the fourth step, which was arbitration, the union filed an unfair labor practice charge alleging violation of the employer's duty to bargain. The Board recognized that the employer's unilateral act "gave rise to a dispute over the interpretation and administration of the agreement,"[209] but it said that the employer satisfied its obligation to bargain by treating the union's complaint as a grievance and by showing its willingness to process the grievance under the contractual procedure. The Board thus dismissed the complaint.

A somewhat similar situation occurred in *National Dairy Products Corp.*[210] There a dispute arose after the employer had told the union that for reasons of economy it intended to subcontract its milk-hauling operations. The employer refused to consider the union's complaint under the grievance procedure on the ground that the agreed-upon procedure did not cover subcontracting. The union took its case to court in a Section 301 suit and also filed refusal-to-bargain charges under Section 8(a)(5) before the Board. The Board dismissed the complaint, saying "the Board is not the proper forum for parties seeking to remedy an alleged breach of contract."[211]

---

[208]109 NLRB 930, 34 LRRM 1472 (1954). This decision followed Board holdings in Consolidated Aircraft Corp., 47 NLRB 694, 12 LRRM 44 (1943), *enforced as modified*, 141 F2d 785, 14 LRRM 533 (CA 9, 1944), and Crown Zellerbach Corp., 95 NLRB 753, 28 LRRM 1357 (1951), that the Board would refrain from deciding any question of contract interpretation which was capable of being resolved under a contractual grievance-arbitration procedure. *See also* Timken Roller Bearing Co., *supra* note 55 (union electing to pursue the grievance process cannot do so when dissatisfied employees file a §8(a)(5) charge); United Tel. of the W., 112 NLRB 779, 36 LRRM 1097 (1955) (disputes arising out of parties' conflicting contract interpretations should not be resolved by the Board because it does not effectuate the Act for the Board to police contracts).

[209]*Supra* note 208, 109 NLRB at 934.

[210]126 NLRB 434, 45 LRRM 1332 (1960).

[211]*Id.* at 435. This case did not involve deference to arbitration, however. Rather, it indicated that a dispute over whether a grievance is arbitrable is a matter of contract interpretation and is therefore more properly settled in another forum. *National Dairy* must also be evaluated in light of more recent authority. *Cf.* Fibreboard Paper Prods. Corp. v. NLRB, 379 US 203, 57 LRRM 2609 (1964) (bargaining over decision to subcontract); Cloverleaf Div. of Adams Dairy, 147 NLRB 410, 56 LRRM 1321 (1964) (Board as proper forum when arbitration is unavailable); NLRB v. C & C Plywood

On its face, the holding of *Collyer*[212] would seem to lend support to the concept that an employer satisfies its duty to bargain when it simply offers to arbitrate unilateral actions taken without discussion with the union. In *Collyer* the employer had made a number of changes in working conditions and pay rates outside the agreement and over the protest of the union. When the union filed Section 8(a)(5) charges, the Board dismissed the complaint because the subject matter of the dispute could have been settled by the parties' contractual grievance procedure. Unlike the approach taken in *McDonnell Aircraft* and *National Dairy*, however, the Board looked at factors other than mere arbitrability of the dispute. In *Collyer*, it held that deferral was appropriate, despite the unilateral change in working conditions and pay rates, because the arbitral interpretation of the contract was intended to resolve both the unfair labor practice issue and the contract-interpretation issue in a manner compatible with the purposes of the Act. The meaning of the contract was perceived as the very heart of the dispute, however, since the employer would violate its duty to bargain only if it initially did not have the right to take the action claimed under the contract.

Cases subsequent to *Collyer* have reenforced this approach: that the Board will not confine itself simply to determining the arbitrability of a contractual dispute, and that the mere offer to resolve issues involving unilateral conduct through grievance procedures will not necessarily satisfy a party's duty to bargain. The *Alfred M. Lewis, Inc.*,[213] case illustrates the point. There the company had unilaterally established production quota systems with disciplinary sanctions for nonfulfillment. The union arbitrated two grievances over the matter, losing both. While a third grievance was pending, it filed refusal-to-bargain charges under Section 8(a)(5). The Board looked to the merits of the dispute and refused to defer either to the two prior arbitral awards or to the pending grievance, because regardless of the contractual claims the unilateral action was clearly a violation of "well-estab-

---

Corp., *supra* note 30; *but cf.* Crescent Bed Co., Inc., 157 NLRB 296, 61 LRRM 1334, *enforced*, 63 LRRM 2480 (CA DC, 1966); Morton Salt Co., 119 NLRB 1402, 41 LRRM 1312 (1958). *See generally* Chapter 17 *supra* at notes 267-329.

[212]Collyer Insulated Wire, *supra* note 53. *Accord*, Schlitz Brewing Co., *supra* note 69; Vickers, Inc., 153 NLRB 561, 59 LRRM 1516 (1965); Flintkote Co., 149 NLRB 1561, 57 LRRM 1477 (1964); Bemis Bros. Bag Co., 143 NLRB 1311, 53 LRRM 1489 (1963); Montgomery Ward & Co., 137 NLRB 418, 50 LRRM 1162 (1962).

[213]229 NLRB 757, 95 LRRM 1216 (1977), *enforced in pertinent part*, 587 F2d 403, 99 LRRM 2841 (CA 9, 1978). *See* Chapter 17 *supra* at note 219.

lished Board precedent."[214] On appeal, the employer argued that it had fulfilled its duty to bargain by following the grievance procedure, which was in itself a bargaining mechanism. The Ninth Circuit rejected that theory, noting that the grievance procedure was inadequate because the arbitrators' prior decisions had violated clear principles of labor law under the Act. The court also observed:

> An essential aspect of the Union's role in collective bargaining is its right to be consulted by the employer about mandatory subjects of bargaining and to make comments, objections, or suggestions to the employer before action is taken. This is a practical mechanism to insure the stability of industrial relations . . . . It would wholly undercut the duty to bargain if the employer were allowed to act with reference to a mandatory bargaining subject and then simply defend its actions in a later arbitration hearing.[215]

In *Texaco, Inc.*[216] the Board noted other circumstances where deferral was deemed inappropriate as to an employer's unilateral change of working conditions. There the employer had changed the employees' hours of starting work, without consulting the union, and then requested the employees to withdraw their premium pay grievance concerning the change in work schedules. Since there was evidence that the employer would not comply with an arbitrator's award concerning the unilateral change, and since the employer had engaged in direct dealings with the employees concerning their grievances, thereby separately violating Section 8(a)(5), the Board refused deferral. It noted that even if an arbitrator were to find the unilateral changes in the work schedule improper and hold that they must be discussed with the union, it is not likely that the arbitrator would adequately remedy the employer's misconduct in dealing directly with the employees. The Board also took into account potential future misconduct, i.e., that the employer would disregard the arbitration award and continue to violate its bargaining obligation. In such a situation, a Board order rather than

---

[214]*Id.*

[215]587 F2d at 408. *See* NLRB Gen. Counsel Report, Second Quarter, 1980, LABOR RELATIONS YEARBOOK—1980, 303-306 (BNA Books, 1981), discussing a case where deferral to an arbitration award was declined and a complaint was issued regarding an employer's unilateral promulgation of a new rule for employee absences. *Cf.* Keebler Co., 75 LA 975 (1980), where, in a *Collyer-Dubo* case, the arbitrator found the employer's unilateral issuance of absenteeism rules to be a violation of the recognition clause in the collective bargaining agreement; thereupon, deferring to the arbitrator's award, the regional director dismissed the union's charge of refusal to bargain under §8(a)(5). *But cf.* Pet, Inc., Bakery Div., 264 NLRB No. 166, 111 LRRM 1495 (1982). *See* note 309 *infra.*

[216]*Supra* note 130.

an arbitrator's award seemed the more appropriate remedy. Thus, in cases where the Board determines that an arbitrator cannot adequately remedy alleged violations of the duty to bargain, it will not defer.

In addition to refusals to defer where arbitration would provide an inadequate remedy, the Board has also declined to defer to arbitration in cases of union unilateral conduct. In *Western Electric Co.*,[217] shortly after the signing of a collective bargaining agreement, a union allegedly violated Sections 8(b)(3) and 8(d) of the Act when it engaged in a strike in order to secure modification of the contract. The union contended that the propriety of its unilateral action (i.e., the strike) should be determined by arbitration and not by the Board. The Board decided that before deferring to arbitration it must first determine the similarity of the issues to be addressed by the Board and the arbitrators. It determined that the issues before it as to the propriety of the strike would be whether the union had complied with the statutory notice requirements of Section 8(d) and whether the purpose of the strike was to achieve a modification of the agreement; the issue before the arbitrator, on the other hand, would be whether there was a breach of the no-strike clause, and this issue would not depend upon notice requirements or improper purpose to achieve a modification. Since "the necessary parallelism of the arbitrable issue and the statutory issue does not exist,"[218] the Board refused to defer to the arbitration mechanism of the contract. The Board also noted that the union's conduct was not a mere breach of the collective agreement but amounted to a repudiation of that agreement. Additionally, it was unclear to the Board whether the strike issue was arbitrable, since the contract did not expressly provide that the employer could invoke the arbitration clause.

The foregoing post-*Collyer* decisions[219] firmly demonstrate that the Board rejects the thesis that in unilateral action cases an offer to utilize the grievance procedure is an absolute defense to the refusal-to-bargain charge. In addition, if it does not appear

---

[217]Communications Workers (Western Elec. Co.), *supra* note 174.
[218]*Id.*
[219]*See also* Anaconda Co., *supra* note 130 (employer's refusal to sign and abide by apprentice agreement and its unilateral action violates §8(d) and constitutes repudiation of relationship between parties); Harley-Davidson Motor Co., *supra* note 141 (employers contractual contention "patently erroneous"); Electrical Workers (IUE) Local 742 (Randall Bearings, Inc.), *supra* note 174 (concerted refusal of employees to work overtime during §8(d) period should not be deferred).

likely that arbitration will settle the issue, either because the arbitral remedy is inadequate or because resolution of the issue before the arbitrator will not also settle the statutory issue before the Board, the Board will resolve the dispute. On the other hand, where the Board believes that there is a substantial issue of contract interpretation and that arbitration seems likely to resolve the dispute, it will defer.

D. The Board's Continuing Role in *Collyerized* and *Dubo* Cases

When a case is *Collyerized* the Board retains jurisdiction solely for the purpose of entertaining a motion (a) that the dispute has not been promptly settled or arbitrated, or (b) that the arbitration has failed to meet *Spielberg* standards. The General Counsel is responsible for the administration of these requirements where cases are deferred without issuance of a complaint.[220] Upon a determination that a case is properly deferrable under *Collyer,* the General Counsel, through the regional director, notifies both the charged and charging parties that Board deferral is conditioned upon the prompt submission of the dispute to an arbitrator.[221] The General Counsel enforces the deferral decision by notifying the charged party that absent a prompt submission of the dispute to an arbitrator, deferral will be rescinded, the case will be further processed by the General Counsel, and a subsequent attempt by the charged party to seek deferral will be considered belated and will be

---

[220]*See* "First Questions From *Collyer,*" speech delivered by General Counsel Nash, Labor Relations Yearbook—1971, 151 (BNA Books, 1971). Eastman Broadcasting Co., Inc., 199 NLRB 434, 437, 81 LRRM 1257 (1972). General Counsel Nash issued three informational memoranda regarding *Collyer: Arbitration Deferral Policy Under Collyer* (Feb. 28, 1972) (*see* Labor Relations Yearbook—1972, 258 (BNA Books, 1973)); *Arbitration Deferral Policy Under Collyer—Revised Guidelines* (May 10, 1973); and *Collyer Deferral in Disputes Over Refusal to Furnish Information* (Dec. 18, 1973). In his *Revised Guidelines* memorandum, *supra,* he stated that according to Board decisions, "deferral may . . . be appropriate where the dispute raises issues of law and is not dependent upon interpretation of ambiguous contract provisions." *See* Peerless Pressed Metal Corp., 198 NLRB 561, 80 LRRM 1708 (1972).

The Board rarely has the opportunity to review the General Counsel's guidelines on how he will interpret *Collyer.* This is because the Board has no means to review a decision by the General Counsel to defer and to refuse to issue a complaint. *See* Chapter 32 *infra* at note 124. It is only when the General Counsel has refused to defer and has issued a complaint that the Board has the opportunity to review the General Counsel's interpretation of *Collyer.* National Radio Co., *supra* note 94, illustrates the Board's reconsideration of a case which had been originally deferred under the *Collyer* doctrine. Another reported case of Board reconsideration after *Collyerization* is United States Postal Serv., 241 NLRB 1253, 101 LRRM 1074 (1979).

[221]*See* General Counsel's guidelines, *Arbitration Deferral Policy Under Collyer—Revised Guidelines, supra* note 220, at 44-45.

opposed by the General Counsel.[222] In addition, the charging party is notified that its unwillingness to submit the dispute to an arbitrator will result in dismissal of its charge.[223]

Since the Board's *GAT* decision,[224] the General Counsel will only apply the *Collyer* doctrine to cases raising violations of Sections 8(a)(5) and 8(b)(3).[225] However, the General Counsel continues to apply its *Dubo* deferral policy to cases raising violations of Sections 8(a)(1), (3), and (5) and 8(b)(1)(A), (2), and (3).[226] While *Collyer* policy requires a charging party to choose arbitration, where it is available, as the forum for the resolution of his dispute, *Dubo* policy requires that the charging party choose either the Board or arbitration as the forum for resolution of the dispute.[227] Upon a determination that the issues raised by the unfair labor practice charge are presently or could be the subject of a grievance, the General Counsel notifies the charging party that it must choose its forum. If the charging party wishes the General Counsel to issue a complaint and vindicate statutory rights, then it must withdraw from the grievance-arbitration procedure and not take any action inconsistent with that withdrawal.[228] If the charging party wishes to remain within the grievance-arbitration procedure, then the General Counsel will defer pending resolution of the dispute in that procedure. As in a *Collyer* deferral, the General Counsel will review the arbitration award or the settlement of the grievance under *Spielberg* standards.[229]

---

[222]*Id.* at 43. However, there is a substantial unresolved issue of whether the Board will accept the General Counsel's position that a charged party's offer to arbitrate is belated as long as the offer comes no later than at the time of the unfair labor practice hearing. *See* cases cited in note 97 *supra*. In Jack Thompson Oldsmobile, Inc., 256 NLRB No. 14, 107 LRRM 1166 (1981), where there was no deferral, the Board noted that the respondent did not raise the issue of deferral until after the unfair labor practice hearing and, therefore, the issue was not fully litigated. (deferral was deemed inappropriate for the further reason of a §8(a)(3) allegation in the case).

[223]*Id.* at 45.

[224]*Supra* note 96.

[225]*See* Gen. Counsel Memo., No. 77-58, *supra* note 120.

[226]*Id. See* Gen. Counsel Memo., No 79-36, *supra* note 123.

[227]*See* discussion *supra* at notes 121-25.

[228]The General Counsel has acknowledged that its *Dubo* policy may appear to be in conflict with the Board's holding in Youngstown Sheet & Tube Co., *supra* note 124. In *Youngstown* the Board adopted the decision of an ALJ who had found that deferral was inappropriate under the *Dubo* policy even though the charging party had a grievance in the third step of the grievance-arbitration procedure that included the issues raised by the unfair labor practice charges. *Id.* at 575. *See* note 125 *supra*.

[229]*See* Gen. Counsel Memo., No. 79-36, *supra* note 123. For an example of such review, see Keebler Co., *supra* note 215.

III. Post-Arbitral Deferral: Applying the *Spielberg*
Standards

Where the subject of an unfair labor practice has been decided
in an arbitration proceeding, the Board continues to determine
deference to the arbitration award under its *Spielberg*[230] doctrine.
Under *Spielberg* and its progeny there are four standards which
must be satisfied before the Board will defer to the decision of
the arbitral tribunal: (1) the unfair labor practice issue must have
been presented to and considered by the arbitral tribunal;[231] (2)
the arbitral proceedings must "appear to have been fair and
regular"; (3) all parties to the arbitral proceedings must have
"agreed to be bound"; and (4) the decision of the arbitral tribunal must not be "clearly repugnant to the purposes and policies of the Act."[232]

An important procedural corollary to the *Spielberg* standards
is that the burden is upon the party urging deferral to show that
all of the requisite elements of *Spielberg* have been met.[233]

There are some cases where the Board does not defer under
Spielberg because of the nature of the case. These special situations—principally cases involving Section 8(a)(2) charges and
representation issues—are discussed in a later section of this
chapter.[234] The conventional *Spielberg* standards are considered
immediately below.

---

[230]*See supra* at notes 52-62. Two earlier cases that served as forerunners of the doctrine
were Wertheimer Stores Corp., 107 NLRB 1434, 33 LRRM 1398 (1954), and Monsanto
Chem. Co., 97 NLRB 517, 29 LRRM 1126 (1951), *enforced*, 205 F2d 763, 32 LRRM
2435 (CA 8, 1953).
[231]This standard was spelled out some years after *Spielberg* in Raytheon Co., *supra*
note 62; *see also* Monsanto Chem. Co., 130 NLRB 1097, 47 LRRM 1451 (1961). The
other three standards were spelled out in Spielberg Mfg. Co., *supra* note 52.
[232]Although the Board has limited the scope of *Collyer*, individual Board members
have continued to voice support for *Spielberg*. In General Am. Transp. Corp., *supra* note
96, then Chairman Murphy stated that she would honor an arbitration award under
the *Spielberg* guidelines even if the award resulted from deferral by a regional office
under the earlier prevailing *Collyer* policy. In Kansas City Star Co., 236 NLRB 866, 98
LRRM 1320 (1978), Member Truesdale, in a concurring opinion, expressed his support
for post-arbitral deferral pursuant to *Spielberg* standards. *See also* Truesdale, *Is Spielberg
Dead?*, *supra* note 1, which illustrated that throughout the period of debate on and
following the ultimate shrinkage of the *Collyer* doctrine, the Board continued to apply
Spielberg standards. By refusing to issue a complaint, the General Counsel routinely
screens out most of the *Spielberg*-type cases. Complaints are issued only when the General
Counsel concludes that *Spielberg* deferral should not take place.
[233]John Sexton & Co., 213 NLRB 794, 87 LRRM 1241 (1974). *See also* notes 243 and
250 *infra*.
[234]*See infra* at notes 377-408.

A. The Issue Under the Act Was Presented and Considered in Arbitration

The Board holds that it will not defer to an award unless the unfair labor practice issue before the Board was both presented to and considered by the arbitrator.[235] This position was illustrated by the Board's early holdings in *Ford Motor Co.*[236] and *Monsanto Chemical Co.*[237] In the *Ford* case the Board refused to give weight to an award where the unfair labor practice issue had never been presented to the umpire. The case concerned employees who had participated in or instigated a work stoppage during the term of the existing contract. The Board noted that the arbitrator "did not have before him, nor did he pass upon the question, now presented to the Board, whether [the employer] had the legal right to suspend [the employees] . . . ."[238]

In *Monsanto* the Board refused to recognize an award upholding the discharge of an employee. It found that although the issue of whether the employee had been illegally discharged for union activity was presented to the arbitrator, he did not pass upon it. In refusing to defer, the Board stated that "[i]t manifestly could not encourage the voluntary settlement of disputes or effectuate the policies and purposes of the Act to give binding effect . . . to an arbitration award which does not purport to resolve the unfair labor practice issue . . . which is the very issue the Board is called upon to decide . . . ."[239]

In *Raytheon Co.*,[240] the earliest case articulating this deferral criterion, two employees were discharged for inciting or partic-

---

[235]*Early cases:* Hawkins v. NLRB, 358 F2d 281, 61 LRRM 2622 (CA 7, 1966), *denial of petition to set aside* Mitchell Trans., Inc., 152 NLRB 122, 59 LRRM 1028 (1965); Dubo Mfg. Corp., *supra* note 67; Precision Fittings, Inc., 141 NLRB 1034, 52 LRRM 1443 (1963) (trial examiner's report); Raytheon Co., *supra* note 62; Electrical Workers (IBEW) Local 340 (Walsh Constr. Co.), 131 NLRB 260, 48 LRRM 1022 (1961); Ford Motor Co., 131 NLRB 1462, 48 LRRM 1280 (1961); Hamilton-Scheu & Walsh Shoe Co., 80 NLRB 1496, 23 LRRM 1263 (1948). These cases, in which a discriminatory reason for a discharge had been masked behind a lawful reason, are frequently referred to as "pretext" cases. *See generally* Chapter 7 *supra. See also* McCulloch, *The Arbitration Issue in NLRB Decisions,* 19 ARB. J. 134, 137-38 (1964); McCulloch, *Arbitration and/or the NLRB,* 18 ARB. J. 3, 9 (1963); Comment, 38 U. COLO. L. REV. 363, 372-73 (1966). *Later cases: see* note 247 *infra* and cases following. For cases during the interim *Electronic Reproduction* period, *see* note 242-46 *infra.*
[236]131 NLRB 1462, 48 LRRM 1280 (1961).
[237]*Supra* note 231.
[238]*Supra* note 236 at 1462-63. *Accord,* La Prensa, Inc., 131 NLRB 527, 48 LRRM 1076 (1961).
[239]130 NLRB at 1099.
[240]Raytheon Co., *supra* note 62.

ipating in a wildcat strike in a breach of a no-strike clause. Finding that the employees had breached the no-strike clause, the arbitrator upheld the discharges. A Board majority found that the arbitrator had not considered the propriety of the discharges under standards embodied in the Act; indeed, he had not even purported to consider the unfair labor practice issue. The Board therefore declined to defer to his award.[241]

In 1974 the Board made a major shift in emphasis, expanding the role of the arbitral tribunal under the post-arbitral *Spielberg* review standards in *Electronic Reproduction Service Corp.*[242] That expansion, and the subsequent contraction of *Spielberg*, roughly paralleled the Board's expansion and contraction of *Collyer* discussed above.

The union in *Electronic Reproduction* had decided at the arbitration hearing involving the discharge of certain employees that it would not present evidence to the arbitrator in support of its belief that the discharges were discriminatory under the Act. Prior to *Electronic Reproduction*, as noted above, the Board had held that it would not defer under *Spielberg* unless the unfair labor practice issue before the Board was both presented to and considered by the arbitrator.[243] In *Electronic Reproduction* the Board reversed those earlier rulings (insofar as discharge and discipline cases were involved), stating:[244]

> [W]e believe the better application of the underlying principles of *Collyer* and *Spielberg* to be that we should give full effect to arbitration awards dealing with discipline and discharge cases, under *Spielberg*, except when unusual circumstances are shown which demonstrate that there were bona fide reasons, other than a mere desire on the part of one party to try the same set of facts before two forums, which caused the failure to introduce such evidence at the arbitration proceeding.[245]

The Board indicated, however, that the principle of *Electronic Reproduction*, which was designed in part to avoid "piecemeal

---

[241]In Precision Fittings, Inc., *supra* note 235, the Board declined to defer to an arbitral award where, after the award had been issued, additional evidence supporting an unfair labor practice charge and indicating that some of the evidence presented at the arbitration hearing was pretextual was submitted to the administrative law judge.
[242]213 NLRB 758, 87 LRRM 1211 (1974).
[243]In Yourga Trucking, Inc., 197 NLRB 928, 80 LRRM 1498 (1972), the Board held that the party seeking deferral under *Spielberg* had the burden of demonstrating that the statutory issue had been presented in the arbitration proceeding. *See also supra* note 233.
[244]In the majority opinion of Chairman Miller and Members Kennedy and Penello.
[245]Electronic Reproduction Serv. Corp., *supra* note 242 at 762.

litigation," would not be appropriate where the arbitrator specifically declined to pass on "statutory" issues or where the parties by agreement excluded "statutory" issues from the arbitration. Otherwise, for the purpose of *Spielberg* deferral, it would be presumed that the arbitrator had considered the issue of whether the discharge or discipline of the grievant (usually the charging party) was for pretextual reasons, unless there was a bona fide reason for the arbitrator not to receive evidence concerning the theory of pretextual discharge or unless the arbitrator refused or was prohibited from considering that theory.[246]

The *Electronic Reproduction* approach prevailed until 1980, when the Board expressly overruled it in *Suburban Motor Freight, Inc.*[247] The charging party in *Suburban*, after he had been reinstated by an arbitral "Joint Grievance Committee," was fired again for a rule infraction; this time the committee ordered his reinstatement, but with a 60-day suspension. He later filed an unfair labor practice charge alleging that the discharges had been motivated by employer reaction to his complaints to the union about certain employer practices. Such allegations had not been mentioned by him nor by the union to the joint committee. The Board declined to defer. While noting that the approach of *Electronic Reproduction* encouraged settlement under contract procedures—thereby reducing multiple litigation—the Board majority agreed with criticism that it had delegated too much of its responsibility concerning protection of Section 7 rights. The majority opinion stated:

> [W]e will no longer honor the results of an arbitration proceeding under *Spielberg* unless the unfair labor practice issue before the Board was both presented to and considered by the arbitrator. In accord with the rule formerly stated in *Airco Industrial Gases*,[248] we will give no deference to an arbitration award which bears no indication that the arbitrator ruled on the statutory issue of discrimination in determining the propriety of an employer's disciplinary actions. In like accord with the corollary rule stated in *Yourga Trucking*,[249] we shall impose on the parties seeking Board deferral to an arbitration

---

[246]*Id.* Dissenting Members Fanning and Jenkins stated that the majority's holding "means, of course, that the Board for all practical purposes will no longer decide any part of a case which has been or could have been decided by an arbitrator who has issued an award."*Id.* at 1219.

[247]247 NLRB 146, 103 LRRM 1113 (1980), with Chairman Fanning and Members Jenkins and Truesdale as the majority and Member Penello dissenting. *See* Propoco, Inc., 263 NLRB No. 34, 110 LRRM 1496 (1982), discussed at notes 271-77 *infra*.

[248]Airco Indus. Gases, Pacific Div., 195 NLRB 676, 79 LRRM 1497 (1972).

[249]Yourga Trucking, Inc., *supra* note 243.

award the burden to prove that the issue of discrimination was litigated before the arbitrator.[250]

Even before *Suburban Motor Freight,* the Board in many cases had continued to refuse to defer where an arbitrator had not considered the unfair labor practice issue.[251] In *Teamsters Local 46*[252] the union had unilaterally halted its practice of not enforcing the union security clause with respect to casual employees. When the union sought arbitration to enforce its new application of the union security clause, the employer filed an unfair labor practice charge alleging violations of Sections 8(b)(1)(A) and 8(b)(2), which charges were deferred under the *Collyer* doctrine. The arbitrator then found that in spite of a long contrary practice, clear contract language supported the union's position. Citing its decision in *Alfred M. Lewis, Inc.,*[253] the Board refused to defer because the arbitrator had not addressed the unfair labor practice issue. The Board then found the arbitrator's conclusion contrary to Board law.

Determining the extent to which the unfair labor practice issue must have been presented to and considered by the arbitration tribunal in order to satisfy the Board's requirement for deferral is not easy. As the following cases demonstrate, the

---

[250]247 NLRB at 147. *See also supra* at notes 233 and 243.

[251]*E.g.,* in Kroger Co., 226 NLRB 512, 93 LRRM 1315 (1976), the arbitrator had noted that an issue was raised about the employer's failure to furnish information relevant to the grievance, but he did not rule on the matter, leaving it for disposition as part of compliance with his back-pay award against the employer; the Board treated this as a failure to resolve the unfair labor practice issue, holding that the arbitrator's resolution did not provide assurance against future violations of the statute.

In the following cases, deferral was denied because the unfair labor practice issue had not been thoroughly raised or considered by the arbitral tribunal. Ad Art, Inc., 238 NLRB 1124, 99 LRRM 1626 (1978), *enforced,* 645 F2d 667, 107 LRRM 3292 (CA 9, 1981); Davol, Inc., 237 NLRB 431, 99 LRRM 1011, (1978), *enforced,* 597 F2d 782 (CA 1, 1979); Alfred M. Lewis, Inc., *supra* note 213; Machinists District 15 (Burroughs Corp.), 231 NLRB 602, 96 LRRM 1625 (1977); Versi Craft Corp., 227 NLRB 877, 94 LRRM 1207 (1977); A & H Truck Line, Inc., 226 NLRB 1153, 93 LRRM 1480 (1976); Shippers Dispatch, Inc., 223 NLRB 439, 92 LRRM 1252 (1976); Clara Barton Terrace Convalescent Center, 225 NLRB 1028, 92 LRRM 1621 (1976). In United Parcel Serv., *supra* note 62, the arbitral tribunal's decision was based partially on the untimeliness of the grievance. In Gimbel Bros., Inc., 233 NLRB 1235, 97 LRRM 1091 (1977), the Board would not defer to an arbitration award concerning issues "superficially similar to the issues before the Board which arose from a different event." In Mason & Dixon Lines, Inc., 237 NLRB 6, 98 LRRM 1540 (1978), and Greif Bros. Corp., 238 NLRB 240, 99 LRRM 1243 (1978), the arbitral tribunal had not considered the §8(a)(3) questions. In Oakland Scavenger Co., 241 NLRB 1, 100 LRRM 1469 (1979), the arbitrator had found that the discharges were not unjust (the question concerned dangerous work, but the arbitrator had not specifically considered §502 of the Act; consequently, the Board did not defer; it considered the "abnormally dangerous" work question in light of §502 but came to the same conclusions as the arbitrator).

[252]236 NLRB 1175, 98 LRRM 1519 (1978).

[253]*Supra* note 213.

Board's assessment of arbitration awards and its decisions whether to defer have been characterized by a notable lack of consistency. The decided cases present a variety of fact patterns which, nevertheless, provide a general sense of the Board's direction in this area.

1. The Standard for Arbitral Review: The Degree of Required Consideration by the Arbitral Tribunal of the Unfair Labor Practice Charge. In *Kansas City Star Co.*,[254] a pre-*Suburban Motor Freight*[255] case, 97 pressmen had been discharged for engaging in a wildcat strike; the next day the employer rescinded the collective bargaining agreement and refused to rehire the terminated pressmen, who then offered to return. Without passing on the legality of the rescission, an arbitrator upheld the discharges (except for two employees who had not refused to work). A Board majority dismissed the complaint, relying on *Spielberg*.[256] In reaching that decision, all members of the majority expressly stated that they were not relying on *Electronic Reproduction*,[257] which was to be overruled by the Board two years later.

Should an arbitrator "assume" the role of the Board and directly and expressly make rulings on unfair labor practices?

---

[254]*Supra* note 62.

[255]247 NLRB 146, 103 LRRM 1113 (1980).

[256]The dissenters would have found that one union officer was engaged in protected activity in trying to resolve the dispute, rather than inciting the wildcat action or refusing to work himself, so that there would have been a violation of §8(a)(3); they also would have found a violation of §8(a)(5) based on the employer's rescission of the contract. They felt the Board should not defer because "the issue of rescission was not specifically before the arbitrator and that *Spielberg* requires that the legal issue be before the arbitrator. . . ." 236 NLRB at 869.

Member Truesdale, in his concurring opinion, which was also embraced by the other members of the majority, stated:

"[W]hile the arbitrator did not pass on the legality of the rescission, he was required to rule on every factual and legal question necessary to the resolution of this issue, since the legality of rescission as a self-help remedy available to respondent turns on whether respondent could legally discharge the strikers, and whether the strike was legal. Both of these issues were considered fully by the arbitrator in the context of the pending unfair labor practices. . . . Thus, my decision to concur rests on the unique relationship between the issues decided and the one omitted—since all of the factual and legal findings necessary to the resolution of the 8(a)(5) allegation concerning rescission were also necessary to a determination of the legality of the discharges. These issues were vigorously litigated before the arbitrator, and he reached his decision on the basis of the full record. No more is required." *Id.*

[257]*Supra* note 242. In Atlantic Steel Co., 245 NLRB 814, 102 LRRM 1247 (1979), *infra* at notes 258-59, the Board noted that deferral had been appropriate on the rescission issue in *Kansas City Star* because the arbitrator's findings were "both complete and comprehensive and factually parallel to the unfair labor practice question." 245 NLRB at 815.

The Board suggested an answer in *Atlantic Steel Co.*[258] There the arbitrator had sustained, under the contract, the discharge of an employee who had been terminated for his past record of discipline and for publicly calling his foreman derogatory names. At the arbitration hearing, the grievant claimed that he had been harassed by the foreman for circulating an employee petition concerning certain benefits. The Board's administrative law judge refused to defer, giving as reasons the fact that the arbitrator had not decided the underlying unfair labor practice and, alternatively, that the arbitrator's conclusion was not consistent with Board law. The Board disagreed, deferring to the arbitrator's award and dismissing the complaint. In explaining its ruling, the Board stated:

> Must the arbitrator actually discuss the unfair labor practice, or is it sufficient that he or she considered all of the evidence relevant to the unfair labor practice in determining whether the discharge was lawful under the contract? . . . [W]hile it may be preferable for the arbitrator to pass on the unfair labor practice directly, the Board generally has not required that he or she do so. Rather, it is necessary only that the arbitrator has considered all of the evidence relevant to the unfair labor practice in reaching his or her decision.[259]

2. The Standard for Arbitral Review: The Board's Application of *Suburban Motor Freight*. The Board remains sharply divided on deferral, and its decisions applying *Suburban Motor Freight*[260] reflect the intensity of the differences among the Board Members. In the first cases decided by panel majorities immediately following *Suburban,* it appeared that comprehensive and express consideration of the unfair labor practice issue by the arbitrator was not a requisite for deferral. However by mid-1982, as indicated by the full Board decision in *Propoco, Inc.,*[261] the Board's approach had become more demanding of both the arbitrator and the parties as to the kind of arbitral record and consideration that would be required for deferral of NLRB action.

In *Bay Shipbuilding Co.*[262] the employer had unilaterally changed its welfare benefit program from an insured program with one carrier to a self-insured program with another carrier. The collective bargaining agreement stated that the existing insur-

---

[258]*Supra* note 257.
[259]*Id.* at 815. *See infra* at notes 271-76.
[260]*Supra* note 247.
[261]263 NLRB No. 34, 110 LRRM 1496 (1982).
[262]251 NLRB 809, 105 LRRM 1376 (1980).

ance coverage was to continue during the term of the agreement. The arbitrator decided that the term "coverage" meant welfare benefits and that these had not been changed by the employer; therefore there was no violation of the collective bargaining agreement. In response to a Section 8(a)(5) charge alleging that the change in insurance arrangements had occurred without good-faith bargaining, the Board panel majority[263] ruled that the Board should defer to the arbitrator's decision, even though he had stated that he had not considered the unfair labor practice issue. The Board deemed his holding that the contract permitted the change as necessarily a ruling that there was no unfair labor practice. Concurring Member Truesdale saw the case as similar to *Atlantic Steel Co.*,[264] where it was not necessary for the arbitrator to expressly rule on the unfair labor practice because he considered the related facts and decided the underlying issue.[265]

In *Chemical Leaman Tank Lines*[266] a truck driver had been discharged for refusing to drive a truck with a defective spring assembly while the truck was loaded with nitrogen. The collective bargaining agreement stated that equipment must not be taken out in an unsafe condition. A joint labor-management arbitration panel denied the grievance. The ALJ found that the statutory issue—whether the employee had been engaged in protected concerted activity based on reasonable safety considerations—had not been presented to nor considered by the arbitration panel. The panel, which had made no written findings, had considered only the safety clause. The Board majority[267] ruled that the ALJ should have deferred because, applying the approach used in *Atlantic Steel,* the arbitration panel had necessarily considered facts parallel to those needed to decide the unfair labor practice charge.[268]

---

[263]Members Penello and Truesdale.

[264]*Supra* note 257.

[265]Dissenting Member Jenkins noted that *Suburban Motor Freight* explicitly stated that the facts relating to the unfair labor practice must be *both* presented to and considered by the arbitrator, and that in unfair labor practice cases involving a change of carrier, the Board considers such matters as the financial stability of the successor carrier and comparability of service being provided; there was no evidence that these factors had been presented to the arbitrator.

[266]251 NLRB 1058, 105 LRRM 1276 (1980).

[267]The same majority as in *Bay Shipbuilding, supra* note 262.

[268]Member Jenkins, in dissent, said that *Atlantic Steel Co.* itself stated that there must be a comprehensive record showing the parallelism; here there were no written findings by the arbitration panel. He also contended that there was no express consideration of the unfair labor practice charge, seemingly required by *Suburban Motor Freight.* He concluded therefore that the decision effectively overruled *Suburban Motor Freight.*

In *Magnetics International, Inc.,*[269] however, a Board panel majority of Chairman Fanning and Member Jenkins refused to defer to an arbitration award which had upheld the disciplinary suspension and discharge of a union steward for activity which they found to be protected. They noted that the "arbitrator considered only the contractual constraints upon the Respondent, not the statutory."[270] Member Penello dissented.

In 1982, in the *Propoco, Inc.,*[271] decision, the reconstituted Board, still split three-to-two,[272] reaffirmed and tightened the *Surburban Motor Freight*[273] doctrine. The case involved a cleaning service company which had discharged an employee who had written and signed a complaint letter, which was also signed by nine other employees. The grievant was fired after she refused to apologize for writing the letter. In the arbitration which followed, the union attorney submitted no evidence as to whether the discharge was an unfair labor practice; his only contention was that the discharge was discriminatory in view of the failure of the employer to impose discipline on any of the other letter signers. Although a copy of the NLRB complaint was submitted to the arbitrator, he indicated that he did not consider the complaint to be before him. However, he did conclude that the grievant was not discharged because of union activity or any other conduct protected by the Act.

The Board majority found that the latter statement was merely gratuitous and that the unfair labor practice issue had neither been presented to nor considered by the arbitrator. Reversing the ALJ, the Board accordingly declined to defer to the arbitration award, which had found the discharge to have been for just cause under the collective agreement. In reaffirming *Suburban,* the Board made clear that a grievant could consciously choose not to present the unfair labor practice issue to the arbitrator.[274] It stated:

---

[269]254 NLRB 520, 106 LRRM 1133 (1981).

[270]*Id.* at 522. *See also* Triple A Mach. Shop, 245 NLRB 136, 102 LRRM 1559 (1979), where the arbitrator failed to pass on statutory issues involved in the discharge of employees for strike misconduct. Concluding that the arbitrator had "in effect rendered 'compromise awards,' " the Board refused to defer.

[271]*Supra* note 261.

[272]Members Fanning, Jenkins, and Zimmerman in the majority; Chairman Van de Water and Member Hunter in dissent.

[273]*Supra* note 247. *But cf.* Pet, Inc., Bakery Div., *supra* note 215.

[274]According to the majority opinion, a "single litigation requirement might actually discourage resort to contractual grievance and arbitration proceedings." 110 LRRM at 1498.

A grievant may choose to challenge disciplinary action solely on the ground that discipline invoked for the stated offense was inconsistent with the employer's past practice or otherwise violated contractual provisions unrelated to the Act. The election to proceed in the contractually created arbitration forum provides no basis, in and of itself, for depriving an alleged discriminatee of the statutorily created forum for adjudication of unfair labor practice charges.[275]

The dissenters would have deferred to the arbitrator's award, contending that it met all of the *Spielberg* standards. Chairman Van de Water used the occasion to charge that the *Suburban Motor Freight* doctrine departs from sound deferral policy:

> The arbitral forum is the one selected through collective bargaining by the parties to resolve their disputes and once that forum has been invoked the grievant should be required to raise any statutory issues before the arbitrator or be precluded from subsequently raising them before the Board.[276]

The judicial response to *Suburban Motor Freight* will be examined in the general discussion of appellate decisions in *Spielberg* cases.[277] These appellate cases will be treated together because, at the appellate level, the Board's standard of arbitral review and its concept of arbitration awards that are repugnant to the policies of the Act tend to merge or become intertwined in the process of judicial analysis.

B. Fair and Regular Proceedings

1. The Arbitral Procedure. The Board's criteria for fairness and regularity are intended to establish minimum due-process-type standards for the conduct of arbitration proceedings. Thus, deferral has been denied where evidence was deliberately withheld from the arbitrator,[278] where the grievant was

---

[275]110 LRRM at 1498. The decision also commented, in response to criticism by Chairman Van de Water, on the matter of how thoroughly the statutory issue must be presented: "This problem, to the extent that it exists, will be no greater in the context of arbitration proceedings than when presented in the context of summary judgment proceedings, motions for reconsideration, or unfair labor practice proceedings relevant to conduct not specifically alleged as unlawful in the complaint." *Id.* And in response to Member Hunter's criticism that the decision requires litigation of the unfair labor practice issue in exactly the same manner as if it were before the Board, the majority stated: "Other than in *Spielberg* itself, the Board has imposed no special rules concerning the manner in which such an issue can be litigated in arbitration proceedings." 110 LRRM at 1499 n. 8.

[276]110 LRRM at 1503. The Chairman also wrote: "Absent evidence to the contrary, the Board should be willing to assume that arbitrators have considered the issue presented to them, including any unfair labor practice issue."

[277]*See infra* at notes 377-408.

[278]Precision Fittings, Inc., *supra* note 235.

given insufficient time to prepare,[279] or was not afforded an opportunity to confront witnesses,[280] or to cross-examine them.[281] Abrasive demeanor by the arbitrator, however, has not prevented deferral.[282]

Deferral did not occur where the union did not present any evidence on the grievant's behalf.[283] And deferral was not granted where one of the parties affected by the award was not represented in the arbitration proceeding.[284]

The Board has stated that, consistent with the Act's policy of permitting parties to resolve their disputes in the manner which they deem best, it will consider the decisions of joint union-employer committees to be similar to those of other arbitral tribunals,[285] regardless of whether a public member participates.[286]

---

[279]Gateway Transp. Co., 137 NLRB 1763, 50 LRRM 1495 (1962) (grievant was pressed to arbitration two days after notice). *But cf.* Raytheon Co. v. NLRB, *supra* note 62, where the Board refused to honor an award because, among other reasons, the grievant was not granted a requested continuance. The Court said: "[W]e cannot think the Board would have expected us to rule it unfair if a trial examiner, rather than an arbitrator, had refused to grant a further continuance on this record." 326 F.2d at 473.

[280]Honolulu Star-Bulletin, 123 NLRB 395, 43 LRRM 1449 (trial examiner's decision), *enforcement denied on other grounds*, 274 F2d 567, 45 LRRM 2184 (CA DC, 1959).

[281]Versi Craft Corp., *supra* note 251.

[282]In Denver-Chicago Trucking Co., Inc., 132 NLRB 1416, 48 LRRM 1524 (1961), the Board deferred to a joint committee award despite testimony that members of the joint committee had given the grievant and his witnesses a tongue lashing. In United States Postal Serv., 241 NLRB 1253, 101 LRRM 1074 (1979), the charging party sought to *de-Collyerize* the case after the arbitrator's award had been handed down. A Board majority refused. The dissenting members would have found the procedure irregular because of the arbitrator's alleged shouting and abusive comments (directed towards the charging party, her counsel, and her witnesses) and because of his refusal to proceed with the arbitration unless the charging party's counsel returned a certain document to respondent.

[283]General Iron Corp., 218 NLRB 707, 89 LRRM 1788 (1975) (Board also noted that no interpreter was available at arbitration, although grievant did not speak English).

[284]Retail Clerks Local 324 (Esgro, Inc.), 206 NLRB 931, 84 LRRM 1431 (1973).

[285]"Where . . . the parties have found the machinery which they have created for the amicable resolution of their disputes has adequately served its purpose, we shall accept such a resolution absent evidence of irregularity, collusion or inadequate provisions for the taking of testimony." Denver-Chicago Trucking Co., *supra* note 282. *Accord*, Terminal Transport Co., 185 NLRB 672, 75 LRRM 1130 (1970). *See also* Modern Motor Express, Inc., 149 NLRB 1507, 58 LRRM 1005 (1964); Gen. Counsel Rul. No. SR-2614, 52 LRRM 1405 (1963). *But cf.* Herman Bros., Inc. v. NLRB, 658 F2d 201, 108 LRRM 2327 (CA 3, 1981), *enforcing* 252 NLRB 848, 105 LRRM 1374 (1980), where the Board did not defer because the arbitration proceedings were not deemed fair and regular. The arbitration panel consisted only of union and management representatives, both of whose interests appeared aligned against the charging-party grievant. *But see* Comment, *Concurrent Jurisdiction of Arbitrators and the NLRB*, 28 U. Colo. L. Rev. 363, 376 (1966). The Supreme Court has ruled that a final decision of such a committee may be enforced under §301(a). Teamsters Local 89 v. Riss & Co., 372 US 517, 52 LRRM 2623 (1963).

[286]Denver-Chicago Trucking Co., *supra* note 282.

Arbitration which is held before discipline is made effective does not preclude deferral, such as in a case where the collective bargaining agreement required the employer to continue employees on the payroll until the issue was resolved by an arbitrator.[287]

2. Hostility of the Tribunal or Union Representative Toward the Grievant. Where the arbitrator may be predisposed against the grievant, deferral to the award will not result. This situation has occasionally occurred under contracts where the machinery provides for final judgment by a joint labor-management committee and where one or more of the committee members may have reason to rule against the grievant regardless of the merits of the dispute. In *Roadway Express, Inc.*,[288] for example, the grievant was the leader of the opposition to incumbent union officials and was also well known for his attacks upon the employing industry; the Board refused to honor an award that was adverse to him.[289] Also, the Board will not defer to an arbitration award where the charging party's interest could not have been properly represented because of his representative's hostility toward him.[290]

C. Agreement of All Parties to Be Bound

The *Spielberg* requirement that all parties agree to be bound by the award has received little attention; usually all parties, by virtue of the collective bargaining agreement, have explicitly agreed to be bound by the contractual arbitral procedure. There have been only a few cases concerning this standard.

---

[287]American Bakeries Co., 249 NLRB 1249, 104 LRRM 1305 (1980). The arbitrator permitted the discharge of two of six employees charged with a work stoppage for refusing to work overtime; the two were union stewards whom the arbitrator found to be instigators. Member Jenkins, dissenting from the panel majority of Members Penello and Truesdale, stated that this pre-discharge arbitration was not what *Spielberg* was intended to cover. He contended that by agreeing to this kind of system for arbitral review before a discharge takes effect, the company had surrendered its management prerogative to effect a discharge.

[288]145 NLRB 513, 54 LRRM 1419 (1963).

[289]Likewise, in Youngstown Cartage Co., 146 NLRB 305, 55 LRRM 1301 (1964), it refused to honor such an award where the grievant had been a dissident within the union. In *Mason & Dixon Lines, Inc.*, supra note 251, union officials on the grievance committee had opposed the dissident faction of which the grievant was a member, and the union official who represented the grievant before the grievance committee had not discussed the case with him prior to the hearing; deferral was refused. However, it did not take such a strong showing for the Board to refuse to defer to a joint labor-management committee in Brown Co., 243 NLRB 769, 101 LRRM 1608 (1979).

[290]Longshoremen & Warehousemen Local 27 (Morris R. Bond), 205 NLRB 1141, 84 LRRM 1546 (1973), *enforced*, 514 F2d 481, 89 LRRM 2113 (CA 9, 1975). *See also* Russ Togs, Inc., 106 LRRM 1067, 253 NLRB 1398 (1980).

In *Wertheimer Stores Corp.*,[291] a case which preceded *Spielberg*, an employee had been discharged for his activities in urging other employees to vote against the employer's proposal to reschedule working hours. The arbitrator found that the discharge was not discriminatory. The Board refused to honor the award, in part because the arbitration proceedings were initiated and carried through despite the opposition of the grievant employee.

The Board refused to give effect to an arbitration award in *Hershey Chocolate Corp.*[292] where none of the employees involved had agreed to be bound by the award. The Board held that the award was "contrary to law."

On the other hand, in *International Harvester Co.*,[293] an early case under the *Spielberg* doctrine, the arbitration award was honored despite the fact that the employee involved had been given no notice and was not present at the arbitration hearing. The Board did not find that circumstance controlling, however, for in its view the employer had adequately championed the employee's interest.[294]

The Board deferred to an arbitration procedure under a labor contract which did not contain specific language stating that the procedure was final and binding in *Champlin Petroleum Co.*[295] The Board pointed out, however, that "it is reasonable to infer that [such finality] was the intention of the parties. Otherwise, the arbitral procedure would be illusory, and resort thereto an exercise in futility."[296]

Where a lessee was not a party to the arbitration proceeding which had been initiated by the union to enforce a subcontracting clause against the lessee's operations, the Board did not

---

[291]107 NLRB 1434, 33 LRRM 1398 (1954).

[292]129 NLRB 1052, 47 LRRM 1130 (1960), *enforcement denied on other grounds,* 297 F2d 286, 49 LRRM 2173 (CA 3, 1961) (*Hershey* also had an element of adverse relation between the union and the charging parties).

[293]*Supra* note 50.

[294]*See* Edward Axel Roffman Assocs., Inc., 147 NLRB 717, 56 LRRM 1268 (1964) (employer withdrew from arbitration following arbitrator's ruling that the matter was arbitrable; the trial examiner ruled: "Despite Respondent's voluntary withdrawal . . . the arbitration proceedings . . . appear to have been fair and regular."). In T.I.M.E.-DC, Inc., 215 NLRB 1175, 93 LRRM 1270 (1976), the Board declined to defer to an award assigning contested work to one union where the union which claimed the work was not party to the arbitration.

[295]201 NLRB 83, 82 LRRM 1388 (1973).

[296]*Id.* at 90.

defer.[297] And where a successor-employer was not a party to the bargaining agreement nor to the arbitration proceeding, the Board would not defer.[298]

Dicta in *Great Scott Supermarkets*[299] suggest that the *Spielberg* reference to agreement of the "parties" to be bound does not refer to individual discriminatees but to the union and the employer.[300]

D. The Award Is Not Repugnant to the Policies of the Act

The "repugnancy" factor accounts for a large volume of the cases in which the Board refuses to defer to the award of an arbitral tribunal.

1. The Standard for Board Review. As one of the three members supporting deferral in *Kansas City Star*,[301] Member Truesdale[302] used the decision to express his strong support of *Spielberg* policy and to define his view of the Board's proper reviewing role under that policy. He likened the Board's role to that of a reviewing court—which should avoid engaging in *de novo* review of the record evidence. Commending the majority in the case, he said:

> The majority reviews the record evidence, sees no irregularities in the proceedings and no facial errors in the arbitrator's factual findings, and then examines the arbitrator's legal conclusion to see if, on the facts he has found, it is consistent with Board law. Finding that it is, and that the arbitrator actually considered Board Law in ruling on all of the discharges . . . the majority defers to the arbitrator's decision. This approach is more consistent not only with past *Spielberg* decisions, but also with the strong labor policy which favors voluntary arbitration.[303]

---

[297]Federated Dep't Stores, Inc., 235 NLRB 69, 97 LRRM 1556 (1978).

[298]Retail, Wholesale & Dep't Store Union Dist. 1199E (Greater Pa. Ave. Nursing Center, Inc.), 238 NLRB 9, 99 LRRM 1194 (1978), *remanded sub nom.* Hospital & Health Care Employees v. NLRB, 613 F2d 1102, 103 LRRM 2001 (CA DC, 1979); the court disagreed on this and other points on which the Board had relied.

[299]206 NLRB 447, 452-53, 84 LRRM 1563 (1973) (ALJ's decision).

[300]"[T]here should not be a broad rule that deferral under *Collyer* can be vetoed by the Charging Party or alleged discriminatees who were not parties to the contract." 206 NLRB at 452. "[T]he policy . . . should be that where the individuals object to arbitration because the interest of their bargaining representative is adverse to the individual's interest, deferral to arbitration should not be had." *Id.* at 453.

[301]Kansas City Star Co., *supra* note 62.

[302]Members Penello and Murphy were the other two members of the majority. Chairman Fanning and Member Jenkins dissented in part.

[303]236 NLRB at 869.

He then chided his dissenting colleagues for refusing to defer to part of the arbitrator's award, charging that they had in fact engaged in exhaustive *de novo* review in which they had substituted "their judgment for that of the arbitrator."[304]

In *Atlantic Steel Co.*,[305] as previously noted, the Board deferred to an arbitral award, finding that it was not repugnant to the Act because "the arbitrator thoroughly considered all of the evidence and made factual findings that are clearly supported by the evidence." And significantly, he "considered the factors which the Board considers. . . ."[306]

The Board, in *Pincus Brothers, Inc.-Maxwell*,[307] expressly left undefined the circumstances under which it would accept an arbitrator's findings of fact as its own and when it would require separate findings of fact after proceedings before an administrative law judge.[308] But in *Inland Steel Co.* the Board said that "[t]he test of repugnancy under Spielberg is not whether the Board would have reached the same results as an arbitrator, but whether the arbitrator's award is palpably wrong as a matter of law."[309]

---

[304]*Id.* at 868. The dissenters reviewed the evidence and the award in great detail, agreeing with the arbitrator in part and disagreeing in part, relying on Banyard v. NLRB, 505 F2d 342, 345, 87 LRRM 2001 (CA DC, 1974), to the effect that the *Spielberg* doctrine is appropriately applied "only where the resolution of the contractual issues is congruent with the resolution of the statutory unfair labor practice issues." *See infra* at note 377.

[305]*Supra* note 257.

[306]245 NLRB at 816. Member Penello, concurring, chided his colleagues (Members Murphy and Truesdale) for their view of the "repugnancy" standard, i.e., "whether the award is in accord with the Act and Board precedent." In his view, his colleagues " 'adopted' [the award] as if the arbitrator were some sort of unofficial administrative law judge. Deferral under such a standard furthers neither the aim nor the efficient administration of the Act but encourages full litigation before the Board of deferrable disputes." *Id.* at 817. *See also* Babcock & Wilcox Co., 249 NLRB 739, 104 LRRM 1199 (1980), and Member Penello's dissent therein.

[307]237 NLRB 1063, 99 LRRM 1099 (1978) (refusing deferral and declining to rule on a record comprised only of the arbitration award), 241 NLRB 805, 100 LRRM 1630 (1979), *enforcement denied*, 620 F2d 367, 104 LRRM 2001 (CA 3, 1980) (because of Board's failure to apply its own *Spielberg* standards). In NLRB v. Wilson Freight Co., 604 F2d 712, 102 LRRM 2269 (CA 1, 1979), *denying enforcement to* 234 NLRB 844, 97 LRRM 1412, the First Circuit held the Board must defer to some of the factual issues decided by the arbitral tribunal. *See infra* at notes 383-84 and 389-90.

[308]This issue had also been left open in Dreis & Krump Mfg. Co., 221 NLRB 309, 90 LRRM 1647 (1975), *enforced*, 544 F2d 320, 93 LRRM 2739 (CA 7, 1976), where an administrative law judge had relied on the arbitrator's findings but where the Board itself relied on the record made before the administrative law judge.

[309]263 NLRB No. 147, 111 LRRM 1193, 1193 (1982), with Member Jenkins dissenting. In Pet, Inc., Bakery Div., *supra* note 215, the Board majority said: "It is not the Board's function to determine whether the arbitrator made the correct decision, and deferral is appropriate even though the Board might not decide the matter as the arbitrator did." 111 LRRM at 1497-98, with Members Fanning and Jenkins in dissent.

In *Max Factor & Co.*[310] the Board stated that it would not defer to an arbitration award rendered *after* an administrative law judge's decision has been issued.

2. Types of Cases. The Board has refused to defer to arbitration awards which have failed to apply, have misapplied, or should not have attempted to apply certain principles embodied in the Act. The following cases illustrate the types of awards which have been found repugnant to various provisions of the Act.

The most common types of cases in which the Board has refused to defer are those which have involved the infringement of protected rights of individual employees. The Board thus has refused to defer to arbitration awards in the following situations: where the discharge of an employee was based partly on the employee's refusal to be questioned without union representation;[311] where the arbitrator had upheld the discharge of an employee based in part on the employee's use of the contract grievance procedure;[312] where part of the arbitrator's award required the employee to waive future rights under Section 7 of the Act;[313] where the arbitration award upheld discharge or discipline based upon verbal abuse of an employer in the course of an employee's exercise of Section 7 rights;[314] and where an arbitrator upheld the discharge of an employee who had refused to cross a picket line, finding, contrary to established precedent, that the right to engage in sympathy strikes had been waived by the contractual no-strike clause, even though that clause did not expressly prohibit such strikes.[315] Additional instances follow.

---

[310]239 NLRB 804, 100 LRRM 1023 (1978), *enforced*, 640 F2d 197, 105 LRRM 2765 (CA 9, 1980).

[311]Illinois Bell Tel. Co., 221 NLRB 159, 91 LRRM 1116 (1975). *See* Chapter 6 *supra* at notes 427-65.

[312]Sea-Land Service, 240 NLRB 1146, 100 LRRM 1406 (1979); Shippers Dispatch, Inc., 223 NLRB 439, 92 LRRM 1252 (1976).

[313]Ford Motor Co. (Rouge Complex), 233 NLRB 698, 96 LRRM 1513 (1977).

[314]Hawaiian Hauling Serv., 219 NLRB 765, 90 LRRM 1011 (1975), *enforced*, 545 F2d 674, 93 LRRM 2952 (CA 9, 1976); Dreis & Krump Mfg. Co., *supra* note 308; Union Fork & Hoe Co., 241 NLRB 907, 101 LRRM 1014 (1979); Ad Art, Inc. *supra* note 251; Clara Barton Terrace Convalescent Center, 225 NLRB 1028, 92 LRRM 1621 (1976). But the Board upheld an award sustaining a discharge for verbal abuse where the unprotected language was not found to be related to the processing of a grievance. Atlantic Steel Co., *supra* note 257. *See also* AMF Voit, Inc., 223 NLRB 363, 92 LRRM 1335 (1976).

[315]United States Steel Corp., 264 NLRB No. 10, 111 LRRM 1200 (1982), with Chairman Van de Water and Member Hunter dissenting. *See also* Inland Steel Co., 264 NLRB No. 11, 111 LRRM 1222 (1982), with Chairman Van de Water and Member Hunter dissenting.

In *Pincus Brothers, Inc.-Maxwell*[316] deferral to an award was refused where the Board found that the discharged employee had been engaged in protected Section 7 activities. However, the Third Circuit reversed that decision, holding that the Board had abused its discretion by applying the wrong standard. The court said that since the employee's "conduct was arguably unprotected," the arbitration award upholding his discharge should have prevailed: "Where there are two arguable interpretations of an arbitration award, one permissible and one impermissible, the Board must defer to the decision rendered by the arbitrator."[317]

In *Kansas City Star Co.*[318] the Board upheld an arbitrator's award which had found that employees' concerted refusal to work in support of a grievance was not protected activity where the conduct violated a prohibition in the contract against work stoppages. In another case,[319] deferral was refused as to an award upholding the discharge of a union steward who had participated in a walkout—he had initially urged the employees to return to work, without success, and then became a spokesman for their grievance. In *American Bakeries Co.*,[320] however, the Board deferred to an arbitral award which had upheld the discharge of two stewards who had acted as spokesmen for a group of employees who had refused to work overtime. The Board also deferred to an award which upheld the discharge of a shop steward who had been charged with insubordination when he advised employees not to fill out their timecards until the employer had furnished the union with certain requested information.[321]

Awards which impair employee right of access to NLRB process are deemed repugnant to the Act. Thus, the Board refused

---

[316]*Supra* note 307.
[317]620 F2d at 368.
[318]*Supra* note 62.
[319]Babcock & Wilcox Co., *supra* note 306 (Chairman Fanning and Member Jenkins, in the majority, with Member Penello dissenting). *See also* Consolidation Coal Co., 263 NLRB No. 188, 111 LRRM 1205 (1982), with Chairman Van de Water and Member Hunter dissenting. The Board's refusal to defer to an arbitrator's determination that the employer has the right to impose selective discipline on striking union officials was reversed in Fournelle v. NLRB, 670 F2d 331, 109 LRRM 2441 (CA DC, 1982). *See also* note 404 *infra* this chapter and Chapter 7 *supra* at notes 302-307.
[320]American Bakeries Co., *supra* note 287 (Members Penello and Truesdale, in the majority, with Member Jenkins dissenting).
[321]G & H Prods., Inc., 261 NLRB No. 47, 110 LRRM 1036 (1982) (panel of Chairman Van de Water and Member Zimmerman, in the majority, and Member Jenkins in dissent).

to defer where the arbitrator's award involved a waiver by the employee of his right to file an unfair labor practice charge,[322] and where an arbitrator upheld a discharge for disloyalty to the employer when the disloyalty consisted of seeking Board assistance in the dispute between the grievant and the employer.[323]

The Board also refused deferral to an award in which the arbitrator had required former members of a superceded union to maintain membership in the new union.[324]

Cases which have not properly enforced a party's bargaining obligation have been found "repugnant"—such as where the employer had instituted unilateral changes in the application of certain provisions in the collective bargaining contract,[325] where the arbitrator failed to consider the issue of the employer's failure to provide information requested by the union,[326] and where the arbitrator's award was ruled to be binding upon a successor-employer.[327]

Additional instances of "repugnant" awards have involved cases where the contractual clause which the arbitrator upheld involved violation of Section 8(e)—the "hot cargo" provision—of the Act,[328] and where the arbitration award involved an accretion to a collective bargaining unit.[329]

IV. OTHER FACTORS AFFECTING THE BOARD'S POST-ARBITRAL DEFERRAL POLICY

There are a number of specific types of cases involving arbitral awards and other final settlements between parties in which the Board may choose not to apply its *Spielberg* deferral policy.

---

[322]Super Valu Stores, Inc., 228 NLRB 1254, 95 LRRM 1444 (1977); Texaco, *supra* note 130; Douglas Aircraft Co., 234 NLRB 578, 97 LRRM 1242 (1978).
[323]Virginia-Carolina Freight Lines, Inc., 155 NLRB 447, 60 LRRM 1331 (1965).
[324]Hershey Chocolate Corp., *supra* note 292.
[325]Alfred M. Lewis, Inc., *supra* note 213; Teamsters Local 46 (Port Distrib. Corp.), *supra* note 252. But *cf*. Machinists Lodge 87 (Valley Ford Sales, Inc.) v. NLRB, 530 F2d 849, 91 LRRM 2832 (CA 9, 1976), *aff'g* 211 NLRB 834, 86 LRRM 1407 (1974), where the Board did defer to an award, finding no unfair labor practice in an employer's unilateral revision of a wage incentive plan.
[326]Kroger Co., *supra* note 251.
[327]Retail, Wholesale & Dep't Store Union Dist. 1199E (Greater Pa. Ave. Nursing Center), *supra* note 298.
[328]Retail Clerks Local 324 (Federated Dep't Stores, Inc.), 235 NLRB 711, 97 LRRM 1556 (1978).
[329]St. Luke's Hosp. Center, 221 NLRB 1314, 91 LRRM 1150, *enforced*, 551 F2d 476, 94 LRRM 2083 (CA 2, 1976); Teamsters Local 814 (Morgan & Bro.-Manhattan Storage Co.), 223 NLRB 527, 91 LRRM 1592 (1976). *See* further discussion of representation issues *infra* at notes 330-46.

A. Representation Cases

For many years the "leading case" dealing with the Board's deference to arbitral awards in representation cases was *Raley's, Inc.*[330] In *Raley's* the issue before the arbitrator was whether certain employees were covered by the contract between the parties to the arbitration proceeding. The arbitrator held that they were. Subsequently, a rival union filed a petition with the Board seeking representation of the employees in question. At the Board hearing, the union which had prevailed in arbitration intervened, contending that its contract with the employer covered the employees in question, that the petitioner was therefore not timely filed with respect to the contract, that the contract should act as a bar,[331] and that the petition should be dismissed. Agreeing with the intervenor, the Board dismissed the petition, holding that:

> The same considerations which moved the Board to honor arbitration awards in unfair labor practice cases are equally persuasive to a similar acceptance of the arbitral process in a representation proceeding such as the instant one. Thus, where, as here, a question of contract interpretation is in issue . . . and an award has already been rendered which meets Board requirements applicable to arbitration awards, we think that it would further the underlying objectives of the Act to promote industrial peace and stability to give effect thereto.[332]

Following the approach which it had used in *International Harvester Co.*,[333] the Board disposed of the argument that the petitioner had not been represented before the arbitrator. The Board in *Raley's* found that "[w]hile the petitioner was not a party to the arbitration . . . its position was vigorously defended by the Employer. . . ."[334]

Impetus was given to the *Raley's* concept by the Supreme Court's decision the following year in *Carey* v. *Westinghouse*,[335] where the Court held a dispute to be arbitrable whether viewed as a representation or as a work-assignment dispute, notwith-

---

[330]143 NLRB 256, 53 LRRM 1347 (1963).
[331]*See generally* Chapter 10 *supra* at notes 117-200.
[332]*Supra* note 330 at 258-59.
[333]*Supra* note 50 (a discrimination case).
[334]*Supra* note 330 at 260 n. 17. *But see* Hotel Employers Ass'n, 159 NLRB 143, 148 n. 7, 62 LRRM 1215 (1966); Hamilton-Scheu & Walsh Shoes Co., 80 NLRB 1496, 23 LRRM 1263 (1948).
[335]*Supra* note 29.

standing that the Board also had jurisdiction over the matter.[336] The Court's order bound only the employer and one of the two unions involved in the dispute. Nevertheless, since arbitration might have resolved the dispute, the Court required the parties to abide by the contractual agreement to arbitrate.

The further history of *Carey* v. *Westinghouse* is enlightening. When the case was submitted to arbitration the arbitrator partially agreed with the grieving union, ordering the company to recognize the Electrical Workers (IUE) as the collective bargaining representative of certain specified employees.[337] His decision, in effect, divided the employees between two collective bargaining units based on salary criteria. But when the Board considered the case, it retreated perceptibly from *Raley's,* refusing to defer to the arbitrator's award.[338] It stated:

> Here . . . the ultimate issue of representation could not be decided by the Arbitrator on the basis of his interpreting the contract under which he was authorized to act, but could only be resolved by utilization of Board criteria for making unit determinations. In such cases, the Arbitrator's award must clearly reflect the use of and be consonant with Board standards. In this case apparently not all the evidence concerning all these standards was available to the arbitrator for his consideration and appraisal, and his award reflects this deficiency.[339]

Almost immediately, the Board began placing limits on *Raley's.* Initially these limits were considered under the *Spielberg* criterion of whether the arbitral award was in keeping with and therefore not repugnant to the Act.[340] But by 1974, in *Hershey Foods Corp.,*[341] the Board was actually suggesting that it would not defer to an arbitral award in a representation matter. In response to the argument that the arbitration award had made a final and binding determination of the issue, the Board stated: "The short answer to that contention is that to do so would be contrary to controlling Board precedent."[342] Finding that pre-

---

[336]*See* note 330 *supra* at 259 n. 13. For the view that the Board's jurisdiction in this field should be exclusive, *see* Feinberg, *The Arbitrator's Responsibility Under the Taft Hartley Act,* 18 ARB. J. 77, 86 (1963); Cummings, *NLRB Jurisdiction and Labor Arbitration: "Uniformity" v. "Industrial Peace,"* 12 LAB. L. J. 425, 433 (1961).

[337]Westinghouse Elec. Corp., 45 LA 161 (1965).

[338]Westinghouse Elec. Corp., 162 NLRB 768, 64 LRRM 1082 (1967).

[339]*Id.* at 771.

[340]Westinghouse Elec. Corp., *supra* note 338. The initial limitations appear in Hotel Employers Ass'n, *supra* note 334; Warm Springs Lumber Co., 181 NLRB 600, 73 LRRM 1429 (1970).

[341]208 NLRB 452, 85 LRRM 1312 (1974), *enforced,* 506 F2d 1052, 90 LRRM 2890 (CA 3, 1974).

[342]*Id.* at 457.

vailing Board law did not warrant deferral, it held that the respondent union's claim, which alleged an accretion to the unit, must be examined on its merits. *Raley's* was distinguished as standing for the proposition that the Board would defer only when the question before both it and the arbitral tribunal was solely one of contract interpretation.

The Board's broad expression in *Raley's*[343] regarding accommodation to arbitral awards involving representation issues has been slowly reversed, with meager explicit reference to *Raley's*. Thus, by 1975, in *Commonwealth Gas Co.*,[344] the Board was stating, without citation: "[I]t is well established that the Board will not defer to arbitration or an arbitration award concerning representation issues such as the ones involved herein as opposed to questions of contract interpretation." Circuit Judge Friendly cogently commented: "We do not think it profitable to engage in lengthy discussion of decisions, notably *Raley's* . . . . [T]he Board seems to have become rather disenchanted with *Raley's*."[345]

In representation cases, regardless of *Collyer* and *Dubo*, the Board will normally proceed and not wait for an arbitrator to render an award, and its deferral policy as to existing awards, as noted, is rarely to defer.[346]

---

[343]143 NLRB 256, 52 LRRM 1347 (1963).

[344]218 NLRB 857, 858, 89 LRRM 1613 (1975).

[345]Long Island College Hosp. v. NLRB, 566 F2d 833, 845 n.5, 96 LRRM 3119 (CA 2, 1977).

[346]*See* Libby, McNeill & Libby, 159 NLRB 677, 62 LRRM 1276 (1966) (suit to compel arbitration stayed pending Board decision); Humble Oil & Ref. Co., 153 NLRB 1361, 1363, 59 LRRM 1632 (1965) ("[Union's] contractual right to arbitrate disputes . . . does not preclude the Board from determining a question concerning the appropriateness of unit"); Standard Register Co., 146 NLRB 1042, 56 LRRM 1003 (1964); Savage Arms Corp., 144 NLRB 1323, 1324, 54 LRRM 1253 (1963). The Second Circuit subsequently reversed a district court order compelling arbitration of the same issues involved in the *Humble* Board case, *supra*, on the ground that the Board had effectively decided all of the issues. McGuire v. Humble Oil & Ref. Co., 355 F2d 352, 61 LRRM 2410 (CA 2, 1966), *cert. denied*, 384 US 988, 62 LRRM 2339 (1966). *But see* A. Seltzer & Co. v. Livingston, 253 F Supp 509, 61 LRRM 2581 (SD NY, 1966) (arbitration with one union not stayed, despite company's contract with another union for same unit and pendency of representation petition); *cf.* Electrical Workers (IBEW) Local 51 v. Illinois Power Co., 357 F2d 916, 61 LRRM 2613 (CA 7, 1966), *cert. denied*, 387 US 850, 63 LRRM 2235 (1966). Nevertheless, an employer's claim that the NLRB has sole and exclusive jurisdiction over the subject matter of an arbitration proceeding is not grounds for a court to refuse to enforce an award. *See* Teamsters Local 745 v. Braswell Motor Freight Lines, 392 F2d 1, 68 LRRM 2143, *reh'g denied*, 395 F2d 655, 68 LRRM 2632 (CA 5, 1968); *cf.* Carey v. Westinghouse, *supra* note 29.

B. Certain Unfair Labor Practices: Sections 8(a)(2) and 8(a)(4)

The Board has declined to defer to arbitration awards involving Section 8(a)(2) (unlawful assistance to a union) and Section 8(a)(4) (discrimination for filing NLRB charges or giving testimony). In *Servair, Inc.*[347] the employer admitted that it had violated Section 8(a)(2) by assisting the Operating Engineers in an election which the Teamsters lost. Shortly after the election a Teamster supporter was discharged, as were 19 employees who stopped work in protest over his discharge. An arbitrator considered the discharge of the strikers under the collective bargaining agreement and found most of the discharges to be for cause. The administrative law judge would not defer to the award because the arbitrator had considered the discharges solely with reference to Section 8(a)(3) of the Act, without taking into account the background and tie-in of the Section 8(a)(2) unlawful assistance charges. He thus found violations of Sections 8(a)(1), (2), and (3) and ordered reinstatement of the strikers. The Board affirmed, declaring that arbitration was not appropriate in this case because the discharges were "so closely intertwined with, and indeed, a part of the 8(a)(2) allegations, which types of allegations never have been and cannot be delegated to an arbitrator . . . ."[348] The Ninth Circuit Court of Appeals, however, showed little patience with the Board's putting the case in a special category because of the Section 8(a)(2) violations; it therefore denied enforcement with respect to reinstatement of the strikers because of the Board's failure to follow its own *Spielberg* standards.[349] The court thus viewed the issue as a factual one—whether the motive for the discharge was unlawful—an issue which the arbitrator had resolved in favor of the employer. The court noted that if the motive had been unlawful, there would be little difference in characterizing the action as a violation of Section 8(a)(2) as well as of Section 8(a)(3).

In a case involving a charge of Section 8(a)(4) violation, *Filmation Associates, Inc.*,[350] the Board stated:

The prohibition expressed in Section 8(a)(4) against discharging or otherwise discriminating against an employee because he has

---

[347]236 NLRB 1278, 98 LRRM 1259 (1978), *enforced in part*, 102 LRRM 2705 (CA 9, 1979). *See infra* at notes 385-87 for subsequent history of the case.
[348]*Id.* at 2707.
[349]*See also infra* at notes 377-408.
[350]227 NLRB 1721, 94 LRRM 1470 (1977).

filed charges or given testimony under the Act is a fundamental guarantee to employees that they may invoke or participate in the investigative procedures of this Board without fear of reprisal and is clearly required in order to safeguard the integrity of the Board's processes. In our view the duty to preserve the Board's processes from abuse is a function of this Board and may not be delegated to the parties or to an Arbitrator. Accordingly, as we conclude that issues involving Section 8(a)(4) of the Act are solely within the Board's province to decide we will not apply the *Spielberg* doctrine to such issues.[351]

C. Work-Assignment Disputes—Deferral by Statute

Section 10(k) is the only section of the Act specifically authorizing the Board to stay its hand if the parties can demonstrate that they have an agreed-upon means of settling their dispute. In relevant part, this section provides:

> Whenever it is charged that any person has engaged in an unfair labor practice within the meaning of paragraphs (4)(D) of Section 8(b), the Board is empowered and directed to hear and determine the dispute out of which such unfair labor practice shall have arisen, unless . . . the parties to such dispute submit to the Board satisfactory evidence that they have . . . agreed upon methods for the voluntary adjustment of the dispute.

This is obviously a different kind of deferral from that involved in *Spielberg* and *Collyer*. If an agreed-upon method for voluntary adjustment of the dispute exists, the Board lacks jurisdiction to consider the dispute—whether before or after the voluntary adjustment occurs. This subject is covered elsewhere in detail.[352] In quashing a notice of hearing, the Board stated in *Mine Workers Local 1269:*

> The *Spielberg* deferral criteria are inapplicable to our assessment of a jurisdictional dispute settlement mechanism because Section 10(k) provides that the existence of an agreed-upon method deprives the Board of jurisdiction to determine the dispute. This is in direct contrast to the *Spielberg* situation where the Board, in its discretion, declines to exercise its jurisdiction and defers to an arbitration decision. The issue before us, therefore, is whether or not all parties to the dispute have agreed to be bound to a method for settlement of the dispute.[353]

---

[351]*Id.* at 1721. *Accord,* Art Steel of Calif., Inc., 256 NLRB 816, 107 LRRM 1325 (1981). *See* NLRB v. Wilson Freight Co., *supra* note 307, where the court noted but did not comment on *Filmation;* it did not deny enforcement because of the Board's failure to defer to the arbitral award as such, but declared that the Board was bound to defer to some of the factual issues decided in arbitration. *See infra* at notes 383-84.

[352]*See generally* Chapter 27 *infra.*

[353]241 NLRB 231, 232, 100 LRRM 1496 (1979). Member Jenkins dissented as to the conclusion that there was an agreed-upon method.

The Board's requirement that all of the parties to the dispute must be bound by the agreed-upon method for adjustment has been approved by the Supreme Court.[354] Where all parties are not so bound and an arbitral decision has been rendered, the question then becomes not one of deferral, but to what degree the Board will give weight to the arbitral award in arriving at its own decision.[355]

D. Settlement or Other Disposition Under a Grievance Procedure Short of an Arbitral Award

Many grievances are resolved by the parties short of arbitration. Will the Board defer to the parties' settlement or other nonimposed disposition of the grievance? While the Board has not explicitly stated that it will apply *Spielberg* standards to grievance settlements, one appellate court believes that the Board has done so and that it is obligated to do so. The rationale for applying the deferral doctrine to voluntary settlements arrived at under a grievance procedure is, simply, that the opposite policy would require that every grievance involving a potential unfair labor practice charge would have to be taken to arbitration whenever a party desired that the Board defer. This would be a result contrary to the underlying purposes of *Collyer* and *Spielberg:* the encouragement of private dispute resolution and the reduction of litigation.[356]

1. Voluntary Grievance Settlements. In *Central Storage Co.*,[357] a 1973 case, the grievant-employee had filed a charge with the Board and in due course the administrative law judge issued a decision, under *Collyer,* deferring consideration to the arbitral process. The matter was then privately settled. Subsequently, the General Counsel requested that the Board consider the original charge. The Board declined, asserting not only that all of the issues involved had been considered and resolved, but also that none of the parties directly involved had challenged

---

[354]NLRB v. Plasterer's Local 79, 404 US 116, 78 LRRM 2897 (1971). *See* Chapter 27 *infra* at note 67.
[355]Newspaper & Mail Deliverers Union of N.Y. v. News Syndicate Co., Inc., 141 NLRB 578, 52 LRRM 1339 (1963); *see also* McLeod v. Newspaper Deliverer's Union, 209 F2d 434, 51 LRRM 2292 (SD NY, 1962). *See* Chapter 27 *infra* at notes 82-126.
[356]*See* NLRB Gen. Counsel Memo., No. 81-39 (July 17, 1981), which implicitly recognizes this point. The memo deals generally with *Dubo* deferral where the aggrieved individual has chosen not to use the contract grievance procedure but the union is pursuing the issue on its own through that procedure.
[357]206 NLRB 337, 84 LRRM 1273 (1973).

the terms of the settlement. And in *Coca-Cola Bottling Co.*[358] the Board held that an employer had not violated Section 8(a)(1) by entering into a private settlement in which the employee had agreed to withdraw his claim with the Board in exchange for a reduction of his discipline. The Board rejected the argument that deferral was inappropriate because it deprived the employee of his right to use the Board's processes. It found instead that the agreement was the product of negotiations in which both sides had compromised.

In *Super Value Xenia,*[359] however, the Board refused deferral to the result reached in Step 4 of a bipartite grievance procedure, because the employee-grievants had not been present at the meeting, no testimony had been taken, and no transcript was available.

In spite of the *Central Cartage* and *Coca-Cola* cases, the Board on several occasions has indicated that it will not defer to private settlements. For example, in *Laredo Packing Co.*[360] the Board declined to defer to a grievance settlement that resulted in withdrawal of a reprimand, for the stated reason that the grievance was settled short of arbitration. In *Owens-Corning Fiberglas Co.*[361] a union steward had been singled out by the employer from a group of employees who had been drinking on duty and discharged because the employer expected the union steward to meet a higher standard of conduct; an informal settlement was reached during the grievance procedure, reducing the penalty to an 11-day suspension without pay. The Board declined to defer on the grounds that the settlement agreement had been "entered into by the parties without the Board's participation or approval"[362] and also because the settlement clearly did not consider the Section 8(a)(3) aspect of the case. The Board has also indicated that it will not apply *Spielberg* to awards reached short of arbitration because in such cases there is no award by an impartial tribunal.[363]

---

[358]243 NLRB 501, 101 LRRM 1456 (1979).

[359]228 NLRB 1254, 95 LRRM 1444 (1977). There were other reasons for refusing to defer.

[360]254 NLRB 1, 106 LRRM 1350 (1981), before Chairman Fanning and Member Jenkins, in the majority, and Member Penello, in dissent.

[361]236 NLRB 479, 98 LRRM 1234 (1978).

[362]*Id.* at 479.

[363]*See* United States Postal Serv., 237 NLRB 117, 99 LRRM 1431 (1978) (ALJ stated that *Spielberg* was inapplicable because the grievance was settled short of arbitration); Pontiac Motors Div., General Motors, 132 NLRB 413, 48 LRRM 1368 (1961) (noting the absence of an arbitral award to review). *See also* Whirlpool Corp., *supra* note 128.

THE DEVELOPING LABOR LAW CH. 20

In *Ford Motor Co. (Rouge Complex)*[364] the charging parties had been disciplined for distributing literature at the plant; their grievances were adjusted at an early stage of the grievance procedure and were not submitted to arbitration. In rejecting the employer's request for deferral under *Spielberg* to this final and binding resolution through the contractual grievance machinery, the Board cited its decision in *Whirlpool*[365] and *Pontiac Motor Division*,[366] indicating that it would not defer to grievance settlements. It also noted that, in any event, the settlement was repugnant to the Act.[367]

In *Roadway Express, Inc.*[368] the Board refused to defer to the voluntary settlement of the discharge of an employee for engaging in union activities. The Board noted that the legality of the discharge had not been discussed, and that the employee was dissatisfied with the settlement, which included reinstatement but no back pay. The full Board split, with the Board's plurality opinion[369] asserting that the Board has discretion to defer to a private settlement that has been voluntarily arrived at by the parties, covers all pertinent issues, and effectuates the policies of the Act; but deferral was deemed inappropriate in this instance. The Fourth Circuit reversed. That court found that substantial evidence failed to support the Board's findings—the validity of the discharge had been considered and the employee-grievant had knowingly agreed to the settlement.

2. Grievances Dropped by the Union. In *Electric Motors & Specialties, Inc.*,[370] grievances had been processed through several steps of the grievance procedure but not to arbitration. The employer argued that since its contract provided that where arbitration was not requested a grievance would be deemed abandoned, the Board's *Spielberg* rule should be applicable just as if the matter had been fully arbitrated. The Board rejected this argument.[371] *Whirlpool Corp.*[372] involved a similar situation.

---

[364]233 NLRB 698, 96 LRRM 1513 (1977).
[365]Whirlpool Corp., *supra* note 128.
[366]Pontiac Motors Div., General Motors, *supra* note 363. The grievance settlement required the waiver by the charging parties of their rights to distribute literature in the future.
[367]See generally *supra* at notes 301-29.
[368]246 NLRB 174, 102 LRRM 1391 (1979), *supplemented in* 250 NLRB 393, 104 LRRM 1349 (1980), *enforcement denied*, 647 F2d 415 (CA 4, 1981), 107 LRRM 2155.
[369]Members Jenkins and Murphy. Member Truesdale concurred in the result.
[370]149 NLRB 131, 57 LRRM 1258 (1964).
[371]See also Pontiac Motors Div., General Motors, *supra* note 363; Dant & Russell, Ltd., 92 NLRB 307, 27 LRRM 1088 (1950) (trial examiner's decision), *set aside on other grounds*,

A terminated employee, after having his grievance processed by the union, filed an unfair labor practice charge. The regional director had initially deferred to the grievance procedure under *Collyer;* but later, after the employee complained that the union had failed to take his case to arbitration, a complaint was issued. Deferral was refused because "[i]t is undisputed that the full range of the mechanism for the determination of the dispute has not been utilized and there is no award that may be examined for conformity with *Spielberg* requirements."[373]

E. Failure to Abide by an Arbitral Award

Failure of a respondent to comply with an arbitration award may be a factor in the Board's determination whether to defer and/or whether to issue a formal Board order.

In *Malrite of Wisconsin, Inc.,*[374] the collective bargaining contract provided that the employer was to assign only one person to a given classification. Ignoring the union and soliciting written consents from individual employees, the employer nevertheless assigned additional employees to the classification. An arbitrator then held that the action violated the agreement, and he directed the employer to cease assigning more than one person to the classification. When the employer refused to comply, the union sought court enforcement of the arbitration award. The Board, deferring to the award under *Spielberg* principles, dismissed the complaint. The majority opinion noted that "direct Court enforcement of arbitrators' awards can provide more prompt and effective action" than can the various steps of the Board's unfair labor practice procedures. Two years later, however, in *Electronic Reproduction*[375] the Board limited *Malrite*. The employer had refused to accept an arbitration award concerning various terms of a new agreement, and Chairman Miller and Member Kennedy agreed that there should be no deferral with respect to the employer's alleged violation of Section 8(a)(5). In their

---

195 F2d 299, 29 LRRM 2585 (CA 9, 1952), *rev'd,* 344 US 375, 31 LRRM 2303 (1953), *enforced,* 207 F2d 165, 32 LRRM 2740 (CA 9, 1953).

[372]216 NLRB 183, 88 LRRM 1329 (1975).

[373]*Id.* at 186 (from the ALJ decision). *See also* NLRB v. Maxwell, d/b/a Pioneer Concrete Co., 637 F2d 698, 106 LRRM 2387 (CA 9, 1981), *enforcing* 241 NLRB 264, 101 LRRM 1012 (1979).

[374]198 NLRB 241, 80 LRRM 1593 (1972), *enforced sub nom.* Electrical Workers (IBEW) Local 1715 v. NLRB, 494 F2d 1136, 85 LRRM 2823 (CA DC, 1974).

[375]*Supra* note 242, on a point presumably not affected by the Board's later overruling of the more controversial aspect of the case in *Suburban Motor Freight, Inc., supra* note 247.

view, the administrative law judge had correctly distinguished this situation, which involved rejection of all of the terms of the contract, from the situation in *Malrite,* which involved only one term of the contract:

> In these circumstances, in which respondents in effect have repudiated the Collective Bargaining process, judicial enforcement of the arbitrator's Award will not serve to remedy the unfair labor practices and the desirability of encouraging resort to arbitration must yield to the Board's duty to protect the bargaining process. This can be done . . . only by an effective Board Order. . . ."[376]

V. RESPONSE OF THE REVIEWING COURT TO THE BOARD'S DEFERRAL STANDARDS

As reflected throughout this chapter, the appellate courts have approved the Board's general approach on deferring to arbitration awards, both as to the *Collyer* pre-arbitral doctrine and the *Spielberg* standards. In specific cases, however, the courts have frequently disagreed with the Board in the implementation of both *Collyer* and *Spielberg.* And in some instances the courts have sought to refine or modify the Board's deferral standards. Although many of the appellate cases have already been noted, it will be instructive to review here some major decisions that reflect the development of judicial response to the Board's deferral policies.

In 1974 the District of Columbia Circuit, in *Banyard v. NLRB,*[377] announced two additional prerequisites to the *Spielberg* checklist of requirements for deferral to arbitral awards. The court stated that its approval of deferral by the Board was "conditional upon the resolution by the arbitral tribunal of *congruent* statutory and contractual issues."[378] The court reversed the Board because of the failure of the arbitral tribunals to consider Section 8(a)(1) issues, and in the process announced two new prerequisites for deferral: that *Spielberg* applies only if the arbitral tribunal "clearly decided the issue on which it is later urged that the Board should give deference, and . . . the arbitral tribunal decided an issue within its competence."[379]

---

[376]213 NLRB at 759.
[377]Banyard v. NLRB (McLean Trucking Co.), 505 F2d 342, 87 LRRM 2001 (CA DC, 1974), *remanding* 202 NLRB 710, 82 LRRM 1652 (1973), and 203 NLRB 157, 83 LRRM 1149 (1973), *supplemented by* 216 NLRB 925, 88 LRRM 1649 (1975).
[378]505 F2d at 348 (emphasis in original).
[379]*Id.* at 343.

The Ninth Circuit, in *Stephenson (Fikse Bros., Inc.)* v. *NLRB*,[380] approved the addition of the two *Banyard* requirements and also suggested, as a refinement of the "clearly decided" component, that "[the arbitrator] must specifically deal with the statutory issue.[381] Seeking further delineation of the *Banyard* "competence" prerequisite, the court noted that deference assumes a "congruence between the statutory and contractual issues." It stated:

> Where the question of unfair labor practice depends on contract interpretation, the expertise of arbitrators (or at least its recognition by the parties to the collective bargaining agreement) is held to be superior to that of the Board which primarily considers the statutory issues. Thus, deference in situations where the statutory and contractual issues are congruent is entirely reasonable. Likewise, where resolution of the unfair labor practice charge involves mainly factual rather than statutory issues, the arbitrator is in as good a position to make a correct decision as is the Board, given the former's access to the facts and to the current practices of the industry. . . . However, where the decision to be made rests primarily on issues of public law rather than on contractual or factual determinations, the arbitrator possesses no special expertise and there is no reason for allowing his decision to determine the statutory rights of the parties. . . . Therefore, the "competence" requirement requires the Board to ascertain the underlying issues in the unfair labor practice charge and to determine whether arbitral expertise and institutional competence justify deferral to arbitration of a particular statutory dispute.[382]

In *NLRB* v. *Wilson Freight Co.*[383] the First Circuit denied enforcement in a case where the Board had refused to defer to an award of a labor-management joint board which had sustained the discharge of a union steward. The court charged that "the Board exceeded its authority to the extent it redecided in [the grievant's] favor factual matters determined by the arbitrators. . . ."[384]

Servair, Inc. v. *NLRB*,[385] previously noted, was another case where the Ninth Circuit refused to enforce parts of a Board

[380]550 F2d 535, 94 LRRM 3224 (CA 9, 1977), *remanding* 220 NLRB 1301, 90 LRRM 1354 (1975).
[381]550 F2d at 536. This requirement has probably become moot as a result of the Board's reversal of *Electronic Reproduction, supra* note 242, in *Suburban Motor Freight, supra* note 247.
[382]550 F2d at 538 n. 4.
[383]*Supra* notes 307 and 351.
[384]604 F2d at 722.
[385]236 NLRB 1278, 99 LRRM 1259 (1978), *enforced in part and remanded*, 102 LRRM 2705 (CA 9, 1979), *opinion withdrawn and case remanded*, 624 F2d 92, 105 LRRM 2649 (CA 9, 1980). *See supra* at notes 347-49.

order which had found that 19 employees, who had walked off the job, were discharged in violation of Section 8(a)(2). The Board acknowledged that the arbitrator had before him the issue of the legality of the discharge under Section 8(a)(3). In the court's view: "The Board simply chose to proceed on the basis of 8(a)(2) in addition to 8(a)(3). That choice does not justify ignoring the arbitration award,"[386] which had upheld the discharges. The court declared that "[if] the alleged contractual breach is also capable of being alleged as a statutory breach, and if the resolution of the contractual breach by the arbitrator also resolves the underlying issues of the statutory breach, then the arbiter's judgment should be respected."[387] The court subsequently withdrew its opinion and simply instructed the Board to reconsider its decision under the *Spielberg* standards.

Again, in *Douglas Aircraft* v. *NLRB*,[388] the Ninth Circuit criticized the Board for failing to defer to an arbitral award which had denied a grievant back pay on each of two grounds. One ground was his abusive and uncivil conduct, the other his rejection of a grievance settlement conditioned on his withdrawing his NLRB charge. The court agreed that the second reason for denying back pay was violative of the Act. Nevertheless, because the arbitrator, in clarifying his award, had stated there was no evidence that the discharge was for protected activities and that abusive conduct was independently sufficient to deny back pay, the court concluded that the Board should have deferred.

Less than a year later, the Third Circuit, in *NLRB* v. *Pincus Brothers, Inc.,-Maxwell*,[389] cited *Douglas Aircraft* with approval in refusing enforcement of a Board order which had failed to defer to an arbitral award, stating "that where there are two arguable interpretations of an arbitration award, one permissible and one impermissible, the Board must defer to the decision rendered by the arbitrator."[390]

In *Retail, Wholesale & Dep't Store Union District 1199E (Greater Pennsylvania Ave. Nursing Center)* v. *NLRB*,[391] the D.C. Circuit addressed the question of whether the Board is required to give

---

[386]102 LRRM at 2709.
[387]*Id.*
[388]609 F2d 352, 102 LRRM 2811 (CA 9, 1979), *denying enforcement to* 238 NLRB 668, 99 LRRM 1274 (1978).
[389]*Supra* note 307.
[390]*Id.*, 620 F2d at 368.
[391]613 F2d 1102, 103 LRRM 2001 (CA DC, 1979).

an adequate explanation of its refusal to defer to an arbitral award. The court's answer was "yes." It recognized that in terms of absolute power—unless the Board's differing construction of the contract from that of the arbitrator is arbitrary and capricious—the Board's interpretation is entitled to precedence. "Nonetheless," said the court, "it is important that disputants continue to be attracted to arbitration for resolution of differences that are susceptible to arbitration."[392] The dispute concerned contracting-out of work, about which the court said that

> before the Board reached a result contrary to the Arbitrator, it should have spoken directly and fully to the issue [to be] decided. . . .
>
> . . .
>
> [W]hatever the final result, the Board should explicitly discuss the implications of the collective bargaining agreement as interpreted by the arbitrator, both because adequate review of the Board's decision cannot be completed without a full explanation of its reasoning and because the respect due the arbitral process requires as much.[393]

The court remanded the case for further explication of the Board's failure to defer.

Most of the later appellate cases, primarily post-*Suburban Motor Freight*[394] decisions—or decisions which have commented favorably on the Board's policy in *Suburban*—have enforced orders where the Board denied deference to arbitral awards, although the D.C. Circuit in one case refused to do so where the Board declined to defer to an arbitrator's interpretation of a no-strike clause.[395]

In *St. Luke's Memorial Hospital* v. *NLRB*[396] the Seventh Circuit agreed with the Board's refusal to defer to an arbitral award where the arbitrator had been selected by a dubious process and where the award did not reflect an appreciation of Board policy or clearly adjudicate the unfair labor practice issues. The court also noted the adoption of the *Suburban Motor Freight* rule, stating that the Board had "properly declined to follow the *Electronic Reproduction* approach in this case."[397]

---

[392]*Id*. at 1109.
[393]*Id*.
[394]*Supra* note 247.
[395]Fournelle v. NLRB, *supra* note 319. *See also* note 404 *infra*.
[396]623 F2d 1173, 104 LRRM 2788 (CA 7, 1980), *enforcing* 240 NLRB 1180, 100 LRRM 1393 (1979).
[397]623 F2d at 1178.

In *NLRB* v. *Max Factor & Co.*[398] the Sixth Circuit enforced an order where the Board had declined to defer to an arbitration award, asserting that the Board's duty to prevent unfair labor practices outweighs the policy of encouraging arbitration.

In three decisions, the Third Circuit enforced Board orders in cases in which deferral had been refused: *NLRB* v. *General Warehouse Corp.*,[399] *Hammermill Paper Co.* v. *NLRB*[400] and *Herman Brothers* v. *NLRB*.[401]

The Ninth Circuit, in upholding the Board's refusal to defer to an arbitration award in *Ad Art, Inc.*,[402] presented its conception of the abuse-of-discretion test applicable to the Board in deferral cases, saying: "The Board only abuses its wide discretion if it fails to follow its own deferral standards or if the standards themselves are invalid."[403]

Courts, moreover, continue to examine each deferral case on its own merits. Rejecting the Board's refusal to defer in *Fournelle* v. *NLRB*,[404] the D.C. Circuit ruled that the Board was not free to substitute its own interpretation of the contract for a permanent umpire's "authoritative construction of a no-strike clause to impose a higher duty on union officials to obey its requirements." In *Distillery Workers Local 2 (Charmer Industries, Inc.)*[405] v. *NLRB*, the Second Circuit held that the Board had abused its discretion in declining to defer to an arbitrator's award that had found a unilateral change in sales procedure for liquor salesmen not to be a change in work rules under the collective agreement—a determination which the court said was necessarily dispositive of the Section 8(a)(5) statutory issue. The court, however, recognized the Board's wide discretion in defining the

---

[398]640 F2d 197, 105 LRRM 2765 (CA 9, 1980), *enforcing* 239 NLRB 804, 100 LRRM 1023 (1978).

[399]643 F2d 965, 106 LRRM 2729 (CA 3, 1981), *enforcing* 247 NLRB 1073, 103 LRRM 1294 (1980).

[400]658 F2d 155, 108 LRRM 2001 (CA 3, 1981), *enforcing* 252 NLRB 1236, 105 LRRM 1409 (1980).

[401]658 F2d 201, 108 LRRM 2327 (CA 3, 1981), *enforcing* 252 NLRB 848, 105 LRRM 1374 (1980).

[402]*Supra* note 251.

[403]645 F2d at 675.

[404]*Supra* note 319. *See also* Metropolitan Edison Co. v. NLRB, 663 F2d 478, 108 LRRM 3020 (CA 3, 1981) (refusing to rule on application of *Spielberg* standards because arbitration award had not been issued on facts of case; Szewczuga v. NLRB, 110 LRRM 3289 (CA DC, 1982)) (failure to raise *Spielberg* deferral issue before the Board precludes its assertion before the reviewing court).

[405]664 F2d 318, 107 LRRM 3137 (CA 2, 1981) *denying enforcement to* 250 NLRB 293, 104 LRRM 1368 (1980).

circumstances under which it will defer, noting that the Board is not required by statute to defer. But "[o]nce the Board has announced a particular set of rules," the court indicated, "some constraints necessarily arise to limit its discretion in individual cases. The Board cannot lightly change the rules on a case by case basis."[406] The Ninth Circuit, in refusing enforcement in *Albertson's, Inc. v. NLRB,*[407] charged that the Board had failed to consider evidence that the grievant would have been fired for incompetence despite any union activity on her part.

VI. *COLLYER* AND *SPIELBERG* IN RETROSPECT

The full impact of the *Collyer, Spielberg,* and *Dubo* doctrines is difficult to perceive, because so many of the basic decisions applying those doctrines are made by the General Counsel through regional offices—decisions as to whether to defer to an arbitral award, to issue a complaint, to pursue or encourage settlement, or to recommend withdrawal or dismissal of a charge. These relatively informal and unpublished decisions, which give meaning to the doctrines, defy quantification. Only a small portion of the cases in which deferral takes place result in reported decisions. The regional offices will not issue a complaint on a charge otherwise meritorious if the subject matter of the dispute has resulted in an arbitral award which the regional office views as meeting *Spielberg* requisites. Thus, it is at the regional office level, where charges originate, that the real effect of *Spielberg* in avoiding litigation of the same dispute in two forums occurs. When a case in which the respondent is seeking deferral to an arbitration award results in a reported Board decision, ordinarily it will have been fully litigated for a second time before the Board—even in those cases where the Board ultimately decides to defer to the arbitral award.

Some of the arguments supporting *Collyer* are the following: (1) avoidance of litigation of the same dispute in two forums— the arbitration tribunal and the Board; (2) the national labor policy favoring the use of private dispute-resolution machinery agreed upon by the parties; (3) "the societal rewards of arbitration outweigh a need for uniformity of result or a correct res-

---

[406]664 F2d at 326.
[407]661 F2d 939, 108 LRRM 2714 (CA 9, 1981), *rev'g & remanding* 252 NLRB 529, 105 LRRM 1443 (1980).

olution of the dispute in every case";[408] (4) the concept that the individual should exhaust his contractual remedies before pursuing relief in another forum; (5) the desirability of limiting government intervention into labor disputes; (6) the reduction in demands upon the limited resources of the National Labor Relations Board; (7) the more expeditious resolution of disputes under grievance-arbitration machinery; (8) the usual finality attached to arbitration awards; and (9) through *Spielberg* review, the Board can still intervene subsequent to the arbitration award to maintain adequate protection of statutory rights.

Some of the arguments on the other side are the following: (1) only the Board has the investigative and legal resources and the knowledge and expertise to process complaints concerning violations of the statute; (2) arbitrators frequently lack the competence or willingness to deal with statutory violations; (4) there is often an absence of congruity between the contractual and statutory issues, resulting in an absence of arbitral authority to decide fully the statutory issue; (5) the inability of an arbitrator to provide an effective remedy, particularly for continuing violations; (6) the greater difficulty posed for the Board in protecting statutory rights if it must await the outcome of the arbitral process, and evidence is no longer fresh; (7) the delay that may occur in providing a necessary statutory remedy; and (8) the possible antipathy or unenthusiastic response by the union to an individual's claim of statutory violations.

The *Spielberg* doctrine itself has not been seriously challenged. However, some of the arguments used against *Collyer* are also arguments against any form of deferral. The overruling of the 1974 *Electronic Reproduction*[409] decision by *Suburban Motor Freight*[410] reflected a narrowing of the application of *Spielberg*. And the 1977 contraction of *Collyer* in *General American Transportation*[411] signalled a more limited policy of deferral in cases involving alleged violations of the rights of individual employees.

Since *Spielberg*, there has been a lack of agreement among Board members as to the weight to be accorded an arbitrator's findings and the appropriate standard of review of the arbitrator's award. Consequently, a broad area of uncertainty remains

---

[408]J. Rosenn in the lead opinion in Pincus Bros., *supra* note 307, 620 F2d at 374.
[409]*Supra* note 242.
[410]*Supra* note 247.
[411]*Supra* note 96.

concerning the degree of restraint which the Board will or should exercise in performing its function of "reviewing" arbitral awards under *Spielberg*. The groping for firmer ground appears likely to continue, with attendant uncertainties for employees, employers, and unions.